THE FIREFLY ITALIAN/ENGLISH VISUAL DICTIONARY

Jean-Claude **Corbeil**
Ariane **Archambault**

FIREFLY BOOKS

Published by Firefly Books Ltd. 2010

First printing

Publisher Cataloging-in-Publication Data (U.S.)

Corbeil, Jean Claude.
The Firefly Italian/English visual dictionary / Jean-Claude Corbeil ; Ariane Archambault.
[592] p. : col. ill., col. maps ; cm.
Includes index.
Summary: A comprehensive general reference visual dictionary featuring terms in English and Italian, including sections on astronomy, geography, the animal and vegetable kingdoms, human biology, the home, clothing and accessories, art and architecture, communication, transportation, energy, science, society and sports.
ISBN-13: 978-1-55407-716-8
ISBN-10: 1-55407-716-8
1. Picture dictionaries, Italian. 2. Picture dictionaries, English. 3. Italian language — Dictionaries — English. 4. English language — Dictionaries — Italian. I. Archambault, Ariane. II. Title.
453.21 dc22 PC1640.C6736 2010

Library and Archives Canada Cataloguing in Publication

Corbeil, Jean-Claude, 1932–
The Firefly Italian/English visual dictionary / Jean-Claude Corbeil and Ariane Archambault.
Includes index.
ISBN-13: 978-1-55407-716-8
ISBN-10: 1-55407-716-8
1. Picture dictionaries, Italian. 2. Picture dictionaries, English. 3. Italian language – Dictionaries – English. 4. English language – Dictionaries – Italian. I. Archambault, Ariane, 1936–2006 II. Title.
AG250.C66373 2010 453'.21 C2010-901138-4

Published in the United States by
Firefly Books (U.S.) Inc.
P.O. Box 1338, Ellicott Station
Buffalo, New York 14205

Published in Canada by
Firefly Books Ltd.
66 Leek Crescent
Richmond Hill, Ontario L4B 1H1

Cover design: Gareth Lind

Printed in China
10 9 8 7 6 5 4 3 2 1 13 12 11 10
429, Version 3.5.4

The publisher gratefully acknowledges the financial support for our publishing program by the Government of Canada through the Canada Book Fund as administered by the Department of Canadian Heritage

ACKNOWLEDGMENTS

Our deepest gratitude to the individuals, institutions, companies and businesses that have provided us with the latest technical documentation for use in preparing *The Firefly Italian/English Visual Dictionary*.

Arcand, Denys (réalisateur); Association Internationale de Signalisation Maritime, Association canadienne des paiements (Charlie Clarke); Association des banquiers canadiens (Lise Provost); Automobiles Citroën; Automobiles Peugeot; Banque du Canada (Lyse Brousseau); Banque Royale du Canada (Raymond Chouinard, Francine Morel, Carole Trottier); Barrett Xplore inc.; Bazarin, Christine;Bibliothèque du Parlement canadien (Service de renseignements); Bibliothèque nationale du Québec (Jean-François Palomino); Bluechip Kennels (Olga Gagne); Bombardier Aéronautique; Bridgestone-Firestone; Brother (Canada); Canadien National; Casavant Frères ltée; C.O.J.O. ATHENES 2004 (Bureau des Médias Internationaux); Centre Eaton de Montréal; Centre national du Costume (Recherche et de Diffusion); Cetacean Society International (William R. Rossiter); Chagnon, Daniel (architecte D.E.S. – M.E.Q.); Cohen et Rubin Architectes (Maggy Cohen); Commission Scolaire de Montréal (École St-Henri); Compagnie de la Baie d'Hudson (Nunzia Iavarone, Ron Oyama); Corporation d'hébergement du Québec (Céline Drolet); École nationale de théâtre du Canada (Bibliothèque); Élevage Le Grand Saphir (Stéphane Ayotte); Énergie atomique du Canada ltée; Eurocopter; Famous Players; Fédération bancaire française (Védi Hékiman); Fontaine, PierreHenry (biologiste); Future Shop; Garaga; Groupe Jean Coutu; Hôpital du Sacré-Cœur de Montréal; Hôtel Inter-Continental; Hydro-Québec; I.P.I.Q. (Serge Bouchard); IGA Barcelo; International Entomological Society (Dr. Michael Geisthardt); Irisbus; Jérôme, Danielle (O.D.); La Poste (Colette Gouts); Le Groupe Canam Manac inc.; Lévesque, Georges (urgentologue); Lévesque, Robert (chef machiniste); Manutan; Marriot Spring Hill suites; MATRA S.A.; Métro inc.; ministère canadien de la Défense nationale (Affaires publiques); ministère de la Défense, République Française; ministère de la Justice du Québec (Service de la gestion immobilière – Carol Sirois); ministère de l'Éducation du Québec (Direction de l'équipement scolaire- Daniel Chagnon); Muse Productions (Annick Barbery); National Aeronautics and Space Administration; National Oceanic and Atmospheric Administration; Nikon Canada inc.; Normand, Denis (consultant en télécommunications); Office de la langue française du Québec (Chantal Robinson); Paul Demers & Fils inc.; Phillips (France); Pratt & Whitney Canada inc.; Prévost Car inc.; Radio Shack Canada ltée; Réno-Dépôt inc.; Robitaille, Jean-François (Département de biologie, Université Laurentienne); Rocking T Ranch and Poultry Farm (Pete and Justine Theer); RONA inc.; Sears Canada inc.; Secrétariat d'État du Canada : Bureau de la traduction ; Service correctionnel du Canada; Société d'Entomologie Africaine (Alain Drumont); Société des musées québécois (Michel Perron); Société Radio-Canada; Sony du Canada ltée; Sûreté du Québec; Théâtre du Nouveau Monde; Transports Canada (Julie Poirier); Urgences-Santé (Éric Berry); Ville de Longueuil (Direction de la Police); Ville de Montréal (Service de la prévention des incendies); Vimont Lexus Toyota; Volvo Bus Corporation; Yamaha Motor Canada Ltd.

QA International wishes to extend a special thank you to the following people for their contribution to *The Firefly Italian/English Visual Dictionary*:

Jean-Louis Martin, Marc Lalumière, Jacques Perrault, Stéphane Roy, Alice Comtois, Michel Blais, Christiane Beauregard, Mamadou Togola, Annie Maurice, Charles Campeau, Mivil Deschênes, Jonathan Jacques, Martin Lortie, Frédérick Simard, Yan Tremblay, Mathieu Blouin, Sébastien Dallaire, Hoang Khanh Le, Martin Desrosiers, Nicolas Oroc, François Escalmel, Danièle Lemay, Pierre Savoie, Benoît Bourdeau, Marie-Andrée Lemieux, Caroline Soucy, Yves Chabot, Anne-Marie Ouellette, Anne-Marie Villeneuve, Anne-Marie Brault, Nancy Lepage, Daniel Provost, François Vézina, Brad Wilson, Michael Worek, Lionel Koffler, Maraya Raduha, Dave Harvey, Mike Parkes, George Walker, Anna Simmons, Guylaine Houle, Sophie Pellerin, Tony O'Riley.

The Firefly Italian/English Visual Dictionary was created and produced by
QA International
329, rue de la Commune Ouest, 3e étage
Montréal (Québec) H2Y 2E1 Canada
T 514.499.3000 F 514.499.3010
www.qa-international.com

EDITORIAL STAFF

Publisher: Jacques Fortin
Authors: Jean-Claude Corbeil and Ariane Archambault
Editorial Director: François Fortin
Editor-in-Chief: Serge D'Amico
Graphic Design: Anne Tremblay

PRODUCTION

Guy Bonin
Salvatore Parisi

TERMINOLOGICAL RESEARCH

Sophie Ballarin
Jean Beaumont
Catherine Briand
Nathalie Guillo
Anne Rouleau

ILLUSTRATIONS

Art Directors: Jocelyn Gardner, Anouk Noël
Jean-Yves Ahern
Rielle Lévesque
Alain Lemire
Mélanie Boivin
Yan Bohler
Claude Thivi,erge
Pascal Bilodeau
Michel Rouleau
Carl Pelletier
Raymond Martin

LAYOUT

Pascal Goyette
Janou-Ève LeGuerrier
Véronique Boisvert
Josée Gagnon
Karine Raymond
Geneviève Théroux Béliveau

DOCUMENTATION

Gilles Vézina
Kathleen Wynd
Stéphane Batigne
Sylvain Robichaud
Jessie Daigle

DATA MANAGEMENT

Programmer: Daniel Beaulieu
Éric Gagnon
Gabriel Trudeau St-Hilaire

REVISION

Marie-Nicole Cimon
Liliane Michaud
Veronica Schami

PREPRESS

Julien Brisebois
François Hénault
Karine Lévesque
Patrick Mercure

Jean-Claude Corbeil is an expert in linguistic planning, with a world-wide reputation in the fields of comparative terminology and socio-linguistics. He serves as a consultant to various international organizations and governments.

Ariane Archambault, a specialist in applied linguistics, has taught foreign languages and is now a terminologist and editor of dictionaries and reference books.

Introduction to *The Firefly Italian/English Visual Dictionary*

A DICTIONARY FOR ONE AND ALL

The Firefly Italian/English Visual Dictionary uses pictures to define words. With thousands of illustrations and thousands of specialist and general terms, it provides a rich source of knowledge about the world around you.

Designed for the general reader and students of language, *The Firefly Italian/English Visual Dictionary* responds to the needs of anyone seeking precise, correct terms for a wide range of objects. Using illustrations enables you to "see" immediately the meaning of each term.

You can use *The Firefly Italian/English Visual Dictionary* in several ways:

By going from an idea to a word. If you are familiar with an object but do not know the correct name for it, you can look up the object in the dictionary and you will find the various parts correctly named.

By going from a word to an idea. If you want to check the meaning of a term, refer to the index where you will find the term and be directed to the appropriate illustration that defines the term.

For sheer pleasure. You can flip from one illustration to another or from one word to another, for the sole purpose of enjoying the illustrations and enriching your knowledge of the world around us.

STRUCTURE

The Firefly Italian/English Visual Dictionary is divided into CHAPTERS, outlining subjects from astronomy to sports.

More complex subjects are divided into THEMES; for example, the Animal Kingdom chapter is divided into themes including insects and arachnids, mollusks, and crustaceans.

The TITLES name the object and, at times, the chief members of a class of objects are brought together under the same SUBTITLE.

The ILLUSTRATIONS show an object, a process or a phenomenon, and the most significant details from which they are constructed. It serves as a visual definition for each of the terms presented.

TERMINOLOGY

Each word in *The Firefly Italian/English Visual Dictionary* has been carefully chosen and verified. Sometimes different words are used to name the same object, and in these cases the word most commonly used was chosen.

COLOR REFERENCE

On the spine and back of the book this identifies and accompanies each theme to facilitate quick access to the corresponding section in the book.

TITLE

It is highlighted in English, and the Italian equivalent is placed underneath in smaller characters. If the title runs over a number of pages, it is printed in gray on the pages subsequent to the first page on which it appears.

SUB-THEME

Most themes are subdivided into sub-themes. The sub-theme is given both in English and in Italian.

NARROW LINES

These link the word to the item indicated. Where too many lines would make reading difficult, they have been replaced by color codes with captions or, in rare cases, by numbers.

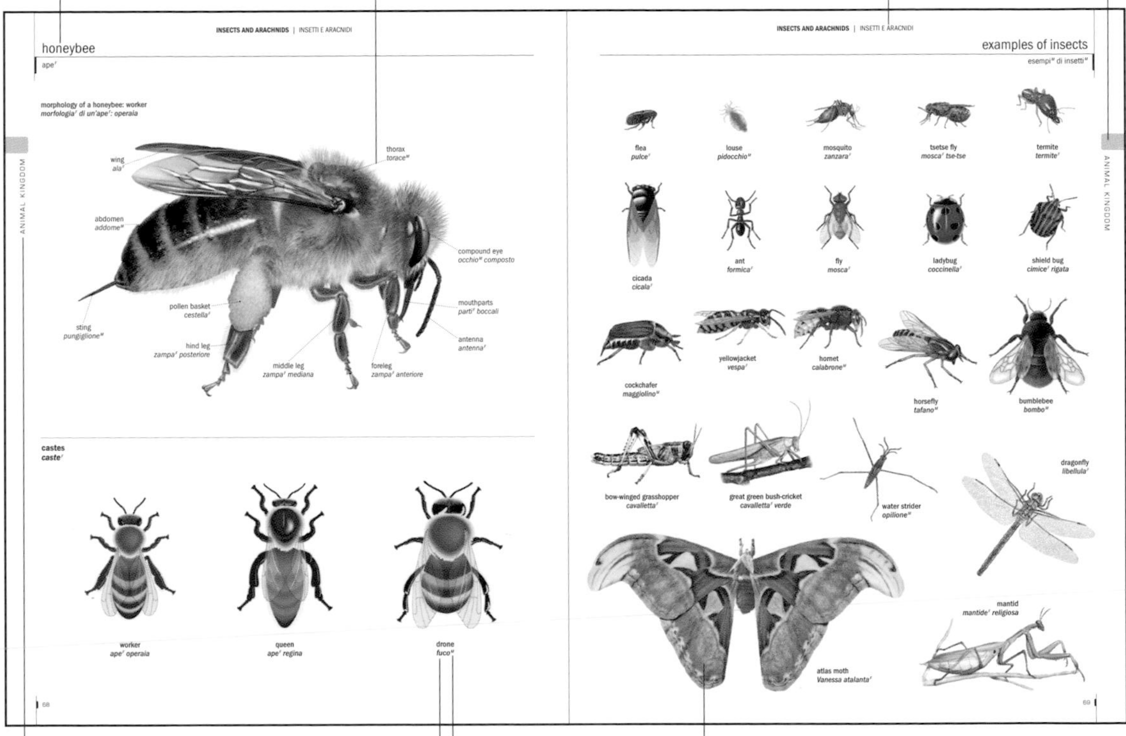

THEME

It is always unilingual, in English.

ILLUSTRATION

It serves as the visual definition for the terms associated with it.

GENDER INDICATION

F: feminine M: masculine N: neuter

The gender of each word in a term is indicated.

The characters shown in the dictionary are men or women when the function illustrated can be fulfilled by either. In these cases, the gender assigned to the word depends on the illustration; in fact, the word is either masculine or feminine depending on the sex of the person.

TERM

Each term appears in the index with a reference to the pages on which it appears. It is given in both languages, with English as the main index entry.

Contents

ASTRONOMY 2

Celestial bodies 2
Astronomical observation 7
Astronautics 10

EARTH 14

Geography 14
Geology 26
Meteorology 37
Environment 44

VEGETABLE KINGDOM 50

ANIMAL KINGDOM 66

Simple organisms and echinoderms 66
Insects and arachnids 67
Crustaceans 71
Mollusks 72
Fishes 74
Amphibians 75
Reptiles 76
Birds 78
Rodents and lagomorphs 82
Ungulate mammals 83
Carnivorous mammals 86
Marine mammals 90
Primate mammals 91

HUMAN BEING 92

Human body 92
Anatomy 96
Sense organs 114

FOOD AND KITCHEN 120

Food 120
Kitchen 162

HOUSE 182

Site 182
Elements of a house 185
Structure of a house 187
Heating 192
Plumbing 194
Electricity 198
House furniture 200

DO-IT-YOURSELF AND GARDENING 216

Do-it-yourself 216
Gardening 230

CLOTHING 238

PERSONAL ADORNMENT AND ARTICLES 264

Personal adornment 264
Personal articles 271

ARTS AND ARCHITECTURE 278

Architecture 278
Performing arts 290
Music 295

COMMUNICATIONS AND OFFICE AUTOMATION 312

Communications 312
Office automation 329

TRANSPORT AND MACHINERY 342

Road transport 342
Rail transport 374
Maritime transport 381
Air transport 388
Handling 396
Heavy machinery 398

ENERGY 402

Geothermal and fossil energy 402
Hydroelectricity 406
Nuclear energy 408
Solar energy 410
Wind energy 412

SCIENCE 414

Chemistry 414
Physics: electricity and magnetism 416
Physics: optics 418
Measuring devices 422
Scientific symbols 426

SOCIETY 430

City 430
Justice 440
Economy and finance 441
Education 444
Religion 446
Politics 448
Safety 454
Health 460

SPORTS AND GAMES 468

Games 468
Track and field 472
Ball sports 474
Racket sports 490
Gymnastics 496
Combat sports 498
Strength sports 500
Precision and accuracy sports 502
Winter sports 506
Aquatic and nautical sports 516
Cycling 522
Motor sports 523
Sports on wheels 526
Outdoor leisure 528

List of chapters

2 **ASTRONOMY**

14 **EARTH**

50 **VEGETABLE KINGDOM**

66 **ANIMAL KINGDOM**

92 **HUMAN BEING**

120 **FOOD AND KITCHEN**

182 **HOUSE**

216 **DO-IT-YOURSELF AND GARDENING**

238 **CLOTHING**

264 **PERSONAL ADORNMENT AND ARTICLES**

278 **ARTS AND ARCHITECTURE**

312 **COMMUNICATIONS AND OFFICE AUTOMATION**

342 **TRANSPORT AND MACHINERY**

402 **ENERGY**

414 **SCIENCE**

430 **SOCIETY**

468 **SPORTS AND GAMES**

539 **INDEX**

solar system

sistema[M] solare

outer planets
pianeti[M] esterni

50,000 astronomical units
50.000 unità[F] astronomiche

Saturn
Saturno

Jupiter
Giove

Uranus
Urano

Neptune
Nettuno

Sun
Sole[M]

50 astronomical units
50 unità[F] astronomiche

Kuiper belt
cintura[F] di Kuiper

Oort cloud
nube[F] di Oort

planets and satellites

pianeti[M] e satelliti[M]

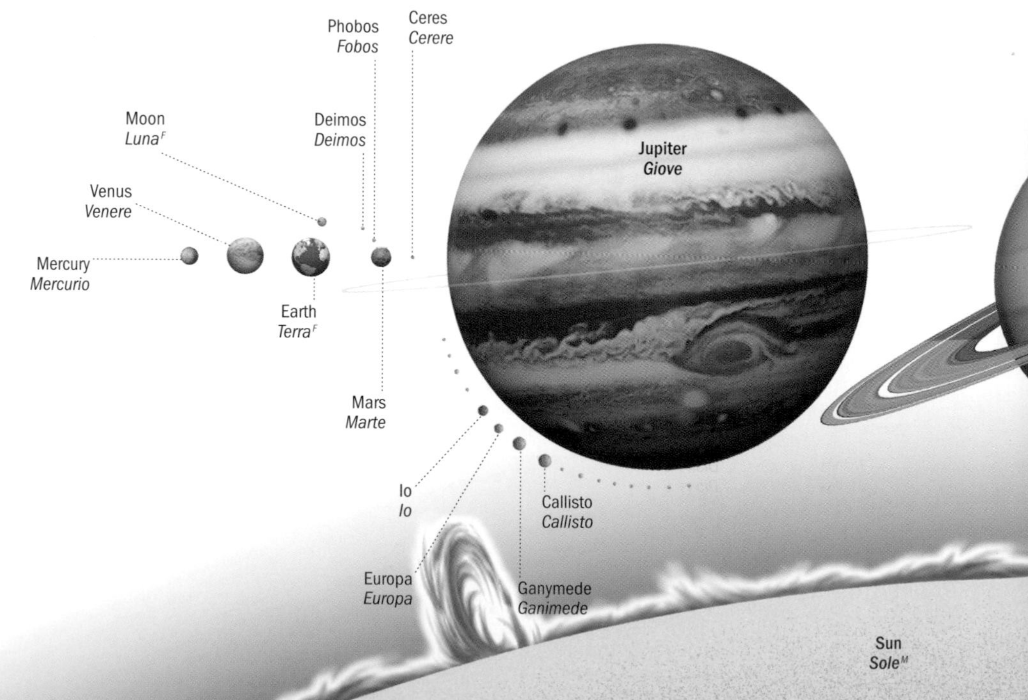

inner planets
pianeti[M] interni

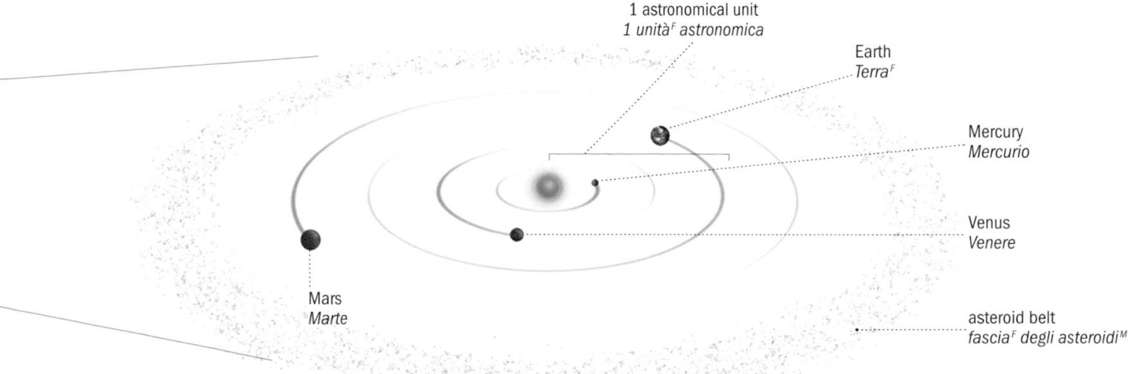

planets and satellites

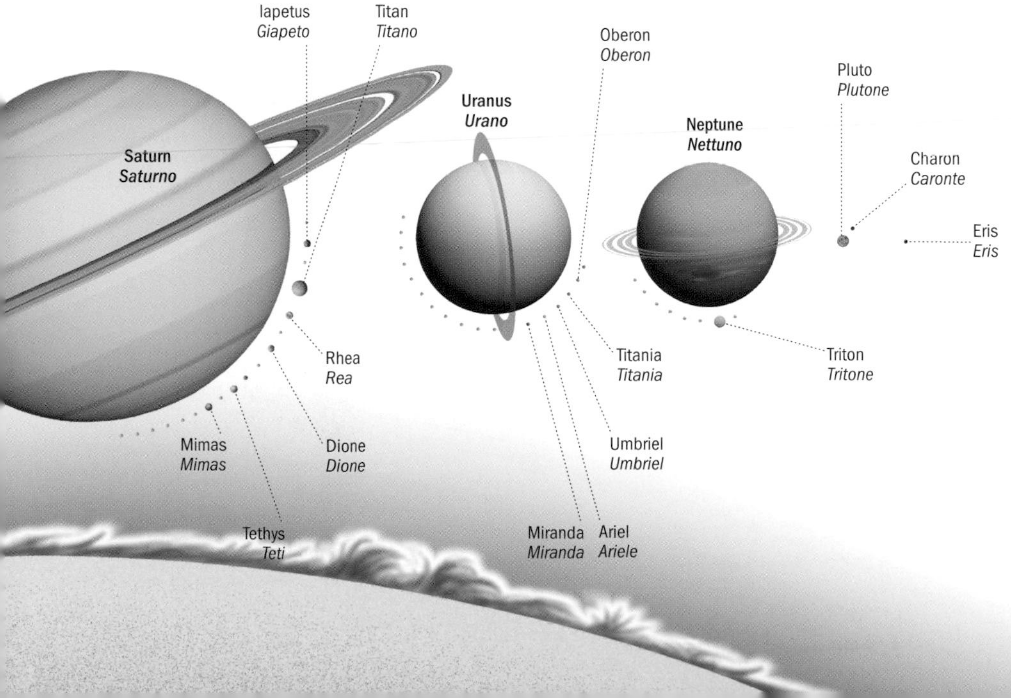

Iapetus *Giapeto*

Titan *Titano*

Oberon *Oberon*

Pluto *Plutone*

Uranus ***Urano***

Neptune ***Nettuno***

Saturn ***Saturno***

Charon *Caronte*

Eris *Eris*

Rhea *Rea*

Titania *Titania*

Triton *Tritone*

Mimas *Mimas*

Dione *Dione*

Umbriel *Umbriel*

Tethys *Teti*

Miranda *Miranda*

Ariel *Ariele*

Sun

Sole[M]

structure of the Sun
struttura[F] del Sole[M]

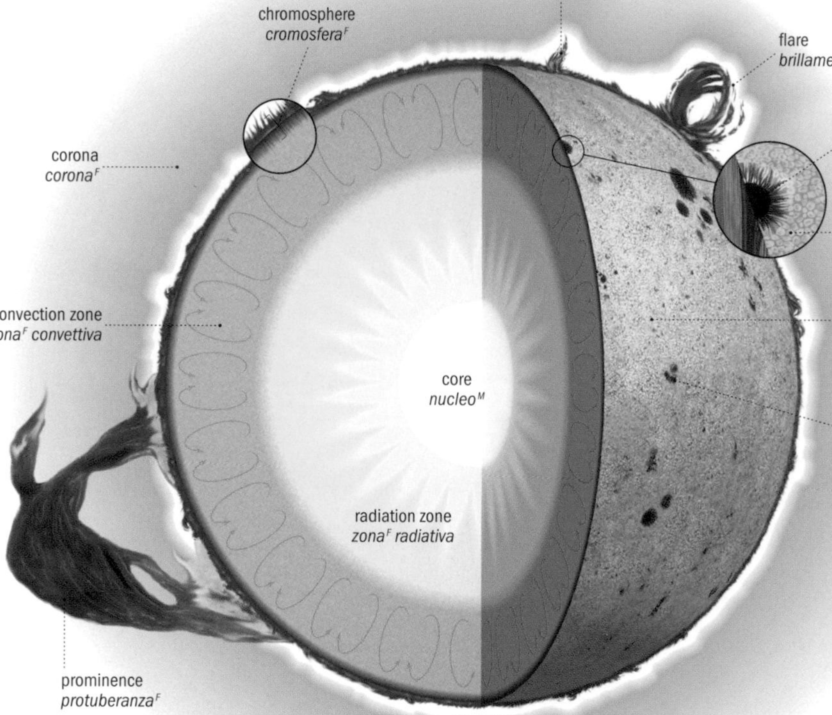

spicules
spicole[F]

chromosphere
cromosfera[F]

flare
brillamento[M]

sunspot
macchia[F] solare

corona
corona[F]

granulation
granulazione[F]

photosphere
fotosfera[F]

convection zone
zona[F] convettiva

core
nucleo[M]

faculae
facole[F]

radiation zone
zona[F] radiativa

prominence
protuberanza[F]

types of eclipses
tipi[M] di eclissi[F]

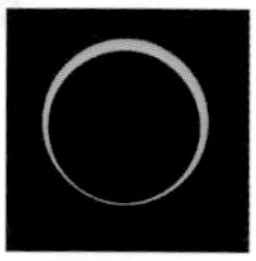

annular eclipse
eclissi[F] anulare

solar eclipse
eclissi[F] di Sole[M]

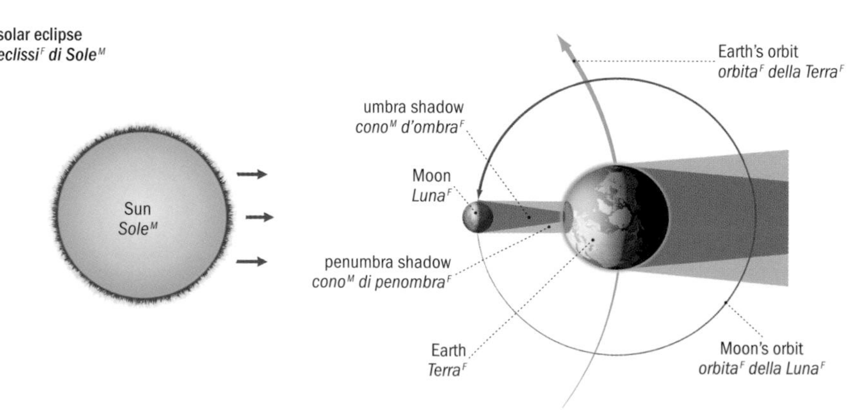

partial eclipse
eclissi[F] parziale

total eclipse
eclissi[F] totale

Moon
Luna[F]

types of eclipses
tipi[M] di eclissi[F]

partial eclipse
eclissi[F] parziale

total eclipse
eclissi[F] totale

lunar features
caratteristiche[F] della Luna[F]

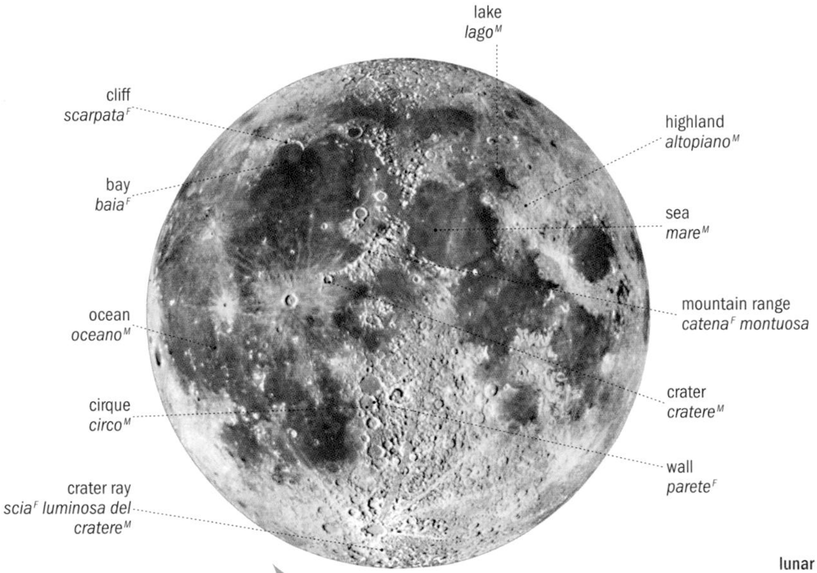

lake
lago[M]

cliff
scarpata[F]

highland
altopiano[M]

bay
baia[F]

sea
mare[M]

mountain range
catena[F] montuosa

ocean
oceano[M]

crater
cratere[M]

cirque
circo[M]

wall
parete[F]

crater ray
scia[F] luminosa del cratere[M]

lunar eclipse
eclissi[F] di Luna[F]

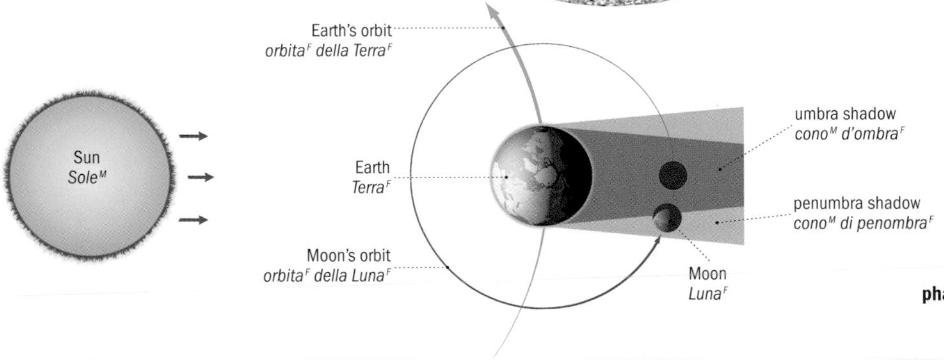

Earth's orbit
orbita[F] della Terra[F]

Sun
Sole[M]

umbra shadow
cono[M] d'ombra[F]

Earth
Terra[F]

penumbra shadow
cono[M] di penombra[F]

Moon's orbit
orbita[F] della Luna[F]

Moon
Luna[F]

phases of the Moon
fasi[F] della Luna[F]

new moon
Luna[F] nuova

new crescent
Luna[F] crescente

first quarter
primo quarto[M]

waxing gibbous
Luna[F] gibbosa crescente

full moon
Luna[F] piena

waning gibbous
Luna[F] gibbosa calante

last quarter
ultimo quarto[M]

old crescent
Luna[F] calante

galaxy

galassia^F

Milky Way
Via^F Lattea

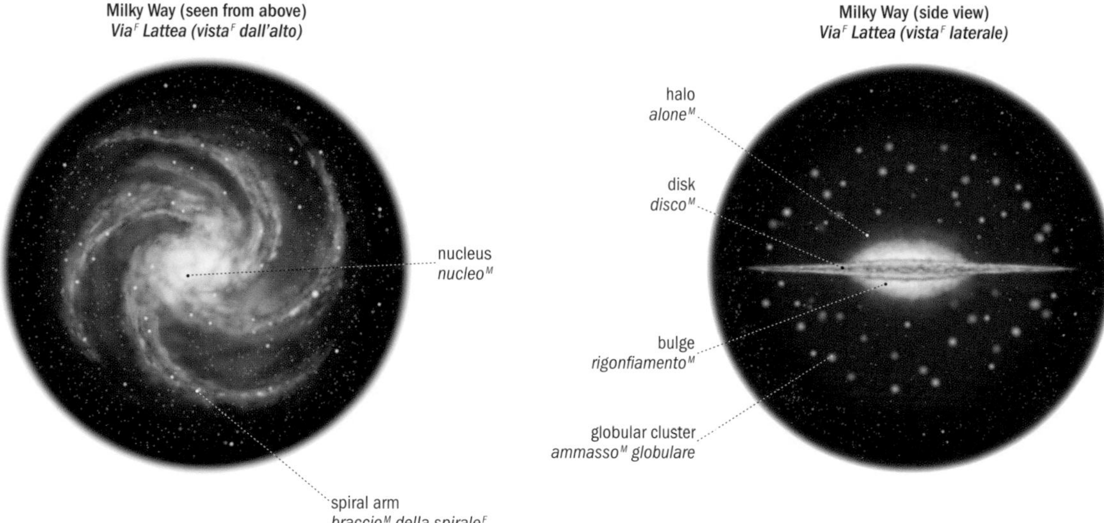

comet

cometa^F

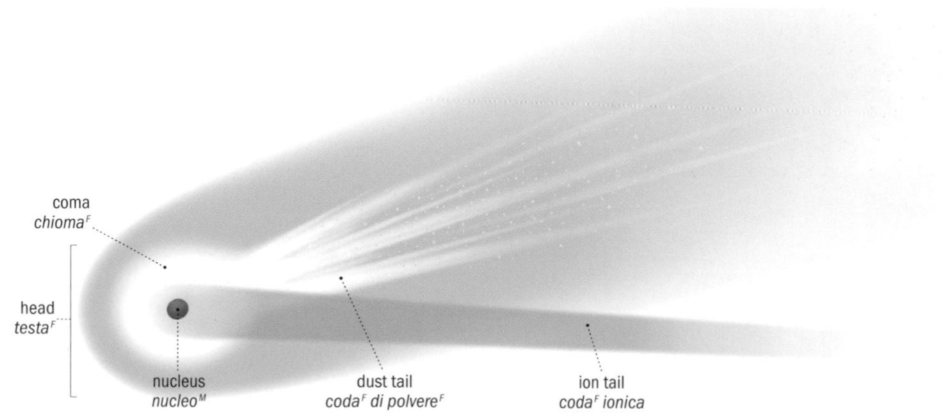

Hubble space telescope

telescopio[M] spaziale Hubble

antenna
antenna[F]
aperture door
portello[M] di apertura[F]
fine guidance system
sistema[M] di guida[F] fine
light shield
schermo[M]
scientific instruments
strumenti[M] scientifici
secondary mirror
specchio[M] secondario
solar panel
pannello[M] solare
primary mirror
specchio[M] primario
aft shroud
protezione[F] posteriore

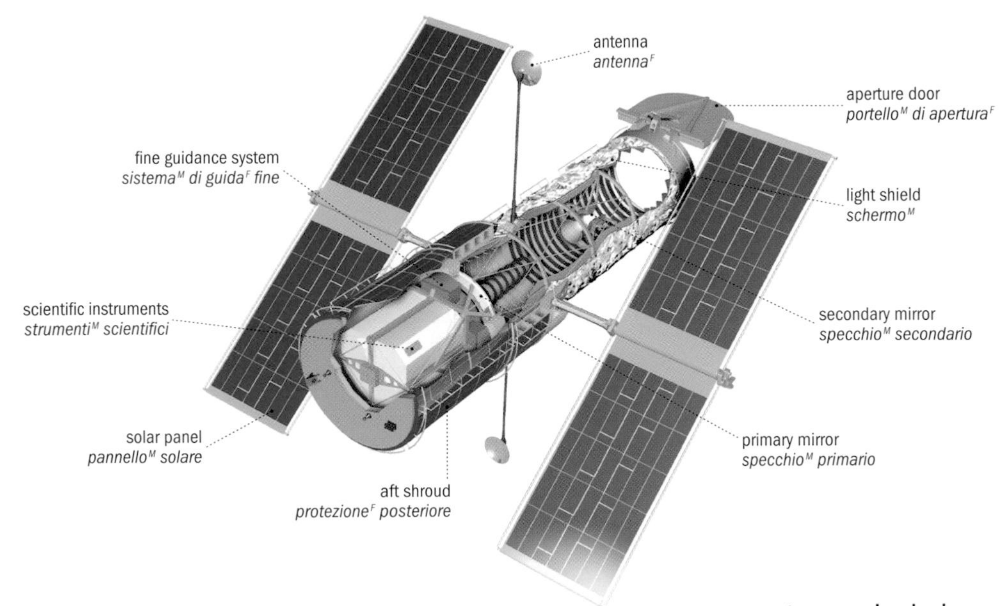

astronomical observatory

osservatorio[M] astronomico

cross section of an astronomical observatory
sezione[F] trasversale di un osservatorio[M] astronomico

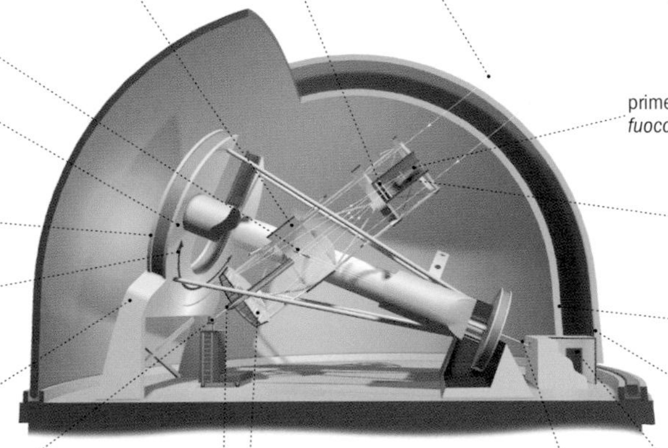

secondary mirror
specchio[M] secondario
telescope
telescopio[M]
light
luce[F]
flat mirror
specchio[M] piano
horseshoe mount
montatura[F] a ferro[M] di cavallo[M]
prime focus
fuoco[M] primario
prime focus observing capsule
cabina[F] di osservazione[F] del fuoco[M] primario
hour angle gear
ingranaggio[M] per il moto[M] orario
polar axis
asse[M] polare
interior dome shell
volta[F] interna della cupola[F]
telescope base
basamento[M] del telescopio[M]
exterior dome shell
volta[F] esterna della cupola[F]
observation post
punto[M] di osservazione[F]
Cassegrain focus
fuoco[M] Cassegrain
primary mirror
specchio[M] primario
coudé focus
fuoco[M] coudé
laboratory
laboratorio[M]

observatory
osservatorio[M]

dome shutter
portellone[M] della cupola[F]
rotating dome
cupola[F] rotante

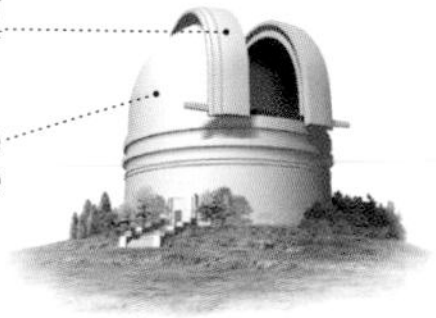

refracting telescope

cannocchiale^M

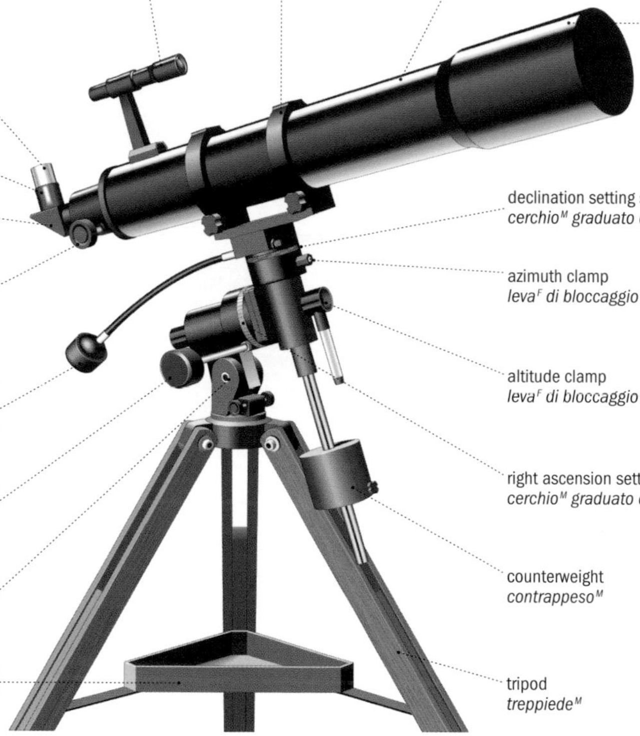

finderscope
cannocchiale^M cercatore
cradle
giogo^M di supporto^M
main tube
tubo^M principale
dew shield
paraluce^M
eyepiece
oculare^M
eyepiece holder
portaoculare^M
star diagonal
prisma^M astronomico
declination setting scale
cerchio^M graduato della declinazione^F
azimuth clamp
leva^F di bloccaggio^M dell'asse^M orizzontale
focusing knob
manopola^F della messa^F a fuoco^M
altitude clamp
leva^F di bloccaggio^M dell'altezza^F
azimuth fine adjustment
regolazione^F micrometrica dell'asse^M orizzontale
right ascension setting scale
cerchio^M graduato dell'ascensione^F retta
altitude fine adjustment
regolazione^F micrometrica dell'altezza^F
counterweight
contrappeso^M
fork
forcella^F
tripod accessories shelf
mensola^F portaccessori
tripod
treppiede^M

cross section of a refracting telescope
sezione^F di un cannocchiale^M

light
luce^F
eyepiece
oculare^M
objective lens
obiettivo^M
main tube
tubo^M principale

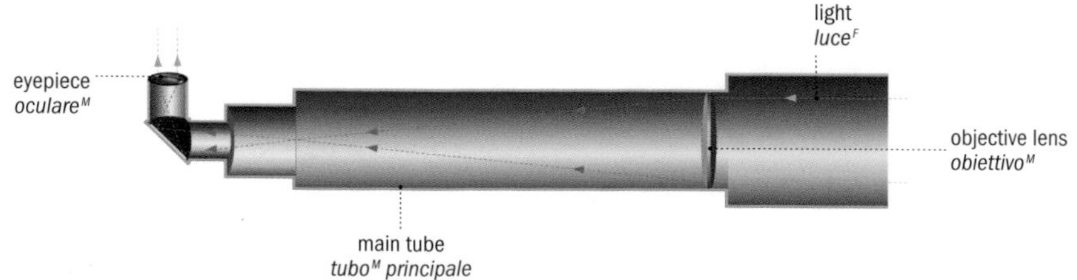

reflecting telescope

telescopio^M

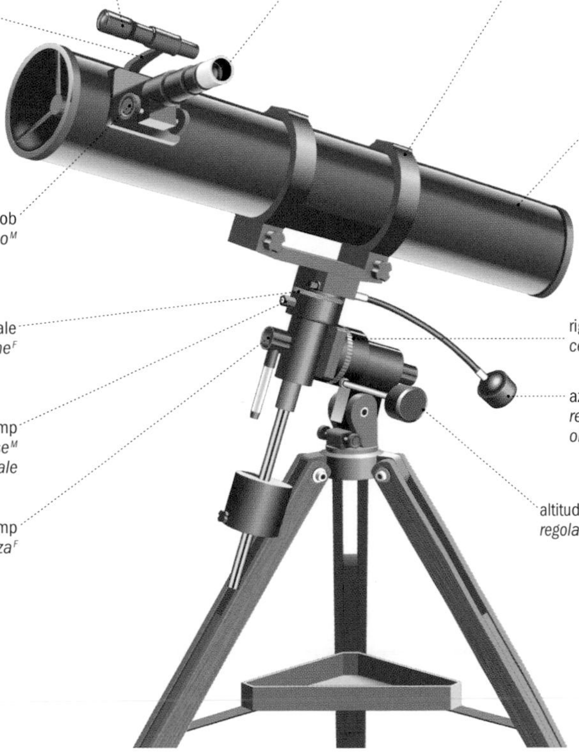

finderscope
cannocchiale^M cercatore
eyepiece
oculare^M
cradle
giogo^M di supporto^M
support
supporto^M
main tube
tubo^M principale
focusing knob
manopola^F della messa^F a fuoco^M
declination setting scale
cerchio^M graduato della declinazione^F
right ascension setting scale
cerchio^M graduato dell'ascensione^F retta
azimuth fine adjustment
regolazione^F micrometrica dell'asse^M orizzontale
azimuth clamp
leva^F di bloccaggio^M dell'asse^M orizzontale
altitude fine adjustment
regolazione^F micrometrica dell'altezza^F
altitude clamp
leva^F di bloccaggio^M dell'altezza^F

cross section of a reflecting telescope
sezione^F di un telescopio^M

eyepiece
oculare^M
secondary mirror
specchio^M secondario
concave primary mirror
specchio^M primario concavo
light
luce^F
main tube
tubo^M principale

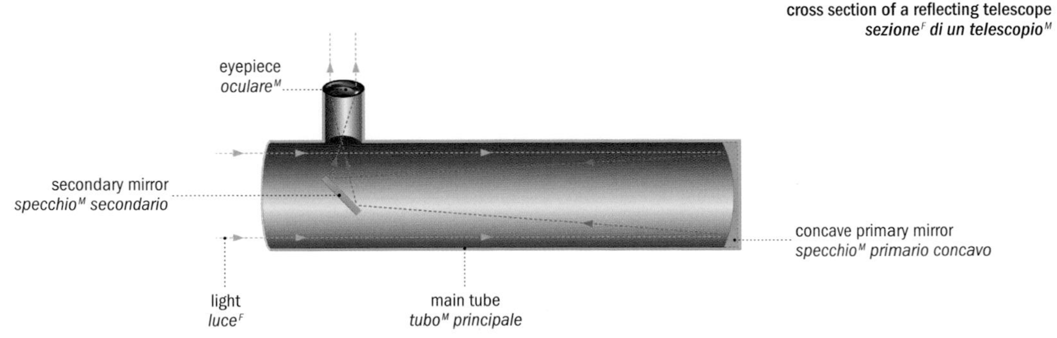

spacesuit

tuta[F] spaziale

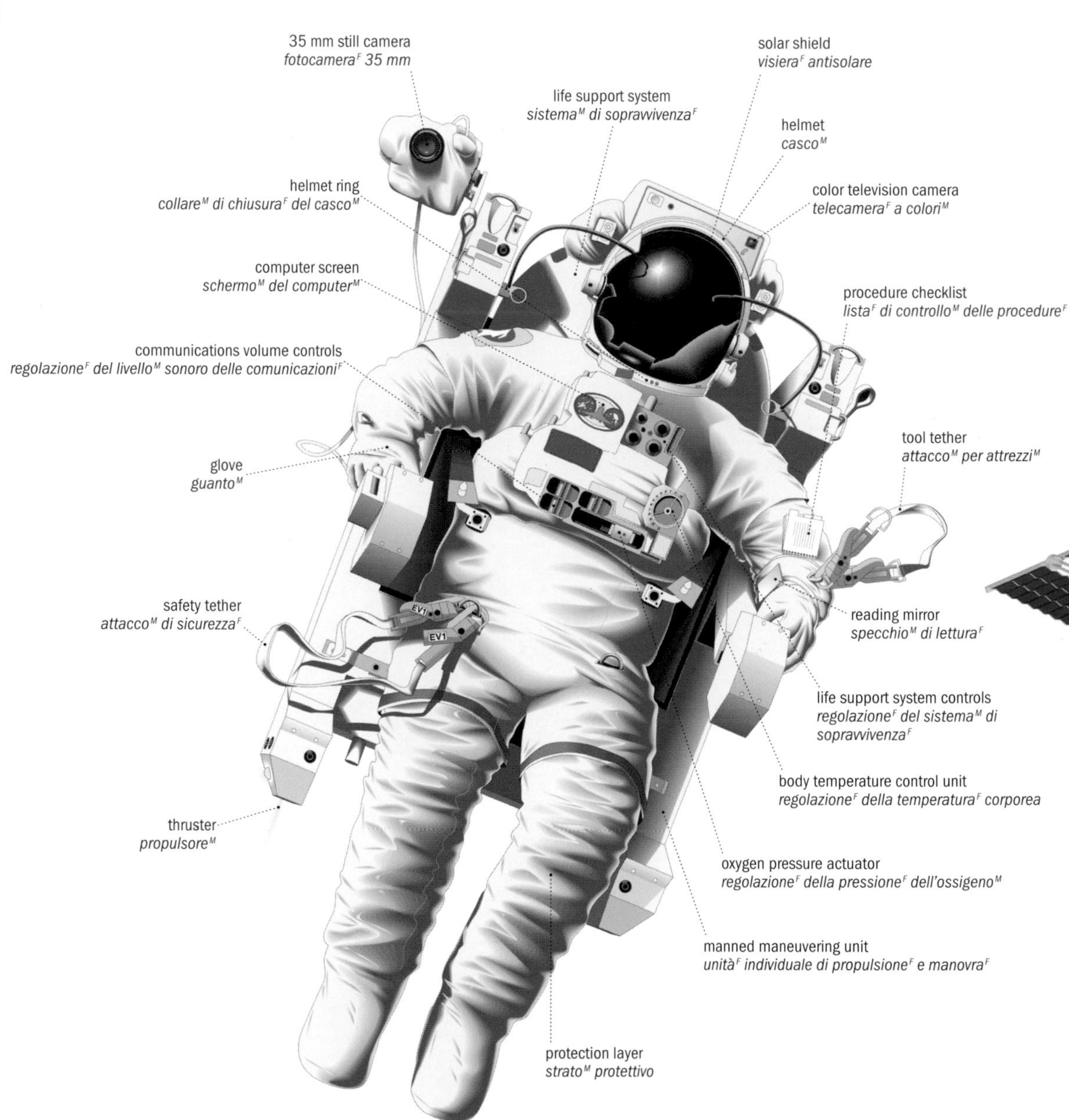

international space station

stazione^F spaziale internazionale

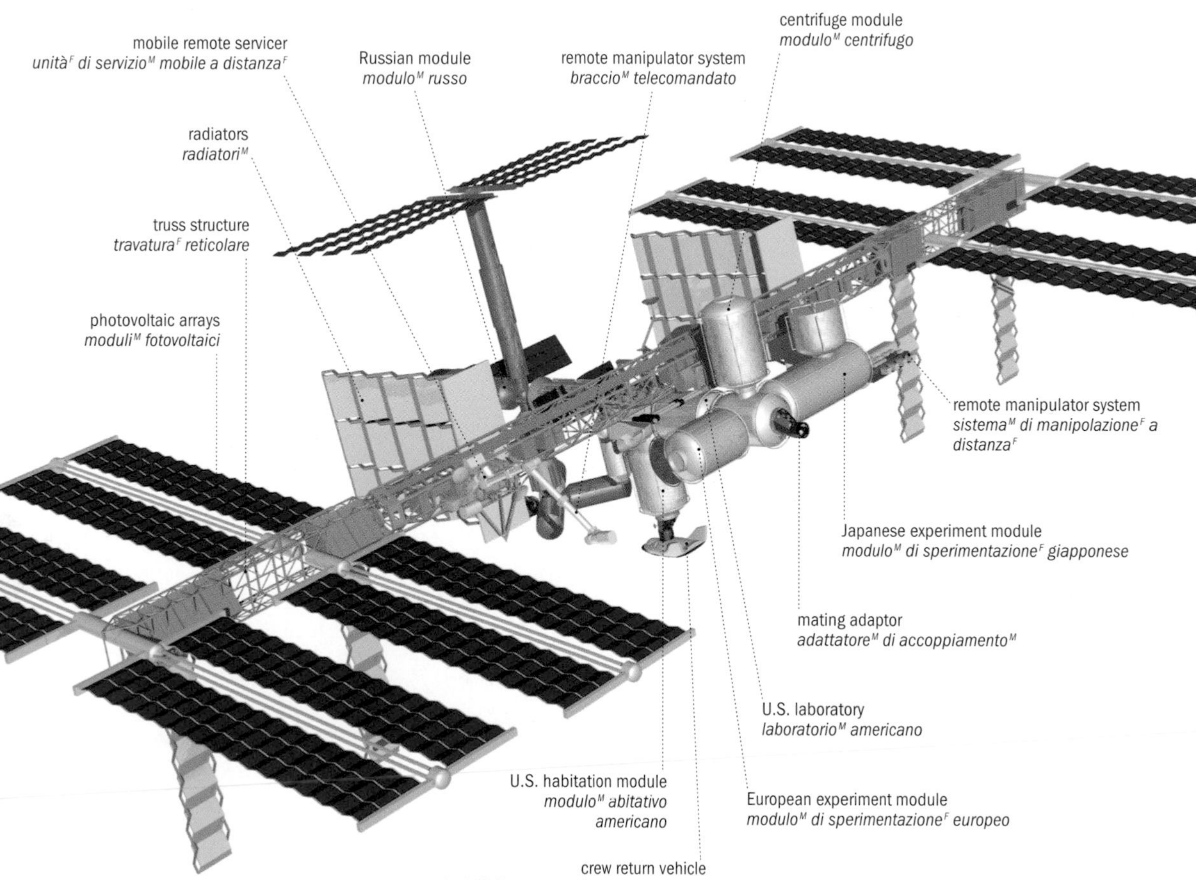

space shuttle

navetta[F] spaziale

space shuttle at takeoff
navetta[F] spaziale al decollo[M]

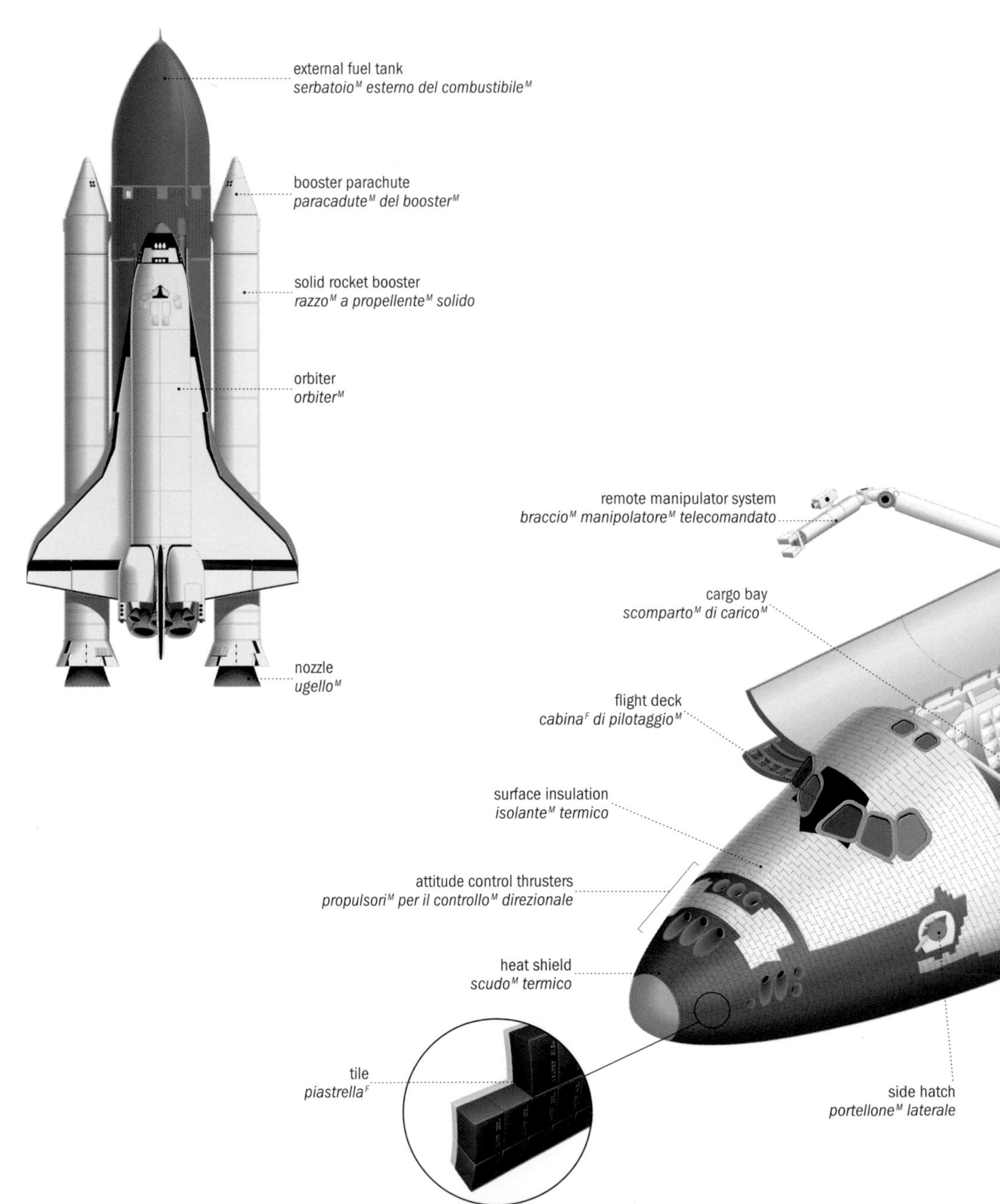

orbiter
*orbiter*M

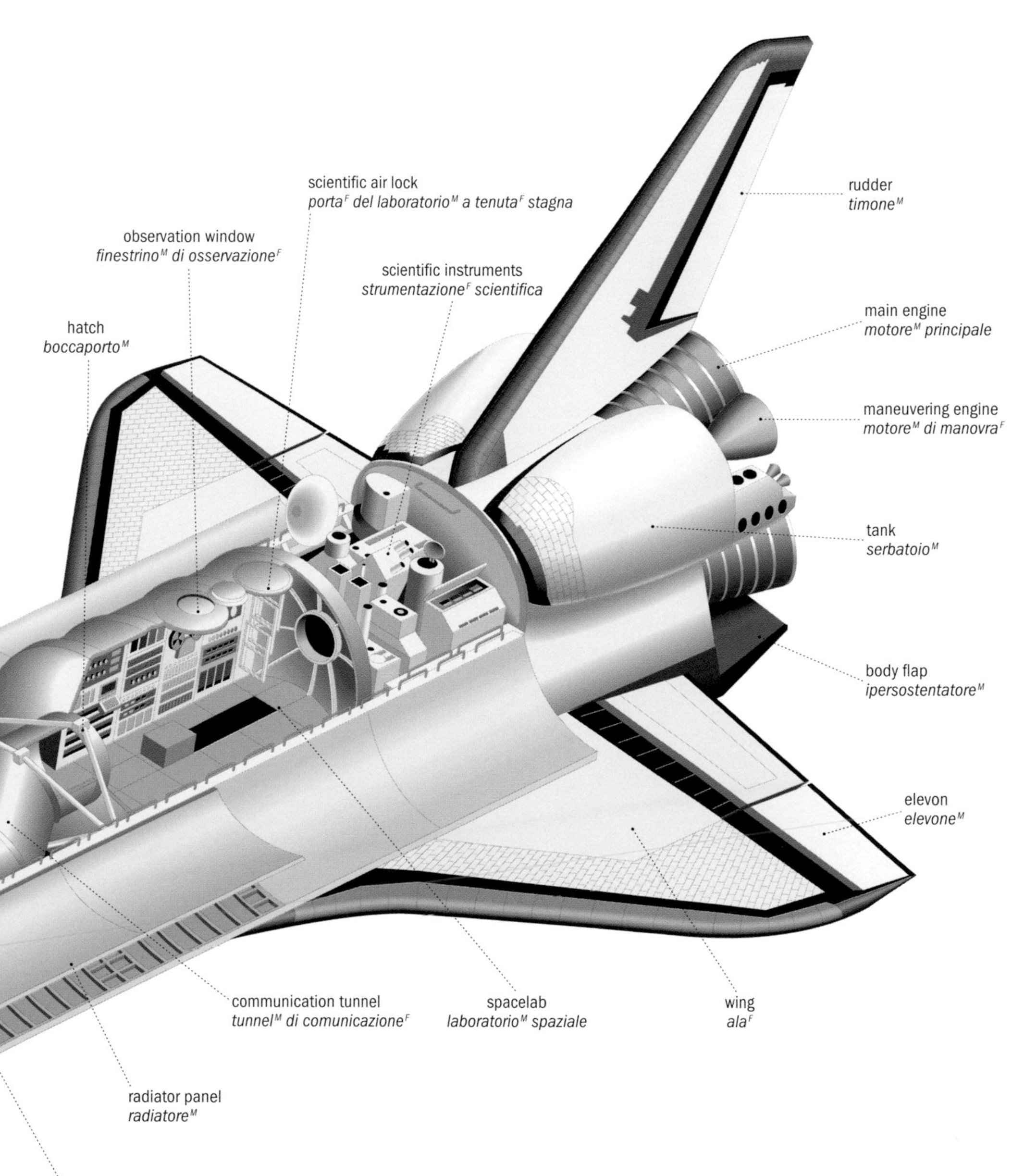

configuration of the continents

carta[F] dei continenti[M]

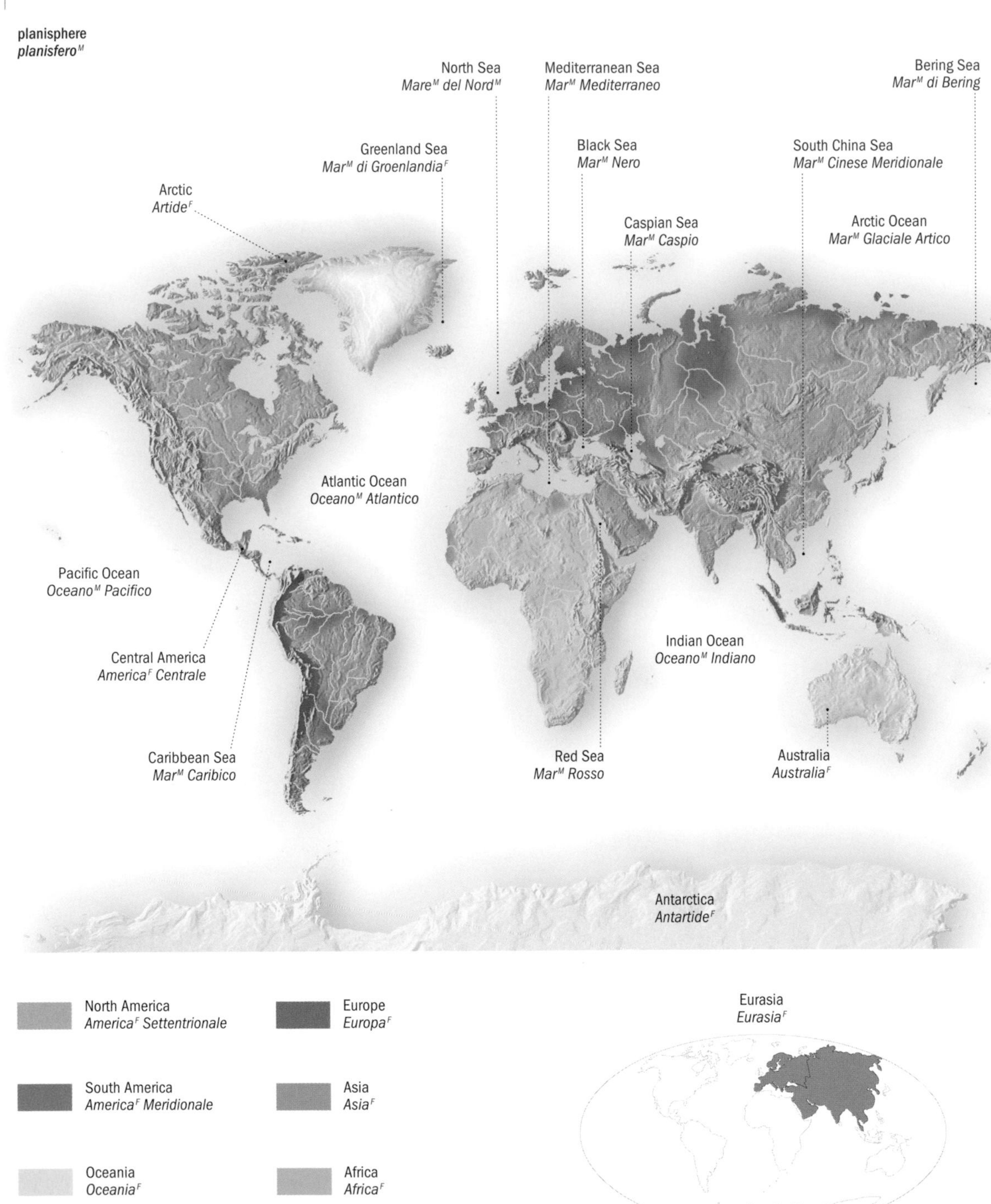

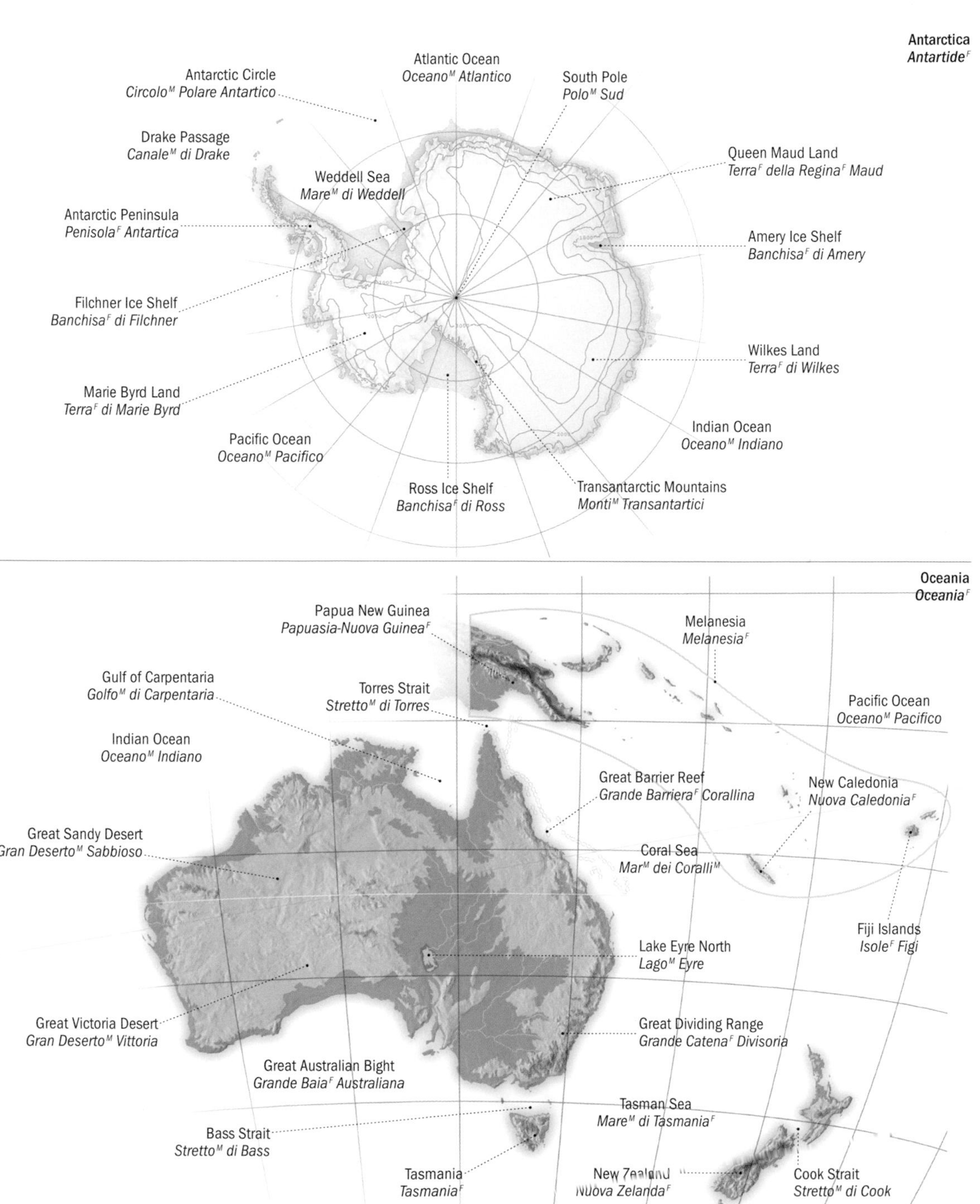
Antarctica
Antartide[F]
Atlantic Ocean
Oceano[M] *Atlantico*
Antarctic Circle
Circolo[M] *Polare Antartico*
South Pole
Polo[M] *Sud*
Drake Passage
Canale[M] *di Drake*
Weddell Sea
Mare[M] *di Weddell*
Queen Maud Land
Terra[F] *della Regina*[F] *Maud*
Antarctic Peninsula
Penisola[F] *Antartica*
Amery Ice Shelf
Banchisa[F] *di Amery*
Filchner Ice Shelf
Banchisa[F] *di Filchner*
Wilkes Land
Terra[F] *di Wilkes*
Marie Byrd Land
Terra[F] *di Marie Byrd*
Indian Ocean
Oceano[M] *Indiano*
Pacific Ocean
Oceano[M] *Pacifico*
Ross Ice Shelf
Banchisa[F] *di Ross*
Transantarctic Mountains
Monti[M] *Transantartici*
Oceania
Oceania[F]
Papua New Guinea
Papuasia-Nuova Guinea[F]
Melanesia
Melanesia[F]
Gulf of Carpentaria
Golfo[M] *di Carpentaria*
Torres Strait
Stretto[M] *di Torres*
Pacific Ocean
Oceano[M] *Pacifico*
Indian Ocean
Oceano[M] *Indiano*
Great Barrier Reef
Grande Barriera[F] *Corallina*
New Caledonia
Nuova Caledonia[F]
Great Sandy Desert
Gran Deserto[M] *Sabbioso*
Coral Sea
Mar[M] *dei Coralli*[M]
Fiji Islands
Isole[F] *Figi*
Lake Eyre North
Lago[M] *Eyre*
Great Victoria Desert
Gran Deserto[M] *Vittoria*
Great Dividing Range
Grande Catena[F] *Divisoria*
Great Australian Bight
Grande Baia[F] *Australiana*
Tasman Sea
Mare[M] *di Tasmania*[F]
Bass Strait
Stretto[M] *di Bass*
Tasmania
Tasmania[F]
New Zealand
Nuova Zelanda[F]
Cook Strait
Stretto[M] *di Cook*

North America
America^F Settentrionale

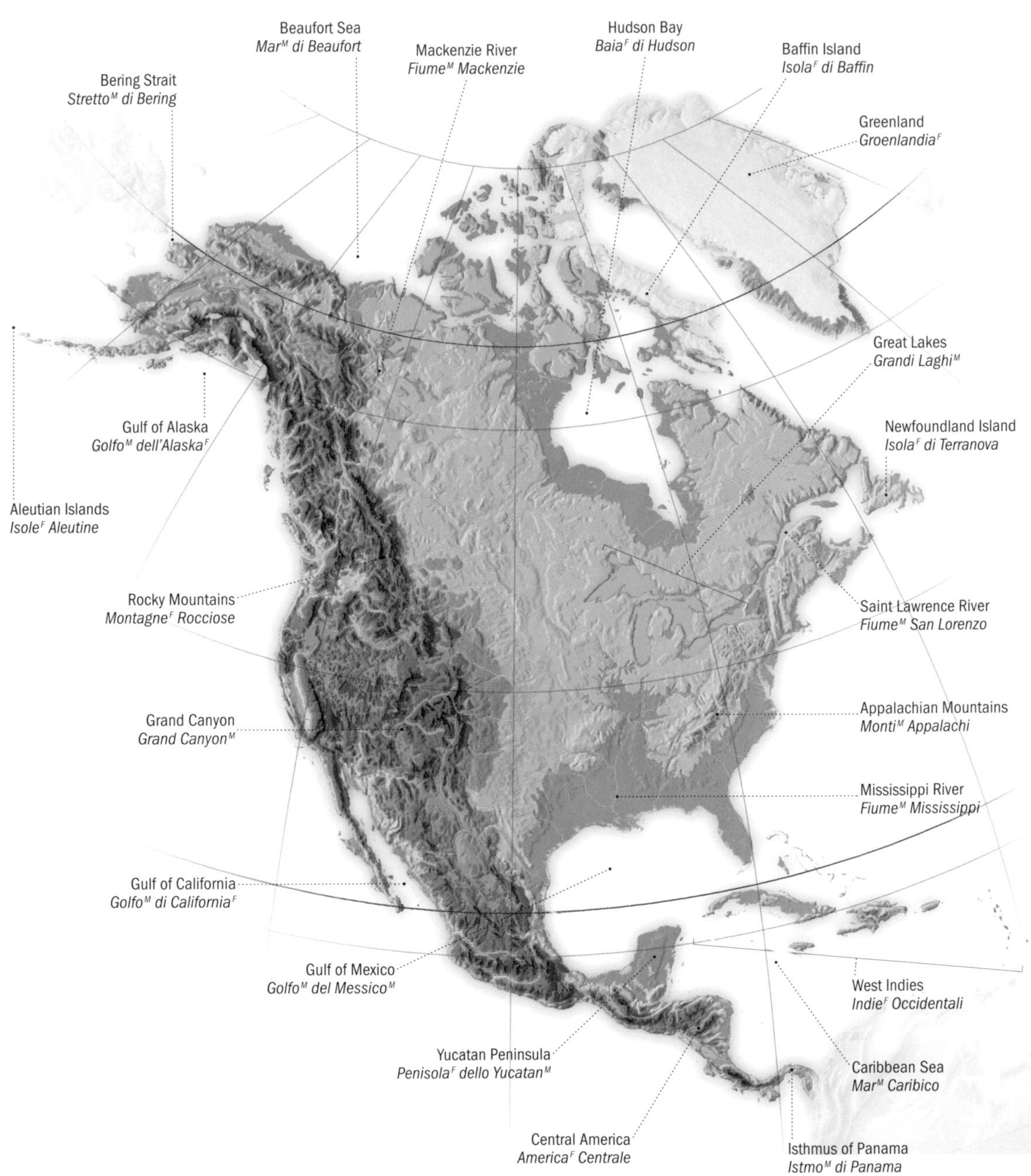

South America
America^F Meridionale

configuration of the continents

EARTH

Europe
EuropaF

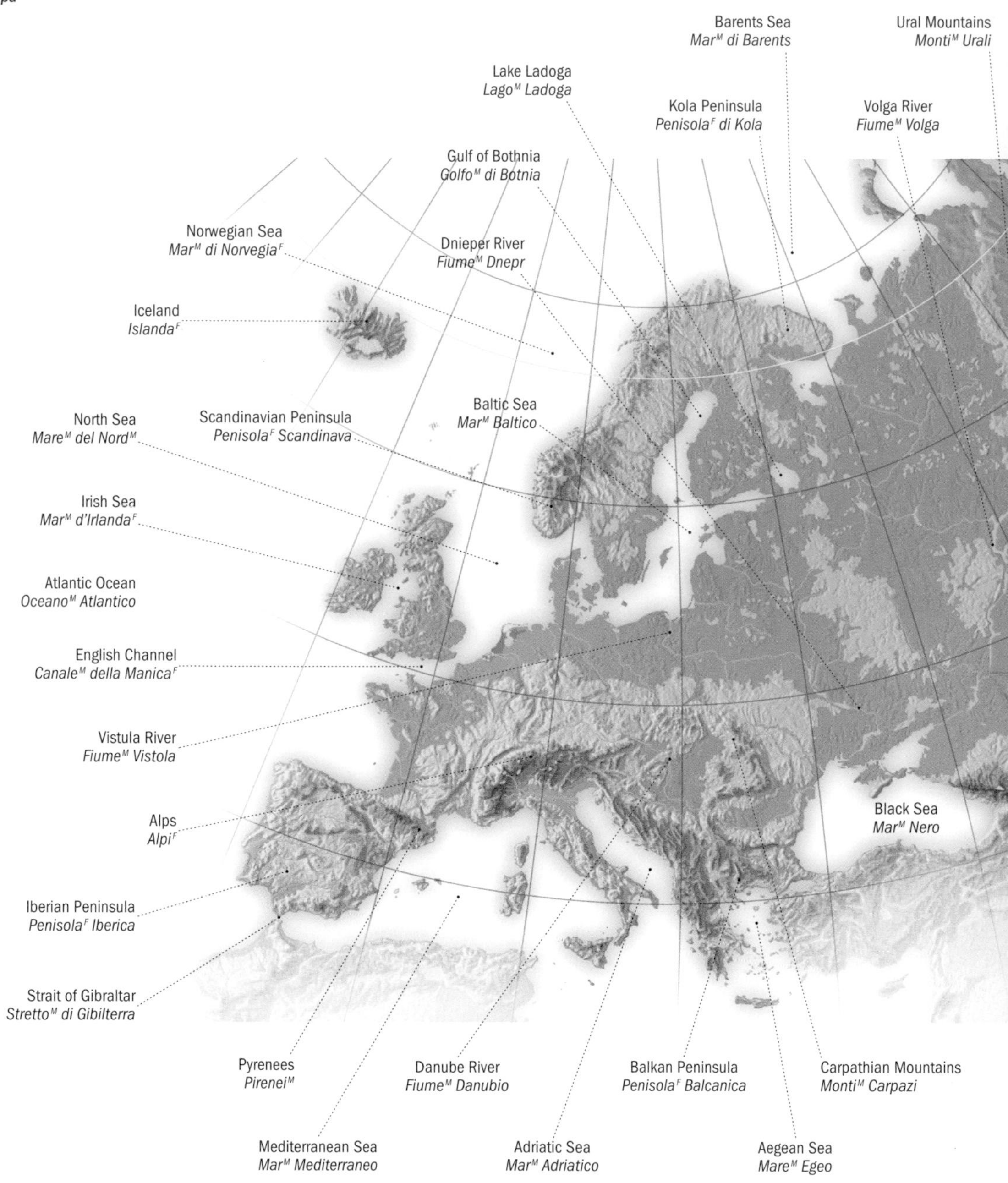

Asia
Asia[F]

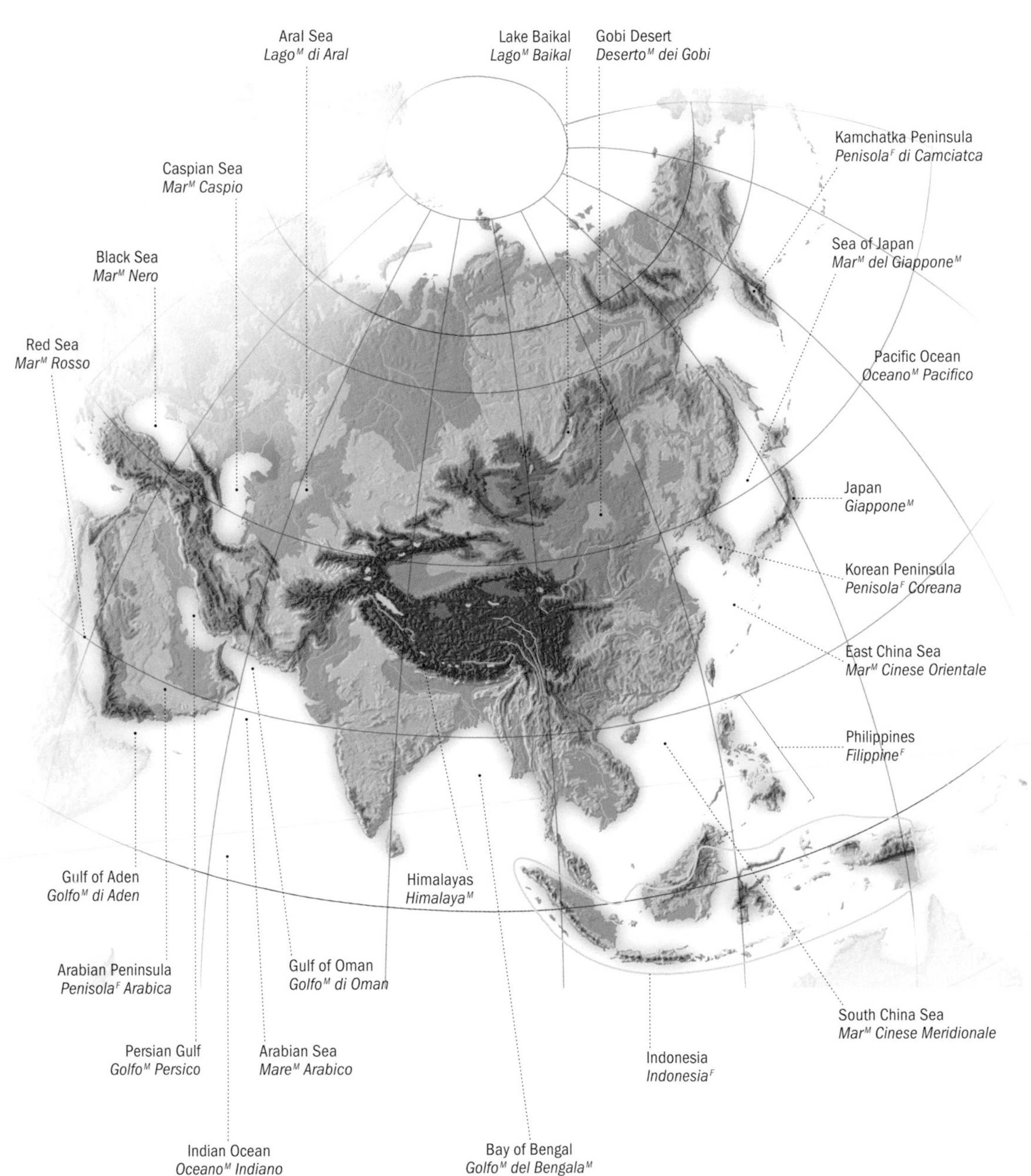
Aral Sea
Lago[M] di Aral
Lake Baikal
Lago[M] Baikal
Gobi Desert
Deserto[M] dei Gobi
Caspian Sea
Mar[M] Caspio
Kamchatka Peninsula
Penisola[F] di Camciatca
Black Sea
Mar[M] Nero
Sea of Japan
Mar[M] del Giappone[M]
Red Sea
Mar[M] Rosso
Pacific Ocean
Oceano[M] Pacifico
Japan
Giappone[M]
Korean Peninsula
Penisola[F] Coreana
East China Sea
Mar[M] Cinese Orientale
Philippines
Filippine[F]
Gulf of Aden
Golfo[M] di Aden
Himalayas
Himalaya[M]
Arabian Peninsula
Penisola[F] Arabica
Gulf of Oman
Golfo[M] di Oman
South China Sea
Mar[M] Cinese Meridionale
Persian Gulf
Golfo[M] Persico
Arabian Sea
Mare[M] Arabico
Indonesia
Indonesia[F]
Indian Ocean
Oceano[M] Indiano
Bay of Bengal
Golfo[M] del Bengala[M]

Africa
Africa[F]

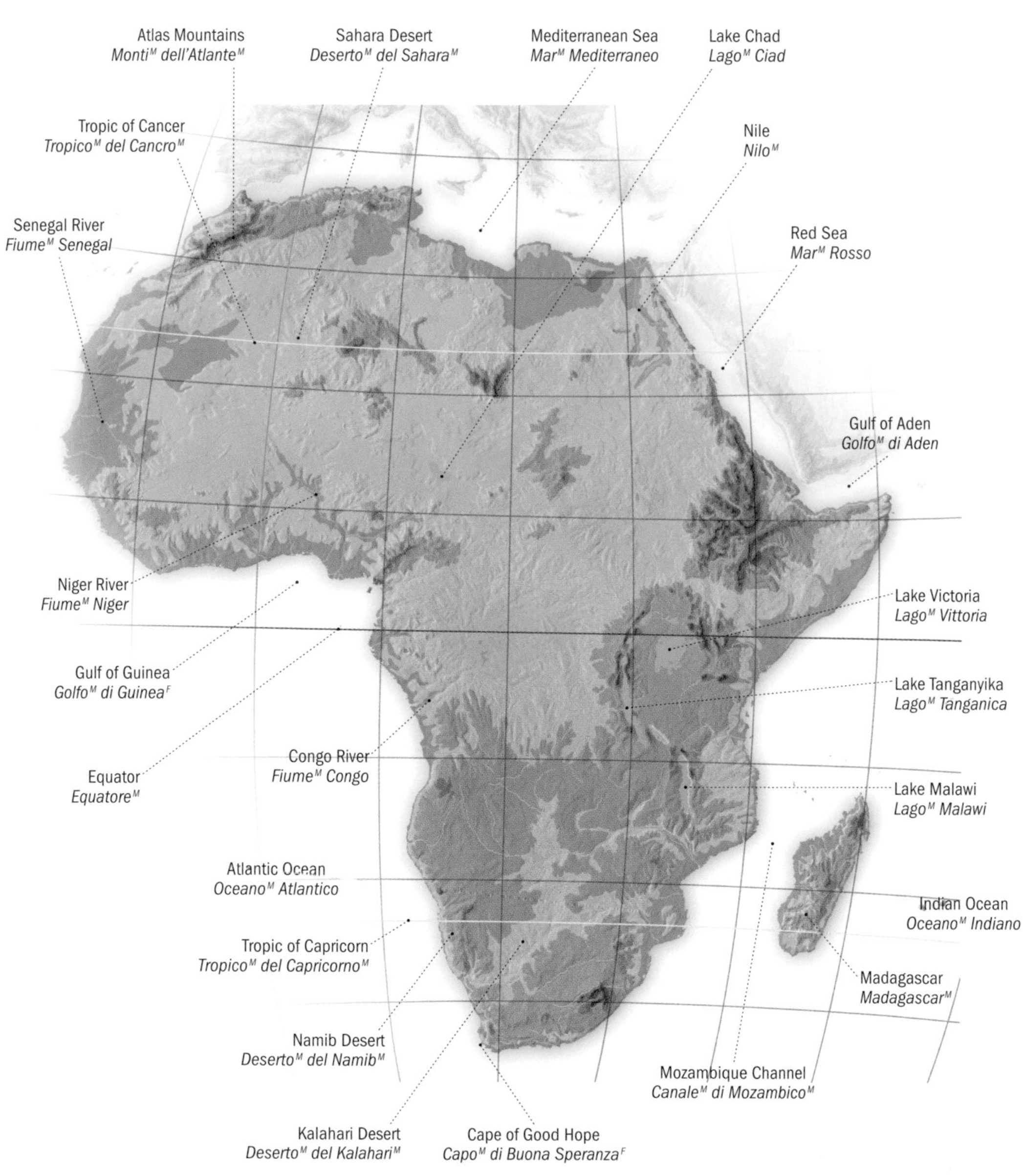

cartography
cartografia[F]

Earth coordinate system
sistema[M] di coordinate[F] terrestri

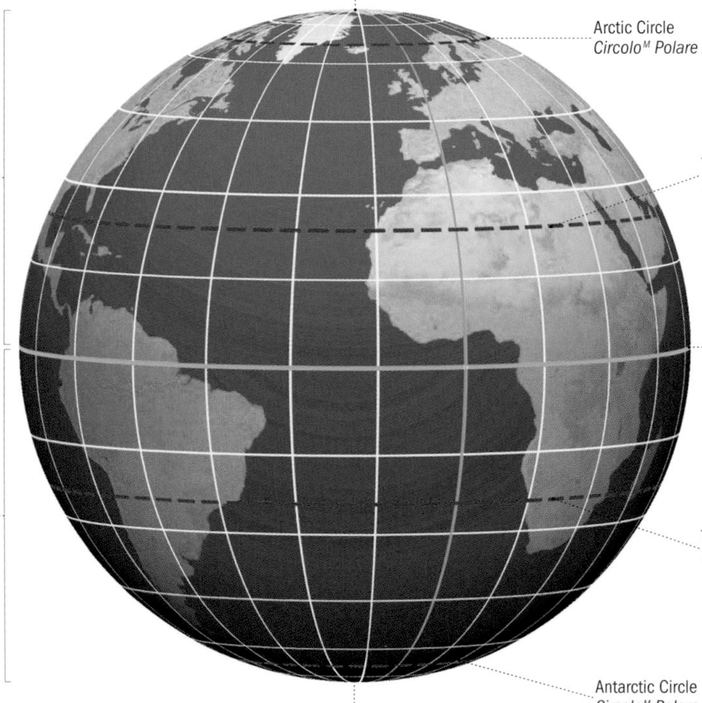

North Pole
Polo[M] Nord
Arctic Circle
Circolo[M] Polare Artico
Northern hemisphere
emisfero[M] settentrionale
Tropic of Cancer
Tropico[M] del Cancro[M]
Equator
Equatore[M]
Southern hemisphere
emisfero[M] meridionale
Tropic of Capricorn
Tropico[M] del Capricorno[M]
Antarctic Circle
Circolo[M] Polare Antartico
South Pole
Polo[M] Sud

hemispheres
emisferi[M]

Northern hemisphere
emisfero[M] settentrionale
Southern hemisphere
emisfero[M] meridionale

Western hemisphere
emisfero[M] occidentale
Eastern hemisphere
emisfero[M] orientale

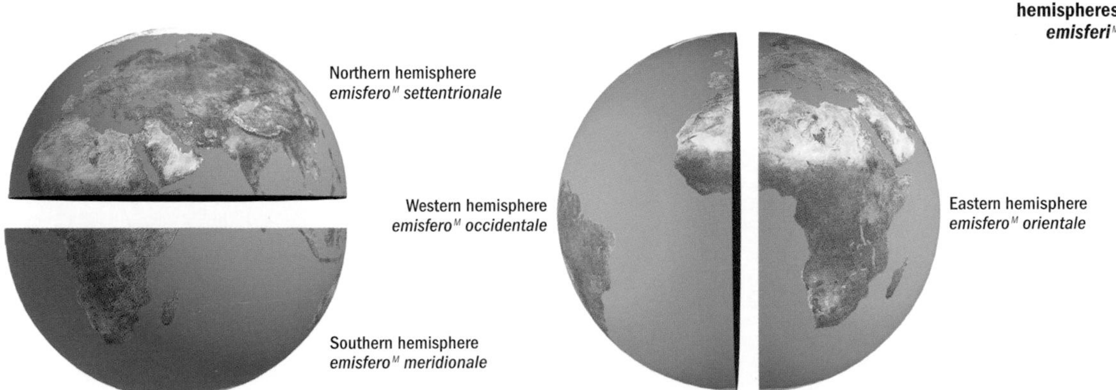

grid system
reticolato^M geografico

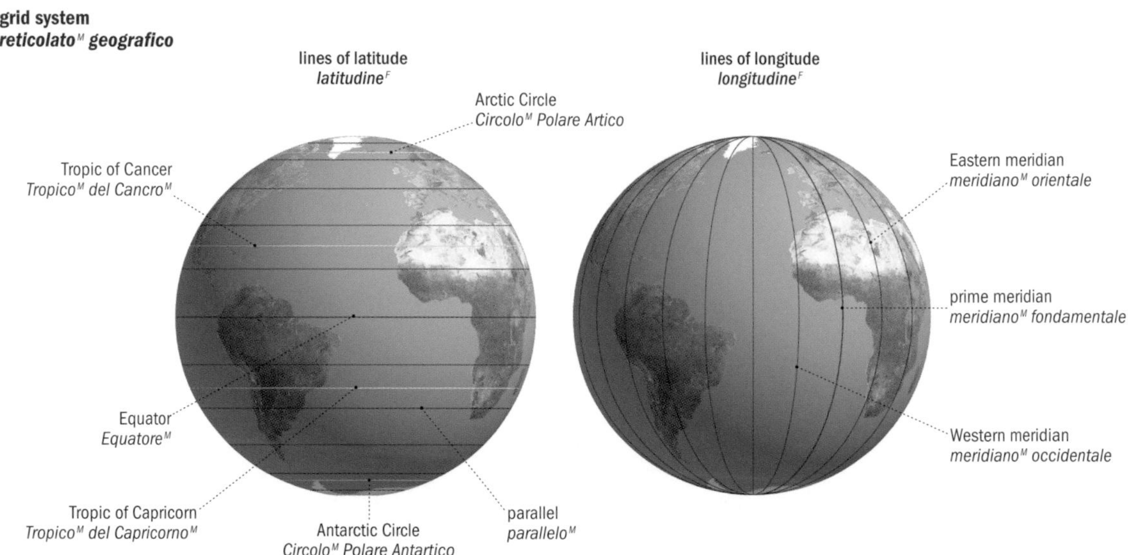

map projections
proiezioni^F cartografiche

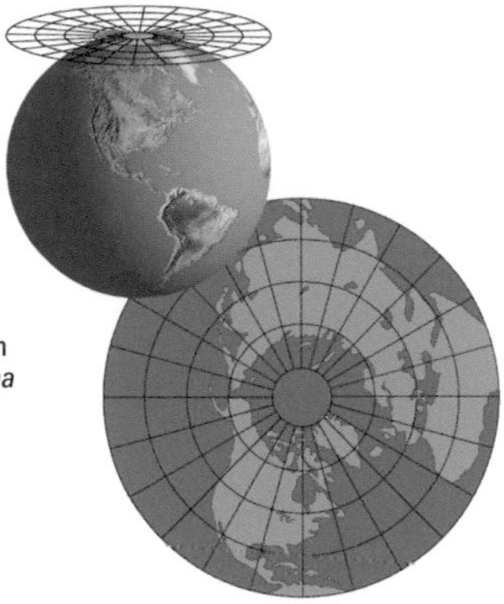

plane projection
proiezione^F piana

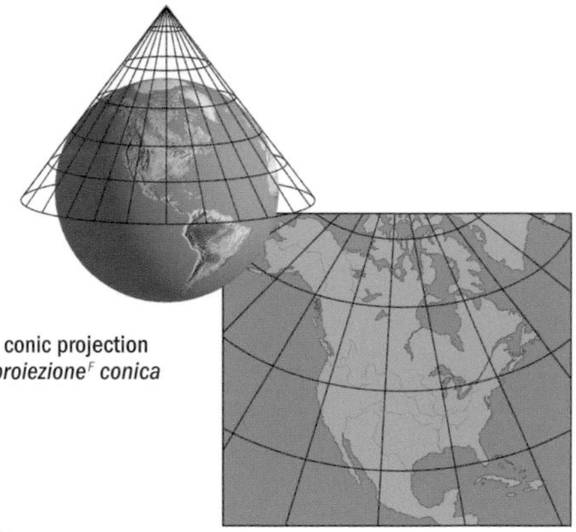

conic projection
proiezione^F conica

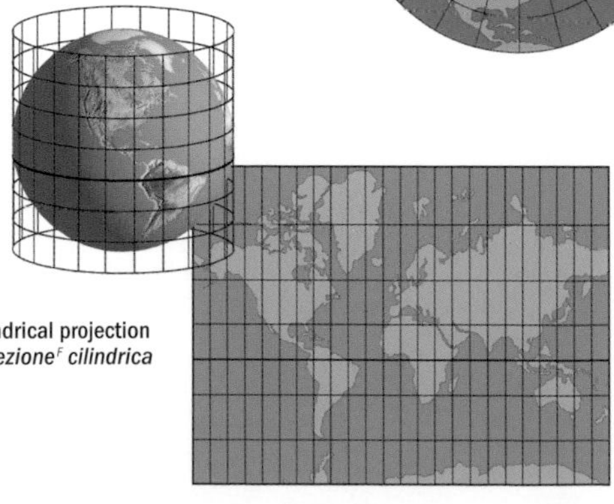

cylindrical projection
proiezione^F cilindrica

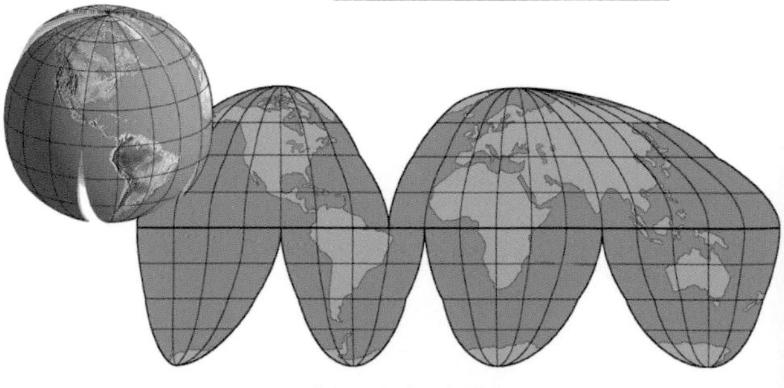

interrupted projection
proiezione^F interrotta

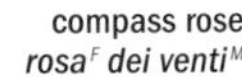

compass rose
***rosa*[F] *dei venti*[M]**

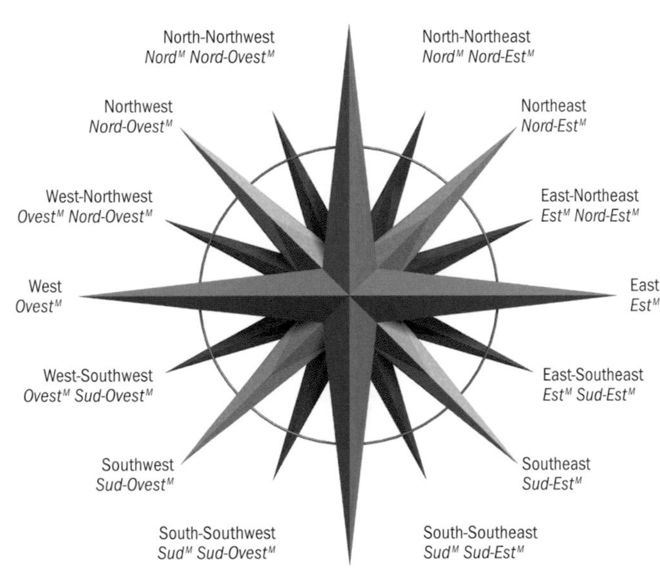

political map
carta*[F] *politica

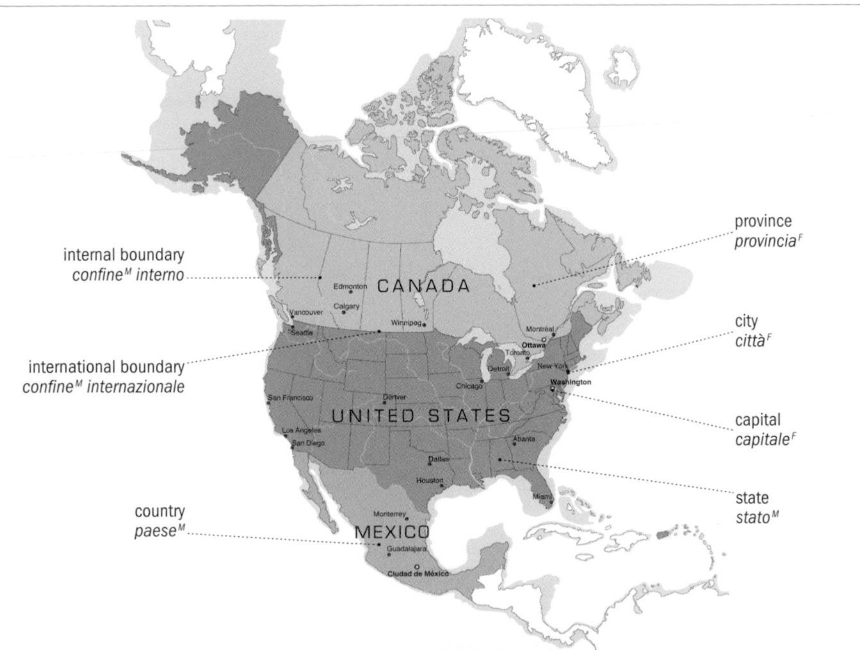

physical map
carta*[F] *fisica

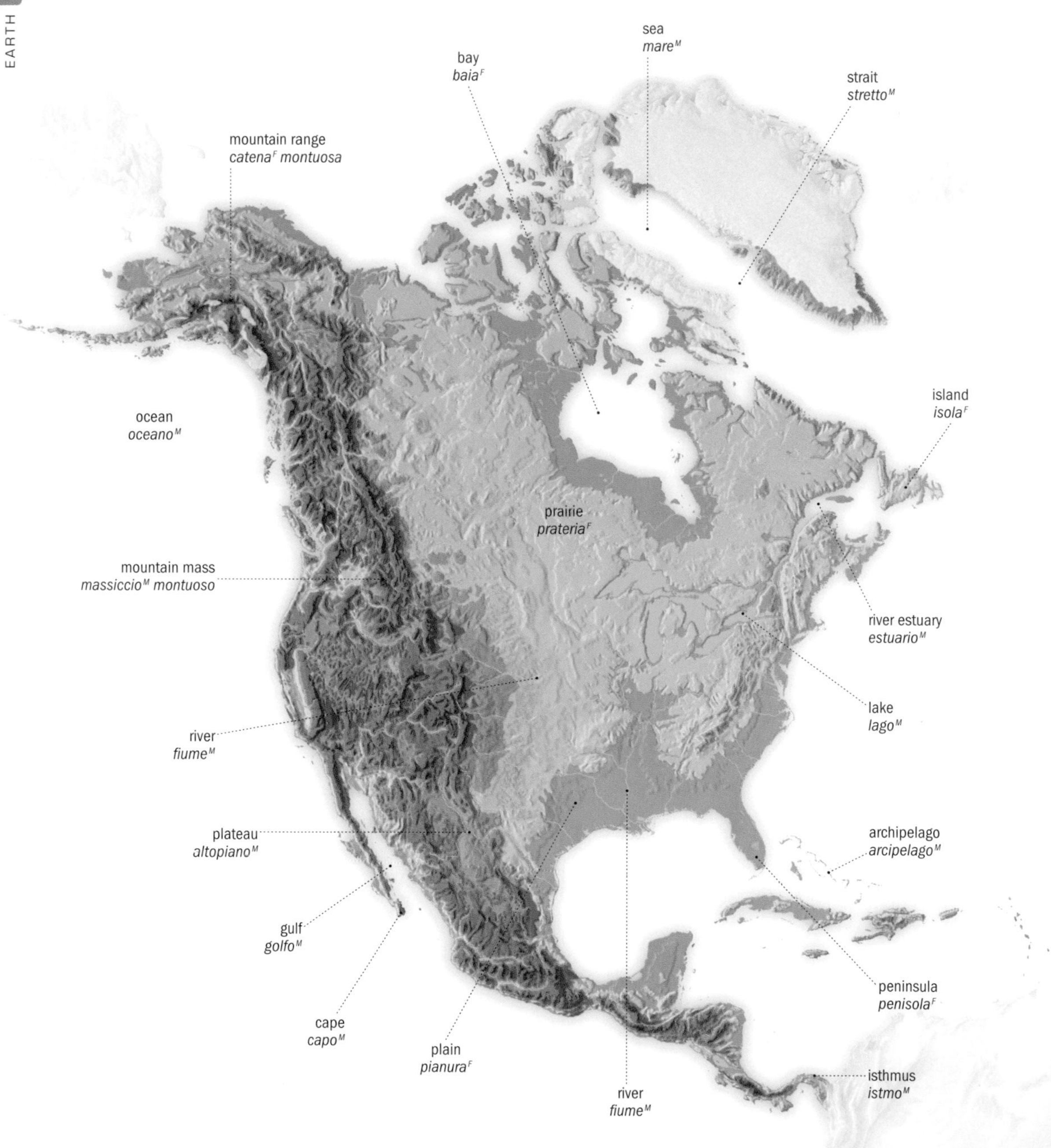

urban map
***pianta*[F] *di città*[F]**

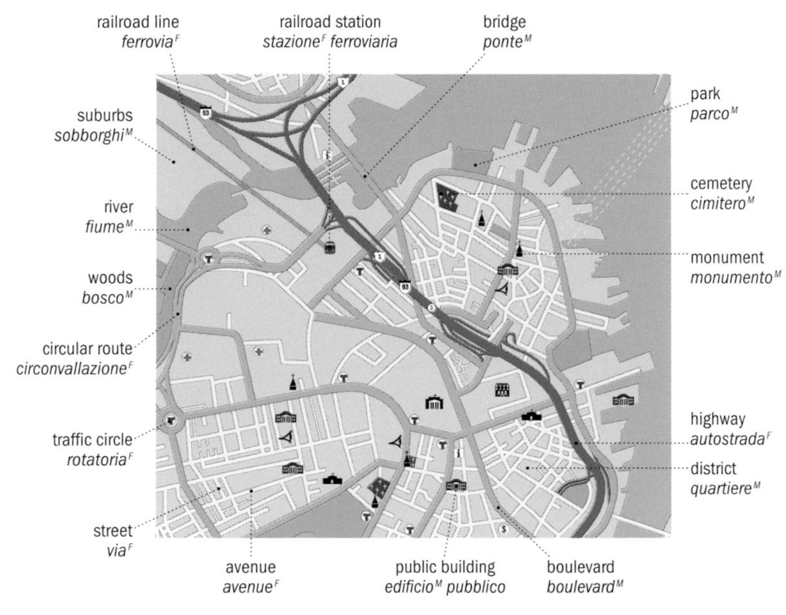

road map
carta*[F] *stradale

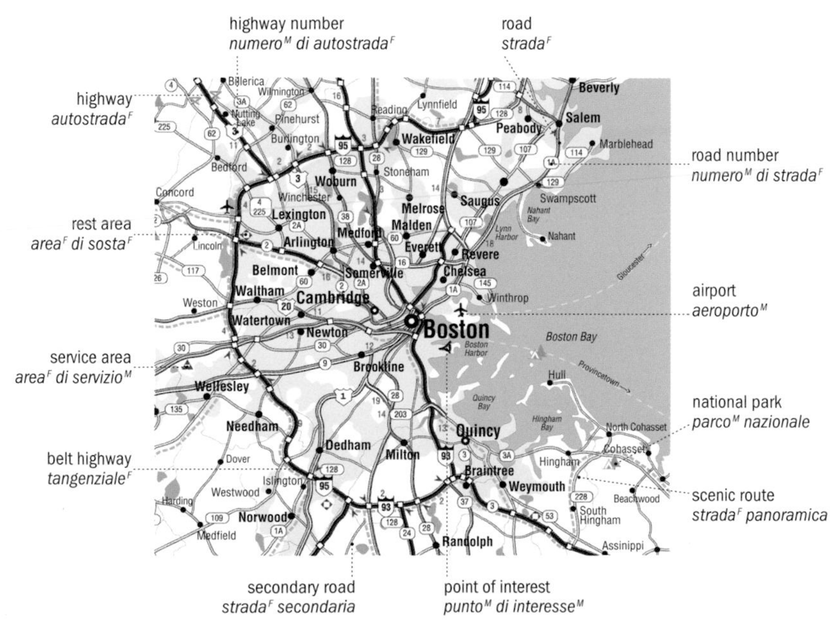

section of the Earth's crust

sezione[F] della crosta[F] terrestre

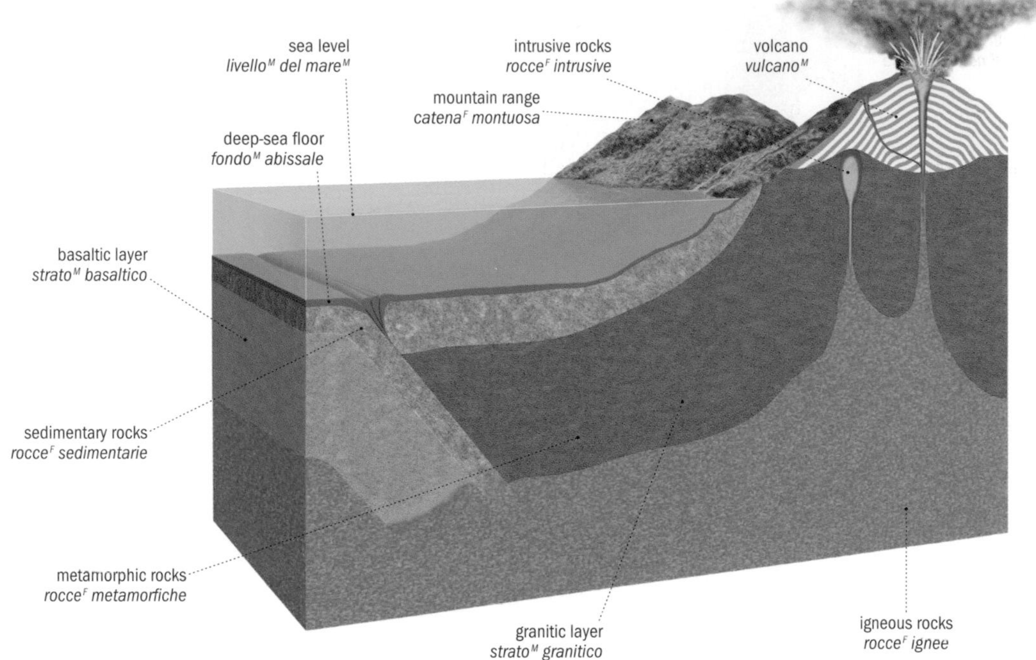

structure of the Earth

struttura[F] della Terra[F]

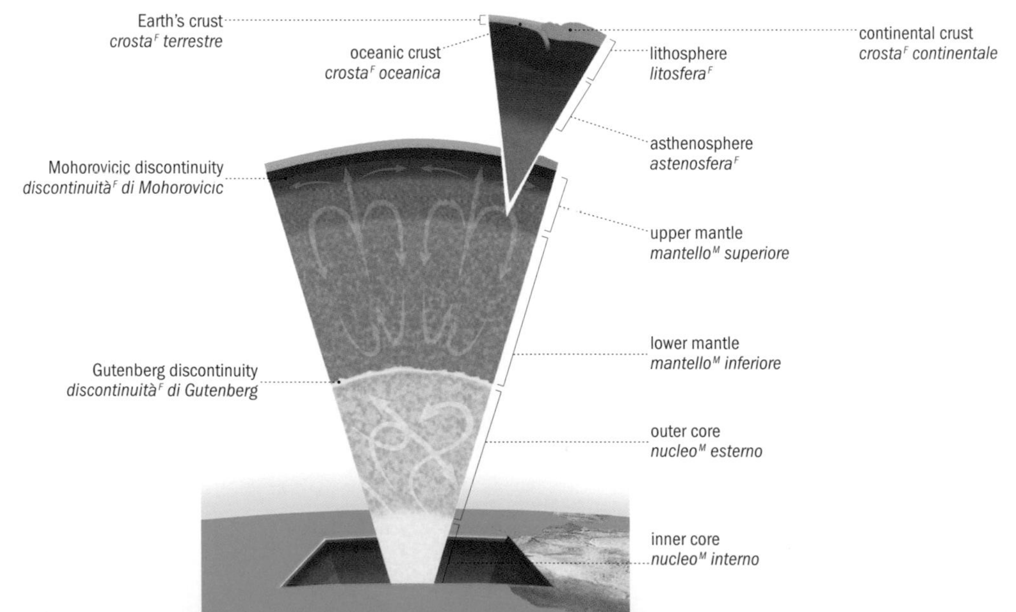

tectonic plates

placche^F tettoniche

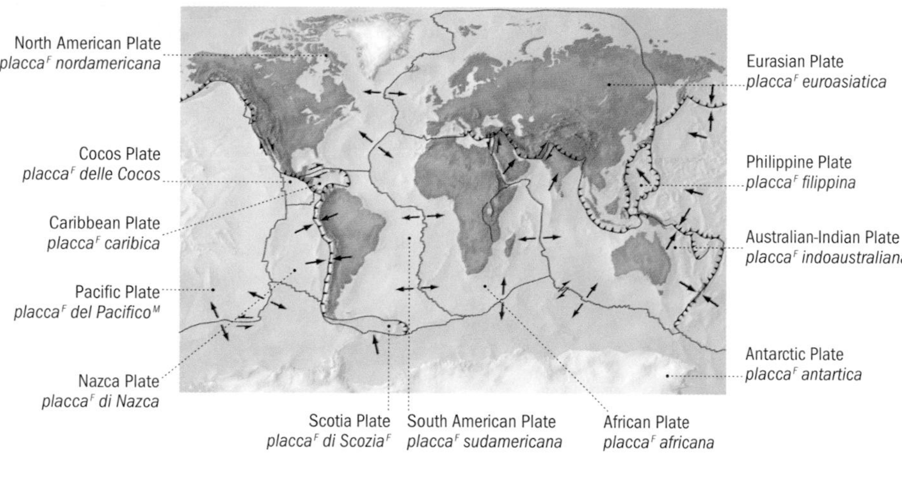

North American Plate
placca^F nordamericana

Cocos Plate
placca^F delle Cocos

Caribbean Plate
placca^F caribica

Pacific Plate
placca^F del Pacifico^M

Nazca Plate
placca^F di Nazca

Scotia Plate
placca^F di Scozia^F

South American Plate
placca^F sudamericana

African Plate
placca^F africana

Eurasian Plate
placca^F euroasiatica

Philippine Plate
placca^F filippina

Australian-Indian Plate
placca^F indoaustraliana

Antarctic Plate
placca^F antartica

subduction
subduzione^F

divergent plate boundaries
placche^F divergenti

convergent plate boundaries
placche^F convergenti

transform plate boundaries
placche^F trasformi

earthquake

terremoto^M

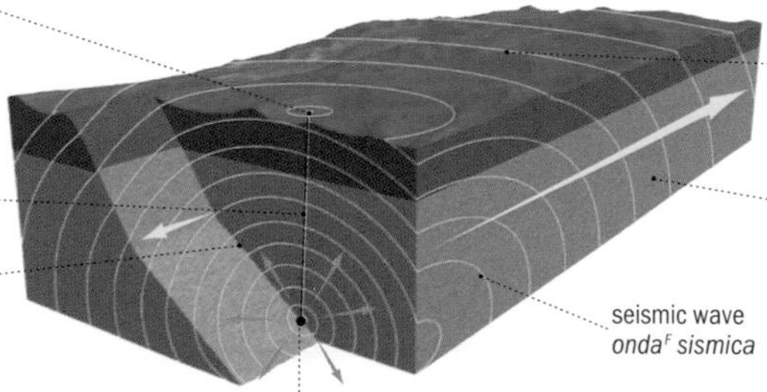

epicenter
epicentro^M

isoseismal line
linea^F isosismica

depth of focus
profondità^F del fuoco^M

Earth's crust
crosta^F terrestre

fault
faglia^F

seismic wave
onda^F sismica

focus
fuoco^M

seismographs
sismografi^M

vertical seismograph
sismografo^M verticale

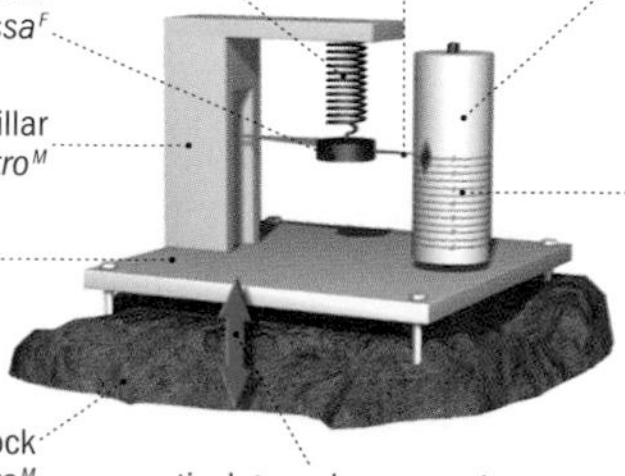

spring
molla^F

pen
pennino^M

rotating drum
tamburo^M rotante

mass
massa^F

pillar
pilastro^M

seismogram
sismogramma^M

stand
piastra^F di base^F

bedrock
basamento^M

vertical ground movement
movimento^M verticale del suolo^M

horizontal seismograph
sismografo^M orizzontale

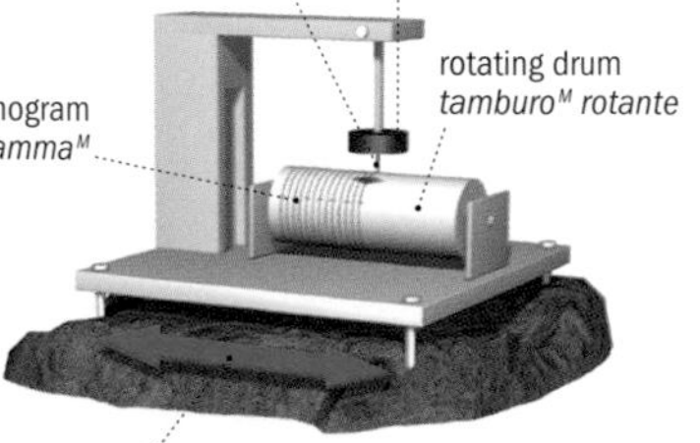

mass
massa^F

pen
pennino^M

rotating drum
tamburo^M rotante

seismogram
sismogramma^M

horizontal ground movement
movimento^M orizzontale del suolo^M

EARTH

volcano

vulcano[M]

volcano during eruption
vulcano[M] in eruzione[F]

crater
cratere[M]

cloud of volcanic ash
nube[F] di ceneri[F] vulcaniche

volcanic bomb
bomba[F] vulcanica

fumarole
fumarola[F]

lava layer
strato[M] di lava[F]

geyser
geyser[M]

lava flow
colata[F] lavica

main vent
camino[M] principale

side vent
cono[M] avventizio

ash layer
strato[M] di ceneri[F]

laccolith
laccolite[M/F]

magma chamber
camera[F] magmatica

dike
dicco[M]

magma
magma[M]

sill
filone strato[M]

examples of volcanoes
esempi[M] di vulcani[M]

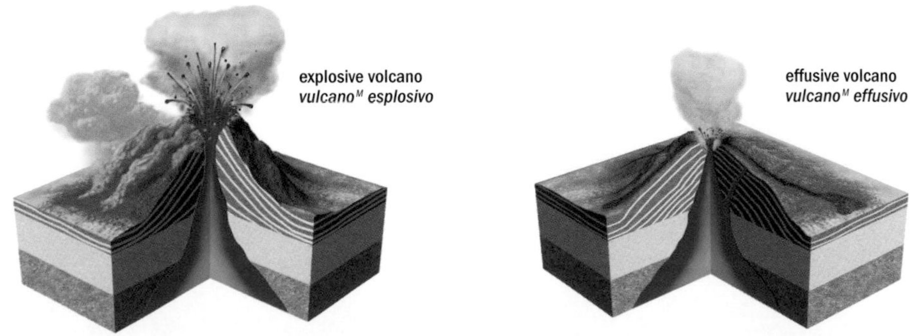

mountain

montagna^F

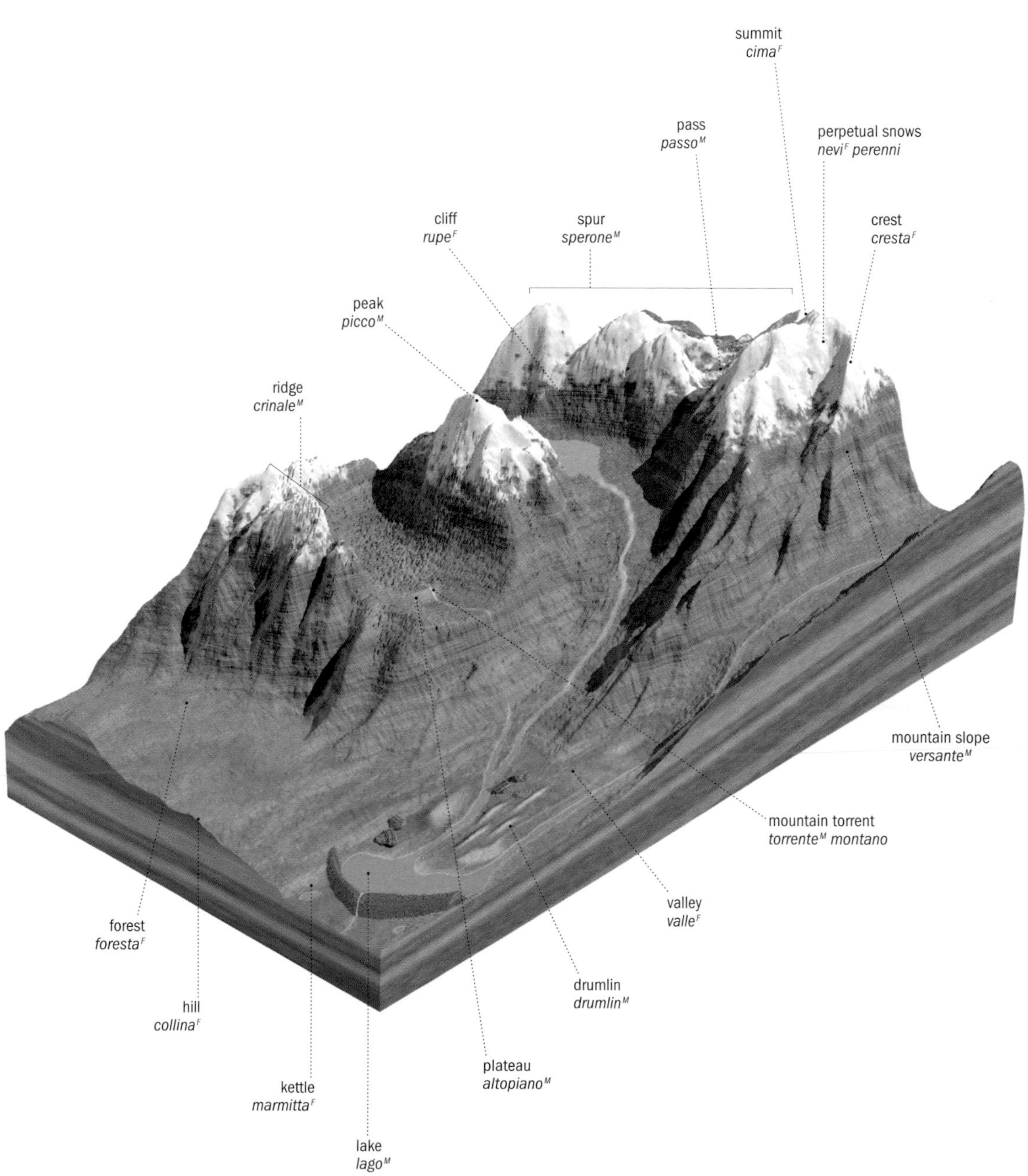

glacier

ghiacciaio^M

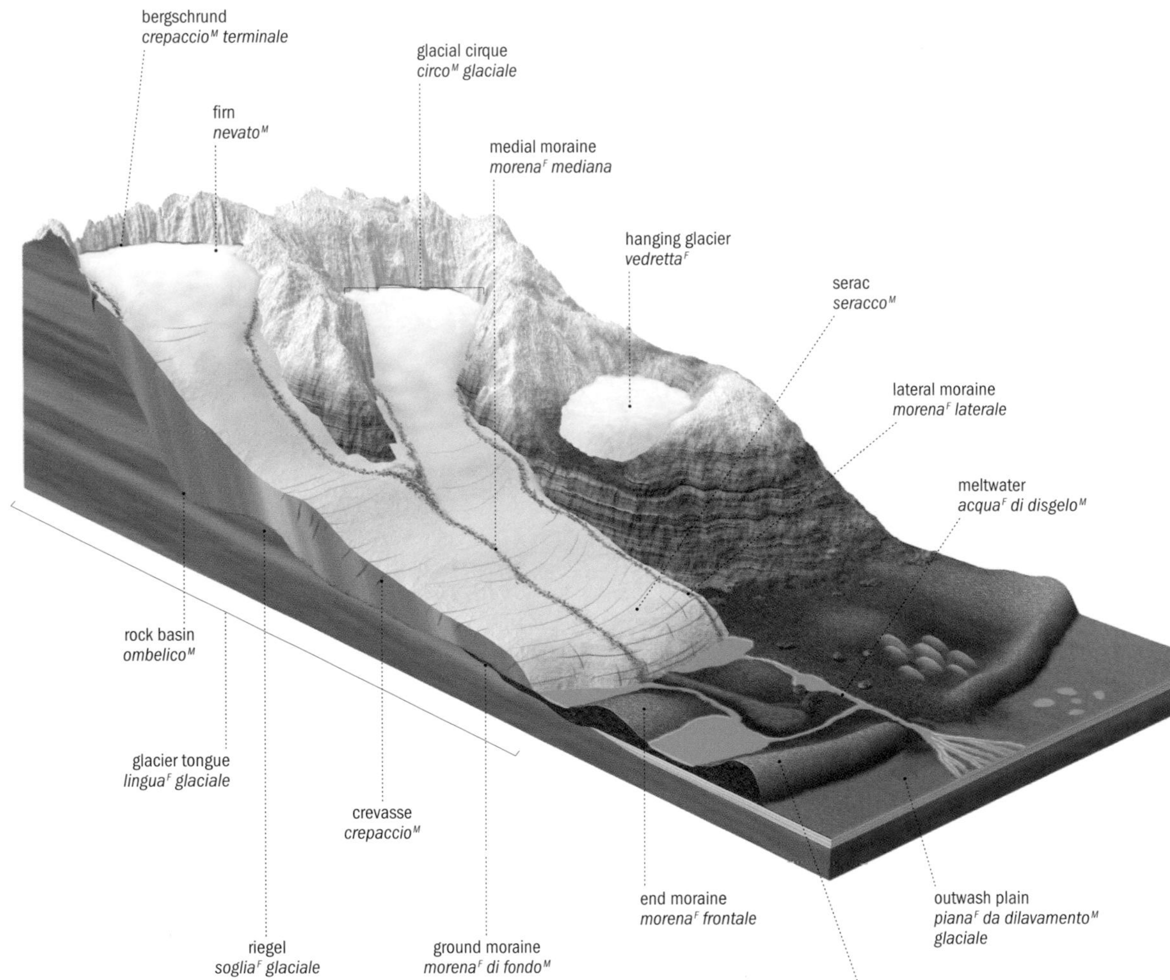

cave

grotta[F]

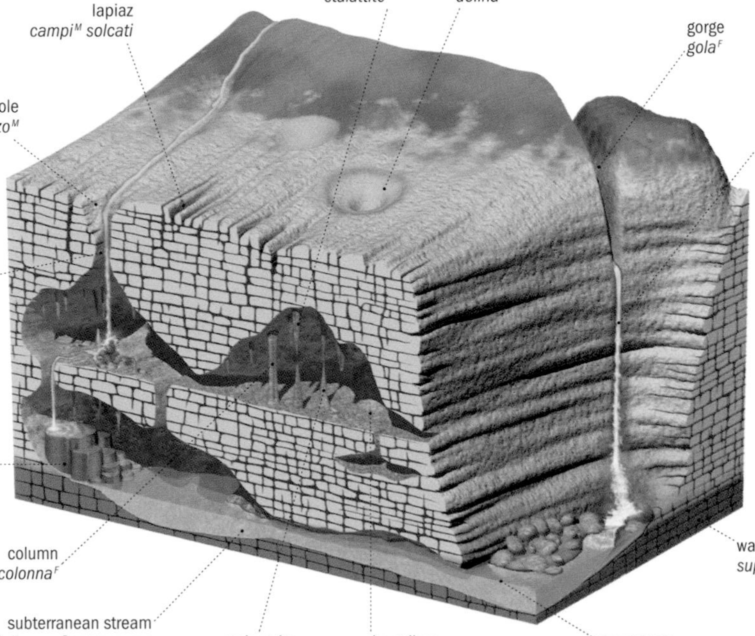

stalactite
stalattite[F]

sinkhole
dolina[F]

lapiaz
campi[M] solcati

gorge
gola[F]

pothole
pozzo[M]

waterfall
cascata[F]

swallow hole
inghiottitoio[M]

gour
conca[F] di concrezione

column
colonna[F]

water table
superficie[F] freatica

subterranean stream
corso[M] d'acqua[F] sotterraneo

stalagmite
stalagmite[F]

dry gallery
galleria[F] secca

resurgence
risorgiva[F]

landslides

movimenti[M] del terreno[M]

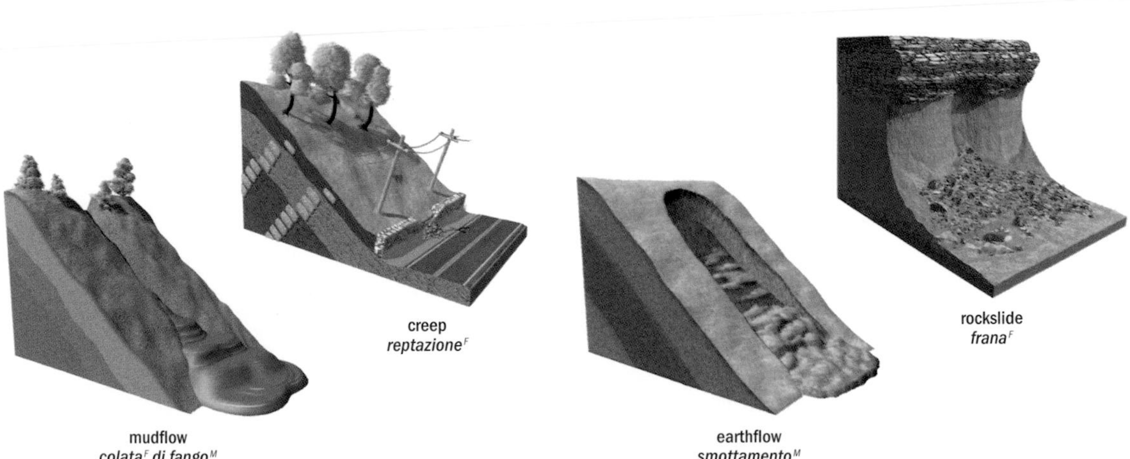

creep
reptazione[F]

rockslide
frana[F]

mudflow
colata[F] di fango[M]

earthflow
smottamento[M]

watercourse

corso[M] d'acqua[F]

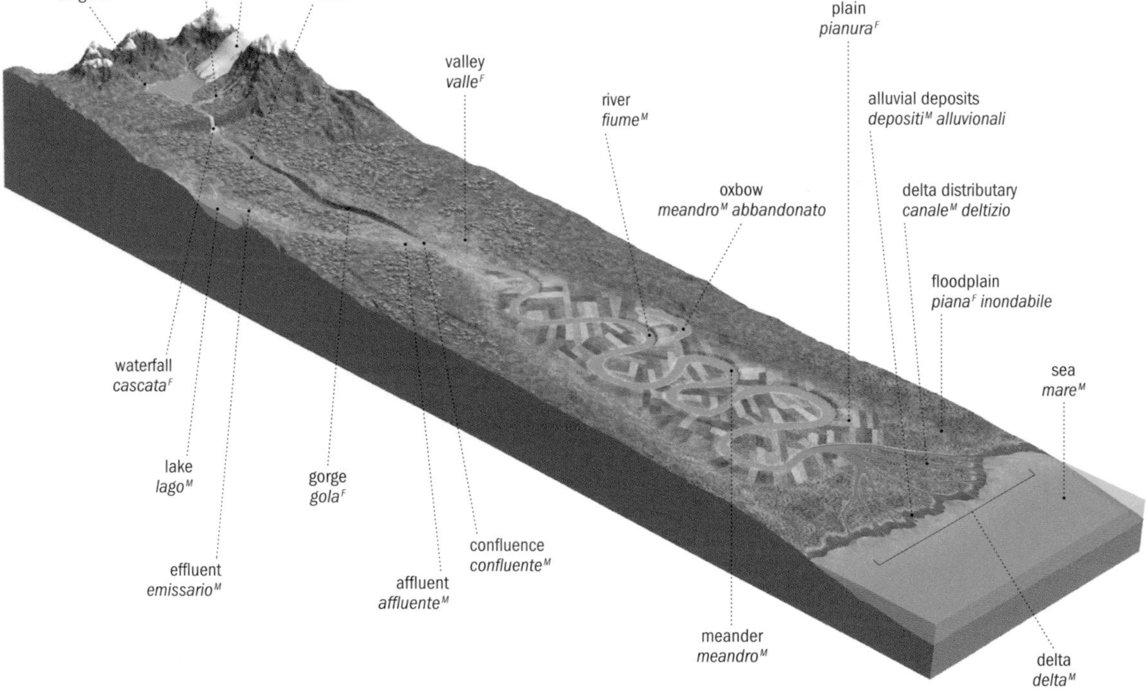
brook
ruscello[M]
glacier
ghiacciaio[M]
spring
sorgente[F]
river
fiume[M]
valley
valle[F]
plain
pianura[F]
river
fiume[M]
alluvial deposits
depositi[M] alluvionali
oxbow
meandro[M] abbandonato
delta distributary
canale[M] deltizio
floodplain
piana[F] inondabile
sea
mare[M]
waterfall
cascata[F]
lake
lago[M]
gorge
gola[F]
confluence
confluente[M]
effluent
emissario[M]
affluent
affluente[M]
meander
meandro[M]
delta
delta[M]

lakes

laghi[M]

glacial lake
lago[M] glaciale

volcanic lake
lago[M] vulcanico

tectonic lake
lago[M] tettonico

oxbow lake
lago[M] di meandro[M] abbandonato

oasis
oasi[F]

artificial lake
lago[M] artificiale

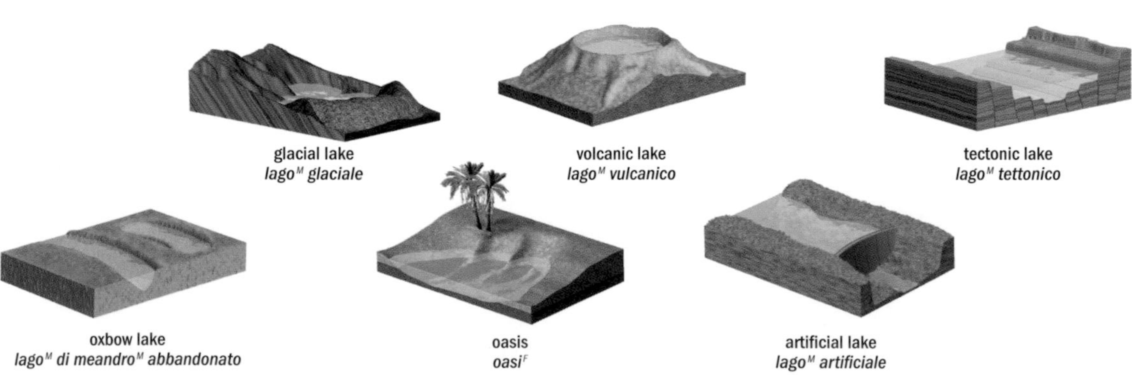

wave

onda[F]

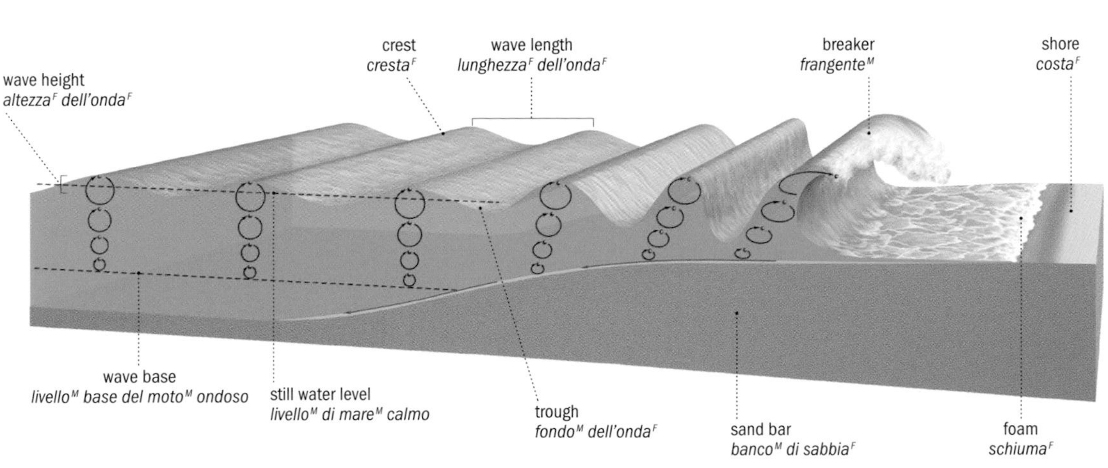

ocean floor

fondale[M] oceanico

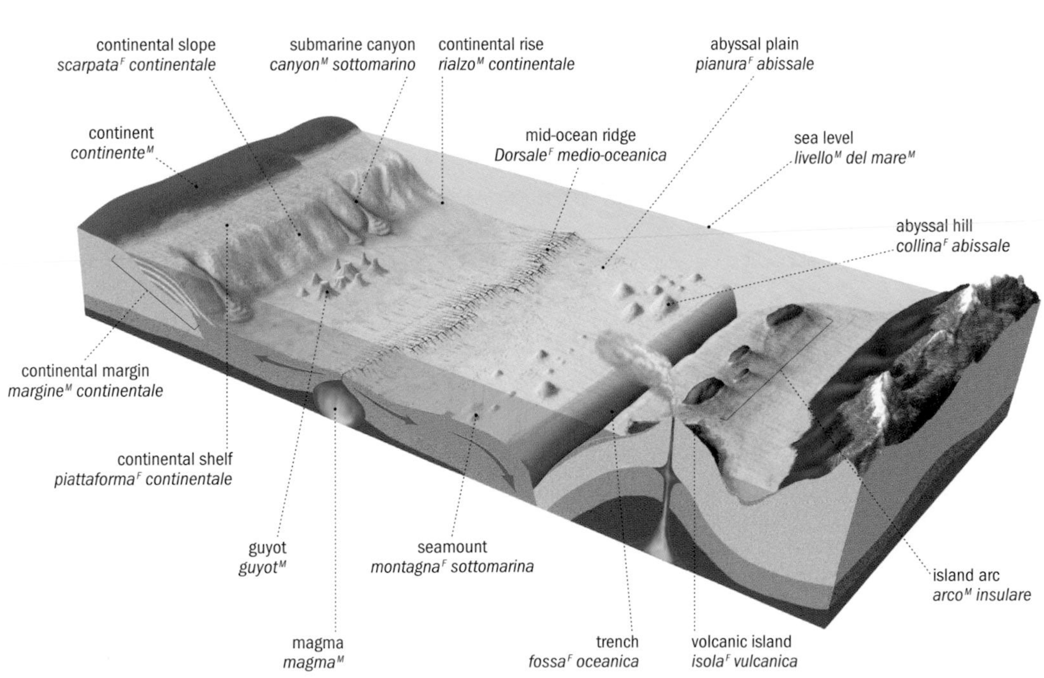

ocean trenches and ridges

fosse^F e dorsali^F oceaniche

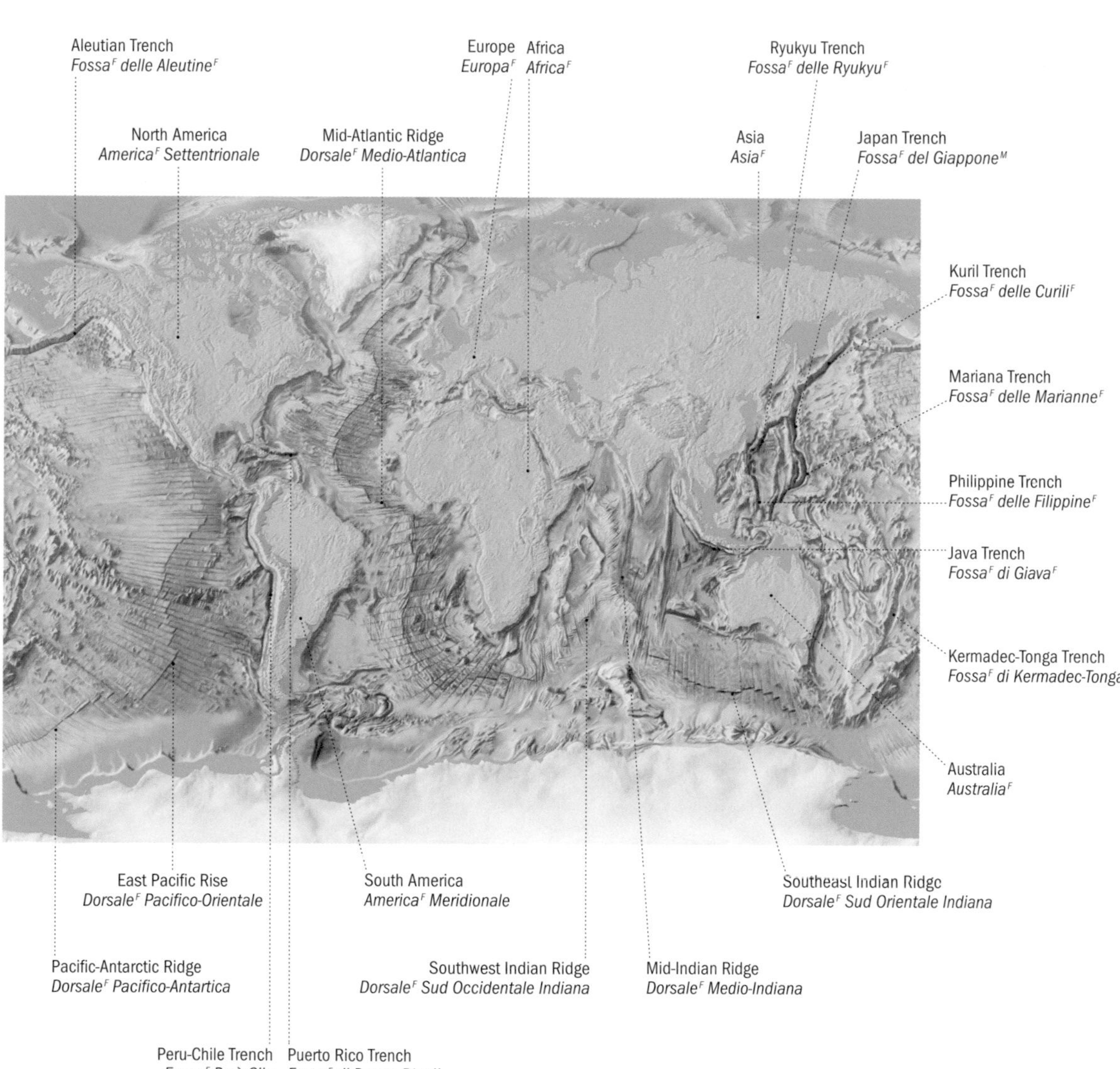

common coastal features

caratteristiche^F della costa^F

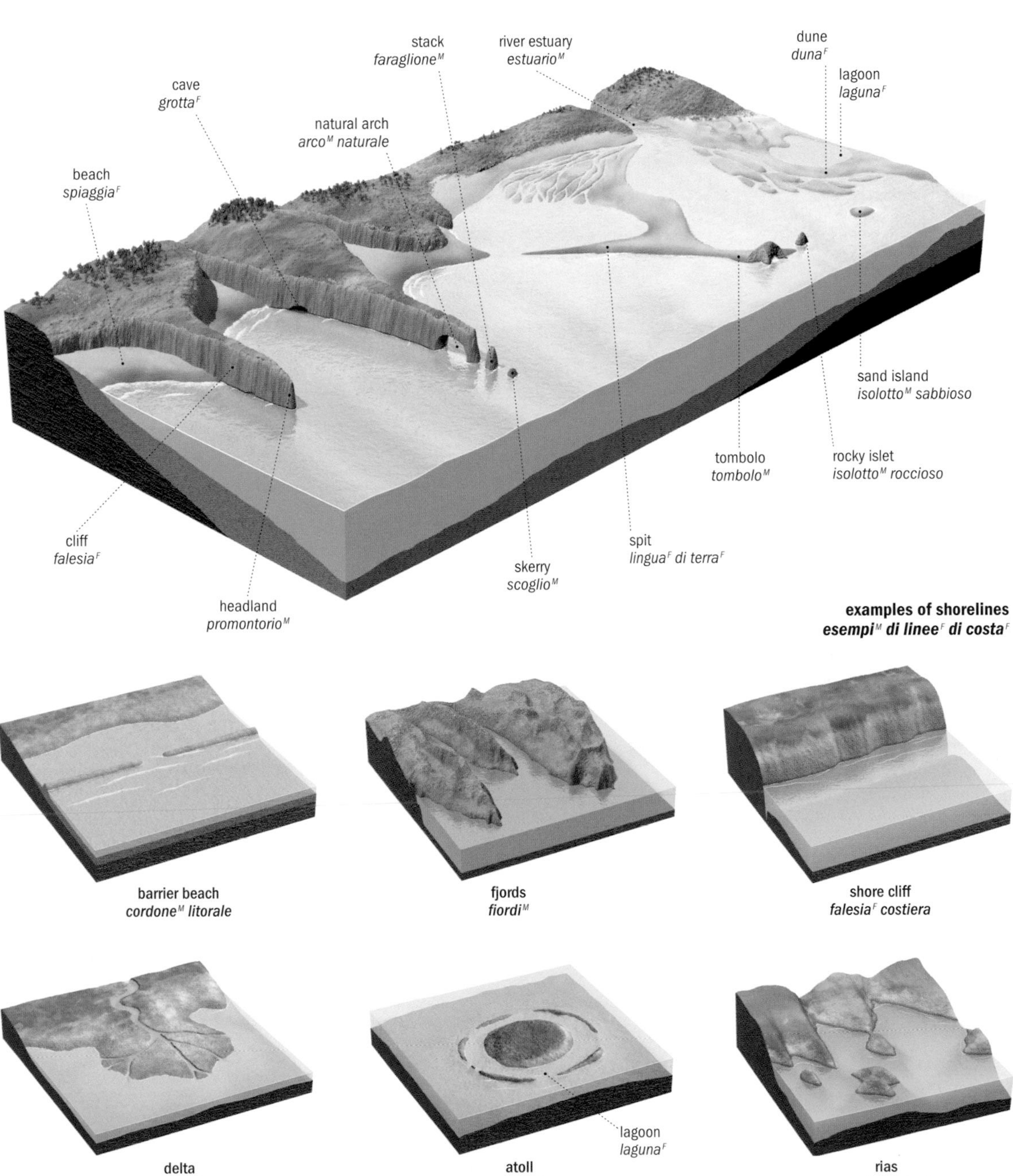

desert

deserto[M]

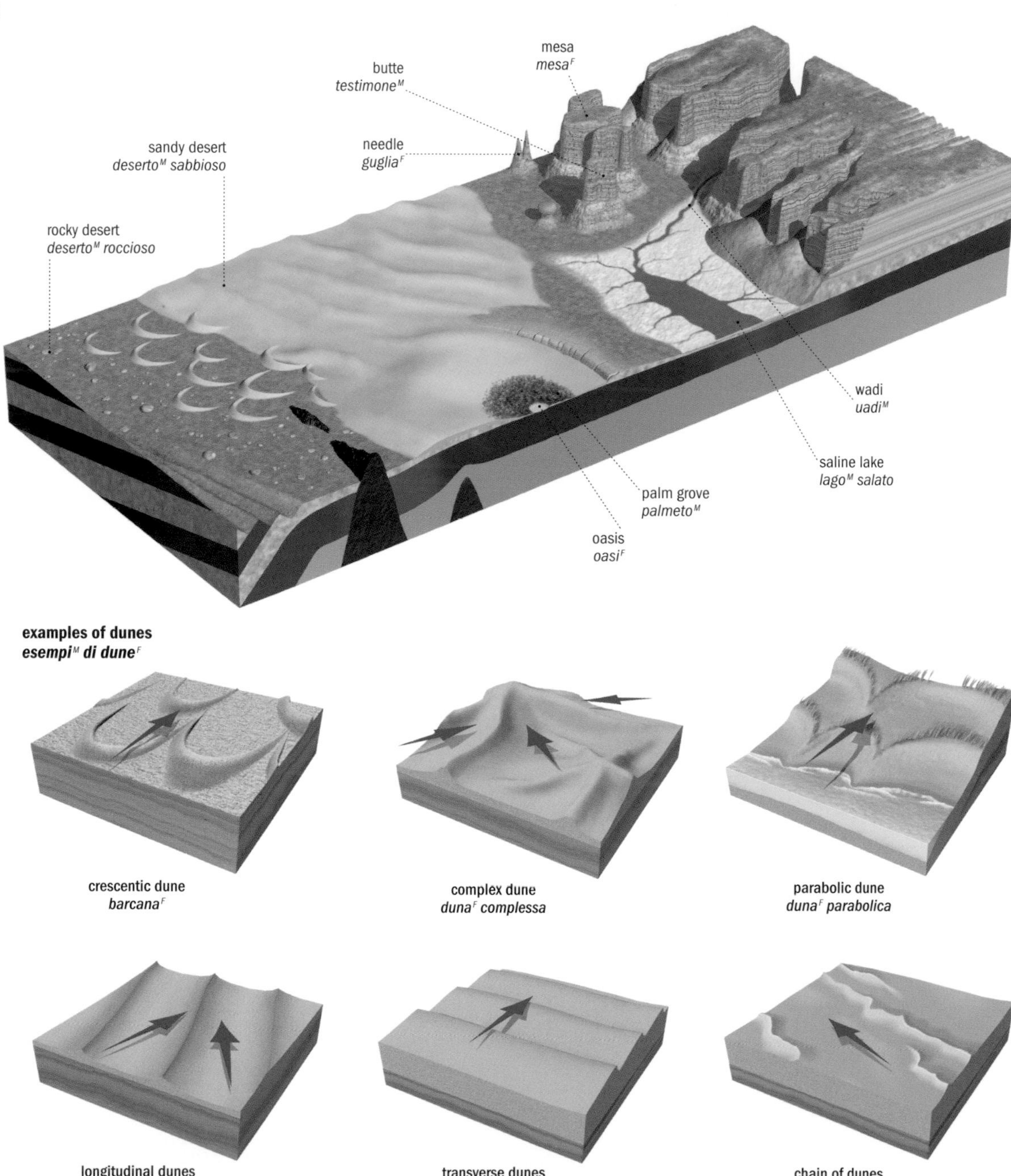

profile of the Earth's atmosphere

profilo[M] dell'atmosfera[F] terrestre

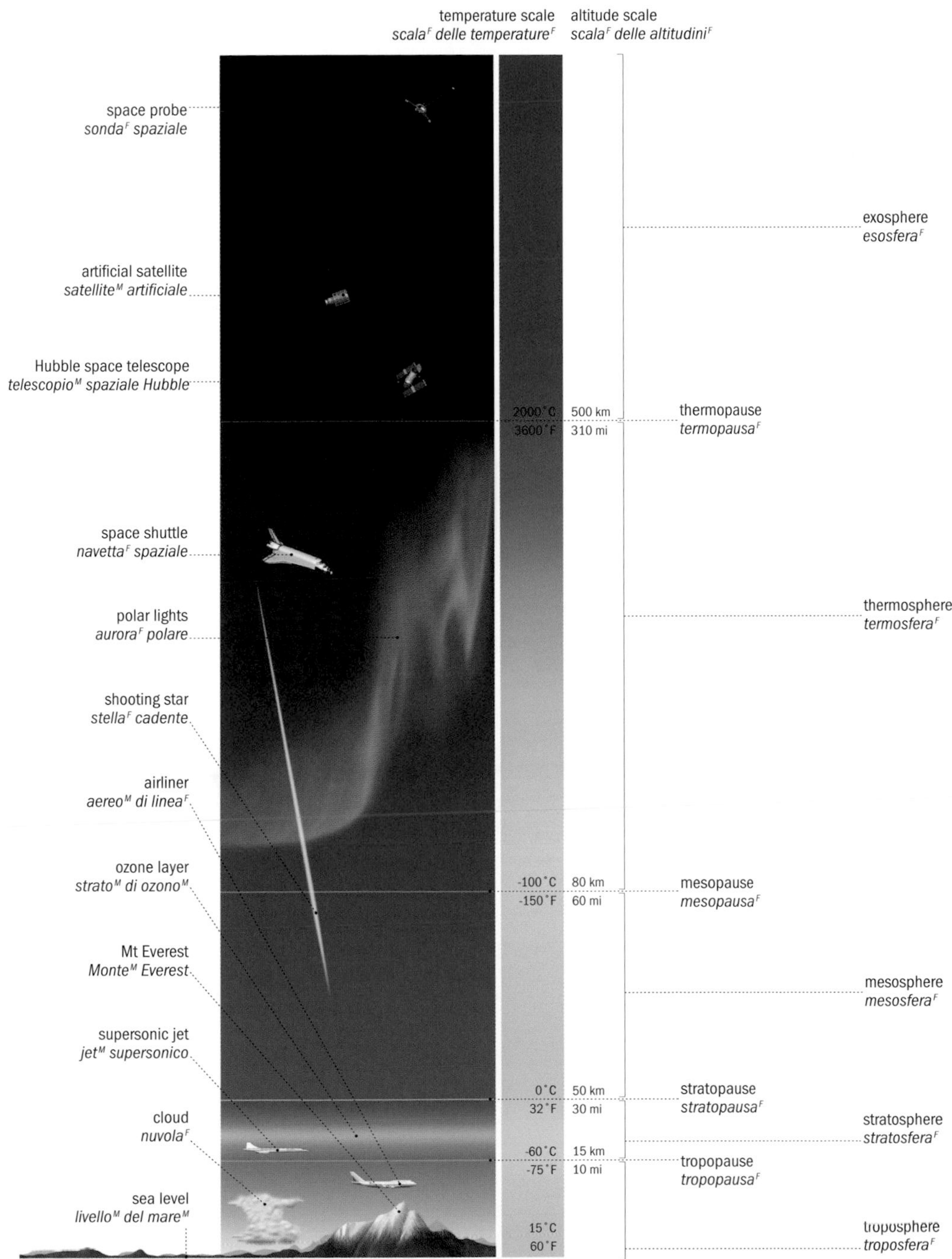

seasons of the year

stagioni^F dell'anno^M

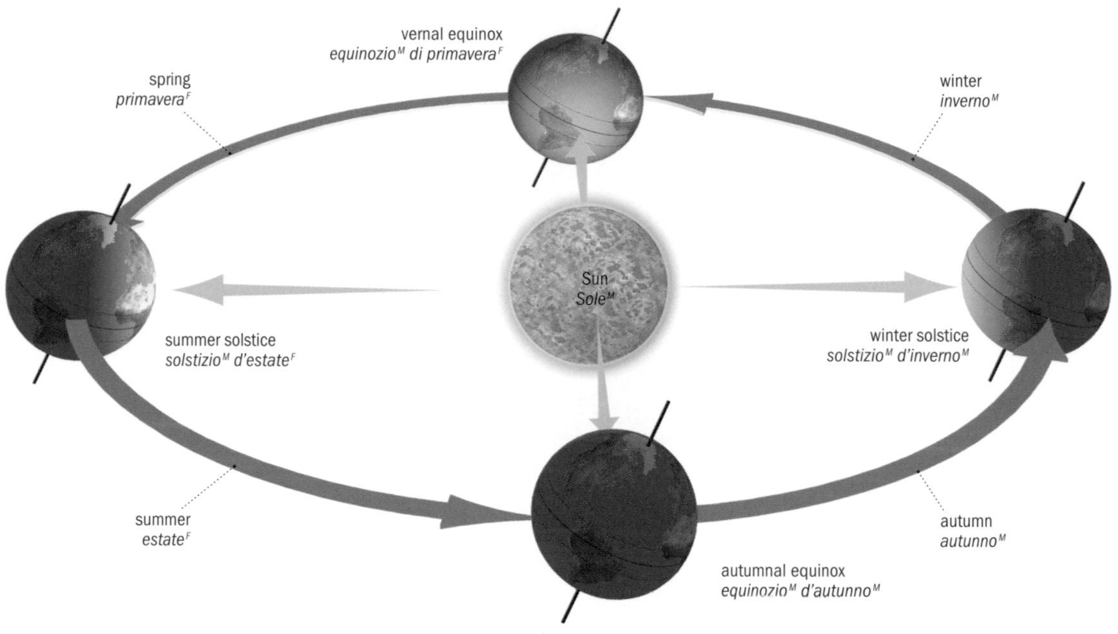

meteorological forecast

previsioni^F meteorologiche

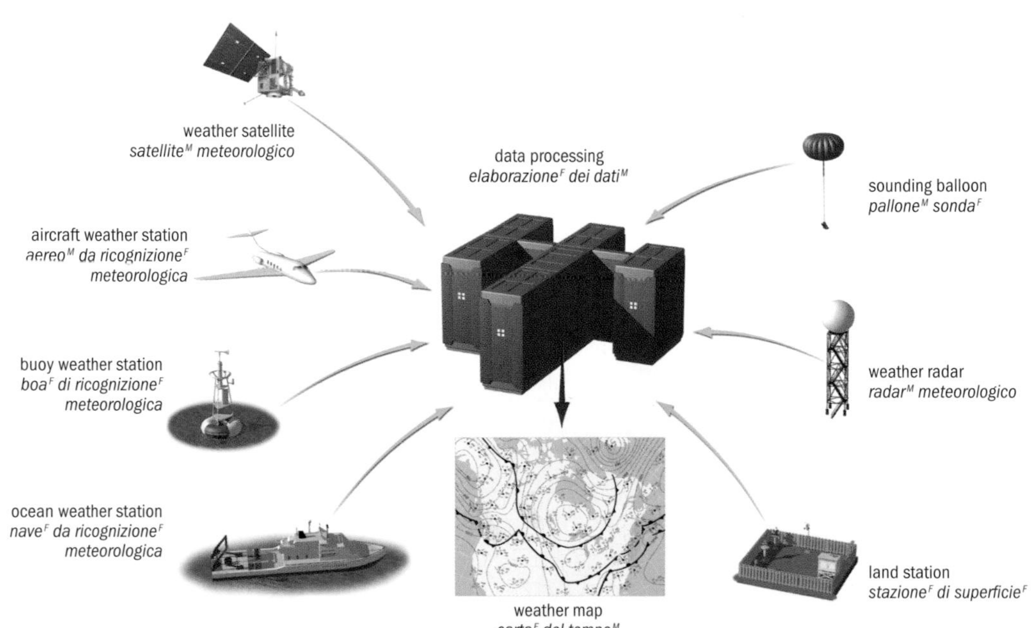

weather map

cartaF del tempoM

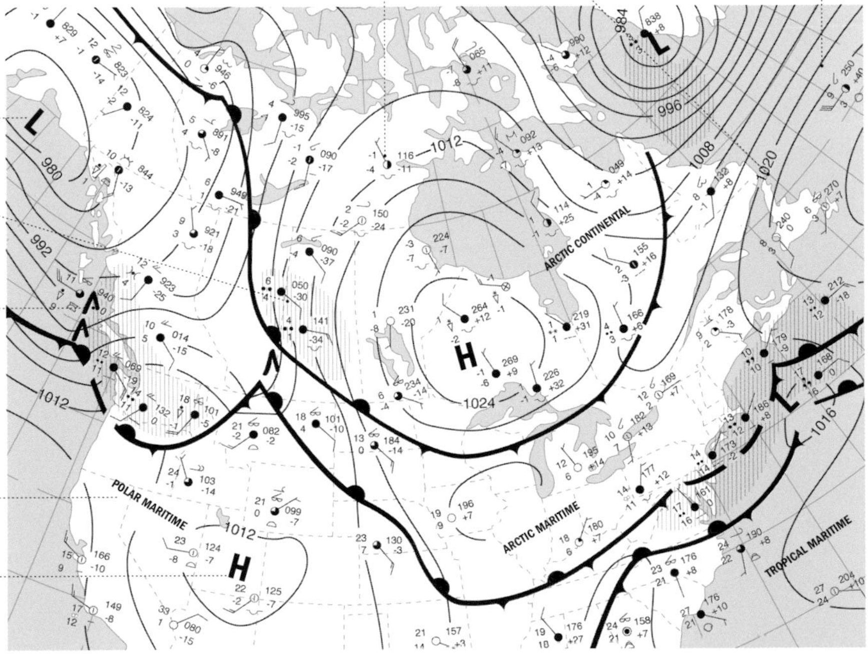

wind direction and speed
direzioneF e forzaF del ventoM
barometric pressure
pressioneF atmosferica
isobar
isobaraF
low-pressure center
centroM di bassa pressioneF
precipitation area
areaF di precipitazioneF
trough
saccaturaF
type of the air mass
tipoM di massaF d'ariaF
high-pressure center
centroM di alta pressioneF
ARCTIC CONTINENTAL
POLAR MARITIME
ARCTIC MARITIME
TROPICAL MARITIME
1012
1024
996
1008
1020
1016
980
992
984
H
L

station model

modelloM di stazioneF

type of high cloud
tipoM di nubeF alta
type of middle cloud
tipoM di nubeF media
wind speed
forzaF del ventoM
station circle
cerchioM di stazioneF
air temperature
temperaturaF dell'ariaF
-2
995
sea-level pressure
pressioneF a livelloM del mareM
sky coverage
coperturaF del cieloM
wind direction
direzioneF del ventoM
+16
barometric tendency
tendenzaF barometrica
present state of weather
statoM presente del tempoM
-6
temperature of dew point
temperaturaF di rugiadaF
type of low cloud
tipoM di nubeF bassa
pressure change
variazioneF di pressioneF

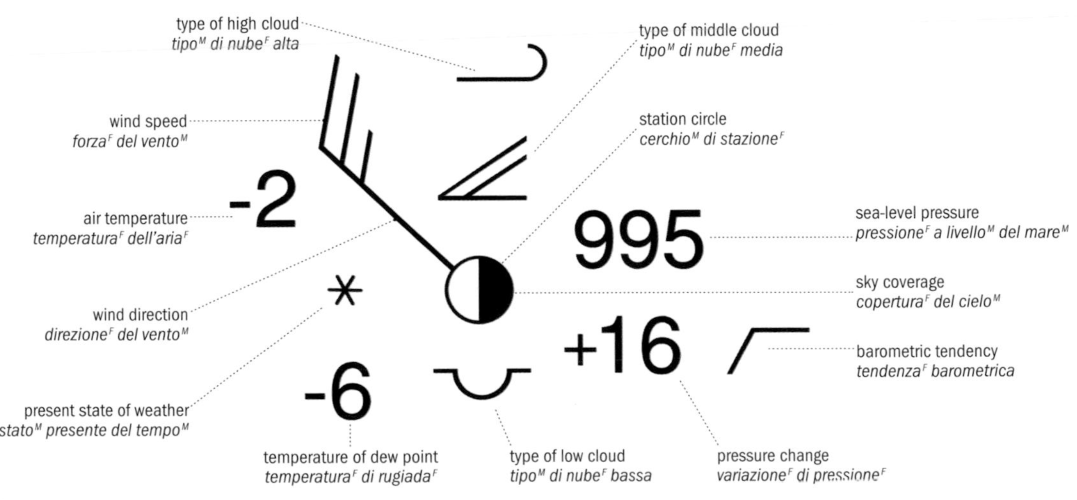

climates of the world

climi[M] del mondo[M]

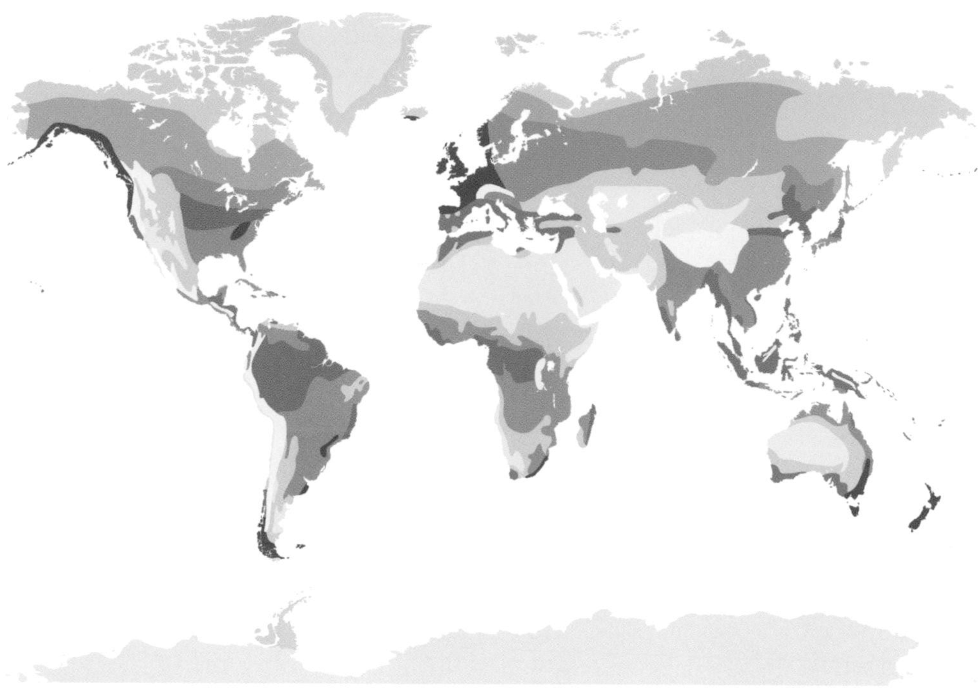

tropical climates
climi[M] tropicali

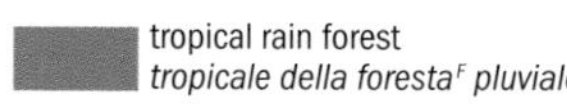
tropical rain forest
tropicale della foresta[F] pluviale

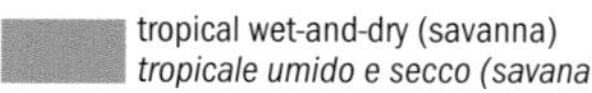
tropical wet-and-dry (savanna)
tropicale umido e secco (savana[F])

dry climates
climi[M] aridi

steppe
steppico

desert
desertico

cold temperate climates
climi[M] temperati freddi

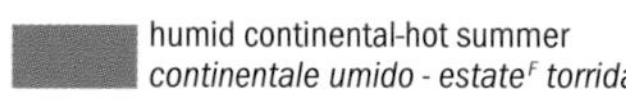
humid continental-hot summer
continentale umido - estate[F] torrida

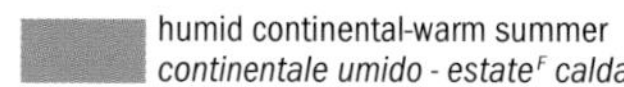
humid continental-warm summer
continentale umido - estate[F] calda

subarctic
subartico

warm temperate climates
climi[M] temperati caldi

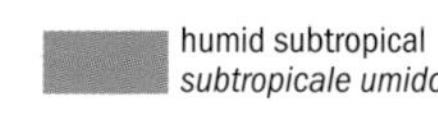
humid subtropical
subtropicale umido

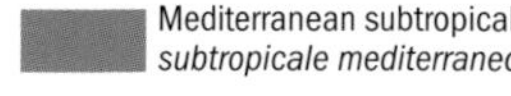
Mediterranean subtropical
subtropicale mediterraneo

marine
marino

polar climates
climi[M] polari

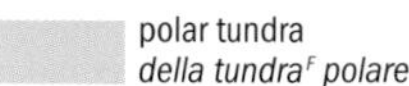
polar tundra
della tundra[F] polare

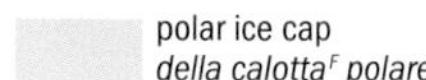
polar ice cap
della calotta[F] polare

highland climates
climi[M] di montagna[F]

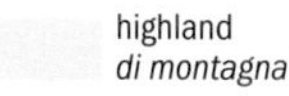
highland
di montagna[F]

precipitation

precipitazioni[F]

winter precipitation
precipitazioni[F] invernali

warm air
aria[F] calda

cold air
aria[F] fredda

rain
pioggia[F]

freezing rain
pioggia[F] congelantesi

sleet
nevischio[M]

snow
neve[F]

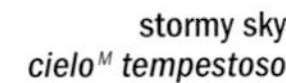

stormy sky
cielo[M] tempestoso

cloud
nube[F]

lightning
fulmine[M]

rainbow
arcobaleno[M]

rain
pioggia[F]

dew
rugiada[F]

mist
foschia[F]

fog
nebbia[F]

rime
brina[F]

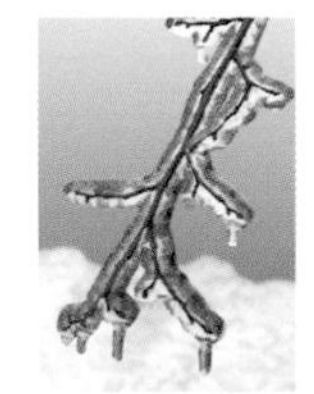

frost
vetrone[M]

clouds

nuvole^{F}

high clouds
nubi^{F} alte

middle clouds
nubi^{F} medie

low clouds
nubi^{F} basse

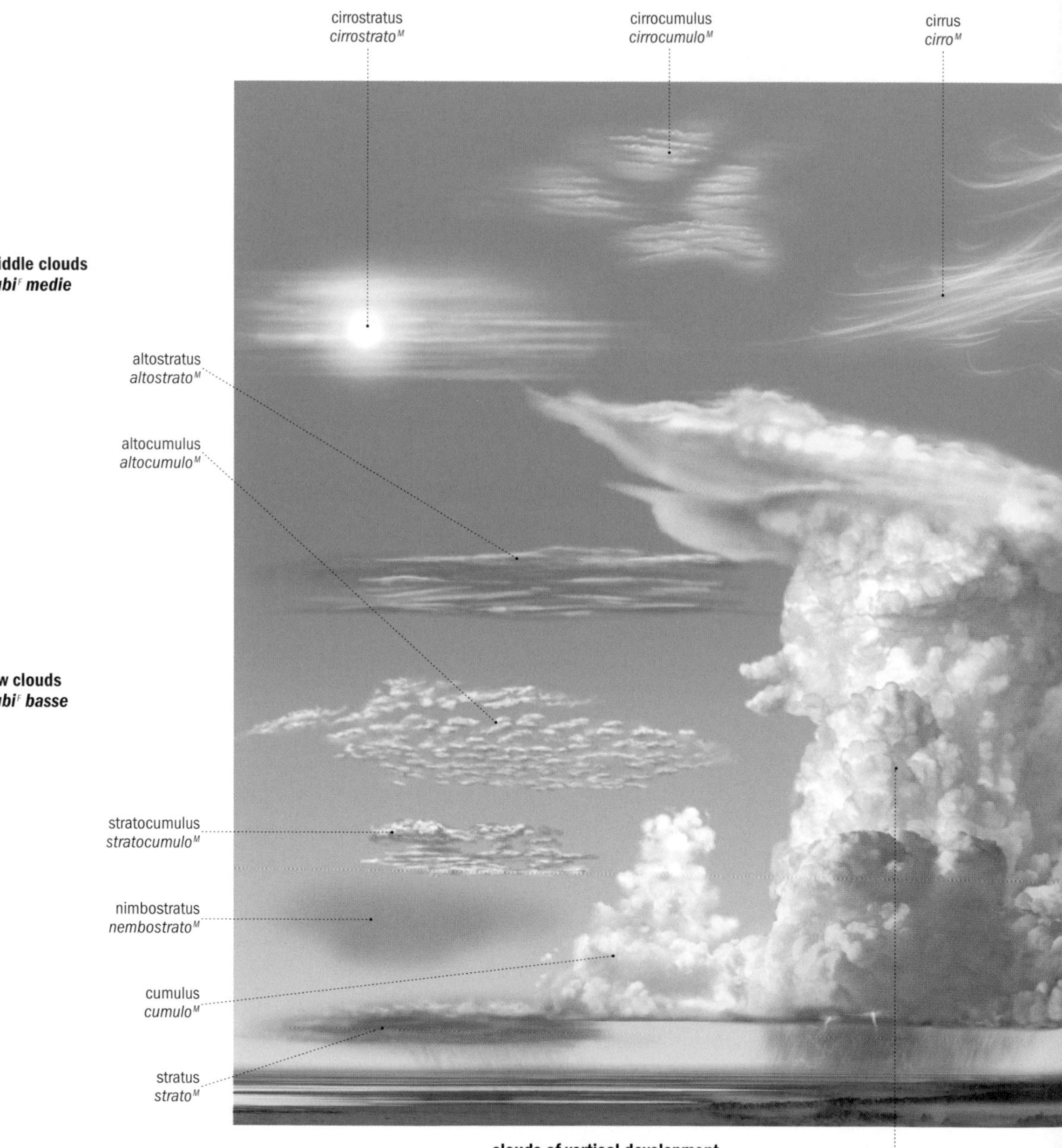

clouds of vertical development
nubi^{F} a sviluppo^{M} verticale

tornado and waterspout

tornado[M] e tromba[F] marina

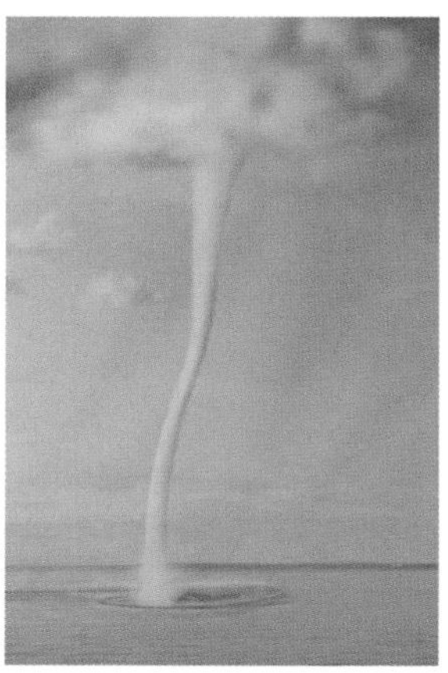

waterspout
tromba[F] marina

wall cloud
parete[F] di nuvole[F]
funnel cloud
nube[F] a proboscide[F]
debris
detriti[M]

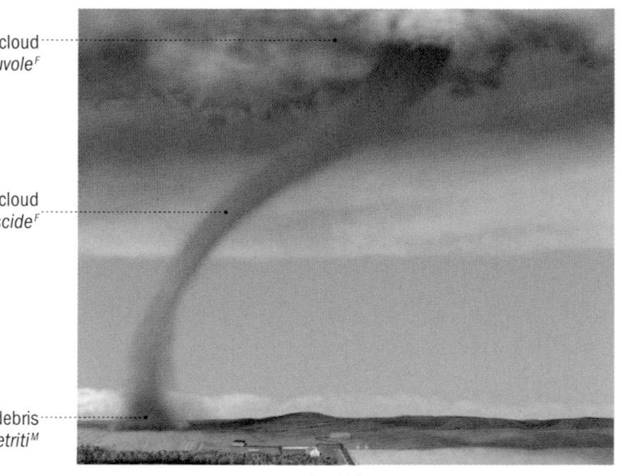

tornado
tornado[M]

tropical cyclone

ciclone[M] tropicale

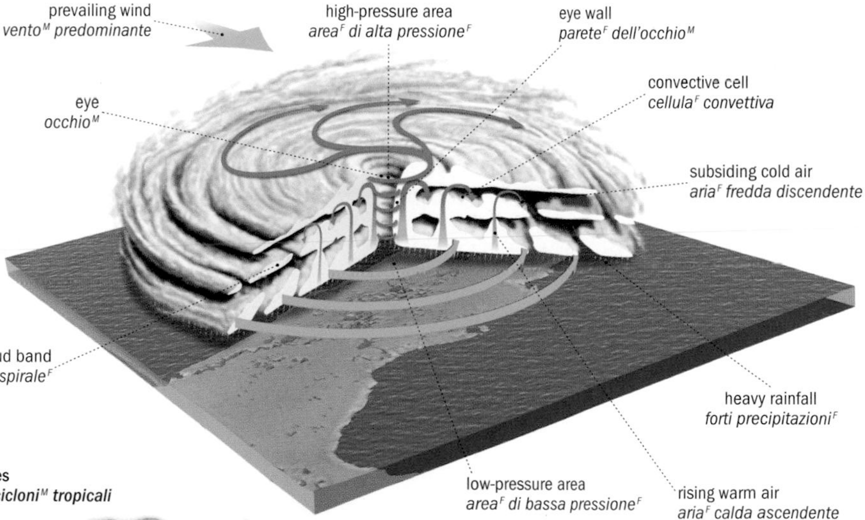
prevailing wind
vento[M] predominante
high-pressure area
area[F] di alta pressione[F]
eye wall
parete[F] dell'occhio[M]
convective cell
cellula[F] convettiva
eye
occhio[M]
subsiding cold air
aria[F] fredda discendente
spiral cloud band
banda[F] nuvolosa a spirale[F]
heavy rainfall
forti precipitazioni[F]
low-pressure area
area[F] di bassa pressione[F]
rising warm air
aria[F] calda ascendente

tropical cyclone names
denominazione[F] dei cicloni[M] tropicali

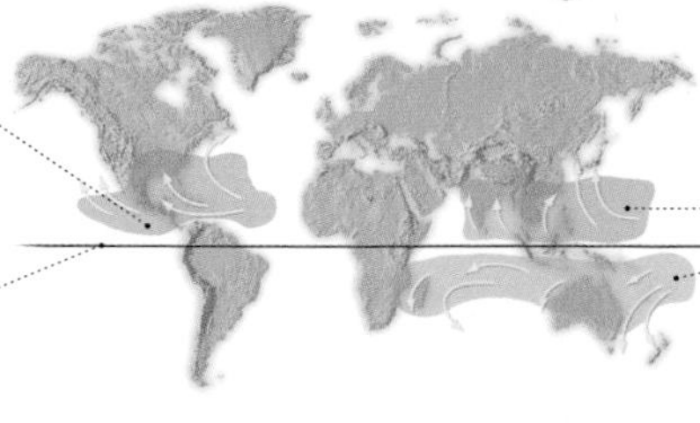
hurricane
uragano[M]
typhoon
Tifone[M]
Equator
Equatore[M]
cyclone
ciclone[M]

vegetation and biosphere

vegetazione[F] e biosfera[F]

vegetation regions
distribuzione[F] della vegetazione[F]

tundra
tundra[F]

temperate forest
foresta[F] temperata

tropical rain forest
foresta[F] pluviale tropicale

desert
deserto[M]

boreal forest
foresta[F] boreale

grassland
prateria[F]

savanna
savana[F]

maquis
macchia[F]

elevation zones and vegetation
altitudine[F] e vegetazione[F]

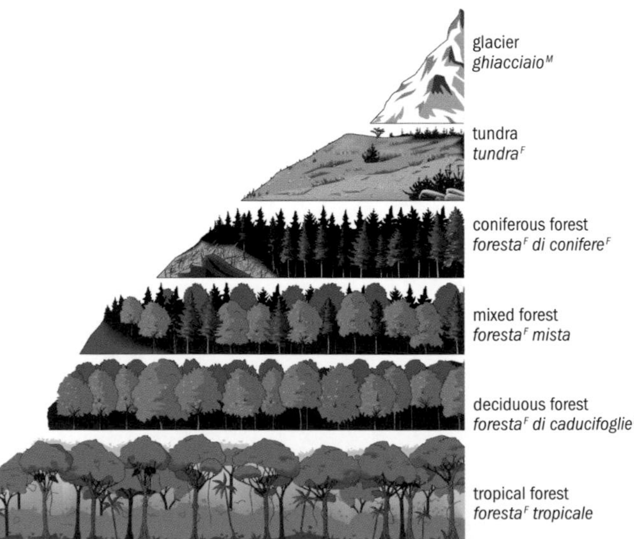

structure of the biosphere
struttura[F] della biosfera[F]

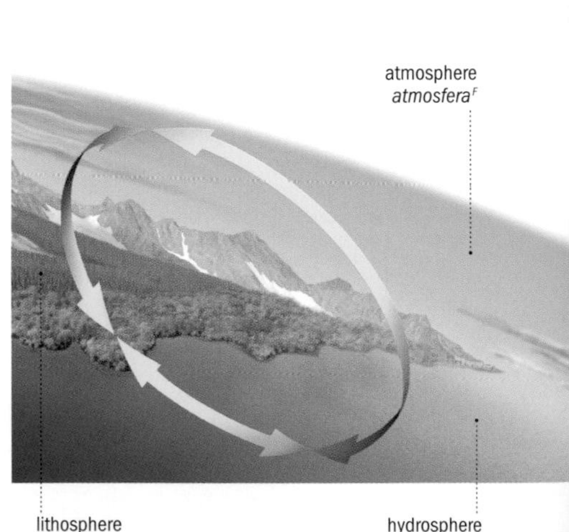

food chain

catena^F alimentare

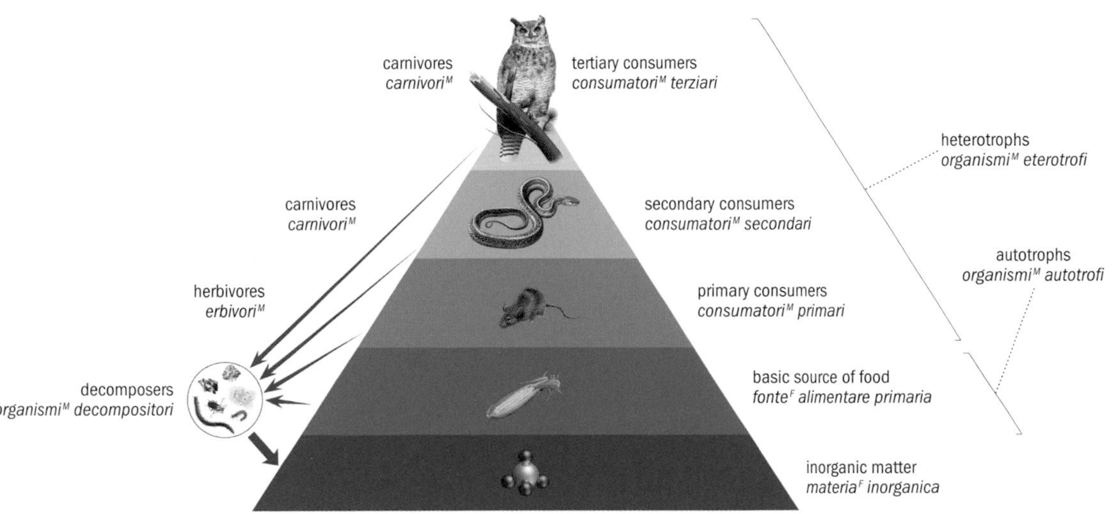

hydrologic cycle

ciclo^M idrologico

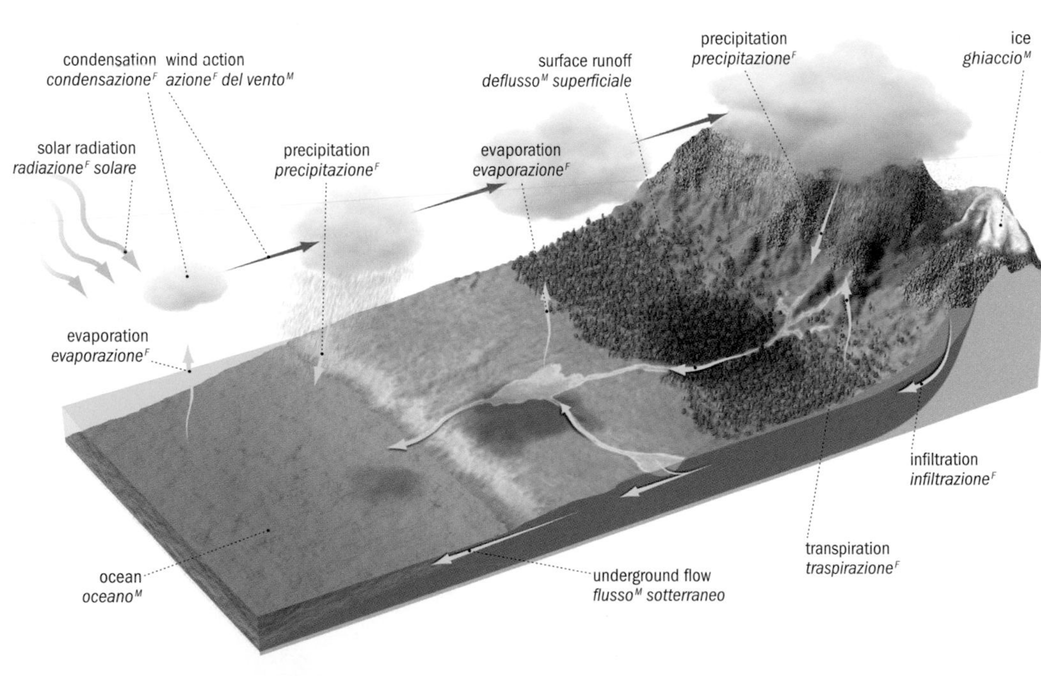

greenhouse effect

effetto^M serra^F

natural greenhouse effect
effetto^M serra^F naturale

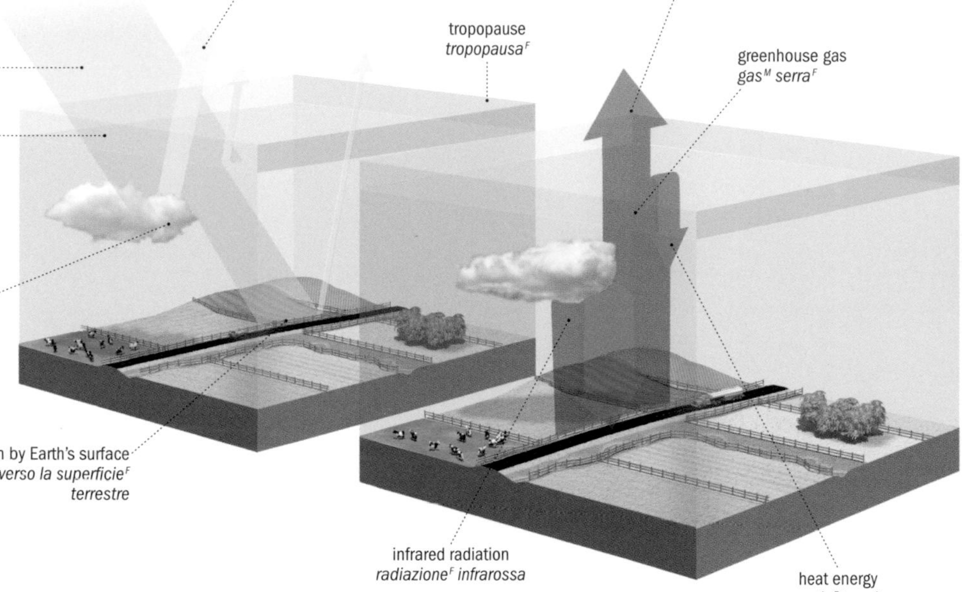

reflected solar radiation
radiazione^F solare riflessa

heat loss
dispersione^F di calore^M

tropopause
tropopausa^F

solar radiation
radiazione^F solare

greenhouse gas
gas^M serra^F

absorbed solar radiation
radiazione^F solare assorbita

absorption by clouds
assorbimento^M attraverso le nuvole^F

absorption by Earth's surface
assorbimento^M attraverso la superficie^F terrestre

infrared radiation
radiazione^F infrarossa

heat energy
energia^F termica

enhanced greenhouse effect
incremento^M dell'effetto^M serra^F

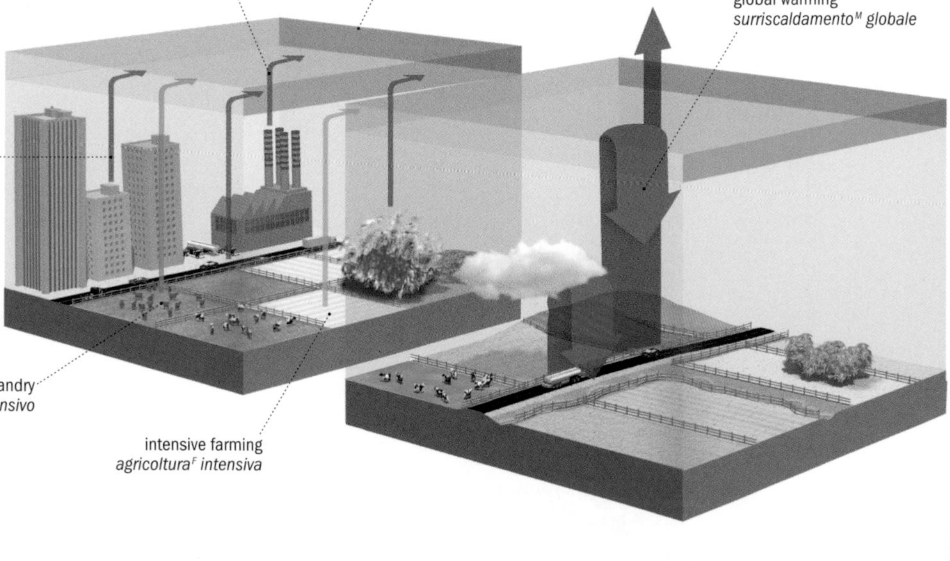

fossil fuel
combustibile^M fossile

greenhouse gas concentration
concentrazione^F di gas^M serra^F

global warming
surriscaldamento^M globale

air conditioning system
sistema^M di climatizzazione^F

intensive husbandry
allevamento^M intensivo

intensive farming
agricoltura^F intensiva

air pollution

inquinamento^M dell'aria^F

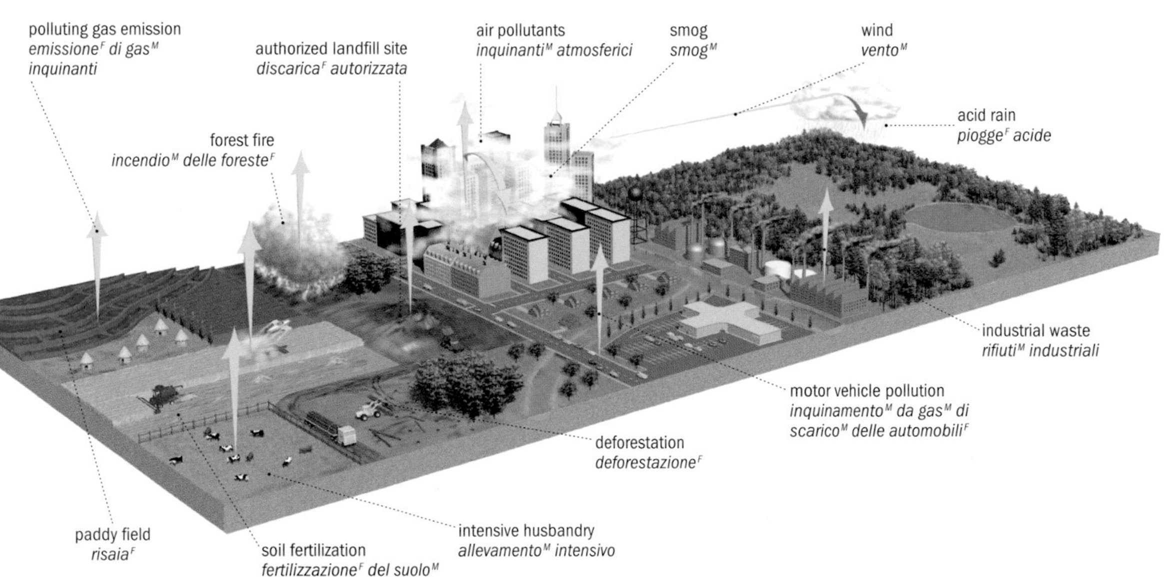

land pollution

inquinamento^M del suolo^M

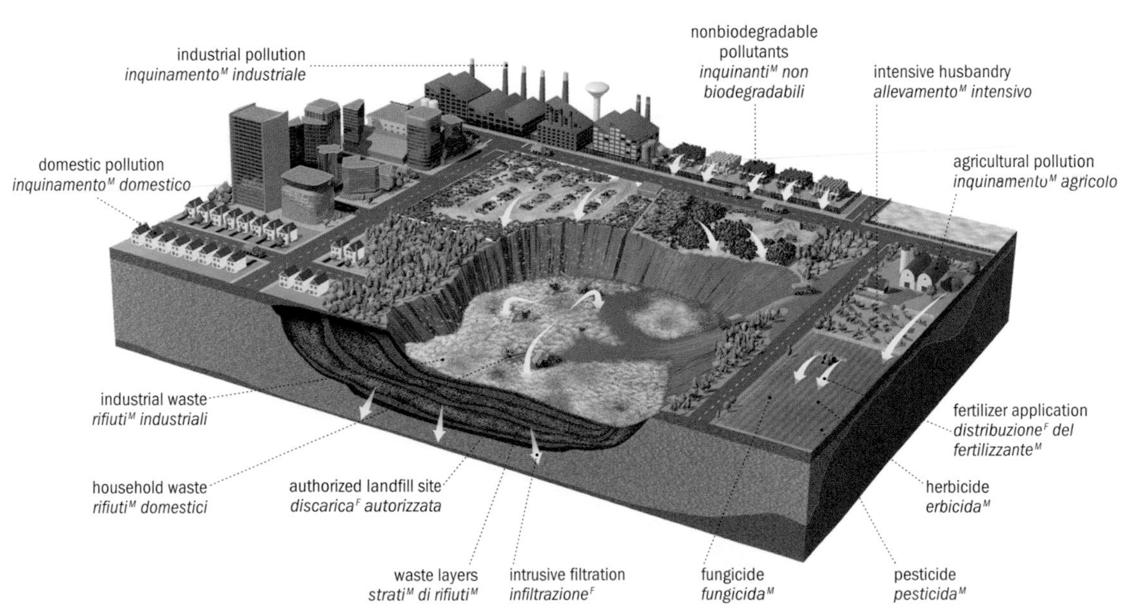

water pollution

inquinamento[M] dell'acqua[F]

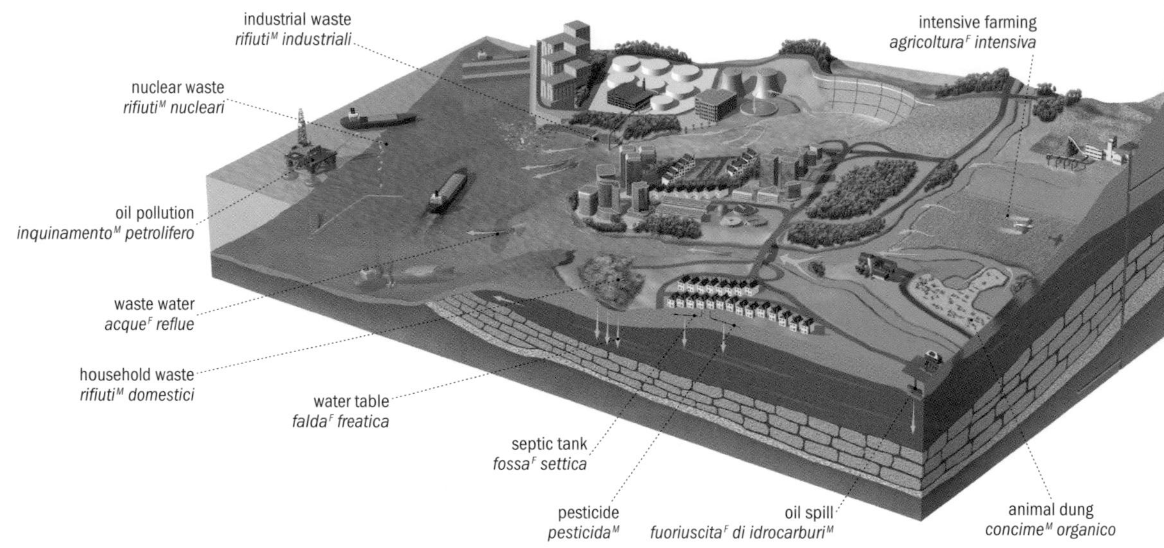

acid rain

piogge[F] acide

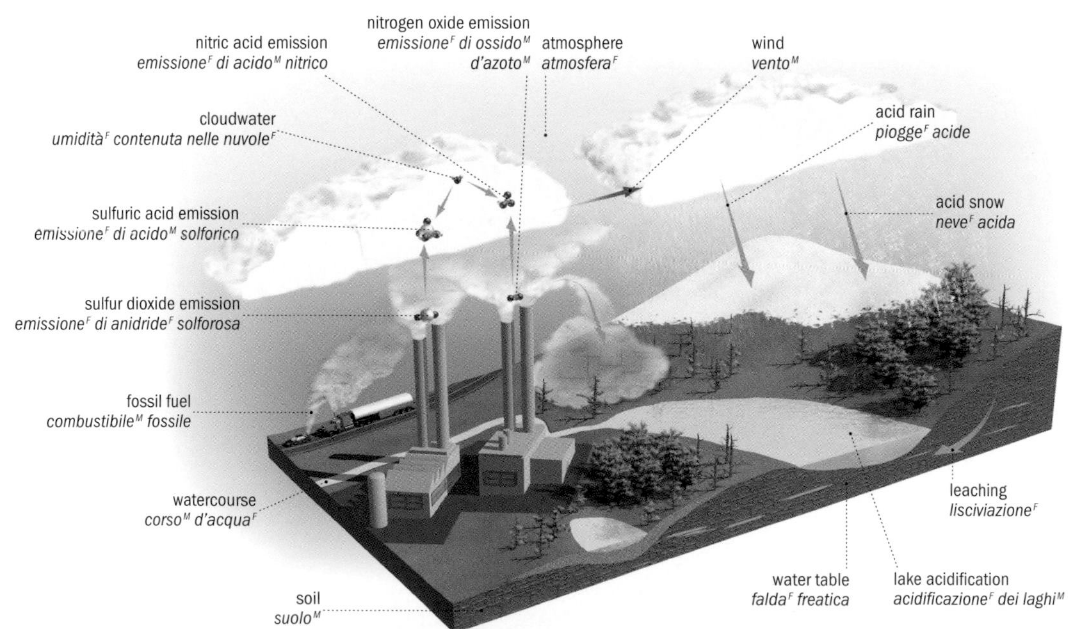

selective sorting of waste

smistamento^{M} selettivo dei rifiuti^{M}

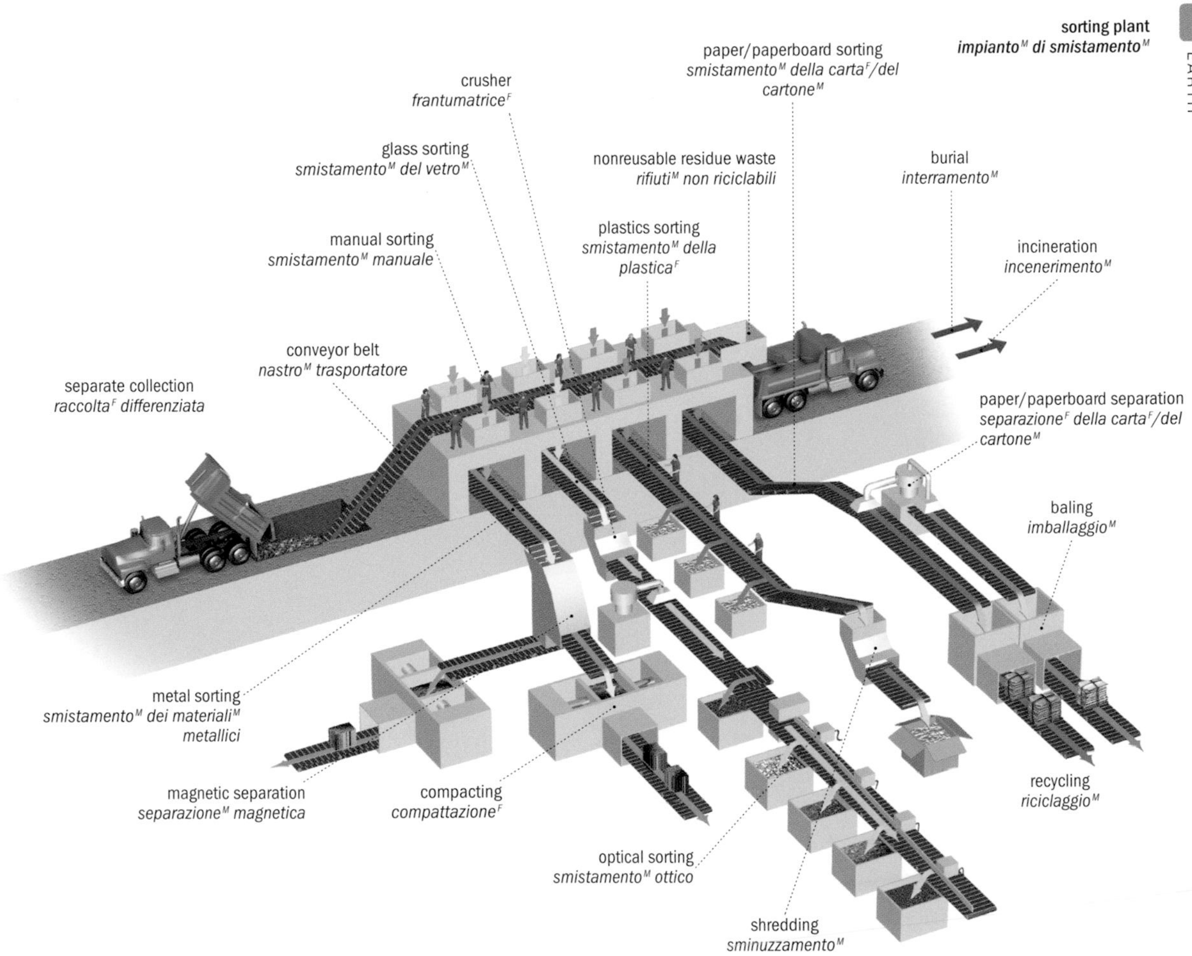

sorting plant
impianto^{M} di smistamento^{M}

paper/paperboard sorting
smistamento^{M} della carta^{F}/del cartone^{M}

crusher
frantumatrice^{F}

glass sorting
smistamento^{M} del vetro^{M}

nonreusable residue waste
rifiuti^{M} non riciclabili

burial
interramento^{M}

manual sorting
smistamento^{M} manuale

plastics sorting
smistamento^{M} della plastica^{F}

incineration
incenerimento^{M}

conveyor belt
nastro^{M} trasportatore

separate collection
raccolta^{F} differenziata

paper/paperboard separation
separazione^{F} della carta^{F}/del cartone^{M}

baling
imballaggio^{M}

metal sorting
smistamento^{M} dei materiali^{M} metallici

magnetic separation
separazione^{M} magnetica

compacting
compattazione^{F}

recycling
riciclaggio^{M}

optical sorting
smistamento^{M} ottico

shredding
sminuzzamento^{M}

recycling containers
contenitori^{M} per la raccolta^{F} differenziata

paper recycling container
bidone^{M} carrellato per il riciclaggio^{M} della carta^{F}

glass recycling container
bidone^{M} carrellato per il riciclaggio^{M} del vetro^{M}

aluminum recycling container
bidone^{M} carrellato per il riciclaggio^{M} dell'alluminio^{M}

paper collection unit
campana^{F} per la raccolta^{F} della carta^{F}

glass collection unit
campana^{F} per la raccolta^{F} del vetro^{M}

recycling bin
contenitore^{M} per il riciclaggio^{M}

plant cell

cellula[F] vegetale

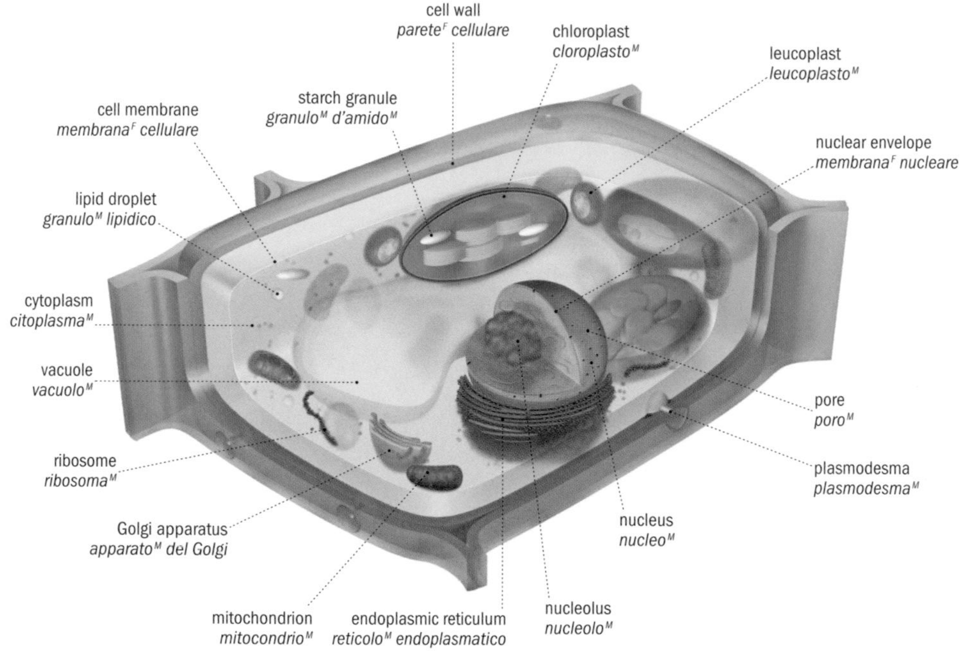

lichen

lichene[M]

structure of a lichen
struttura[F] di un lichene[M]

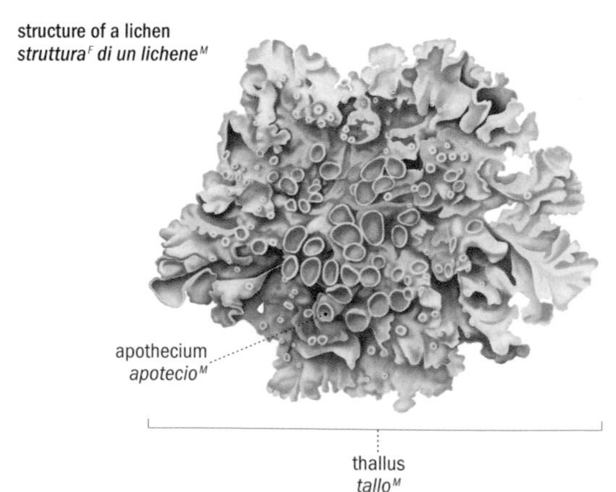

examples of lichens
esempi[M] di licheni[M]

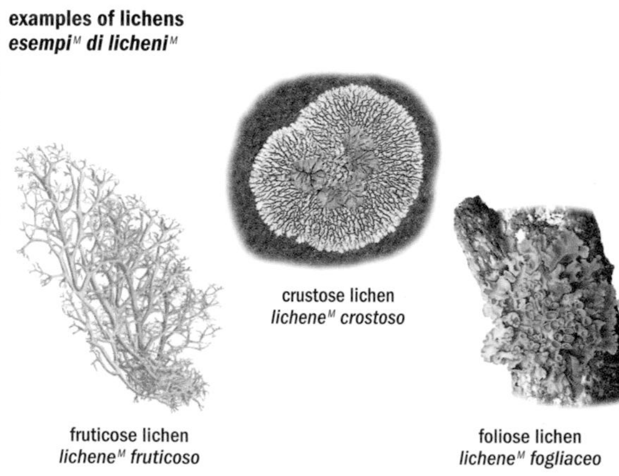

moss

muschio^{M}

structure of a moss
struttura^{F} di un muschio^{M}

capsule
capsula^{F}
stalk
stelo^{M}
leaf
foglia^{F}
stem
gambo^{M}
rhizoid
rizoide^{M}

examples of mosses
esempi^{M} di muschi^{M}

prickly sphagnum
sfagno^{M} pungente

common hair cap moss
politrico^{M} comune

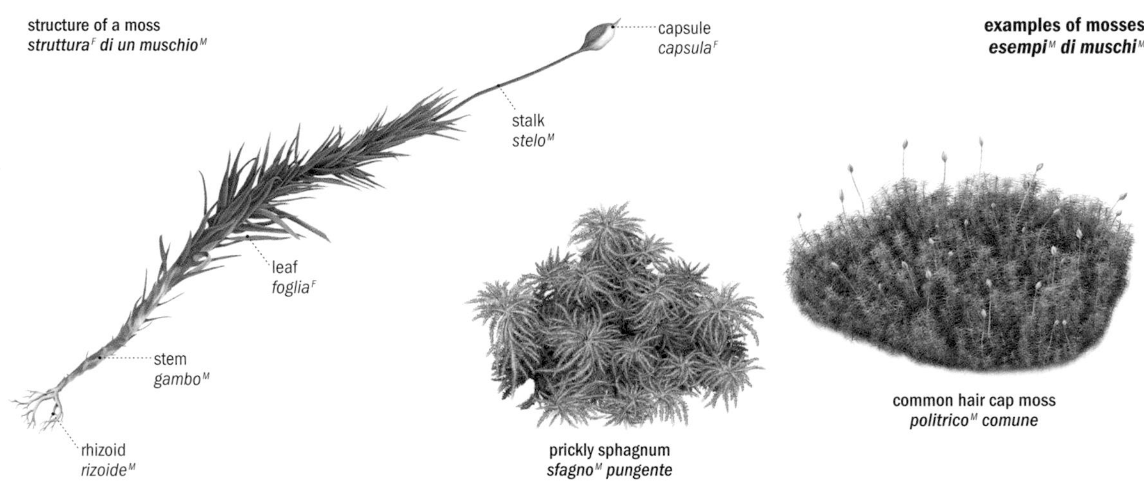

algae

alghe^{F}

structure of an alga
struttura^{F} di un'alga^{F}

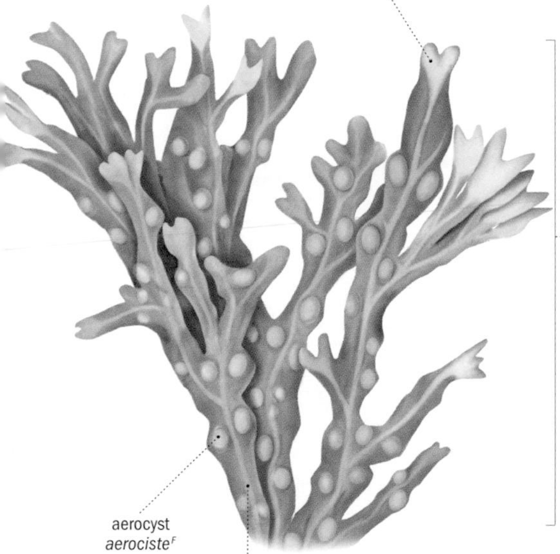

receptacle
ricettacolo^{M}
thallus
tallo^{M}
aerocyst
aerociste^{F}
midrib
nervatura^{F} centrale

examples of algae
esempi^{M} di alghe^{F}

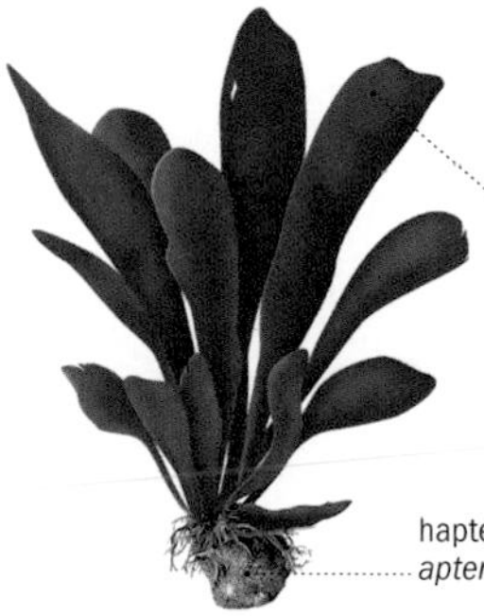

lamina
lamina^{F}
hapteron
aptero^{M}

red alga
alga^{F} rossa

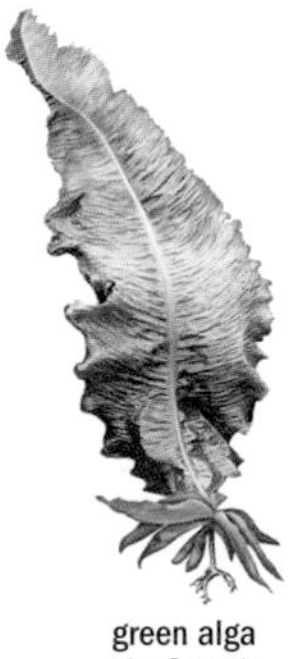

green alga
alga^{F} verde

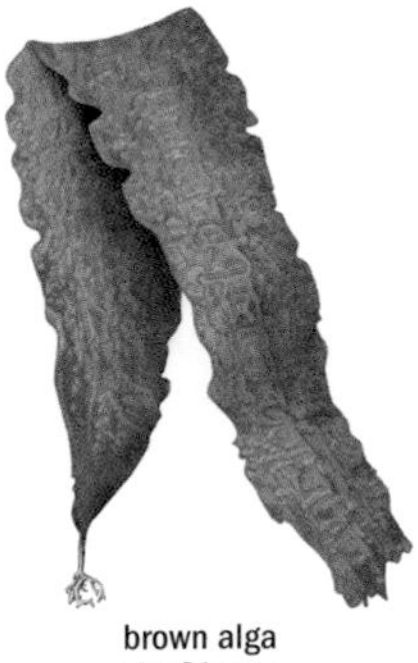

brown alga
alga^{F} bruna

mushroom

fungo^M

structure of a mushroom
struttura^F di un fungo^M

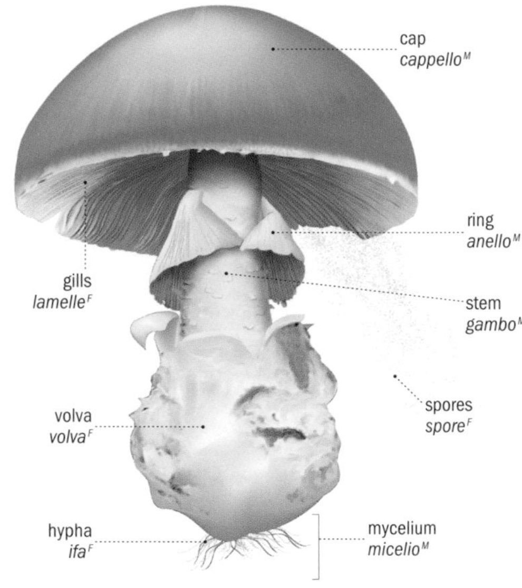

deadly poisonous mushroom
fungo^M velenoso e mortale

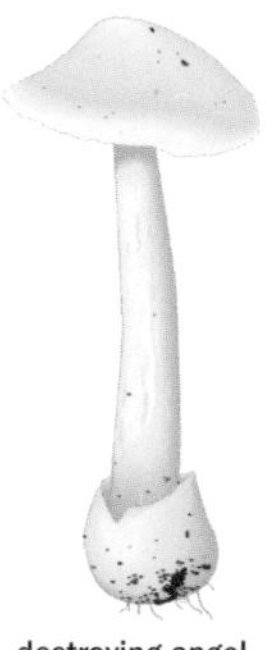

destroying angel
amanita^F virosa

poisonous mushroom
fungo^M velenoso

fly agaric
amanita^F muscaria

fern

felce^F

structure of a fern
struttura^F di una felce^F

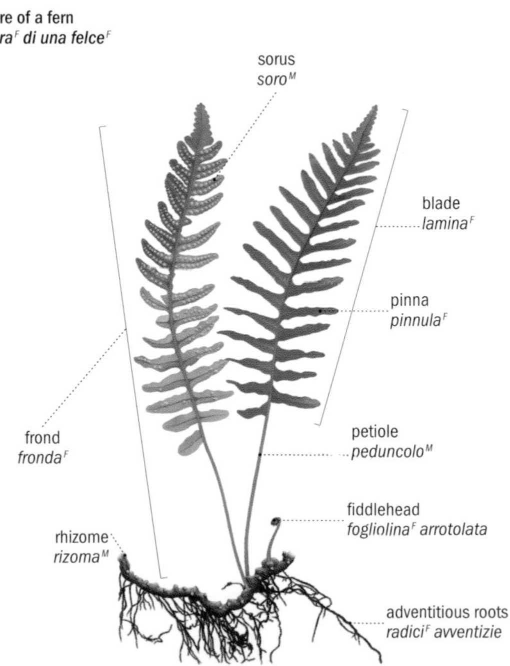

examples of ferns
esempi^M di felci^F

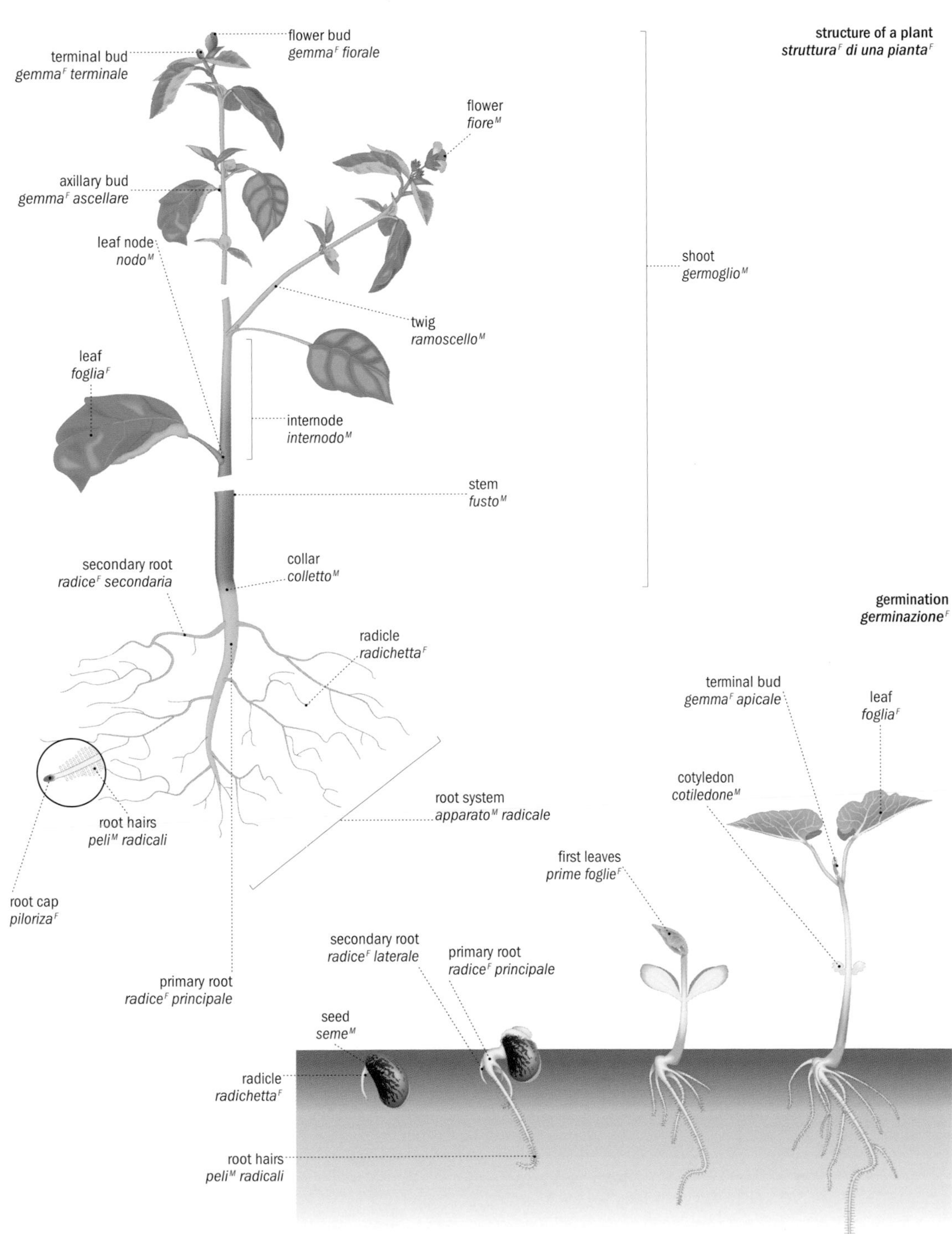
structure of a plant
strutturaF di una piantaF
flower bud
gemmaF fiorale
terminal bud
gemmaF terminale
flower
fioreM
axillary bud
gemmaF ascellare
leaf node
nodoM
shoot
germoglioM
twig
ramoscelloM
leaf
fogliaF
internode
internodoM
stem
fustoM
secondary root
radiceF secondaria
collar
collettoM
radicle
radichettaF
root system
apparatoM radicale
root hairs
periM radicali
root cap
pilorizaF
primary root
radiceF principale
germination
germinazioneF
terminal bud
gemmaF apicale
leaf
fogliaF
cotyledon
cotiledoneM
first leaves
prime foglieF
secondary root
radiceF laterale
primary root
radiceF principale
seed
semeM
radicle
radichettaF
root hairs
periM radicali

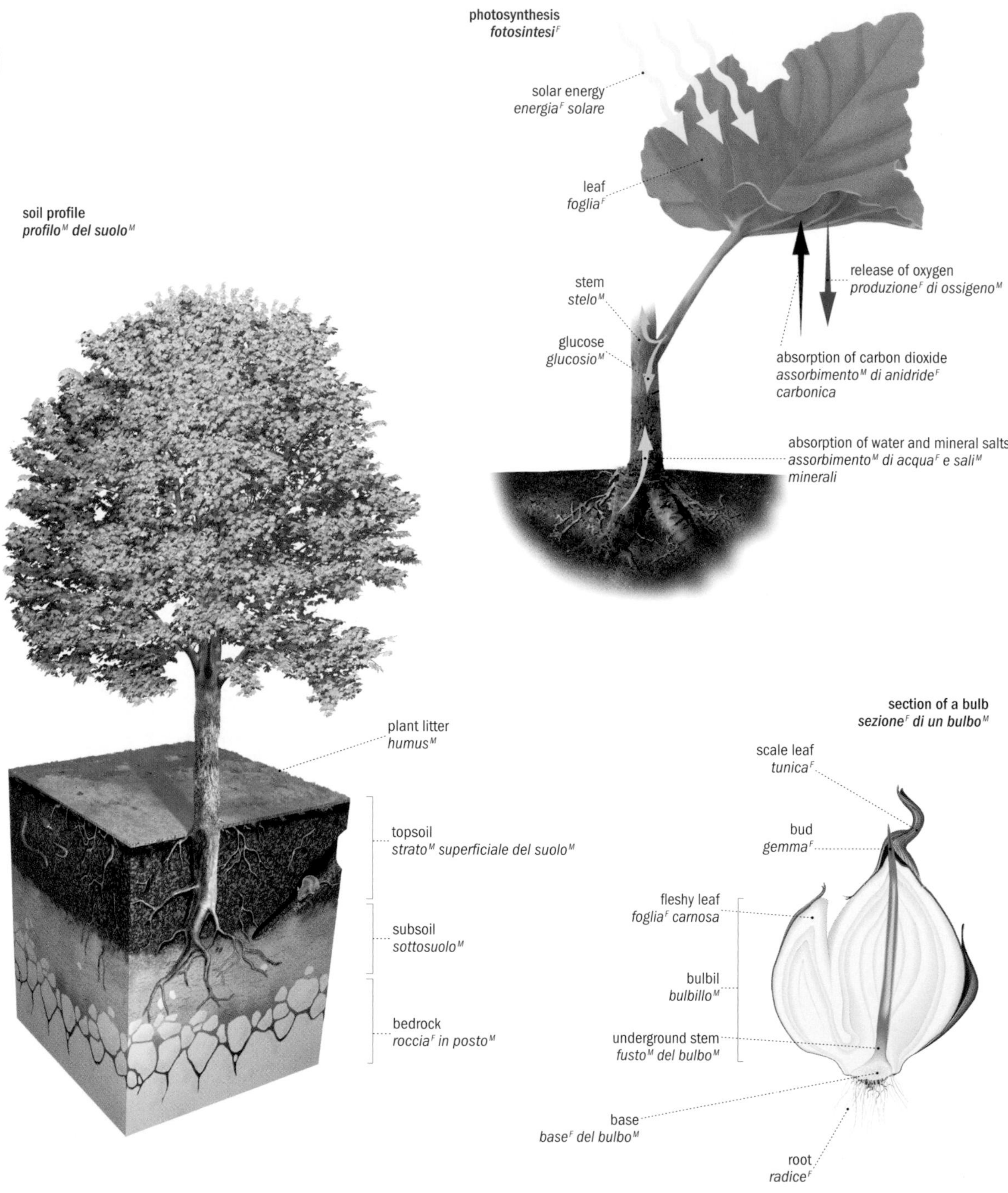
photosynthesis
fotosintesi[F]
solar energy
energia[F] solare
leaf
foglia[F]
stem
stelo[M]
glucose
glucosio[M]
release of oxygen
produzione[F] di ossigeno[M]
absorption of carbon dioxide
assorbimento[M] di anidride[F] carbonica
absorption of water and mineral salts
assorbimento[M] di acqua[F] e sali[M] minerali
soil profile
profilo[M] del suolo[M]
plant litter
humus[M]
topsoil
strato[M] superficiale del suolo[M]
subsoil
sottosuolo[M]
bedrock
roccia[F] in posto[M]
section of a bulb
sezione[F] di un bulbo[M]
scale leaf
tunica[F]
bud
gemma[F]
fleshy leaf
foglia[F] carnosa
bulbil
bulbillo[M]
underground stem
fusto[M] del bulbo[M]
base
base[F] del bulbo[M]
root
radice[F]

simple leaves
foglie*F *semplici

cordate
cordata

reniform
reniforme

orbiculate
orbicolare

spatulate
spatolata

linear
lineare

hastate
astata

ovate
ovata

lanceolate
lanceolata

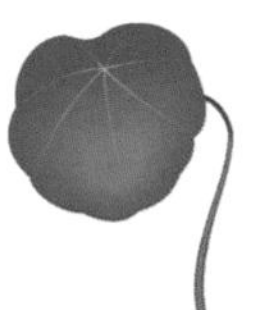

peltate
peltata

structure of a leaf
***struttura*F *di una foglia*F**

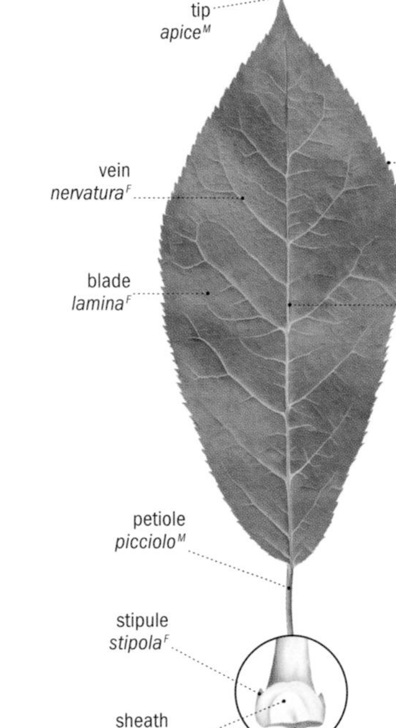

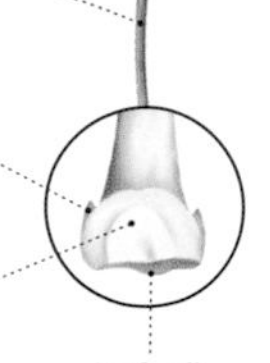

compound leaves
foglie*F *composte

trifoliolate
trifogliata

pinnatifid
pennatifida

palmate
palmata

abruptly pinnate
paripennata

odd pinnate
imparipennata

leaf margins
margine*M *fogliare

dentate
dentato

doubly dentate
doppiamente dentato

crenate
crenato

ciliate
ciliato

entire
liscio

lobate
lobato

flower

fiore[M]

structure of a flower
struttura[F] di un fiore[M]

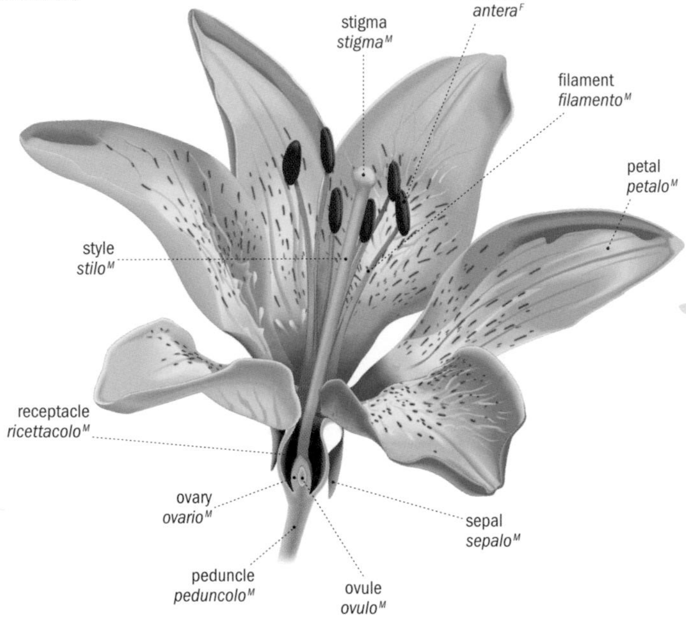

anther *antera[F]*

stigma *stigma[M]*

filament *filamento[M]*

petal *petalo[M]*

style *stilo[M]*

receptacle *ricettacolo[M]*

ovary *ovario[M]*

sepal *sepalo[M]*

peduncle *peduncolo[M]*

ovule *ovulo[M]*

pistil ***pistillo[M]***

corolla ***corolla[F]***

stamen ***stame[M]***

calyx ***calice[M]***

examples of flowers
esempi[M] di fiori[M]

orchid *orchidea[F]*

daffodil ***trombone[M]***

poppy ***papavero[M]***

tulip ***tulipano[M]***

lily of the valley ***mughetto[M]***

carnation ***garofano[M]***

rose ***rosa[F]***

begonia ***begonia[F]***

lily ***giglio[M]***

violet ***viola[F]***

crocus ***croco[M]***

sunflower ***girasole[M]***

types of inflorescences
***tipi**[M] **di infiorescenze**[F]*

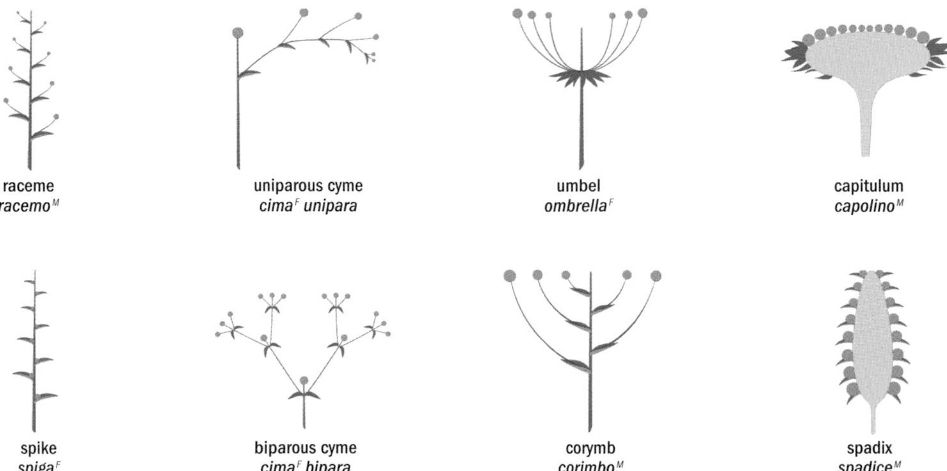

fruit

frutti[M]

fleshy fruit: stone fruit
***drupa**[F]*

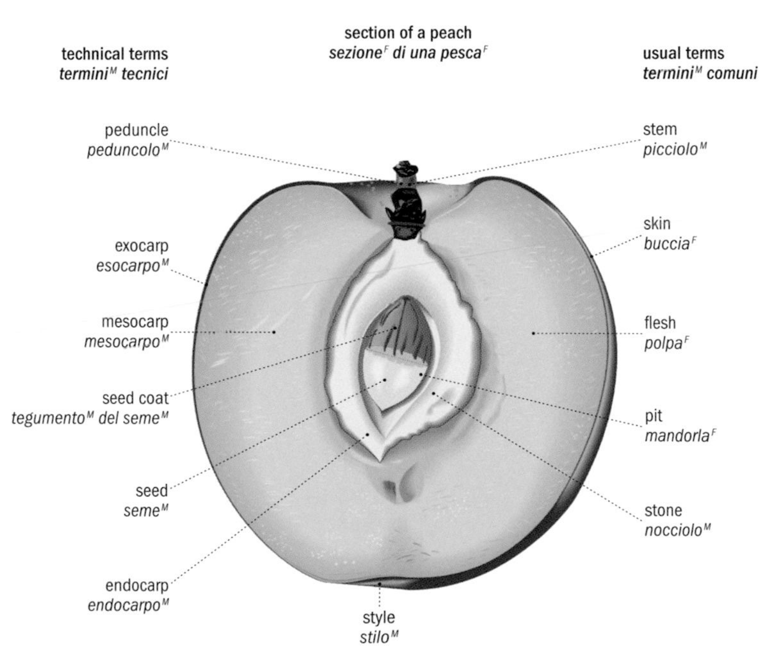

fleshy fruit: pome fruit
*frutto*ᴹ *carnoso: mela*ᶠ

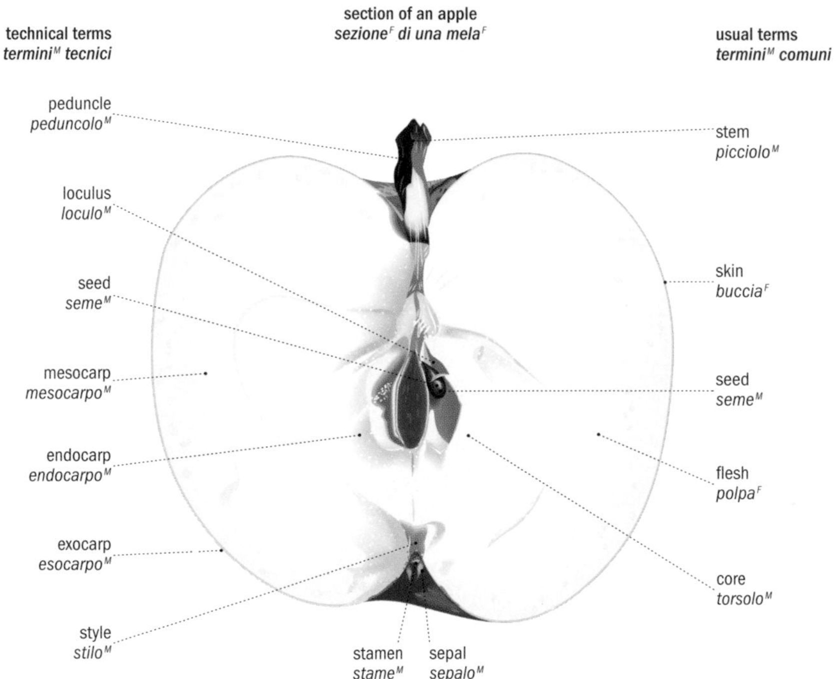

fleshy fruit: citrus fruit
*frutto*ᴹ *carnoso: agrume*ᴹ

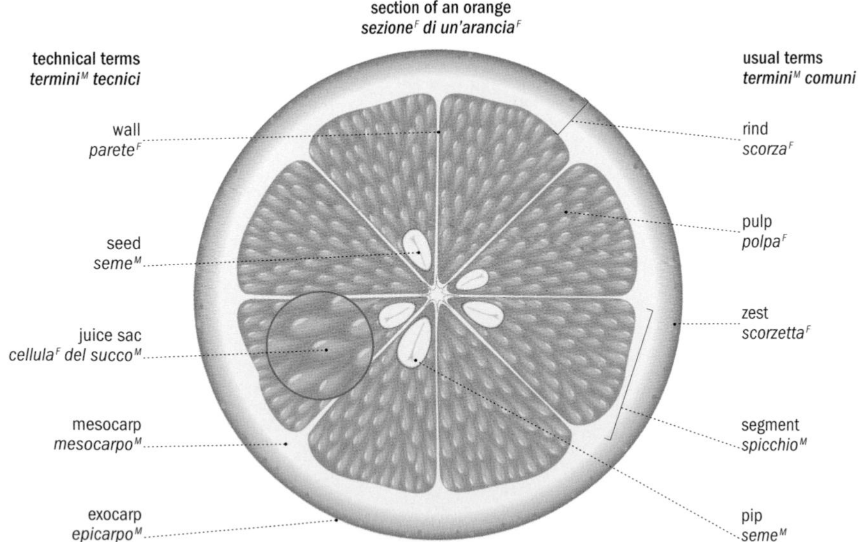

fleshy fruit: berry fruit
frutto[M] carnoso: bacca[F]

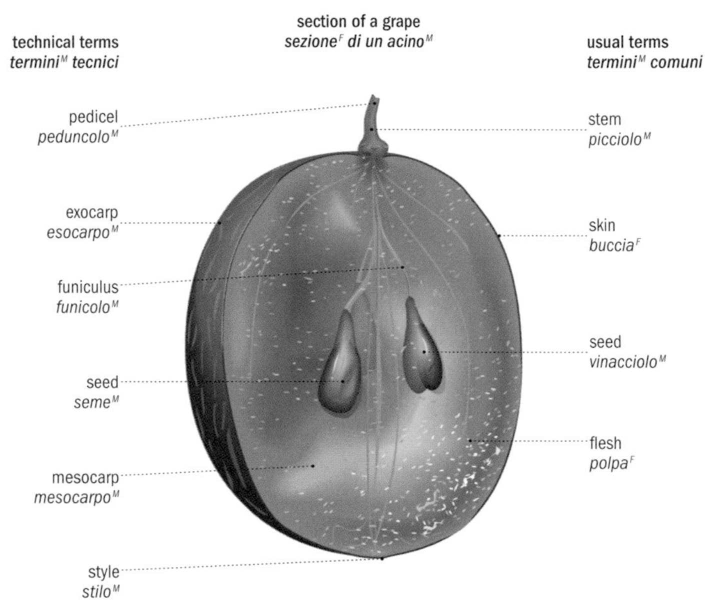

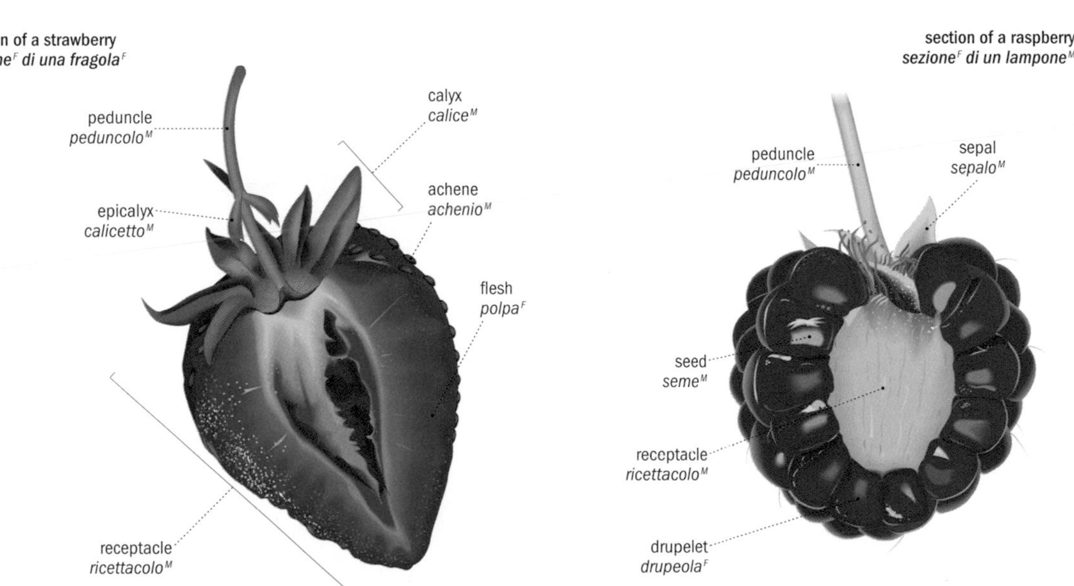

dry fruits
frutti^M secchi

husk
mallo^M

section of a follicle: star anise
sezione^F di un follicolo^M: anice^M stellato

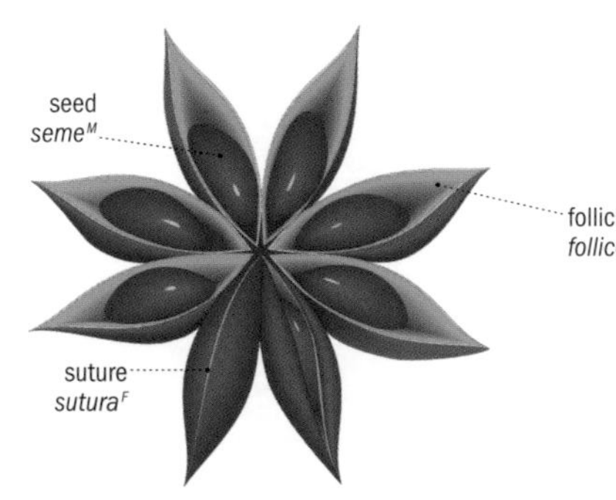

section of a silique: mustard
sezione^F di una siliqua^F: senape^F nera

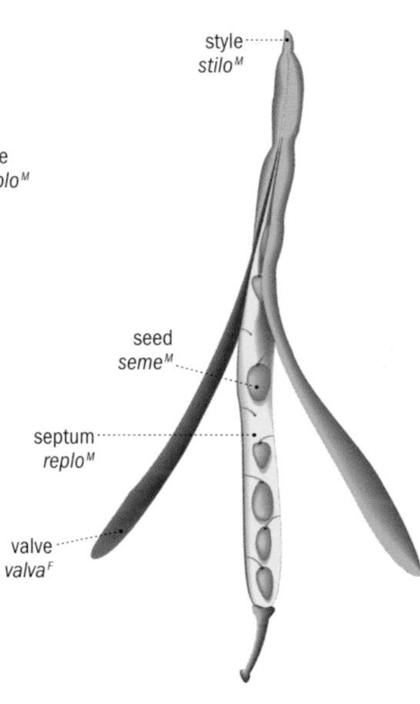

section of a hazelnut
sezione^F di una nocciola^F

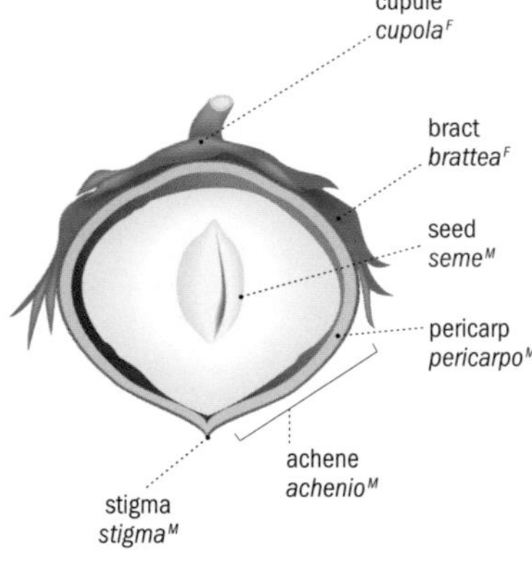

section of a legume: pea
sezione^F di un legume^M: pisello^M

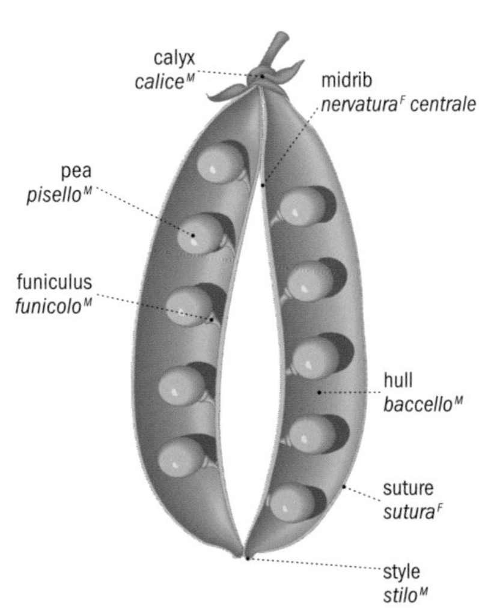

section of a capsule: poppy
sezione^F di una capsula^F: papavero^M

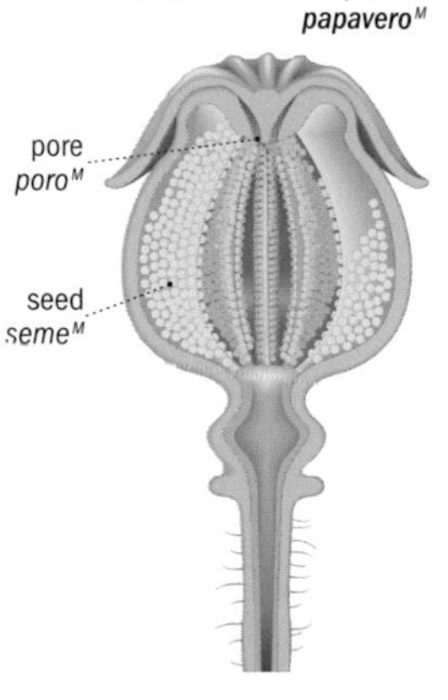

section of a walnut
sezione^F di una noce^F

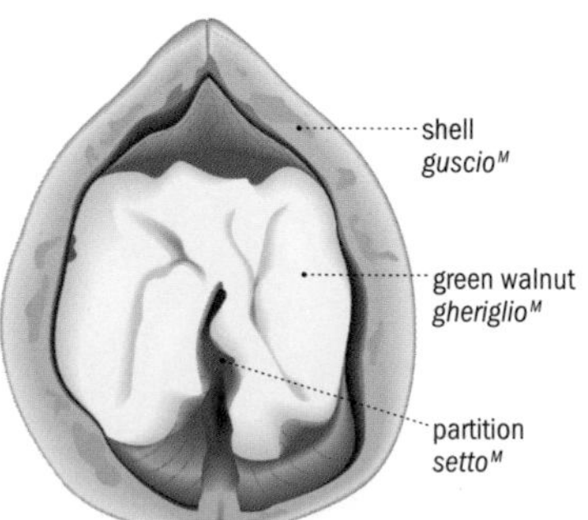

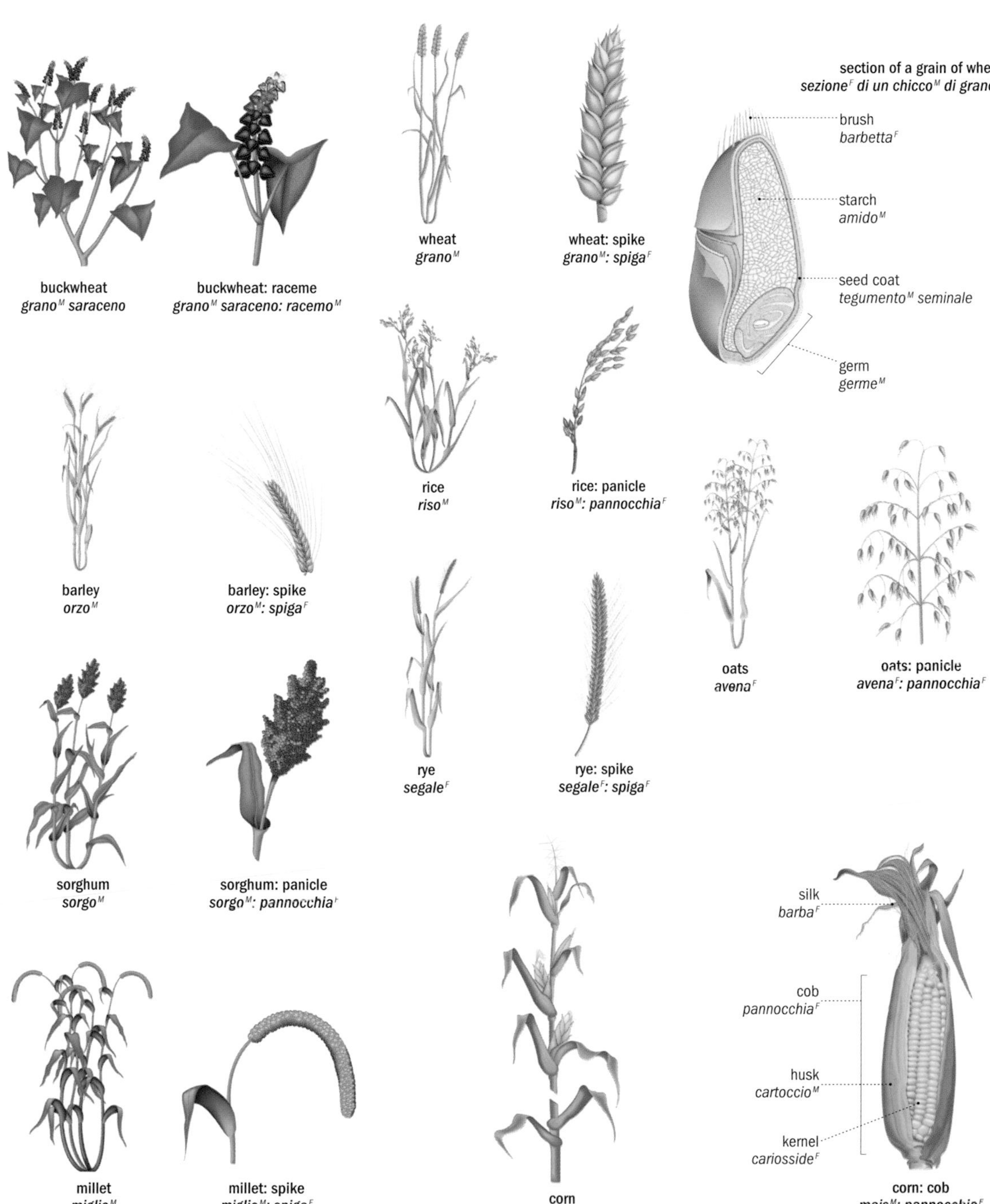

buckwheat
grano[M] saraceno
buckwheat: raceme
grano[M] saraceno: racemo[M]
wheat
grano[M]
wheat: spike
grano[M]: spiga[F]
section of a grain of wheat
sezione[F] di un chicco[M] di grano[M]
brush
barbetta[F]
starch
amido[M]
seed coat
tegumento[M] seminale
germ
germe[M]
rice
riso[M]
rice: panicle
riso[M]: pannocchia[F]
barley
orzo[M]
barley: spike
orzo[M]: spiga[F]
oats
avena[F]
oats: panicle
avena[F]: pannocchia[F]
rye
segale[F]
rye: spike
segale[F]: spiga[F]
sorghum
sorgo[M]
sorghum: panicle
sorgo[M]: pannocchia[F]
silk
barba[F]
cob
pannocchia[F]
husk
cartoccio[M]
kernel
cariosside[F]
millet
miglio[M]
millet: spike
miglio[M]: spiga[F]
corn
mais[M]
corn: cob
mais[M]: pannocchia[F]

grape

vite[F]

bunch of grapes
grappolo[M] d'uva[F]

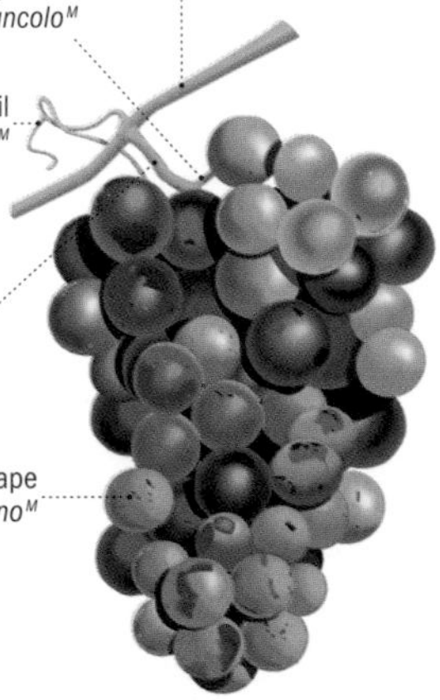

branch
ramo[M]

pedicel
peduncolo[M]

tendril
viticcio[M]

peduncle
rachide[F]

grape
acino[M]

vine stock
albero[M] della vite[F]

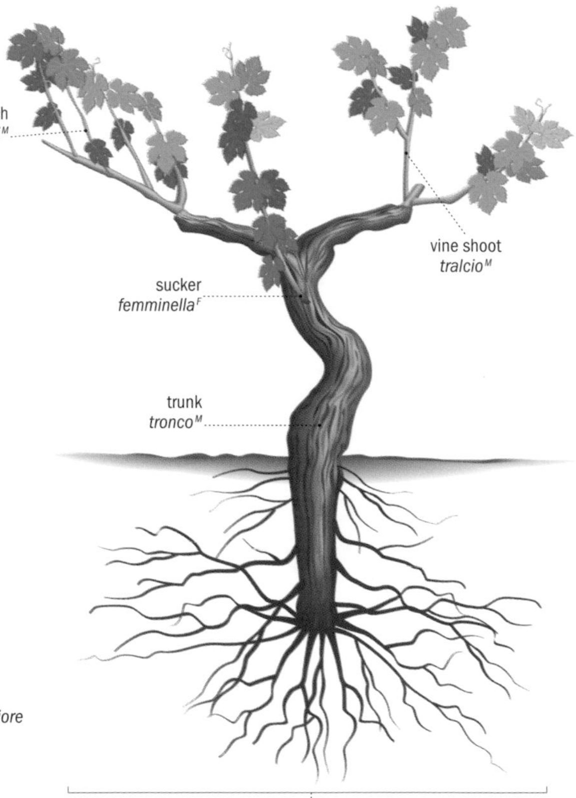

fruit branch
ramo[M] con frutti[M]

vine shoot
tralcio[M]

sucker
femminella[F]

trunk
tronco[M]

root system
apparato[M] radicale

grape leaf
pampino[M]

upper lateral lobe
lobo[M] laterale superiore

terminal lobe
lobo[M] terminale

upper lateral sinus
seno[M] laterale superiore

lower lateral lobe
lobo[M] laterale inferiore

lower lateral sinus
seno[M] laterale inferiore

petiolar sinus
seno[M] peziolato

steps in maturation
stadi[M] di maturazione[F]

flowering
fioritura[F]

fruition
fruttificazione[F]

ripening
maturazione[F]

ripeness
maturità[F]

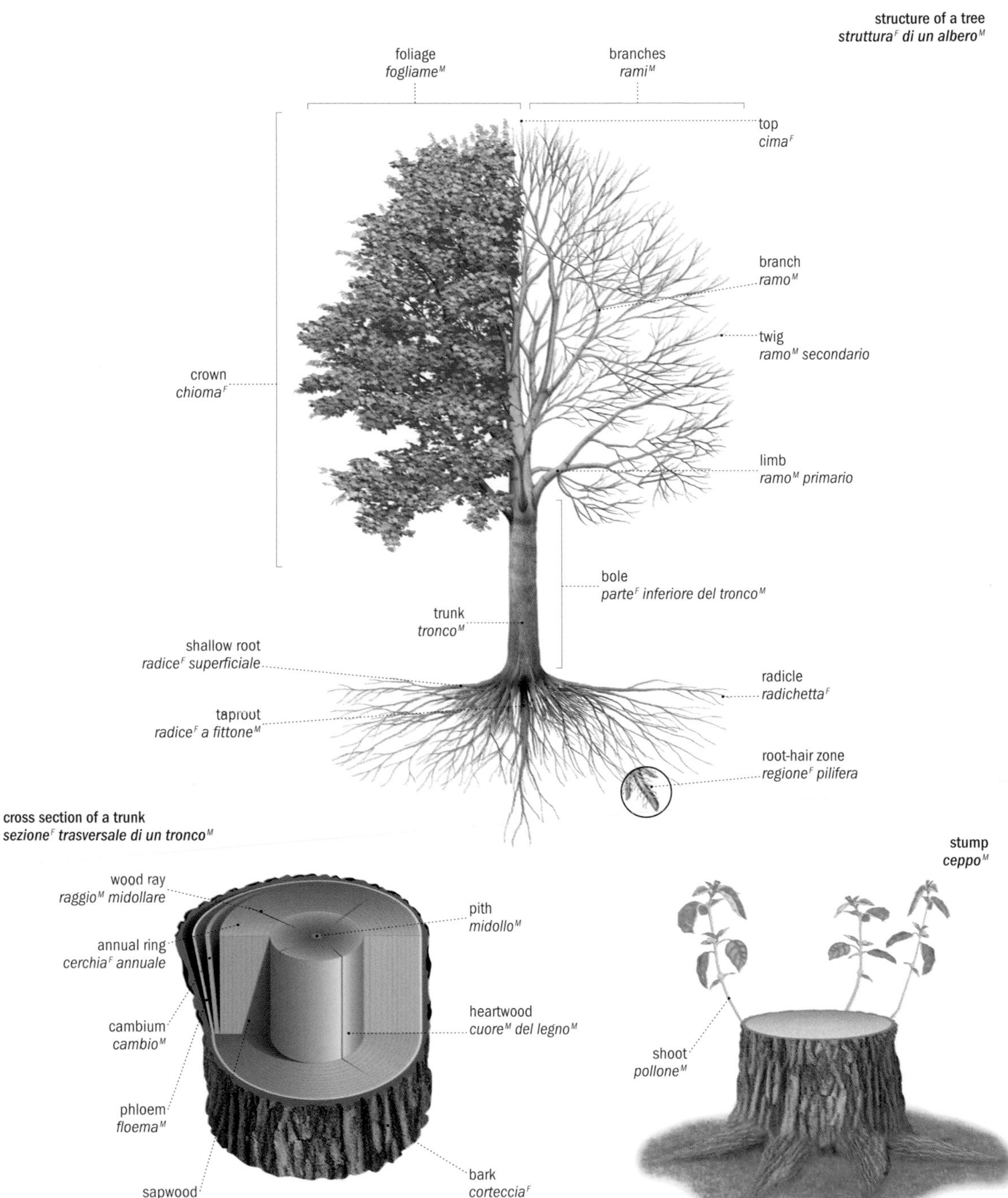

structure of a tree
struttura[F] di un albero[M]
foliage
fogliame[M]
branches
rami[M]
top
cima[F]
branch
ramo[M]
twig
ramo[M] secondario
crown
chioma[F]
limb
ramo[M] primario
bole
parte[F] inferiore del tronco[M]
trunk
tronco[M]
shallow root
radice[F] superficiale
radicle
radichetta[F]
taproot
radice[F] a fittone[M]
root-hair zone
regione[F] pilifera
cross section of a trunk
sezione[F] trasversale di un tronco[M]
stump
ceppo[M]
wood ray
raggio[M] midollare
pith
midollo[M]
annual ring
cerchia[F] annuale
heartwood
cuore[M] del legno[M]
cambium
cambio[M]
shoot
pollone[M]
phloem
floema[M]
bark
corteccia[F]
sapwood
alburno[M]

examples of broadleaved trees
***esempi*[M] *di latifoglie*[F]**

conifer

conifera[F]

pinecone
cono[M]

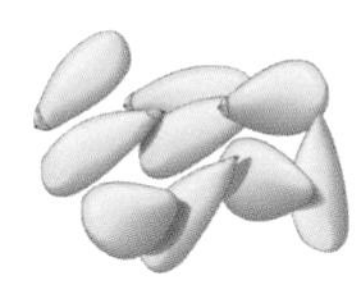

pine seed
pinolo[M]

branch
ramo[M]

examples of leaves
***esempi*[M] *di foglie*[F]**

fir needles
aghi[M] *d'abete*[M]

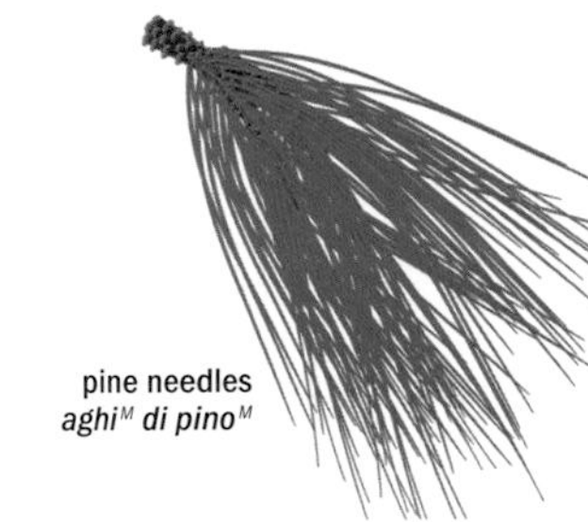

pine needles
aghi[M] *di pino*[M]

cypress scalelike leaves
foglie[F] *squamiformi del cipresso*[M]

examples of conifers
***esempi*[M] *di conifere*[F]**

umbrella pine
pino[M] *domestico*

cedar of Lebanon
cedro[M] *del Libano*[M]

spruce
picea[F]

larch
larice[M]

fir
abete[M]

animal cell

cellula^F animale

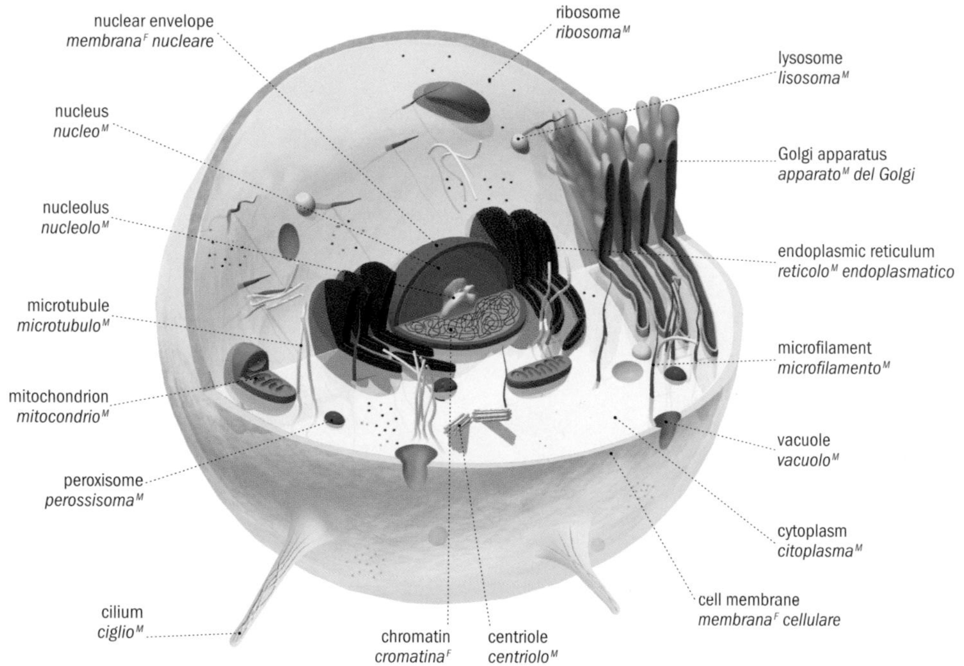

unicellulars

unicellulari^M

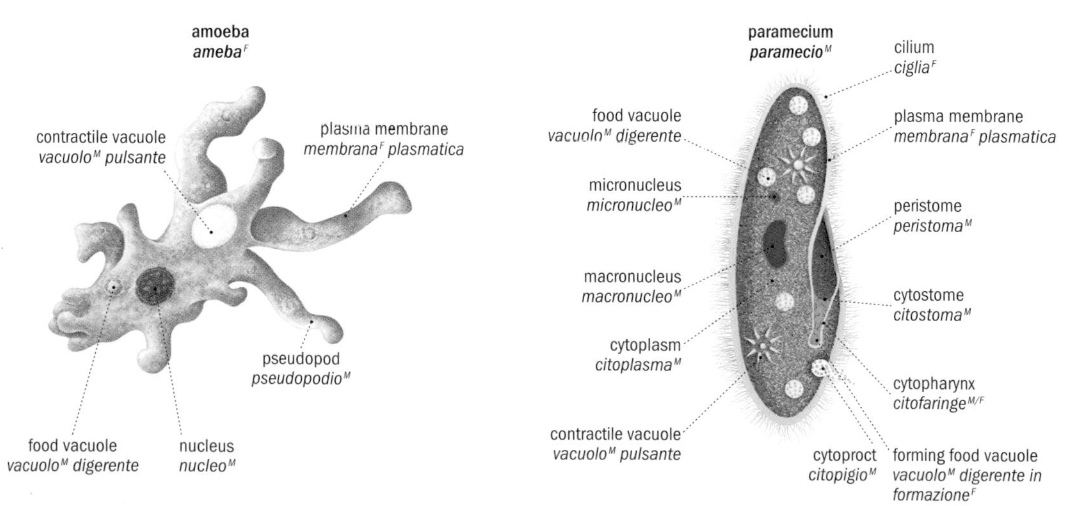

butterfly

farfalla[F]

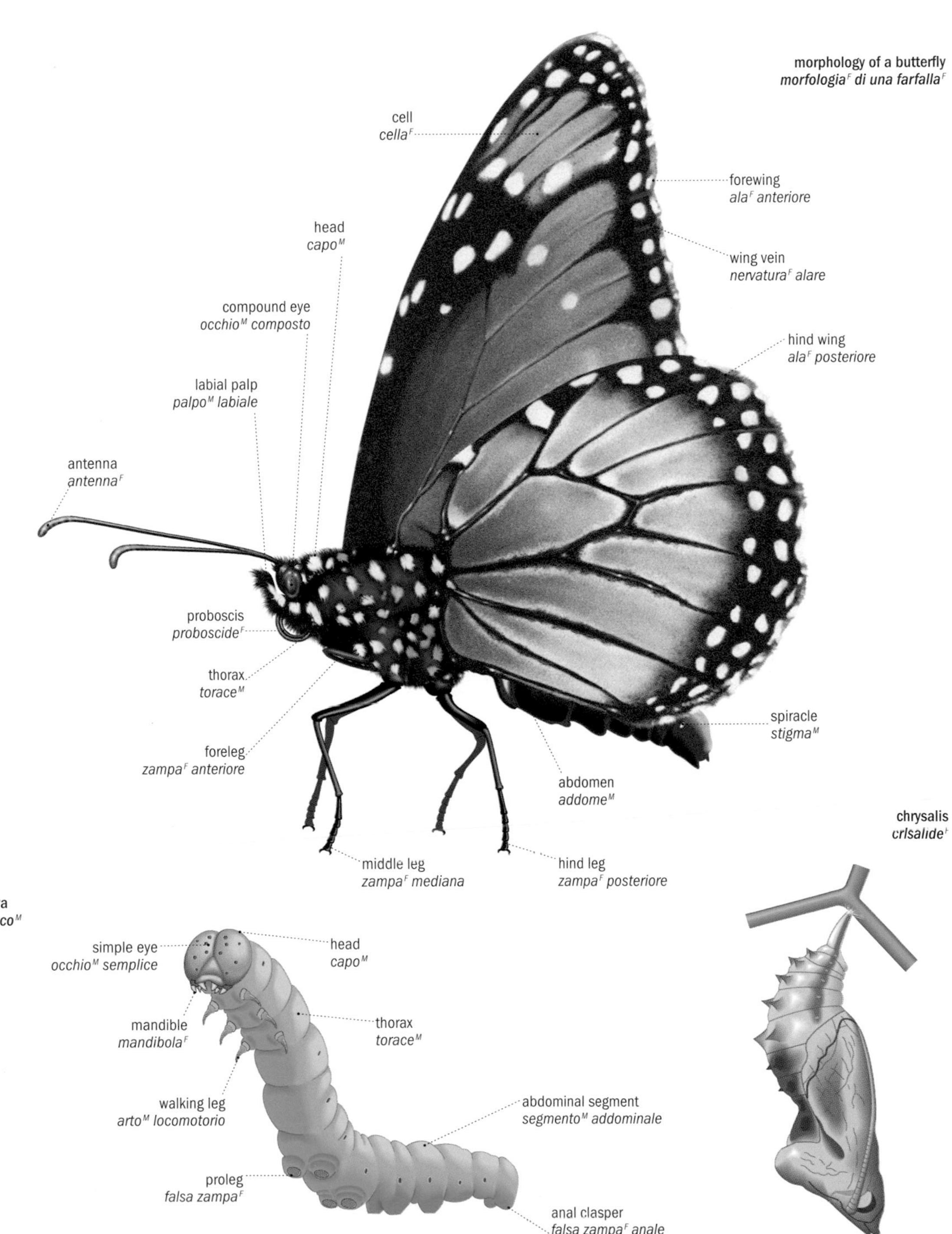

honeybee

apeF

morphology of a honeybee: worker
morfologiaF di un'apeF: operaia

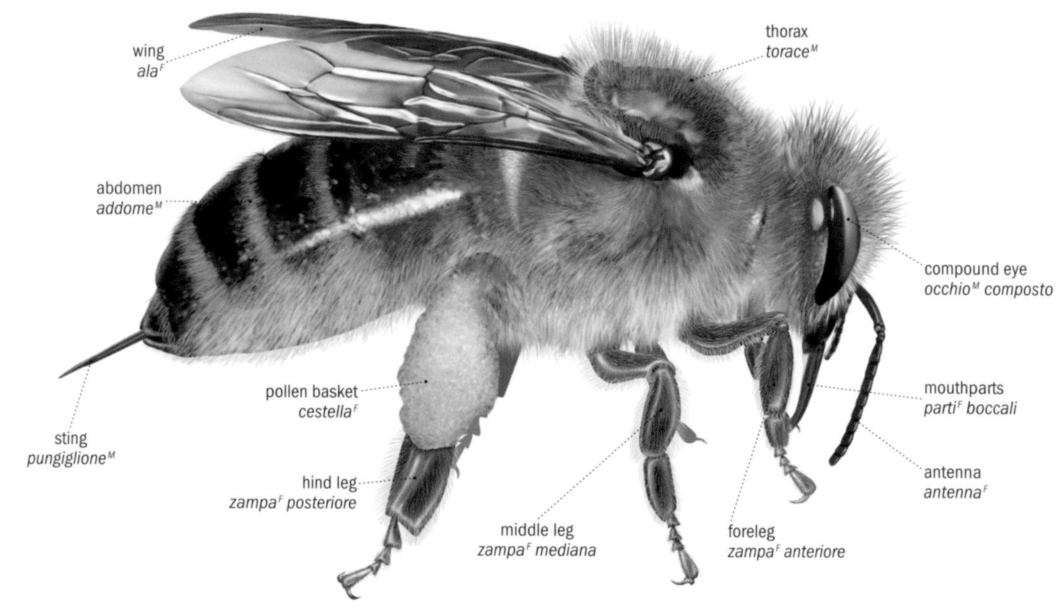

castes
casteF

examples of insects

esempi^M di insetti^M

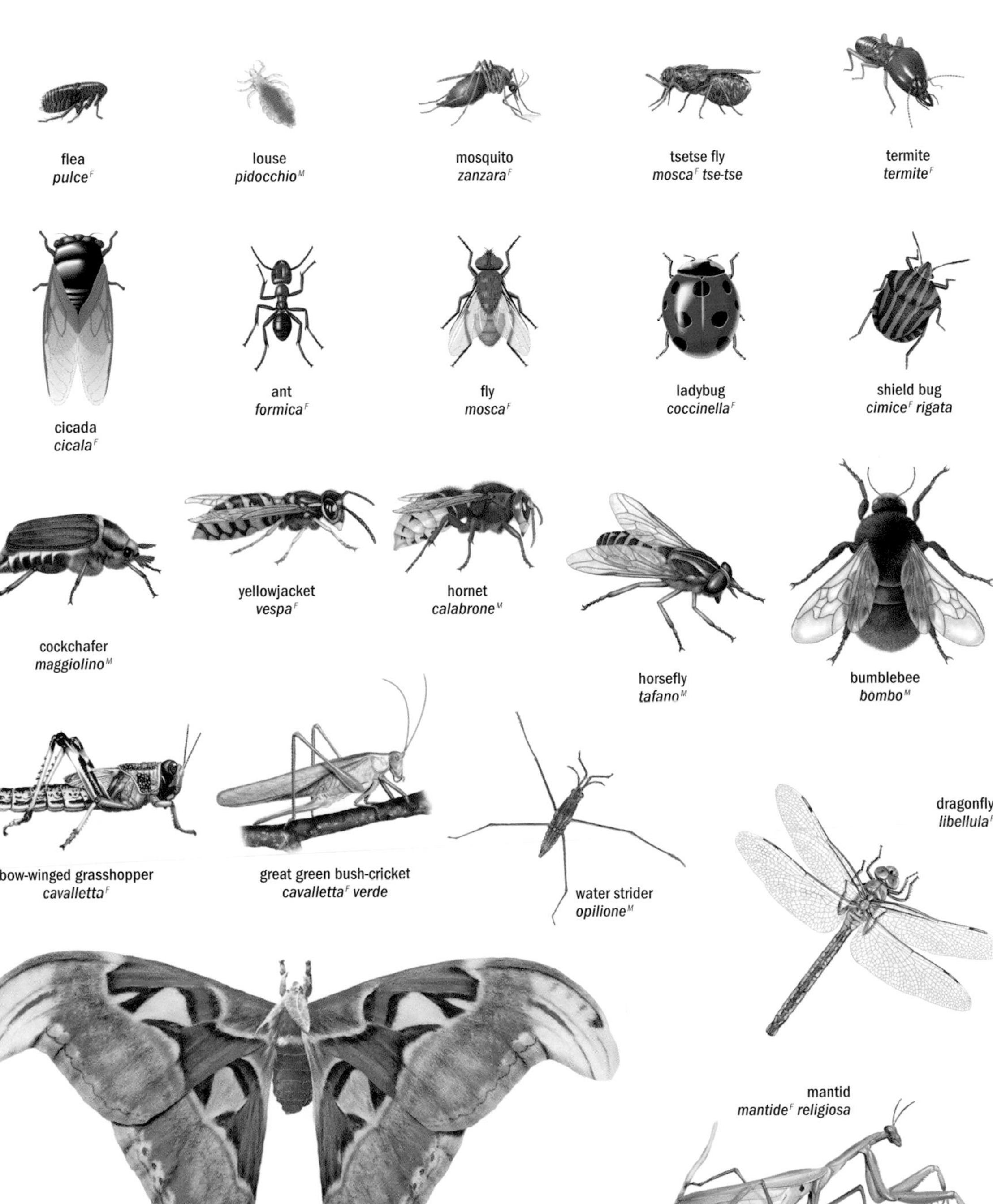

spider

ragno[M]

spider web
ragnatela[F]

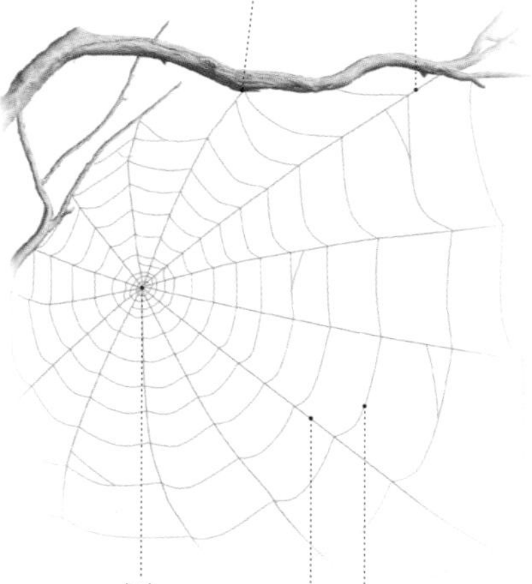

anchor point
punto[M] d'appoggio[M]
support thread
filo[M] d'appoggio[M]
hub
centro[M] della ragnatela[F]
spiral thread
filo[M] spirale
radial thread
filo[M] radiale

morphology of a spider
morfologia[F] di un ragno[M]

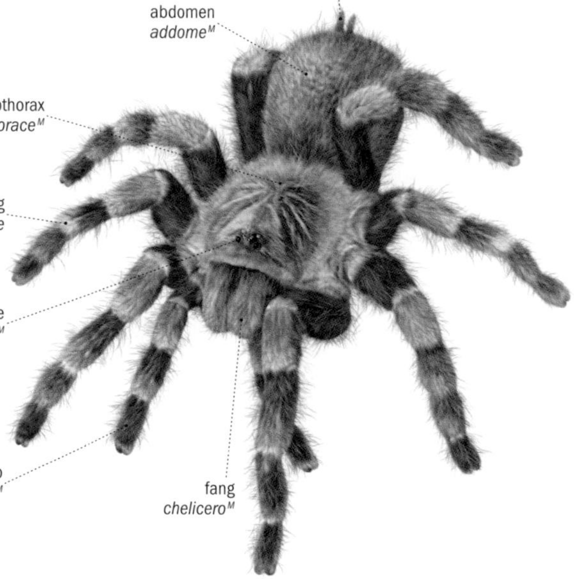

spinneret
filiere[F]
abdomen
addome[M]
cephalothorax
cefalotorace[M]
leg
arto[M] locomotore
eye
occhio[M]
pedipalp
pedipalpo[M]
fang
chelicero[M]

examples of arachnids

esempi[M] di aracnidi[M]

crab spider
ragno[M]-granchio[M]
garden spider
epeira[F]
scorpion
scorpione[M]
tick
zecca[F]
water spider
ragno[M] acquatico
red-kneed tarantula
migale[F] del Messico[M]

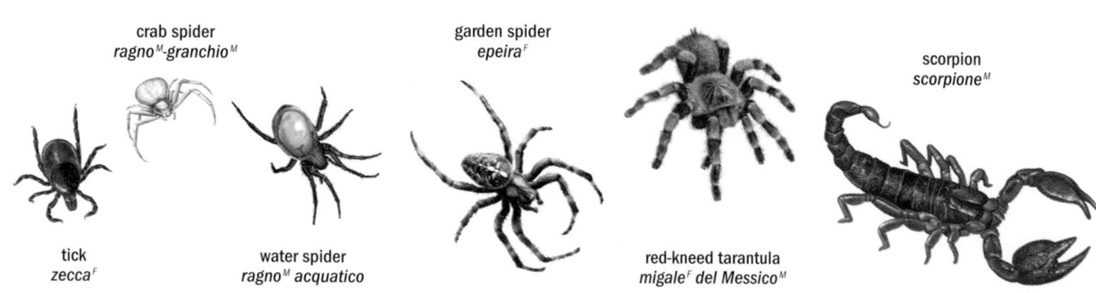

lobster

astice^M

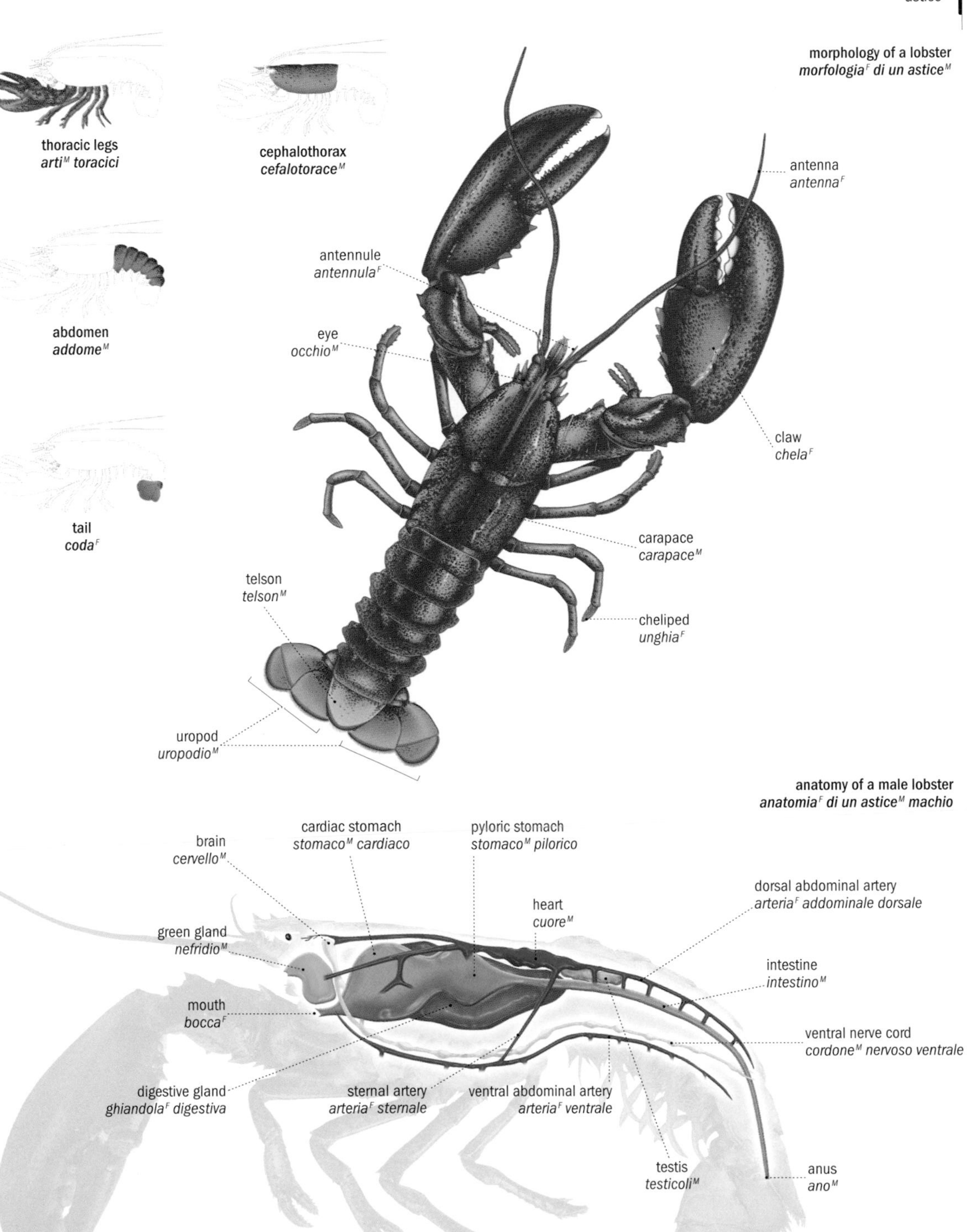

snail

chiocciola^F

morphology of a snail
morfologia^F di una chiocciola^F

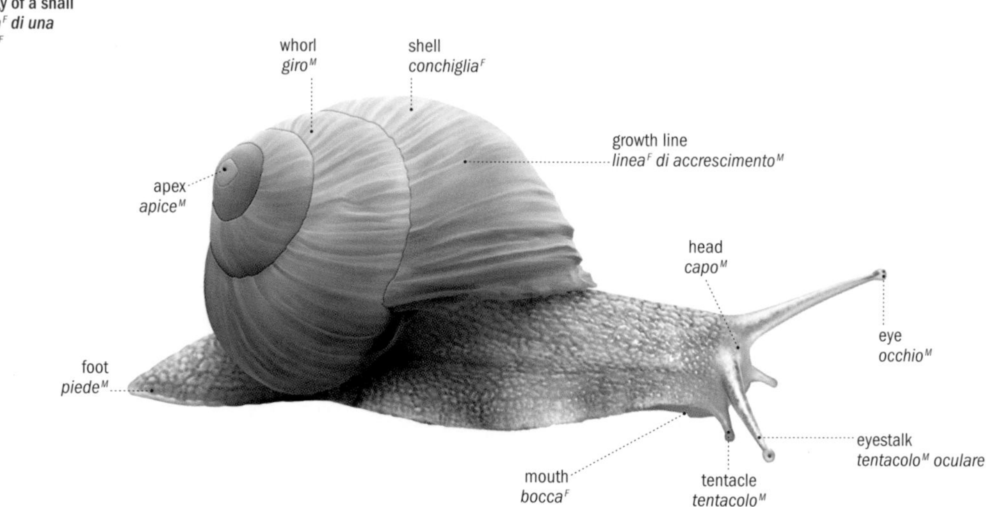

octopus

polpo^M

morphology of an octopus
morfologia^F di un polpo^M

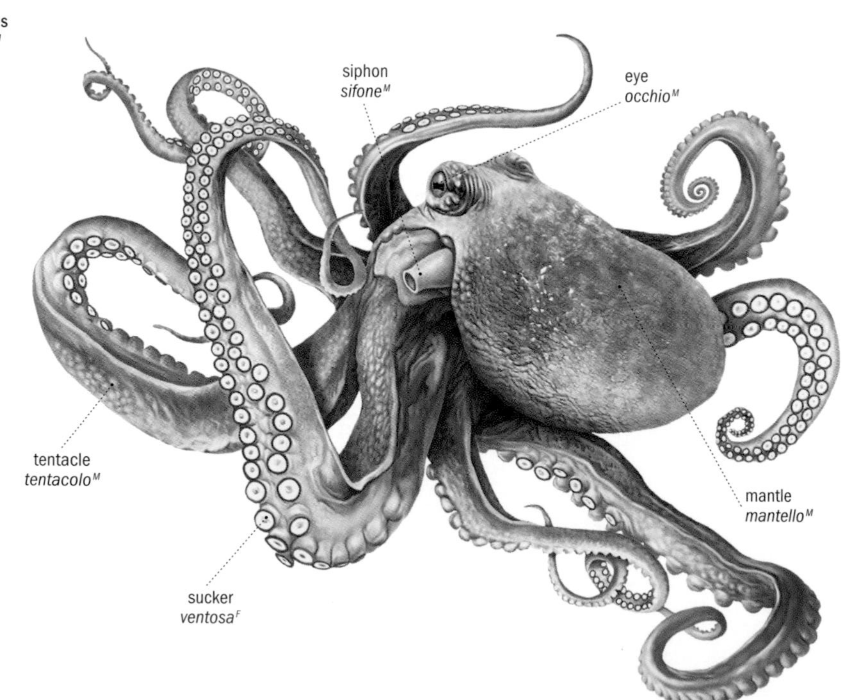

univalve shell

conchiglia^F univalve

morphology of a univalve shell
morfologia^F di una conchiglia^F univalve

apex
apice^M
nuclear whorl
giro^M embrionale
columella
columella^F
whorl
giro^M della spira^F
axial rib
costa^F assiale
suture
sutura^F
spiral rib
costa^F spirale
aperture
apertura^F
outer lip
labbro^M esterno
columella fold
piega^F della columella^F
inner lip
labbro^M interno
siphonal canal
canale^M del sifone^M

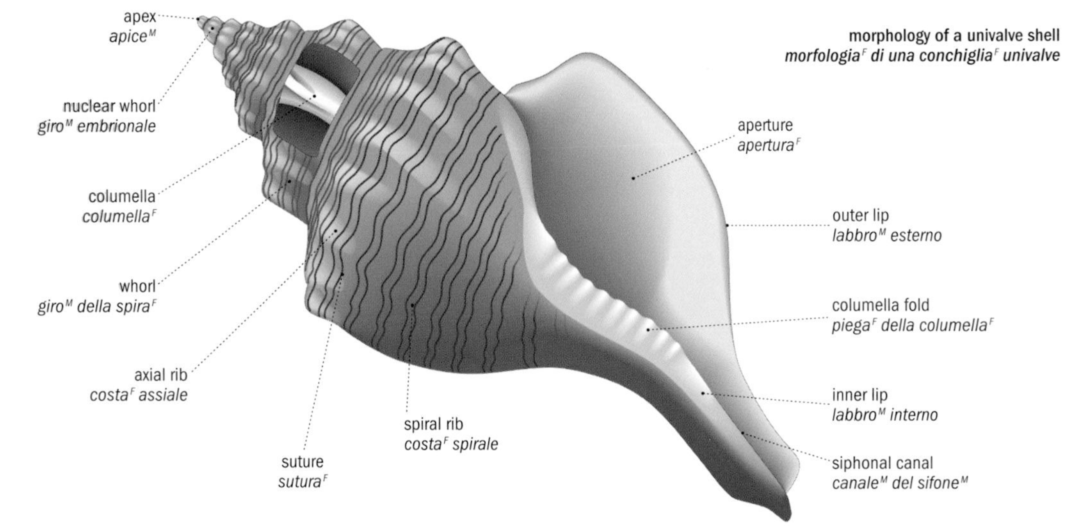

bivalve shell

conchiglia^F bivalve

anatomy of a bivalve shell
anatomia^F di una conchiglia^F bivalve

kidney
rene^M
shell
conchiglia^F
heart
cuore^M
umbo
cerniera^F
ligament
legamento^M
posterior adductor muscle
muscolo^M adduttore posteriore
digestive gland
ghiandola^F digestiva
anus
ano^M
stomach
stomaco^M
anterior adductor muscle
muscolo^M adduttore anteriore
visceral ganglion
ganglio^M viscerale
gills
branchie^F
labial palp
palpo^M
mantle
mantello^M
gonad
gonade^F
mouth
bocca^F
intestine
intestino^M
foot
piede^M
cerebropleural ganglion
ganglio^M cerebropleurale

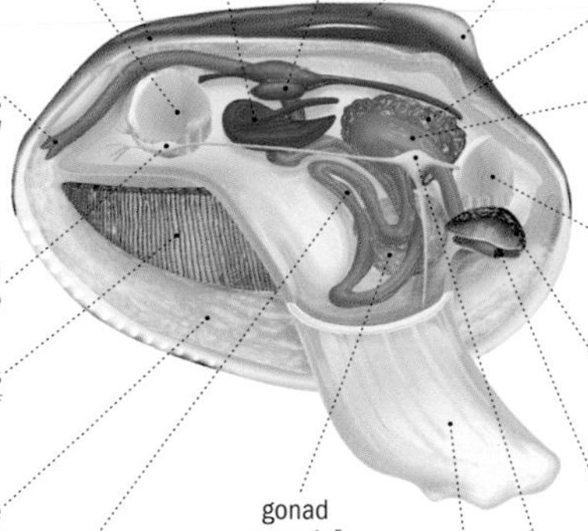

morphology of a bivalve shell
morfologia^F di una conchiglia^F bivalve

anterior end
margine^M anteriore
lunule
lunula^F
umbo
umbone^M
ligament
legamento^M
escutcheon
scutello^M
growth line
linea^F di accrescimento^M
valve
valva^F
posterior end
margine^M posteriore

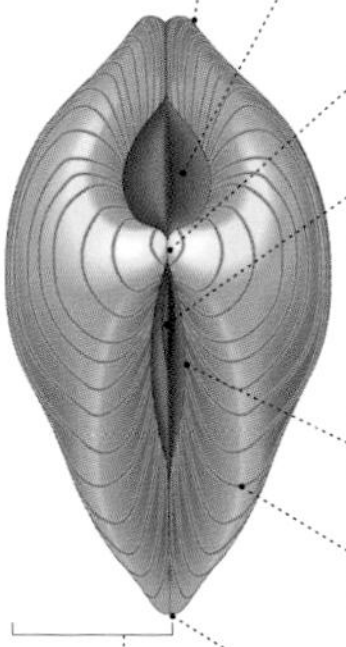

cartilaginous fish

pesce^M cartilagineo

morphology of a female shark
morfologia^F di uno squalo^M femminile

first dorsal fin
prima pinna^F dorsale
carina
carena^F
second dorsal fin
seconda pinna^F dorsale
snout
rostro^M
caudal fin
pinna^F caudale
nostril
narice^F
tooth
dente^M
pelvic fin
pinna^F pelvica
gill slits
fessure^F branchiali
pectoral fin
pinna^F pettorale
anal fin
pinna^F anale

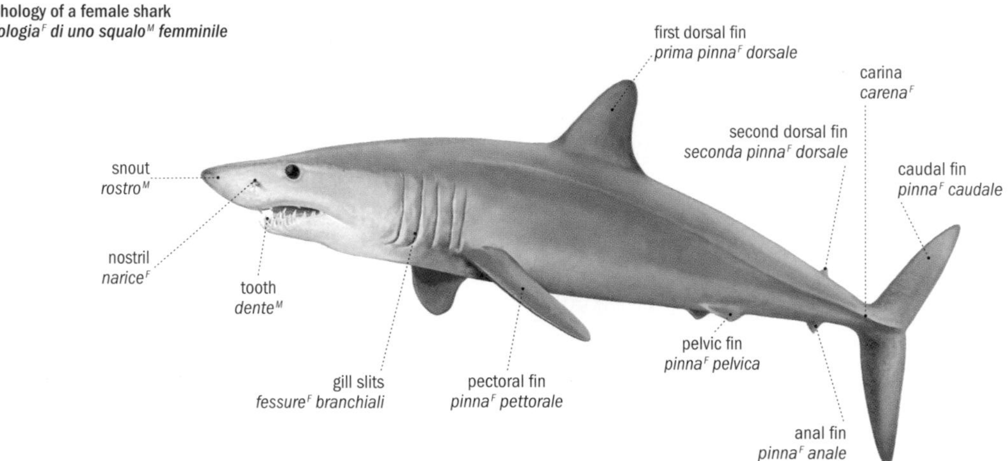

bony fish

pesce^M osseo

morphology of a perch
morfologia^F di un persico^M

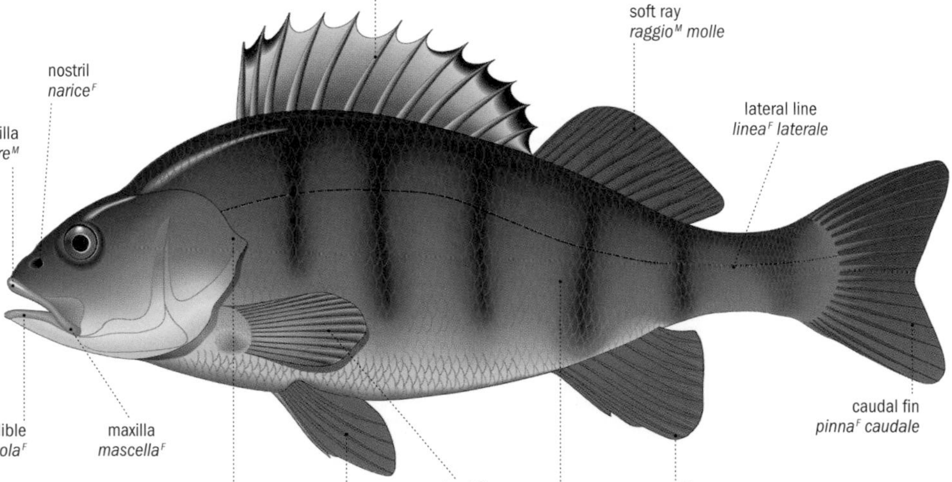

spiny ray
raggio^M spinoso
soft ray
raggio^M molle
nostril
narice^F
lateral line
linea^F laterale
premaxilla
premascellare^M
caudal fin
pinna^F caudale
mandible
mandibola^F
maxilla
mascella^F
pectoral fin
pinna^F pettorale
anal fin
pinna^F anale
operculum
opercolo^M
pelvic fin
pinna^F pelvica
scale
scaglia^F

ANIMAL KINGDOM

frog

rana[F]

morphology of a frog
morfologia[F] di una rana[F]

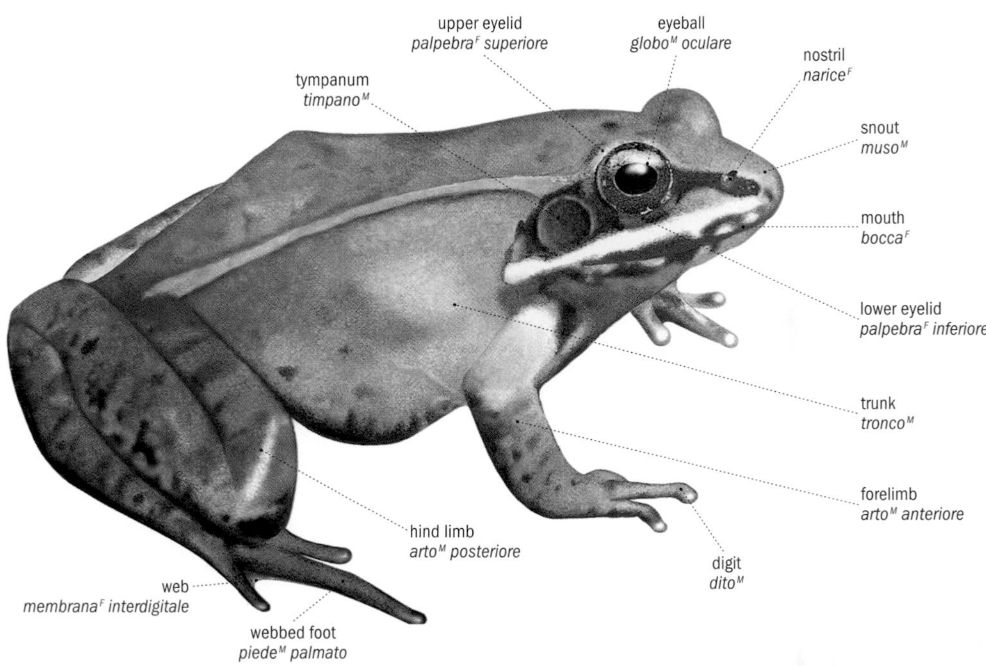

examples of amphibians

esempi[M] di anfibi[M]

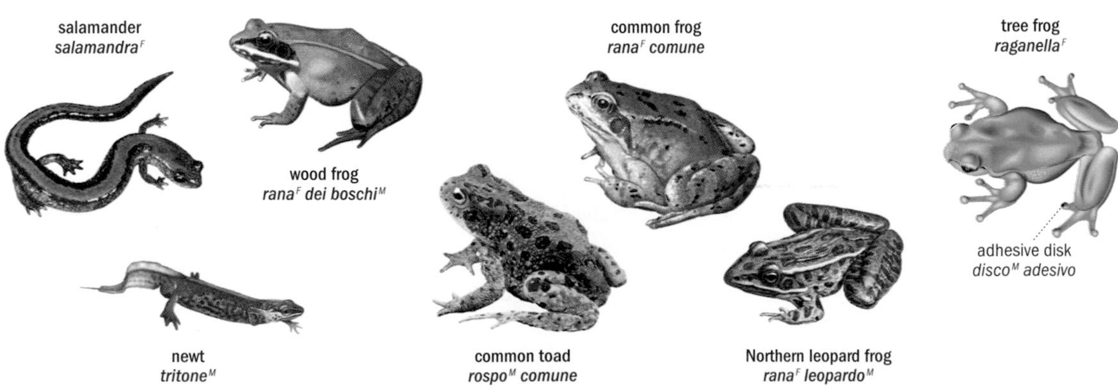

snake

serpente[M]

morphology of a venomous snake: head
morfologia[F] di un serpente[M] velenoso: testa[F]

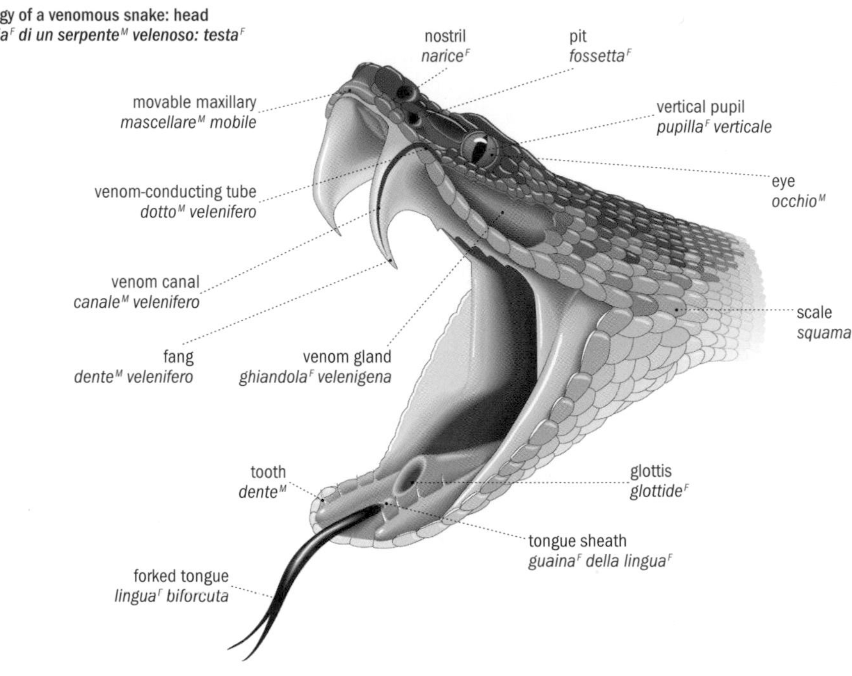

turtle

tartaruga[F]

morphology of a turtle
morfologia[F] di una tartaruga[F]

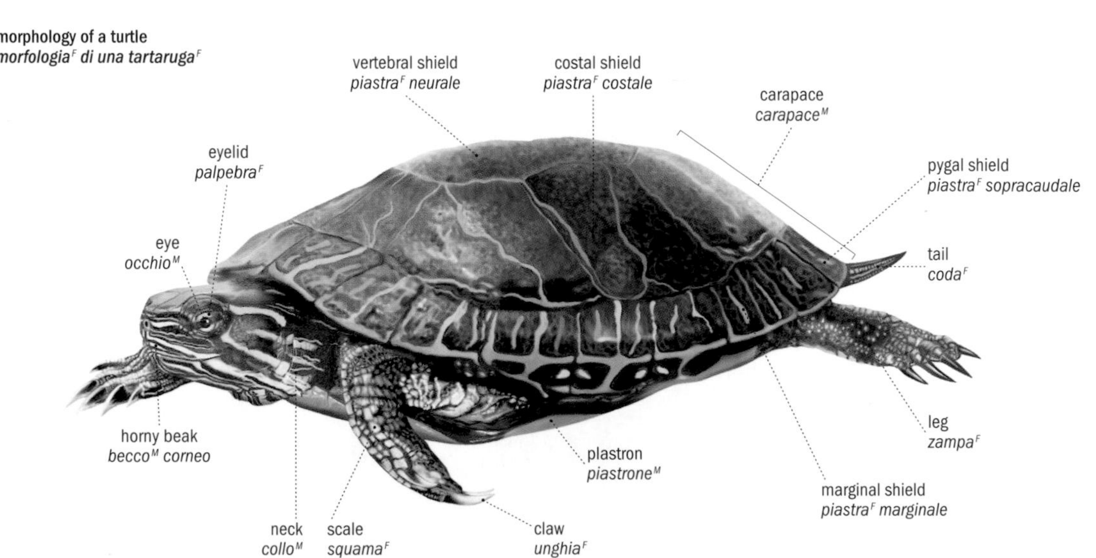

examples of reptiles

esempi[M] di rettili[M]

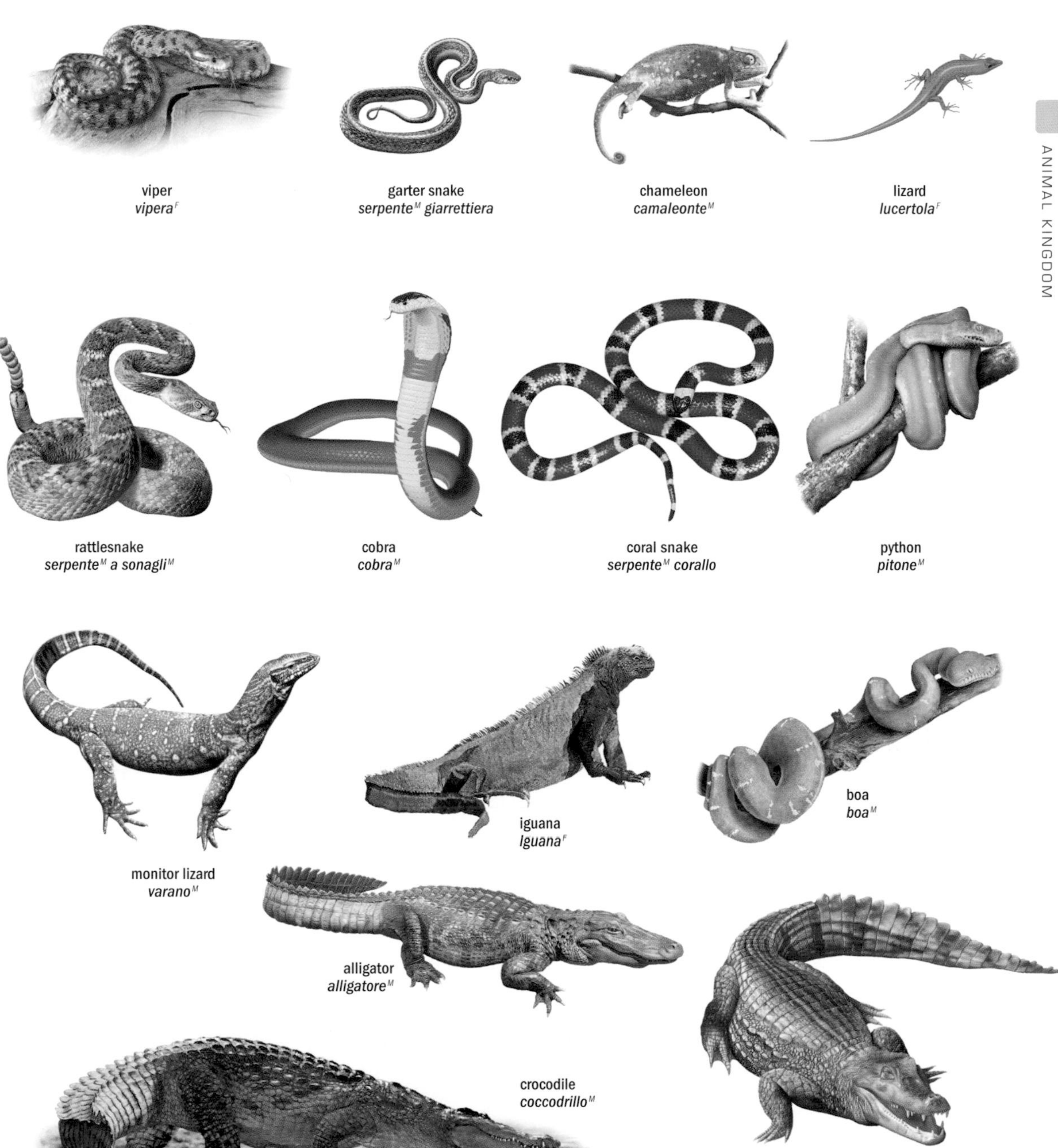

bird

uccello[M]

morphology of a bird
morfologia[F] di un uccello[M]

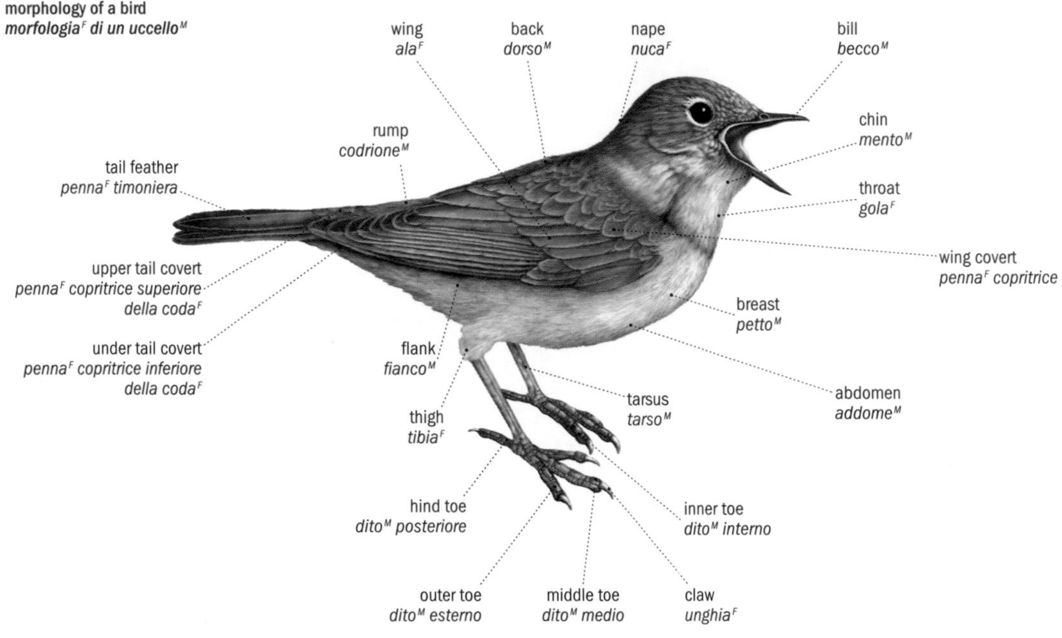

head
capo[M]

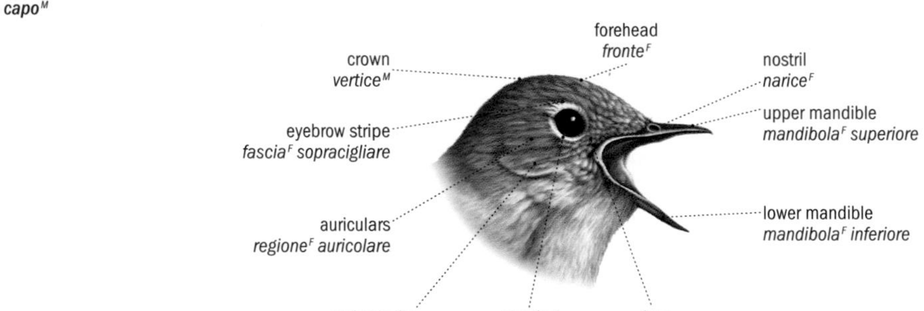

wing
ala[F]

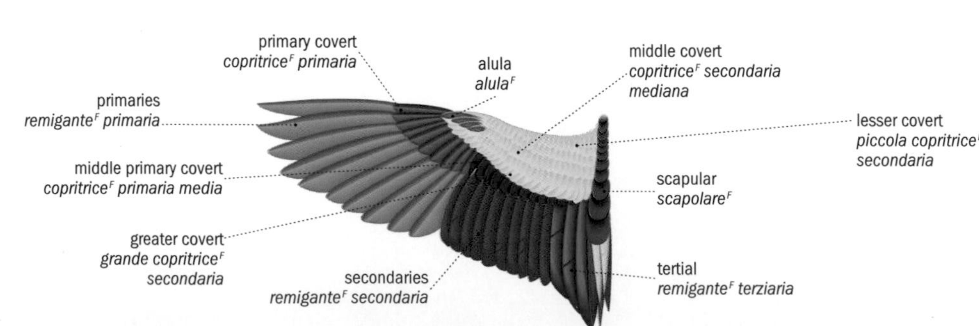

egg
uovo[M]

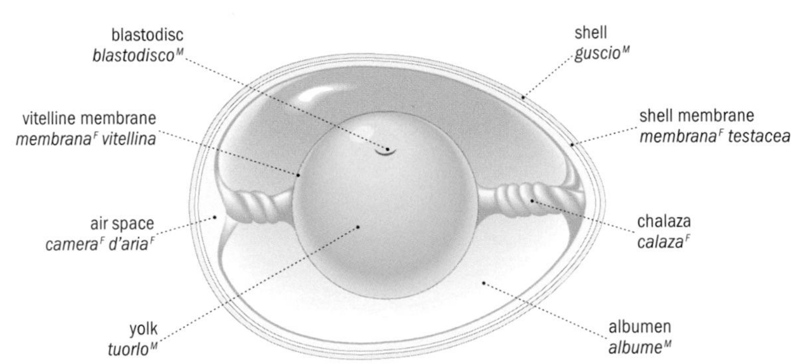

examples of bills
***esempi*[M] *di becchi*[M]**

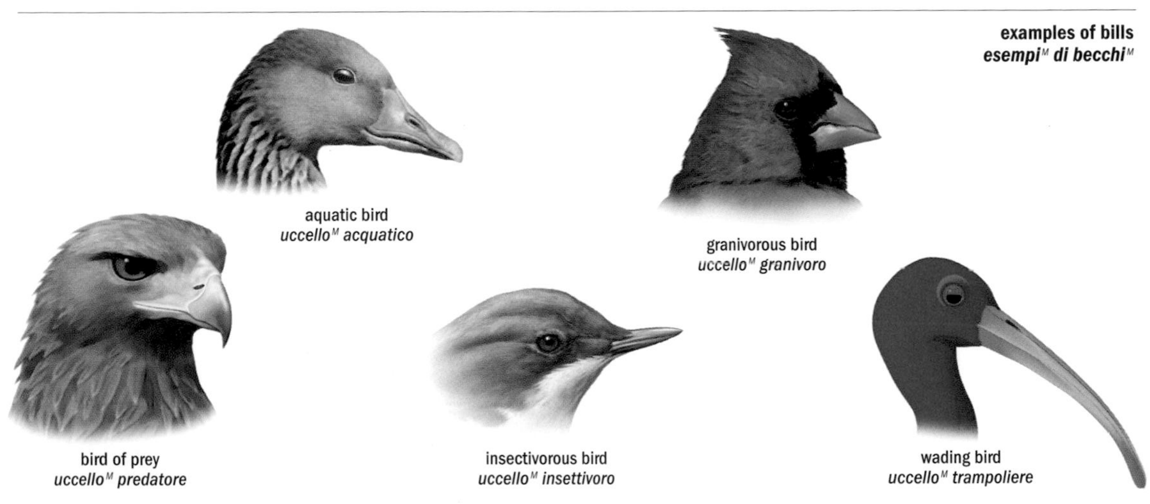

examples of feet
***esempi*[M] *di zampe*[F]**

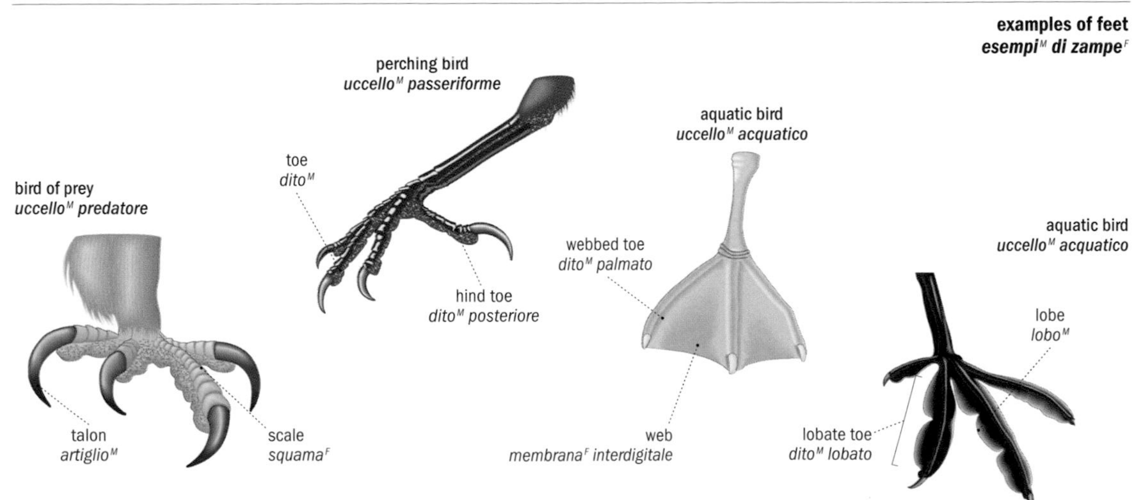

examples of birds

esempi[M] di uccelli[M]

pheasant
fagiano M
great horned owl
gufo M reale
falcon
falco M
quail
quaglia F
eagle
aquila F
duck
anatra F
hen
gallina F
pigeon
piccione M
turkey
tacchino M
guinea fowl
faraona F
goose
oca F
rooster
gallo M
ostrich
struzzo M
peacock
pavone M
flamingo
fenicottero M

rodent

roditore[M]

examples of rodents

esempi[M] di roditori[M]

examples of lagomorphs

esempi[M] di lagomorfi[M]

horse

cavallo[M]

morphology of a horse
morfologia[F] di un cavallo[M]

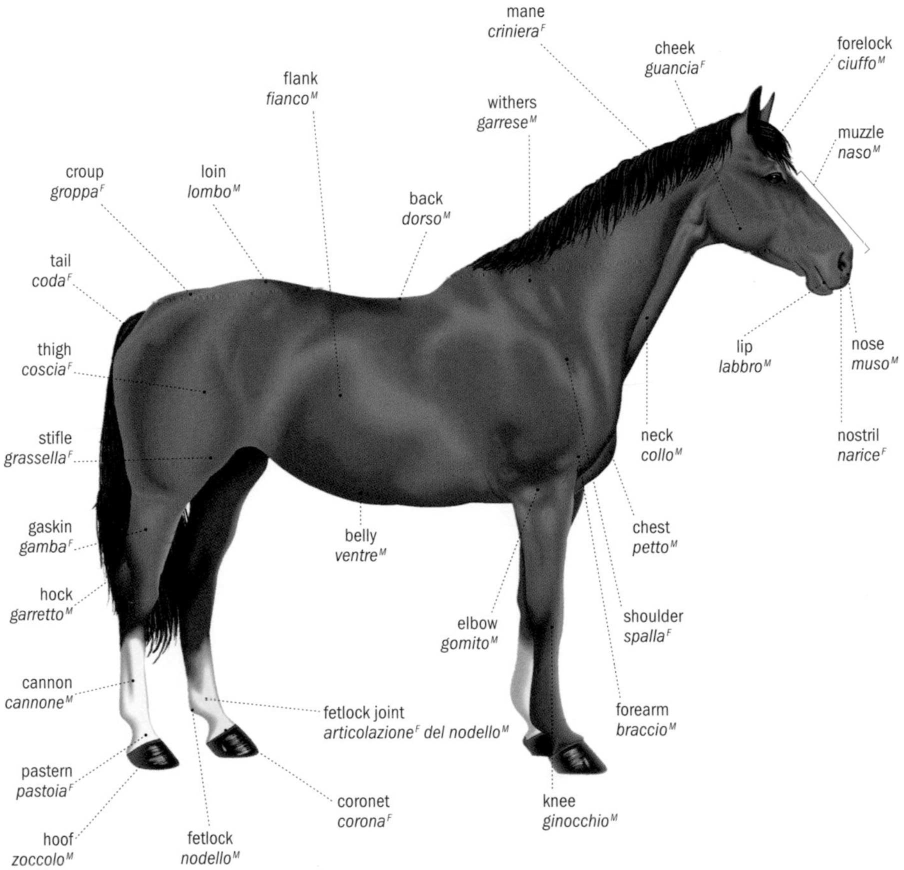

mane
criniera[F]

cheek
guancia[F]

forelock
ciuffo[M]

flank
fianco[M]

withers
garrese[M]

muzzle
naso[M]

croup
groppa[F]

loin
lombo[M]

back
dorso[M]

tail
coda[F]

thigh
coscia[F]

lip
labbro[M]

nose
muso[M]

stifle
grassella[F]

neck
collo[M]

nostril
narice[F]

gaskin
gamba[F]

belly
ventre[M]

chest
petto[M]

hock
garretto[M]

elbow
gomito[M]

shoulder
spalla[F]

cannon
cannone[M]

fetlock joint
articolazione[F] del nodello[M]

forearm
braccio[M]

pastern
pastoia[F]

coronet
corona[F]

knee
ginocchio[M]

hoof
zoccolo[M]

fetlock
nodello[M]

gaits
andature[F]

walk
passo[M]

pace
ambio[M]

trot
trotto[M]

canter
galoppo[M]

examples of ungulate mammals

esempi[M] di mammiferi[M] ungulati

peccary
pecari[M]

wild boar
cinghiale[M]

pig
maiale[M]

goat
capra[F]

antelope
antilope[F]

sheep
pecora[F]

calf
vitello[M]

white-tailed deer
cervo[M] dalla coda[F] bianca

mouflon
muflone[M]

caribou
renna[F]

wapiti (elk)
wapiti[M] (elk[M])

okapi
okapi[M]

donkey
asino[M]

mule
mulo[M]

cow
mucca[F]

zebra
zebra[F]

llama
lama[M]

bison
bisonte[M]

buffalo
bufalo[M]

examples of ungulate mammals

ox
bue[M]

yak
yak[M]

horse
cavallo[M]

moose
alce[F]

bactrian camel
cammello[M]

dromedary camel
dromedario[M]

rhinoceros
rinoceronte[M]

hippopotamus
ippopotamo[M]

giraffe
giraffa[F]

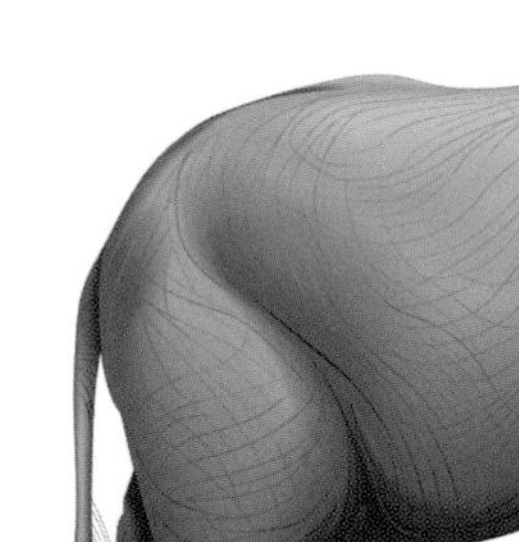
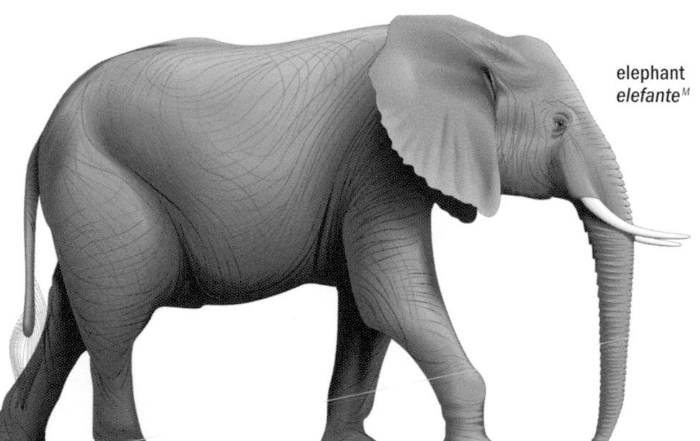

elephant
elefante[M]

dog

cane^M

morphology of a dog
morfologia^F di un cane^M

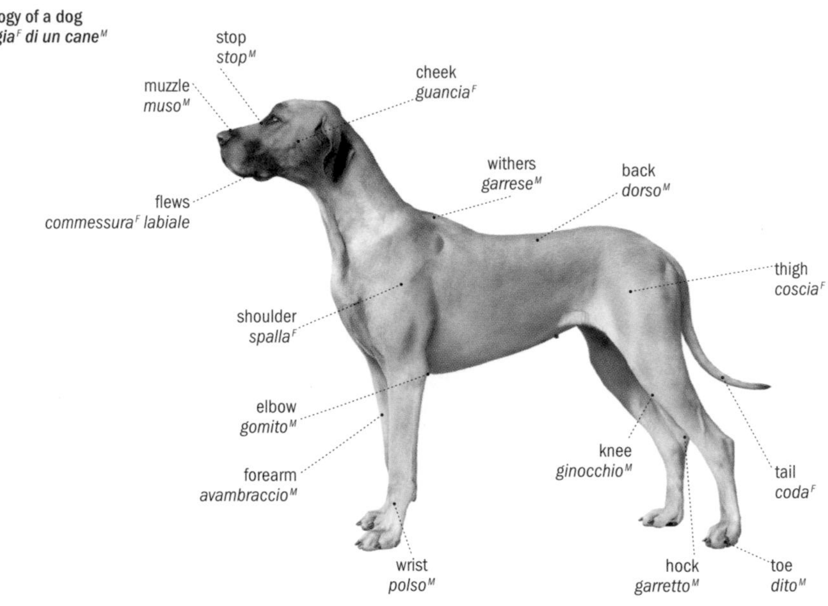

examples of dog breeds

razze^F canine

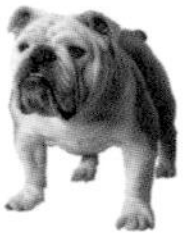

bulldog
bulldog^M

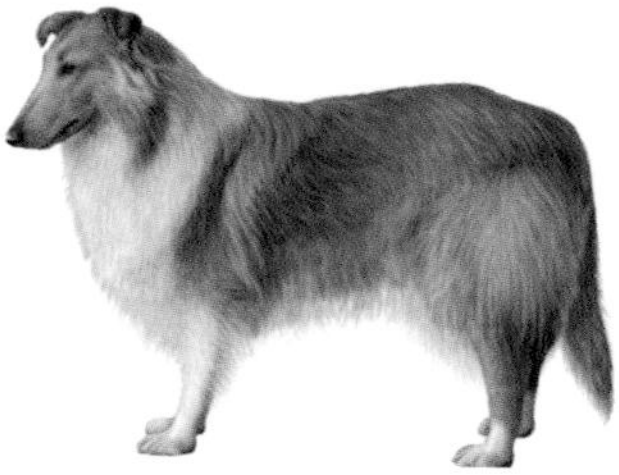

collie
collie^M

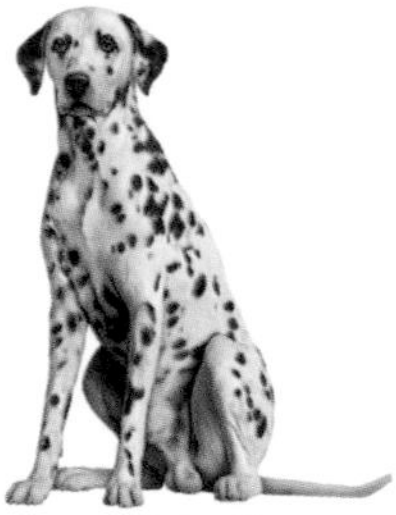

Dalmatian
dalmata^M

poodle
barbone^M

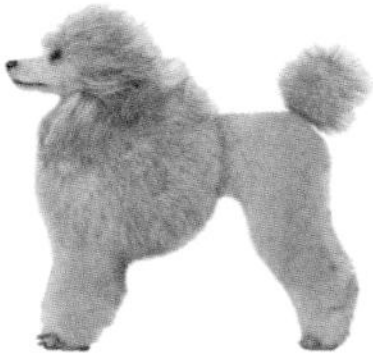

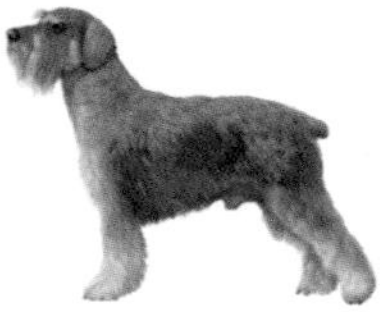

schnauzer
schnauzer^M

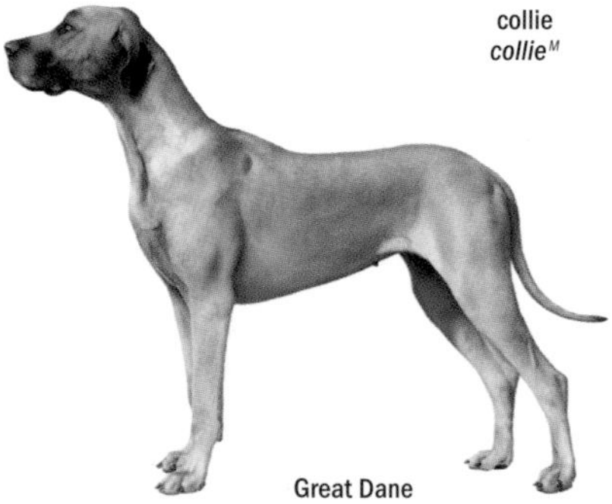

Great Dane
alano^M

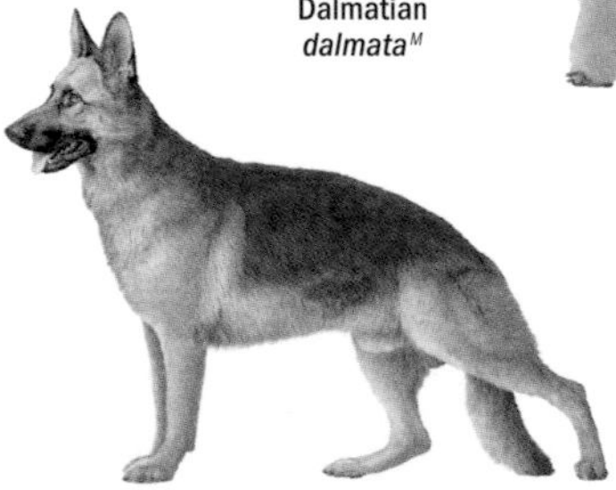

German shepherd
pastore^M tedesco

Saint Bernard
sanbernardo^M

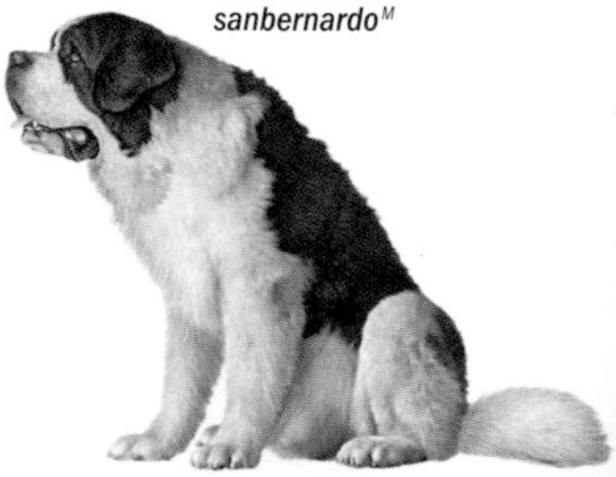

cat

gatto^M

cat's head
testa^F di gatto^M

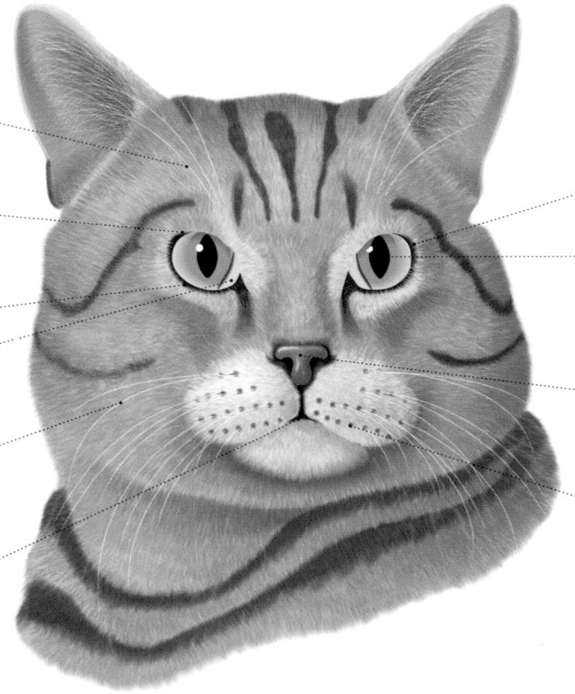
whisker
vibrisse^F
upper eyelid
palpebra^F superiore
lower eyelid
palpebra^F inferiore
nictitating membrane
membrana^F nittitante
whisker
vibrisse^F
lip
labbro^M
eyelashes
ciglia^F
pupil
pupilla^F
nose leather
rinario^M
muzzle
muso^M

examples of cat breeds

razze^F di gatti^M

Siamese
siamese^M

Abyssinian
abissino^M

Persian
persiano^M

Maine coon
gatto^M del Maine^M

Manx
gatto^M dell'isola^F di Man

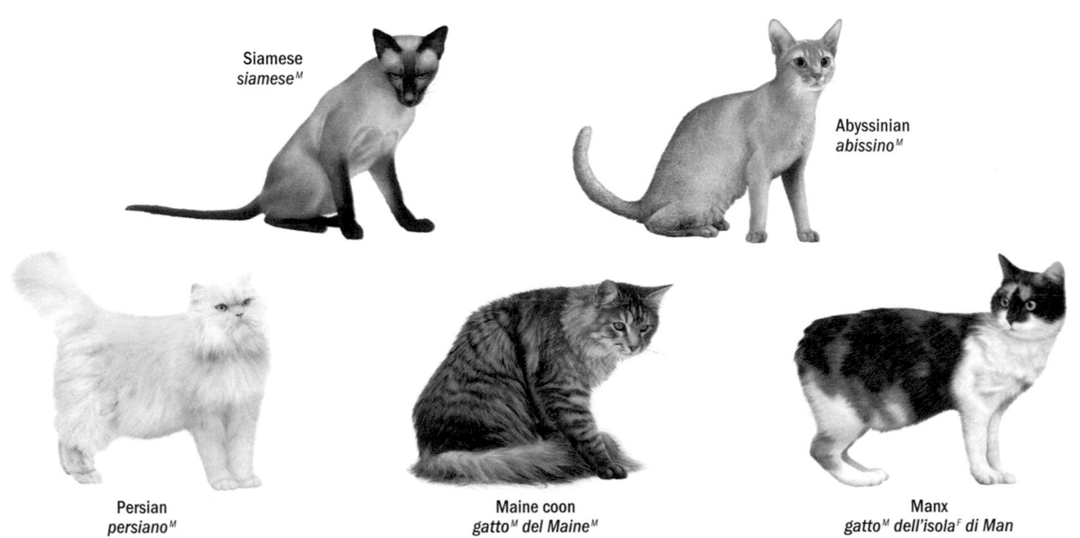

examples of carnivorous mammals

esempi[M] di mammiferi[M] carnivori

cheetah
ghepardo[M]
leopard
leopardo[M]
lion
leone[M]
jaguar
giaguaro[M]
tiger
tigre[F]
polar bear
orso[M] *polare*
black bear
orso[M] *bruno*

dolphin

delfino[M]

morphology of a dolphin
morfologia[F] di un delfino[M]

blowhole
sfiatatoio[M]
dorsal fin
pinna[F] dorsale
beak
bocca[F]
tail
coda[F]
eye
occhio[M]
caudal fin
pinna[F] caudale
pectoral fin
pinna[F] pettorale

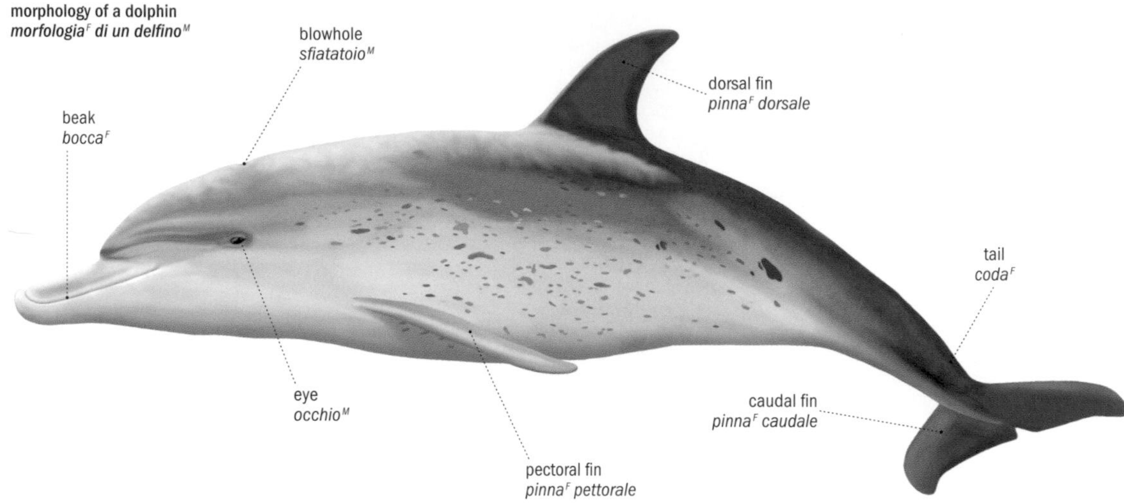

examples of marine mammals

esempi[M] di mammiferi[M] marini

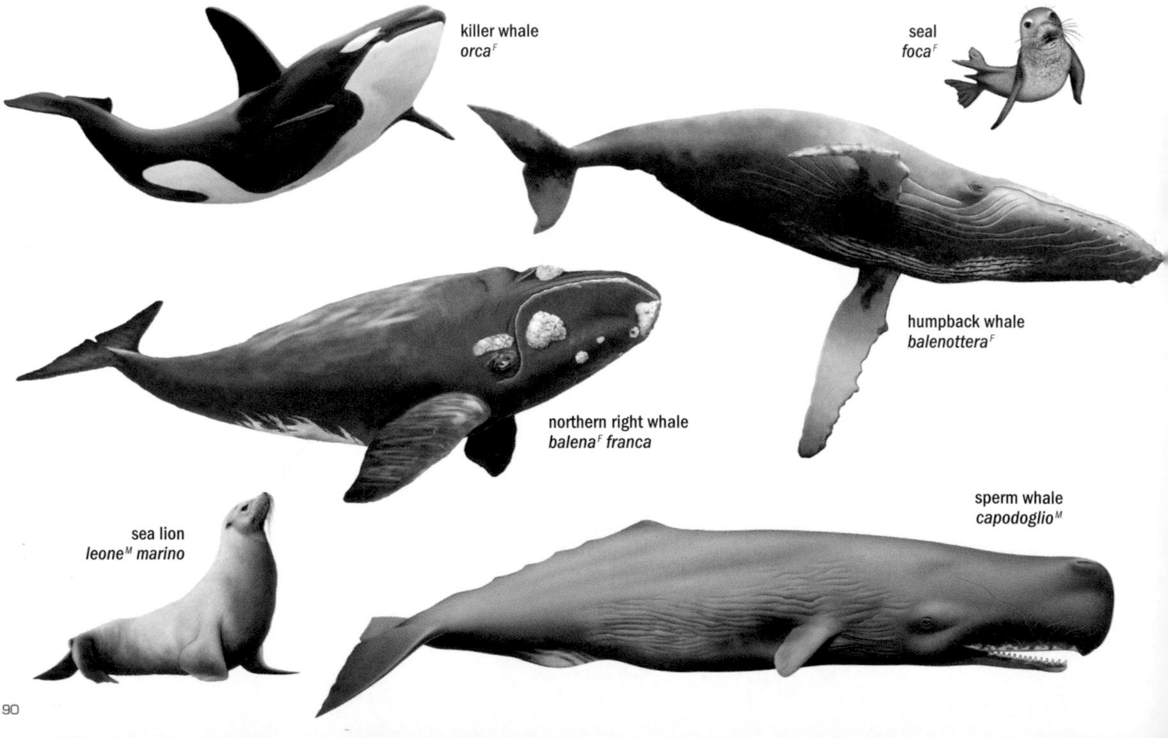

killer whale
orca[F]
seal
foca[F]
humpback whale
balenottera[F]
northern right whale
balena[F] franca
sperm whale
capodoglio[M]
sea lion
leone[M] marino

gorilla

gorilla[M]

morphology of a gorilla
morfologia[F] di un gorilla[M]

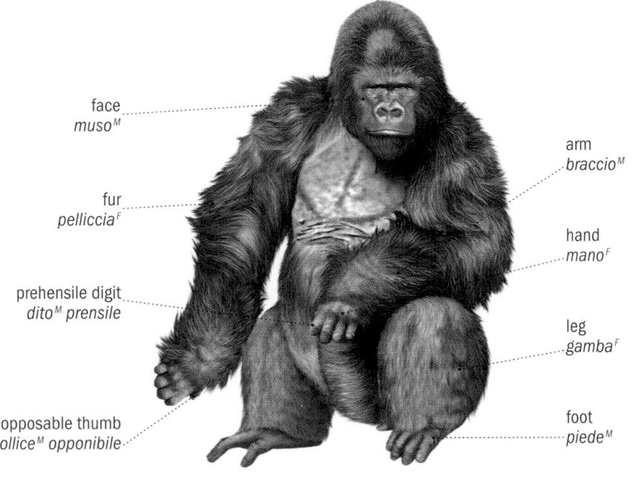

examples of primates

esempi[M] di primati[M]

tamarin
tamarino[M]

baboon
babbuino[M]

macaque
macaco[M]

marmoset
uistitì[M]

orangutan
orangotango[M]

chimpanzee
scimpanzé[M]

lemur
lemure[M]

gibbon
gibbone[M]

man

uomo^M

anterior view
vista^F anteriore

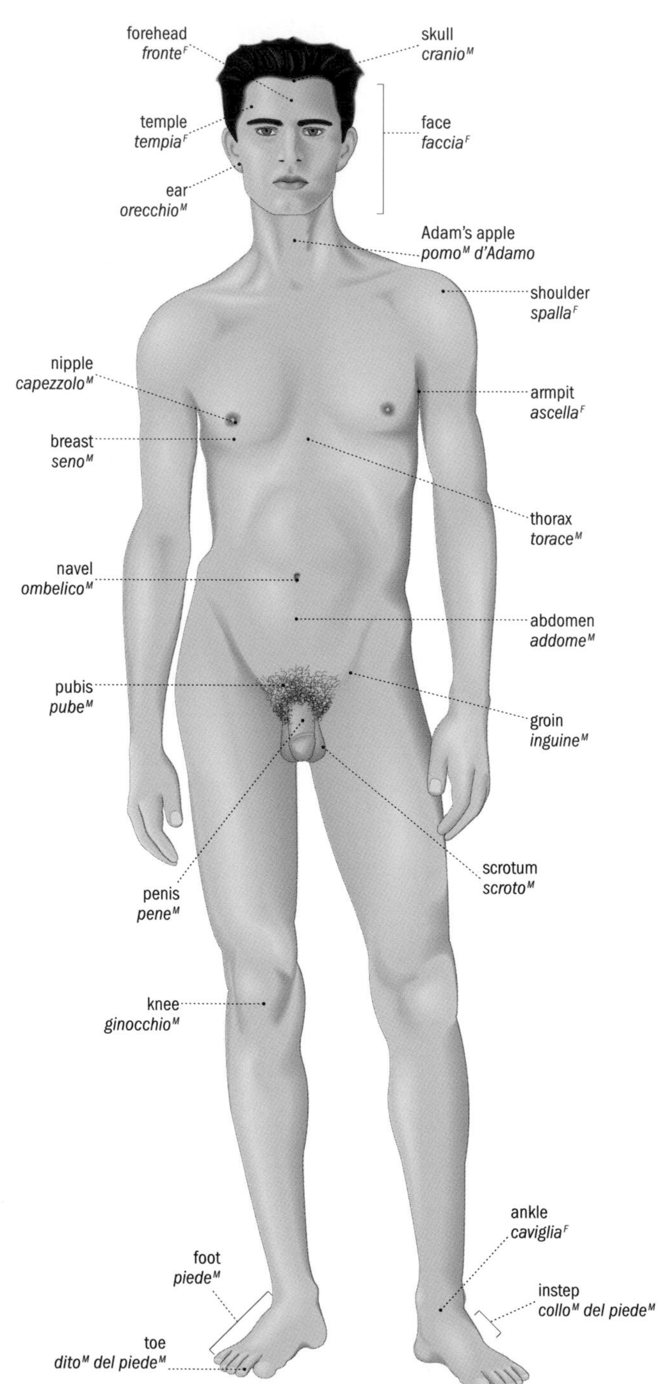

posterior view
vista[F] *posteriore*

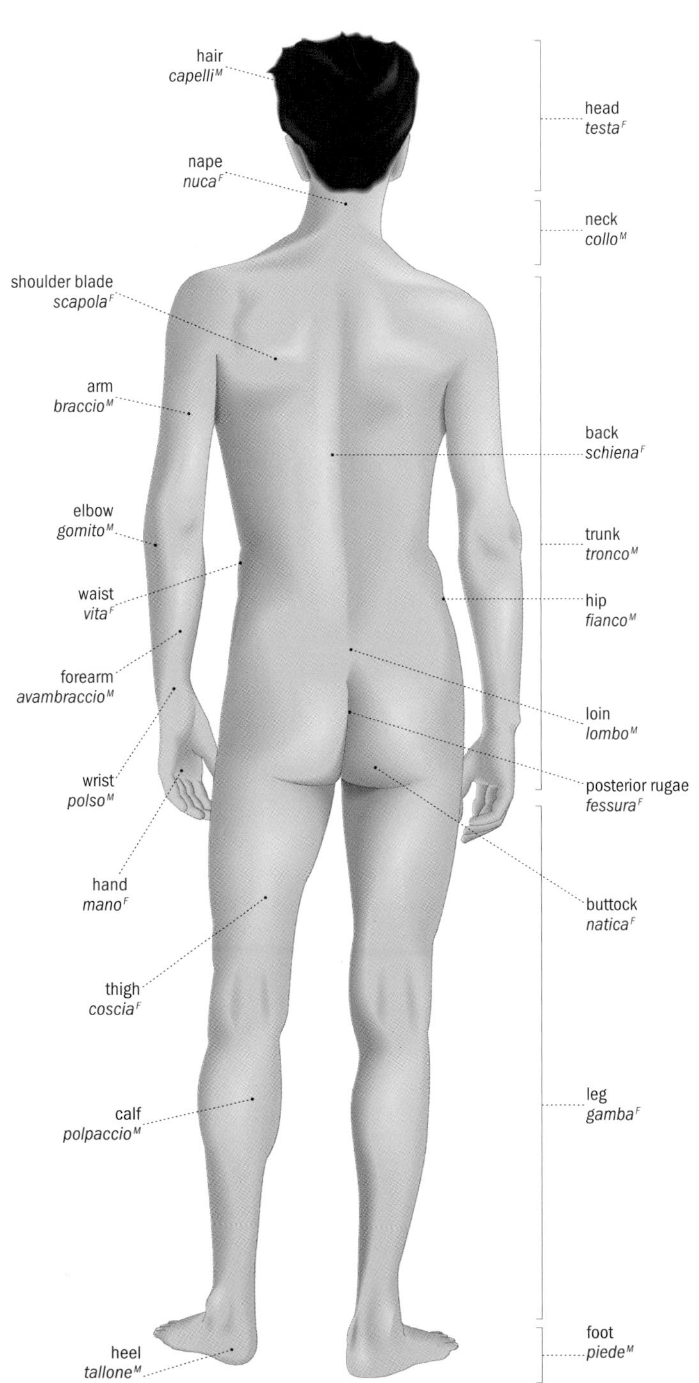

woman

donna[F]

anterior view
vista[F] anteriore

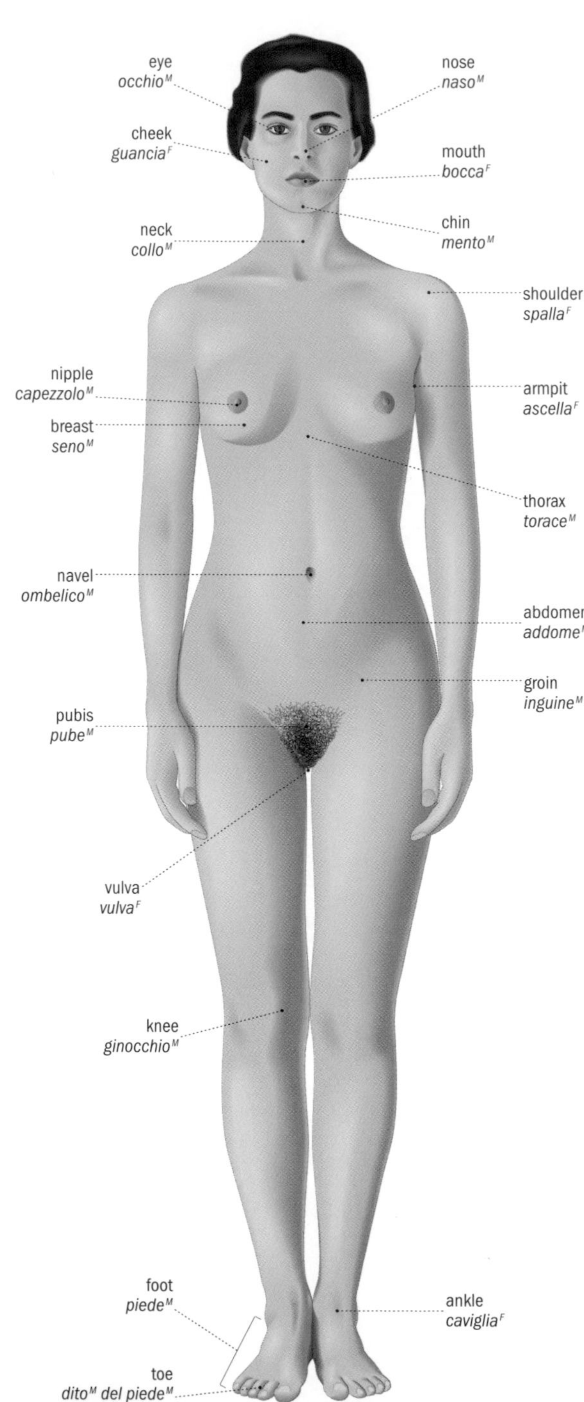

posterior view
vista[F] posteriore

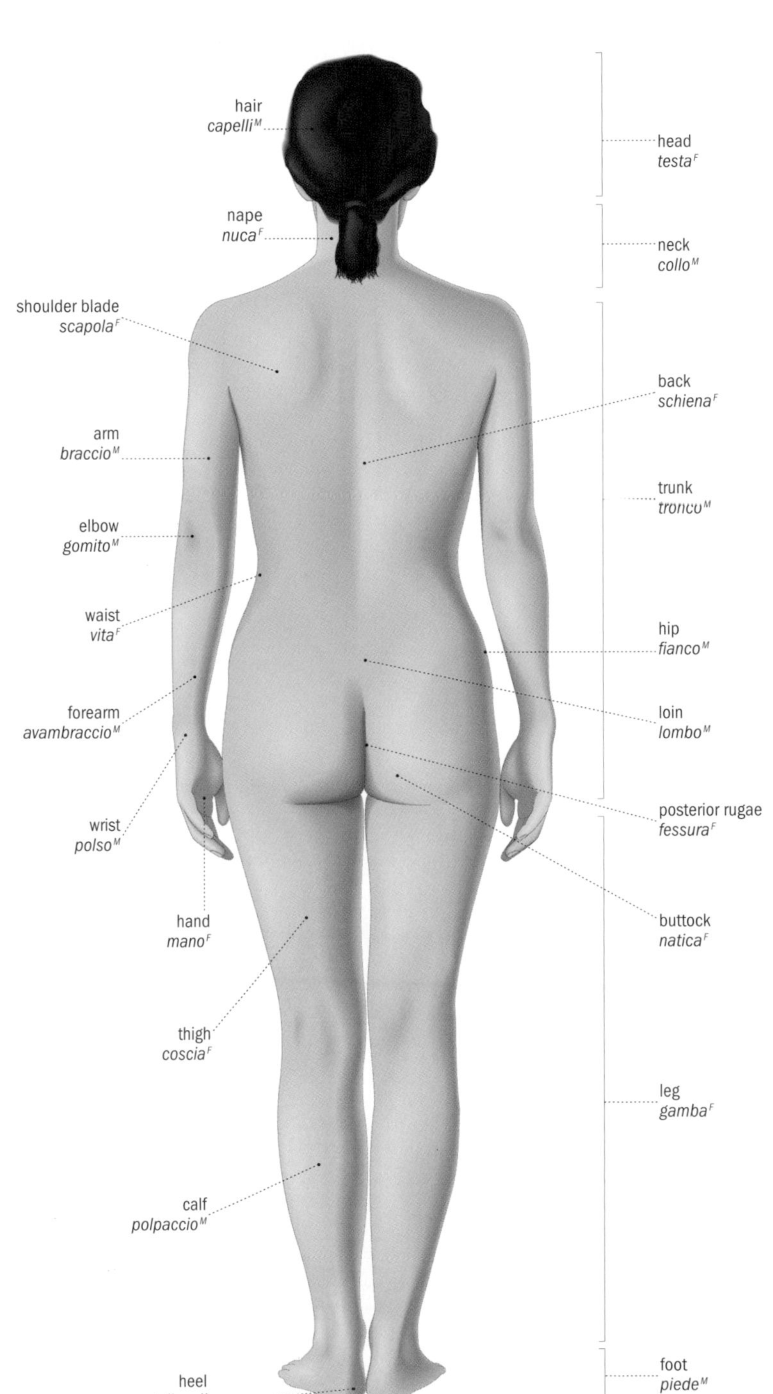

muscles

muscoli[M]

anterior view
vista[F] anteriore

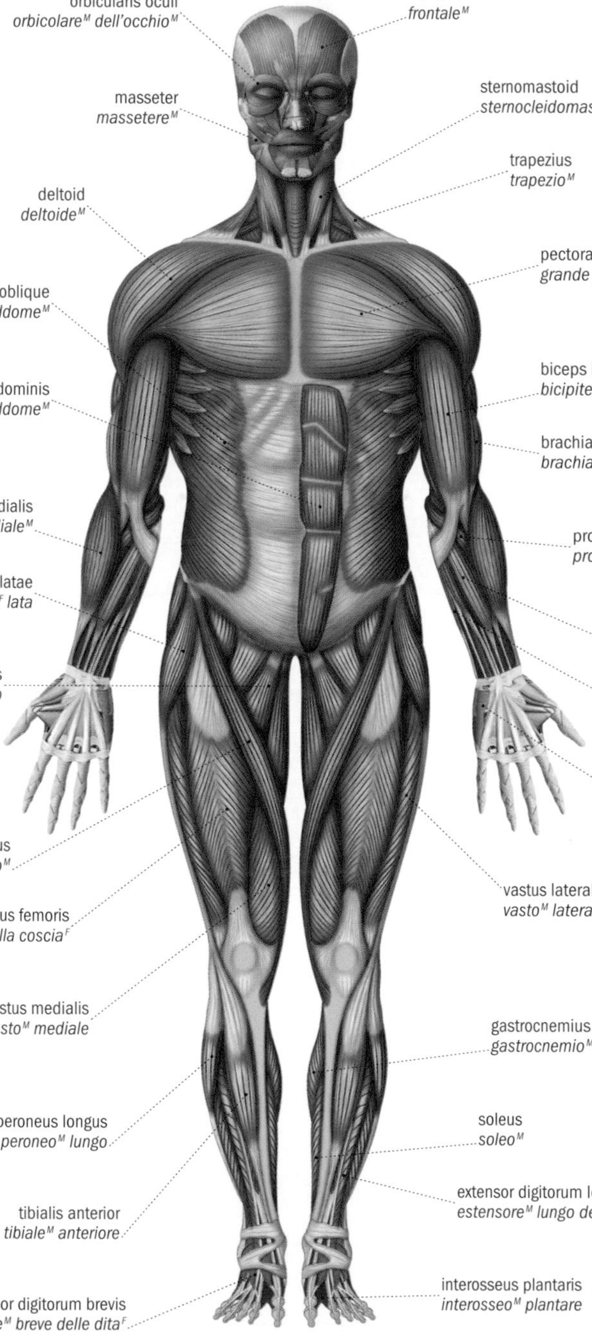

orbicularis oculi
orbicolare[M] dell'occhio[M]

masseter
massetere[M]

deltoid
deltoide[M]

external oblique
obliquo[M] esterno dell'addome[M]

rectus abdominis
retto[M] dell'addome[M]

brachioradialis
brachioradiale[M]

tensor fasciae latae
tensore[M] della fascia[F] lata

adductor longus
adduttore[M] lungo

sartorius
sartorio[M]

rectus femoris
retto[M] della coscia[F]

vastus medialis
vasto[M] mediale

peroneus longus
peroneo[M] lungo

tibialis anterior
tibiale[M] anteriore

extensor digitorum brevis
estensore[M] breve delle dita[F]

frontalis
frontale[M]

sternomastoid
sternocleidomastoideo[M]

trapezius
trapezio[M]

pectoralis major
grande pettorale[M]

biceps brachii
bicipite[M] brachiale

brachialis
brachiale[M]

pronator teres
pronatore[M] rotondo

palmaris longus
palmare[M] lungo

flexor carpi ulnaris
flessore[M] ulnare del carpo[M]

palmaris brevis
palmare[M] breve

vastus lateralis
vasto[M] laterale

gastrocnemius
gastrocnemio[M]

soleus
soleo[M]

extensor digitorum longus
estensore[M] lungo delle dita[F]

interosseus plantaris
interosseo[M] plantare

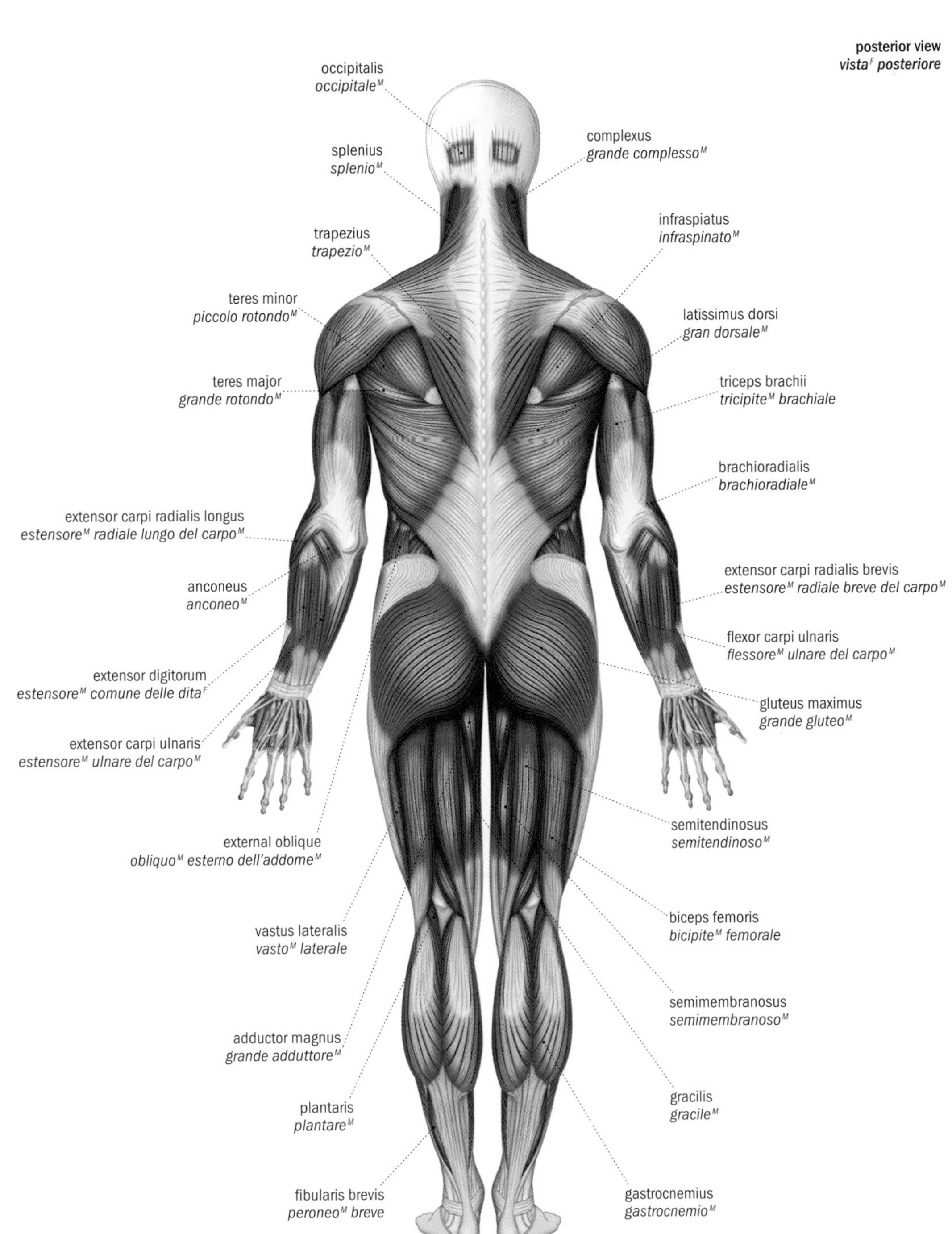
posterior view
vista^F posteriore
occipitalis
occipitale^M
complexus
grande complesso^M
splenius
splenio^M
infraspiatus
infraspinato^M
trapezius
trapezio^M
teres minor
piccolo rotondo^M
latissimus dorsi
gran dorsale^M
teres major
grande rotondo^M
triceps brachii
tricipite^M brachiale
brachioradialis
brachioradiale^M
extensor carpi radialis longus
estensore^M radiale lungo del carpo^M
extensor carpi radialis brevis
estensore^M radiale breve del carpo^M
anconeus
anconeo^M
flexor carpi ulnaris
flessore^M ulnare del carpo^M
extensor digitorum
estensore^M comune delle dita^F
gluteus maximus
grande gluteo^M
extensor carpi ulnaris
estensore^M ulnare del carpo^M
semitendinosus
semitendinoso^M
external oblique
obliquo^M esterno dell'addome^M
biceps femoris
bicipite^M femorale
vastus lateralis
vasto^M laterale
semimembranosus
semimembranoso^M
adductor magnus
grande adduttore^M
gracilis
gracile^M
plantaris
plantare^M
fibularis brevis
peroneo^M breve
gastrocnemius
gastrocnemio^M

skeleton

scheletro^M

anterior view
vista^F anteriore

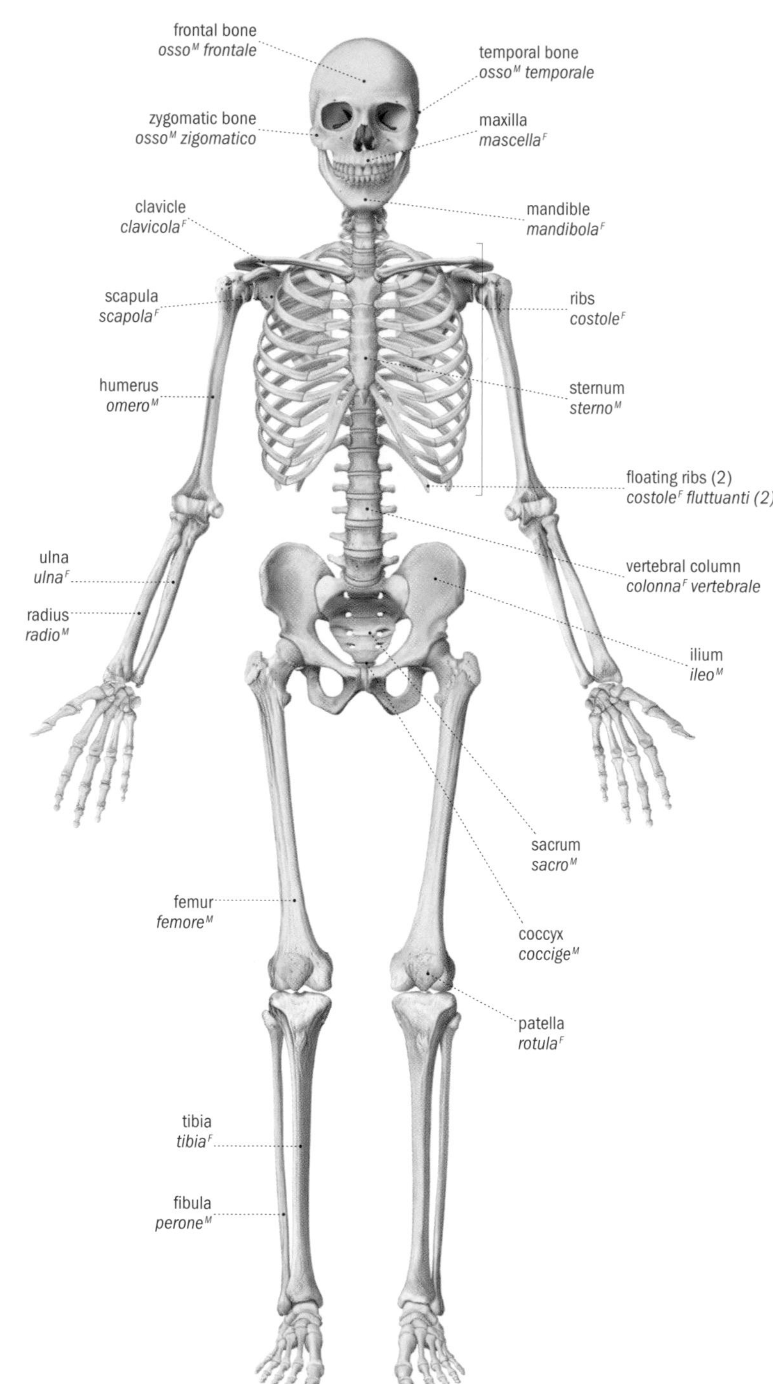

posterior view
vista^F posteriore

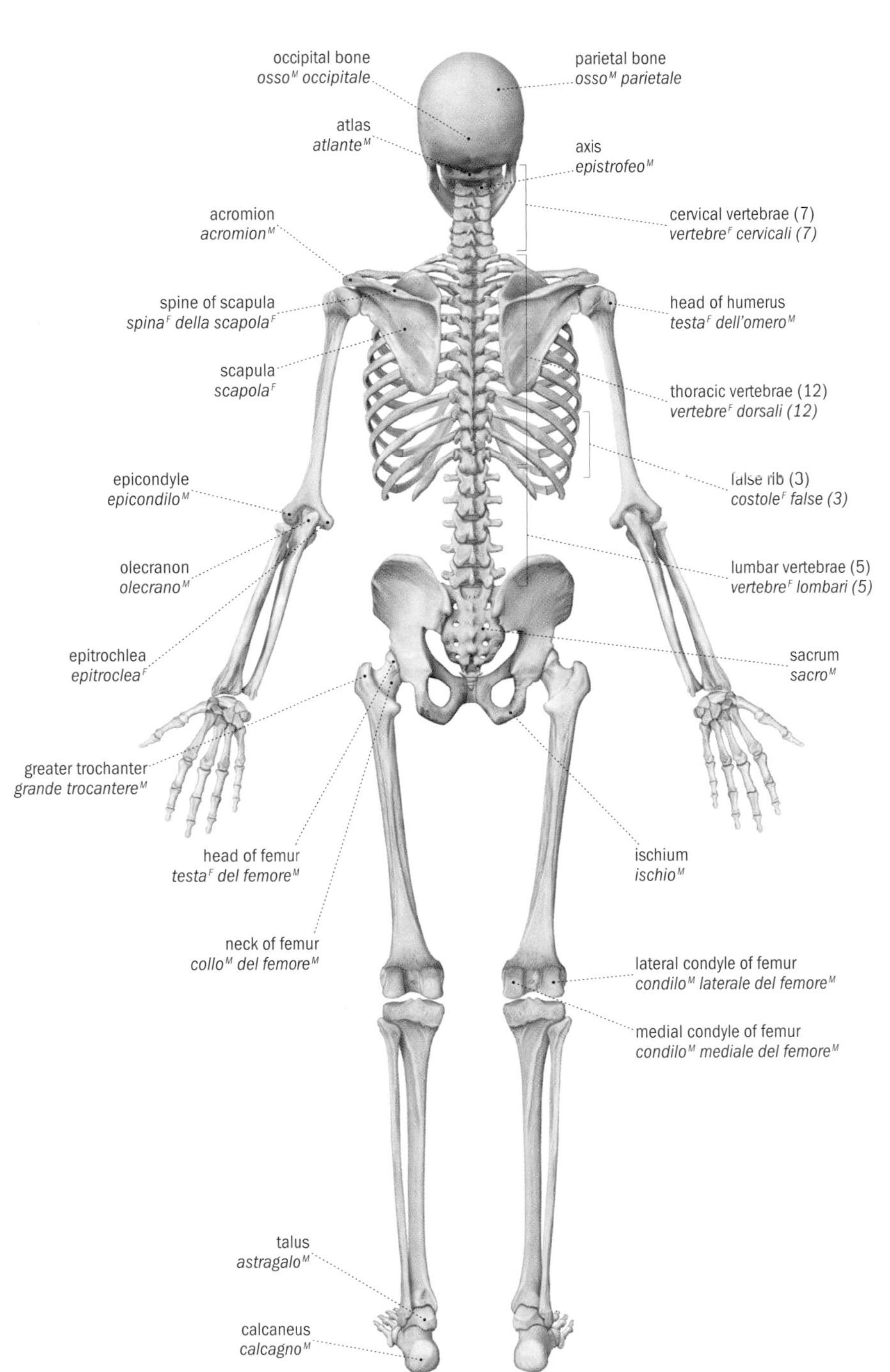

lateral view of adult skull
vista^F laterale del cranio^M adulto

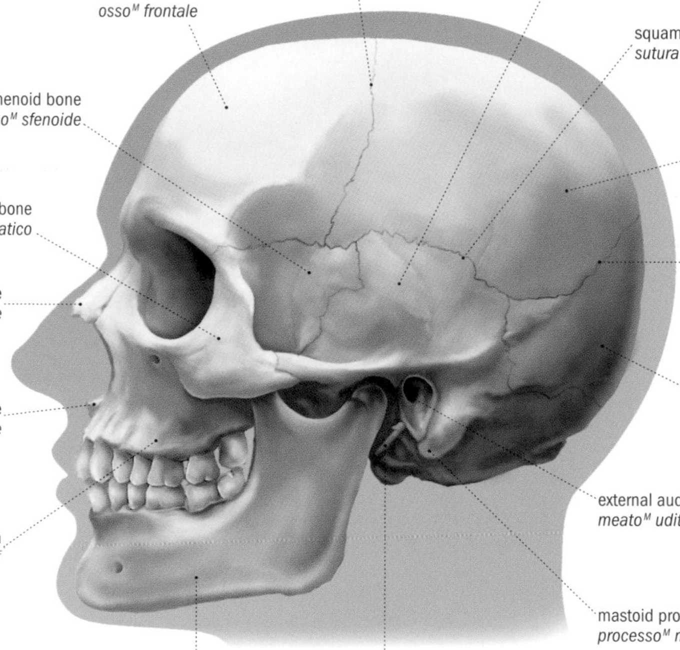

coronal suture
sutura^F coronale
temporal bone
osso^M temporale
frontal bone
osso^M frontale
squamous suture
sutura^F squamosa
sphenoid bone
osso^M sfenoide
parietal bone
osso^M parietale
zygomatic bone
osso^M zigomatico
lambdoid suture
sutura^F lambdoidea
nasal bone
osso^M nasale
occipital bone
osso^M occipitale
anterior nasal spine
spina^F nasale anteriore
external auditory meatus
meato^M uditivo esterno
maxilla
mascella^F
mastoid process
processo^M mastoideo
mandible
mandibola^F
styloid process
processo^M stiloideo

lateral view of child's skull
vista^F laterale del cranio^M di bambino^M

anterior fontanelle
fontanella^F anteriore
parietal bone
osso^M parietale
coronal suture
sutura^F coronaria
posterior fontanelle
fontanella^F posteriore
frontal bone
osso^M frontale
occipital bone
osso^M occipitale
sphenoidal fontanelle
fontanella^F sfenoidale
mastoid fontanelle
fontanella^F mastoidea

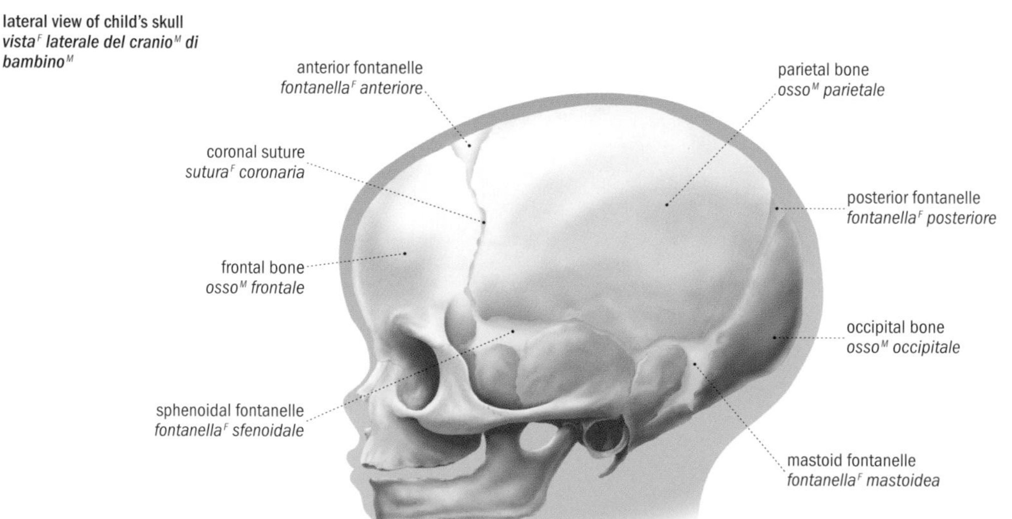

teeth

denti^M

human denture
dentatura^F nell'uomo^M

incisors
incisivi^M
canine
canino^M
premolars
premolari^M
molars
molari^M
first molar
primo molare^M
third molar
dente^M del giudizio^M
central incisor
incisivo^M centrale
lateral incisor
incisivo^M laterale
first premolar
primo premolare^M
second premolar
secondo premolare^M
second molar
secondo molare^M

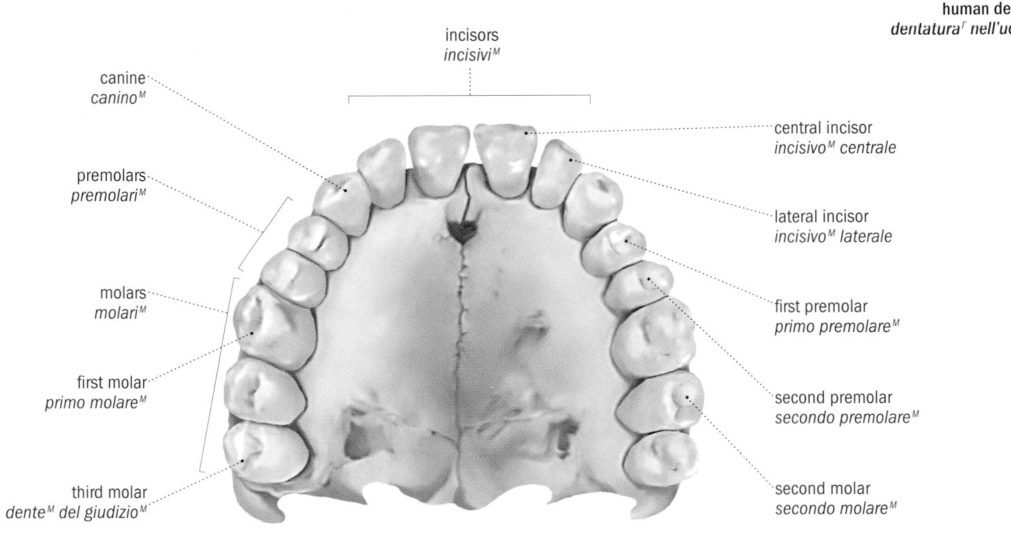

cross section of a molar
sezione^F trasversale di un molare^M

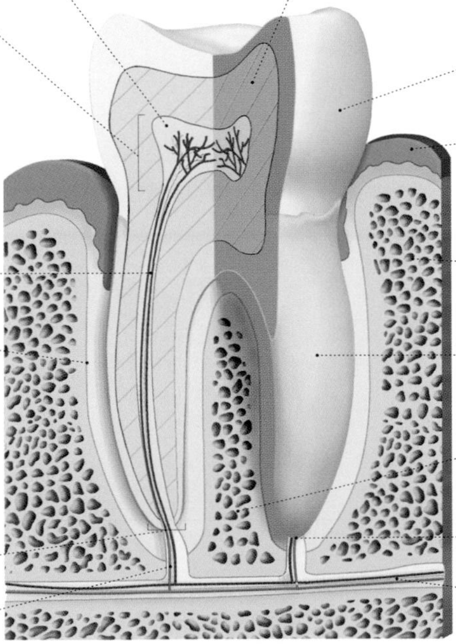

pulp chamber
camera^F pulpare
pulp
polpa^F
dentin
dentina^F
crown
corona^F
neck
colletto^M
root canal
canale^M della radice^F
periodontal ligament
legamento^M periodontale
root
radice^F
dental alveolus
alveolo^M dentario
apical foramen
foro^M apicale
enamel
smalto^M
gum
gengiva^F
maxillary bone
osso^M mascellare
cementum
cemento^M
alveolar bone
osso^M alveolare
apex
apice^M
plexus of nerves
plesso^M dentale

HUMAN BEING

blood circulation

circolazione[F] del sangue[M]

principal veins and arteries
principali vene[F] e arterie[F]

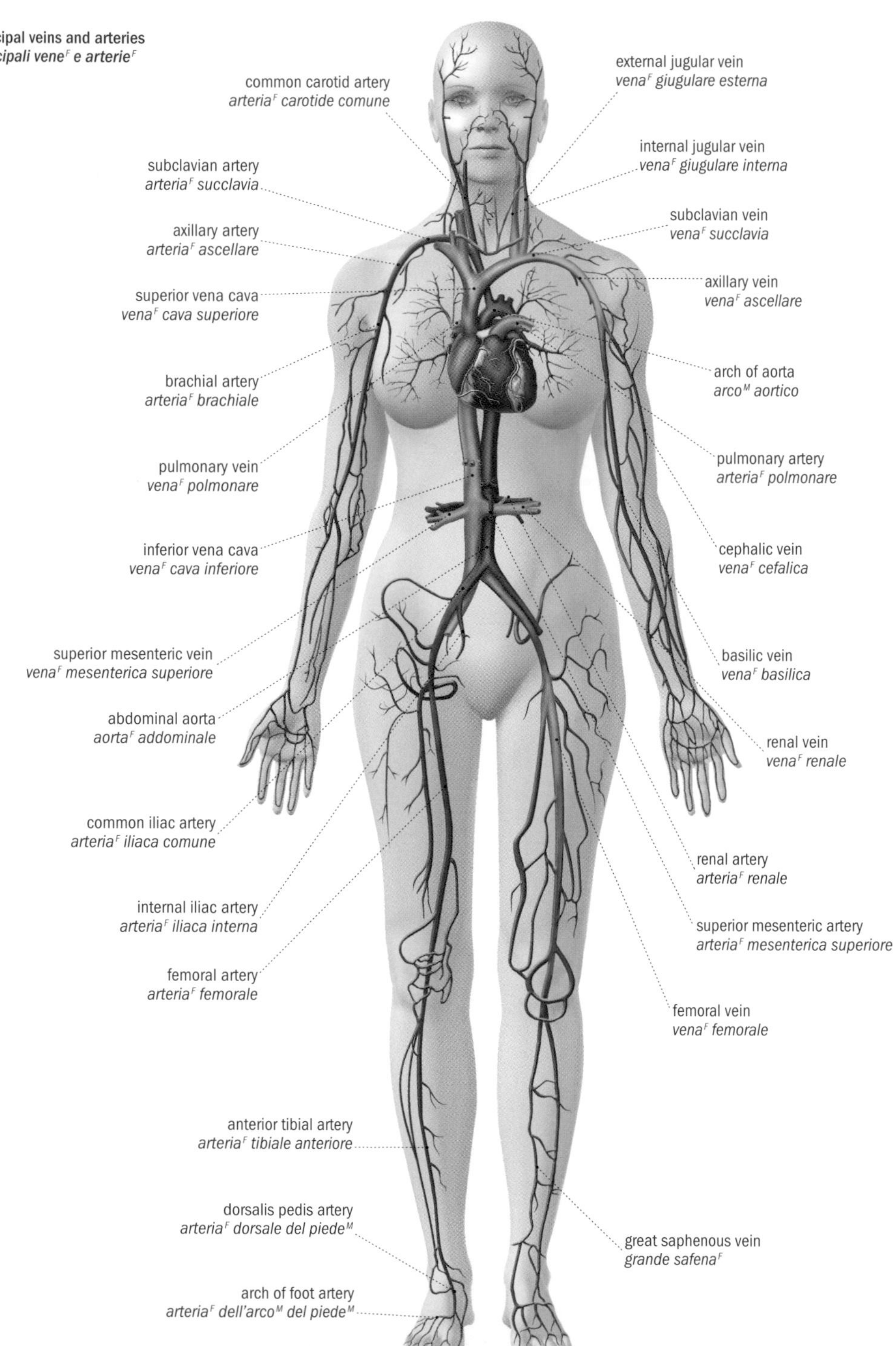

schema of circulation
schemaᴹ della circolazioneᶠ

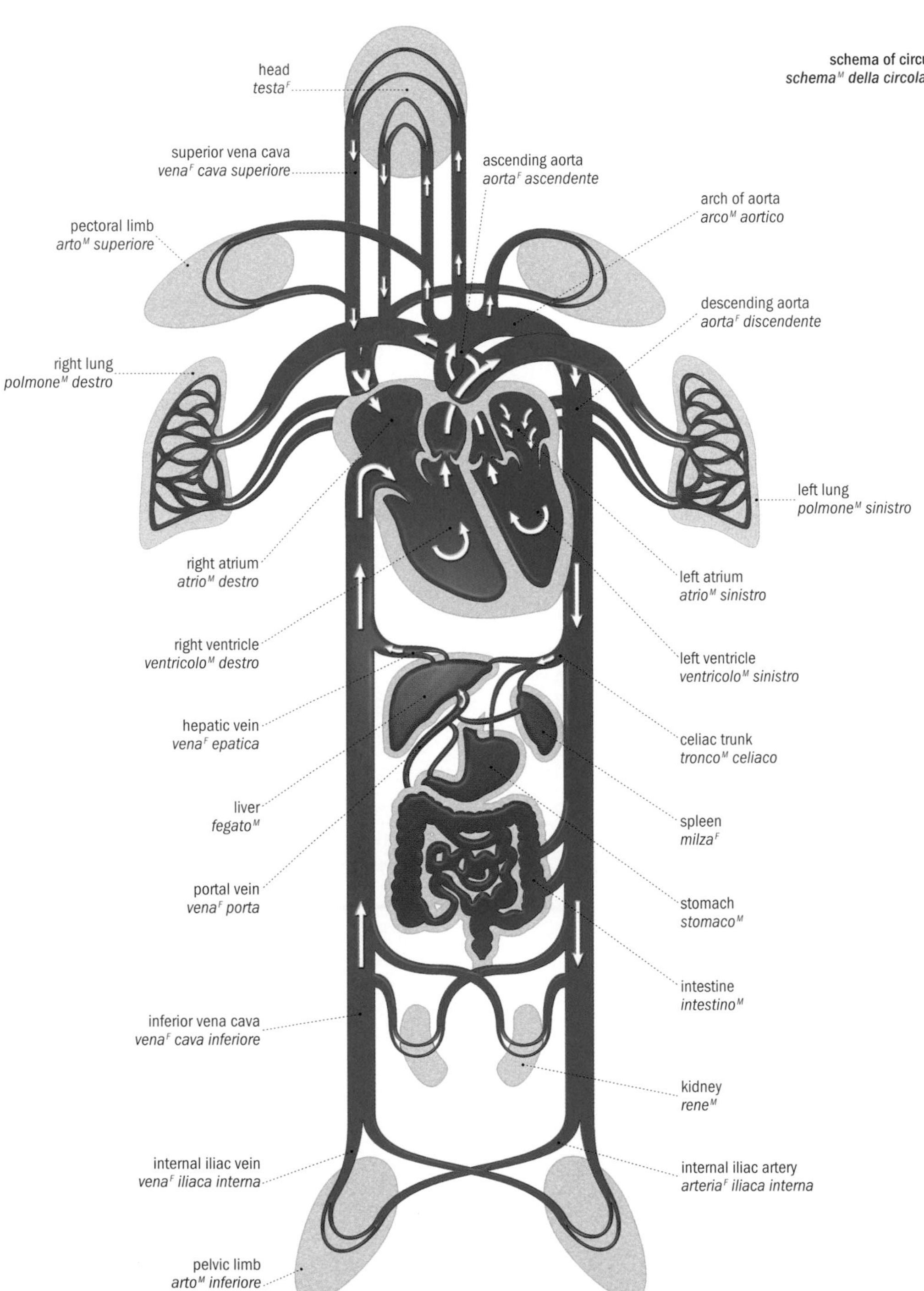

blood circulation

composition of the blood
composizione^F del sangue^M

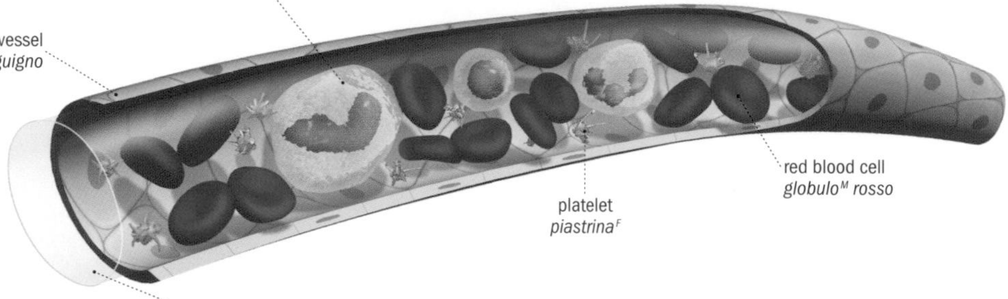

white blood cell
globulo^M bianco

blood vessel
vaso^M sanguigno

red blood cell
globulo^M rosso

platelet
piastrina^F

plasma
plasma^M

heart
cuore^M

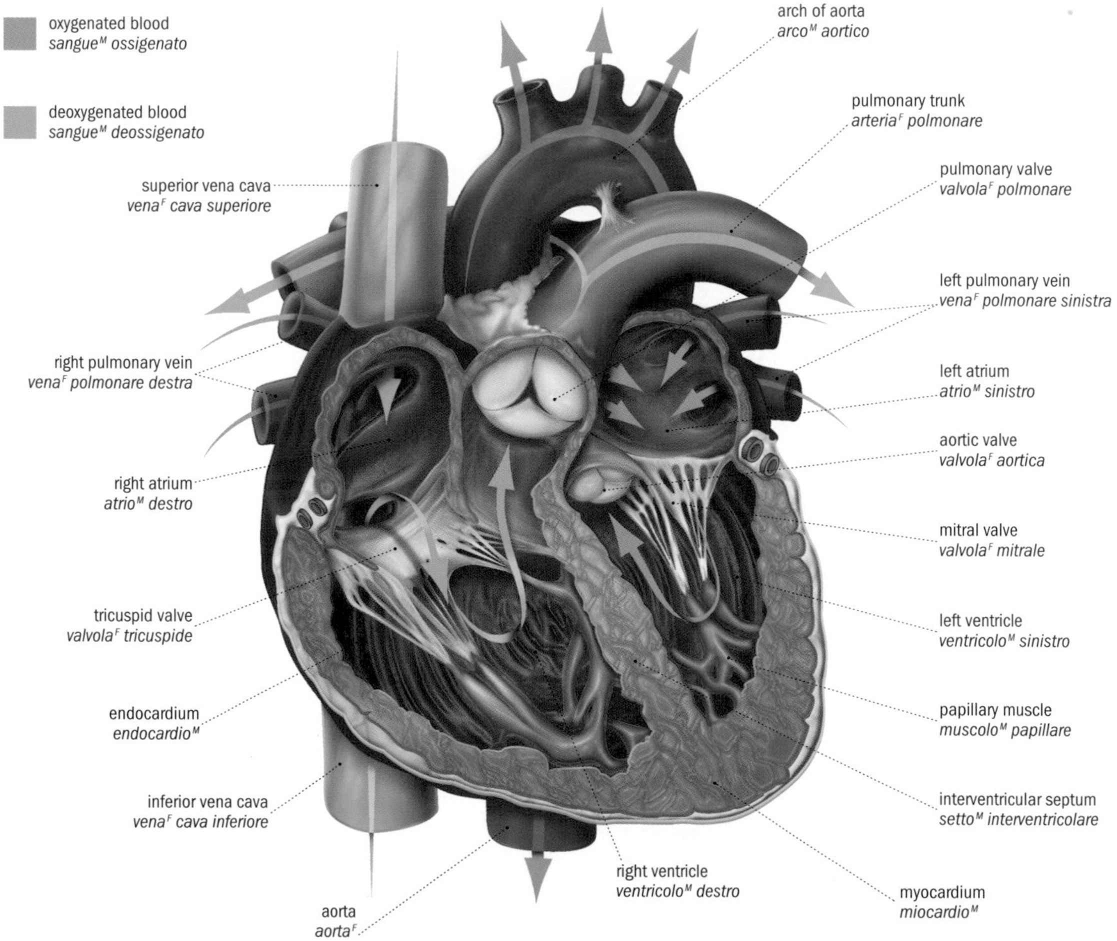

oxygenated blood
sangue^M ossigenato

deoxygenated blood
sangue^M deossigenato

arch of aorta
arco^M aortico

pulmonary trunk
arteria^F polmonare

pulmonary valve
valvola^F polmonare

superior vena cava
vena^F cava superiore

left pulmonary vein
vena^F polmonare sinistra

right pulmonary vein
vena^F polmonare destra

left atrium
atrio^M sinistro

aortic valve
valvola^F aortica

right atrium
atrio^M destro

mitral valve
valvola^F mitrale

tricuspid valve
valvola^F tricuspide

left ventricle
ventricolo^M sinistro

papillary muscle
muscolo^M papillare

endocardium
endocardio^M

interventricular septum
setto^M interventricolare

inferior vena cava
vena^F cava inferiore

right ventricle
ventricolo^M destro

myocardium
miocardio^M

aorta
aorta^F

respiratory system

apparato^M respiratorio

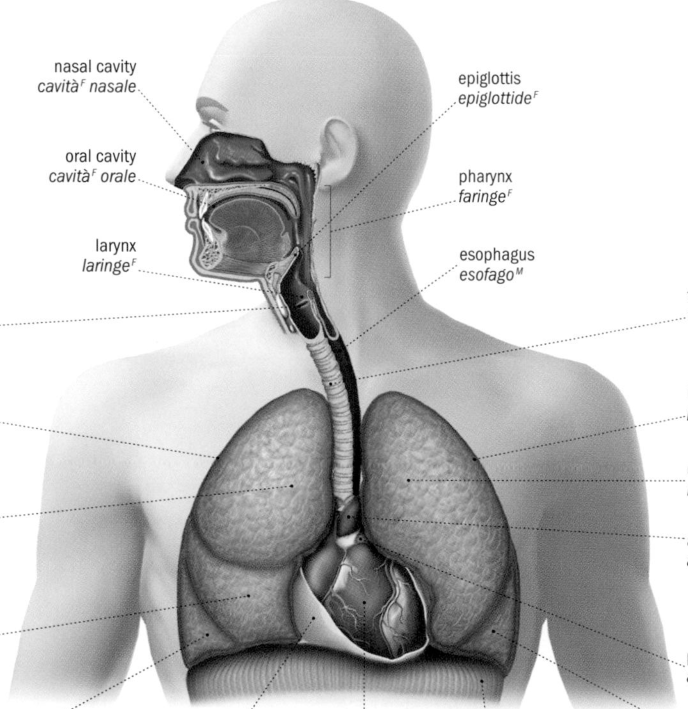

nasal cavity
cavità^F nasale
oral cavity
cavità^F orale
larynx
laringe^F
vocal cord
corda^F vocale
right lung
polmone^M destro
upper lobe
lobo^M superiore
middle lobe
lobo^M medio
lower lobe
lobo^M inferiore
pericardium
pericardio^M
heart
cuore^M
diaphragm
diaframma^M
epiglottis
epiglottide^F
pharynx
faringe^F
esophagus
esofago^M
trachea
trachea^F
left lung
polmone^M sinistro
upper lobe
lobo^M superiore
aorta
aorta^F
pulmonary artery
arteria^F polmonare
lower lobe
lobo^M inferiore

lungs
polmoni^M

upper lobe
lobo^M superiore
trachea
trachea^F
main bronchus
bronco^M principale
lobe bronchus
bronco^M lobare
terminal bronchiole
bronchiolo^M terminale
parietal pleura
pleura^F parietale
pleural cavity
cavità^F pleurica
visceral pleura
pleura^F viscerale
oblique fissure
scissura^F obliqua
lower lobe
lobo^M inferiore

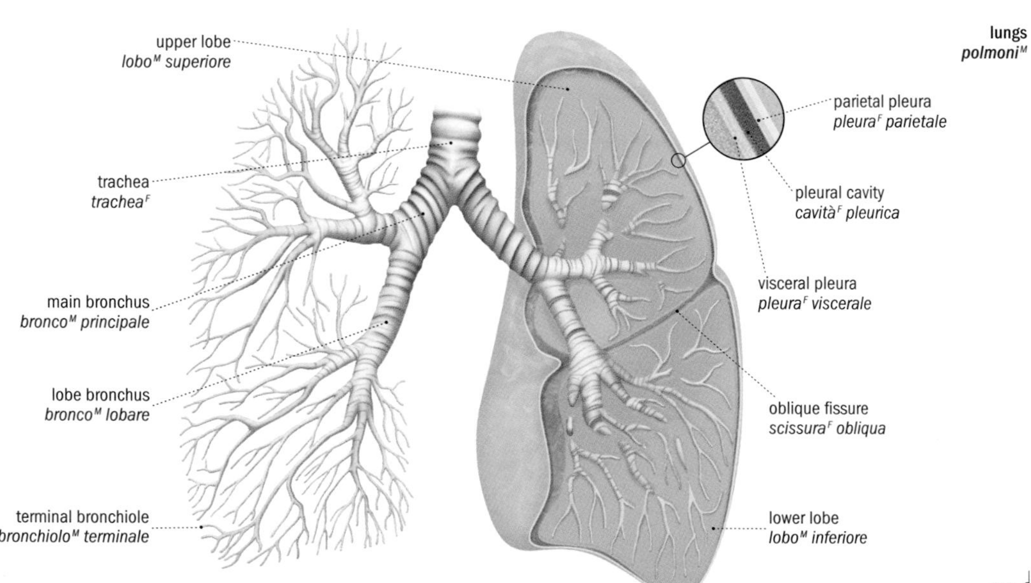

digestive system

apparato[M] digerente

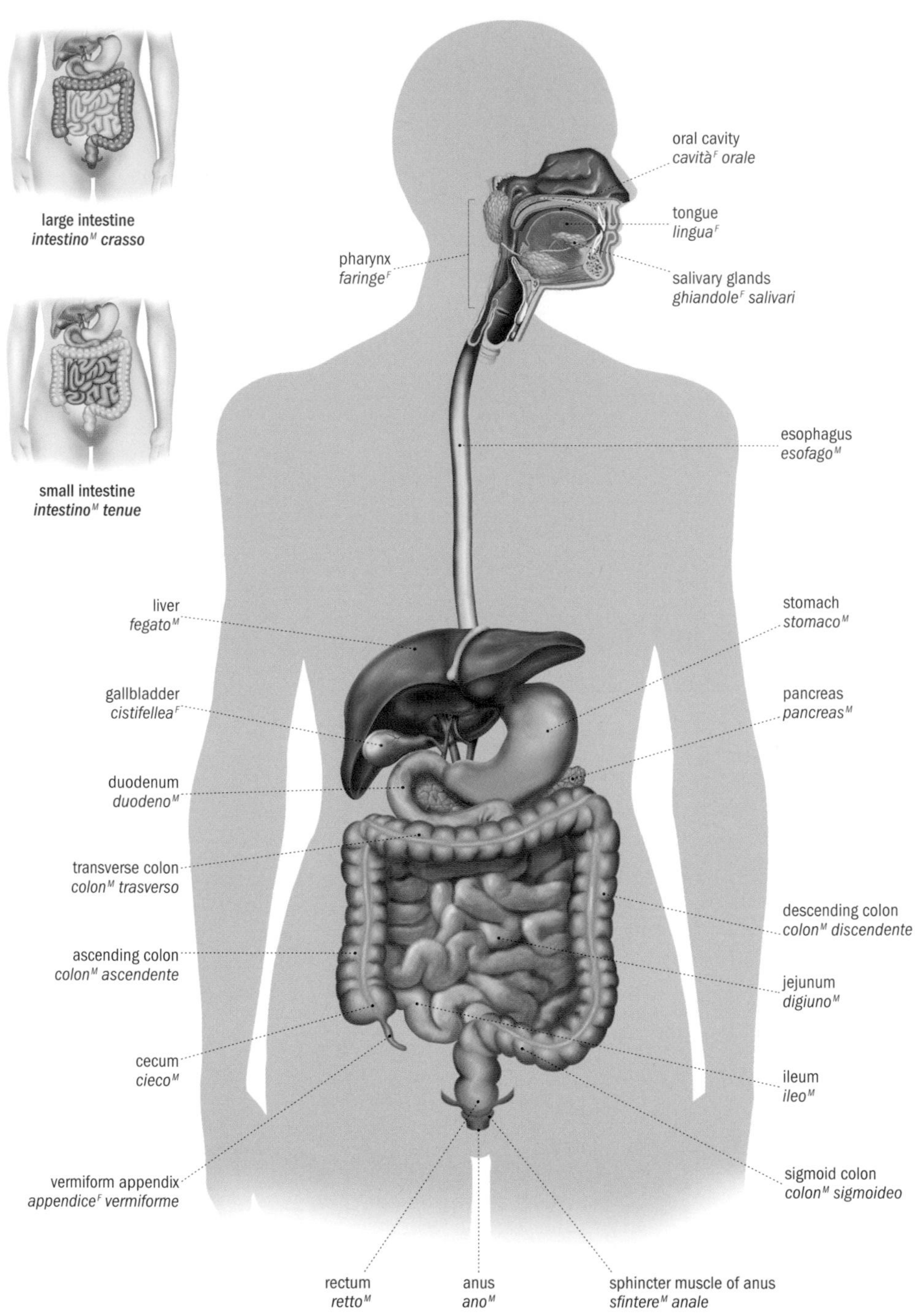

urinary system

apparato[M] urinario

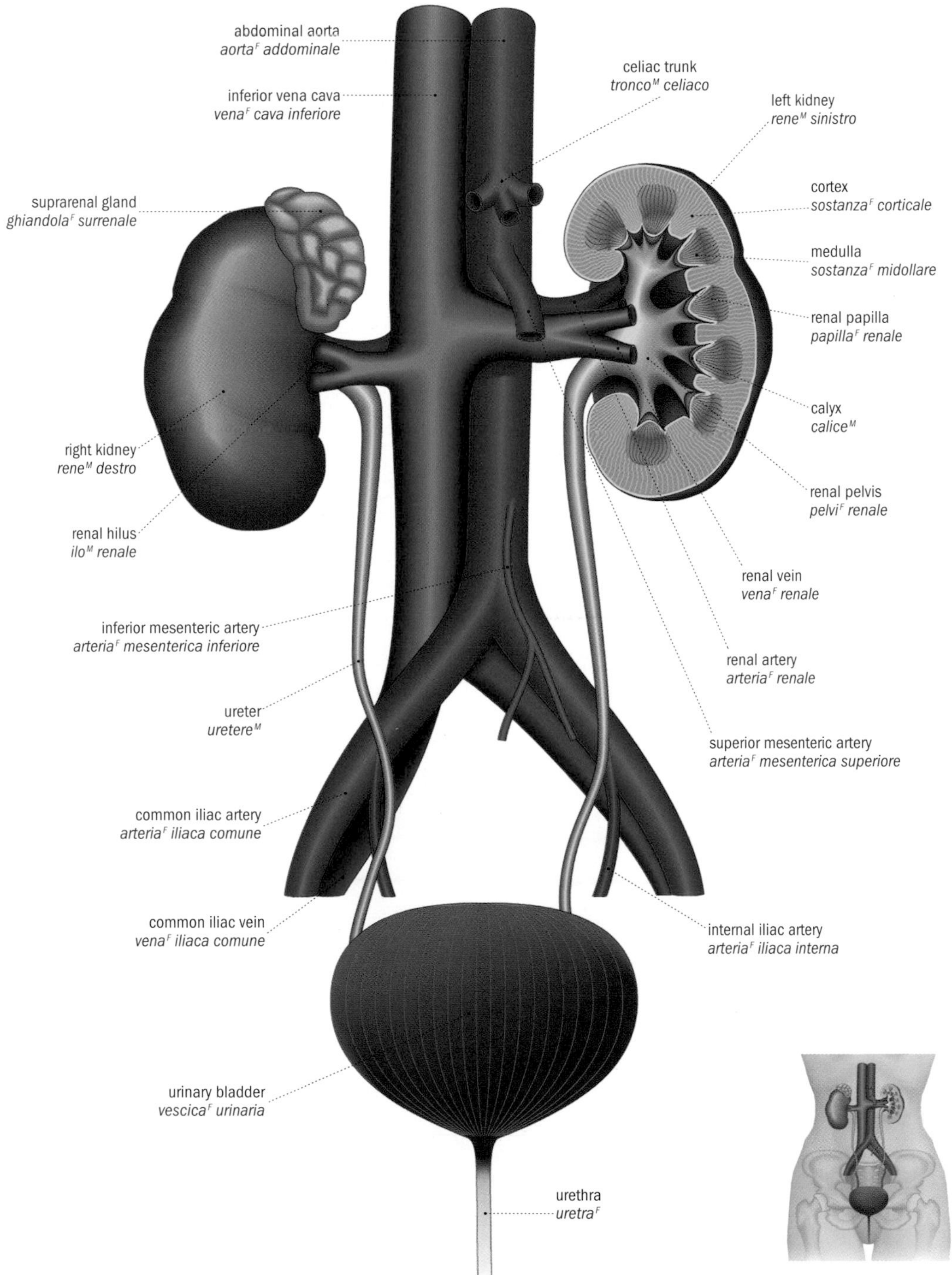

HUMAN BEING

nervous system

sistema[M] nervoso

peripheral nervous system
sistema[M] nervoso periferico

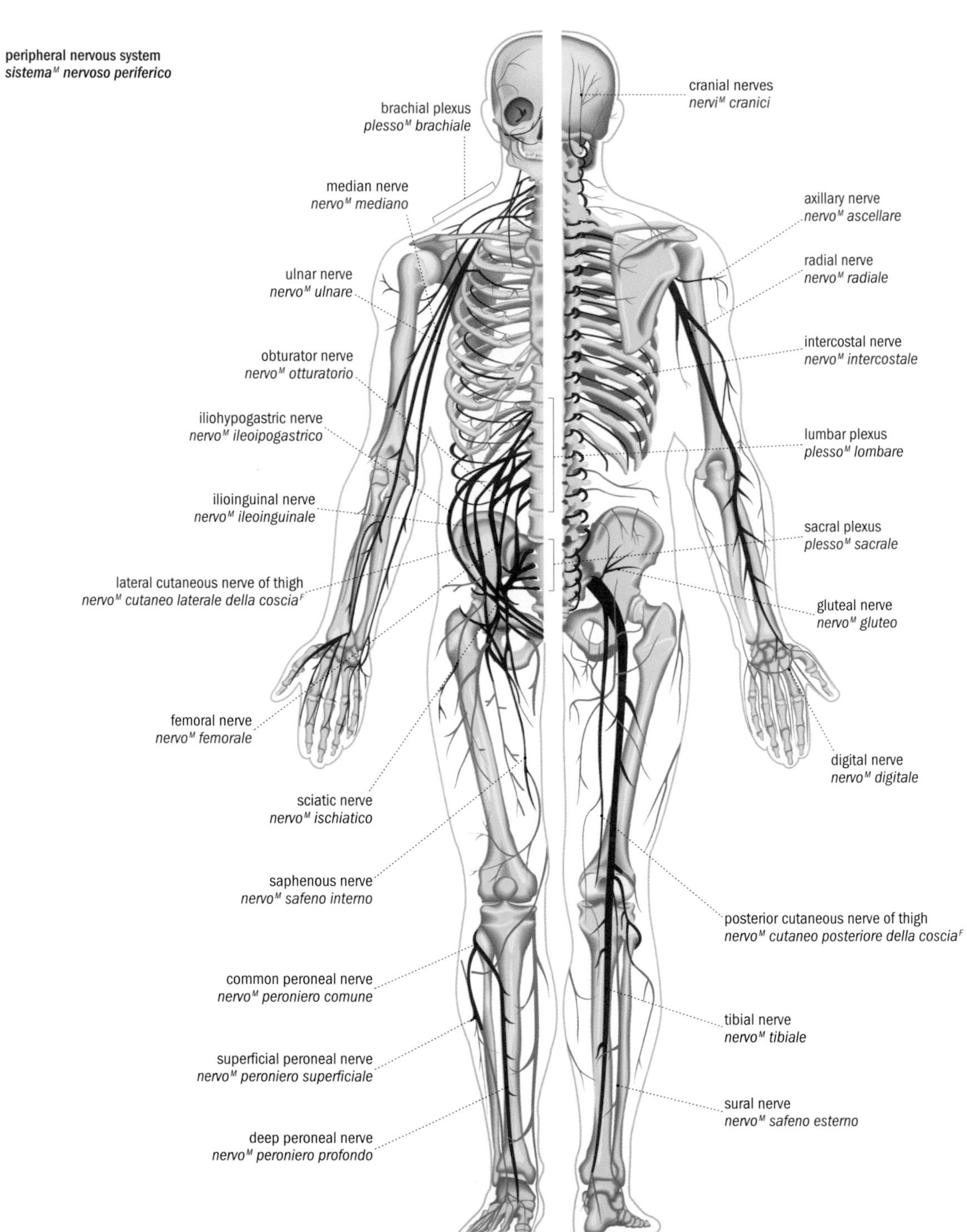

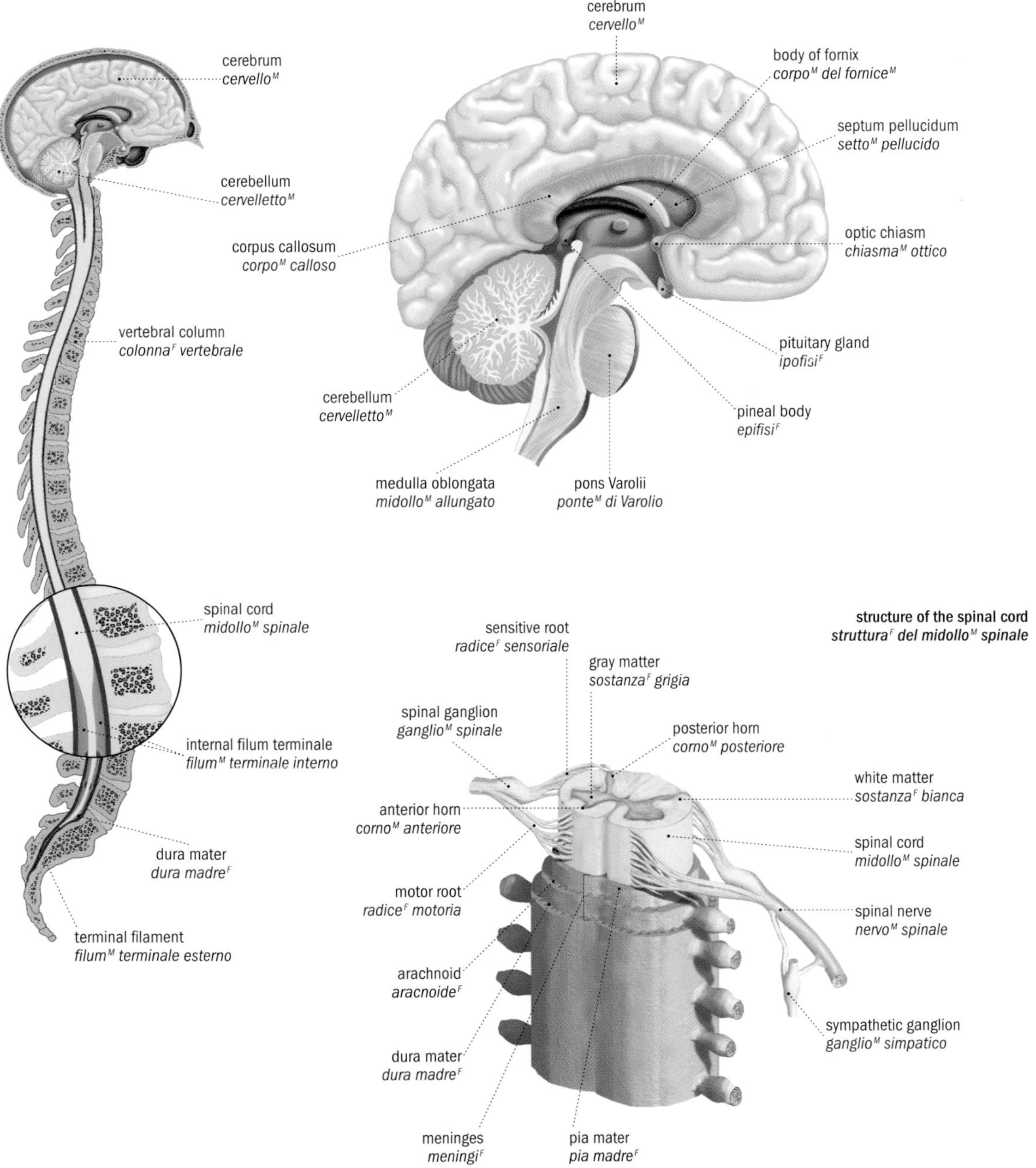
central nervous system
sistemaM nervoso centrale
cerebrum
cervelloM
cerebellum
cervellettoM
corpus callosum
corpoM calloso
vertebral column
colonnaF vertebrale
spinal cord
midolloM spinale
internal filum terminale
filumM terminale interno
dura mater
dura madreF
terminal filament
filumM terminale esterno
cerebrum
cervelloM
body of fornix
corpoM del forniceM
septum pellucidum
settoM pellucido
optic chiasm
chiasmaM ottico
pituitary gland
ipofisiF
pineal body
epifisiF
cerebellum
cervellettoM
medulla oblongata
midolloM allungato
pons Varolii
ponteM di Varolio
structure of the spinal cord
strutturaF del midolloM spinale
sensitive root
radiceF sensoriale
gray matter
sostanzaF grigia
spinal ganglion
ganglioM spinale
posterior horn
cornoM posteriore
white matter
sostanzaF bianca
anterior horn
cornoM anteriore
spinal cord
midolloM spinale
motor root
radiceF motoria
spinal nerve
nervoM spinale
arachnoid
aracnoideF
sympathetic ganglion
ganglioM simpatico
dura mater
dura madreF
meninges
meningiF
pia mater
pia madreF

nervous system

HUMAN BEING

chain of neurons
***catena*^{F} *di neuroni*^{M}**

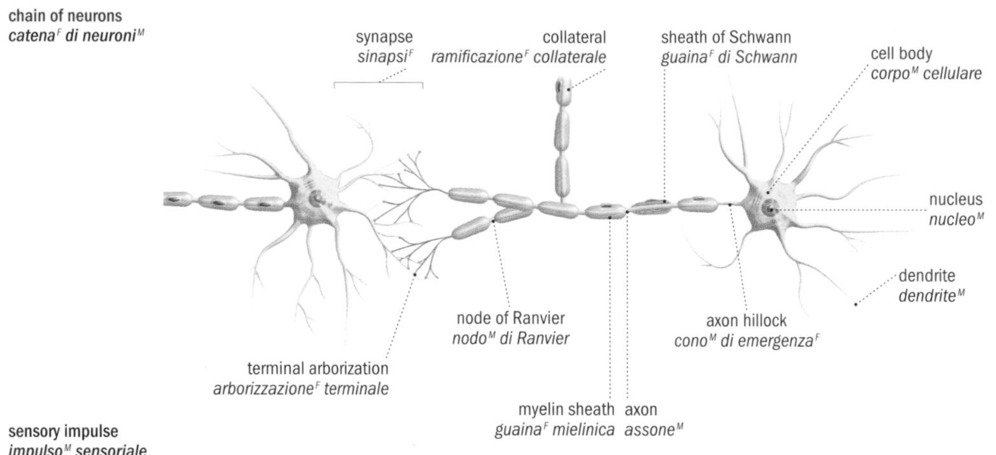

sensory impulse
impulso*^{M} *sensoriale

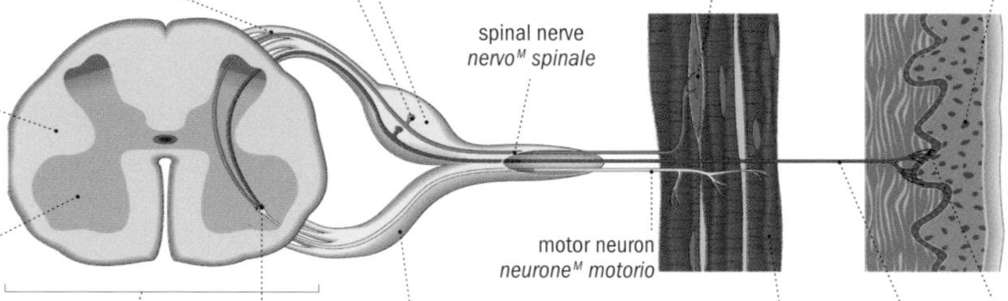

sensory root
radice^F *sensoriale*

protoneuron
protoneurone^M

spinal ganglion
ganglio^M *spinale*

motor end plate
placca^F *motrice*

skin
cute^F

white matter
sostanza^F *bianca*

spinal nerve
nervo^M *spinale*

gray matter
sostanza^F *grigia*

motor neuron
neurone^M *motorio*

sense receptor
recettore^M *sensoriale*

spinal cord
midollo^M *spinale*

synapse
sinapsi^F

motor root
radice^F *motoria*

muscle fiber
fibra^F *muscolare*

sensory neuron
neurone^M *sensoriale*

cervical vertebra
vertebre*^{F} *cervicali

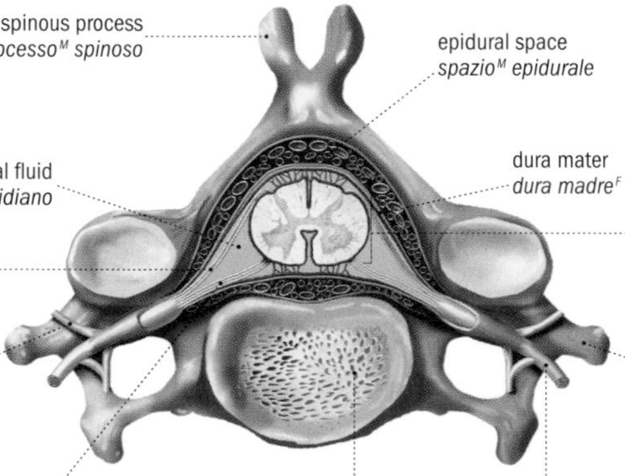

spinous process
processo^M *spinoso*

epidural space
spazio^M *epidurale*

cerebrospinal fluid
liquido^M *cefalorachidiano*

dura mater
dura madre^F

spinal cord
midollo^M *spinale*

posterior root
radice^F *posteriore*

transverse process
processo^M *trasverso*

communicating ramus
ramo^M *comunicante*

anterior root
radice^F *anteriore*

vertebral body
corpo^M *vertebrale*

spinal nerve
nervo^M *spinale*

male reproductive organs

organi^M genitali maschili

sagittal section
sezione^F sagittale

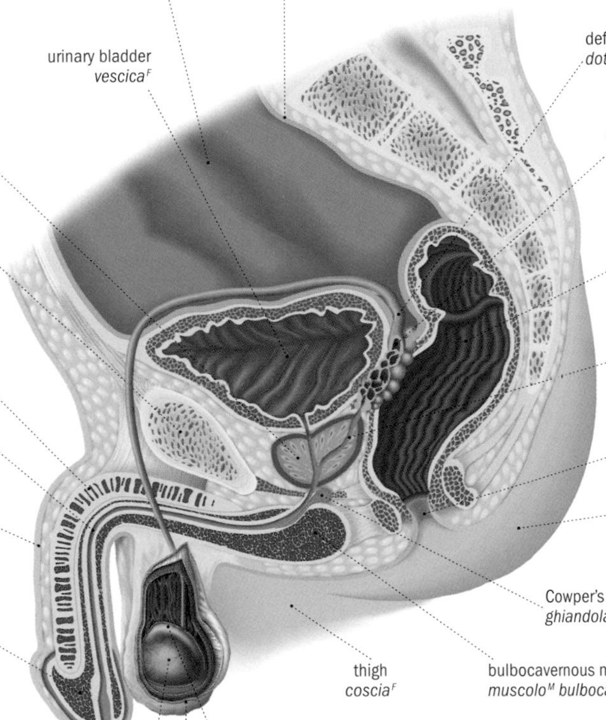

abdominal cavity
cavità^F addominale
peritoneum
peritoneo^M
urinary bladder
vescica^F
deferent duct
dotto^M deferente
prostate
prostata^F
seminal vesicle
vescichetta^F seminale
symphysis pubis
sinfisi^F pubica
rectum
retto^M
cavernous body
corpo^M cavernoso
ejaculatory duct
dotto^M eiaculatore
male urethra
uretra^F
anus
ano^M
penis
pene^M
buttock
natica^F
Cowper's gland
ghiandola^F di Cowper
glans penis
glande^M
thigh
coscia^F
bulbocavernous muscle
muscolo^M bulbocavernoso
prepuce
prepuzio^M
epididymis
epididimo^M
urinary meatus
meato^M urinario
testicle
testicolo^M
scrotum
scroto^M

spermatozoon
spermatozoo^M

head
testa^F
end piece
parte^F terminale
tail
coda^F
neck
collo^M
middle piece
parte^F intermedia

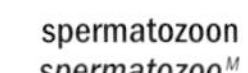

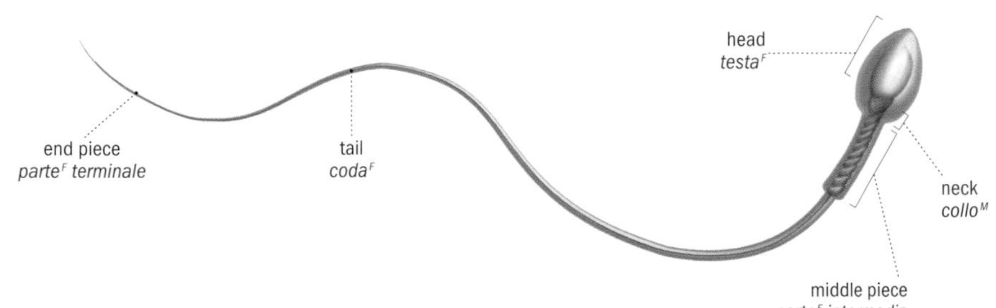

female reproductive organs

organi[M] genitali femminili

sagittal section
sezione[F] sagittale

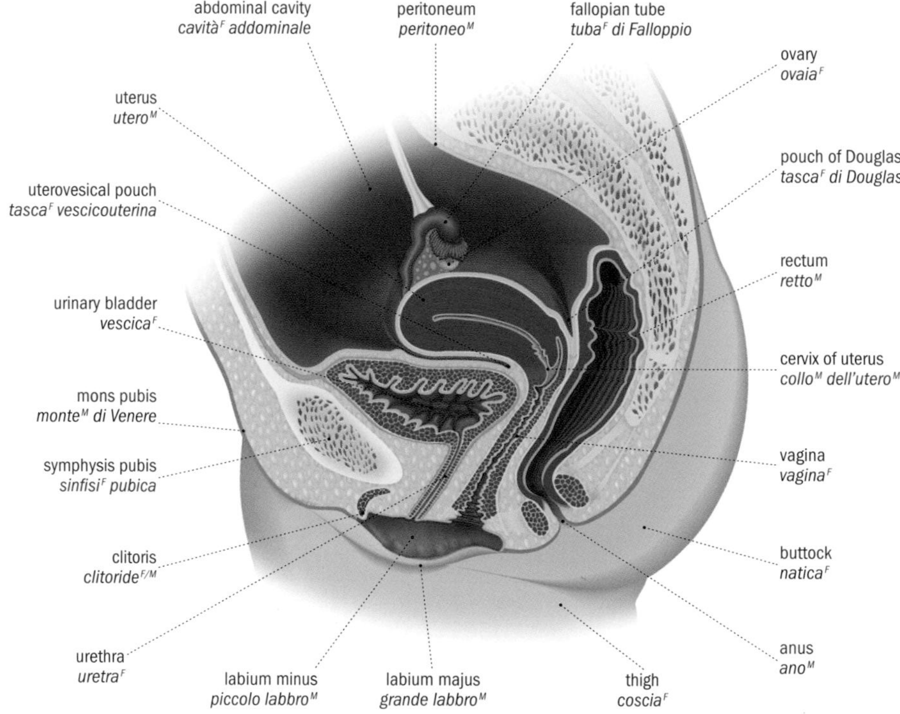

egg
ovulo[M]

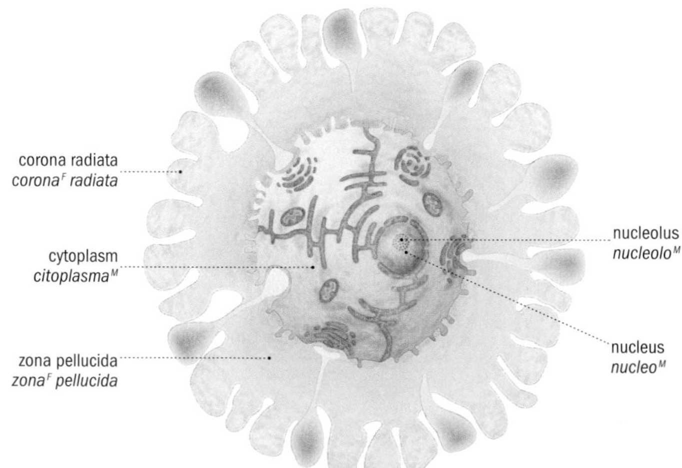

posterior view
vista^F posteriore

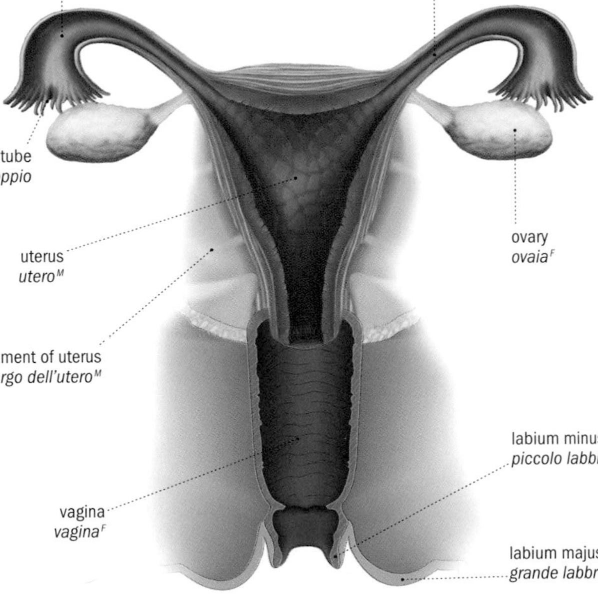

ampulla of fallopian tube
ampolla^F della tuba^F di Falloppio
isthmus of fallopian tube
istmo^M della tuba^F di Falloppio
infundibulum of fallopian tube
infundibolo^M della tuba^F di Falloppio
uterus
utero^M
ovary
ovaia^F
broad ligament of uterus
legamento^M largo dell'utero^M
labium minus
piccolo labbro^M
vagina
vagina^F
labium majus
grande labbro^M

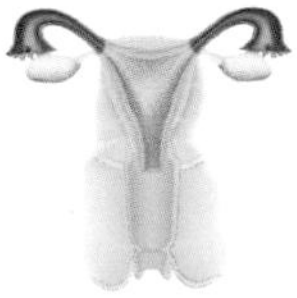

fallopian tubes
tube^F di Falloppio

vulva
vulva^F

breast

seno^M

adipose tissue
tessuto^M adiposo
areola
areola^F
nipple
capezzolo^M
mammary gland
ghiandola^F mammaria
lactiferous duct
dotto^M galattoforo

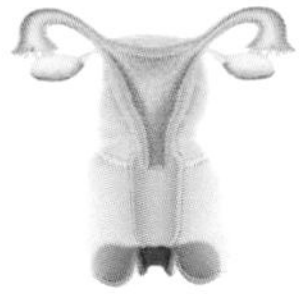

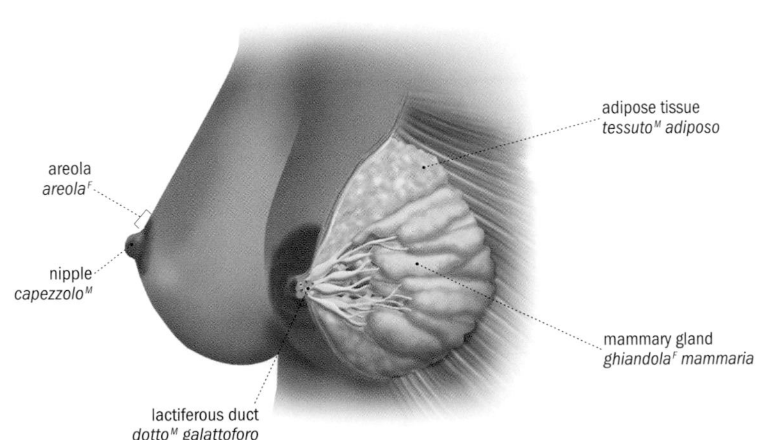

touch

tatto[M]

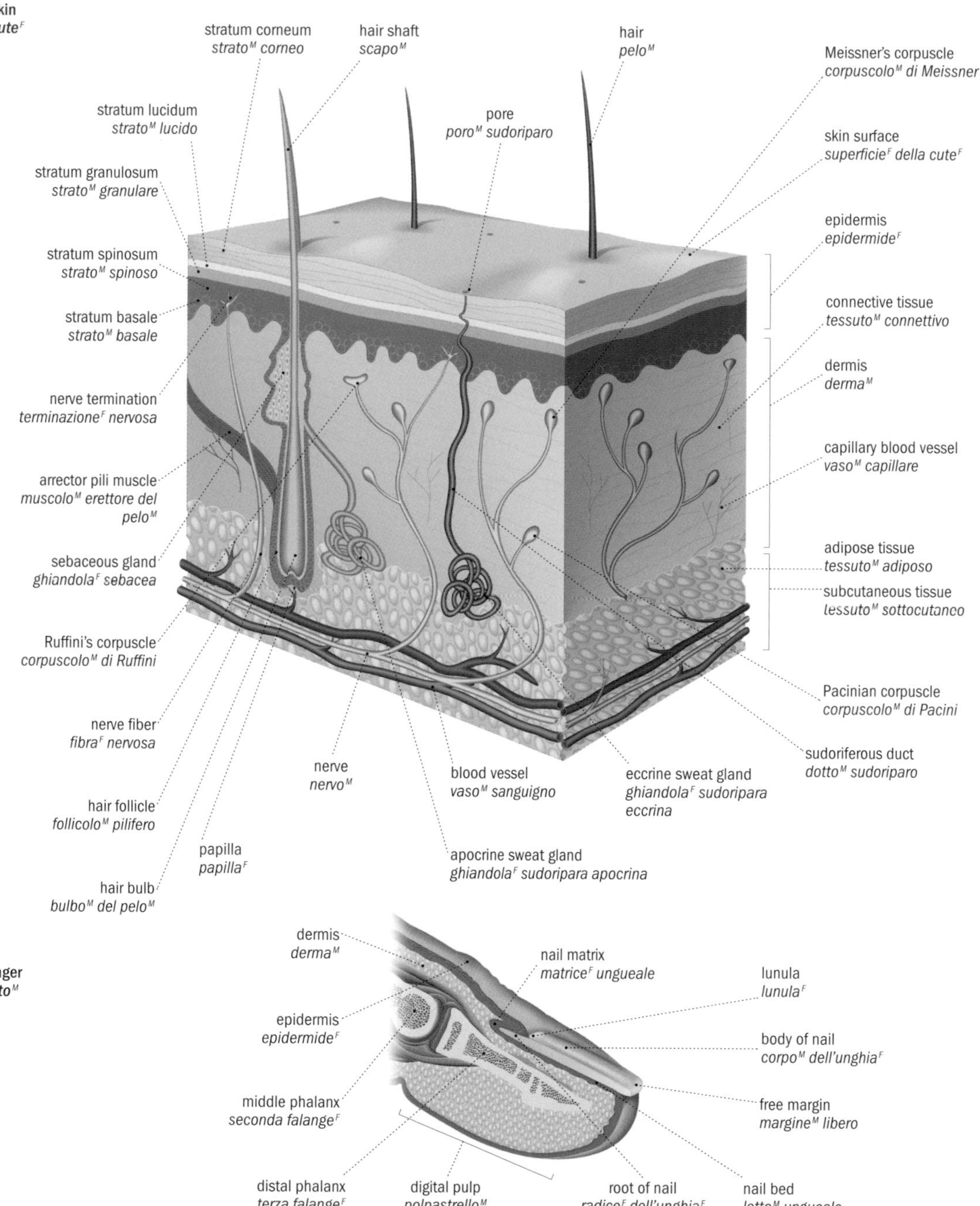

touch

hand
mano[F]

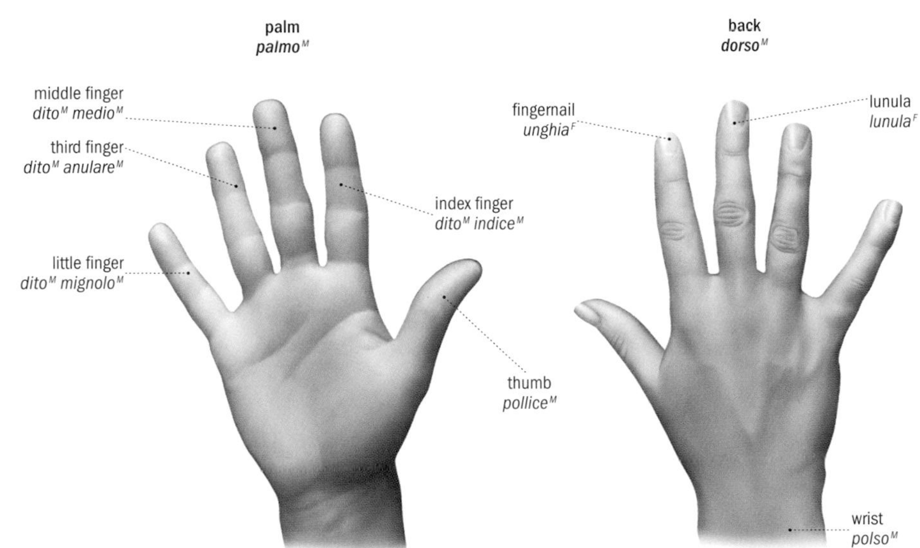

hearing

udito[M]

auricle
padiglione[M] *auricolare*

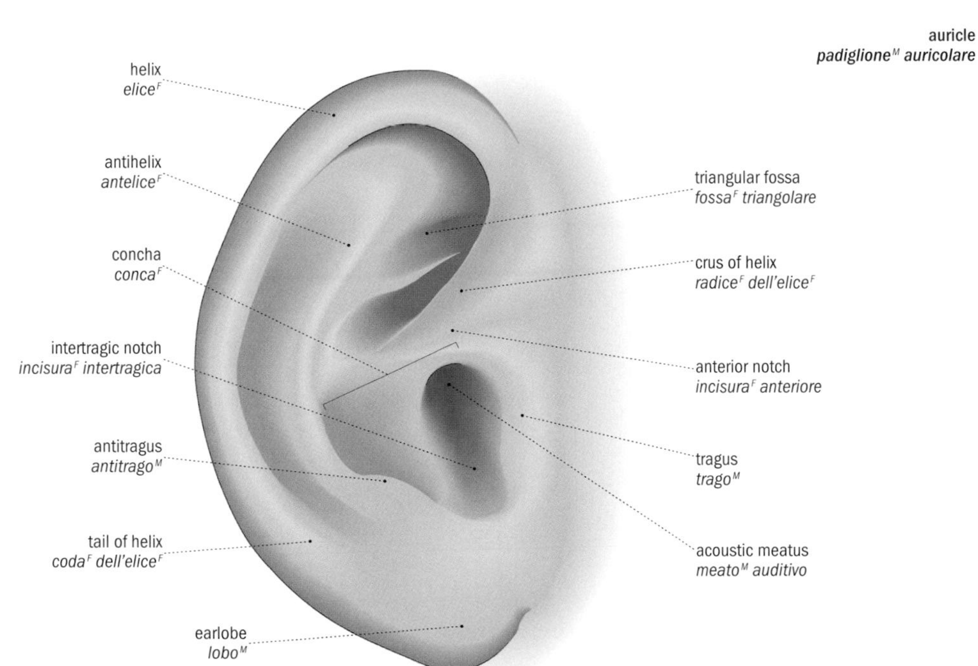

hearing

structure of the ear
struttura[F] dell'orecchio[M]

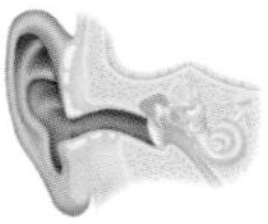

external ear
orecchio[M] esterno

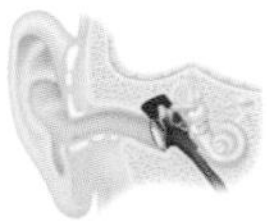

middle ear
orecchio[M] medio

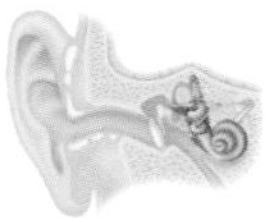

internal ear
orecchio[M] interno

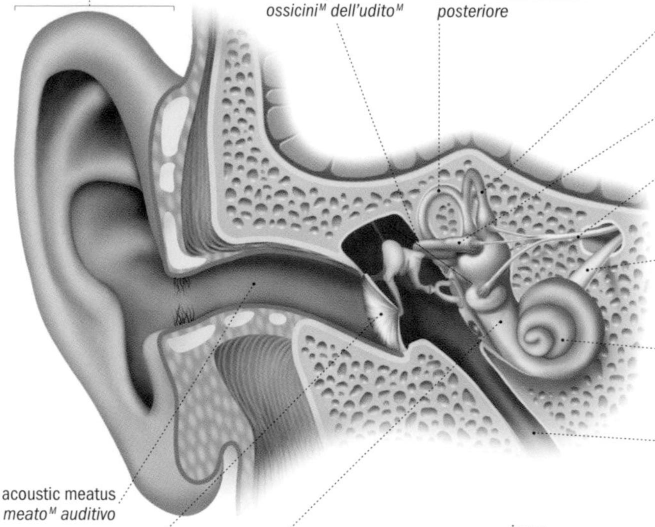

auricle
padiglione[M]

auditory ossicles
ossicini[M] dell'udito[M]

posterior semicircular canal
canale[M] semicircolare posteriore

superior semicircular canal
canale[M] semicircolare superiore

lateral semicircular canal
canale[M] semicircolare laterale

vestibular nerve
nervo[M] vestibolare

cochlear nerve
nervo[M] cocleare

cochlea
coclea[F]

Eustachian tube
tuba[F] di Eustachio

acoustic meatus
meato[M] auditivo

ear drum
membrana[F] del timpano[M]

vestibule
vestibolo[M]

auditory ossicles
ossicini[M] dell'udito[M]

incus
incudine[F]

malleus
martello[M]

stapes
staffa[F]

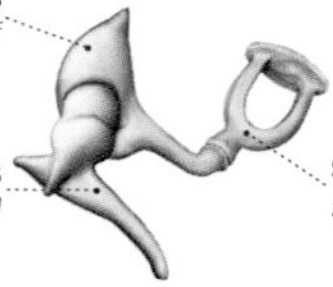

smell and taste

olfatto[M] e gusto[M]

mouth
bocca[F]

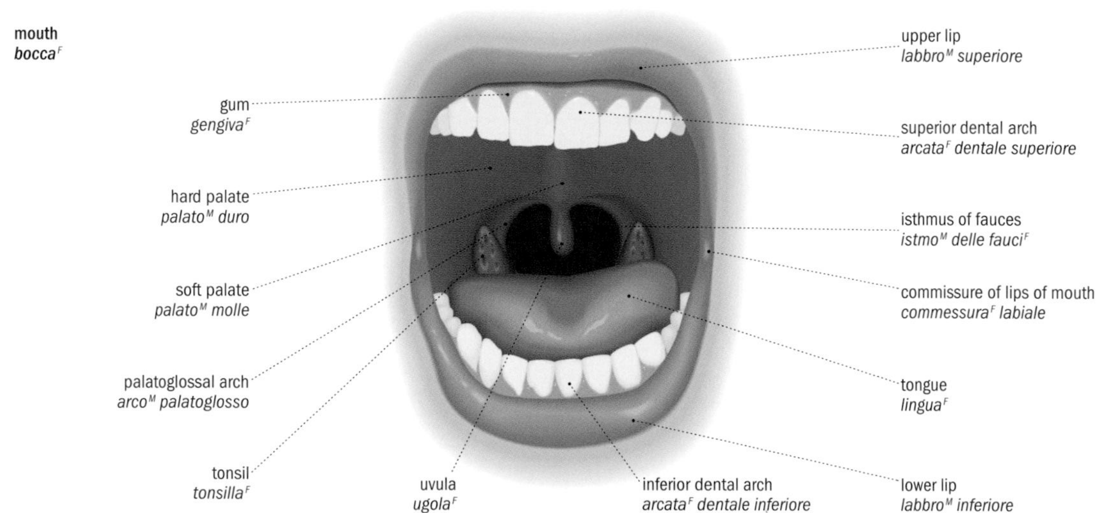

external nose
naso*[M] *esterno

root of nose
radice[F] *del naso*[M]
dorsum of nose
dorso[M] *del naso*[M]
tip of nose
punta[F] *del naso*[M]
ala
ala[F]
nostril
narice[F]
philtrum
filtro[M]
septum
setto[M]

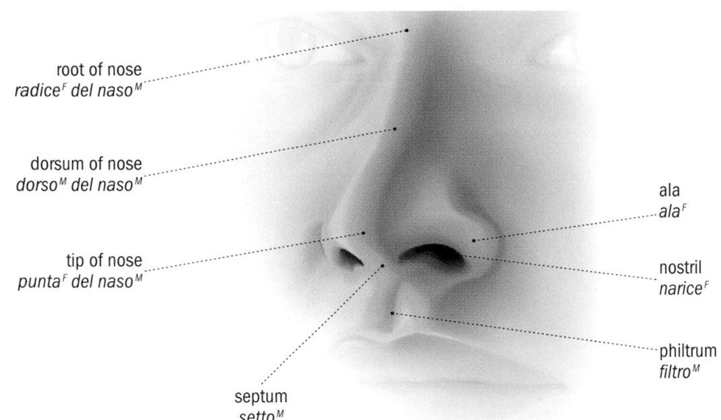

nasal fossae
fosse*[F] *nasali

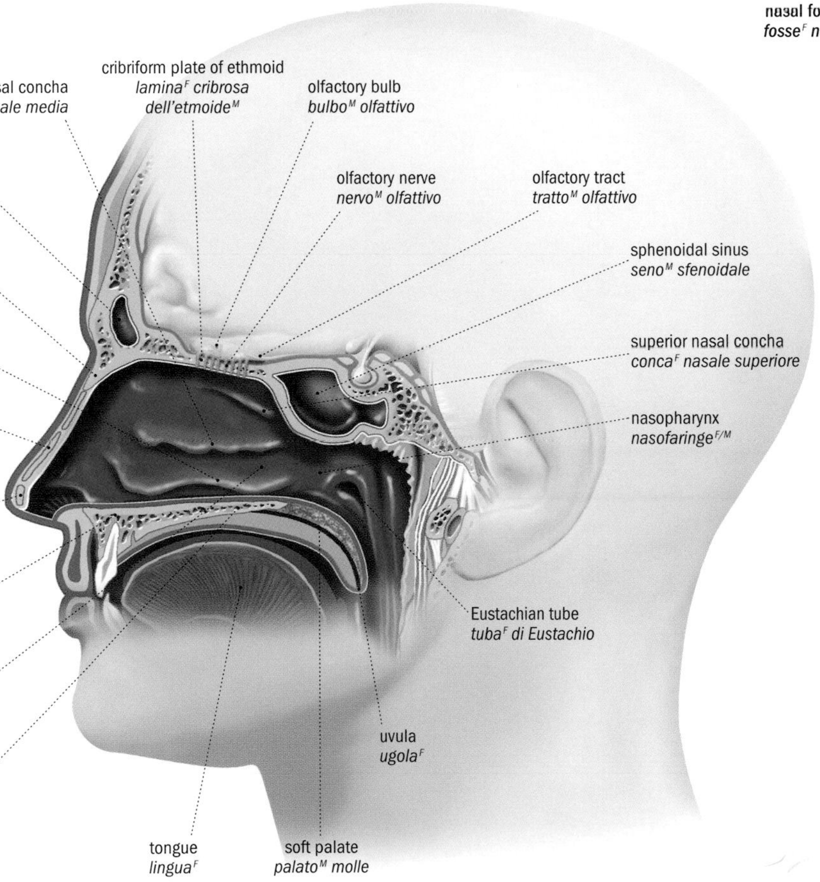

middle nasal concha
conca[F] *nasale media*
cribriform plate of ethmoid
lamina[F] *cribrosa dell'etmoide*[M]
olfactory bulb
bulbo[M] *olfattivo*
frontal sinus
seno[M] *frontale*
olfactory nerve
nervo[M] *olfattivo*
olfactory tract
tratto[M] *olfattivo*
nasal bone
osso[M] *nasale*
sphenoidal sinus
seno[M] *sfenoidale*
inferior nasal concha
conca[F] *nasale inferiore*
superior nasal concha
conca[F] *nasale superiore*
septal cartilage of nose
cartilagine[F] *del setto*[M] *nasale*
nasopharynx
nasofaringe[F/M]
greater alar cartilage
cartilagine[F] *alare maggiore*
maxilla
mascella[F]
Eustachian tube
tuba[F] *di Eustachio*
olfactory mucosa
mucosa[F] *olfattiva*
uvula
ugola[F]
hard palate
palato[M] *duro*
tongue
lingua[F]
soft palate
palato[M] *molle*

dorsum of tongue
dorso[M] della lingua[F]

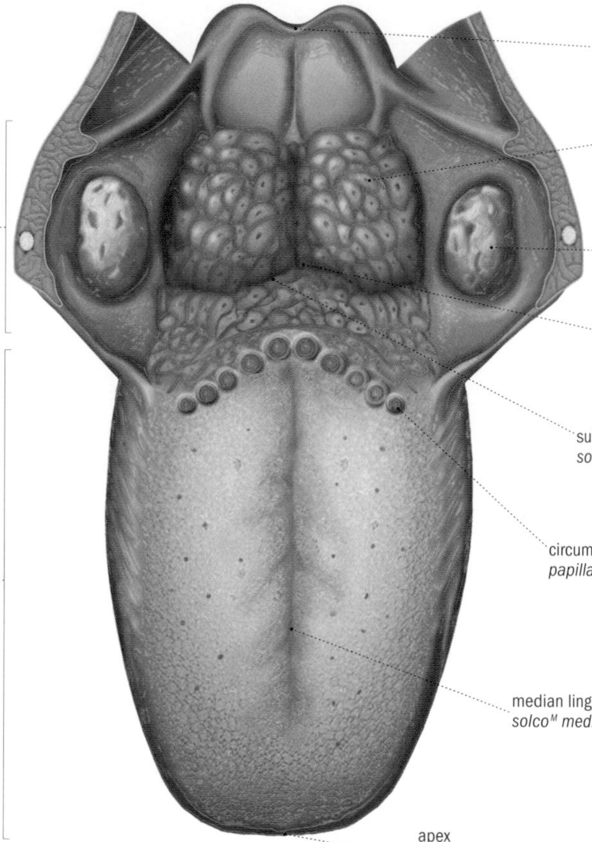

epiglottis
epiglottide[F]

lingual tonsil
tonsilla[F] linguale

root
radice[F]

palatine tonsil
tonsilla[F] palatina

foramen cecum
forame[M] cieco

sulcus terminalis
solco[M] terminale

circumvallate papilla
papilla[F] circumvallata

body
corpo[M]

median lingual sulcus
solco[M] mediano

apex
apice[M]

taste receptors
recettori[M] gustativi

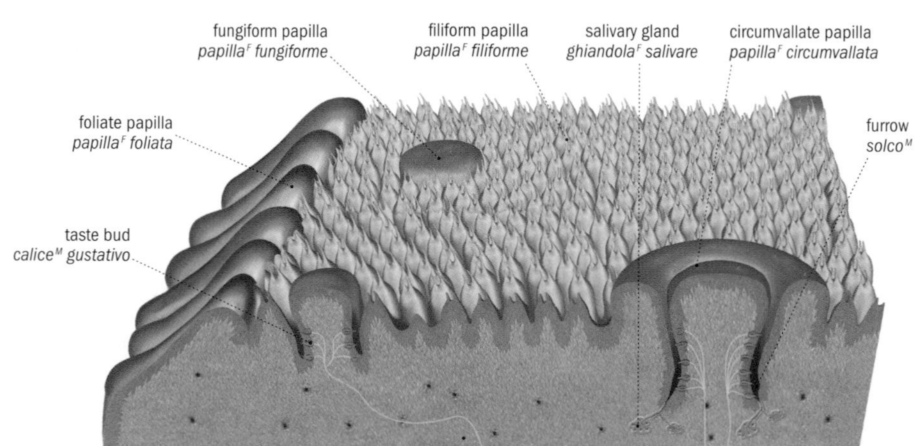

sight
vista[F]

eye
occhio[M]

upper eyelid
palpebra[F] *superiore*
eyelash
ciglio[M]
lachrymal caruncle
caruncola[F] *lacrimale*
lachrymal canal
canale[M] *lacrimale*
iris
iride[F]
lower eyelid
palpebra[F] *inferiore*
lachrymal gland
ghiandola[F] *lacrimale*
pupil
pupilla[F]
sclera
sclera[F]

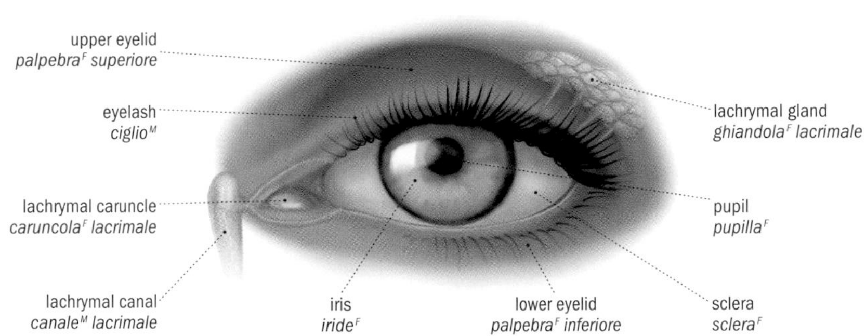

eyeball
globo[M] ***oculare***

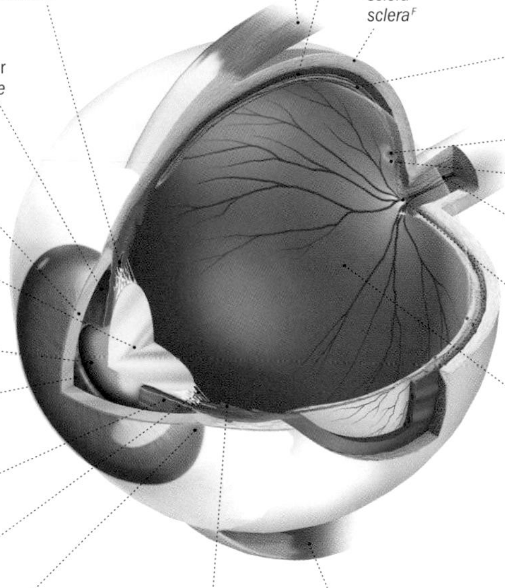

superior rectus muscle
muscolo[M] *retto superiore*
choroid
coroide[F]
posterior chamber
camera[F] *posteriore*
sclera
sclera[F]
retina
retina[F]
anterior chamber
camera[F] *anteriore*
fovea
fovea[F]
cornea
cornea[F]
macula
macula[F]
lens
cristallino[M]
optic nerve
nervo[M] *ottico*
pupil
pupilla[F]
papilla
papilla[F] *ottica*
aqueous humor
umor[M] *acqueo*
vitreous body
corpo[M] *vitreo*
iris
iride[F]
suspensory ligament
legamento[M] *sospensore*
conjunctiva
congiuntiva[F]
ciliary body
corpo[M] *ciliare*
inferior rectus muscle
muscolo[M] *retto inferiore*

photoreceptors
fotorecettori[M]

cone
cono[M]

rod
bastoncello[M]

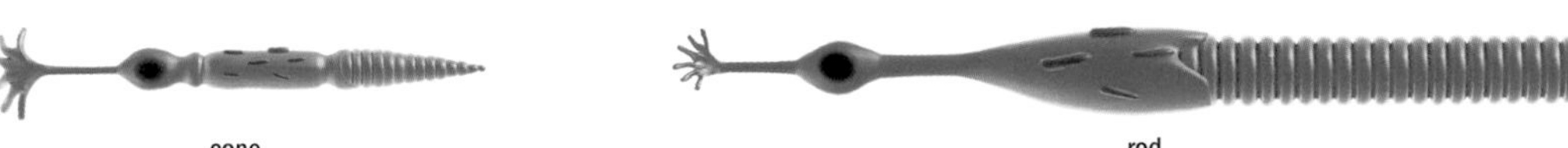

supermarket

supermercato[M]

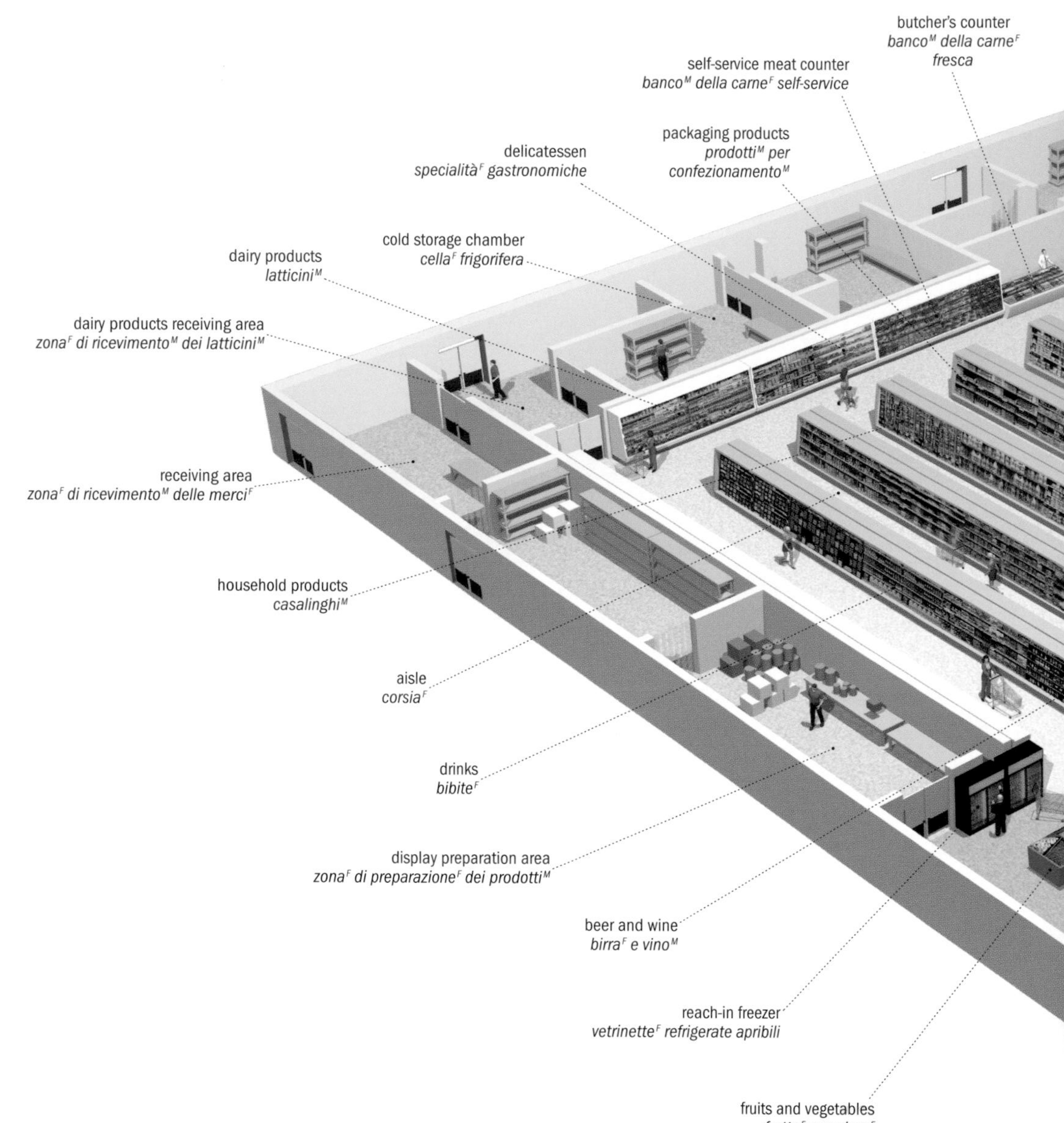

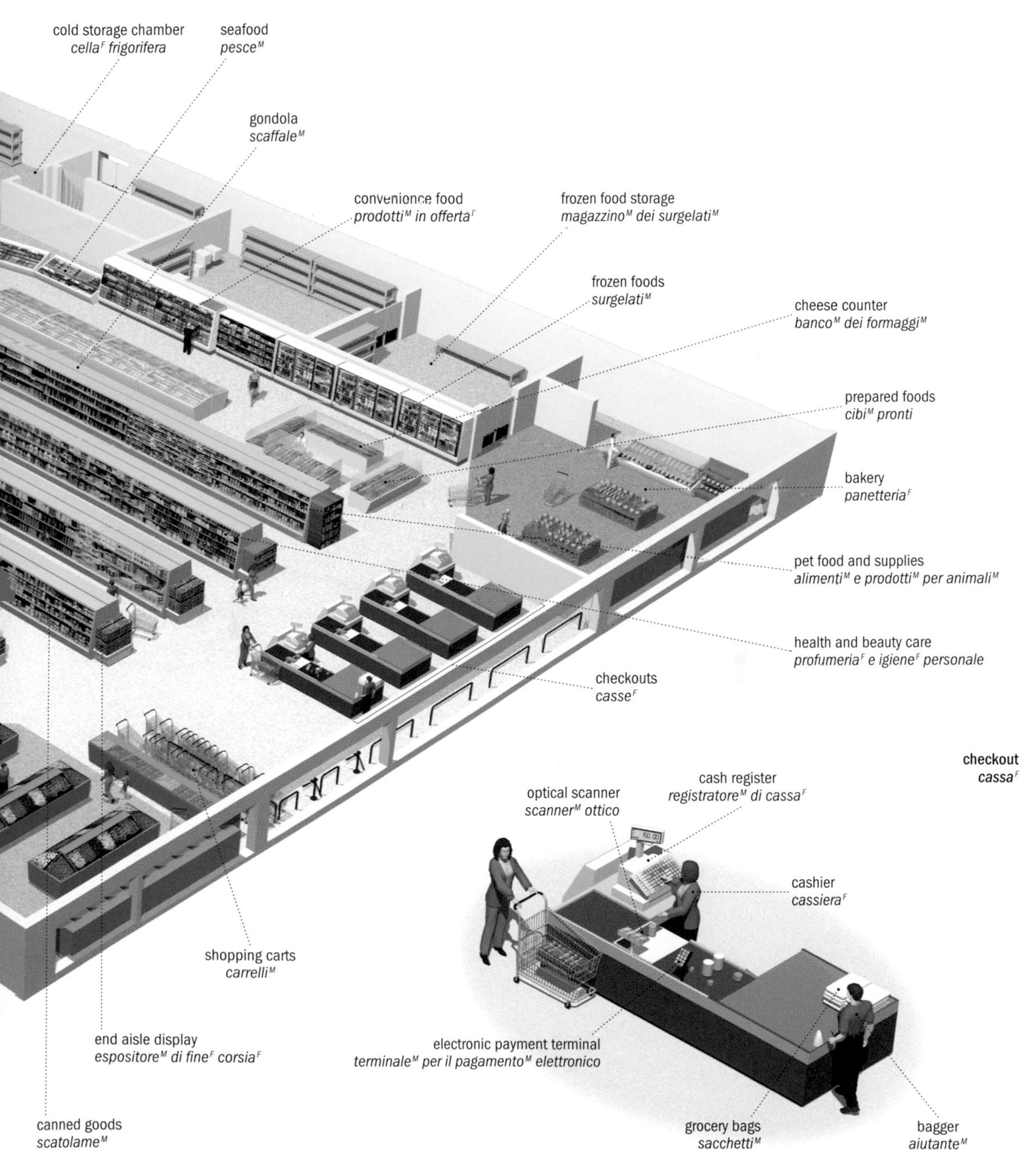
cold storage chamber
cella^F frigorifera
seafood
pesce^M
gondola
scaffale^M
convenience food
prodotti^M in offerta^F
frozen food storage
magazzino^M dei surgelati^M
frozen foods
surgelati^M
cheese counter
banco^M dei formaggi^M
prepared foods
cibi^M pronti
bakery
panetteria^F
pet food and supplies
alimenti^M e prodotti^M per animali^M
health and beauty care
profumeria^F e igiene^F personale
checkouts
casse^F
checkout
cassa^F
cash register
registratore^M di cassa^F
optical scanner
scanner^M ottico
cashier
cassiera^F
shopping carts
carrelli^M
end aisle display
espositore^M di fine^F corsia^F
electronic payment terminal
terminale^M per il pagamento^M elettronico
canned goods
scatolame^M
grocery bags
sacchetti^M
bagger
aiutante^M

farmstead

fattoria[F]

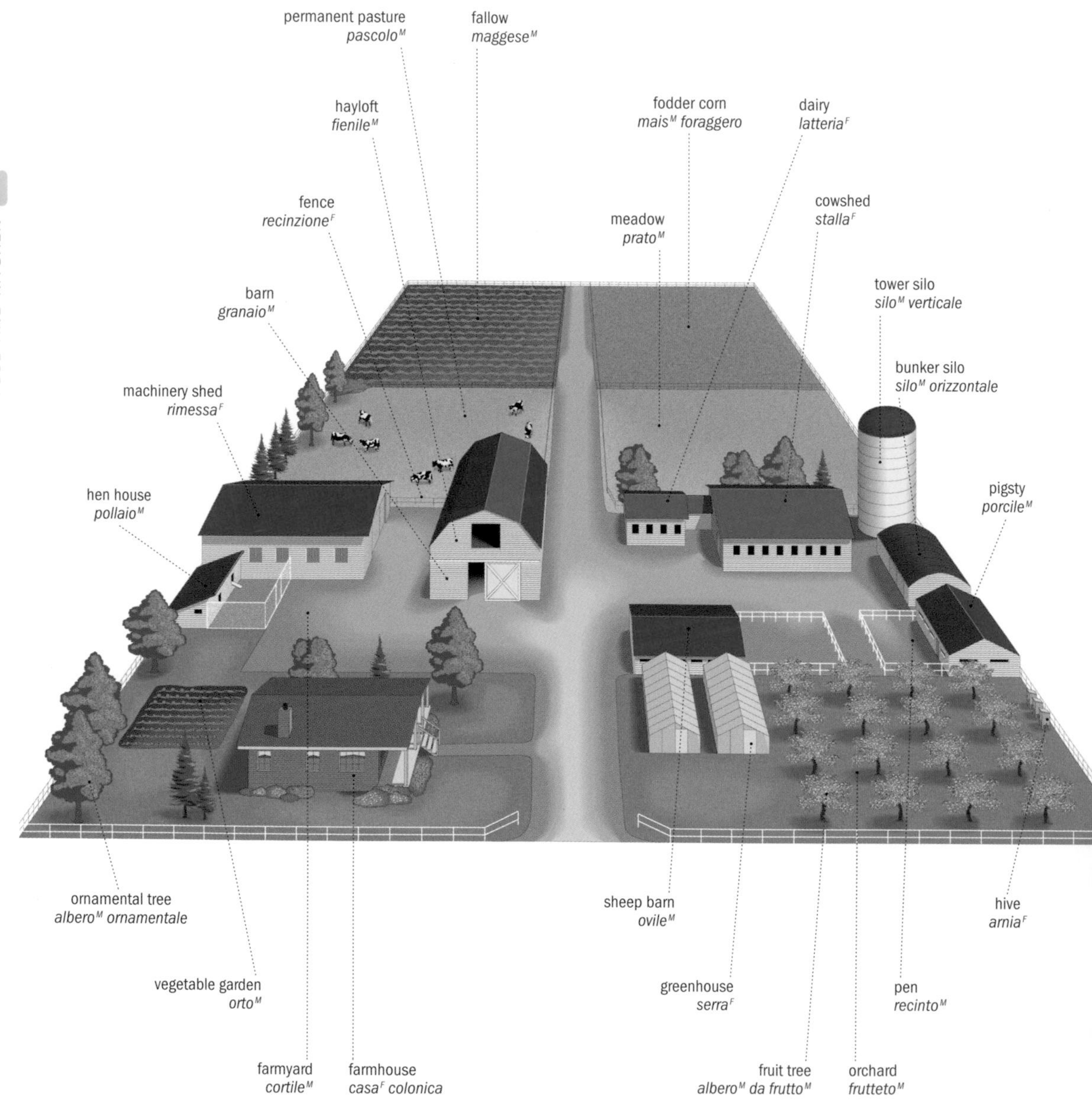

mushrooms

funghi^M^

truffle
tartufo^M^

wood ear
orecchio^M^ *di Giuda*

royal agaric
ovolo^M^ *buono*

delicious lactarius
agarico^M^ *delizioso*

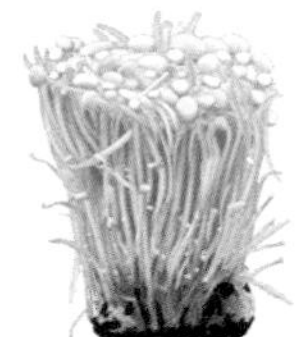

enoki
collibia^F^

oyster
gelone^M^

cultivated mushrooms
fungo^M^ *coltivato*

green russula
verdone^M^

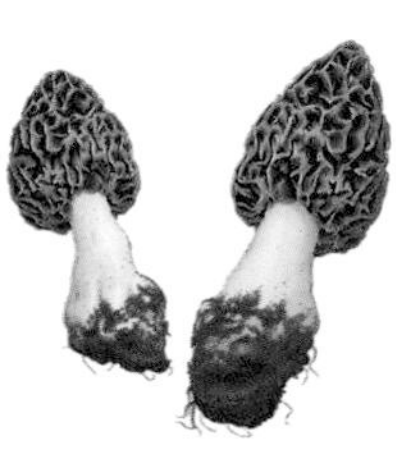
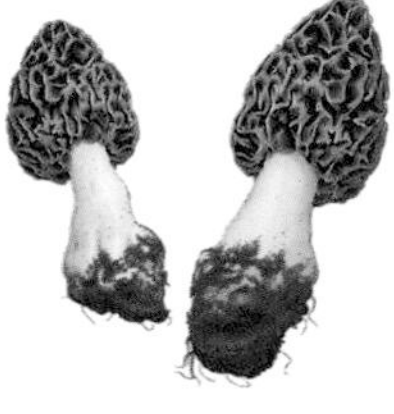

morels
spugnola^F^

edible boletus
porcino^M^

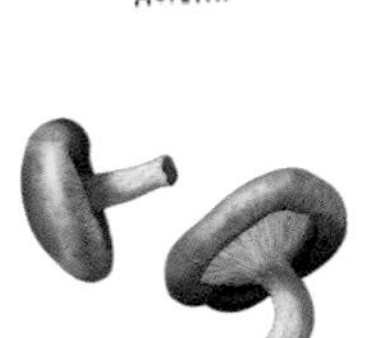

shitake
shiitake^M^

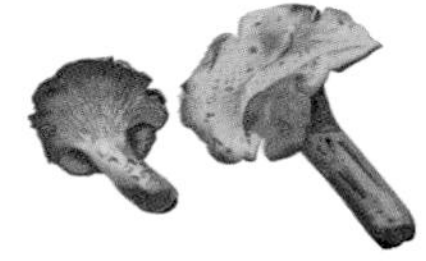

chanterelles
cantarello^M^

seaweed

alga^F^ marina

arame
arame^F^

wakame
wakame^F^

kombu
kombu^F^

spirulina
spirulina^F^

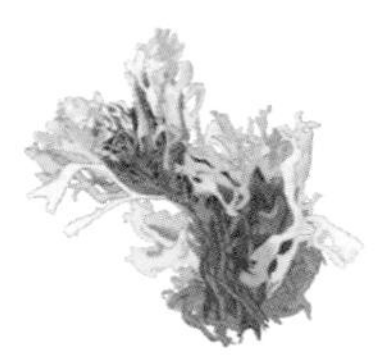
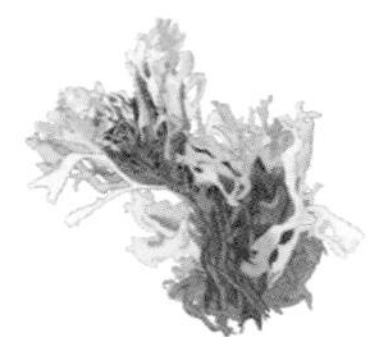

Irish moss
muschio^M^ *d'Irlanda*^F^

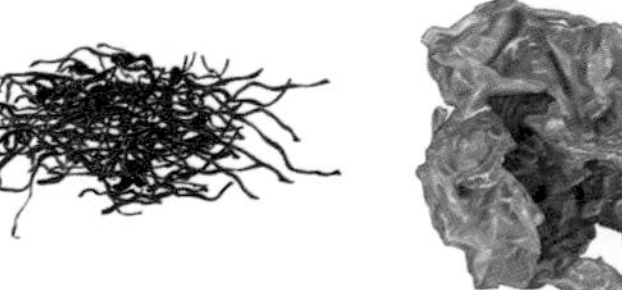

hijiki
hijiki^F^

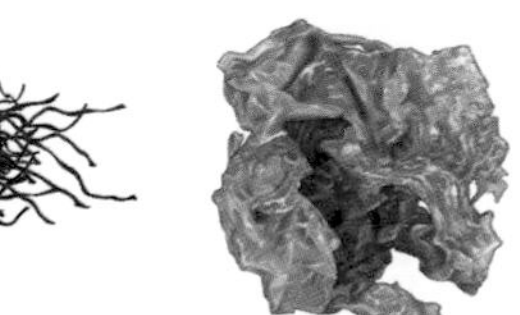
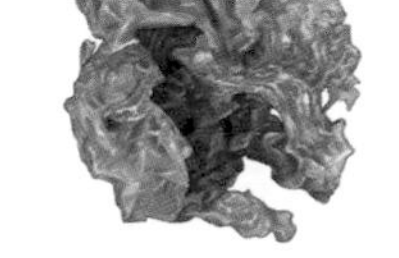

sea lettuce
lattuga^F^ *marina*

agar-agar
agar-agar^M^

nori
nori^F^

dulse
dulse^F^

vegetables

ortaggi[M]

bulb vegetables
ortaggi[M] da bulbo[M]

shallot
scalogno[M]

water chestnut
castagna[F] d'acqua[F]

green onion
cipolla[F] verde

scallion
cipolla[F] d'inverno[M]

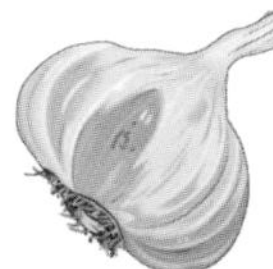

garlic
aglio[M]

chives
erba[F] cipollina

leeks
porri[M]

yellow onion
cipolla[F] di Spagna[F]

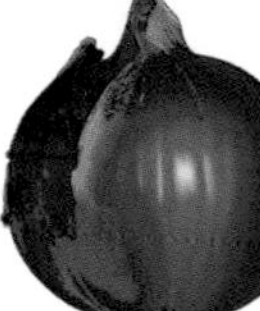

red onion
cipolla[F] rossa

white onion
cipolla[F] bianca

pickling onions
cipolline[F]

tuber vegetables
ortaggi[M] da tubero[M]

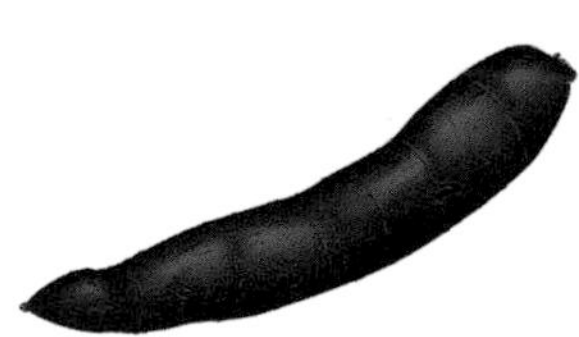

cassava
manioca[F]

crosne
crosne[M]

taro
taro[M]

jicama
jicama[F]

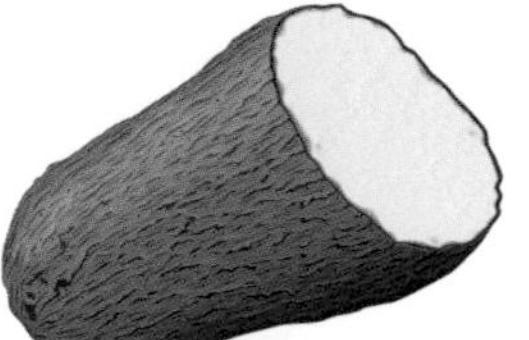

tropical yam
igname[M]

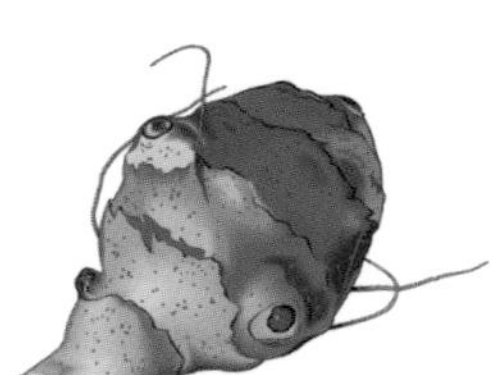

Jerusalem artichoke
topinambur[M]

sweet potato
patata[F] americana

potatoes
patate[F]

stalk vegetables
ortaggi[M] da fusto[M]

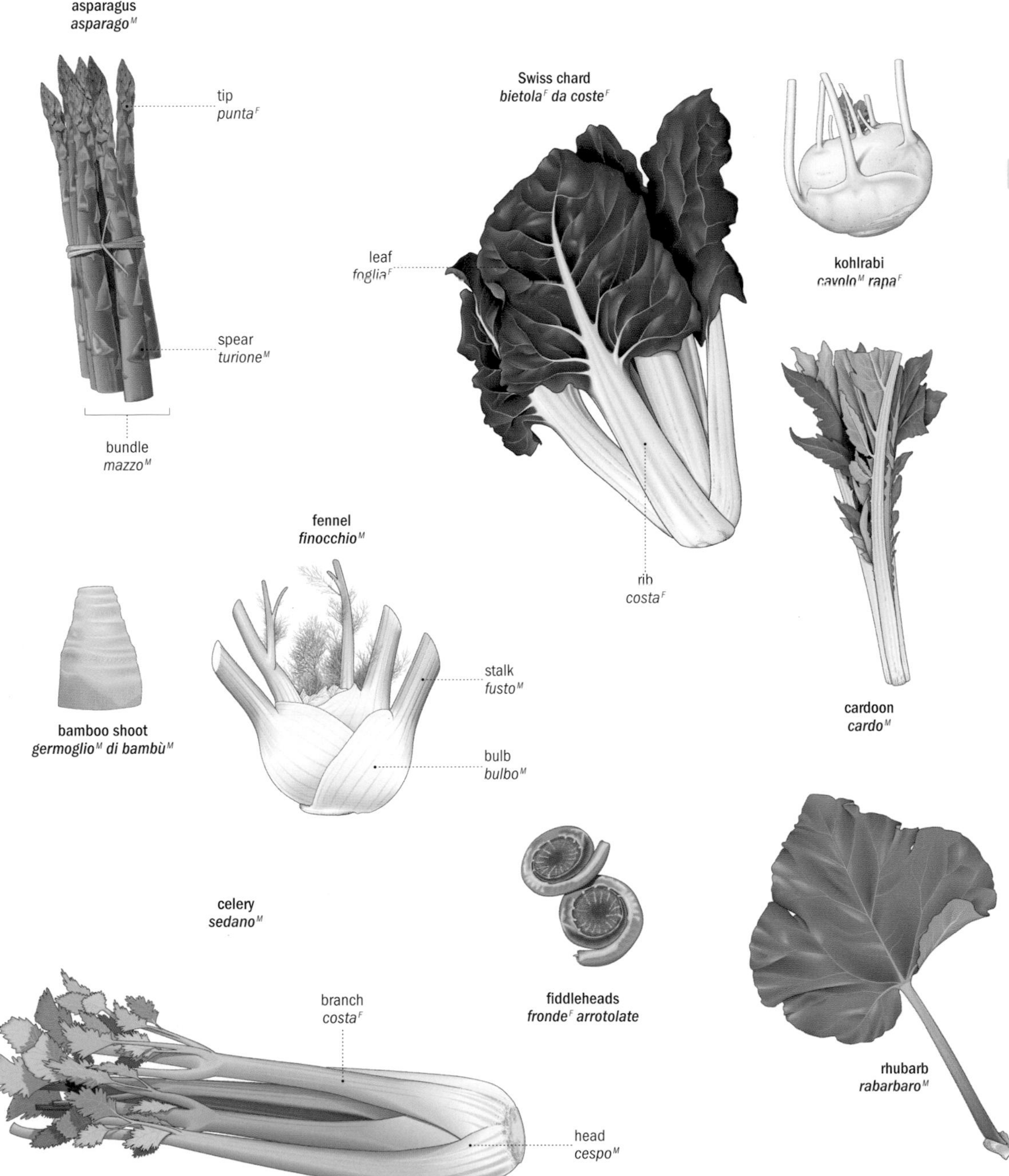

vegetables

FOOD AND KITCHEN

leaf vegetables
ortaggi^M da foglia^F

leaf lettuce
insalata^F riccia

romaine lettuce
lattuga^F romana

celtuce
lattuga^F asparago^M

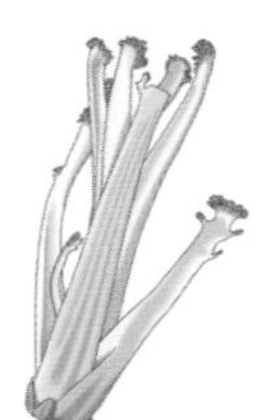
sea kale
cavolo^M marittimo

collards
gramigna^F crestata

escarole
scarola^F

butter lettuce
lattuga^F cappuccina

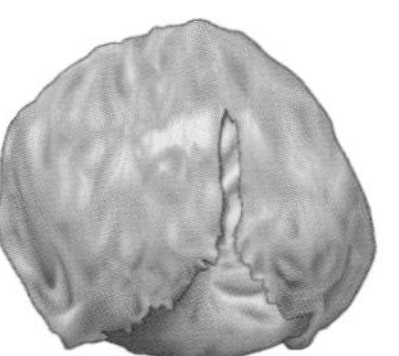
iceberg lettuce
lattuga^F iceberg^M

radicchio
radicchio^M

ornamental kale
cavolo^M ornamentale

curly kale
cavolo^M riccio

grape leaves
pampino^M

brussels sprouts
cavolini^M di Bruxelles

red cabbage
cavolo^M rosso

white cabbage
cavolo^M bianco

savoy cabbage
cavolo^M verzotto

green cabbage
cavolo^M verza^F

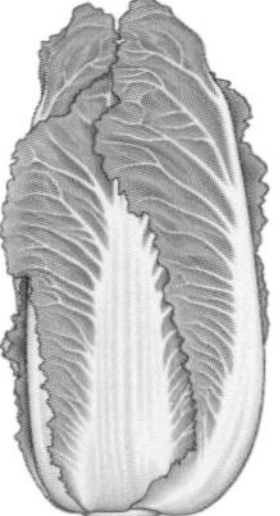
pe-tsai
pe-tsai^M

bok choy
pak-choi^M

purslane
porcellana[F]

nettle
ortica[F]

watercress
crescione[M]

dandelion
dente[M] *di leone*[M]

corn salad
valerianella[F]

arugula
rucola[F]

spinach
spinacio[M]

garden cress
crescione[M] *d'orto*[M]

garden sorrel
acetosa[F]

curly endive
indivia[F] *riccia*

Belgian endive
insalata[F] *belga*

inflorescent vegetables
ortaggi[M] *da infiorescenza*[F]

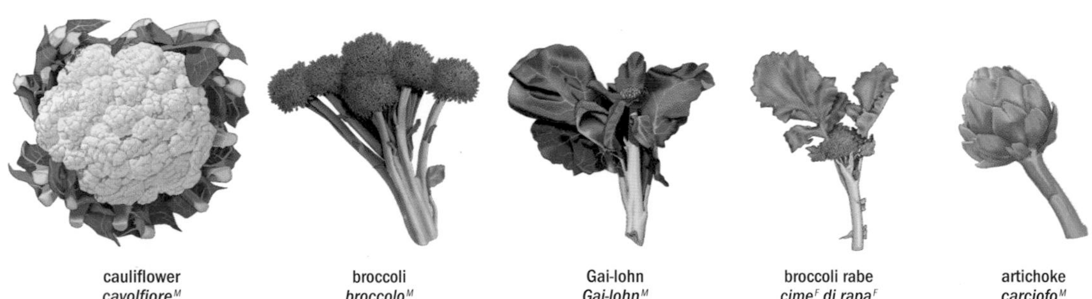

cauliflower
cavolfiore[M]

broccoli
broccolo[M]

Gai-lohn
Gai-lohn[M]

broccoli rabe
cime[F] *di rapa*[F]

artichoke
carciofo[M]

fruit vegetables
***ortaggi*[M] *da frutto*[M]**

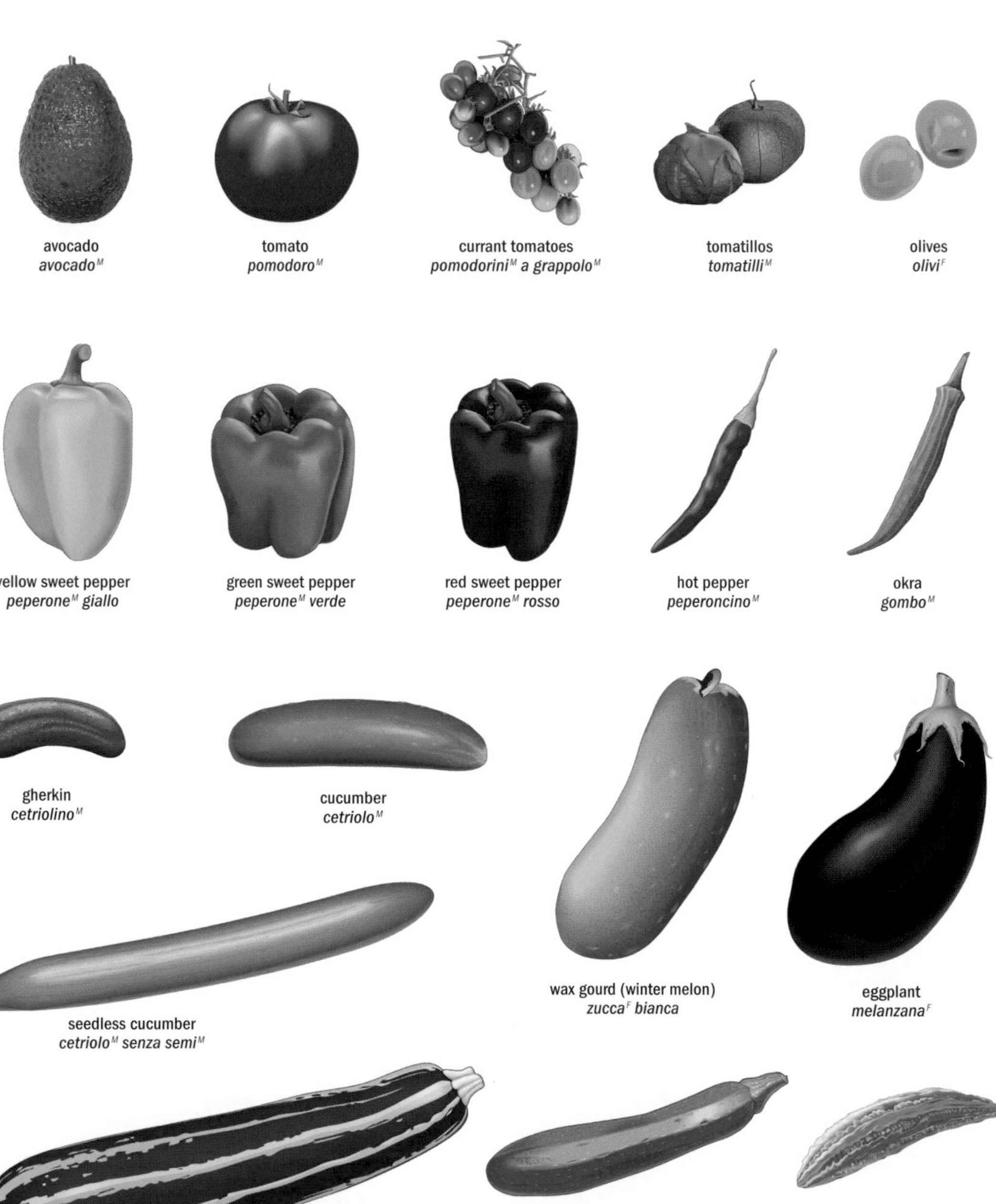

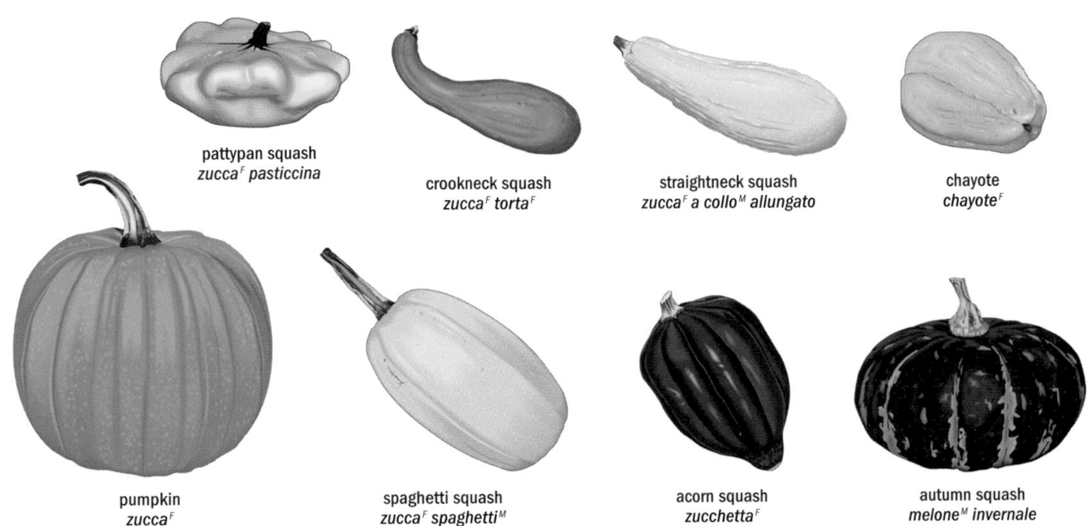

pattypan squash
zucca[F] pasticcina

crookneck squash
zucca[F] torta[F]

straightneck squash
zucca[F] a collo[M] allungato

chayote
chayote[F]

pumpkin
zucca[F]

spaghetti squash
zucca[F] spaghetti[M]

acorn squash
zucchetta[F]

autumn squash
melone[M] invernale

root vegetables
ortaggi[M] da radice[F]

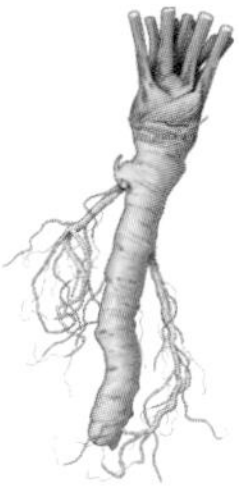

horseradish
barbaforte[M]

black radishes
ravenelli[M] neri

radish
ravanello[M]

salsify
salsefica[F]

carrot
carota[F]

black salsify
scorzonera[F]

parsnip
pastinaca[F]

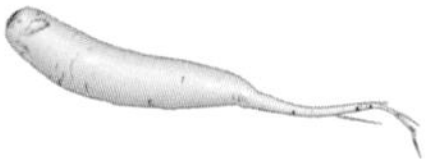

daikon
rafano[M] giapponese

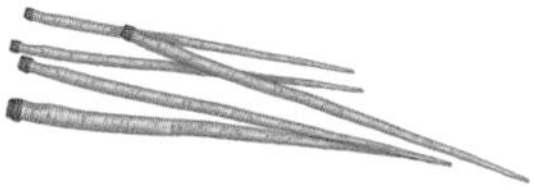

burdock
bardana[F]

beet
barbabietola[F]

turnip
rapa[F]

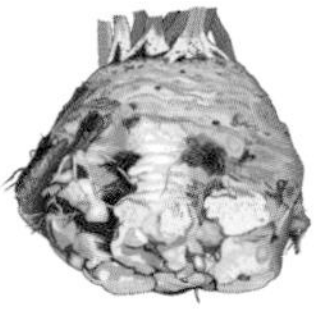

celeriac
sedano[M] rapa[F]

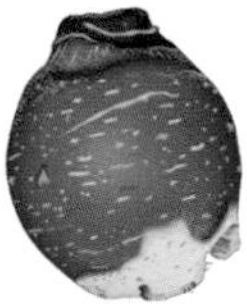

rutabaga
navone[M]

malanga
malanga[F]

legumes

legumi[M]

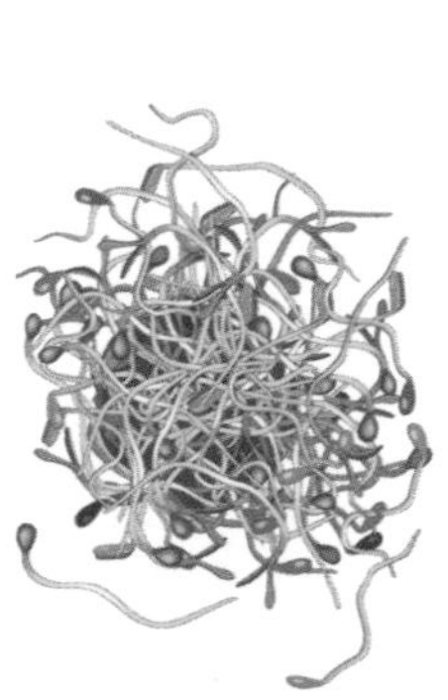

alfalfa sprouts
erba[F] medica

lupines
lupino[M]

lentils
lenticchie[F]

peanut
arachide[F]

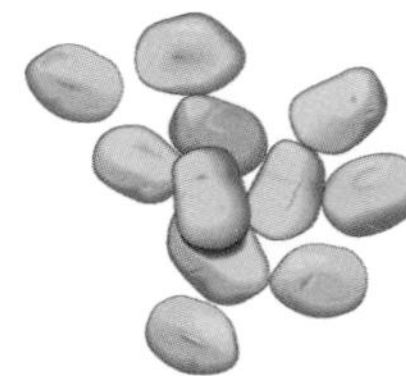

broad beans
fave[F]

peas
piselli[M]

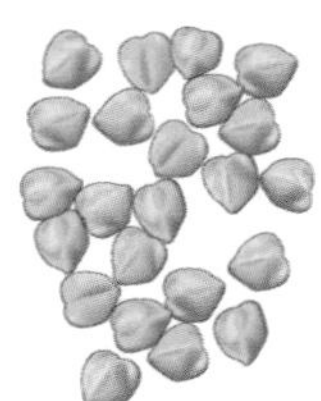

chick peas
ceci[M]

split peas
piselli[M] secchi spaccati

green peas
piselli[M]

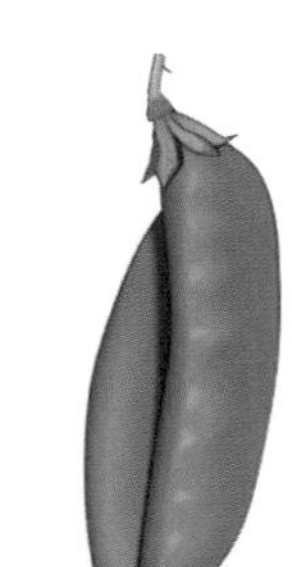

snow peas
piselli[M] mangiatutto

dolichos beans
dollchi[M]

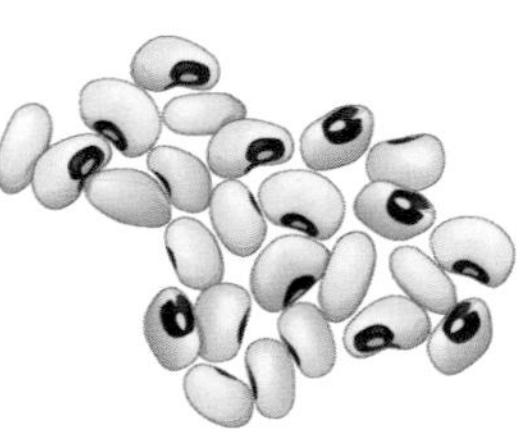

black-eyed peas
fagiolo[M] dall'occhio[M] nero

lablab beans
fagiolo[M] egiziano

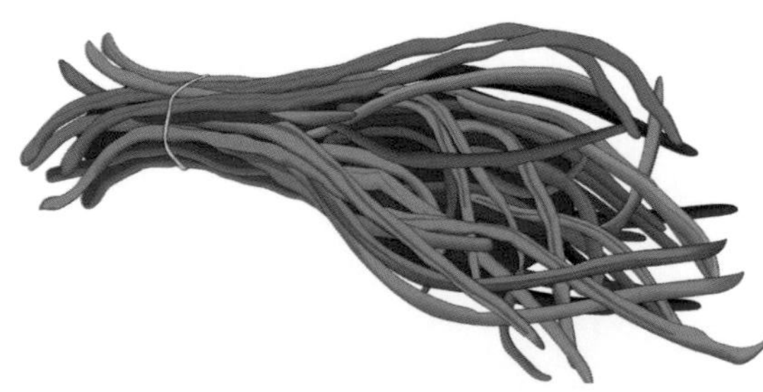

yard-long beans
fagiolo[M] asparagio[M]

beans
***fagioli**[M]*

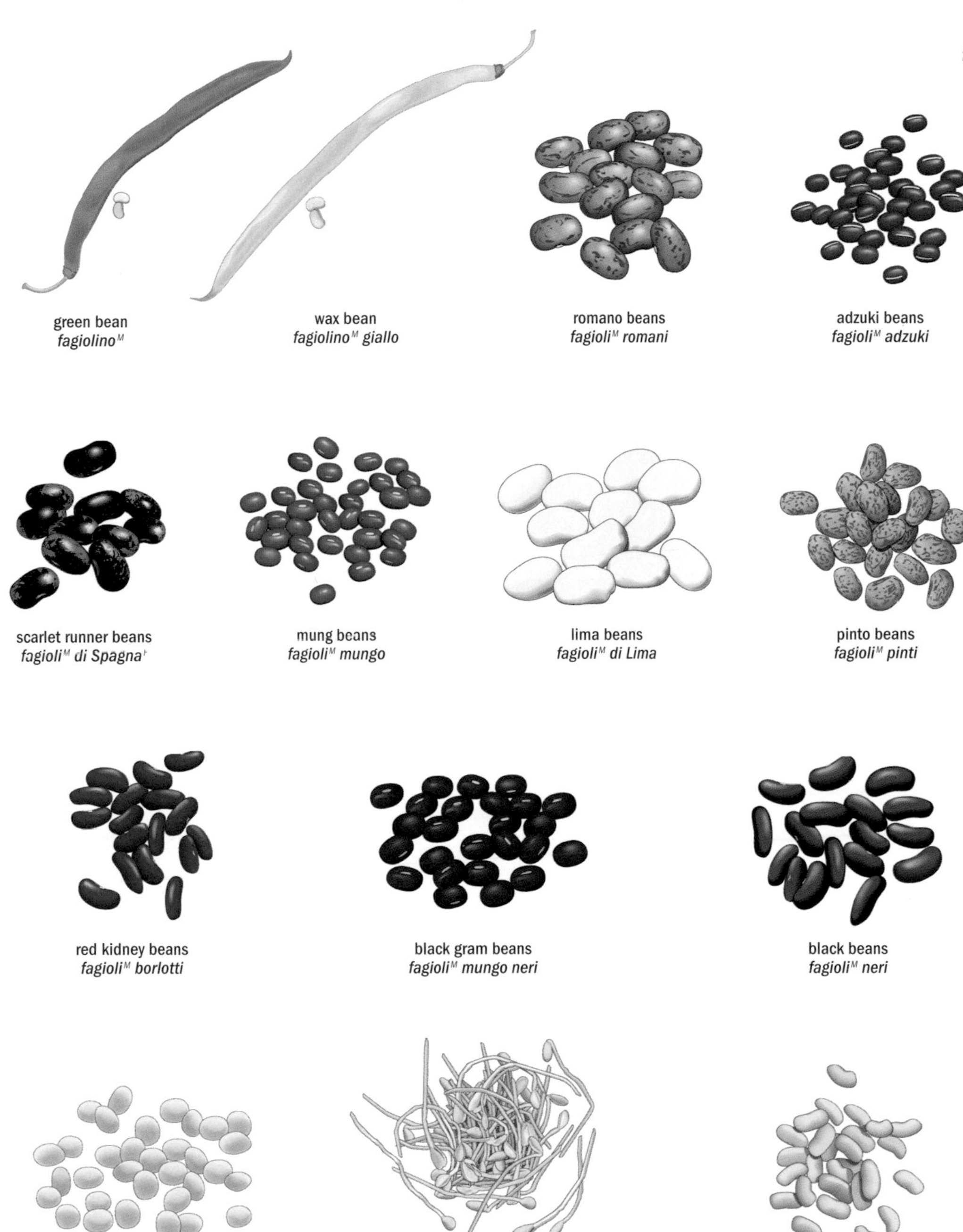

green bean
fagiolino[M]

wax bean
fagiolino[M] giallo

romano beans
fagioli[M] romani

adzuki beans
fagioli[M] adzuki

scarlet runner beans
fagioli[M] di Spagna[F]

mung beans
fagioli[M] mungo

lima beans
fagioli[M] di Lima

pinto beans
fagioli[M] pinti

red kidney beans
fagioli[M] borlotti

black gram beans
fagioli[M] mungo neri

black beans
fagioli[M] neri

soybeans
semi[M] di soia[F]

soybean sprouts
germogli[M] di soia[F]

flageolets
fagioli[M] cannellini[M]

fruits
frutti M

berries
bacche F

currants
ribes M

black currants
ribes M *nero*

gooseberries
uvaspine F

grapes
uve F

blueberries
mirtilli M

bilberries
mirtilli M

red whortleberries
mirtilli M *rossi*

alkekengi
alchechengi M

cranberries
mirtilli M *palustri*

raspberries
lampone M

blackberries
more F

strawberries
fragole F

stone fruits
drupe F

plums
prugne F

peach
pesca F

nectarine
nettarina F

apricot
albicocca F

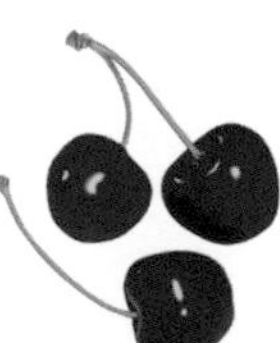

cherries
ciliegie F

dates
datteri M

dry fruits
frutti^M secchi

macadamia nuts
noce^F di macadamia^F

ginkgo nuts
noce^F di ginco^M

pistachio nuts
pistacchii^M

pine nuts
pinoli^M

cola nuts
noce^F di cola^F

pecan nuts
noce^F di pecan^M

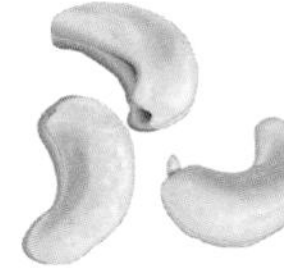
cashews
noce^F di acagiù^M

almonds
mandorle^F

hazelnuts
nocciole^F

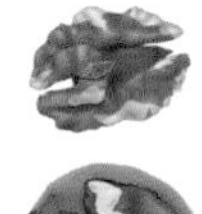
walnut
noce^F

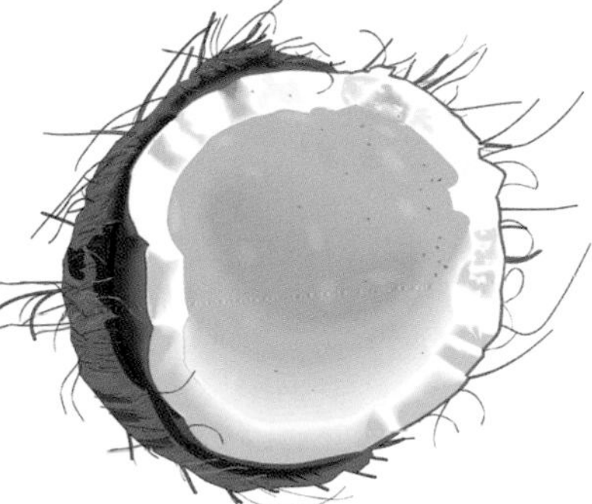
coconut
noce^F di cocco^M

chestnuts
castagne^F

beechnut
faggiola^F

Brazil nuts
noce^F del Brasile^M

pome fruits
pomi^M

pear
pera^F

quince
mela^F cotogna

apple
mela^F

Japanese plums
nespole^F del Giappone^M

citrus fruits
agrumi[M]

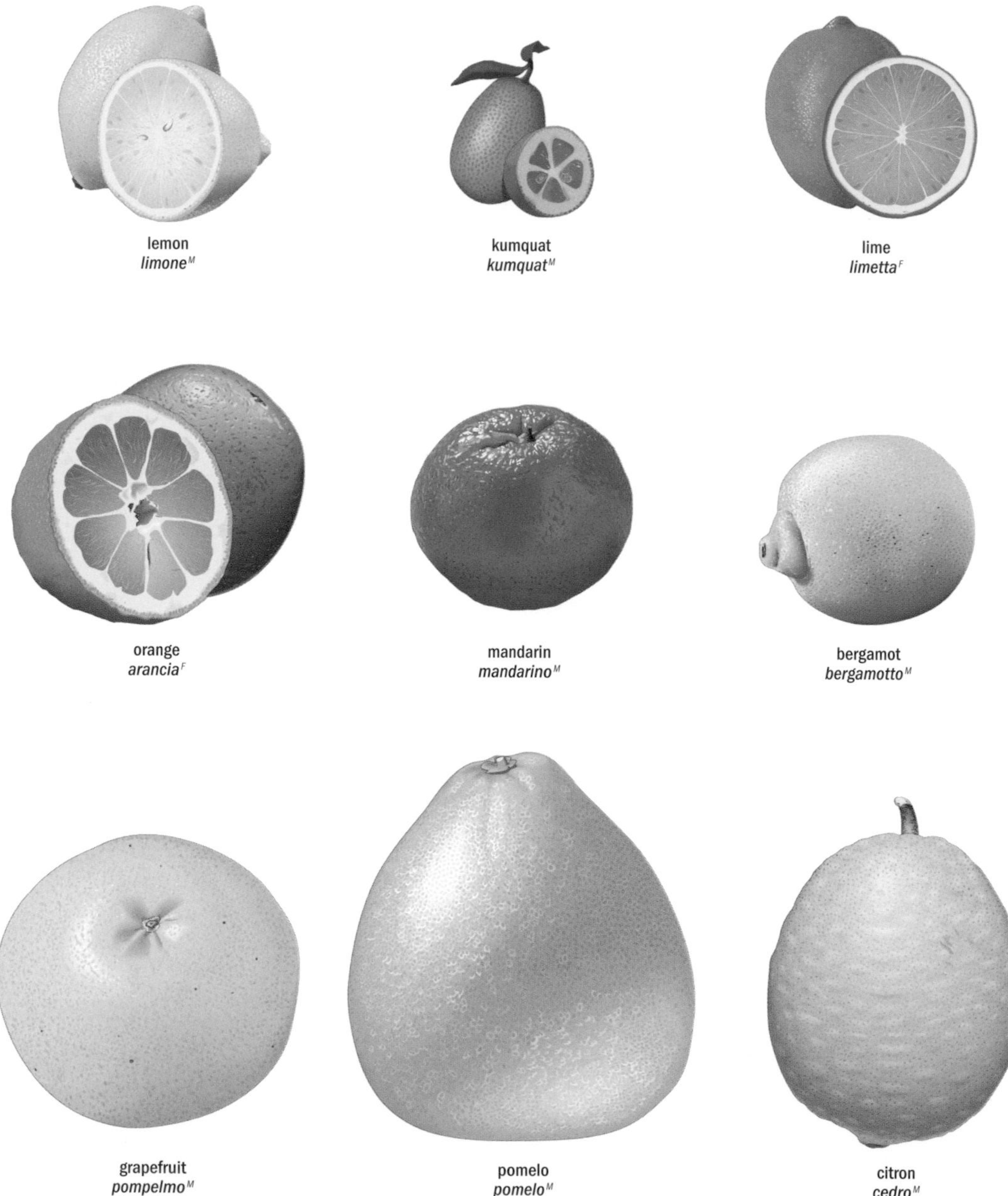

lemon
limone[M]

kumquat
kumquat[M]

lime
limetta[F]

orange
arancia[F]

mandarin
mandarino[M]

bergamot
bergamotto[M]

grapefruit
pompelmo[M]

pomelo
pomelo[M]

citron
cedro[M]

melons
meloni[M]

cantaloupe
cantalupo[M]

casaba melon
melone[M] *invernale*

honeydew melon
melone[M] *mieloso*

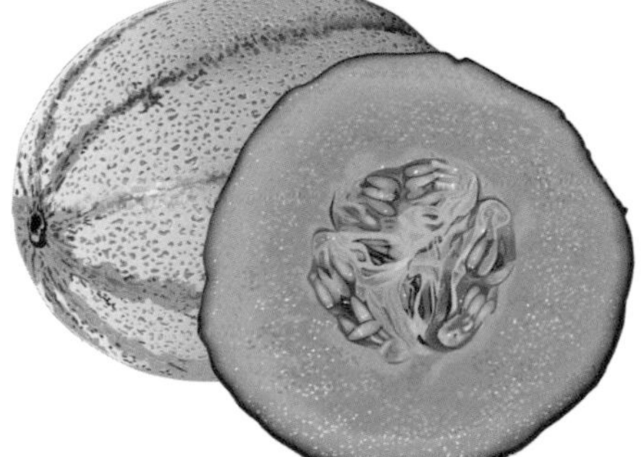

muskmelon
melone[M] *retato*

canary melon
melone[M] *giallo canario*

watermelon
cocomero[M]

Ogen melon

melone[M] *Ogen*

tropical fruits
frutti*^M *tropicali

plantain
banana^F *plantain*

banana
banana^F

longan
longan^M

tamarillo
tamarillo^M

passion fruit
maracuja^F

horned melon
kiwano^M

mangosteen
mangostano^M

kiwi
kiwi^M

pomegranate
melograno^M

cherimoya
cerimolia^F

jackfruit
frutto^M *del jack*

pineapple
ananas^M

jaboticabas
jaboticaba[F]

litchi
litchi[M]

fig
fico[M]

Chinese dates
giuggiola[F]

sapodilla
sapotiglia[F]

guava
guaiava[F]

rambutan
rambutan[M]

Japanese persimmon
cachi[M]

prickly pear
fico[M] *d'India*[F]

carambola
carambola[F]

Asian pear
nashi[M]

mango
mango[M]

durian
durian[M]

papaya
papaia[F]

pepino
pepino[M]

feijoa
feijoa[F]

spices

spezie[F]

juniper berries
bacce[F] di ginepro[M]

cloves
chiodi[M] di garofano[M]

allspice
pepe[M] della Giamaica[F]

white mustard
senape[F] bianca

black mustard
senape[F] nera

black pepper
pepe[M] nero

white pepper
pepe[M] bianco

pink pepper
pepe[M] rosa

green pepper
pepe[M] verde

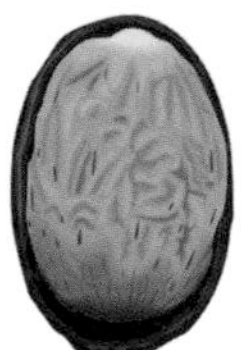

nutmeg
noce[F] moscata

caraway
carvi[M]

cardamom
cardamomo[M]

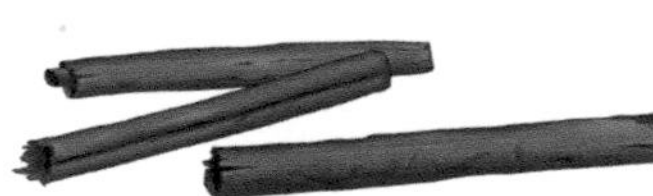

cinnamon
cannella[F]

saffron
zafferano[M]

cumin
cumino[M]

curry
curry[M]

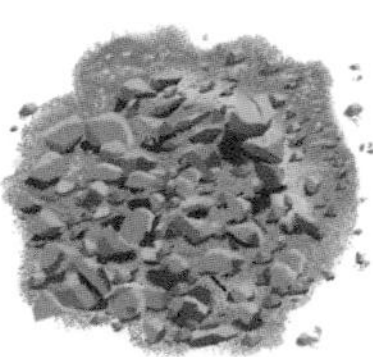

turmeric
curcuma[F]

fenugreek
fieno[M] greco

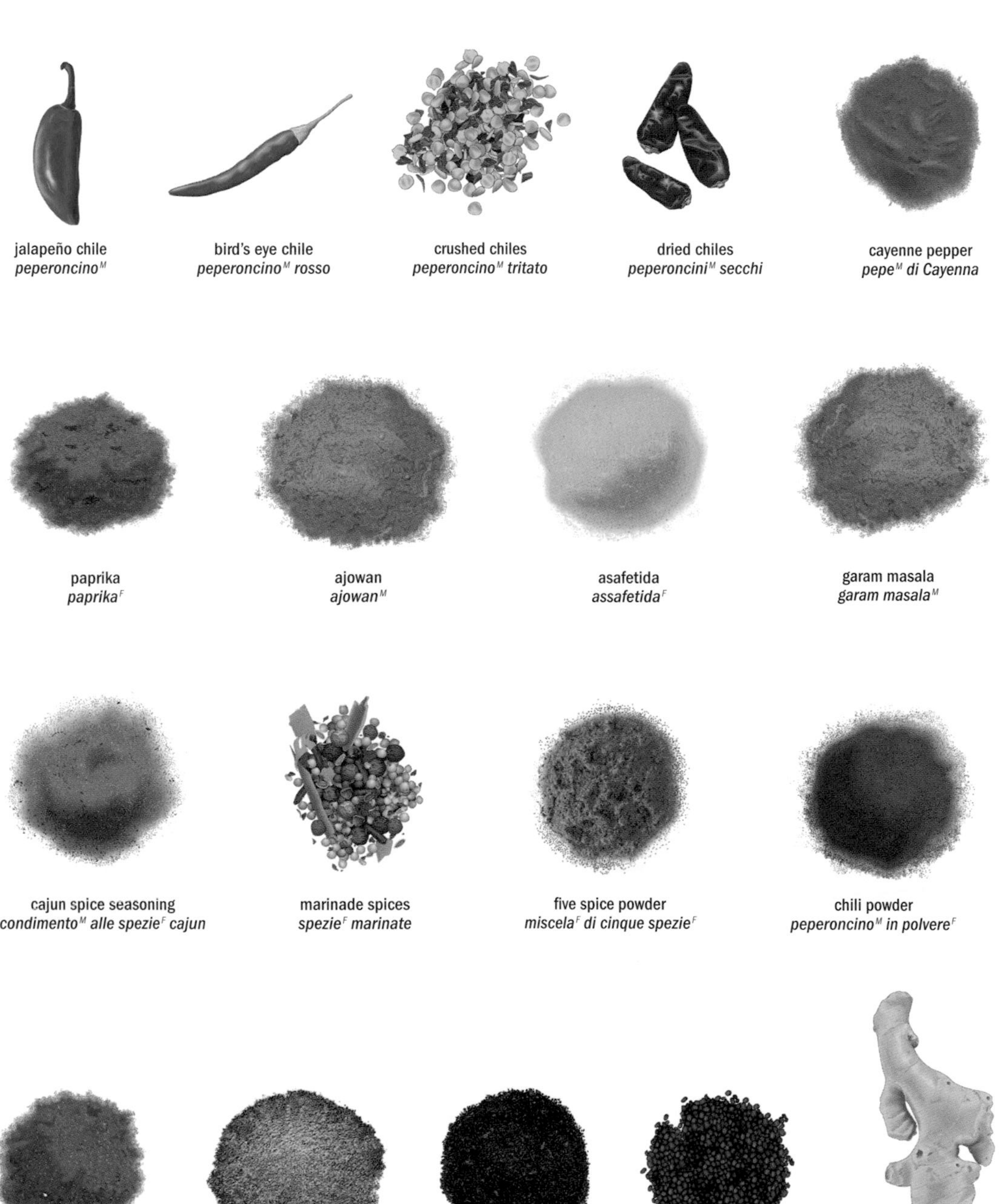

jalapeño chile
peperoncino[M]

bird's eye chile
peperoncino[M] *rosso*

crushed chiles
peperoncino[M] *tritato*

dried chiles
peperoncini[M] *secchi*

cayenne pepper
pepe[M] *di Cayenna*

paprika
paprika[F]

ajowan
ajowan[M]

asafetida
assafetida[F]

garam masala
garam masala[M]

cajun spice seasoning
condimento[M] *alle spezie*[F] *cajun*

marinade spices
spezie[F] *marinate*

five spice powder
miscela[F] *di cinque spezie*[F]

chili powder
peperoncino[M] *in polvere*[F]

ground pepper
pepe[M] *macinato*

ras el hanout
ras el hanout[M]

sumac
sumac[M]

poppy seeds
semi[M] *di papavero*[M]

ginger
zenzero[M]

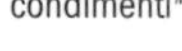

condiments

condimenti[M]

Tabasco® sauce
salsa[F] Tobasco®[M]

Worcestershire sauce
salsa[F] Worcestershire

tamarind paste
pasta[F] di tamarindo[M]

vanilla extract
estratto[M] di vaniglia[F]

tomato paste
concentrato[M] di pomodoro[M]

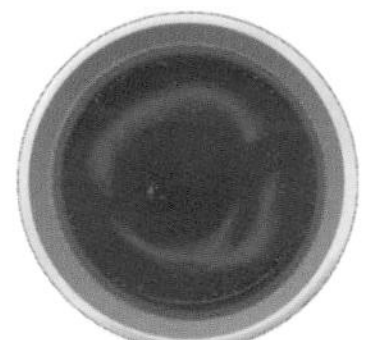

tomato sauce
passata[F] di pomodoro[M]

hummus
hummus[M]

tahini
tahini[M]

hoisin sauce
salsa[F] hoisin

soy sauce
salsa[F] di soia[F]

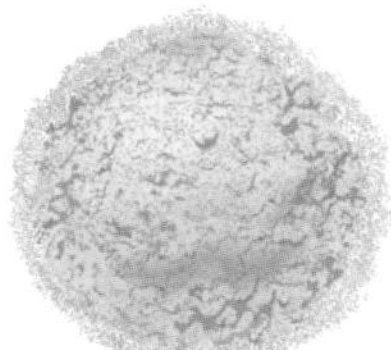

powdered mustard
senape[F] in polvere[F]

wholegrain mustard
senape[F] in granuli[M]

Dijon mustard
senape[F] di Digione

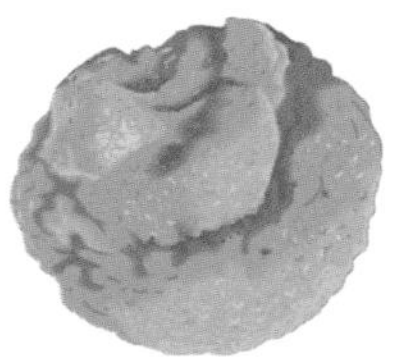

German mustard
senape[F] tedesca

English mustard
senape[F] inglese

American mustard
senape[F] americana

plum sauce
salsa^F di prugne^F

mango chutney
chutney^M al mango^M

harissa
harissa^F

sambal oelek
sambal oelek^M

ketchup
ketchup^M

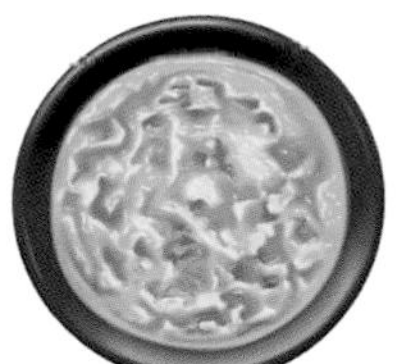
wasabi
wasabi^M

table salt
sale^M fino

coarse salt
sale^M grosso

sea salt
sale^M marino

balsamic vinegar
aceto^M balsamico

rice vinegar
aceto^M di riso^M

apple cider vinegar
aceto^M di mele^F

malt vinegar
aceto^M di malto^M

wine vinegar
aceto^M di vino^M

herbs

piante[F] aromatiche

cereal

cereali[M]

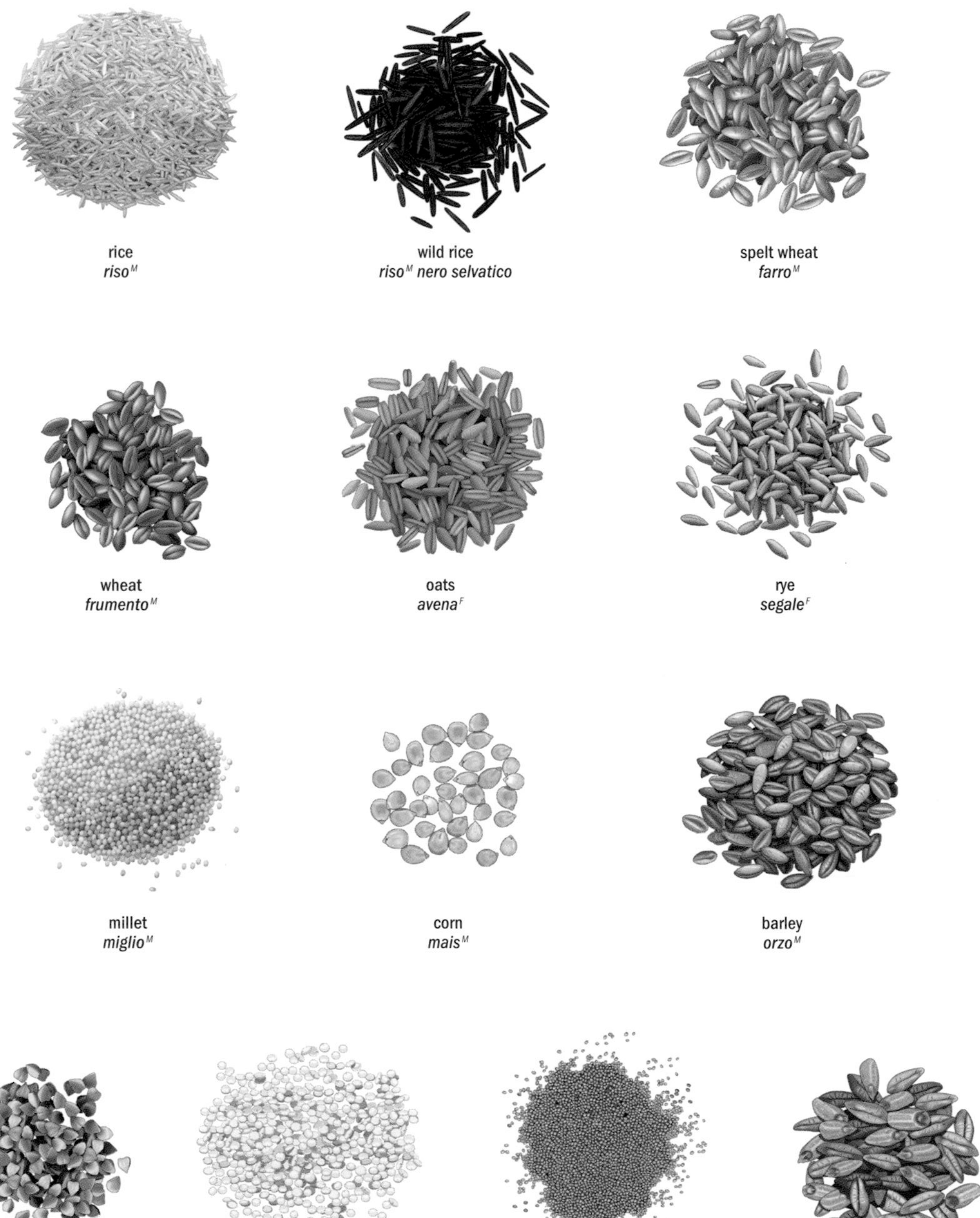

cereal products

prodotti[M] cerealicoli

flour and semolina
farina[F] e semolino[M]

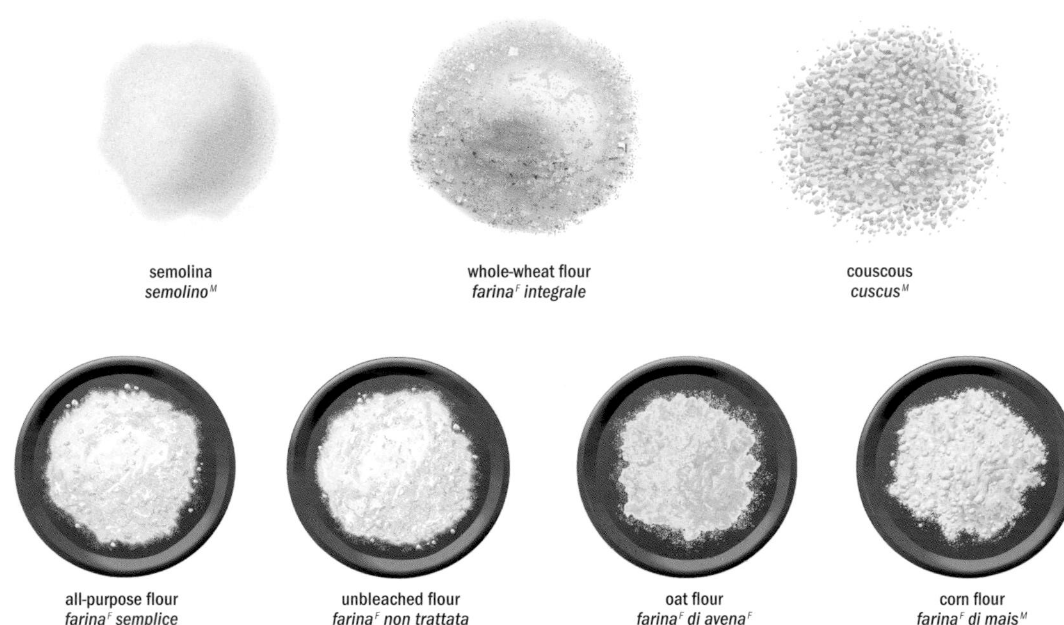

semolina
semolino[M]

whole-wheat flour
farina[F] integrale

couscous
cuscus[M]

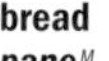

all-purpose flour
farina[F] semplice

unbleached flour
farina[F] non trattata

oat flour
farina[F] di avena[F]

corn flour
farina[F] di mais[M]

bread
pane[M]

croissant
croissant[M]

black rye bread
pane[M] nero di segale[F]

bagel
ciambella[F]

Greek bread
pane[F] greco

baguette
filone[M] francese

ear loaf
spiga[F]

French bread
baguette[F]

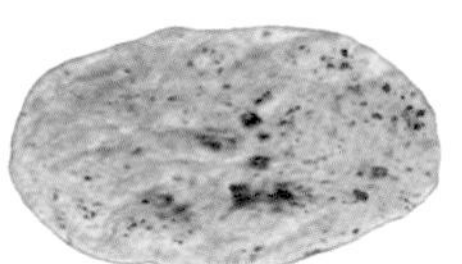
chapati
pane[M] chapati indiano

tortillas
tortilla[F]

pita bread
pane[M] pita

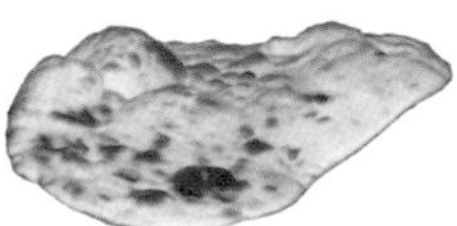
naan
pane[M] naan indiano

unleavened bread
pane[M] azzimo

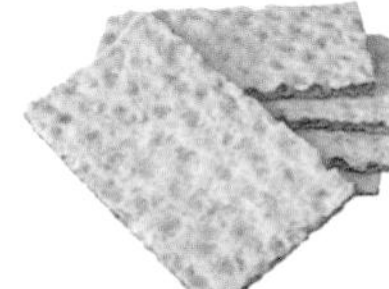
cracked rye bread
galletta[F] di segale[F]

Scandinavian cracked bread
galletta[F] scandinava

phyllo dough
pasta[F] sfoglia[F]

Danish rye bread
pane[M] di segale[F] danese

American corn bread
pane[M] di mais[M] americano

multigrain bread
pane[M] multicereali

Russian pumpernickel
Pumpernickel[M] russo

German rye bread
pane[M] di segale[F] tedesco

challah
pane[M] ebraico

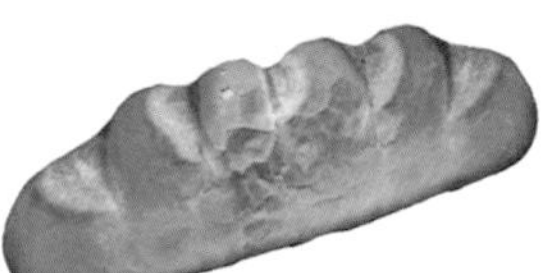
white bread
pane[M] bianco

wholemeal bread
pane[M] integrale

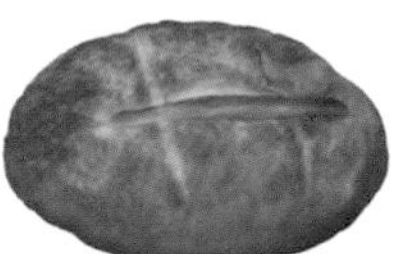
farmhouse bread
pane[M] casereccio

Irish soda bread
pane[M] irlandese

English loaf
pagnottella[F] inglese

pasta
pasta [F]

rigatoni
rigatoni [M]

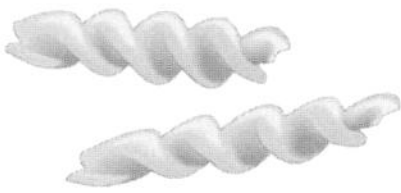

rotini
eliche [F]

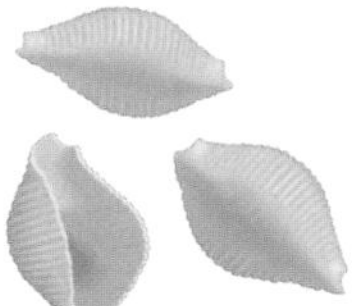

conchiglie
conchiglie [F]

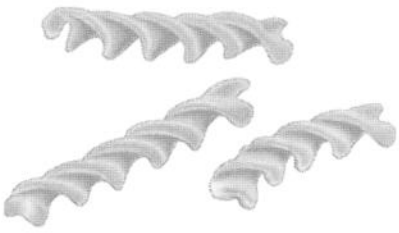

fusilli
fusilli [M]

spaghetti
spaghetti [M]

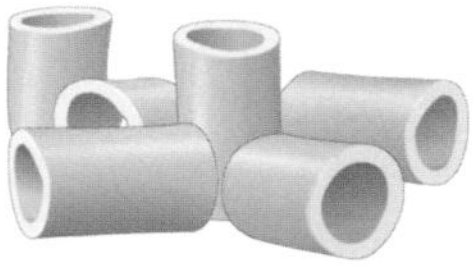

ditali
ditali [M]

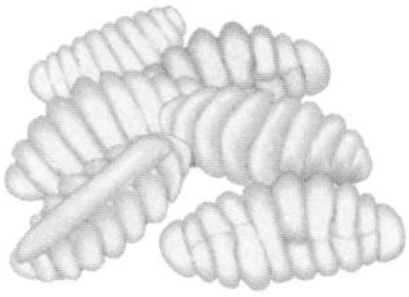

gnocchi
gnocchi [M]

tortellini
tortellini [M]

spaghettini
spaghettini [M]

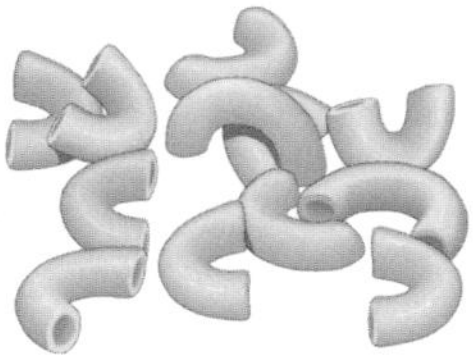

elbows
gomiti [M]

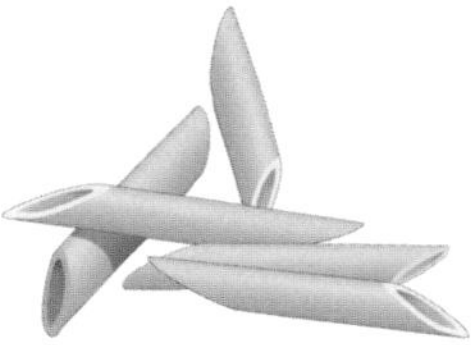

penne
penne [F]

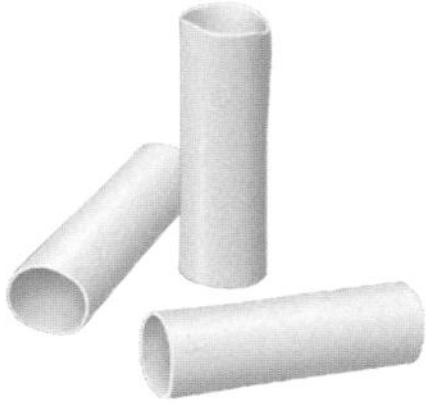

cannelloni
cannelloni [M]

lasagna
lasagne [F]

ravioli
ravioli [M]

spinach tagliatelle
tagliatelle [F] *verdi*

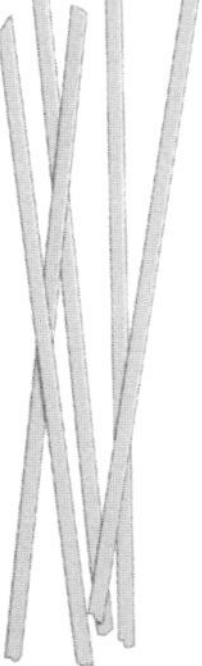

fettucine
fettuccine [F]

Asian noodles
spaghetti[M] asiatici

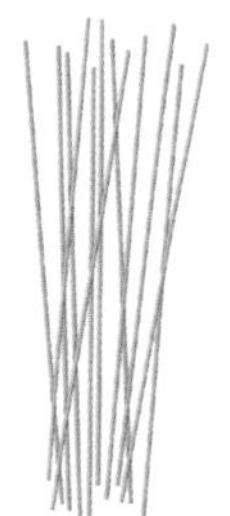
soba noodles
spaghetti[M] soba

somen noodles
spaghetti[M] somen

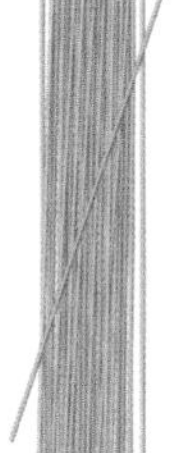
udon noodles
spaghetti[M] udon

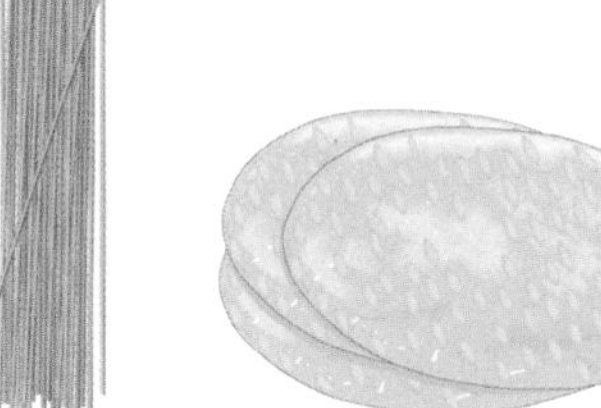
rice paper
gallette[F] di riso[M]

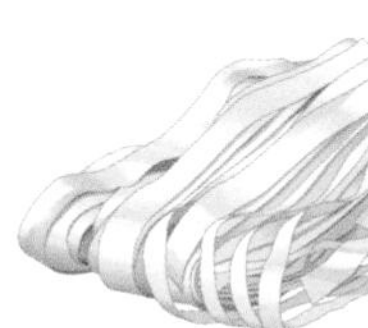
rice noodles
spaghetti[M] di riso[M]

bean thread cellophane noodles
spaghetti[M] di fagioli[M] mungo

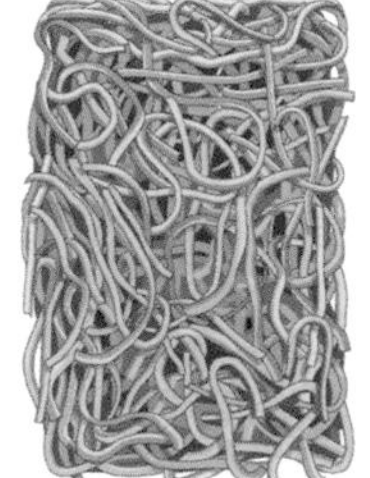
egg noodles
spaghetti[M] all'uovo[M]

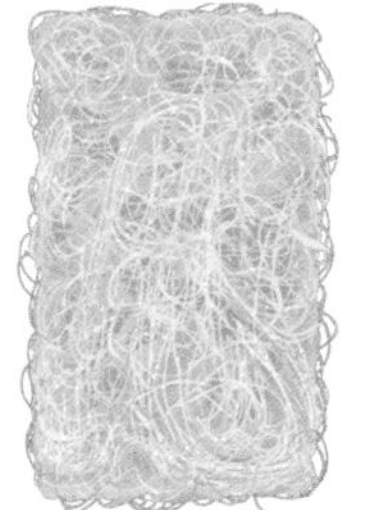
rice vermicelli
vermicelli[M] di riso[M]

won ton skins
pasta[F] won ton

rice
riso[M]

white rice
riso[M] bianco

brown rice
riso[M] integrale

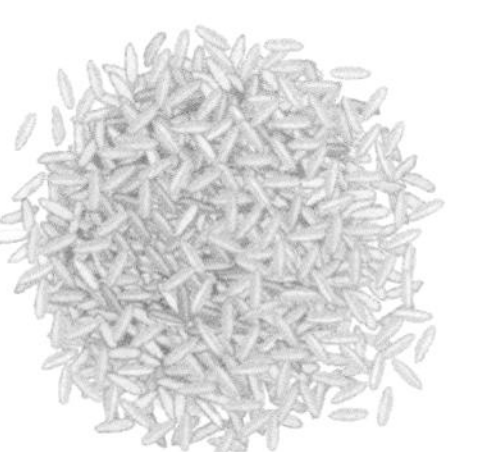
parboiled rice
riso[M] parboiled

basmati rice
riso[M] basmati

coffee and infusions

caffè[M] e infusi[M]

coffee
caffè[M]

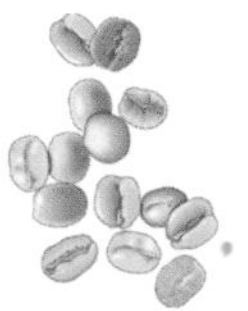

green coffee beans
chicchi[M] *di caffè*[M] *verdi*

roasted coffee beans
chicchi[M] *di caffè*[M] *tostati*

herbal teas
tisane[F]

linden
tiglio[M]

chamomile
camomilla[F]

verbena
verbena[F]

tea
_tè_[M]

green tea
tè[M] *verde*

black tea
tè[M] *nero*

oolong tea
tè[M] *oolong*

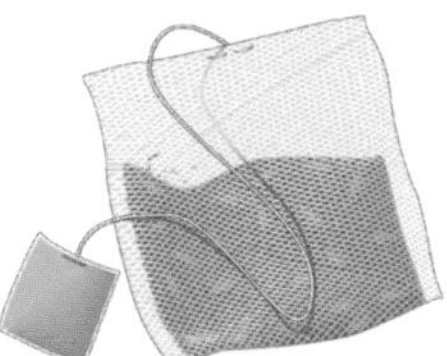

tea bag
bustina[F] *di tè*[M]

chocolate

cioccolato[M]

dark chocolate
cioccolato[M] *fondente*

milk chocolate
cioccolato[M] *al latte*[M]

cocoa
cacao[M]

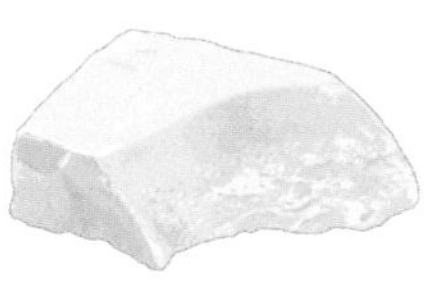

white chocolate
cioccolato[M] *bianco*

sugar

zuccheroM

granulated sugar
zuccheroM in graniM

powdered sugar
zuccheroM a veloM

brown sugar
zuccheroM di cannaF

rock candy
zuccheroM candito

molasses
melassaF

corn syrup
sciroppoM di maisM

maple syrup
sciroppoM d'aceroM

honey
mieleM

fats and oils

grassiM e oliM

corn oil
olioM di maisM

olive oil
olioM d'olivaF

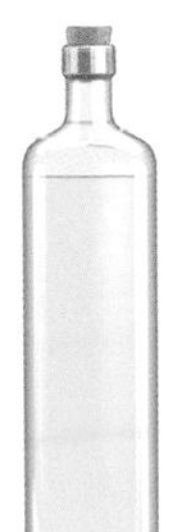
sunflower-seed oil
olioM di semi M di girasoleM

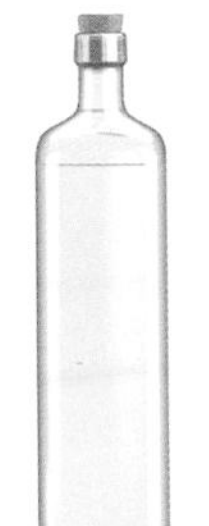
peanut oil
olioM di arachidiF

sesame oil
olioM di sesamoM

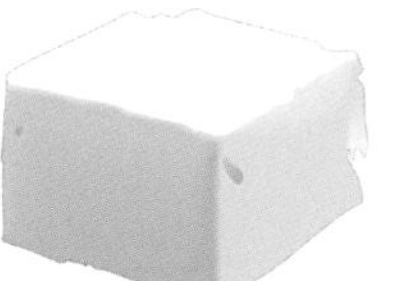
shortening
grassoM alimentare

lard
lardoM

margarine
margarinaF

dairy products

prodotti[M] caseari

yogurt
yogurt[M]

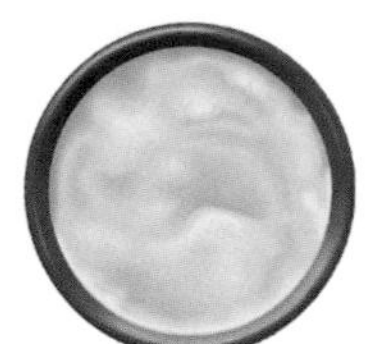
ghee
ghi[M]

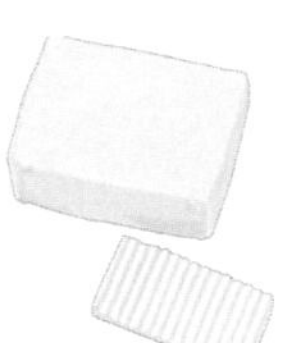
butter
burro[M]

cream
panna[F]

whipping cream
panna[F] *da montare*

sour cream
panna[F] *acida*

milk
latte[M]

homogenized milk
latte[M] *omogeneizzato*

goat's milk
latte[M] *di capra*[F]

evaporated milk
latte[M] *evaporato*

buttermilk
latticello[M]

powdered milk
latte[M] *in polvere*[F]

fresh cheeses
formaggi[M] *freschi*

cottage cheese
cottage cheese[M]

mozzarella
mozzarella[F]

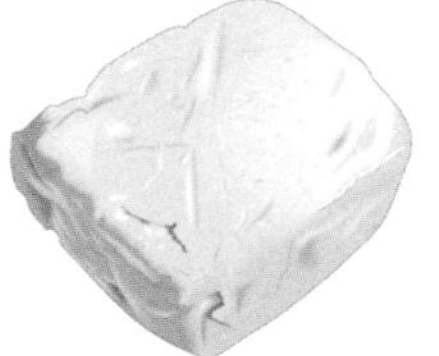
ricotta
ricotta[F]

cream cheese
formaggio[M] *cremoso*

goat's-milk cheeses
formaggi[M] *di capra*[F]

chèvre cheese
formaggio[M] *fresco di capra*[F]

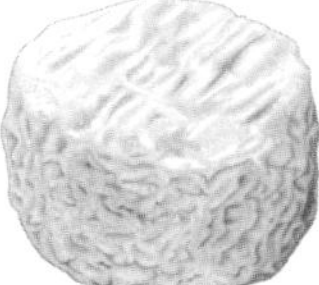
Crottin de Chavignol
crottin[M] *de chavignol*

pressed cheeses
formaggi[M] a pasta[F] dura

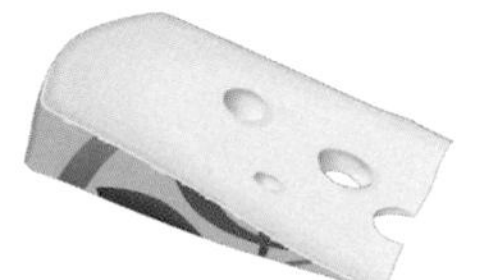

Jarlsberg
jarlsberg[M]

Emmenthal
emmental[M]

raclette
raclette[F]

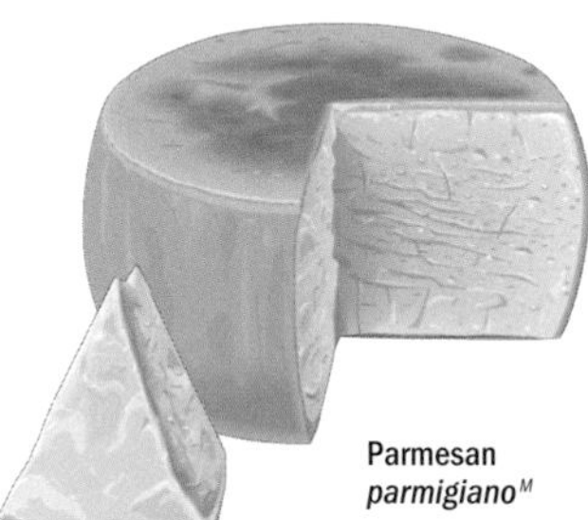

Parmesan
parmigiano[M]

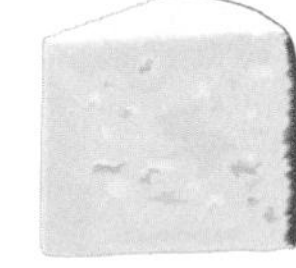

Romano
pecorino[M] romano

Gruyère
groviera[M/F]

blue-veined cheeses
formaggi[M] erborinati

Roquefort
roquefort[M]

Stilton
stilton[M]

Gorgonzola
gorgonzola[M]

Danish Blue
danish blue[M]

soft cheeses
formaggi[M] a pasta[F] molle

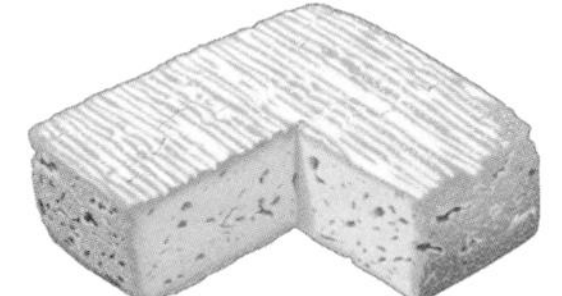

Pont-l'Évêque
pont-l'évêque[M]

Coulommiers
coulommiers[M]

Munster
munster[M]

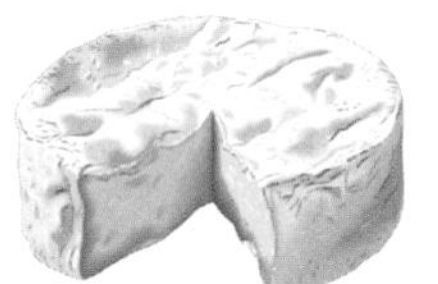

Camembert
camembert[M]

Brie
brie[M]

meat

carne[F]

cuts of beef
tagli[M] di manzo[M]

steak
bistecca[F]

beef cubes
spezzatino[M]

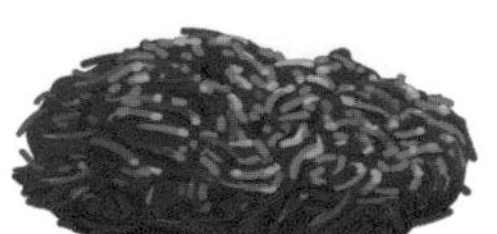

ground beef
macinato[M]

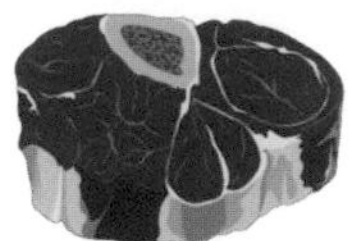

shank
ossobuco[M]

tenderloin roast
filetto[M]

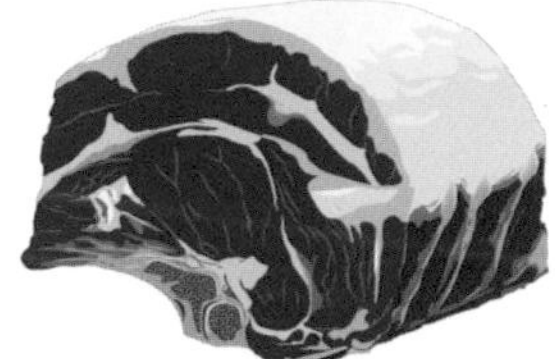

rib roast
costate[F]

back ribs
costine[F]

cuts of veal
tagli[M] di vitello[M]

veal cubes
spezzatino[M]

ground veal
macinato[M]

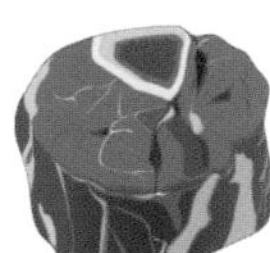

shank
ossobuco[M]

roast
arrotolato[M]

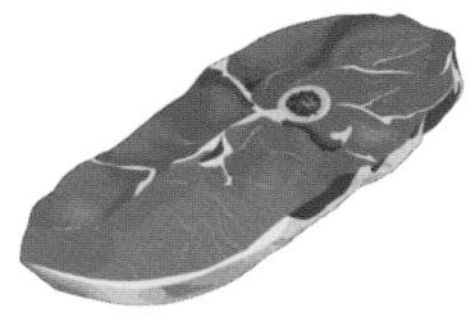

steak
bistecca[F]

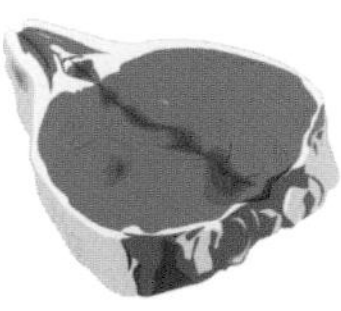

chop
braciola[F]

cuts of lamb
tagli^M *di agnello*^M

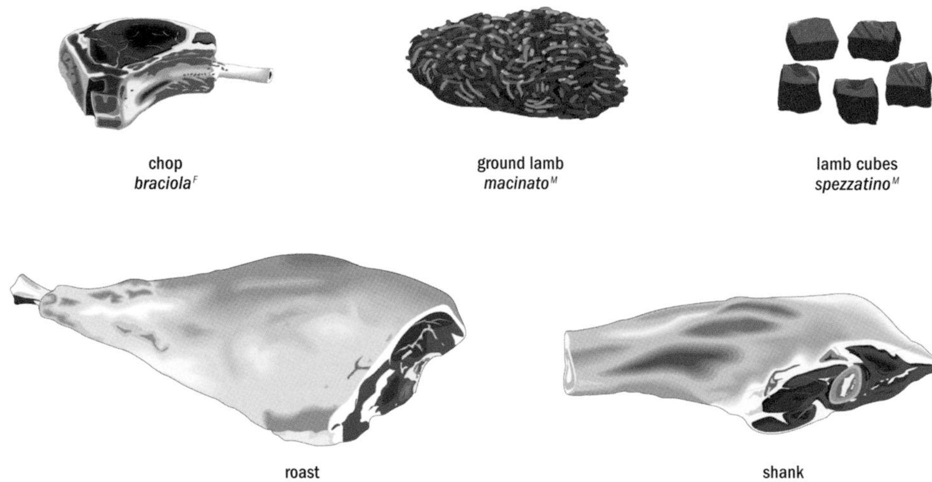

chop
braciola^F

ground lamb
macinato^M

lamb cubes
spezzatino^M

roast
arrosto^M

shank
stinco^M

cuts of pork
tagli^M *di maiale*^M

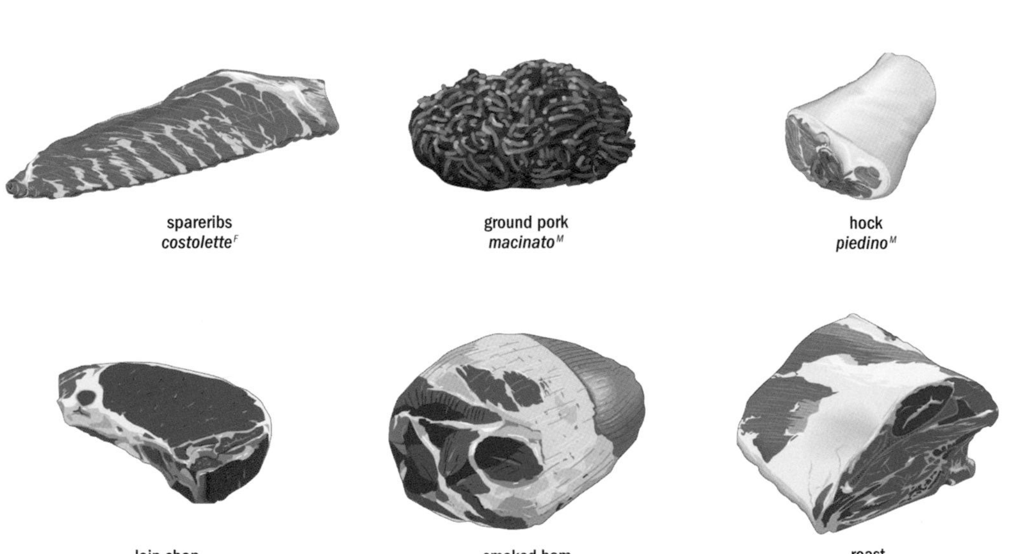

spareribs
costolette^F

ground pork
macinato^M

hock
piedino^M

loin chop
lonza^F

smoked ham
prosciutto^M *affumicato*

roast
arrosto^M

organ meat

interiora[F]

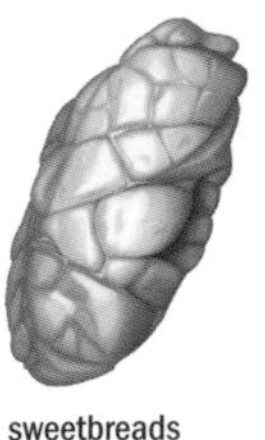

sweetbreads
animelle[F]

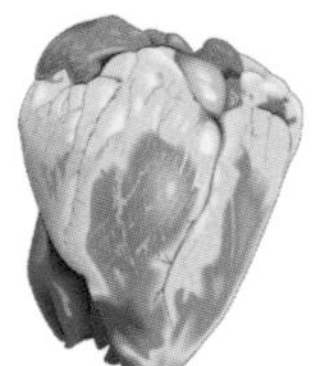

heart
cuore[M]

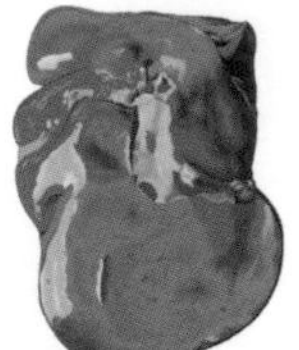

liver
fegato[M]

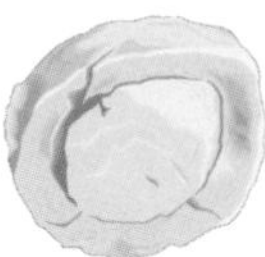

marrow
midollo[M]

tongue
lingua[F]

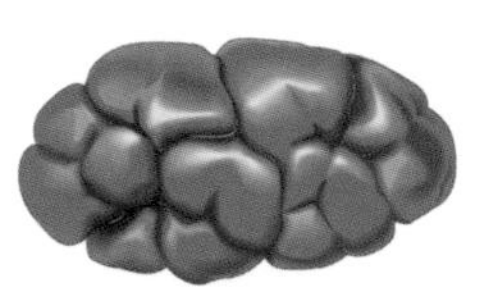

kidney
rognone[M]

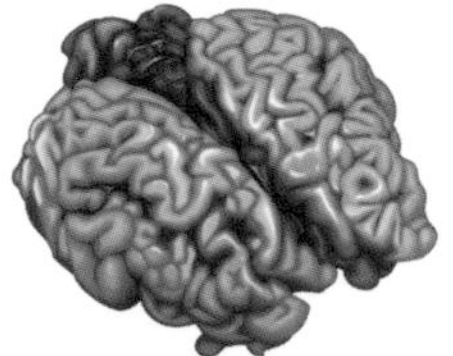

brains
cervella[F]

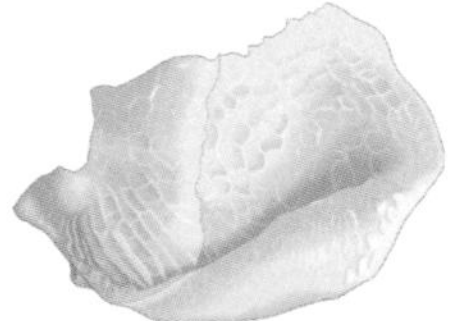

tripe
trippa[F]

game

selvaggina[F]

quail
quaglia[F]

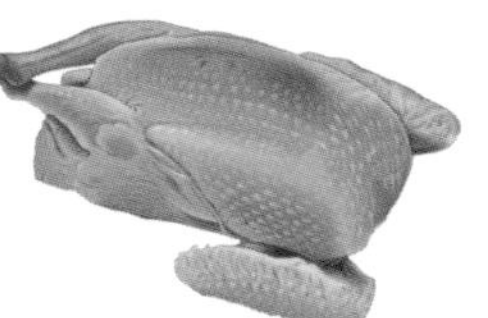

pigeon
piccione[M]

guinea fowl
faraona[F]

pheasant
fagiano[M]

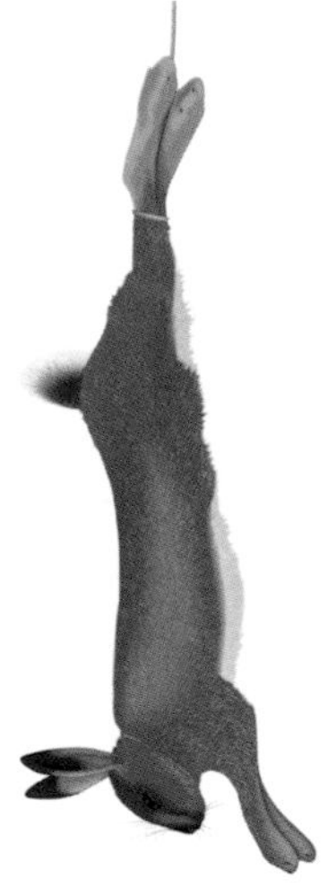

hare
lepre[F]

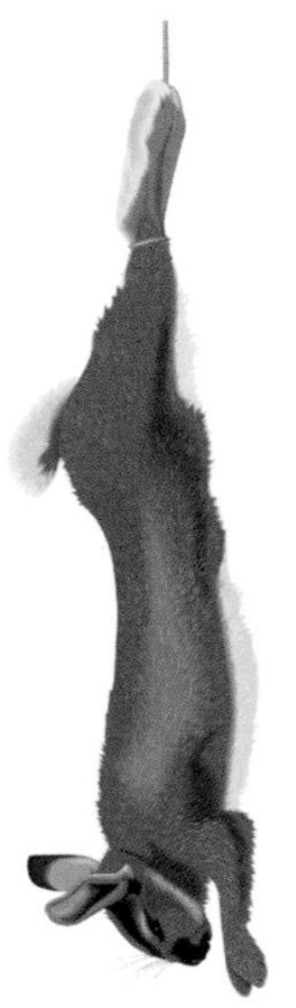

rabbit
coniglio[M]

poultry

volatili[M]

chicken
pollo[M]

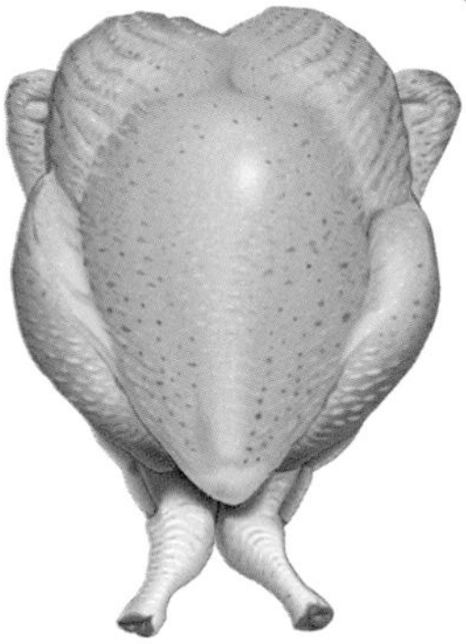

duck
anatra[F]

capon
cappone[M]

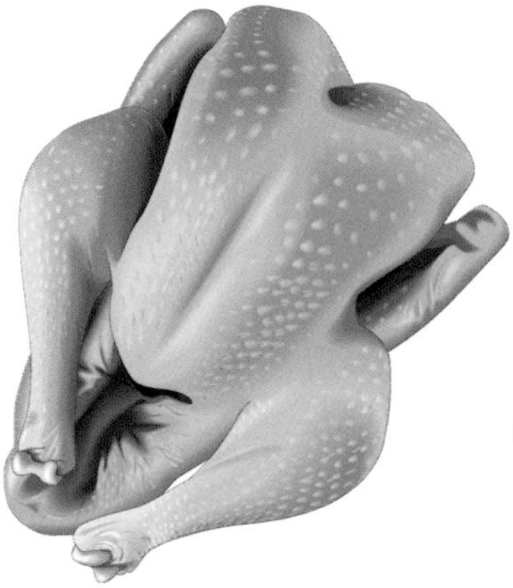

turkey
tacchino[M]

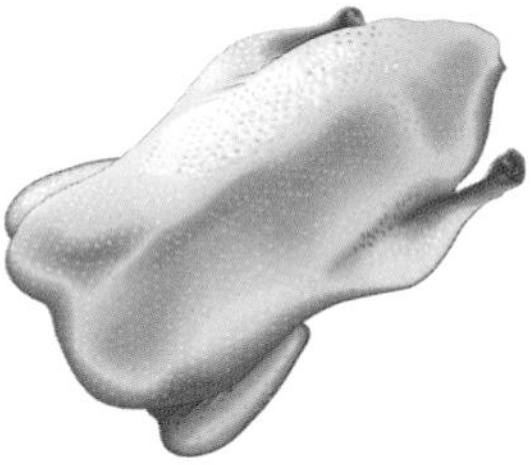

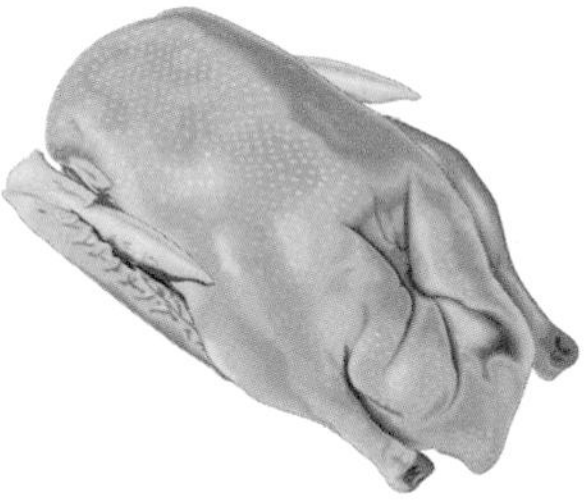

goose
oca[F]

eggs

uova[F]

quail egg
uovo[M] *di quaglia*[F]

pheasant egg
uovo[M] *di fagiano*[M]

goose egg
uovo[M] *di oca*[F]

ostrich egg
uovo[M] *di struzzo*[M]

duck egg
uovo[M] *di anatra*[F]

hen egg
uovo[M] *di gallina*[F]

delicatessen

gastronomia[F]

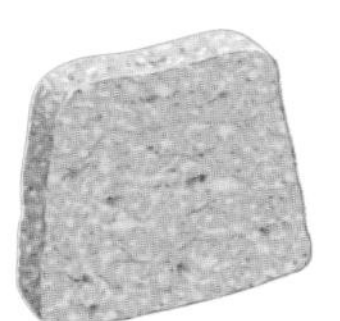

rillettes
ciccioli[M]

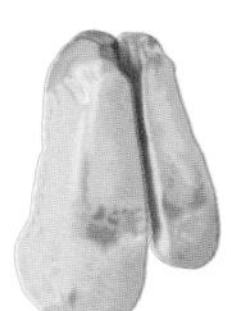

foie gras
foie-gras[M]

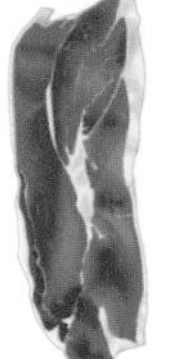

prosciutto
prosciutto[M]

kielbasa sausage
salsiccia[F] kielbasa

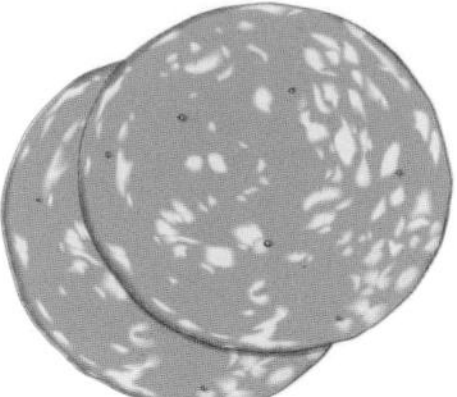

mortadella
mortadella[F]

blood sausage
sanguinaccio[M]

chorizo
chorizo[M]

pepperoni
salsiccia[F] piccante

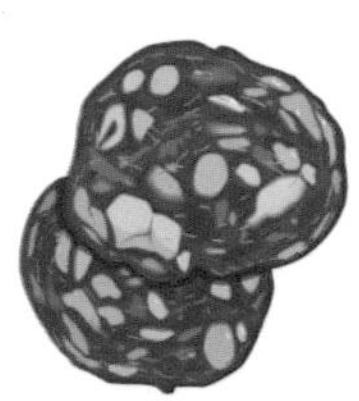

Genoa salami
salame[M] di Genova

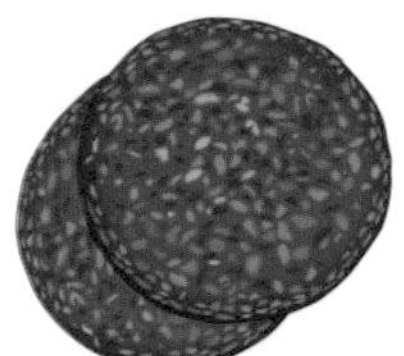

German salami
salame[M] tedesco

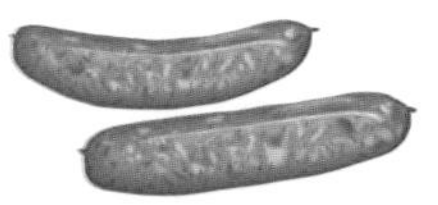

Toulouse sausages
salame[M] di Tolosa

merguez sausages
merguez[F]

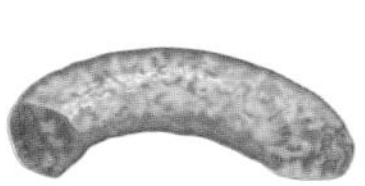

andouillette
salsiccia[F] di trippa[F]

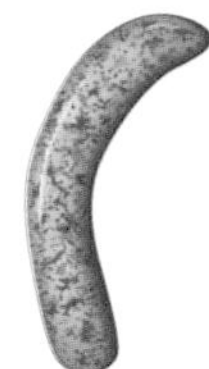

chipolata sausage
salsiccia[F] alle cipolle[F]

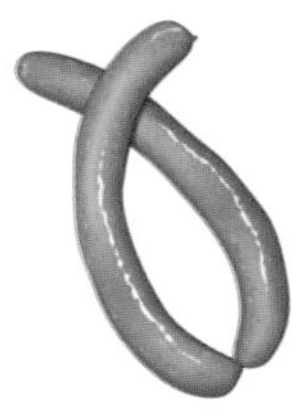

frankfurters
salsiccia[F] di Francoforte

pancetta
pancetta[F]

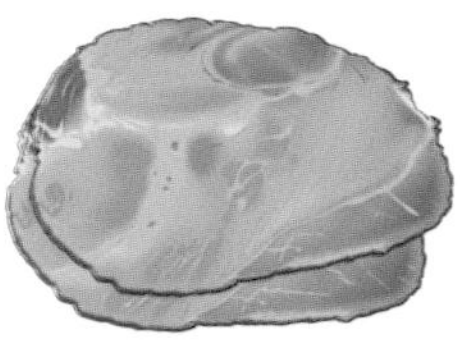

cooked ham
prosciutto[M] cotto

American bacon
bacon[M] americano

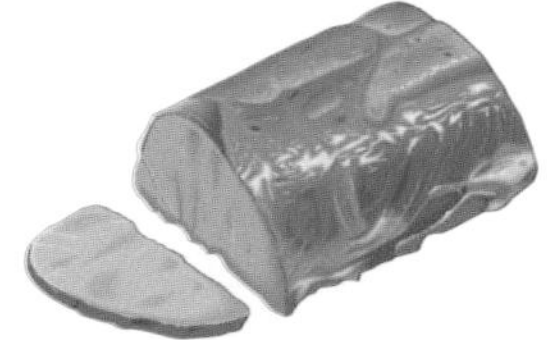

Canadian bacon
bacon[M] canadese

mollusks

molluschi[M]

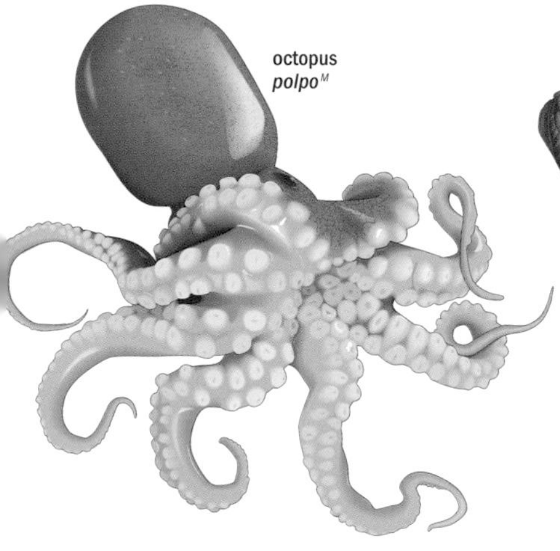

octopus
polpo[M]

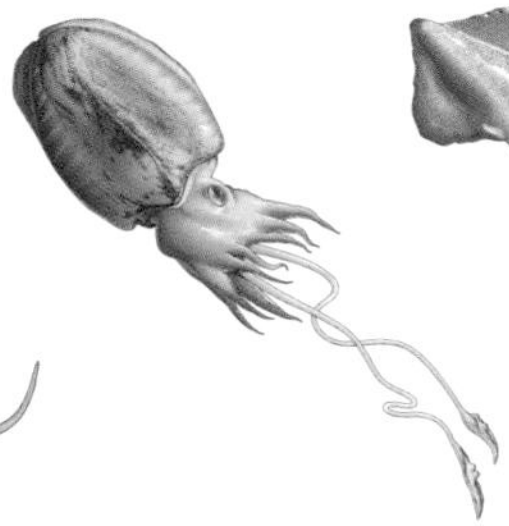

cuttlefish
seppia[F]

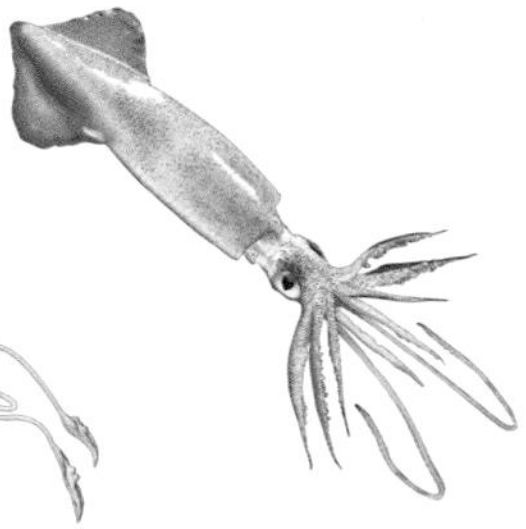

squid
calamaro[M]

scallop
pettine[M]

hard-shell clams
tartufo[M] di mare[M]

soft shell clam
vongola[F] molle

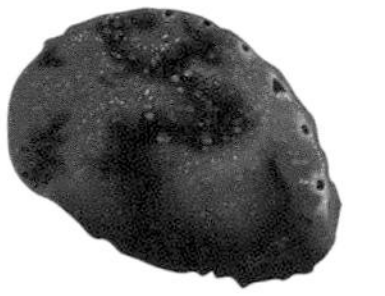

abalone
orecchia[F] di mare[M]

great scallop
capasanta[F]

snail
chiocciola[F]

limpet
patella[F]

common periwinkles
littorine[F]

clams
vongole[F]

cockles
cardii[M]

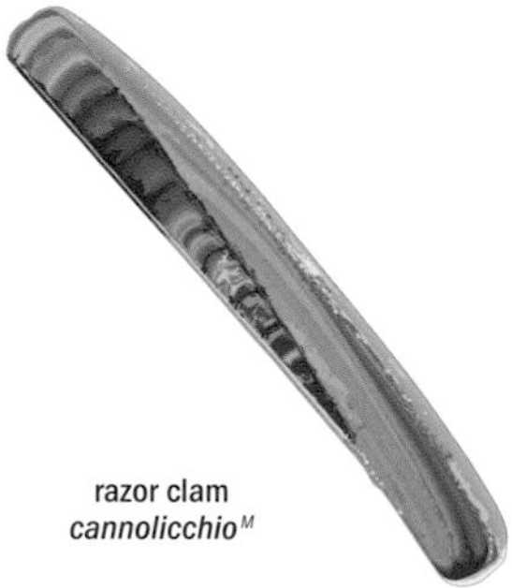

razor clam
cannolicchio[M]

flat oyster
ostrica[F]

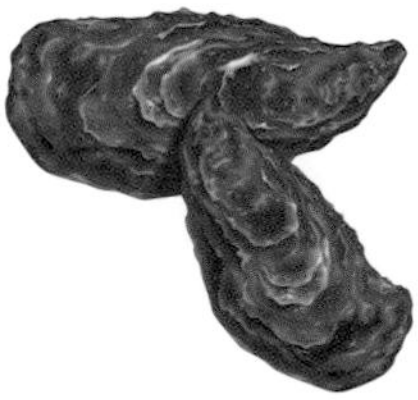

cupped Pacific oysters
ostrice[F]

blue mussels
mitili[M]

whelk
buccino[M]

crustaceans

crostacei[M]

lobster
astice[M]

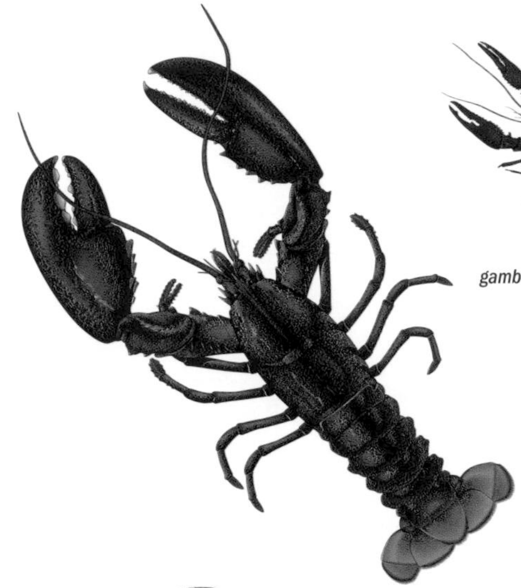

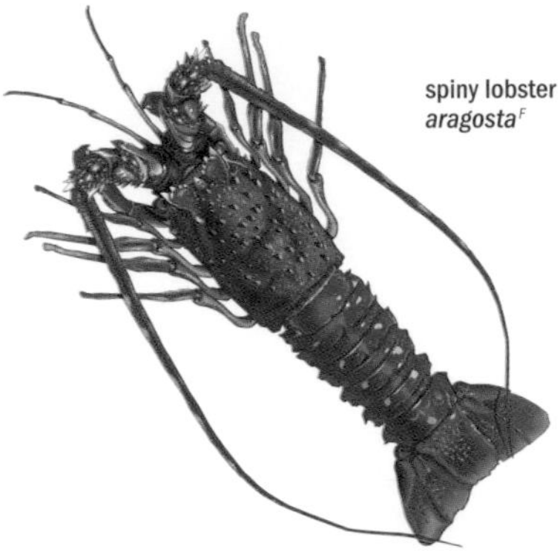

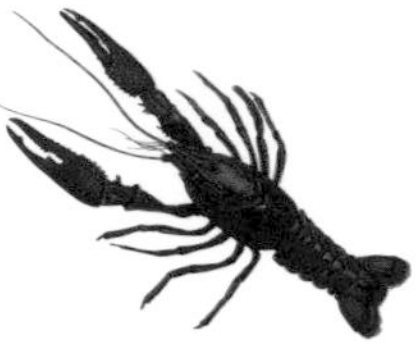

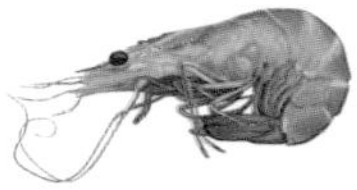

crayfish
gambero[M] di acqua[F] dolce

spiny lobster
aragosta[F]

shrimp
gamberetto[M]

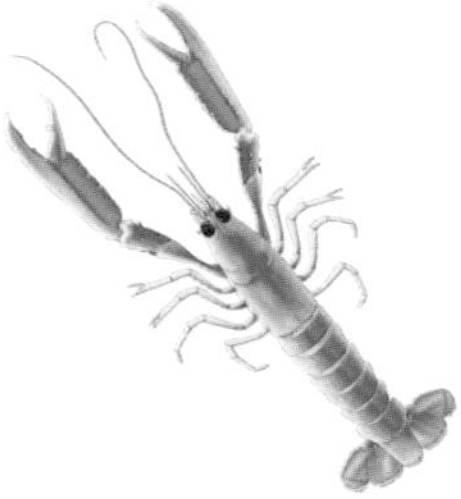

scampi
scampo[M]

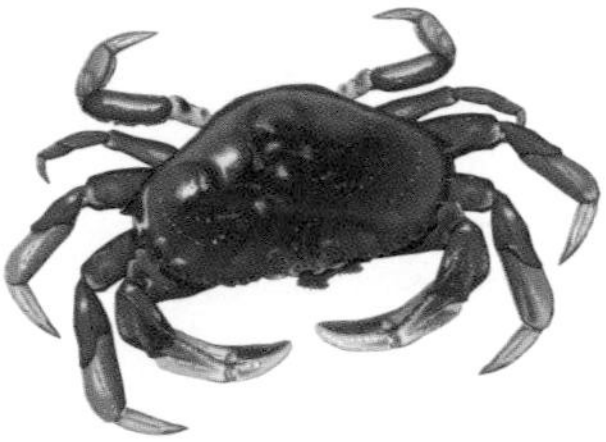

crab
granchio[M]

cartilaginous fishes

pesci[M] cartilaginei

larger spotted dogfish
gattuccio[M] stellato

skate
razza[F]

smooth hound
palombo[M] liscio

sturgeon
storione[M]

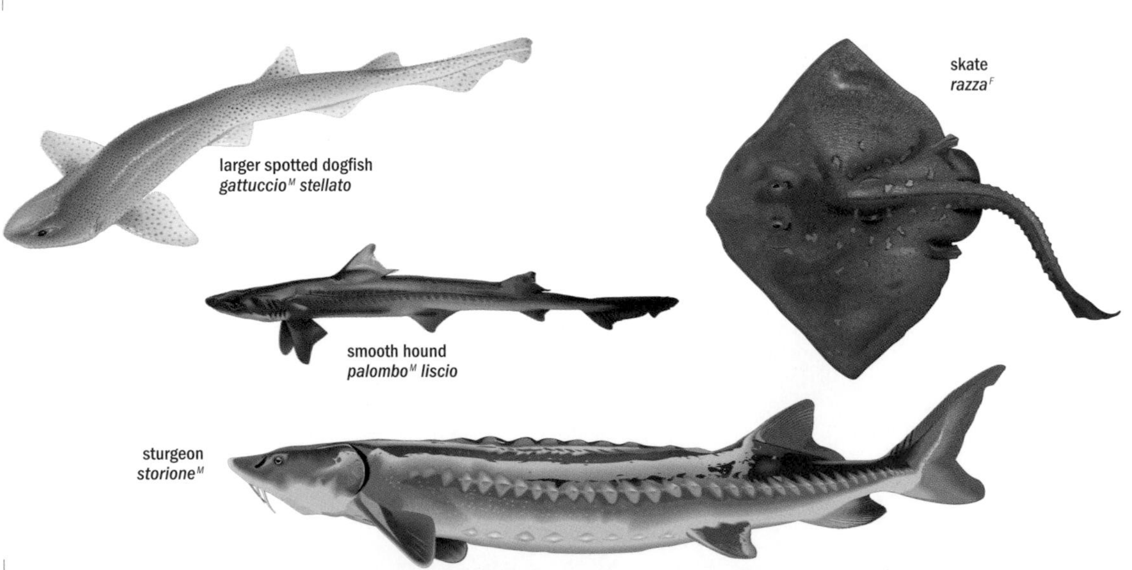

bony fishes

pesci[M] ossei

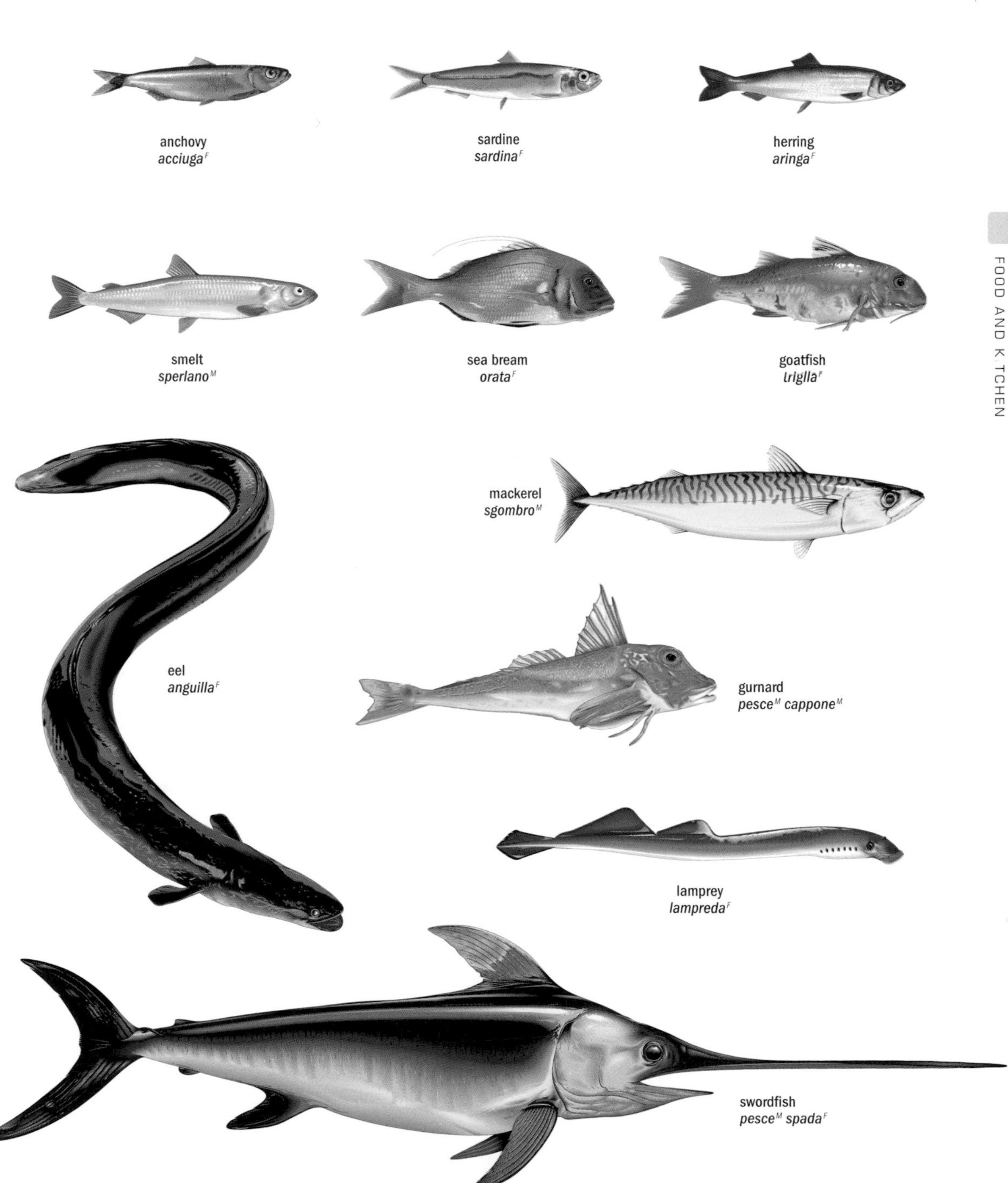

bony fishes

bass
persico[M] *trota*[F]
mullet
cefalo[M]
carp
carpa[F]
perch
persico[M]
shad
alosa[F]
pike
luccio[M]
pike perch
lucioperca[F]
bluefish
ballerino[M]
sea bass
branzino[M]
monkfish
pesce[M] *rospo*[M]
tuna
tonno[M]

redfish
salmone^M rosso
whiting
merlano^M
haddock
eglefino^M
black pollock
merlano^M nero
Atlantic cod
merluzzo^M dell'Atlantico^M
trout
trota^F
Pacific salmon
salmone^M del Pacifico^M
Atlantic salmon
salmone^M dell'Atlantico^M
brook trout
salmerino^M di fontana^F
John Dory
pesce^M San Pietro
halibut
ippoglosso^M
turbot
rombo^M
common plaice
passera^F di mare^M
sole
sogliola^F

packaging

confezioni[F]

pouch
sacchetto[M]

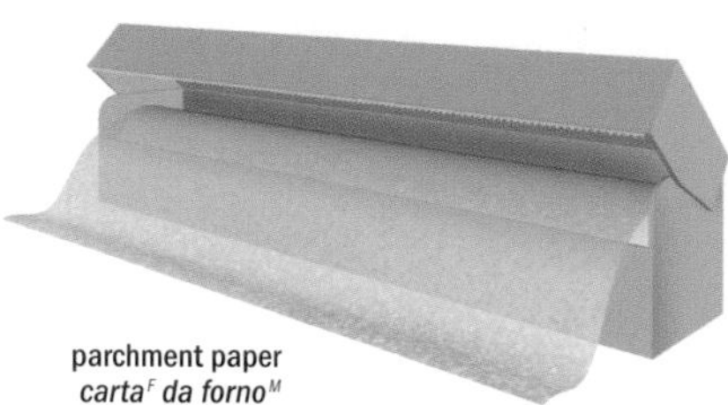

parchment paper
carta[F] da forno[M]

aluminum foil
pellicola[F] d'alluminio[M]

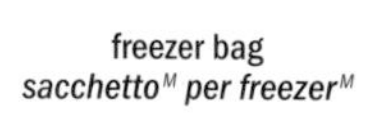

freezer bag
sacchetto[M] per freezer[M]

waxed paper
carta[F] cerata

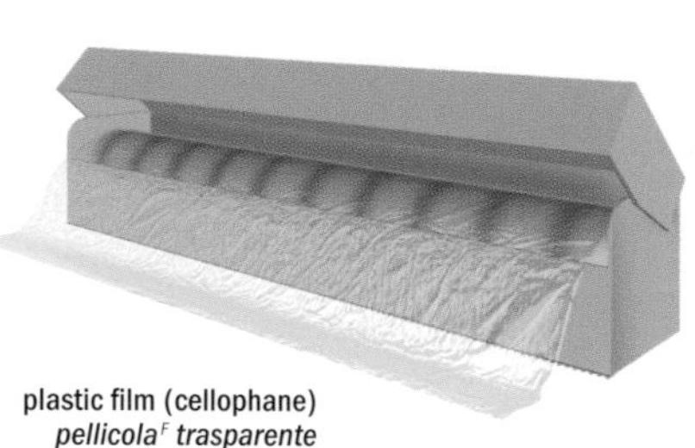

plastic film (cellophane)
pellicola[F] trasparente

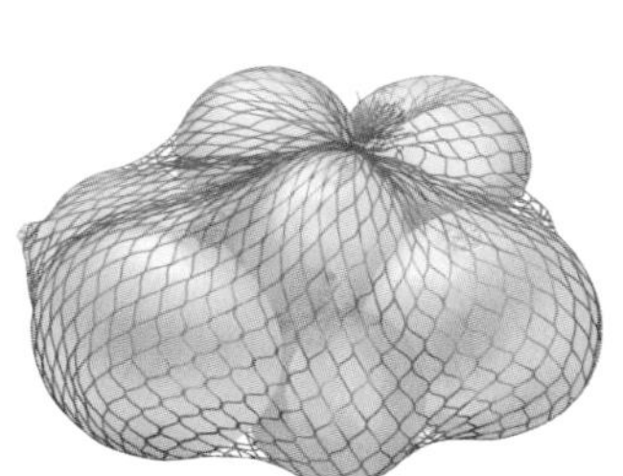

mesh bag
rete[F] per alimenti[M]

canisters
barattoli[M]

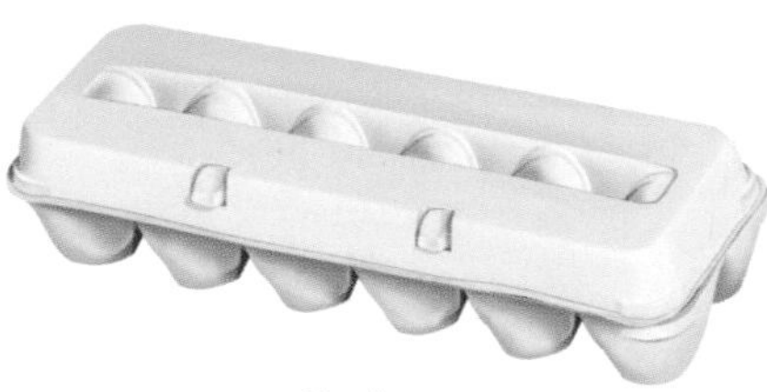

egg carton
confezione[F] in cartone[M] per uova[F]

food tray
vaschetta[F] per alimenti[M]

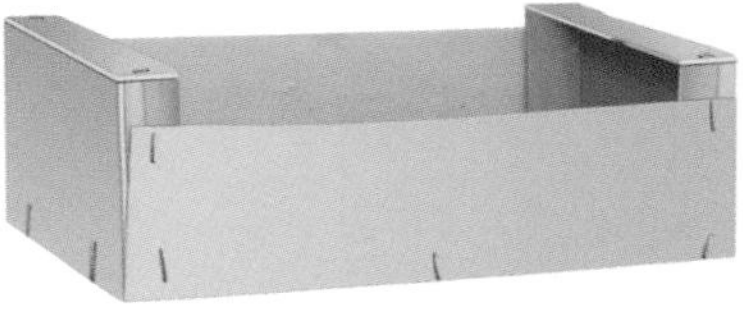

small crate
cassetta[F] piccola

small open crate
cassetta[F] aperta

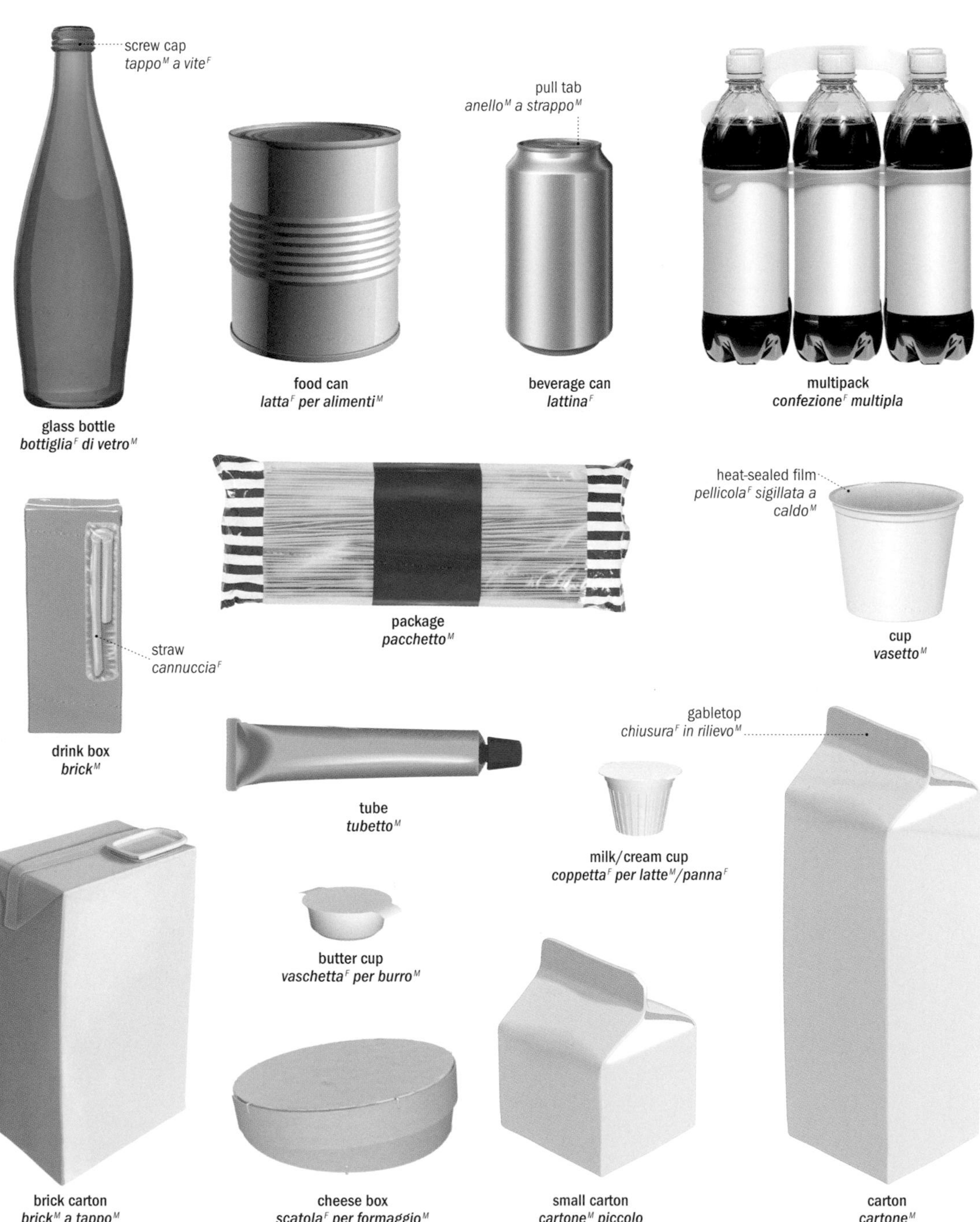

glass bottle
bottiglia F di vetro M

food can
latta F per alimenti M

beverage can
lattina F

multipack
confezione F multipla

drink box
brick M

package
pacchetto M

cup
vasetto M

tube
tubetto M

milk/cream cup
coppetta F per latte M/panna F

butter cup
vaschetta F per burro M

brick carton
brick M a tappo M

cheese box
scatola F per formaggio M

small carton
cartone M piccolo

carton
cartone M

kitchen

cucina[F]

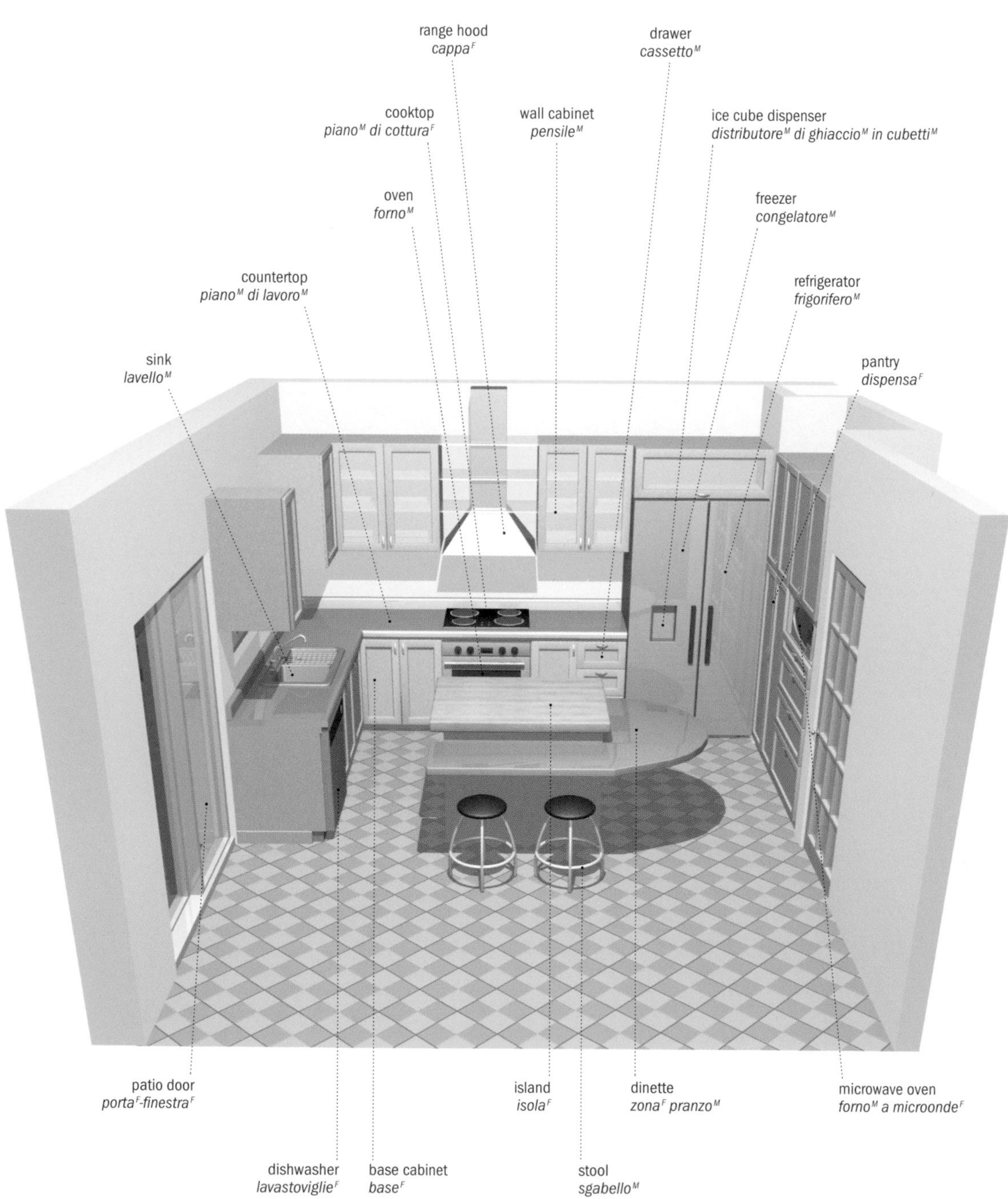

glassware

cristalleria[F]

liqueur glass
bicchierino[M] da liquore[M]

port glass
bicchiere[M] da porto[M]

sparkling wine glass
coppa[F] da spumante[M]

brandy snifter
bicchiere[M] da brandy[M]

Alsace glass
bicchiere[M] da vino[M] alsaziano

burgundy glass
bicchiere[M] da Borgogna[M]

bordeaux glass
bicchiere[M] da Bordeaux[M]

white wine glass
bicchiere[M] da vino[M] bianco

water goblet
bicchiere[M] da acqua[F]

cocktail glass
calice[M] da cocktail[M]

highball glass
bicchiere[M] da bibita[F]

old-fashioned glass
tumbler[M]

beer mug
boccale[M] da birra[F]

champagne flute
flûte[M]

small decanter
caraffa[F]

decanter
bottiglia[F] da tavola[F]

dinnerware

vasellame[M] da tavola[F]

demitasse
tazzina[F] da caffè[M]

cup
tazza[F] da tè[M]

coffee mug
tazza[F] alta da caffè[M]

creamer
bricco[M] del latte[M]

sugar bowl
zuccheriera[F]

salt shaker
saliera[F]

pepper shaker
pepaiola[F]

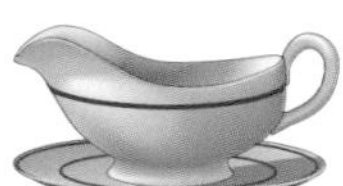
gravy boat
salsiera[F]

butter dish
burriera[F]

ramekin
formina[F] da forno[M]

soup bowl
scodella[F]

rim soup bowl
piatto[M] fondo

dinner plate
piatto[M] piano

salad plate
piatto[M] frutta[F] / insalata[F]

bread and butter plate
piattino[M] per pane[M] e burro[M]

teapot
teiera[F]

platter
piatto[M] da portata[F]

vegetable bowl
legumiera[F]

fish platter
piatto[M] per il pesce[M]

hors d'oeuvre dish
antipastiera[F]

water pitcher
caraffa[F]

salad bowl
insalatiera[F]

salad dish
coppetta[F] per l'insalata[F]

soup tureen
zuppiera[F]

silverware

posateria^F

knife
coltello^M

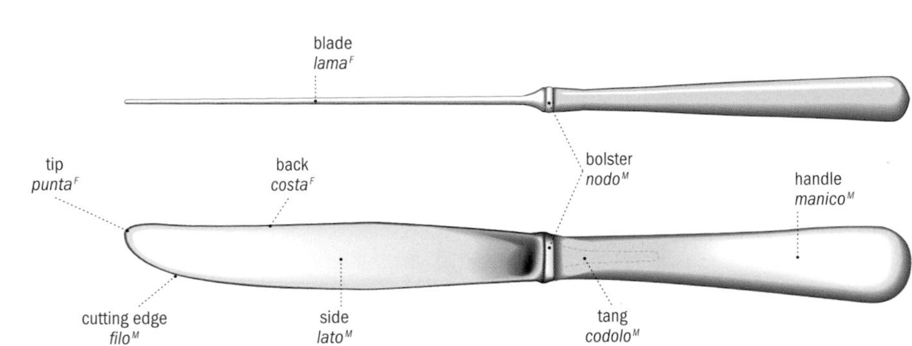

fork
forchetta^F

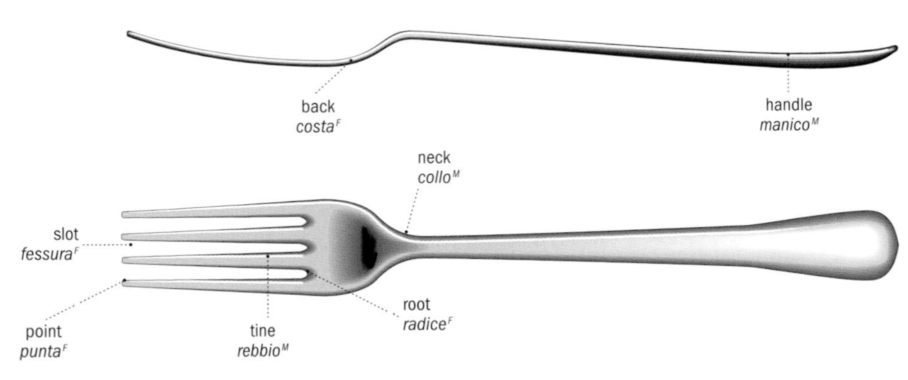

spoon
cucchiaio^M

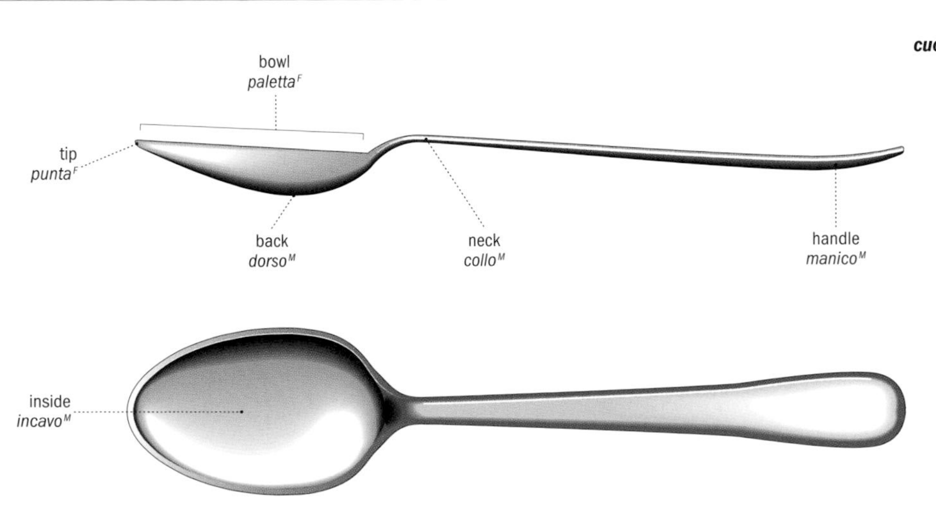

silverware

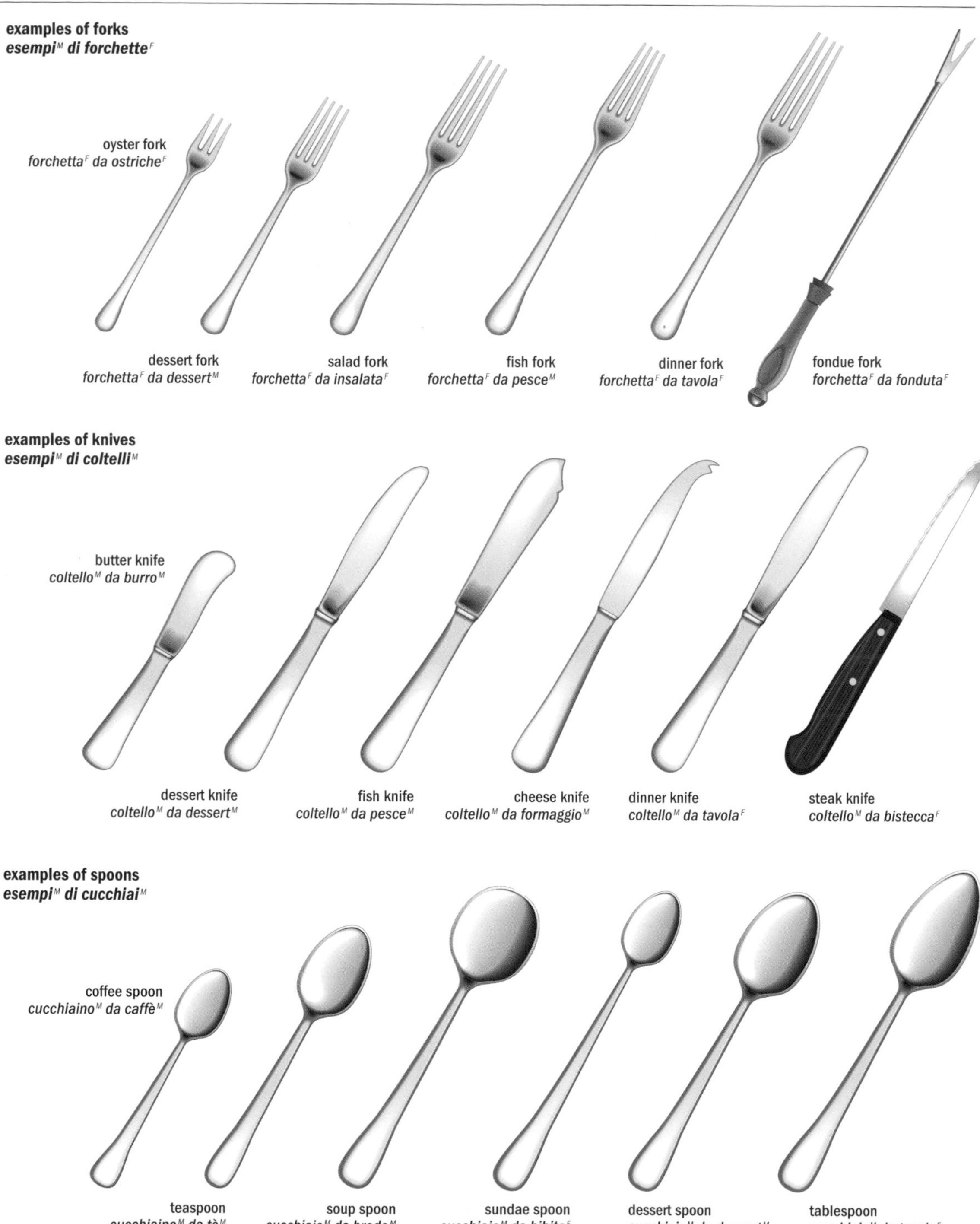
examples of forks
esempi^M di forchette^F
oyster fork
forchetta^F da ostriche^F
dessert fork
forchetta^F da dessert^M
salad fork
forchetta^F da insalata^F
fish fork
forchetta^F da pesce^M
dinner fork
forchetta^F da tavola^F
fondue fork
forchetta^F da fonduta^F
examples of knives
esempi^M di coltelli^M
butter knife
coltello^M da burro^M
dessert knife
coltello^M da dessert^M
fish knife
coltello^M da pesce^M
cheese knife
coltello^M da formaggio^M
dinner knife
coltello^M da tavola^F
steak knife
coltello^M da bistecca^F
examples of spoons
esempi^M di cucchiai^M
coffee spoon
cucchiaino^M da caffè^M
teaspoon
cucchiaino^M da tè^M
soup spoon
cucchiaio^M da brodo^M
sundae spoon
cucchiaio^M da bibita^F
dessert spoon
cucchiaio^M da dessert^M
tablespoon
cucchiaio^M da tavola^F

kitchen utensils

utensili[M] da cucina[F]

kitchen knife
coltello[M] da cucina[F]

half handle
mezzo manico[M]
bolster
nodo[M]
tang
codolo[M]
back
costa[F]
point
punta[F]
heel
tallone[M]
guard
guardia[F]
blade
lama[F]
cutting edge
filo[M]
rivet
rivetto[M]

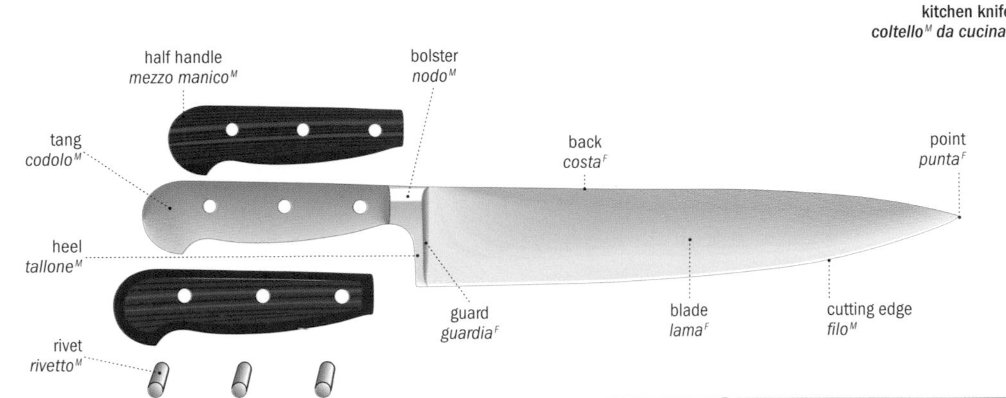

examples of utensils for cutting
esempi[M] di coltelli[M] da cucina[F]

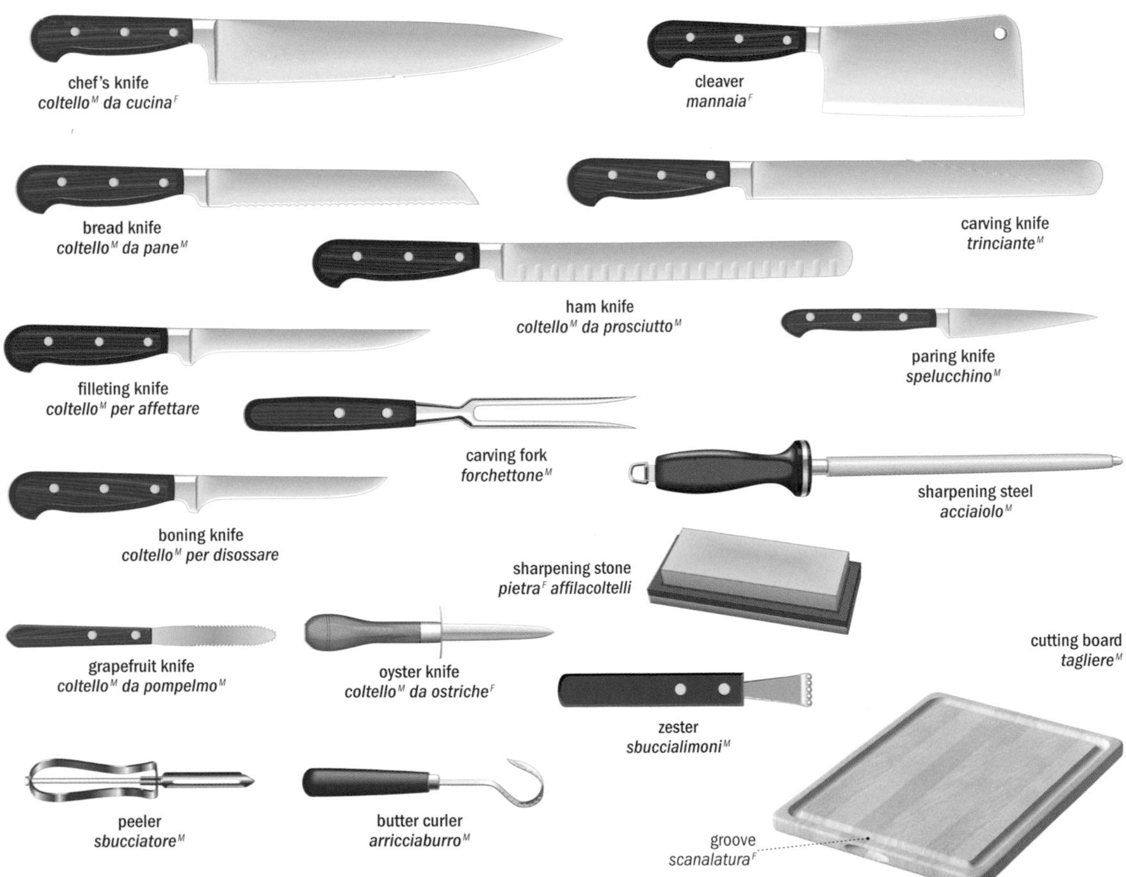

chef's knife
coltello[M] da cucina[F]
cleaver
mannaia[F]
bread knife
coltello[M] da pane[M]
carving knife
trinciante[M]
ham knife
coltello[M] da prosciutto[M]
paring knife
spelucchino[M]
filleting knife
coltello[M] per affettare
carving fork
forchettone[M]
sharpening steel
acciaiolo[M]
boning knife
coltello[M] per disossare
sharpening stone
pietra[F] affilacoltelli
cutting board
tagliere[M]
grapefruit knife
coltello[M] da pompelmo[M]
oyster knife
coltello[M] da ostriche[F]
zester
sbuccialimoni[M]
peeler
sbucciatore[M]
butter curler
arricciaburro[M]
groove
scanalatura[F]

kitchen utensils

for opening
per aprire

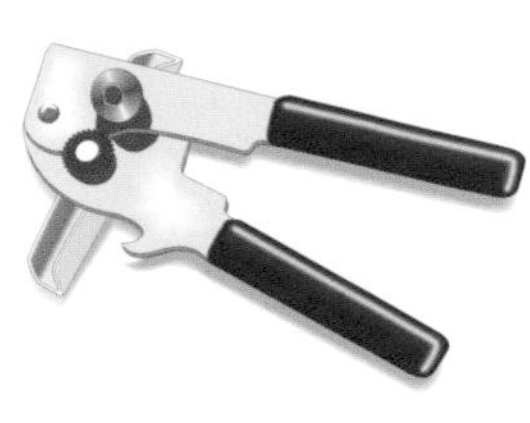

can opener
apriscatole[M]

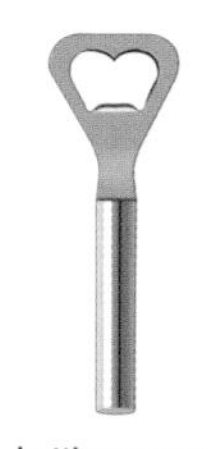

bottle opener
apribottiglie[M]

waiter's corkscrew
cavatappi[M] *da cameriere*[M]

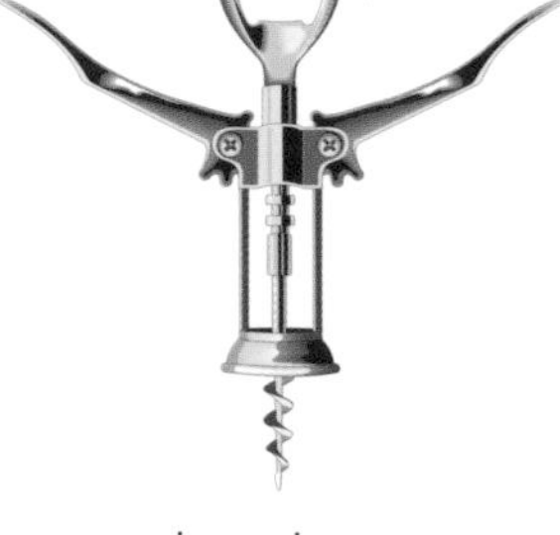

lever corkscrew
cavatappi[M] *a leva*[F]

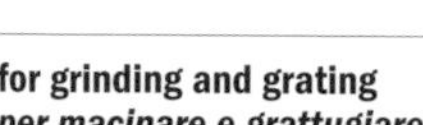

for grinding and grating
per macinare e grattugiare

nutcracker
schiaccianoci[M]

mortar
mortaio[M]

pestle
pestello[M]

meat grinder
tritacarne[M]

garlic press
spremiaglio[M]

citrus juicer
spremiagrumi[M]

nutmeg grater
grattugia[F] *per noce*[F] *moscata*

grater
grattugia[F]

rotary cheese grater
grattugiaformaggio[M]

pusher
pigiatore[M]

crank
levetta[F]

drum
tamburo[M]

handle
impugnatura[F]

pasta maker
macchina[F] *per fare la pasta*[F]

food mill
passaverdure[M]

mandoline
affettaverdure[M]

for measuring
per misurare

measuring spoons
cucchiai[M] dosatori

measuring cups
misurini[M]

candy thermometer
termometro[M] per zucchero[M]

instant-read thermometer
termometro[M] a lettura[F] istantanea

measuring cup
tazza[F] graduata

meat thermometer
termometro[M] per carne[F]

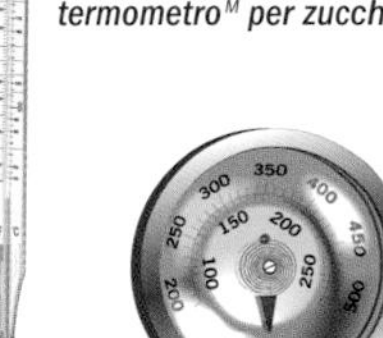
oven thermometer
termometro[M] del forno[M]

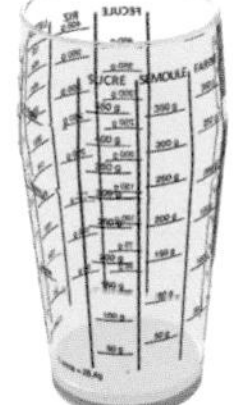
measuring beaker
recipiente[M] graduato

kitchen timer
contaminuti[M]

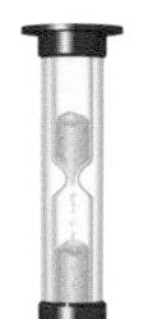
egg timer
clessidra[F] per uova[F] alla coque

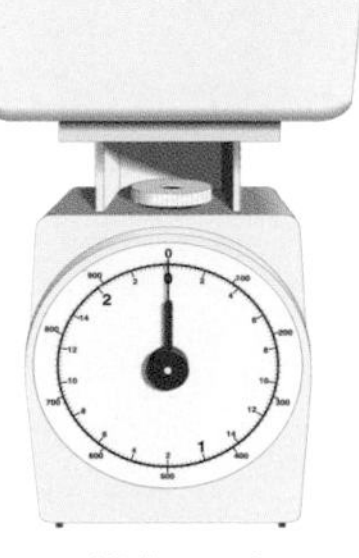
kitchen scale
bilancia[F] da cucina[F]

for straining and draining
per scolare e filtrare

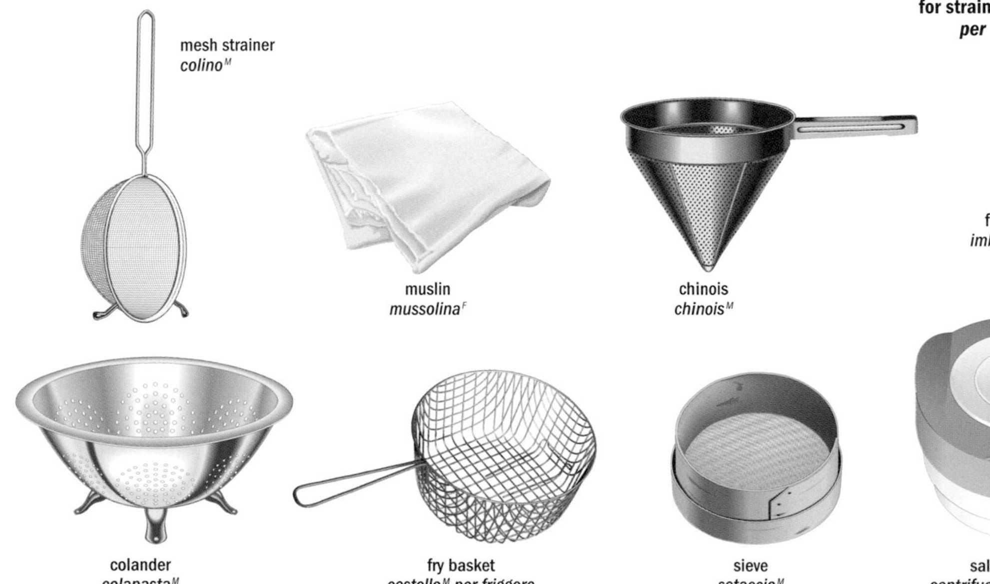
mesh strainer
colino[M]

muslin
mussolina[F]

chinois
chinois[M]

funnel
imbuto[M]

colander
colapasta[M]

fry basket
cestello[M] per friggere

sieve
setaccio[M]

salad spinner
centrifuga[F] scolainsalata

baking utensils
utensili[M] per dolci[M]

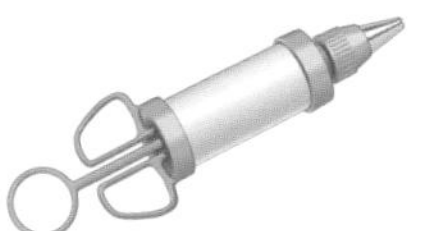
icing syringe
siringa[F] per decorazioni[F]

pastry cutting wheel
rotella[F] tagliapasta

pastry brush
pennello[M] per dolci[M]

egg beater
frullino[M]

whisk
frusta[F]

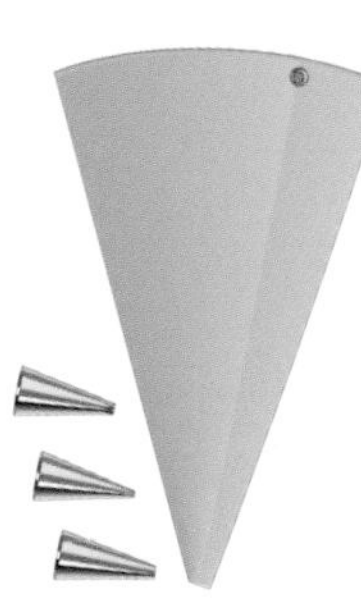
pastry bag and nozzles
tasca[F] e bocchette[F]

sifter
setaccio[M]

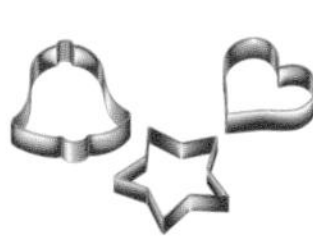
cookie cutters
tagliabiscotti[M]

dredger
spolverino[M]

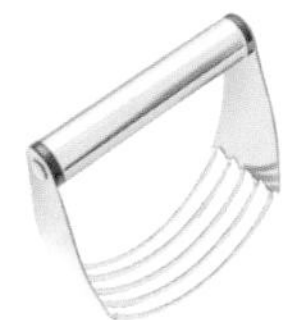
pastry blender
miscelatore[M] per dolci[M]

mixing bowls
ciotole[F] per mescolare

rolling pin
matterello[M]

baking sheet
teglia[F] da forno[M]

muffin pan
stampini[M] per dolci[M]

soufflé dish
tegamino[M] per sufflè[M]

charlotte mold
stampo[M] per charlotte[F]

spring-form pan
teglia[F] con fondo[M] staccabile

pie pan
teglia[F] per torta[F]

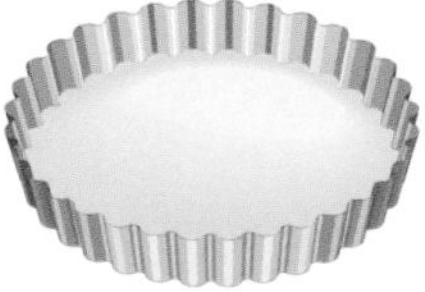
quiche plate
stampo[M] per crostata[F]

cake pan
tortiera[F]

set of utensils
set[M] di utensili[M]

skimmer *schiumaiola[F]*

draining spoon *cucchiaio[M] forato*

spatula *spatola[F]*

turner *paletta[F]*

ladle *mestolo[M]*

potato masher *schiacciapatate[M]*

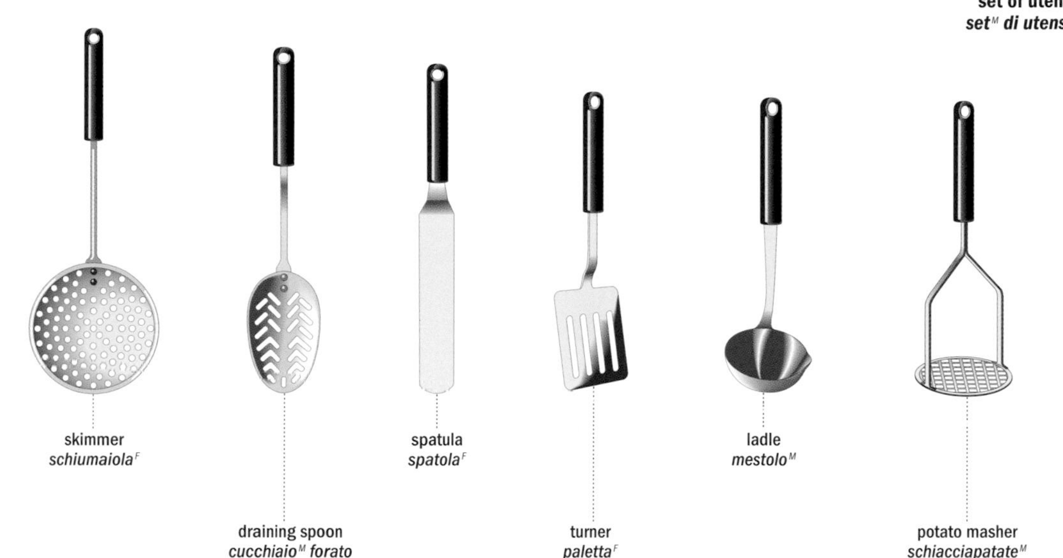

miscellaneous utensils
utensili[M] vari

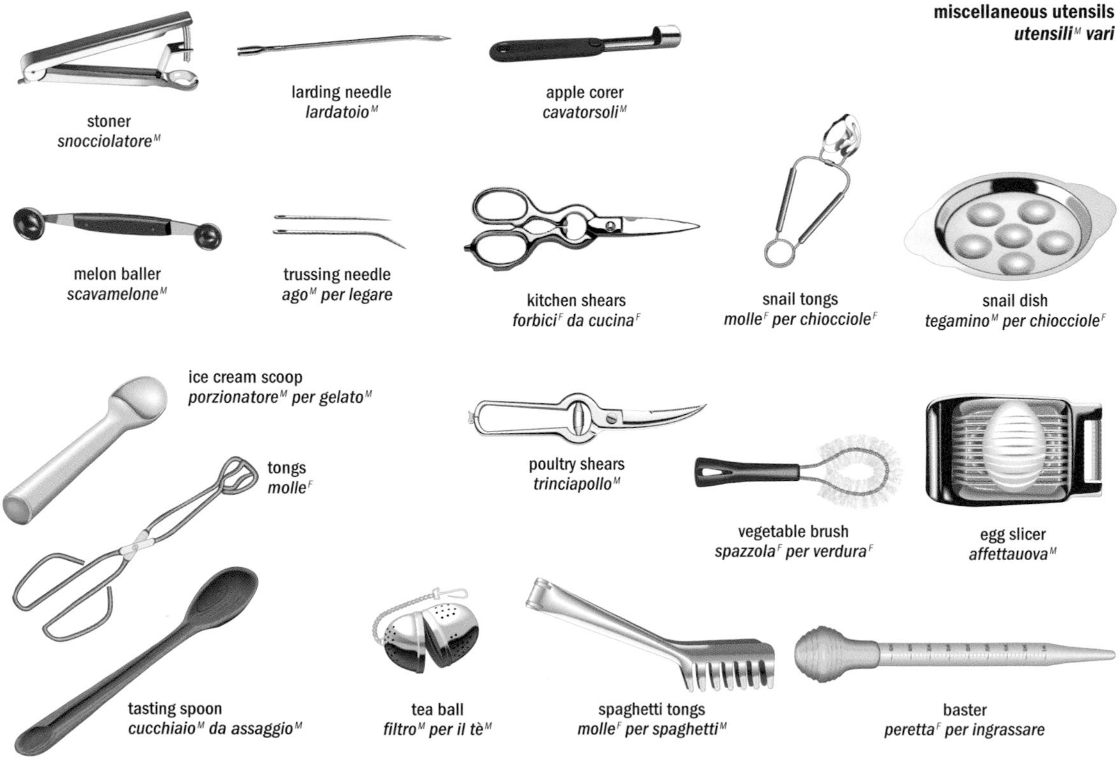

stoner *snocciolatore[M]*

larding needle *lardatoio[M]*

apple corer *cavatorsoli[M]*

melon baller *scavamelone[M]*

trussing needle *ago[M] per legare*

kitchen shears *forbici[F] da cucina[F]*

snail tongs *molle[F] per chiocciole[F]*

snail dish *tegamino[M] per chiocciole[F]*

ice cream scoop *porzionatore[M] per gelato[M]*

tongs *molle[F]*

poultry shears *trinciapollo[M]*

vegetable brush *spazzola[F] per verdura[F]*

egg slicer *affettauova[M]*

tasting spoon *cucchiaio[M] da assaggio[M]*

tea ball *filtro[M] per il tè[M]*

spaghetti tongs *molle[F] per spaghetti[M]*

baster *peretta[F] per ingrassare*

cooking utensils

utensili^M per cucinare

raclette with grill
grigliaF per racletteF
dish
piattoM
cooking plate
piastraF di cotturaF
base
baseF
electric steamer
pentolaF a vaporeM elettrica
cooking dishes
piattiM di cotturaF
water level indicator
indicatoreM del livelloM d'acquaF
signal lamp
spiaF luminosa
timer
contaminutiM
indoor electric grill
grigliaF elettrica per interniM
insulated handle
manigliaF isolata
drip pan
leccardaF
cooking surface
pianoM di cotturaF
adjustable thermostat
termostatoM regolabile
bread machine
impastatriceF
lid
coperchioM
control panel
quadroM di comandoM
window
finestraF di controlloM
loaf pan
stampoM per paneM
electric griddle
piastraF elettrica
cooking surface
pianoM di cotturaF
handle
manigliaF
detachable control
regolatoreM staccabile
grease well
bacinellaF raccogligrasso

miscellaneous domestic appliances

elettrodomestici[M] vari

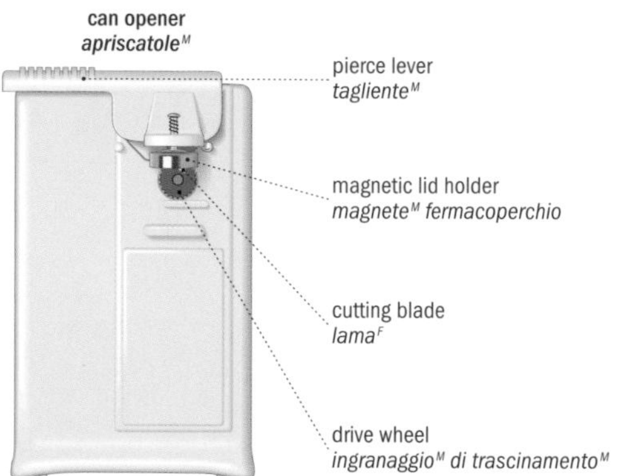

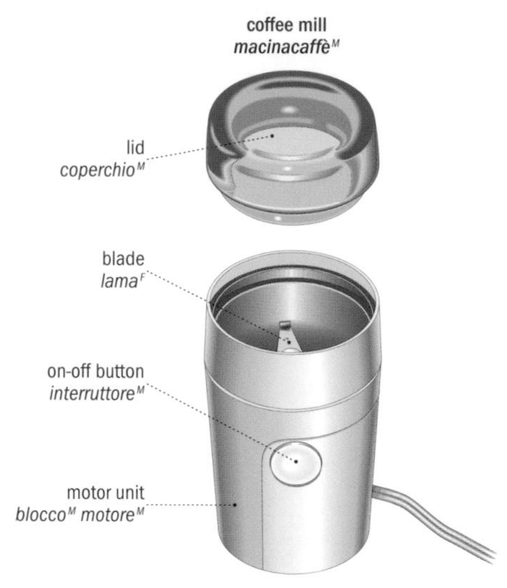

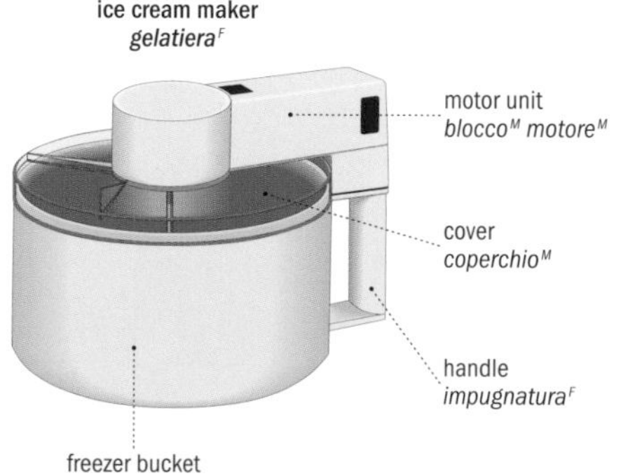

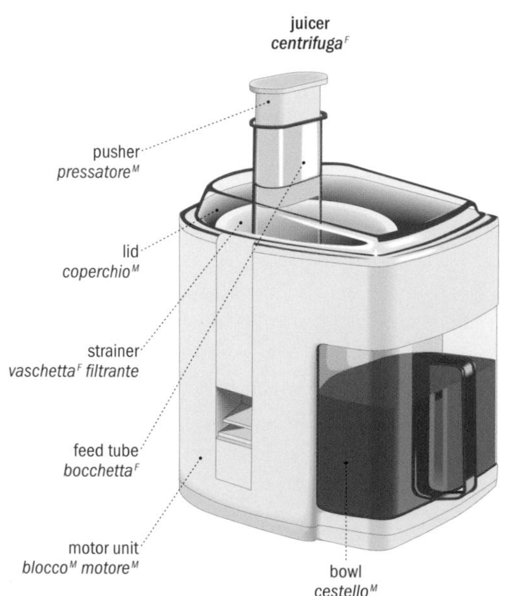

coffee makers

macchine^F da caffè^M

automatic drip coffee maker
macchina^F da caffè^M a filtro^M

Neapolitan coffee maker
caffettiera^F napoletana

espresso machine
macchina^F per espresso^M

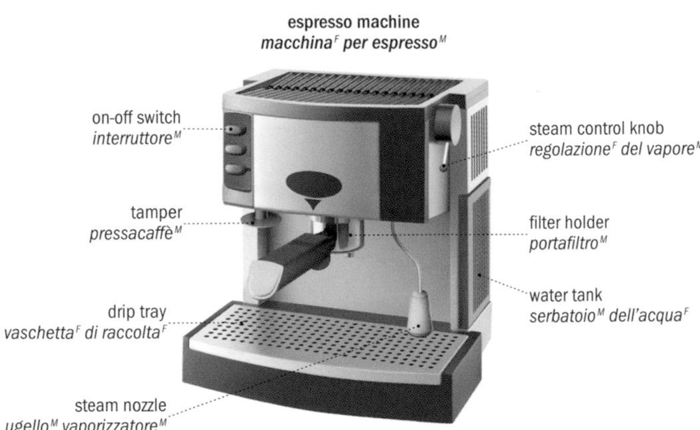

vacuum coffee maker
caffettiera^F a infusione^F

French press
caffettiera^F a pistone^M

espresso maker
caffettiera^F per espresso^M

percolator
caffettiera^F a filtro^M

FOOD AND KITCHEN

exterior of a house

esterno^M di una casa^F

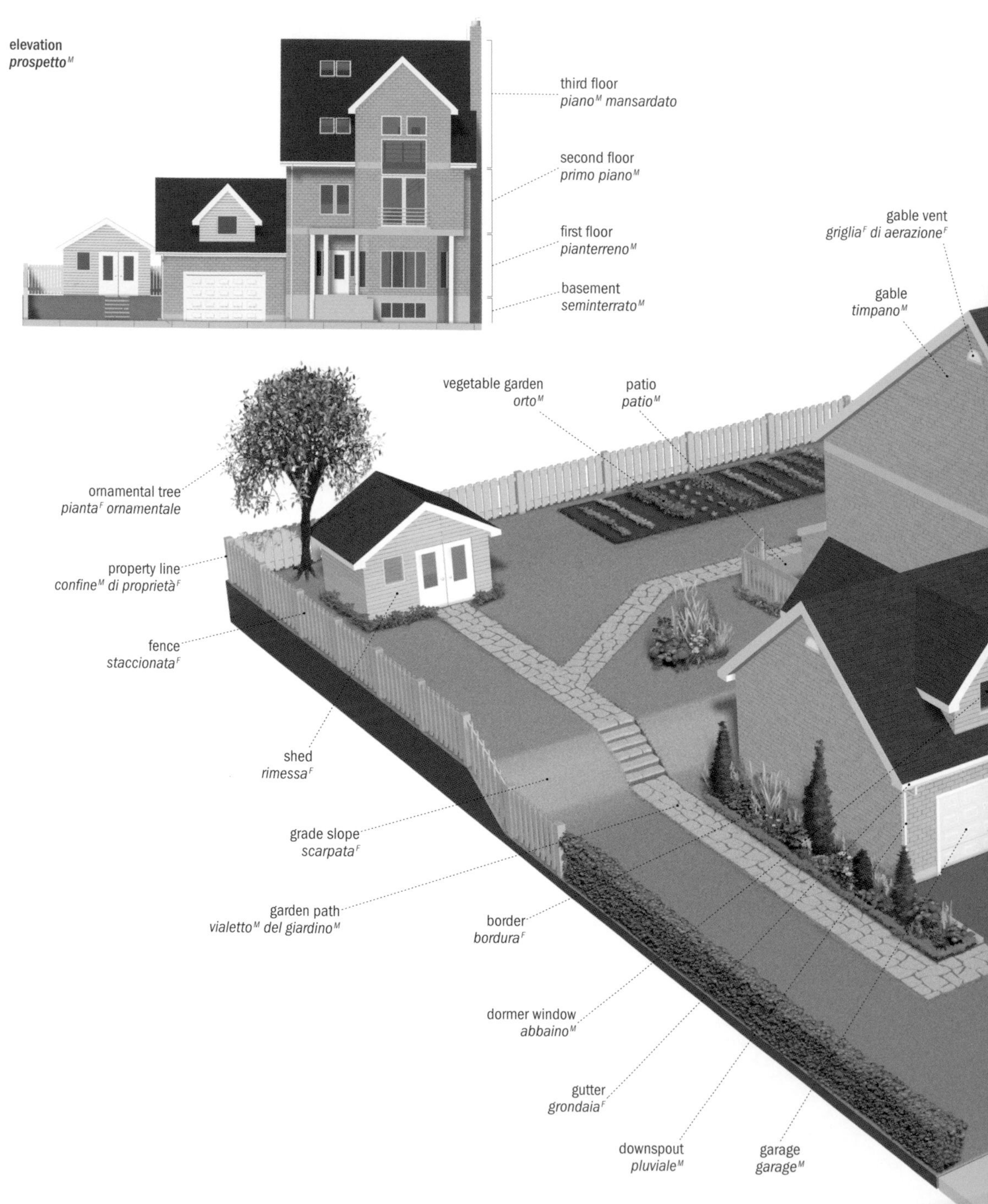

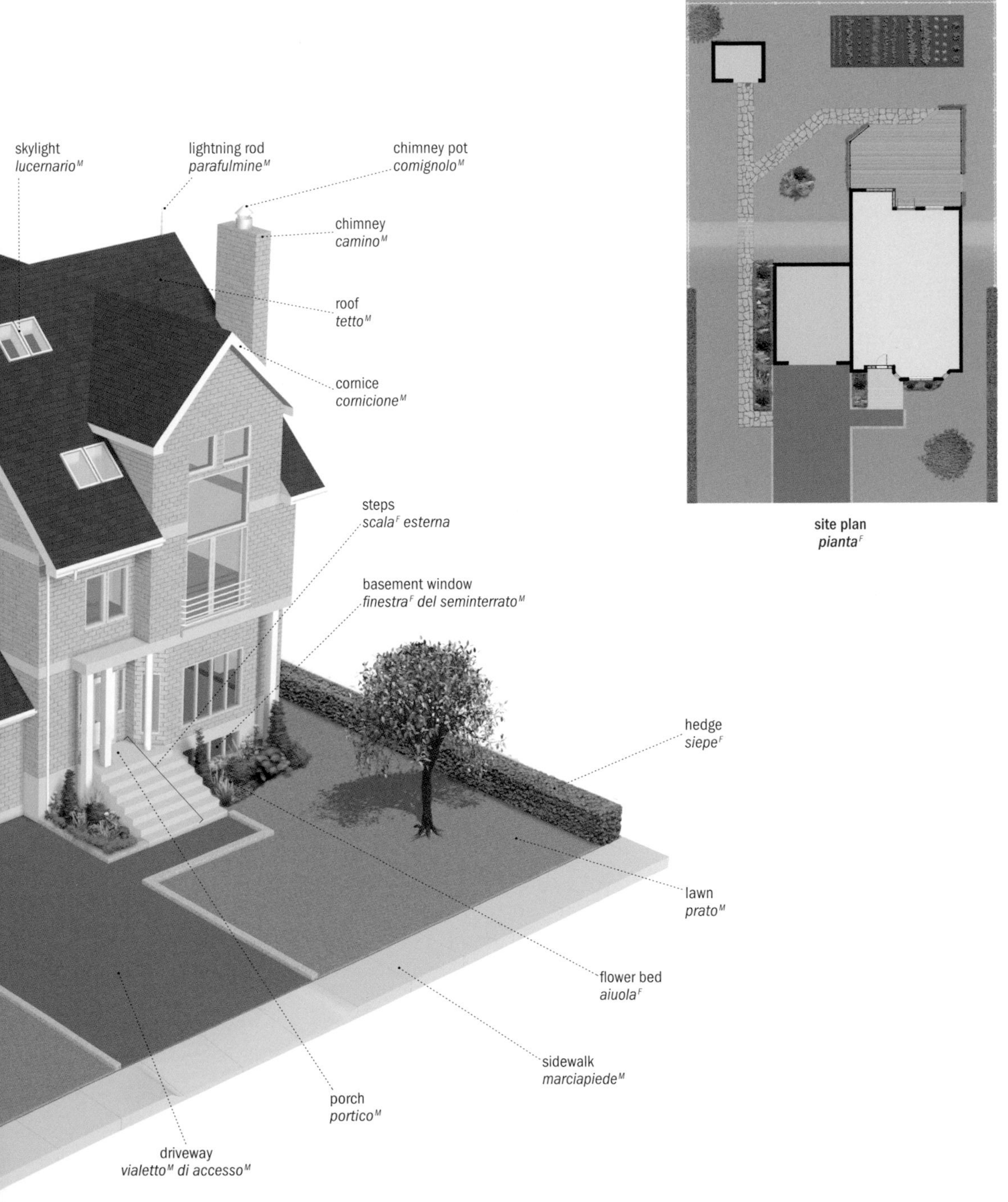

site plan
pianta^F

pool

piscina^F

hot tub
vasca^F idromassaggio^M

above-ground swimming pool
piscina^F fuori terra^F

in-ground swimming pool
piscina^F interrata

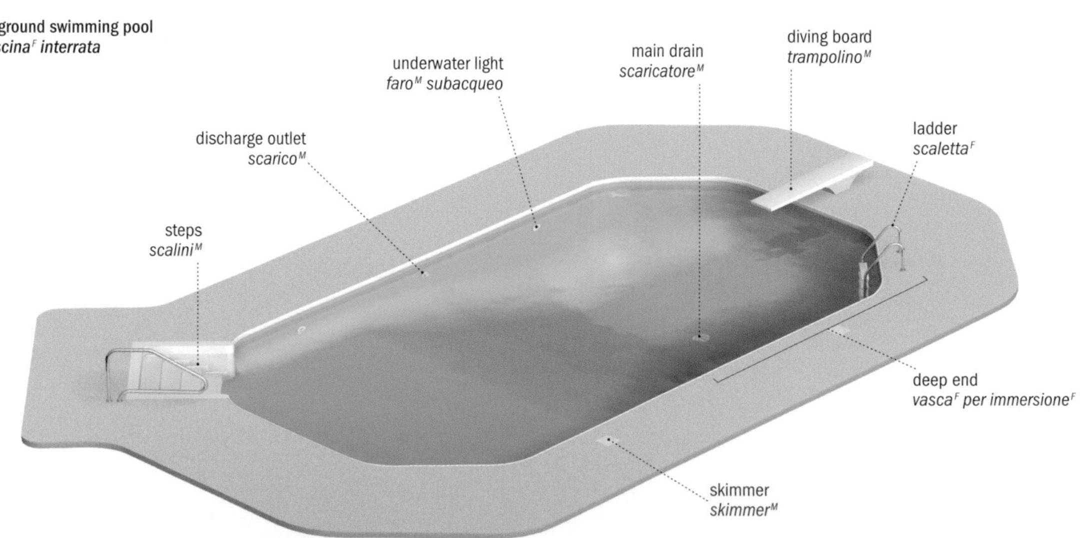

exterior door

porta^F esterna

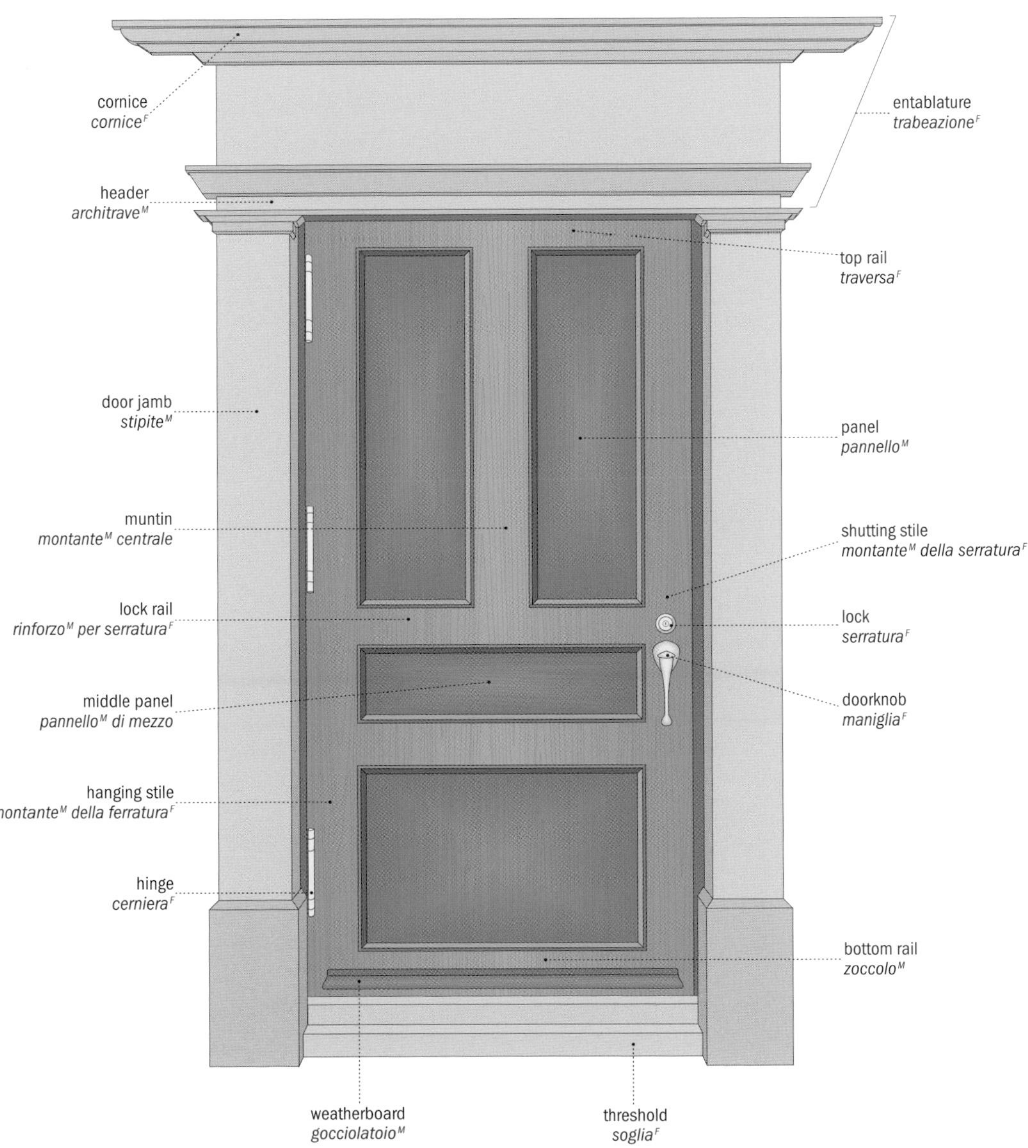

lock

serratura[F]

general view
visione[F] di insieme[M]

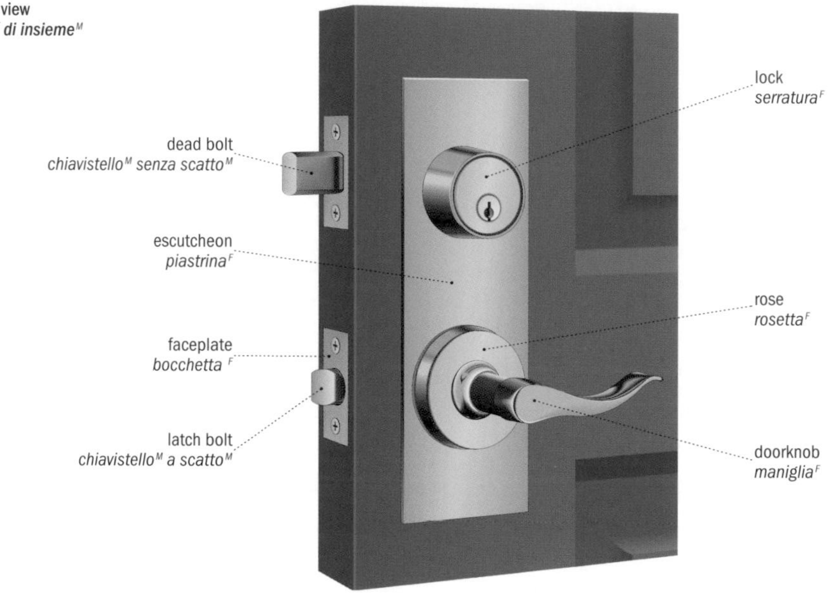

window

finestra[F]

structure
struttura[F]

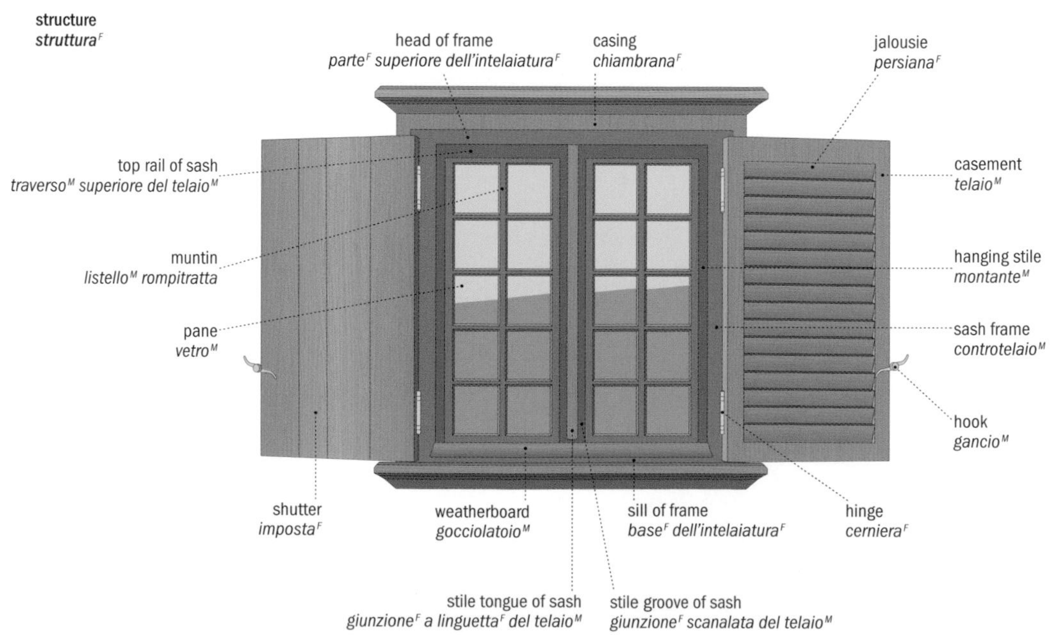

frame

struttura[F]

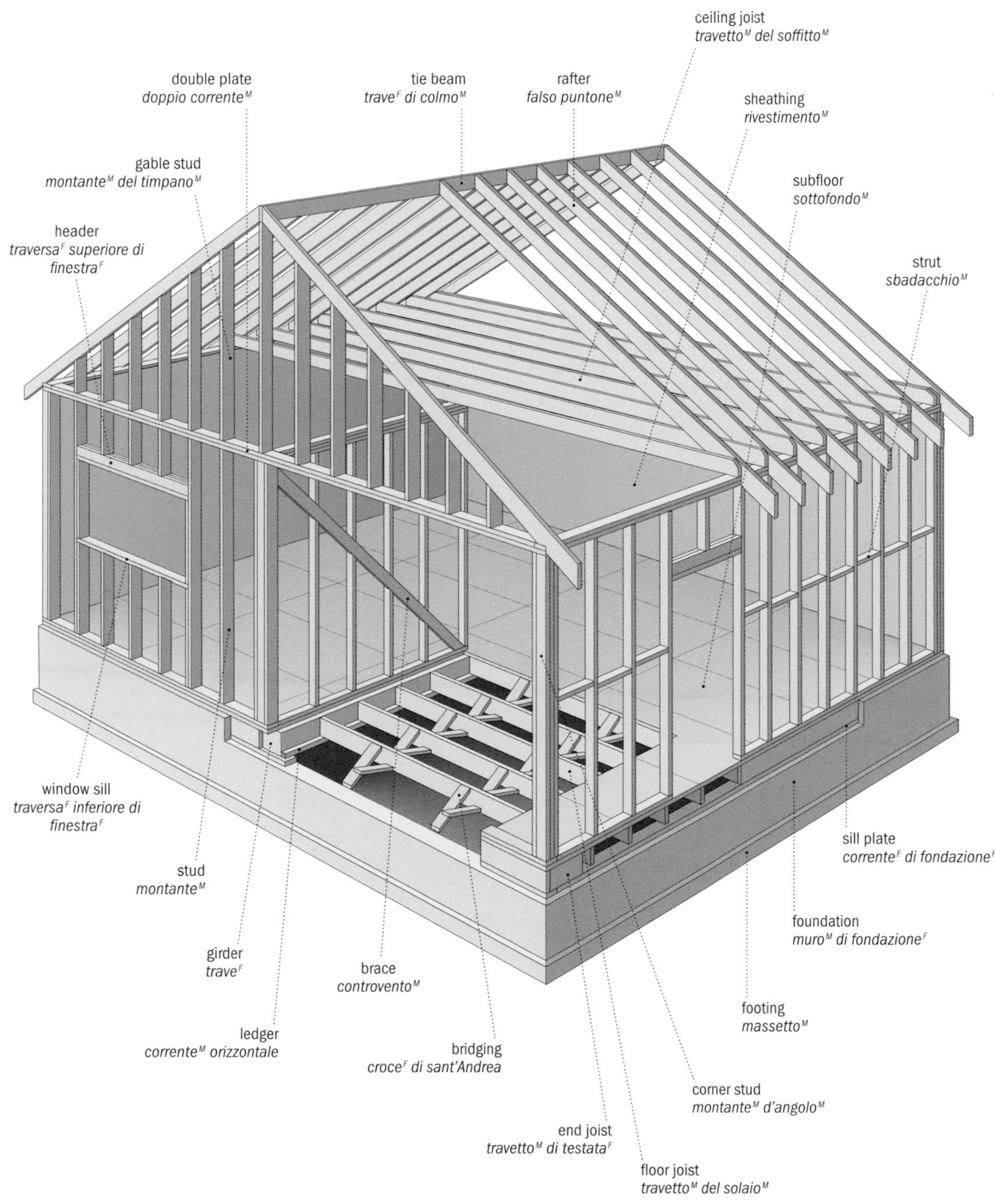

main rooms

stanze^F principali

first floor
pianterreno^M

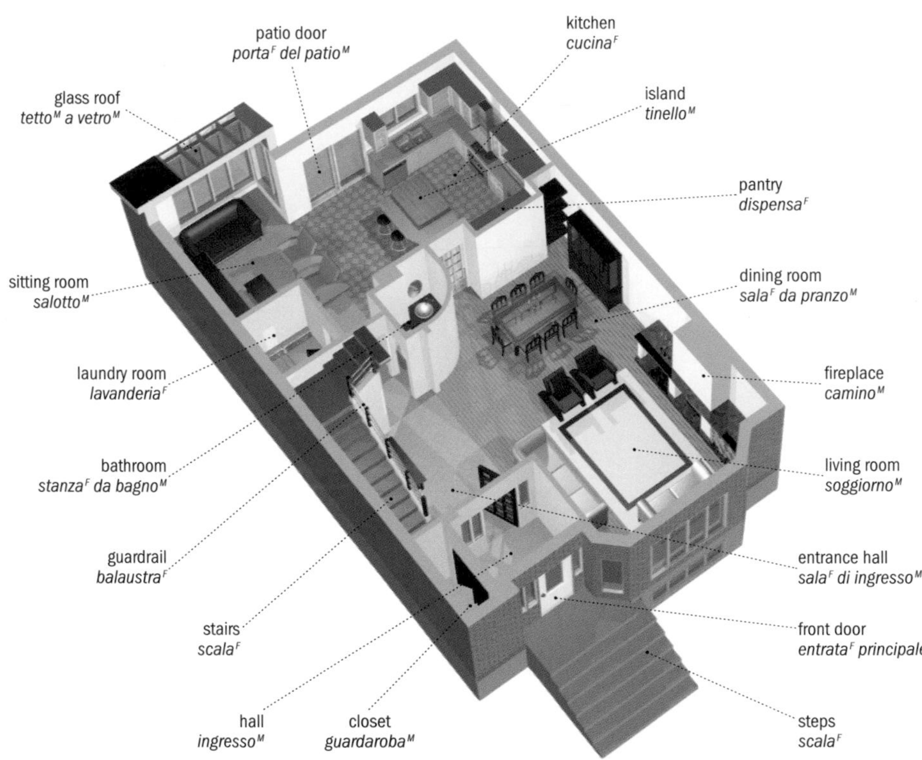

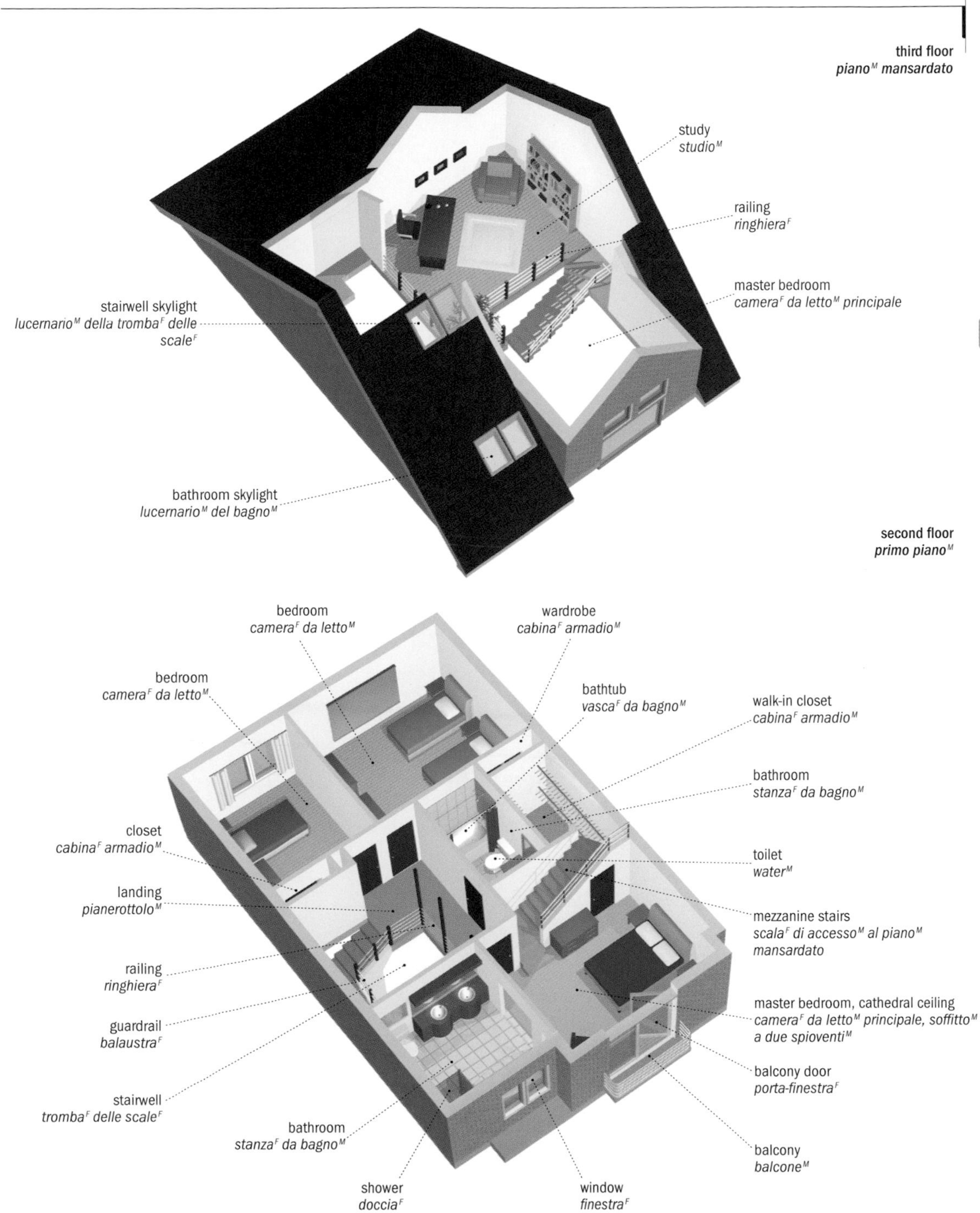
third floor
piano^M mansardato
study
studio^M
railing
ringhiera^F
master bedroom
camera^F da letto^M principale
stairwell skylight
lucernario^M della tromba^F delle scale^F
bathroom skylight
lucernario^M del bagno^M
second floor
primo piano^M
bedroom
camera^F da letto^M
wardrobe
cabina^F armadio^M
bedroom
camera^F da letto^M
bathtub
vasca^F da bagno^M
walk-in closet
cabina^F armadio^M
bathroom
stanza^F da bagno^M
closet
cabina^F armadio^M
toilet
water^M
landing
pianerottolo^M
mezzanine stairs
scala^F di accesso^M al piano^M mansardato
railing
ringhiera^F
master bedroom, cathedral ceiling
camera^F da letto^M principale, soffitto^M a due spioventi^M
guardrail
balaustra^F
balcony door
porta-finestra^F
stairwell
tromba^F delle scale^F
bathroom
stanza^F da bagno^M
balcony
balcone^M
shower
doccia^F
window
finestra^F

wood flooring

parquet[M]

wood flooring on cement screed
parquet[M] su sottofondo[M] di cemento[M]

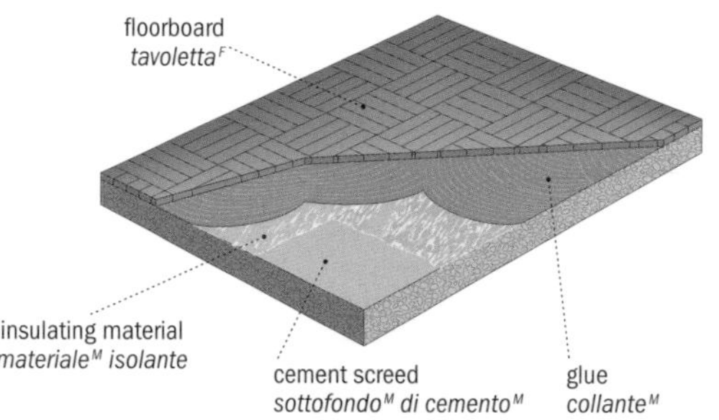

wood flooring on wooden structure
parquet[M] su struttura[F] lignea

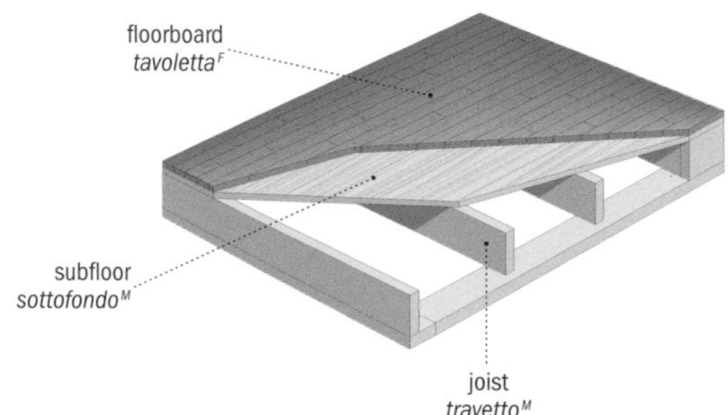

wood flooring arrangements
tipi[M] di parquet[M]

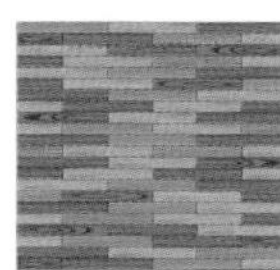

overlay flooring
parquet[M] a listoni[M]

strip flooring with alternate joints
parquet[M] a listelli[M]

herringbone parquet
parquet[M] a spina[F] di pesce[M]

herringbone pattern
parquet[M] a spina[F] di pesce[M]

inlaid parquet
parquet[M] a mosaico[M]

basket weave pattern
parquet[M] a tessitura[F] di vimini[M]

Arenberg parquet
parquet[M] Arenberg

Chantilly parquet
parquet[M] Chantilly

Versailles parquet
parquet[M] Versailles

textile floor coverings

rivestimenti[M] in tessuto[M] per pavimento[M]

rug
tappeto[M]

pile carpet
moquette[F]

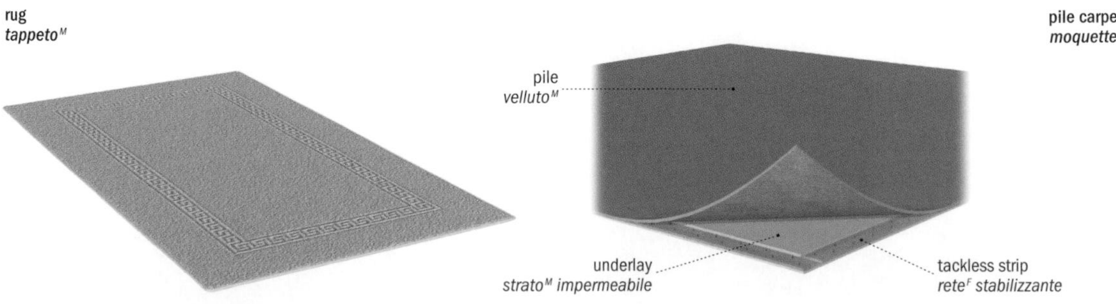

stairs
scale^F

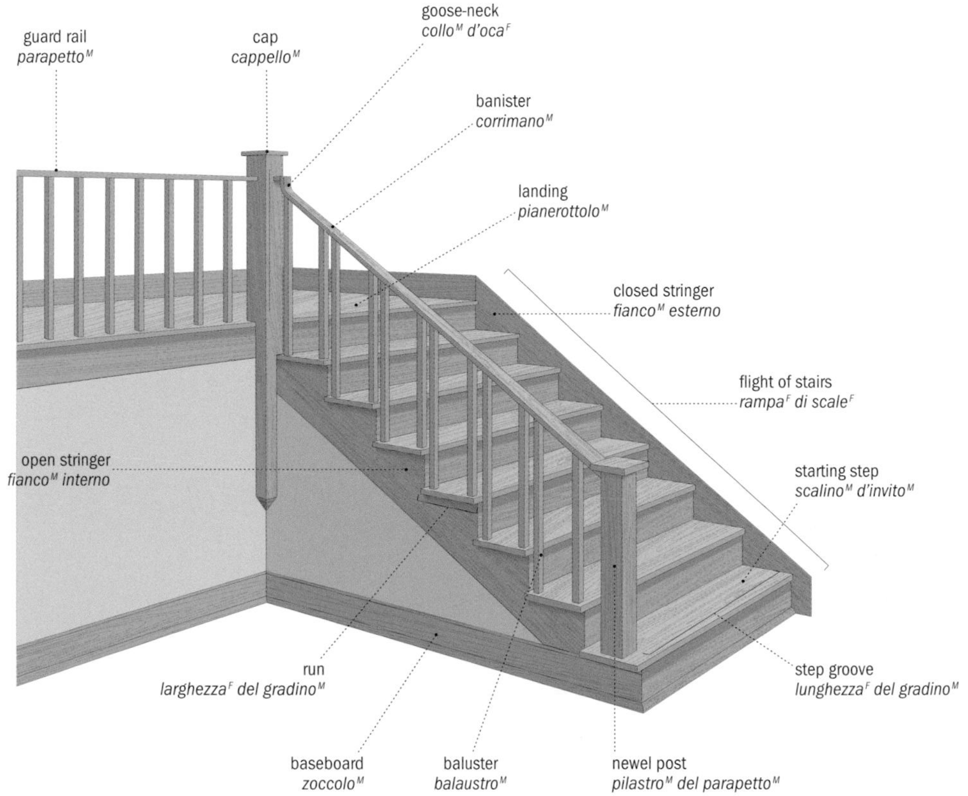

guard rail
parapetto^M
cap
cappello^M
goose-neck
collo^M d'oca^F
banister
corrimano^M
landing
pianerottolo^M
closed stringer
fianco^M esterno
flight of stairs
rampa^F di scale^F
open stringer
fianco^M interno
starting step
scalino^M d'invito^M
run
larghezza^F del gradino^M
step groove
lunghezza^F del gradino^M
baseboard
zoccolo^M
baluster
balaustro^M
newel post
pilastro^M del parapetto^M

step
gradino^M

tread
pedata^F
riser
frontale^M
rise
alzata^F
nosing
sporgenza^F

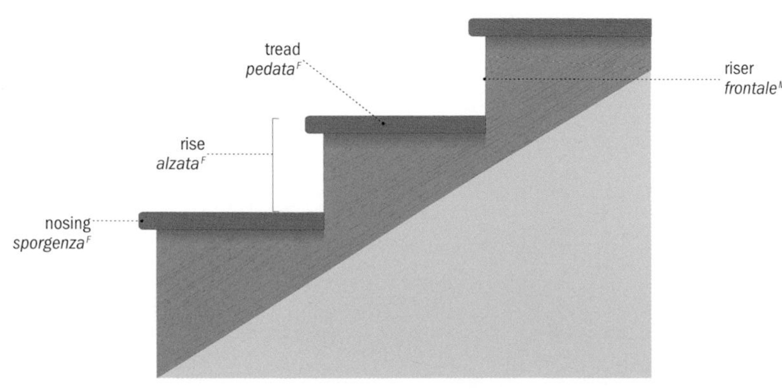

wood burning

riscaldamento[M] a legna[F]

fireplace
camino[M]

hood
cappa[F]

mantel shelf
mensola[F]

corbel piece
mensolone[M]

mantel
caminiera[F]

lintel
architrave[M]

jamb
stipite[M]

frame
intelaiatura[F]

firebrick back
fondo[M] refrattario

base
base[F]

inner hearth
focolare[M]

woodbox
cassone[M] per legna[F] da ardere

slow-burning wood stove
stufa[F] a combustione[F] lenta

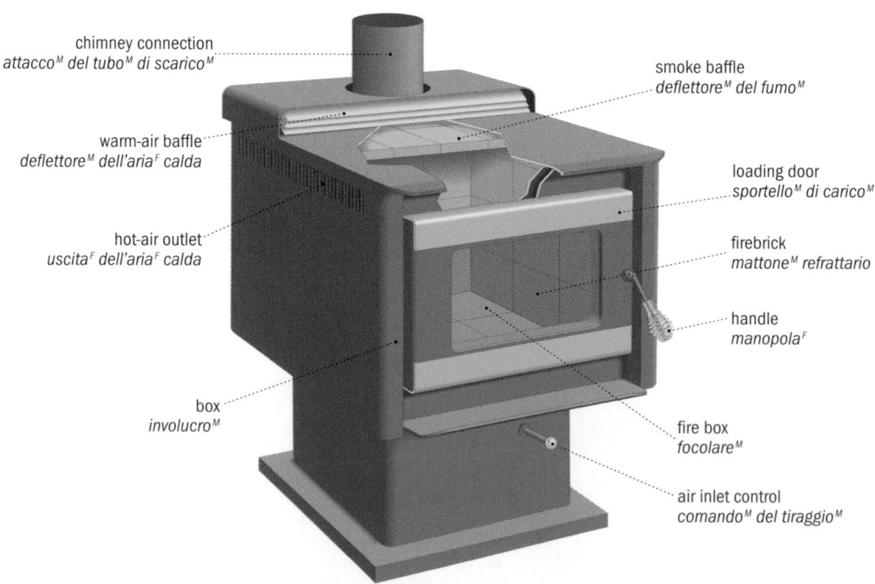

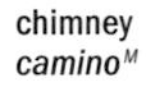

chimney
camino[M]

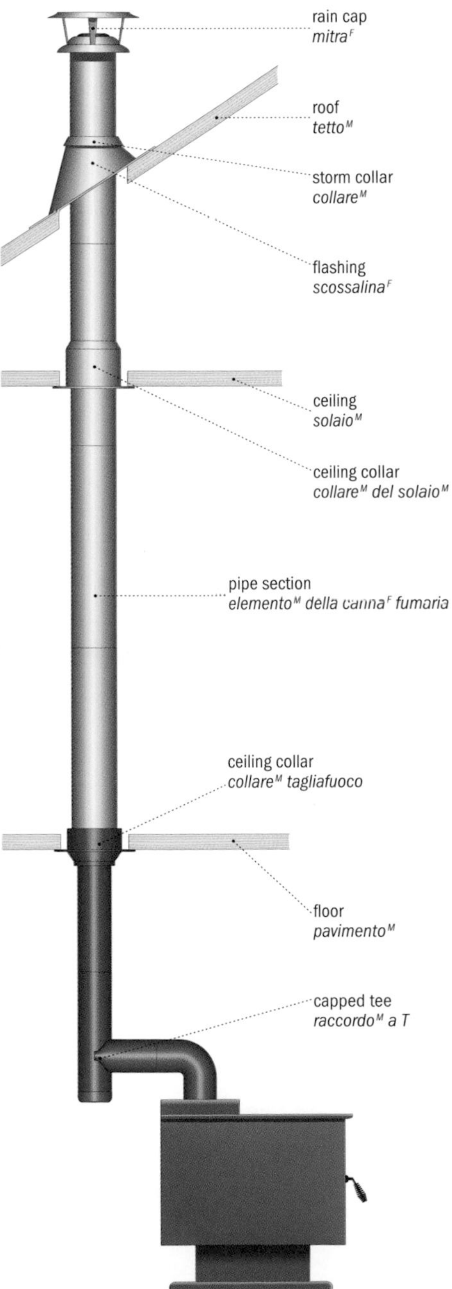

fire irons
***ferri*[M] *per il camino*[M]**

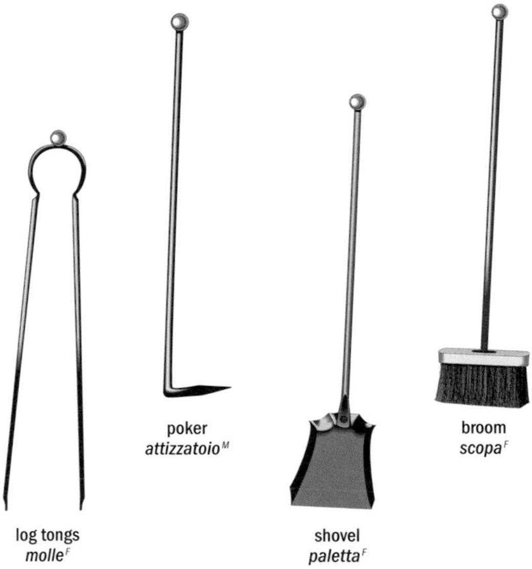

log tongs
molle[F]

poker
attizzatoio[M]

shovel
paletta[F]

broom
scopa[F]

andirons
alari[M]

log carrier
portaceppi[M]

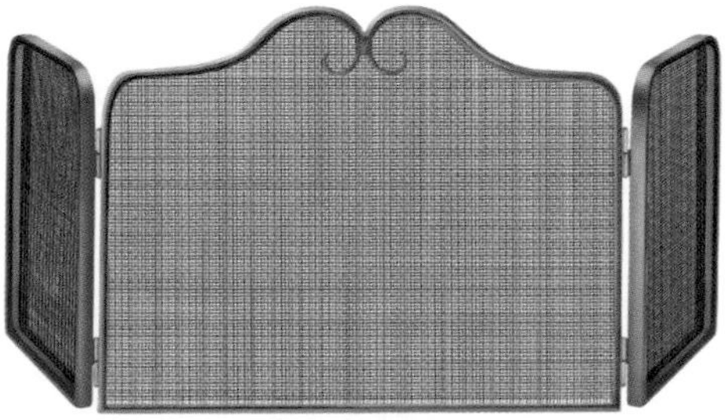

fireplace screen
parafuoco[M]

plumbing system

impianto[M] idraulico

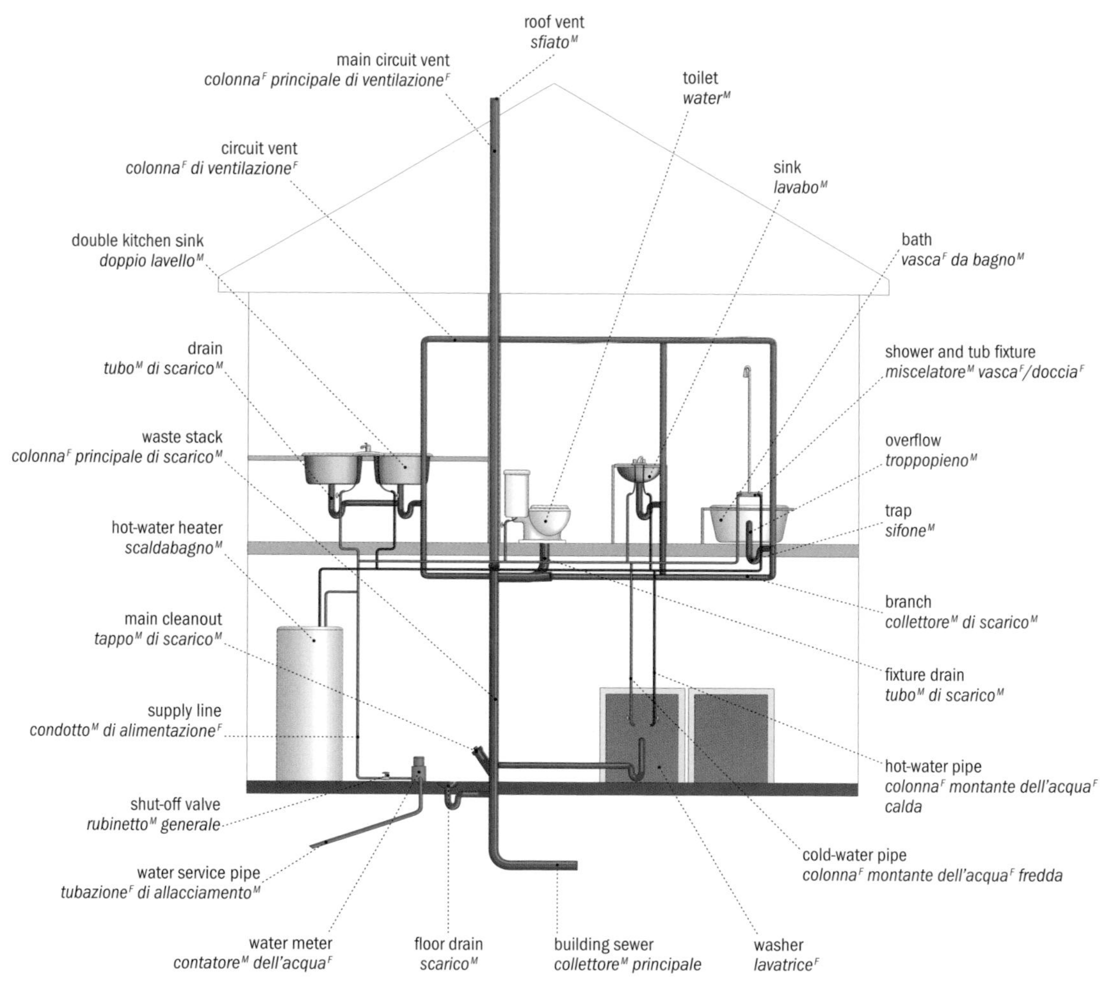

ventilating circuit
rete[F] di ventilazione[F]

draining circuit
rete[F] di scarico[M]

cold-water circuit
rete[F] di distribuzione[F] dell'acqua[F] fredda

hot-water circuit
rete[F] di distribuzione[F] dell'acqua[F] calda

bathroom

stanza[F] da bagno[M]

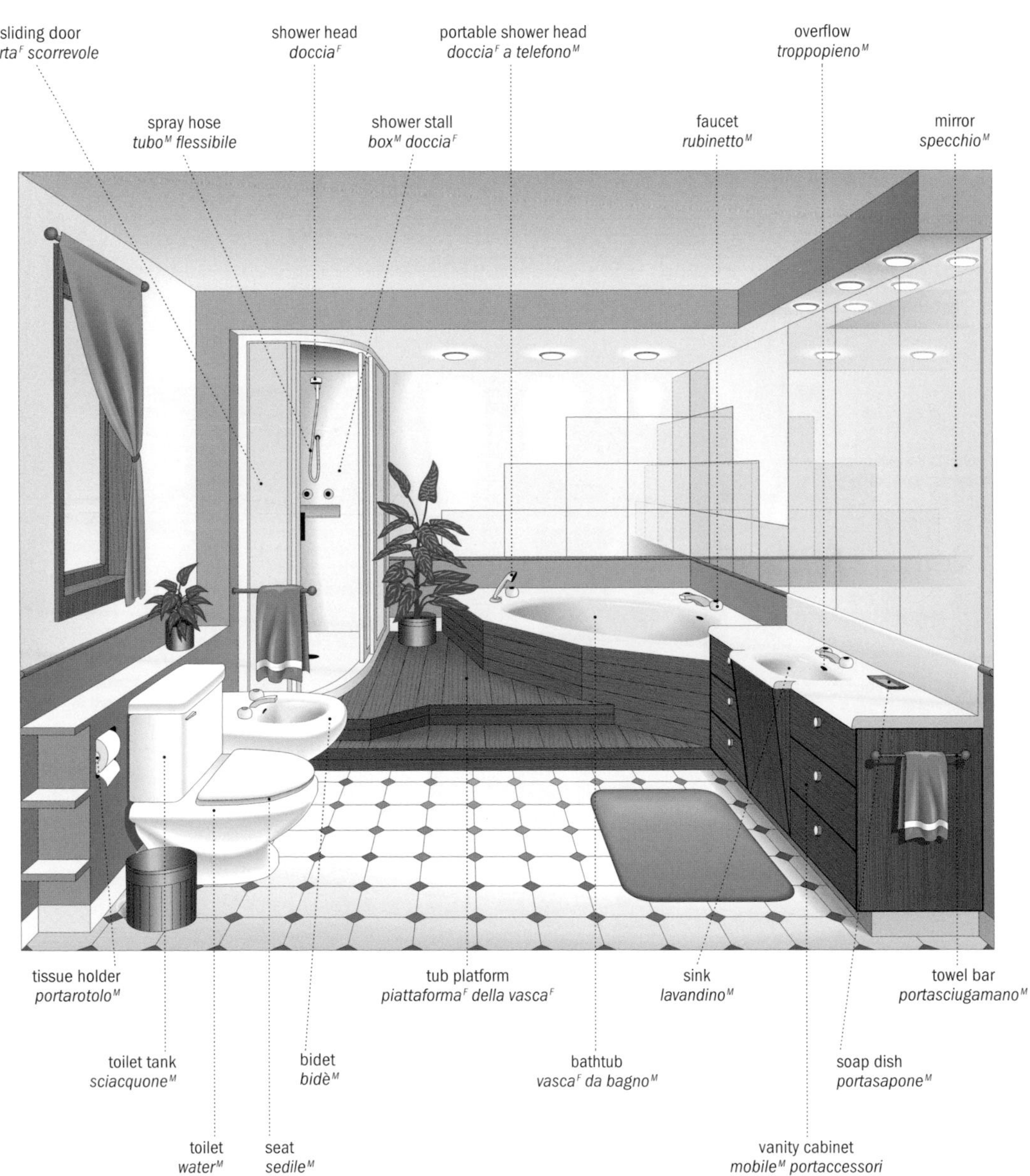

network connection

allacciamento^M alla rete^F

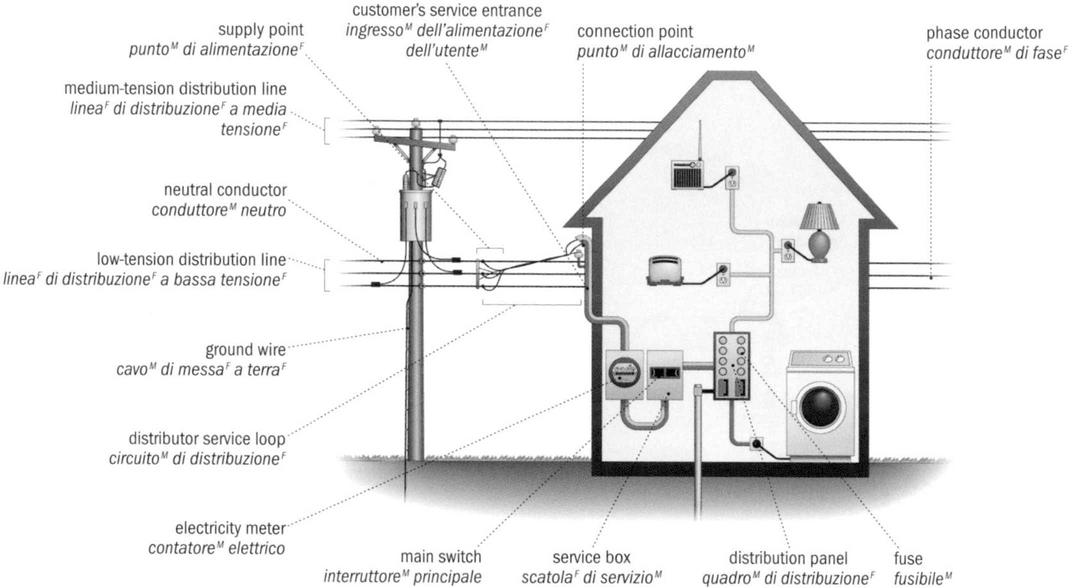

contact devices

dispositivi^M di contatto^M

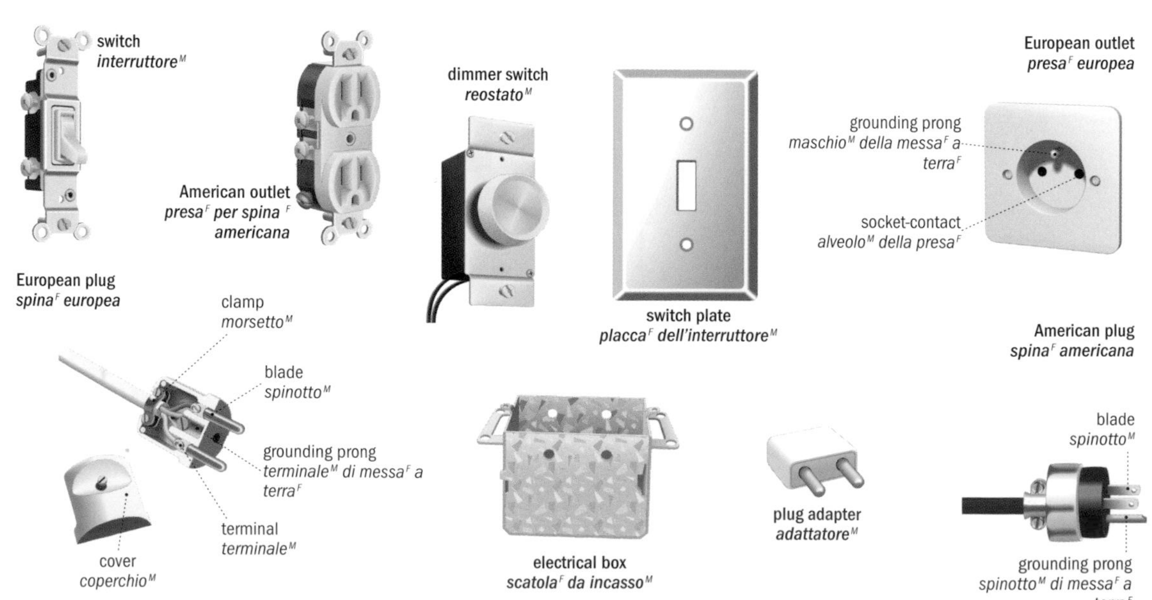

lighting

illuminazione[F]

incandescent lightbulb
lampadina[F] a incandescenza[F]

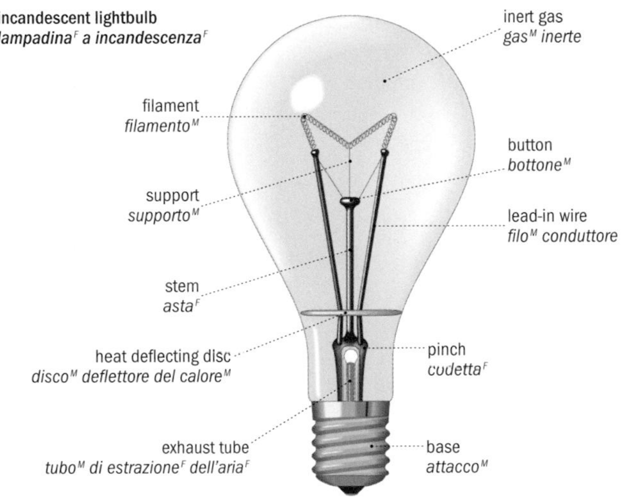

lamp socket
portalampada[M]

energy-saving bulb
lampadina[F] a risparmio[M] di energia[F]

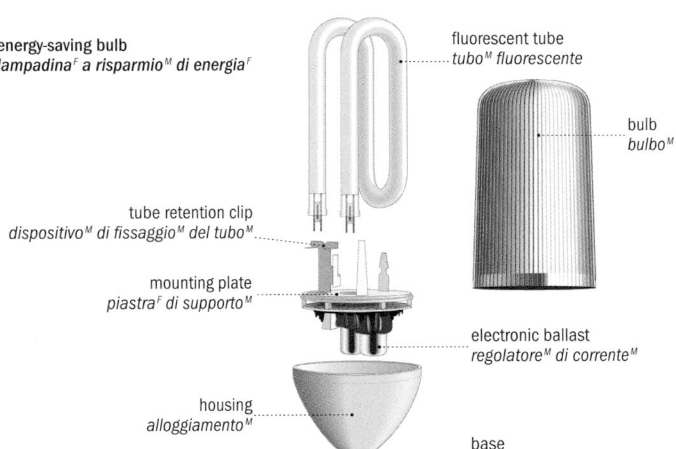

screw base
attacco[M] a vite[F]

bayonet base
attacco[M] a baionetta[F]

fluorescent tube
tubo[M] fluorescente

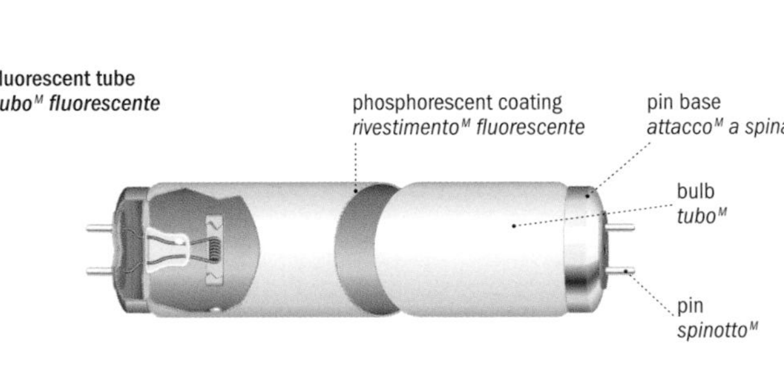

tungsten-halogen lamp
lampada[F] alogena al tungsteno[M]

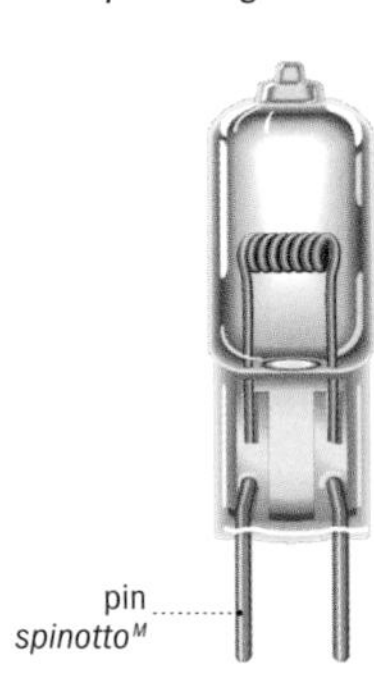

HOUSE

armchair

poltrona^F

parts
parti^F

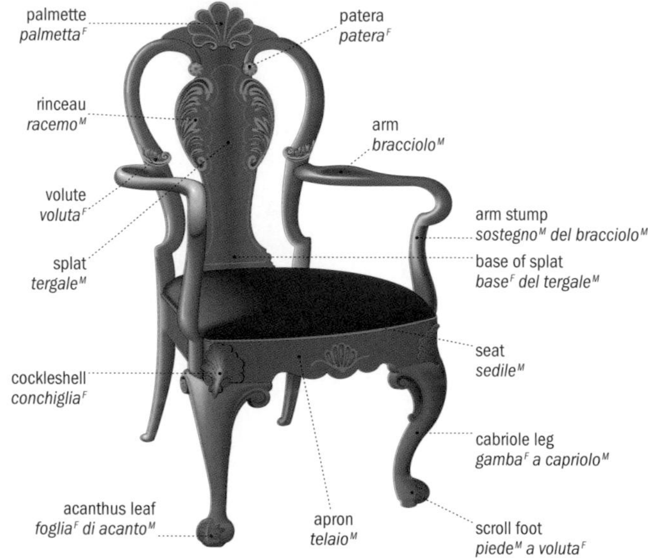

examples of armchairs
esempi^M di poltrone^F e divani^M

Wassily chair
poltrona^F Wassily

director's chair
sedia^F da regista^M

rocking chair
sedia^F a dondolo^M

cabriolet
cabriolet^F

méridienne
méridienne^F

récamier
agrippina^F

club chair
poltrona^F da salotto^M

bergère
bergère^F

sofa
divano^M

love seat
divano^M a due posti^M

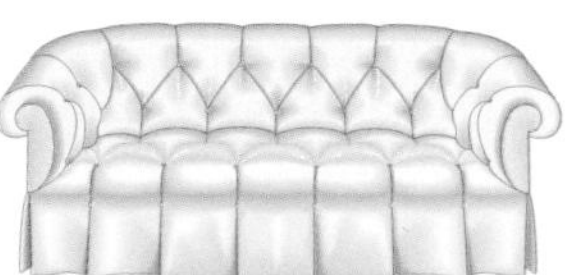

chesterfield
divano^M Chesterfield

side chair

sedia^F

parts
parti^F

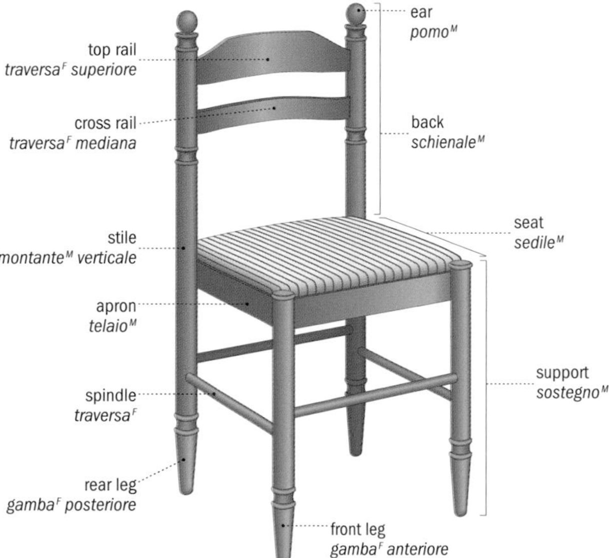

examples of chairs
esempi^M di sedie^F

rocking chair
sedia^F a dondolo^M

stacking chairs
sedie^F impilabili

folding chairs
sedia^F pieghevole

chaise longue
sedia^F a sdraio^M

seats

sedili^M

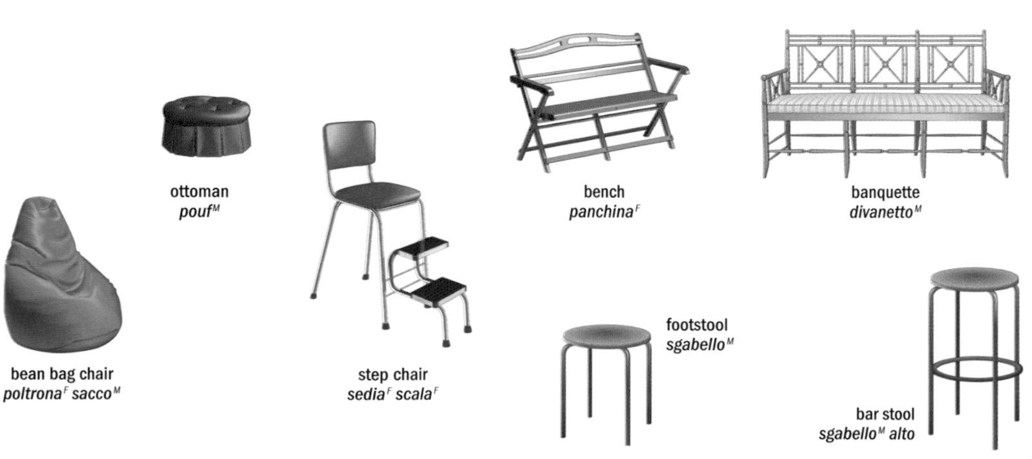

table

tavolo[M]

gate-leg table
tavolo[M] a cancello[M]

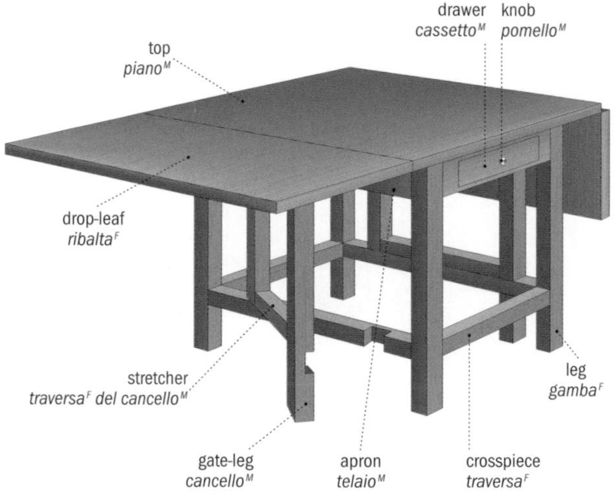

examples of tables
esempi[M] di tavoli[M]

extension table
tavolo[M] allungabile

nest of tables
tavolini[M] sovrapponibili

serving cart
carrello[M] portavivande

storage furniture

mobili[M] contenitori

armoire
armadio[M]

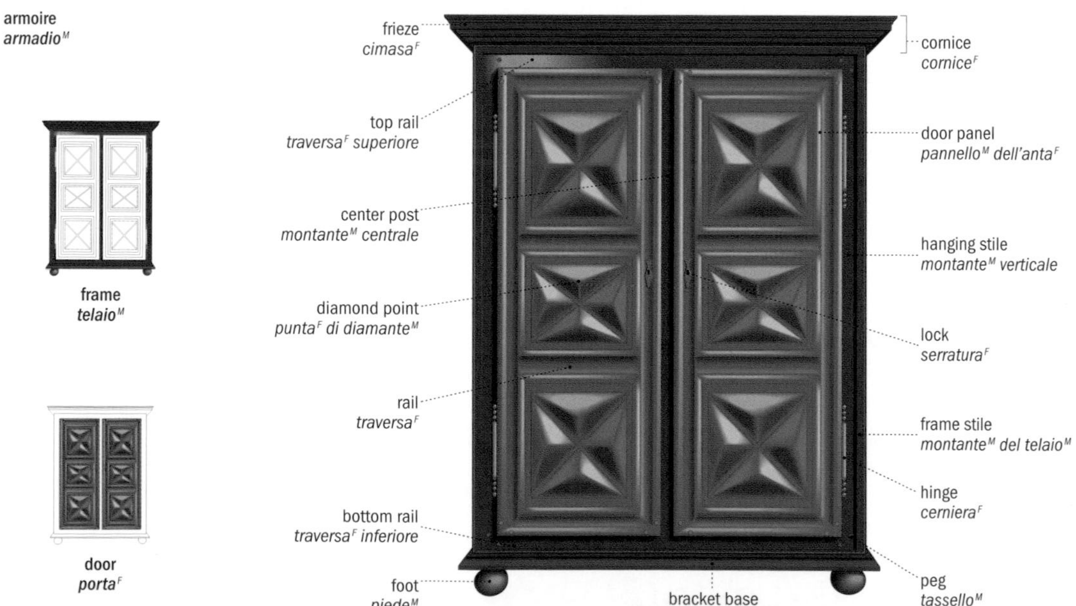

compartment
scompartoM
fall front
ribaltaF
linen chest
cassapancaF
closet
armadioM appendiabiti
shelf
ripianoM
secretary
secrétaireM
dresser
comòM
wardrobe
guardarobaM
drawer
cassettoM
chiffonier
cassettieraF
display cabinet
vetrinaF
corner cupboard
angolieraF
glass-fronted display cabinet
credenzaF con vetrinaF
buffet
credenzaF
cocktail cabinet
mobileM barM

bed

letto^M

sofa bed
divano-letto^M

parts
parti^F

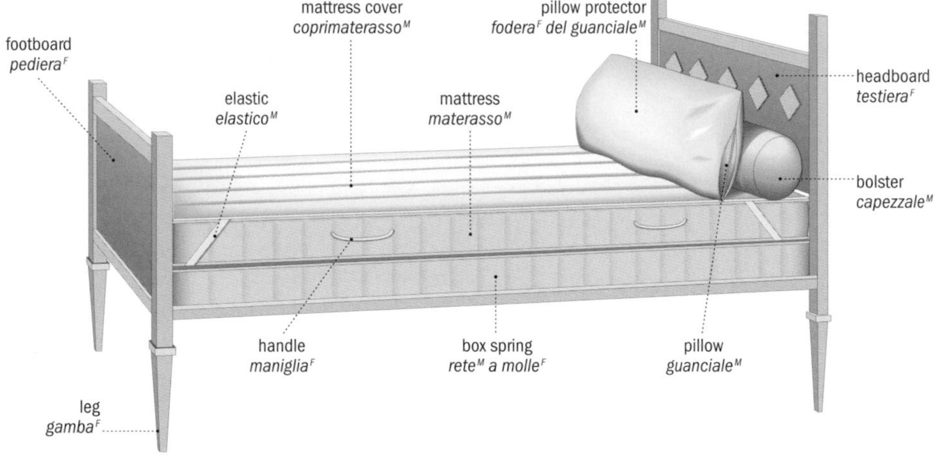

linen
biancheria^F da letto^M

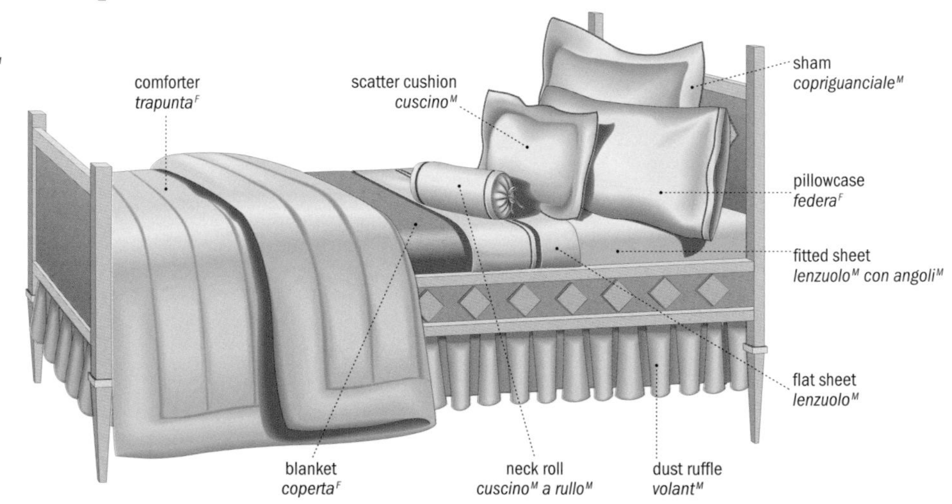

children's furniture

mobili^M per bambini^M

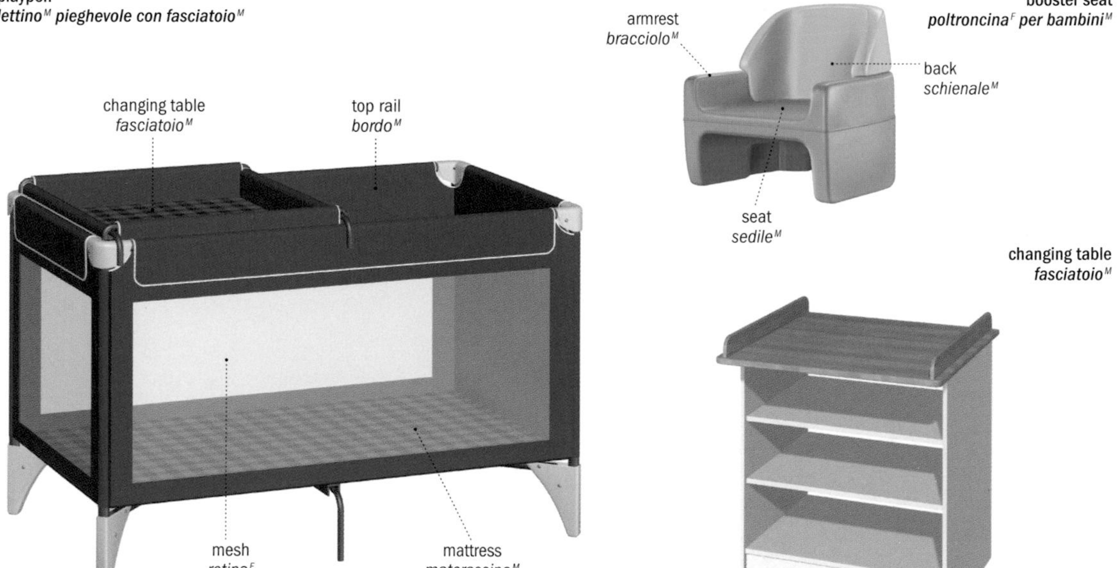

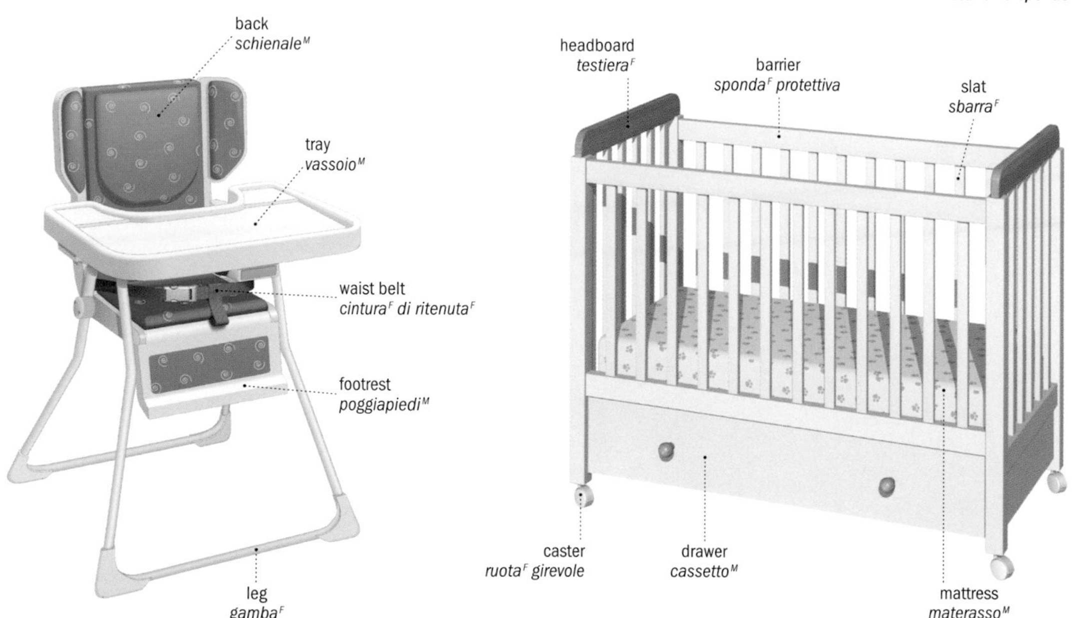

lights

luci[F]

clamp spotlight
faretto[M] a pinza[F]

ceiling fixture
plafoniera[F]

hanging pendant
lampada[F] a sospensione[F]

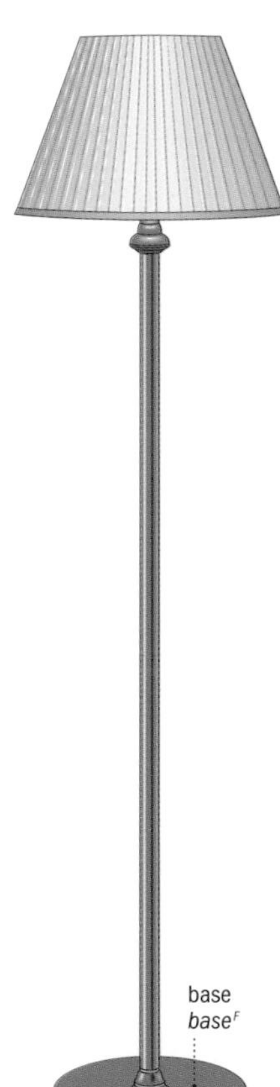

floor lamp
lampada[F] a stelo[M]

halogen desk lamp
lampada[F] alogena da tavolo[M]

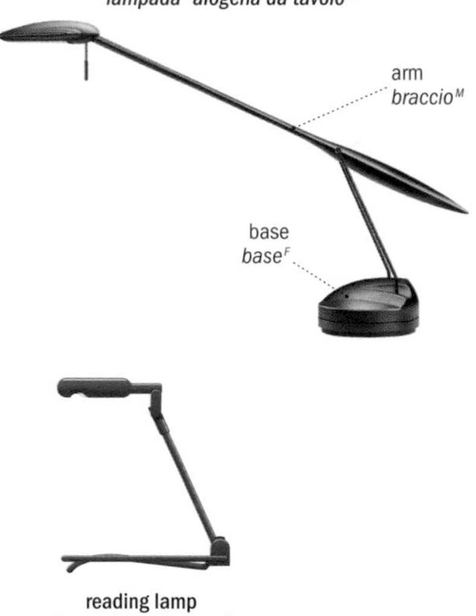

reading lamp
lampada[F] da lettura[F]

table lamp
lampada[F] da tavolo[M]

adjustable lamp
lampada[F] a braccio[M] regolabile

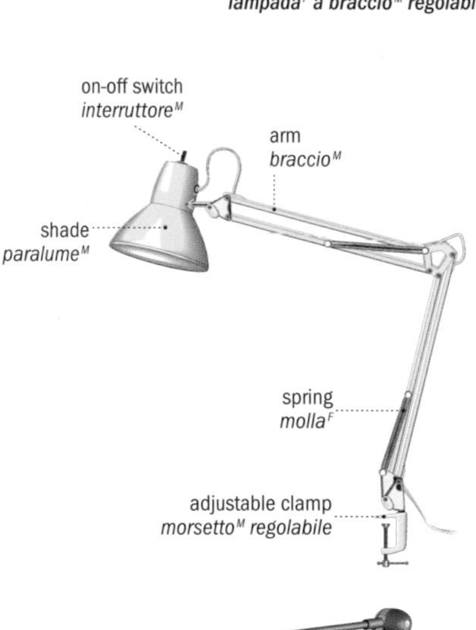

desk lamp
lampada[F] da tavolo[M]

HOUSE

chandelier
lampadario^M
bobeche
coppetta^F
crystal drop
goccia^F di cristallo^M
crystal button
perlina^F di cristallo^M
column
colonna^F
track lighting
faretto^M da binario^M
bar frame
binario^M
transformer
trasformatore^M
contact lever
leva^F di contatto^M
spot
faretto^M orientabile
wall lantern
lampione^M da parete^F
wall sconce
lampada^F da parete^F
swivel wall lamp
lampada^F da parete^F con braccio^M estensibile
strip lights
lampade^F in serie^F
post lantern
lampione^M

domestic appliances

elettrodomestici^M

steam iron
ferro^M da stiro^M a vapore^M

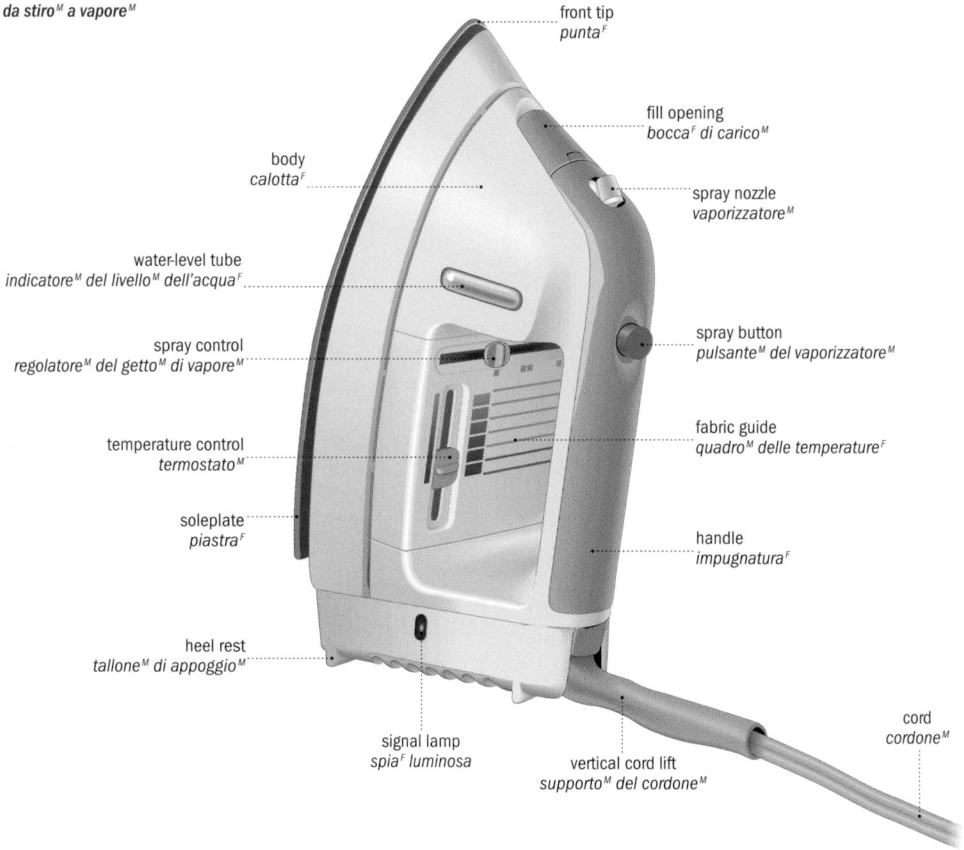

front tip
punta^F
fill opening
bocca^F di carico^M
body
calotta^F
spray nozzle
vaporizzatore^M
water-level tube
indicatore^M del livello^M dell'acqua^F
spray control
regolatore^M del getto^M di vapore^M
spray button
pulsante^M del vaporizzatore^M
fabric guide
quadro^M delle temperature^F
temperature control
termostato^M
soleplate
piastra^F
handle
impugnatura^F
heel rest
tallone^M di appoggio^M
cord
cordone^M
signal lamp
spia^F luminosa
vertical cord lift
supporto^M del cordone^M

hand held vacuum cleaner
miniaspiratutto^M

locking button
pulsante^M di bloccaggio^M
on-off switch
interruttore^M
dust receiver
vano^M raccoglipolvere
recharging base
presa^F per ricarica^F
motor unit
blocco^M motore^M

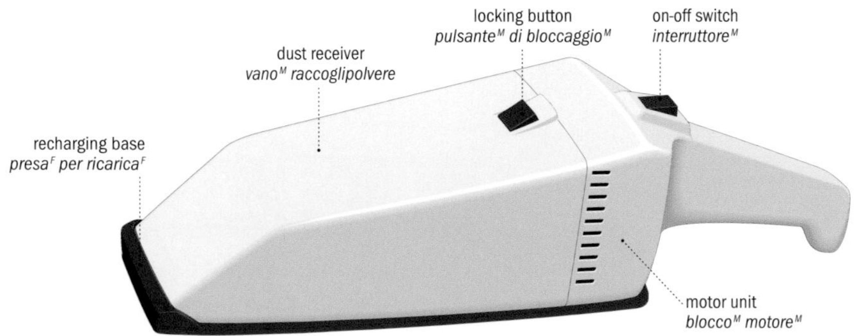

upright vacuum cleaner
aspirapolvere[M] verticale

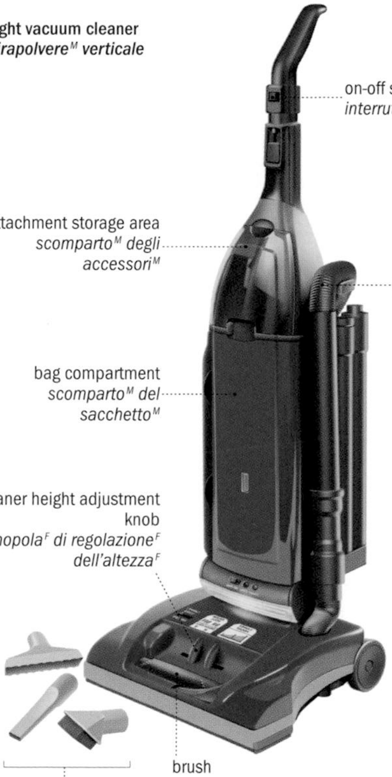

on-off switch
interruttore[M]

attachment storage area
scomparto[M] degli accessori[M]

hose
tubo[M] flessibile

bag compartment
scomparto[M] del sacchetto[M]

cleaner height adjustment knob
manopola[F] di regolazione[F] dell'altezza[F]

attachments
accessori[M]

brush
spazzola[F]

cylinder vacuum cleaner
aspirapolvere[M]

locking device
dispositivo[M] di bloccaggio[M]

pipe
tubo[M] rigido

flexible hose
tubo[M] flessibile

ventilating grille
griglia[F] di ventilazione[F]

on-off switch
interruttore[M]

bumper
protezione[F] antiurto

extension pipe
tubo[M] rigido di prolunga[F]

caster
ruota[F] orientabile

cord
cordone[M]

handle
maniglia[F]

rug and floor brush
spazzola[F] per tappeti[M] e pavimenti[M]

hood
calotta[F]

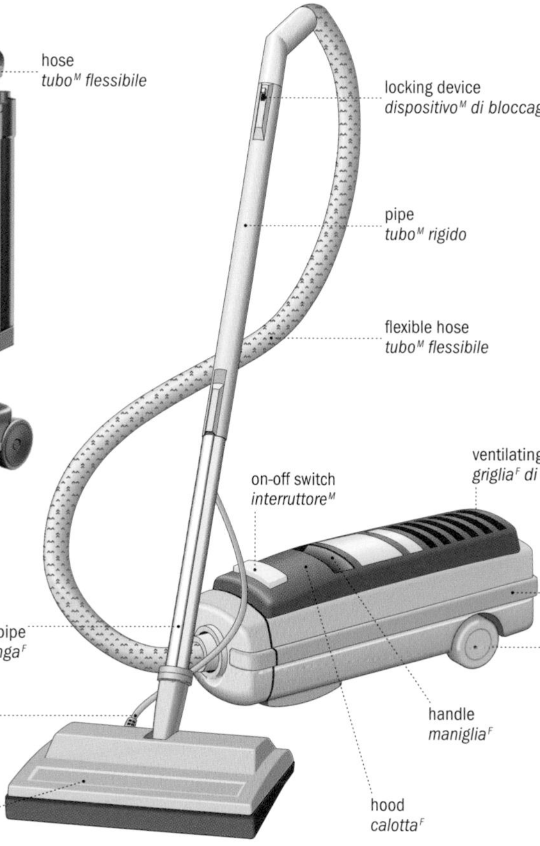

vacuum cleaner attachments
accessori[M] di pulitura[F]

upholstery nozzle
bocchetta[F] per tappezzeria[F]

dusting brush
spazzola[F] a pennello[M]

crevice tool
bocchetta[F] per fessure[F]

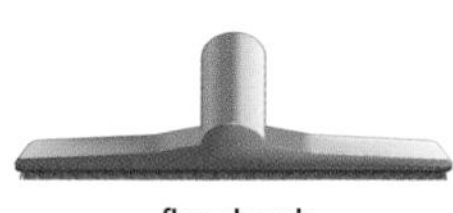

floor brush
spazzola[F] per pavimenti[M]

domestic appliances

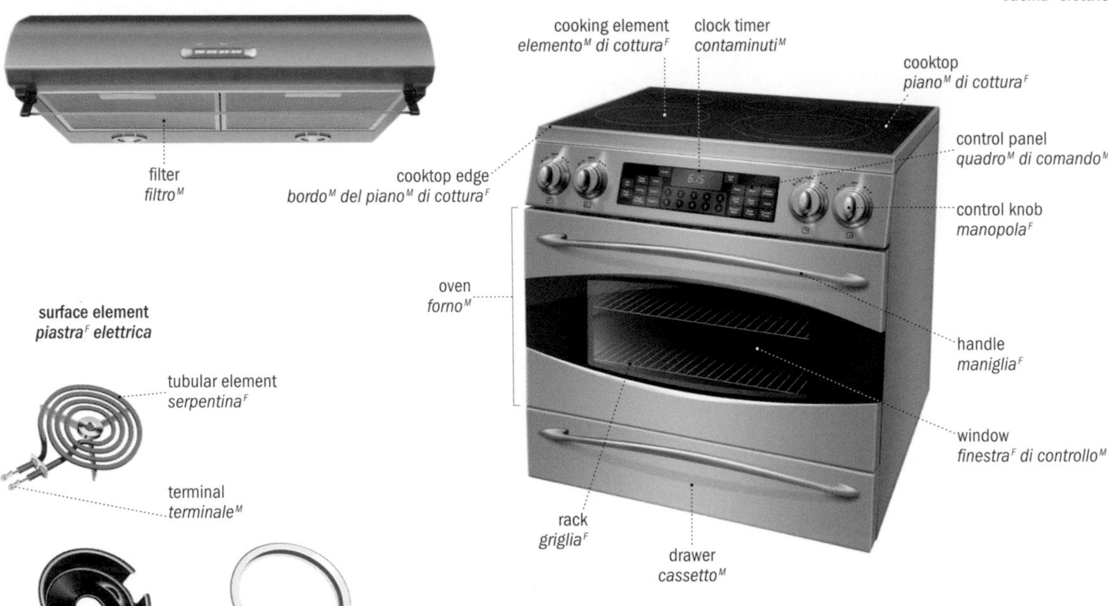

HOUSE

chest freezer
congelatore[M] orizzontale

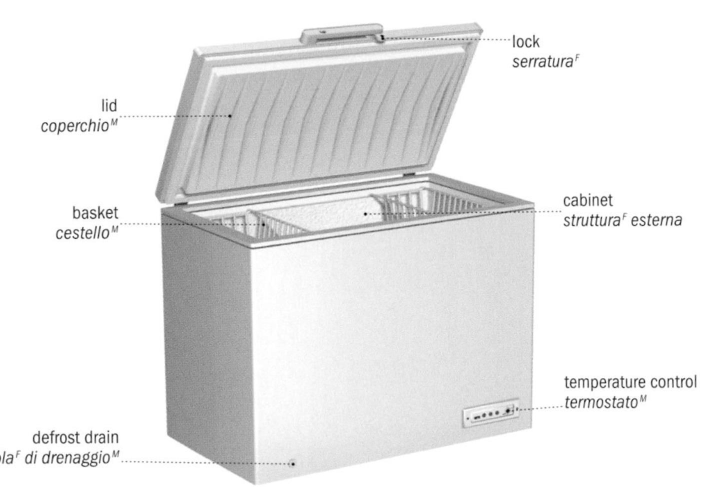

refrigerator
frigorifero[M]

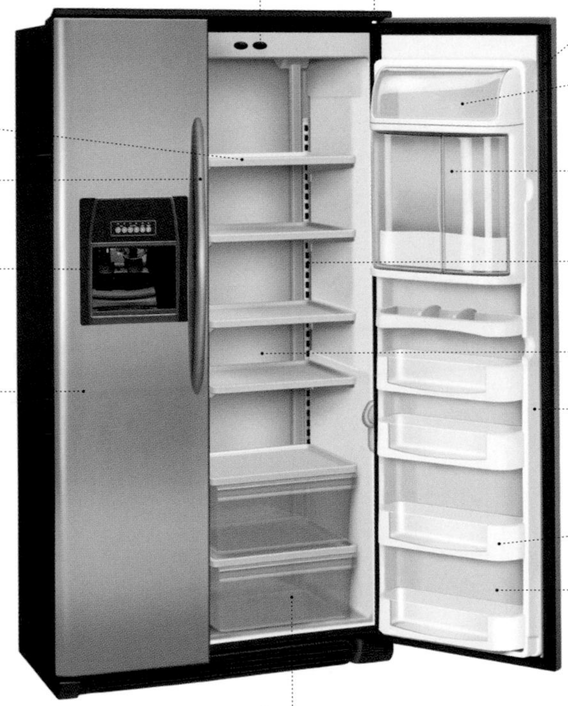

switch
interruttore[M]

door stop
fermaporta[M]

magnetic gasket
guarnizione[F] magnetica

shelf
ripiano[M]

butter compartment
scomparto[M] per il burro[M]

handle
maniglia[F]

meat keeper
cassetto[M] per la carne[F]

water dispenser
distributore[M] automatico d'acqua[F]

shelf channel
griglia[F] dei ripiani[M]

refrigerator compartment
scomparto[M] del frigorifero[M]

freezer compartment
scomparto[M] del congelatore[M]

storage door
controporta[F] attrezzata

guard rail
listarella[F]

dairy compartment
scomparto[M] per i latticini[M]

crisper
cassetto[M] per la verdura[F]

domestic appliances

front-loading washer
lavabiancheria[F] a carica[F] frontale

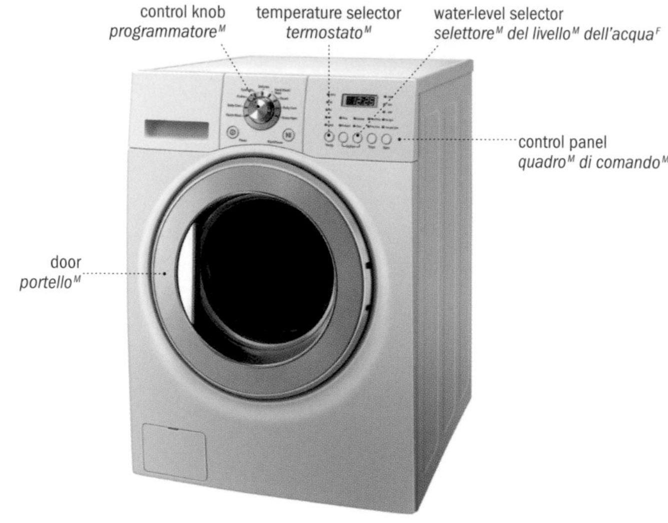

top-loading washer
lavabiancheria[F] a carica[F] verticale

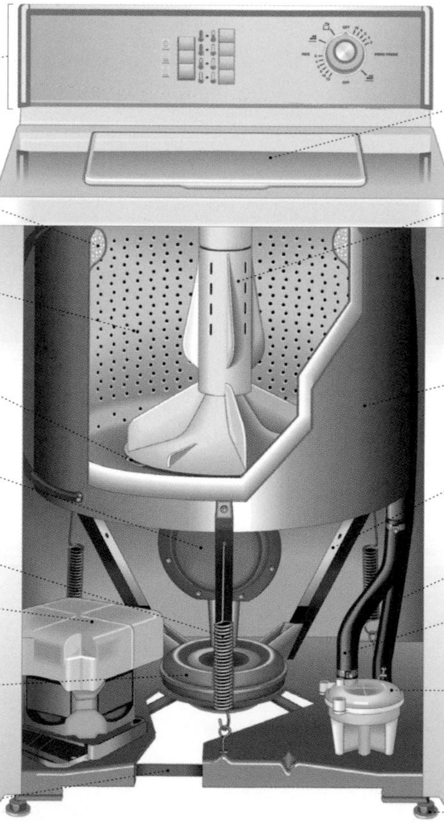

backguard
alzata[F]

lid
coperchio[M]

tub rim
orlo[M] della vasca[F]

agitator
centrifuga[F]

basket
cestello[M]

cabinet
struttura[F] esterna

lint filter
filtro[M] per lanugine[F]

tub
vasca[F]

transmission
trasmissione[F]

suspension arm
braccio[M] di sospensione[F]

spring
molla[F]

drain hose
tubo[M] di drenaggio[M]

motor
motore[M]

emptying hose
tubo[M] di scarico[M]

torque converter
convertitore[M] di coppia[F]

pump
pompa[F]

drive belt
cinghia[F] di tramissione[F]

leveling foot
piedino[M] regolabile

dryer
***asciugatrice*[F]**

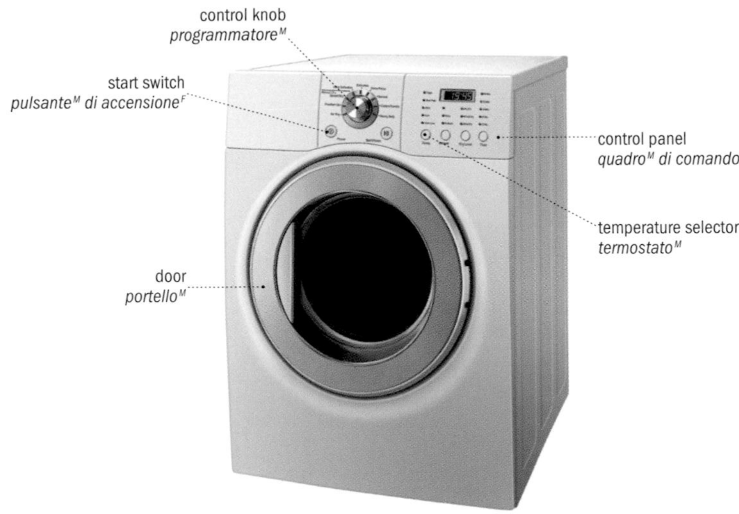

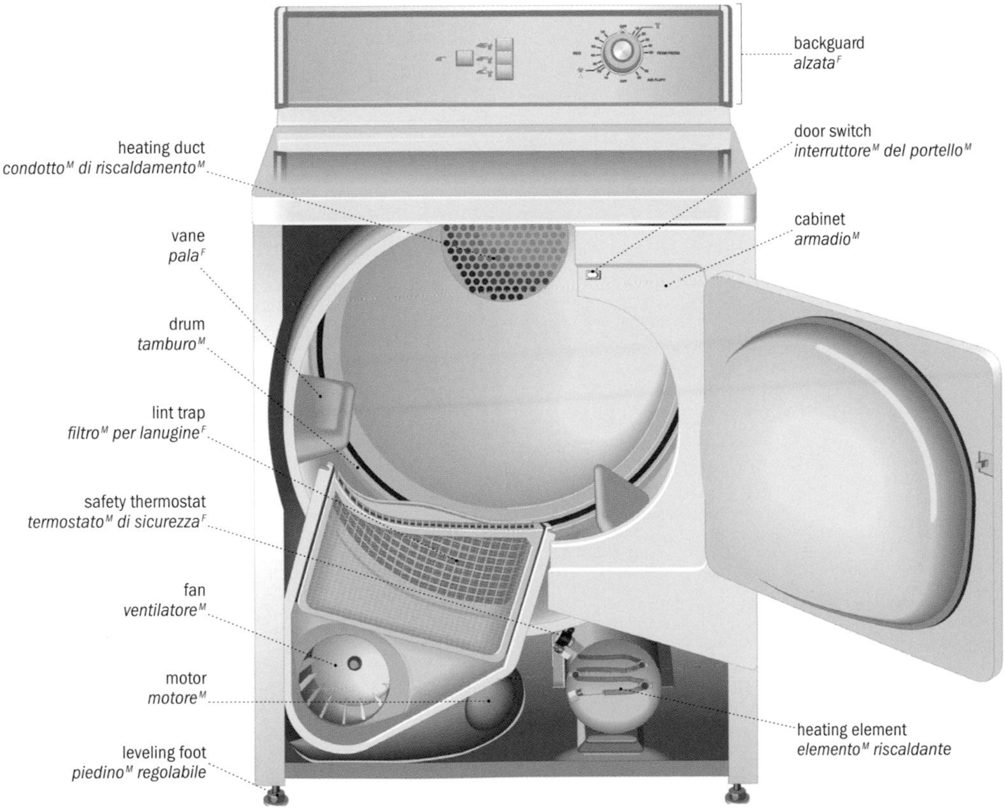

backguard
alzata[F]

heating duct
condotto[M] *di riscaldamento*[M]

door switch
interruttore[M] *del portello*[M]

cabinet
armadio[M]

vane
pala[F]

drum
tamburo[M]

lint trap
filtro[M] *per lanugine*[F]

safety thermostat
termostato[M] *di sicurezza*[F]

fan
ventilatore[M]

motor
motore[M]

heating element
elemento[M] *riscaldante*

leveling foot
piedino[M] *regolabile*

HOUSE

control panel: dishwasher
***quadro*[M] *di comando*[M]**

control buttons
tasti[M] di comando[M]
signal lamp
spia[F] luminosa
air vent
sfiatatoio[M]
handle
maniglia[F]

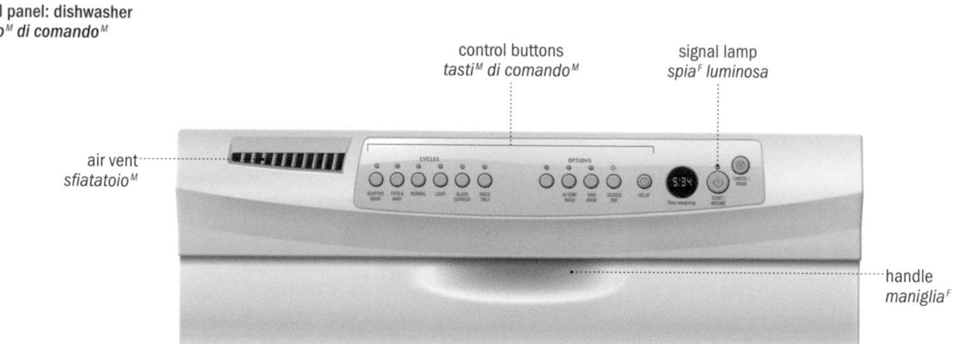

dishwasher
***lavastoviglie*[F]**

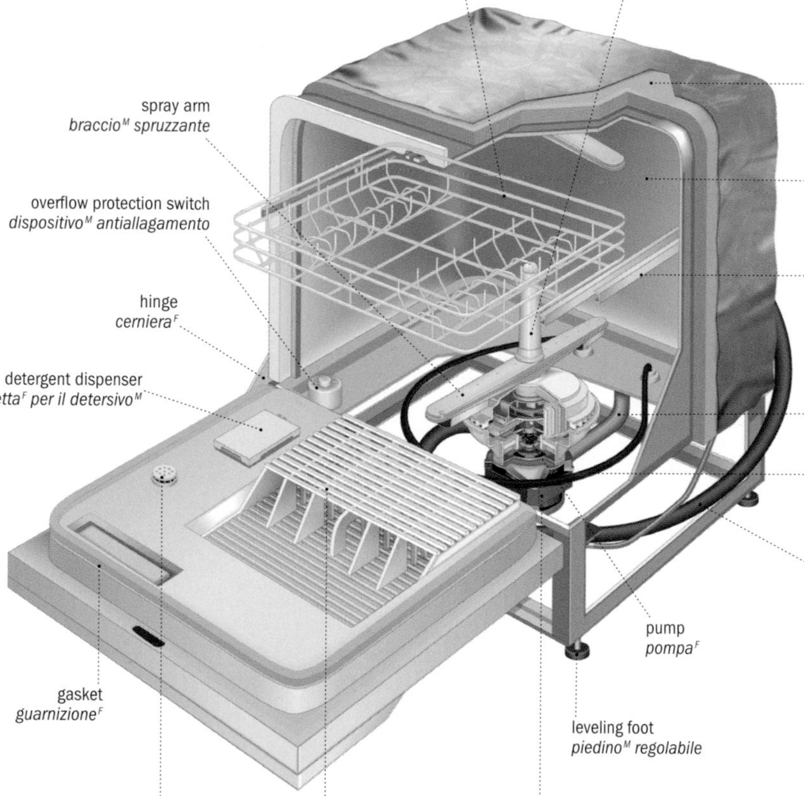

rack
cestello[M]
wash tower
torre[F] di lavaggio[M]
insulating material
materiale[M] isolante
spray arm
braccio[M] spruzzante
tub
vasca[F]
overflow protection switch
dispositivo[M] antiallagamento
slide
guida[F]
hinge
cerniera[F]
water hose
tubo[M] di alimentazione[F] dell'acqua[F]
detergent dispenser
vaschetta[F] per il detersivo[M]
heating element
elemento[M] riscaldante
drain hose
tubo[M] di drenaggio[M]
pump
pompa[F]
gasket
guarnizione[F]
leveling foot
piedino[M] regolabile
rinse-aid dispenser
serbatoio[M] per il brillantante[M]
cutlery basket
cestello[M] per le posate[F]
motor
motore[M]

household equipment

attrezzi[M] domestici

plumbing tools

attrezzi^{M} idraulici

plunger
sturalavandini^{M}

plumber's snake
molla^{F} sturatrice per scarichi^{M}

Teflon® tape
nastro^{M} di Teflon®^{M}

wrenches
chiavi^{F}

basin wrench
chiave^{F} regolabile da lavandino^{M}

pipe wrench
giratubi^{M}

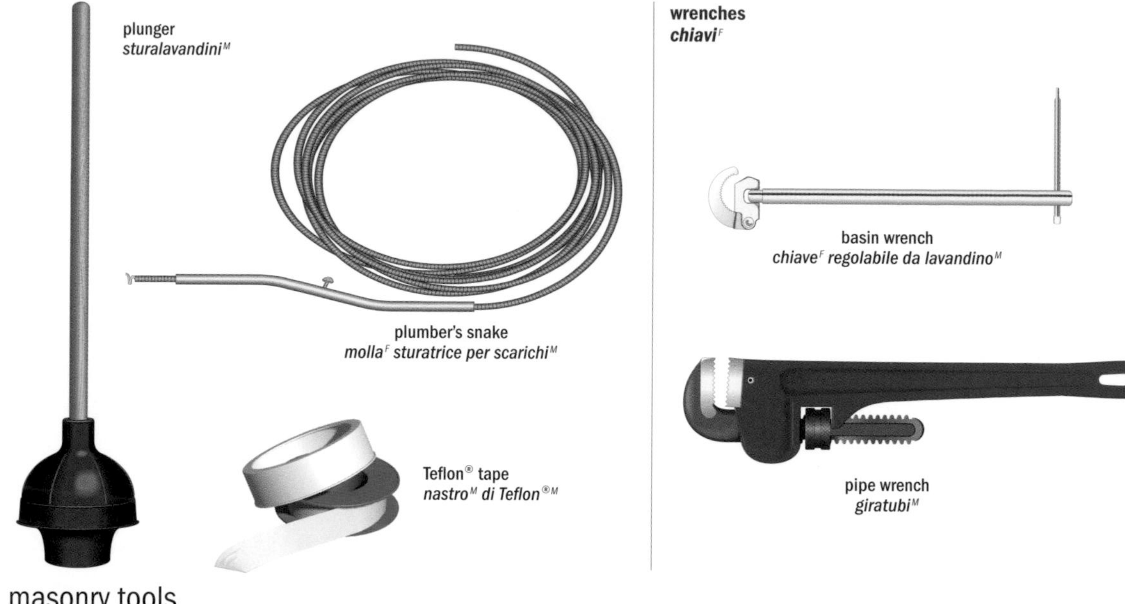

masonry tools

attrezzi^{M} da muratore^{M}

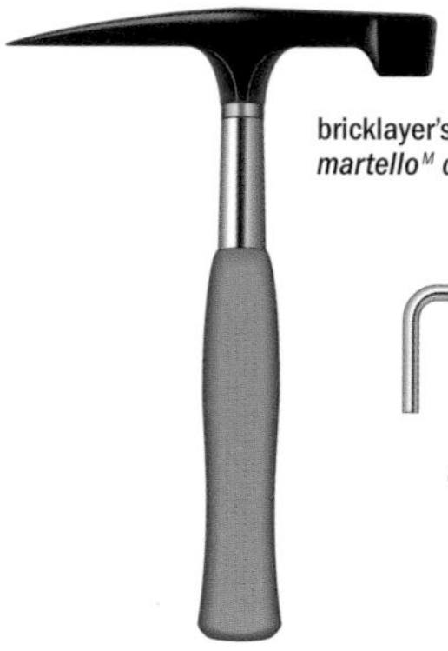

bricklayer's hammer
martello^{M} da muratore^{M}

caulking gun
pistola^{F} turapori

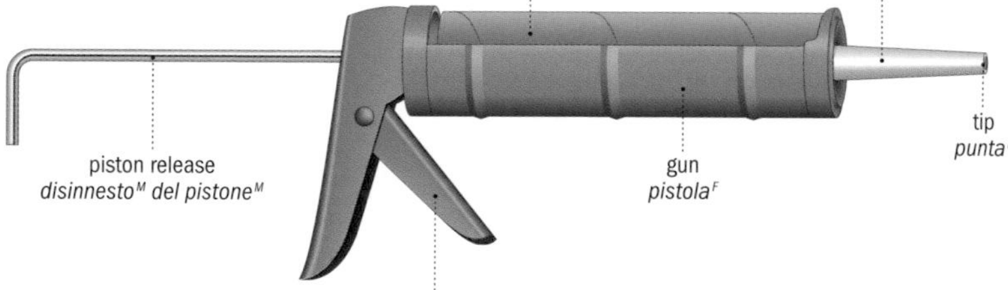

cartridge
cartuccia^{F}
nozzle
ugello^{M}
piston release
disinnesto^{M} del pistone^{M}
gun
pistola^{F}
tip
punta^{F}
piston lever
leva^{F} del pistone^{M}

hawk
sparviero^{M}

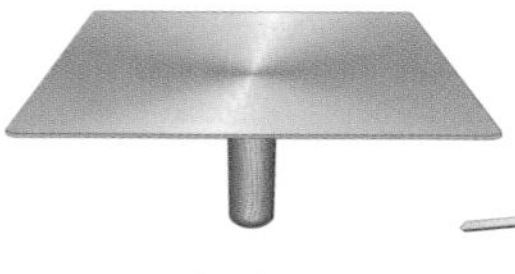

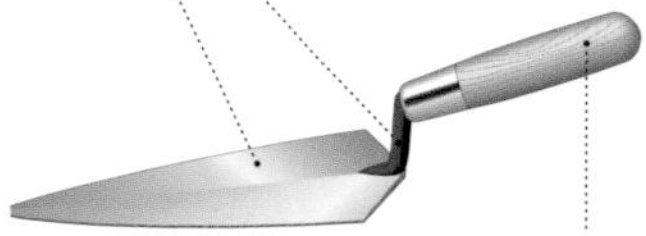

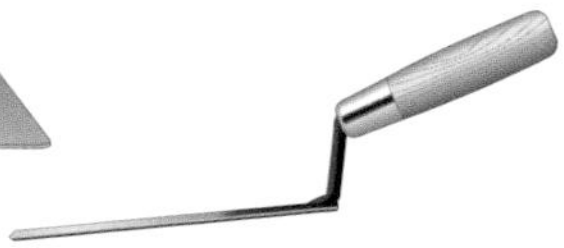

joint filler
paletta^{F} riempigiunti

square trowel
frattazzo^{M}

mason's trowel
cazzuola^{F} da muratore^{M}

blade
lama^{F}
tang
codolo^{M}
handle
manico^{M}

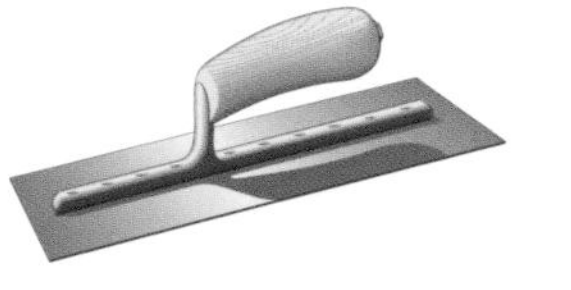

electricity tools

attrezzatura^F elettrica

drop light
lampada^F portatile a gabbia^F

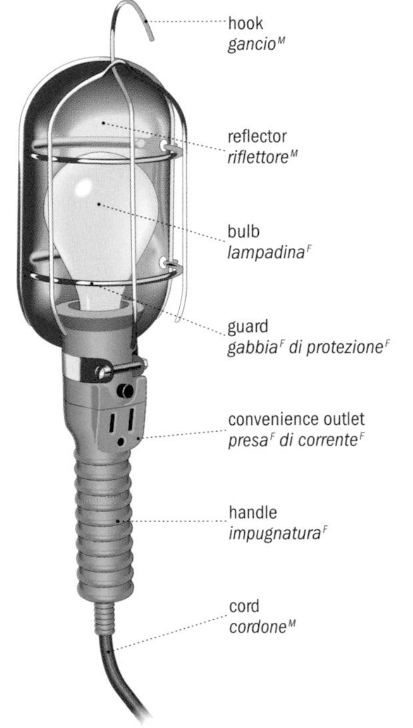

neon tester
lampada^F provacircuiti

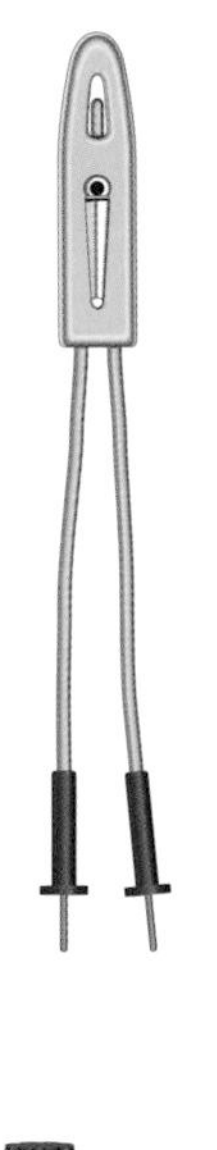

voltage tester
cercafase^M

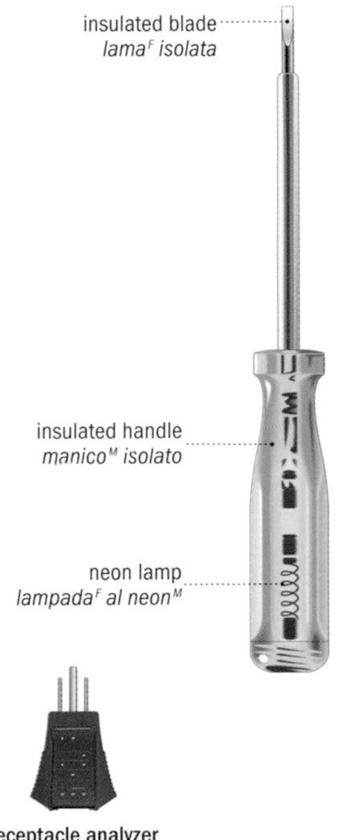

wire nut
proteggicavo^M

receptacle analyzer
tester^M di presa^F

multipurpose tool
pinza^F multiuso

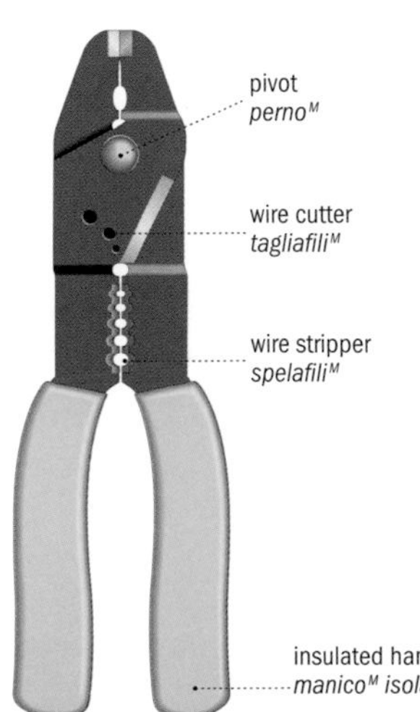

needle-nose pliers
pinza^F a becchi^M lunghi

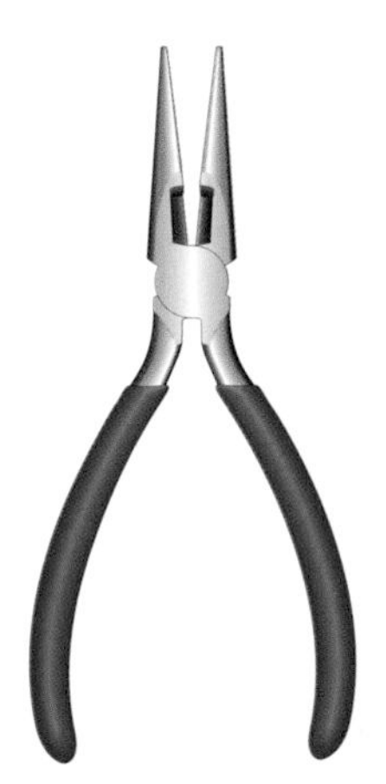

lineman's pliers
pinza^F universale

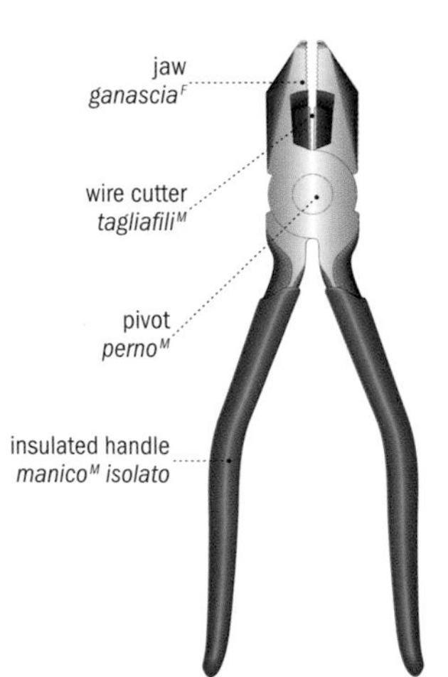

soldering and welding tools

attrezzi[M] di brasatura[F] e saldatura[F]

soldering gun
saldatore[M] a pistola[F]

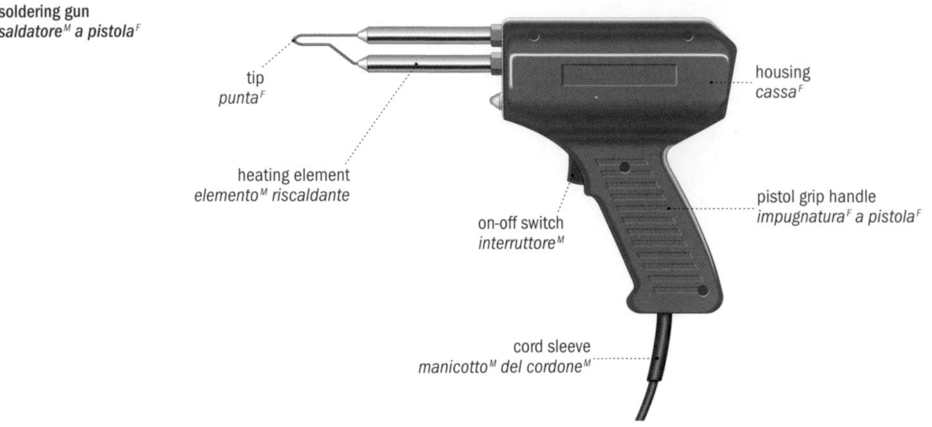

striker
acciarino[M]

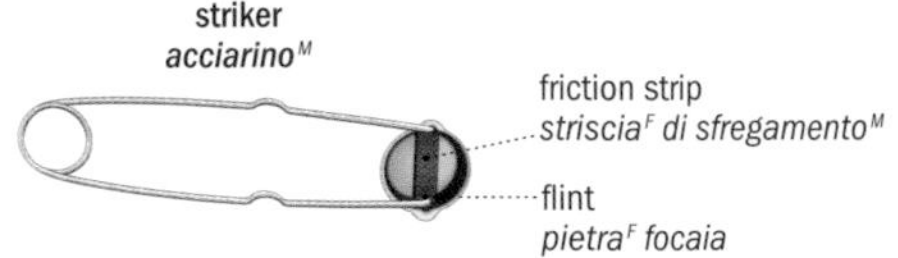

solder
filo[M] per saldatura[F]

tip cleaners
alesatori[M] per la pulizia[F] degli ugelli[M]

soldering torch
lampada[F] per saldare

pencil-point tip
ugello[M]

disposable fuel cylinder
bombola[F] del gas[M]

flame spreader tip
diffusore[M] della fiamma[F]

goggles
occhiali[M] di protezione[F]

soldering iron
saldatore[M] elettrico

wrenches
chiavi[F]

crescent wrench
chiave[F] *a rullino*[M]

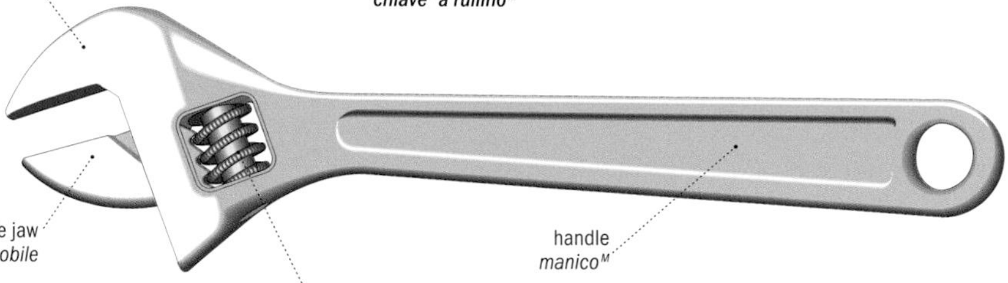
fixed jaw
ganascia[F] fissa
movable jaw
ganascia[F] mobile
thumbscrew
rullino[M]
handle
manico[M]

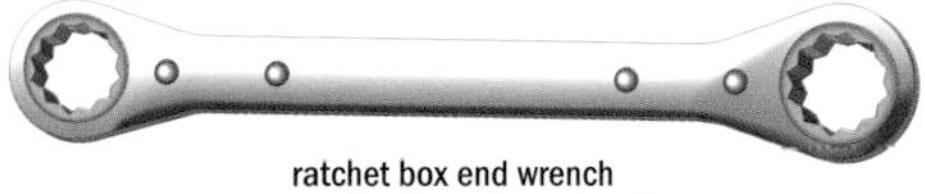
ratchet box end wrench
chiave[F] *poligonale a cricco*[M]

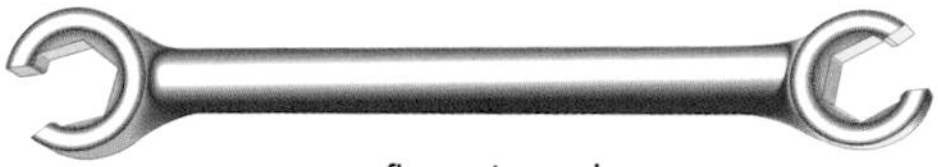
flare nut wrench
chiave[F] *poligonale doppia ad anello*[M] *aperto*

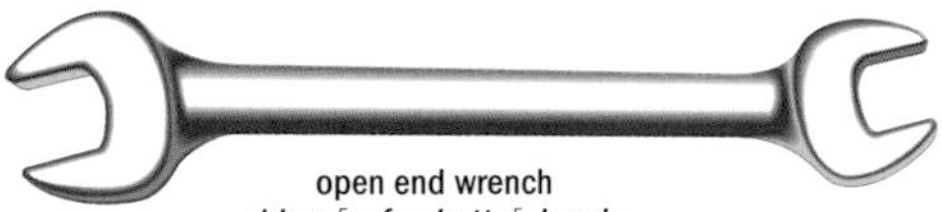
open end wrench
chiave[F] *a forchetta*[F] *doppia*

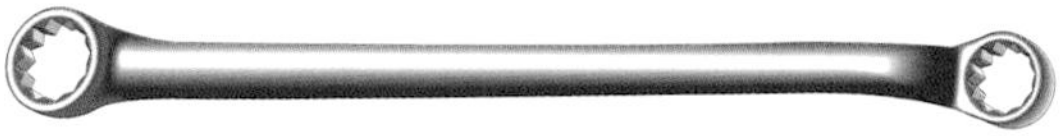
box end wrench
chiave[F] *poligonale doppia*

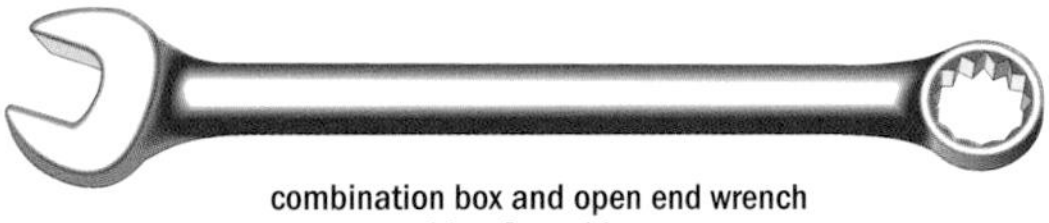
combination box and open end wrench
chiave[F] *combinata*

ratchet socket wrench
chiave[F] *a bussola*[F] *a cricchetto*[M]

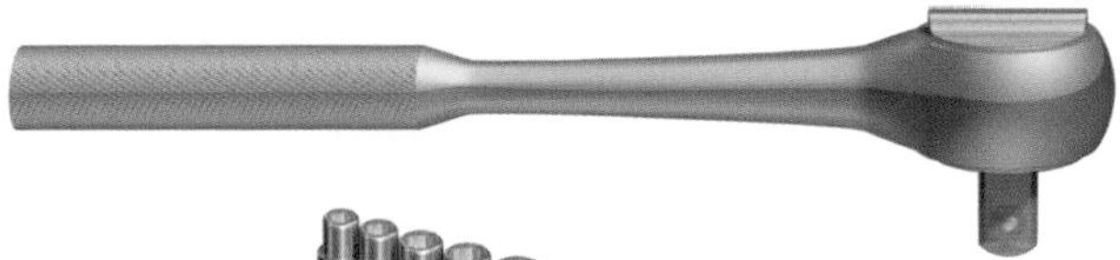

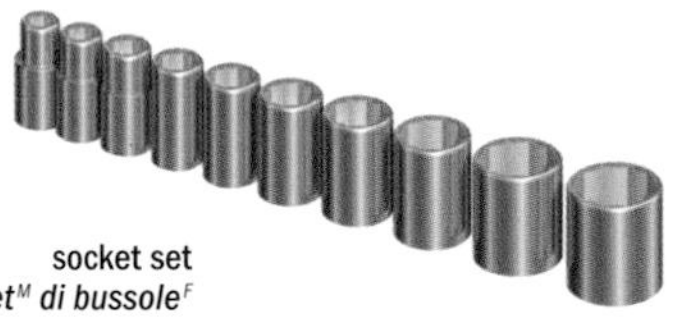
socket set
set[M] *di bussole*[F]

nuts
dadi[M]

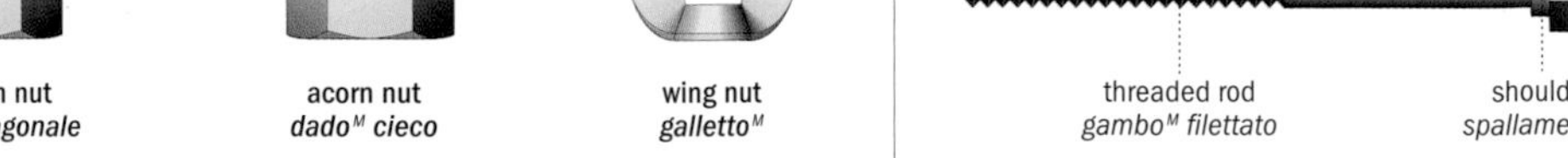

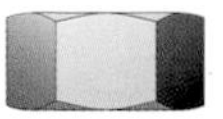
hexagon nut
dado[M] *esagonale*

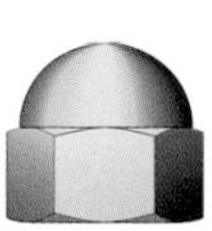
acorn nut
dado[M] *cieco*

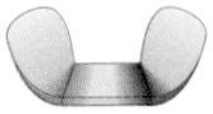
wing nut
galletto[M]

bolts
bulloni[M]

bolt
bullone[M]

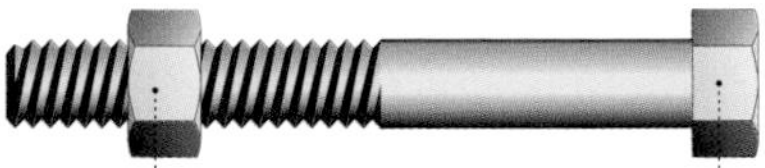
nut
dado[M]
head
testa[F]

shoulder bolt
bullone[M] *di spallamento*[M]

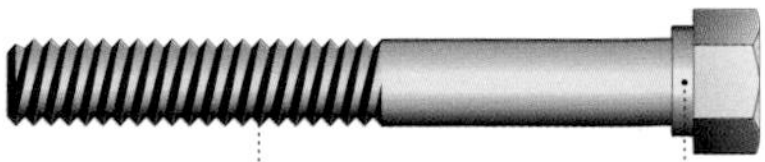
threaded rod
gambo[M] filettato
shoulder
spallamento[M]

DO-IT-YOURSELF AND GARDENING

carpentry: gripping and tightening tools

C-clamp
morsetto*[M] *a C

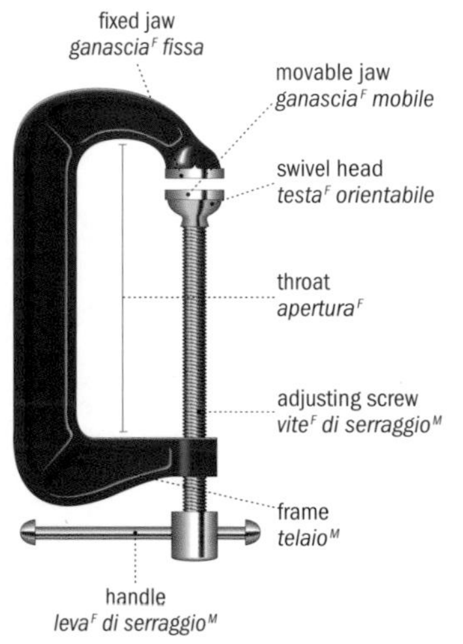

vise
***morsa*[F]**

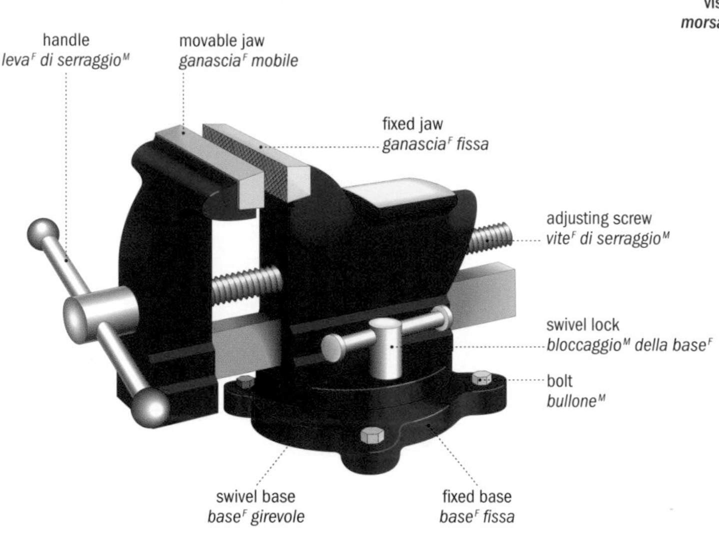

pipe clamp
***morsa*[F] *serratubi*[M]**

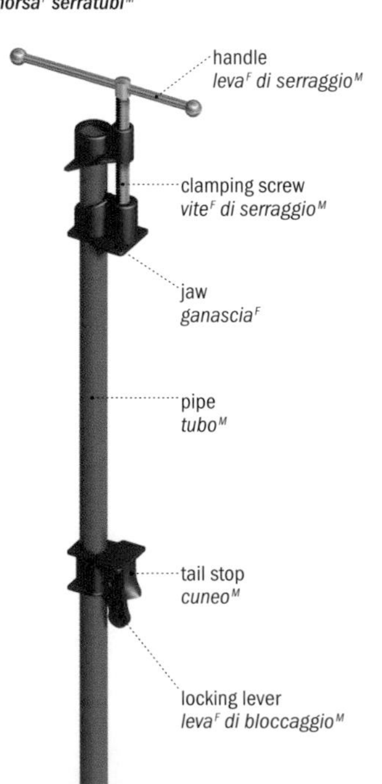

work bench and vise
***piano*[M] *di lavoro*[M] *a morsa*[F]**

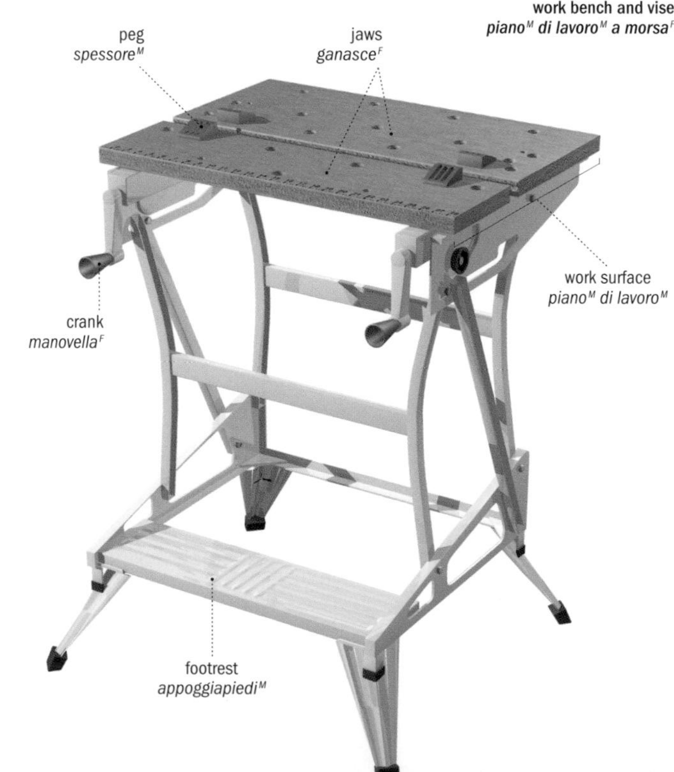

carpentry: measuring and marking tools

carpenteria^{F}: strumenti^{M} di misurazione^{F} e tracciamento^{M}

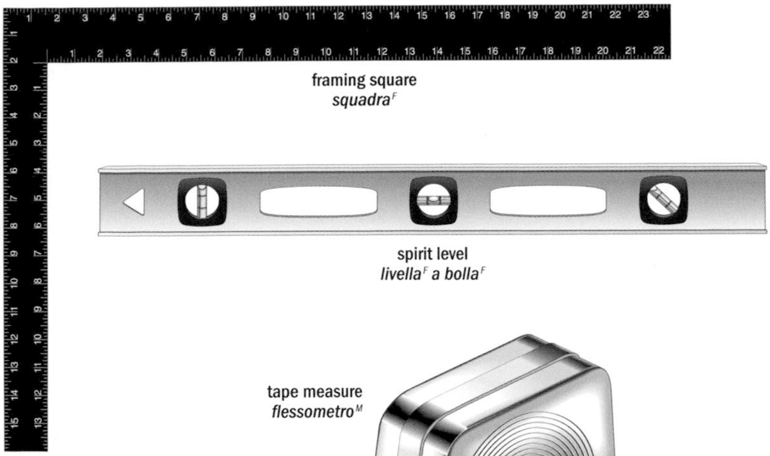

framing square
squadra^{F}

spirit level
livella^{F} a bolla^{F}

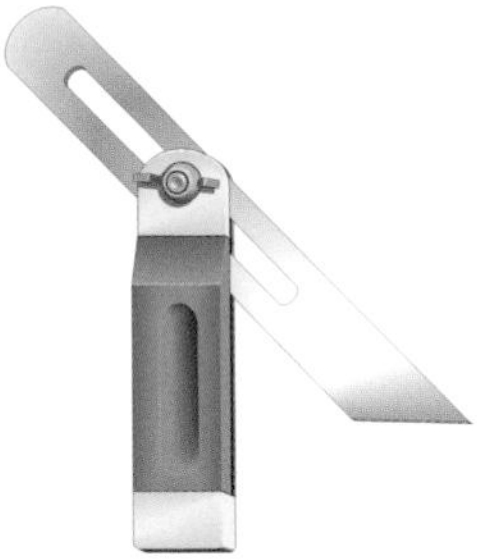

bevel square
squadra^{F} falsa

tape measure
flessometro^{M}

tape lock
fermo^{M} del nastro^{M}
scale
scala^{F}
hook
gancio^{M}
tape
nastro^{M}
case
involucro^{M}

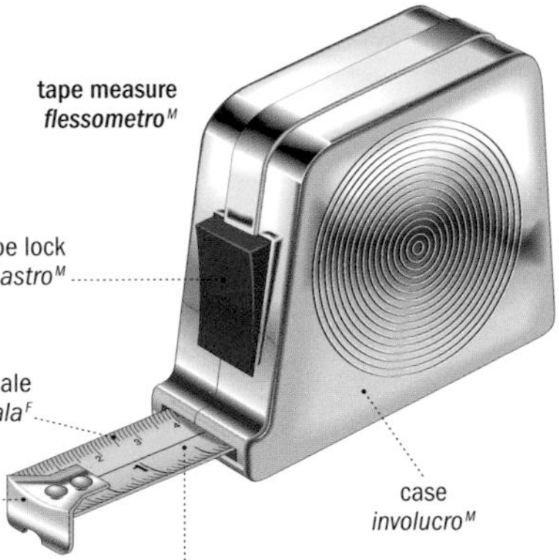

chalk line
filo^{M} di tracciamento^{M}

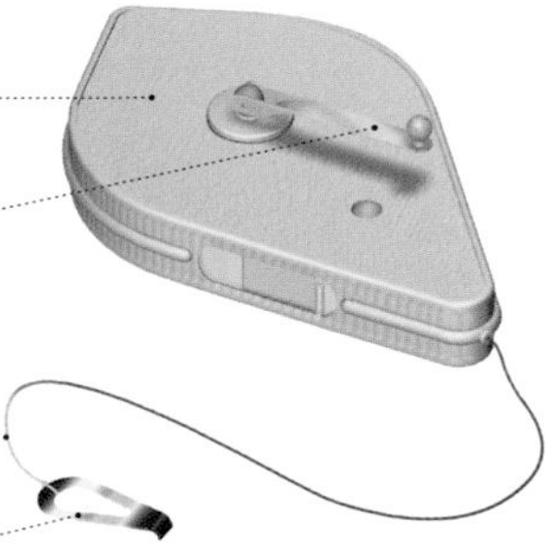

case
involucro^{M}
crank handle
manovella^{F} d'avvolgimento^{M}
line
filo^{M}
hook
gancio^{M}

carpentry: miscellaneous material

carpenteria^{F}: materiale^{M} vario

tool box
cassetta^{F} degli attrezzi^{M}

handle
maniglia^{F}
lid
coperchio^{M}
tray
piano^{M} a scomparti^{M}

tool belt
cintura^{F} portautensili

belt
cintura^{F}
hammer loop
portamartello^{M}
pocket
tasca^{F}

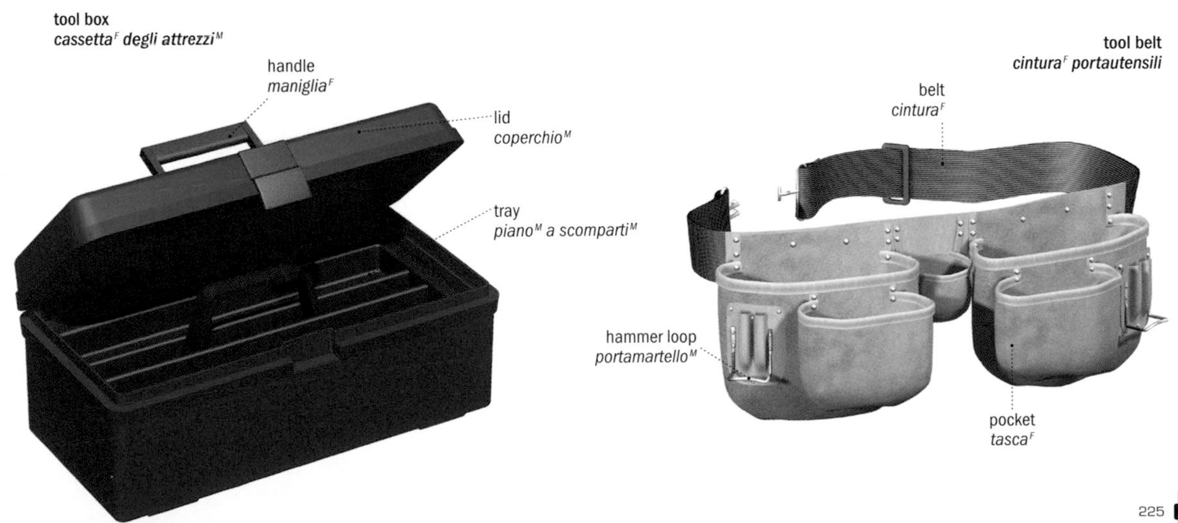

carpentry: sawing tools

carpenteria[F]: utensili[M] per segare

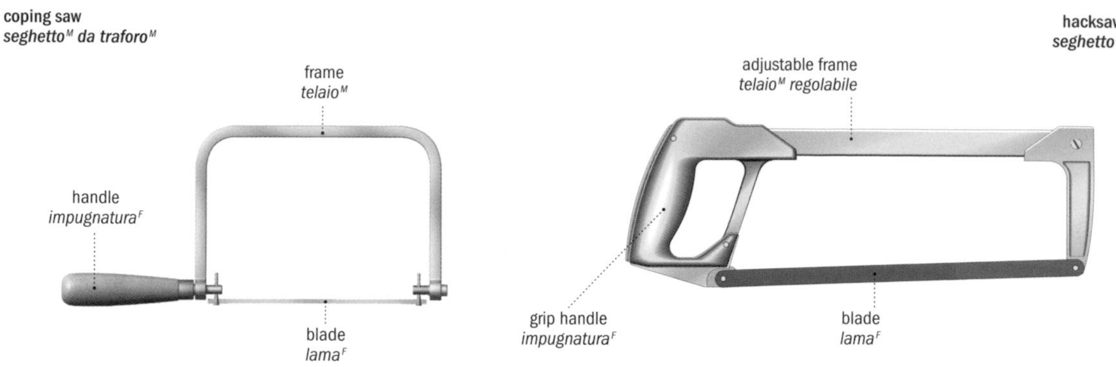

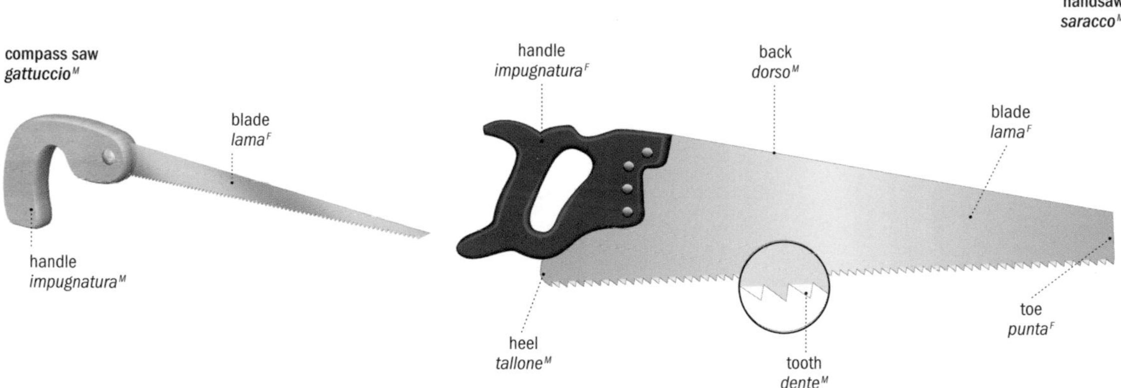

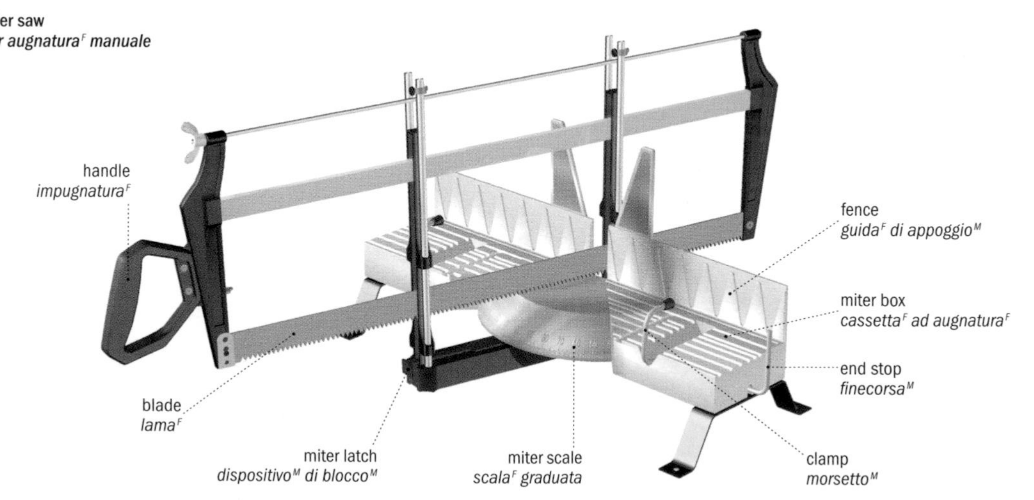

jig saw
seghetto[M] alternativo

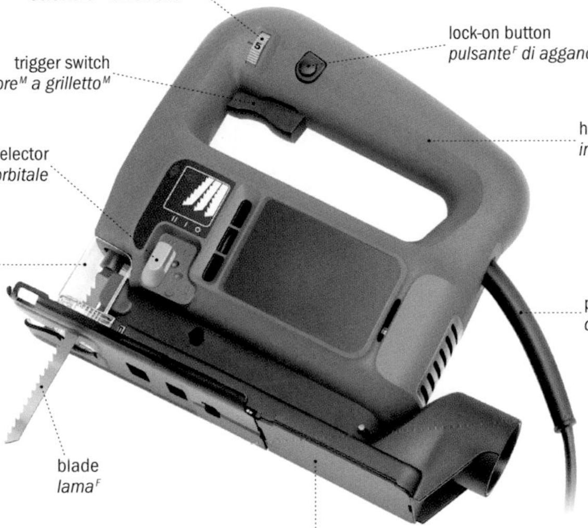

speed selector switch
selettore[M] di velocità[F]
lock-on button
pulsante[F] di aggancio[M]
trigger switch
interruttore[M] a grilletto[M]
handle
impugnatura[F]
orbital-action selector
selettore[M] del movimento[M] orbitale
chip cover
paratrucioli[M]
power cord
cavo[M] di alimentazione[F]
blade
lama[F]
base
basamento[M]

circular saw blade
lama[F] di sega[F] circolare

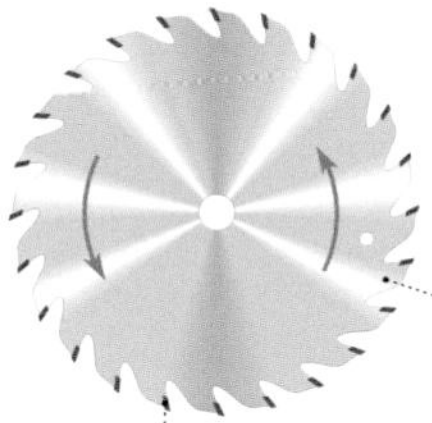

tooth
dente[M]
tip
punta[F]

circular saw
sega[F] circolare

handle
impugnatura[F]
trigger switch
interruttore[M] a grilletto[M]
upper blade guard
paralama[M] superiore
height adjustment scale
indice[M] di regolazione[F] dell'altezza[F]
blade
lama[F]
motor
motore[M]
lower guard retracting lever
leva[F] per togliere il paralama[M] inferiore
blade tilting mechanism
regolatore[M] dell'inclinazione[F] della lama[F]
knob handle
poggiamano[M]
blade locking bolt
vite[F] di blocco[M] della lama[F]
lower blade guard
paralama[M] inferiore
blade tilting lock
dispositivo[M] di blocco[M] dell'inclinazione[F] della lama[F]
rip fence
guida[F] parallela
base plate
piastra[F] di base[F]

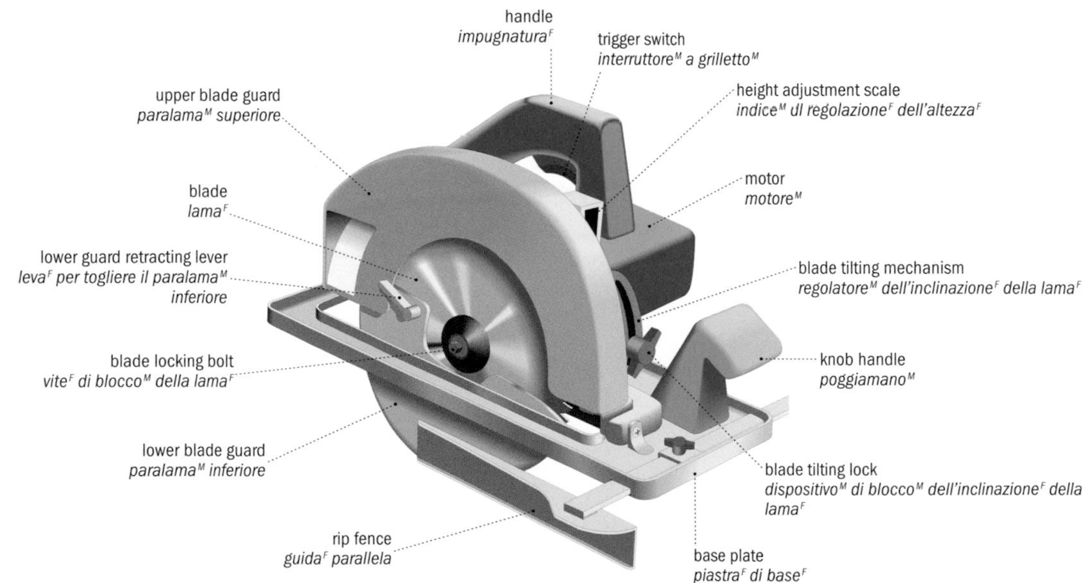

carpentry: drilling tools

carpenteria^F: attrezzi^M per trapanare

cordless drill
trapano^M senza fili^M

electric drill
trapano^M elettrico

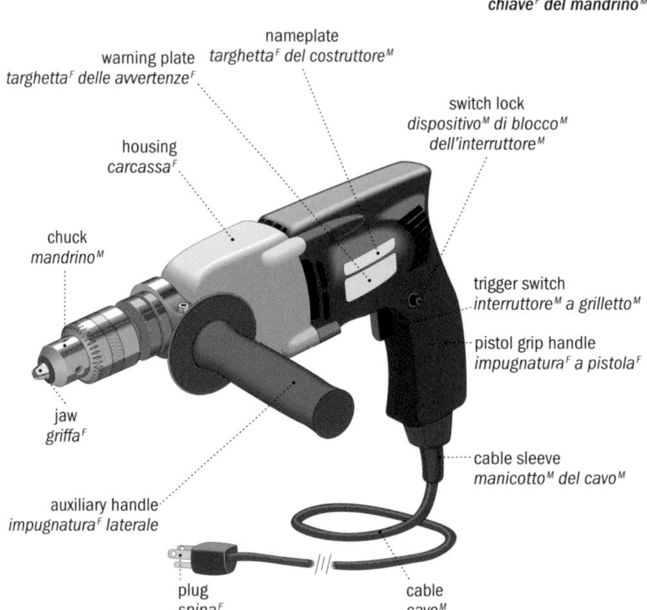

examples of bits and drills
esempi^M di mecchie^F e punte^F da trapano^M

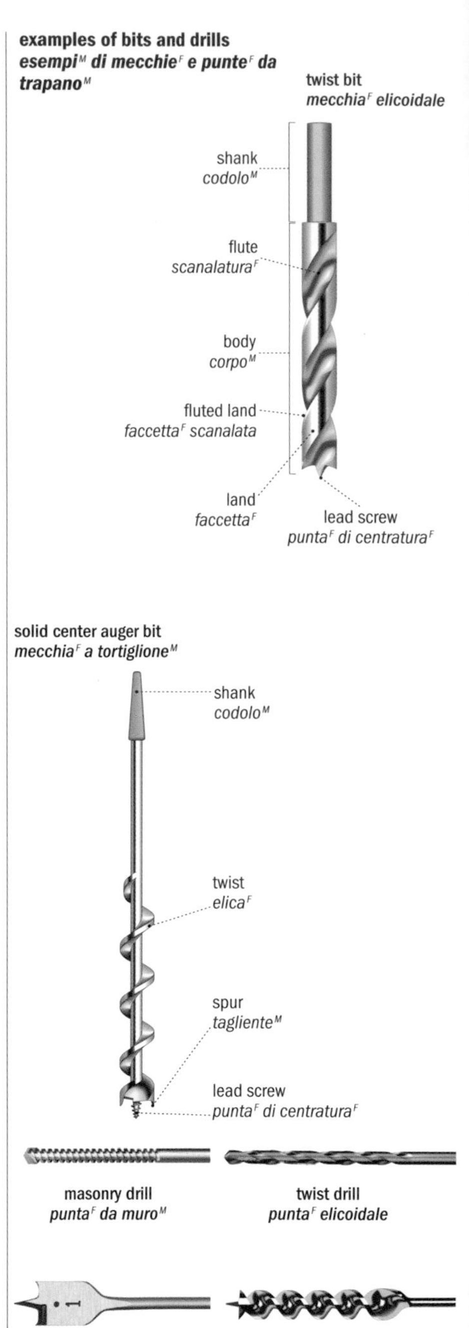

DO-IT-YOURSELF AND GARDENING

carpentry: shaping tools

carpenteria[F]: attrezzi[M] per sagomare

plane
pialla[F]

lateral-adjustment lever
leva[F] di regolazione[F] laterale
wedge lever
leva[F] di serraggio[M]
handle
impugnatura[F]
lever cap
blocco[M] d'arresto[M]
depth-of-cut adjustment knob
manopola[F] di regolazione[F] dell'aggetto[M]
knob
pomolo[M]
heel
tallone[M]
toe
punta[F]
sole
piastra[F] d'appoggio[M]
frog-adjustment screw
vite[F] di regolazione[F]
blade
ferro[M]
cap iron
controferro[M]

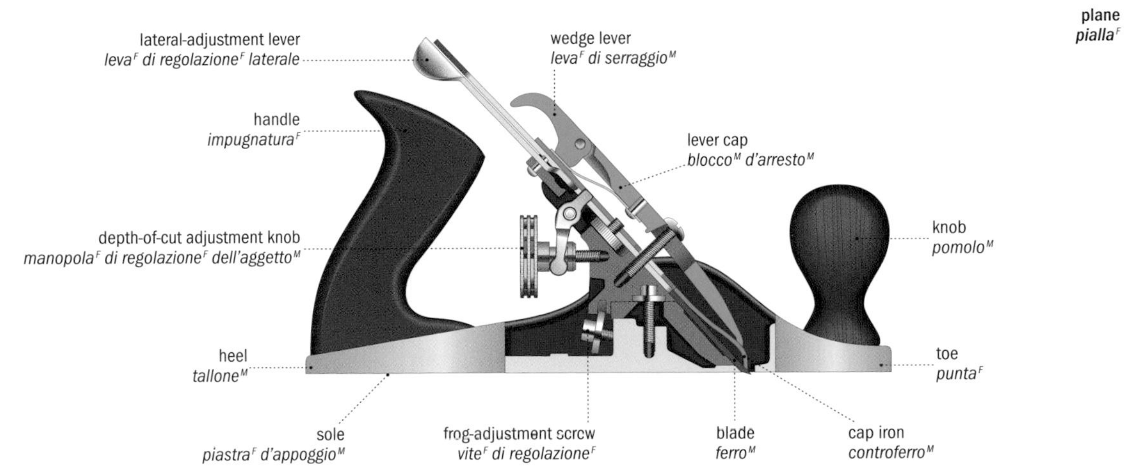

random orbit sander
smerigliatrice[F] eccentrica

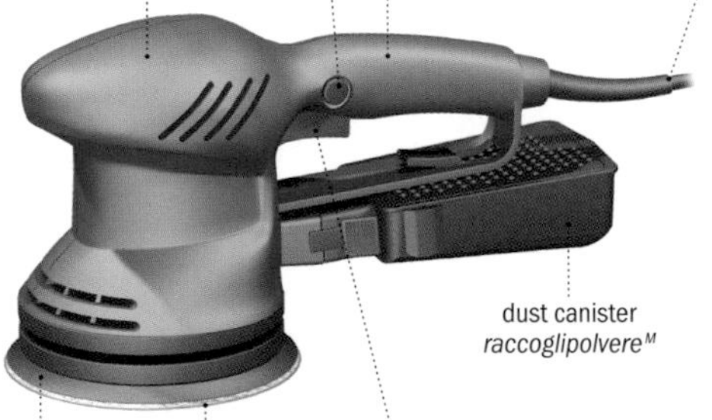

lock-on button
pulsante[M] di arresto[M]
power cord
cavo[M] d'alimentazione[F]
housing
carcassa[F]
handle
impugnatura[F]
dust canister
raccoglipolvere[M]
sanding disk
disco[M] abrasivo
trigger switch
interruttore[M] a grilletto[M]
sanding pad
supporto[M] del disco[M] abrasivo

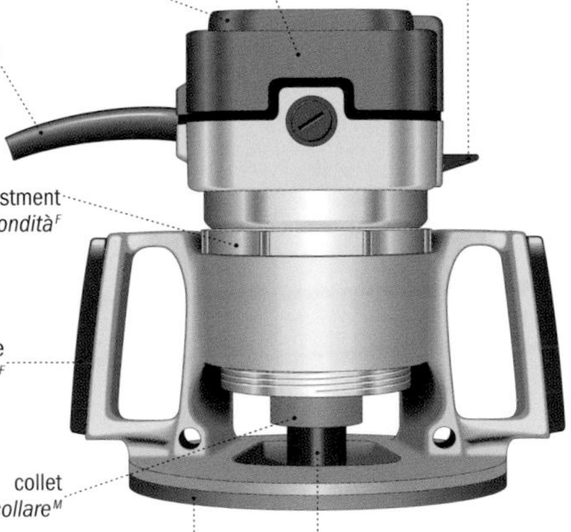

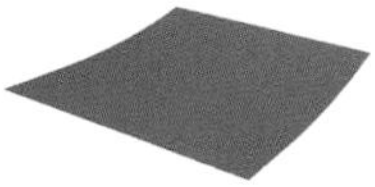

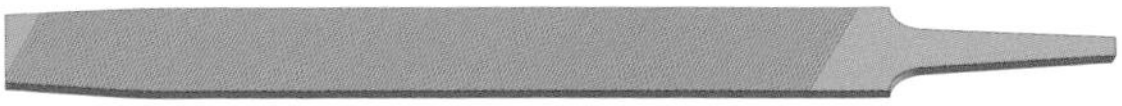

router
fresatrice[F] verticale

motor
motore[M]
head
testa[F]
switch
interruttore[M]
cord sleeve
manicotto[M] del cordone[M]
depth adjustment
regolatore[M] di profondità[F]
guide handle
impugnatura[F]
collet
collare[M]
base
base[F]
tool holder
portautensili[M]

sand paper
carta[F] vetrata

file
lima[F]

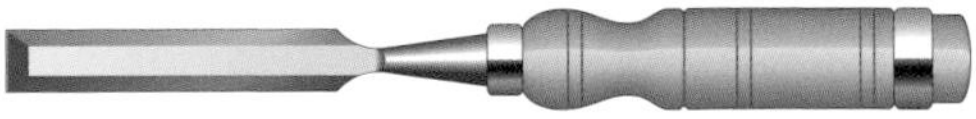

wood chisel
scalpello[M] da falegname[M]

pleasure garden

giardino[M]

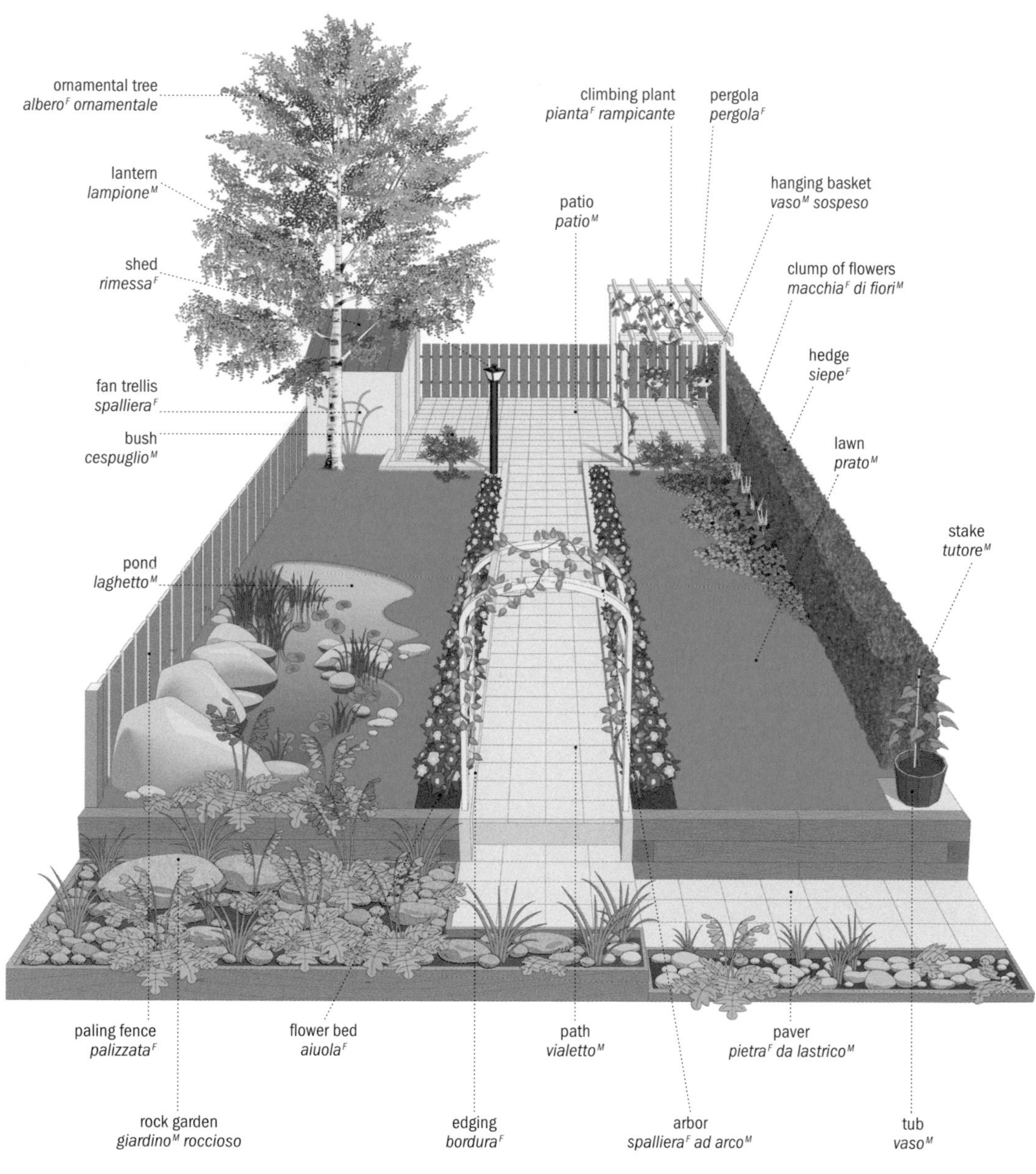

miscellaneous equipment

attrezzatura[F] varia

compost bin
contenitore[M] della composta[F]

wheelbarrow
carriola[F]

seeding and planting tools

attrezzi[M] per seminare e piantare

garden line
filo[M] da giardino[M]

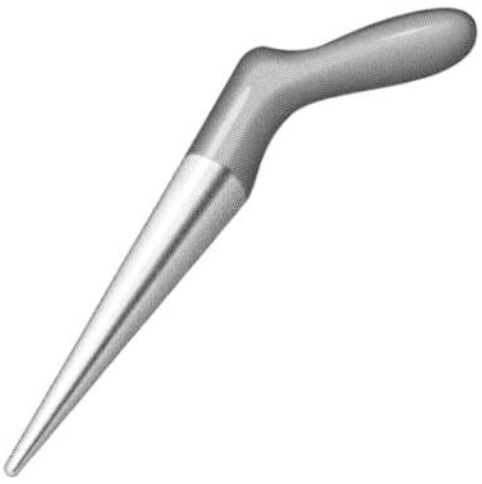

dibble
piantatoio[M]

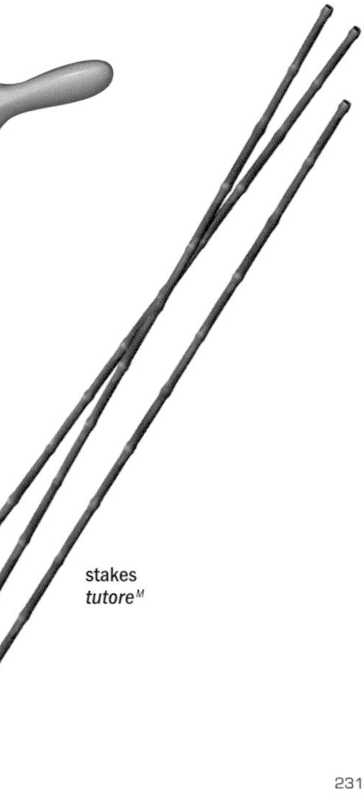

stakes
tutore[M]

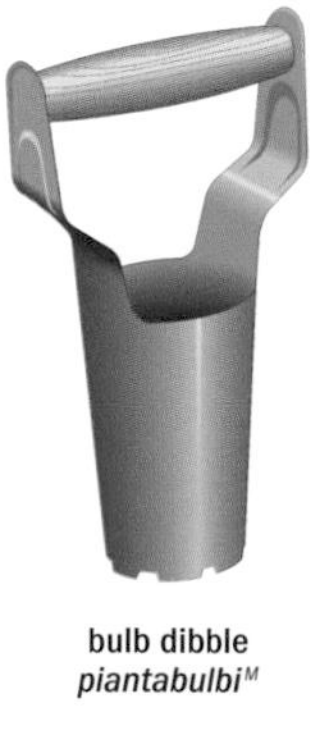

bulb dibble
piantabulbi[M]

seeder
seminatoio[M] a mano[F]

hand tools

attrezzi[M] per piccoli lavori[M] di giardinaggio[M]

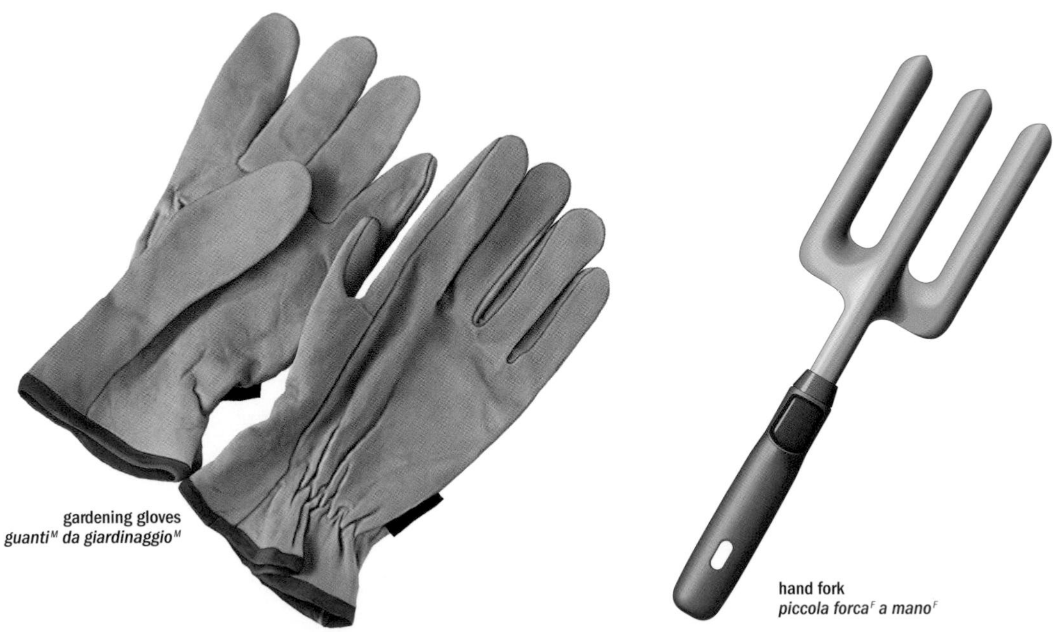

tools for loosening the earth

attrezzi[M] per smuovere la terra[F]

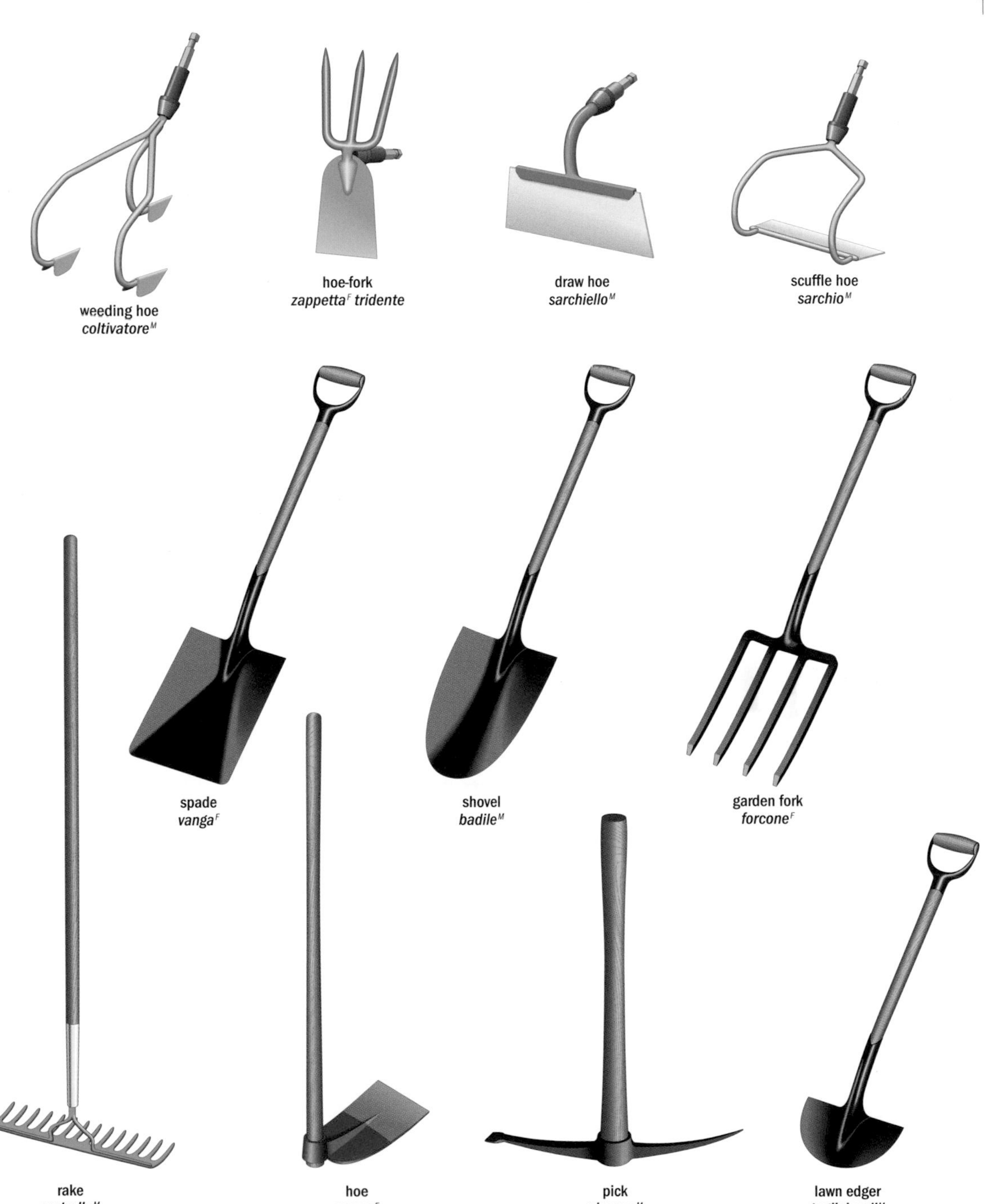

pruning and cutting tools

attrezzi[M] per potare e tagliare

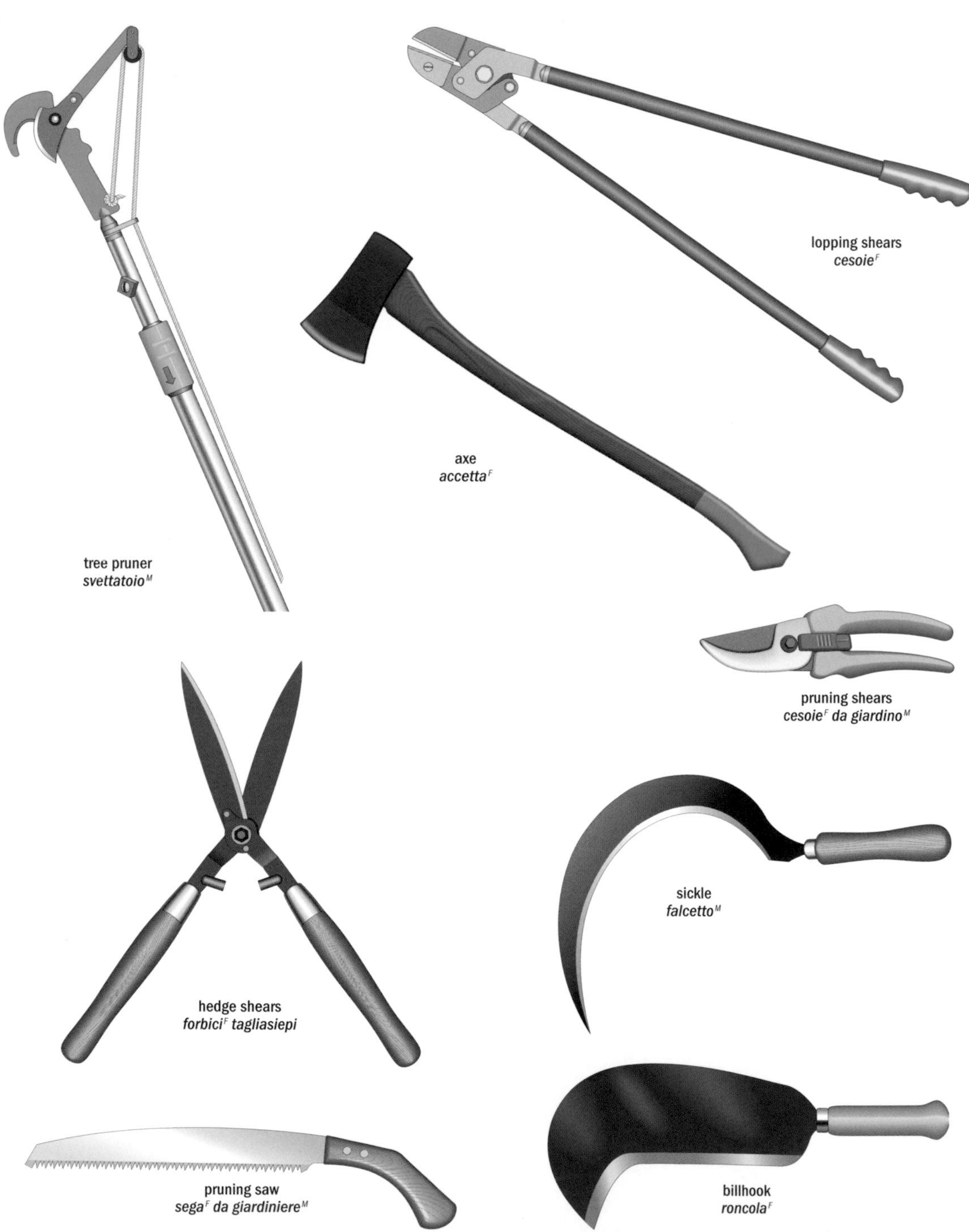

hedge trimmer
*tagliasiepi^M/F^*

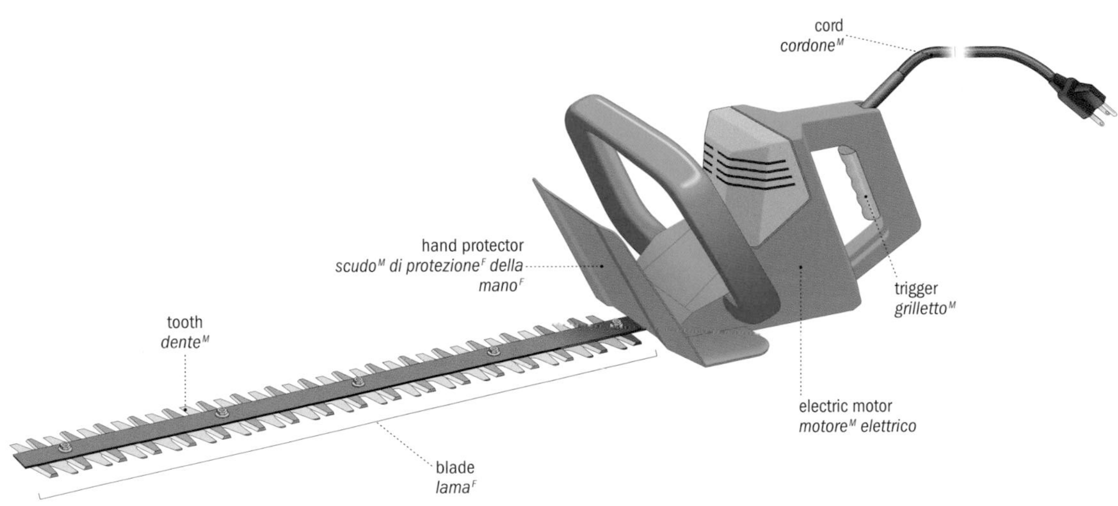

chainsaw
*motosega^F^*

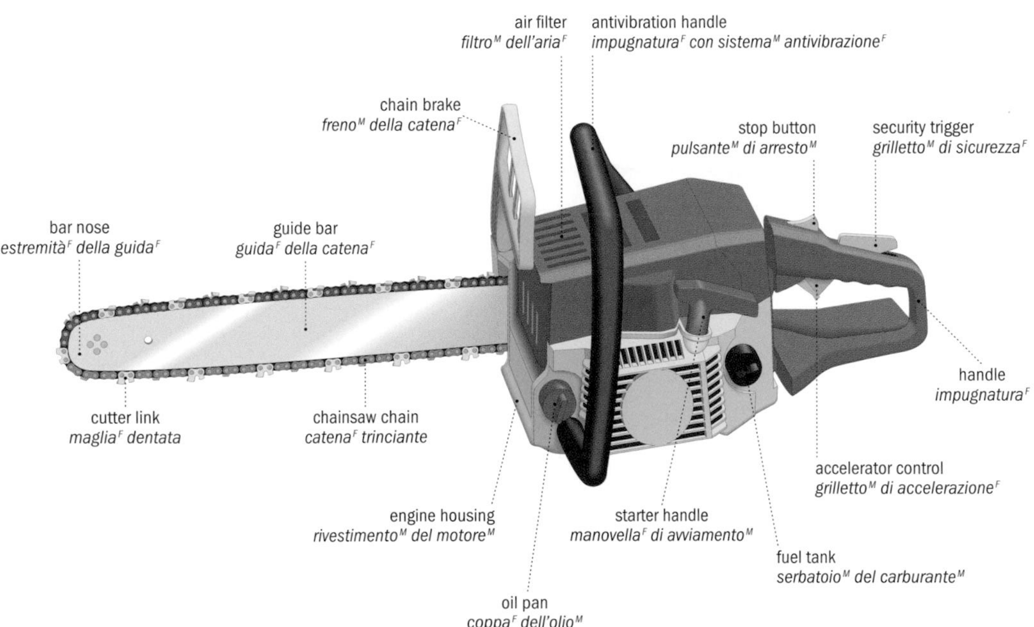

watering tools

attrezzi^M per annaffiare

lawn care

cura[F] del prato[M]

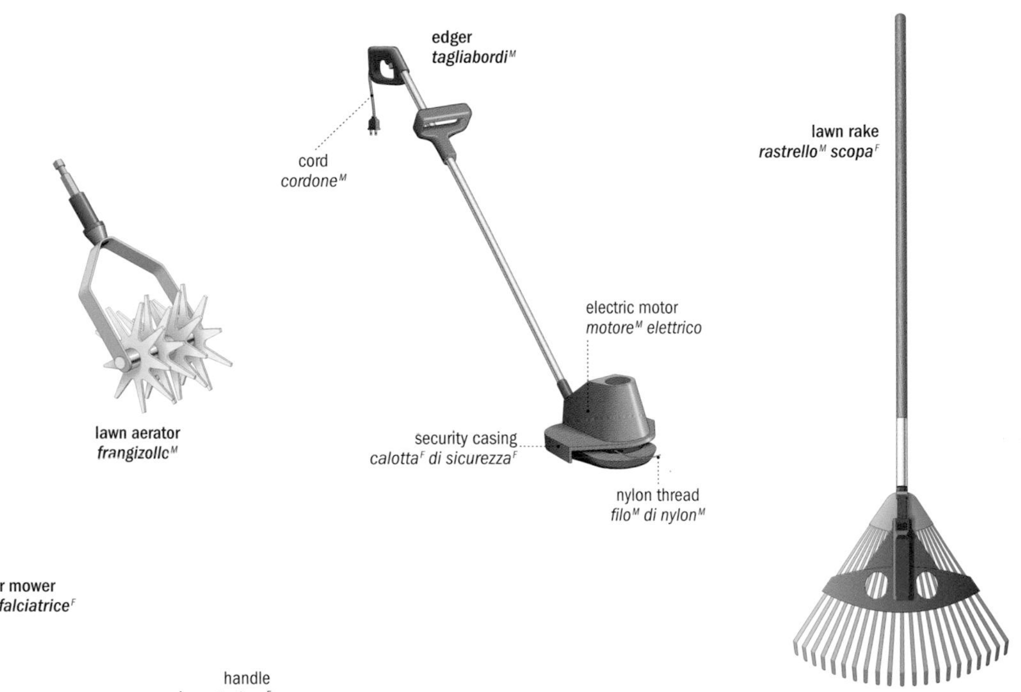

power mower
motofalciatrice[F]

headgear

copricapi[M]

women's headgear
copricapi[M] femminili

pillbox hat
tocco[M]

cartwheel hat
cappello[M] a falda[F] larga

cloche
cloche[F]

toque
toque[F]

gob hat
cappello[M] da marinaio[M]

crown
calotta[F]

brim
tesa[F]

turban
turbante[M]

sou'wester
berretto[M] impermeabile

unisex headgear
copricapi[M] unisex

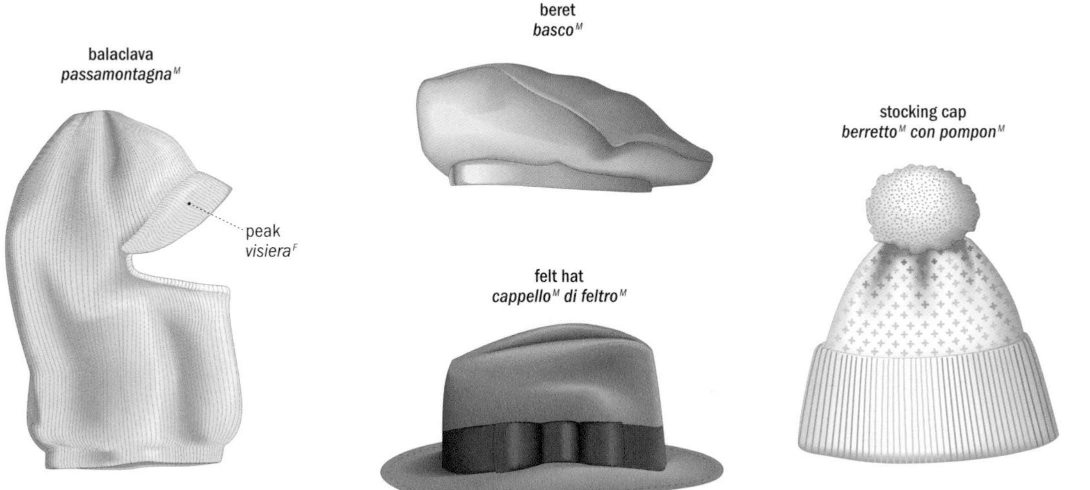

men's shoes
scarpe^F da uomo^M
parts of a shoe
parti^F di una scarpa^F
lining
fodera^F
shoelace
stringa^F
cuff
collo^M
tongue
linguetta^F
vamp
tomaia^F
heel grip
rinforzo^M interno del calcagno^M
stitch
impuntura^F
quarter
quartiere^M
punch hole
foro^M
outside counter
rinforzo^M esterno del calcagno^M
heel
tacco^M
top lift
salvatacchi^M
waist
fiosso^M
nose of the quarter
parte^F anteriore del quartiere^M
eyelet tab
lunetta^F
tag
puntale^M
outsole
suola^F
perforated toe cap
mascherina^F perforata
eyelet
occhiello^M
welt
guardolo^M
heavy duty boot
scarpone^M
chukka
scarpa^F a collo^M alto
rubber
galoscia^F
bootee
scarponcino^M
oxford shoe
scarpa^F oxford
blucher oxford
scarpa^F stringata

CLOTHING

women's shoes
scarpe[F] da donna[F]

unisex shoes
scarpe*^{F} *unisex

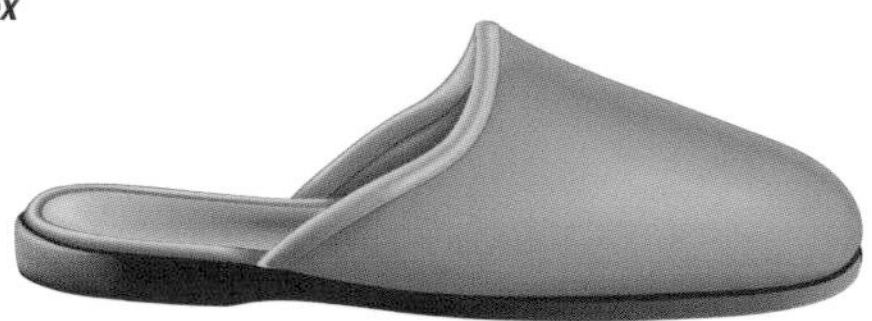

mule
pianella^F

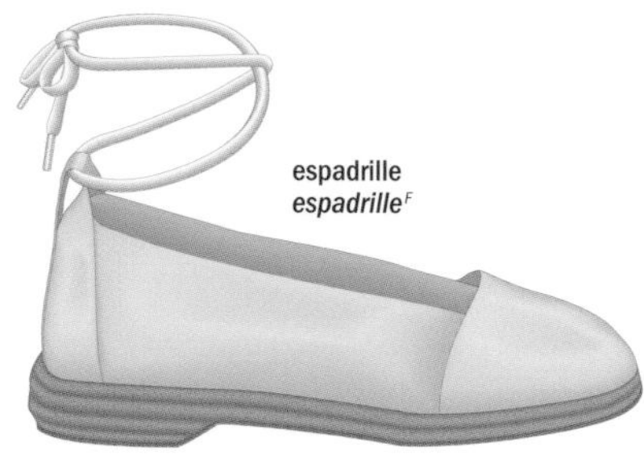

espadrille
espadrille^F

tennis shoe
scarpa^F *da tennis*^{M}

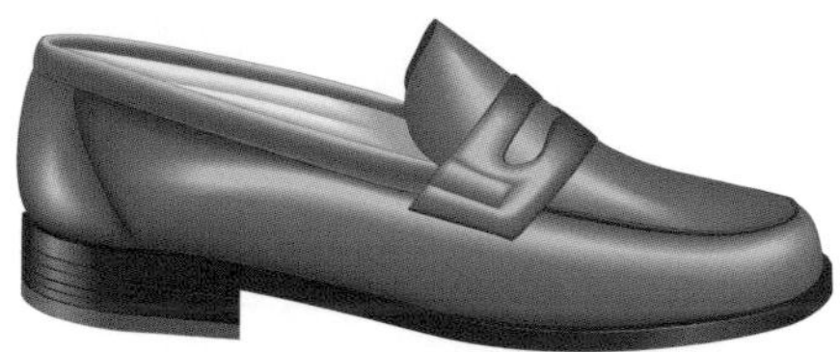

loafer
mocassino^M *classico*

sandal
sandalo^M *indiano*

moccasin
mocassino^M

thong
infradito^M

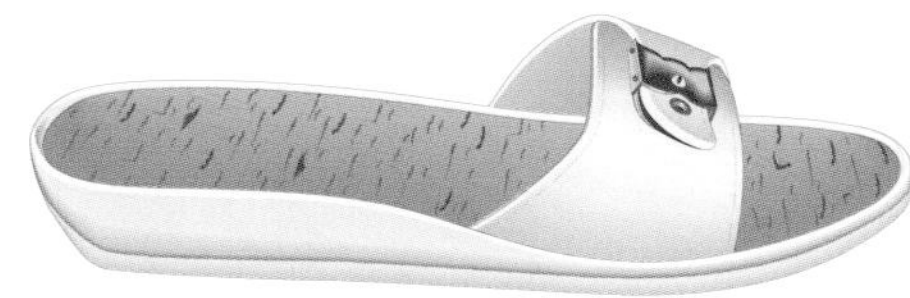

clog
zoccolo^M

sandal
sandalo^M

hiking boot
pedula^F

gloves
guanti[M]

men's gloves
guanti[M] da uomo[M]

back of a glove
dorso[M] del guanto[M]

stitching
impuntura[F]

palm of a glove
palmo[M] del guanto[M]

fourchette
linguella[F]

glove finger
dito[M] del guanto[M]

thumb
pollice[M]

palm
palmo[M]

seam
cucitura[F]

snap fastener
bottone[M] a pressione[F]

opening
apertura[F]

perforation
foro[M]

driving glove
guanto[M] da guida[F]

mitten
muffola[F]

women's gloves
guanti[M] da donna[F]

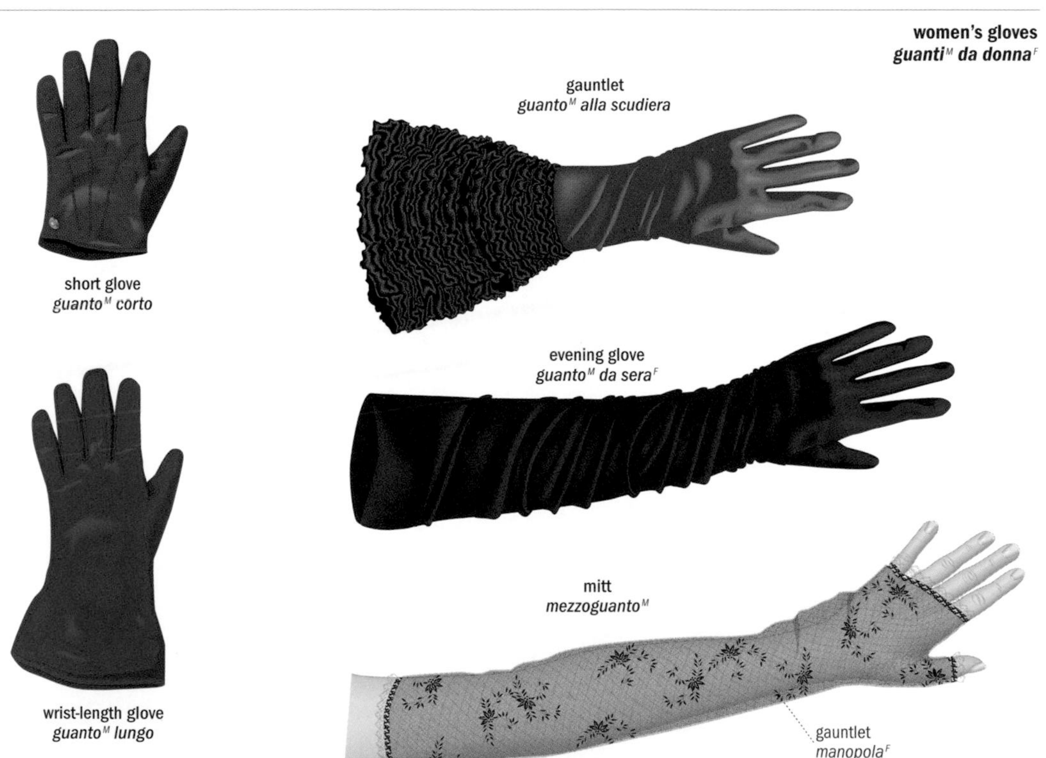

jackets
giacche^F e gilè^M

shirt
***camicia*[F]**

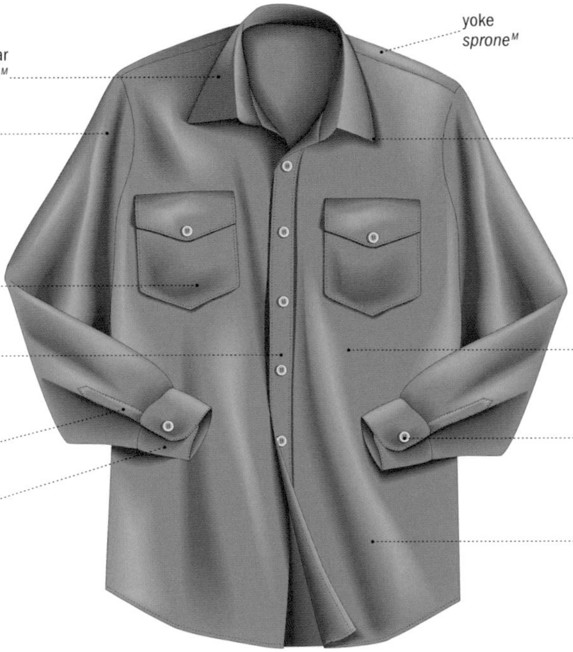

collar
colletto[M]
yoke
sprone[M]
set-in sleeve
manica[F] *a giro*[M]
collar point
punta[F] *del colletto*[M]
breast pocket
tasca[F] *applicata con aletta*[F]
front
davanti[M]
buttoned placket
cannoncino[M]
button
bottone[M]
pointed tab end
profilo[M] *dello spacco*[M]
cuff
polsino[M]
shirttail
lembo[M] *della camicia*[F]

buttondown collar
collo*[M] *button-down

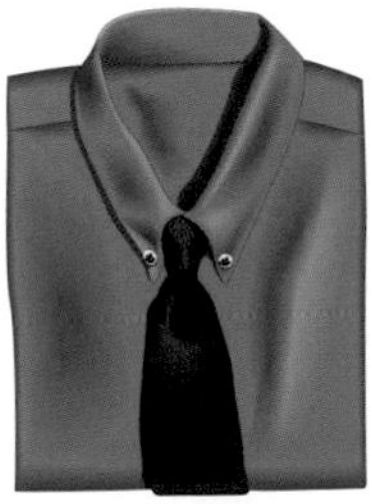

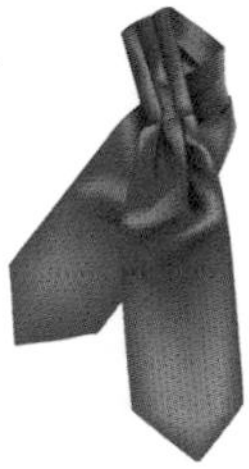

ascot tie
***lavallière*[F]**

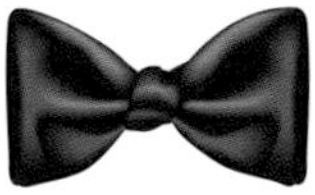

bow tie
***papillon*[M]**

collar stay
tendicollo[M]

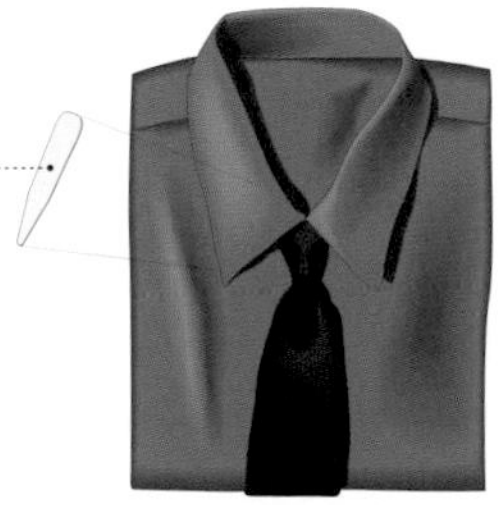

spread collar
***collo*[M] *a camicia*[F]**

necktie
***cravatta*[F]**

front apron
lembo[M] *anteriore*
neck end
annodatura[F]
rear apron
lembo[M] *posteriore*
lining
fodera[F]
loop
passante[M]
slip-stitched seam
cucitura[F] *a sottopunto*[M]

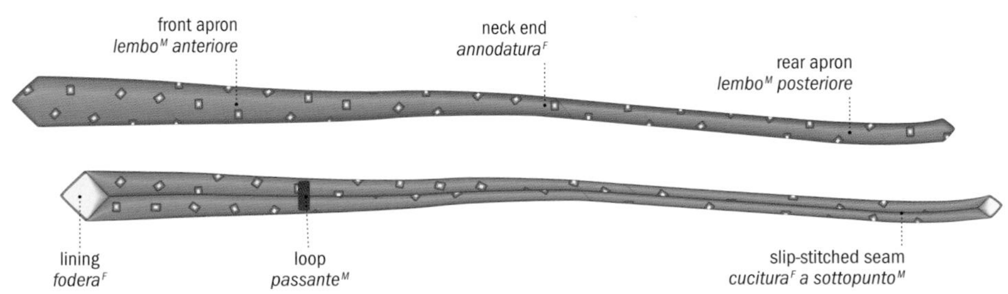

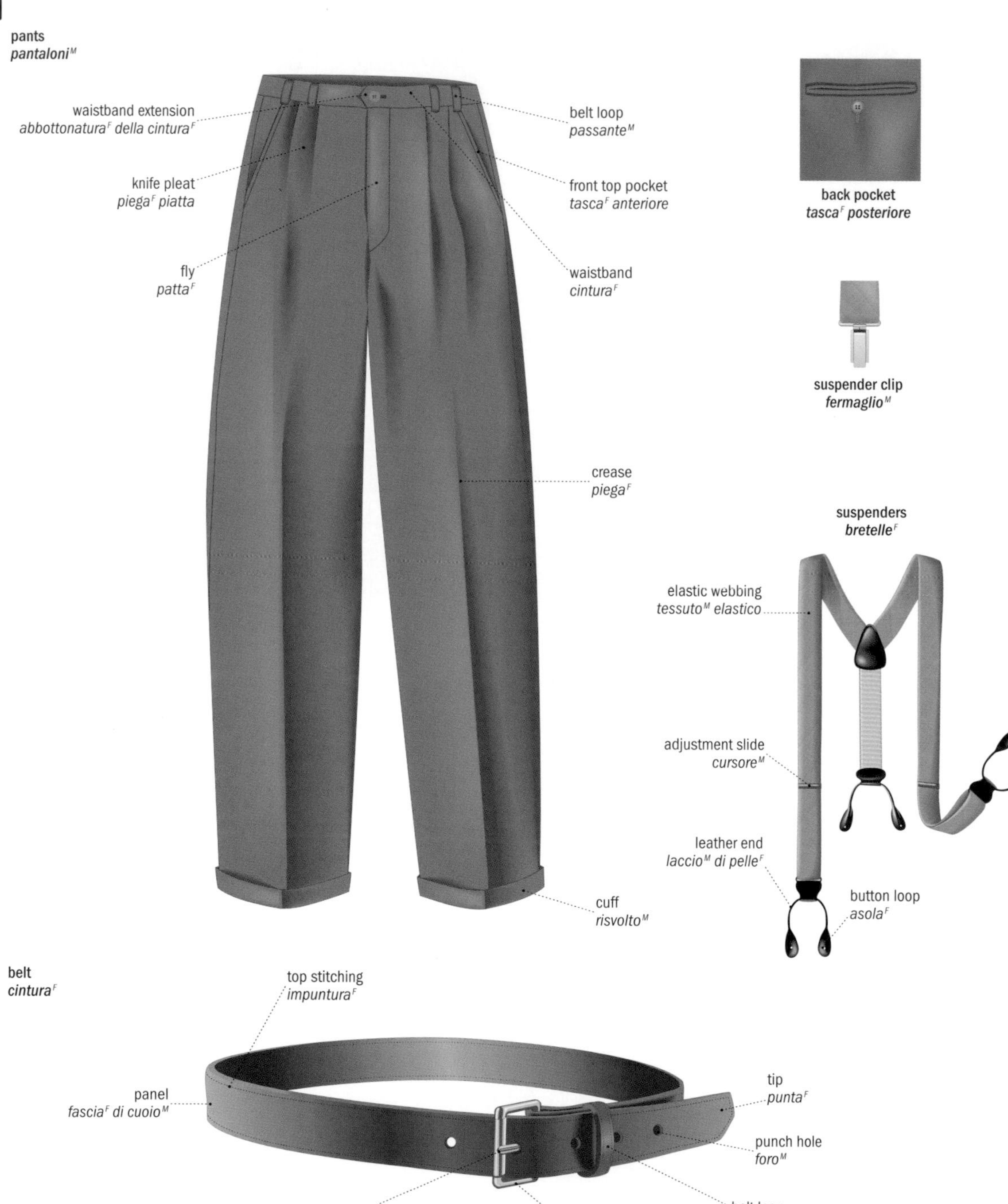
pants
pantaloni[M]
waistband extension
abbottonatura[F] della cintura[F]
knife pleat
piega[F] piatta
fly
patta[F]
belt loop
passante[M]
front top pocket
tasca[F] anteriore
waistband
cintura[F]
crease
piega[F]
cuff
risvolto[M]
back pocket
tasca[F] posteriore
suspender clip
fermaglio[M]
suspenders
bretelle[F]
elastic webbing
tessuto[M] elastico
adjustment slide
cursore[M]
leather end
laccio[M] di pelle[F]
button loop
asola[F]
belt
cintura[F]
top stitching
impuntura[F]
panel
fascia[F] di cuoio[M]
tip
punta[F]
punch hole
foro[M]
belt loop
passante[M]
tongue
ardiglione[M]
buckle
fibbia[F]

underwear
biancheria^F intima

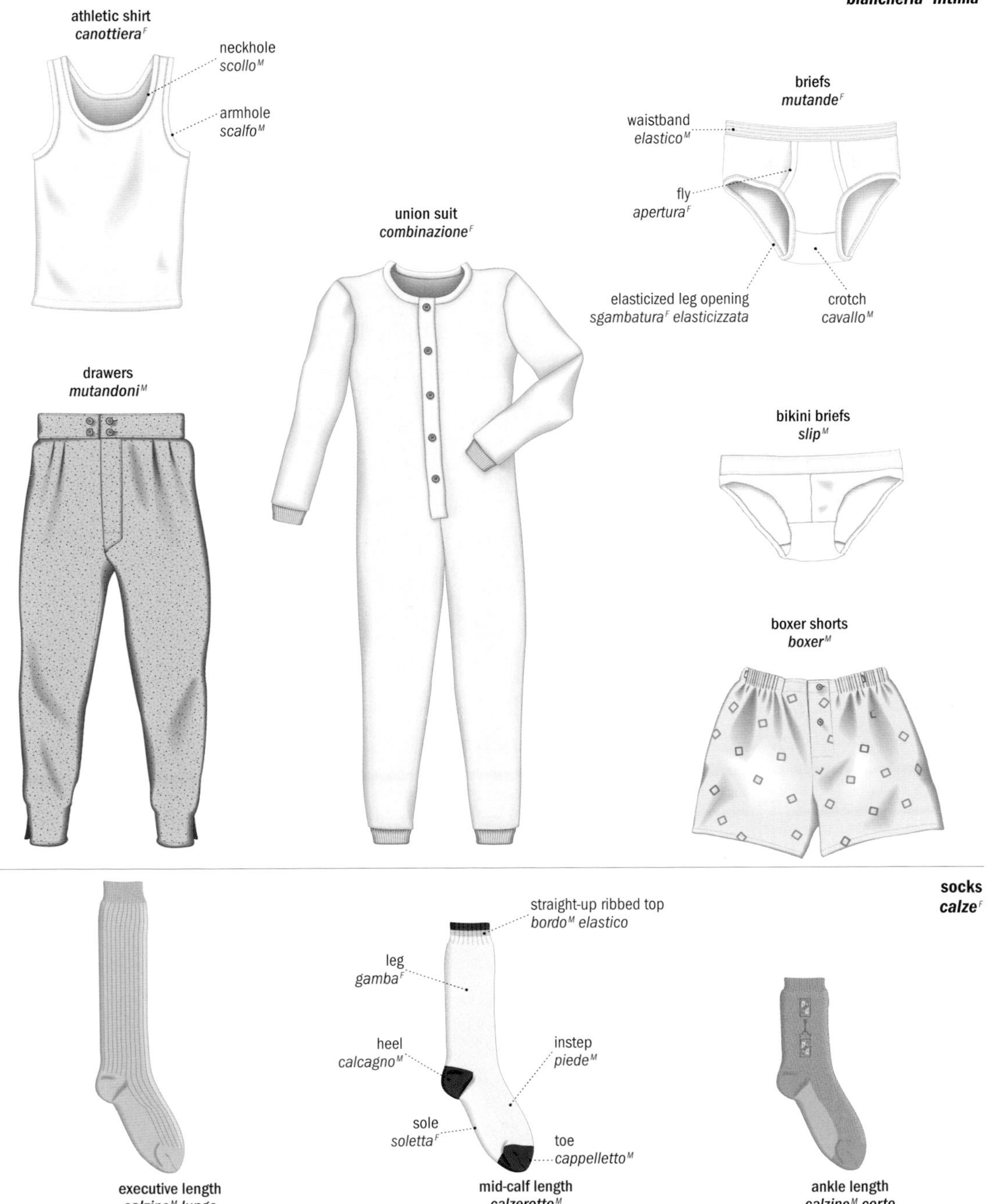

coats
***esempi*[M] *di giacconi*[M] *e cappotti*[M]**

parka
parka^M
snap-fastening tab
allacciatura^F con bottoni^M a pressione^F
zipper
chiusura^F lampo
sheepskin jacket
montone^M
duffle coat
montgomery^M
hood
cappuccio^M
yoke
carré^M
frog
alamaro^M
patch pocket
tasca^F applicata
toggle fastening
olivetta^F
jacket
giacca^F a vento^M
snap fastener
bottone^M a pressione^F
hand-warmer pocket
tasca^F interna con aletta^F
elastic waistband
fascia^F elastica
windbreaker
giacca^F a vento^M
waistband
coulisse^F
drawstring
cordoncino^M

sweaters

maglioni[M]

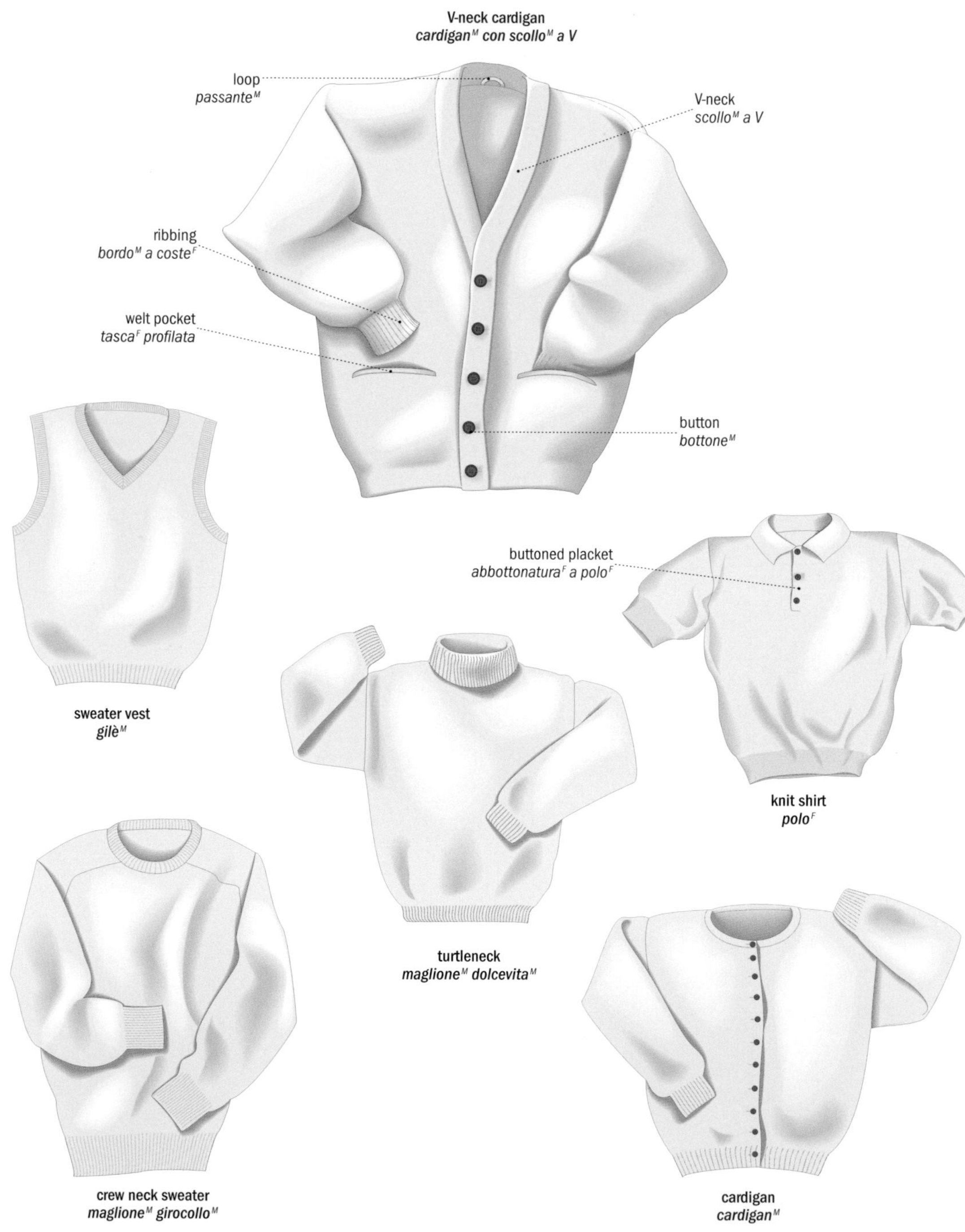

coats
esempi[M] di giacche[F] e cappotti[M]

suit
tailleur[M]

jacket
giacca[F]

skirt
gonna[F]

raglan
cappotto[M] alla raglan

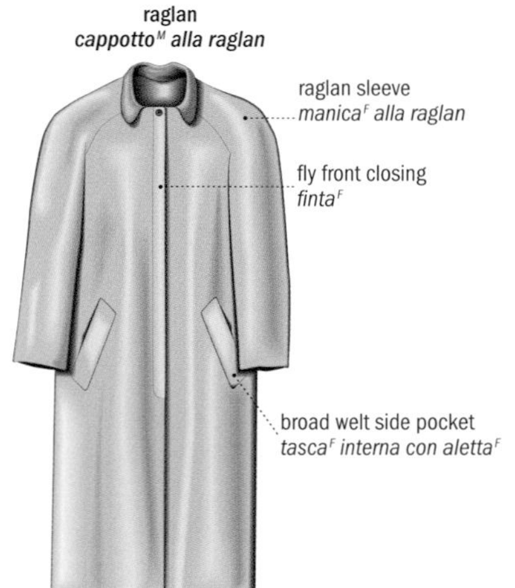

top coat
redingote[F]

pelerine
cappotto[M] con pellegrina[F]

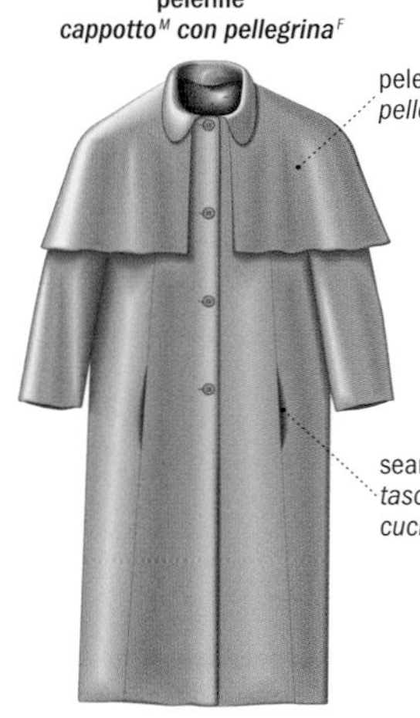

cape
mantella[F]

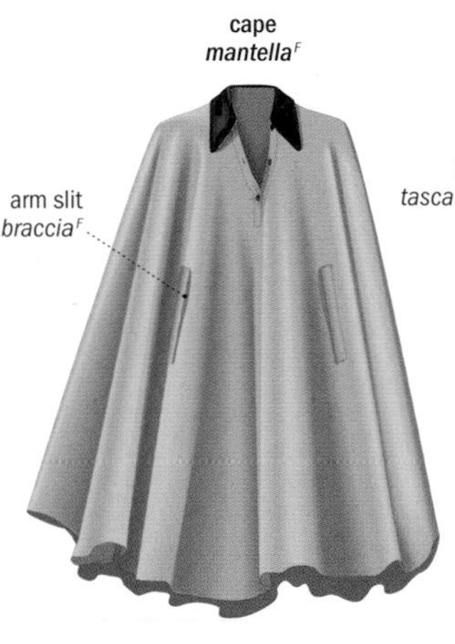

pea jacket
giacca[F] alla marinara

overcoat
cappotto[M]

car coat
giaccone[M]

jacket
giacca[F]

poncho
poncho[M]

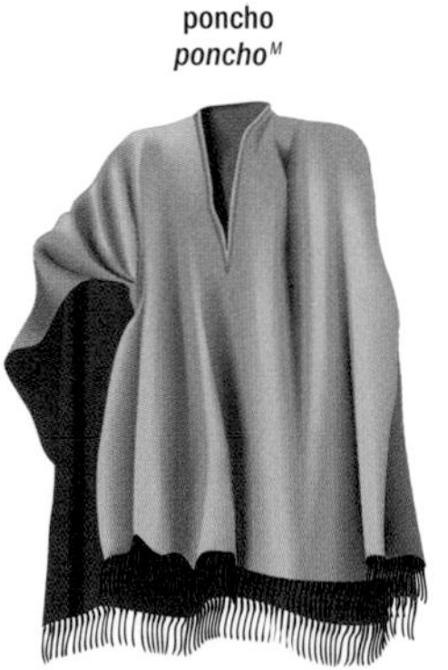

examples of dresses
esempi[M] *di abiti*[M]

sheath dress
tubino[M]

princess-seamed dress
princesse[F]

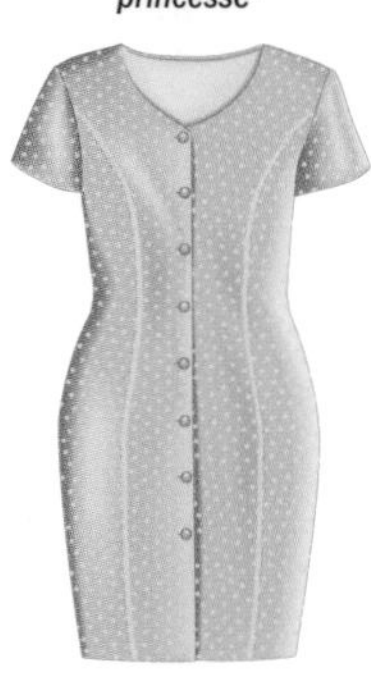

coat dress
robe-manteau[F/M]

polo dress
abito[M] *a polo*[F]

housedress
abito[M] *da casa*[F]

shirtwaist dress
chemisier[M]

drop-waist dress
abito[M] *a vita*[F] *bassa*

trapeze dress
abito[M] *a trapezio*[M]

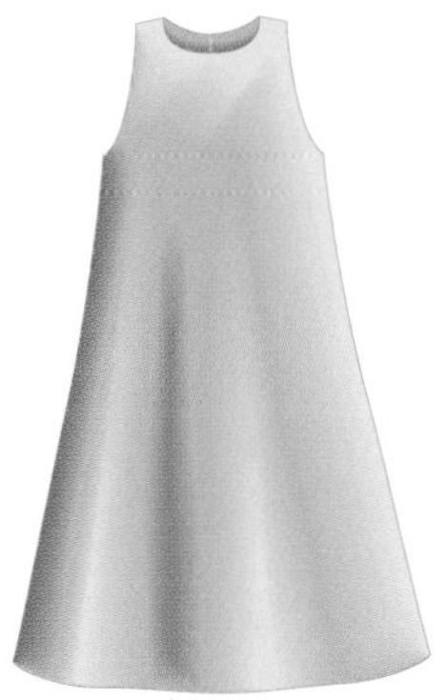

sundress
prendisole[M]

wraparound dress
abito[M] *a vestaglia*[F]

tunic dress
abito[M] *a tunica*[F]

jumper
scamiciato[M]

examples of skirts
esempi[M] di gonne[F]

gored skirt
gonna[F] a teli[M]

kilt
gonnelino[M] scozzese

sarong
sarong[M]

wraparound skirt
gonna[F] a portafoglio[M]

sheath skirt
gonna[F] ad anfora[F]

ruffled skirt
gonna[F] a balze[F]

straight skirt
gonna[F] diritta

yoked skirt
gonna[F] con baschina[F]

gathered skirt
gonna[F] arricciata

culottes
gonna[F] pantalone[M]

examples of pleats
esempi[M] di pieghe[F]

inverted pleat
piega[F] invertita

kick pleat
piega[F] sovrapposta

accordion pleat
plissé[M]

top-stitched pleat
piega[F] impunturata

knife pleat
piega[F] a coltello[M]

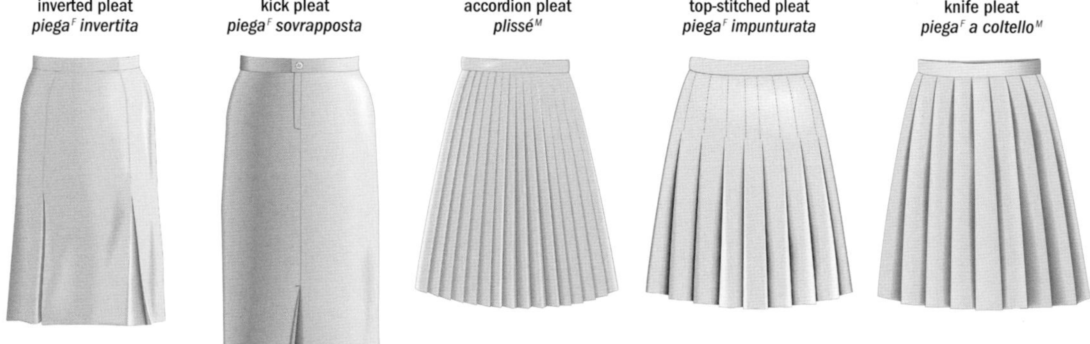

examples of pants
esempi[M] di pantaloni[M]

shorts
shorts[M]

Bermuda shorts
bermuda[M]

knickers
pantaloni[M] alla zuava

pedal pushers
pantaloni[M] alla pescatora

jeans
jeans[M]

ski pants
fuseau[M]

footstrap
staffa[F]

jumpsuit
tuta[F]

overalls
salopette[F]

bell bottoms
pantaloni[M] a zampa[F] di elefante[M]

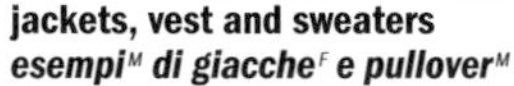

jackets, vest and sweaters
esempi[M] di giacche[F] e pullover[M]

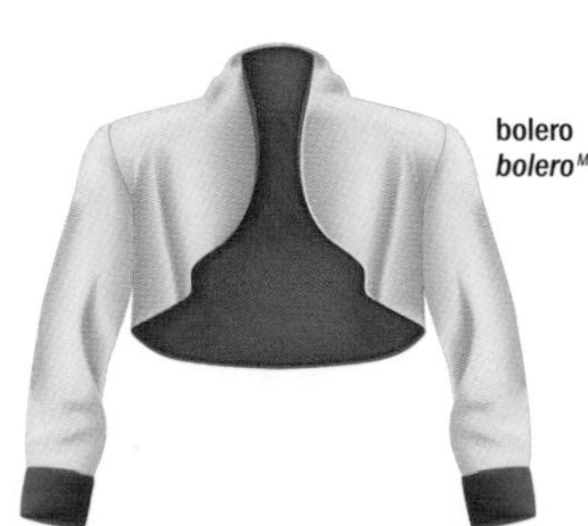

bolero
bolero[M]

spencer
spencer[M]

blazer
blazer[M]

safari jacket
sahariana^F
gusset pocket
tasca^F applicata a soffietto^M
vest
gilè^M
twin-set
twin-set^M
crew neck sweater
maglia^F girocollo^M
cardigan
cardigan^M
examples of shirts
esempi^M di camicette^F
body suit
body^M
crotch piece
cavallo^M
middy
maglietta^F alla marinara
yoke
carré^M
gather
arricciatura^F
shirttail
lembo^M
oversized shirt
camicione^M
classic blouse
camicetta^F classica
smock
sopravveste^F a grembiule^M
tunic
camiciotto^M
wrapover top
camicetta^F incrociata
polo shirt
polo^F
over-blouse
casacca^F

nightwear
***biancheria*[F] *da notte*[F]**

kimono
kimono[M]

nightgown
camicia[F] *da notte*[F]

baby doll
baby-doll[M]

pajamas
pigiama[M]

negligee
vestaglia[F]

bathrobe
accappatoio[M]

hose
calze[F]

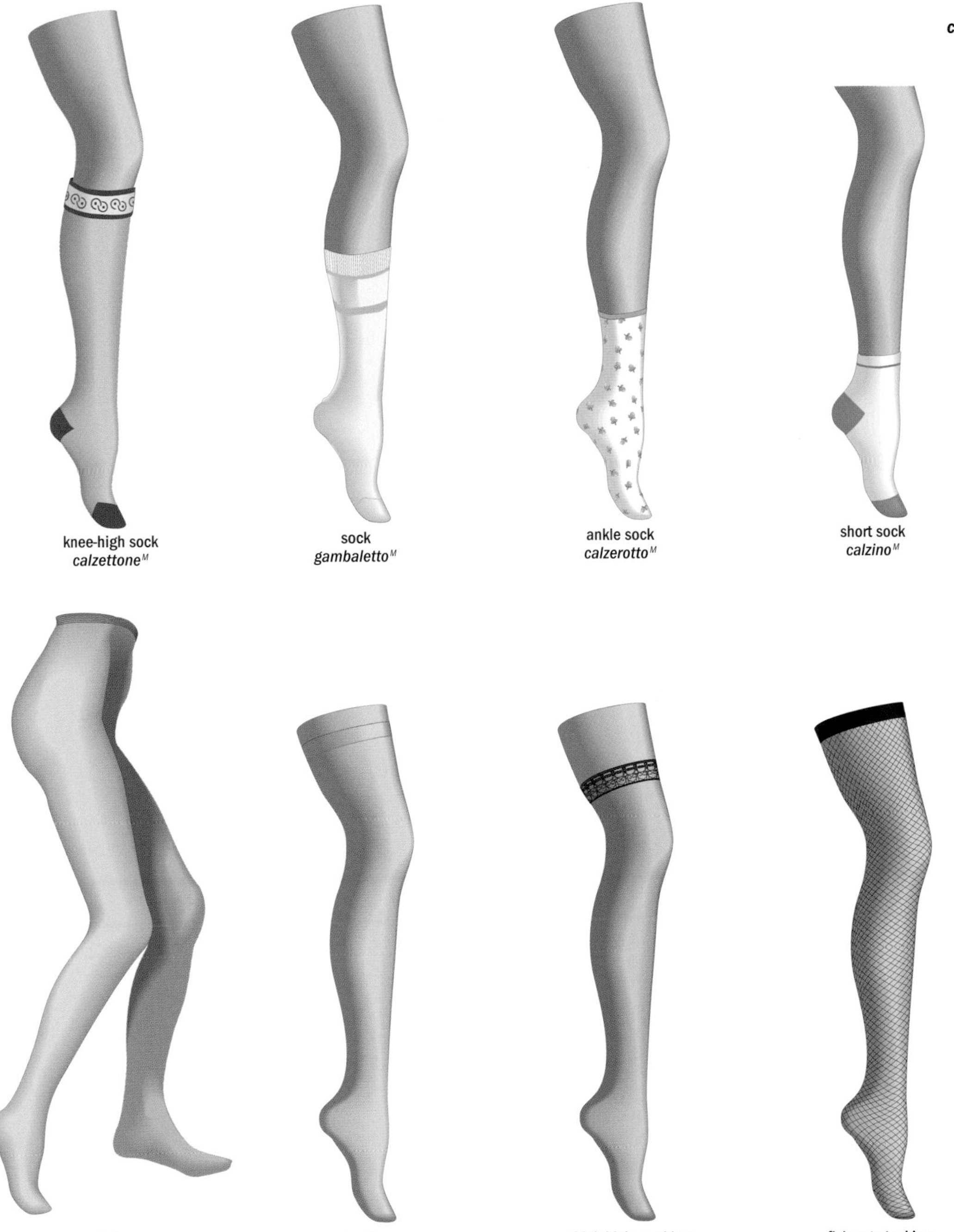

knee-high sock
calzettone[M]

sock
gambaletto[M]

ankle sock
calzerotto[M]

short sock
calzino[M]

panty hose
collant[M]

stocking
calza[F]

thigh-high stocking
calza[F] *autoreggente*

fish net stocking
calza[F] *a rete*[F]

underwear
biancheria*[F] *intima

corselette
modellatore[M] *aperto*

camisole
top[M]

teddy
pagliaccetto[M]

body suit
body[M]

panty corselette
modellatore[M] *sgambato*

half-slip
sottogonna[F]

foundation slip
sottoveste[F]

slip
sottoveste[F] *con reggiseno*[M]

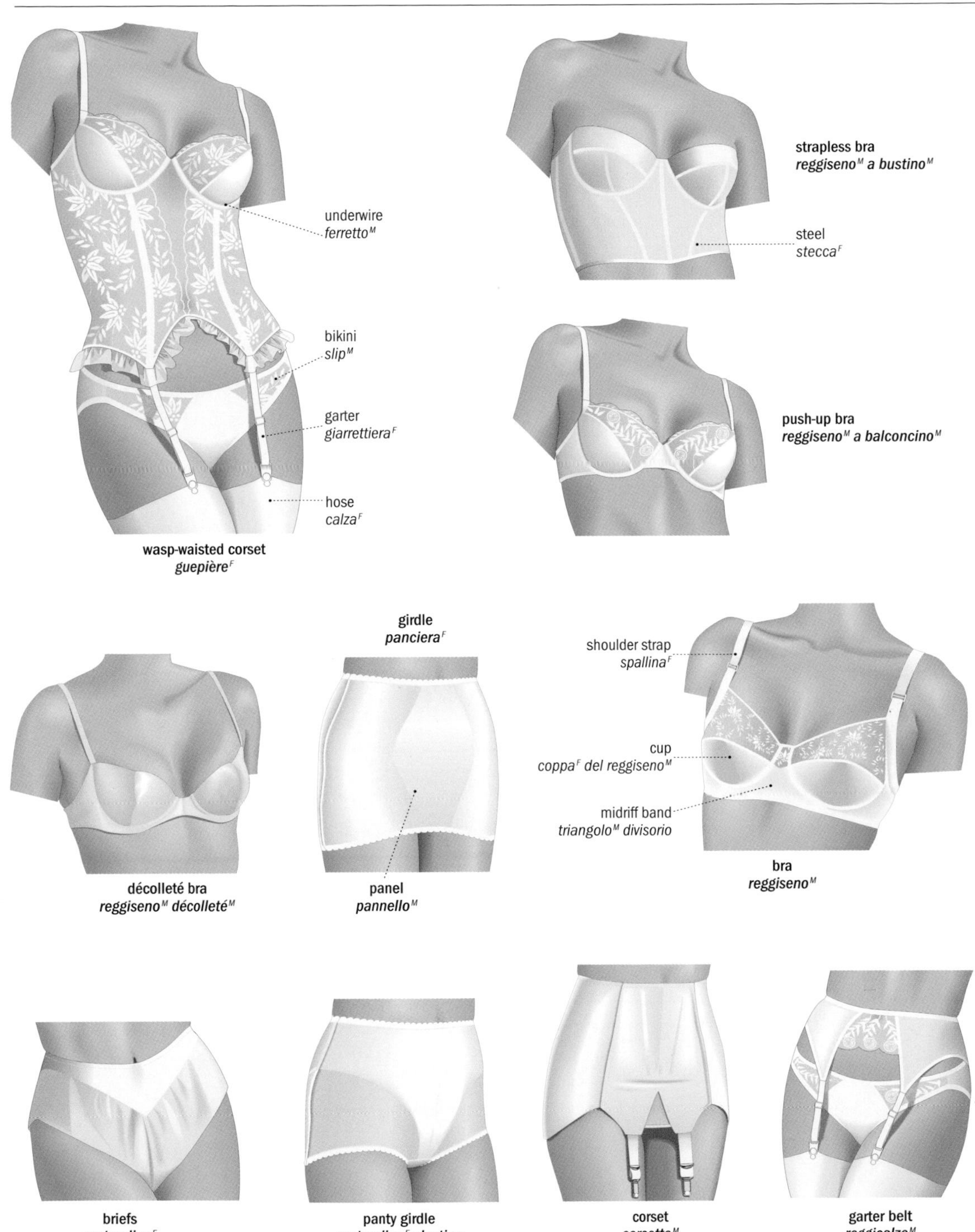

wasp-waisted corset
guepière[F]

girdle
panciera[F]

décolleté bra
reggiseno[M] *décolleté*[M]

bra
reggiseno[M]

briefs
mutandina[F]

panty girdle
mutandina[F] *elastica*

corset
corsetto[M]

garter belt
reggicalze[M]

newborn children's clothing

vestiti[M] per neonati[M]

jumpsuit
salopette[F] a tutina[F]

bunting bag
tutina[F] a sacco[M]

mittens
manopole[F]

bootees
scarponcino[M]

bathing wrap
telo[M] di spugna[F] con cappuccio[M]

hood
cappuccio[M]
decorative braid
guarnizione[F]
false tuck
profilo[M] sbieco

bodysuit
body[M]

rumba tights
ghettina[F] con ruches[F]

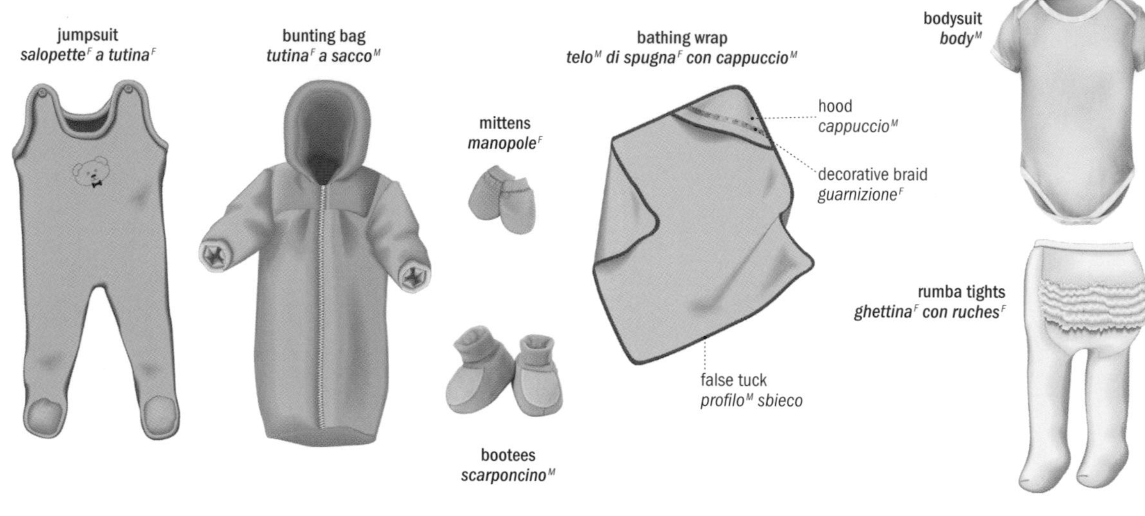

grow sleepers
pigiamino[M] a due pezzi[M]

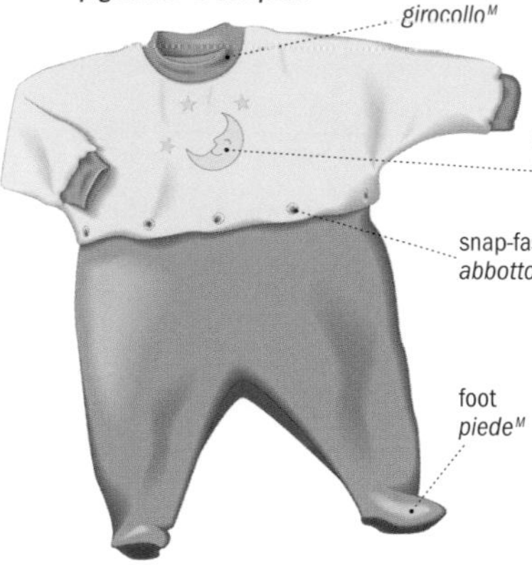

crew neck
girocollo[M]
screen print
disegno[M] stampato
snap-fastening waist
abbottonatura[F] a pressione[F]
foot
piede[M]

overalls
salopette[F]

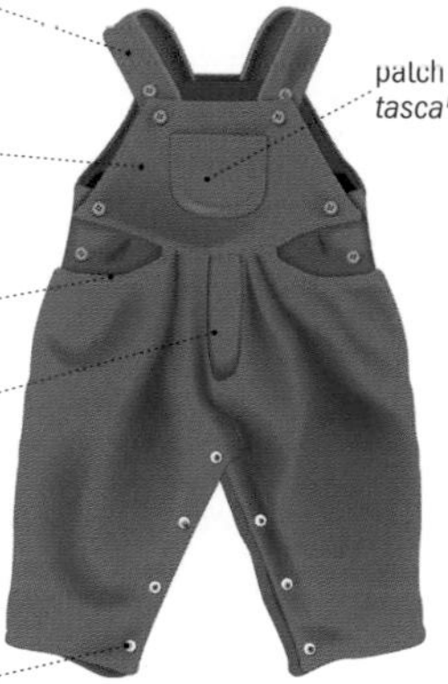

adjustable strap
bretella[F] regolabile
patch pocket
tasca[F] applicata
bib
pettorina[F]
top-stitching
impuntura[F]
fly
patta[F]
inside-leg snap-fastening
interno[M] gamba[F] con abbottonatura[F] a pressione[F]

shirt
maglietta[F] intima

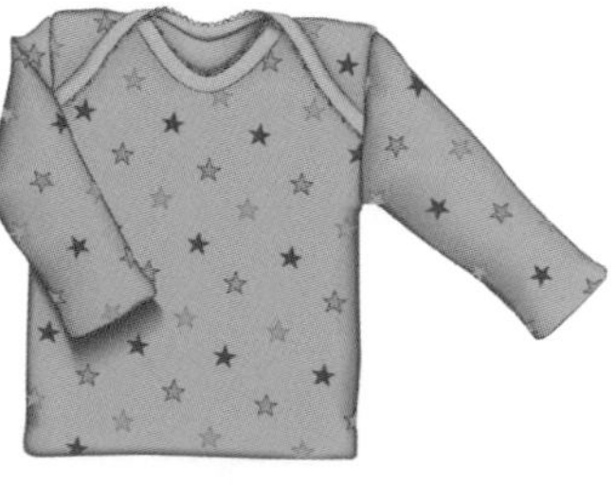

diaper
pannolino[M]

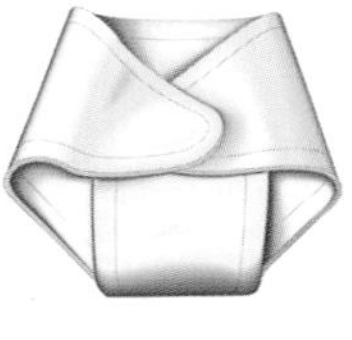

bib
bavaglino[M]

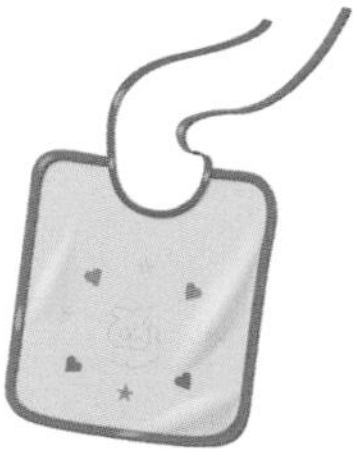

ruffled rumba pants
mutandina[F] con ruches[F]

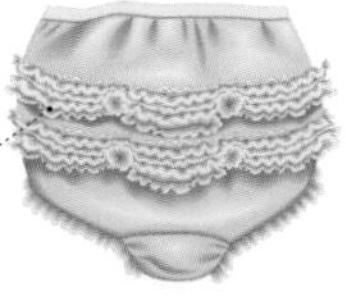

ruching
ruches[F]

disposable diaper
pannolino[F] usa e getta

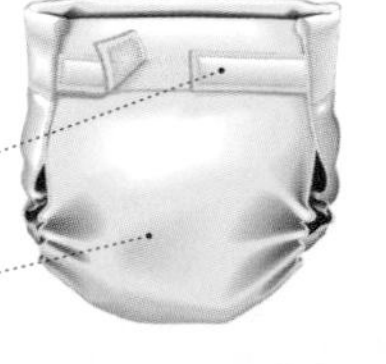

Velcro closure
velcro®[M]
waterproof pants
mutandina[F] impermeabile

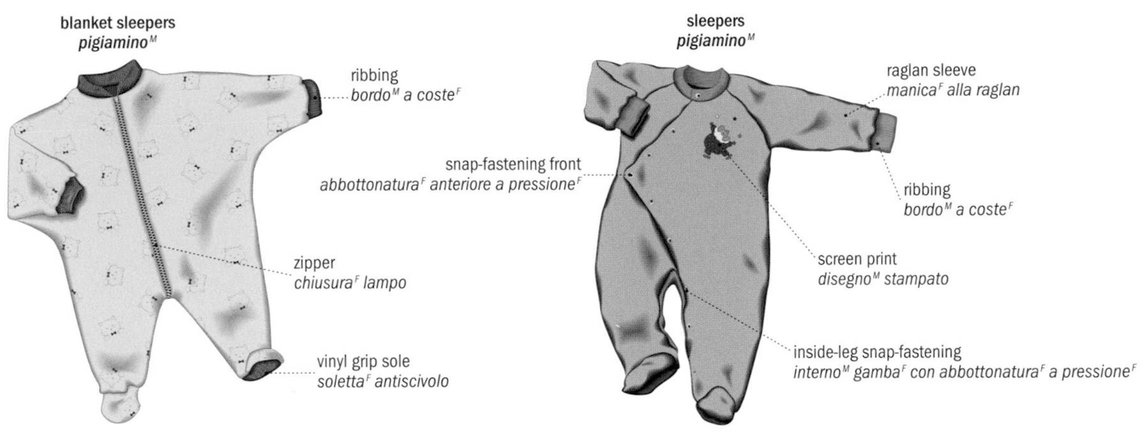

children's clothing

vestiti[M] per bambini[M]

overalls
salopette[F] con bretelle[F] incrociate

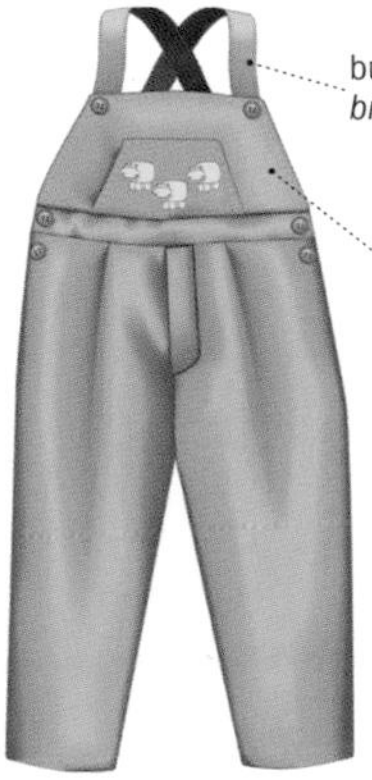

button strap
bretella[F] abbottonabile

bib
pettorina[F]

snowsuit
tuta[F] da sci[M]

hood
cappuccio[M]

overalls
salopette[F]

pajamas
pigiama[M]

T-shirt dress
abito[M] a T-shirt[F]

rompers
pagliaccetto[M]

training set
completo[M] da ginnastica[F]

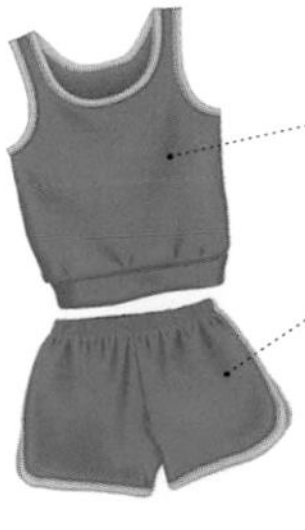

tank top
canottiera[F]

shorts
pantaloncini[M]

jumpsuit
tuta[F]

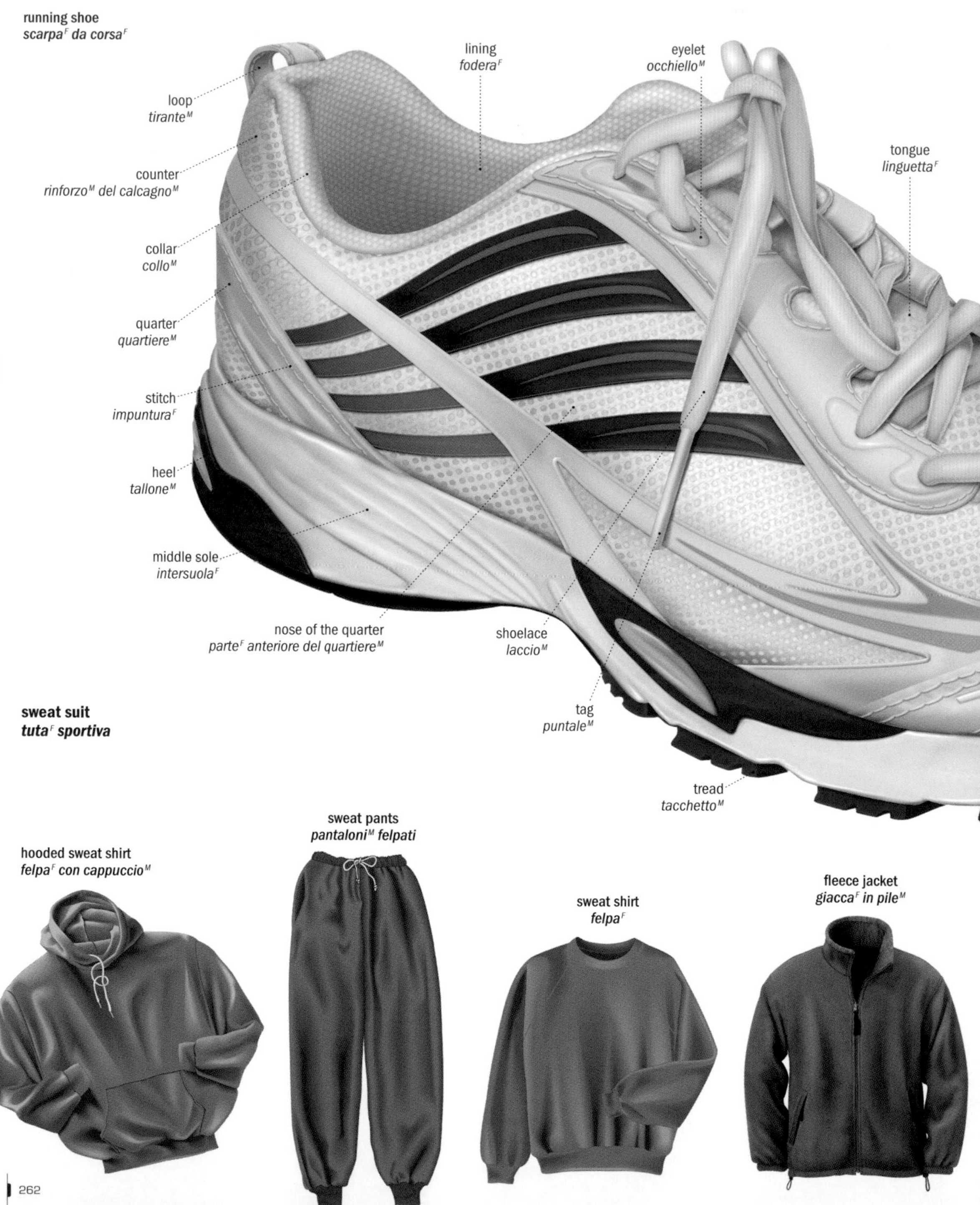
running shoe
scarpa^F da corsa^F
loop
tirante^M
counter
rinforzo^M del calcagno^M
collar
collo^M
quarter
quartiere^M
stitch
impuntura^F
heel
tallone^M
middle sole
intersuola^F
nose of the quarter
parte^F anteriore del quartiere^M
lining
fodera^F
eyelet
occhiello^M
tongue
linguetta^F
shoelace
laccio^M
tag
puntale^M
tread
tacchetto^M
sweat suit
tuta^F sportiva
hooded sweat shirt
felpa^F con cappuccio^M
sweat pants
pantaloni^M felpati
sweat shirt
felpa^F
fleece jacket
giacca^F in pile^M

swimming trunks
slip^M da bagno^M

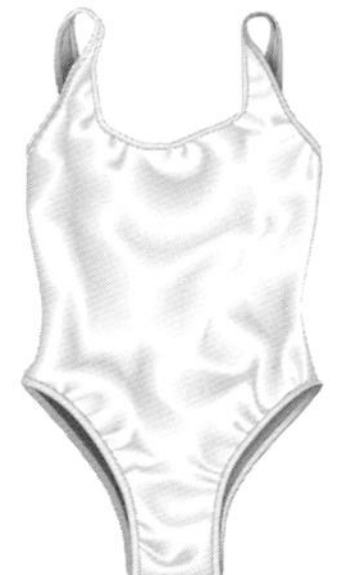

swimsuit
costume^M da bagno^M

footless tights
pantacollant^M

exercise wear
abbigliamento^M da ginnastica^F

leotard
body^M

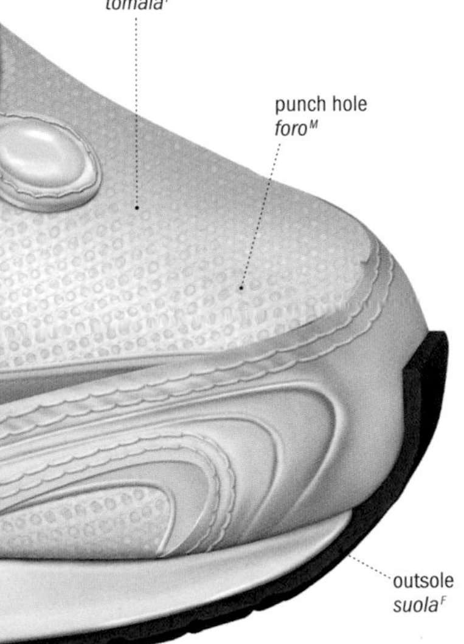

tank top
canottiera^F

T-shirt
T-shirt^F

leg-warmer
scaldamuscoli^M

pants
pantaloni^M

anorak
giacca^F avento^M

boxer shorts
pantaloncini^M da corsa^F

shorts
pantaloncini^M da ciclista^F

jewelry

gioielli^M

earrings
orecchini^M

clip earrings
orecchini^M a clip^F

screw earring
orecchini^M a vite^F

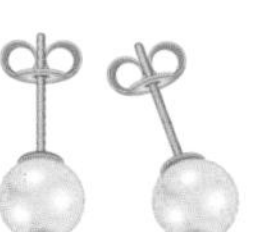
pierced earrings
orecchini^M a perno^M

drop earrings
orecchini^M pendenti

hoop earrings
orecchini^M ad anello^M

necklaces
collane^F

matinee-length necklace
collana^F

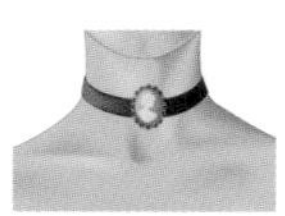
velvet-band choker
collarino^M di velluto^M

pendant
pendenti^M

rope necklace
collana^F lunga alla vita^F

opera-length necklace
collana^F lunga

bib necklace
collana^F a cinque giri^M

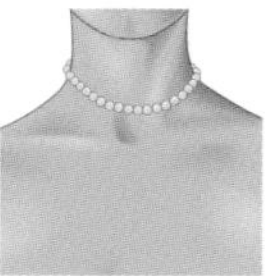
choker
girocollo^M

locket
medaglione^M

bracelets
bracciali^M

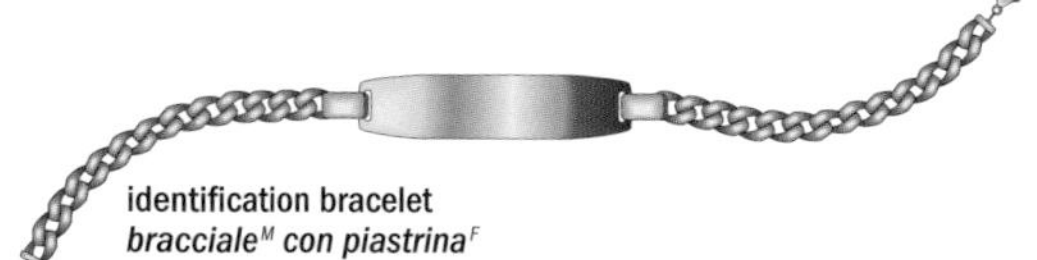
identification bracelet
bracciale^M con piastrina^F

charm bracelet
bracciale^M con ciondoli^M

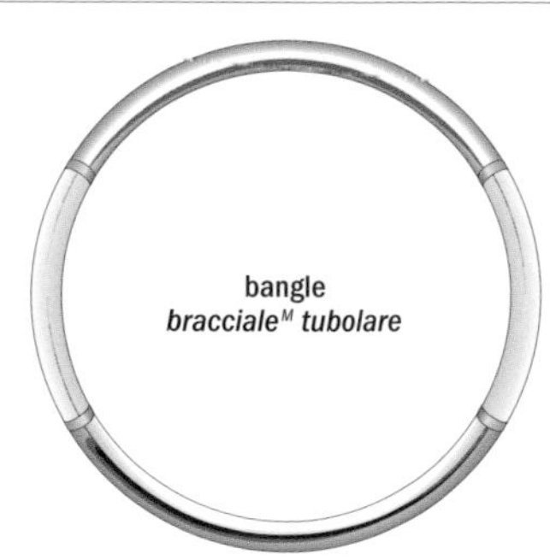
bangle
bracciale^M tubolare

rings
anelli^M

band ring
anello^M a fascia^F

signet ring
anello^M con sigillo^M

solitaire ring
solitario^M

engagement ring
anello^M di fidanzamento^M

wedding ring
fede^F nuziale

nail care

manicure[F]

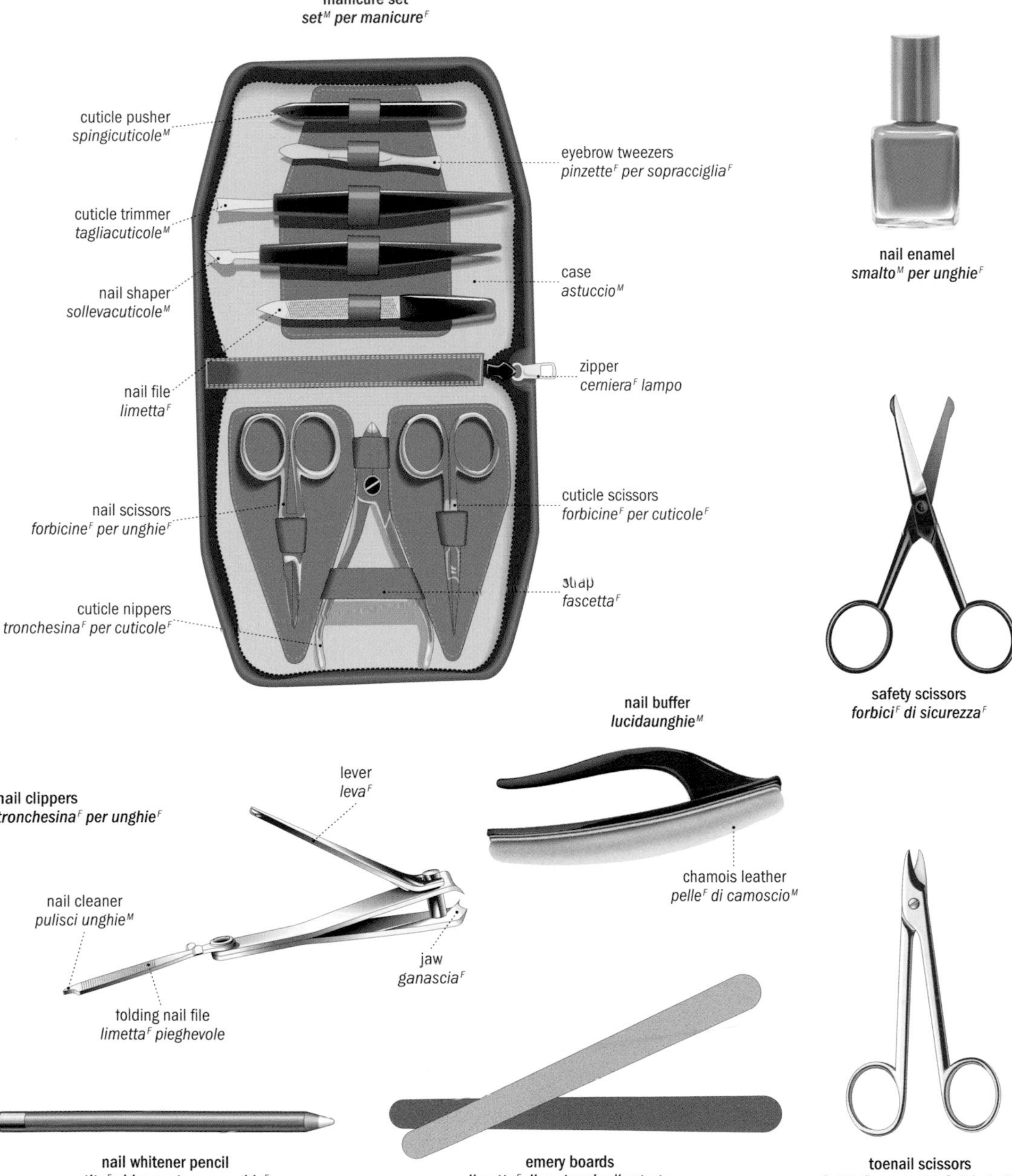

makeup

trucco[M]

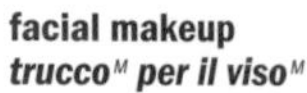

facial makeup
trucco[M] per il viso[M]

fan brush
pennello[M] a ventaglio[M]

powder puff
piumino[M] da cipria[F]

blusher brush
pennello[M] da fard[M]

powder blusher
fard[M] in polvere[F]

compact
portacipria[M]

pressed powder
cipria[F] compatta

synthetic sponge
spugna[F] sintetica

loose powder
cipria[F] in polvere[F]

loose powder brush
pennello[M] da cipria[F] in polvere[F]

liquid foundation
fondotinta[M] fluido

eye makeup
trucco[M] per gli occhi[M]

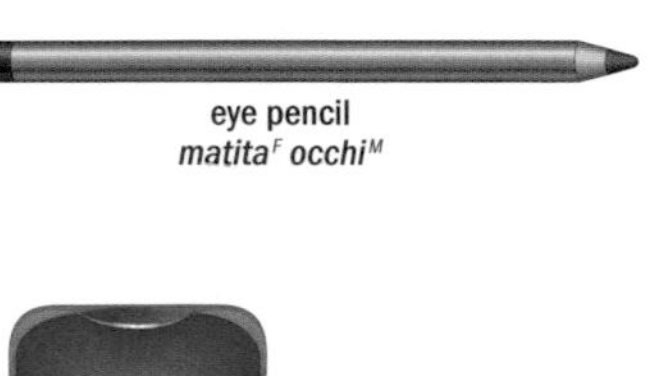

eye pencil
matita[F] occhi[M]

eyelash curler
piegaciglia[M]

brow brush and lash comb
pettinino[M] per ciglia[F] e spazzolino[M] per sopracciglia[F]

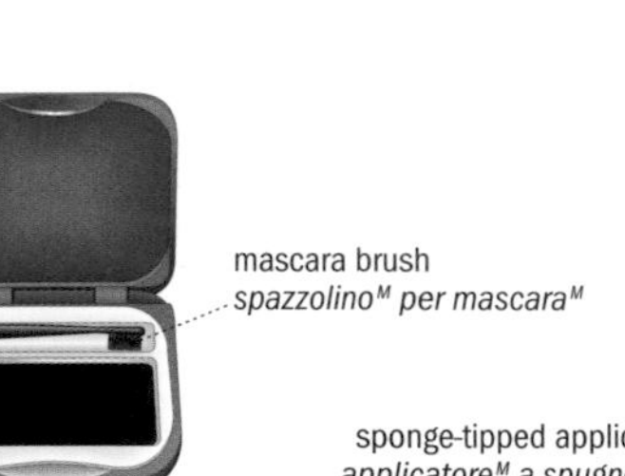

mascara brush
spazzolino[M] per mascara[M]

cake mascara
mascara[M] compatto

sponge-tipped applicator
applicatore[M] a spugnetta[F]

eyeshadow
ombretto[M]

liquid eyeliner
eye-liner[M]

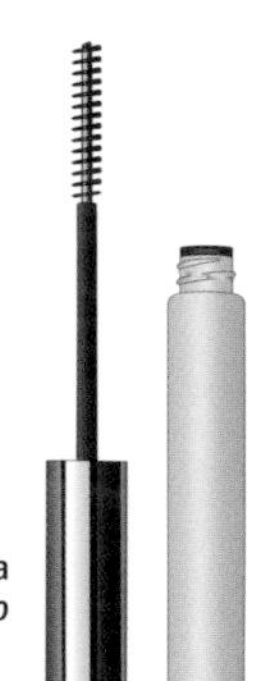

liquid mascara
mascara[M] liquido

lip makeup
trucco[M] per le labbra[F]

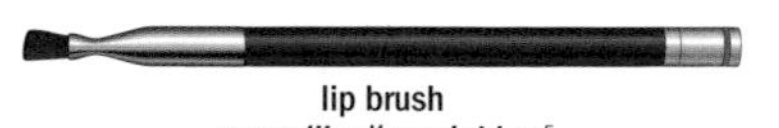

lip brush
pennellino[M] per labbra[F]

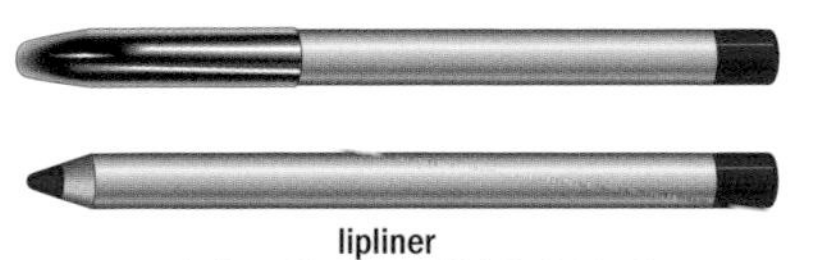

lipliner
matite[F] per il contorno[M] delle labbra[F]

lipstick
rossetto[M]

body care

cura[F] del corpo[M]

eau de parfum
profumo[M]

toilet soap
saponetta[F]

hair conditioner
balsamo[M] *per capelli*[M]

shampoo
shampoo[M]

haircolor
tintura[F] *per capelli*[M]

deodorant
deodorante[M]

eau de toilette
eau de toilette[F]

bubble bath
bagnoschiuma[M]

washcloth
manopola[F]

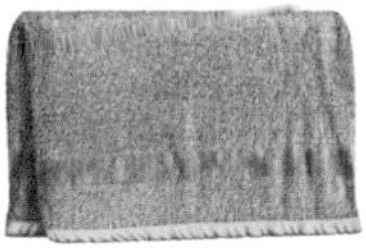

washcloth
ospite[M]

massage glove
guanto[M] *di crine*[M]

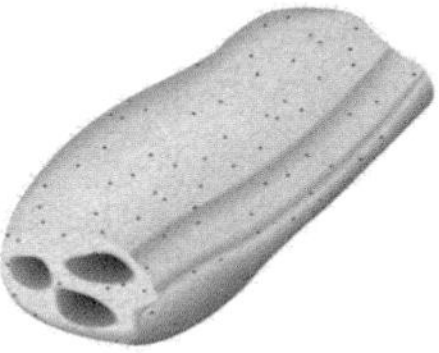

vegetable sponge
spugna[F] *vegetale*

natural sponge
spugna[F] *naturale*

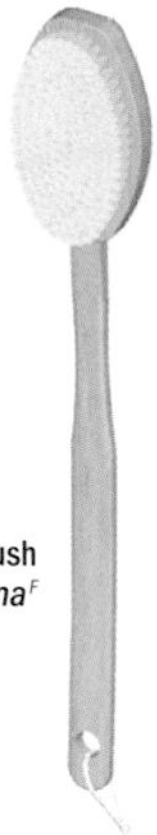

back brush
spazzola[F] *per la schiena*[F]

bath sheet
asciugamano[M] *da bagno*[M]

bath towel
asciugamano[M]

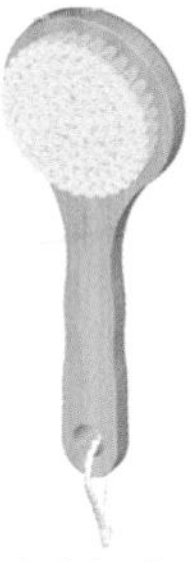

bath brush
spazzola[F] *da bagno*[M]

hairdressing

articoli[M] per acconciatura[F]

hairbrushes
spazzole[F] per capelli[M]

flat-back brush
spazzola[F] a dorso[M] piatto

round brush
spazzola[F] rotonda

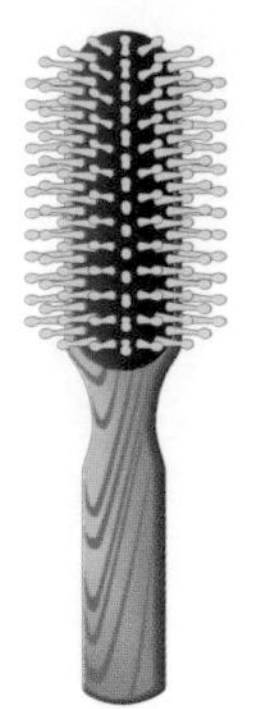

quill brush
spazzola[F] antistatica

vent brush
spazzola[F] ragno

combs
pettini[M]

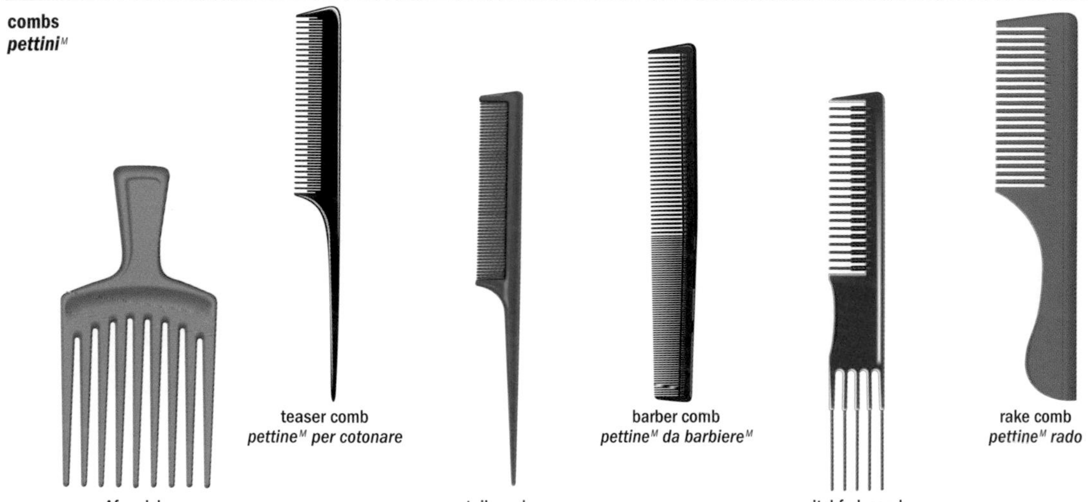

teaser comb
pettine[M] per cotonare

barber comb
pettine[M] da barbiere[M]

rake comb
pettine[M] rado

Afro pick
pettine[M] afro

tail comb
pettine[M] a coda[F]

pitchfork comb
pettine[M] a forchetta[F]

hair roller
bigodino[M]

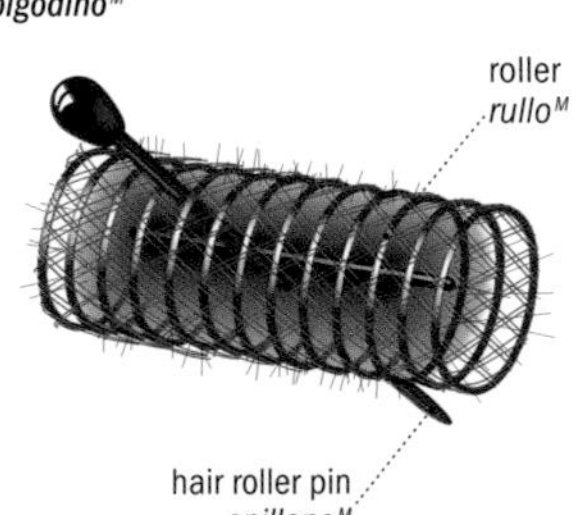

wave clip
pinza[F] per capelli[M]

hairpin
forcina[F]

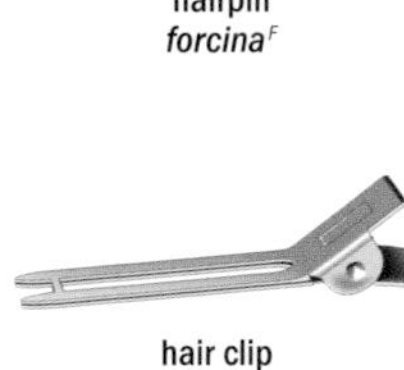

hair clip
beccuccio[M]

bobby pin
molletta[F]

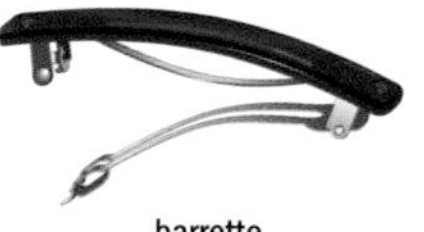

barrette
fermacapelli[M]

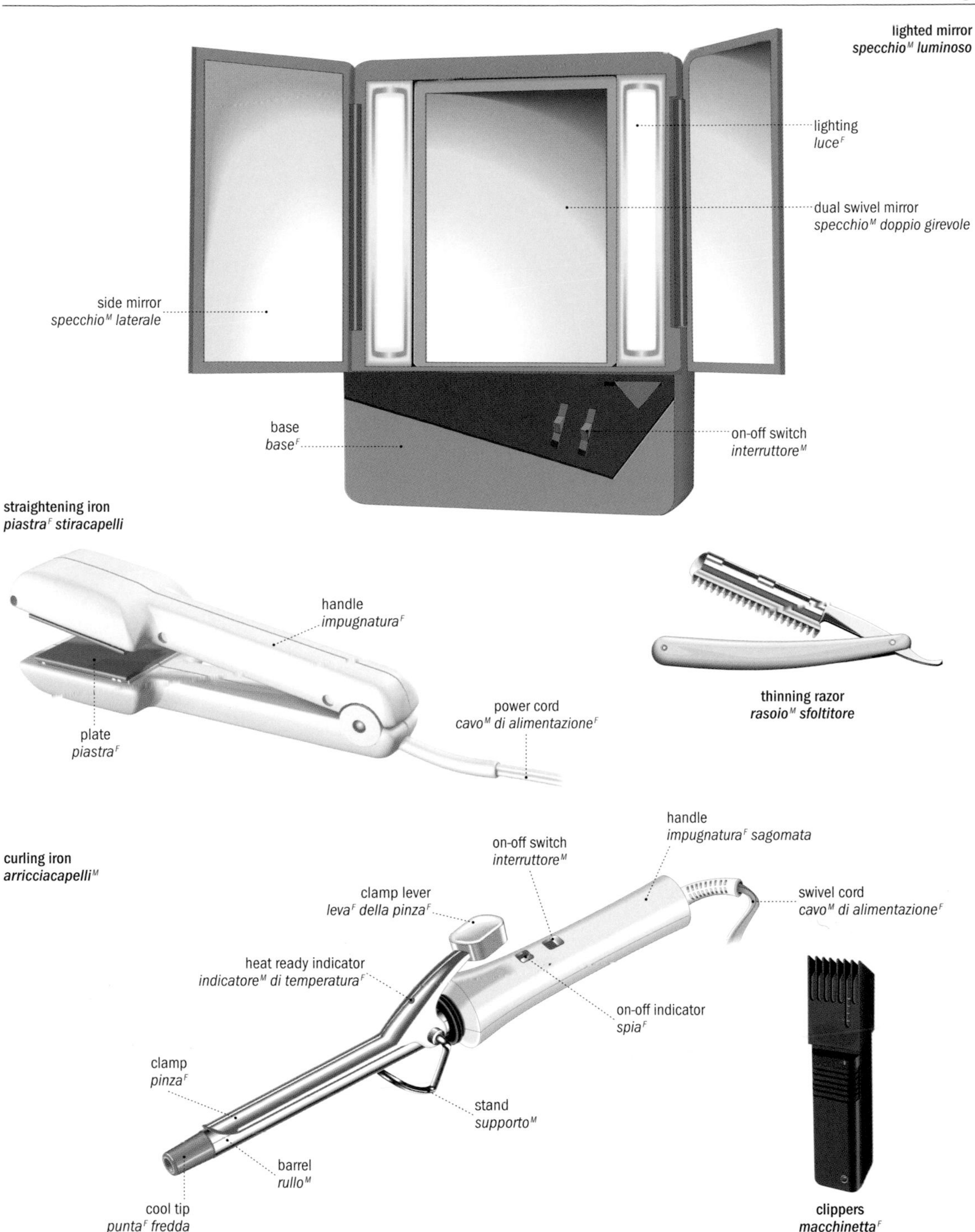
lighted mirror
specchio luminoso
lighting
luce
dual swivel mirror
specchio doppio girevole
side mirror
specchio laterale
base
base
on-off switch
interruttore
straightening iron
piastra stiracapelli
handle
impugnatura
plate
piastra
power cord
cavo di alimentazione
thinning razor
rasoio sfoltitore
curling iron
arricciacapelli
handle
impugnatura sagomata
on-off switch
interruttore
clamp lever
leva della pinza
swivel cord
cavo di alimentazione
heat ready indicator
indicatore di temperatura
on-off indicator
spia
clamp
pinza
stand
supporto
barrel
rullo
cool tip
punta fredda
clippers
macchinetta

hairdressing

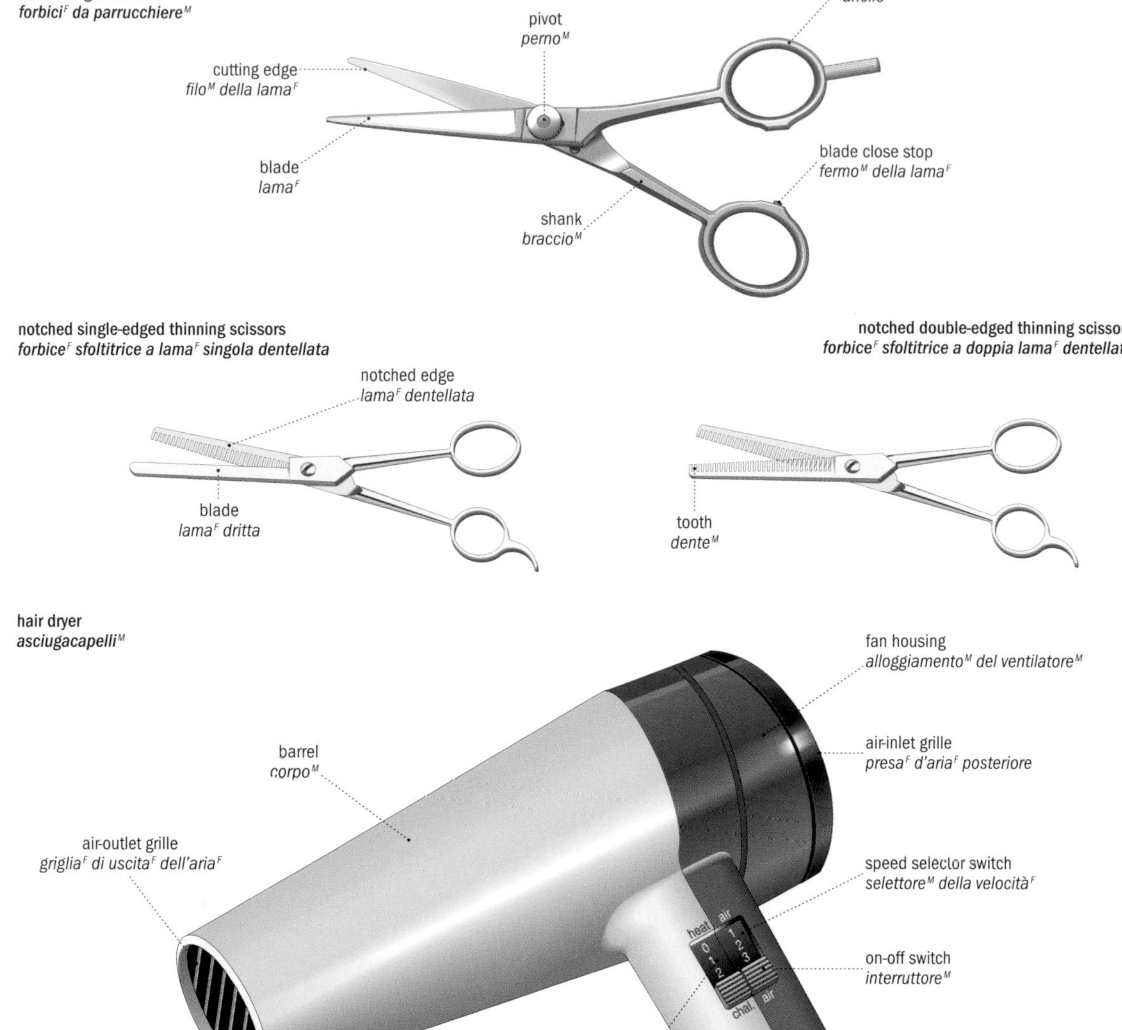

shaving

rasatura[F]

shaving foam
schiuma[F] da barba[F]

power cord
cordone[M] dell'alimentazione[F]

cleaning brush
spazzolino[M] di pulizia[F]

electric razor
rasoio[M] elettrico

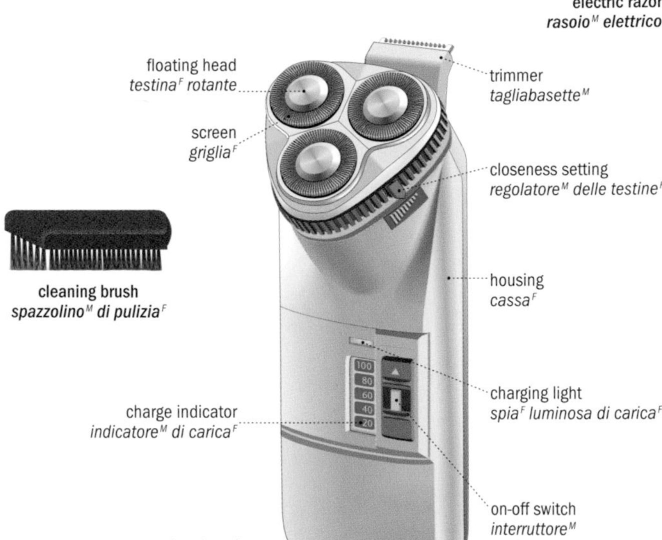

shaving brush
pennello[M] da barba[F]

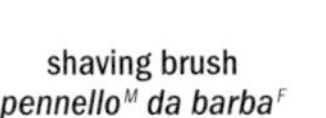

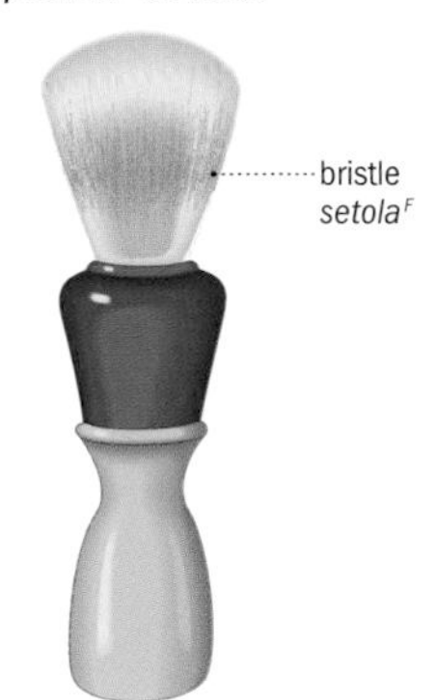

plug adapter
adattatore[M]

straight razor
rasoio[M] a mano[F] libera

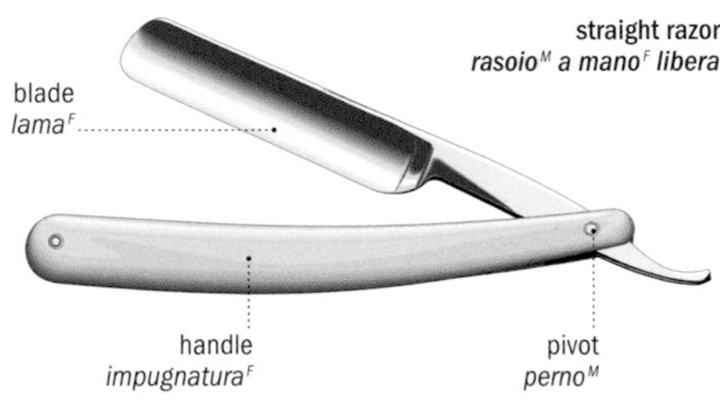

aftershave
dopobarba[M]

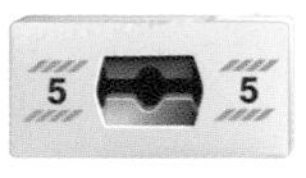

blade injector
caricatore[M] di lamette[F]

shaving mug
tazza[F] per sapone[M] da barba[F]

double-edged blade
lametta[F] a due tagli[M]

double-edged razor
rasoio[M] di sicurezza[F]

disposable razor
rasoio[M] usa e getta

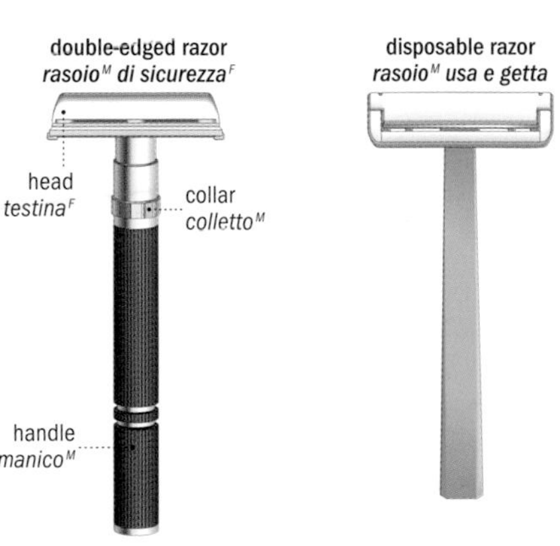

PERSONAL ADORNMENT AND ARTICLES

dental care

igiene^F orale

toothbrush
spazzolino^M da denti^M

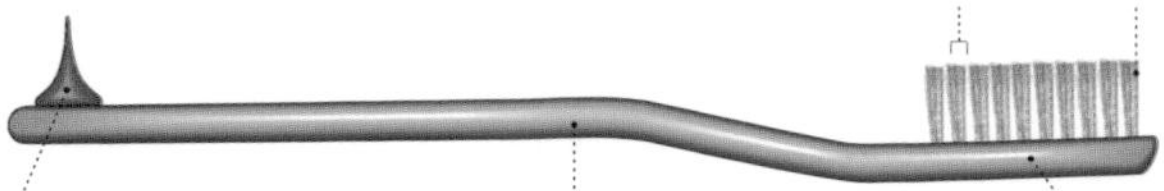

row
fila^F
bristle
setola^F
stimulator tip
stimolatore^M gengivale
handle
manico^M
head
testa^F

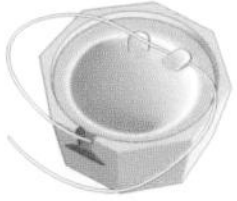

dental floss
filo^M interdentale

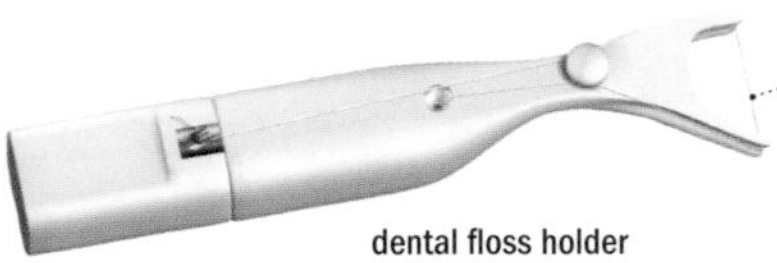

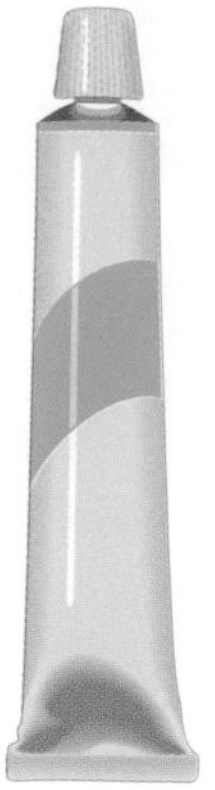

toothpaste
dentifricio^M

dental floss
filo^M interdentale

dental floss holder
contenitore^M per filo^M interdentale

oral hygiene center
spazzolino^M da denti^M elettrico

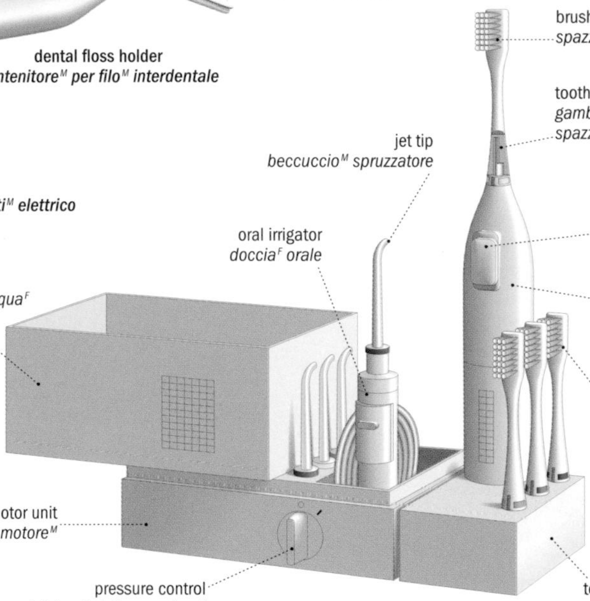

brush
spazzola^F
toothbrush shaft
gambo^M a innesto^M dello spazzolino^M
jet tip
beccuccio^M spruzzatore
on-off switch
interruttore^M
oral irrigator
doccia^F orale
water tank
serbatoio^F dell'acqua^F
handle
impugnatura^F
toothbrush
spazzolino^M da denti^M
motor unit
blocco^M motore^M
pressure control
regolatore^M della pressione^F
toothbrush well
vano^M portaspazzolini

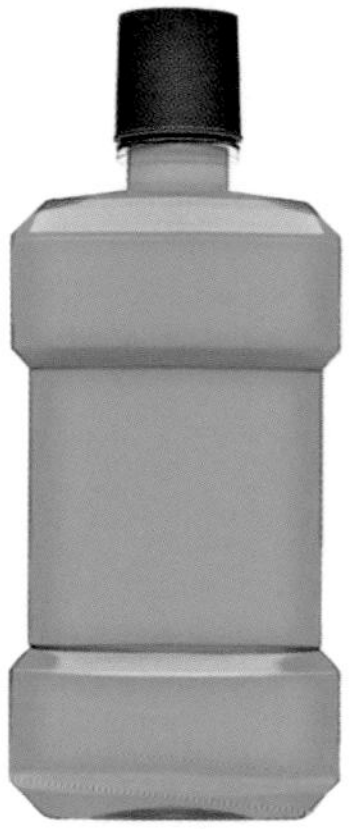

mouthwash
collutorio^M

contact lenses

lenti^F a contatto^M

multipurpose solution
soluzione^F multiuso

lubricant eye drops
gocce^F oftalmiche lubrificanti

soft contact lens
lente^F a contatto^M morbida

disposable contact lens
lente^F a contatto^M monouso

hard contact lens
lente^F a contatto^M rigida

left side
lato^M sinistro
right side
lato^M destro

lens case
portalenti^M

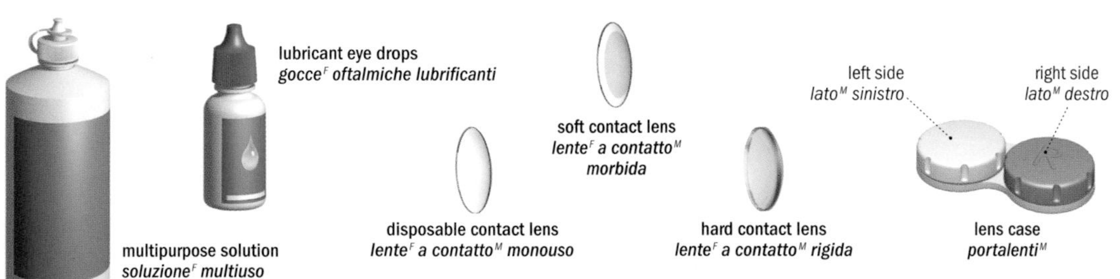

eyeglasses

occhiali^M

eyeglasses parts
parti^F degli occhiali^M

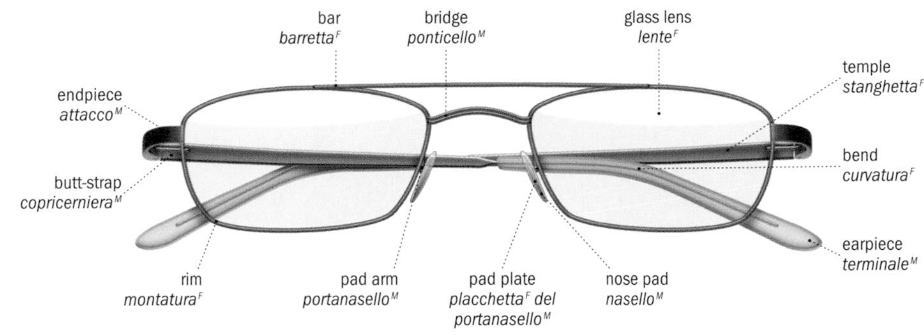

examples of eyeglasses
esempi^M di occhiali^M

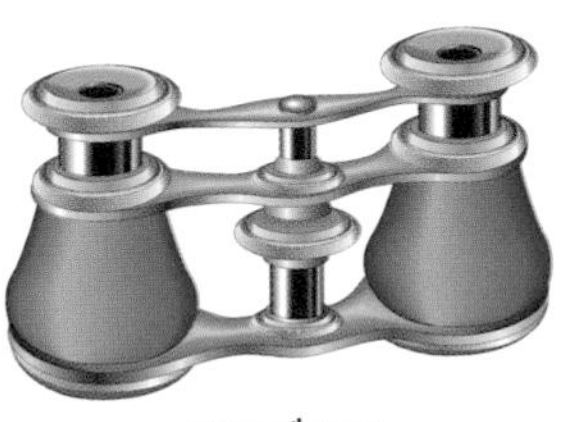

opera glasses
binocolo^M da teatro^M

sunglasses
occhiali^M da sole^M

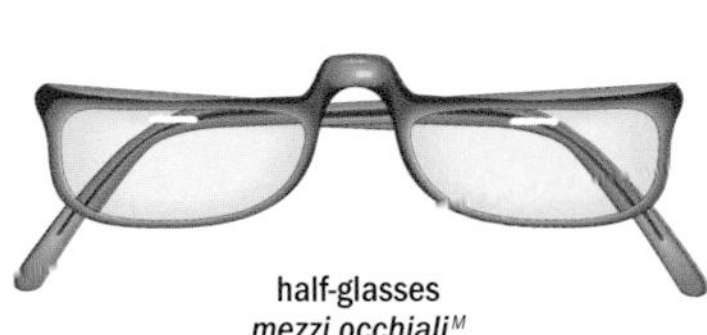

half-glasses
mezzi occhiali^M

umbrellas and stick

ombrelli^M e bastone^M

umbrellas
ombrelli^M

umbrella stand
portaombrelli^M

walking stick
bastone^M da passeggio^M

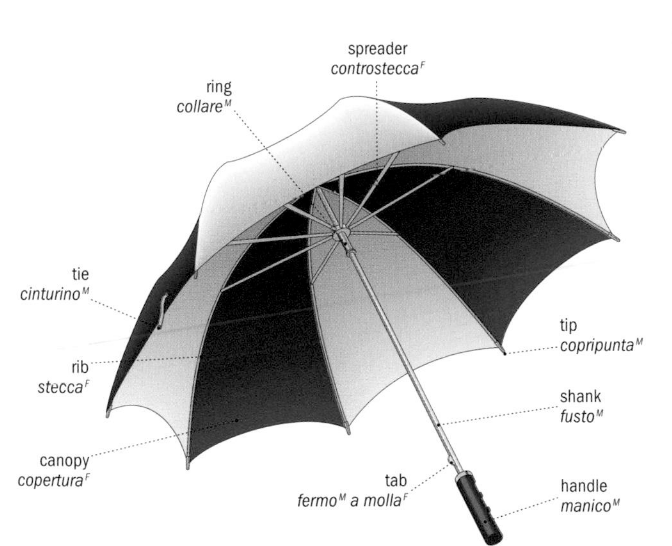

leather goods

articoli[M] di pelletteria[F]

attaché case
ventiquattrore[F]

clasp
chiusura[F]

divider
pannello[M] divisorio

expandable file pouch
scomparto[M] portadocumenti

pocket
tasca[F]

pen holder
portapenne[M]

hinge
reggicoperchio[M]

lining
fodera[F]

frame
telaio[M]

handle
manico[M]

combination lock
serratura[F] a combinazione[F]

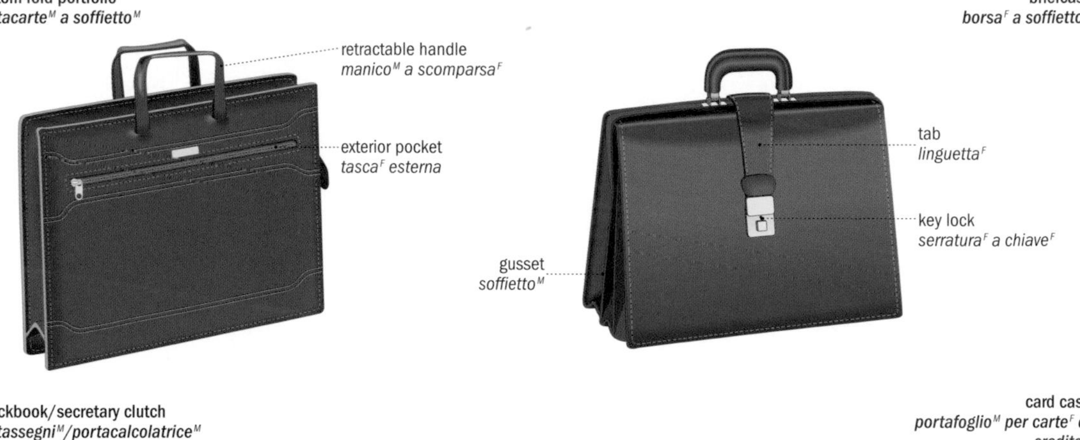

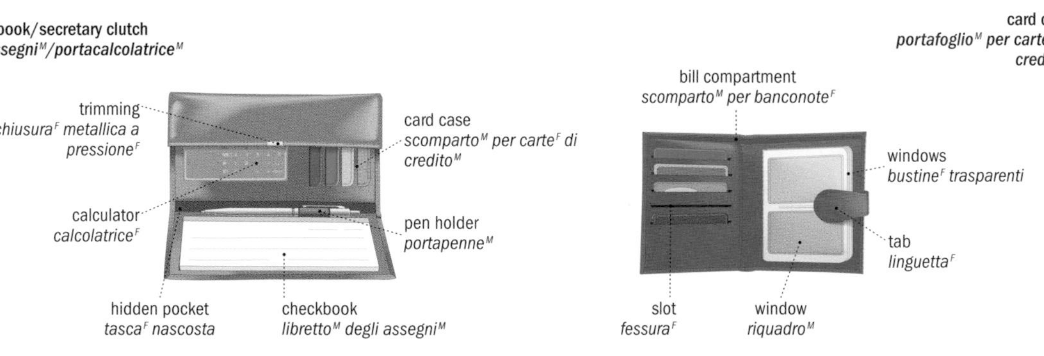

leather goods

wallet
*portafoglio*ᴹ

coin purse
*portamonete*ᴹ

key case
*portachiavi*ᴹ

purse
*borsellino*ᴹ

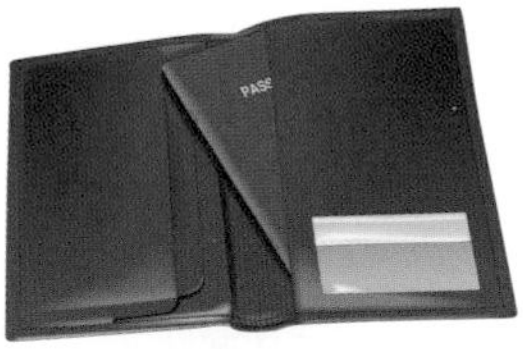

passport case
*portapassaporto*ᴹ

billfold
*portafoglio*ᴹ

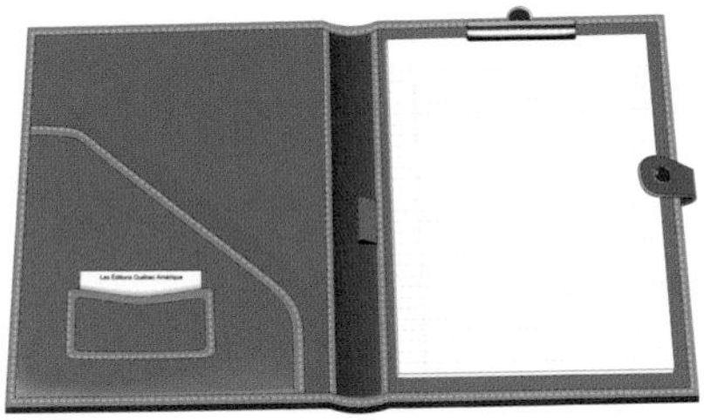

writing case
*portablocco*ᴹ

checkbook
*portassegni*ᴹ

eyeglasses case
*astuccio*ᴹ *per occhiali*ᴹ

underarm portfolio
*busta*ᶠ *portadocumenti*

handbags

borse^F

drawstring bag
secchiello^M *con cordoncino*^M

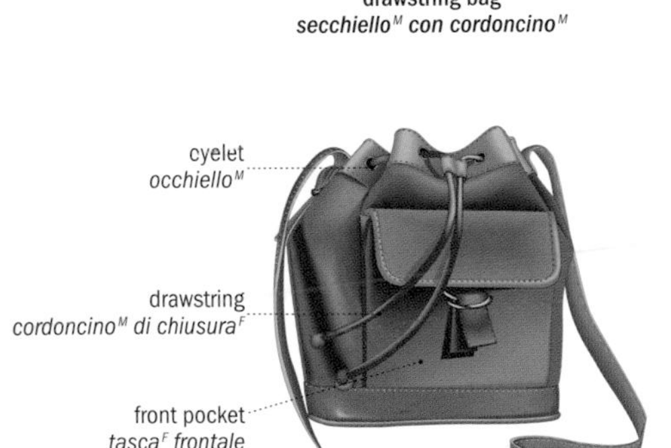

satchel bag
cartella^F

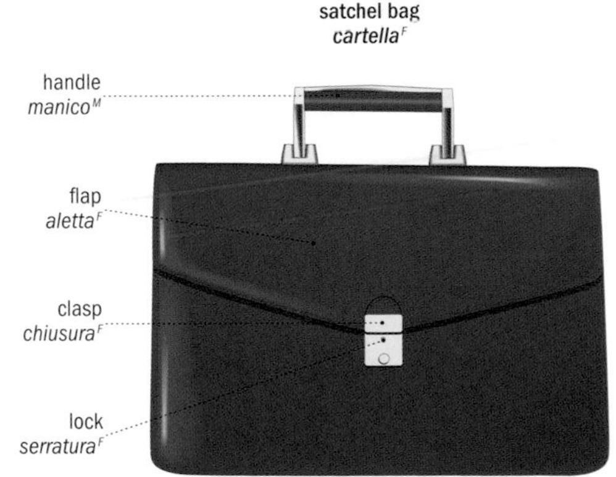

handbags

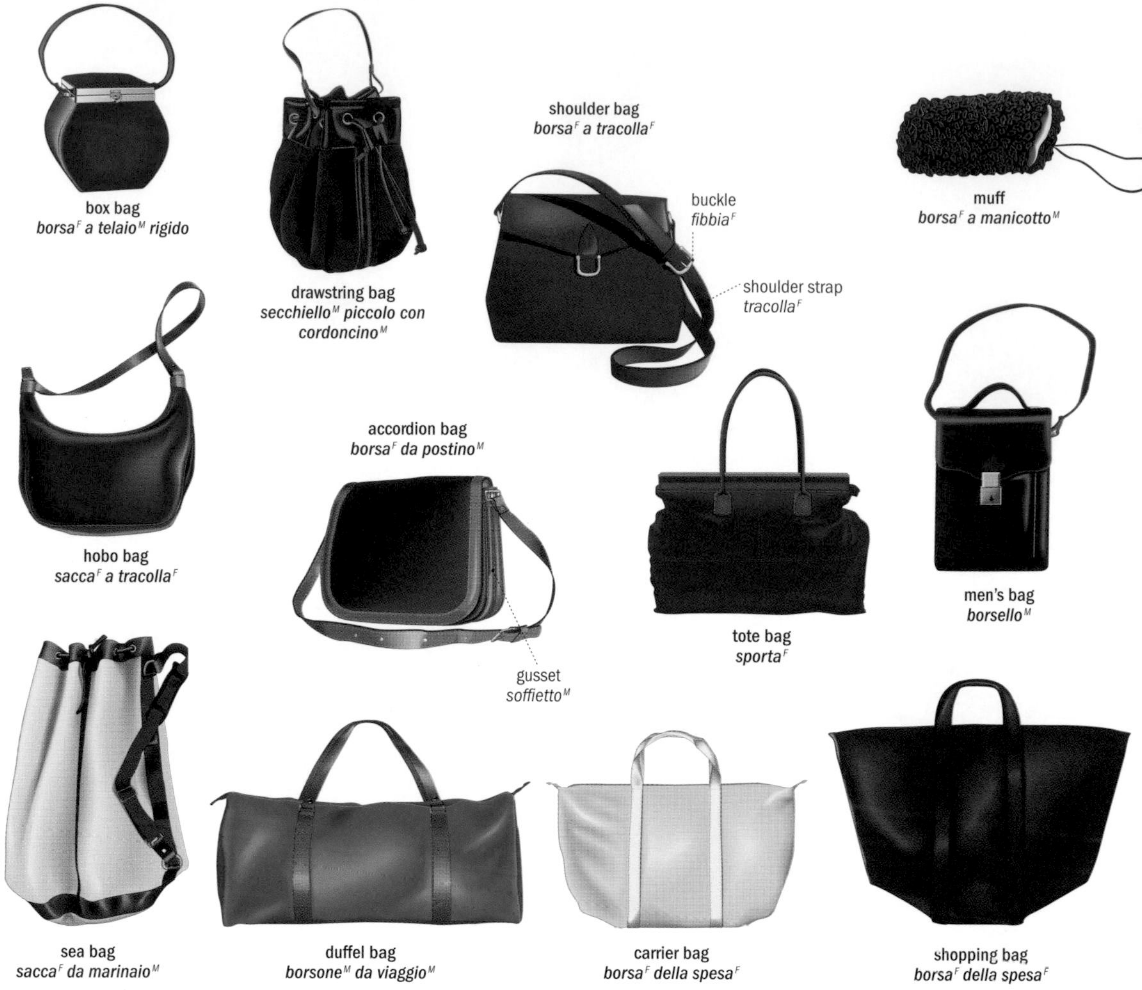

box bag
borsa^{F} a telaio^{M} rigido
drawstring bag
secchiello^{M} piccolo con cordoncino^{M}
shoulder bag
borsa^{F} a tracolla^{F}
buckle
fibbia^{F}
shoulder strap
tracolla^{F}
muff
borsa^{F} a manicotto^{M}
hobo bag
sacca^{F} a tracolla^{F}
accordion bag
borsa^{F} da postino^{M}
gusset
soffietto^{M}
tote bag
sporta^{F}
men's bag
borsello^{M}
sea bag
sacca^{F} da marinaio^{M}
duffel bag
borsone^{M} da viaggio^{M}
carrier bag
borsa^{F} della spesa^{F}
shopping bag
borsa^{F} della spesa^{F}

luggage

bagagli^{M}

utility case
trousse^{F}
carry-on bag
borsa^{F} da viaggio^{M}
handle
manico^{M}
exterior pocket
tasca^{F} esterna
shoulder strap
tracolla^{F}
tote bag
bagaglio^{M} a mano^{F}

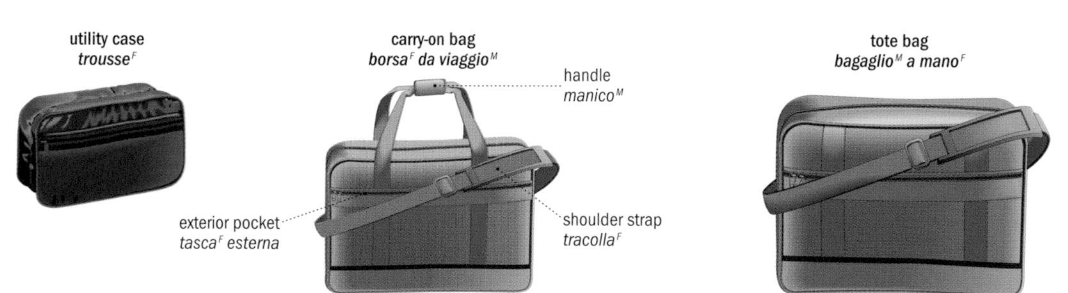

Roman amphitheater

anfiteatro^M romano

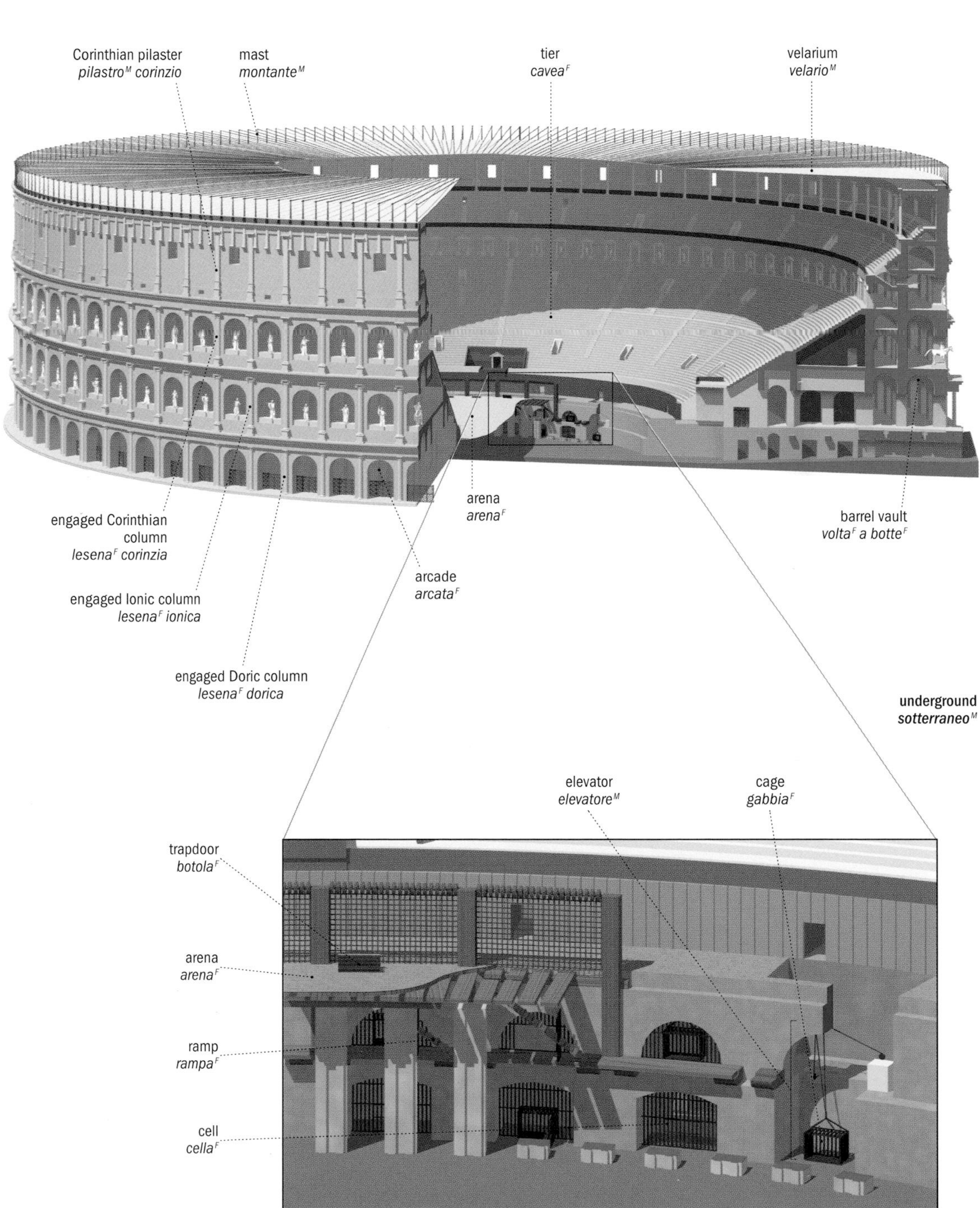

castle

castello[M]

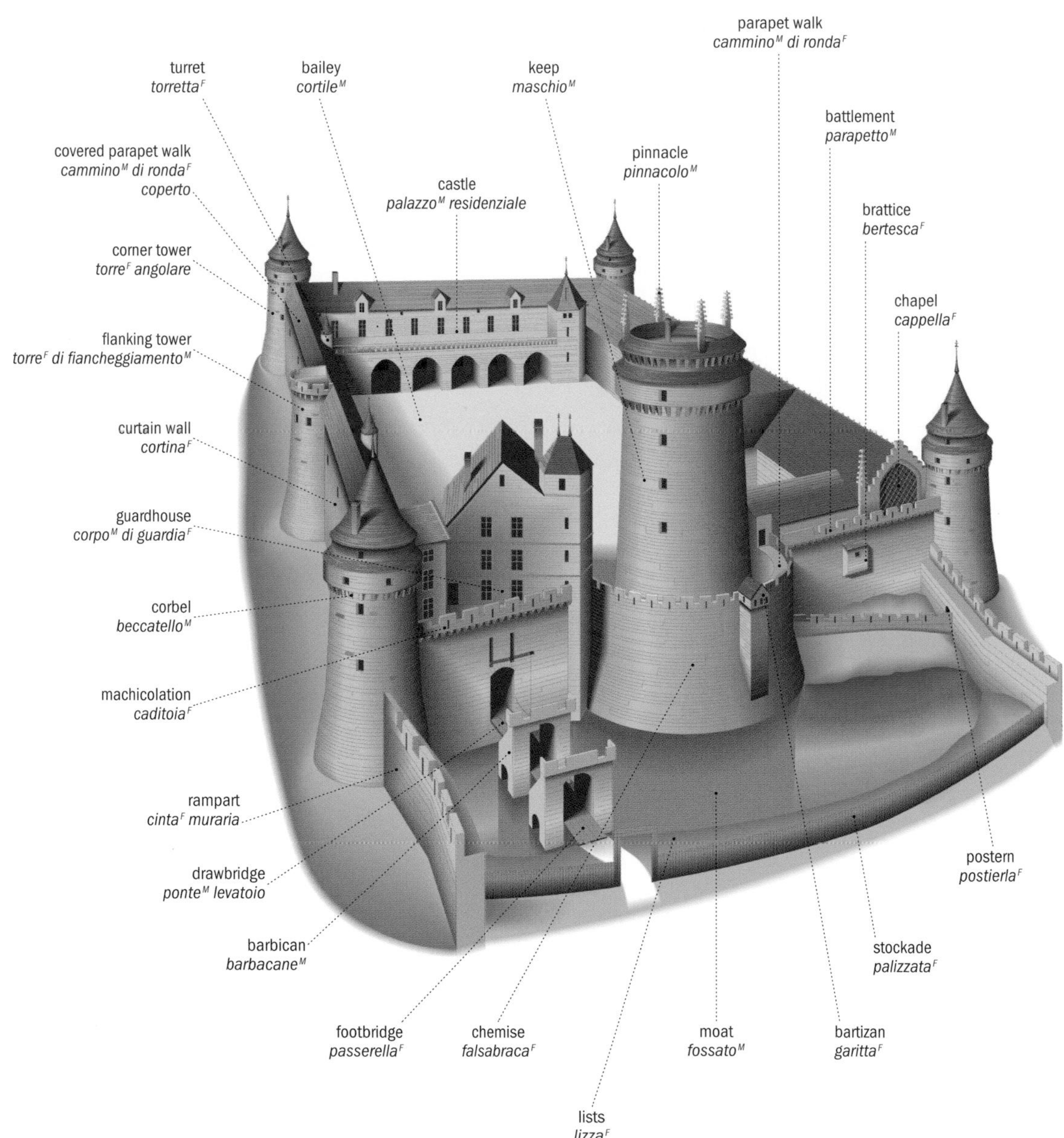

pagoda

pagoda[F]

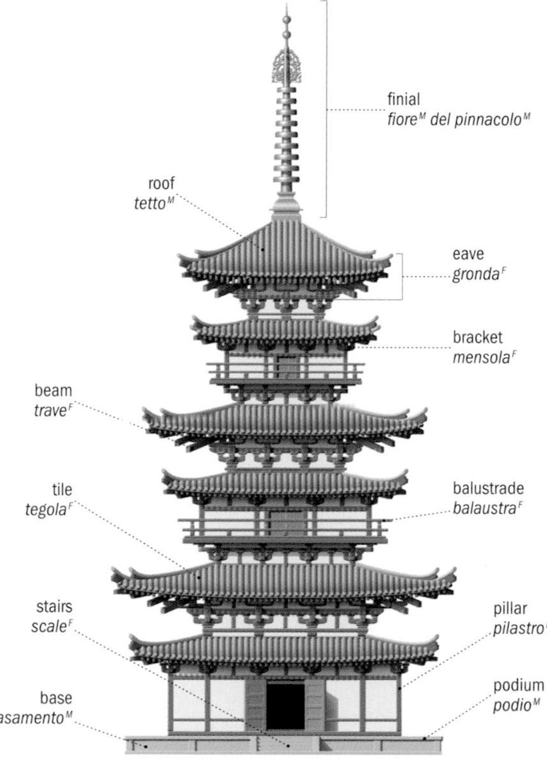

Aztec temple

tempio[M] azteco

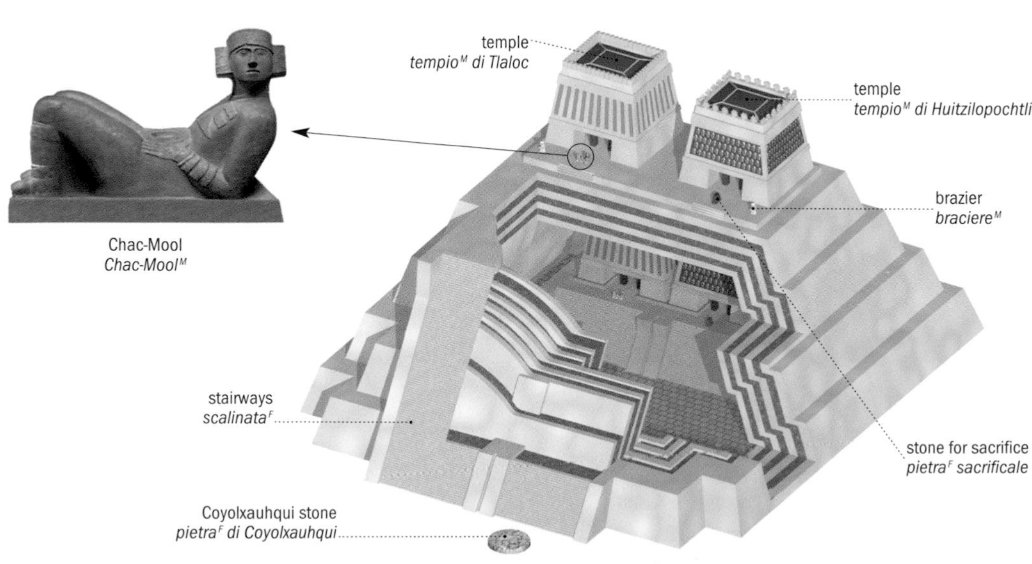

cathedral

cattedrale^F

Gothic cathedral
cattedrale^F gotica

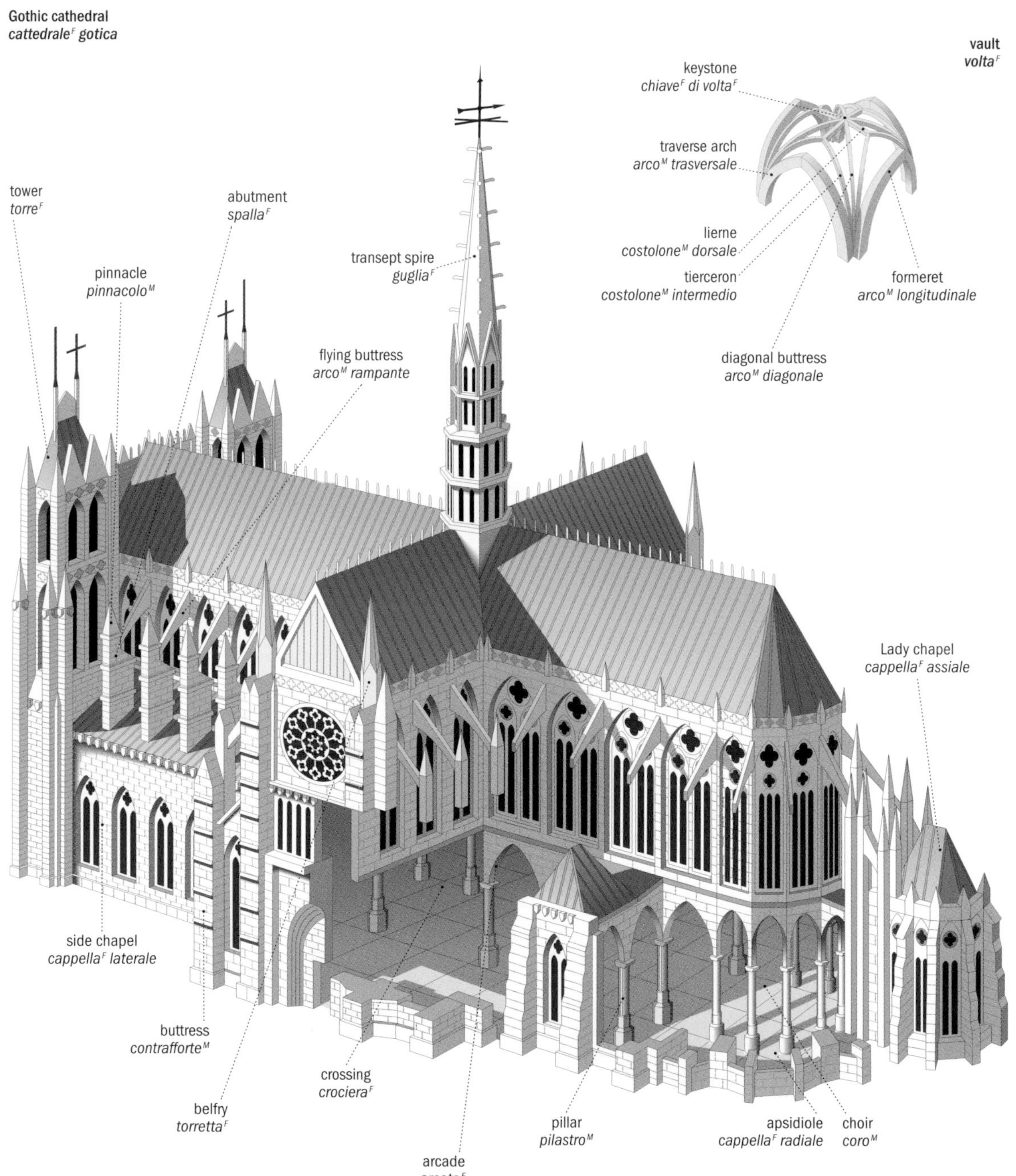

cathedral

façade
*facciata*F

louver-board
abat-son M
bell tower
torre F campanaria
gallery
galleria F
rose window
rosone M
spire
guglia F
tracery
traforo M
belfry
torretta F
stained glass
vetro M colorato
gable
gattone M
flying buttress
arco M rampante
trefoil
decorazione F a trifoglio M
order
archivolto M
tympanum
timpano M
lintel
architrave M
splay
strombatura F
pier
trumeau M
portal
portale M
pier
piedritto M

plan
*pianta*F

transept
transetto M
ambulatory
deambulatorio M
apsidiole
cappella F radiale
aisle
navata F laterale
chevet
capocroce M
nave
navata F centrale
Lady chapel
cappella F assiale
porch
portico M
crossing
crociera F
choir
coro M
apse
abside F

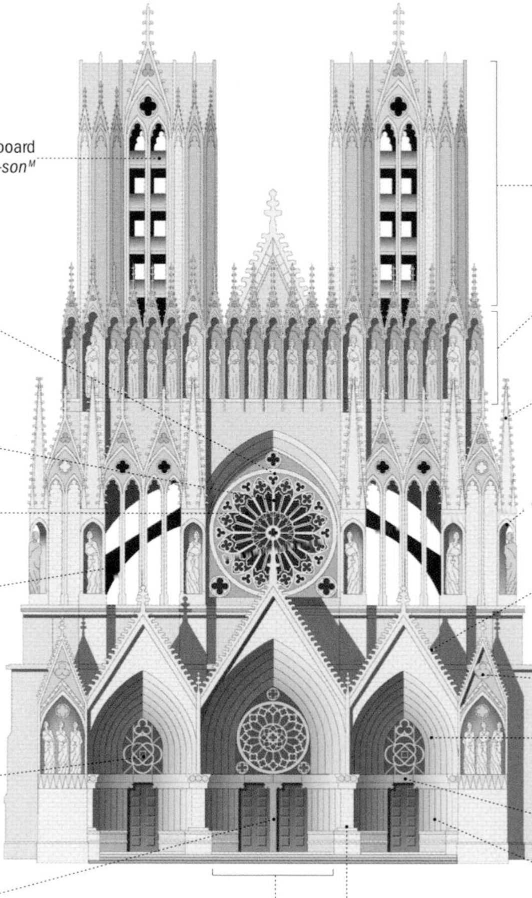

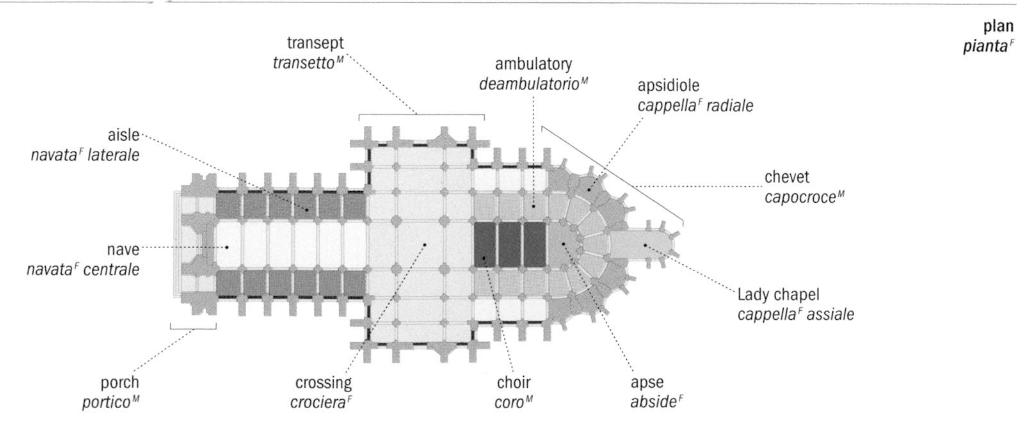

elements of architecture

elementi^M architettonici

examples of doors
esempi^M di porte^F

manual revolving door
porta^F girevole manuale

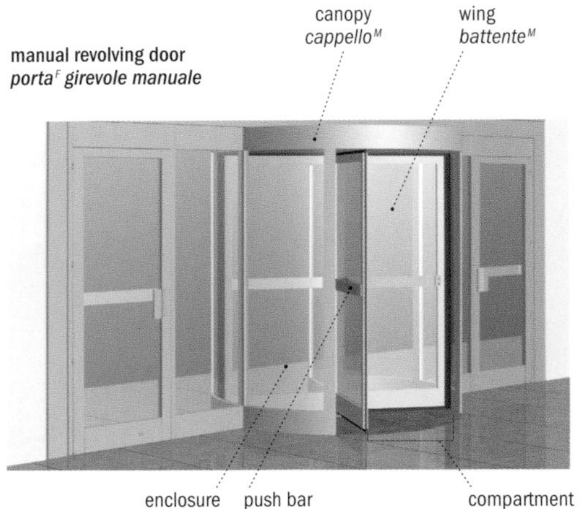

automatic sliding door
porta^F scorrevole automatica

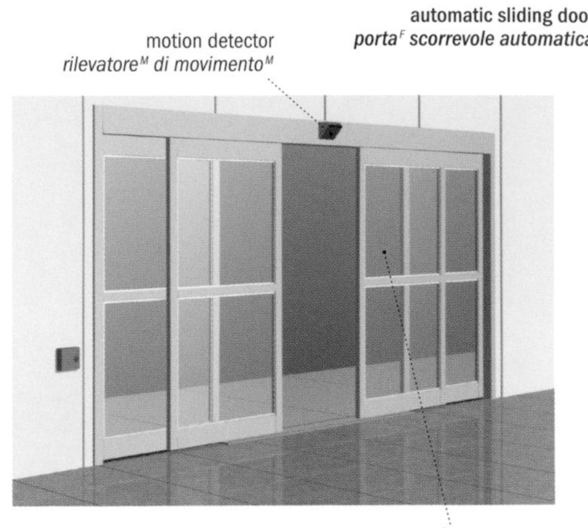

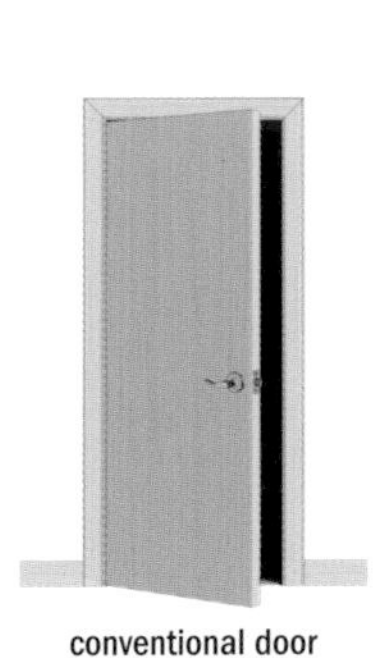

conventional door
porta^F a un battente^M

folding door
porta^F a libro^M

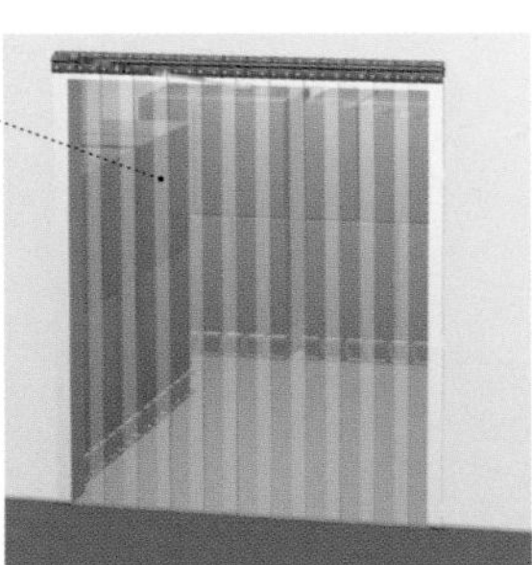

strip door
porta^F a bande^F verticali

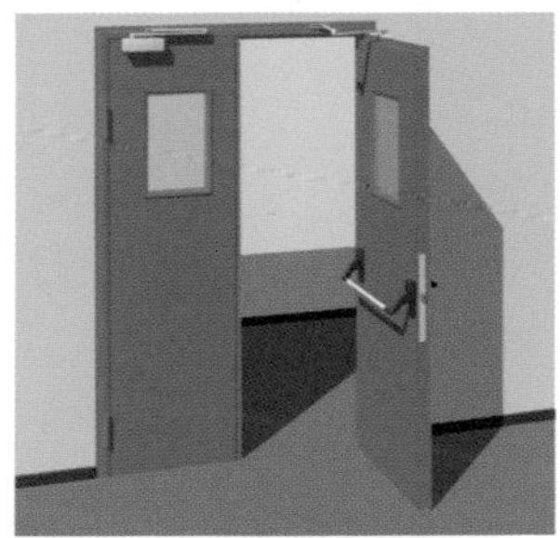

fire door
porta^F antincendio

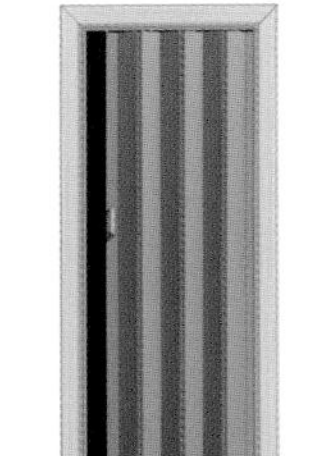

sliding folding door
porta^F a fisarmonica^F

sliding door
porta^F scorrevole

sectional garage door
porta^F sezionale del garage^M

up and over garage door
porta^F basculante del garage^M

examples of windows
esempi[M] di finestre[F]

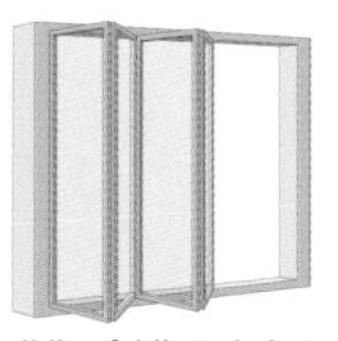

sliding folding window
finestra[F] a libro[M]

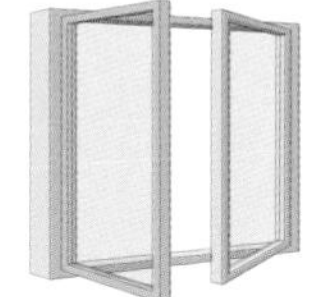

French window
finestra[F] a battenti[M] con apertura[F] all'interno[M]

casement window
finestra[F] a battenti[M]

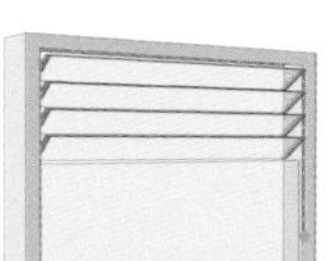

louvered window
finestra[F] a gelosia[F]

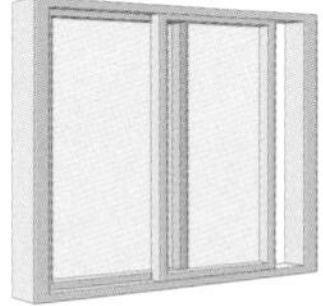

sliding window
finestra[F] scorrevole

sash window
finestra[F] a ghigliottina[F]

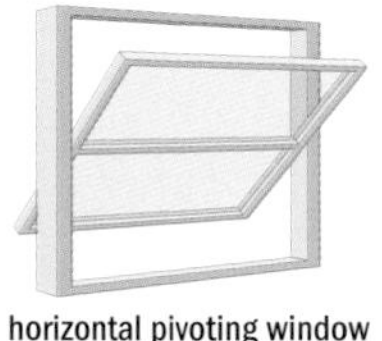

horizontal pivoting window
finestra[F] a bilico[M] orizzontale

vertical pivoting window
finestra[F] a bilico[M] verticale

elevator

ascensore[M]

elevator car
cabina[F] dell'ascensore[M]

position indicator
indicatore[M] del piano[M]

car ceiling
soffitto[M] della cabina[F]

operating panel
pannello[M] di funzionamento[M]

handrail
corrimano[M]

car floor
pavimento[M] della cabina[F]

door
porta[F]

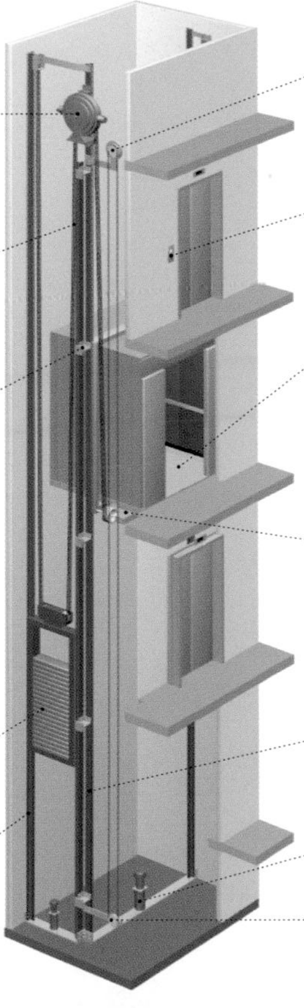

winch
argano[M]

hoisting rope
fune[F] di sollevamento[M]

limit switch
interruttore[M] di fine[F] corsa[F]

counterweight
contrappeso[M]

counterweight guide rail
guida[F] del contrappeso[M]

speed governor
regolatore[M] di velocità[F]

call button
pulsante[M] di chiamata[F]

elevator car
cabina[F] dell'ascensore[M]

car safety
paracadute[M]

car guide rail
guida[F] della cabina[F]

buffer
ammortizzatore[M]

governor tension sheave
puleggia[F] di tensione[F] del regolatore[M]

traditional houses

case^F tradizionali

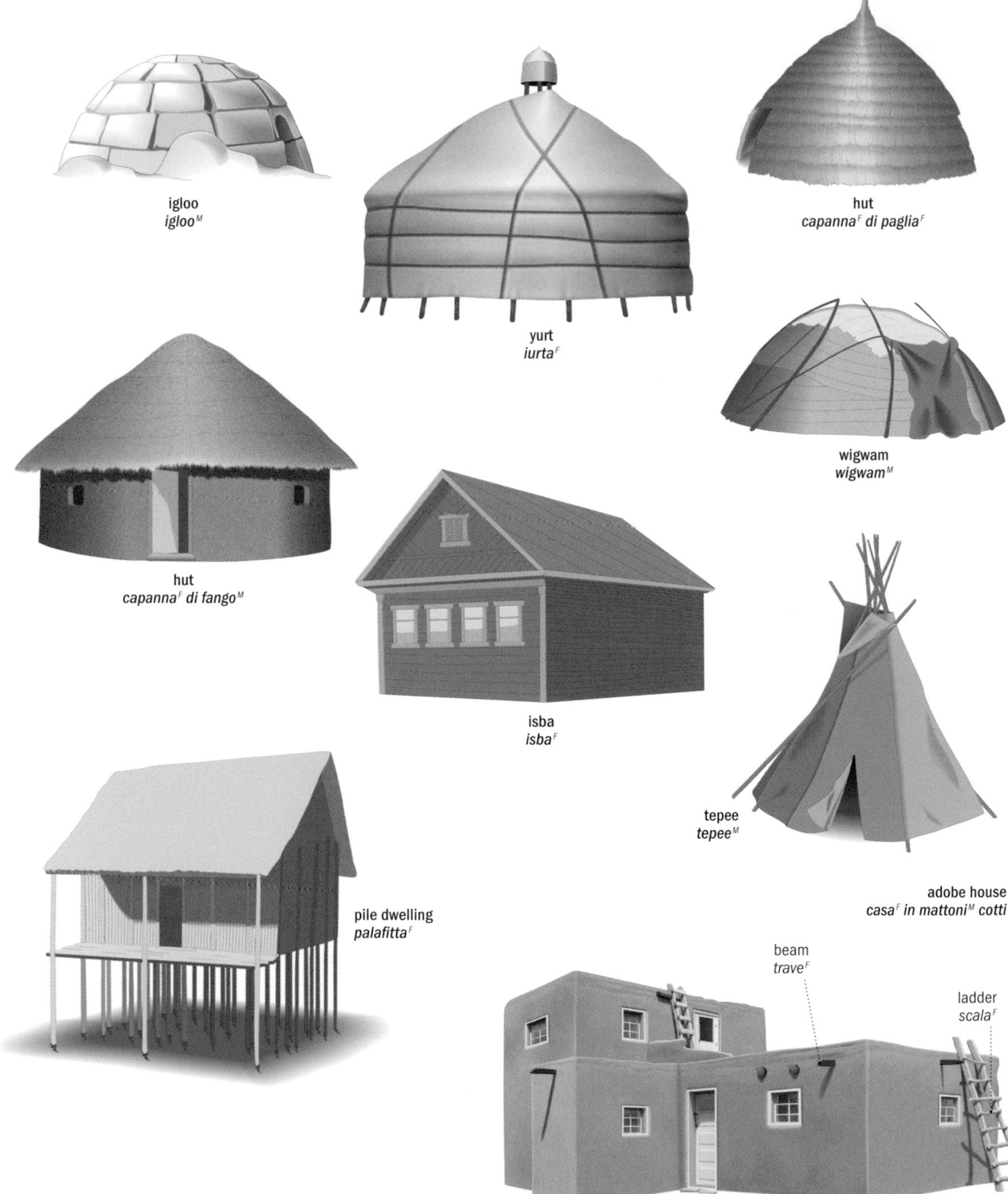

city houses

abitazioni^F urbane

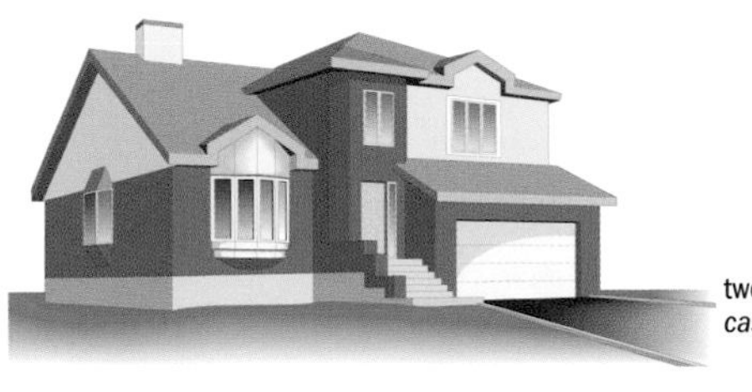

two-storey house
casa^F a due piani^M

one-storey house
casa^F a un piano^M

semidetached house
villetta^F bifamiliare

town houses
case^F a schiera^F

condominiums
palazzo^M in condominio^M

high-rise apartment building
casatorre^F

sound stage

set^M delle riprese^F

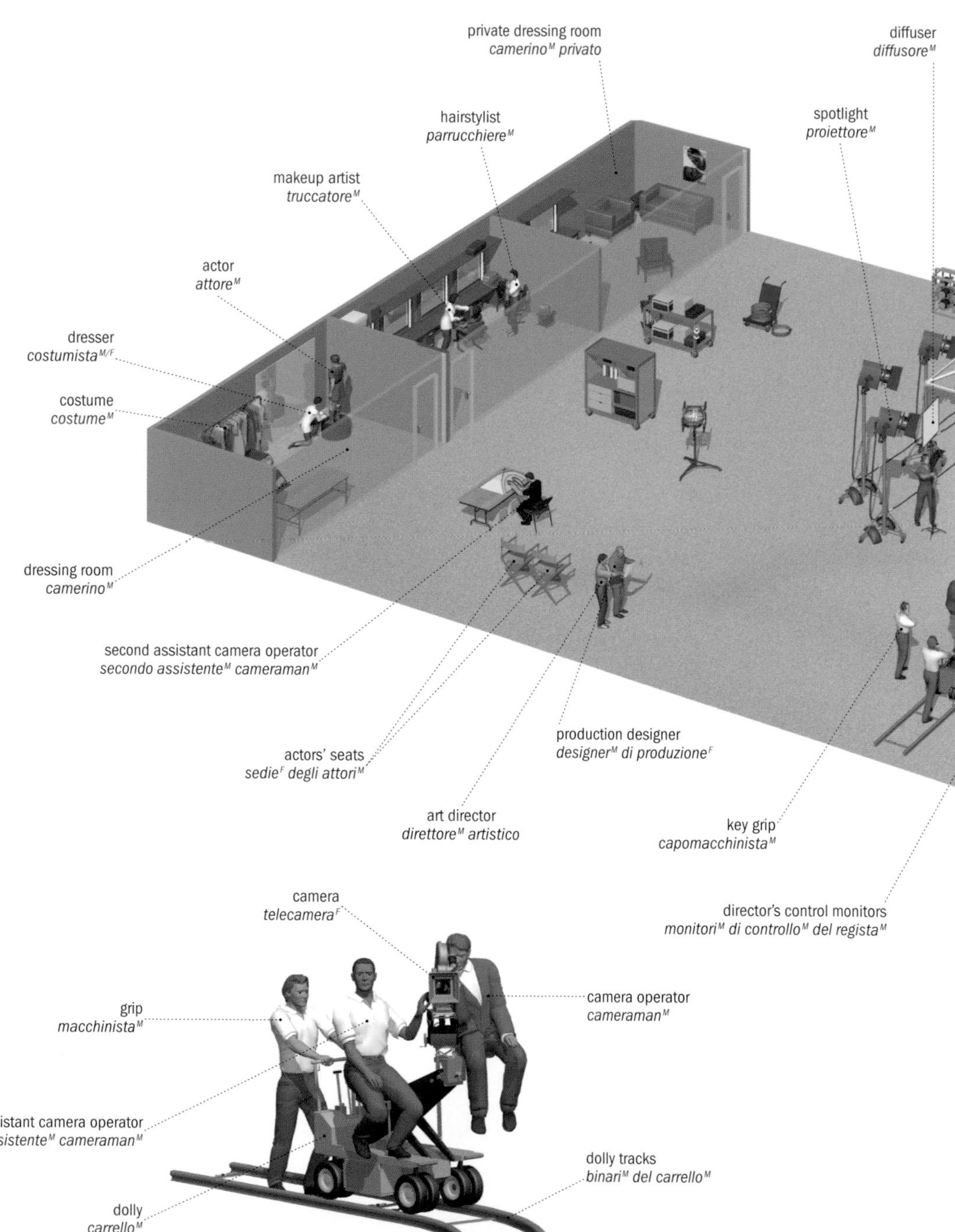

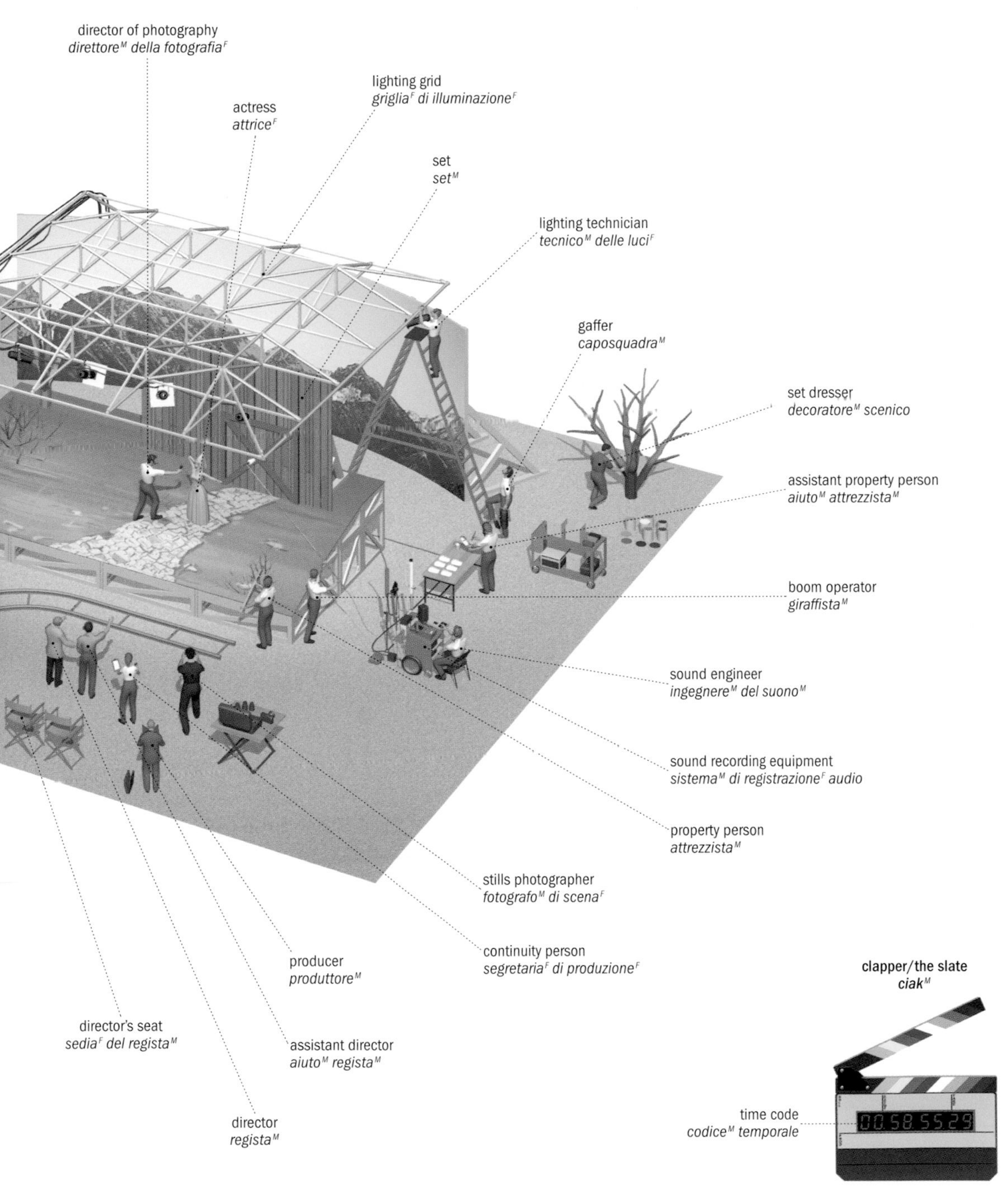

clapper/the slate
*ciak*M

time code
*codice*M *temporale*

theater

teatro^M

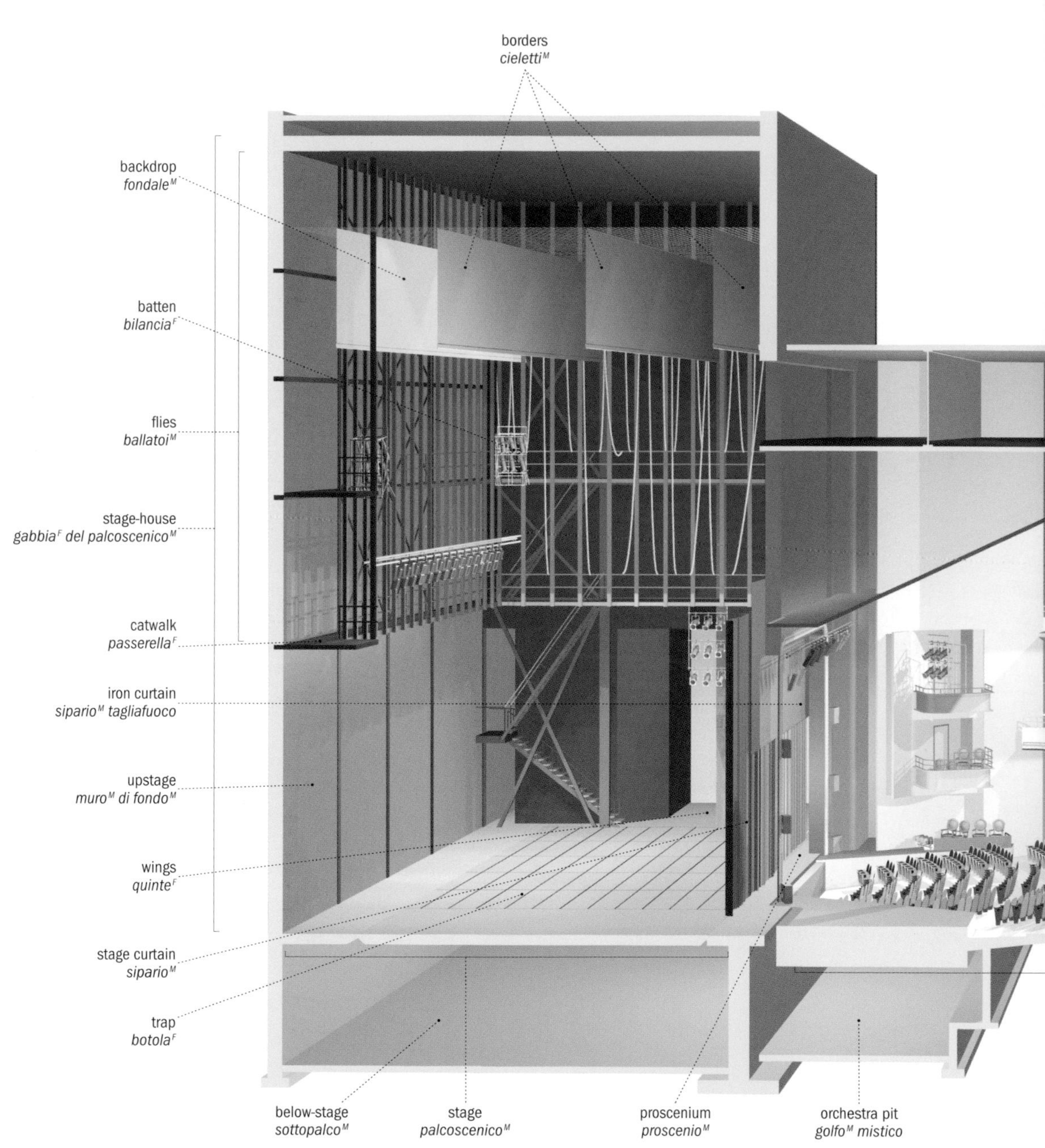

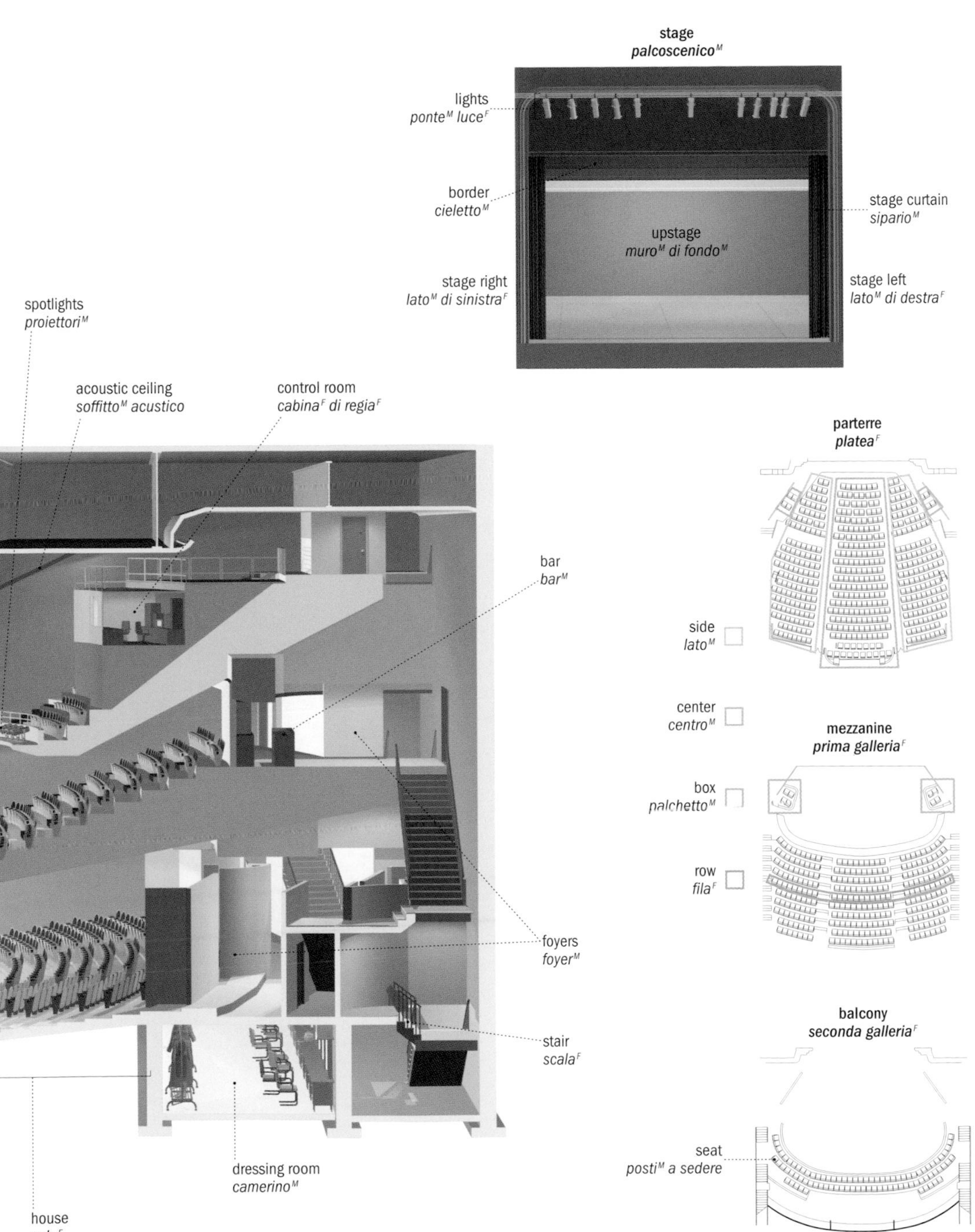
stage
palcoscenico[M]
lights
ponte[M] luce[F]
border
cieletto[M]
stage curtain
sipario[M]
upstage
muro[M] di fondo[M]
stage right
lato[M] di sinistra[F]
stage left
lato[M] di destra[F]
spotlights
proiettori[M]
acoustic ceiling
soffitto[M] acustico
control room
cabina[F] di regia[F]
parterre
platea[F]
bar
bar[M]
side
lato[M]
center
centro[M]
mezzanine
prima galleria[F]
box
palchetto[M]
row
fila[F]
foyers
foyer[M]
stair
scala[F]
balcony
seconda galleria[F]
seat
posti[M] a sedere
dressing room
camerino[M]
house
sala[F]

movie theater

cinema^{M}

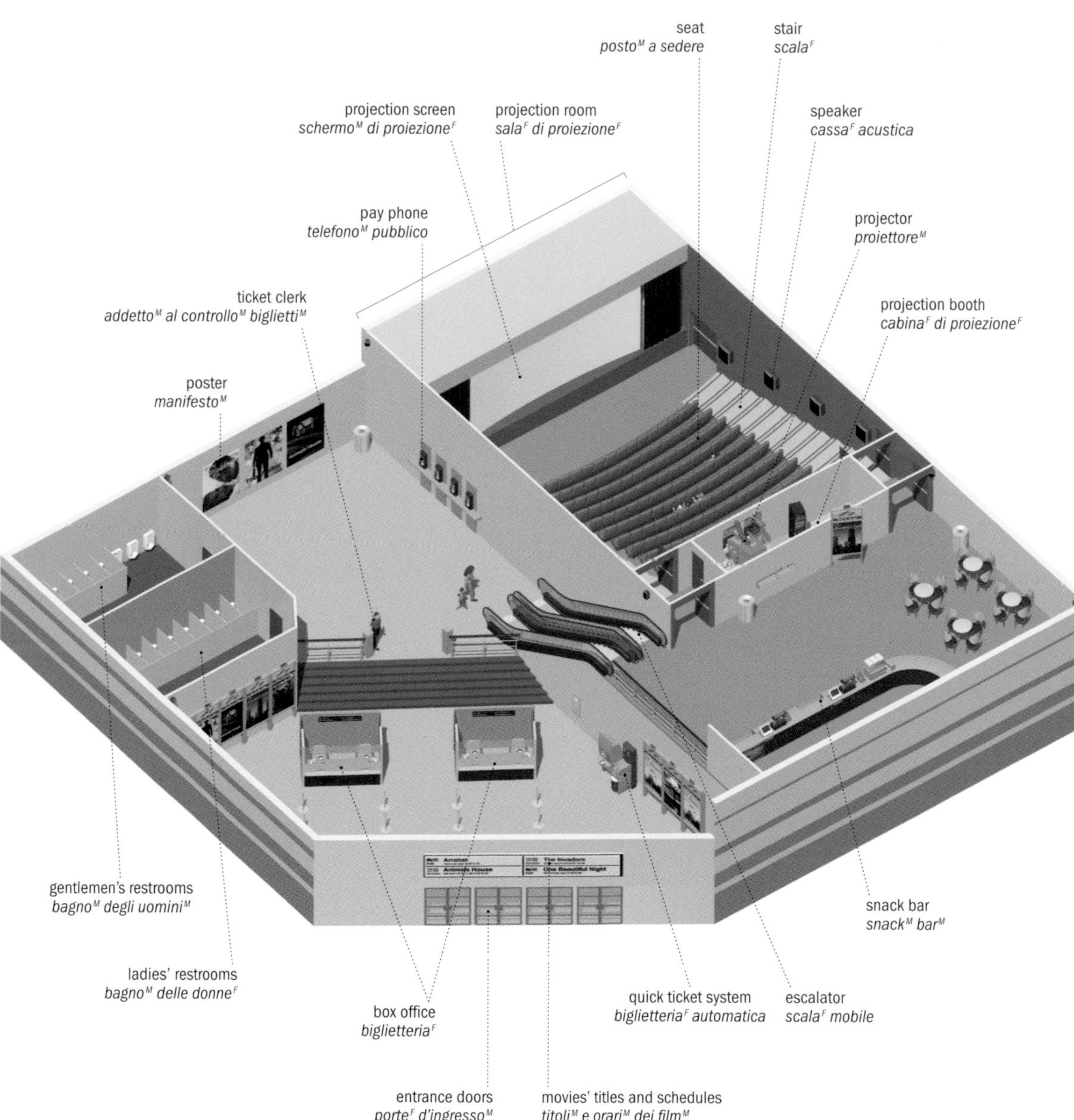

symphony orchestra

orchestra[F] sinfonica

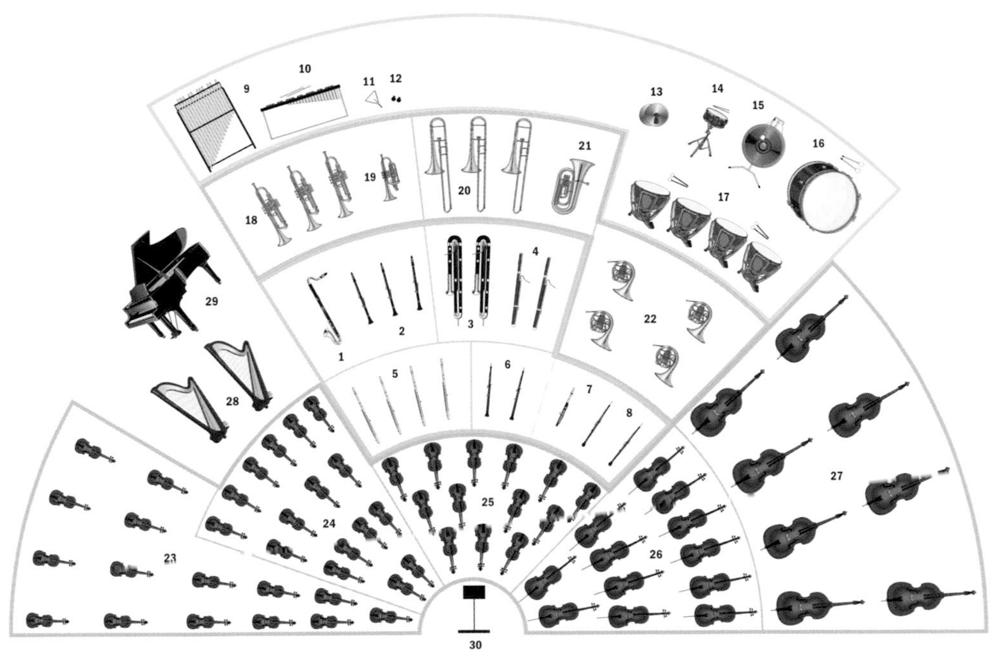

woodwind section
sezione[F] dei legni[M]

1 bass clarinet *clarinetto[M] basso*

2 clarinets *clarinetti[M]*

3 contrabassoons *controfagotti[M]*

4 bassoons *fagotti[M]*

5 flutes *flauti[M]*

6 oboes *oboi[M]*

7 piccolo *ottavino[M]*

8 English horns *corni[M] inglesi*

percussion section
strumenti[M] a percussione[F]

9 tubular bells *campane[F] tubolari*

10 xylophone *xilofono[M]*

11 triangle *triangolo[M]*

12 castanets *nacchere[F]*

13 cymbals *piatti[M]*

14 snare drum *cassa[F] chiara*

15 gong *gong[M]*

16 bass drum *grancassa[F]*

17 timpani *timpani[M]*

28 harps *arpe[F]*

brass section
sezione[F] degli ottoni[M]

18 trumpets *trombe[F]*

19 cornet *cornetta[F]*

20 trombones *tromboni[M]*

21 tuba *tuba[F]*

22 French horns *corni[M]*

29 piano *pianoforte[M]*

string section
sezione[F] degli archi[M]

23 first violins *primi violini[M]*

24 second violins *secondi violini[M]*

25 violas *viole[F]*

26 cellos *violoncelli[M]*

27 double basses *contrabbassi[M]*

30 conductor's podium *podio[M] del direttore[M] d'orchestra[F]*

traditional musical instruments

strumenti^{M} musicali tradizionali

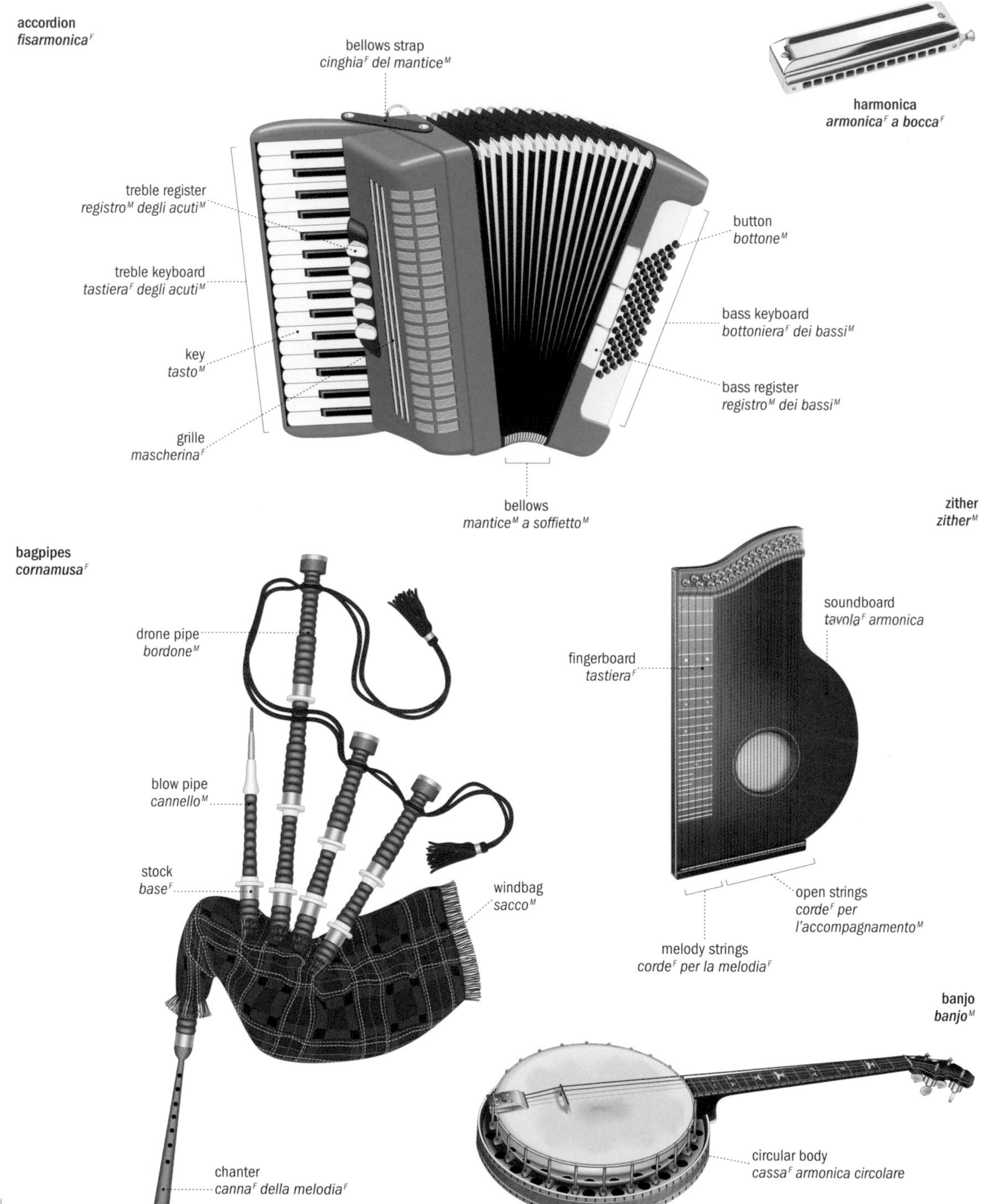

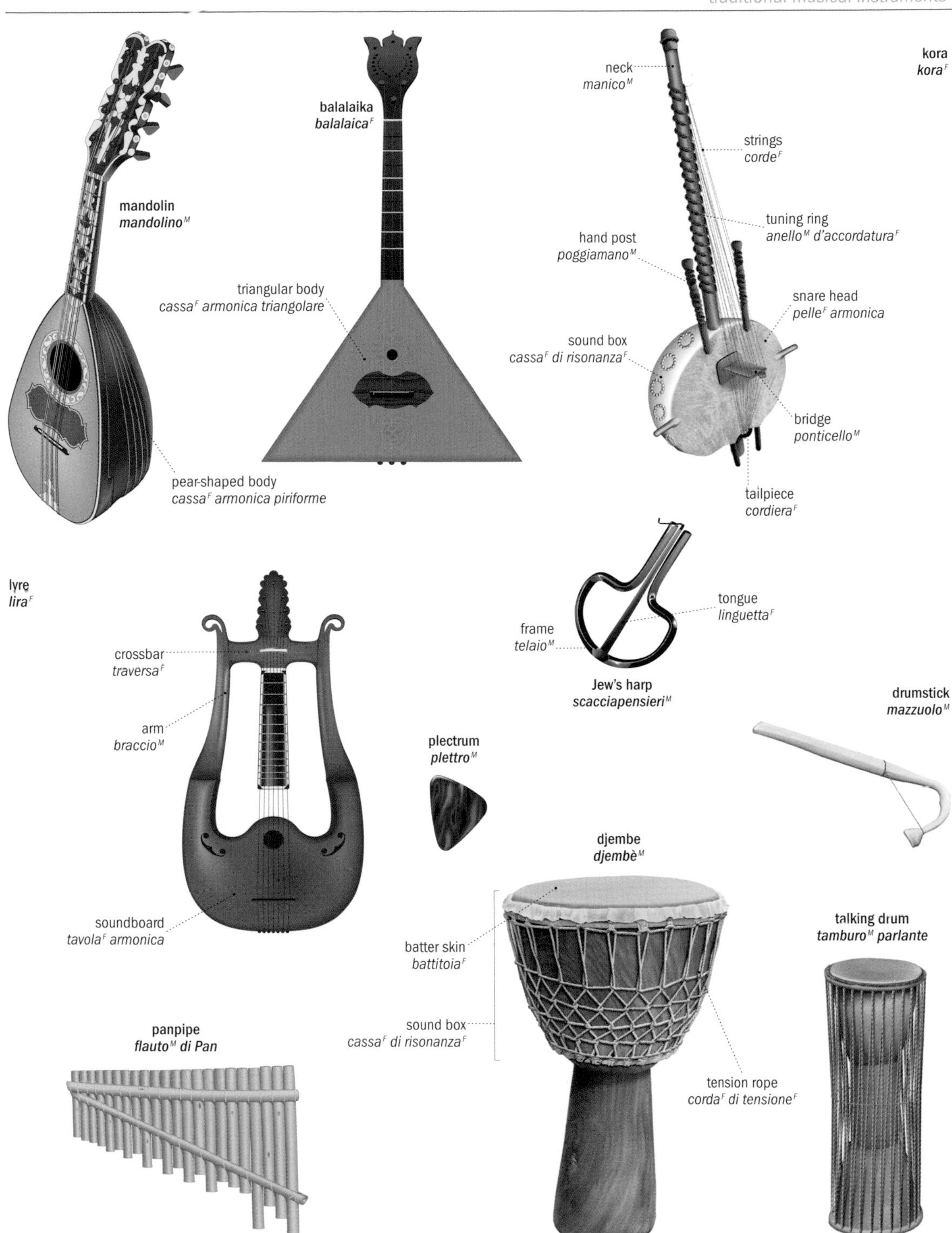
mandolin
mandolino^M
pear-shaped body
cassa^F armonica piriforme
balalaika
balalaica^F
triangular body
cassa^F armonica triangolare
kora
kora^F
neck
manico^M
strings
corde^F
tuning ring
anello^M d'accordatura^F
hand post
poggiamano^M
snare head
pelle^F armonica
sound box
cassa^F di risonanza^F
bridge
ponticello^M
tailpiece
cordiera^F
lyre
lira^F
crossbar
traversa^F
arm
braccio^M
soundboard
tavola^F armonica
plectrum
plettro^M
Jew's harp
scacciapensieri^M
tongue
linguetta^F
frame
telaio^M
drumstick
mazzuolo^M
djembe
djembè^M
batter skin
battitoia^F
sound box
cassa^F di risonanza^F
tension rope
corda^F di tensione^F
talking drum
tamburo^M parlante
panpipe
flauto^M di Pan

musical notation

notazione[F] musicale

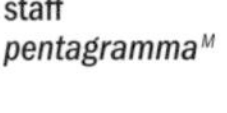

staff
pentagramma[M]

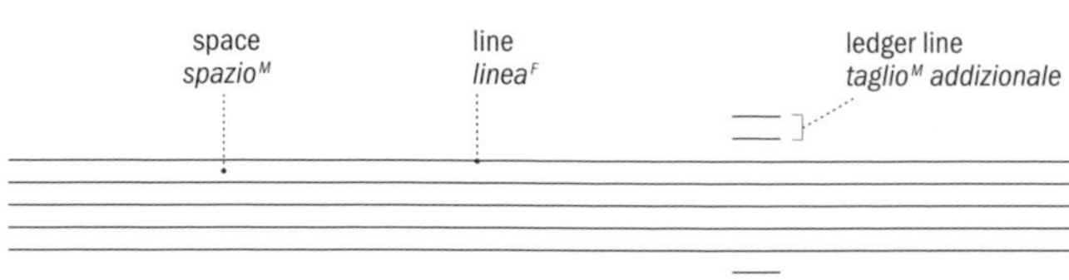

clefs
chiavi[F]

time signatures
indicazioni[F] di tempo[M]

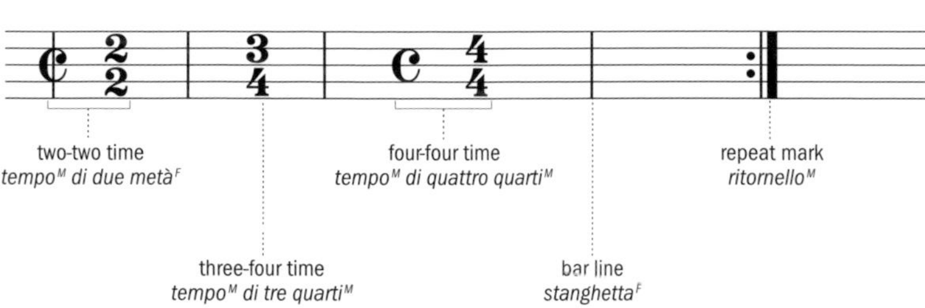

intervals
intervalli[M]

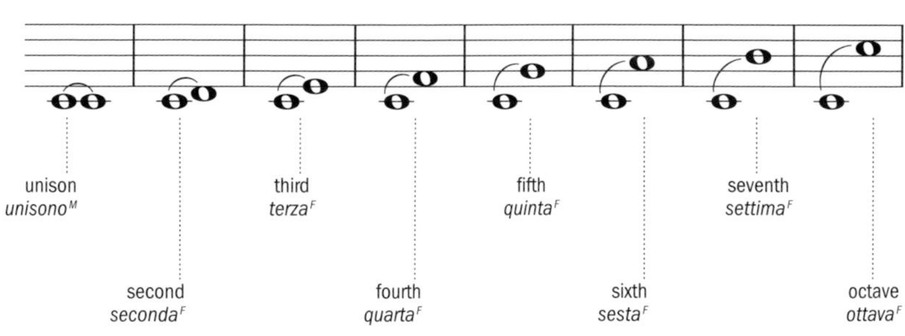

scale
scala[F]

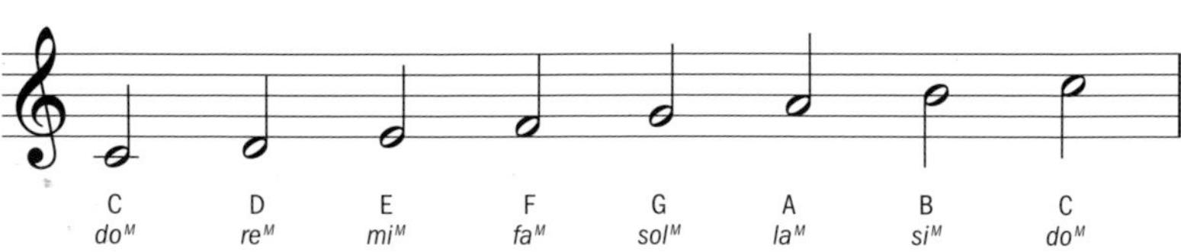

ARTS AND ARCHITECTURE

rest symbols
valori[M] di durata[F] delle pause[F]

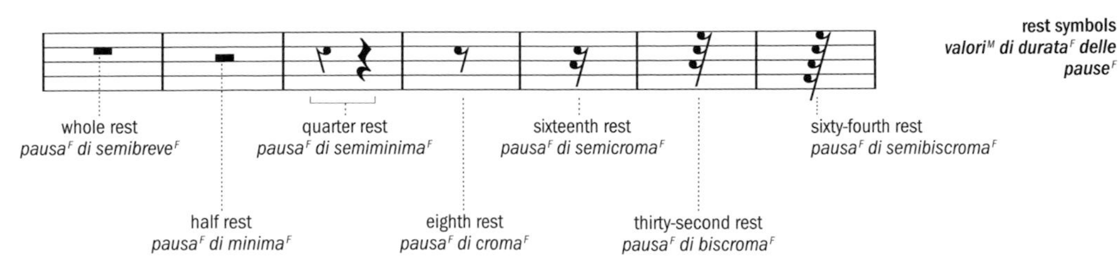

ornaments
abbellimenti[M]

note symbols
valori[M] di durata[F] delle note[F]

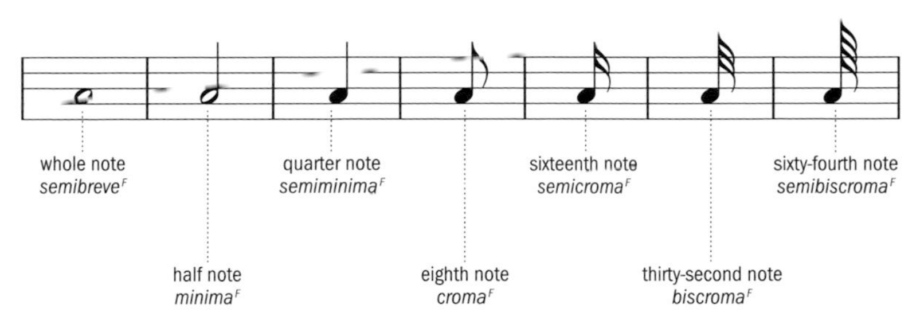

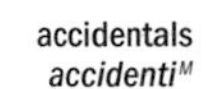

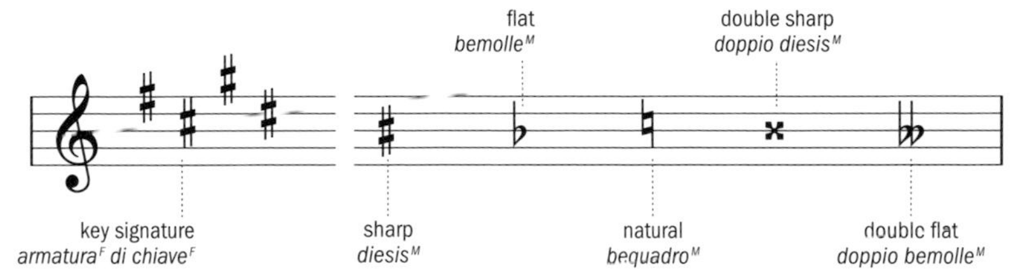

other signs
altri segni[M]

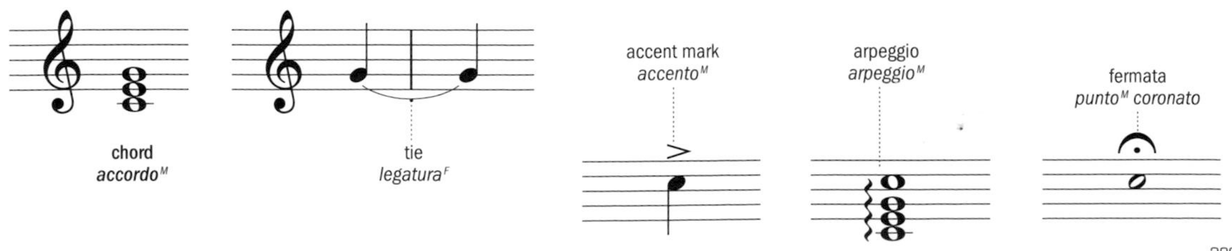

ARTS AND ARCHITECTURE

examples of instrumental groups

esempi^M di gruppi^M strumentali

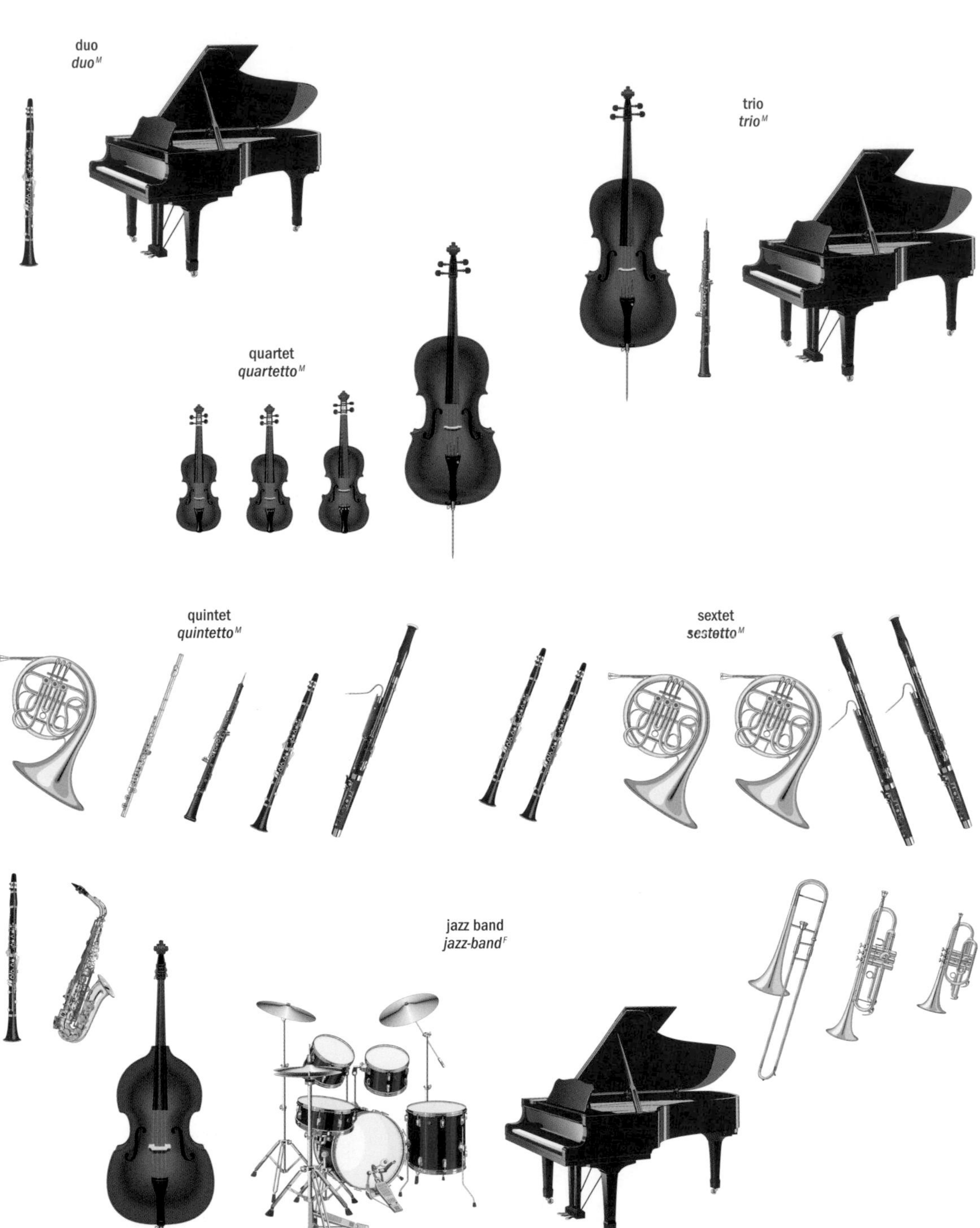

stringed instruments

strumenti[M] a corde[F]

bow
archetto[M]

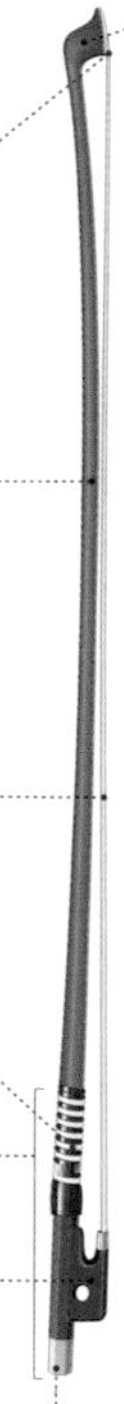

head
testina[F]
point
punta[F]
stick
bacchetta[F]
hair
crine[M]
handle
impugnatura[F]
heel
tallone[M]
frog
bietta[F]
screw
vite[F]

violin
violino[M]

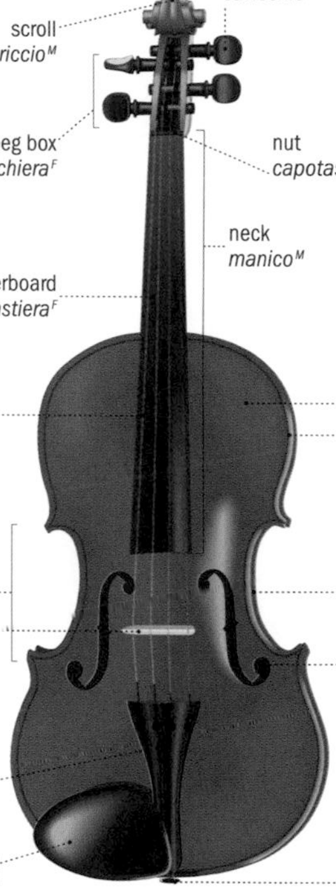

peg
cavicchio[M]
scroll
riccio[M]
peg box
cavicchiera[F]
nut
capotasto[M]
neck
manico[M]
fingerboard
tastiera[F]
soundboard
tavola[F] armonica
string
corda[F]
purfling
filettatura[F]
waist
strozzatura[F]
rib
fascia[F]
bridge
ponticello[M]
sound hole
foro[M] di risonanza[F]
tailpiece
cordiera[F]
chin rest
mentoniera[F]
end button
bottone[M]

violin family
famiglia[F] degli archi[M]

double bass
contrabbasso[M]
cello
violoncello[M]
viola
viola[F]
violin
violino[M]

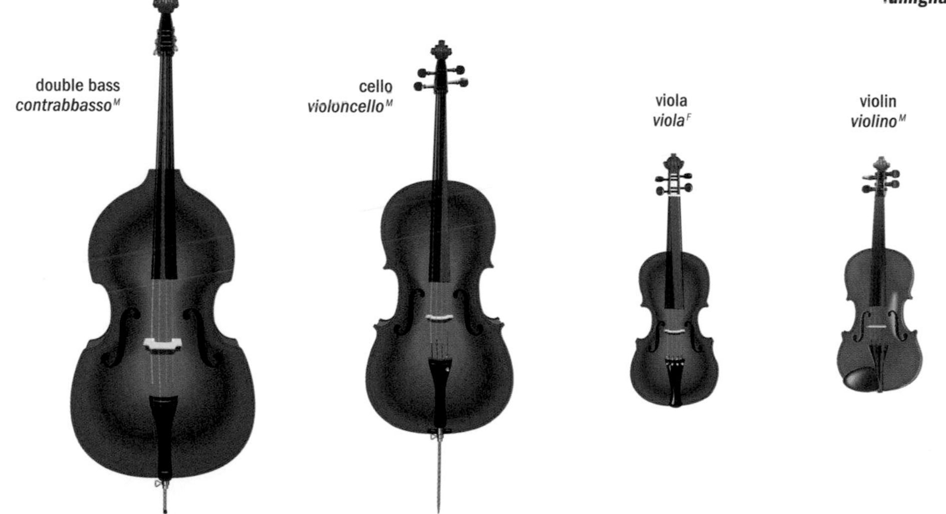

stringed instruments

harp
arpa F

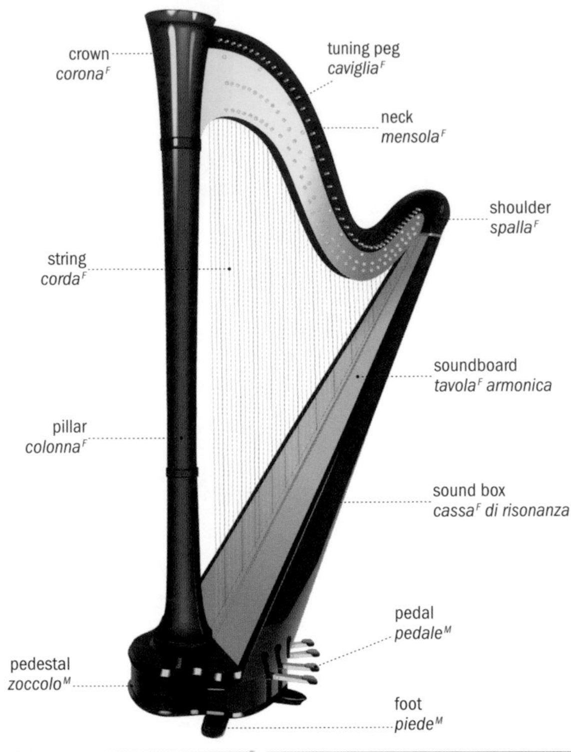

acoustic guitar
chitarra F acustica

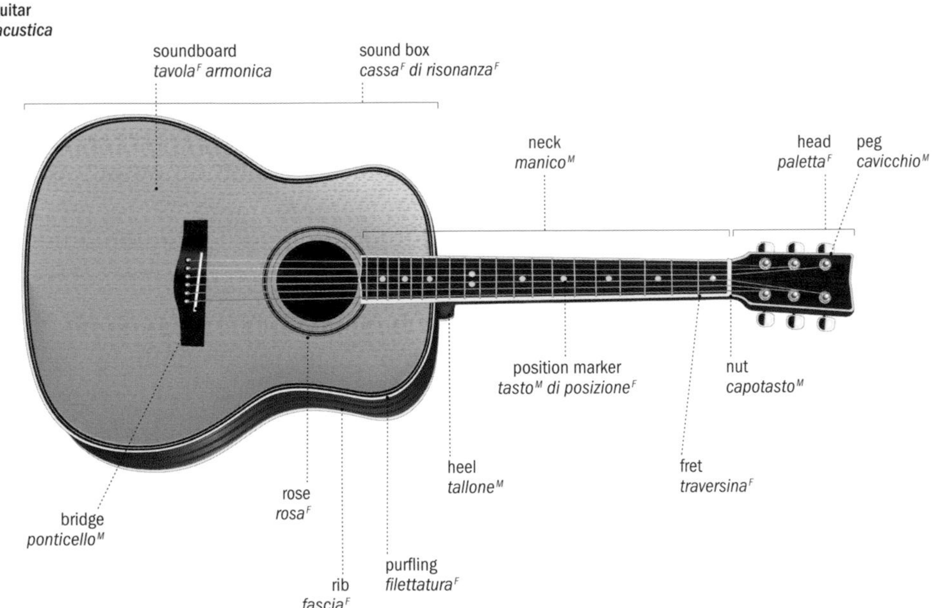

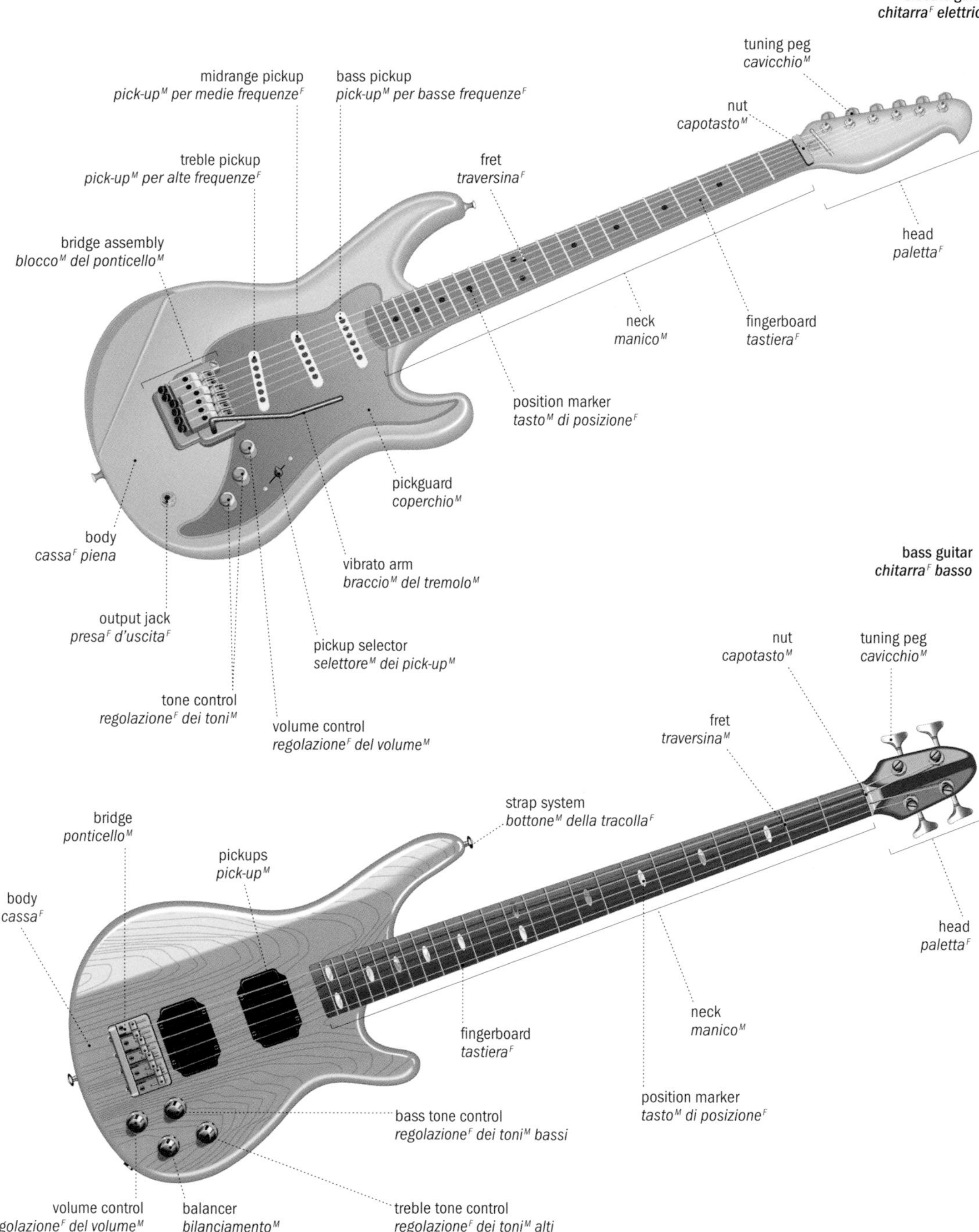
electric guitar
chitarra^F elettrica
tuning peg
cavicchio^M
midrange pickup
pick-up^M per medie frequenze^F
bass pickup
pick-up^M per basse frequenze^F
nut
capotasto^M
treble pickup
pick-up^M per alte frequenze^F
fret
traversina^F
bridge assembly
blocco^M del ponticello^M
head
paletta^F
neck
manico^M
fingerboard
tastiera^F
position marker
tasto^M di posizione^F
pickguard
coperchio^M
body
cassa^F piena
vibrato arm
braccio^M del tremolo^M
output jack
presa^F d'uscita^F
pickup selector
selettore^M dei pick-up^M
tone control
regolazione^F dei toni^M
volume control
regolazione^F del volume^M
bass guitar
chitarra^F basso
nut
capotasto^M
tuning peg
cavicchio^M
fret
traversina^M
strap system
bottone^M della tracolla^F
bridge
ponticello^M
pickups
pick-up^M
body
cassa^F
head
paletta^F
neck
manico^M
fingerboard
tastiera^F
position marker
tasto^M di posizione^F
bass tone control
regolazione^F dei toni^M bassi
volume control
regolazione^F del volume^M
balancer
bilanciamento^M
treble tone control
regolazione^F dei toni^M alti

keyboard instruments

strumenti[M] a tastiera[F]

upright piano
pianoforte[M] verticale

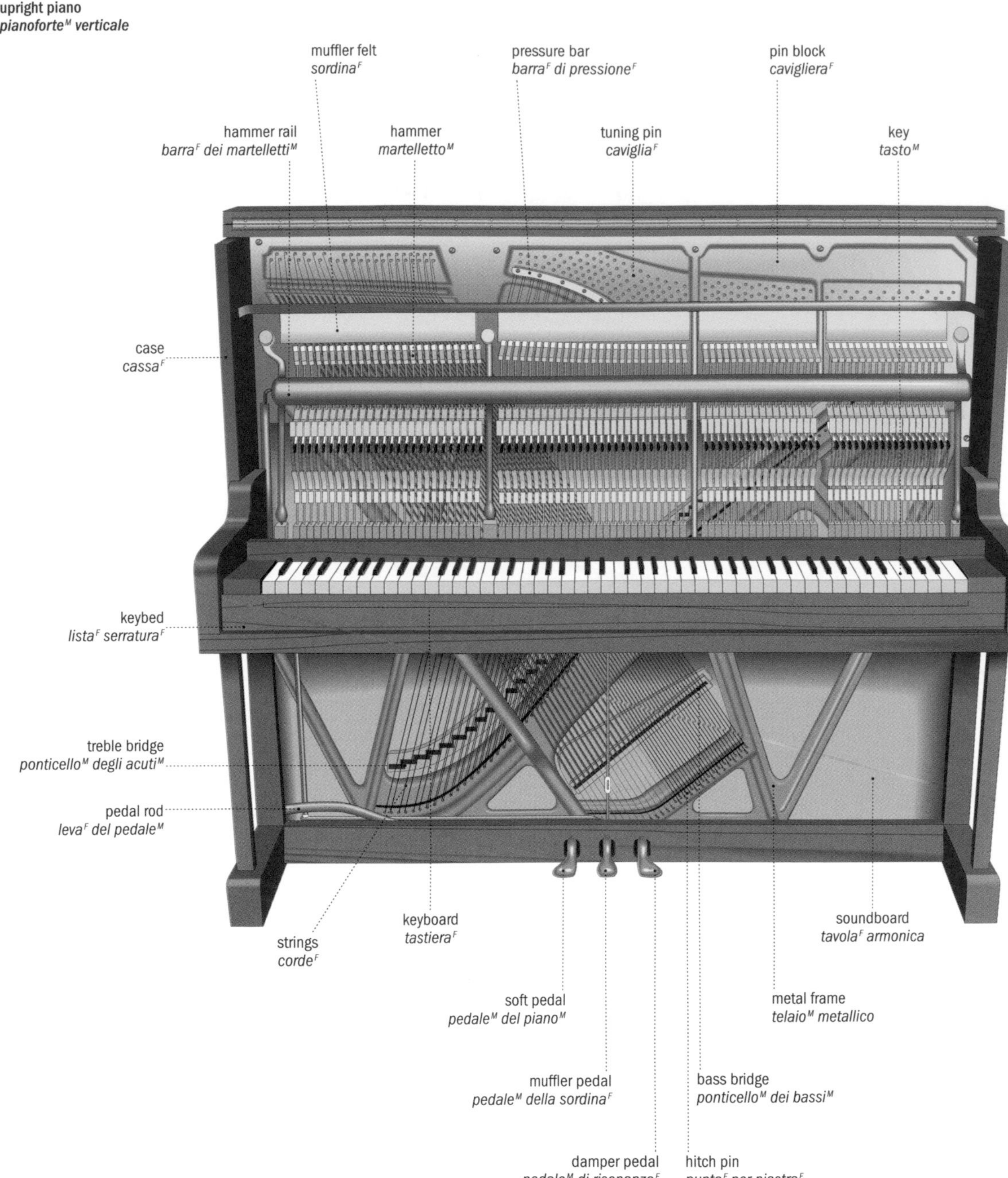

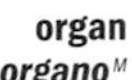

organ
organo[M]

organ console
console[F] dell'organo[M]

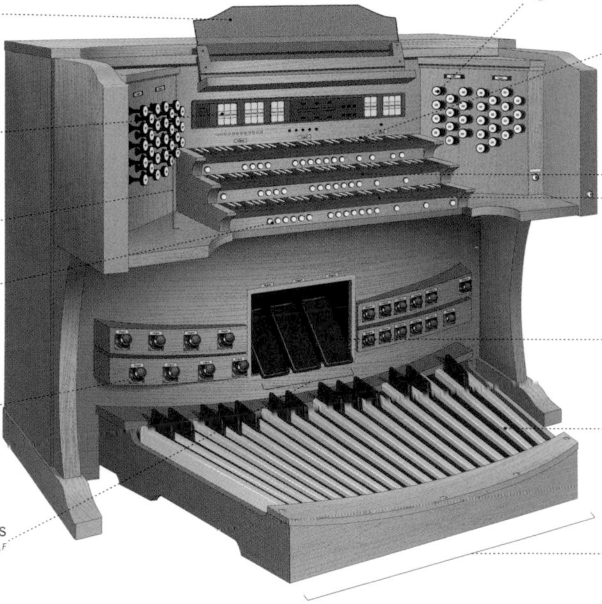

music stand
leggio[M]

stop knob
tasto[M] di registro[M]

swell organ manual
manuale[M] dell'organo[M] espressivo

coupler-tilt tablet
placchetta[F] a bilanciere[M]

choir organ manual
manuale[M] dell'organo[M] positivo

great organ manual
manuale[M] del grand'organo[M]

manuals
manuali[M]

thumb piston
pistoncino[M] del manuale[M]

crescendo pedal
pedale[M] del crescendo[M]

toe piston
pistoncino[M] del pedale[M]

pedal key
pedale[M]

swell pedals
pedali[M] d'espressione[F]

pedal keyboard
pedaliera[F]

reed pipe
canna[F] ad ancia[F]

resonator
padiglione[M]

tuning wire
asta[F] d'accordo[M]

block
blocco[F]

wedge
cuneo[M]

shallot
gola[F]

tongue
ancia[F]

foot
stivale[M]

foot hole
foro[M] del piede[M]

flue pipe
canna[F] ad anima[F]

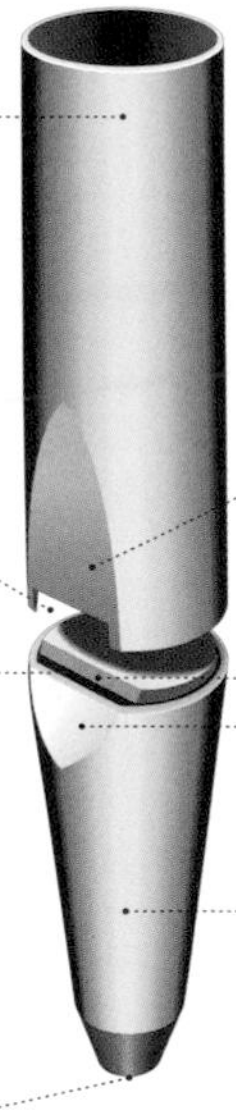

body
corpo[M]

upper lip
labbro[M] superiore

mouth
bocca[F]

languid
anima[F]

flue
fessura[F]

lower lip
labbro[M] inferiore

foot
piede[M]

foot hole
foro[M] del piede[M]

ARTS AND ARCHITECTURE

wind instruments

strumenti^M a fiato^M

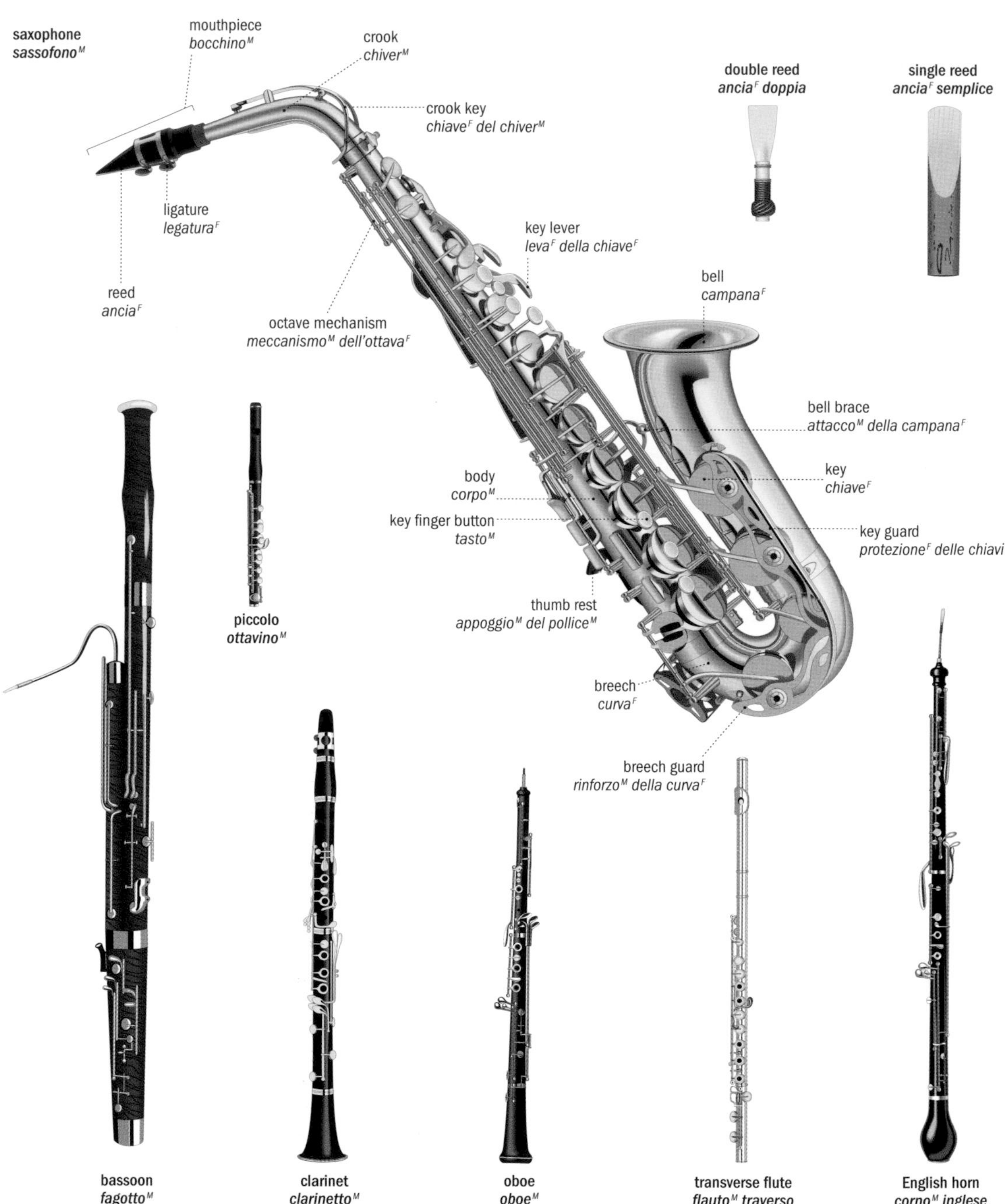

trumpet
tromba F
key
pistone M
little finger hook
appoggio M *del mignolo* M
bell
campana F
mouthpiece receiver
alloggiamento M *del bocchino* M
mouthpipe
canna F *di imboccatura* F
ring
anello M
mouthpiece
bocchino M
tuning slide
tubo M *di accordo* M
first valve slide
tubo M *della prima valvola* F
spit valve
chiave F *dell'acqua* F
third valve slide
tubo M *della terza valvola* F
thumb hook
appoggio M *del pollice* M
valve
valvola F
mute
sordina F
valve casing
corpo M *della valvola* F
second valve slide
tubo M *della seconda valvola* F
French horn
corno M
cornet
cornetta F
bugle
tromba F ***militare***
saxhorn
saxhorn M
tuba
tuba F
trombone
trombone M

percussion instruments

strumenti[M] a percussione[F]

drums
batteria[F]

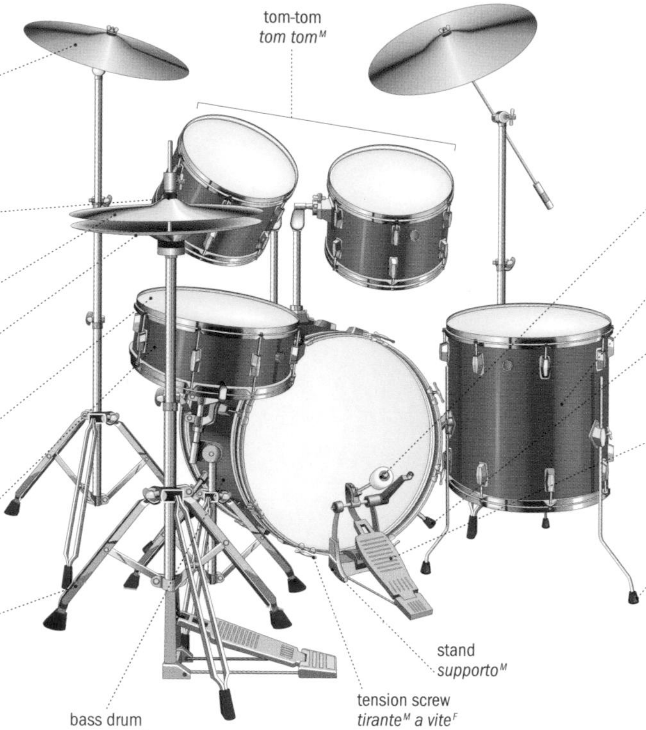

tom-tom
tom tom[M]
cymbal
piatto[M]
high-hat cymbal
charleston[M]
superior cymbal
piatto[M] superiore
inferior cymbal
piatto[M] inferiore
batter head
battitoia[F]
snare drum
cassa[F] chiara
tripod stand
treppiede[M]
bass drum
grancassa[F]
tension screw
tirante[M] a vite[F]
stand
supporto[M]
mallet
mazza[F]
tenor drum
tamburo[M] tenore[M]
spur
piedino[M]
pedal
pedale[M]
leg
piedino[M]

kettledrum
timpano[M]

snare drum
cassa[F] chiara

lug
blocchetto[M]
tension rod
tirante[M]
snare strainer
tirante[M] della cordiera[F]
snare
cordiera[F]
snare head
bordoniera[F]

tie rod
tirante[M] a vite[F]
batter head
battitoia[F]
metal counterhoop
cerchio[M] di serraggio[M]
tuning gauge
chiavi[F] di tensione[F]
shell
caldaia[F]
strut
gabbia[F]
tension rod
tirante[M]
crown
corona[F]
pedal
pedale[M]
caster
rotella[F] orientabile
foot
base[F]

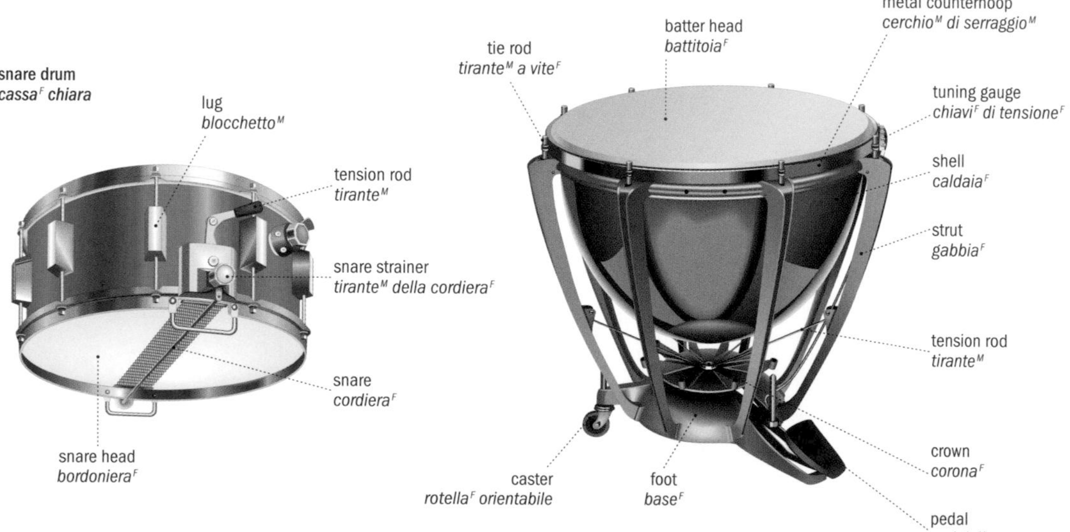

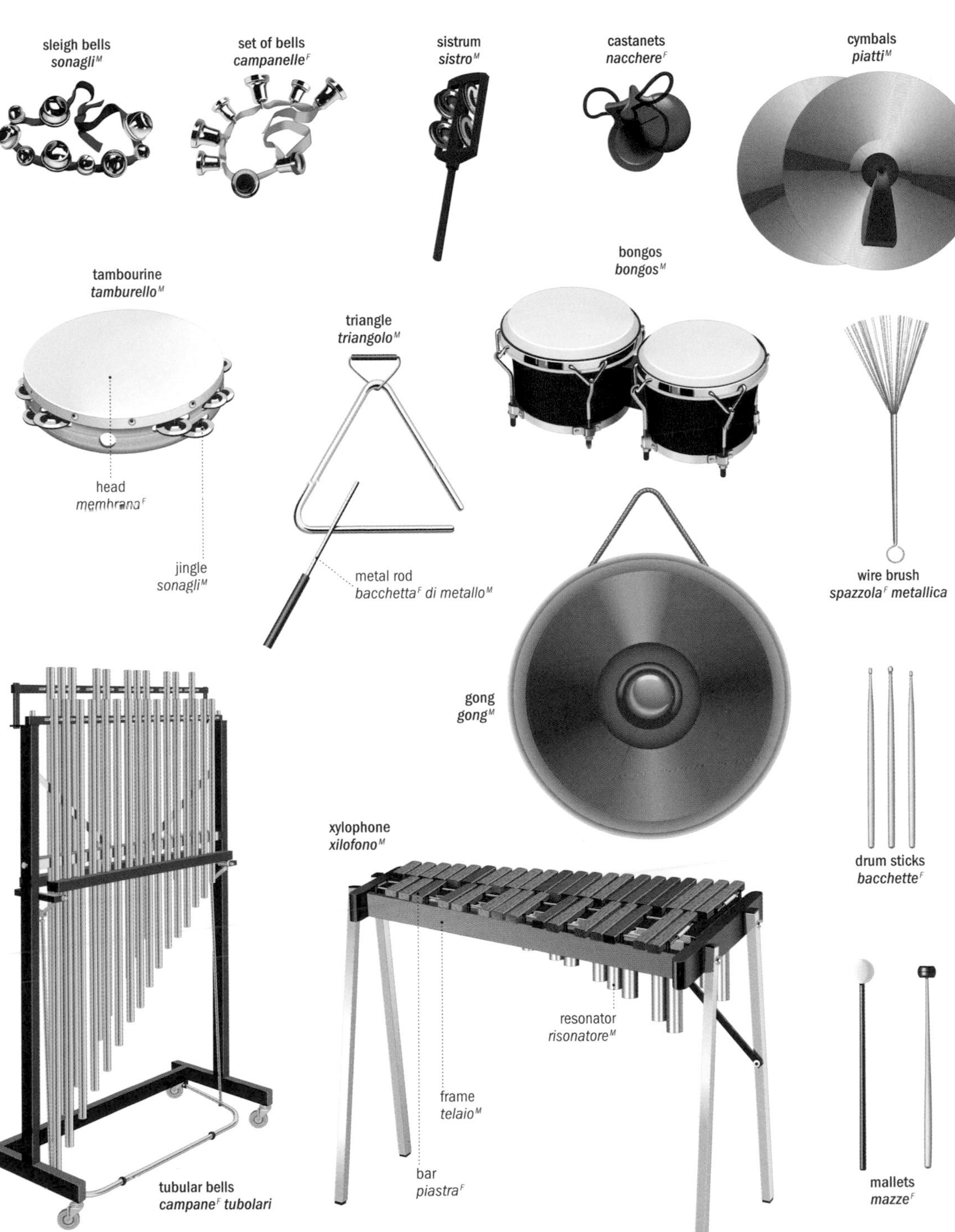
sleigh bells
*sonagli*M
set of bells
*campanelle*F
sistrum
*sistro*M
castanets
*nacchere*F
cymbals
*piatti*M
bongos
*bongos*M
tambourine
*tamburello*M
triangle
*triangolo*M
head
*membrana*F
jingle
*sonagli*M
metal rod
*bacchetta*F *di metallo*M
wire brush
*spazzola*F *metallica*
gong
*gong*M
xylophone
*xilofono*M
drum sticks
*bacchette*F
resonator
*risonatore*M
frame
*telaio*M
bar
*piastra*F
tubular bells
*campane*F *tubolari*
mallets
*mazze*F

electronic instruments

strumenti[M] elettronici

sequencer
sequencer[M]

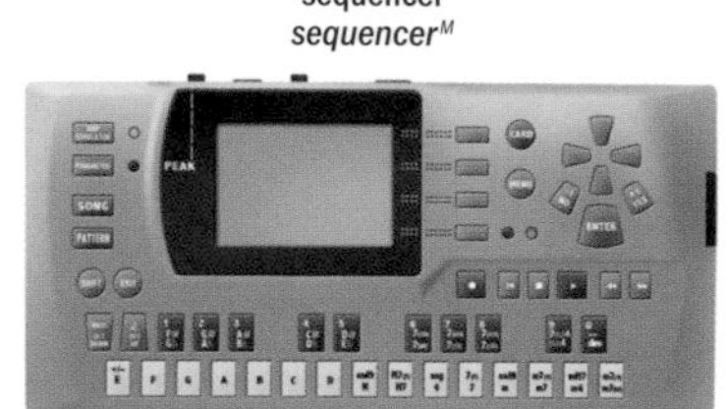

sampler
campionatore[M]

headphone jack
presa[F] per cuffia[F]

function display
display[M] delle funzioni[F]

disk drive
unità[F] a disco[M]

expander
expander[M]

synthesizer
sintetizzatore[M]

system buttons
tasti[M] di sistema[M]

function display
display[M] delle funzioni[F]

program selector
selettore[M] di programma[M]

voice edit buttons
tasti[M] per l'editing[M] del suono[M]

volume control
controllo[M] del volume[M]

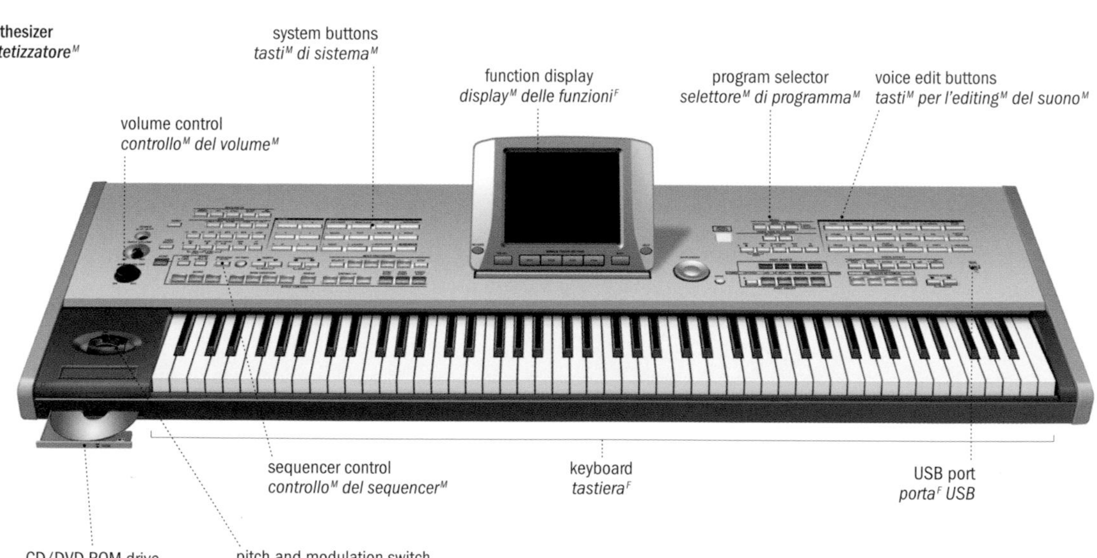

sequencer control
controllo[M] del sequencer[M]

keyboard
tastiera[F]

USB port
porta[F] USB

CD/DVD-ROM drive
lettore[M] CD[M]/DVD-ROM[M]

pitch and modulation switch
modulazione[F] dell'altezza[F] e del timbro[M] del suono[M]

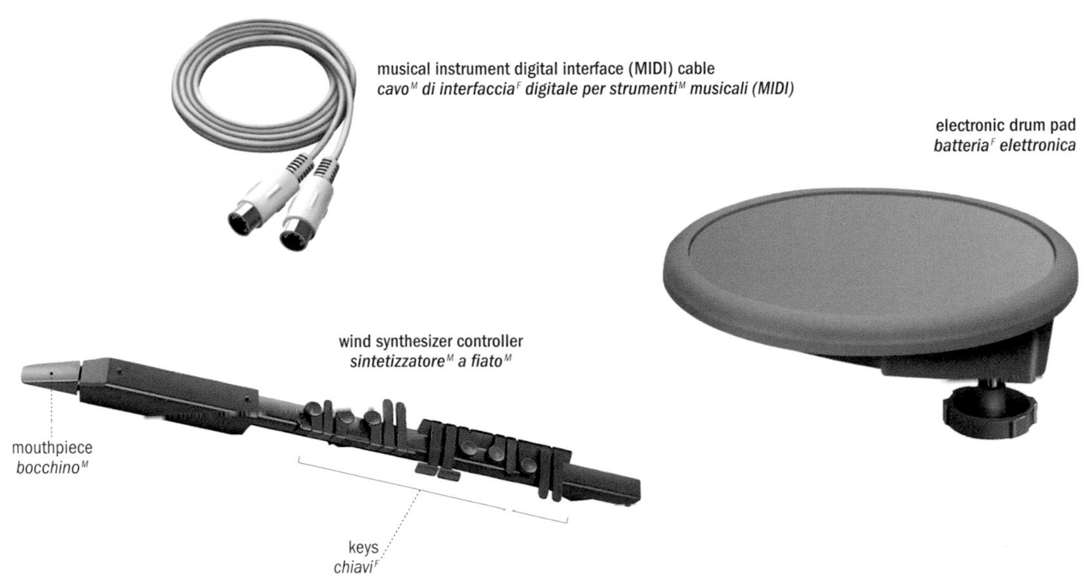

electronic piano
piano[M] elettronico

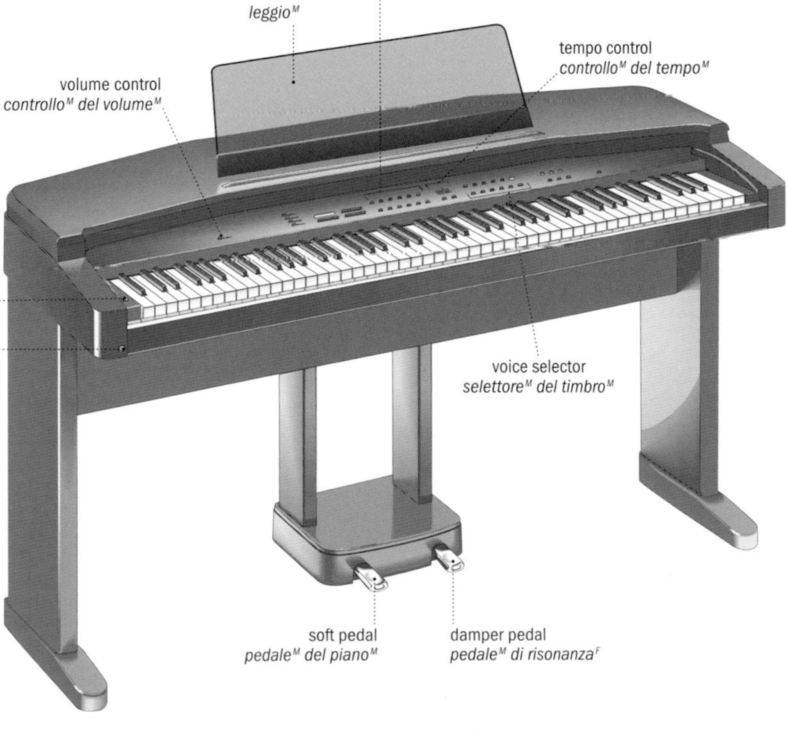

rhythm selector
selettore[M] del ritmo[M]

music stand
leggio[M]

tempo control
controllo[M] del tempo[M]

volume control
controllo[M] del volume[M]

power switch
interruttore[M]

headphone jack
presa[F] per cuffia[F]

voice selector
selettore[M] del timbro[M]

soft pedal
pedale[M] del piano[M]

damper pedal
pedale[M] di risonanza[F]

writing instruments

strumenti[M] scrittori

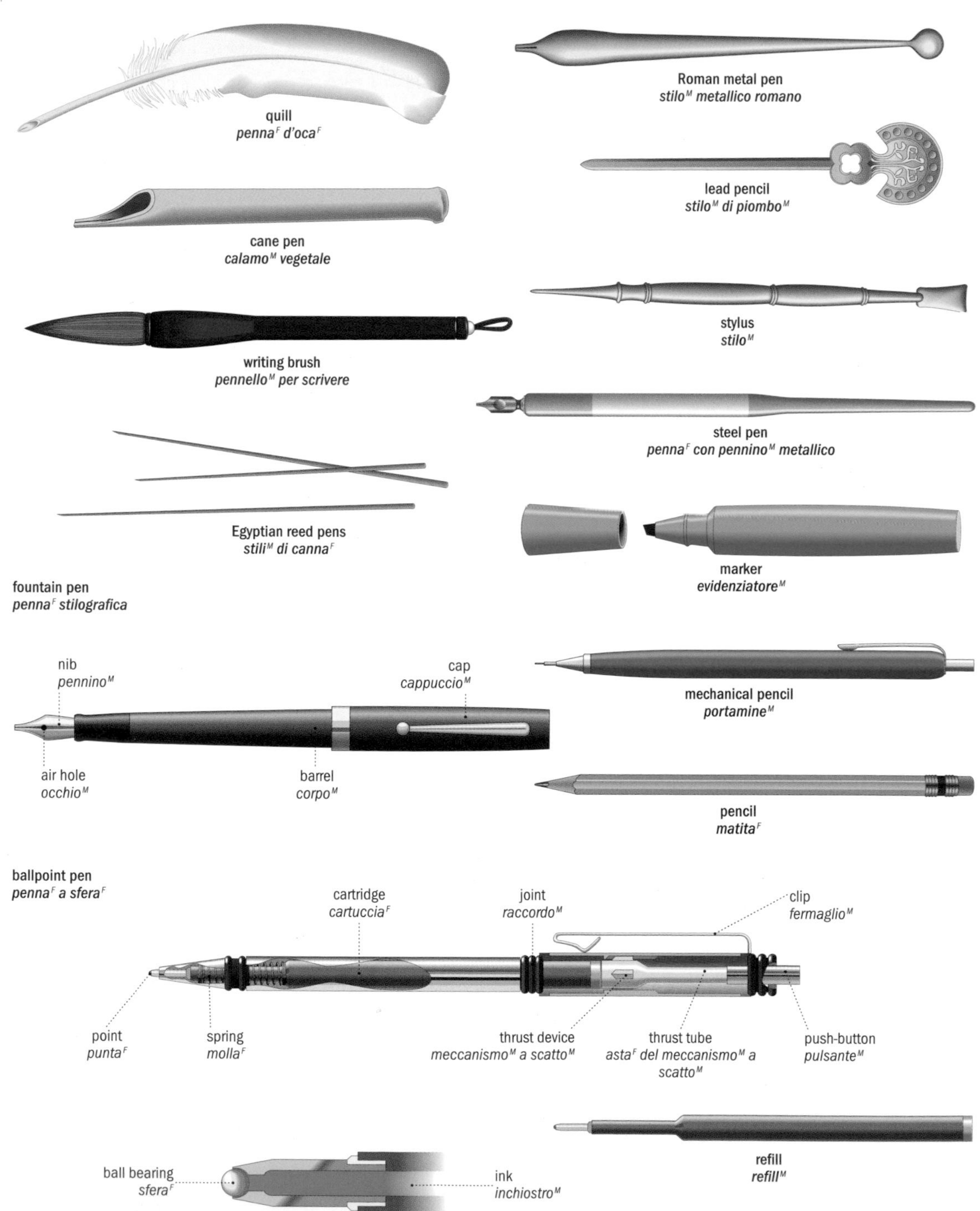

newspaper
giornale[M]

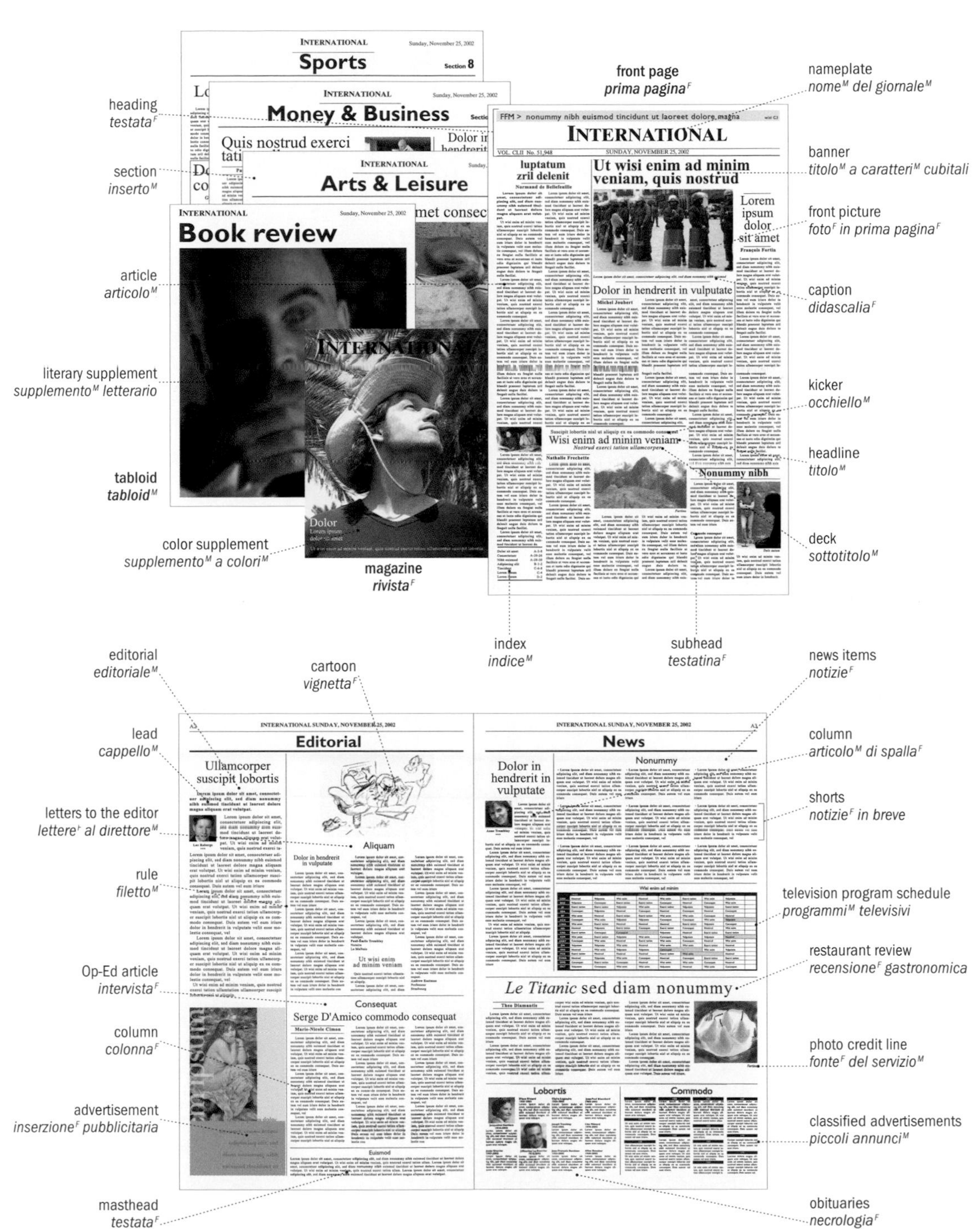

photography

fotografia[F]

single-lens reflex (SLR) camera: front view
macchina[F] fotografica reflex monoculare: vista[F] frontale

exposure adjustment knob
pulsante[M] di compensazione[F] dell'esposizione[F]

accessory shoe
slitta[F] per accessori[M]

hot-shoe contact
contatto[M] caldo

drive mode
modo[M] di acquisizione[F]

control panel
display[M]

exposure mode
tasto[M] per il modo[M] di esposizione[F]

command control dial
selettore[M] dei programmi[M]

multiple exposure mode
tasto[M] per le esposizioni[F] multiple

on-off switch
interruttore[M] di accensione[F]

sensitivity
sensibilità[F]

shutter release button
pulsante[M] di scatto[M]

remote control terminal
presa[F] per il comando[M] a distanza[F]

self-timer indicator
spia[F] luminosa dell'autoscatto[M]

focus mode selector
selettore[M] della messa[F] a fuoco[M]

camera body
corpo[M] della macchina[F] fotografica

lens release button
pulsante[M] di sblocco[M] dell'obiettivo[M]

objective lens
obiettivo[M]

depth-of-field preview button
pulsante[M] di controllo[M] della profondità[F] di campo[M]

lenses
obiettivi[M]

telephoto lens
teleobiettivo[M]

zoom lens
obiettivo[M] zoom

wide-angle lens
obiettivo[M] grandangolare

macro lens
obiettivo[M] macro

lens accessories
accessori[M] dell'obiettivo[M]

lens cap
coperchio[M] di protezione[F] dell'obiettivo[M]

lens hood
paraluce[M]

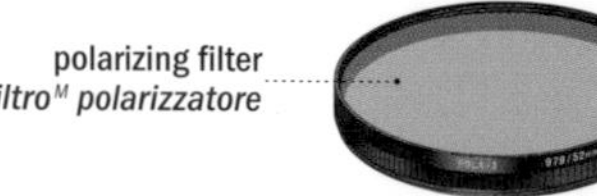

polarizing filter
filtro[M] polarizzatore

digital reflex camera: camera back
macchina[F] fotografica reflex digitale: dorso[M]

still cameras
macchine[F] fotografiche

Polaroid® camera
Polaroid®[F]

medium-format SLR (6 x 6)
macchina[F] fotografica reflex (6x6)

ultracompact camera
macchina[F] ultracompatta

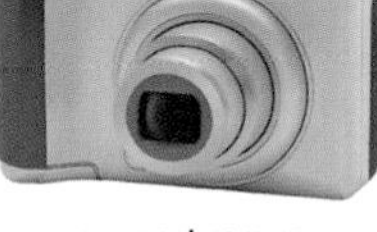

compact camera
macchina[F] compatta

disposable camera
macchina[F] fotografica usa e getta

view camera
macchina[F] fotografica a banco[M] ottico

broadcast satellite communication

trasmissione^F via satellite^M

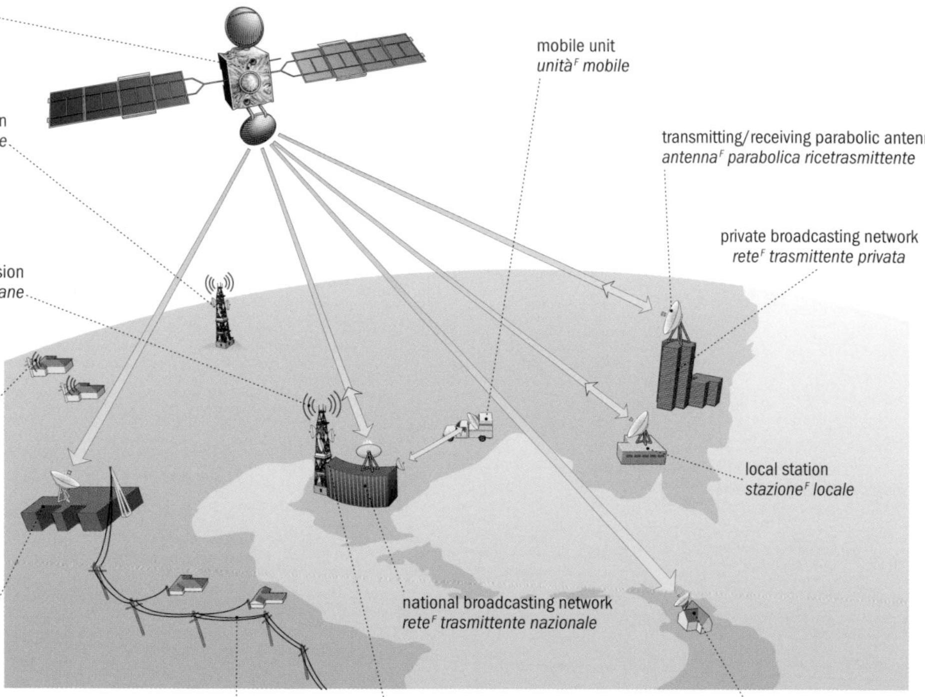

satellite
satellite^M
mobile unit
unità^F mobile
relay station
stazione^F ripetitrice
transmitting/receiving parabolic antenna
antenna^F parabolica ricetrasmittente
private broadcasting network
rete^F trasmittente privata
Hertzian wave transmission
trasmissione^F a onde^F hertziane
home antenna
antenna^F di casa^F
local station
stazione^F locale
national broadcasting network
rete^F trasmittente nazionale
cable distributor
distributore^M via cavo^M
distribution by aerial cable network
trasmissione^F via cavo^M aereo
transmitting tower
torre^F trasmittente
direct home reception
ricezione^F privata diretta

telecommunication satellites

satelliti^M per telecomunicazioni^F

Eutelsat
Eutelsat

transmitting/receiving dish
antenna^F di trasmissione^F/ricezione^F
solar reflectors
riflettori^M solari
communication module
modulo^M di comunicazione^F
service module
modulo^M di servizio^M
solar array
pannello^M solare
propulsion module
modulo^M di propulsione^F
transmission dish
antenna^F emittente

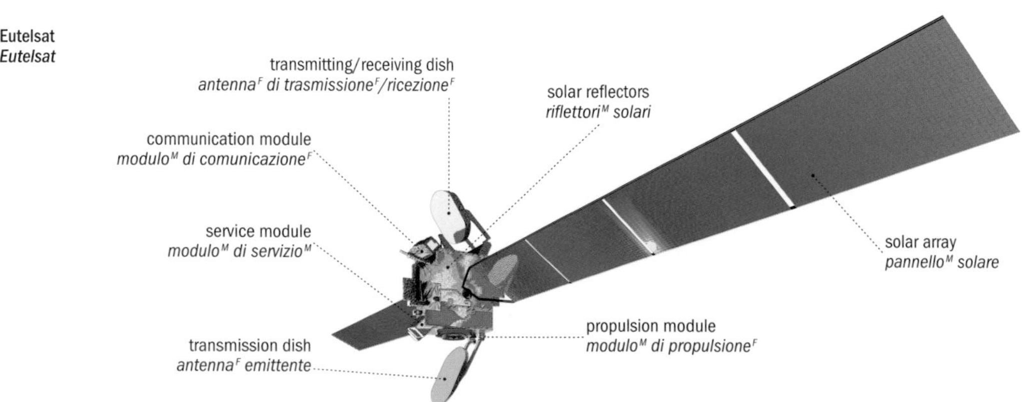

telecommunications by satellite

telecomunicazioni^F via satellite^M

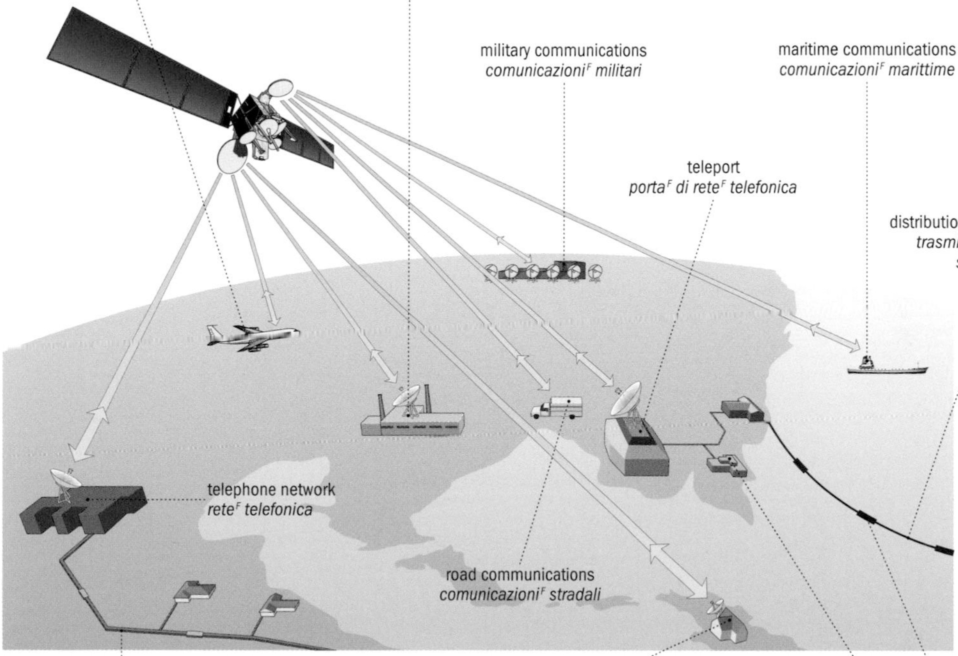

air communications
comunicazioni^F aeree
industrial communications
comunicazioni^F industriali
military communications
comunicazioni^F militari
maritime communications
comunicazioni^F marittime
teleport
porta^F di rete^F telefonica
distribution by submarine cable
trasmissione^F via cavo^M sottomarino
telephone network
rete^F telefonica
road communications
comunicazioni^F stradali
distribution by underground cable network
trasmissione^F via cavo^M sotterraneo
personal communications
comunicazioni^F private
consumer
utente^M
repeater
ripetitore^M

telecommunication satellites

Anik
Anik

Intelsat
Intelsat

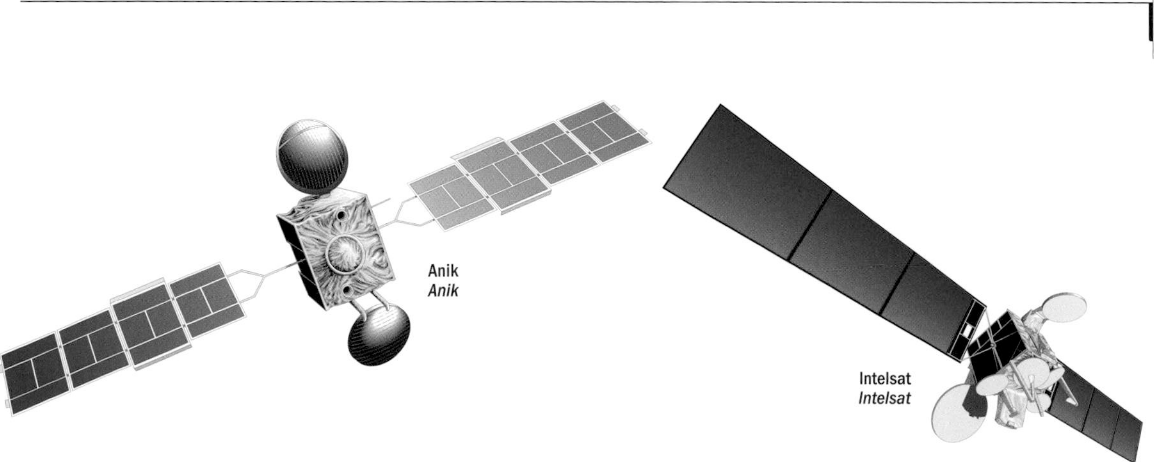

television

televisione^F

liquid crystal display (LCD) television
televisore^M a cristalli^M liquidi

plasma television
televisore^M al plasma^M

cathode ray tube (CRT) television
televisore^M a tubo^M catodico

picture tube
cinescopio^M

electron gun
cannone^M elettronico

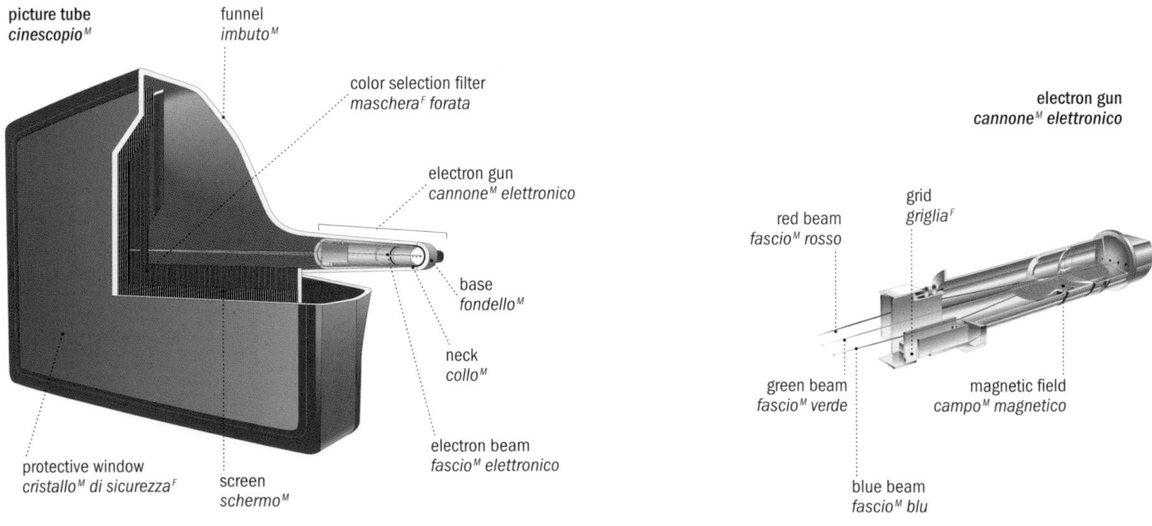

remote control
telecomando

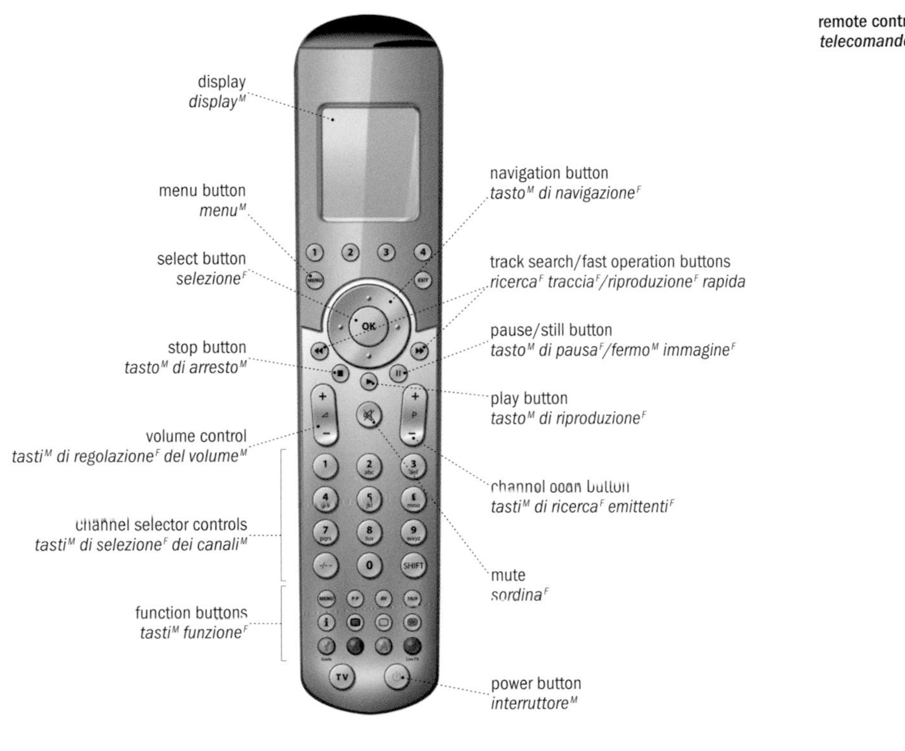

DVD recorder
registratore DVD

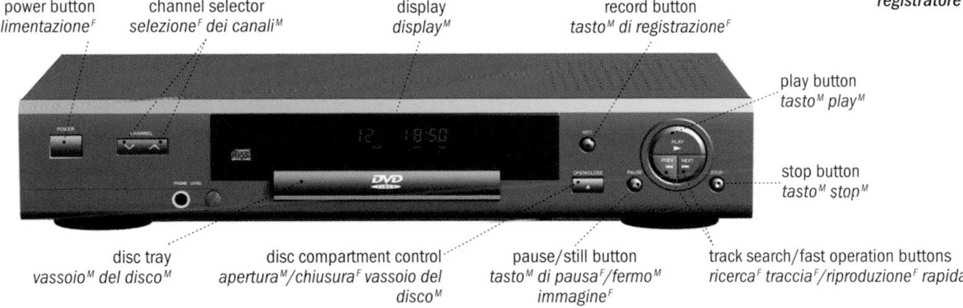

recording media
supporti di registrazione

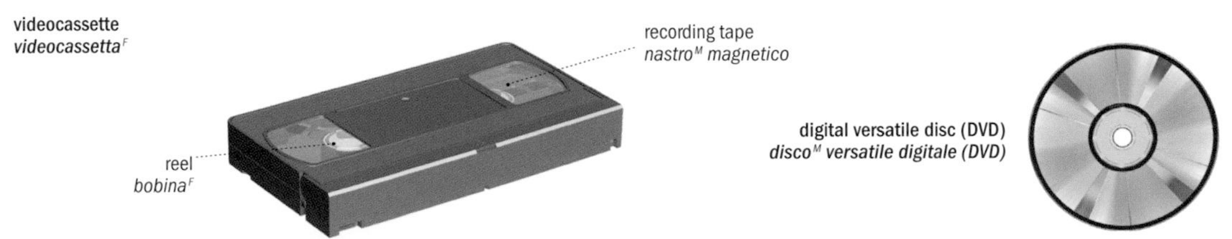

mini-DV camcorder: front view
videocamera^F mini-DV: vista^F frontale

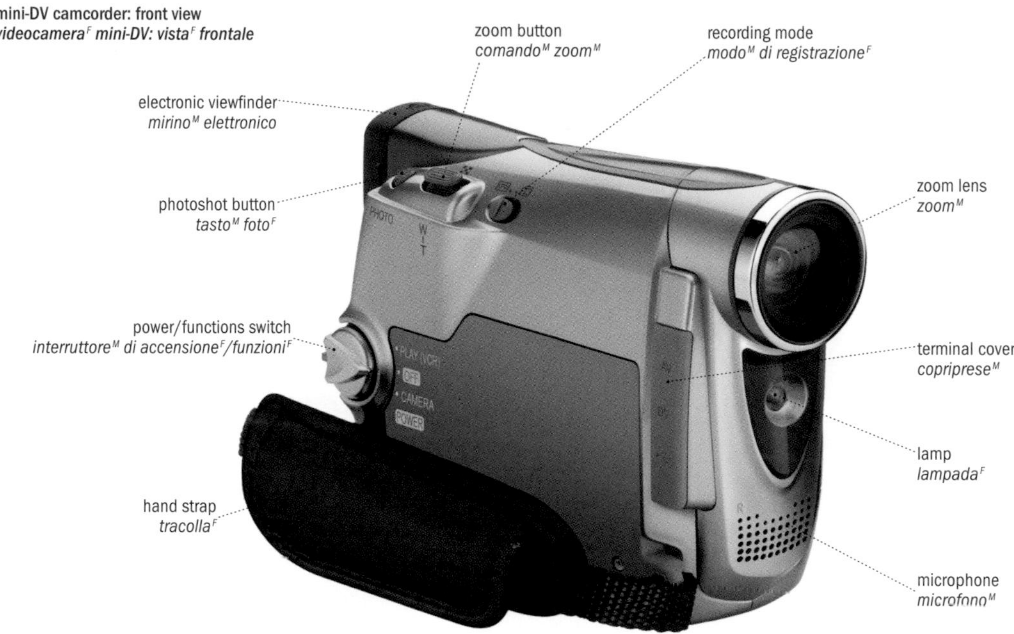

mini-DV camcorder: rear view
videocamera^F mini-DV: vista^F posteriore

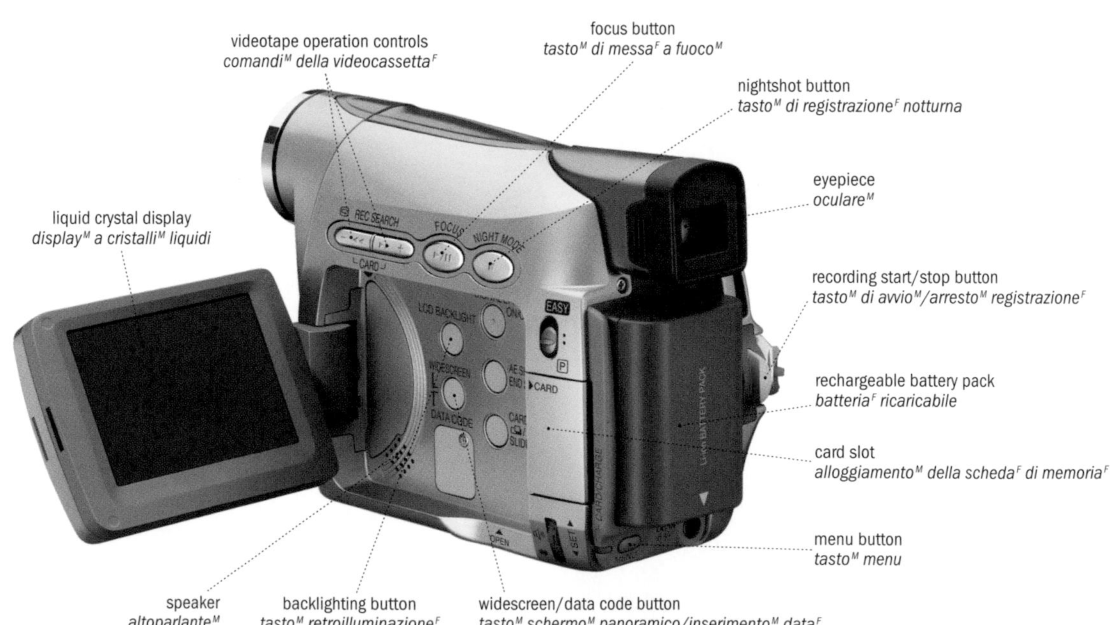

dish antenna
antenna*[F] *parabolica

receiver
***ricevitore*[M]**

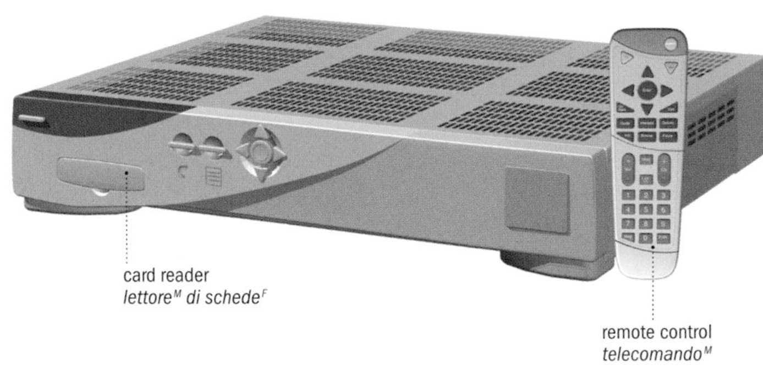

home theater
***home theatre*[M]**

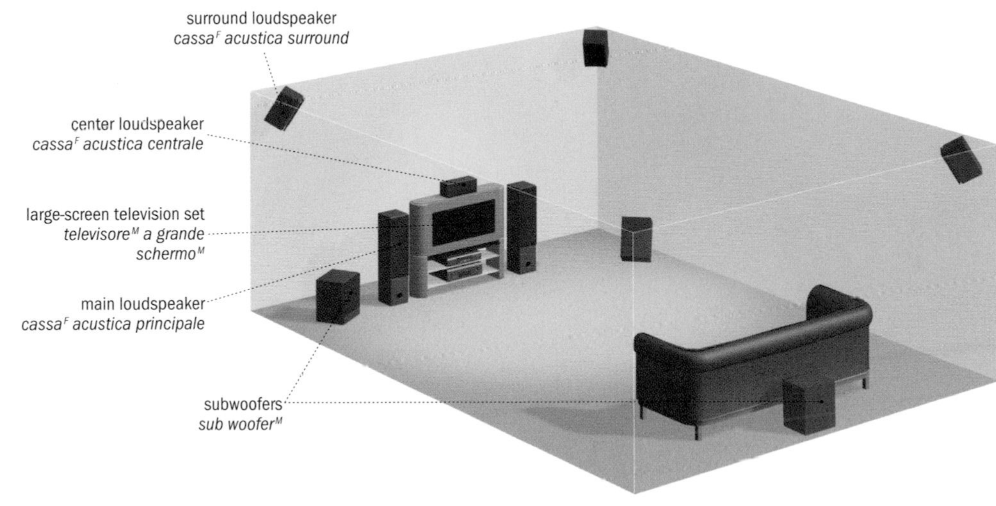

videocassette recorder (VCR)
***videoregistratore*[M]**

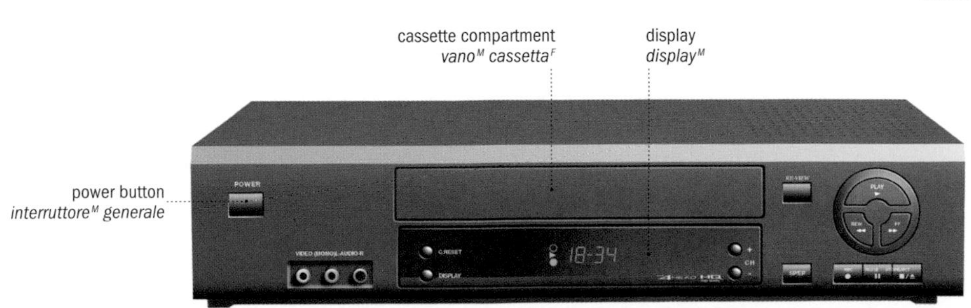

sound reproducing system

impianto[M] hi-fi di riproduzione[F] del suono[M]

ampli-tuner: front view
sintoamplificatore[M]: vista[F] frontale

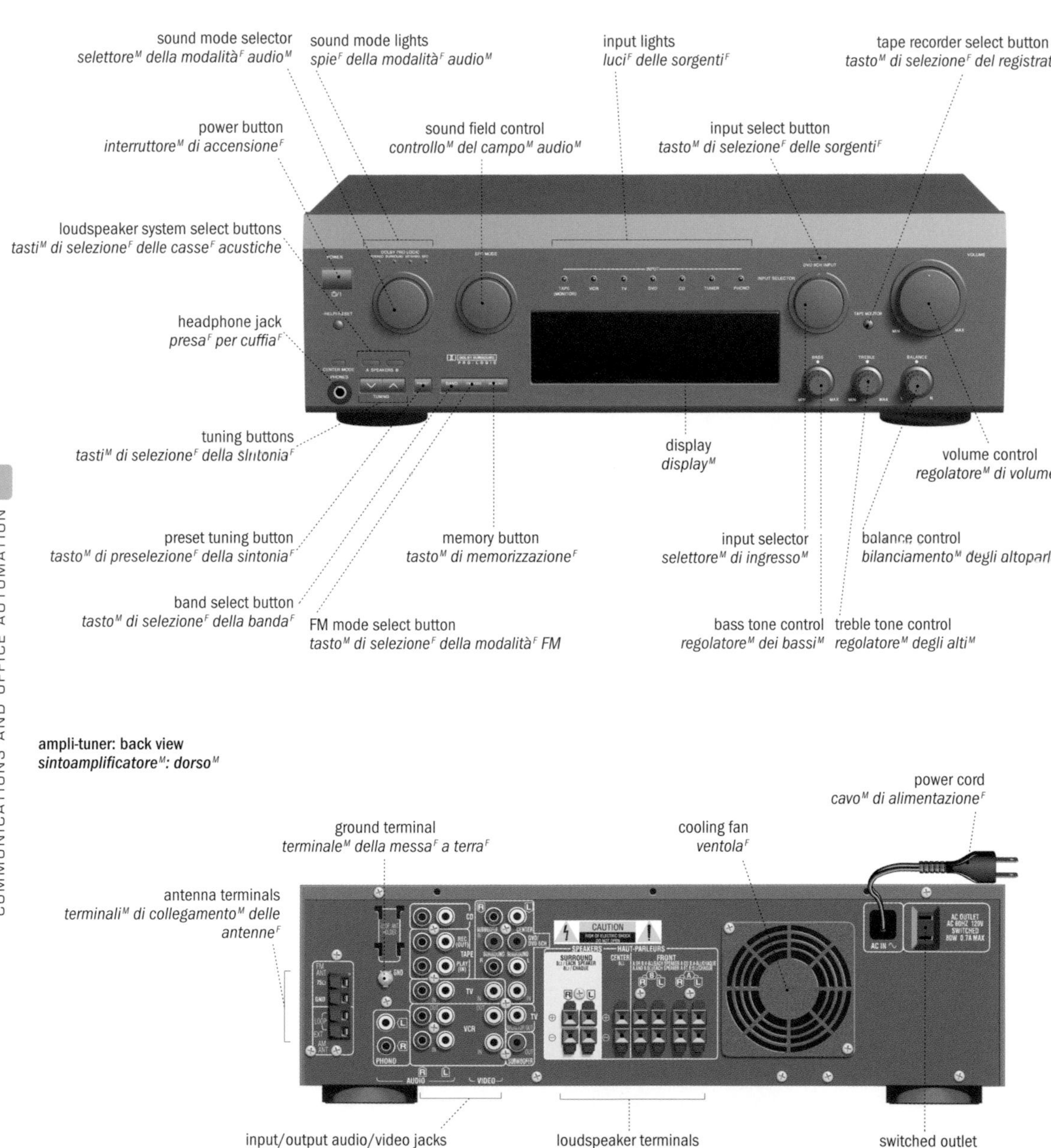

cassette tape deck
piastra[F] di registrazione[F]

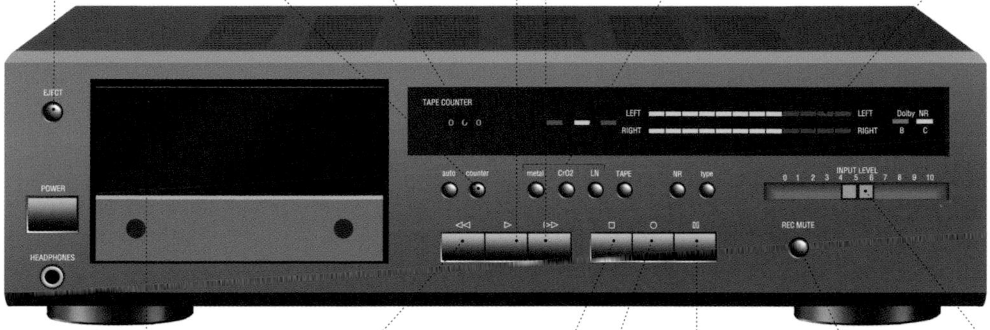

counter reset button
tasto[M] di azzeramento[M] del contatore[M]
play button
tasto[M] di riproduzione[F]
fast-forward button
tasto[M] di avanzamento[M] rapido
eject button
tasto[M] di espulsione[F]
tape counter
contatore[M]
tape selector
selettore[M] del nastro[M]
peak-level meter
LED[M] indicatore[M] del livello[M] di picco[M]
cassette holder
vano[M] della cassetta[F]
stop button
tasto[M] di arresto[M]
record muting button
muting[M]
rewind button
tasto[M] di riavvolgimento[M]
record button
tasto[M] di registrazione[F]
pause button
tasto[M] di pausa[F]
recording level control
selettore[M] del livello[M] di registrazione[F]

compact disc player
lettore[M] di compact disc[M]

power button
interruttore[M] di accensione[F]
shuffle play
riproduzione[F] casuale
direct disc access buttons
tasti[M] di accesso[M] diretto
repeat button
tasto[M] di ripetizione[F]
track search/fast operation buttons
ricerca[F] traccia[F]/riproduzione[F] rapida
stop button
stop[M]
pause button
pausa[F]
play button
riproduzione[F]
disc skip
cambio[M] disco[M]
headphone jack
presa[F] cuffie
disc compartment
vano[M] del disco[M]
display
display[M]
disc compartment control
tasto[M] di espulsione[F]

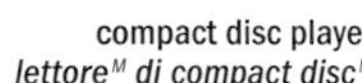

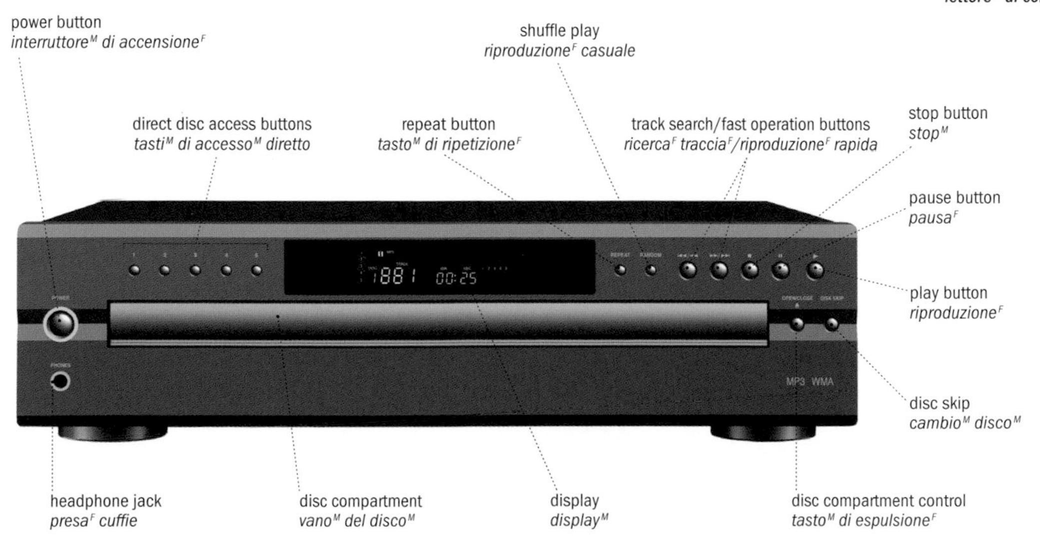

sound reproducing system

headphones
cuffia[F]

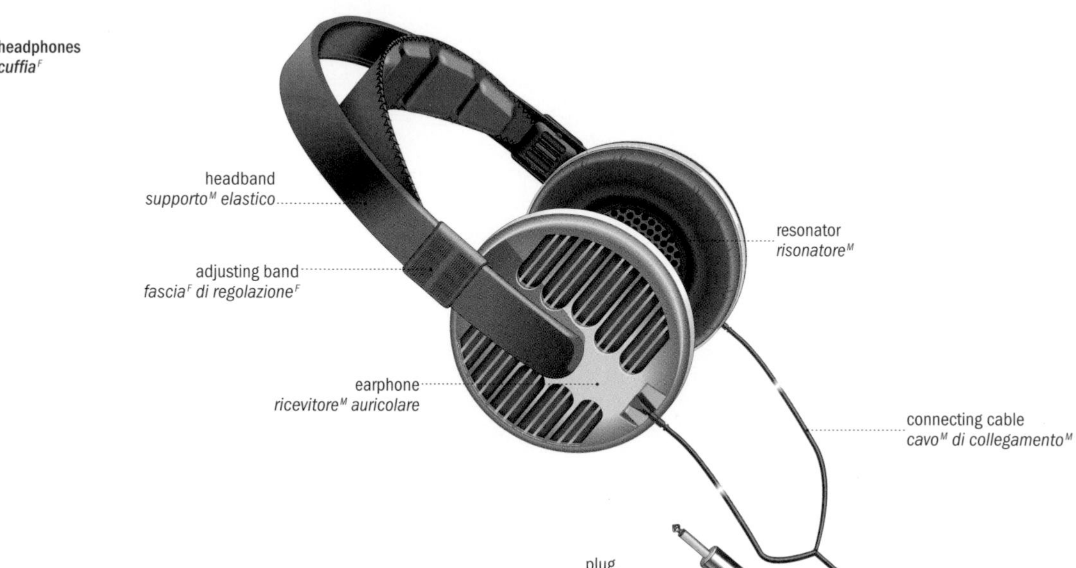

loudspeakers
cassa[F] acustica

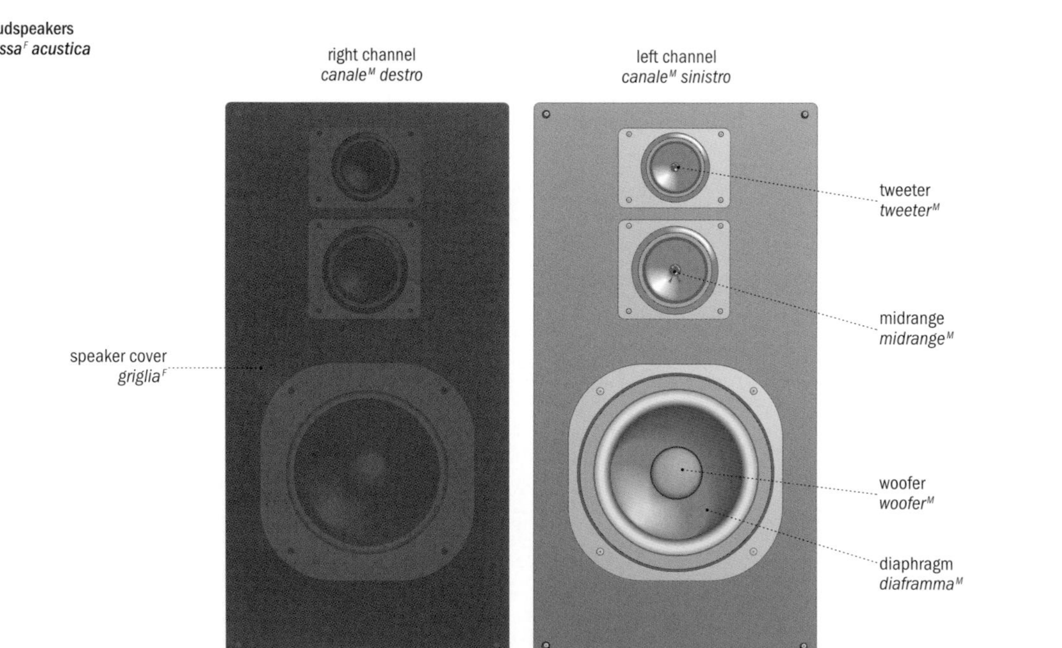

mini stereo sound system

mini impianto[M] hi-fi

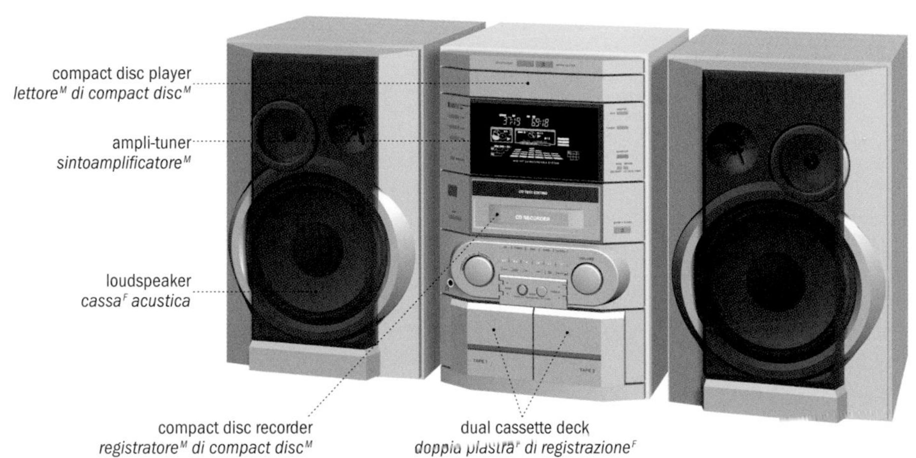

portable sound systems

riproduttori[M] portatili

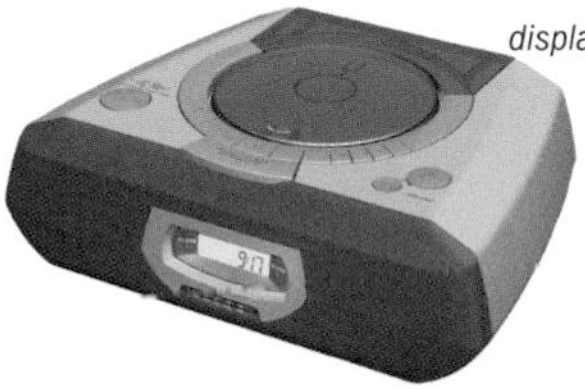

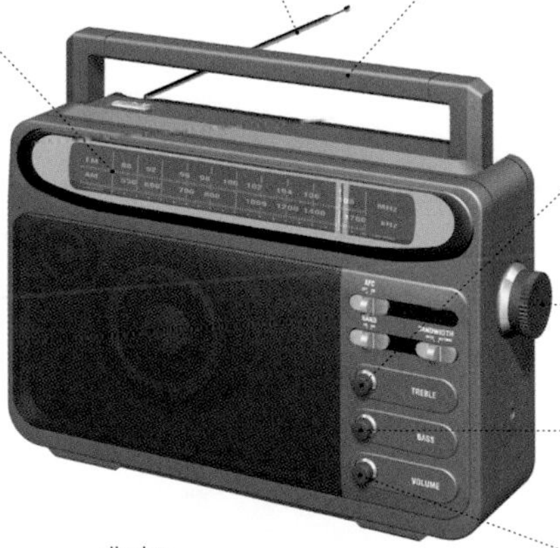

portable radio
radio[F] portatile

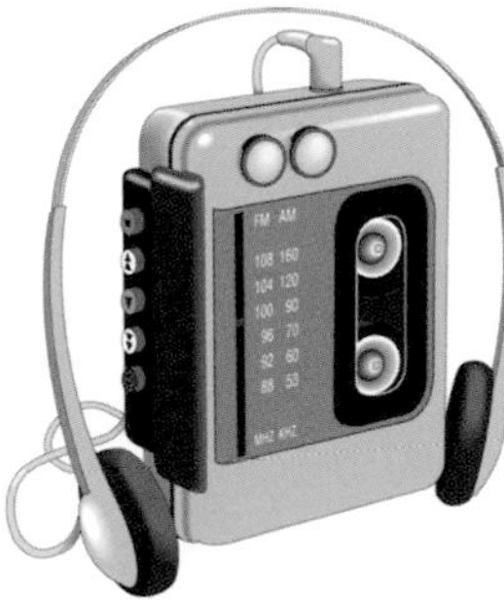

telescoping antenna
antenna[F] telescopica

handle
maniglia[F]

frequency display
display[M] delle frequenze[F]

treble tone control
regolatore[M] dei toni[M] alti

tuning control
manopola[F] di sintonizzazione[F]

bass tone control
regolatore[M] dei toni[M] bassi

volume control
manopola[F] del volume[M]

clock radio
radiosveglia[F]

display
display[M]

earphones
auricolare[M]

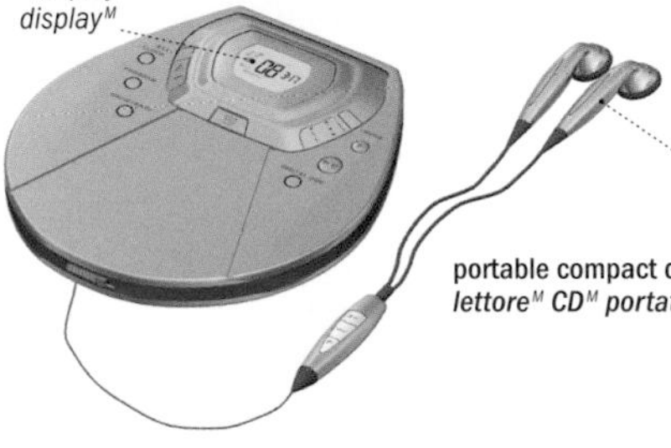

portable compact disc player
lettore[M] CD[M] portatile

personal radio cassette player
Walkman[®M]

portable sound systems

portable digital audio player
lettore[M] audio digitale portatile

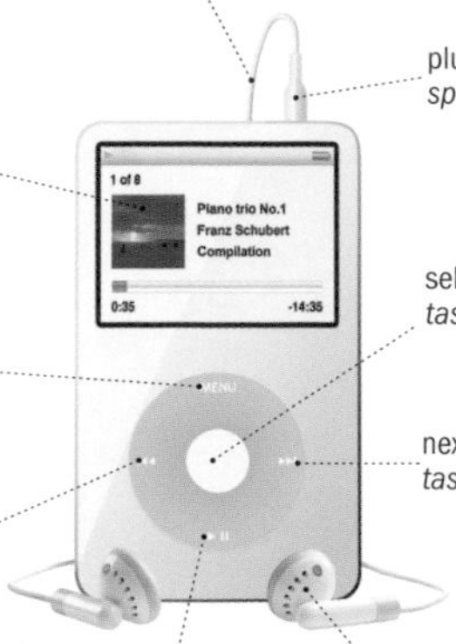

cable
cavo[M]

plug
spina[F]

display
display[M]

select button
tasto[M] di selezione

menu button
tasto[M] menu

next/fast-forward button
tasto[M] successivo/avanti veloce

previous/rewind button
tasto[M] precedente/indietro veloce

play/pause button
tasto[M] riproduzione[F]/pausa[F]

earphones
cuffie[F]

satellite radio receiver
ricevitore[M] radio[F] satellitare

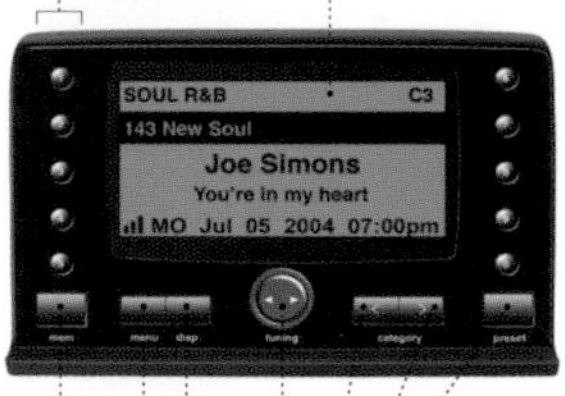

number buttons
tasti[M] numerici

liquid crystal display
display[M] a cristalli[M] liquidi

memory button
tasto[M] memoria[F]

preset button
tasto[M] di preselezione[F]

menu button
tasto[M] menu

category buttons
tasti[M] di categorie[F]

display button
tasto[M] di visualizzazione[F]

tuning control
selettore[M] stazioni[F]

portable CD/radio/cassette recorder
radioregistratore[M] con compact disc[M]

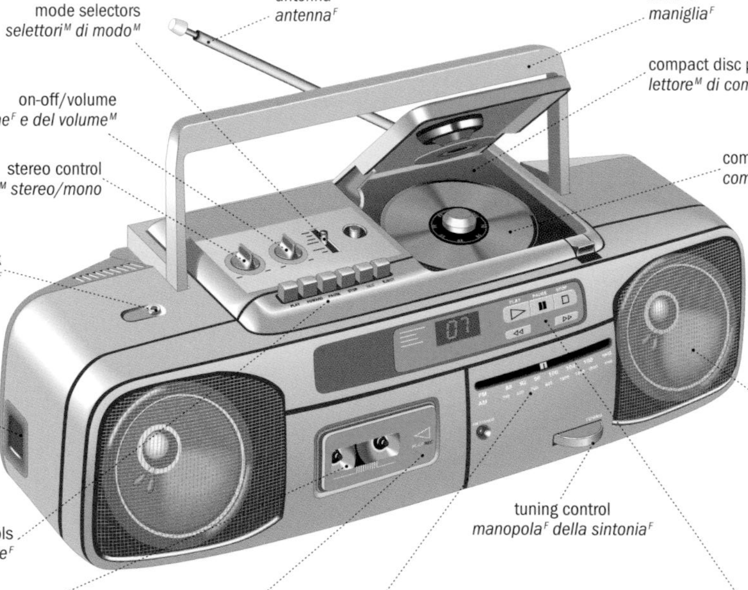

mode selectors
selettori[M] di modo[M]

antenna
antenna[F]

handle
maniglia[F]

compact disc player
lettore[M] di compact disc[M]

on-off/volume
interruttore[M] di accensione[F] e del volume[M]

compact disc
compact disc[M]

stereo control
selettore[M] stereo/mono

headphone jack
presa[F] per cuffia[F]

power plug
presa[F] di alimentazione[F]

speaker
altoparlante[M]

tuning control
manopola[F] della sintonia[F]

cassette player controls
tasti[M] del riproduttore[M] a cassette[F]

cassette
cassetta[F]

cassette player
riproduttore[M] a cassette[F]

tuner
sintonizzatore[M]

compact disc player controls
tasti[M] del lettore[M] di compact disc[M]

communication by telephone

comunicazione^F via telefono^M

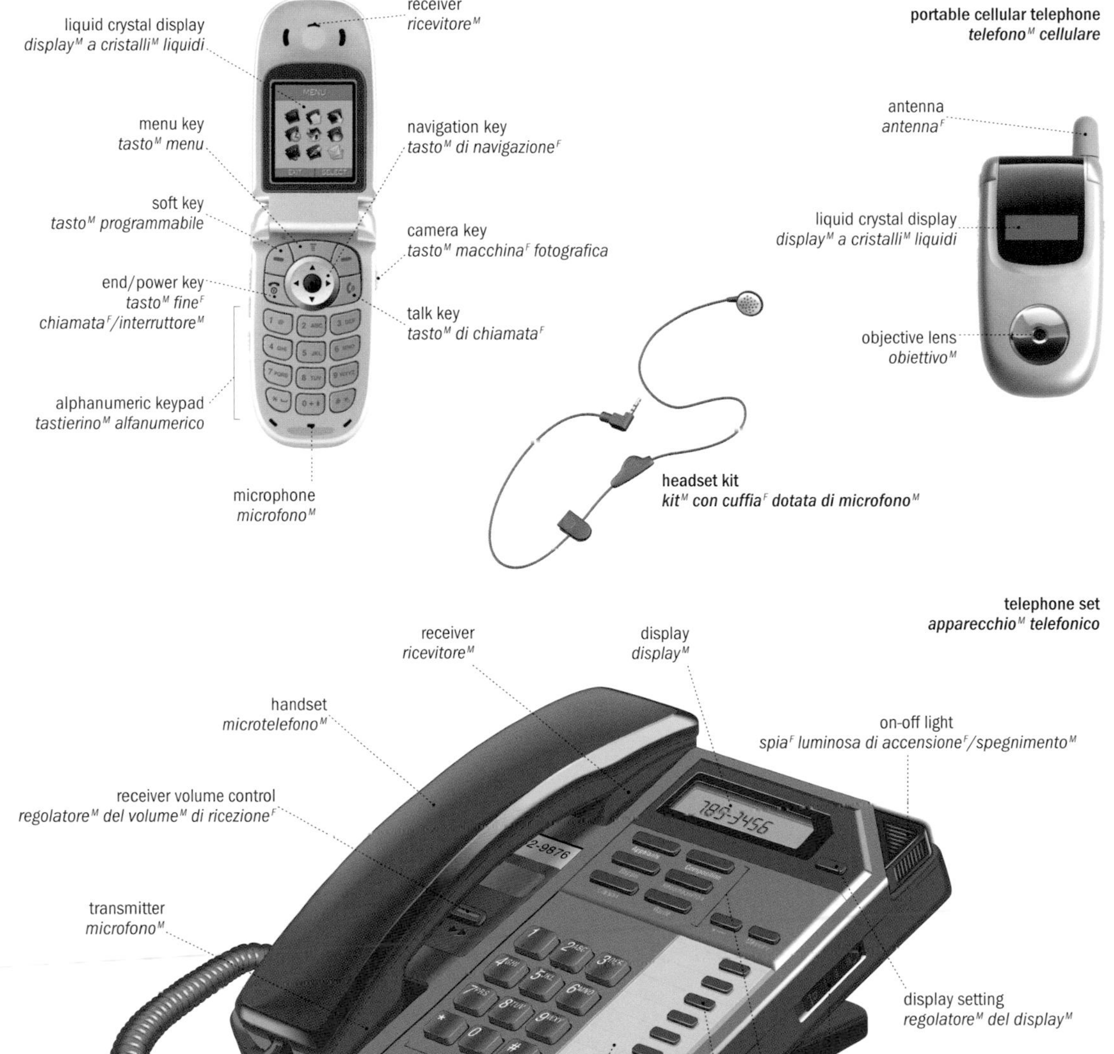

Internet

Internet[F]

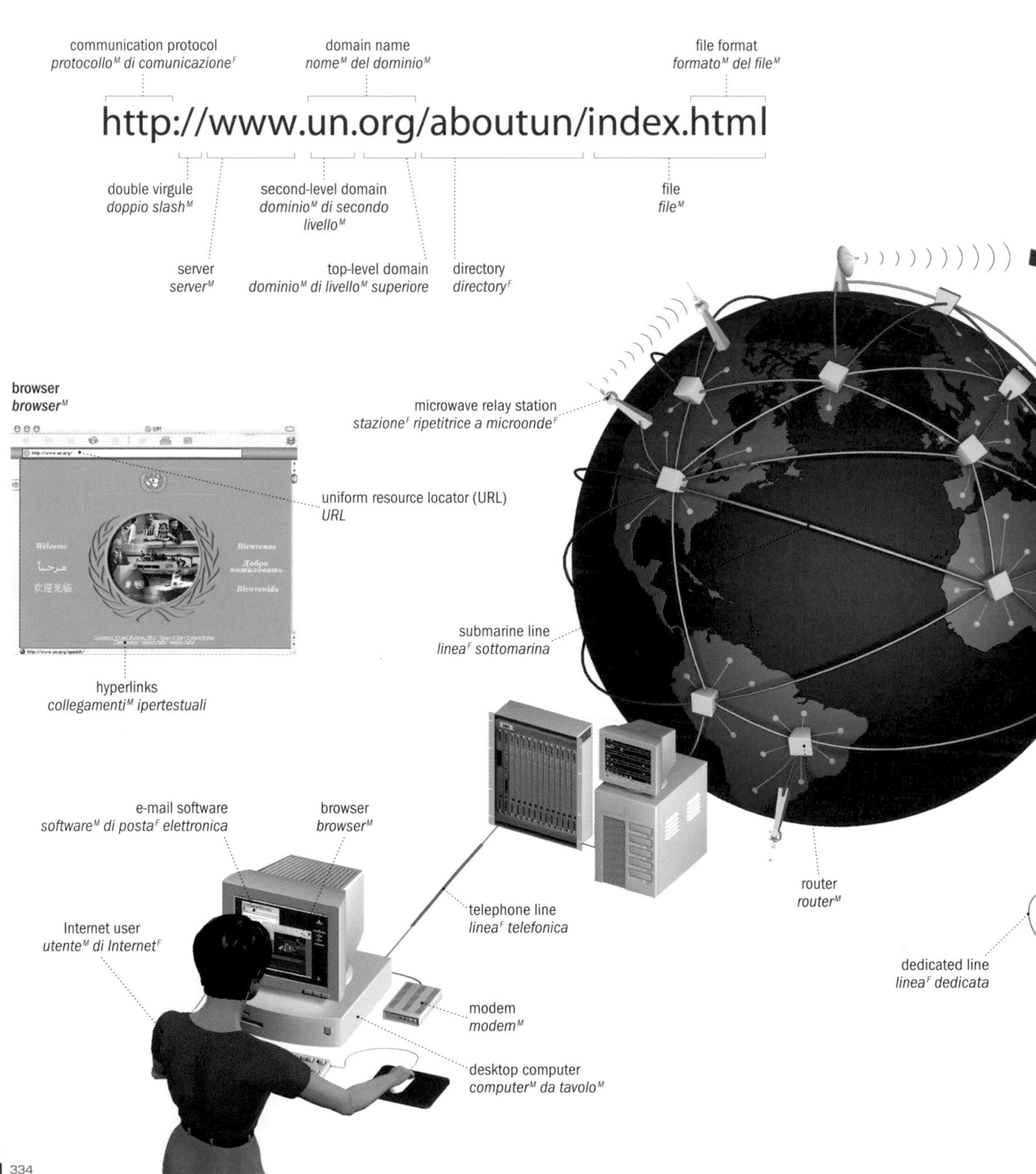

Internet uses
impieghi^M di Internet^F

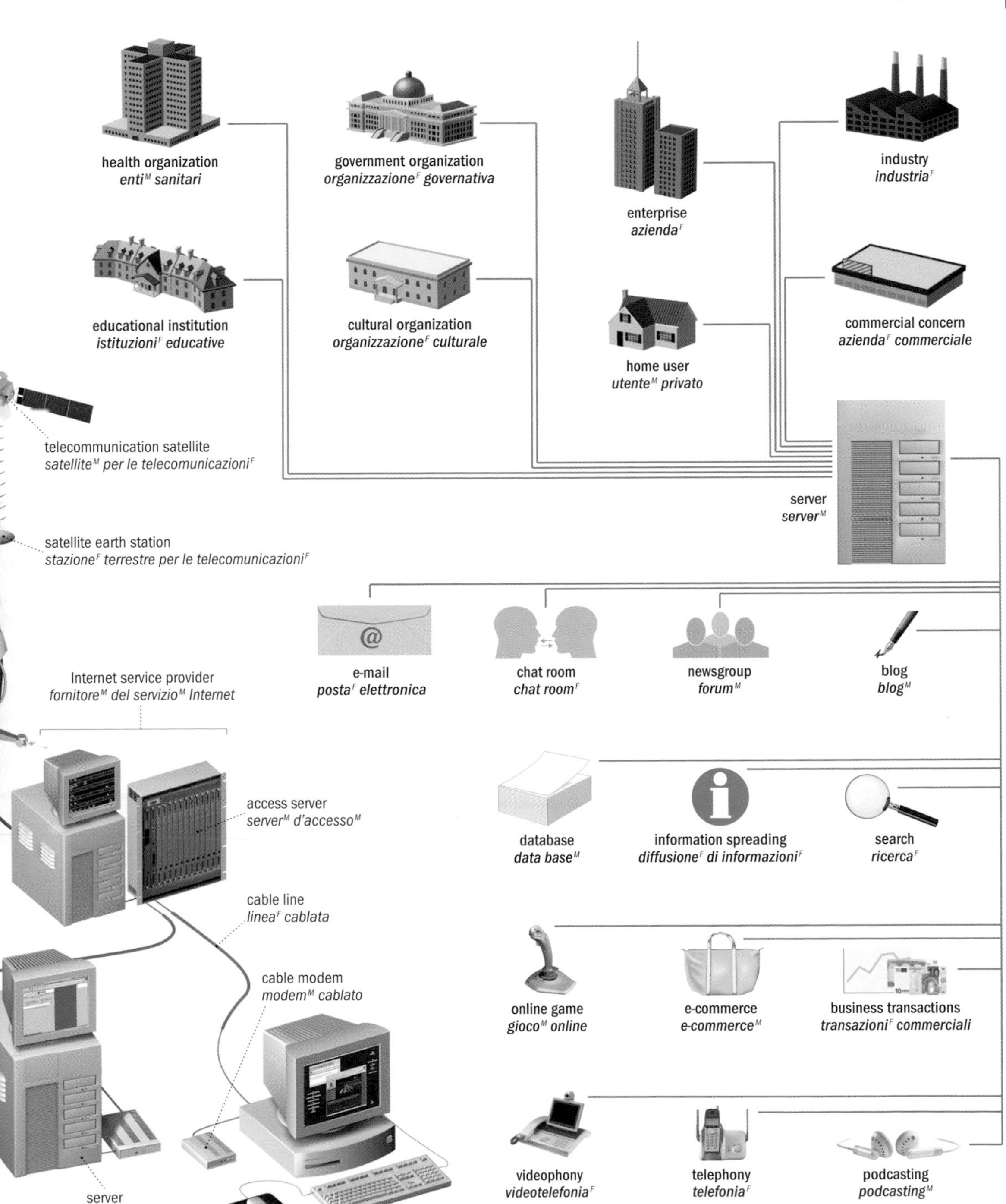

laptop computer

computer[M] portatile

laptop computer: front view
computer[M] portatile: vista[F] frontale

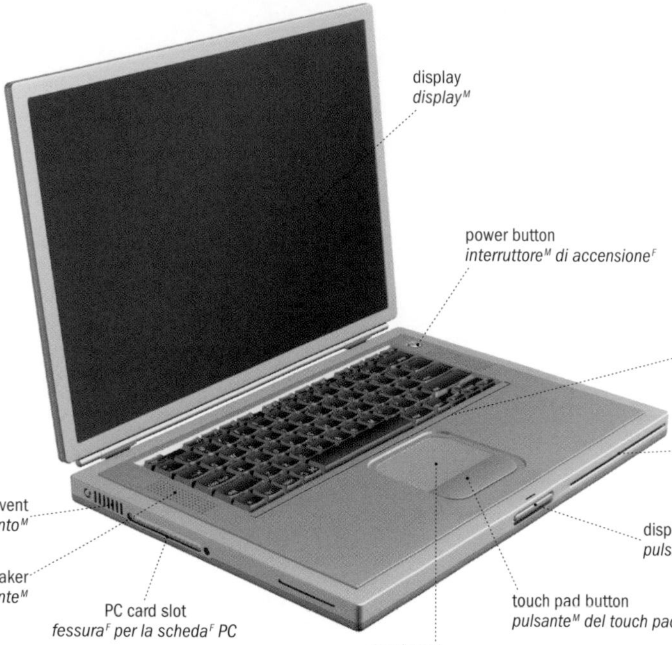

display
display[M]

power button
interruttore[M] di accensione[F]

keyboard
tastiera[F]

CD/DVD-ROM drive
lettore[M] CD[M]/DVD-ROM[M]

cooling vent
ventola[F] di raffreddamento[M]

display release button
pulsante[M] di apertura[F] del display[M]

speaker
altoparlante[M]

PC card slot
fessura[F] per la scheda[F] PC

touch pad button
pulsante[M] del touch pad[M]

touch pad
touch pad[M]

laptop computer: rear view
computer[M] portatile: dorso[M]

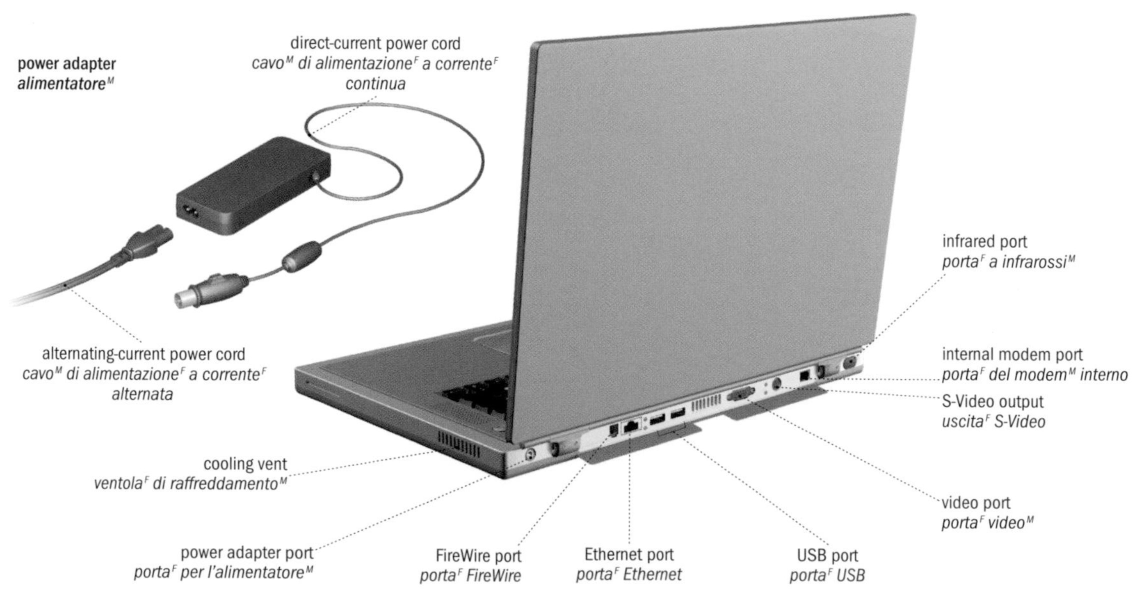

handheld computer/personal digital assistant (PDA)

computer[M] tascabile

audio input/output jack
ingresso[M]/uscita[F] audio[M]
microphone
microfono[M]
infrared port
porta[F] a infrarossi[M]
voice recorder button
pulsante[M] del registratore[M] vocale
alarm/charge indicator light
spia[F] di allarme[M] e di messa[F] in carica[F]
dial/action button
rotella[F] di comando[M]
touch screen
touch screen[M]
exit button
pulsante[M] di uscita[F]
application launch buttons
pulsanti[M] di avvio[M] delle applicazioni[F]
sync cable
cavo[M] di sincronizzazione[F]
power and backlight button
pulsante[M] di alimentazione[F] e di controluce[F]
power plug
spina[F] di alimentazione[F]
docking cradle
alloggiamento[M]
stylus
stilo[F]

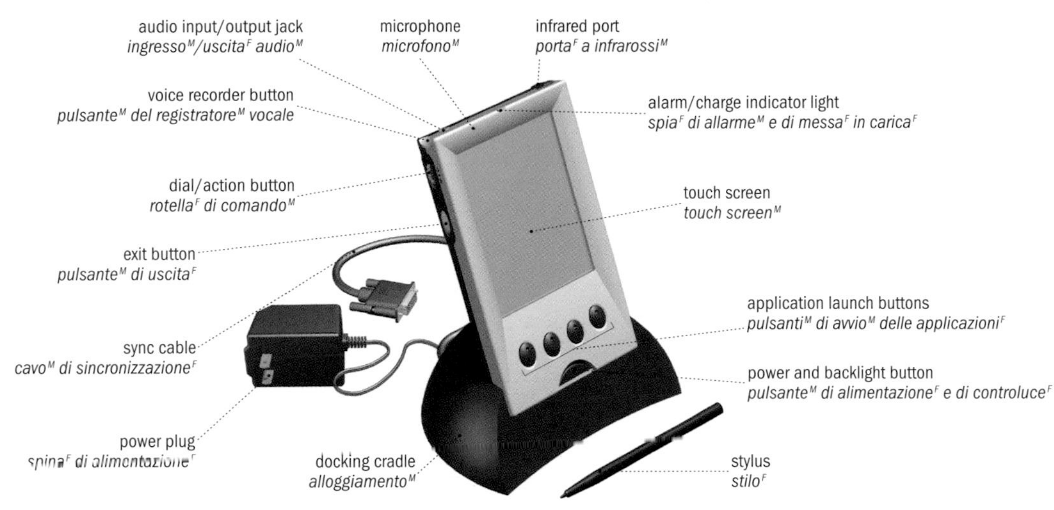

stationery

articoli[M] di cancelleria[F]

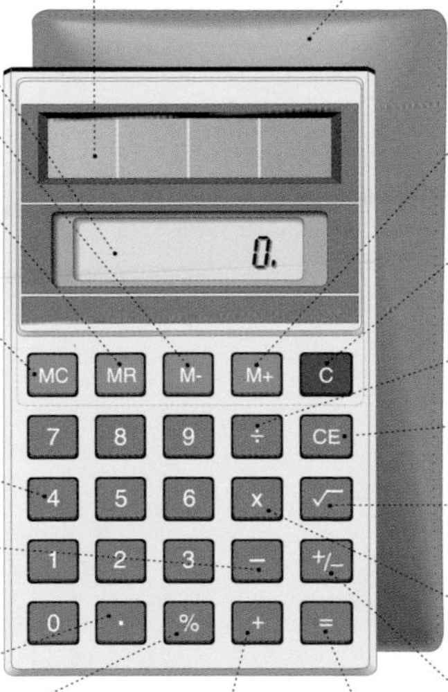

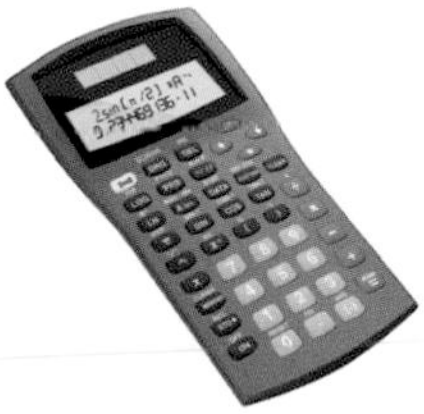

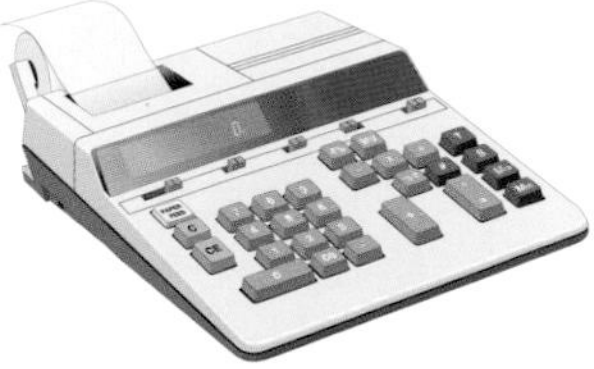

pocket calculator
calcolatrice[F] tascabile

display
display[M]
solar cell
cella[F] solare
wallet
custodia[F]
subtract from memory
tasto[M] di sottrazione[F] in memoria[F]
add to memory
tasto[M] di somma[F] in memoria[F]
memory recall
tasto[M] di richiamo[M] della memoria[F]
clear key
tasto[M] di azzeramento[M]
memory cancel
tasto[M] di cancellazione[F] della memoria[F]
divide key
tasto[M] di divisione[F]
clear-entry key
tasto[M] di azzeramento[M] ultimo dato[M]
number key
tasto[M] numerico
square root key
tasto[M] di radice[F] quadrata
subtract key
tasto[M] di sottrazione[F]
multiply key
tasto[M] di moltiplicazione[F]
decimal key
tasto[M] di punto[M] decimale
percent key
tasto[M] di percentuale[F]
add key
tasto[M] di addizione[F]
equals key
tasto[M] di uguale[M]
change-sign key
tasto[M] di cambio[M] segno[M]
0.
MC
MR
M-
M+
C
7
8
9
÷
CE
4
5
6
x
√
1
2
3
–
+/–
0
.
%
+
=

scientific calculator
calcolatrice[F] scientifica

printing calculator
calcolatrice[F] da tavolo[M]

for time management
per la gestione ***F*** ***del tempo*** ***M***

tear-off calendar
calendario *M* *a fogli* *M* *staccabili*

calendar pad
calendario *M* *da tavolo* *M*

electronic organizer
organizer *M*

display
display *M*

alphabetical keypad
tastierino *M* *alfabetico*

numeric keypad
tastierino *M* *numerico*

appointment book
agenda *F*

self-stick note
post-it *M*

memo pad
bloc-notes *M*

for correspondence
per la corrispondenza ***F***

stamp pad
tampone *M*

rubber stamp
timbro *M* *di gomma* *F*

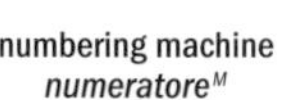

numbering machine
numeratore *M*

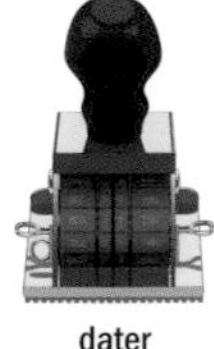

dater
datario *M*

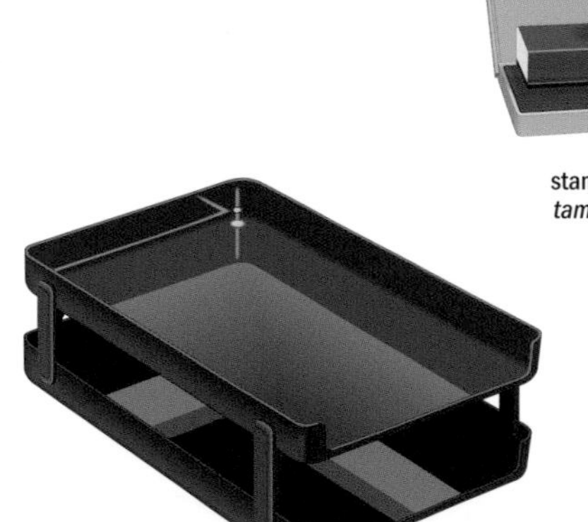

desk tray
vaschetta *F* *portacorrispondenza*

rotary file
schedario *M* *rotativo*

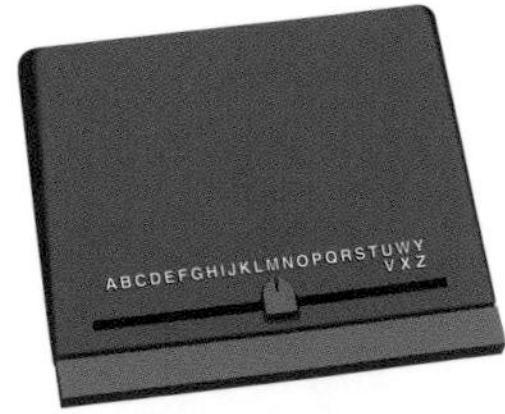

telephone index
rubrica *F* *telefonica*

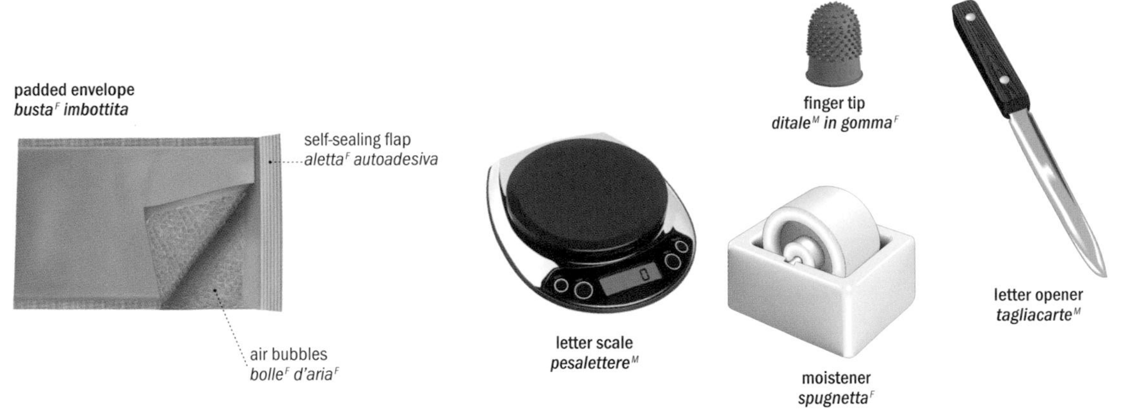

for filing
per l'archiviazione[F]

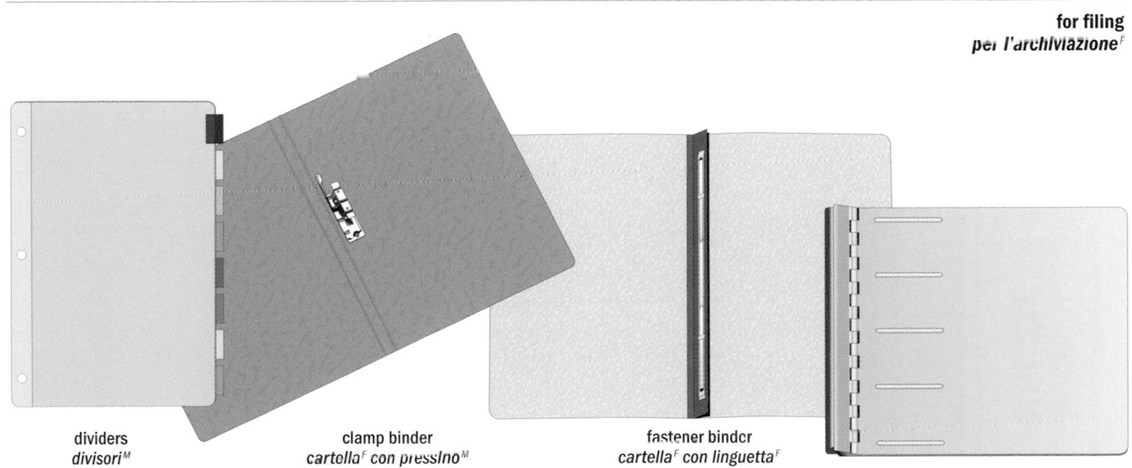

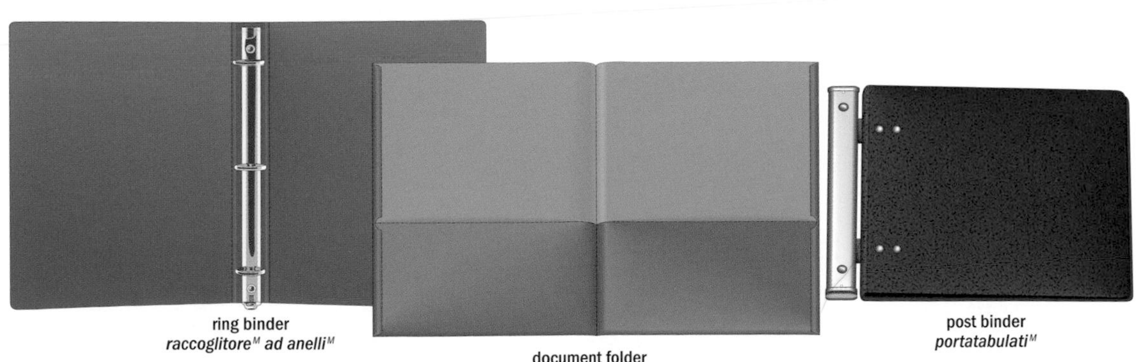

stationery

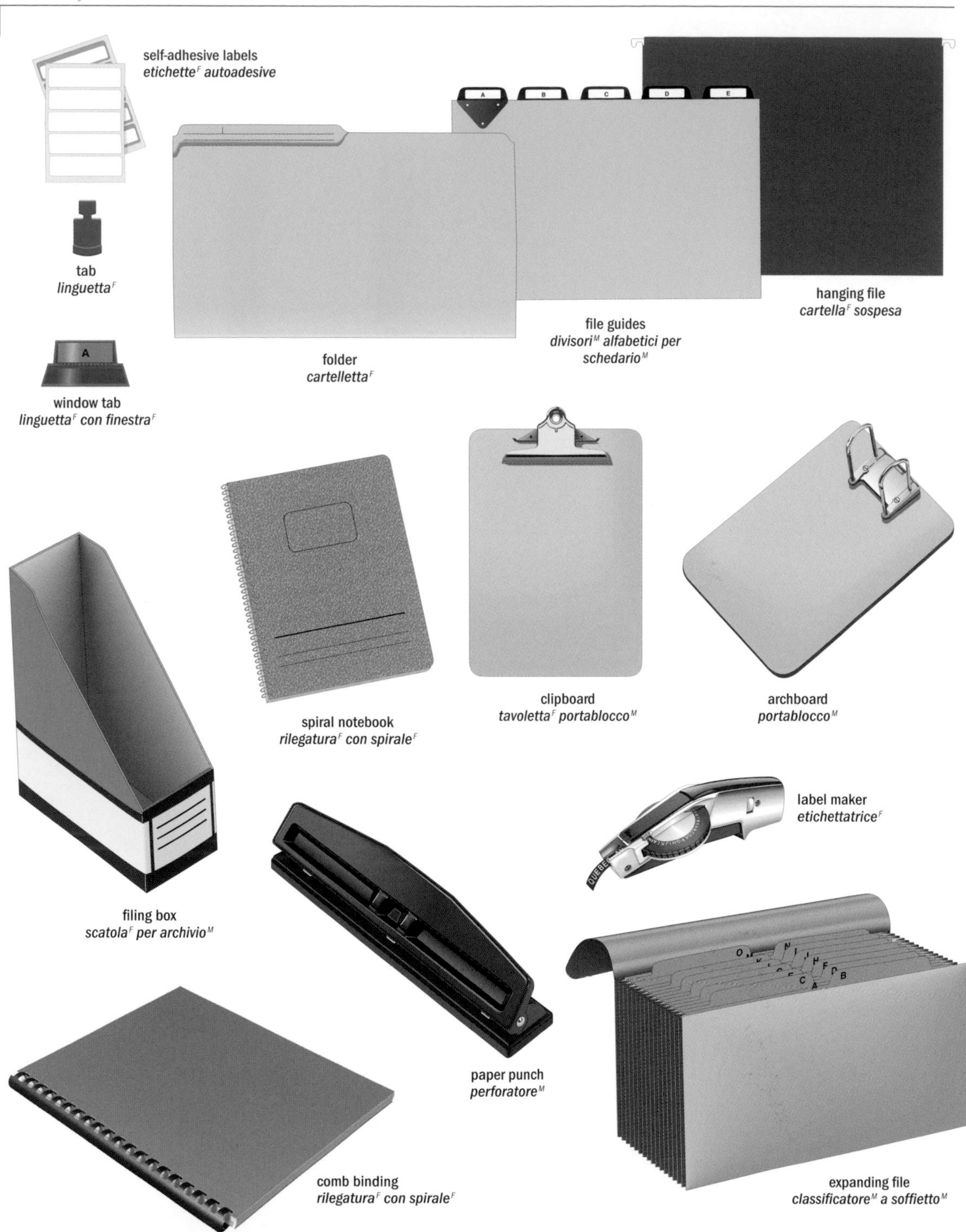
self-adhesive labels
etichette^F autoadesive
tab
linguetta^F
window tab
linguetta^F con finestra^F
folder
cartelletta^F
file guides
divisori^M alfabetici per schedario^M
hanging file
cartella^F sospesa
spiral notebook
rilegatura^F con spirale^F
clipboard
tavoletta^F portablocco^M
archboard
portablocco^M
label maker
etichettatrice^F
filing box
scatola^F per archivio^M
paper punch
perforatore^M
comb binding
rilegatura^F con spirale^F
expanding file
classificatore^M a soffietto^M

miscellaneous articles
articoli[M] *vari*

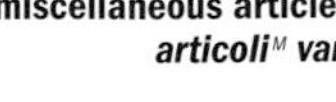

paper clips
fermagli[M]

thumb tacks
puntine[F] *da disegno*[M]

paper fasteners
fermacampioni[M]

packing tape dispenser
nastratrice[F]

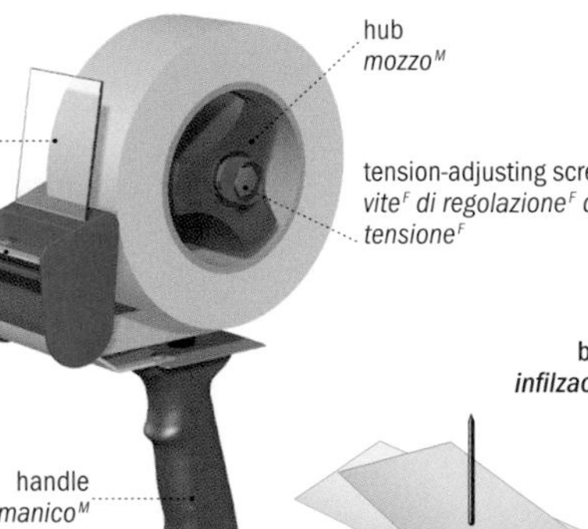

pencil sharpener
temperamatite[M]

eraser
gomma[F]

bill-file
infilzacarte[M]

staple remover
levapunti[M]

tape dispenser
chiocciola[F] *per nastro*[M] *adesivo*

glue stick
colla[F] *in stick*[M]

stapler
cucitrice[F]

staples
punti[M] *metallici*

book ends
reggilibri[M]

paper clip holder
portafermagli[M]

pencil sharpener
temperamatite[M]

bulletin board
bacheca[F]

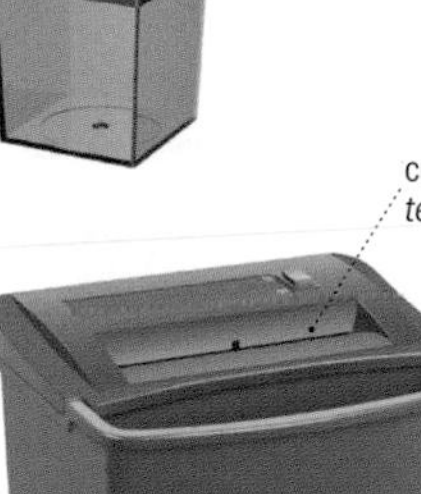

paper shredder
distruggidocumenti[M]

waste basket
cestino[M]

road system

sistema[M] stradale

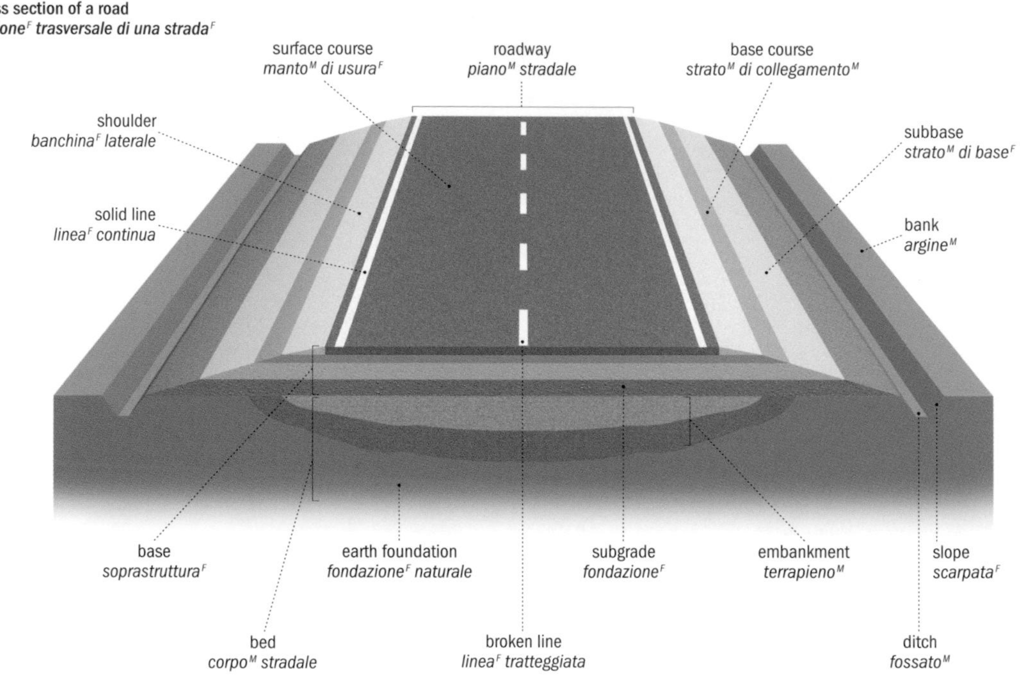

examples of interchanges
esempi[M] di raccordo[M]

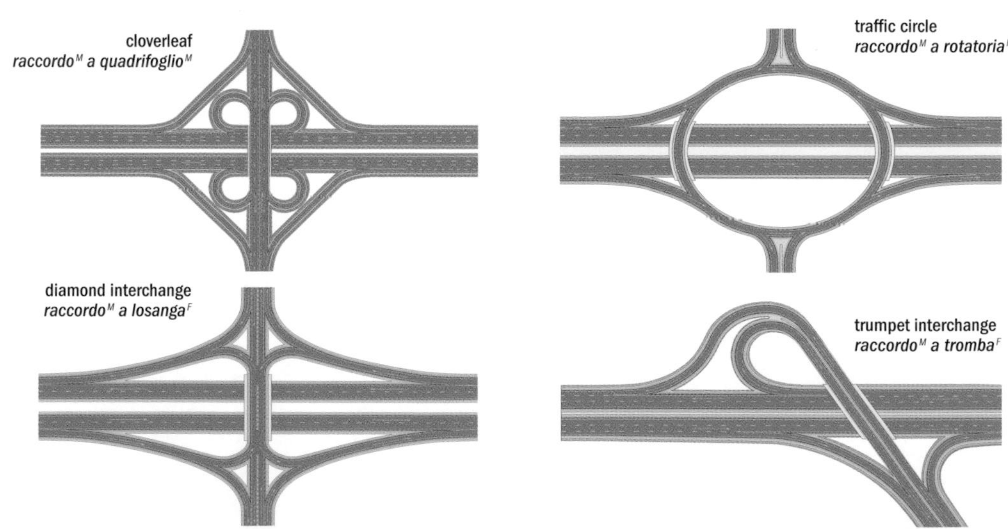

TRANSPORT AND MACHINERY

cloverleaf
raccordo^M a quadrifoglio^M

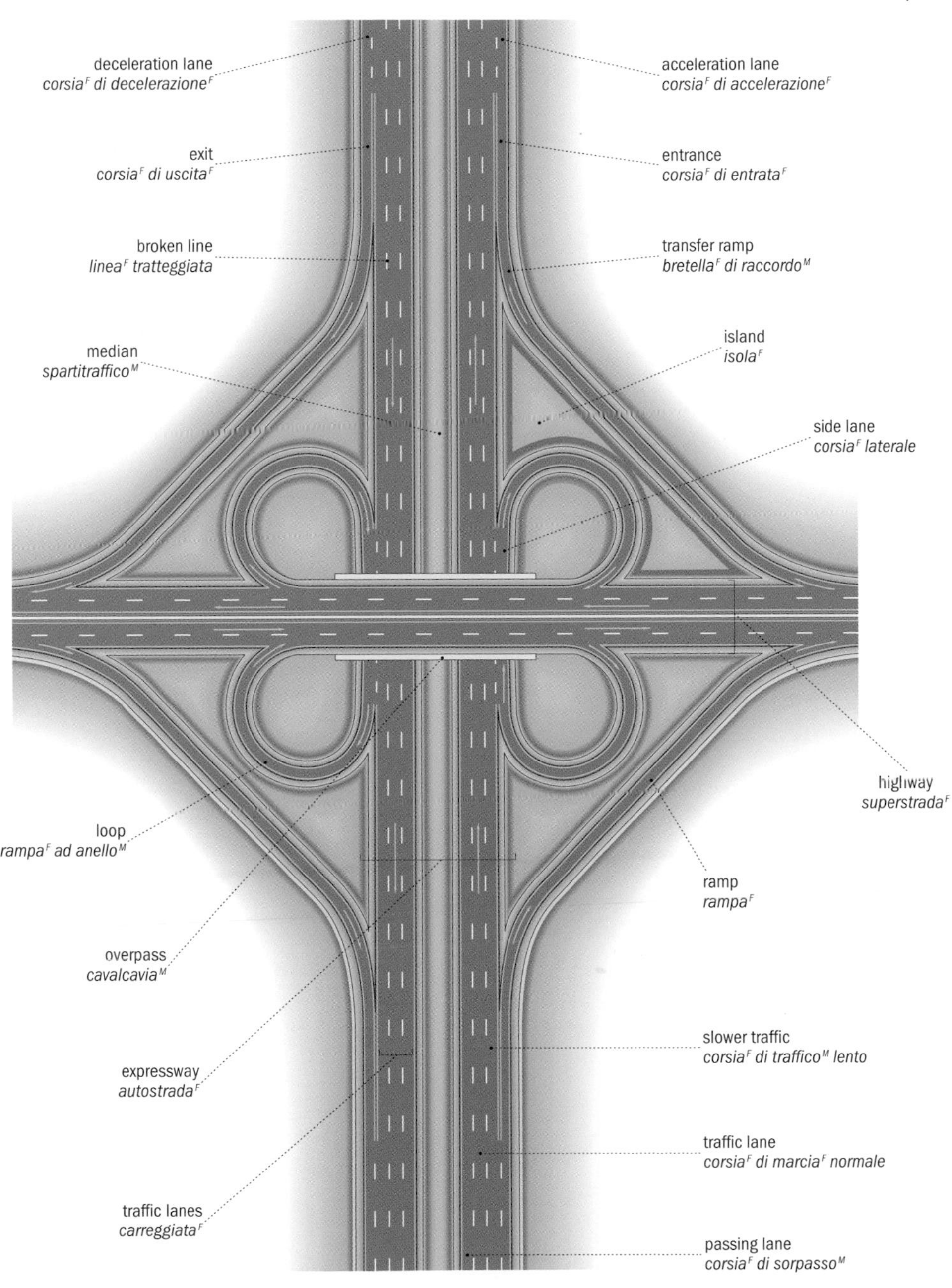

fixed bridges

ponti[M] fissi

beam bridge
ponte[M] a travata[F]

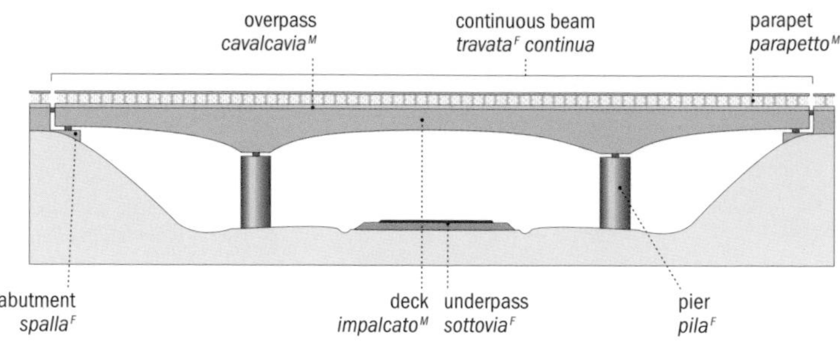

suspension bridge
ponte[M] sospeso

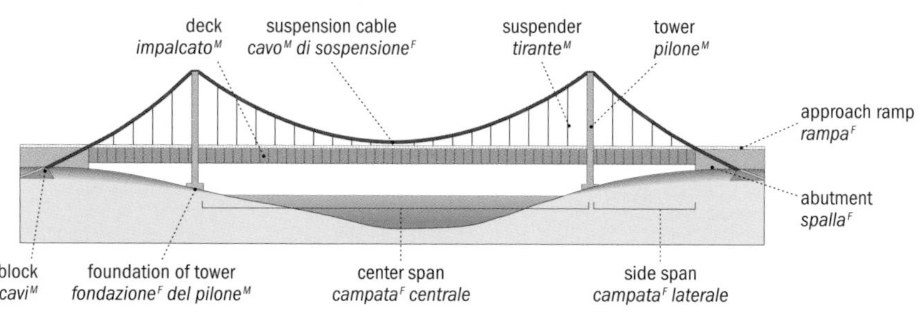

cantilever bridge
ponte[M] a cantilever[M]

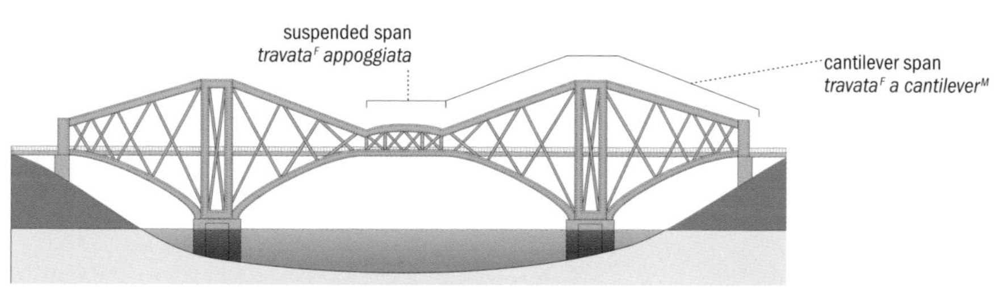

movable bridges

ponti[M] mobili

swing bridge
ponte[M] girevole

movable bridges

counterweight
*contrappeso*ᴹ

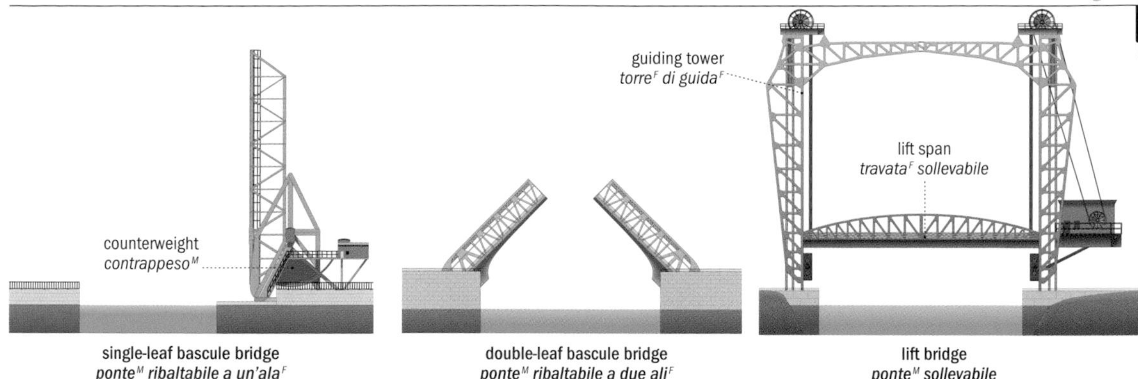

single-leaf bascule bridge
***ponte*ᴹ *ribaltabile a un'ala*ᶠ**

double-leaf bascule bridge
***ponte*ᴹ *ribaltabile a due ali*ᶠ**

guiding tower
*torre*ᶠ *di guida*ᶠ
lift span
*travata*ᶠ *sollevabile*

lift bridge
ponte*ᴹ *sollevabile

road tunnel

galleriaᶠ

connecting gallery
*galleria*ᶠ *di collegamento*ᴹ
emergency station
*stazione*ᶠ *di pronto soccorso*ᴹ
shelter
*rifugio*ᴹ
technical room
*locale*ᴹ *tecnico*
stairs
*scale*ᶠ
pressurized refuge
*camera*ᶠ *pressurizzata*
emergency truck
*mezzo*ᴹ *di pronto intervento*ᴹ
vehicle rest area
*area*ᶠ *di sosta*ᶠ *dei veicoli*ᴹ
safety niche
*nicchia*ᶠ *di sicurezza*ᶠ
roadway
*strada*ᶠ
fresh air duct
*condotto*ᴹ *dell'aria*ᶠ *pulita*
exhaust air duct
*condotto*ᴹ *dell'aria*ᶠ *di scarico*ᴹ
evacuation route
*percorso*ᴹ *di evacuazione*ᶠ

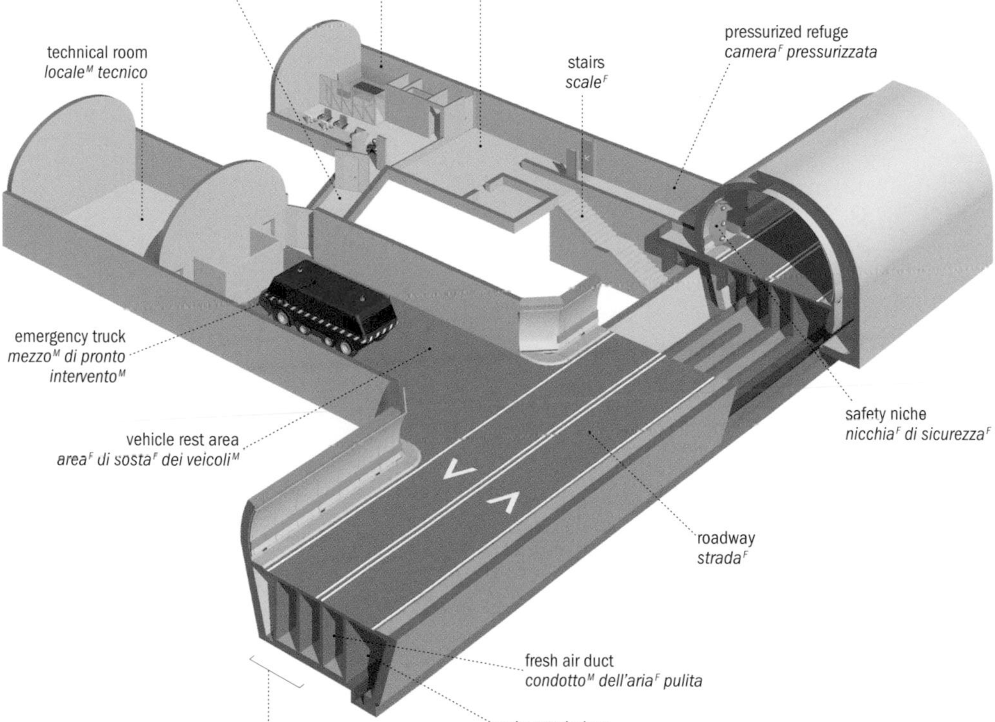

service station

stazione[F] di servizio[M]

gasoline pump
pompa[F] della benzina[F]

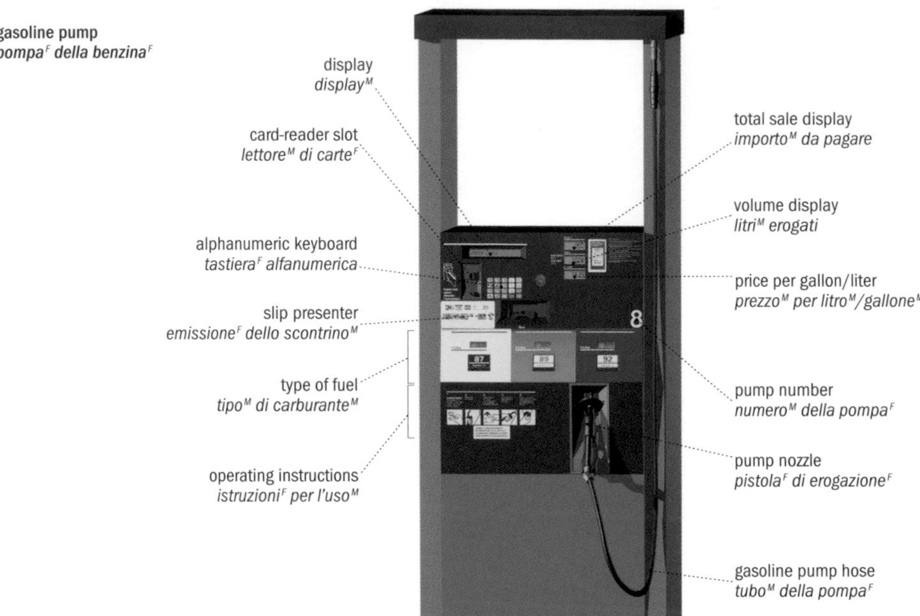

service station
stazione[F] di servizio[M]

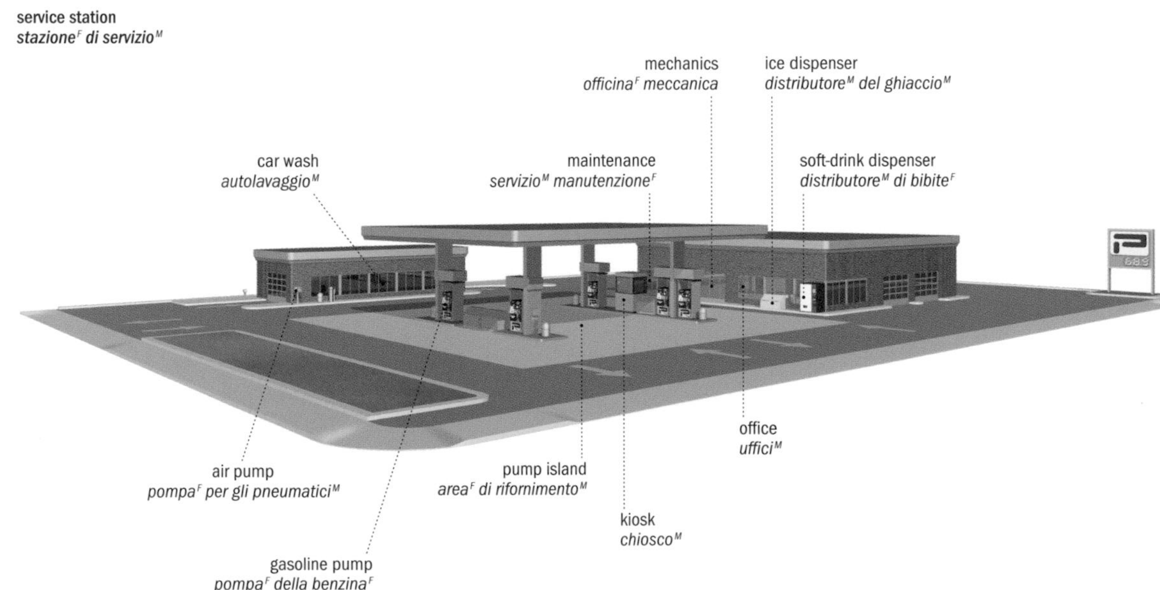

automobile

automobile[F]

examples of bodies
esempi[M] di carrozzerie[F]

sports car
granturismo[F]

micro compact car
microvettura[F] compatta

hatchback
vettura[F] a tre porte[F]

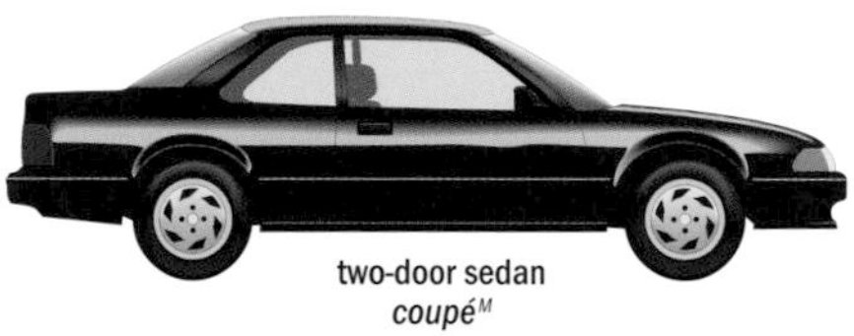

two-door sedan
coupé[M]

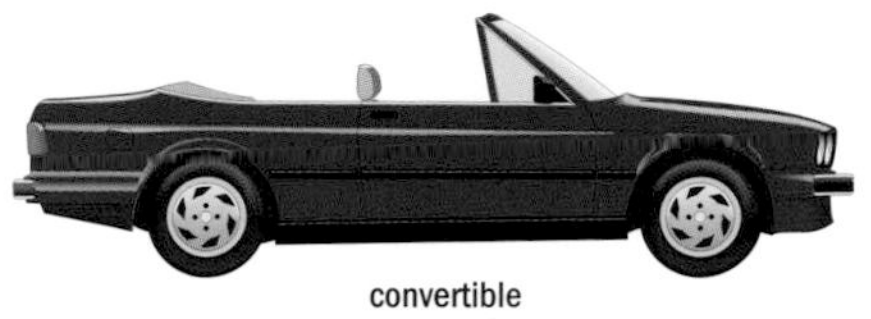

convertible
spider[F]

four-door sedan
berlina[F]

station wagon
station wagon[F]

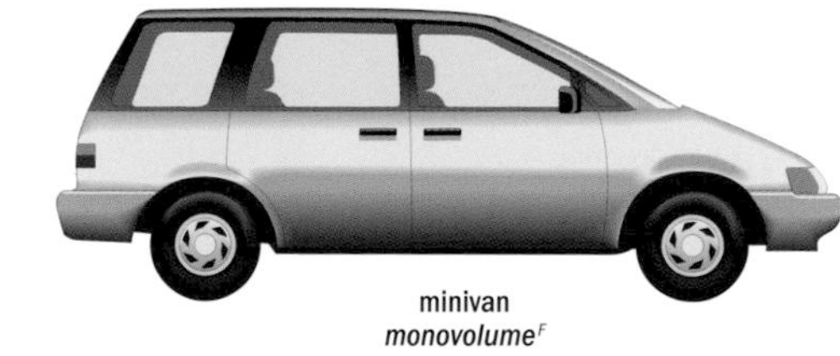

minivan
monovolume[F]

sport-utility vehicle
fuoristrada[M]

pickup truck
pickup[M]

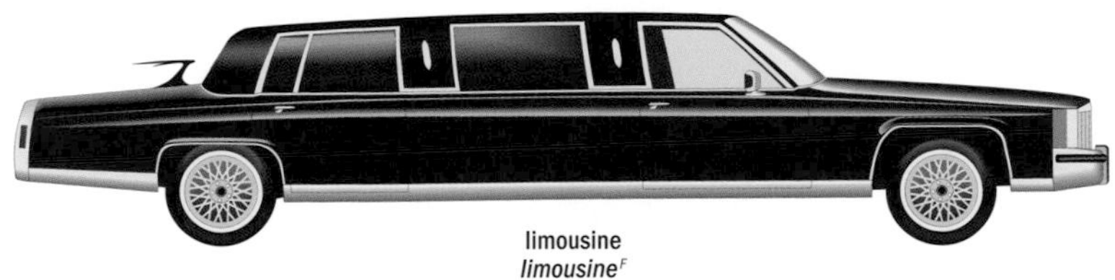

limousine
limousine[F]

body
*carrozzeria*F

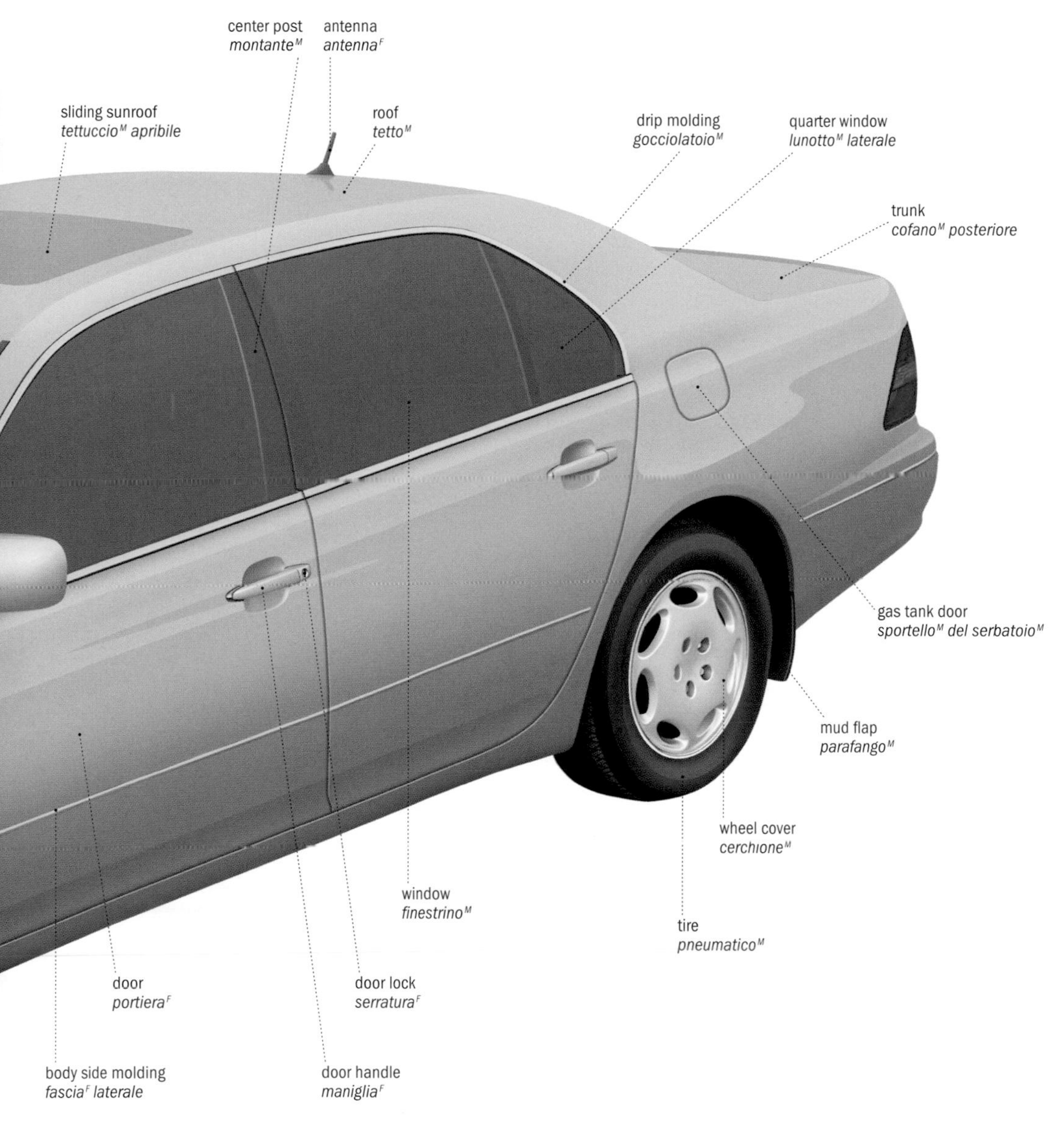
center post
montante^M
antenna
antenna^F
sliding sunroof
tettuccio^M apribile
roof
tetto^M
drip molding
gocciolatoio^M
quarter window
lunotto^M laterale
trunk
cofano^M posteriore
gas tank door
sportello^M del serbatoio^M
mud flap
parafango^M
wheel cover
cerchione^M
window
finestrino^M
tire
pneumatico^M
door
portiera^F
door lock
serratura^F
body side molding
fascia^F laterale
door handle
maniglia^F

automobile

automobile systems: main parts
sistemi^{M} dell'automobile^{F}: componenti^{M} principali

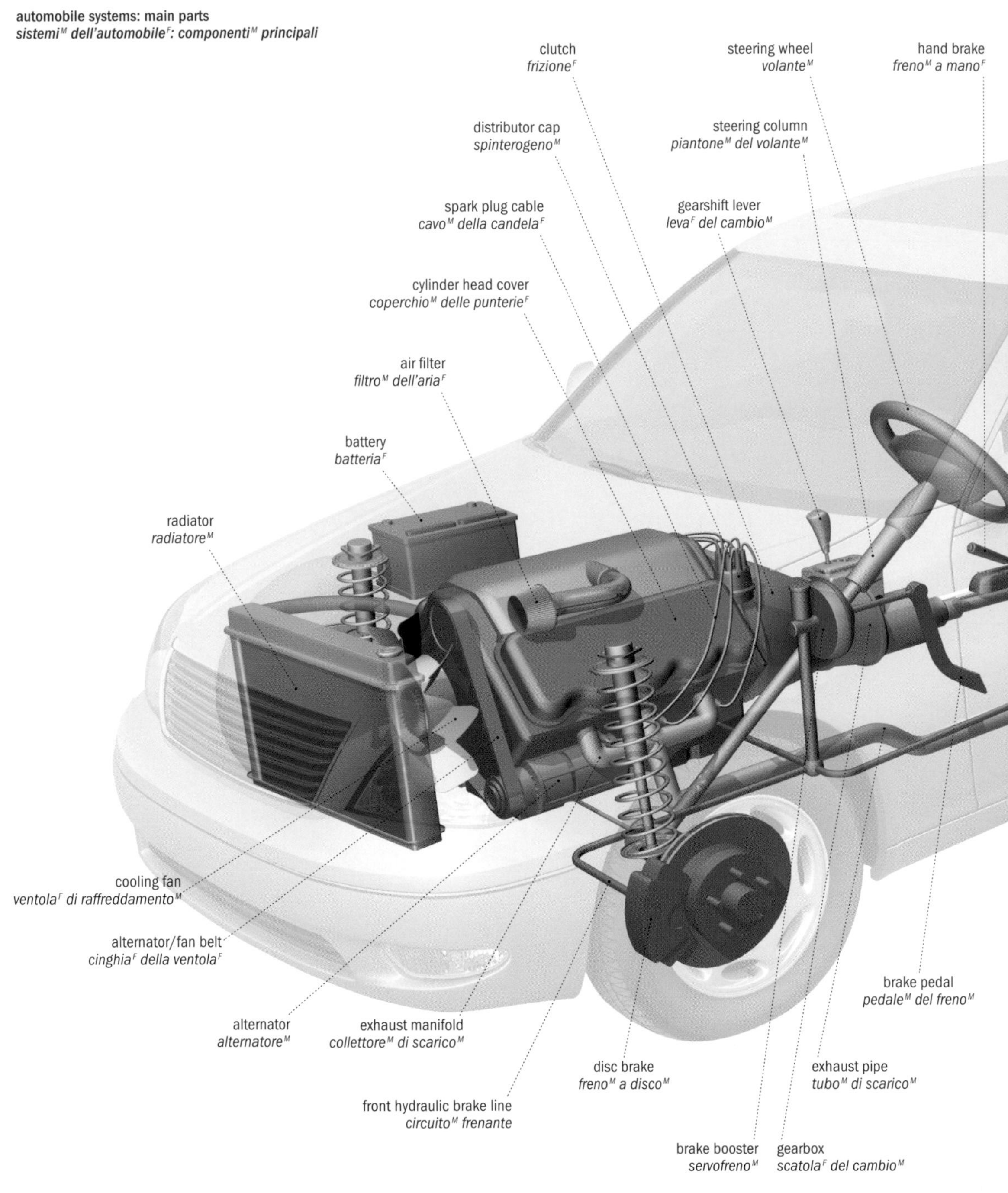

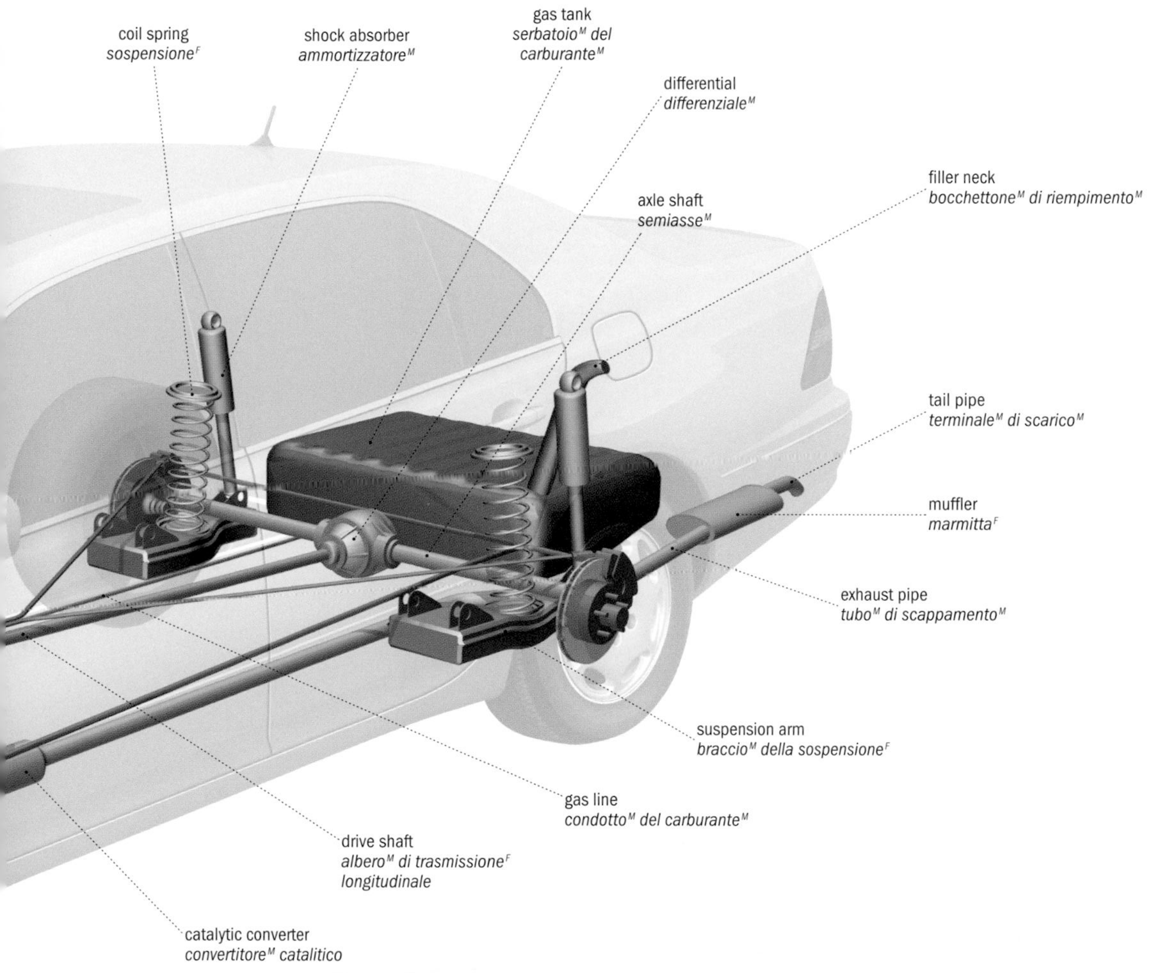

coil spring
sospensione[F]

shock absorber
ammortizzatore[M]

gas tank
serbatoio[M] *del carburante*[M]

differential
differenziale[M]

axle shaft
semiasse[M]

filler neck
bocchettone[M] *di riempimento*[M]

tail pipe
terminale[M] *di scarico*[M]

muffler
marmitta[F]

exhaust pipe
tubo[M] *di scappamento*[M]

suspension arm
braccio[M] *della sospensione*[F]

gas line
condotto[M] *del carburante*[M]

drive shaft
albero[M] *di trasmissione*[F] *longitudinale*

catalytic converter
convertitore[M] *catalitico*

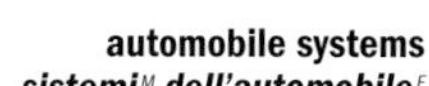

automobile systems
***sistemi*[M] *dell'automobile*[F]**

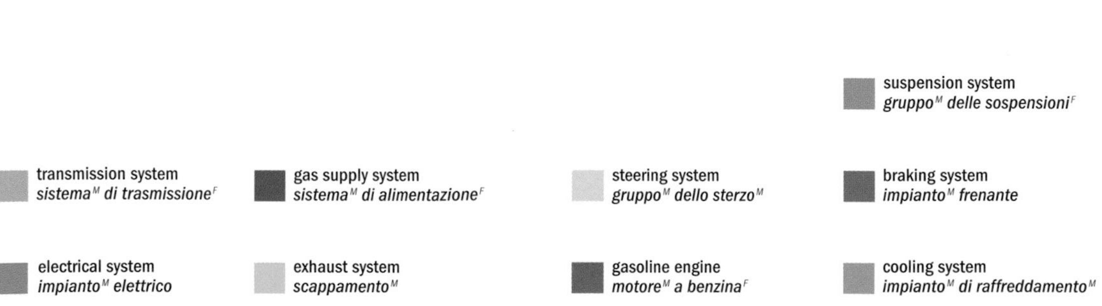

suspension system
***gruppo*[M] *delle sospensioni*[F]**

transmission system
***sistema*[M] *di trasmissione*[F]**

gas supply system
***sistema*[M] *di alimentazione*[F]**

steering system
***gruppo*[M] *dello sterzo*[M]**

braking system
impianto*[M] *frenante

electrical system
impianto*[M] *elettrico

exhaust system
***scappamento*[M]**

gasoline engine
***motore*[M] *a benzina*[F]**

cooling system
***impianto*[M] *di raffreddamento*[M]**

automobile

headlights
luci[F] anteriori

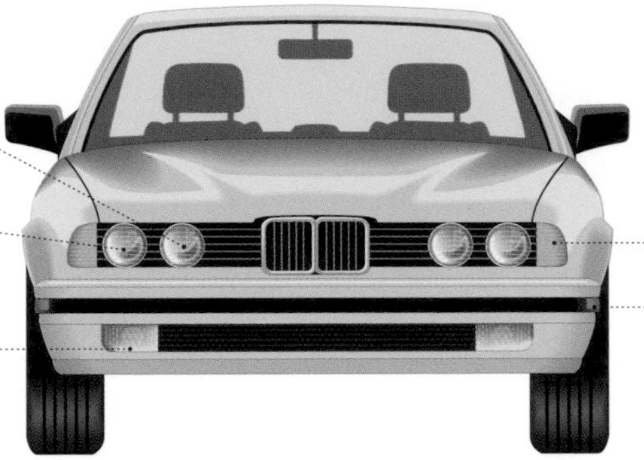

high beam
proiettore[M] abbagliante e anabbagliante
low beam
luce[F] di posizione[F]
fog light
faro[M] fendinebbia
turn signal
indicatore[M] di direzione[F]
side-marker light
luce[F] di ingombro[M] laterale

taillights
luci[F] posteriori

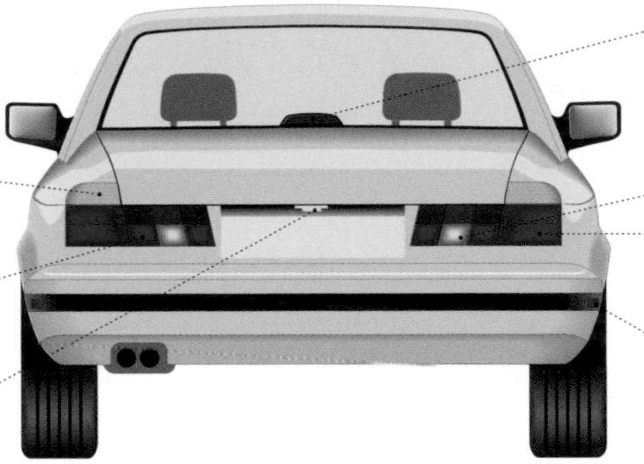

brake light
luce[F] di arresto[M]
turn signal
indicatore[M] di direzione[F]
reverse light
luce[F] di retromarcia[F]
taillight
luce[F] di posizione[F] posteriore
brake light
luce[F] di arresto[M]
side-marker light
luce[F] di ingombro[M] laterale
license plate light
luce[F] della targa[F]

door
portiera[F]

interior door handle
maniglia[F] interna
window
finestrino[M]
assist grip
maniglia[F] fissa
interior door lock button
pomello[M] della sicura[F]
outside mirror control
regolazione[F] dello specchietto[M] retrovisore esterno
armrest
bracciolo[M]
lock
serratura[F]
window regulator handle
manopola[F] alzacristalli
trim panel
pannello[M]
hinge
cardine[M]
accessory pocket
tasca[F] portaoggetti
inner door shell
telaio[M] interno della portiera[F]

TRANSPORT AND MACHINERY

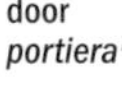

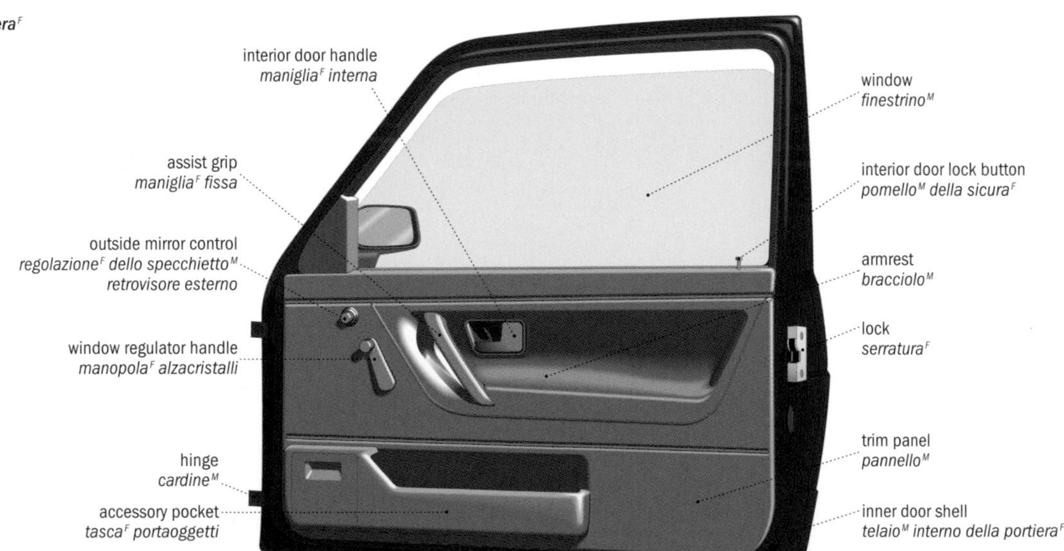

bucket seat: front view
sedile[M]: vista[F] anteriore

bucket seat: side view
sedile[M]: vista[F] laterale

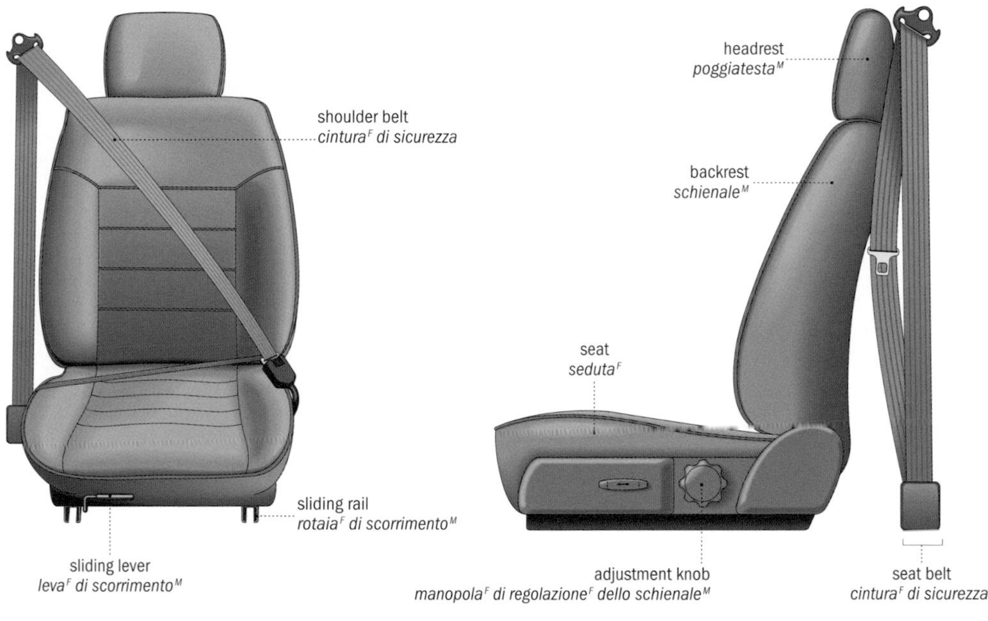

rear seat
divano[M] posteriore

dashboard
***plancia**F*

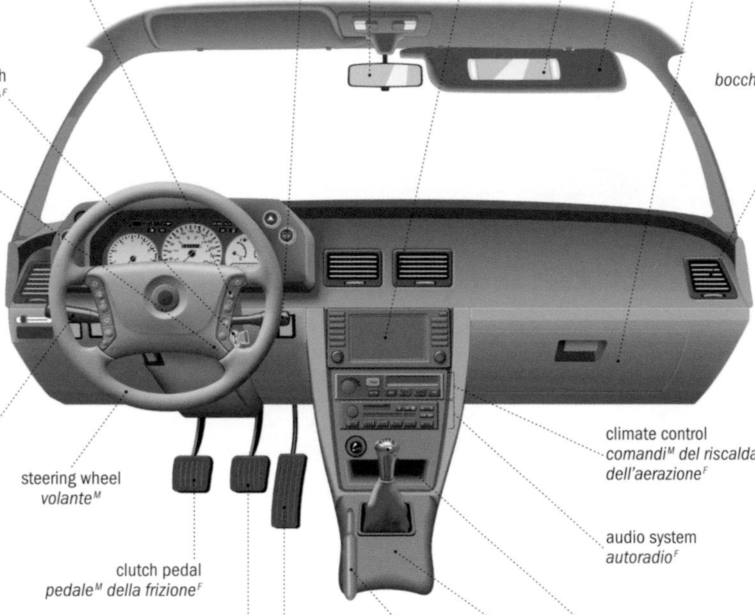

rearview mirror
specchietto M retrovisore
vanity mirror
specchietto M di cortesia F
wiper switch
comando M del tergicristallo M
on-board computer
computer M di bordo M
sun visor
aletta F parasole
cruise control
controllo M della velocità F di crociera F
glove compartment
vano M portaoggetti
ignition switch
blocchetto M di accensione F
vent
bocchetta F di ventilazione F
horn
clacson M
climate control
comandi M del riscaldamento M e dell'aerazione F
steering wheel
volante M
audio system
autoradio F
clutch pedal
pedale M della frizione F
gearshift lever
leva F del cambio M
headlight/turn signal
comando M dei proiettori M e dell'indicatore M di direzione F
parking brake lever
leva F del freno M a mano F
center console
console F centrale
brake pedal
pedale M del freno M
gas pedal
pedale M dell'acceleratore M

air bag restraint system
sistema M di ritenuta F degli air bag M

air bag
air bag M
safing sensor
sensore M di sicurezza F
primary crash sensor
sensore M di collisione F principale
electrical cable
cavo M elettrico

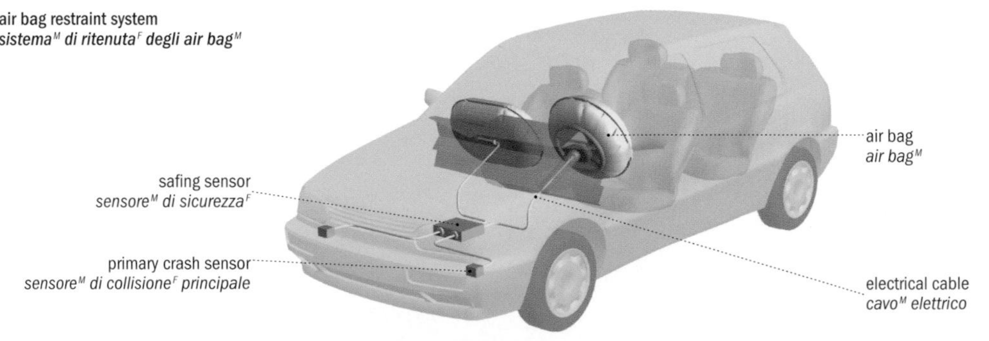

instrument panel
quadro[M] degli strumenti[M] di controllo[M]

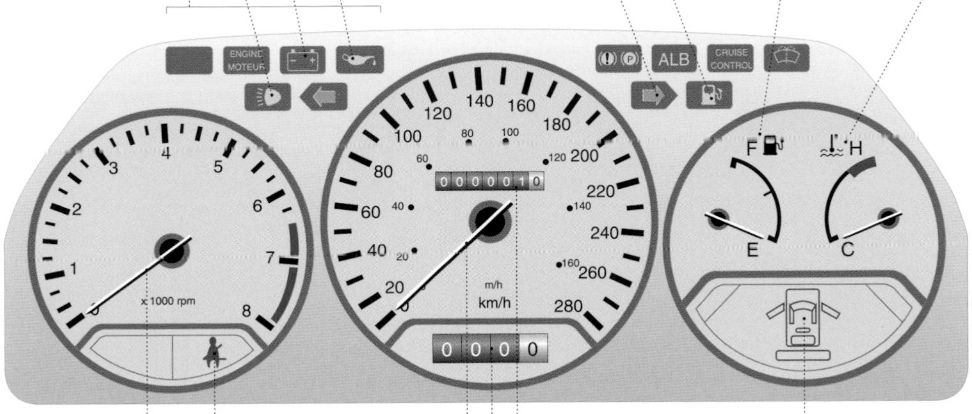

alternator warning light
spia[F] della batteria[F]
oil warning light
spia[F] della pressione[F] dell'olio[M]
temperature indicator
indicatore[M] della temperatura[F] del liquido[M] di raffreddamento[M]
high beam indicator light
spia[F] dei proiettori[M] abbaglianti
low fuel warning light
spia[F] della riserva[F] di carburante[M]
fuel indicator
indicatore[M] del livello[M] di carburante[M]
warning lights
spie[F]
turn signal indicator
spia[F] dell'indicatore[M] di direzione[F]
ENGINE
MOTEUR
ALB
CRUISE
CONTROL
x 1000 rpm
m/h
km/h
F
E
H
C
tachometer
contagiri[M]
speedometer
tachimetro[M]
odometer
contachilometri[M] totale
seat-belt warning light
spia[F] delle cinture[F] di sicurezza[F] non allacciate
trip odometer
contachilometri[M] parziale
door open warning light
spia[F] delle porte[F] aperte

windshield wiper
tergicristallo[M]

windshield wiper blade
spatola[F] metallica
articulation
articolazione[F]
wiper
spazzola[F] di gomma[F]
wiper arm
braccio[M] del tergicristallo[M]
tension spring
molla[F] di tensione[F]
fluted shaft
perno[M] oscillante

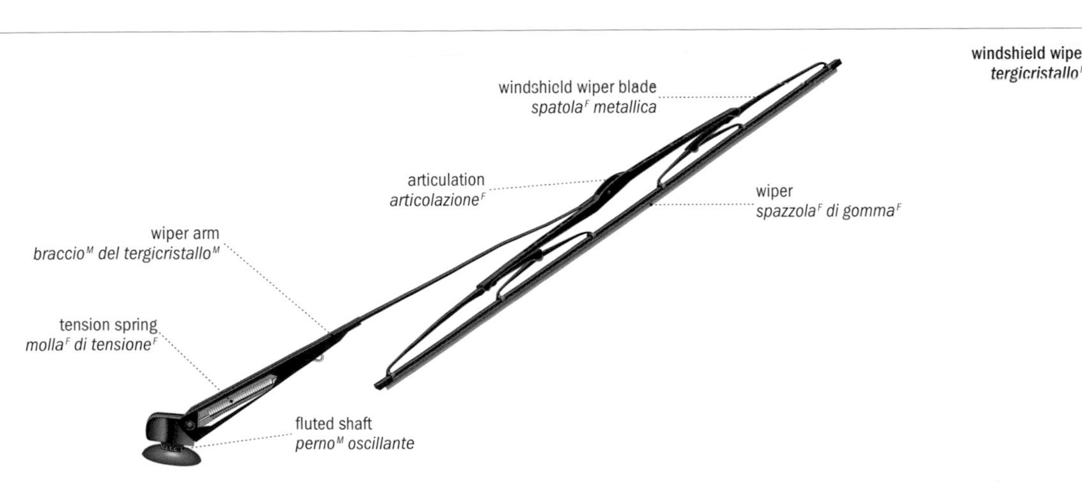

accessories
accessori[M]

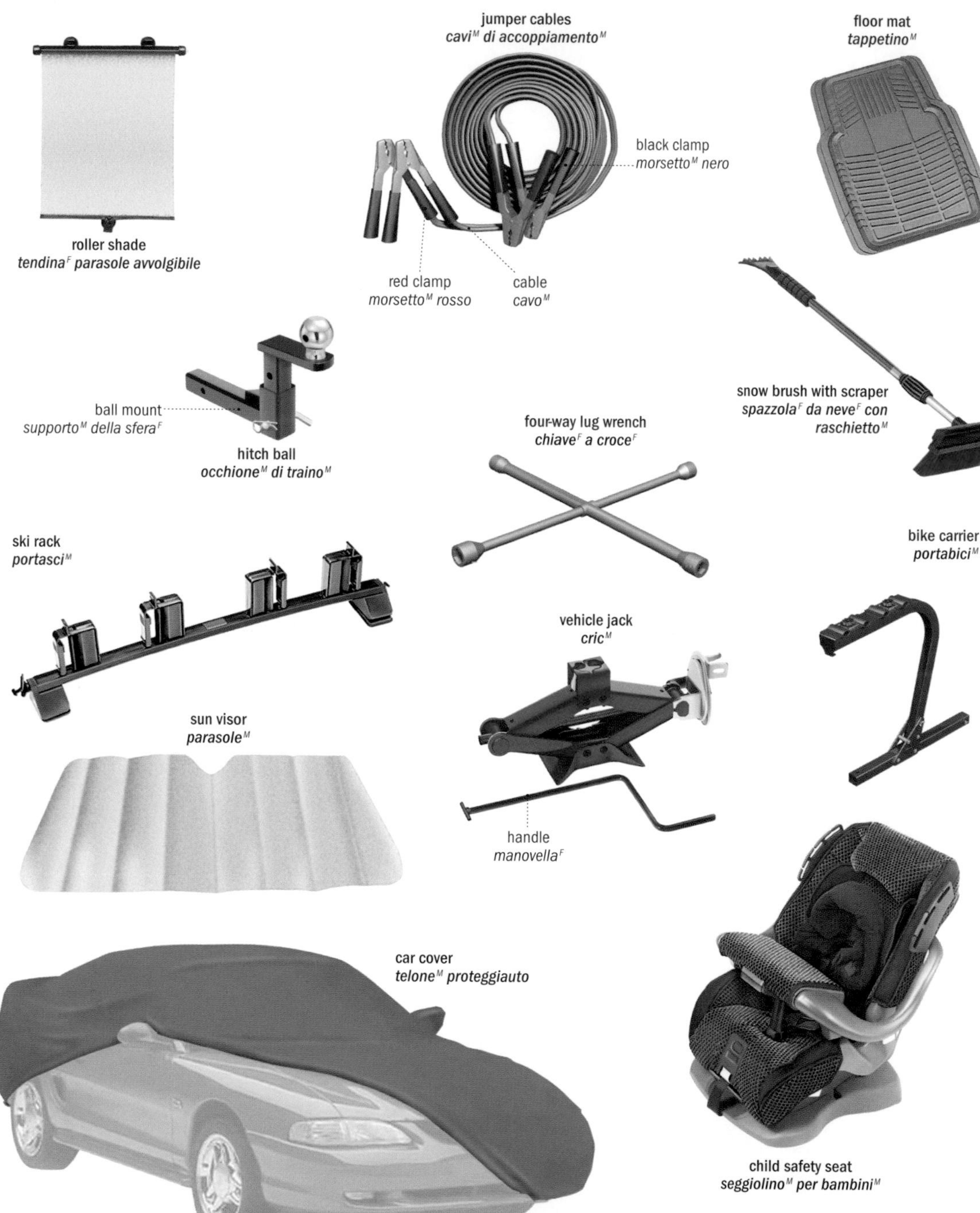

brakes
freni[M]

disc brake
freno[M] a disco[M]

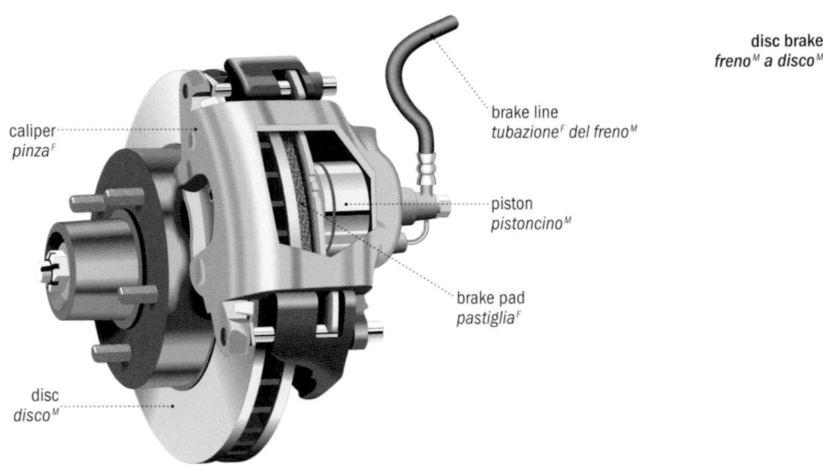

drum brake
freno[M] a tamburo[M]

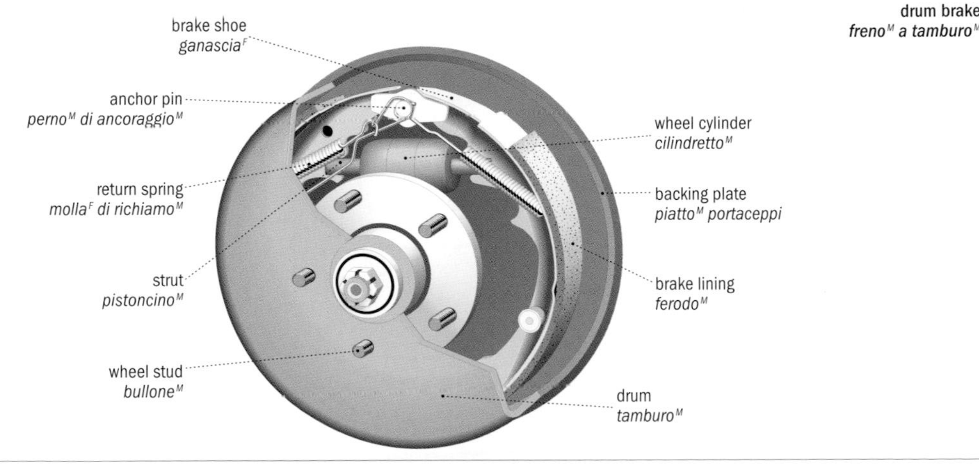

antilock braking system (ABS)
ABS[M], sistema[M] frenante antibloccaggio

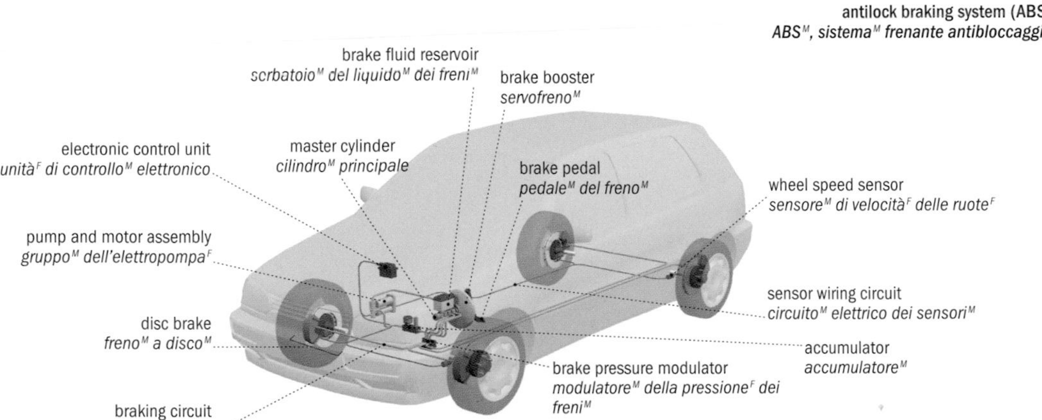

tire

pneumatico[M]

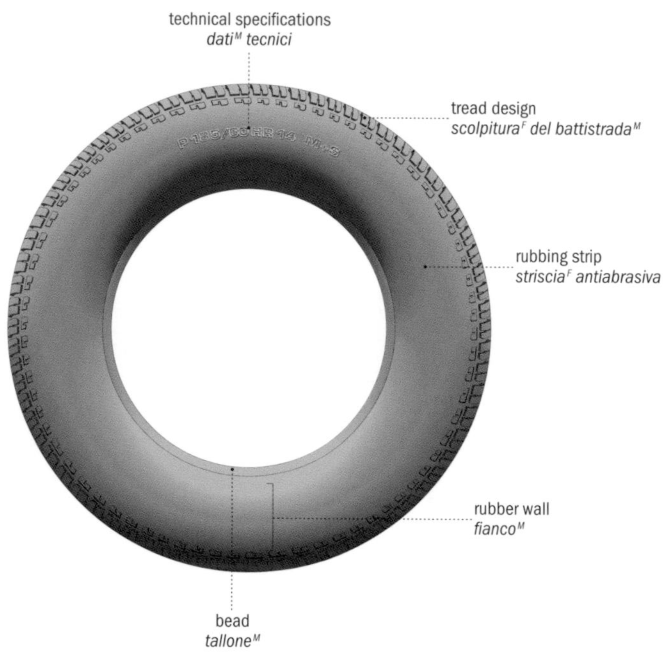

examples of tires
esempi[M] di pneumatici[M]

performance tire
pneumatico[M] sportivo

all-season tire
pneumatico[M] per tutte le stagioni[F]

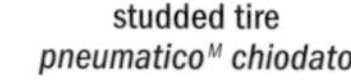

studded tire
pneumatico[M] chiodato

winter tire
pneumatico[M] invernale

touring tire
pneumatico[M] granturismo

radiator

radiatore[M]

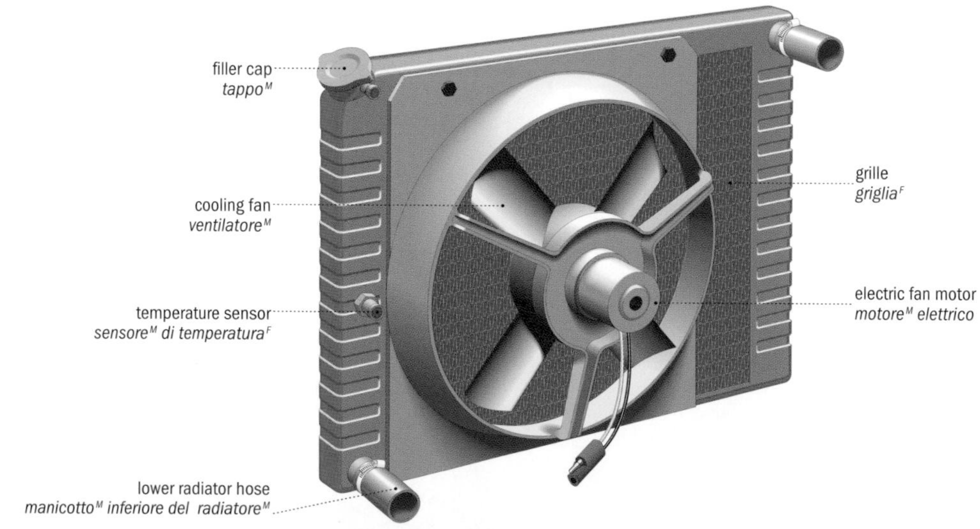

spark plug
candela^F

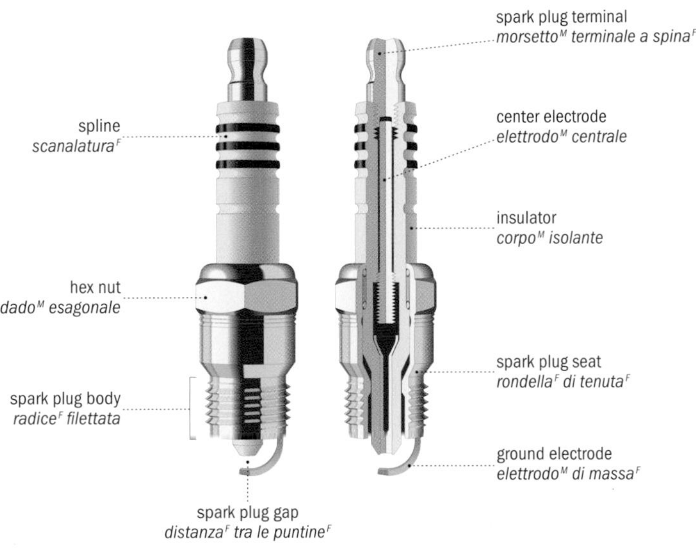

battery
batteria^F

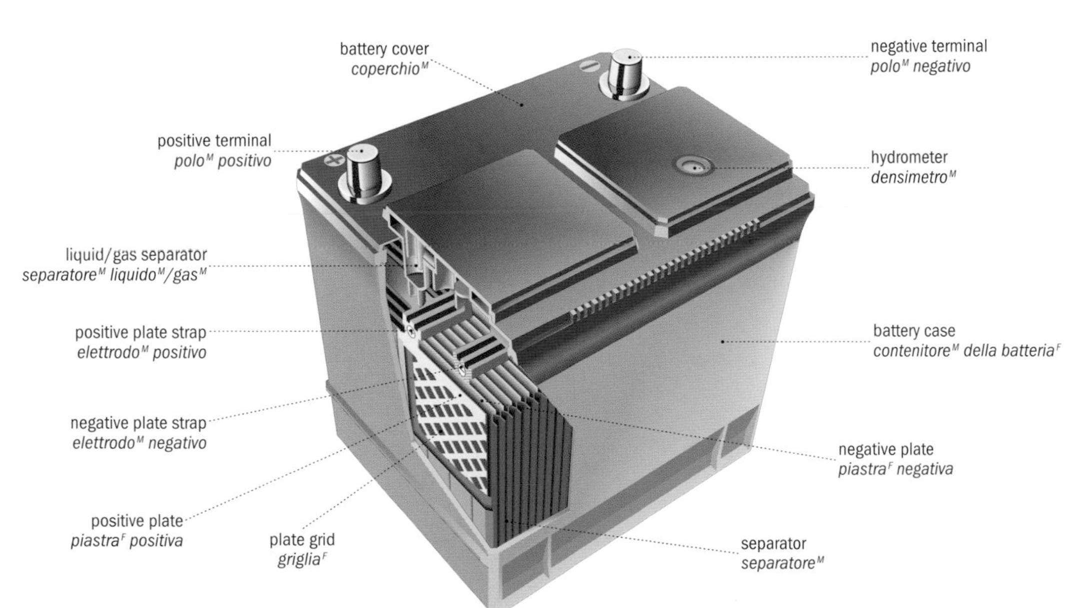

gasoline engine

motore[M] a benzina[F]

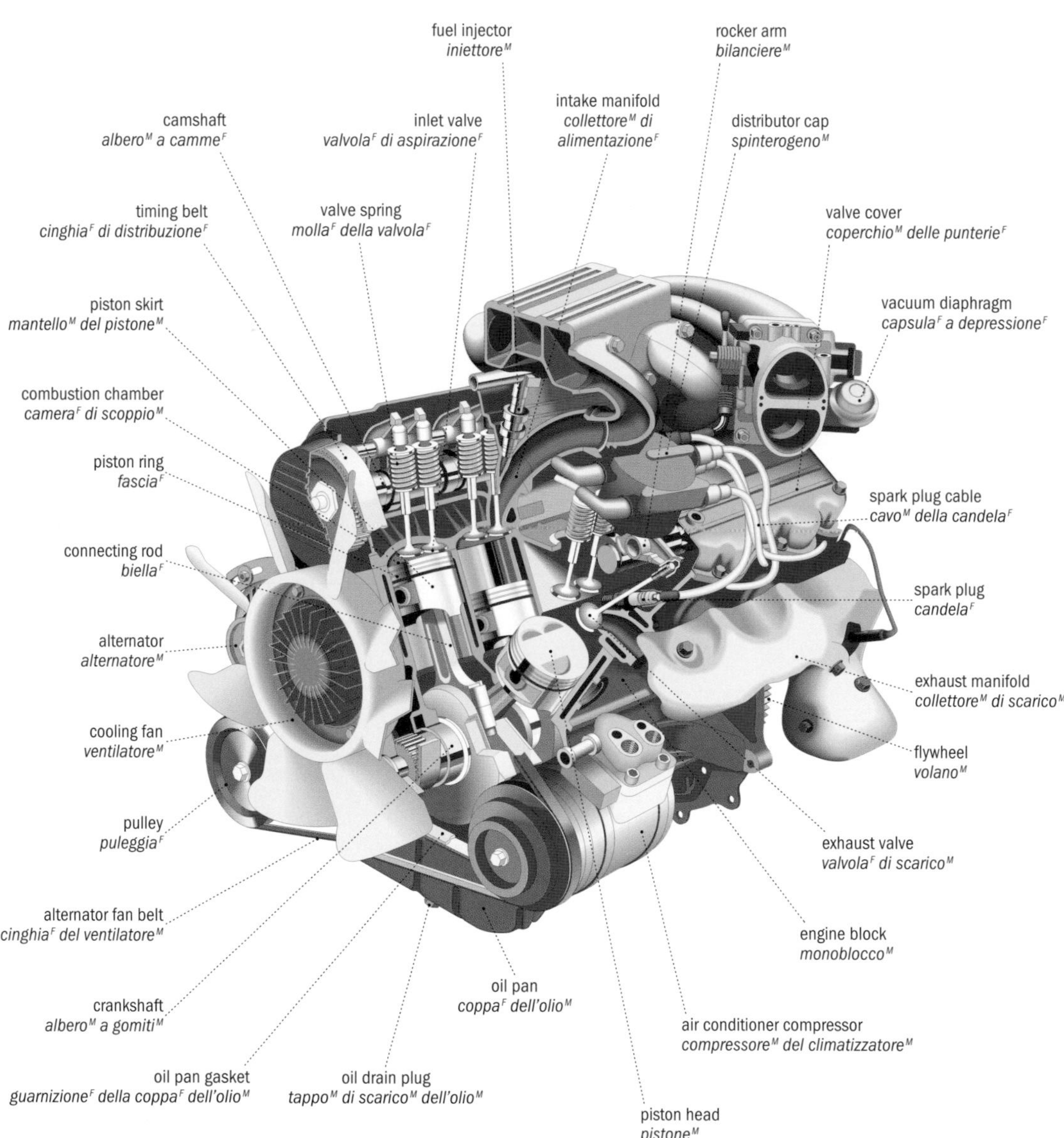

camping trailers

rimorchi^M e autocaravan^M

trailer
roulotte^F

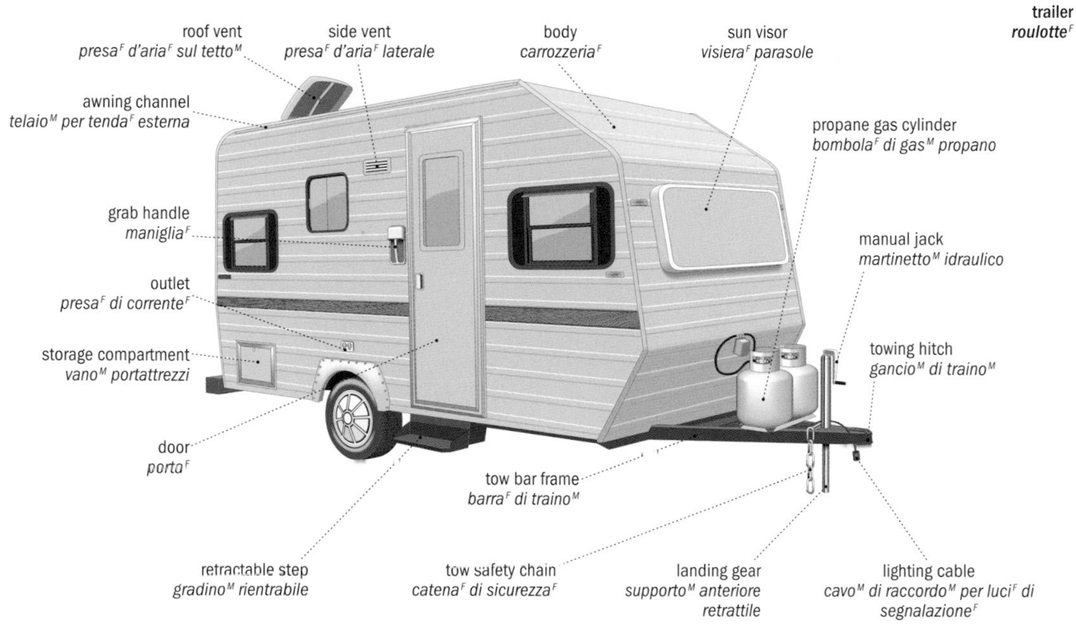

tent trailer
carrello^M tenda^F

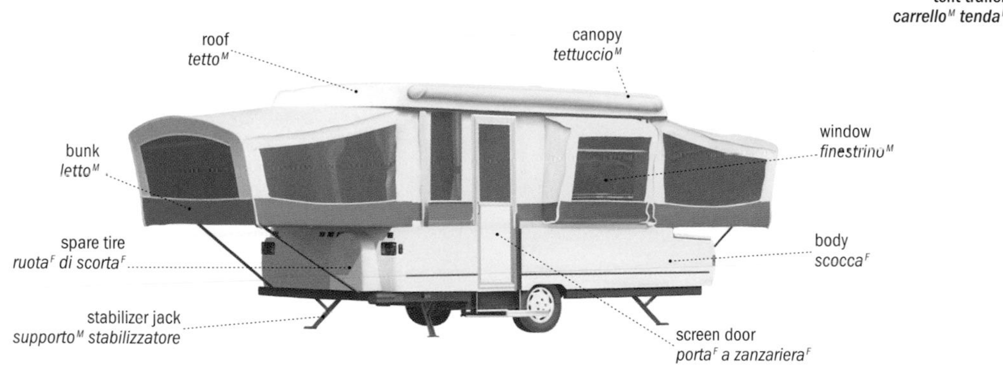

motor home
autocaravan^M

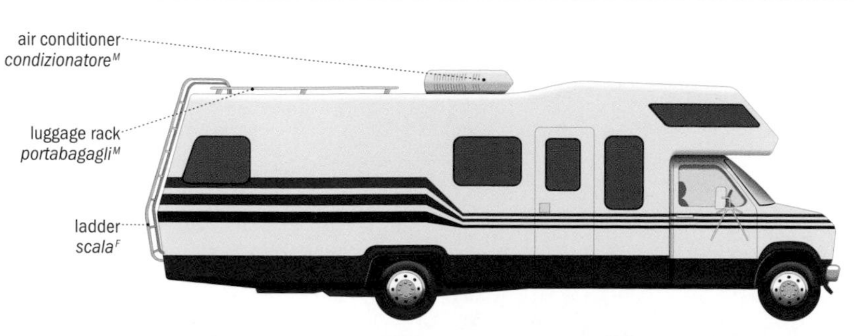

buses

autobus^M

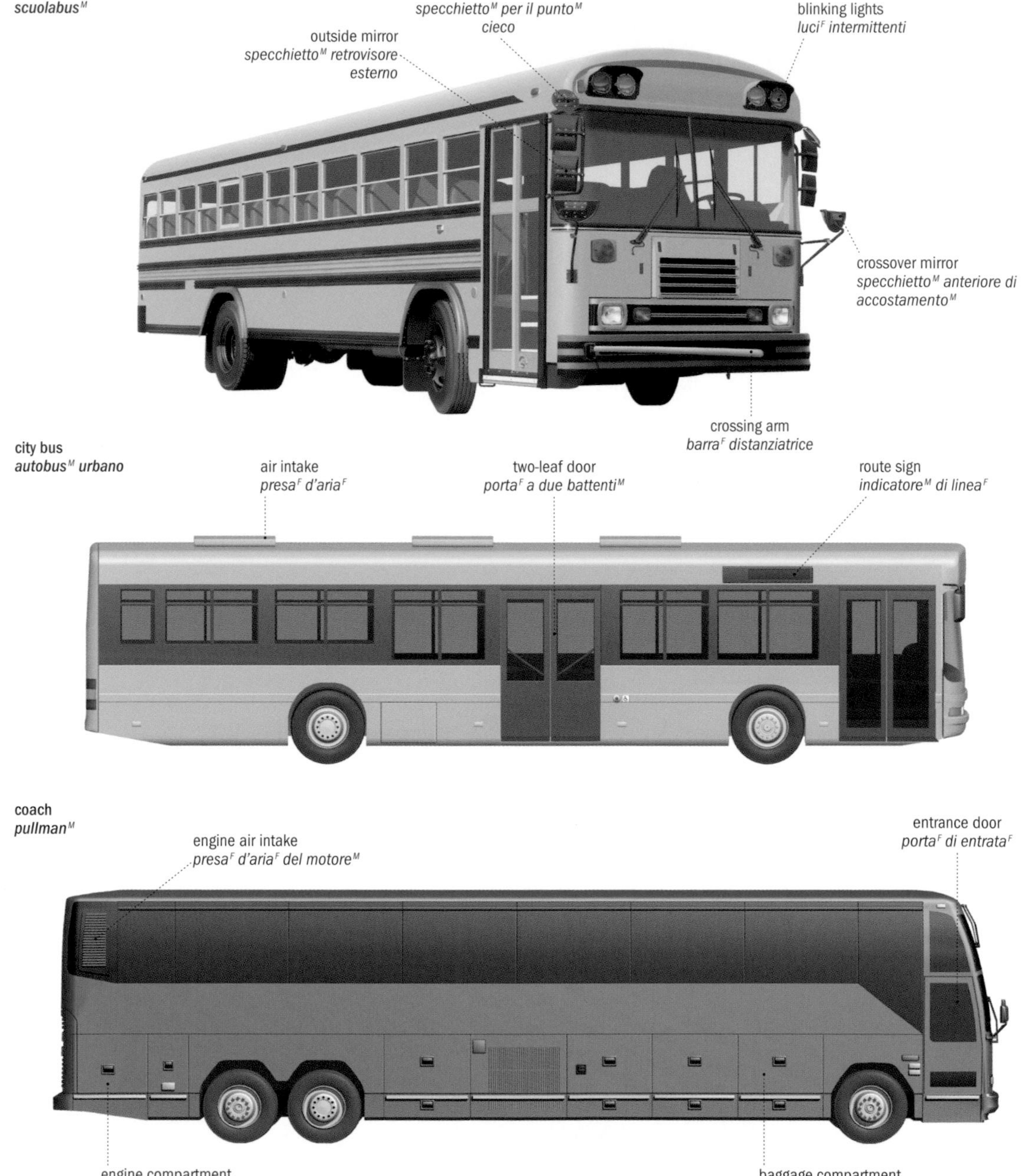

double-decker bus
autobus[M] a due piani[M]

minibus
minibus[M]

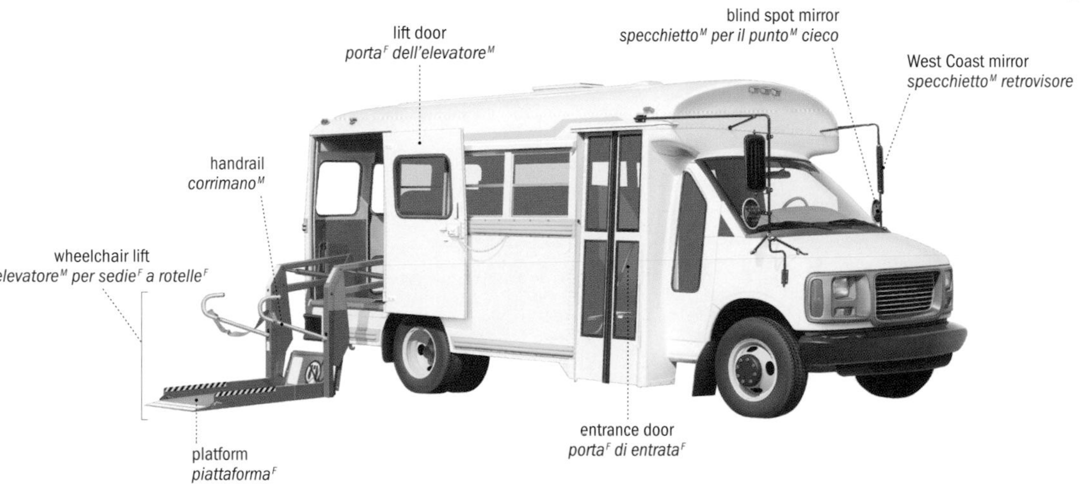

articulated bus
autobus[M] articolato

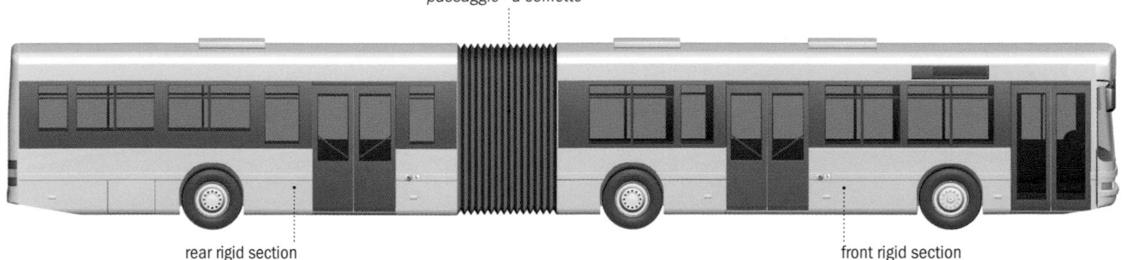

trucking

autoveicoli[M] industriali

truck tractor
motrice[F]

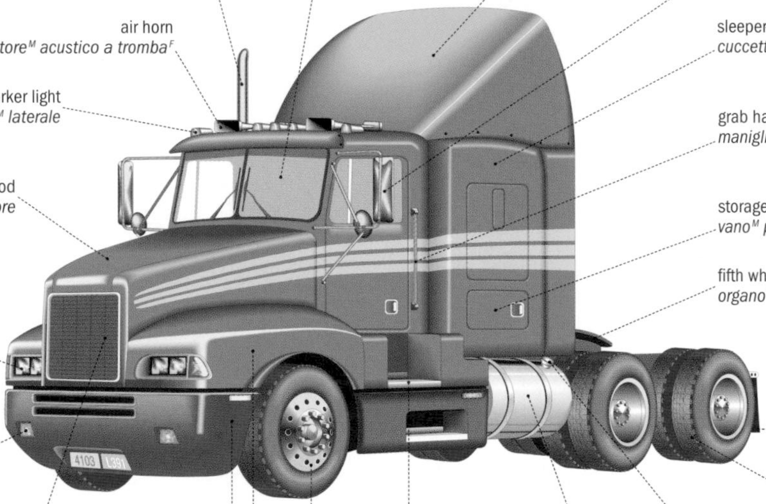

exhaust stack
tubo[M] di scappamento[M]
windshield
parabrezza[M]
wind deflector
spoiler[M]
West Coast mirror
specchietto[M] retrovisore esterno
air horn
avvisatore[M] acustico a tromba[F]
sleeper-cab
cuccetta[F]
marker light
luce[F] di ingombro[M] laterale
grab handle
maniglia[F] di salita[F]
hood
cofano[M] anteriore
storage compartment
vano[M] portaoggetti
fifth wheel
organo[M] di raccordo[M]
headlight
proiettore[M]
mud flap
aletta[F] del parafango[M]
tire
pneumatico[M]
fog light
faro[M] fendinebbia
bumper
paraurti[M]
step
gradino[M]
filler cap
tappo[M] del serbatoio[M]
radiator grille
griglia[F] del radiatore[M]
fender
parafango[F]
wheel
ruota[F]
fuel tank
serbatoio[M] per il carburante[M]

examples of trucks
esempi[M] di camion[M]

tank body
cisterna[F]

tank truck
autobotte[F]

garbage collection truck
compattatore[M]

loading hopper
tramoggia[F] di caricamento[M]
packer body
cassone[M] di compattazione[F]

tow truck
autogrù[F]

boom
braccio[M] di sollevamento[M]
cable
cavo[M]
hook
gancio[M]
towing device
dispositivo[M] di rimorchio[M]
winch controls
comandi[M] del verricello[M]
elevating cylinder
cilindro[M] di sollevamento[M]
winch
verricello[M]

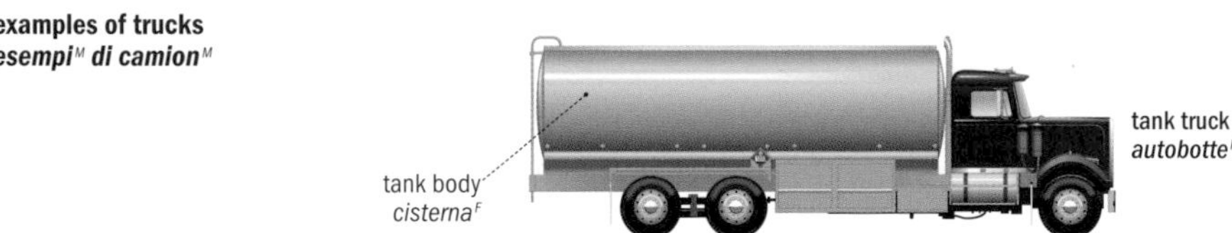

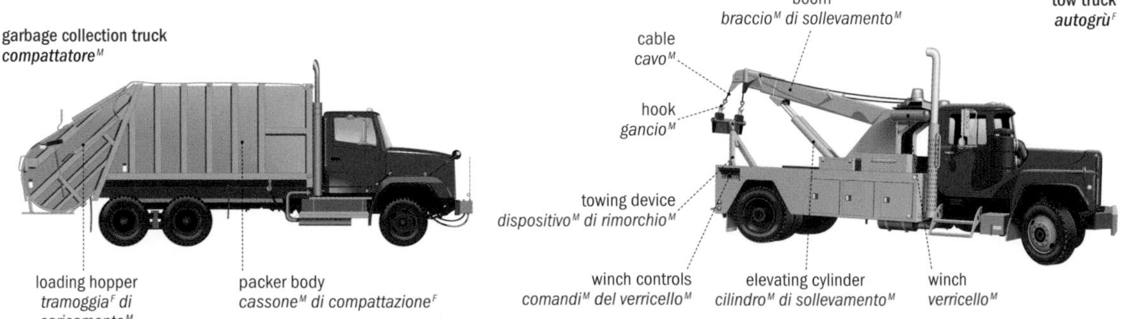

refrigerated semitrailer
semirimorchio[M] frigorifero

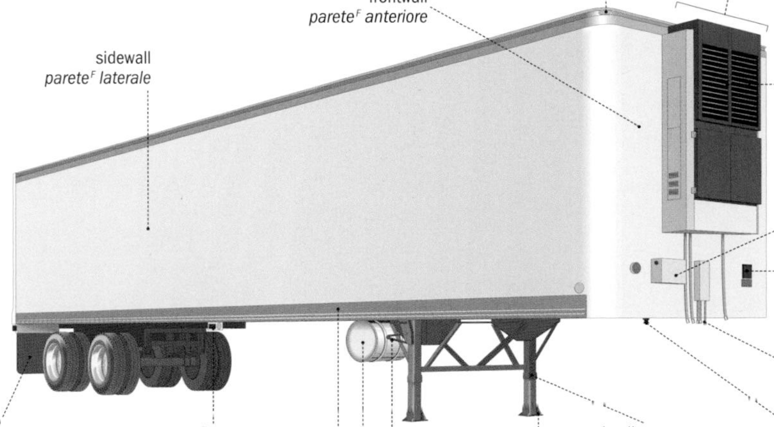

marker light
luce[F] di ingombro[M] laterale
refrigeration unit
gruppo[M] frigorifero
frontwall
parete[F] anteriore
sidewall
parete[F] laterale
vent door
presa[F] d'aria[F]
battery box
cassa[F] portabatteria
partlow chart
diagramma[M] di carico[M]
electrical connection
collegamento[M] elettrico
reflector
catarifrangente[M]
landing gear
supporto[M] retrattile
kingpin
perno[M] di agganciamento[M]
mud flap
alettone[M] parafango[M]
side rail
longherone[M] laterale
sand shoe
piede[M] di appoggio[M]
auxiliary tank
serbatoio[M] ausiliario
landing gear crank
manovella[F] del supporto[M]

van straight truck
furgone[M]

concrete mixer truck
betoniera[F]

street sweeper
spazzatrice[F]

collection body
cassone[M] di raccolta[F] dei rifiuti[M]
central brush
spazzola[F] rotante centrale
lateral brush
spazzola[F] rotante laterale
watering tube
tubo[M] annaffiatore[M]

snowblower
spazzaneve[M] a turbina[F]

projection device
tubo[M] di getto[M] laterale
DANGER
worm
vite[F] senza fine[F]

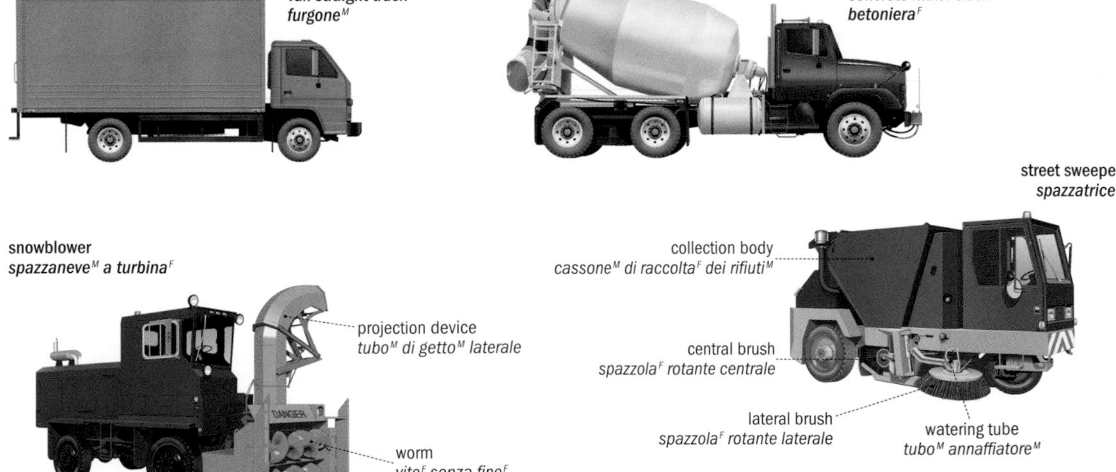

motorcycle

motocicletta[F]

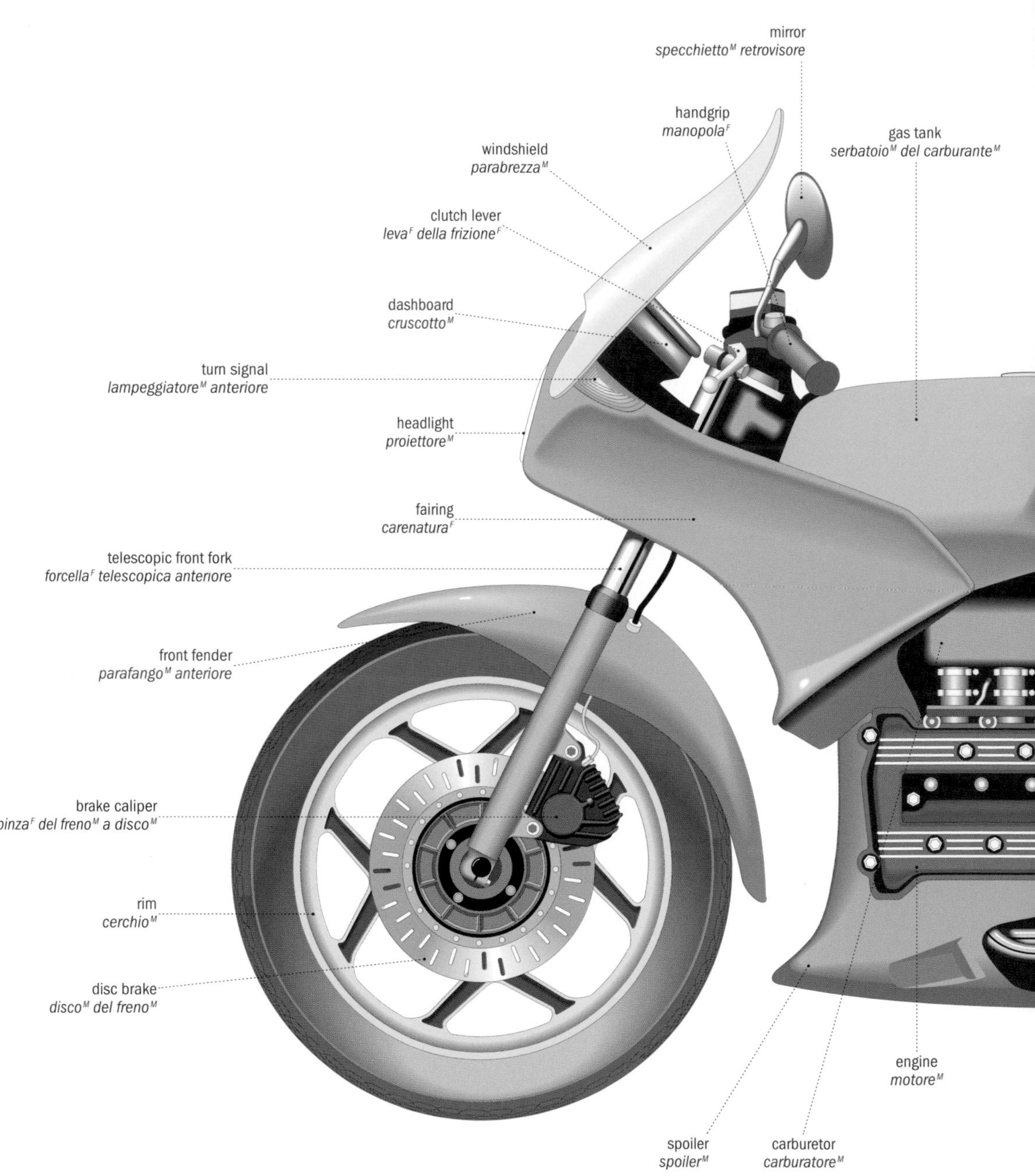

protective helmet
casco[M] di protezione[F]

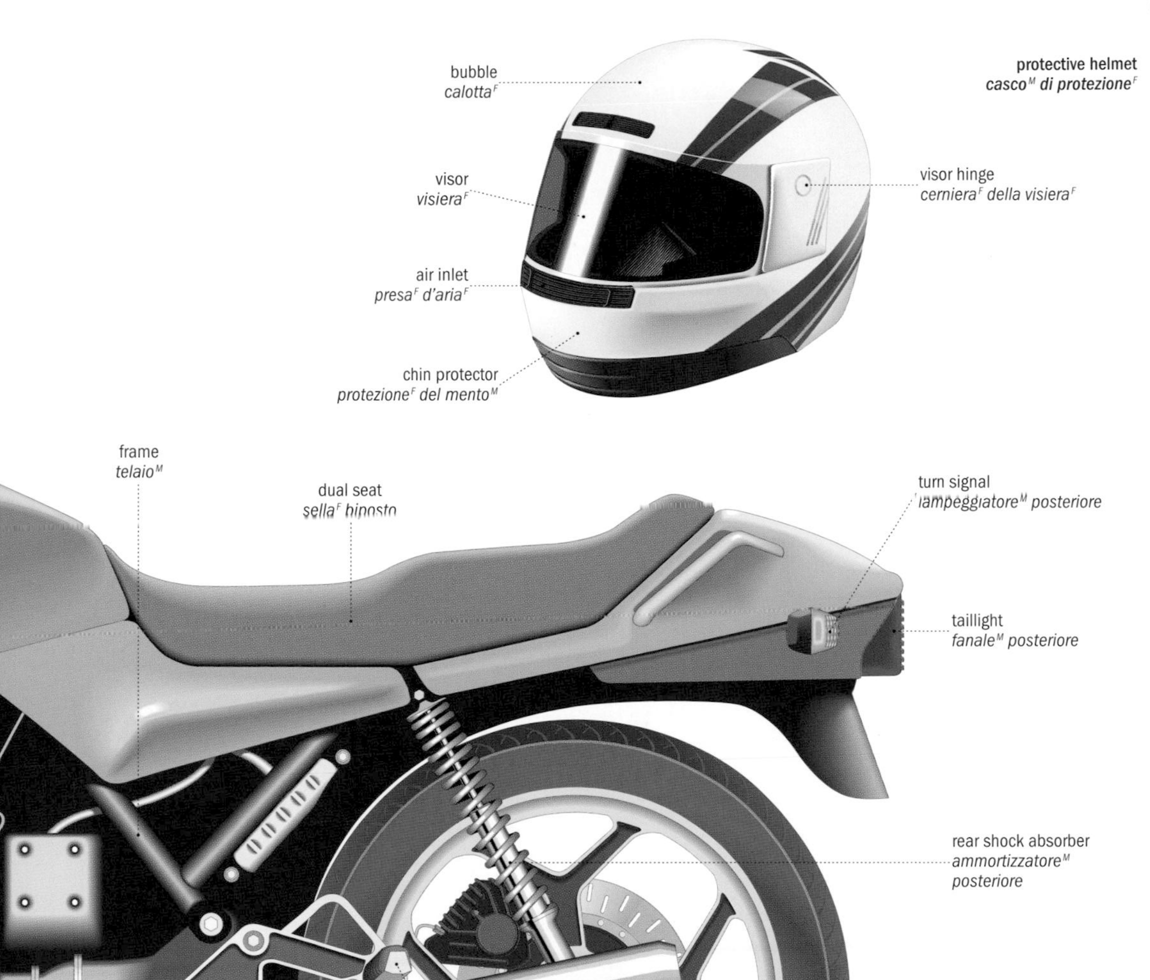

motorcycle

motorcycle dashboard
cruscotto[M]

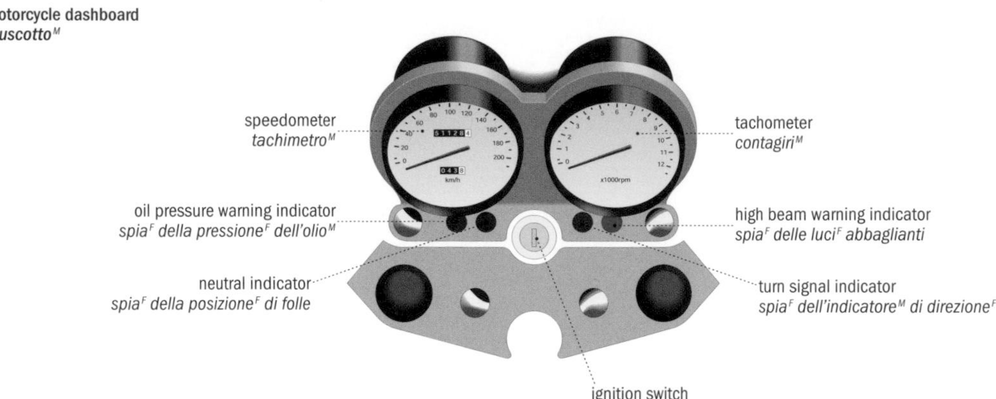

motorcycle: view from above
motocicletta[F]: vista[F] dall'alto[M]

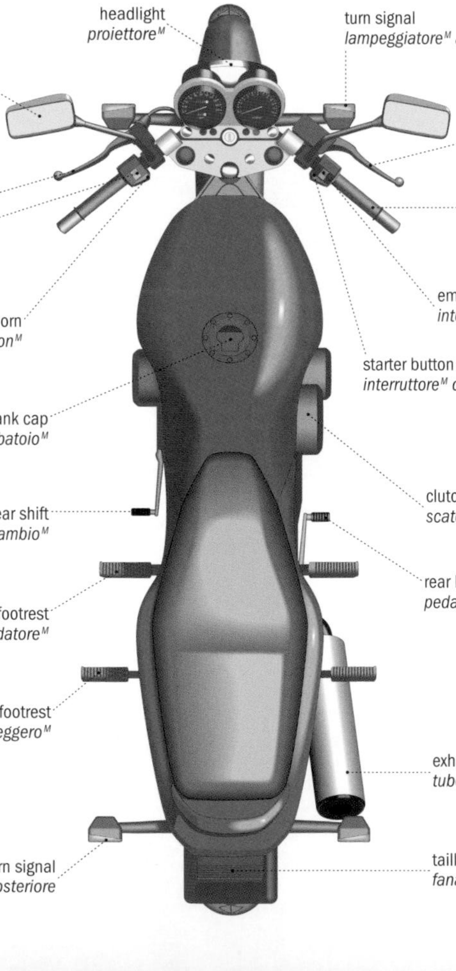

headlight
proiettore[M]

turn signal
lampeggiatore[M] anteriore

mirror
specchietto[M] retrovisore

front brake lever
leva[F] del freno[M] anteriore

clutch lever
leva[F] della frizione[F]

twist grip throttle
manopola[F] dell'acceleratore[M]

dip switch
commutatore[M] delle luci[F]

emergency switch
interruttore[M] di emergenza[F]

horn
clacson[M]

starter button
interruttore[M] di avviamento[M]

gas tank cap
tappo[M] del serbatoio[M]

clutch housing
scatola[F] della frizione[F]

gear shift
pedale[M] del cambio[M]

rear brake pedal
pedale[M] del freno[M] posteriore

front footrest
appoggiapiedi[M] del guidatore[M]

pillion footrest
appoggiapiedi[M] del passeggero[M]

exhaust pipe
tubo[M] di scappamento[M]

turn signal
lampeggiatore[M] posteriore

taillight
fanale[M] posteriore

motorcycle

motor scooter
***scooter*[M]**

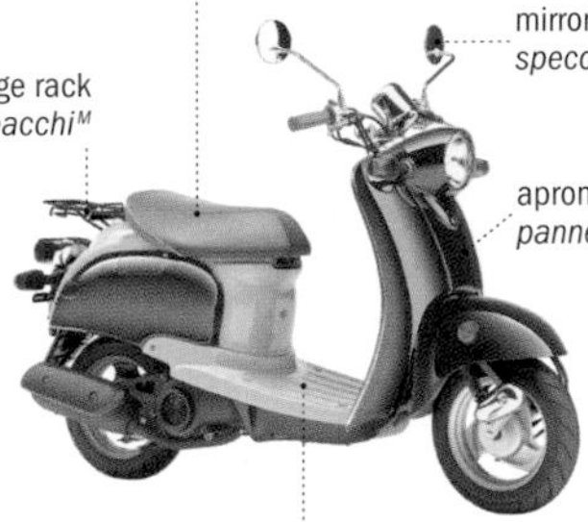

seat
sella[F]

mirror
specchietto[M] *retrovisore*

luggage rack
portapacchi[M]

apron
pannello[M] *di protezione*[F]

floorboard
appoggiapiedi[M]

examples of motorcycles
***esempi*[M] *di motociclette*[F] *e ciclomotore*[M]**

seat
sella[F]

off-road motorcycle (dirtbike)
***motocicletta*[F] *da cross*[M]**

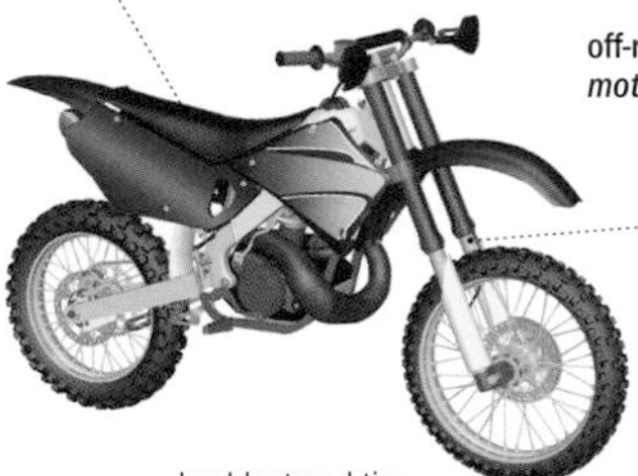

telescopic front fork
forcella[F] *telescopica anteriore*

knobby tread tire
pneumatico[M] *scolpito*

moped
***ciclomotore*[M]**

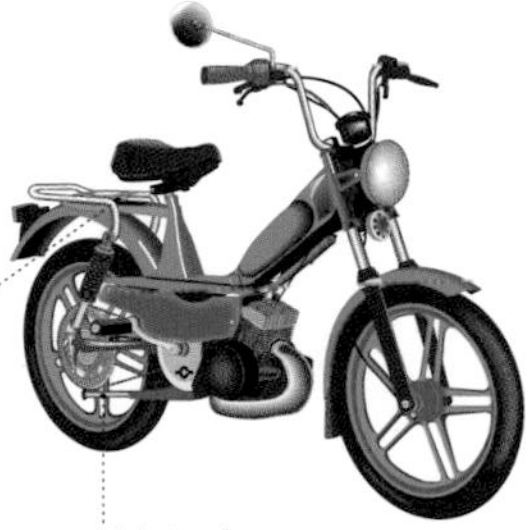

carrier
portapacchi[M]

kickstand
cavalletto[M] *laterale*

touring motorcycle
***motocicletta*[F] *da turismo*[M]**

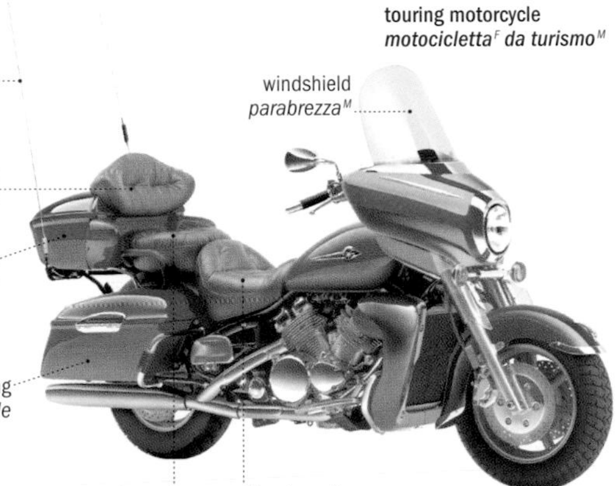

antenna
antenna[F]

windshield
parabrezza[M]

backrest
schienale[M]

top box
bauletto[M]

saddlebag
borsa[F] *laterale*

passenger seat
sella[F] *del passeggero*[M]

driver's seat
sella[F] *del guidatore*[M]

4 X 4 all-terrain vehicle

veicolo[M] a trazione[F] integrale 4x4

bicycle

biciclettaF

parts of a bicycle
componentiM di una biciclettaF

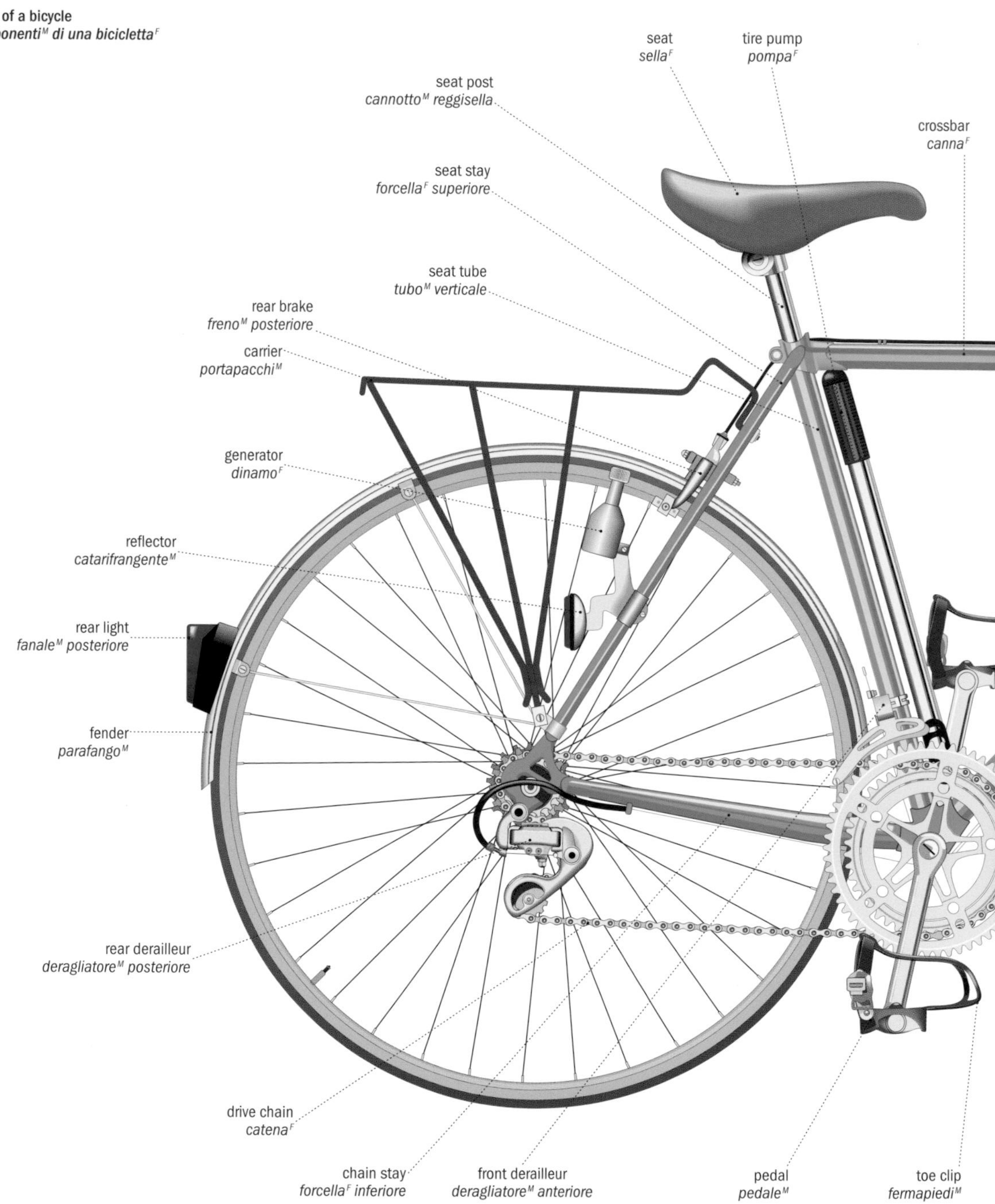

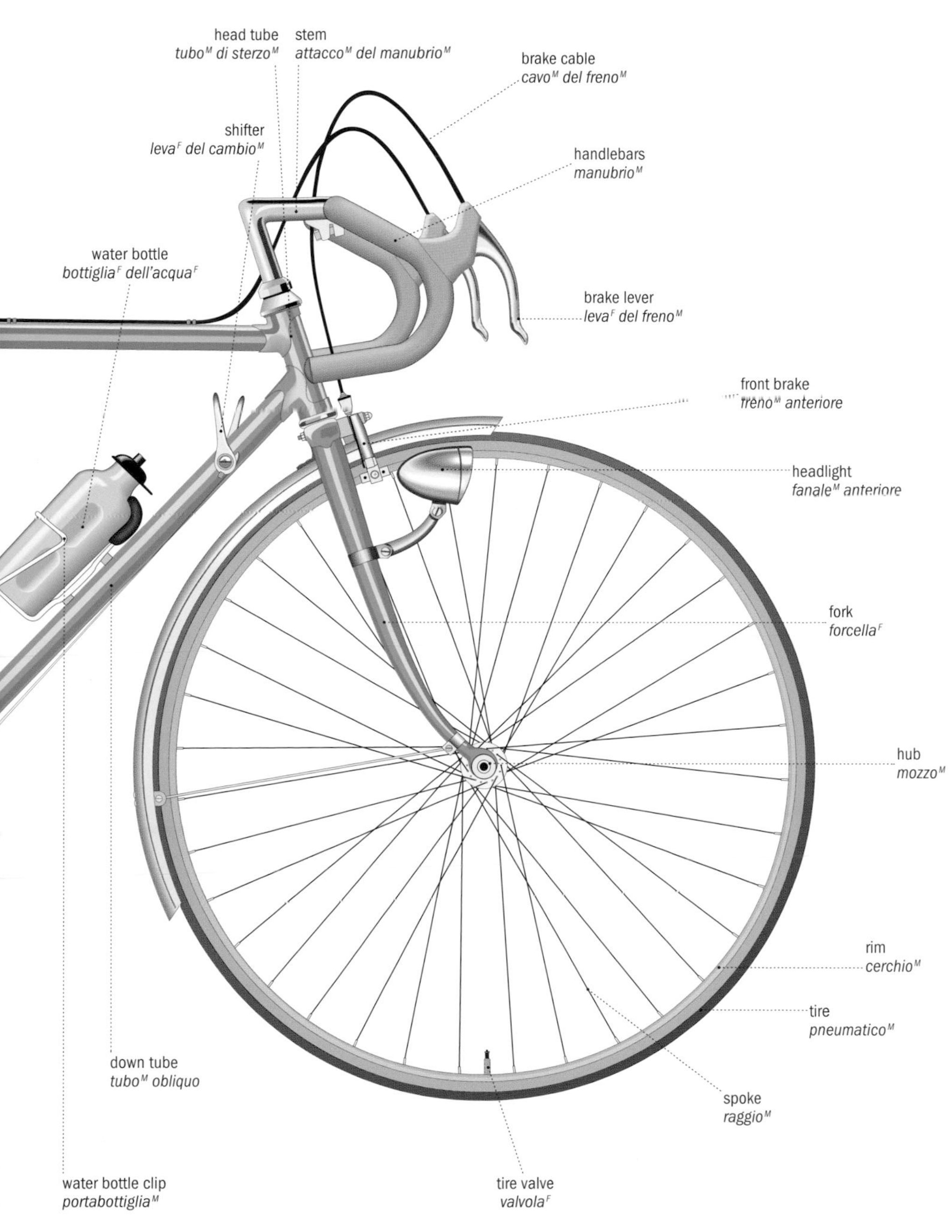
head tube
tubo^M di sterzo^M
stem
attacco^M del manubrio^M
brake cable
cavo^M del freno^M
shifter
leva^F del cambio^M
handlebars
manubrio^M
water bottle
bottiglia^F dell'acqua^F
brake lever
leva^F del freno^M
front brake
freno^M anteriore
headlight
fanale^M anteriore
fork
forcella^F
hub
mozzo^M
rim
cerchio^M
tire
pneumatico^M
down tube
tubo^M obliquo
spoke
raggio^M
water bottle clip
portabottiglia^M
tire valve
valvola^F

bicycle

power train
***organi*[M] *di trasmissione*[F]**

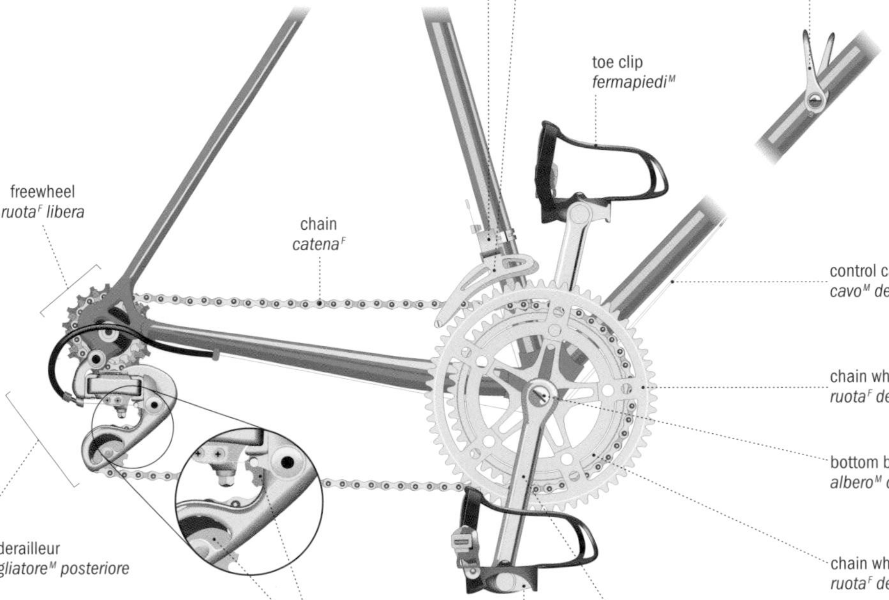

front derailleur
deragliatore[M] *anteriore*

chain guide
guida[F] *della catena*[F]

shifter
leva[F] *del cambio*[M]

toe clip
fermapiedi[M]

freewheel
ruota[F] *libera*

chain
catena[F]

control cable
cavo[M] *del cambio*[M]

chain wheel A
ruota[F] *dentata A*

bottom bracket axle
albero[M] *delle pedivelle*[F]

rear derailleur
deragliatore[M] *posteriore*

chain wheel B
ruota[F] *dentata B*

jockey rollers
rullini[M] *tenditori*[M]

pedal
pedale[M]

crank
pedivella[F]

accessories
***accessori*[M]**

lock
lucchetto[M]

protective helmet
casco[M] *di protezione*[F]

tool kit
kit[M] *di attrezzi*[M]

bicycle bag (pannier)
zaino[M]

child carrier
seggiolino[M] *per bambini*[M]

examples of bicycles
***esempi*[M] *di biciclette*[F]**
child's tricycle
triciclo[M]
BMX bike
mountain bike[F] *da cross*[M]
Dutch bicycle
bicicletta[F] *olandese*
mountain bike
mountain bike[F]
city bicycle
city bike[F]
road bicycle
bicicletta[F] *da corsa*[F]
touring bicycle
bicicletta[F] *da turismo*[M]
tandem bicycle
tandem[M]

passenger station

stazione^F dei viaggiatori^M

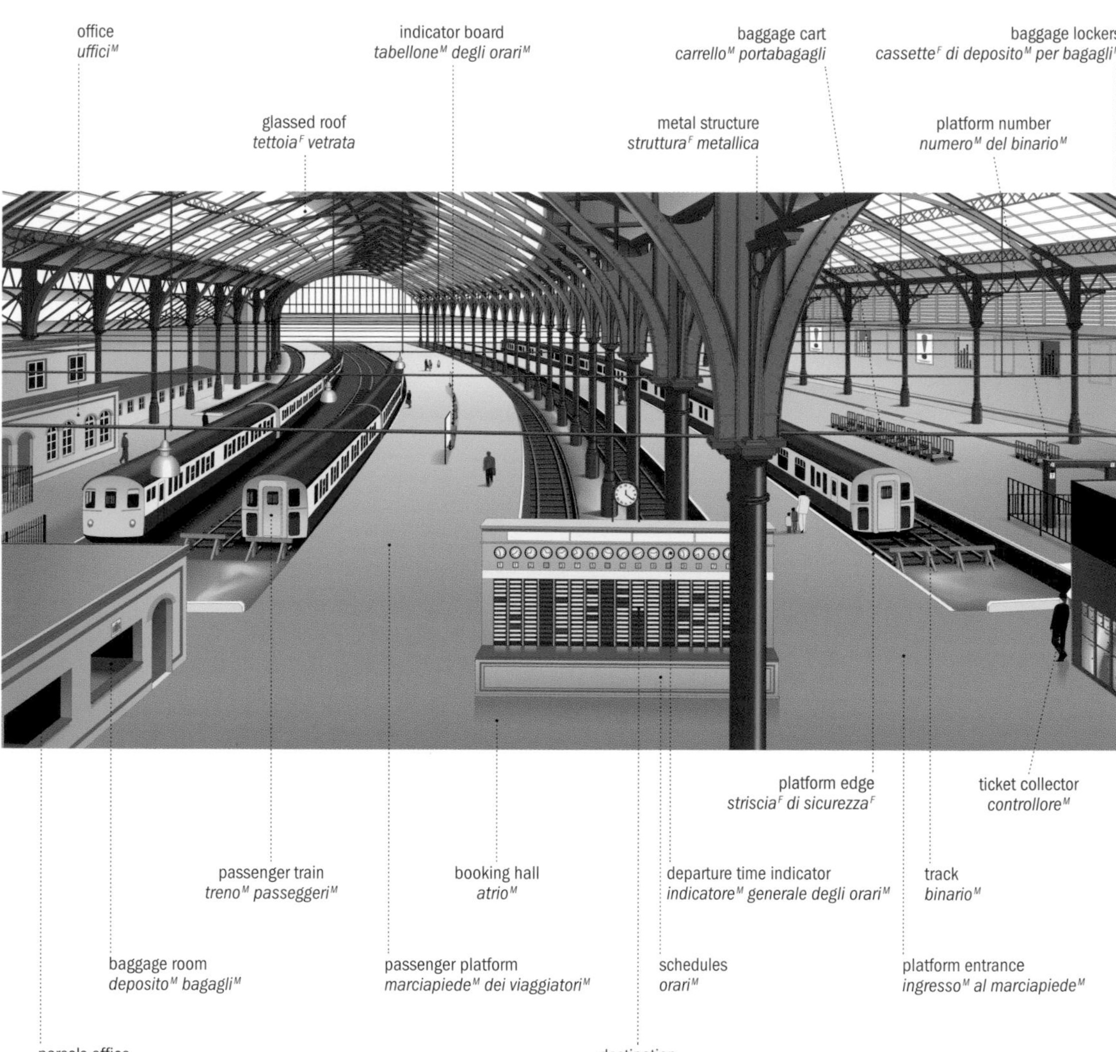

railroad station

stazione^F ferroviaria

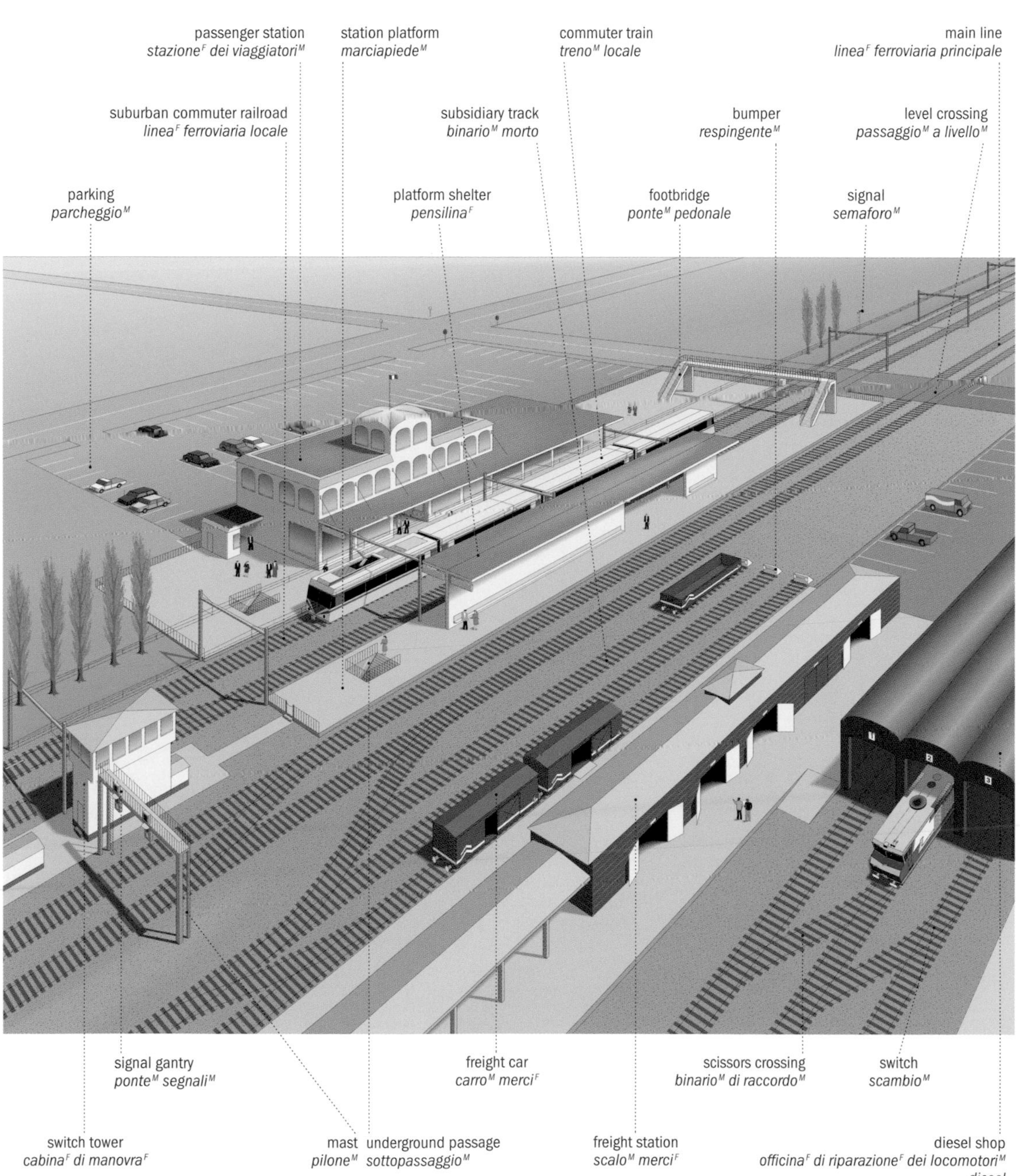

high-speed train

treno[M] ad alta velocità[F]

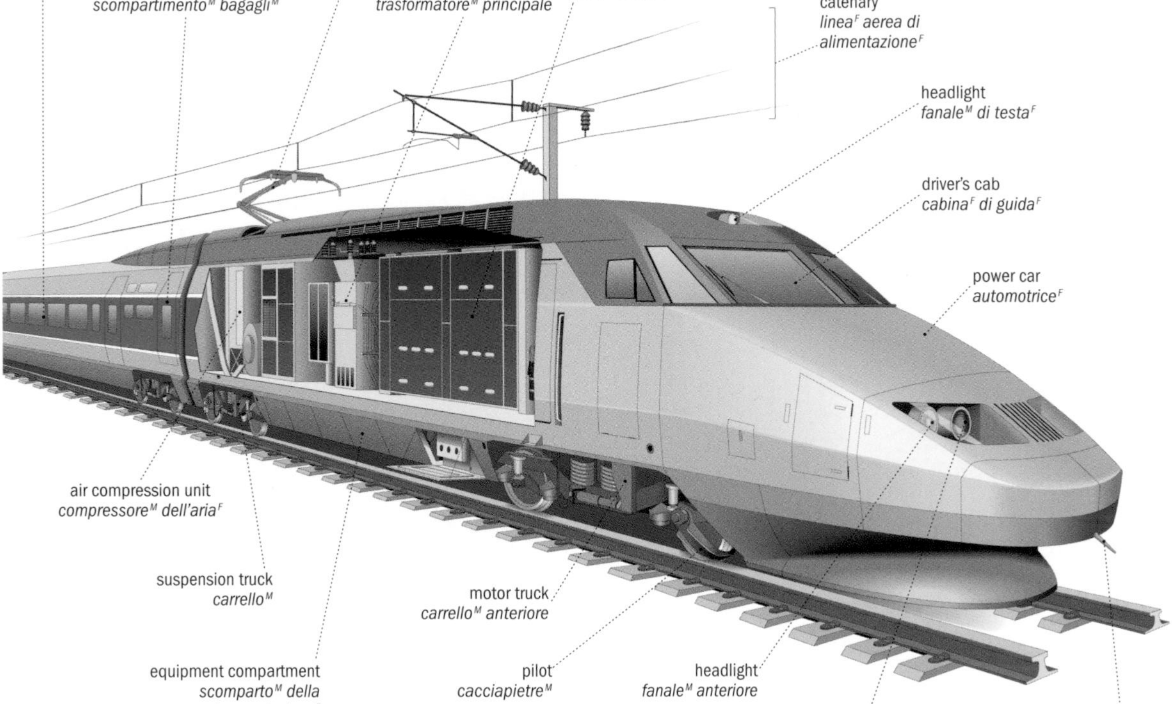

passenger car
vagone[M] viaggiatori[M]

pantograph
pantografo[M]

baggage compartment
scompartimento[M] bagagli[M]

main transformer
trasformatore[M] principale

motor unit
unità[F] motrice

catenary
linea[F] aerea di alimentazione[F]

headlight
fanale[M] di testa[F]

driver's cab
cabina[F] di guida[F]

power car
automotrice[F]

air compression unit
compressore[M] dell'aria[F]

suspension truck
carrello[M]

motor truck
carrello[M] anteriore

equipment compartment
scomparto[M] della strumentazione[F]

pilot
cacciapietre[M]

headlight
fanale[M] anteriore

position light
luce[F] di posizione[F]

coupling guide device
antenna[F] di captazione[F]

types of passenger cars

tipi[M] di vagoni[M] passeggeri[M]

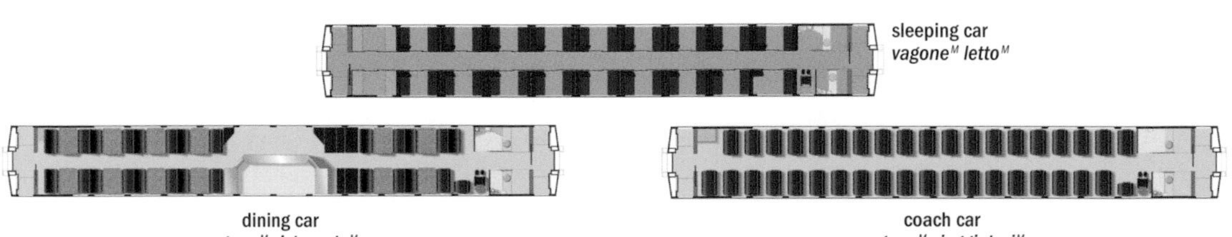

sleeping car
vagone[M] letto[M]

dining car
vagone[M] ristorante[M]

coach car
vagone[M] viaggiatori[M]

diesel-electric locomotive

locomotiva^F diesel-elettrica

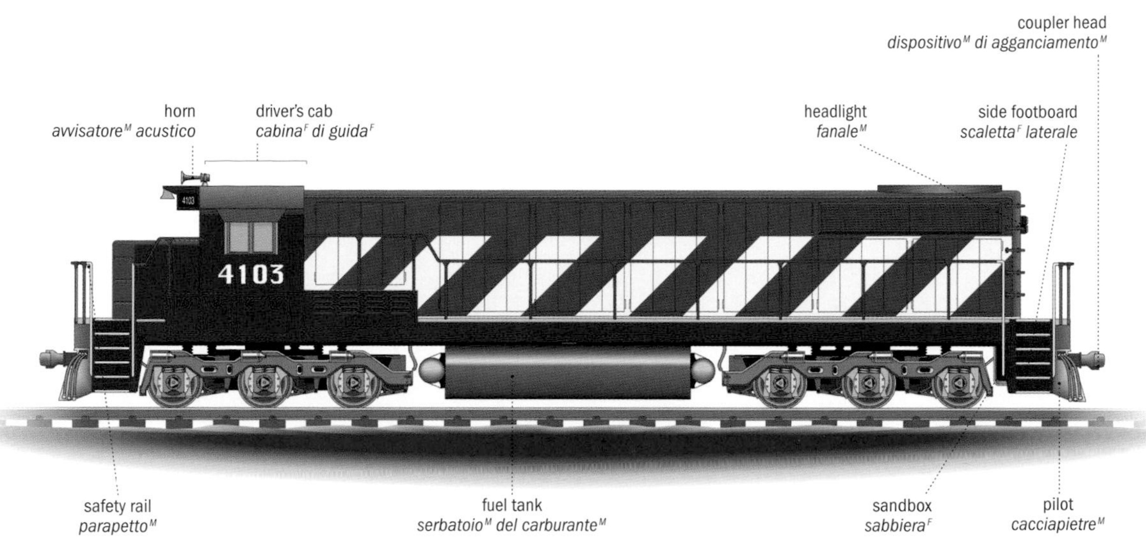

examples of freight cars

esempi^M di carri^M merci^F

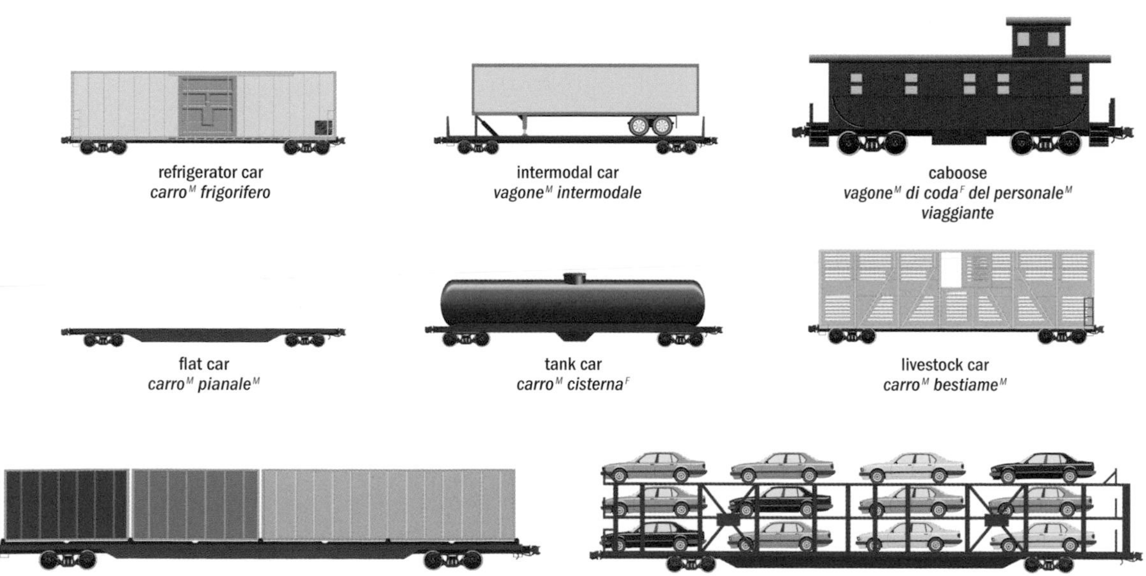

subway

metropolitana[F]

subway station
stazione[F] della metropolitana[F]

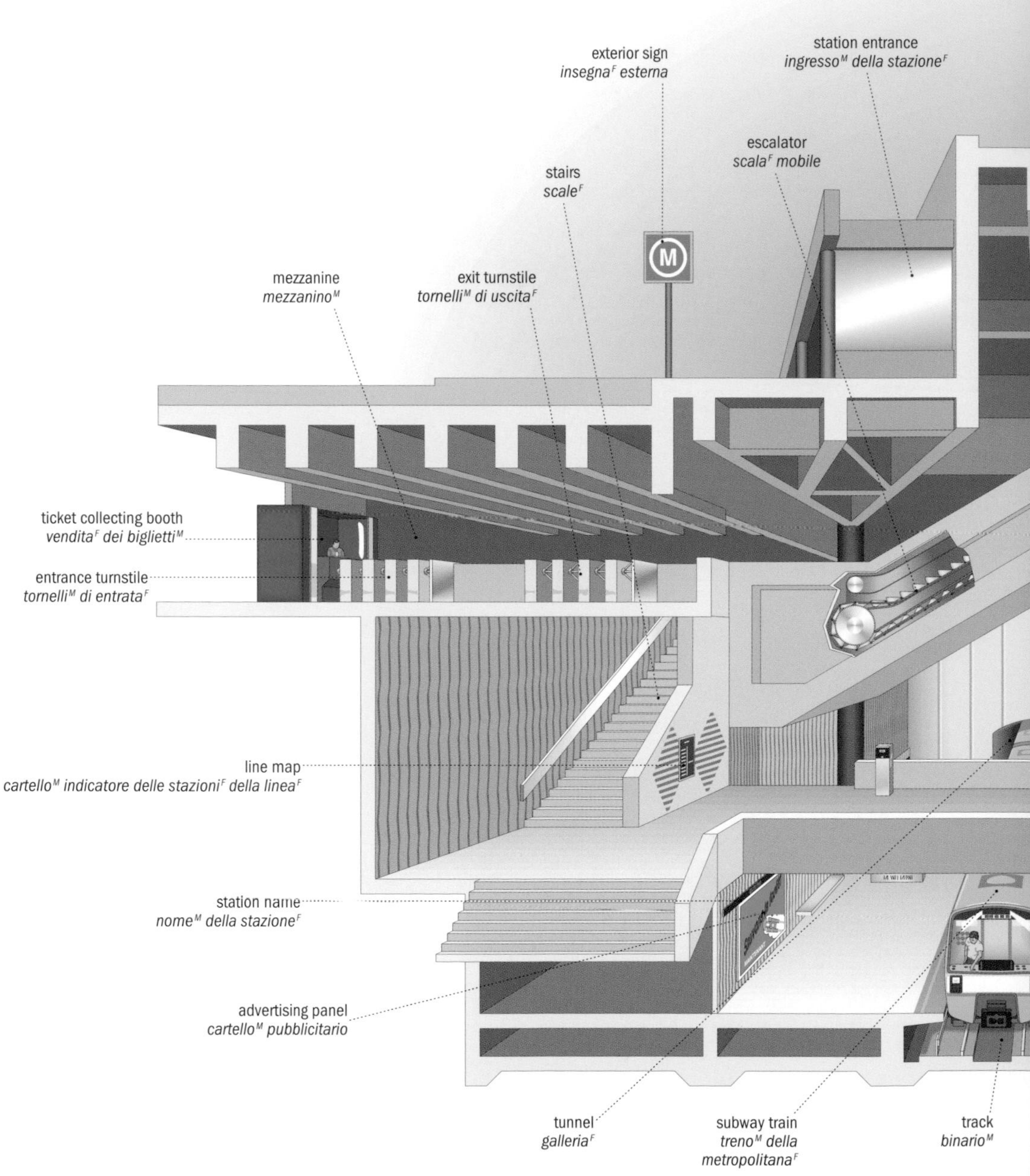

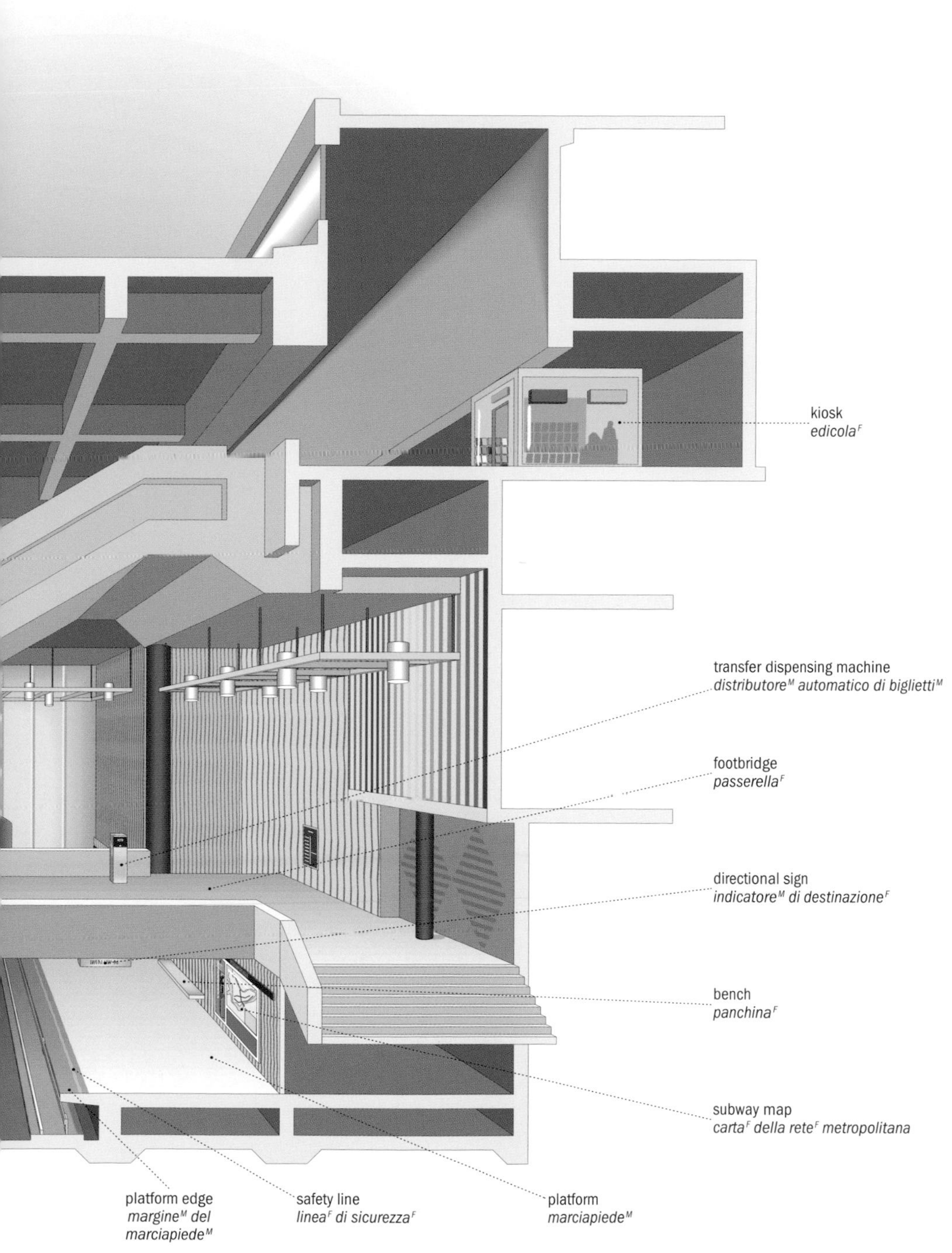
kiosk
edicola^F
transfer dispensing machine
distributore^M automatico di biglietti^M
footbridge
passerella^F
directional sign
indicatore^M di destinazione^F
bench
panchina^F
subway map
carta^F della rete^F metropolitana
platform edge
margine^M del marciapiede^M
safety line
linea^F di sicurezza^F
platform
marciapiede^M

subway

passenger car
carrozza^{F} passeggeri^{M}

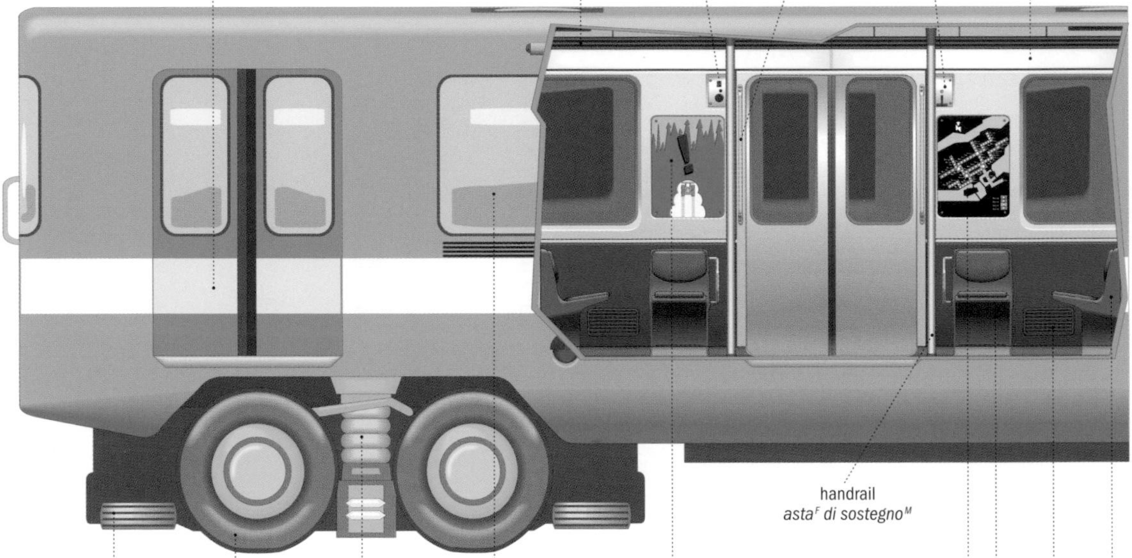

communication set
altoparlante^{M}

emergency brake
freno^{M} di emergenza^{F}

side door
porta^{F}

ventilator
griglia^{F} di aerazione^{F}

side handrail
maniglia^{F} laterale

light
luce^{F}

handrail
asta^{F} di sostegno^{M}

inflated guiding tire
ruota^{F} di guida^{F}

window
finestrino^{M}

subway map
carta^{F} della rete^{F} metropolitana

suspension
sospensione^{F}

advertising poster
cartello^{M} pubblicitario

single seat
sedile^{M} singolo

inflated carrying tire
ruota^{F} portante

heating grille
griglia^{F} del riscaldamento^{M}

double seat
sedile^{M} doppio

subway train
metropolitana^{F}

motor car
motrice^{F}

trailer car
rimorchio^{M}

motor car
motrice^{F}

harbor

porto^M marittimo

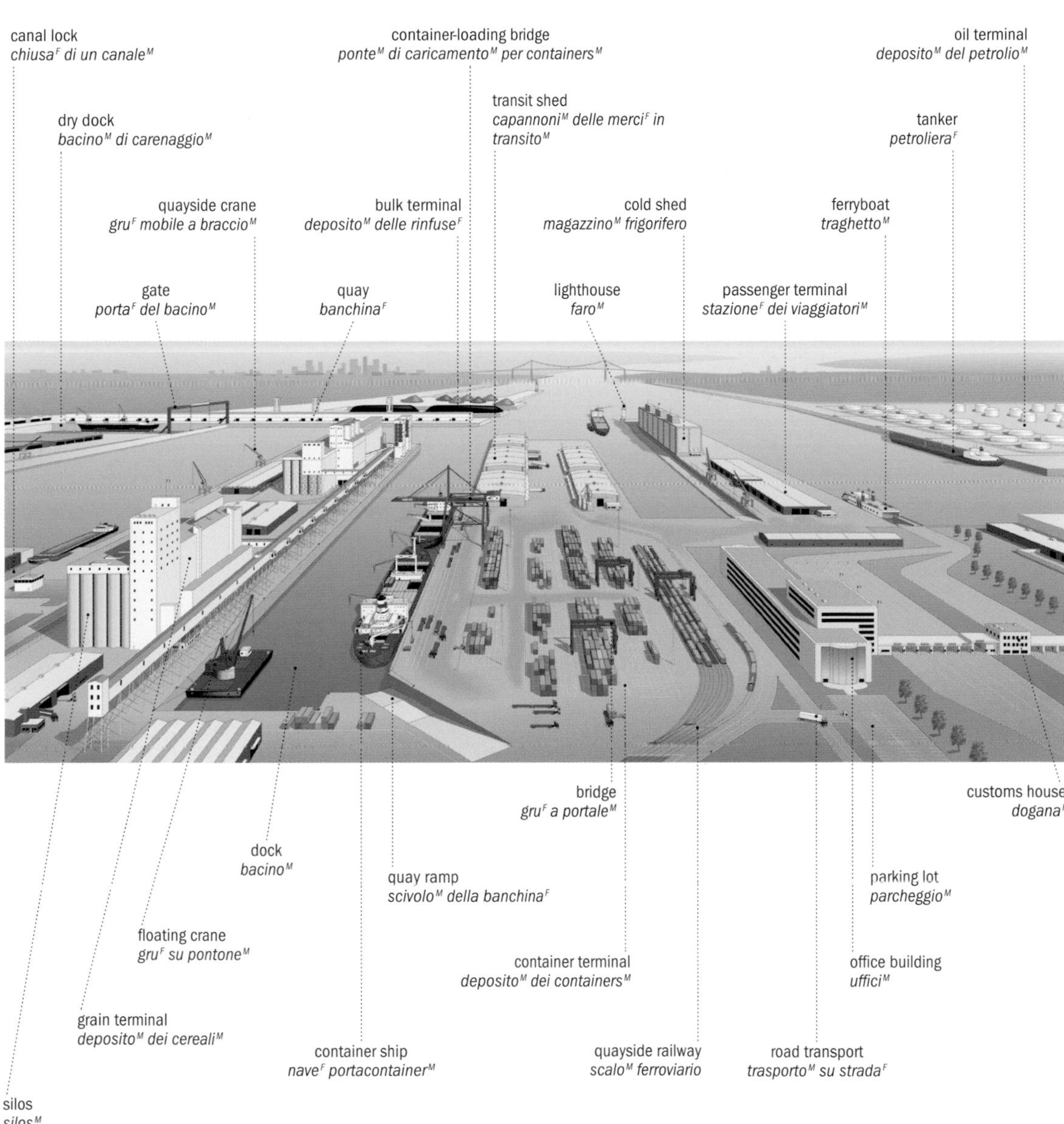

examples of boats and ships

esempi^M di barche^F e navi^F

drill ship
nave^F da perforazione^F

derrick
derrick^M

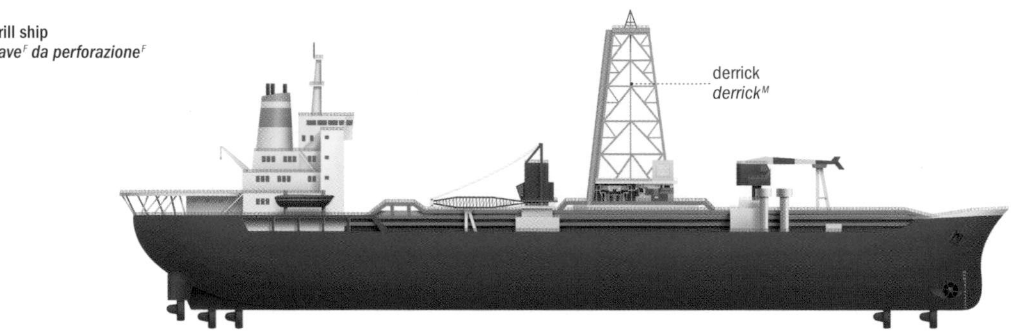

bulk carrier
nave^F per il trasporto^M delle merci^F

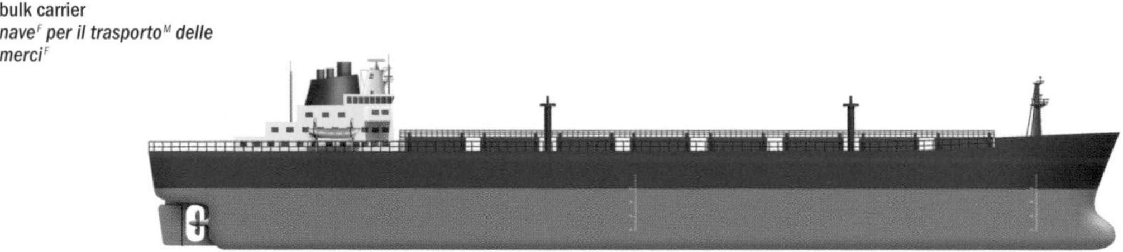

container ship
nave^F portacontainer^M

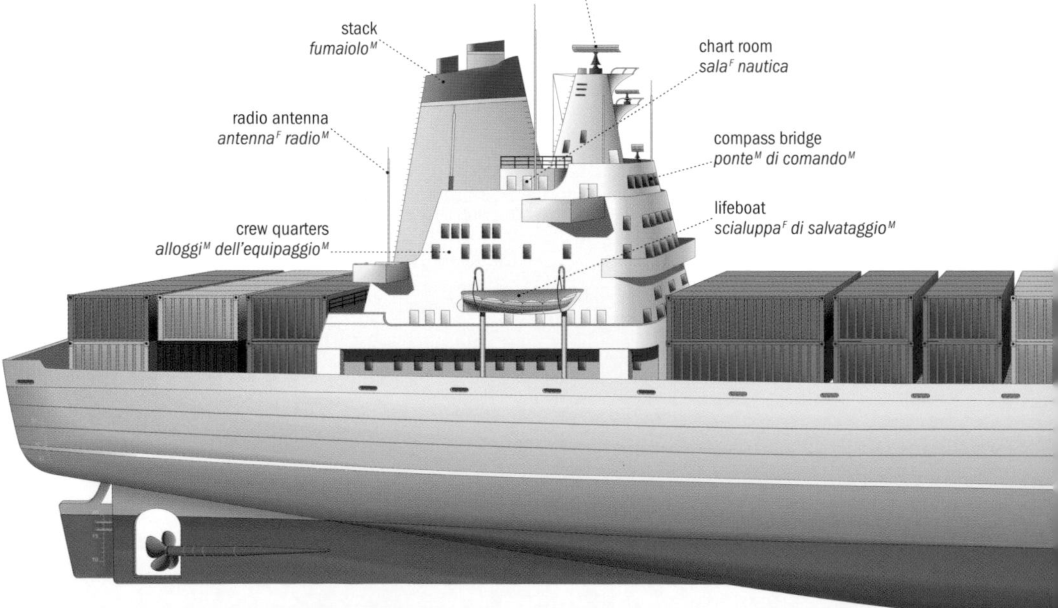

radar
radar^M
stack
fumaiolo^M
chart room
sala^F nautica
radio antenna
antenna^F radio^M
compass bridge
ponte^M di comando^M
lifeboat
scialuppa^F di salvataggio^M
crew quarters
alloggi^M dell'equipaggio^M

hovercraft
hovercraft^{M}

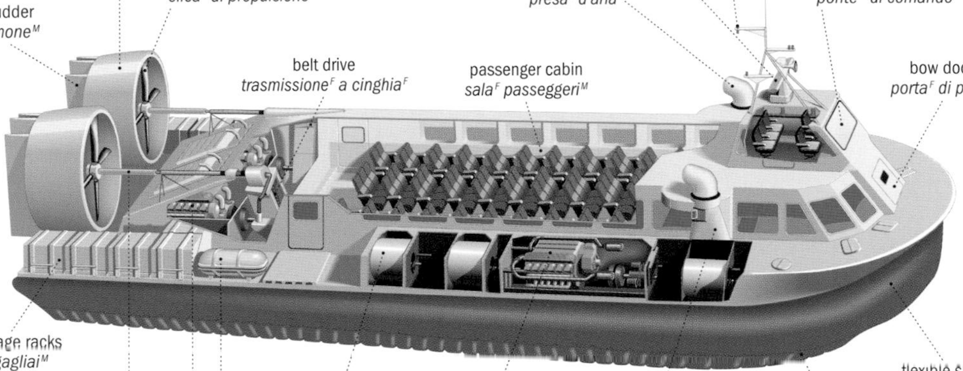

propeller duct
mantello^{M} *d'elica*^{F}
radar
radar^{M}
navigation light
luce^{F} *di navigazione*^{F}
dynamics propeller
elica^{F} *di propulsione*^{F}
air intake
presa^{F} *d'aria*^{F}
control deck
ponte^{M} *di comando*^{M}
rudder
timone^{M}
belt drive
trasmissione^{F} *a cinghia*^{F}
passenger cabin
sala^{F} *passeggeri*^{M}
bow door
porta^{F} *di prua*^{F}
baggage racks
bagagliai^{M}
blade lift fan
ventilatore^{M} *di sostentamento*^{M}
lift-fan air inlet
presa^{F} *d'aria*^{F} *del ventilatore*^{M} *di sostentamento*^{M}
flexible skirt
grembiule^{M}
drive shaft
albero^{M} *di trasmissione*^{F}
skirt finger
gomma^{F} *di tenuta*^{F} *del grembiule*^{M}
life raft
zattera^{F} *di salvataggio*^{M}
diesel lift engine
motore^{M} *diesel del ventilatore*^{M} *di sostentamento*^{M}
diesel propulsion engine
motore^{M} *diesel di propulsione*^{F}

masthead light
fanale^{M} *di testa*^{F} *dell'albero*^{M}
forecastle
castello^{M}
container
container^{M}
container hold
stiva^{F} *per i containers*^{M}
anchor-windlass room
cubia^{F}

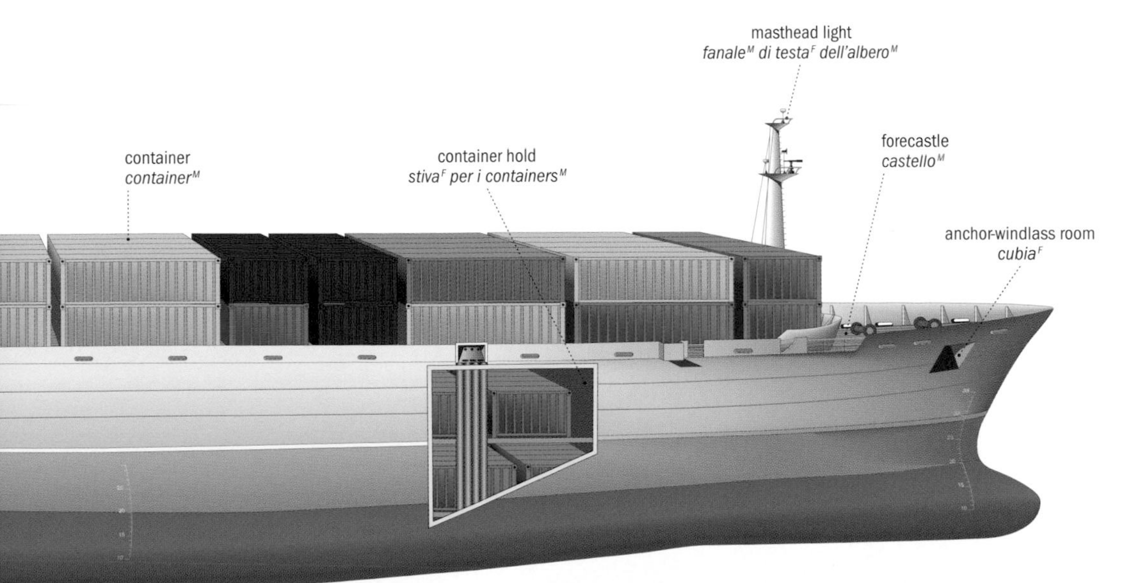

examples of boats and ships

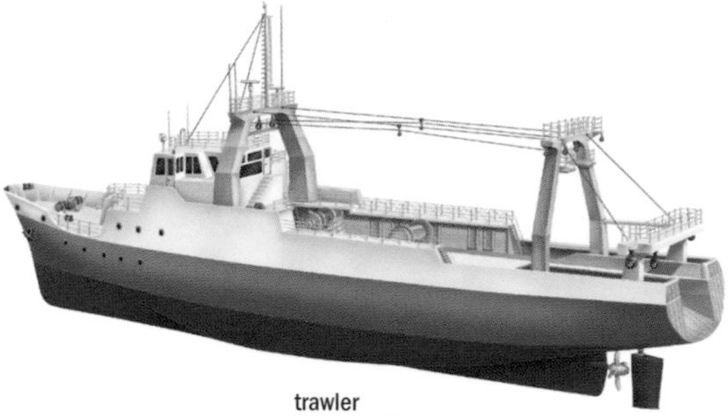

trawler
peschereccio[M]

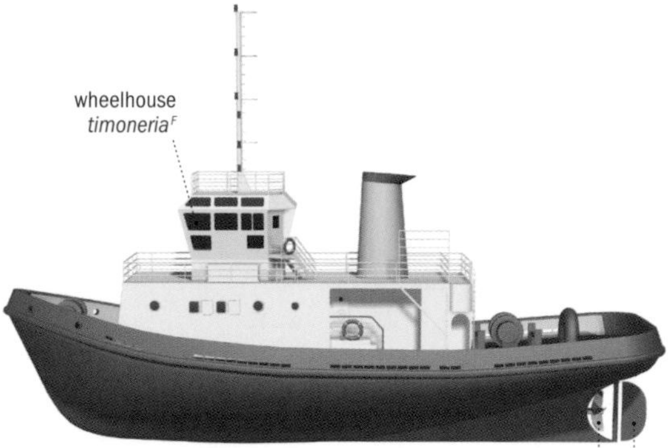

wheelhouse
timoneria[F]

tug
rimorchiatore[M]

propeller
elica[F]

rudder blade
pala[F] *del timone*[M]

stem
prua[F]

stem propeller
elica[F] *di prua*[F]

ice breaker
rompighiaccio[M]

rear propeller
elica[F] *posteriore*

tanker
nave[F] *cisterna*[F]

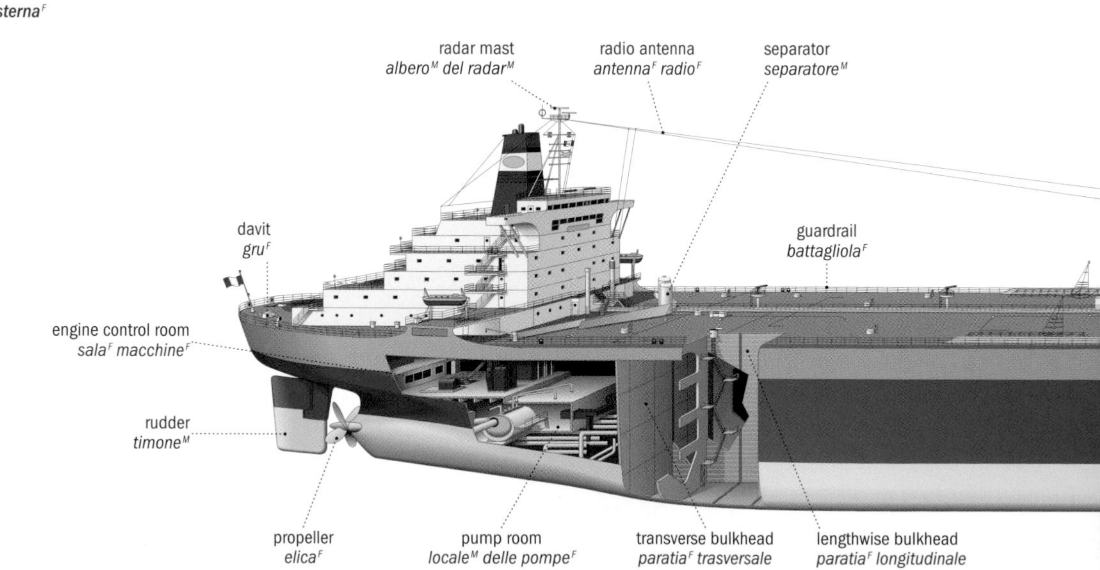

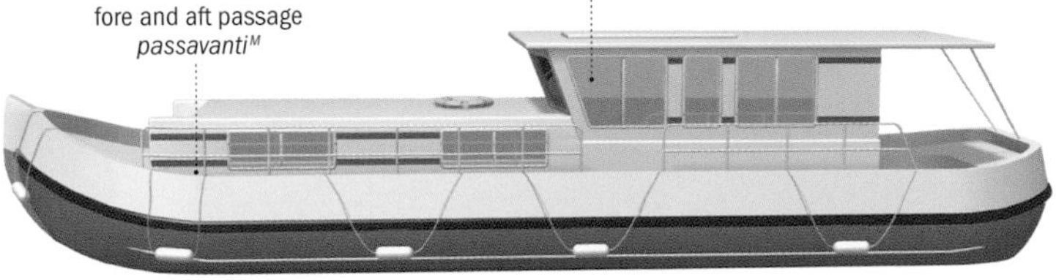

examples of boats and ships

pilot house
cabina[F] di pilotaggio[M]

fore and aft passage
passavanti[M]

houseboat
casa[F] galleggiante

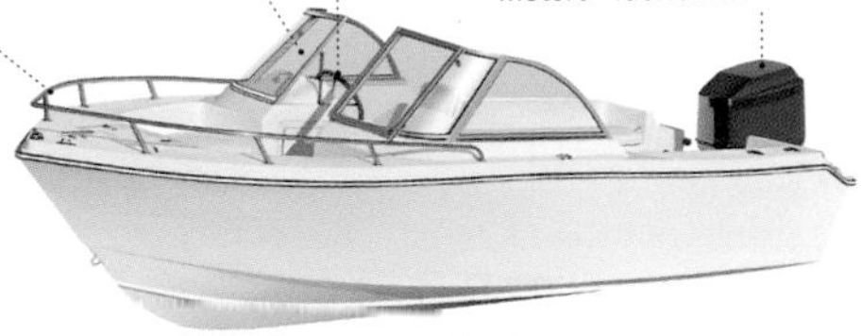

steering wheel
volante[M]

windshield
parabrezza[M]

outboard engine
motore[M] fuoribordo[M]

handrail
corrimano[M]

speedboat
motoscafo[M] da diporto[M]

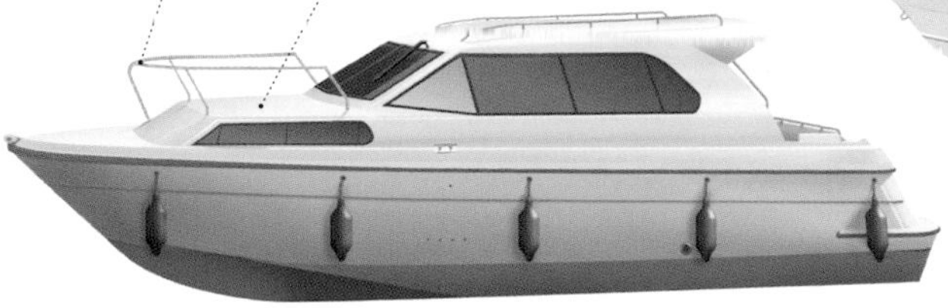

handrail
corrimano[M]

sun deck
solarium[M]

motor yacht
yacht[M] a motore[M]

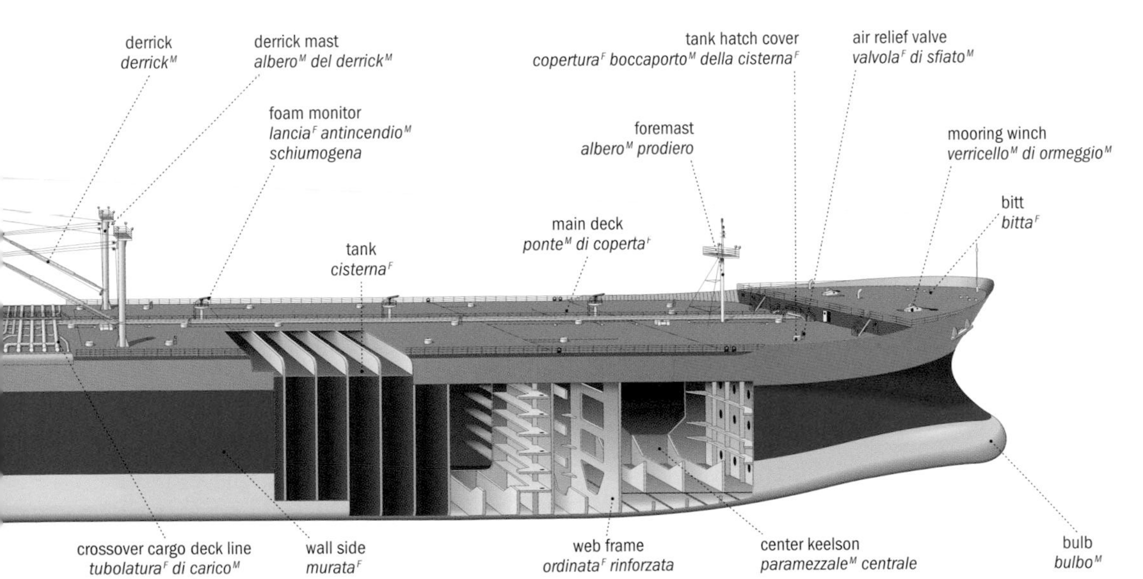

examples of boats and ships

catamaran ferryboat
nave^{F} traghetto^{M}

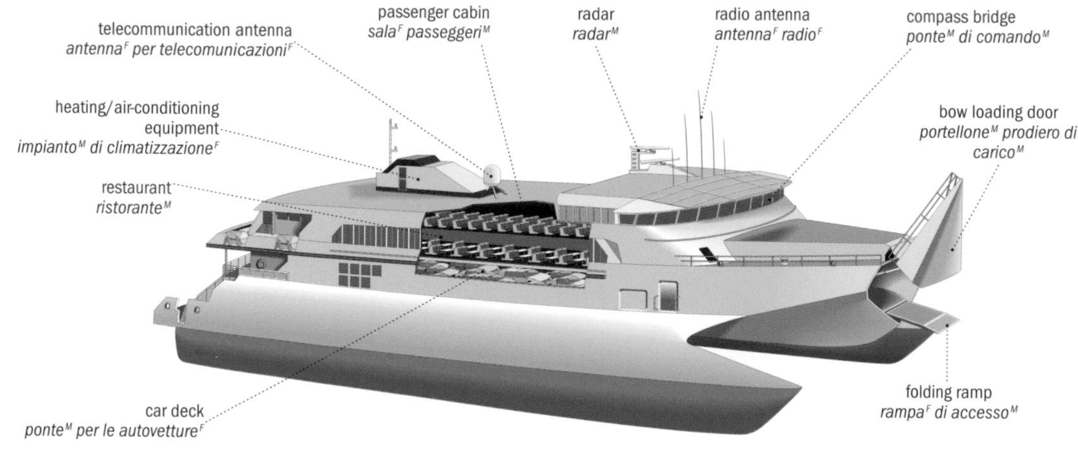

passenger liner
transatlantico^{M}

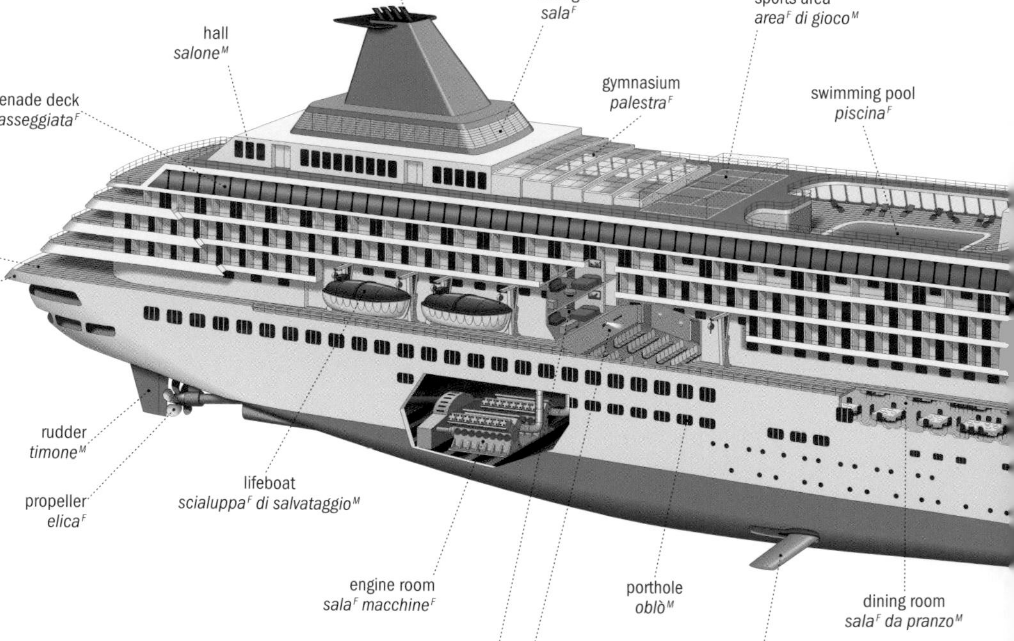

funnel
fumaiolo^{M}
lounge
sala^{F}
sports area
area^{F} di gioco^{M}
hall
salone^{M}
gymnasium
palestra^{F}
swimming pool
piscina^{F}
promenade deck
ponte^{M} di passeggiata^{F}
quarter-deck
cassero^{M} poppiero
stern
poppa^{F}
rudder
timone^{M}
propeller
elica^{F}
lifeboat
scialuppa^{F} di salvataggio^{M}
engine room
sala^{F} macchine^{F}
porthole
oblò^{M}
dining room
sala^{F} da pranzo^{M}
cabin
cabina^{F}
movie theater
cinema^{M}
stabilizer fin
pinna^{F} stabilizzatrice

hydrofoil boat
aliscafo^M

radio antenna
antenna^F radio^F
radar
radar^M
life buoy
salvagente^M
passenger cabin
sala^F passeggeri^M
compass bridge
ponte^M di comando^M
strut
sostegno^M dell'ala^F
surface-piercing foils
ala^F semiimmersa
propeller shaft
albero^M dell'elica^F
rear foil
ala^F poppiera
propeller
elica^F
front foil
ala^F prodiera

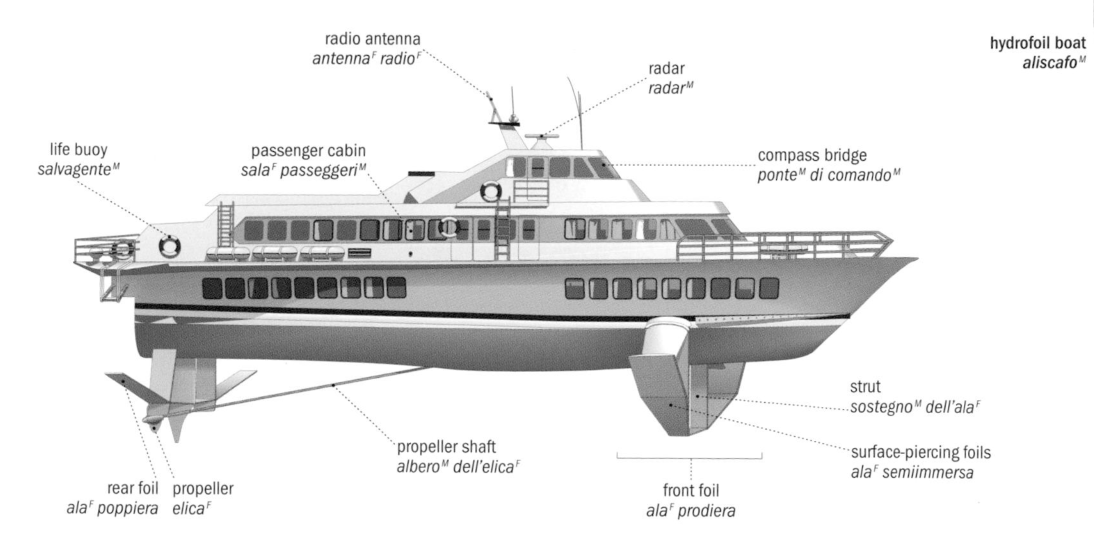

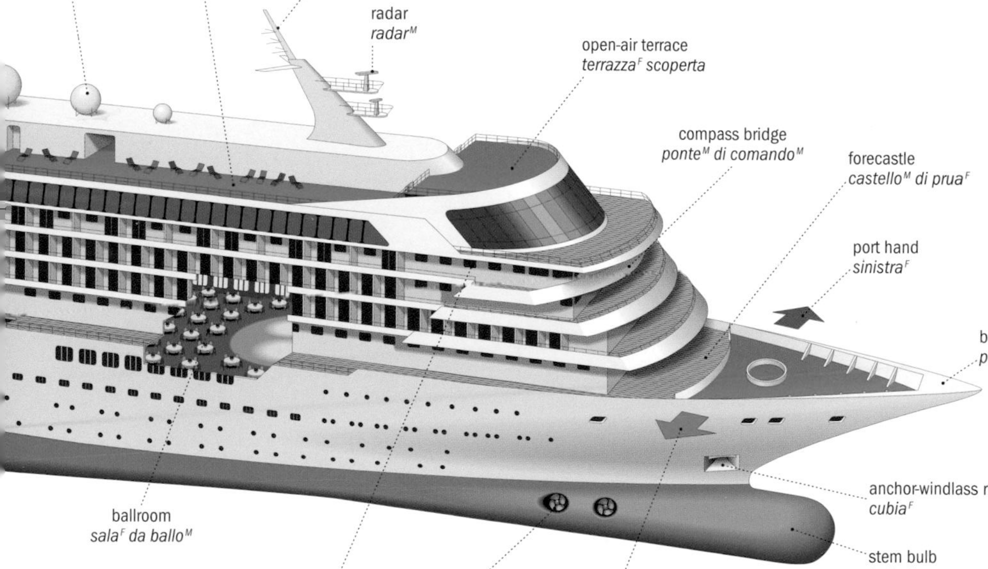

telecommunication antenna
antenna^F per telecomunicazioni^F
radio antenna
antenna^F radio^F
sun deck
solarium^M
radar
radar^M
open-air terrace
terrazza^F scoperta
compass bridge
ponte^M di comando^M
forecastle
castello^M di prua^F
port hand
sinistra^F
bow
prua^F
anchor-windlass room
cubia^F
stem bulb
bulbo^M
ballroom
sala^F da ballo^M
captain's quarters
alloggio^M del comandante^M
bow thruster
propulsore^M di prua^F
starboard hand
dritta^F

airport

aeroporto[M]

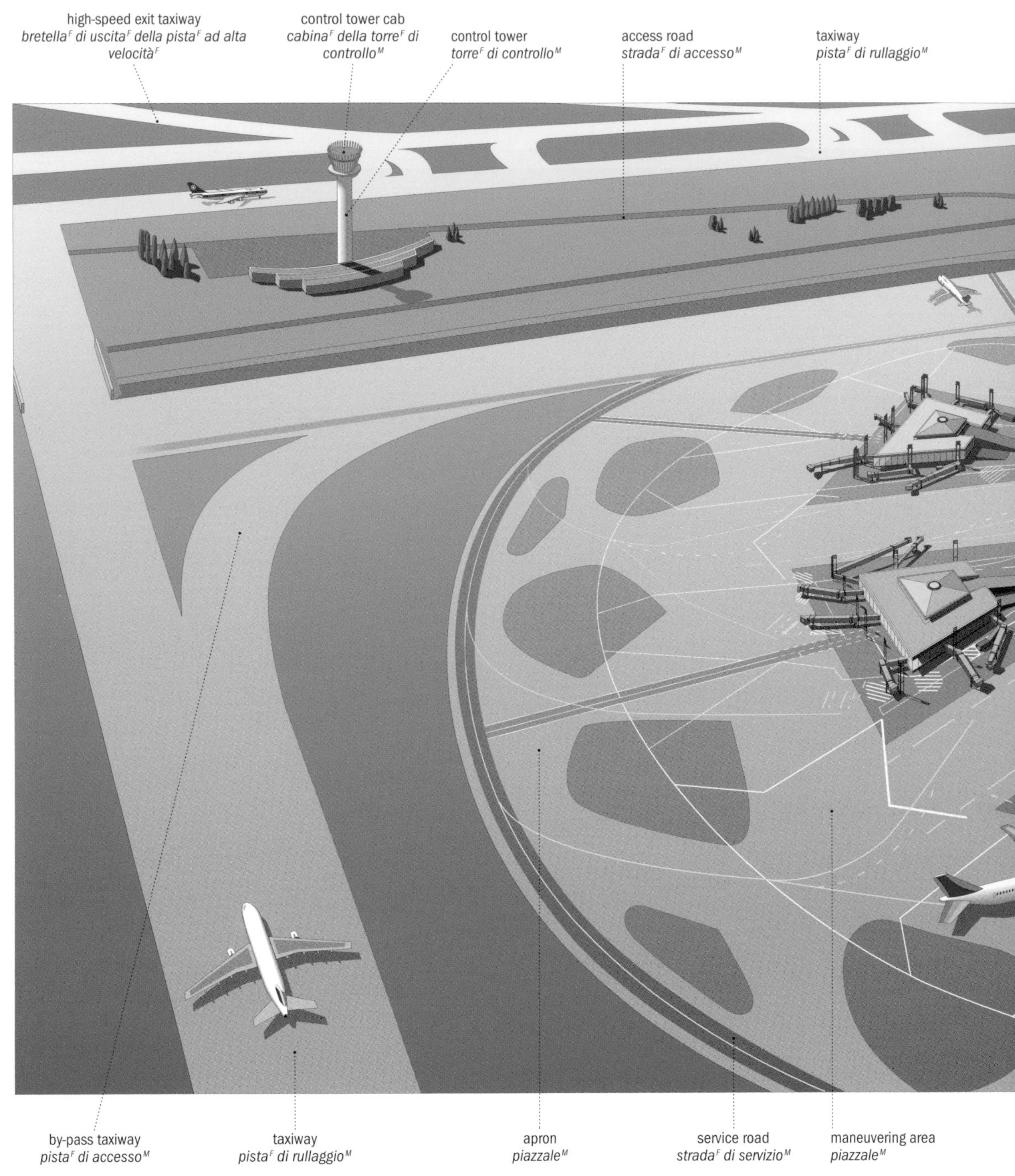

passenger terminal
terminal^M dei passeggeri^M
maintenance hangar
aviorimessa^F
parking area
area^F di parcheggio^M
telescopic corridor
corridoio^M telescopico
service area
area^F di servizio^M
boarding walkway
passerella^F di imbarco^M
taxiway line
linea^F di rullaggio^M
radial passenger-loading area
terminal^M satellite^M dei passeggeri^M

airport

passenger terminal
terminal[M] dei passeggeri[M]

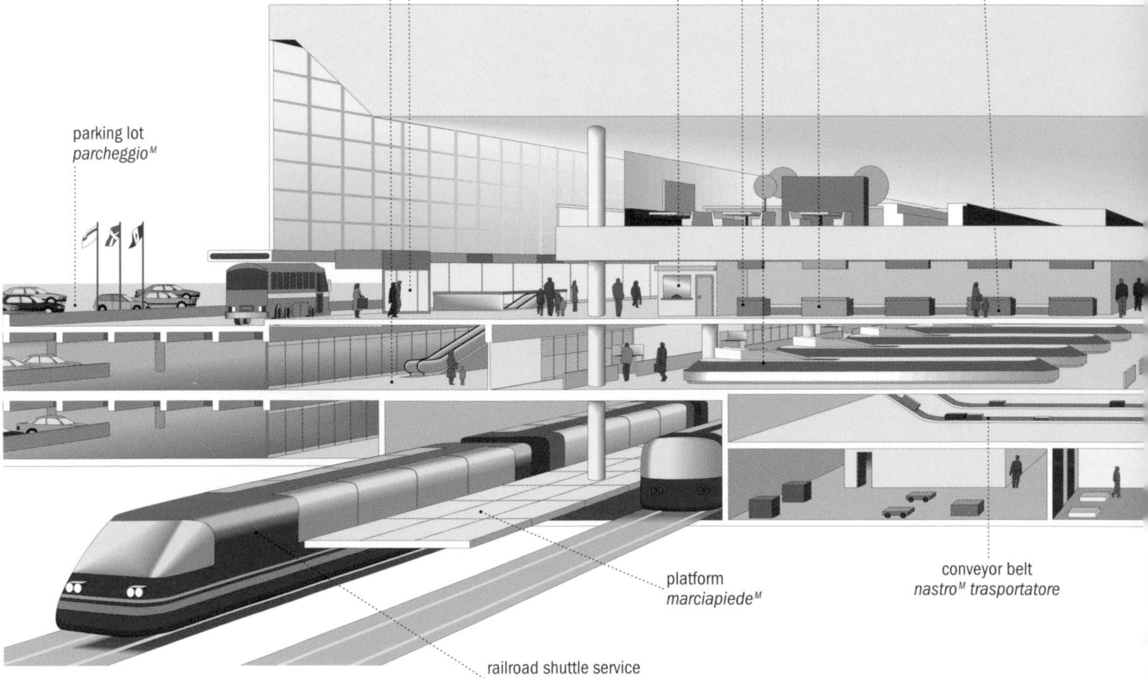

information counter
banco[M] delle informazioni[F]

baggage claim area
area[F] per il ritiro[M] dei bagagli[M]

hotel reservation desk
banco[M] per la prenotazione[F] degli hotel[M]

ticket counter
biglietteria[F]

lobby
salone[M]

automatically controlled door
porta[F] automatica

baggage check-in counter
banco[M] di registrazione[F]

parking lot
parcheggio[M]

platform
marciapiede[M]

conveyor belt
nastro[M] trasportatore

railroad shuttle service
servizio[M] di navetta[F]

runway
pista[F]

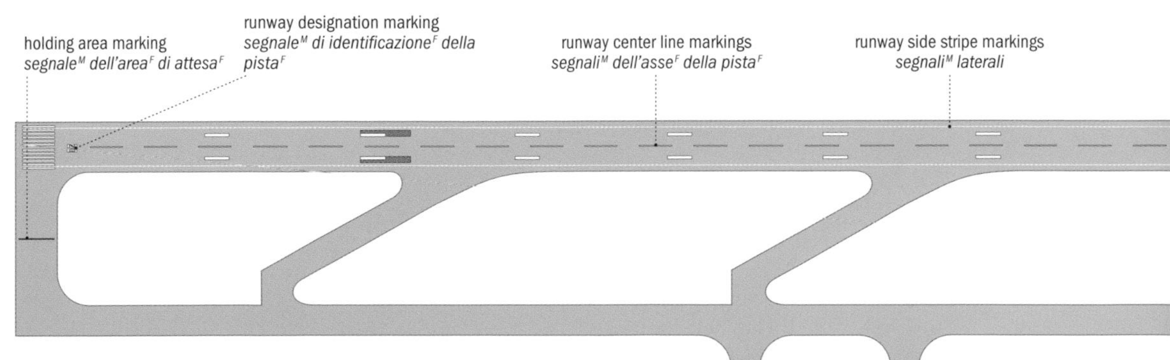

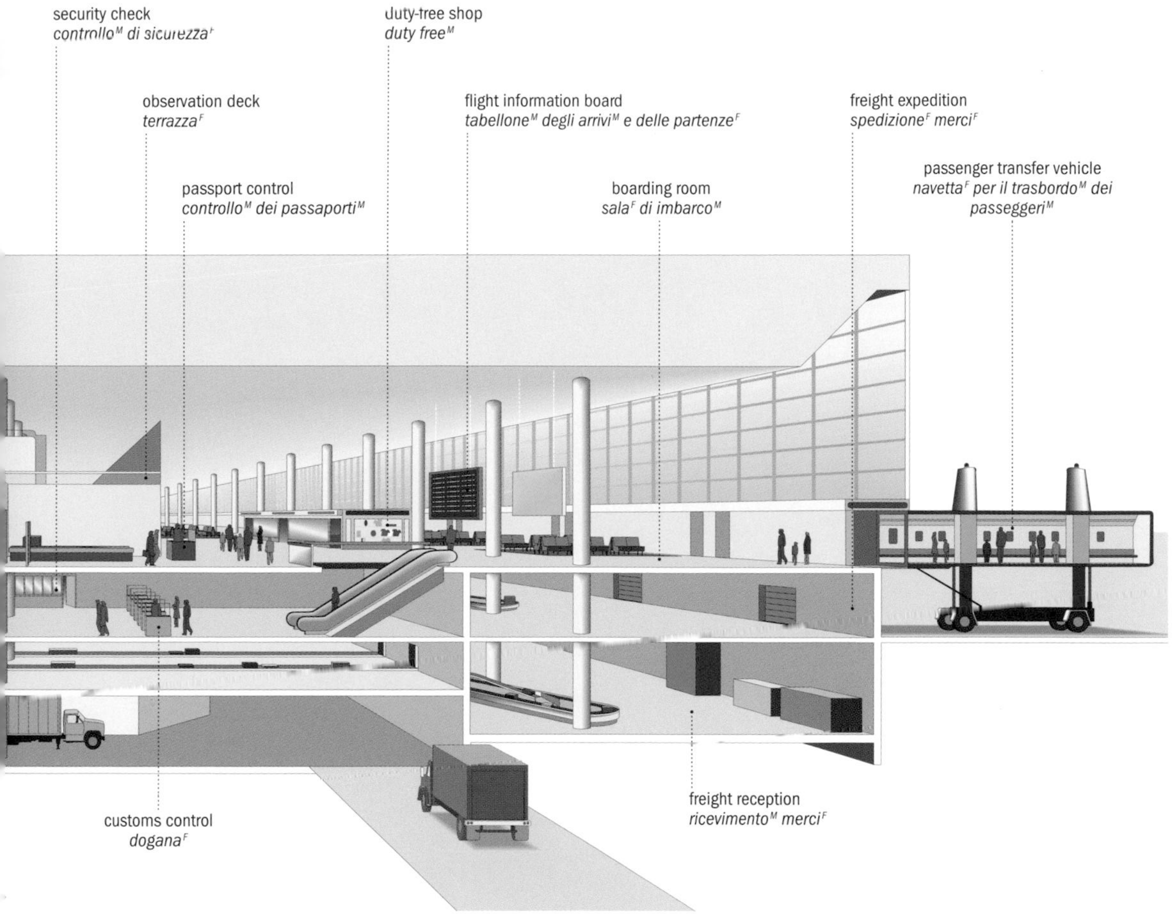

security check
controllo[M] di sicurezza[F]

duty-free shop
duty free[M]

observation deck
terrazza[F]

flight information board
tabellone[M] degli arrivi[M] e delle partenze[F]

freight expedition
spedizione[F] merci[F]

passport control
controllo[M] dei passaporti[M]

boarding room
sala[F] di imbarco[M]

passenger transfer vehicle
navetta[F] per il trasbordo[M] dei passeggeri[M]

customs control
dogana[F]

freight reception
ricevimento[M] merci[F]

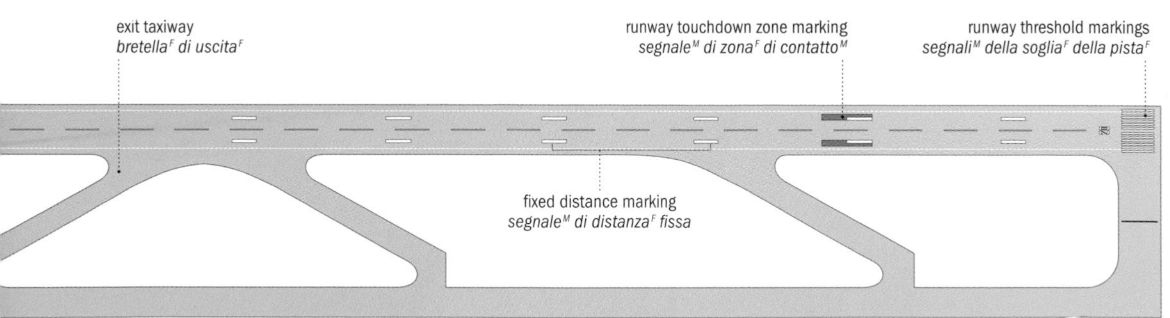

long-range jet

aviogetto^M a lungo raggio^M

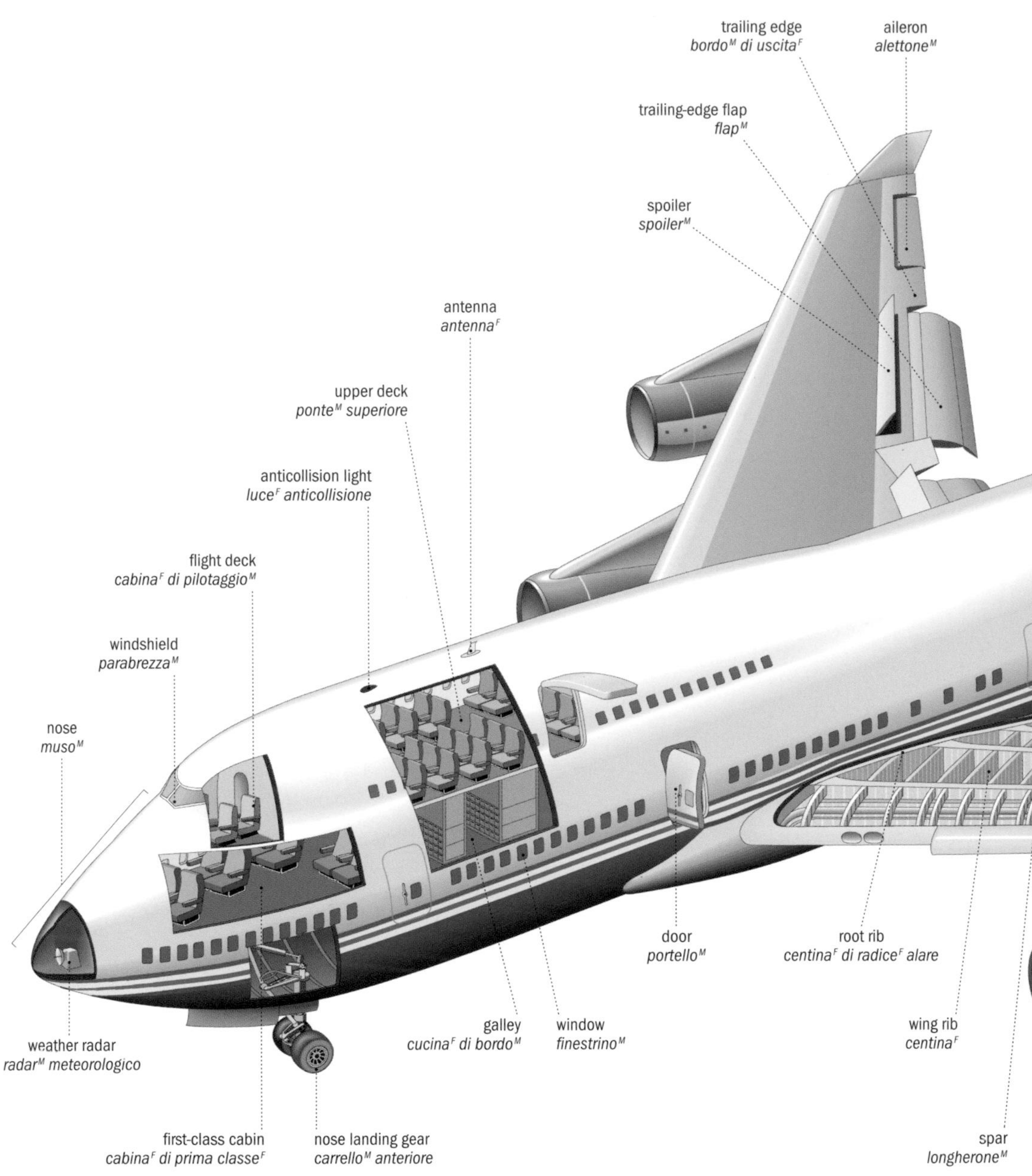

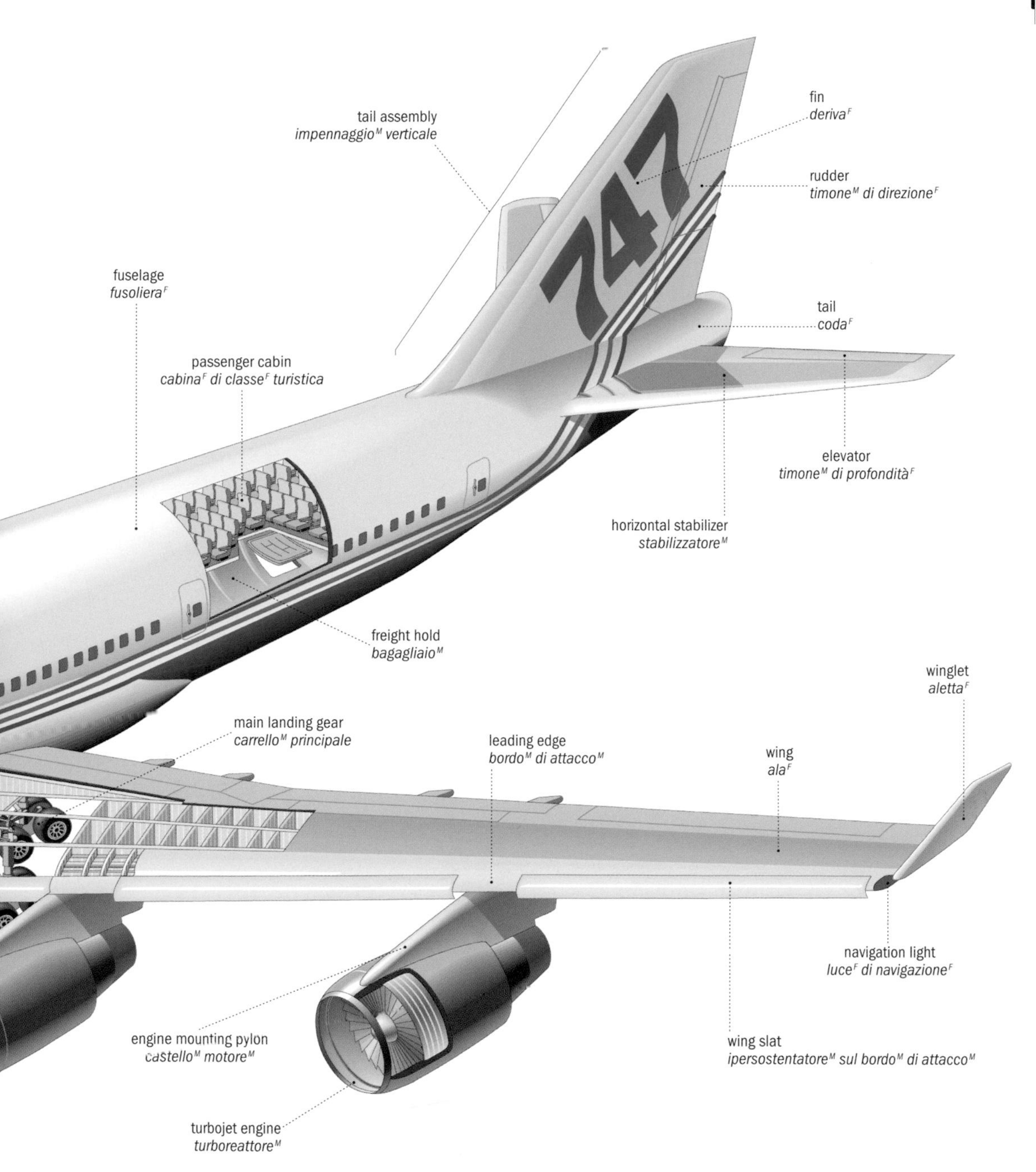
tail assembly
impennaggio[M] verticale
fin
deriva[F]
rudder
timone[M] di direzione[F]
fuselage
fusoliera[F]
tail
coda[F]
passenger cabin
cabina[F] di classe[F] turistica
elevator
timone[M] di profondità[F]
horizontal stabilizer
stabilizzatore[M]
freight hold
bagagliaio[M]
winglet
aletta[F]
main landing gear
carrello[M] principale
leading edge
bordo[M] di attacco[M]
wing
ala[F]
navigation light
luce[F] di navigazione[F]
engine mounting pylon
castello[M] motore[M]
wing slat
ipersostentatore[M] sul bordo[M] di attacco[M]
turbojet engine
turboreattore[M]

examples of airplanes

esempi^M di aeroplani^M

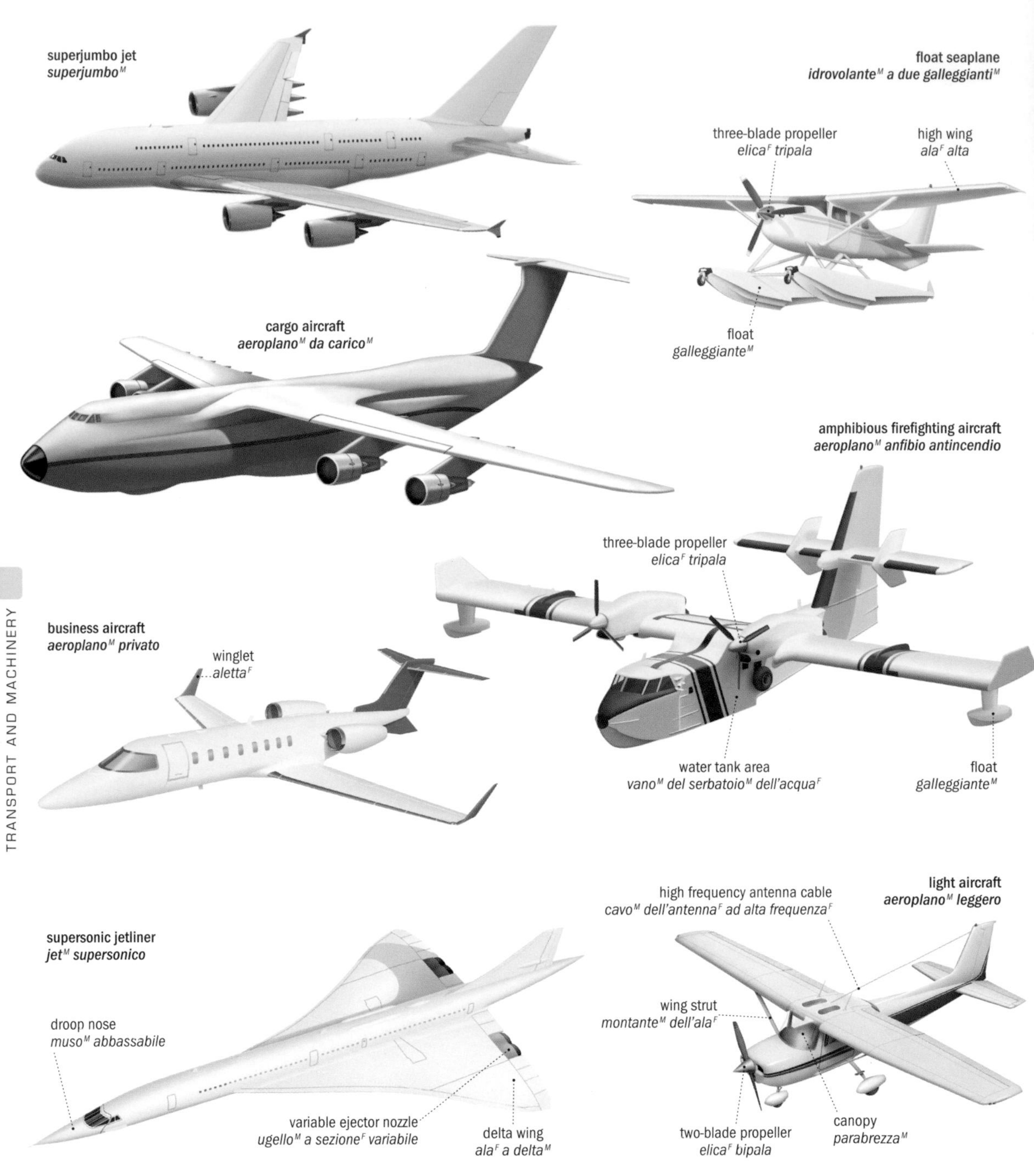

TRANSPORT AND MACHINERY

movements of an airplane

movimenti^M di un aeroplano^M

pitch
beccheggio^M
yaw
imbardata^F
roll
rollio^F

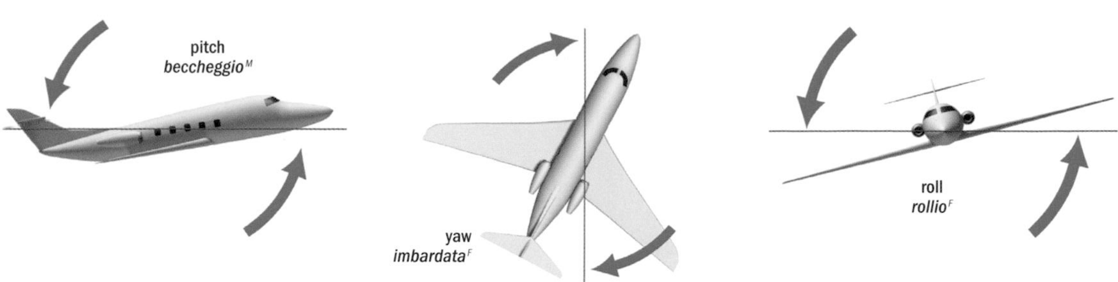

helicopter

elicottero^M

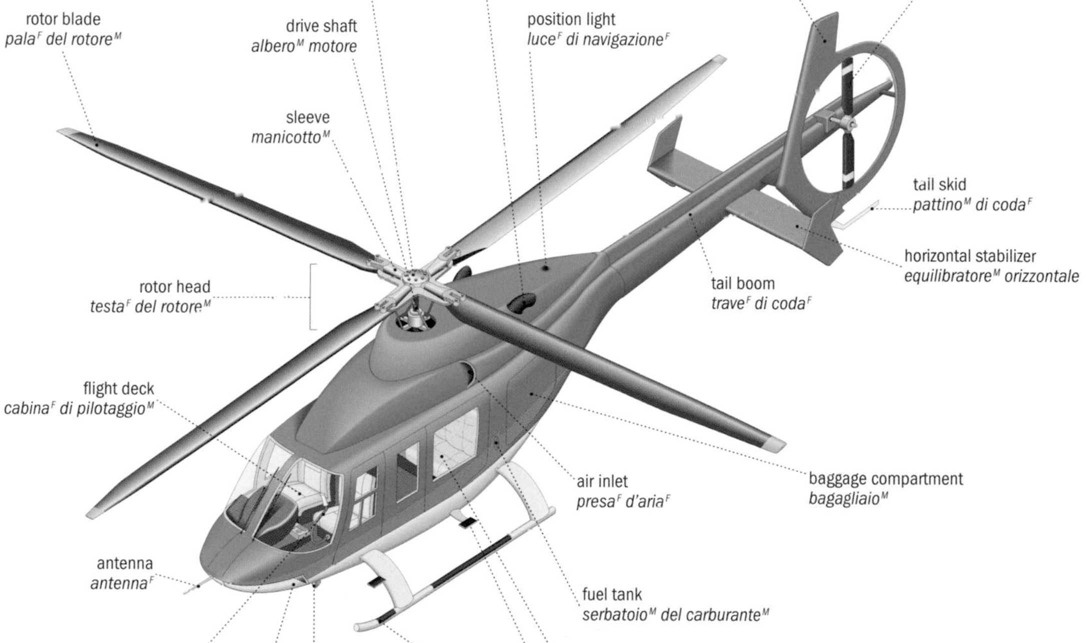

rotor hub
mozzo^M del rotore^M
exhaust pipe
tubo^M di scarico^M
fin
deriva^F
anti-torque tail rotor
rotore^M anticoppia
rotor blade
pala^F del rotore^M
drive shaft
albero^M motore
position light
luce^F di navigazione^F
sleeve
manicotto^M
tail skid
pattino^M di coda^F
horizontal stabilizer
equilibratore^M orizzontale
rotor head
testa^F del rotore^M
tail boom
trave^F di coda^F
flight deck
cabina^F di pilotaggio^M
air inlet
presa^F d'aria^F
baggage compartment
bagagliaio^M
antenna
antenna^F
fuel tank
serbatoio^M del carburante^M
skid
pattino^M
control stick
barra^F di comando^M
cabin
cabina^F passeggeri^M
landing window
finestrino^M di atterraggio^M
landing light
faro^M di atterraggio^M
boarding step
gradino^M di accesso^M

material handling

movimentazione^F dei materiali^M

cranes
gru^F

tower crane
gru^F a torre^F

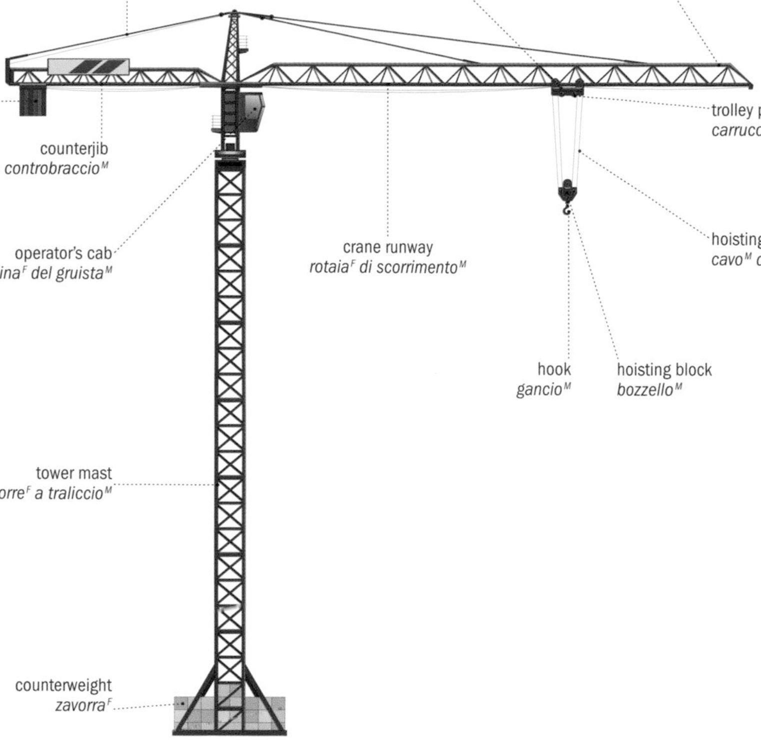

jib tie
tirante^M del braccio^M
trolley
carrello^M
jib
braccio^M
counterjib ballast
contrappeso^M
trolley pulley
carrucola^F del carrello^M
counterjib
controbraccio^M
operator's cab
cabina^F del gruista^M
crane runway
rotaia^F di scorrimento^M
hoisting rope
cavo^M di sollevamento^M
hook
gancio^M
hoisting block
bozzello^M
tower mast
torre^F a traliccio^M
counterweight
zavorra^F

truck crane
autogrù^F

telescopic boom
braccio^M telescopico
elevating cylinder
cilindro^M di sollevamento^M
operator's cab
cabina^F dell'autogruista^M
outrigger
stabilizzatore^M

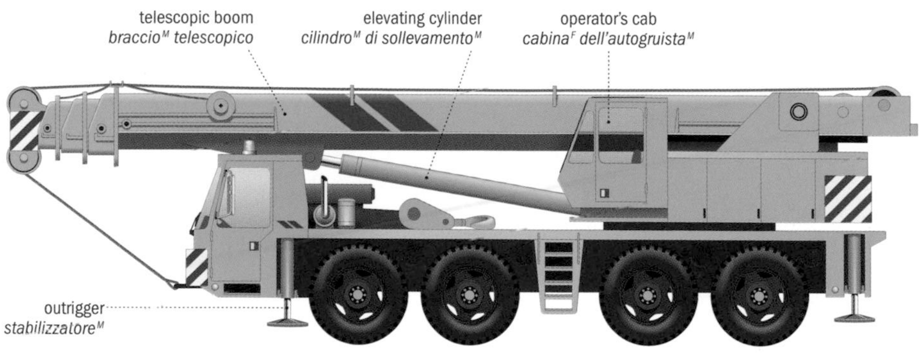

bulldozer

bulldozer[M]

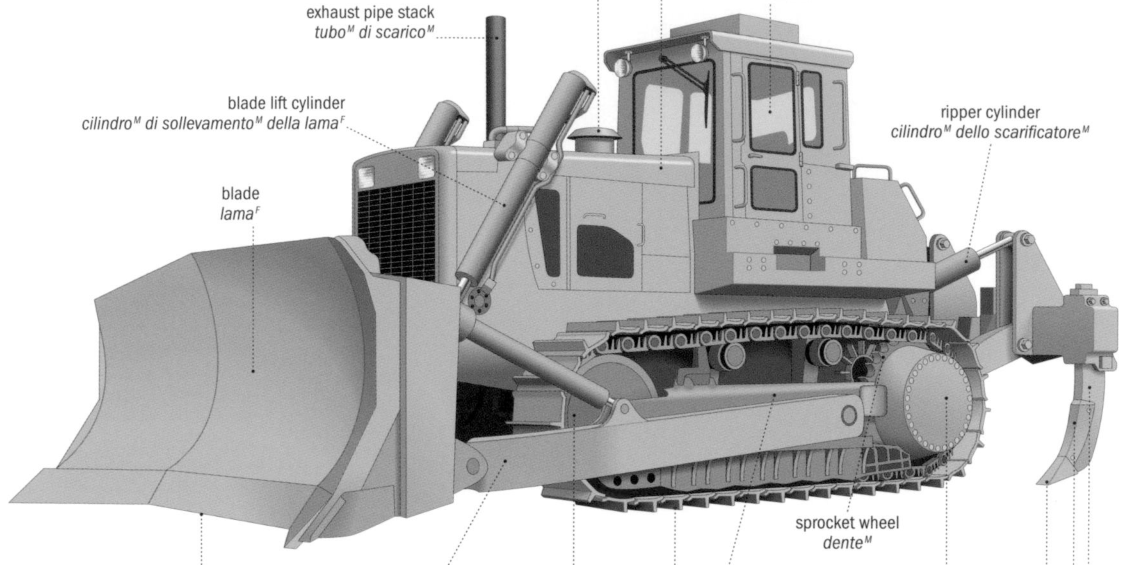

air pre-cleaner filter
filtro[M] dell'aria[F]

diesel motor compartment
vano[M] del motore[M] diesel

cab
cabina[F]

exhaust pipe stack
tubo[M] di scarico[M]

blade lift cylinder
cilindro[M] di sollevamento[M] della lama[F]

ripper cylinder
cilindro[M] dello scarificatore[M]

blade
lama[F]

sprocket wheel
dente[M]

cutting edge
tagliente[M]

push frame
telaio[M] di spinta[F]

track idler
ruota[F] tendicingolo[M]

final drive
ruota[F] motrice

track
cingolo[M]

ripper tip tooth
scalpello[M] dello scarificatore[M]

track roller frame
telaio[M] dei rulli[M] dei cingoli[M]

shank protector
protezione[F] del dente[M]

ripper shank
dente[M] dello scarificatore[M]

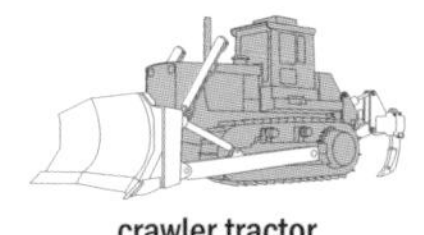
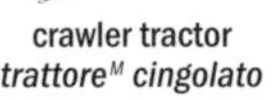

crawler tractor
trattore[M] cingolato

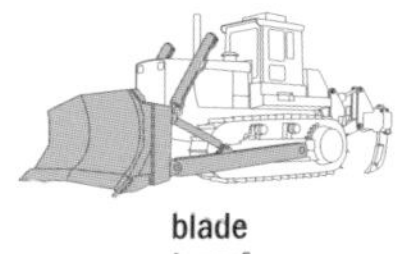

blade
lama[F]

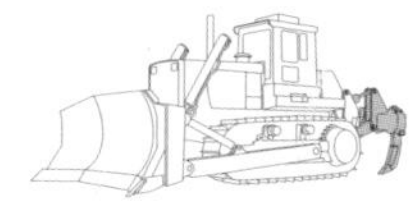

ripper
scarificatore[M]

wheel loader

terna[F]

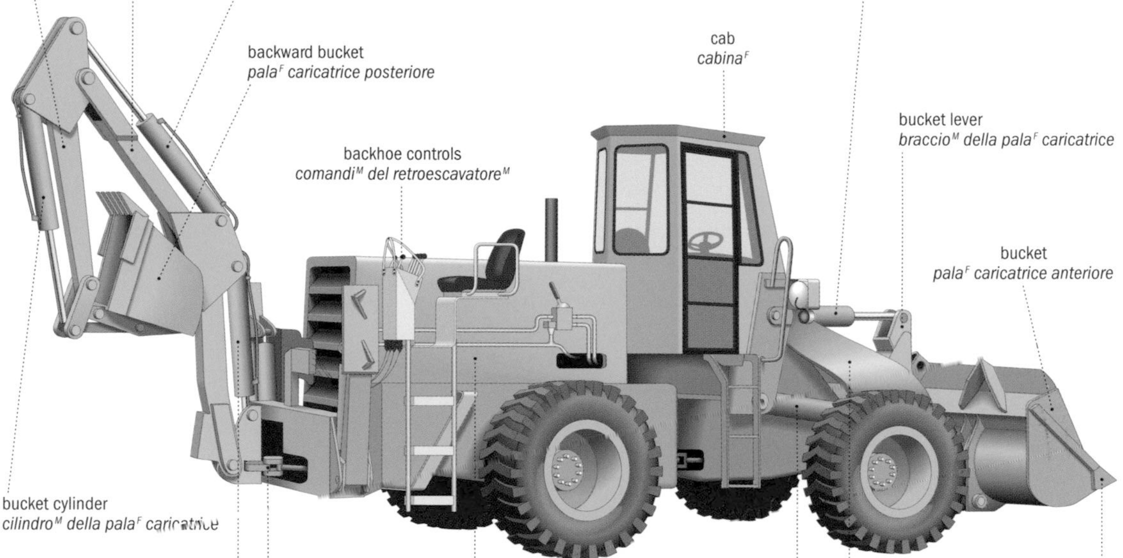

dipper arm
braccio[M] della pala[F] caricatrice

dipper-arm cylinder
cilindro[M] della pala[F] caricatrice

boom
braccio[M] di sollevamento[M]

backward bucket
pala[F] caricatrice posteriore

backhoe controls
comandi[M] del retroescavatore[M]

cab
cabina[F]

bucket cylinder
cilindro[M] della pala[F] caricatrice

bucket lever
braccio[M] della pala[F] caricatrice

bucket
pala[F] caricatrice anteriore

bucket cylinder
cilindro[M] della pala[F] caricatrice

boom cylinder
cilindro[M] di sollevamento[M]

diesel engine compartment
vano[M] del motore[M] diesel

lift arm
braccio[M] di sollevamento[M]

boom swing hinge pin
perno[M] di incernieramento[M] della pala[F] caricatrice

lift-arm cylinder
cilindro[M] del braccio[M] di sollevamento[M]

cutting edge
tagliente[M]

TRANSPORT AND MACHINERY

front-end loader
pala[F] caricatrice anteriore

wheel tractor
trattore[M] gommato

backhoe
retroescavatore[M]

scraper

ruspa^F

hydraulic shovel

escavatore^M idraulico

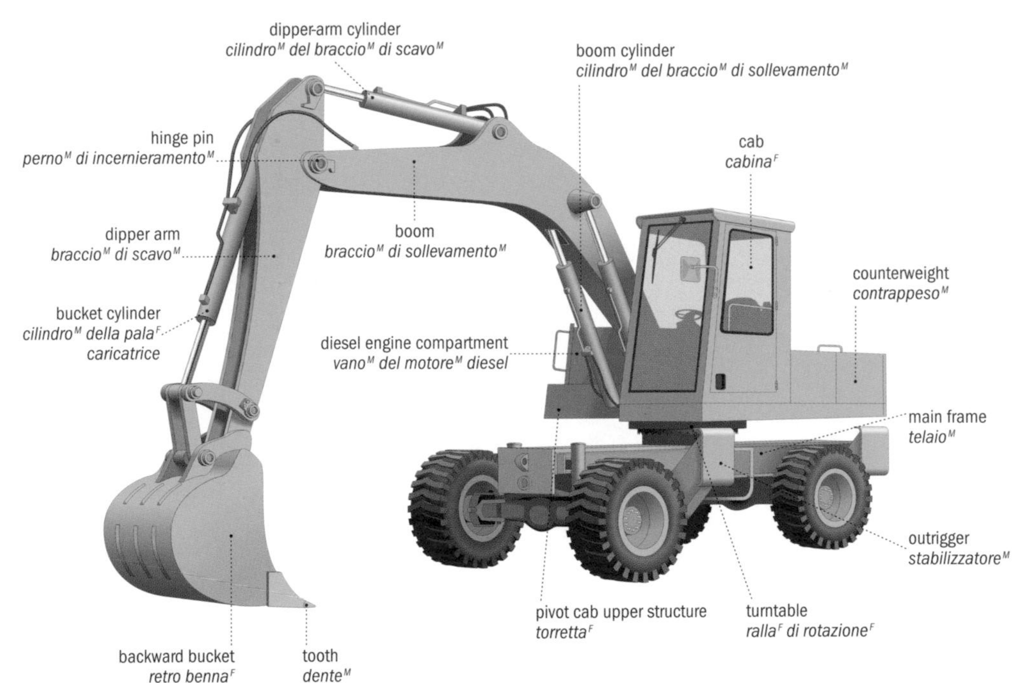

grader

livellatrice^F

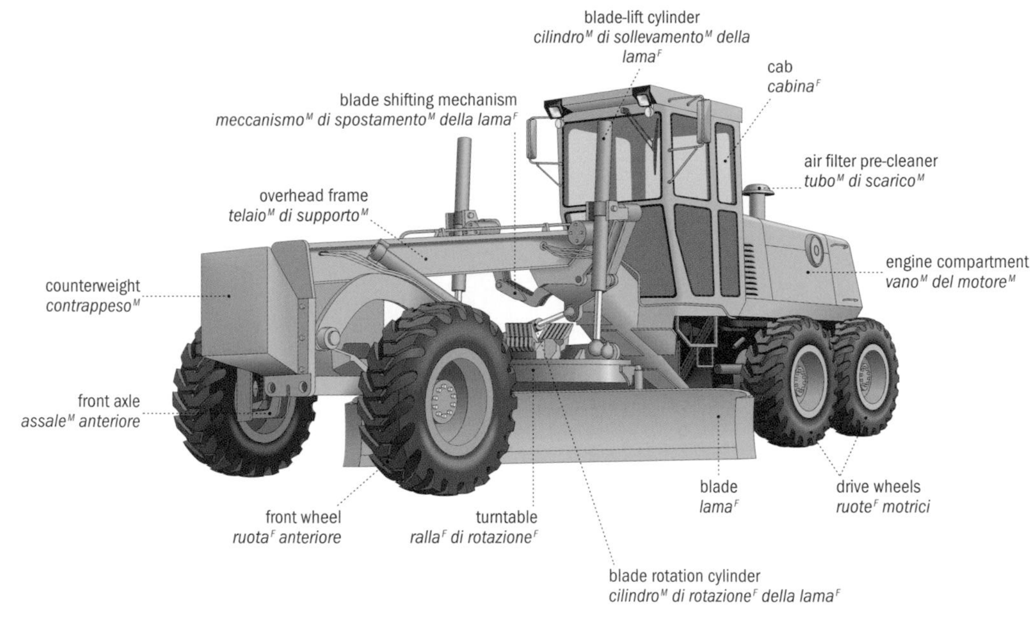

dump truck

autocarro^M a cassone^M ribaltabile

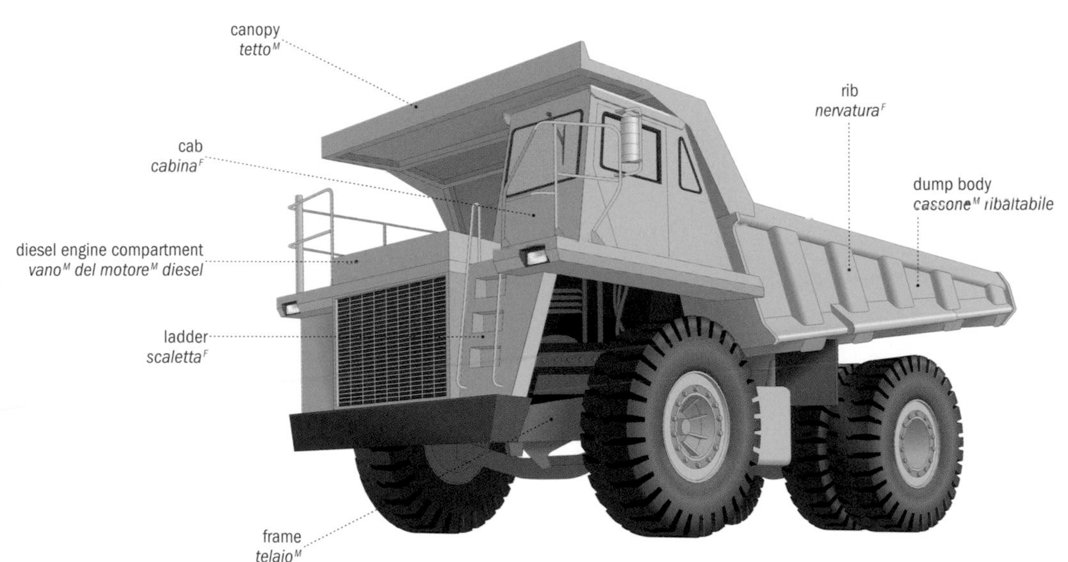

production of electricity from geothermal energy

energia^F geotermica

turbine
turbina^F
generator
alternatore^M
condenser
condensatore^M
steam
vapore^M
separator
separatore^M
high-tension electricity transmission tower
trasmissione^F di elettricità^F ad alta tensione^F
transformer (voltage increase)
aumento^M di tensione^F
water-steam mix
miscela^F di acqua^F e vapore^M
cooling tower
torre^F di raffreddamento^M
upper confining bed
strato^M superiore confinante
water
acqua^F
geothermal field
campo^M geotermico
lower confining bed
strato^M inferiore confinante
production well
pozzo^M di produzione^F
confined aquifer
acquifero^M artesiano
injection well
pozzo^M di iniezione^F
magma chamber
camera^F magmatica

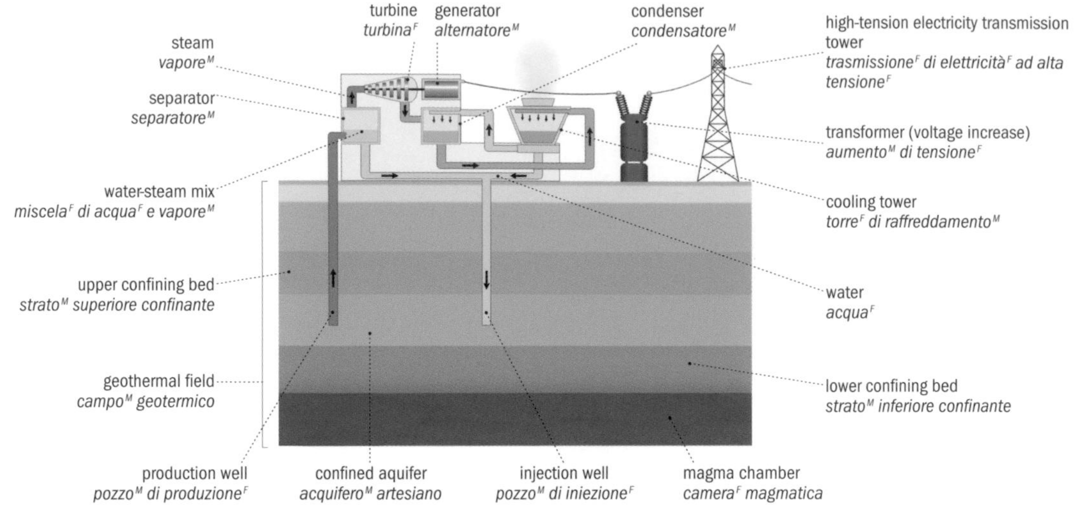

thermal energy

energia^F termica

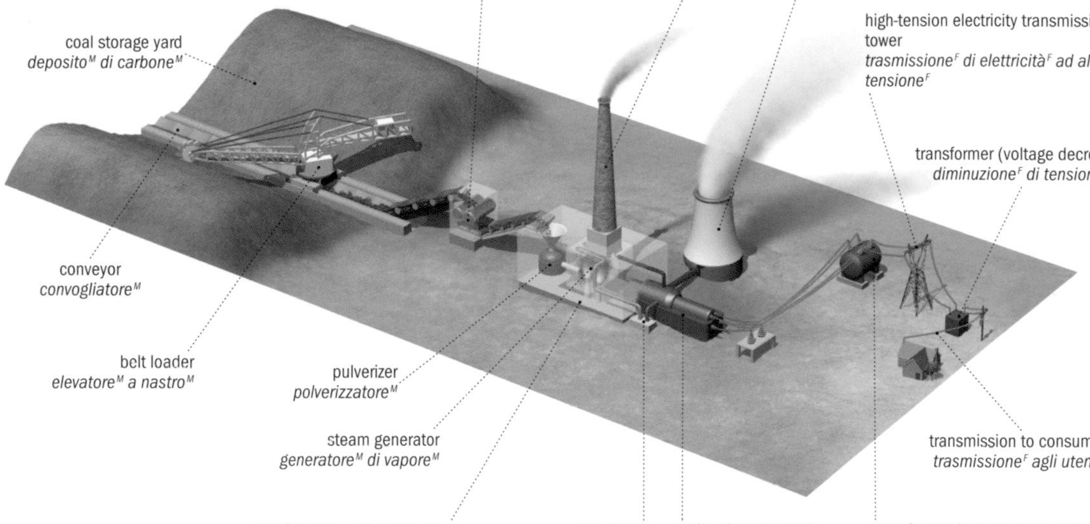

geothermal energy
geotermica
crusher
frantumatore^M
stack
ciminiera^F
cooling tower
torre^F di raffreddamento^M
coal storage yard
deposito^M di carbone^M
high-tension electricity transmission tower
trasmissione^F di elettricità^F ad alta tensione^F
transformer (voltage decrease)
diminuzione^F di tensione^F
conveyor
convogliatore^M
belt loader
elevatore^M a nastro^M
pulverizer
polverizzatore^M
steam generator
generatore^M di vapore^M
transmission to consumers
trasmissione^F agli utenti^M
coal-fired thermal power plant
centrale^F termoelettrica a carbone^M
condenser
condensatore^M
turbo-alternator unit
gruppo^M del turbo-alternatore^M
transformer (voltage increase)
aumento^M di tensione^F

oil

petrolio[M]

surface prospecting
prospezione[F] terrestre

seismographic recording
registrazione[F] sismografica
shock wave
onda[F] d'urto[M]
petroleum trap
trappola[F] petrolifera

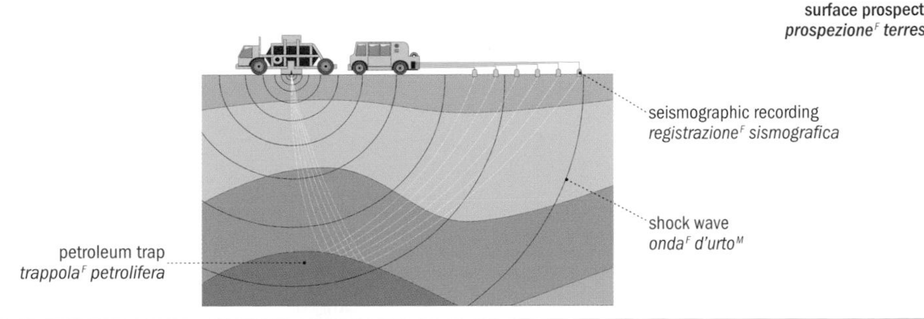

drilling rig
impianto[M] di trivellazione[F]

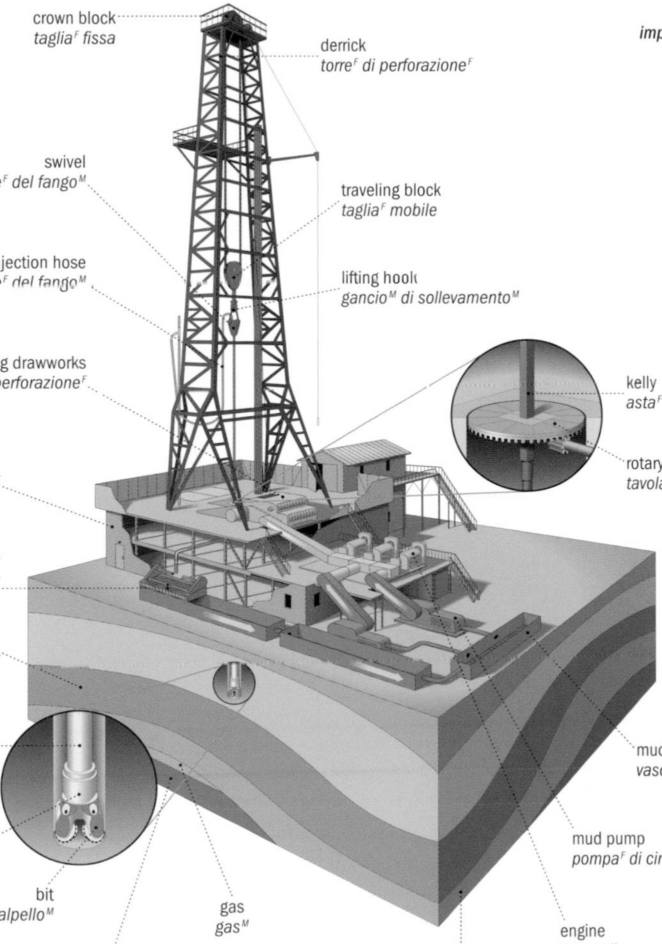

crown block
taglia[F] fissa
derrick
torre[F] di perforazione[F]
swivel
testa[F] di iniezione[F] del fango[M]
traveling block
taglia[F] mobile
mud injection hose
tubo[M] di iniezione[F] del fango[M]
lifting hook
gancio[M] di sollevamento[M]
rotary system
sistema[M] a rotazione[F]
drilling drawworks
argani[M] di perforazione[F]
kelly
asta[F] motrice quadra
substructure
sottostruttura[F]
rotary table
tavola[F] di rotazione[F]
vibrating mudscreen
vibrovaglio[M] per la depurazione[F] del fango[M]
anticline
anticlinale[F]
drill pipe
asta[F] di perforazione[F]
mud pit
vasca[F] del fango[M]
drill collar
manicotto[M] di attacco[M] dello scalpello[M]
mud pump
pompa[F] di circolazione[F] del fango[M]
bit
scalpello[M]
gas
gas[M]
engine
motore[M]
impervious rock
roccia[F] impermeabile
oil
petrolio[M]

oil

floating-roof tank
serbatoio^M a tetto^M galleggiante

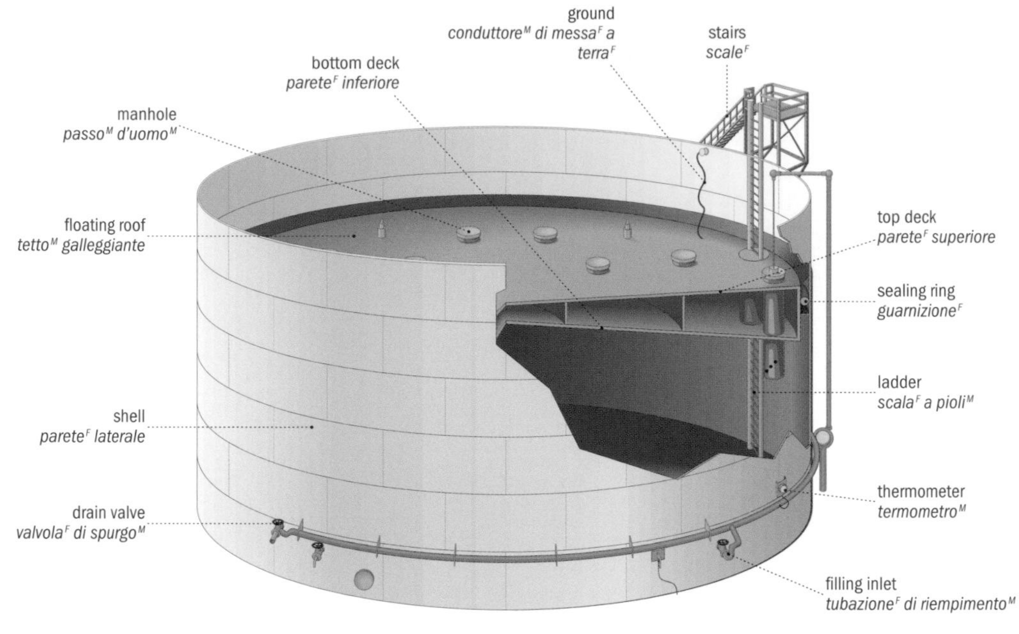

crude-oil pipeline
rete^F di oleodotti^M

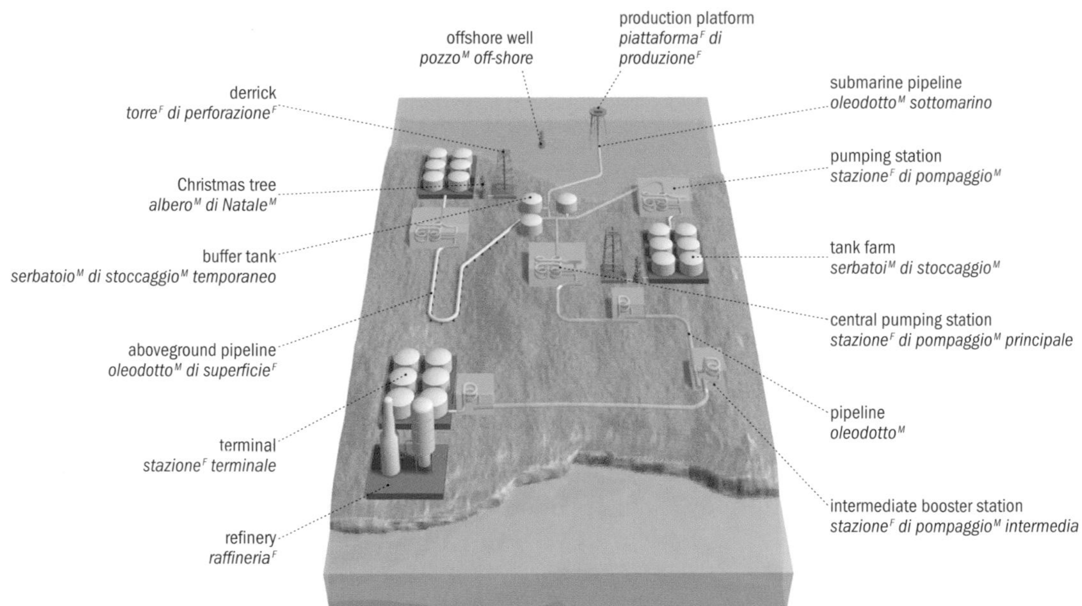

refinery products
***prodotti*[M] *di raffinazione*[F]**

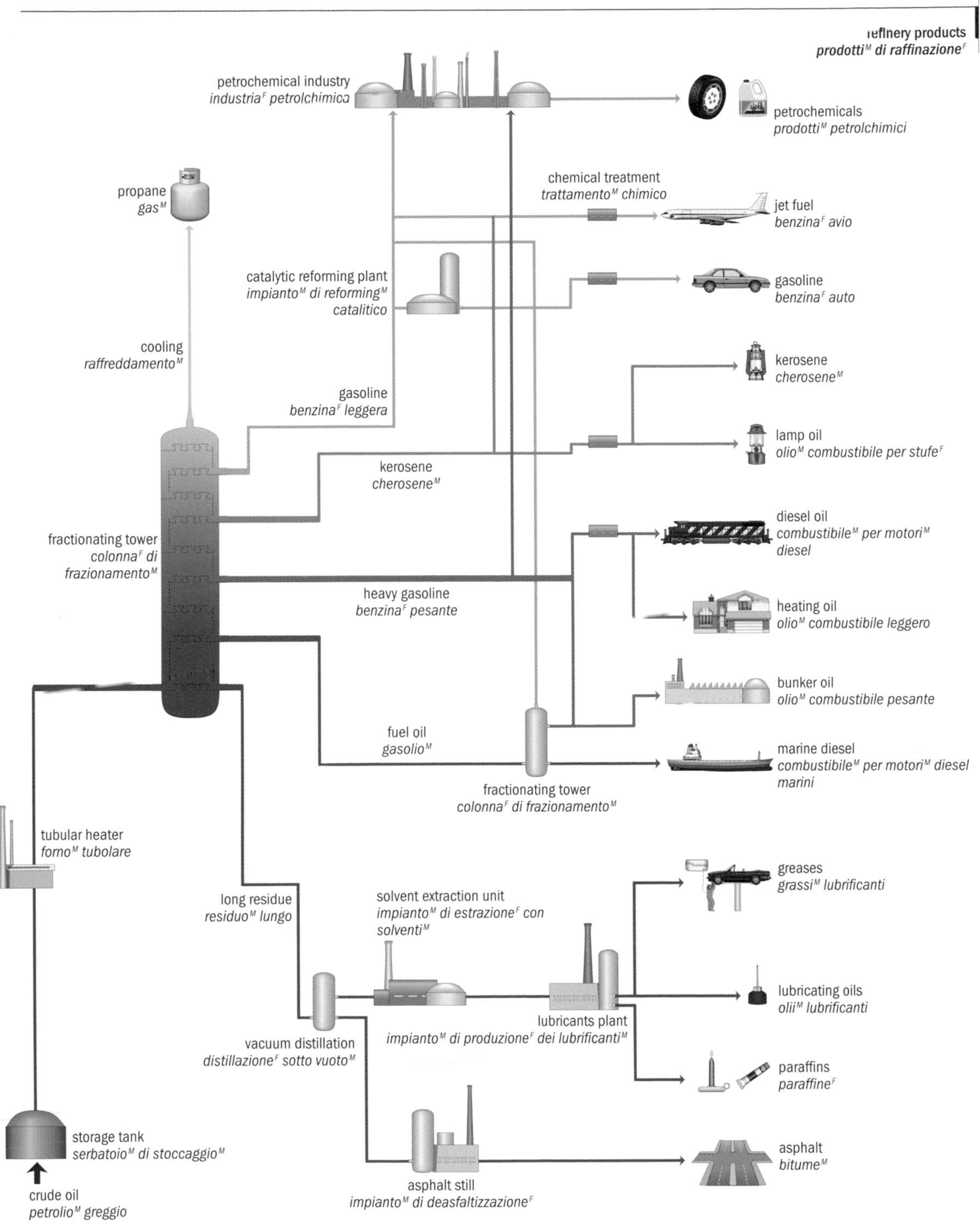

hydroelectric complex

impianto^M idroelettrico

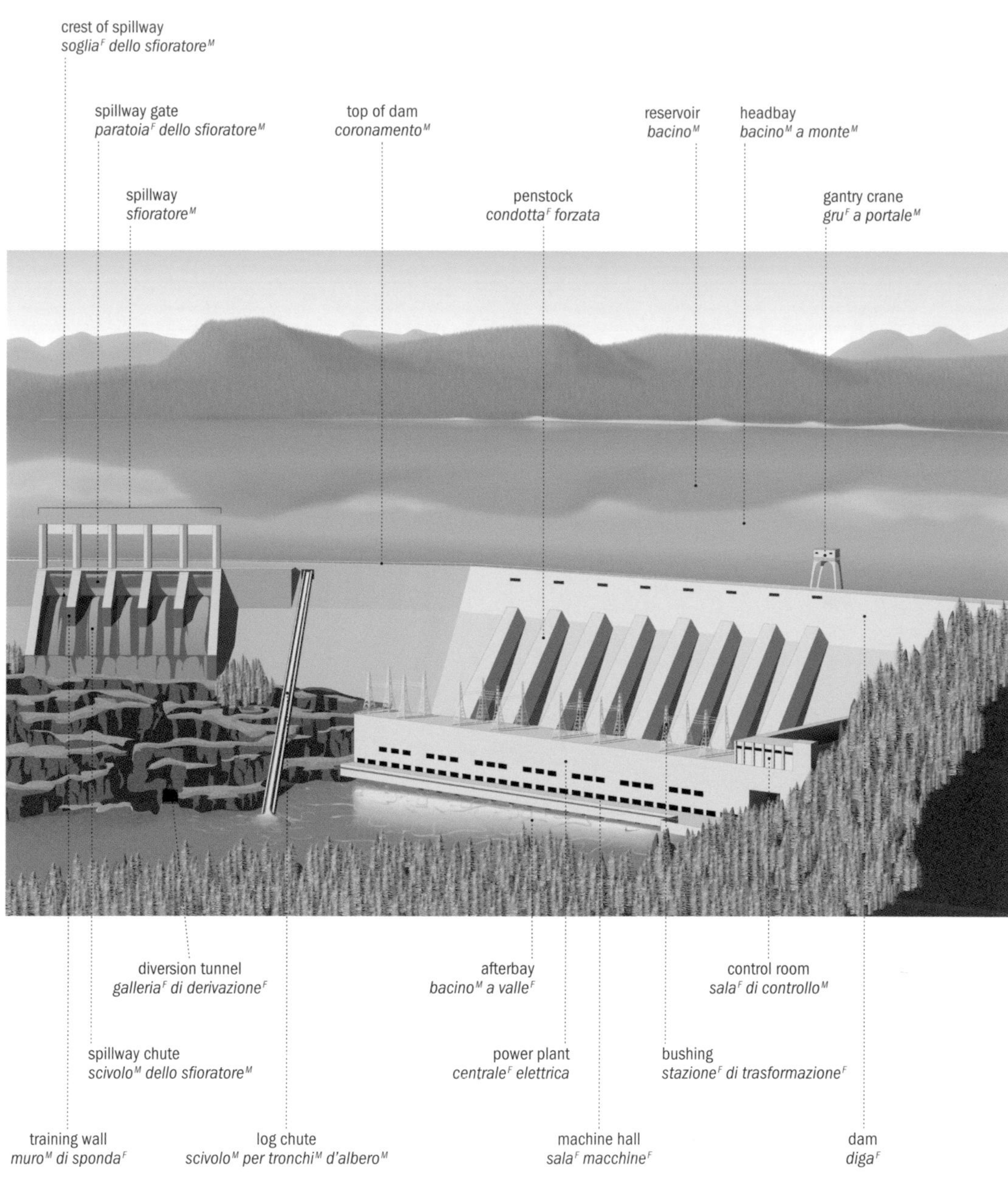

cross section of a hydroelectric power plant
sezione^F trasversale di una centrale^F idroelettrica

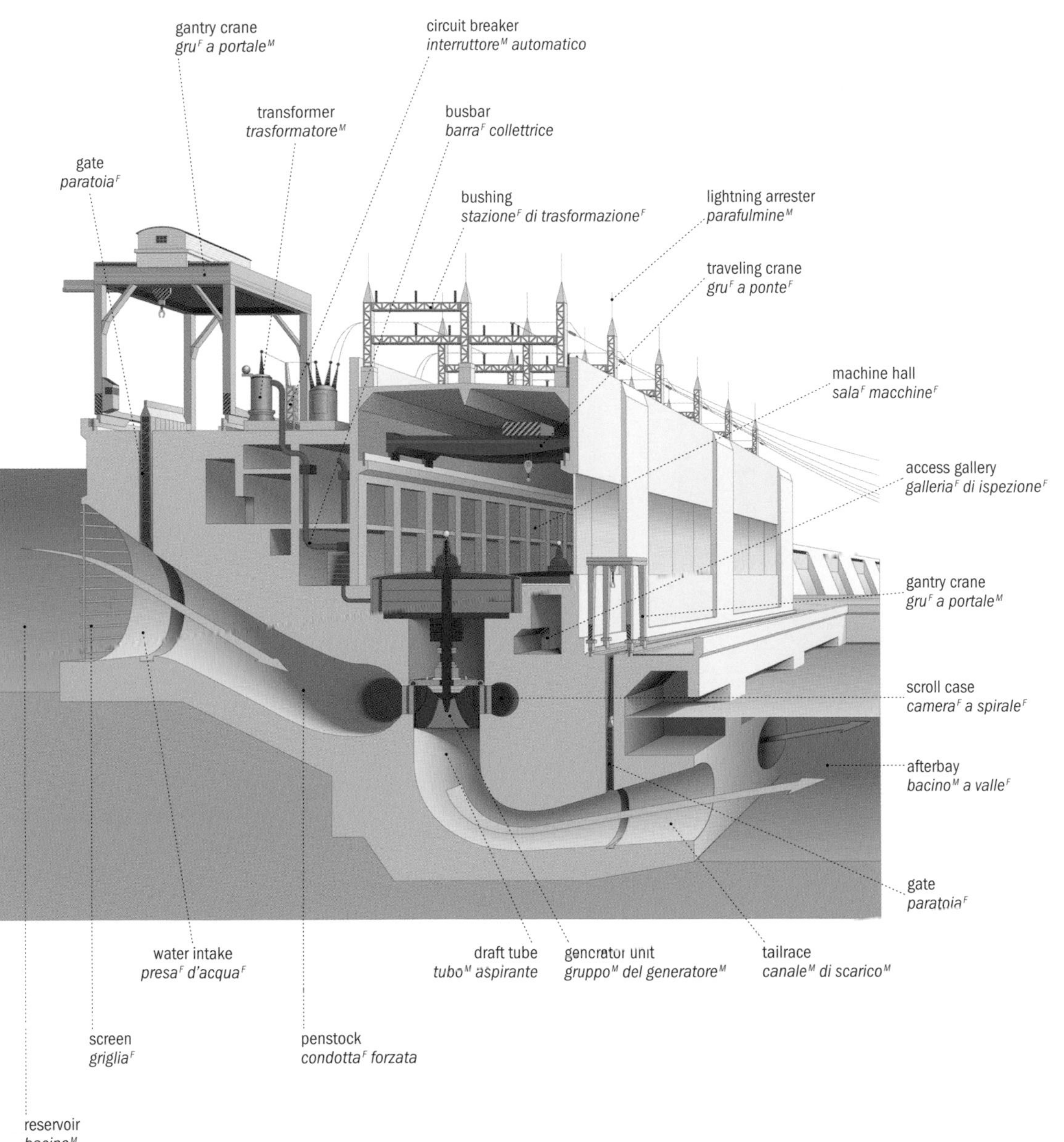

production of electricity from nuclear energy

produzione[F] di elettricità[F] da energia[F] nucleare

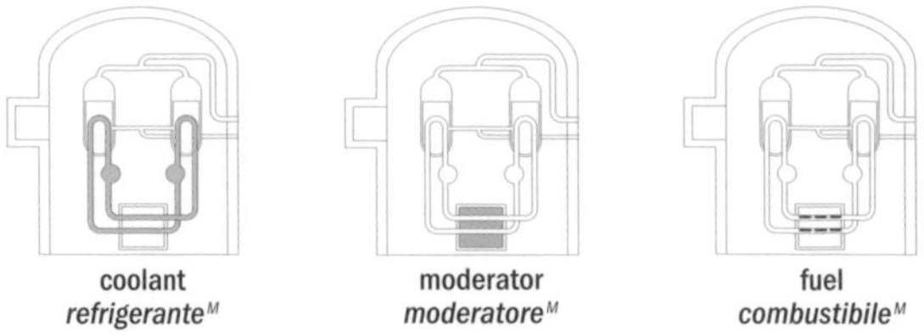

coolant
refrigerante[M]
moderator
moderatore[M]
fuel
combustibile[M]

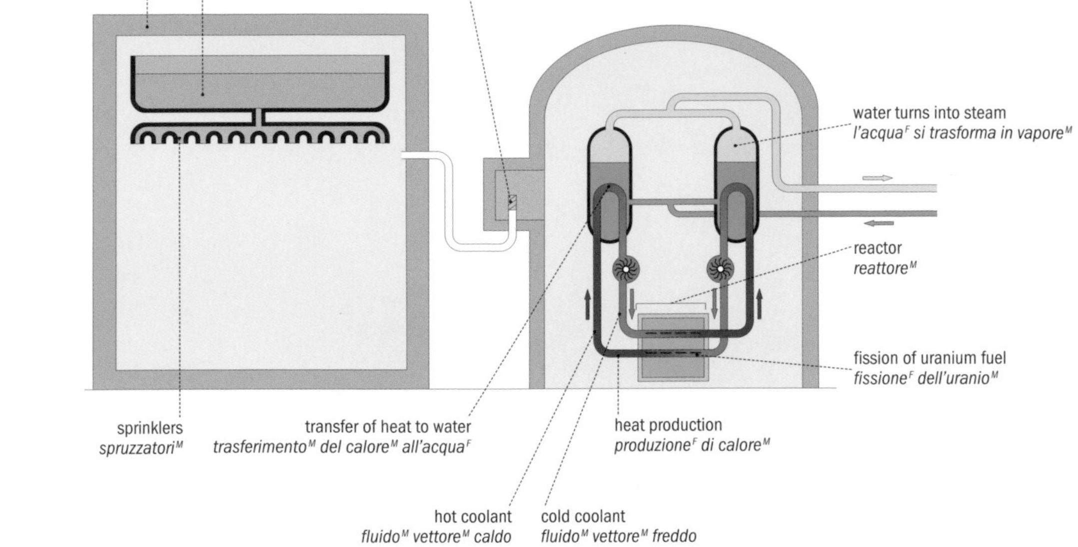

dousing water tank
serbatoio[M] dell'acqua[F] di raffreddamento[M]
containment building
contenitore[M] in calcestruzzo[M]
safety valve
valvola[F] di sicurezza[F]
water turns into steam
l'acqua[F] si trasforma in vapore[M]
reactor
reattore[M]
fission of uranium fuel
fissione[F] dell'uranio[M]
sprinklers
spruzzatori[M]
transfer of heat to water
trasferimento[M] del calore[M] all'acqua[F]
heat production
produzione[F] di calore[M]
hot coolant
fluido[M] vettore[M] caldo
cold coolant
fluido[M] vettore[M] freddo

production of electricity by the generator
produzione[F] di elettricità[F] da alternatore[M]
steam pressure drives turbine
la pressione[F] del vapore[M] aziona la turbina[F]
turbine shaft turns generator
l'albero[M] della turbina[F] fa ruotare il generatore[M]
electricity transmission
trasmissione[F] dell'elettricità[F]
voltage increase
aumento[M] di tensione[F]
water is pumped back into the steam generator
l'acqua[F] di condensazione[F] ritorna nel generatore[M] di vapore[M]
condensation of steam into water
il vapore[M] condensa in acqua[F]
water cools the used steam
l'acqua[F] raffredda il vapore[M] utilizzato

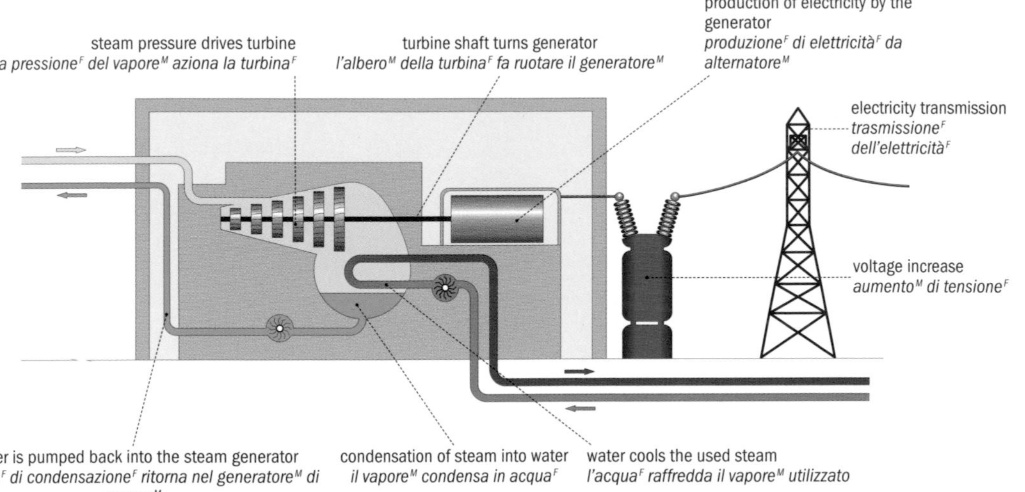

fuel bundle

elemento^{M} di combustibile^{M}

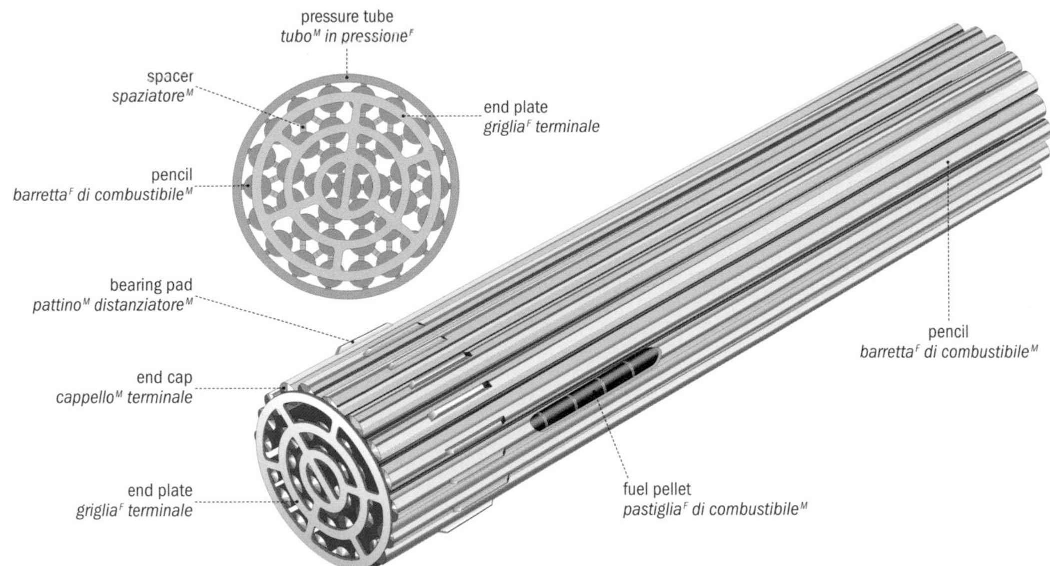

nuclear reactor

reattore^{M} nucleare

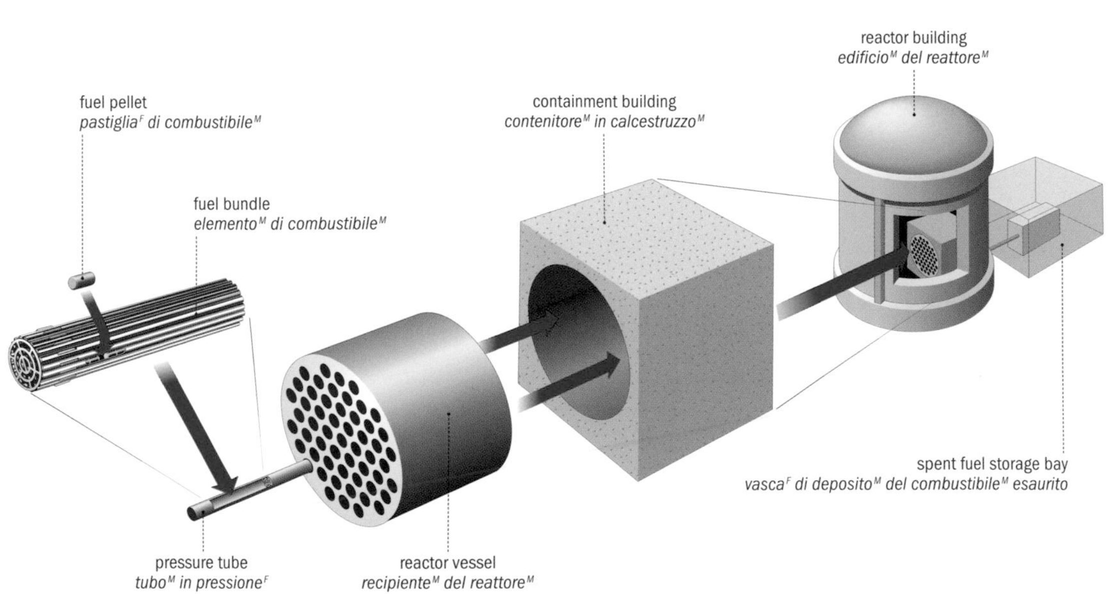

solar cell

cella^F solare

solar radiation
radiazione^F solare
antireflection coating
rivestimento^M antiriflettente
metallic contact grid
griglia^F di contatto^M metallica
negative region
zona^F negativa
negative contact
contatto^M negativo
positive/negative junction
giunzione^F positivo-negativa
positive region
zona^F positiva
positive contact
contatto^M positivo

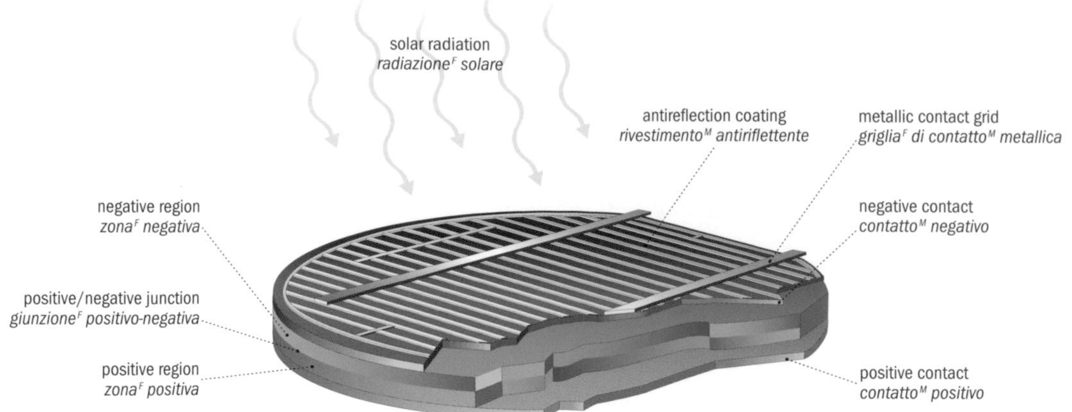

flat-plate solar collector

collettore^M solare piatto

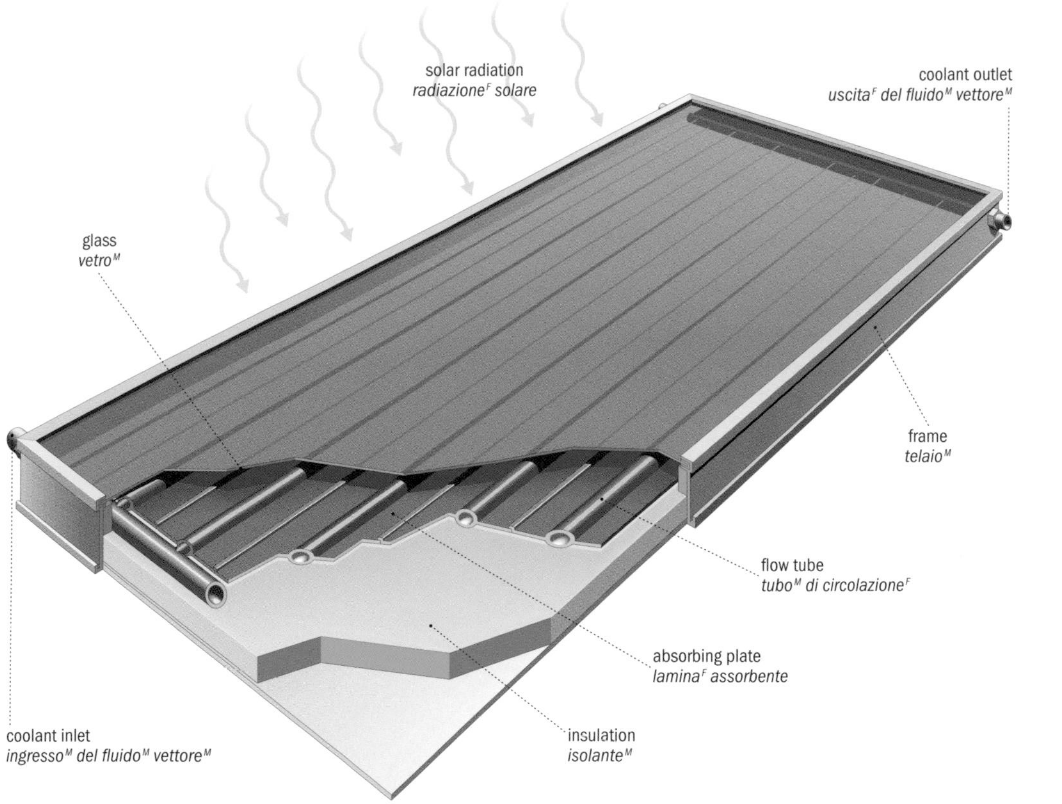

solar radiation
radiazione^F solare
coolant outlet
uscita^F del fluido^M vettore^M
glass
vetro^M
frame
telaio^M
flow tube
tubo^M di circolazione^F
absorbing plate
lamina^F assorbente
coolant inlet
ingresso^M del fluido^M vettore^M
insulation
isolante^M

solar-cell system

sistema[M] a celle[F] solari

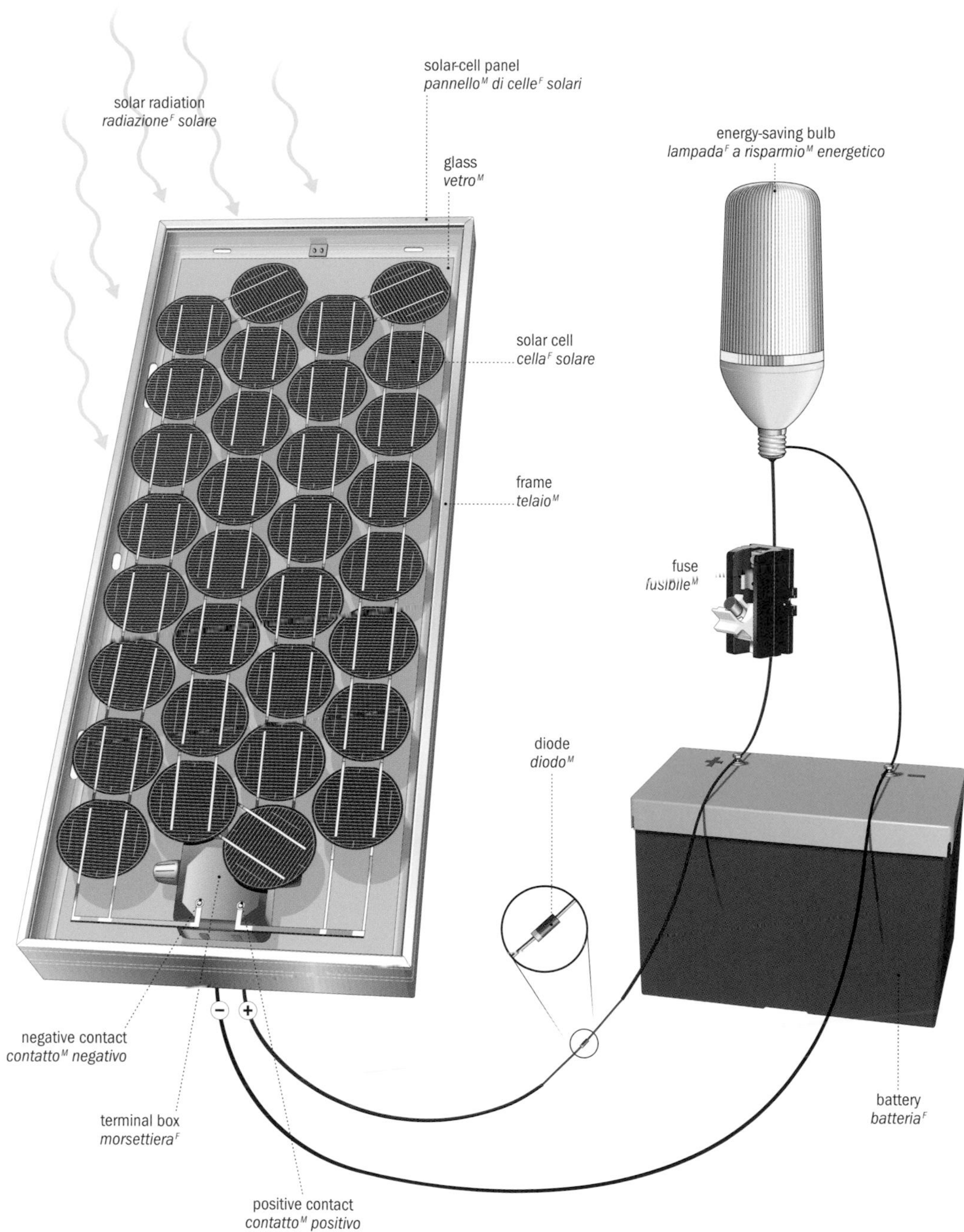

windmill

mulino[M] a vento[M]

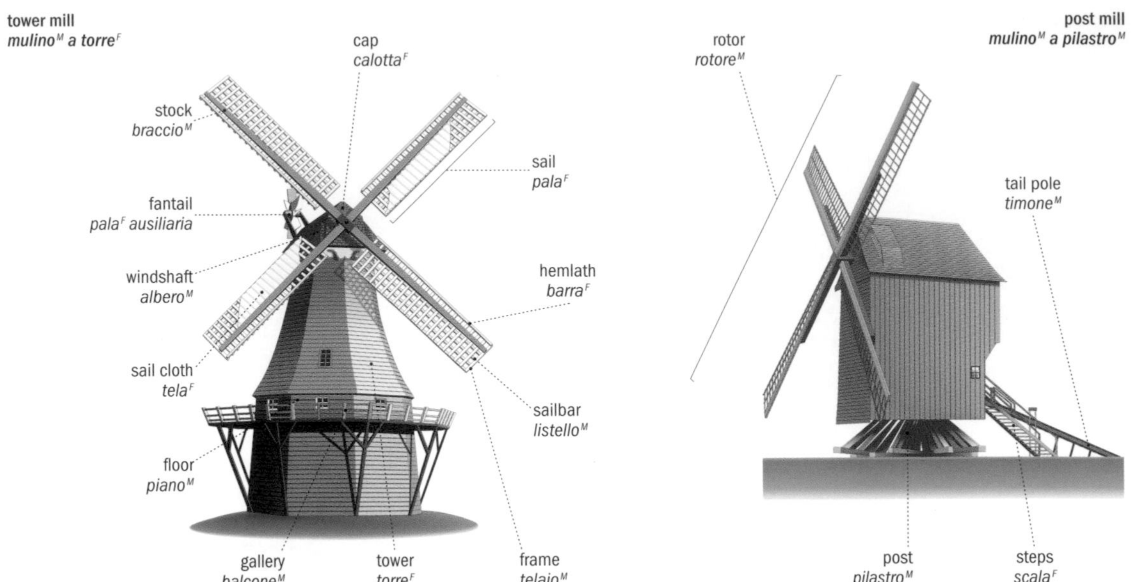

wind turbines and electricity production

turbine[F] eoliche e produzione[F] di elettricità[F]

vertical-axis wind turbine
turbina[F] ad asse[M] verticale

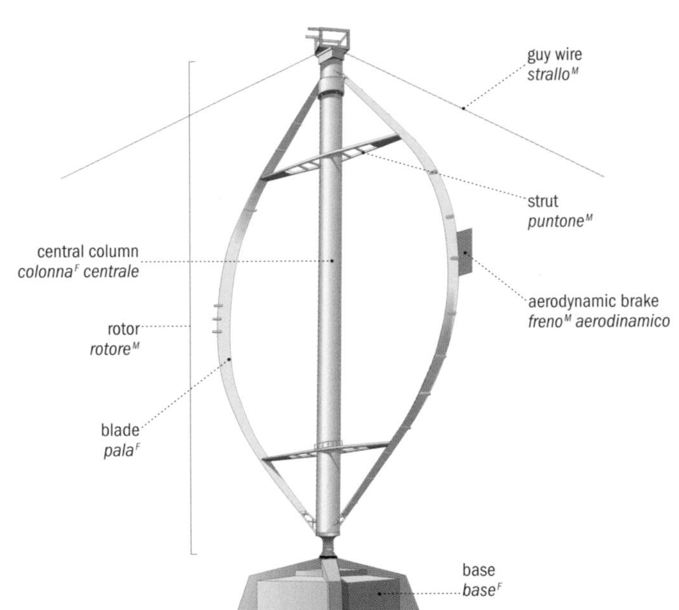

horizontal-axis wind turbine
turbina[F] eolica ad asse[M] orizzontale

nacelle cross-section
sezione[F] trasversale di una navicella[F]

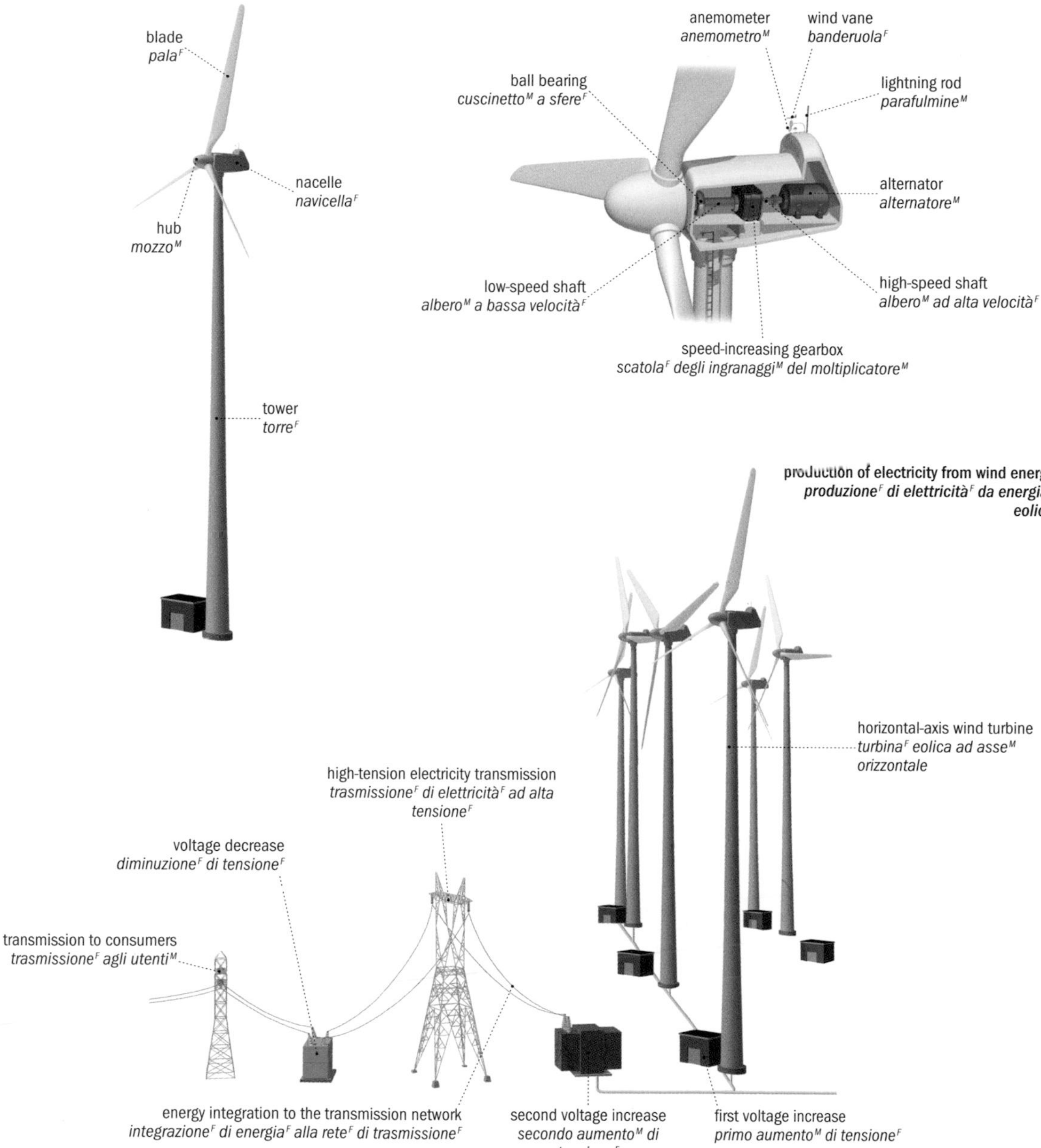

matter

materia[F]

atom
atomo[M]

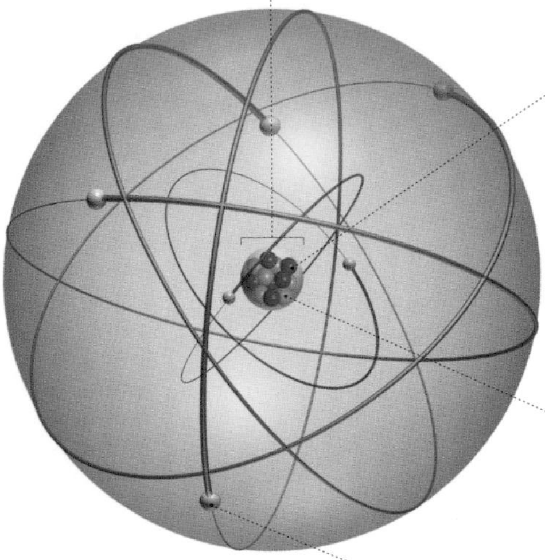

nucleus
nucleo[M]

neutron
neutrone[M]

proton
protone[M]

electron
elettrone[M]

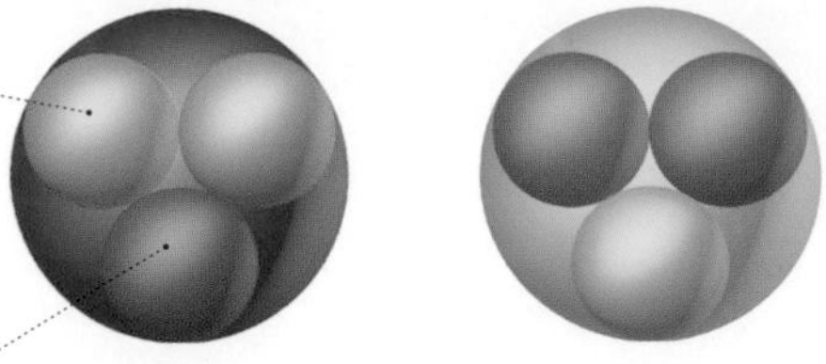

d quark
quark[M] d

u quark
quark[M] u

neutron
neutrone[M]

proton
protone[M]

molecule
molecola[F]

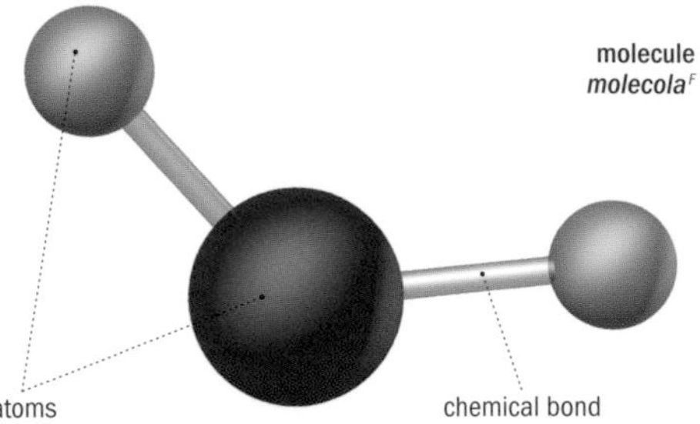

atoms
atomi[M]

chemical bond
legame[M] chimico

states of matter
stati[M] della materia[F]

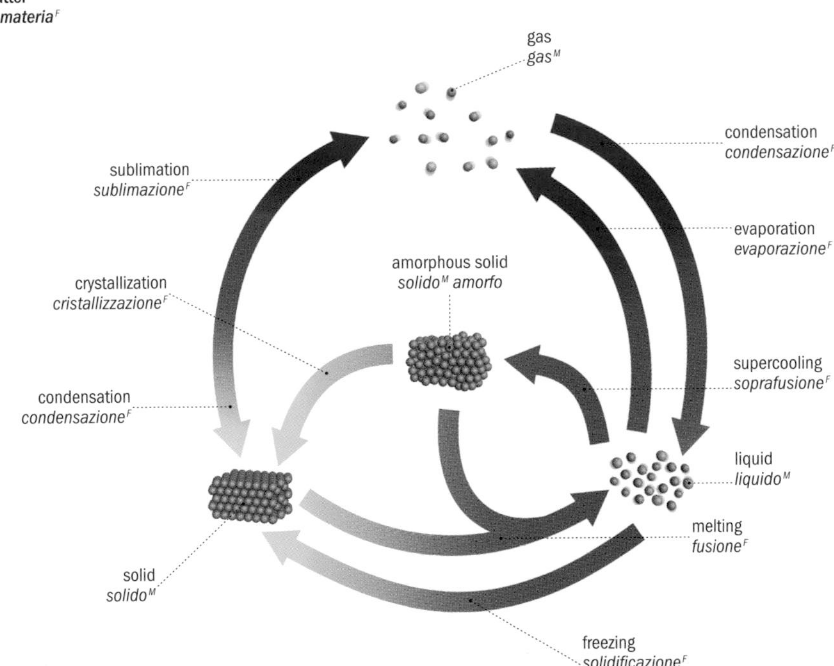

SCIENCE

nuclear fission
fissione^F nucleare

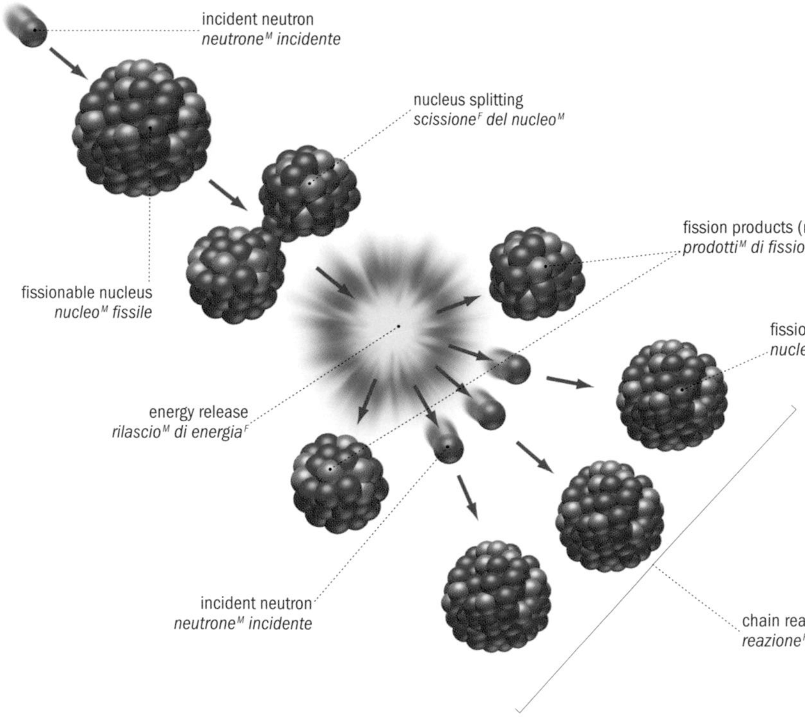

incident neutron
neutrone^M incidente
nucleus splitting
scissione^F del nucleo^M
fission products (radioactive nuclei)
prodotti^M di fissione^F (nuclei^M radioattivi)
fissionable nucleus
nucleo^M fissile
fissionable nucleus
nucleo^M fissile
energy release
rilascio^M di energia^F
incident neutron
neutrone^M incidente
chain reaction
reazione^F a catena^F

heat transfer
trasferimento^M di calore^M

convection
convezione^F
vapor
vapore^M
liquid
liquido^M
radiation
radiazione^F
convection current
corrente^F di convezione^F
solid
solido^M
conduction
conduzione^F
flame
fiamma^F

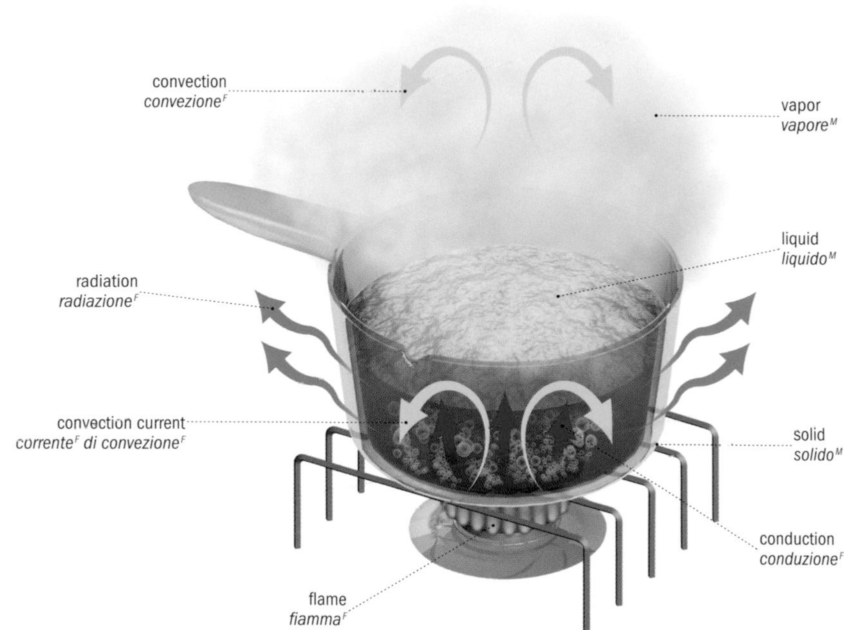

magnetism

magnetismo[M]

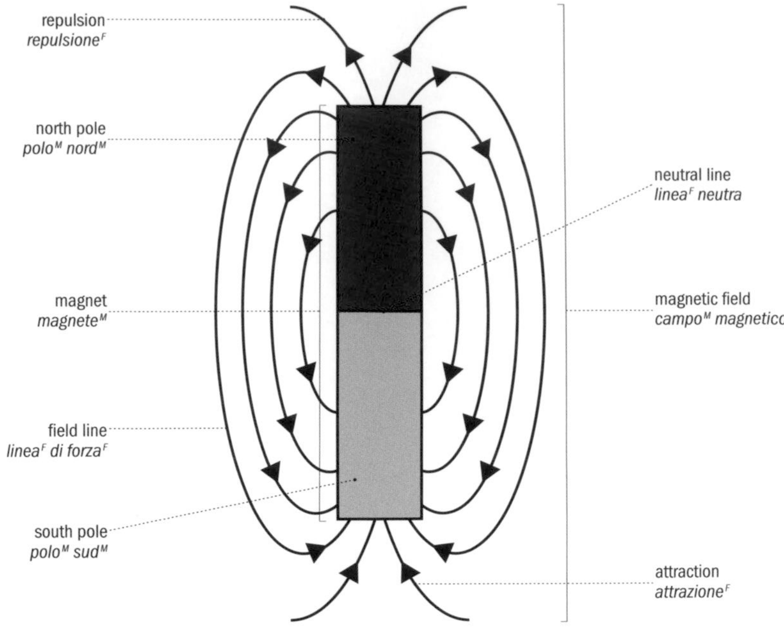

parallel electrical circuit

circuito[M] elettrico parallelo

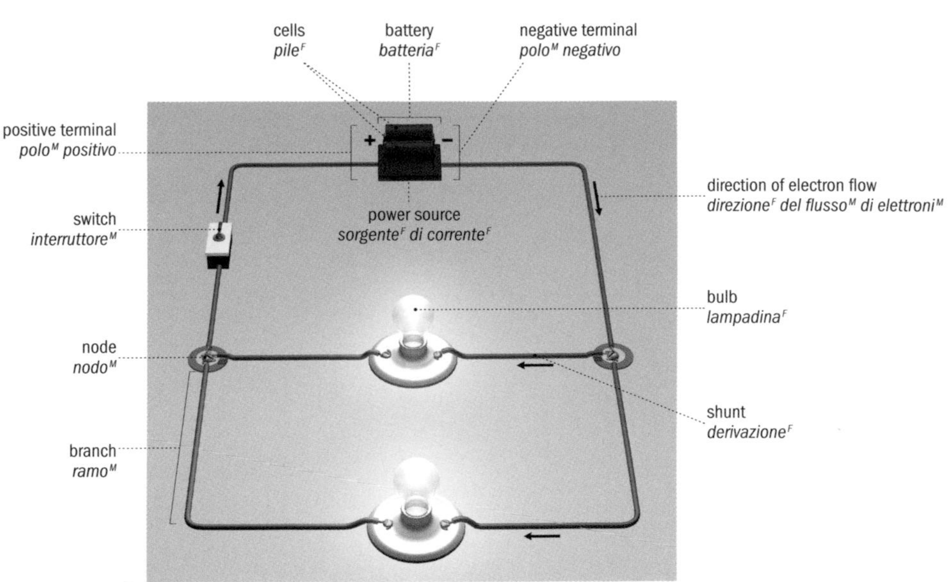

dry cells
pile[F] a secco[M]

carbon-zinc cell
pila[F] a carbone[M]-zinco[M]

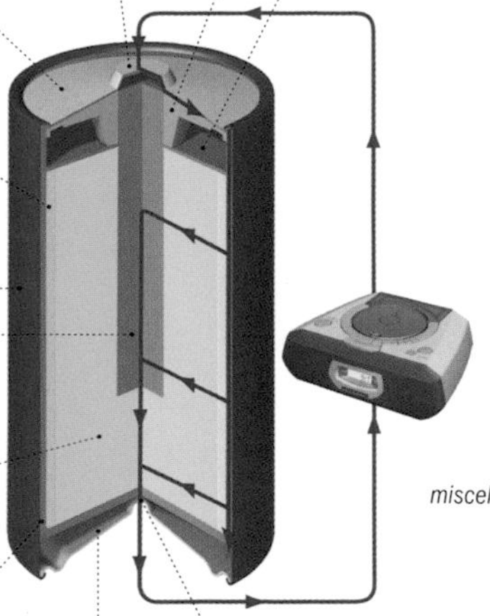

sealing plug
tappo[M] di isolamento[M]
positive terminal
polo[M] positivo
washer
rondella[F]
top cap
coperchio[M] superiore
electrolytic separator
separatore[M] elettrolitico
jacket
rivestimento[M]
carbon rod (cathode)
bastoncino[M] di carbone[M] (catodo[M])
depolarizing mix
miscela[F] di sostanze[F] depolarizzanti
zinc can (anode)
involucro[M] di zinco[M] (anodo[M])
bottom cap
coperchio[M] inferiore
negative terminal
polo[M] negativo

alkaline manganese-zinc cell
pila[F] alcalina a manganese[M]-zinco[M]

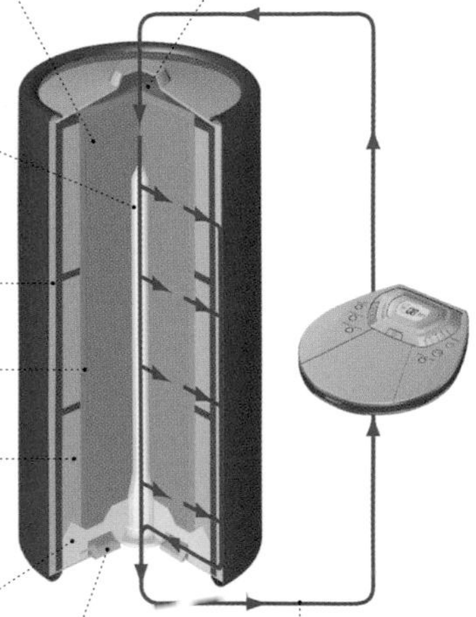

zinc-electrolyte mix (anode)
miscela[F] di zinco[M] ed elettroliti[M] (anodo[M])
sealing material
materiale[M] isolante
electron collector
collettore[M] di elettroni[M]
steel casing
corpo[M] d'acciaio[M]
separator
separatore[M]
manganese mix (cathode)
miscela[F] di manganese[M] (catodo[M])
sealing plug
tappo[M] di isolamento[M]
bottom cap
coperchio[M] inferiore
direction of electron flow
direzione[F] del flusso[M] di elettroni[M]

electronics
elettronica[F]

printed circuit board
scheda[F] del circuito[M] stampato

ceramic capacitor
condensatore[M] di ceramica[F]
electrolytic capacitors
condensatori[M] elettrolitici
plastic film capacitor
condensatore[M] a pellicola[F] plastica
packaged integrated circuit
circuito[M] integrato inscatolato
resistors
resistenze[F]
printed circuit
circuito[M] stampato

packaged integrated circuit
circuito[M] integrato inscatolato

integrated circuit
circuito[M] integrato
lid
coperchio[M]
wire
filo[M]
dual-in-line package
scatola[F] a doppia linea[F] di connessione[F]
connection pin
spinotto[M] di connessione[F]

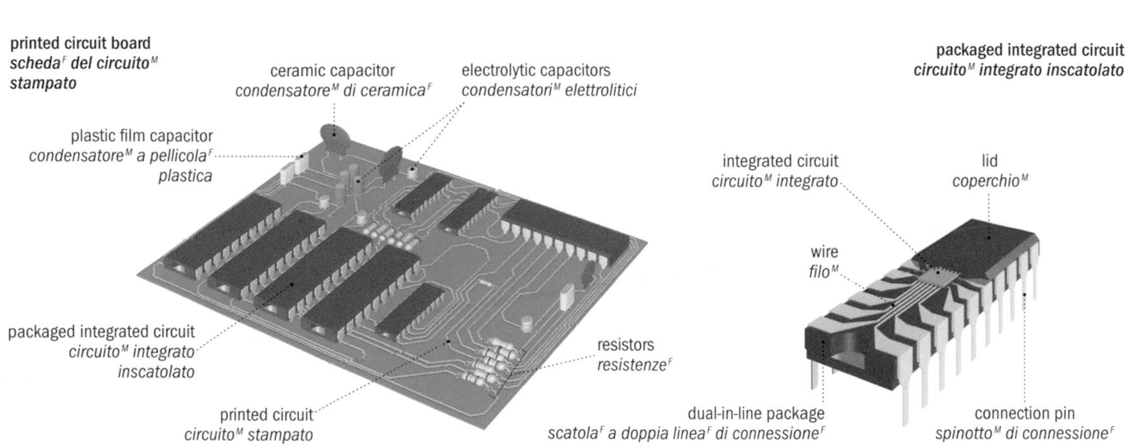

electromagnetic spectrum

spettro[M] elettromagnetico

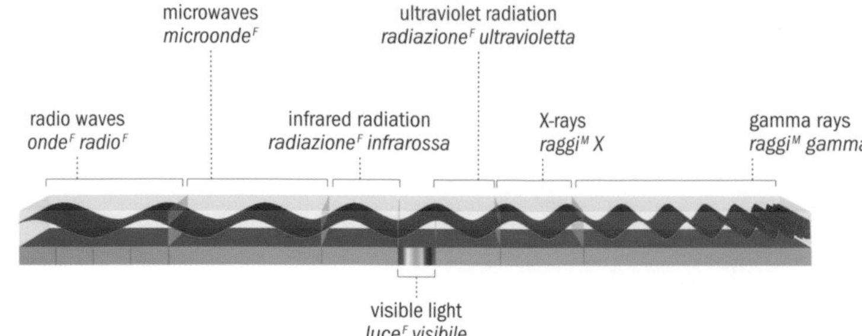

wave

onda[F]

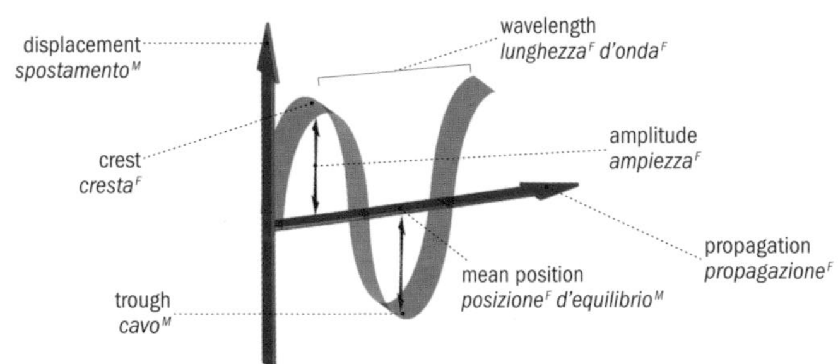

color synthesis

sintesi[F] dei colori[M]

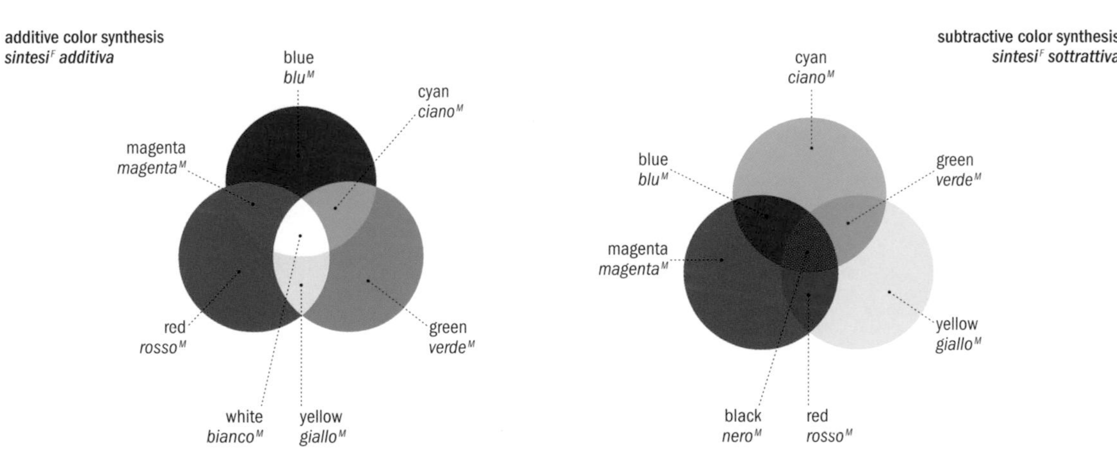

vision

vista[F]

normal vision
vista[F] normale

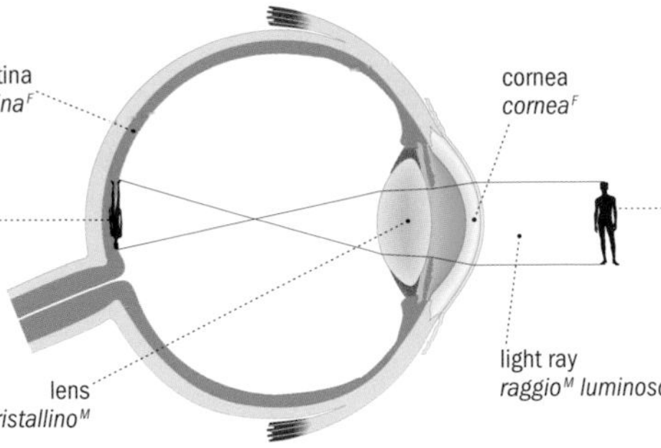

retina
retina[F]
focus
fuoco[M]
lens
cristallino[M]
cornea
cornea[F]
object
oggetto[M]
light ray
raggio[M] luminoso

vision defects and corrective lenses
difetti[M] della vista[F]

myopia
miopia[F]

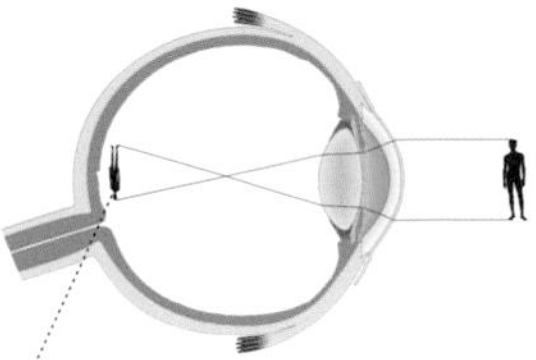

focus
fuoco[M]

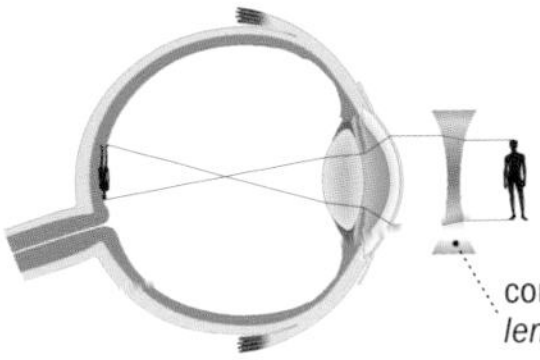

concave lens
lente[F] concava

hyperopia
ipermetropia[F]

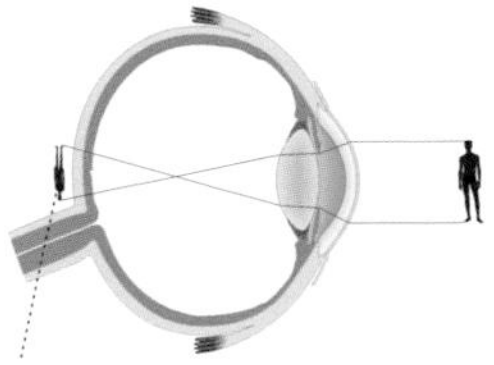

focus
fuoco[M]

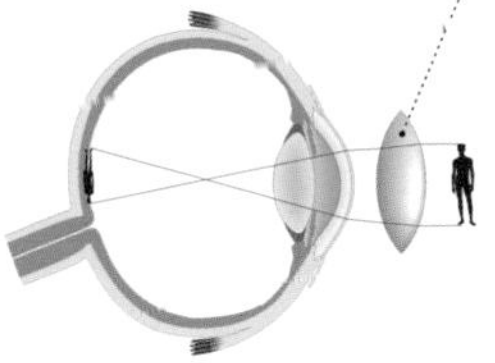

convex lens
lente[F] convessa

astigmatism
astigmatismo[M]

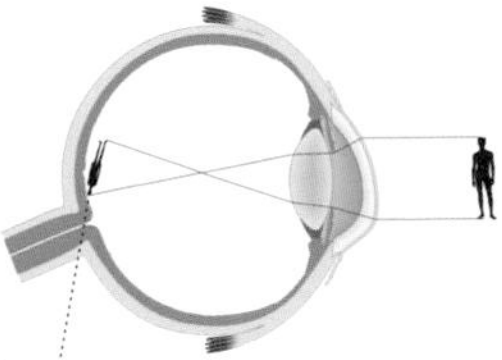

focus
fuoco[M]

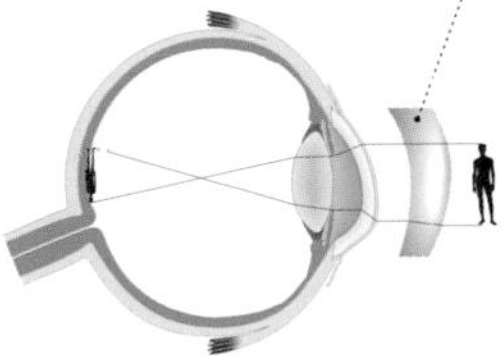

toric lens
lente[F] torica

lenses

lenti[F]

converging lenses
lenti[F] convergenti

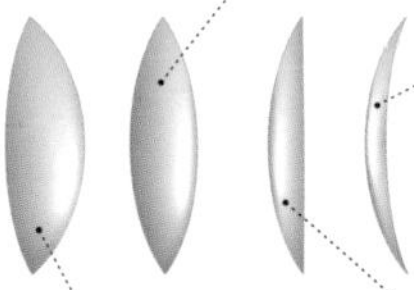

biconvex lens
lente[F] biconvessa
positive meniscus
menisco[M] convergente
convex lens
lente[F] convessa
plano-convex lens
lente[F] piano-convessa

diverging lenses
lenti[F] divergenti

plano-concave lens
lente[F] piano-concava
concave lens
lente[F] concava
biconcave lens
lente[F] biconcava
negative meniscus
menisco[M] divergente

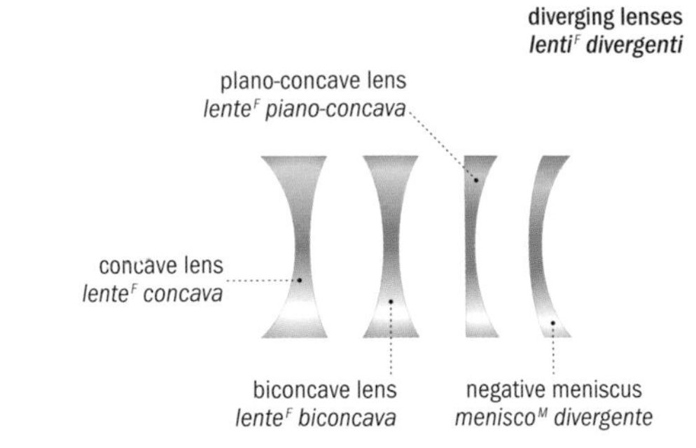

pulsed ruby laser

laser[M] a rubino[M] pulsato

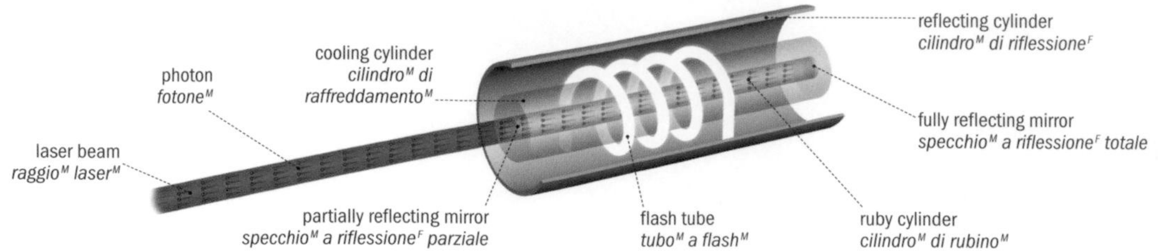

prism binoculars

binocolo[M] prismatico

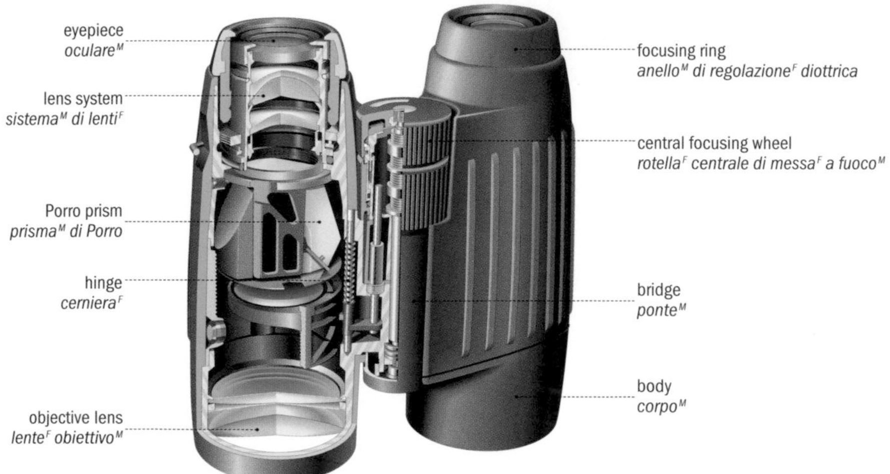

telescopic sight

cannocchiale[M] di mira[F]

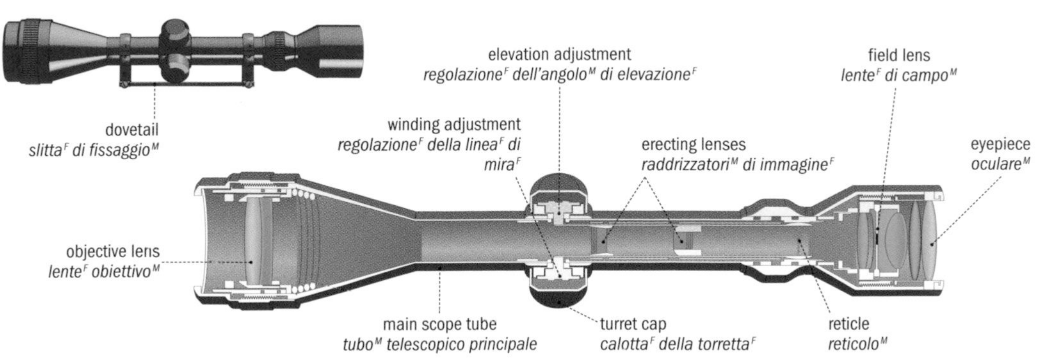

magnifying glass and microscopes

lente[F] di ingrandimento[M] e microscopi[M]

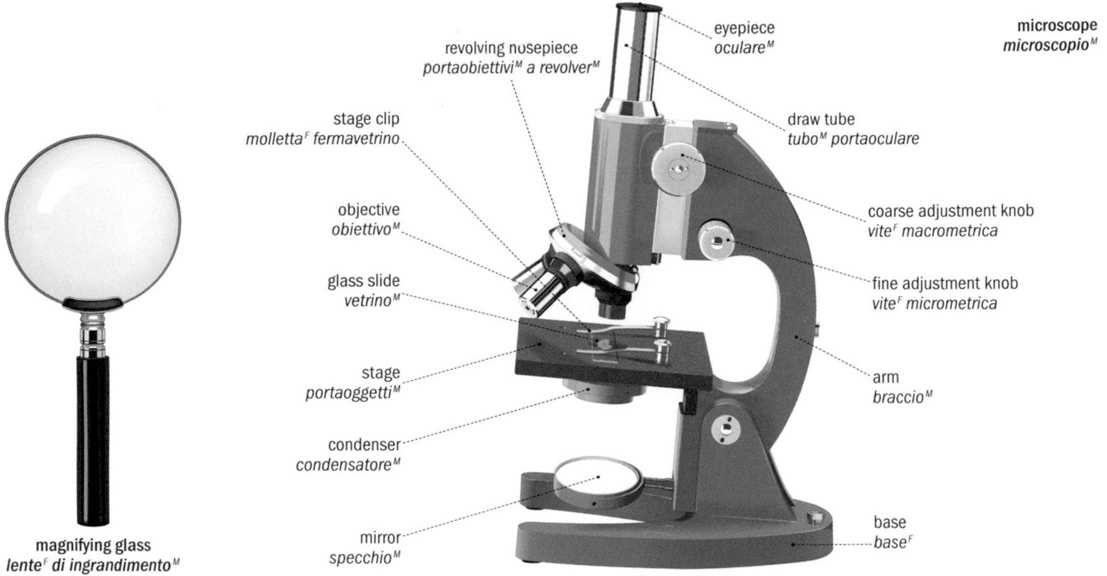

magnifying glass
lente[F] di ingrandimento[M]

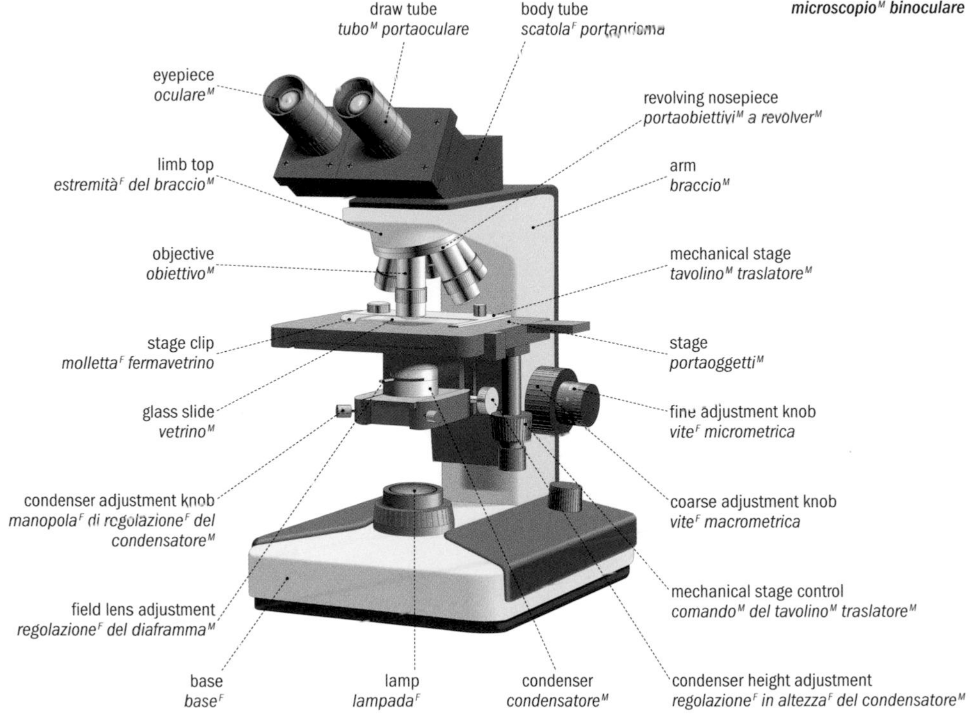

measurement of weight

misura[F] del peso[M]

beam balance
bilancia[F] di precisione[F]

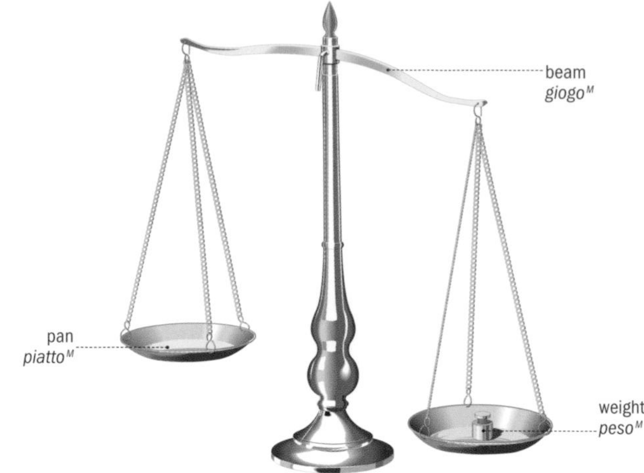

steelyard
stadera[F]

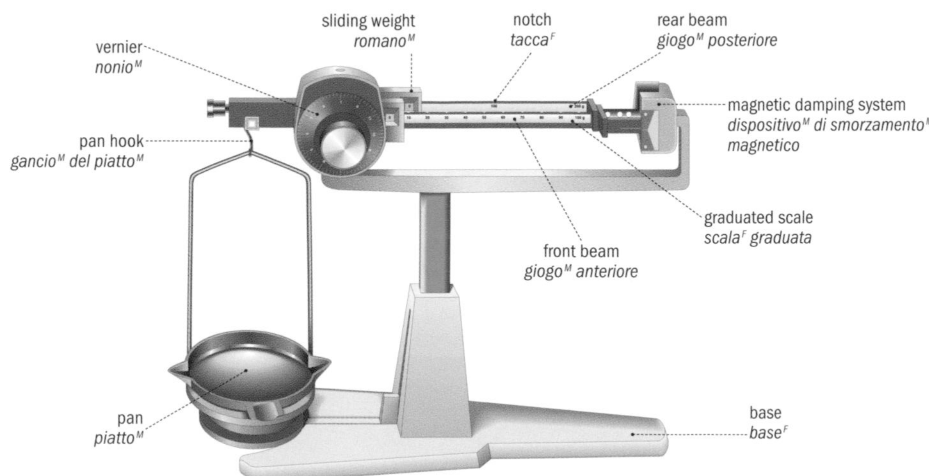

Roberval's balance
bilancia[F] a sospensione[F] inferiore

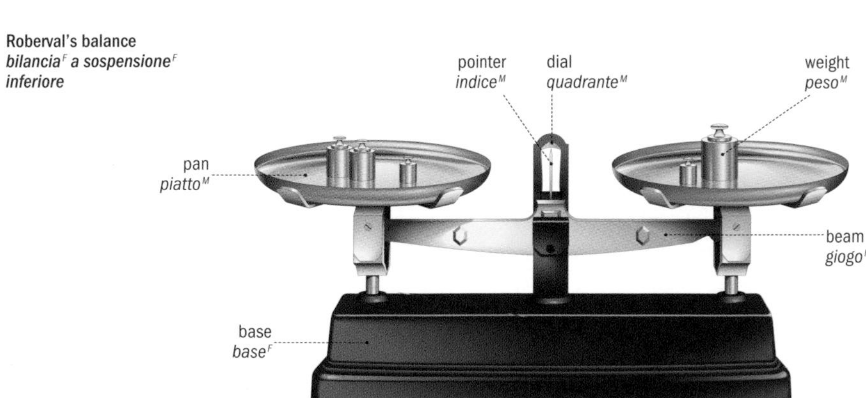

measurement of weight

spring balance
bilancia[F] a molla[F]

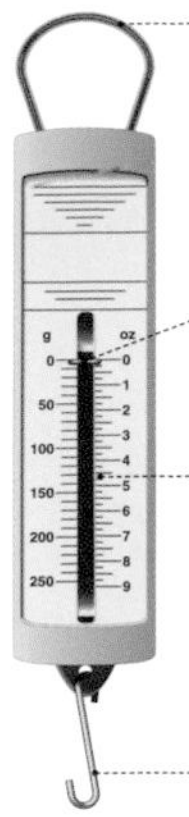

ring
anello[M]
pointer
indice[M]
graduated scale
scala[F] graduata
hook
gancio[M]

electronic scale
bilancia[F] elettronica

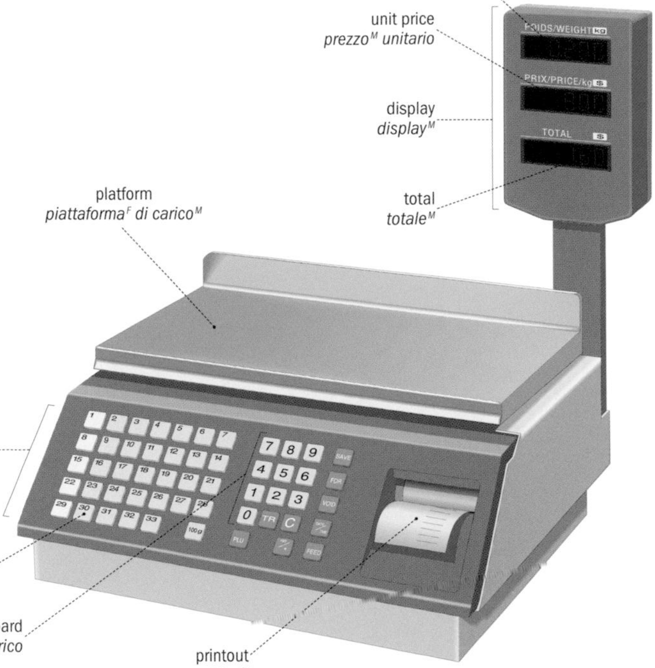

weight
peso[M]
unit price
prezzo[M] unitario
display
display[M]
total
totale[M]
platform
piattaforma[F] di carico[M]
function keys
tasti[M] funzione[F]
product code
codice[M] del prodotto[M]
numeric keyboard
tastierino[M] numerico
printout
scontrino[M]
PRIX/PRICE/kg
TOTAL

bathroom scale
bilancia[F] pesapersone

digital display
display[M] digitale
000
weighing platform
pedana[F]

analytical balance
bilancia[F] da analisi[F]

glass case
custodia[F] a pareti[F] di vetro[M]
access door
sportello[M]
pan
piatto[M]
4.4956 g
leveling screw
vite[F] di livello[M]

SCIENCE

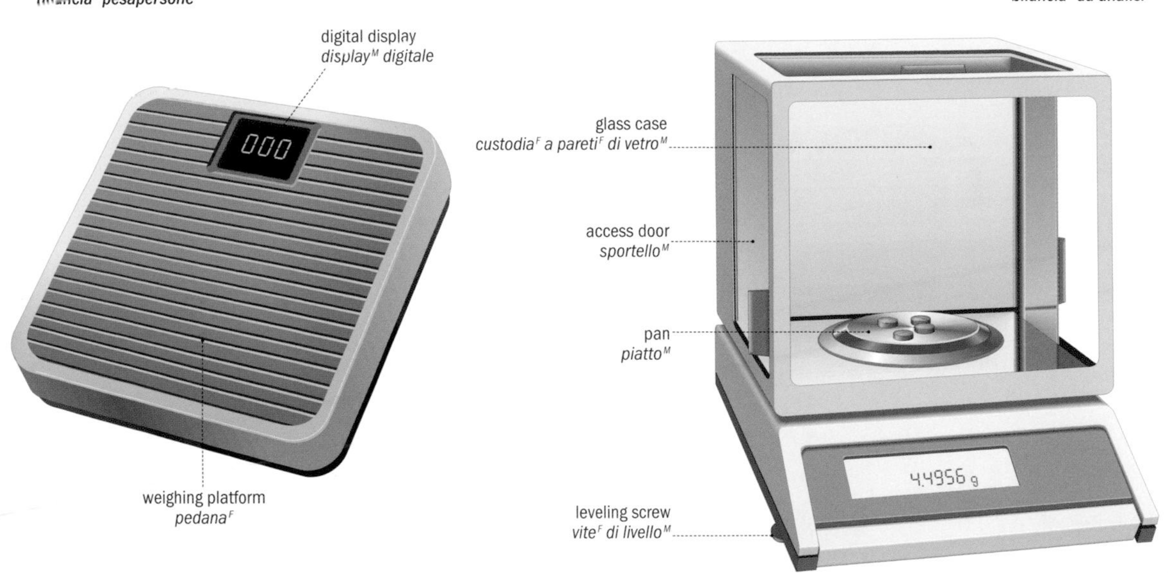

measurement of temperature

misura[F] della temperatura[F]

thermometer
termometro[M]

Fahrenheit scale
scala[F] Fahrenheit
Celsius scale
scala[F] Celsius
temperature measured in Fahrenheit
gradi[M] Fahrenheit
temperature measured in Celsius
gradi[M] Celsius
alcohol column
colonna[F] d'alcool[M]
alcohol bulb
bulbo[M] d'alcool[M]
120
110
100
90
80
70
60
50
40
32
20
10
0
10
20
30
40
50
F
C

clinical thermometer
termometro[M] clinico

capillary tube
tubo[M] capillare
expansion chamber
camera[F] di espansione[F]
scale
scala[F] graduata
column of mercury
colonna[F] di mercurio[M]
stem
asta[F]
constriction
strozzatura[F]
mercury bulb
bulbo[M] di mercurio[M]

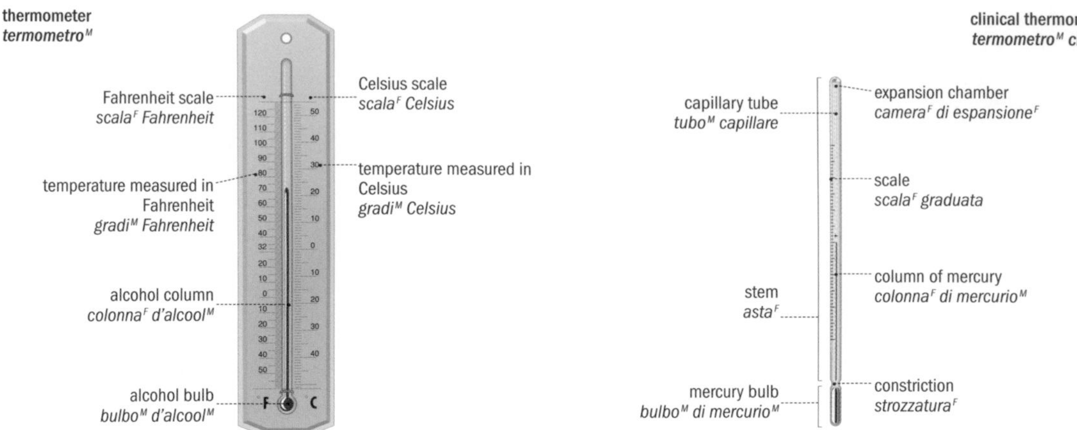

measurement of time

misura[F] del tempo[M]

stopwatch
cronometro[M]

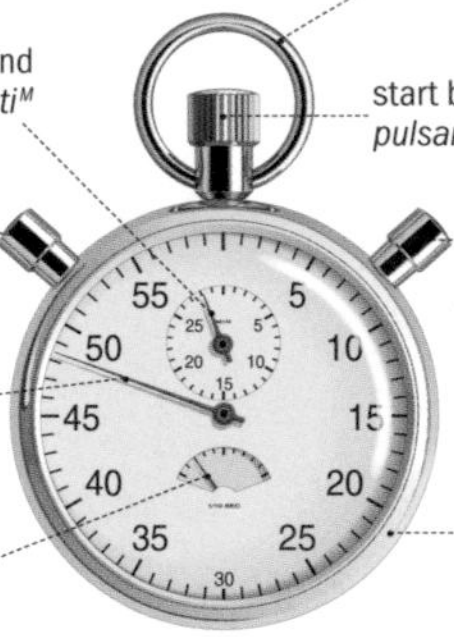

ring
anello[M]
minute hand
lancetta[F] dei minuti[M]
start button
pulsante[M] di partenza[F]
reset button
pulsante[M] di azzeramento[M]
stop button
pulsante[M] di arresto[M]
second hand
lancetta[F] dei secondi[M]
1/10 second hand
lancetta[F] dei decimi[M] di secondo[M]
case
cassa[F]

analog watch
orologio[M] analogico

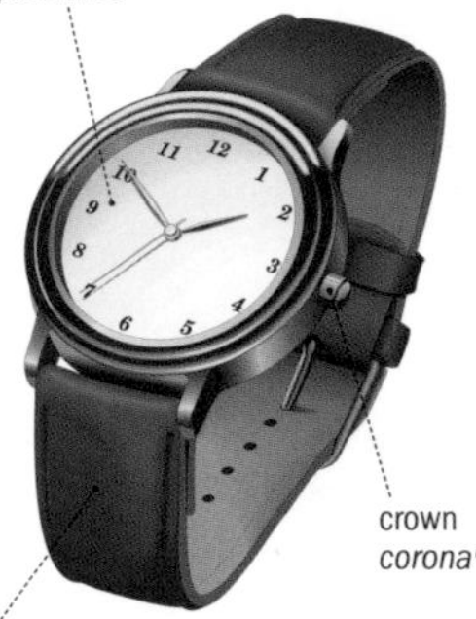

dial
quadrante[M]
crown
corona[F]
strap
cinturino[M]

digital watch
orologio[M] digitale

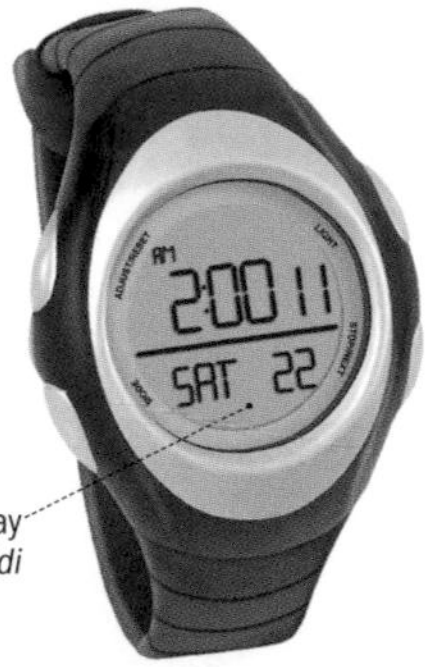

2:00 11
SAT 22
liquid crystal display
quadrante[M] a cristalli[M] liquidi

sundial
meridiana[F]

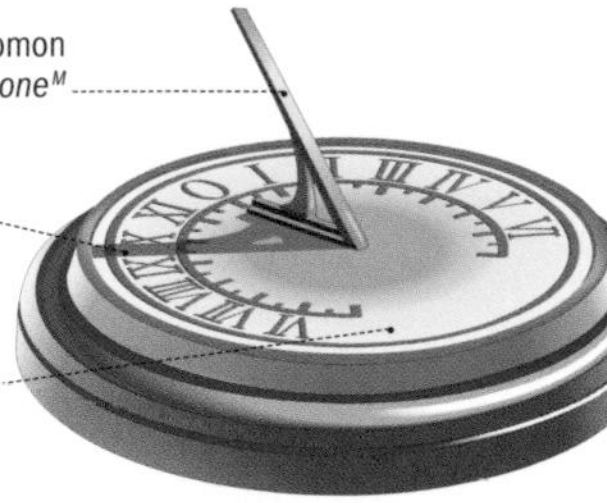

gnomon
gnomone[M]
shadow
ombra[F]
dial
quadrante[M]

SCIENCE

measurement of length

misura^F della lunghezza^F

ruler
righello^M

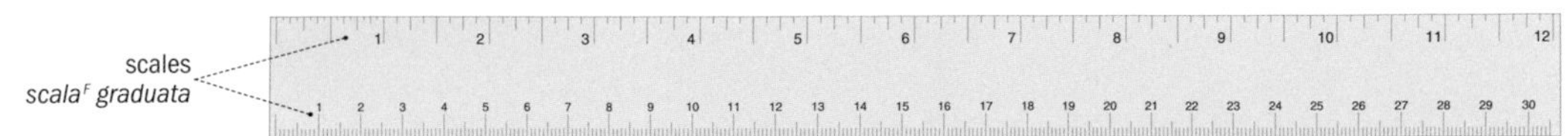

measurement of thickness

misura^F dello spessore^M

vernier caliper
calibro^M a corsoio^M con nonio^M

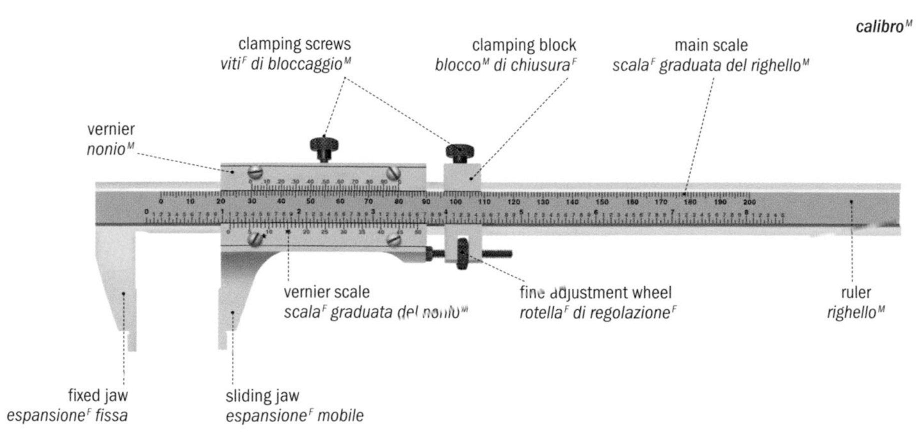

micrometer caliper
micrometro^M a vite^F

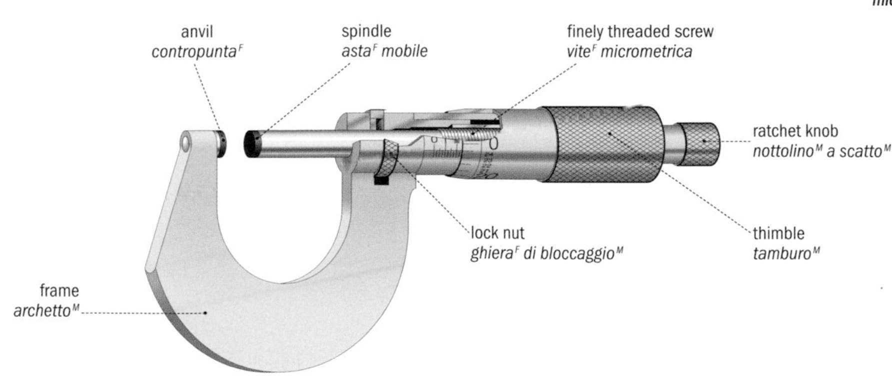

SCIENCE

international system of units

sistema[M] internazionale di unità[F] di misura[F]

unit of frequency
unità[F] di misura[F] della frequenza[F]

Hz

hertz
hertz[M]

unit of electric potential difference
unità[F] di misura[F] della differenza[F] di potenziale[M] elettrico

V

volt
volt[M]

unit of electric charge
unità[F] di misura[F] della carica[F] elettrica

C

coulomb
coulomb[M]

unit of energy
unità[F] di misura[F] dell'energia[F]

J

joule
joule[M]

unit of power
unità[F] di misura[F] della potenza[F] elettrica

W

watt
watt[M]

unit of force
unità[F] di misura[F] della forza[F]

N

newton
newton[M]

unit of electric resistance
unità[F] di misura[F] della resistenza[F] elettrica

Ω

ohm
ohm[M]

unit of electric current
unità[F] di misura[F] della corrente[F] elettrica

A

ampere
ampere[M]

unit of length
unità[F] di misura[F] della lunghezza[F]

m

meter
metro[M]

unit of mass
unità[F] di misura[F] della massa[F]

kg

kilogram
kilogrammo[M]

unit of temperature
unità[F] di misura[F] della temperatura[F]

°C

degree Celsius
grado[M] Celsius

unit of thermodynamic temperature
unità[F] di misura[F] della temperatura[F] termodinamica

K

kelvin
kelvin[M]

unit of amount of substance
unità[F] di misura[F] della quantità[F] di sostanza[F]

mol

mole
mole[F]

unit of radioactivity
unità[F] di misura[F] della radioattività[F]

Bq

becquerel
becquerel[M]

unit of pressure
unità[F] di misura[F] della pressione[F]

Pa

pascal
pascal[M]

unit of luminous intensity
unità[F] di misura[F] dell'intensità[F] luminosa

cd

candela
candela[F]

biology

biologia[F]

♂

male
maschile

female
femminile

Rh+

blood factor RH positive
fattore[M] Rh positivo

Rh-

blood factor RH negative
fattore[M] Rh negativo

death
morte[F]

*

birth
nascita[F]

mathematics

matematica[F]

$-$
minus/negative
sottrazione[F]

$+$
plus/positive
addizione[F]

X
multiplied by
moltiplicazione[F]

$\div$
divided by
divisione[F]

$=$
equals
uguale a

$\neq$
is not equal to
diverso da

$\approx$
is approximately equal to
approssimativamente uguale a

$\sim$
is equivalent to
equivalente a

$\equiv$
is identical to
coincide con

$\not\equiv$
is not identical to
non coincide con

$\pm$
plus or minus
più o meno

$\leqslant$
is less than or equal to
minore o uguale a

$>$
is greater than
maggiore di

$\geqslant$
is greater than or equal to
maggiore o uguale a

$<$
is less than
minore di

$\varnothing$
empty set
insieme[M] *vuoto*

$\cup$
union of two sets
unione[F]

$\cap$
intersection of two sets
intersezione[F]

$\subseteq$
is included in/is a subset of
contenuto in

%
percent
percento[M]

$\in$
is an element of
appartiene a

$\notin$
is not an element of
non appartiene a

$\sum$
sum
sommatoria[F]

$\sqrt{\ }$
square root of
radice[F] *quadrata di*

$1/2$
fraction
frazione[F]

∞
infinity
infinito[M]

$\int$
integral
integrale[M]

!
factorial
fattoriale[M]

Roman numerals

numeri*[M] *romani

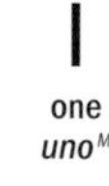
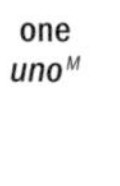
one
uno[M]

five
cinque[M]

ten
dieci[M]

L
fifty
cinquanta[M]

one hundred
cento[M]

five hundred
cinquecento[M]

M
one thousand
mille[M]

SCIENCE

geometry

geometria[F]

°	'	"	π	⊥
degree *grado[M]*	**minute** *primo[M]*	**second** *secondo[M]*	**pi** *pi[M] greco*	**perpendicular** *perpendicolare*
‖	∦	∟		∠
is parallel to *parallelo a*	**is not parallel to** *non parallelo a*	**right angle** *angolo[M] retto*	**obtuse angle** *angolo[M] ottuso*	**acute angle** *angolo[M] acuto*

geometrical shapes

forme[F] geometriche

examples of angles
esempi[M] di angoli[M]

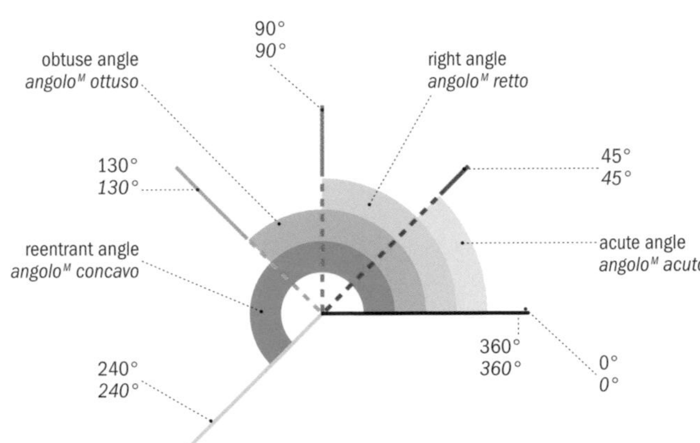

plane surfaces
superfici[F]

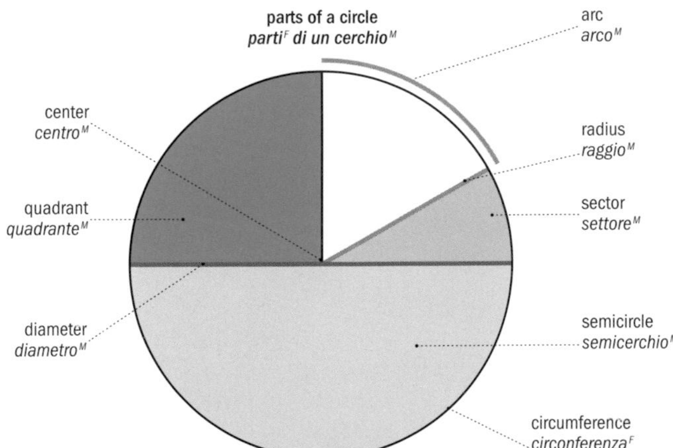

polygons
poligoni[M]

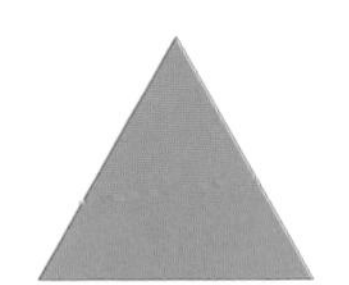

triangle
triangolo[M]

square
quadrato[M]

rectangle
rettangolo[M]

rhombus
rombo[M]

trapezoid
trapezio[M]

parallelogram
parallelogramma[M]

quadrilateral
quadrilatero[M]

regular pentagon
pentagono[M] *regolare*

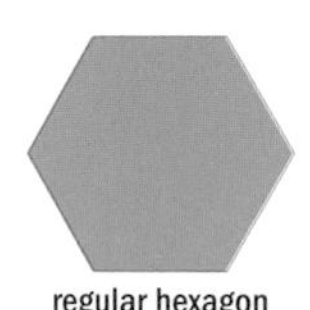

regular hexagon
esagono[M] *regolare*

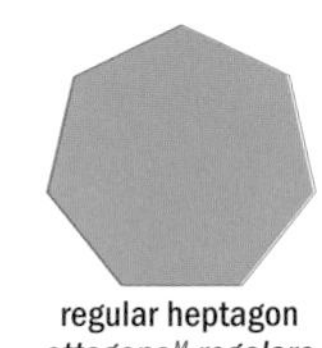

regular heptagon
ettagono[M] *regolare*

regular octagon
ottagono[M] *regolare*

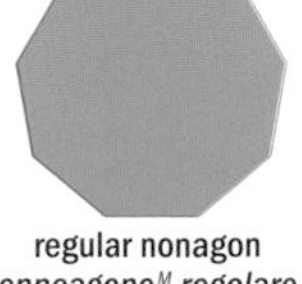

regular nonagon
enneagono[M] *regolare*

regular decagon
decagono[M] *regolare*

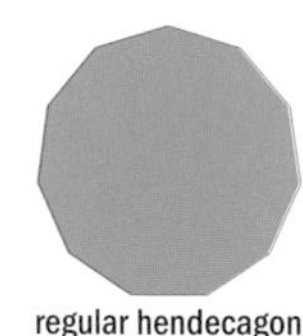

regular hendecagon
endecagono[M] *regolare*

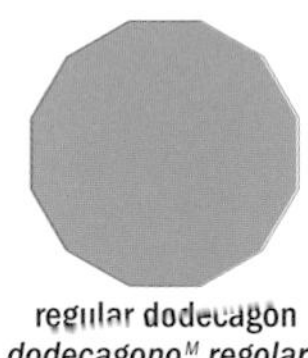

regular dodecagon
dodecagono[M] *regolare*

solids
solidi[M]

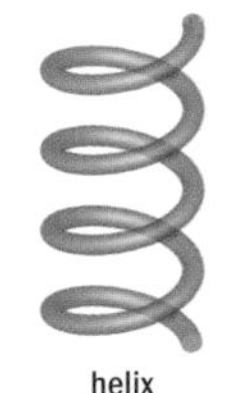

helix
elica[F]

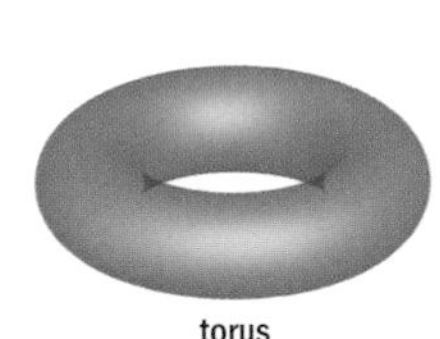

torus
toro[M]

hemisphere
semisfera[F]

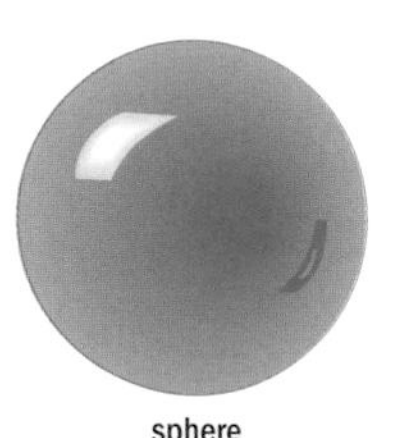

sphere
sfera[F]

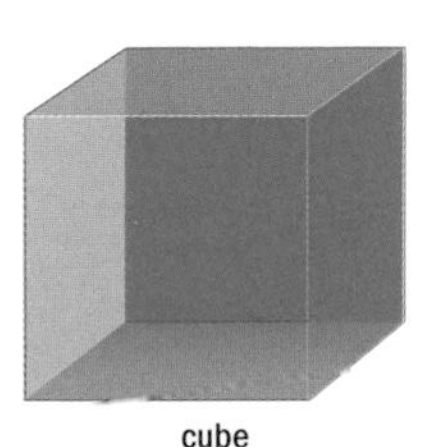

cube
cubo[M]

cone
cono[M]

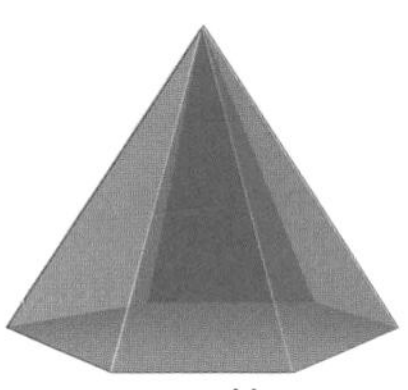

pyramid
piramide[F]

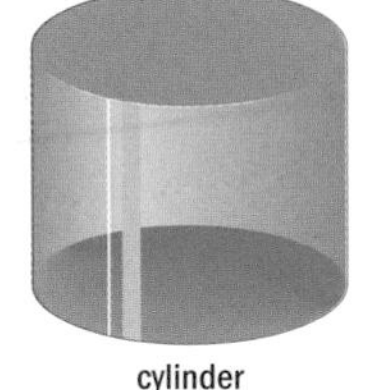

cylinder
cilindro[M]

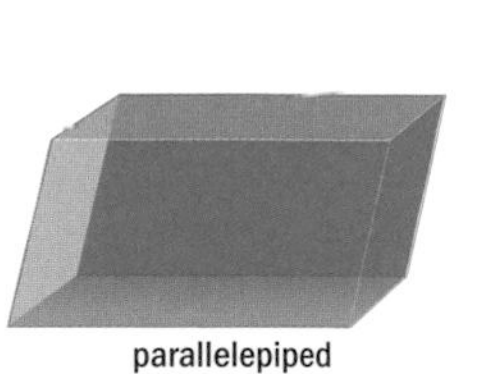

parallelepiped
parallelepipedo[M]

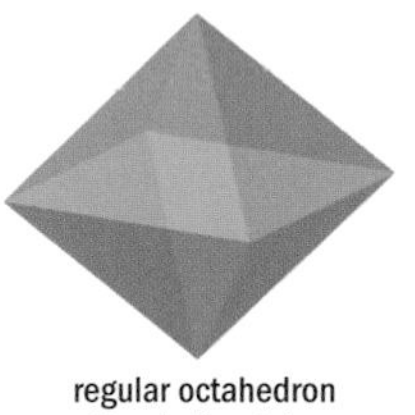

regular octahedron
ottaedro[M] *regolare*

agglomeration

conurbazione[F]

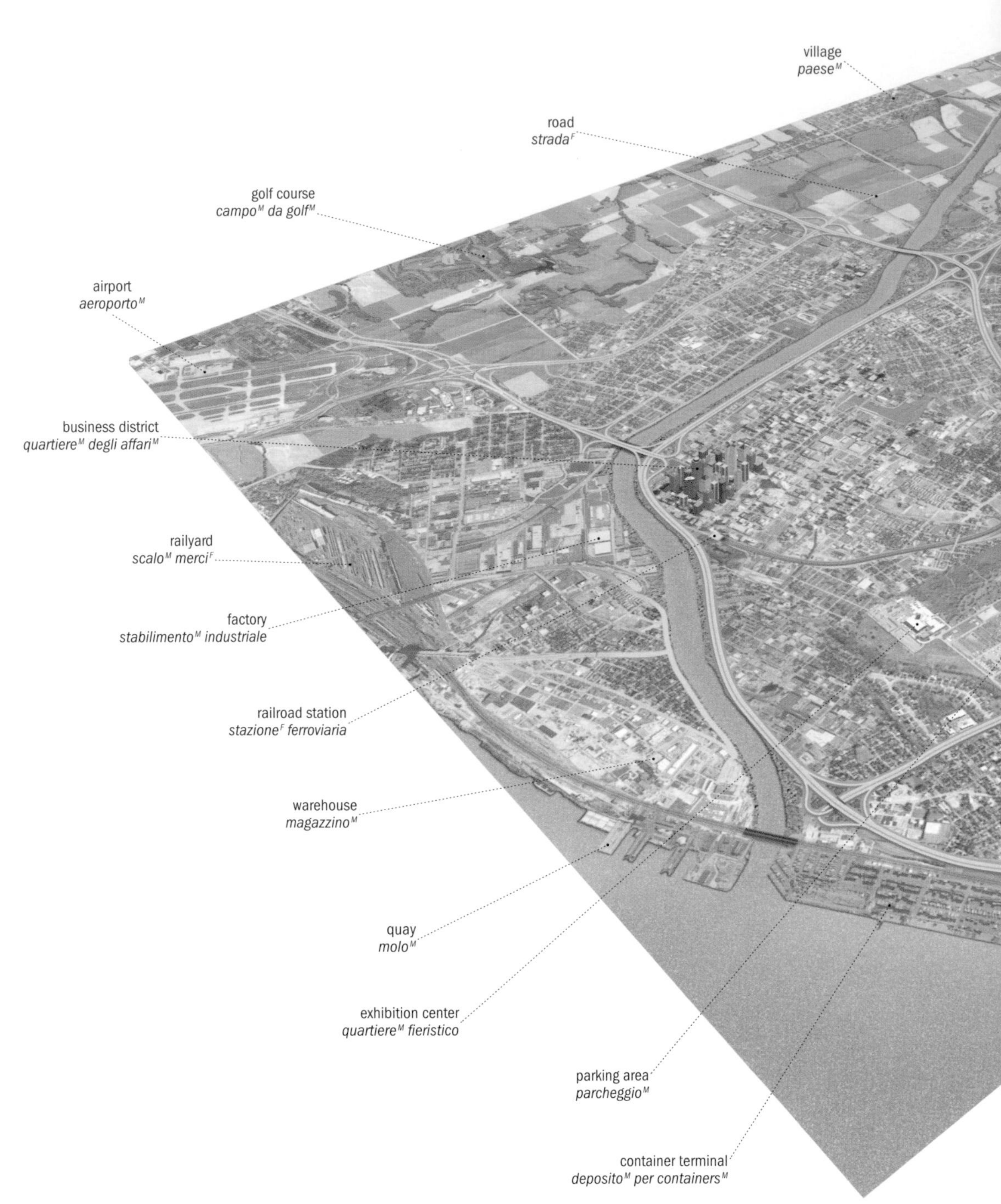

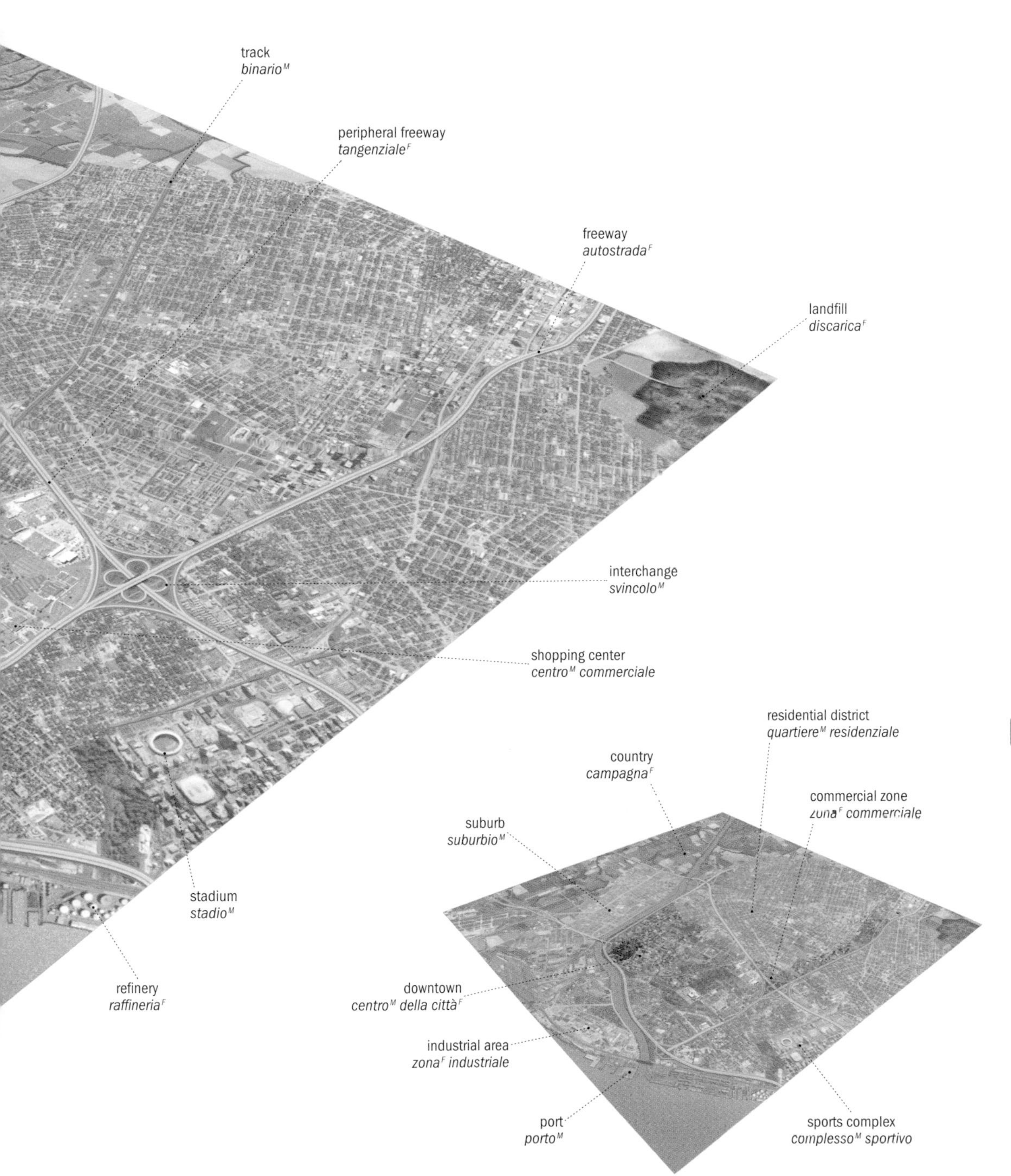
track
binario M
peripheral freeway
tangenziale F
freeway
autostrada F
landfill
discarica F
interchange
svincolo M
shopping center
centro M commerciale
residential district
quartiere M residenziale
country
campagna F
commercial zone
zona F commerciale
suburb
suburbio M
stadium
stadio M
refinery
raffineria F
downtown
centro M della città F
industrial area
zona F industriale
port
porto M
sports complex
complesso M sportivo

downtown

centro[M] della città[F]

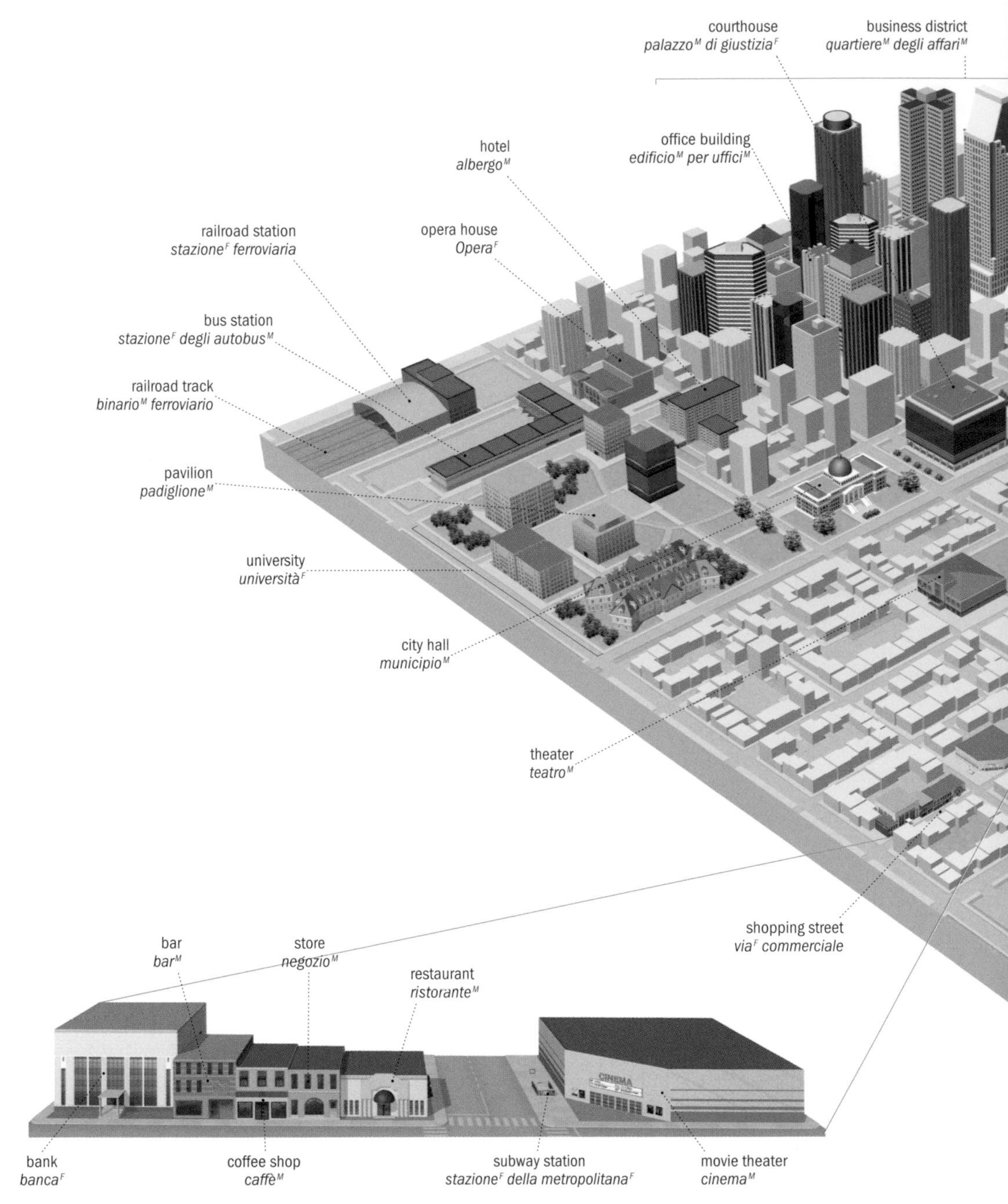

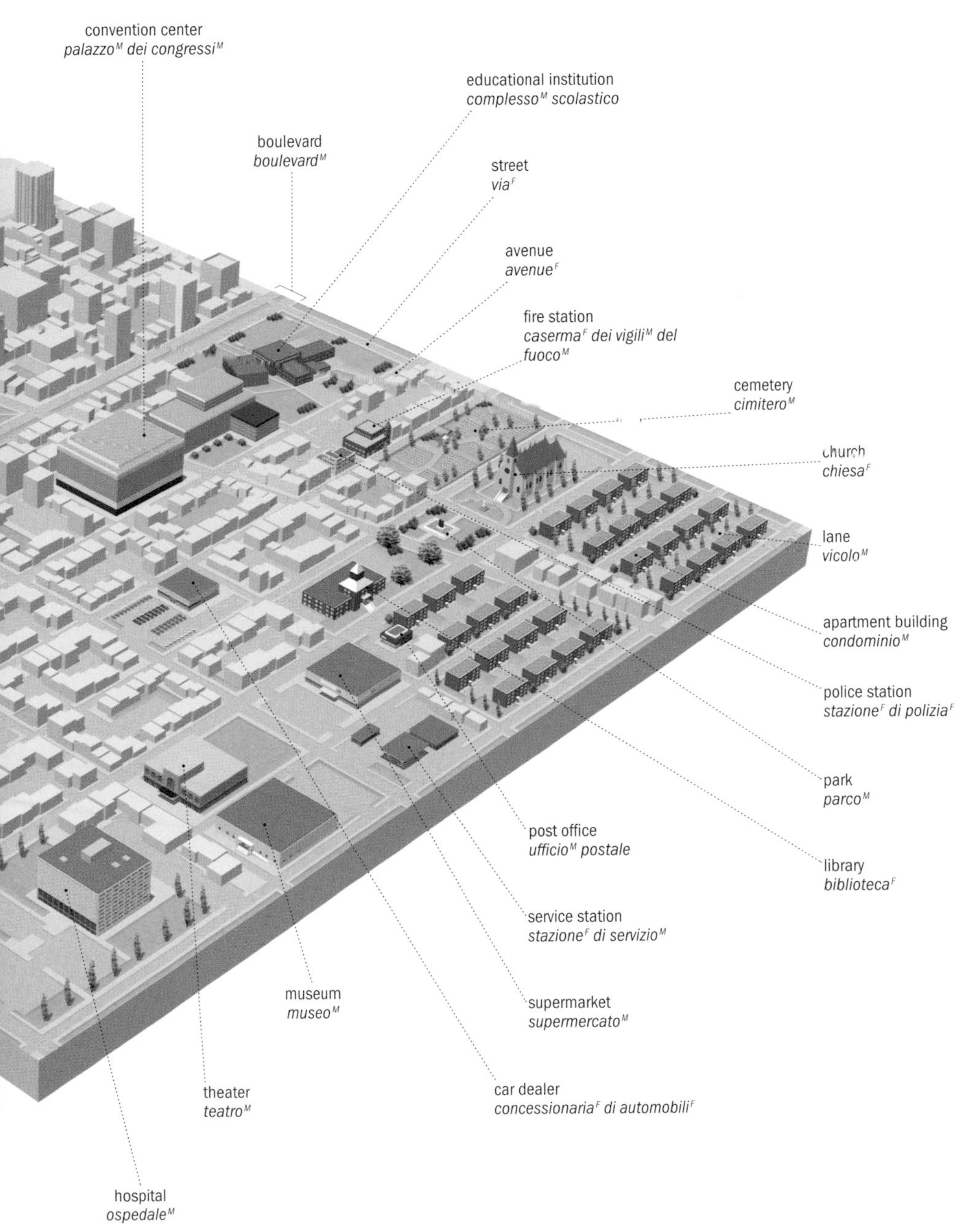
convention center
palazzo^M dei congressi^M
educational institution
complesso^M scolastico
boulevard
boulevard^M
street
via^F
avenue
avenue^F
fire station
caserma^F dei vigili^M del fuoco^M
cemetery
cimitero^M
church
chiesa^F
lane
vicolo^M
apartment building
condominio^M
police station
stazione^F di polizia^F
park
parco^M
post office
ufficio^M postale
library
biblioteca^F
service station
stazione^F di servizio^M
museum
museo^M
supermarket
supermercato^M
theater
teatro^M
car dealer
concessionaria^F di automobili^F
hospital
ospedale^M

cross section of a street

sezione^F trasversale di una strada^F

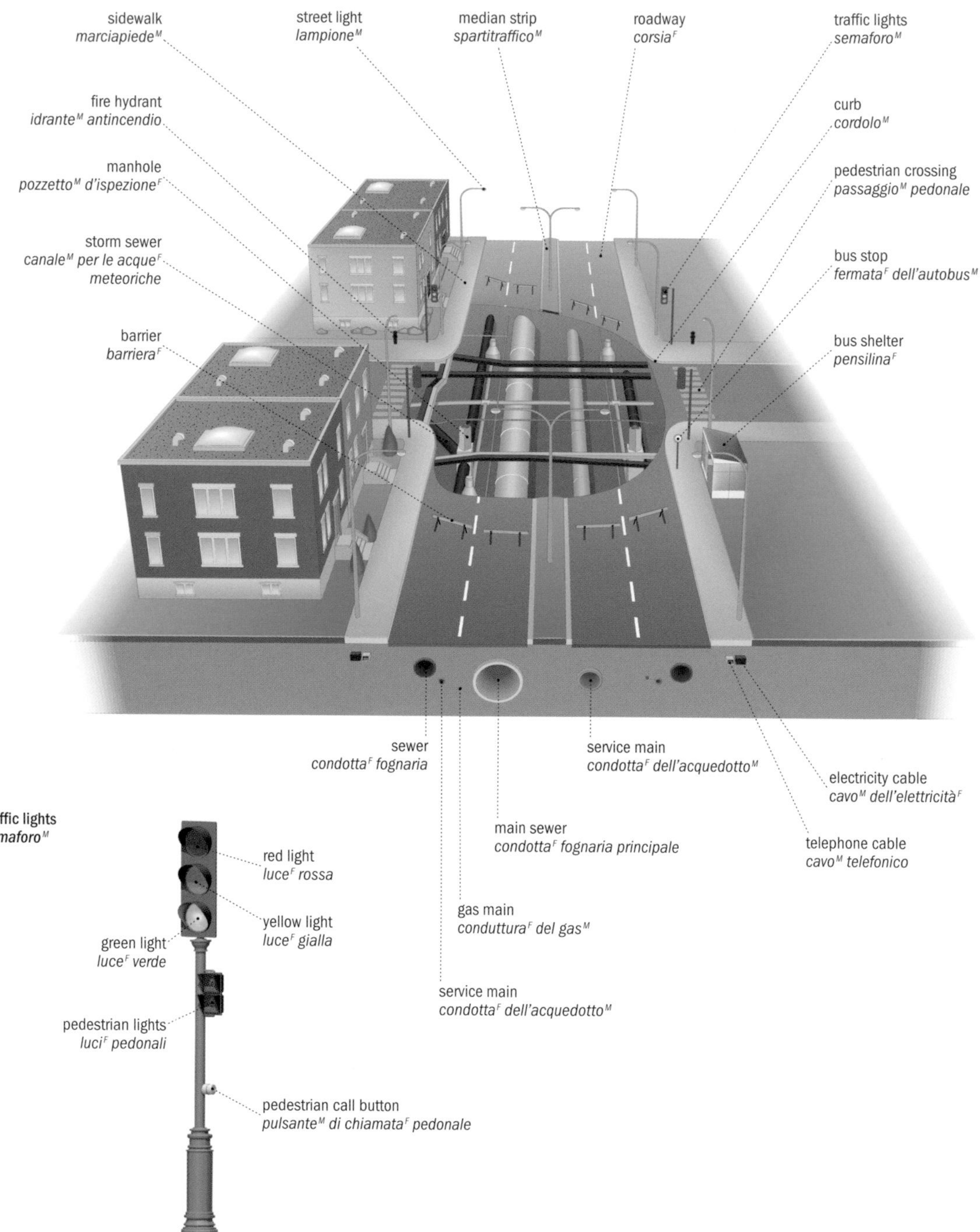

office building
edificio[M] per uffici[M]

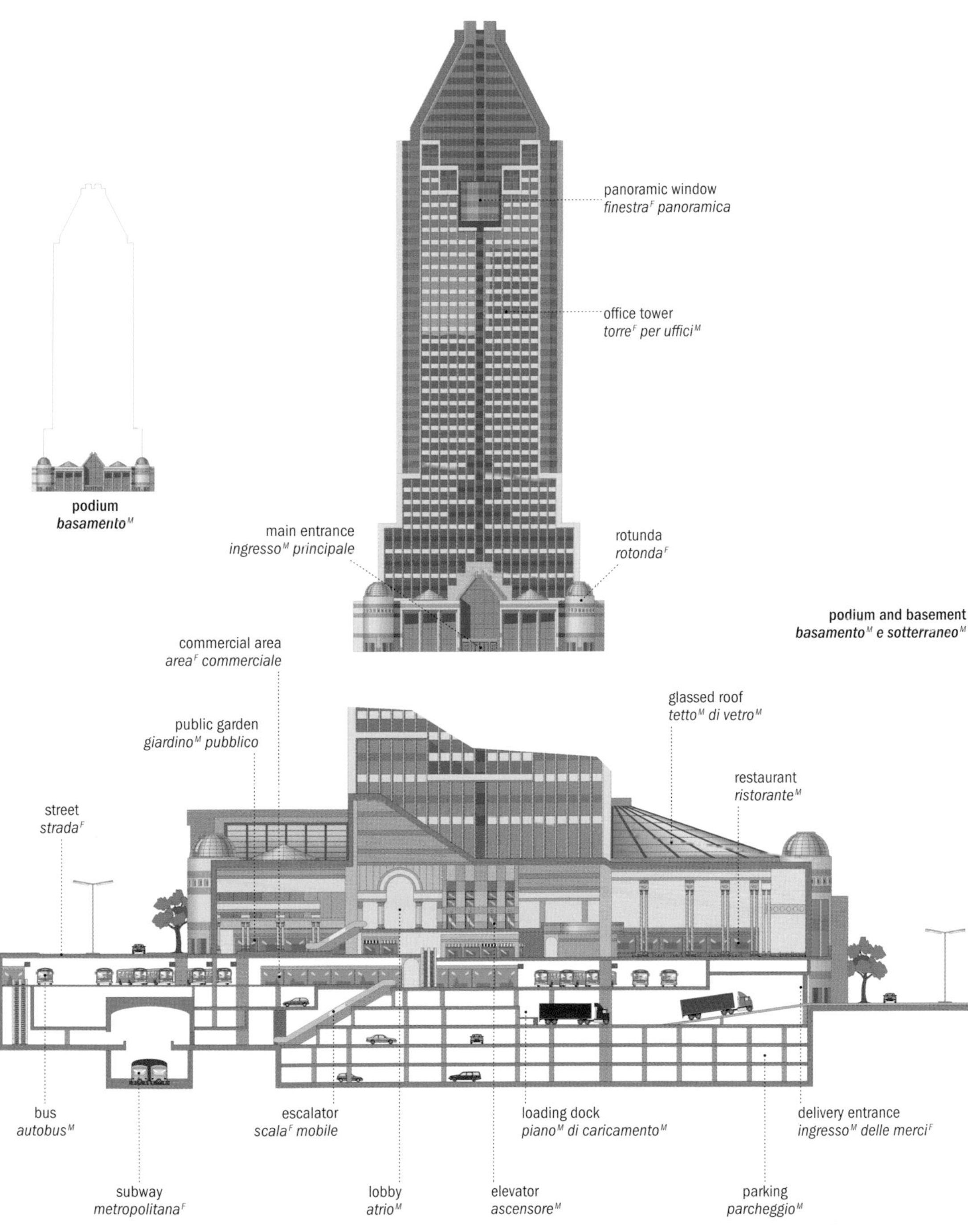

shopping center

centro[M] commerciale

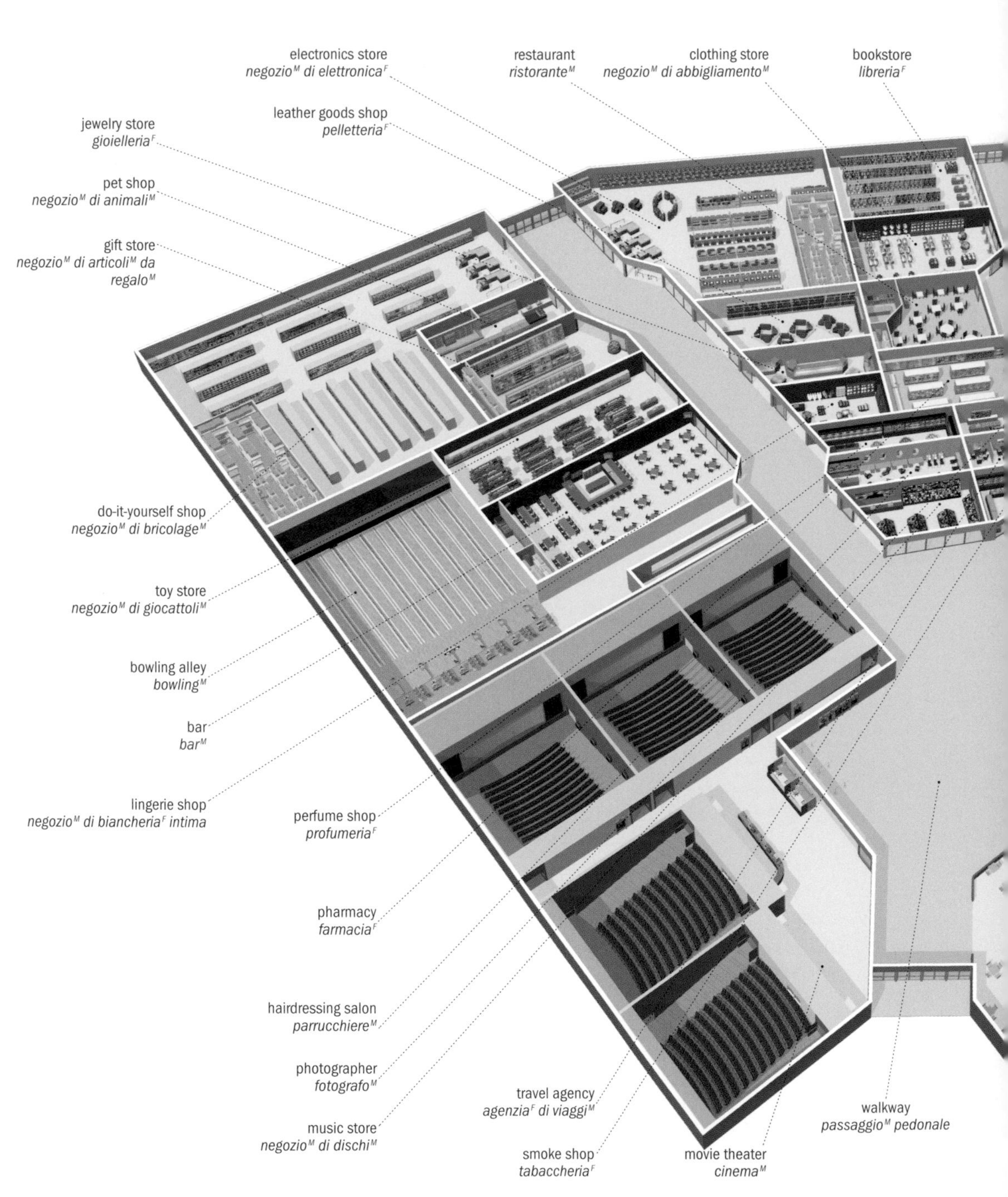

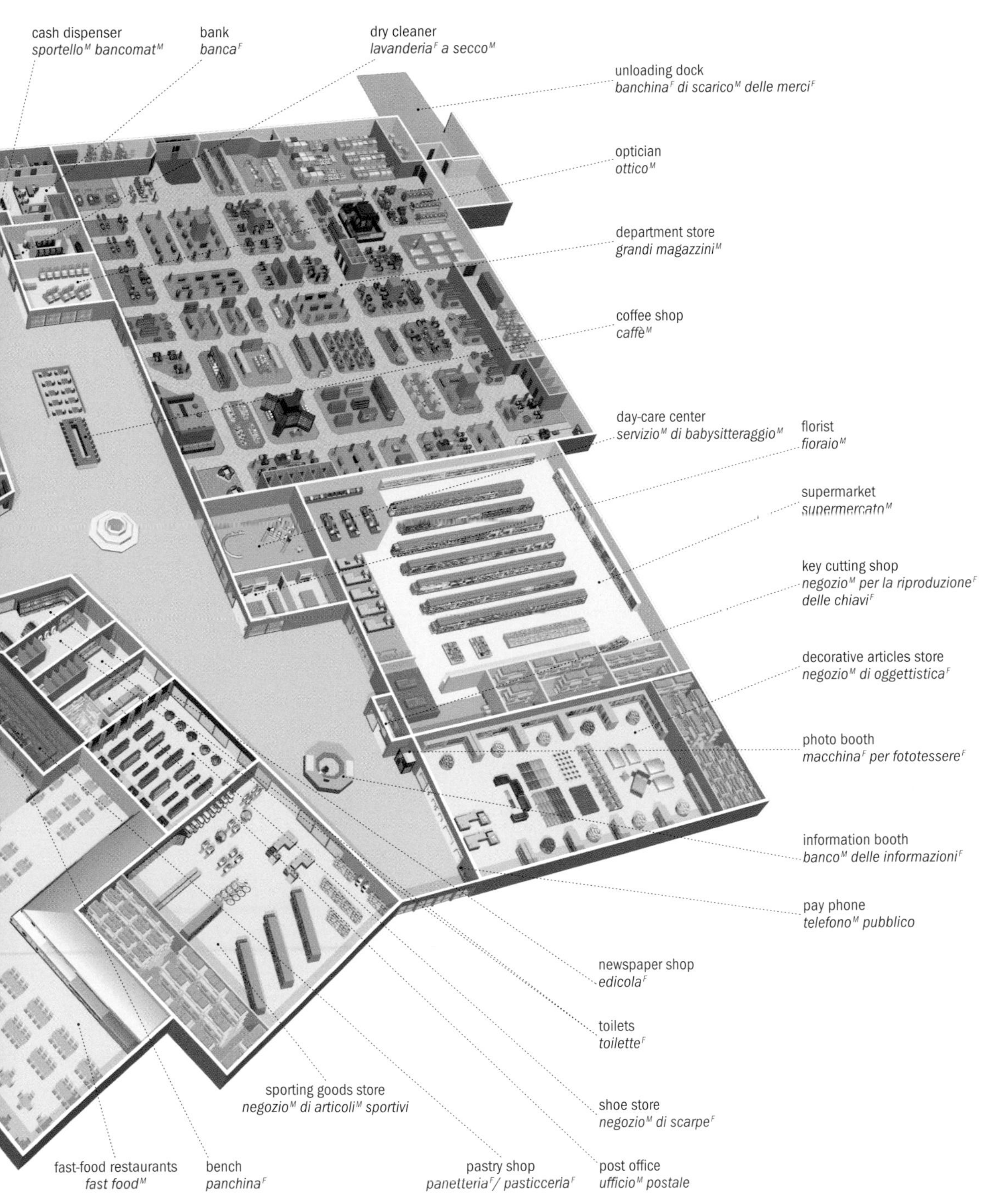
cash dispenser
sportello^M bancomat^M
bank
banca^F
dry cleaner
lavanderia^F a secco^M
unloading dock
banchina^F di scarico^M delle merci^F
optician
ottico^M
department store
grandi magazzini^M
coffee shop
caffè^M
day-care center
servizio^M di babysitteraggio^M
florist
fioraio^M
supermarket
supermercato^M
key cutting shop
negozio^M per la riproduzione^F delle chiavi^F
decorative articles store
negozio^M di oggettistica^F
photo booth
macchina^F per fototessere^F
information booth
banco^M delle informazioni^F
pay phone
telefono^M pubblico
newspaper shop
edicola^F
toilets
toilette^F
sporting goods store
negozio^M di articoli^M sportivi
shoe store
negozio^M di scarpe^F
fast-food restaurants
fast food^M
bench
panchina^F
pastry shop
panetteria^F / pasticceria^F
post office
ufficio^M postale
SOCIETY

restaurant

ristorante[M]

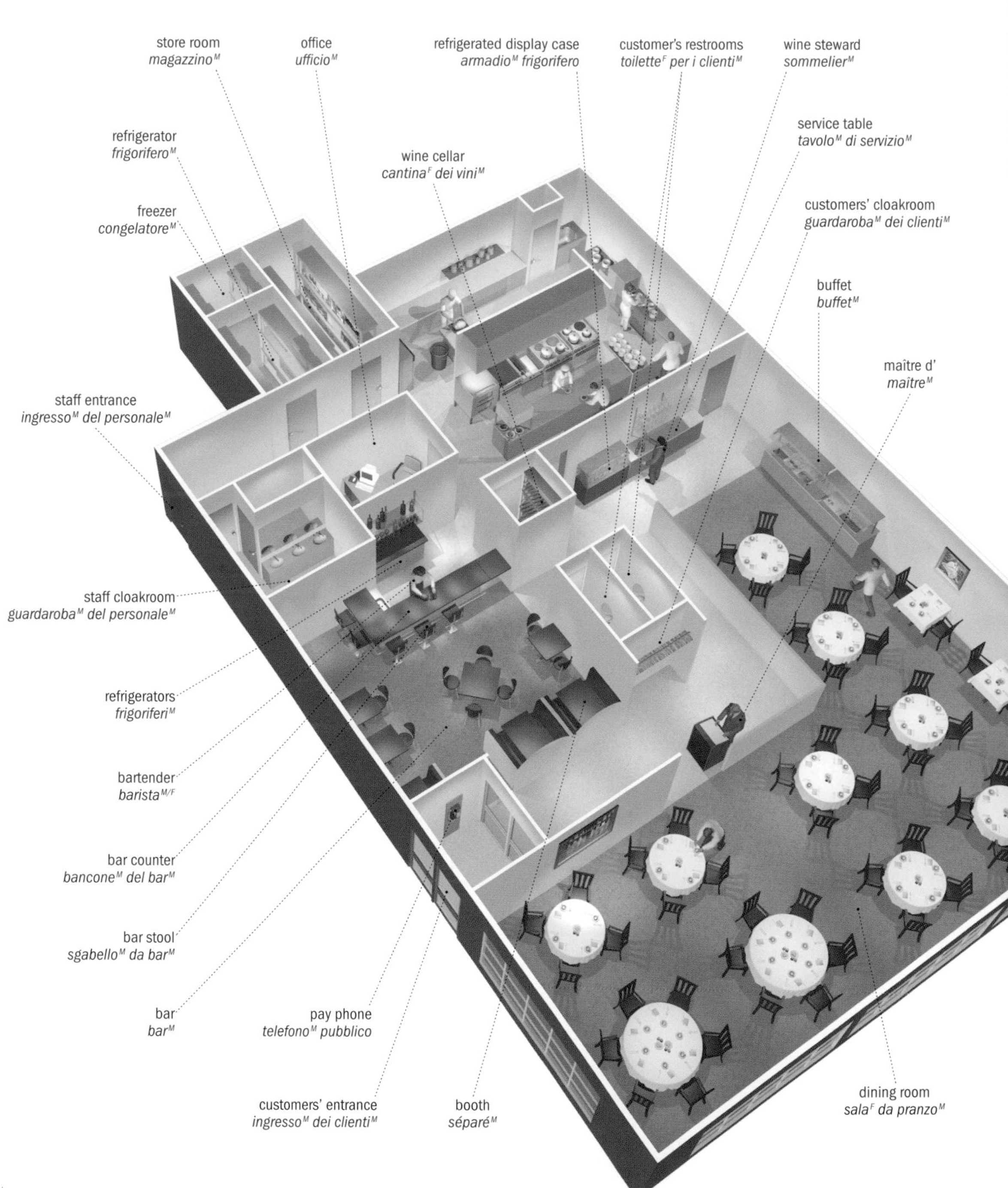

SOCIETY

hotel

albergo[M]

reception level
piano[M] della reception[F]

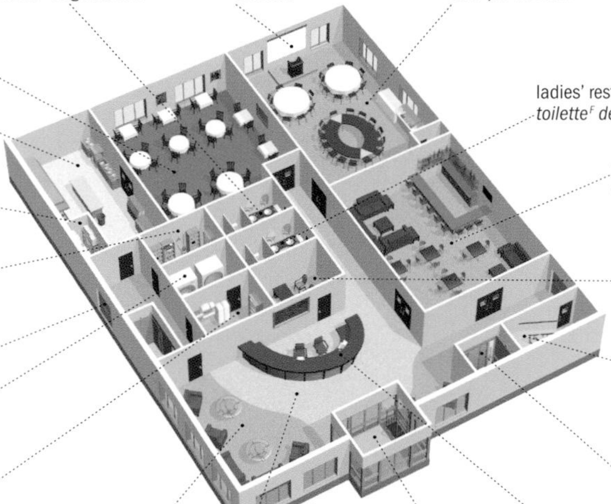

dining room
sala[F] da pranzo[M]

kitchen
cucina[F]

food reserves
dispensa[F]

janitor's closet
stanzino[M] del portiere[M]

unloading dock
banchina[F] di scarico[M] delle merci[F]

laundry
lavanderia[F]

linen room
locale[M] per la biancheria[F]

gentlemen's restroom
toilette[F] degli uomini[M]

screen
schermo[M]

meeting room
sala[F] per riunioni[F]

ladies' restroom
toilette[F] delle donne[F]

cocktail lounge
sala[F] per i cocktail[M]

office
ufficio[M]

stairs
scale[F]

elevator
ascensore[M]

front desk
reception[F]

lounge
salotto[M]

hall
hall[F]

lobby
atrio[M]

hotel rooms
camera[F] d'albergo[M]

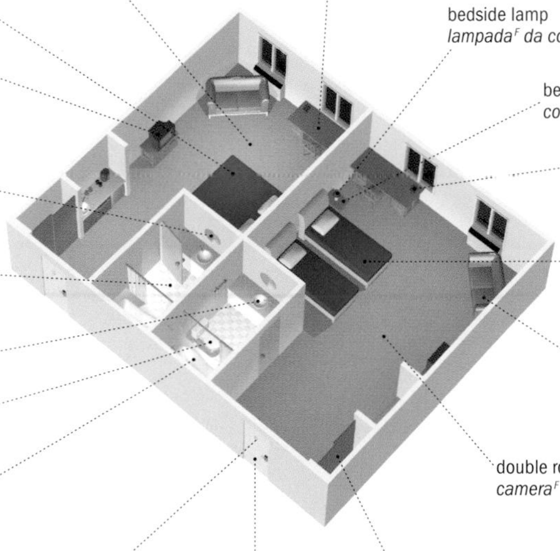

single room
camera[F] matrimoniale

desk
scrivania[F]

double bed
letto[M] matrimoniale

television set
televisione[F]

mirror
specchio[M]

bathroom
stanza[F] da bagno[M]

sink
lavandino[M]

toilet
water[M]

bath and shower
vasca[F] da bagno[M] e doccia[F]

bedside lamp
lampada[F] da comodino[M]

bedside table
comodino[M]

telephone
telefono[M]

single bed
letto[M] singolo

love seat
divano[M] a due posti[M]

double room
camera[F] doppia

room number
numero[M] della camera[F]

door
porta[F]

wardrobe
armadio[M]

court

tribunale[M]

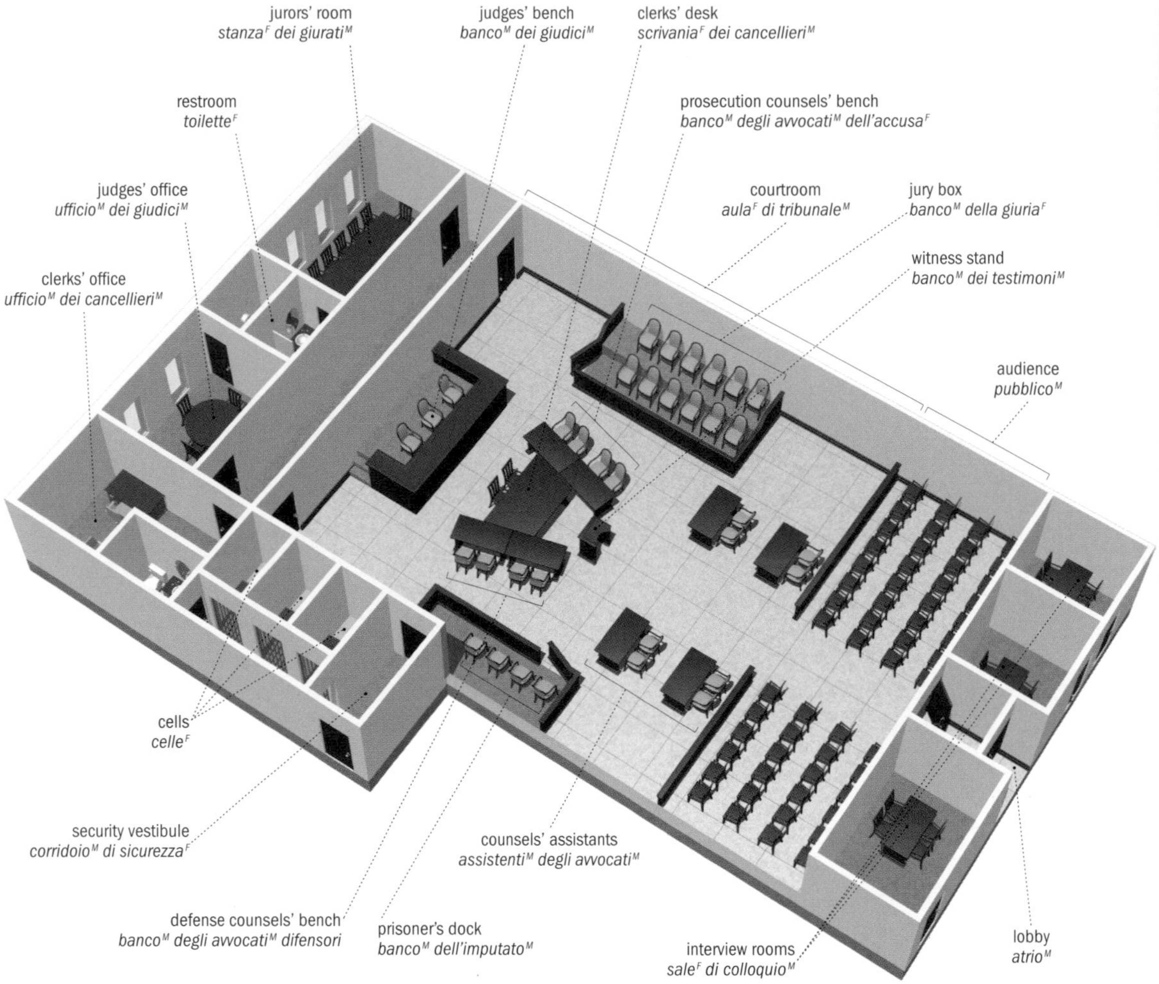

jurors' room
stanza[F] dei giurati[M]

judges' bench
banco[M] dei giudici[M]

clerks' desk
scrivania[F] dei cancellieri[M]

restroom
toilette[F]

prosecution counsels' bench
banco[M] degli avvocati[M] dell'accusa[F]

judges' office
ufficio[M] dei giudici[M]

courtroom
aula[F] di tribunale[M]

jury box
banco[M] della giuria[F]

clerks' office
ufficio[M] dei cancellieri[M]

witness stand
banco[M] dei testimoni[M]

audience
pubblico[M]

cells
celle[F]

security vestibule
corridoio[M] di sicurezza[F]

counsels' assistants
assistenti[M] degli avvocati[M]

defense counsels' bench
banco[M] degli avvocati[M] difensori

prisoner's dock
banco[M] dell'imputato[M]

interview rooms
sale[F] di colloquio[M]

lobby
atrio[M]

examples of currency abbreviations

esempi[M] di simboli[M] di valute[F]

dollar
dollaro[M]

cent
cent[M]

Rs
rupee
rupia[F]

euro
euro[M]

new shekel
nuovo shekel[M]

peso
peso[M]

yen
yen[M]

pound
sterlina[F]

SOCIETY

money and modes of payment

denaro[M] e metodi[M] di pagamento[M]

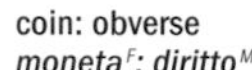

coin: obverse
moneta[F]: diritto[M]

date
anno[M]

edge
contorno[M]

banknote: front
banconota[F]: dritto[M]

initials of the issuing bank
iniziali[F] della banca[F] di emissione[F]

security thread
filo[M] di sicurezza[F]

hologram foil strip
banda[F] olografica

official signature
firma[F] ufficiale

watermark
filigrana[F]

color shifting ink
inchiostro[M] a colori[M] cangianti

portrait
effigie[F]

serial number
numero[M] di serie[F]

coin: reverse
moneta[F]: rovescio[M]

outer ring
corona[F]

denomination
indicazione[F] del valore[M]

banknote: back
banconota[F]: rovescio[M]

flag of the European Union
bandiera[F] dell'Unione[F] Europea

serial number
numero[M] di serie[F]

motto
motto[M]

denomination
indicazione[F] del valore[M]

name of the currency
nome[M] della valuta[F]

checks
assegni[M]

credit card
carta[F] di credito[M]

magnetic stripe
banda[F] magnetica

cardholder's signature
firma[F] del titolare[M]

card number
numero[M] della carta[F]

cardholder's name
nome[M] del titolare[M]

expiration date
data[F] di scadenza[F]

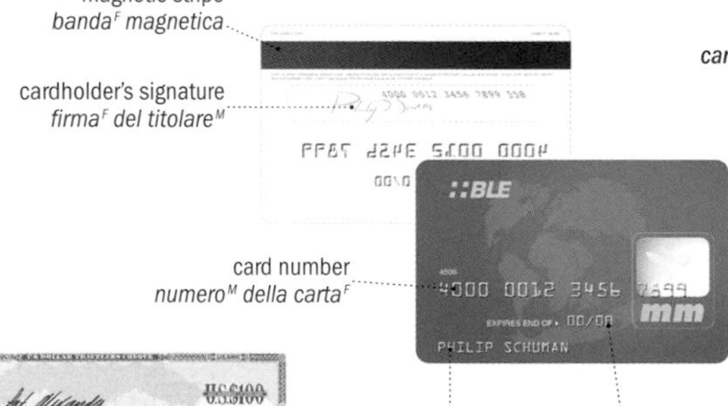

traveler's check
traveller's cheque[M]

SOCIETY

bank

banca[F]

cash dispenser
sportello[M] bancomat[M]

automatic teller machine (ATM)
sportello[M] automatico

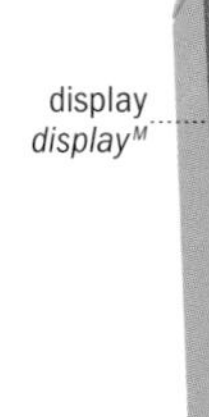

operation keys
tasti[M] funzione[F]

deposit slot
fessura[F] per il deposito[M]

display
display[M]

card reader slot
lettore[M] di carte[F]

transaction record slot
fessura[F] di registrazione[F] della transazione[F]

alphanumeric keyboard
tastiera[F] alfanumerica

bill presenter
emissione[F] di banconote[F]

passbook update slot
fessura[F] di aggiornamento[M] dell'estratto conto[M]

professional training office
ufficio[M] di formazione[F] professionale

waiting area
area[F] d'attesa[F]

insurance services
servizi[M] assicurativi

brochure rack
espositore[M] di brochure[F]

photocopier
fotocopiatrice[F]

financial services
servizi[M] finanziari

information desk
banco[M] delle informazioni[F]

conference room
sala[F] per conferenze[F]

reception desk
banco[M] della reception[F]

loan services
servizi[M] di credito[M]

meeting room
sala[F] per riunioni[F]

security grille
griglia[F] di sicurezza[F]

lobby
atrio[M]

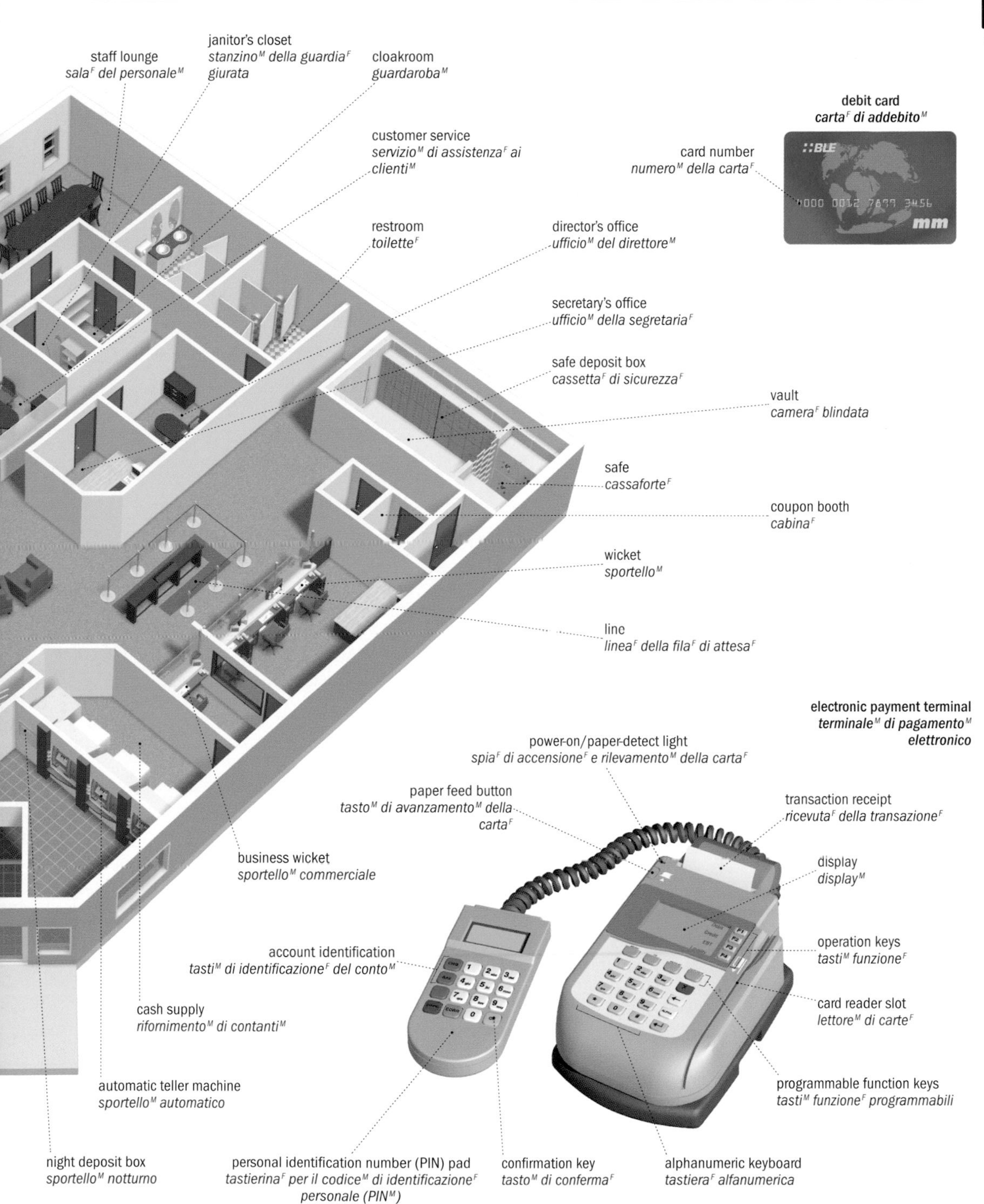
staff lounge
sala^F del personale^M
janitor's closet
stanzino^M della guardia^F giurata
cloakroom
guardaroba^M
customer service
servizio^M di assistenza^F ai clienti^M
restroom
toilette^F
director's office
ufficio^M del direttore^M
secretary's office
ufficio^M della segretaria^F
safe deposit box
cassetta^F di sicurezza^F
vault
camera^F blindata
safe
cassaforte^F
coupon booth
cabina^F
wicket
sportello^M
line
linea^F della fila^F di attesa^F
business wicket
sportello^M commerciale
cash supply
rifornimento^M di contanti^M
automatic teller machine
sportello^M automatico
night deposit box
sportello^M notturno
debit card
carta^F di addebito^M
card number
numero^M della carta^F
electronic payment terminal
terminale^M di pagamento^M elettronico
power-on/paper-detect light
spia^F di accensione^F e rilevamento^M della carta^F
paper feed button
tasto^M di avanzamento^M della carta^F
transaction receipt
ricevuta^F della transazione^F
display
display^M
account identification
tasti^M di identificazione^F del conto^M
operation keys
tasti^M funzione^F
card reader slot
lettore^M di carte^F
programmable function keys
tasti^M funzione^F programmabili
personal identification number (PIN) pad
tastierina^F per il codice^M di identificazione^F personale (PIN^M)
confirmation key
tasto^M di conferma^F
alphanumeric keyboard
tastiera^F alfanumerica

school

scuola^F

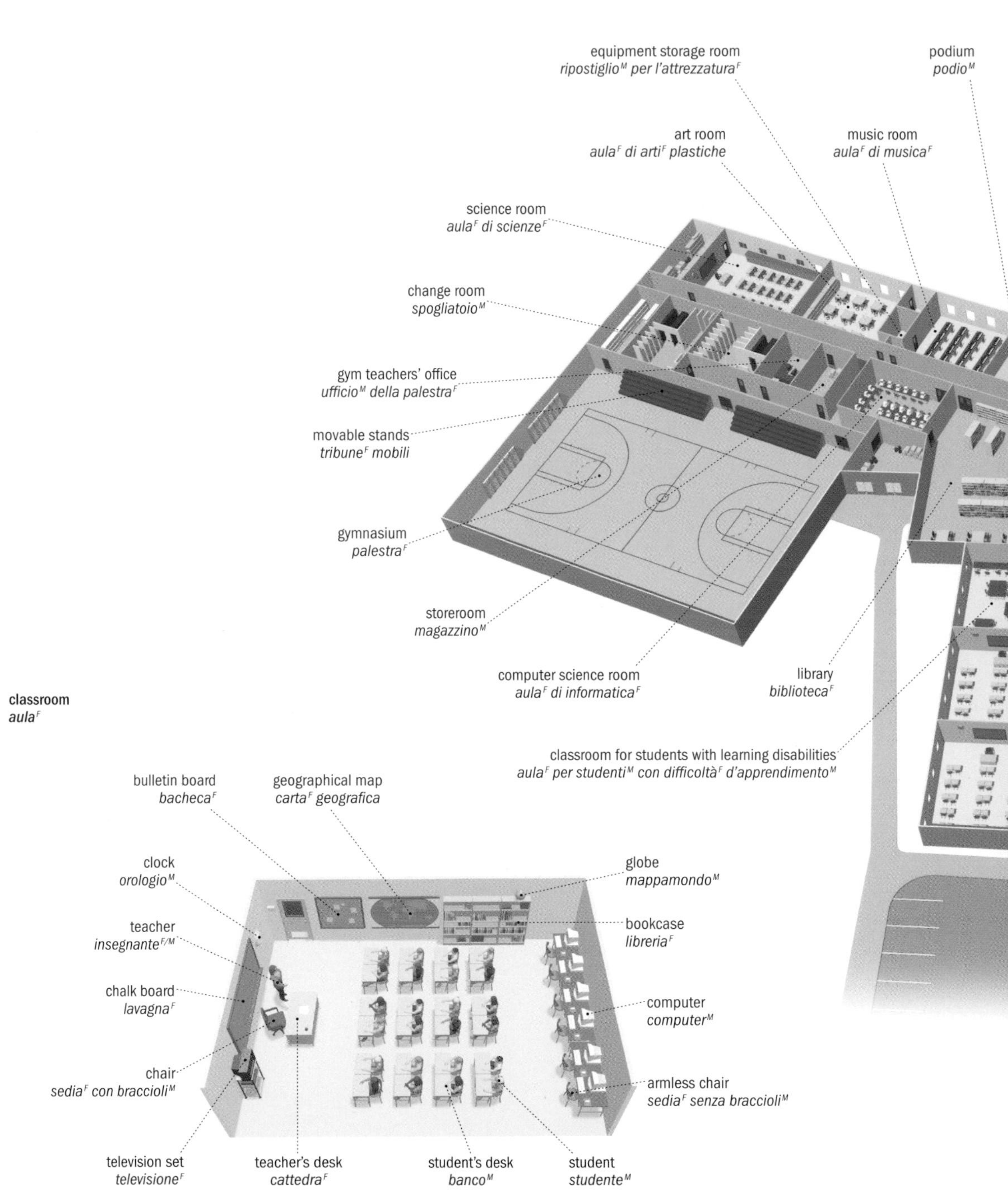

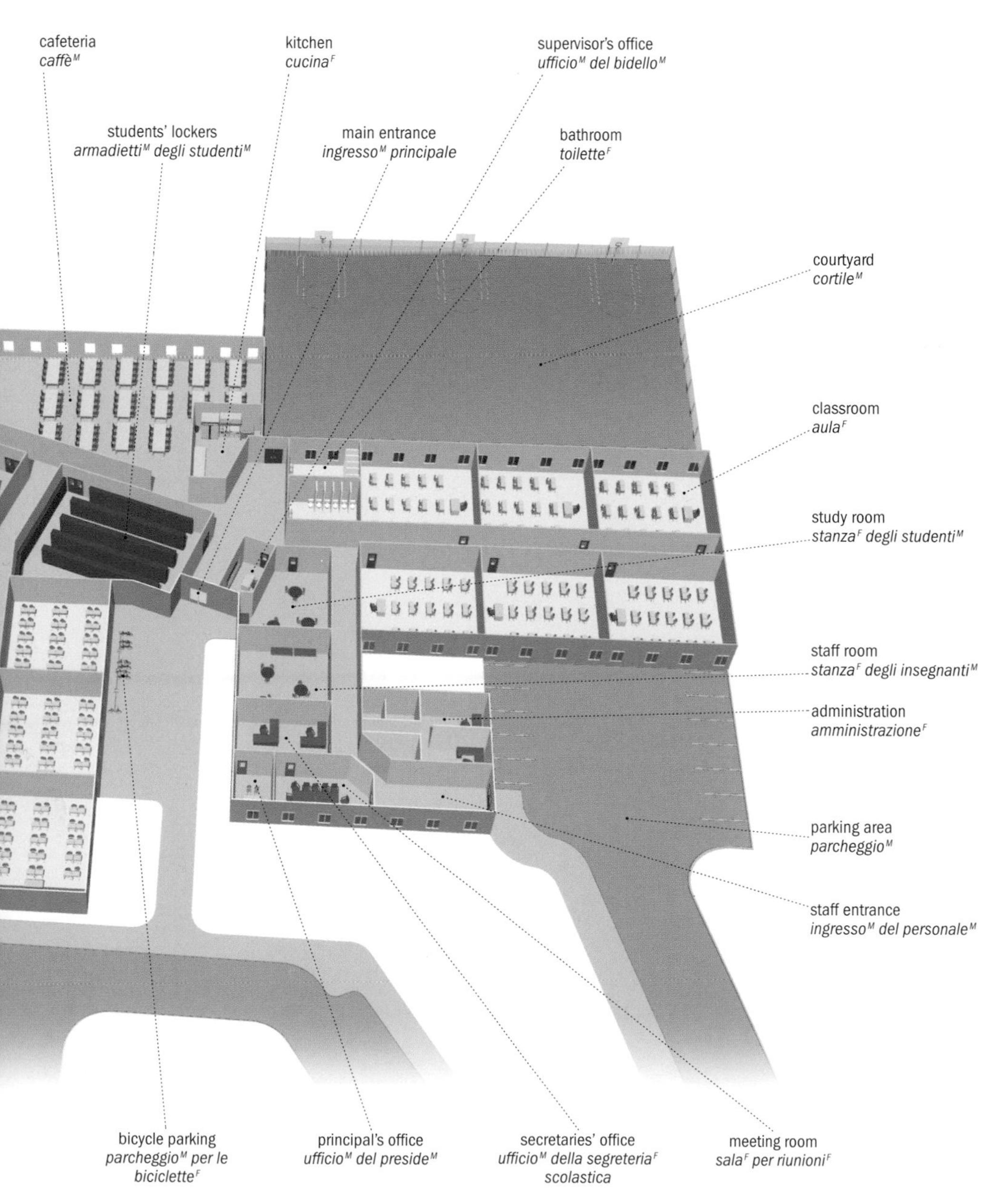
cafeteria
caffè^M
kitchen
cucina^F
supervisor's office
ufficio^M del bidello^M
students' lockers
armadietti^M degli studenti^M
main entrance
ingresso^M principale
bathroom
toilette^F
courtyard
cortile^M
classroom
aula^F
study room
stanza^F degli studenti^M
staff room
stanza^F degli insegnanti^M
administration
amministrazione^F
parking area
parcheggio^M
staff entrance
ingresso^M del personale^M
bicycle parking
parcheggio^M per le biciclette^F
principal's office
ufficio^M del preside^M
secretaries' office
ufficio^M della segreteria^F scolastica
meeting room
sala^F per riunioni^F

Catholic church

chiesa[F]

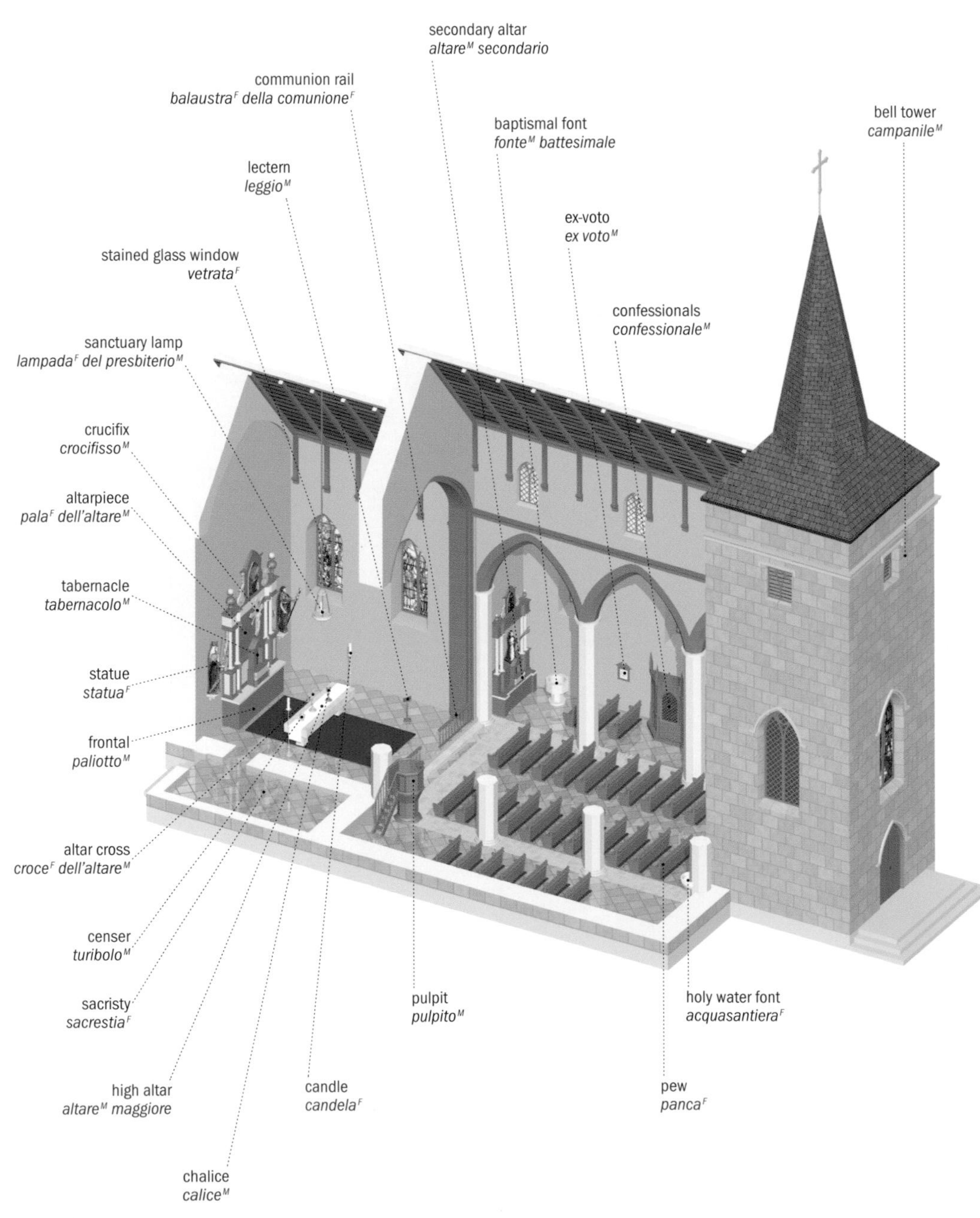

synagogue

sinagoga^F

menorah
menorah^F
balcony
balconata^F
memorial board
lapide^F commemorativa
pulpit
pulpito^M
bimah
bimah^F
eternal light
luce^F perpetua
Torah scrolls
rotoli^M della Torah^F
Star of David
stella^F di David
Ten Commandments
dieci comandamenti^M
ark
arca^F
rabbi's seat
seggio^M del rabbino^M

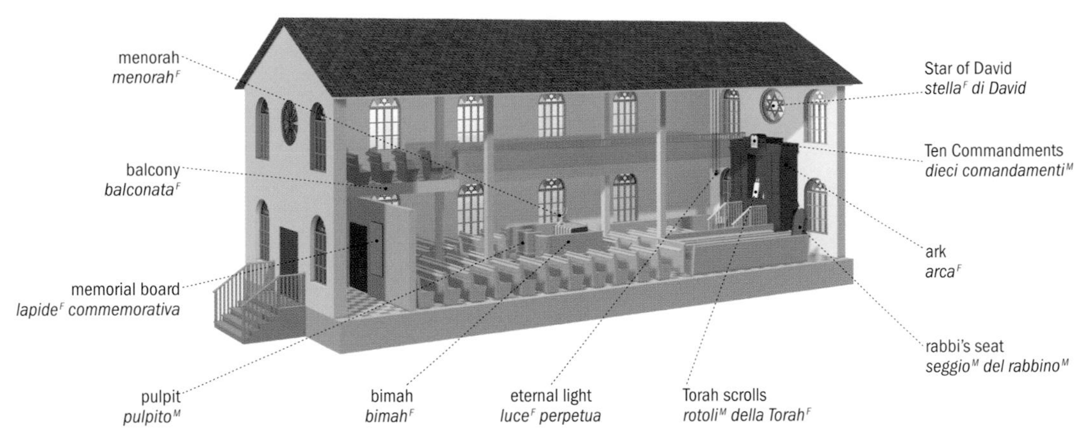

mosque

moschea^F

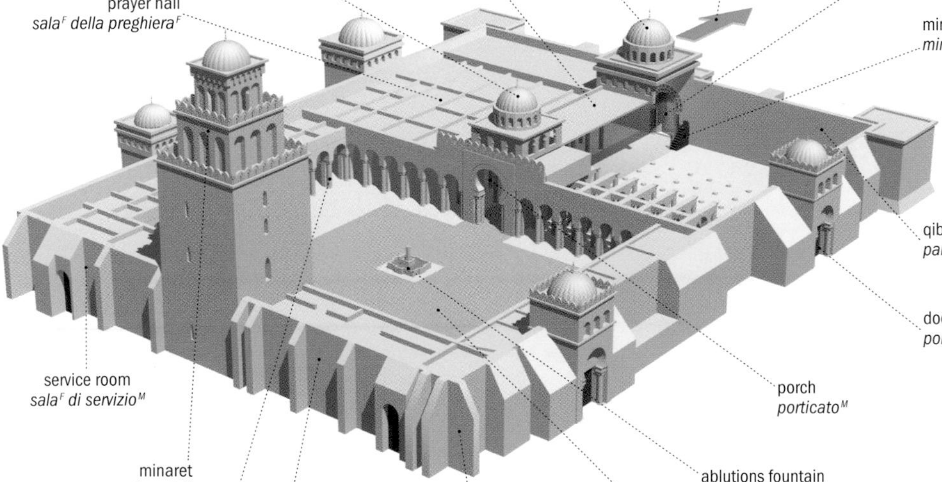

porch dome
cupola^F sul porticato^M
central nave
navata^F centrale
mihrab dome
cupola^F sul mihrab^M
direction of Mecca
direzione^F della Mecca^F
mihrab
mihrab^M
prayer hall
sala^F della preghiera^F
minbar
minbar^M
qibla wall
parete^F della qibla^F
door
porta^F
service room
sala^F di servizio^M
porch
porticato^M
minaret
minareto^M
ablutions fountain
fontana^F per le abluzioni^F
shady arcades
portico^M coperto
reception hall
sala^F di ingresso^M
fortified wall
mura^F fortificate
courtyard
cortile^M

flags

bandiere[F]

Americas
Americhe[F]

1 

Canada
Canada[M]

2 

United States of America
Stati[M] Uniti d'America[F]

3 

Mexico
Messico[M]

4 

Honduras
Honduras[M]

5 

Guatemala
Guatemala[M]

6 

Belize
Belize[M]

7 

El Salvador
El Salvador[M]

8 

Nicaragua
Nicaragua[M]

9 

Costa Rica
Costa Rica[M]

10 

Panama
Panama[M]

11 

Colombia
Colombia[F]

12 

Venezuela
Venezuela[M]

13 

Guyana
Guyana[F]

14 

Suriname
Suriname[M]

15 

Ecuador
Ecuador[M]

16 

Peru
Perù[M]

17 

Brazil
Brasile[M]

18 

Bolivia
Bolivia[F]

19 

Paraguay
Paraguay[M]

20 

Chile
Cile[M]

21 

Argentina
Argentina[F]

22 

Uruguay
Uruguay[M]

Caribbean Islands
Isole[F] delle Antille[F]

23 

The Bahamas
Bahama[F]

24 

Cuba
Cuba[F]

25 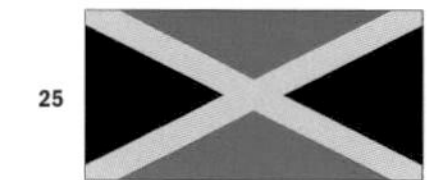

Jamaica
Giamaica[F]

26 

Haiti
Haiti[F]

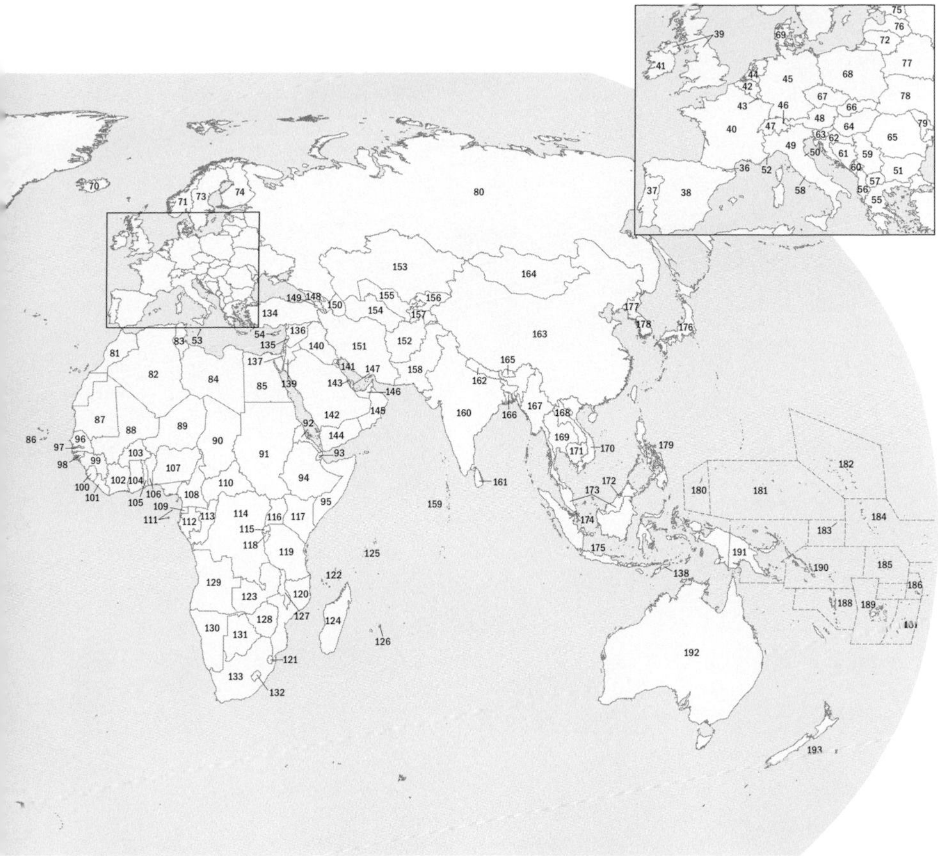

27

Saint Kitts and Nevis
Saint Kitts e Nevis^{F}

28

Antigua and Barbuda
Antigua^{F} *e Barbuda*^{F}

29

Dominica
Dominica^{F}

30

Saint Lucia
Saint Lucia^{F}

31 

Saint Vincent and the Grenadines
Saint Vincent e Grenadine^{F}

32 

Dominican Republic
Repubblica^{F} *Dominicana*

33 

Barbados
Barbados^{F}

34 

Grenada
Grenada^{F}

35 

Trinidad and Tobago
Trinidad^{F} *e Tobago*^{F}

Europe
Europa^{F}

36 

Andorra
Andorra^{F}

37 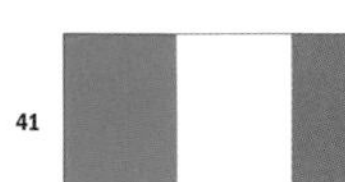

Portugal
Portogallo^{M}

38 

Spain
Spagna^{F}

39 

United Kingdom
Regno^{M} *Unito di Gran Bretagna*^{F} *e Irlanda*^{F} *del Nord*^{M}

40 

France
Francia^{F}

41 

Ireland
Irlanda^{F}

42 

Belgium
Belgio^{M}

43 

Luxembourg
Lussemburgo^{M}

44 

Netherlands
Paesi^{M} *Bassi*

flags

45 
Germany
Germania^F

46 
Liechtenstein
Liechtenstein^M

47 
Switzerland
Svizzera^F

48 
Austria
Austria^F

49 
Italy
Italia^F

50 
San Marino
Repubblica^F di San Marino^M

51 
Bulgaria
Bulgaria^F

52 
Monaco
Principato^M di Monaco^M

53 
Malta
Malta^F

54 
Cyprus
Cipro^F

55 
Greece
Grecia^F

56 
Albania
Albania^F

57 
The Former Yugoslav Republic of Macedonia
Repubblica^F Ex Jugoslava di Macedonia^F

58 
Holy See (Vatican City)
Città^F del Vaticano^M

59 
Serbia
Serbia^F

60 
Montenegro
Montenegro^M

61 
Bosnia and Herzegovina
Bosnia^F ed Erzegovina^F

62 
Croatia
Croazia^F

63 
Slovenia
Slovenia^F

64 
Hungary
Ungheria^F

65 
Romania
Romania^F

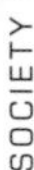

66 
Slovakia
Slovacchia^F

67 
Czech Republic
Repubblica^F Ceca

68 
Poland
Polonia^F

69 
Denmark
Danimarca^F

70 
Iceland
Islanda^F

71 
Norway
Norvegia^F

72 
Lithuania
Lituania^F

73 
Sweden
Svezia^F

74 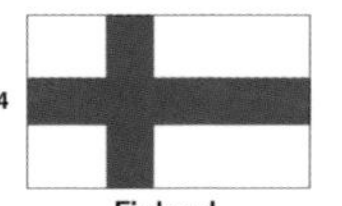
Finland
Finlandia^F

75 
Estonia
Estonia^F

76 
Latvia
Lettonia^F

77 
Belarus
Bielorussia^F

78 
Ukraine
Ucraina^F

79 
Moldova
Moldavia^F

80 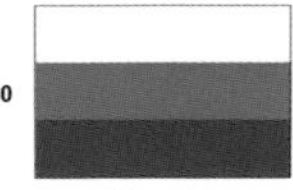
Russia
Federazione^F Russa

Africa
Africa[F]

81 
Morocco
Marocco[M]

82 
Algeria
Algeria[F]

83 
Tunisia
Tunisia[F]

84 
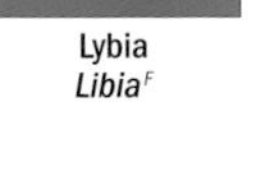
Lybia
Libia[F]

85
Egypt
Egitto[M]

86
Cape Verde
Capo Verde[M]

87
Mauritania
Mauritania[F]

88
Mali
Repubblica[F] *del Mali*[M]

89 
Niger
Niger[M]

90 

Chad
Ciad[M]

91 
Sudan
Sudan[M]

92 
Eritrea
Eritrea[F]

93 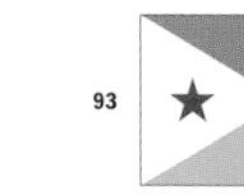
Djibouti
Gibuti[M]

94 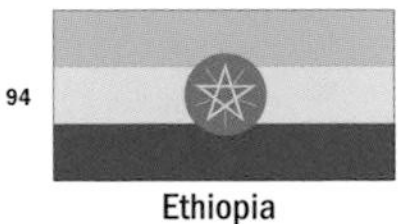
Ethiopia
Etiopia[F]

95 
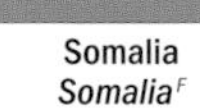
Somalia
Somalia[F]

96 
Senegal
Senegal[M]

97 
The Gambia
Gambia[M]

98 
Guinea-Bissau
Guinea Bissau[F]

99 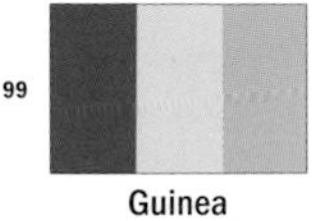
Guinea
Guinea[F]

100 
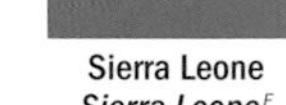
Sierra Leone
Sierra Leone[F]

101 
Liberia
Liberia[F]

102 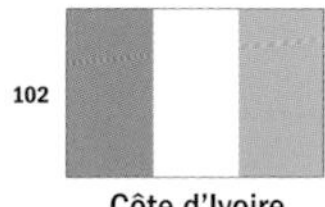
Côte d'Ivoire
Costa d'Avorio[F]

103 
Burkina Faso
Burkina Faso[M]

104 
Ghana
Ghana[M]

105 
Togo
Togo[M]

106 
Benin
Benin[M]

107 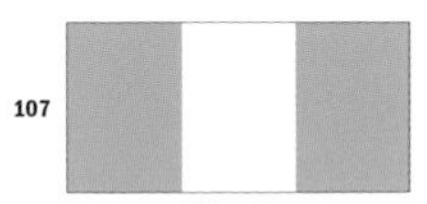
Nigeria
Nigeria[F]

108 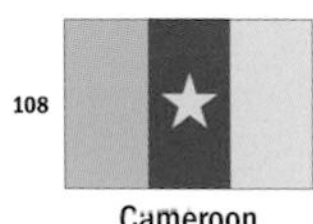
Cameroon
Camerun[M]

109 
Equatorial Guinea
Guinea[F] *Equatoriale*

110 
Central African Republic
Repubblica[F] *Centrafricana*

111 
Sao Tome and Principe
São Tomé e Príncipe[M]

112 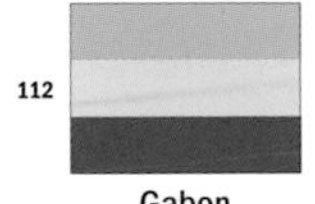
Gabon
Gabon[M]

113 
Republic of the Congo
Congo[M]

114 
Democratic Republic of the Congo
Repubblica[F] *Democratica del Congo*[M]

115 
Rwanda
Ruanda[M]

116 
Uganda
Uganda[F]

117 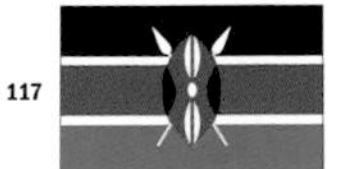
Kenya
Kenya[M]

118 
Burundi
Burundi[M]

119 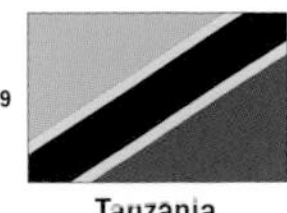
Tanzania
Tanzania[F]

flags

120 
Mozambique
Mozambico[M]

121 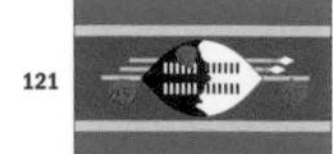
Swaziland
Swaziland[M]

122 
Comoros
Comore[F]

123 
Zambia
Zambia[M]

124 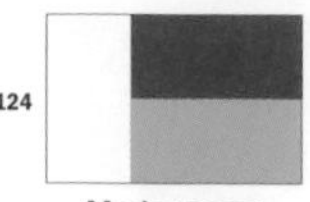
Madagascar
Madagascar[M]

125 
Seychelles
Seychelles[F]

126 
Mauritius
Maurizio[F]

127 
Malawi
Malawi[M]

128 
Zimbabwe
Zimbabwe[M]

129 
Angola
Angola[F]

130 
Namibia
Namibia[F]

131 
Botswana
Botswana[M]

132 
Lesotho
Lesotho[M]

133 
South Africa
Repubblica[F] *Sudafricana*

Asia
Asia[F]

134 
Turkey
Turchia[F]

135 
Lebanon
Libano[M]

136 
Syria
Siria[F]

137 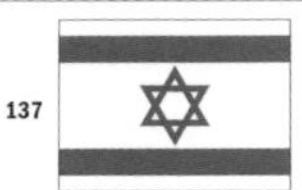
Israel
Israele[M]

138 
East Timor
Timor[M] *Orientale*

139 
Jordan
Giordania[F]

140 
Iraq
Iraq[M]

141 
Kuwait
Kuwait[M]

142 
Saudi Arabia
Arabia Saudita[F]

143 
Bahrain
Bahrein[M]

144 
Yemen
Yemen[M]

145 
Oman
Oman[M]

146 
United Arab Emirates
Emirati Arabi Uniti[M]

147 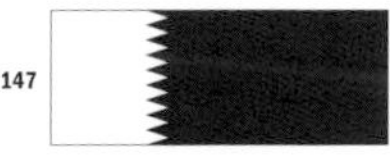
Qatar
Qatar[M]

148 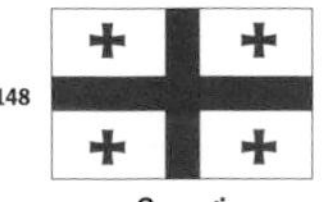
Georgia
Georgia[F]

149 
Armenia
Armenia[F]

150 
Azerbaijan
Azerbaigian[M]

151 
Iran
Iran[M]

152 
Afghanistan
Afghanistan[M]

153 
Kazakhstan
Kazakistan[M]

154 
Turkmenistan
Turkmenistan[M]

155 
Uzbekistan
Uzbekistan[M]

156 
Kyrgyzstan
Kirghizistan[M]

157 
Tajikistan
Tagikistan[M]

158 
Pakistan
Pakistan[M]

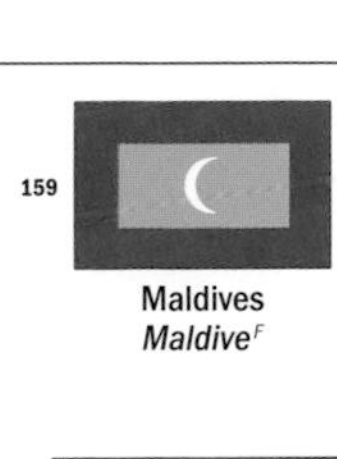
159 Maldives *Maldive[F]*

160 India *India[F]*

161 Sri Lanka *Sri Lanka[M]*

162 Nepal *Nepal[M]*

163 China *Cina[F]*

164 Mongolia *Mongolia[F]*

165 Bhutan *Bhutan[M]*

166 Bangladesh *Bangladesh[M]*

167 Burma *Myanmar[M]*

168 Laos *Laos[M]*

169 Thailand *Tailandia[F]*

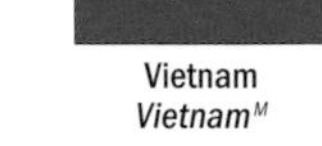
170 Vietnam *Vietnam[M]*

171 Cambodia *Cambogia[F]*

172 Brunei *Brunei[M]*

173 Malaysia *Malaysia[F]*

174 Singapore *Singapore[F]*

175 Indonesia *Indonesia[F]*

176 Japan *Giappone[M]*

177 North Korea *Repubblica[F] Democratica Popolare di Corea[F]*

178 South Korea *Repubblica[F] di Corea[F]*

Oceania and Polynesia
Oceania[F] e Polinesia[F]

179 Philippines *Filippine[F]*

180 Palau *Palau[M]*

181 Federated States of Micronesia *Micronesia[F]*

182 Marshall Islands *Isole Marshall[F]*

183 Nauru *Nauru[M]*

184 Kiribati *Kiribati[M]*

185 Tuvalu *Tuvalu[M]*

186 Samoa *Samoa[F]*

187 Tonga *Tonga[M]*

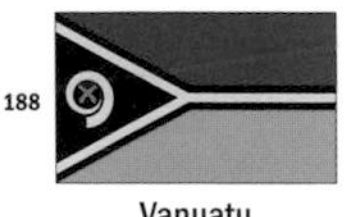
188 Vanuatu *Vanuatu[M]*

189 Fiji *Figi[F]*

190 Solomon Islands *Isole[F] Salomone*

191 Papua New Guinea *Papua Nuova Guinea[F]*

192 Australia *Australia[F]*

193 New Zealand *Nuova Zelanda[F]*

fire prevention

prevenzione^F degli incendi^M

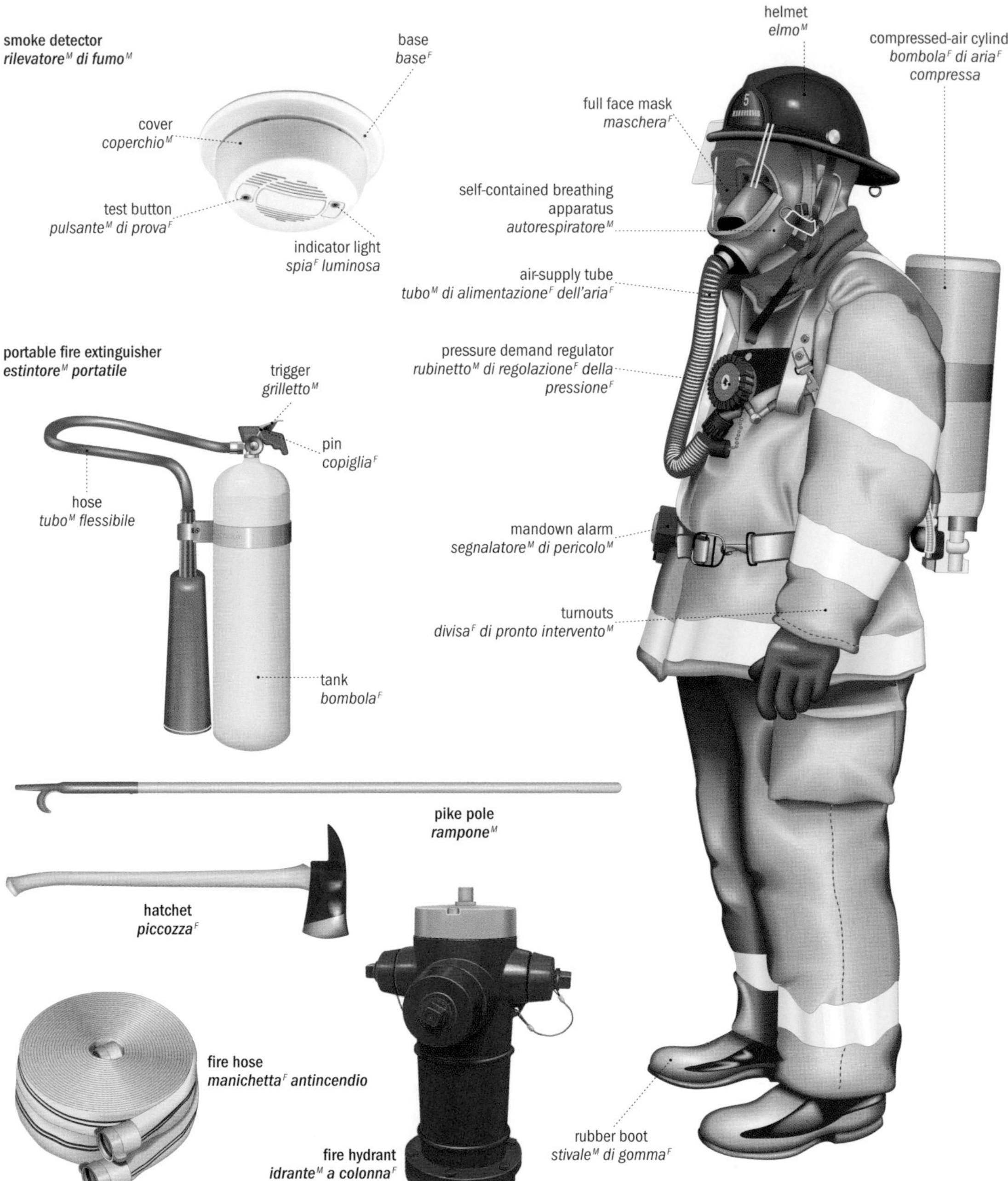

fire trucks
carri^M dei pompieri^M

pumper
autopompa^F

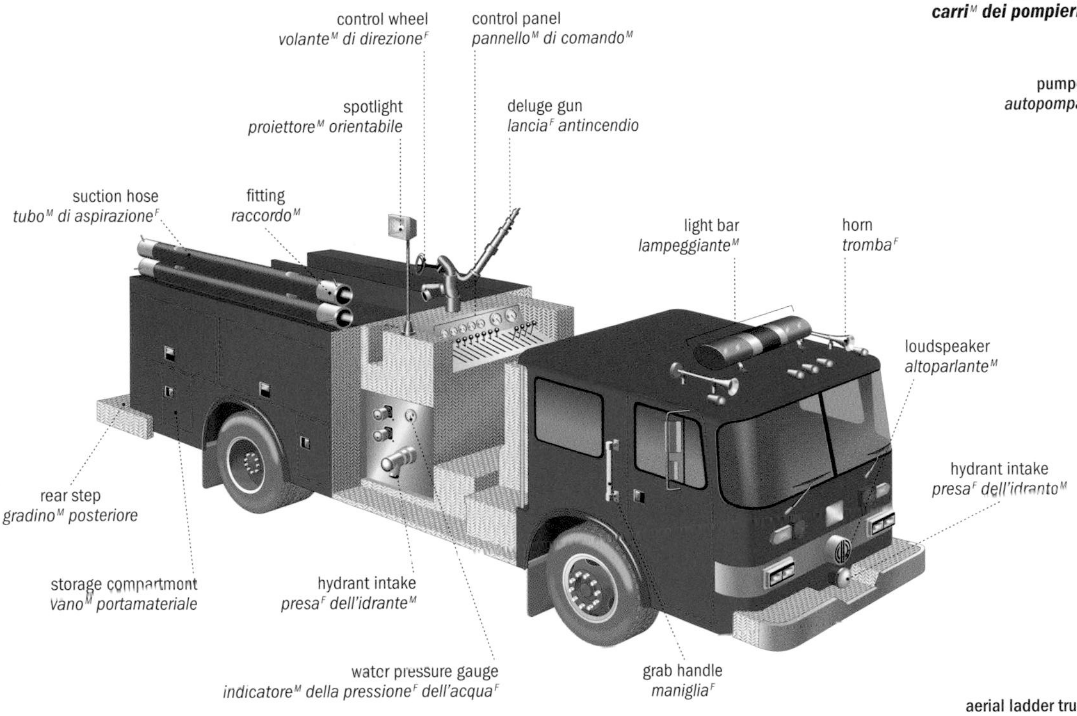

control wheel
volante^M di direzione^F
control panel
pannello^M di comando^M
spotlight
proiettore^M orientabile
deluge gun
lancia^F antincendio
suction hose
tubo^M di aspirazione^F
fitting
raccordo^M
light bar
lampeggiante^M
horn
tromba^F
loudspeaker
altoparlante^M
hydrant intake
presa^F dell'idrante^M
rear step
gradino^M posteriore
storage compartment
vano^M portamateriale
hydrant intake
presa^F dell'idrante^M
water pressure gauge
indicatore^M della pressione^F dell'acqua^F
grab handle
maniglia^F

aerial ladder truck
autoscala^F

ladder pipe nozzle
erogatore^M del tubo^M della scala^F
telescopic boom
braccio^M telescopico
oscillating light
luce^F rotante
elevating cylinder
cilindro^M di sollevamento^M
turntable mounting
piattaforma^F girevole
tower ladder
scala^F aerea
top ladder
tronco^M di testa^F della scala^F
spotlight
proiettore^M orientabile
storage compartment
vano^M portamateriale
outrigger
stabilizzatore^M

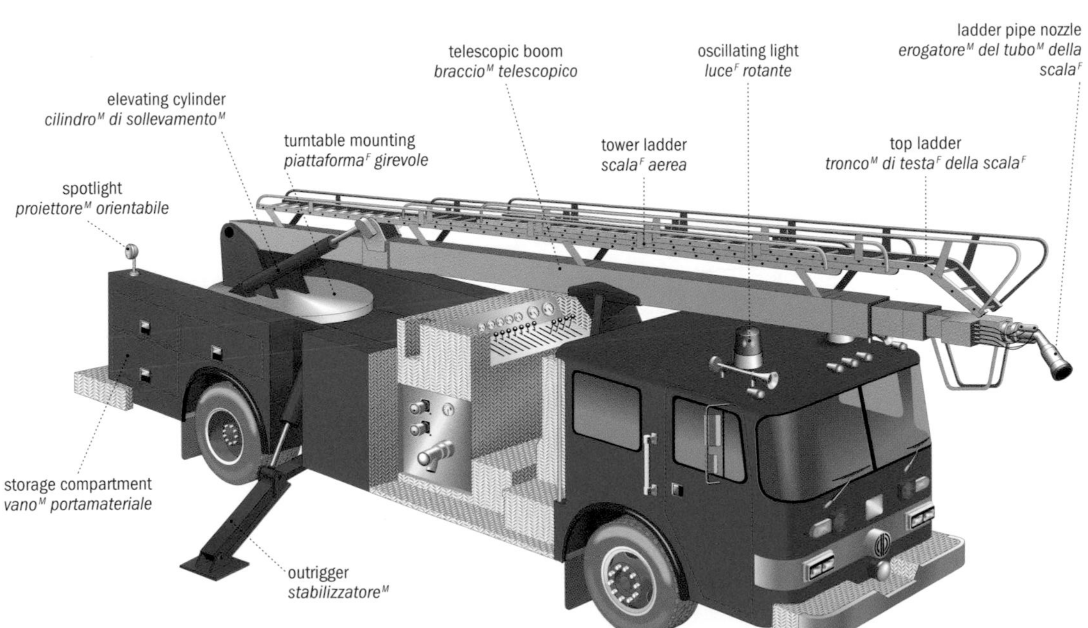

crime prevention

prevenzione[F] del crimine[M]

police officer
agente[M] di polizia[F]

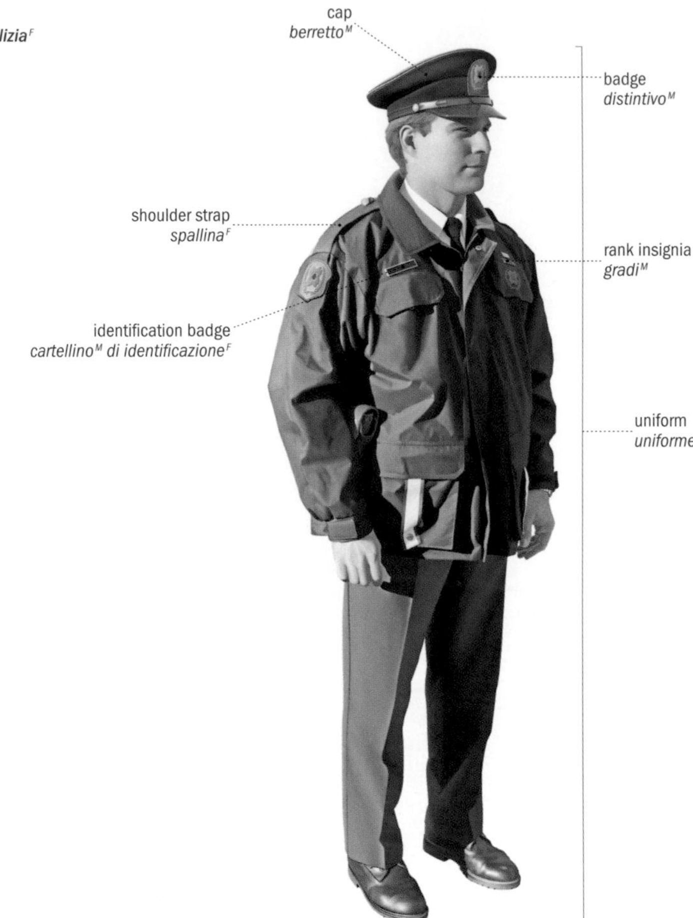

duty belt
cintura[F] di servizio[M]

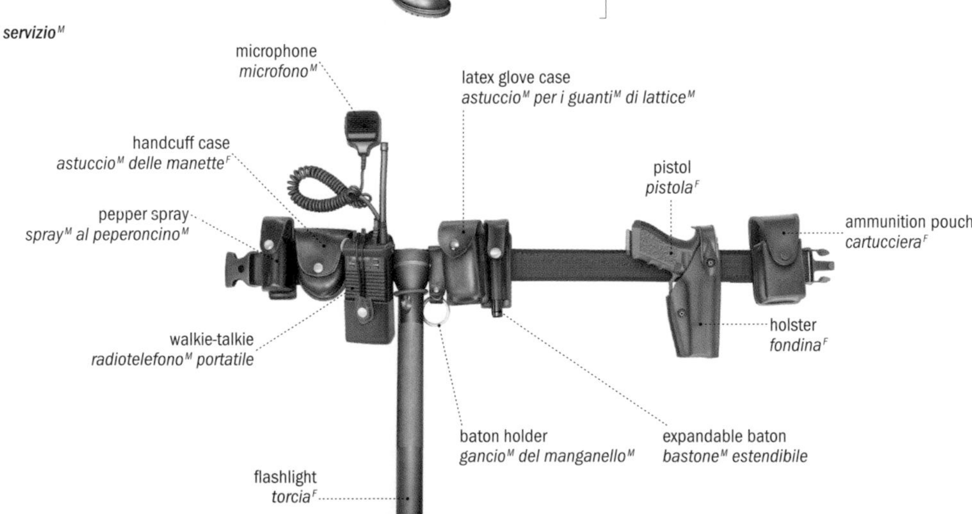

dashboard equipment
***equipaggiamento*^M *del cruscotto*^M**

light bar controller
sistema^M *di controllo*^M *del lampeggiante*^M
radar transceiver
ricetrasmettitore^M *radar*^M
reading light
luce^F *di lettura*^F
microphones
microfoni^M
dashboard computer
computer^M *di bordo*^M
computer programs
programmi^M *del computer*^M
radar display
display^M *del radar*^M
radio
radio^F

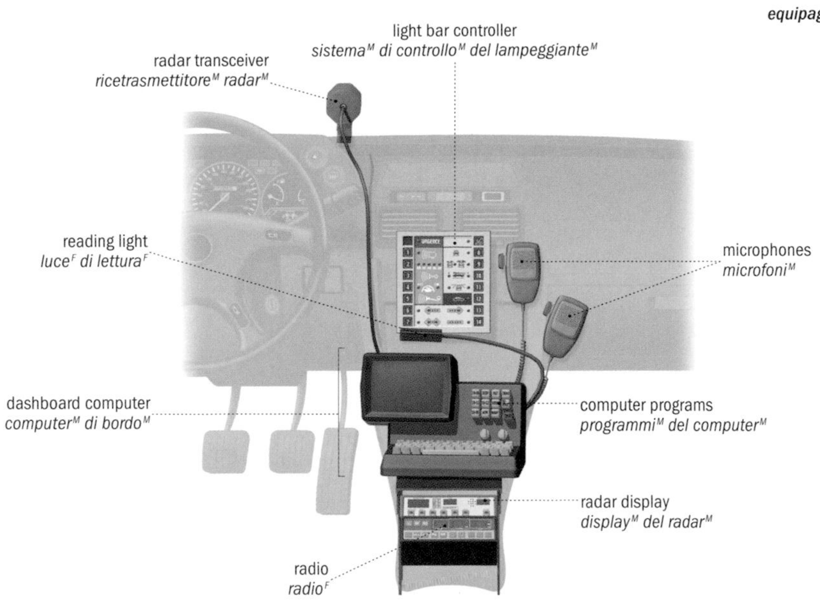

police car
***macchina*^F *della polizia*^F**

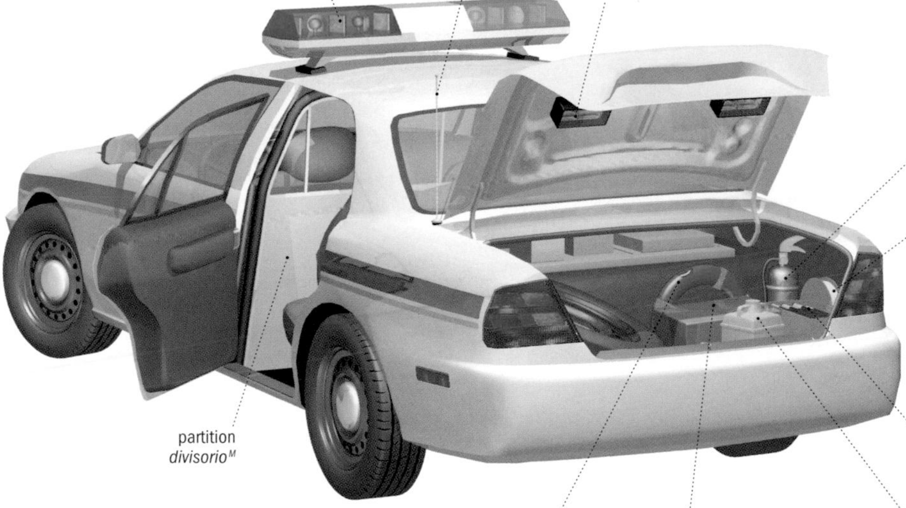

light bar
lampeggiante^M
antenna
antenna^F
safety lighting
luce^F *di sicurezza*^F
fire extinguisher
estintore^M
barrier barricade tape
nastro^M *di delimitazione*^F
partition
divisorio^M
road flare
razzo^M *illuminante*
life buoy
salvagente^M
first aid kit
cassetta^F *di pronto soccorso*^M
used syringe box
contenitore^M *delle siringhe*^F *usate*

ear protection

protezione^F per le orecchie^F

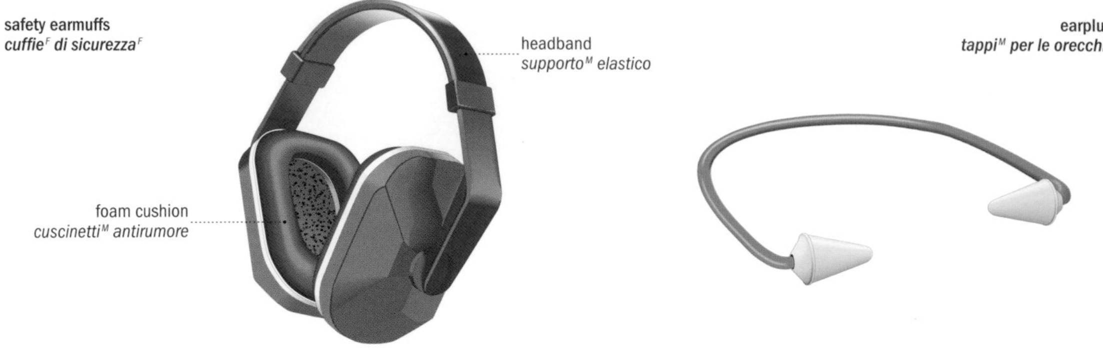

eye protection

protezione^F per gli occhi^M

head protection

protezione^F per la testa^F

SOCIETY

hard hat
elmetto^M

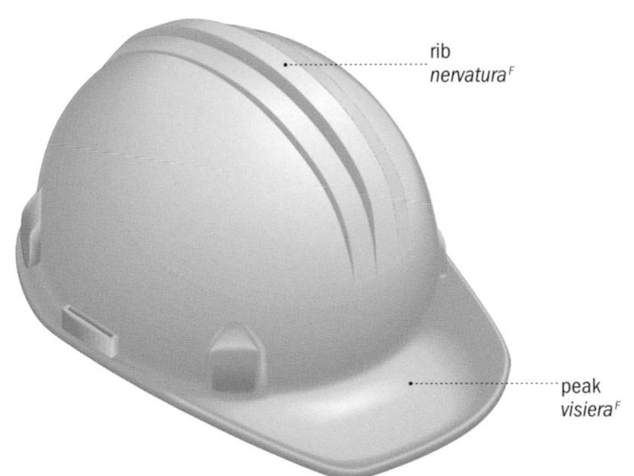

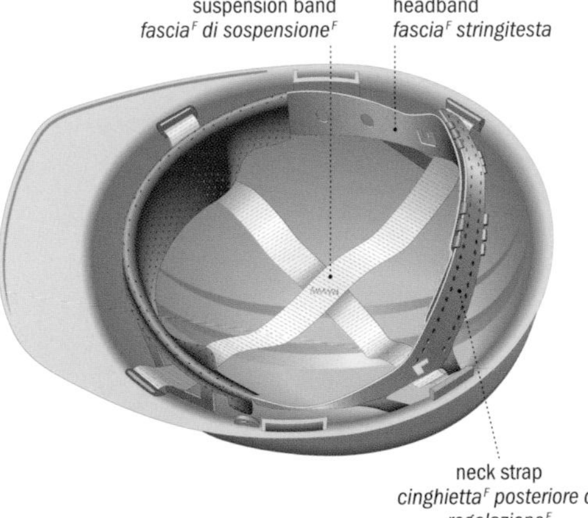

respiratory system protection

protezione[F] per le vie[F] respiratorie

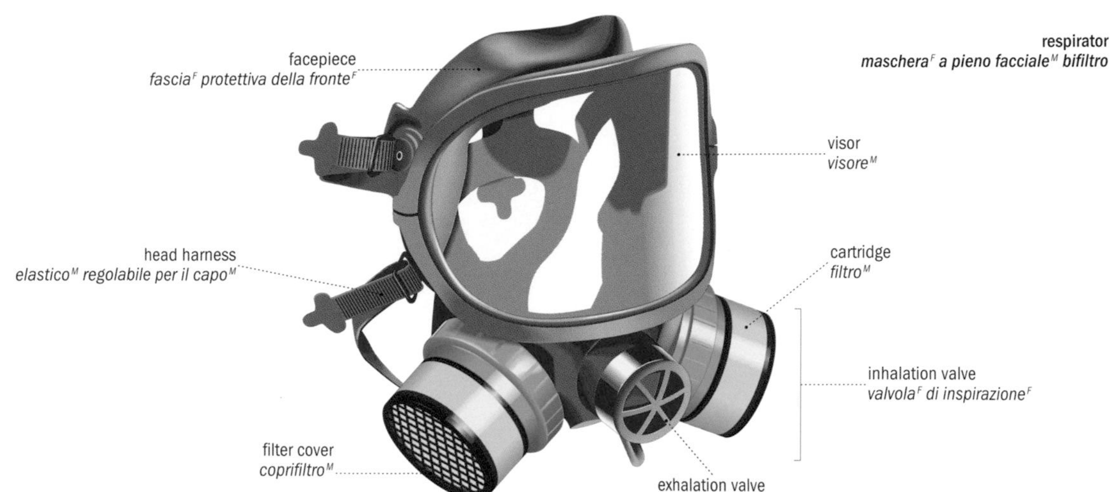

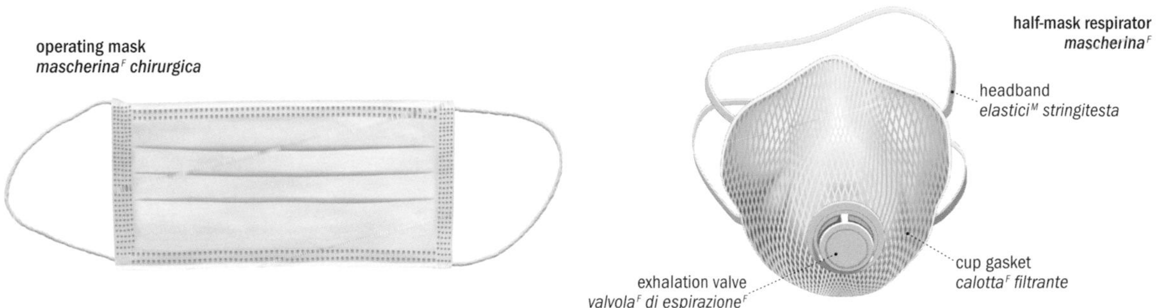

foot protection

protezione[F] per i piedi[M]

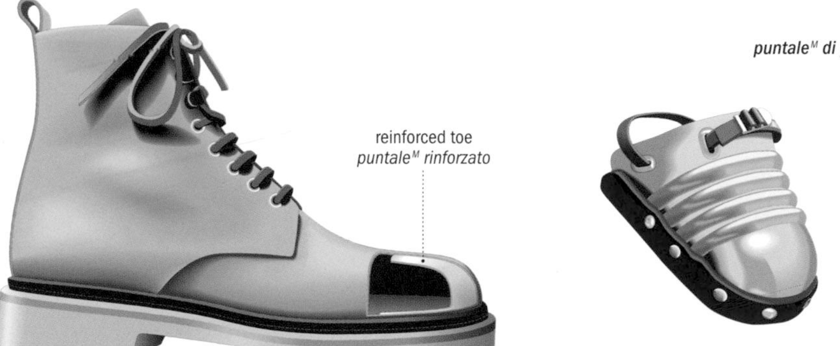

first aid equipment

strumenti[M] per il pronto soccorso[M]

stethoscope
fonendoscopio[M]

Y-tube
raccordo[M] a Y

sound receiver
capsula[F] di risonanza[F]

branch clip
molla[F]

earpiece
oliva[F] auricolare

flexible tube
tubo[M] flessibile

branch
archetto[M]

syringe
siringa[F]

bevel
punta[F]

needle
ago[M]

needle hub
cono[M]

Luer-Lock tip
punta[F] Luer-Lock

hollow barrel
cilindro[M]

tip protector
cappuccio[M] di protezione[F]

rubber bulb
gommino[M]

finger flange
aletta[F]

scale
scala[F] graduata

thumb rest
spingistantuffo[M]

plunger
stantuffo[M]

latex glove
guanto[M] di lattice[M]

syringe for irrigation
schizzetto[M]

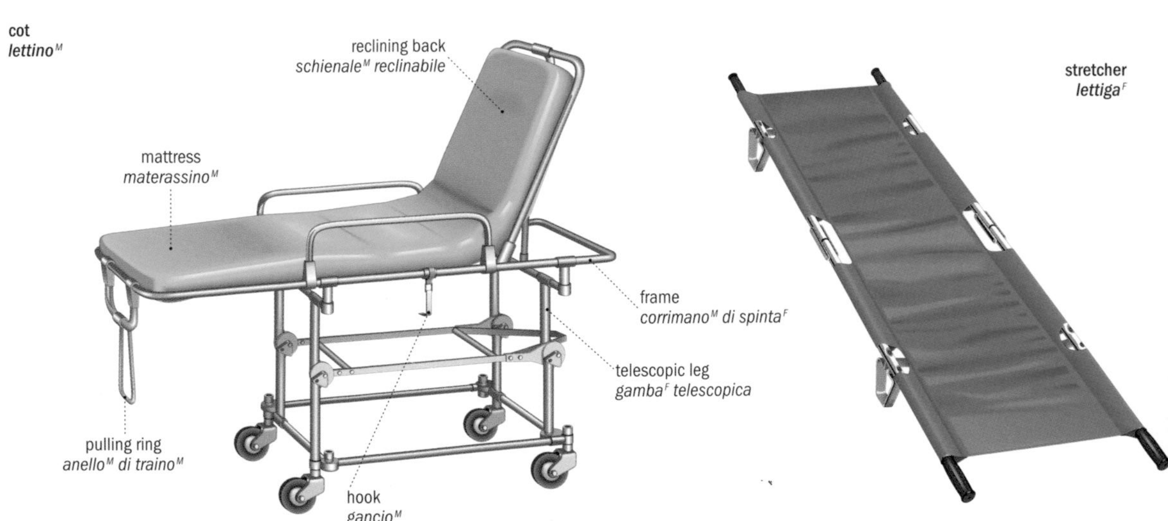

first aid kit

cassetta[F] di pronto soccorso[M]

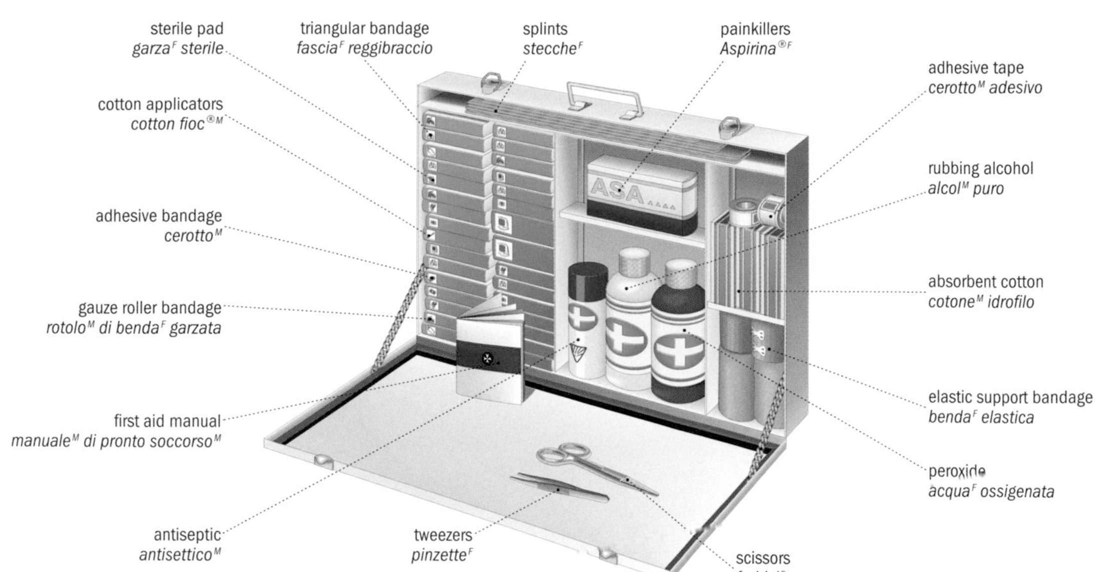

clinical thermometers

termometri[M] clinici

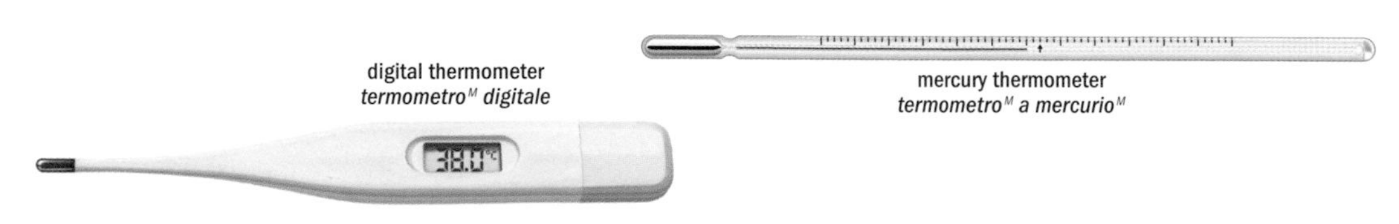

blood pressure monitor

monitor[M] della pressione[F] sanguigna

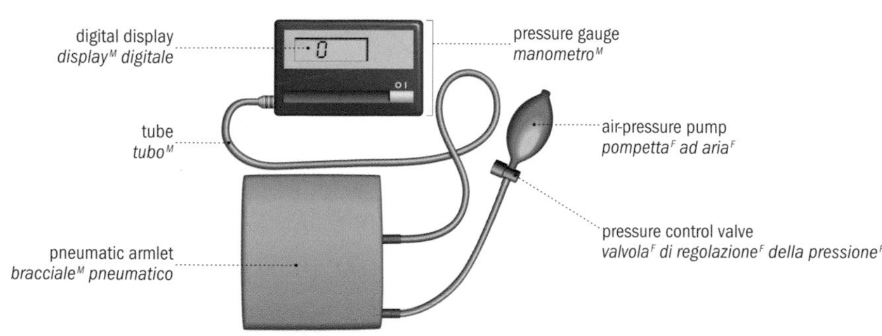

hospital

ospedale[M]

emergency
pronto soccorso[M]

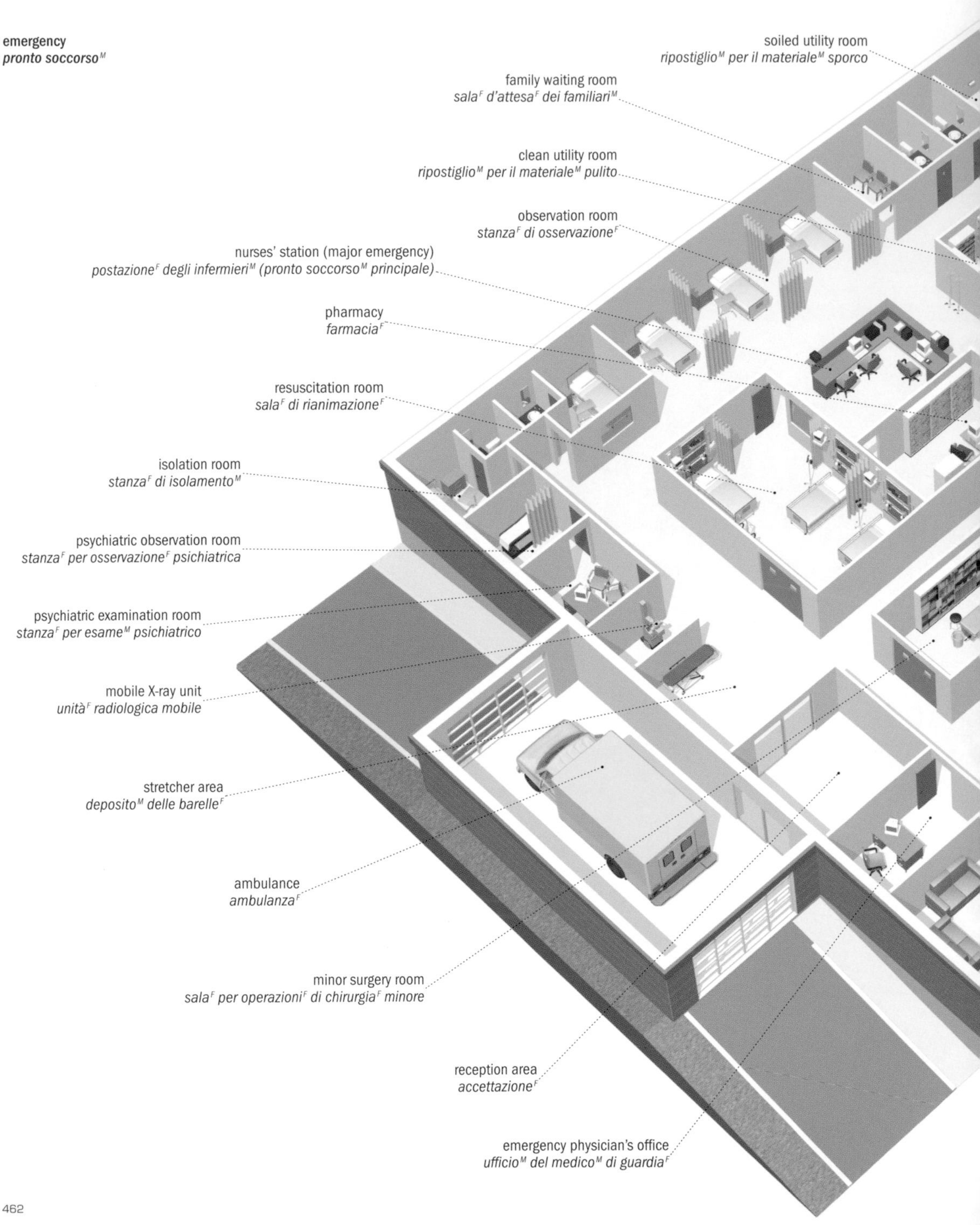

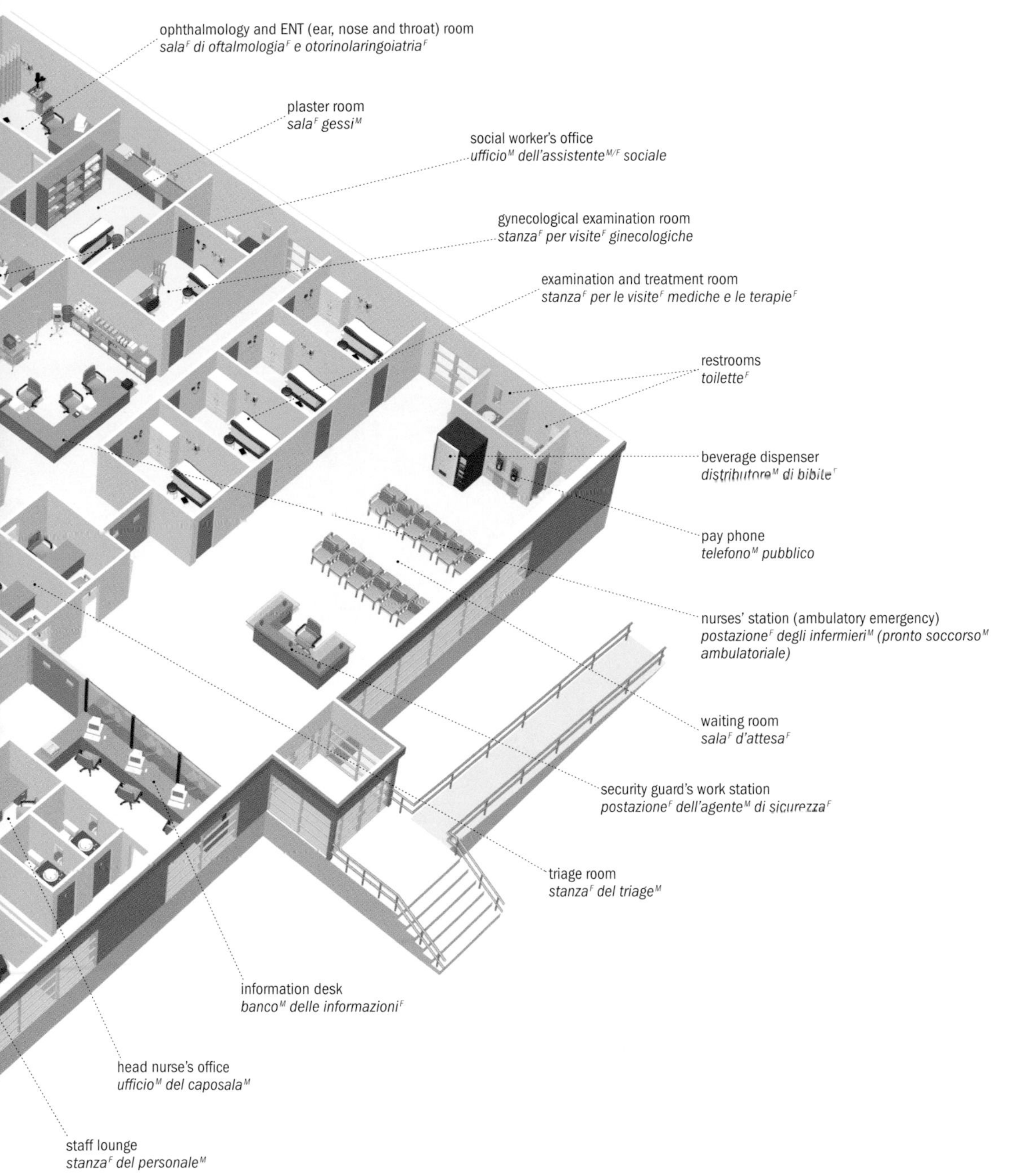
ophthalmology and ENT (ear, nose and throat) room
salaF di oftalmologiaF e otorinolaringoiatriaF
plaster room
salaF gessiM
social worker's office
ufficioM dell'assistenteM/F sociale
gynecological examination room
stanzaF per visiteF ginecologiche
examination and treatment room
stanzaF per le visiteF mediche e le terapieF
restrooms
toiletteF
beverage dispenser
distributoreM di bibiteF
pay phone
telefonoM pubblico
nurses' station (ambulatory emergency)
postazioneF degli infermieriM (pronto soccorsoM ambulatoriale)
waiting room
salaF d'attesaF
security guard's work station
postazioneF dell'agenteM di sicurezzaF
triage room
stanzaF del triageM
information desk
bancoM delle informazioniF
head nurse's office
ufficioM del caposalaM
staff lounge
stanzaF del personaleM

hospital

patient room
***stanza*[F] *di degenza*[F]**

bedside lamp
lampada[F] *da notte*[F]
resident
medico[M] *interno*
intravenous stand
piantana[F] *per fleboclisi*[F]
physician
medico[M]
oxygen outlet
presa[F] *dell'ossigeno*[M]
patient
paziente[M/F]
shower
doccia[F]
overbed table
tavolino[M] *da letto*[M]
bedside table
comodino[M]
privacy curtain
tendina[F] *divisoria*
toilet
water[M]
chair
poltroncina[F] *del paziente*[M]
bathroom
sala[F] *da bagno*[M]
hospital bed
letto[M] *d'ospedale*[M]
nurse
infermiera[F]

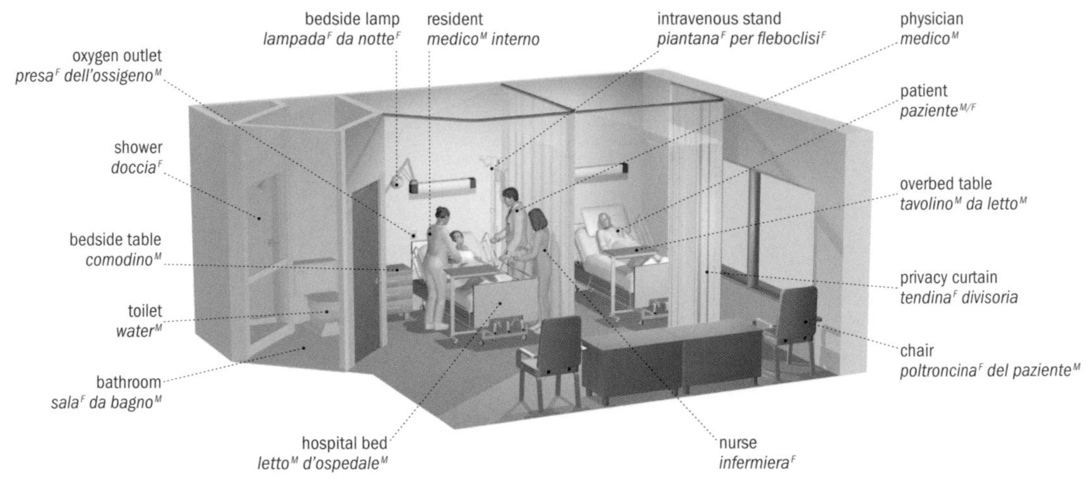

operating suite
blocco*[M] *operatorio

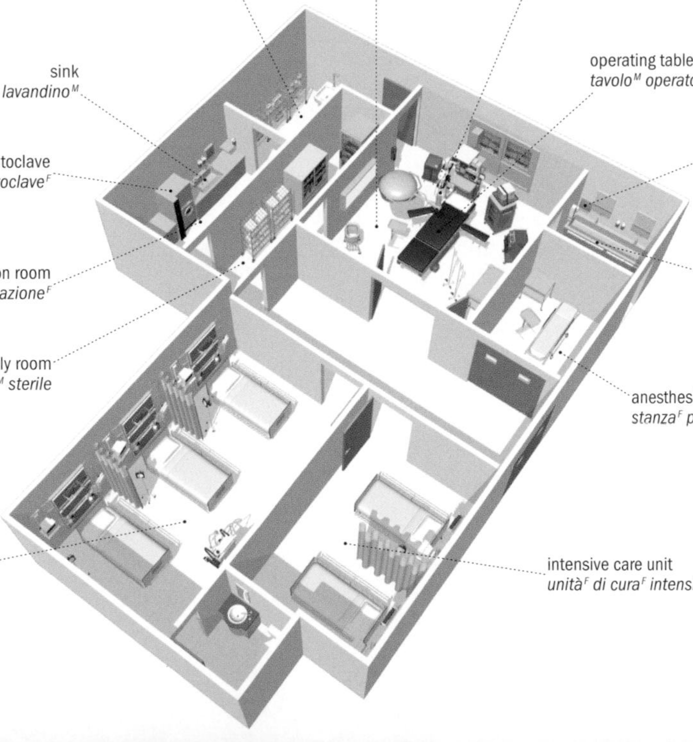

soiled utility room
deposito[M] *del materiale*[M] *sporco*
operating room
sala[F] *operatoria*
medical gas cylinder
bombola[F] *di gas*[M] *medicale*
sink
lavandino[M]
operating table
tavolo[M] *operatorio*
glove storage
scomparto[M] *per i guanti*[M]
autoclave
autoclave[F]
scrub room
stanza[F] *per la preparazione*[F] *chirurgica*
sterilization room
stanza[F] *di sterilizzazione*[F]
supply room
deposito[M] *del materiale*[M] *sterile*
anesthesia room
stanza[F] *per l'anestesia*[F]
recovery room
stanza[F] *di degenza*[F] *postoperatoria*
intensive care unit
unità[F] *di cura*[F] *intensiva*

ambulatory care unit
***poliambulatorio*[M]**

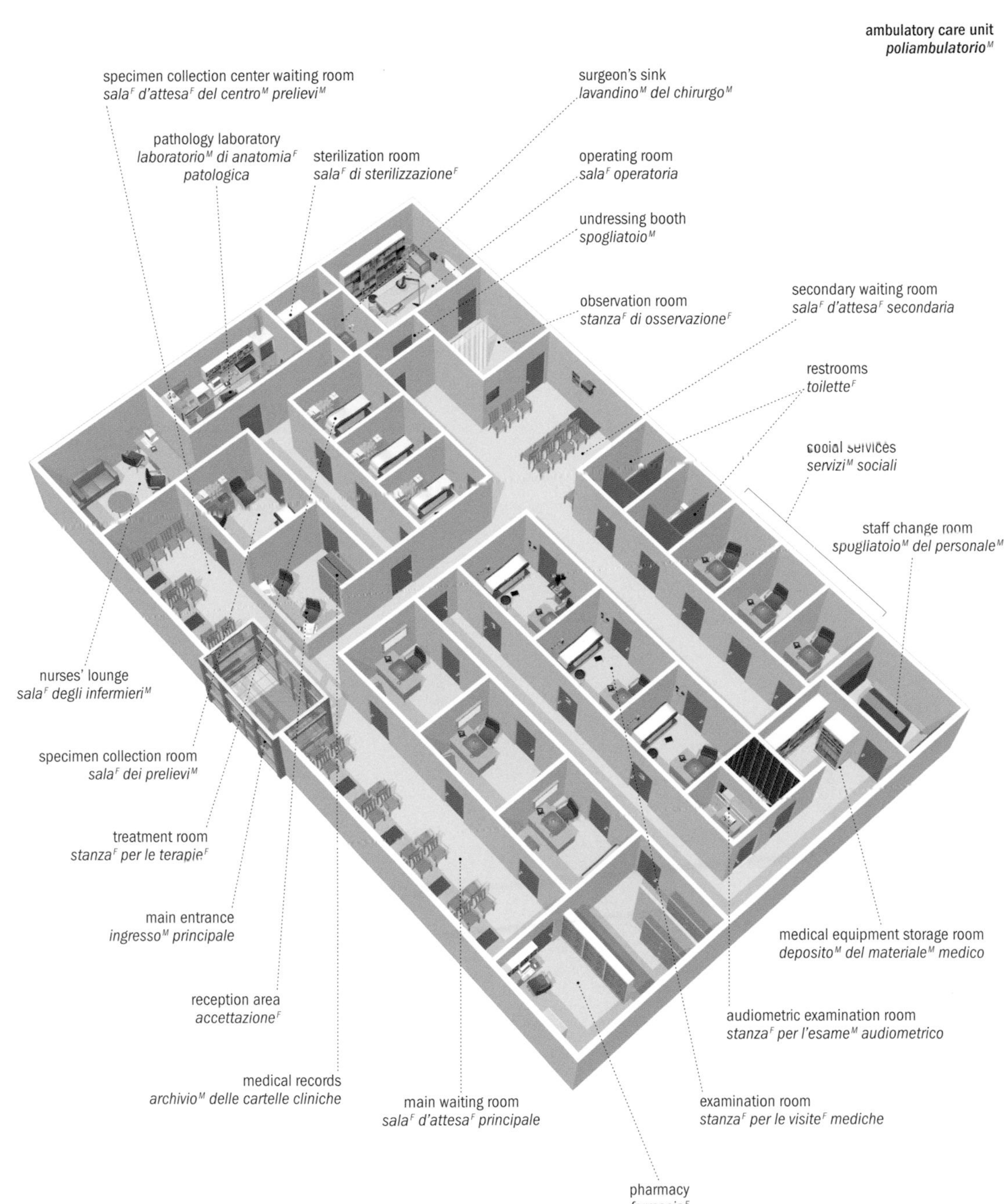

walking aids

supporti[M] per camminare

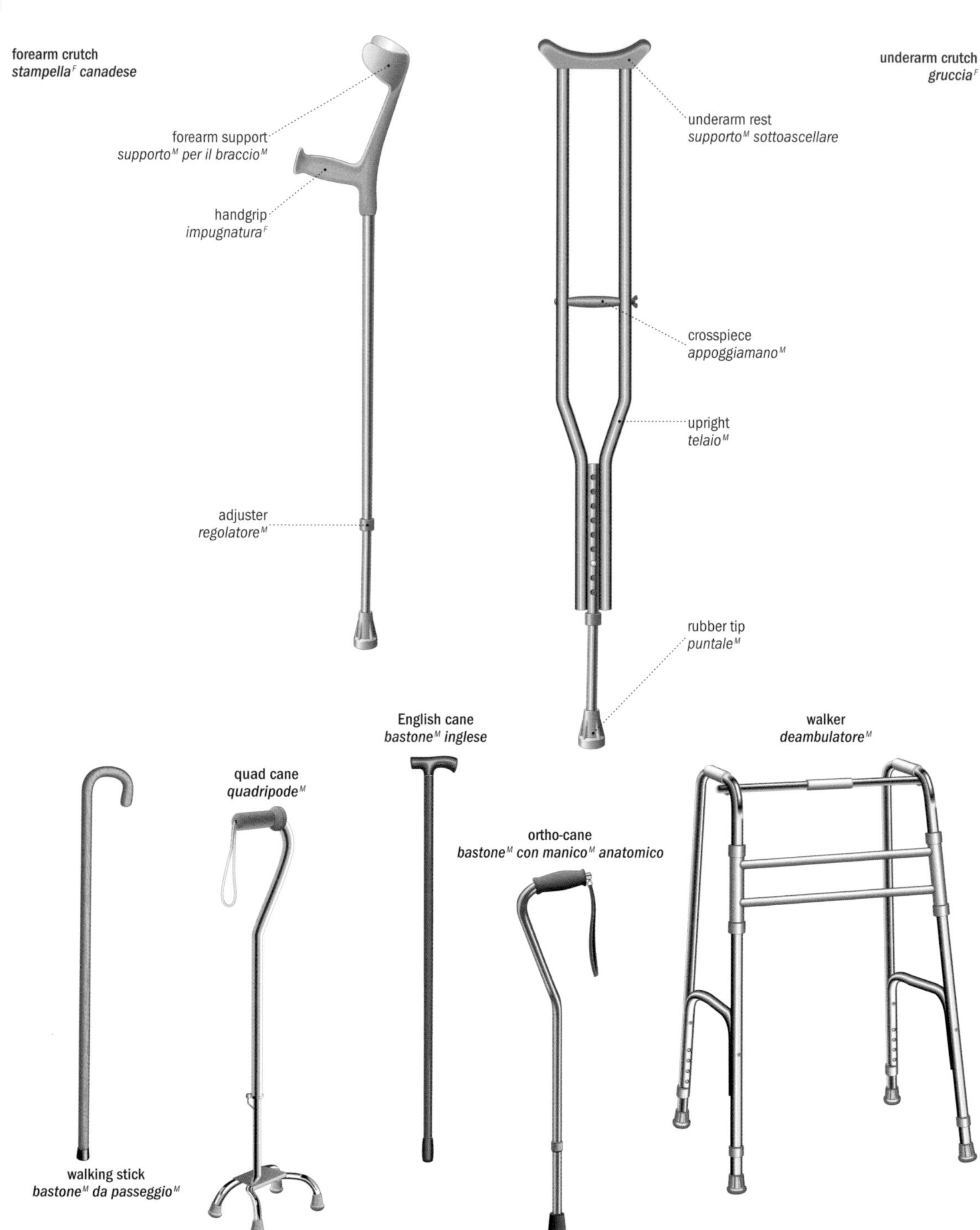

wheelchair

sedia^F a rotelle^F

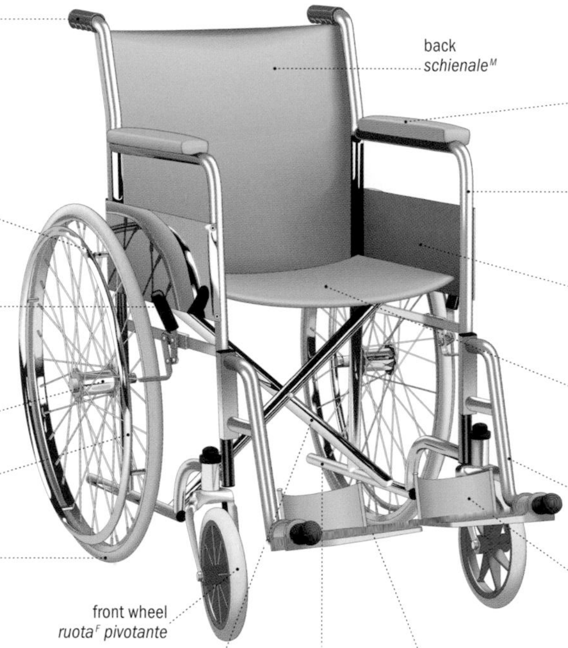

handle
impugnatura^F
back
schienale^M
armrest
bracciolo^M
spacer
distanziatore^M
arm
braccio^M
brake
freno^M
clothing guard
fiancata^F
hub
mozzo^M
seat
seduta^F
push rim
ruota^F di spinta^F
hanger bracket
braccio^M di sospensione^F
large wheel
ruota^F piena o gonfiabile
heel loop
supporto^M per il tallone^M
front wheel
ruota^F pivotante
cross brace
rinforzo^M a crociera^F
tipping lever
pedale^M di sollevamento^M
footrest
appoggiapiedi^M

forms of medications

confezioni^F farmaceutiche di medicinali^M

100 ml

syrup
flacone^M

mouthpiece
boccaglio^M
cap
cappuccio^M

metered dose inhaler
inalatore^M dosimetrico

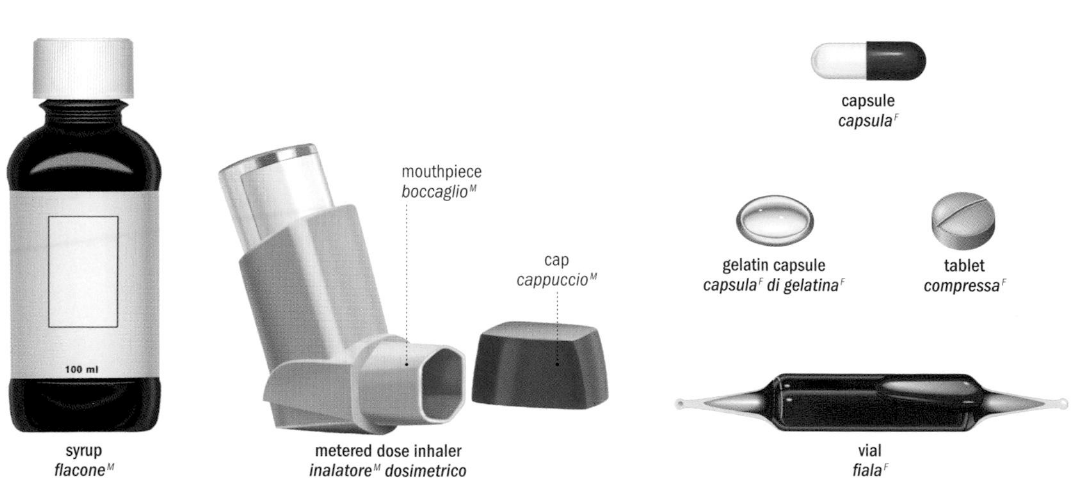

capsule
capsula^F

gelatin capsule
capsula^F di gelatina^F

tablet
compressa^F

vial
fiala^F

dice and dominoes

dadi[M] e domino[M]

ordinary die
dado[M] comune

poker die
dado[M] da poker[M]

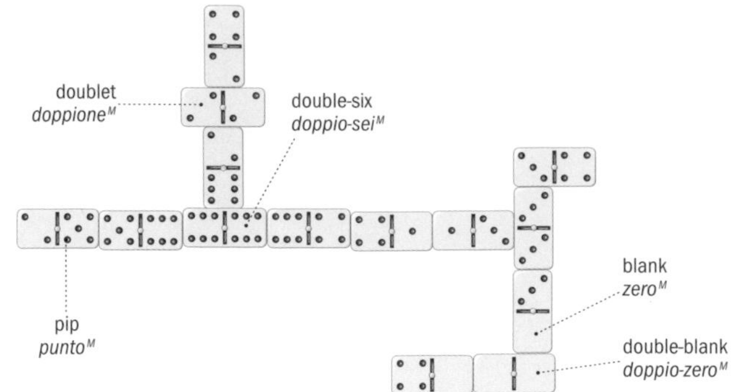

dominoes
domino[M]

doublet
doppione[M]

double-six
doppio-sei[M]

pip
punto[M]

blank
zero[M]

double-blank
doppio-zero[M]

cards

giochi[M] di carte[F]

symbols
simboli[M]

heart
cuori[M]

diamond
quadri[M]

club
fiori[M]

spade
picche[M]

joker
jolly[M]

ace
asso[M]

king
re[M]

queen
donna[F]

jack
fante[M]

standard poker hands
combinazioni[F] del poker[M]

high card
carta[F] più alta

one pair
coppia[F]

two pairs
doppia coppia[F]

three-of-a-kind
tris[M]

straight
scala[F]

flush
colore[M]

full house
full[M]

four-of-a-kind
poker[M]

straight flush
scala[F] reale

royal flush
scala[F] reale massima

board games
giochi[M] da tavola[F]

backgammon
backgammon[M]

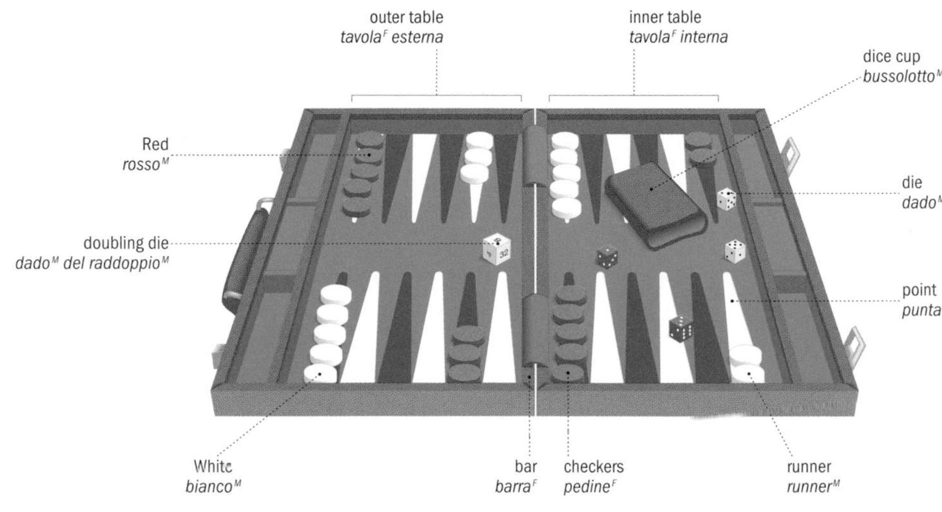

snakes and ladders
serpenti[M] e scale[F]

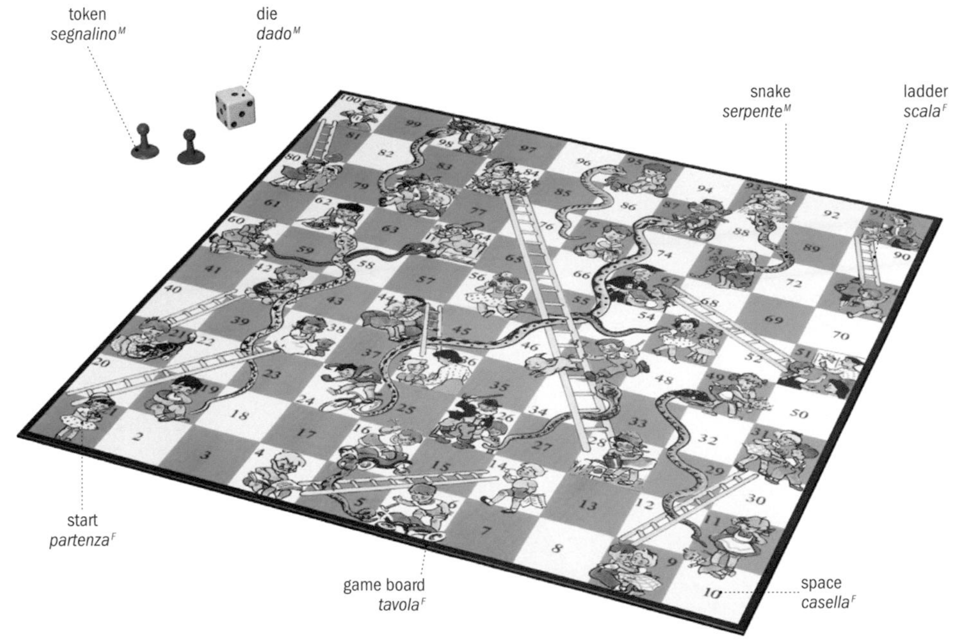

board games

chess
scacchi[M]

chessboard
scacchiera[F]

queen's side
lato[M] *della regina*[F]

king's side
lato[M] *del re*[M]

Black
neri[M]

white square
casella[F] *bianca*

black square
casella[F] *nera*

White
bianchi[M]

chess notation
notazione[F] *degli scacchi*[M]

8
7
6
5
4
3
2
1
a b c d e f g h

chess pieces
pezzi[M]

pawn
pedone[M]

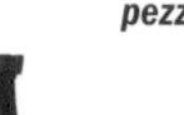

rook
torre[F]

bishop
alfiere[M]

knight
cavallo[M]

types of movements
tipi[M] ***di movimenti***[M]

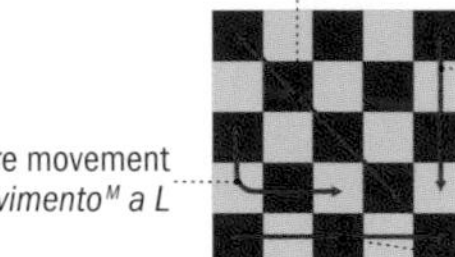

king
re[M]

queen
regina[F]

go
go[M]

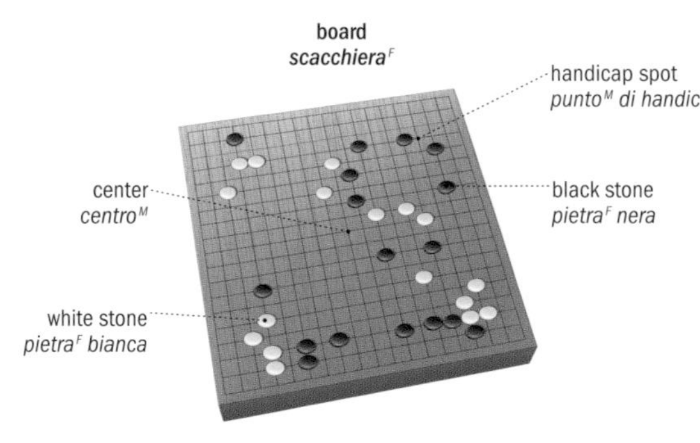

major motions
mosse[F] ***principali***

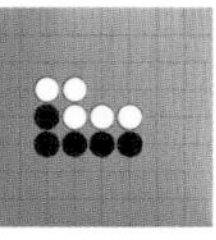

connection
gruppo[M]

contact
contatto[M]

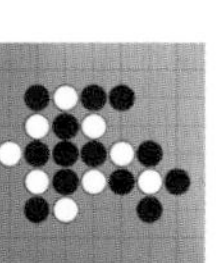

capture
cattura[F]

checkers
dama[F]

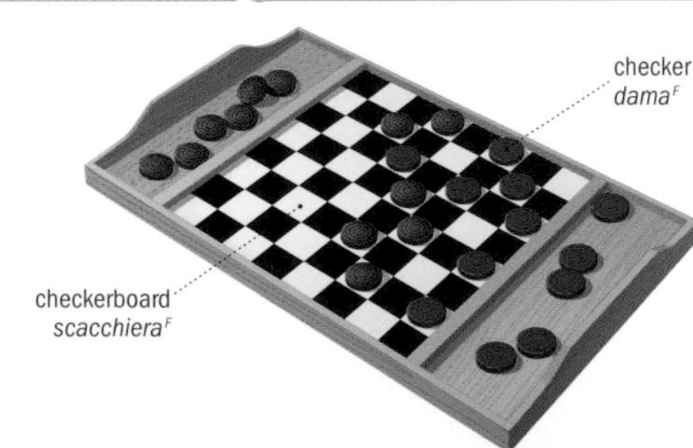

SPORTS AND GAMES

video entertainment system

videogioco[M]

eject button
pulsante[M] di espulsione[F]
CD/DVD player
lettore[M] CD[M]/DVD[M]
game console
console[F]
cover
coperchio[M]
directional buttons
pulsanti[M] direzionali
controller
manopola[F] di controllo[M]
joysticks
joystick[M]
action buttons
pulsanti[M] di azione[F]
reset button
pulsante[M] di reset[M]
monitor
video[M]

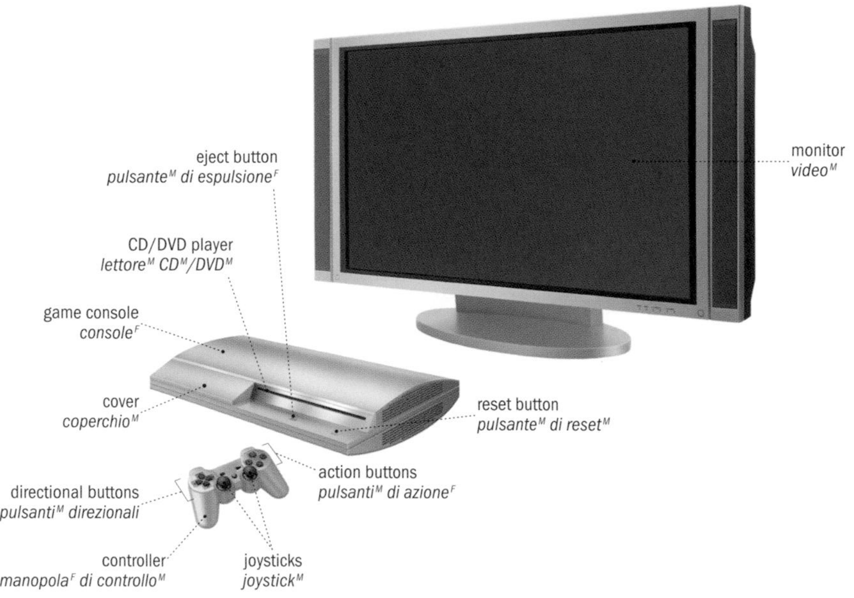

darts

freccette[F]

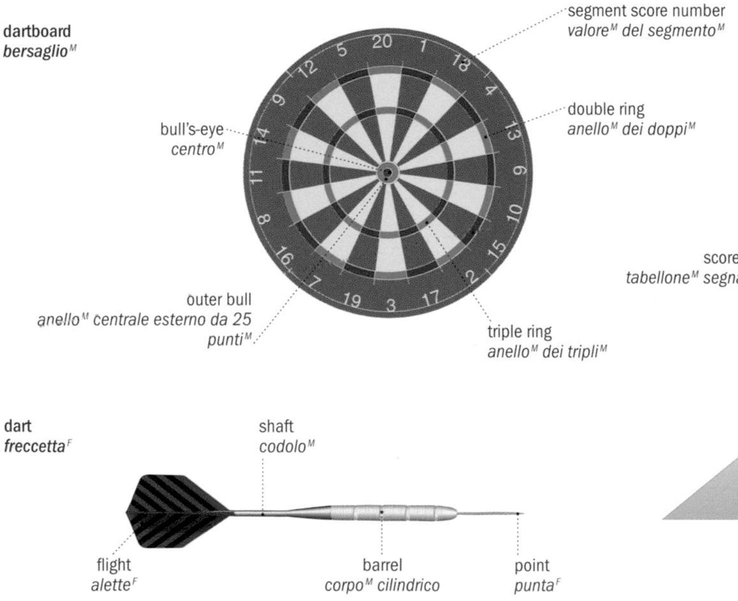

dartboard
bersaglio[M]
segment score number
valore[M] del segmento[M]
double ring
anello[M] dei doppi[M]
bull's-eye
centro[M]
outer bull
anello[M] centrale esterno da 25 punti[M]
triple ring
anello[M] dei tripli[M]
dart
freccetta[F]
shaft
codolo[M]
flight
alette[F]
barrel
corpo[M] cilindrico
point
punta[F]

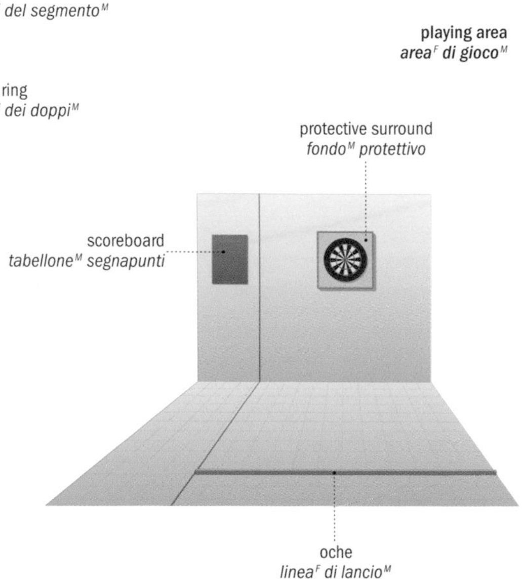

playing area
area[F] di gioco[M]
protective surround
fondo[M] protettivo
scoreboard
tabellone[M] segnapunti
oche
linea[F] di lancio[M]

SPORTS AND GAMES

arena

stadio^{M}

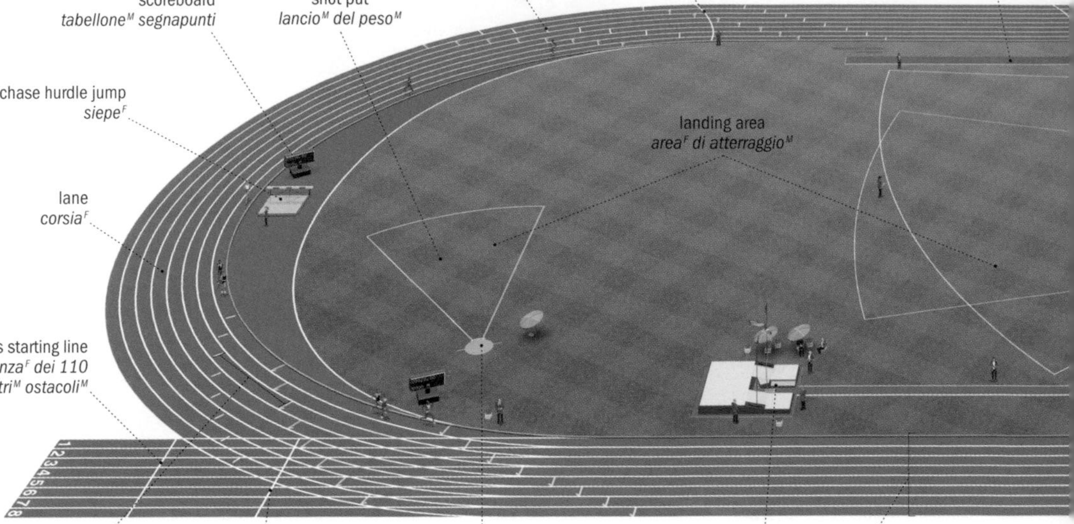

200 m starting line
linea^{F} di partenza^{F} dei 200 metri^{M} piani

5,000 m starting line
linea^{F} di partenza^{F} dei 5000 metri^{M} piani

long jump and triple jump
salto^{M} in lungo e salto^{M} triplo

scoreboard
tabellone^{M} segnapunti

shot put
lancio^{M} del peso^{M}

steeplechase hurdle jump
siepe^{F}

landing area
area^{F} di atterraggio^{M}

lane
corsia^{F}

110 m hurdles starting line
linea^{F} di partenza^{F} dei 110 metri^{M} ostacoli^{M}

takeover zone
zona^{F} del passaggio^{M} del testimone^{M}

100 m and 100 m hurdles starting line
linea^{F} di partenza^{F} dei 100 metri^{M} piani e dei 100 metri^{M} ostacoli^{M}

throwing circle
pedana^{F} di lancio^{M}

pole vault
salto^{M} con l'asta^{F}

track
pista^{F}

equipment
attrezzatura^{F}

starting pistol
pistola^{F} dello starter^{M}

shot
peso^{M}

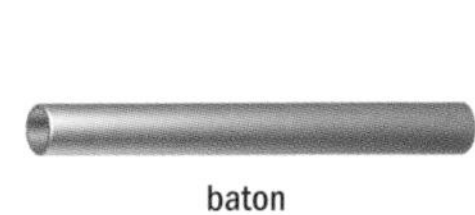

baton
testimone^{M}

discus
disco^{M}

hammer
martello^{M}

javelin
giavellotto^{M}

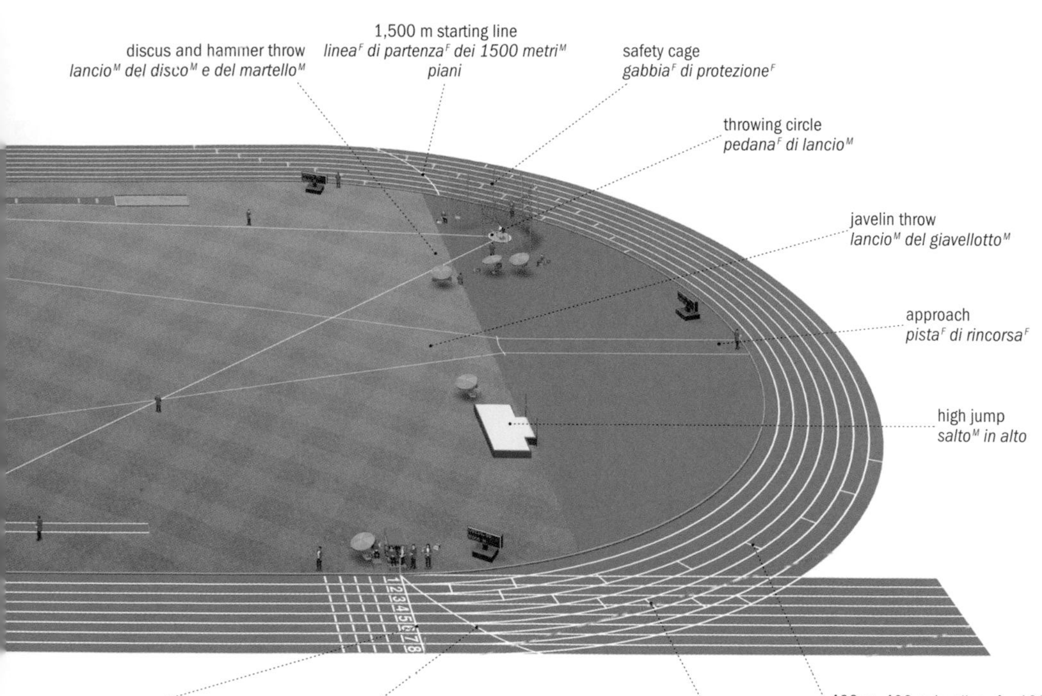

athlete: starting block
atleta$^{M/F}$: blocco^{M} di partenza^{F}

singlet
maglietta^{F}

number
numero^{M}

shorts
pantaloncini^{M}

pedal
pedale^{M}

track shoe
scarpa^{F}

starting line
linea^{F} di partenza^{F}

notch
tacca^{F}

lane line
linea^{F} della corsia^{F}

anchor
ancoraggio^{M}

rack
cremagliera^{F}

spike
chiodo^{M}

block
blocco^{M}

base
base^{F}

baseball

baseball[M]

player positions
posizioni[F] dei giocatori[M]

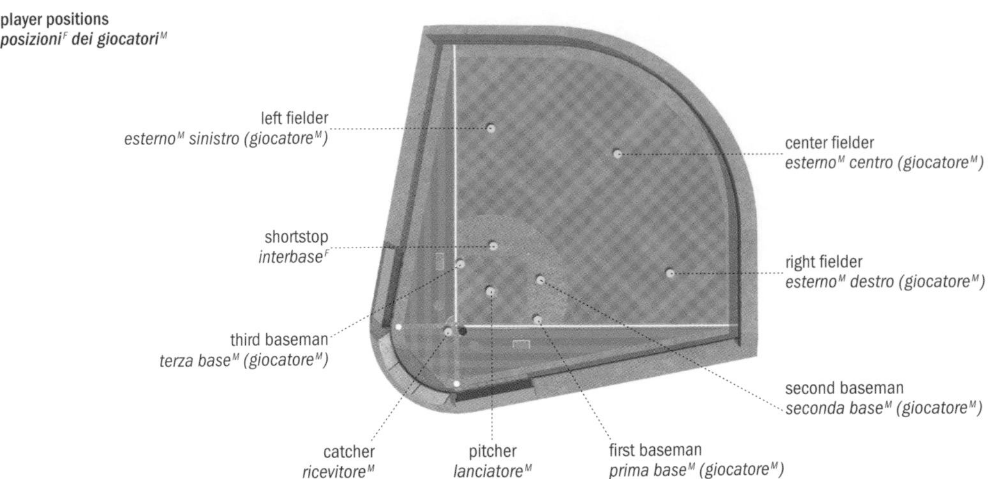

field
campo[M]

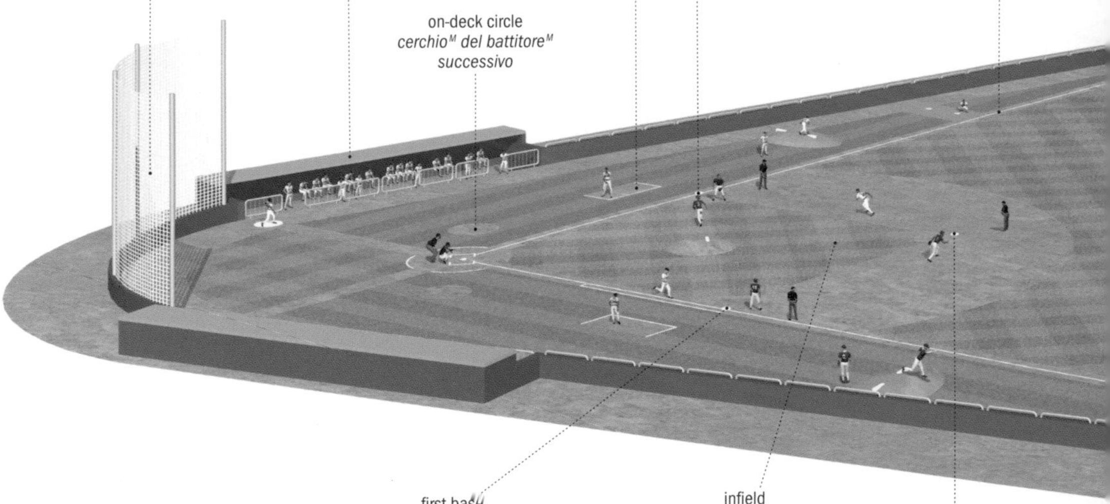

third base
terza base[F] (posizione[F])

foul line
linea[F] di fuoricampo[M]

dugout
panchina[F] dei giocatori[M]

coach's box
zona[F] dell'allenatore[M]

backstop
schermo[M] di protezione[F]

on-deck circle
cerchio[M] del battitore[M] successivo

first base
prima base[F] (posizione[F])

infield
diamante[M]

second base
seconda base[F] (posizione[F])

SPORTS AND GAMES

pitch
lancio[M]

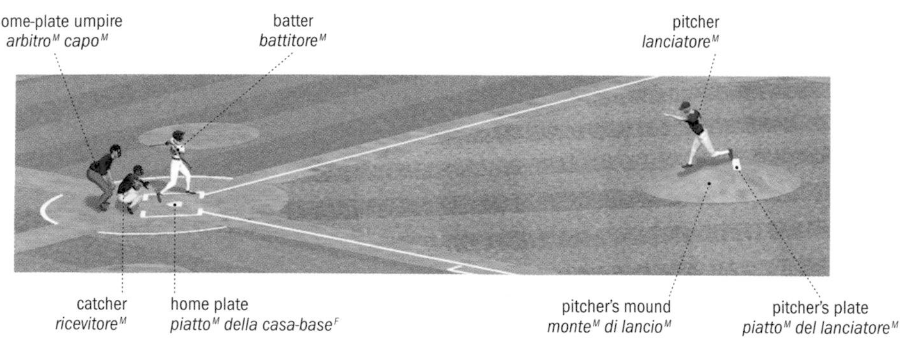

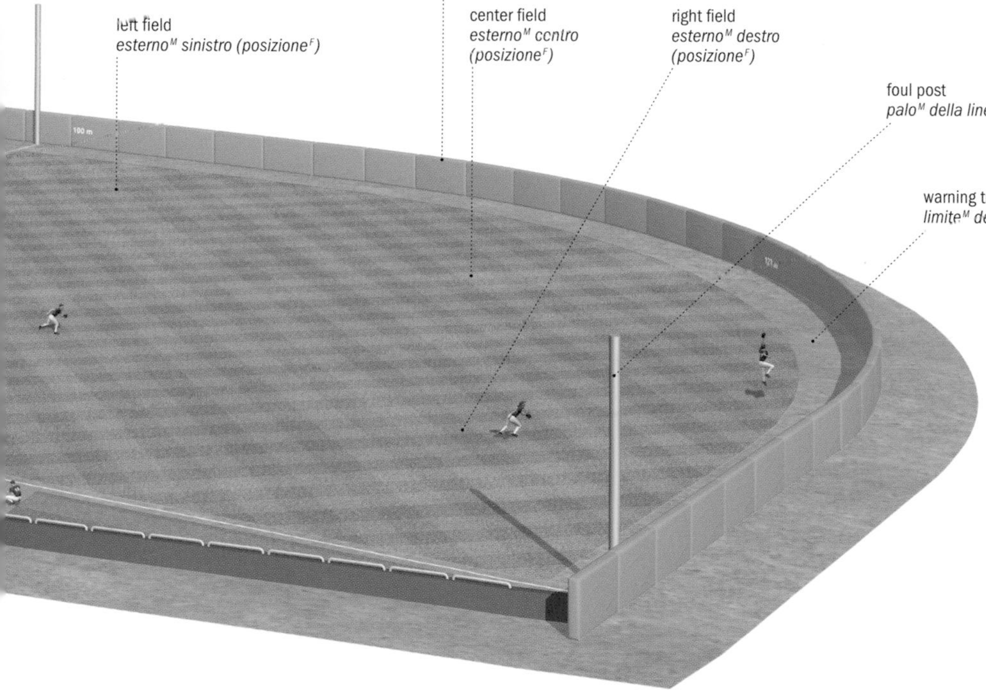

outfield fence
recinzione[F]

left field
esterno[M] sinistro (posizione[F])

center field
esterno[M] centro (posizione[F])

right field
esterno[M] destro (posizione[F])

foul post
palo[M] della linea[F] di fuoricampo[M]

warning track
limite[M] del campo[M]

baseball

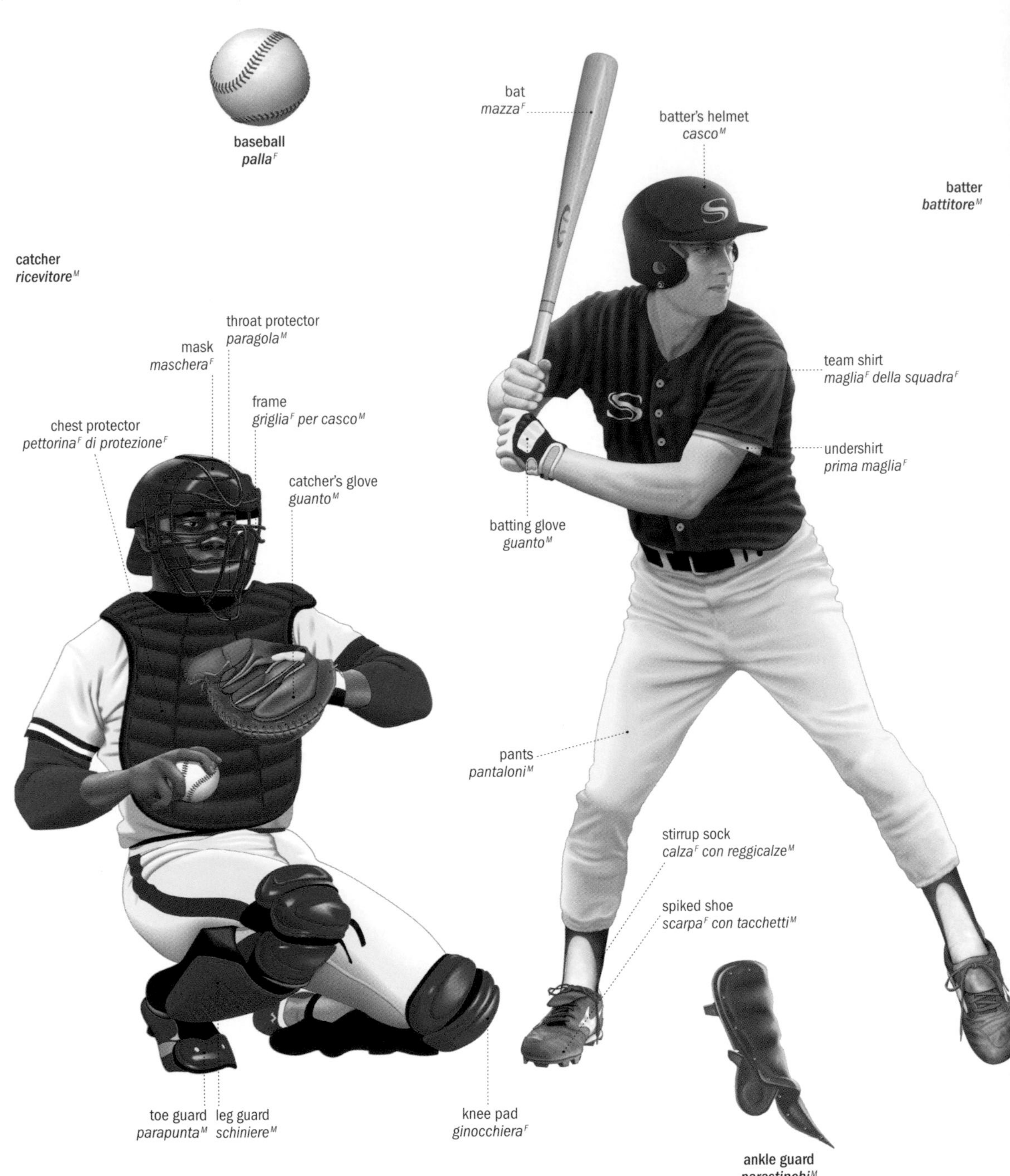
baseball
palla F
bat
mazza F
batter's helmet
casco M
batter
battitore M
catcher
ricevitore M
throat protector
paragola M
mask
maschera F
team shirt
maglia F della squadra F
frame
griglia F per casco M
chest protector
pettorina F di protezione F
undershirt
prima maglia F
catcher's glove
guanto M
batting glove
guanto M
pants
pantaloni M
stirrup sock
calza F con reggicalze M
spiked shoe
scarpa F con tacchetti M
toe guard
parapunta M
leg guard
schiniere M
knee pad
ginocchiera F
ankle guard
parastinchi M

baseball

bat
***mazza*[F]**

knob
pomo[M]
handle
impugnatura[F]
crest
stemma[M]
hitting area
zona[F] *di battuta*[F]

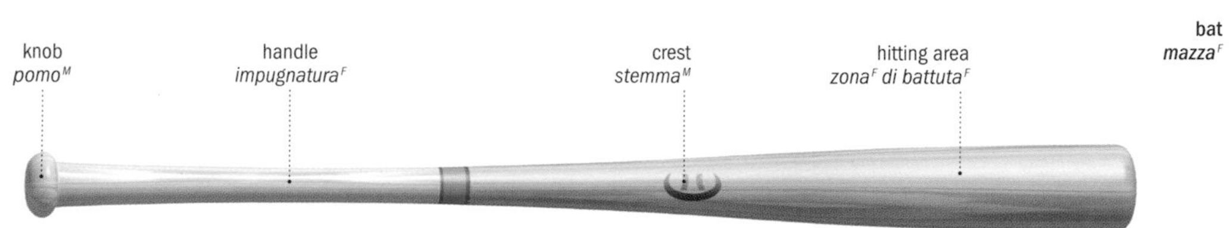

fielder's glove
***guanto*[M] *del difensore*[M]**

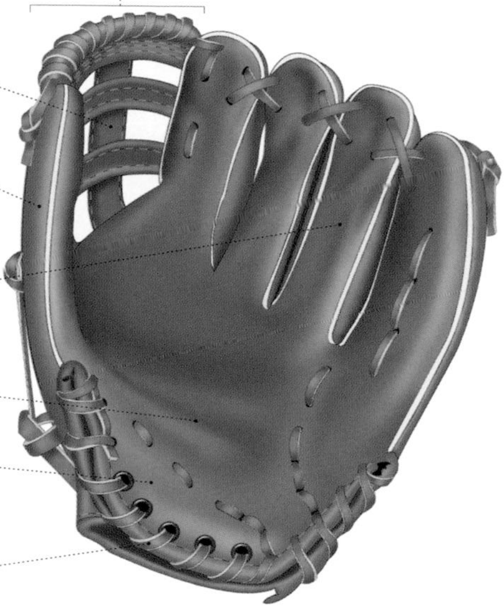

web
finestra[F]
strap
cinturino[M]
thumb
pollice[M]
finger
dito[M]
palm
sacco[M]
heel
tallone[M]
lace
stringa[F]

cross section of a baseball
***sezione*[F] *di una palla*[F]**

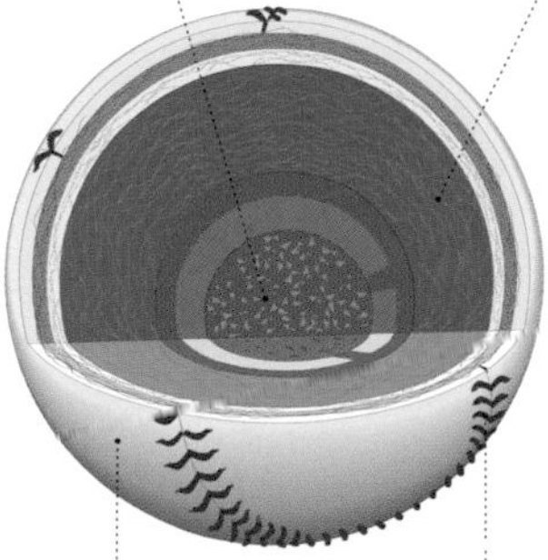

cork ball
palla[F] *di sughero*[M]
yarn
palla[F] *di filo*[M]
cover
rivestimento[M] *esterno*
stitches
cucitura[F]

softball

softball[M]

softball glove
***guanto*[M]**

softball
***palla*[F]**

softball bat
***mazza*[F]**

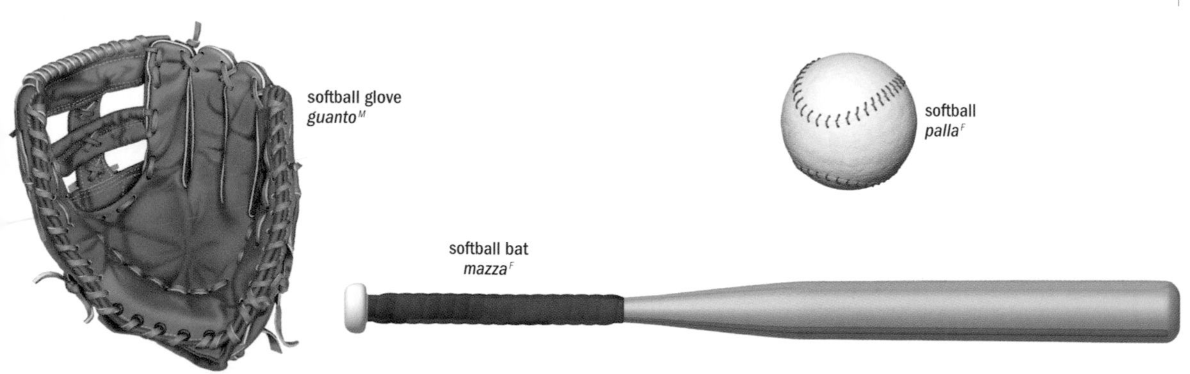

cricket

cricket^{M}

cricket player: batsman
giocatore^{M}: battitore^{M}

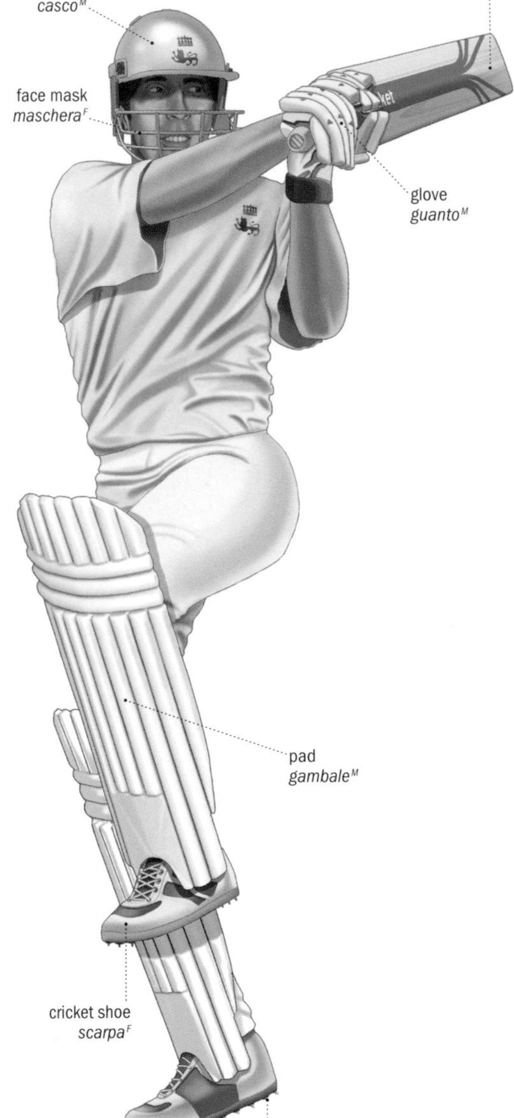

cricket ball
palla^{F}

leather skin
cuoio^{M}

seam
cucitura^{F}

bat
mazza^{F}

handle
impugnatura^{F}

willow
pala^{F}

front view
vista^{F} frontale

side view
vista^{F} laterale

field
campo[M]

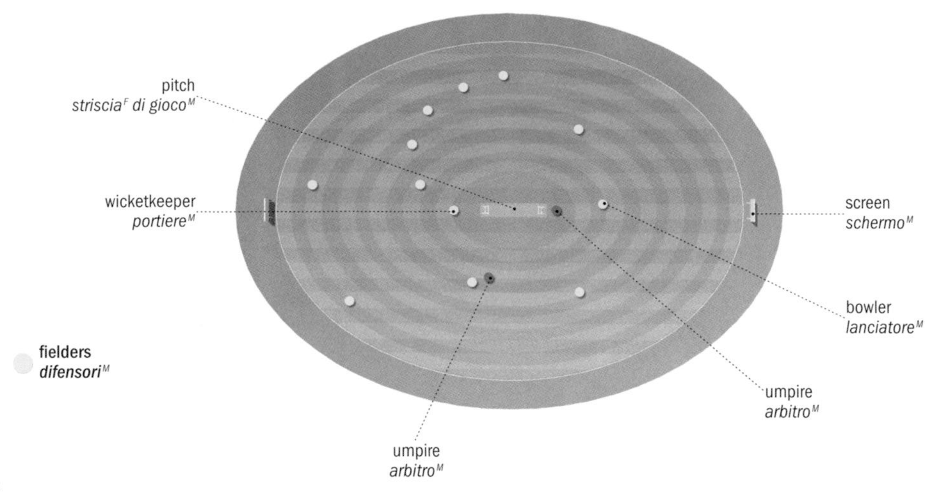

wicket
porta[F]

pitch
striscia[F] ***di gioco***[M]

soccer

calcio^{M}

soccer player
calciatore^{M}

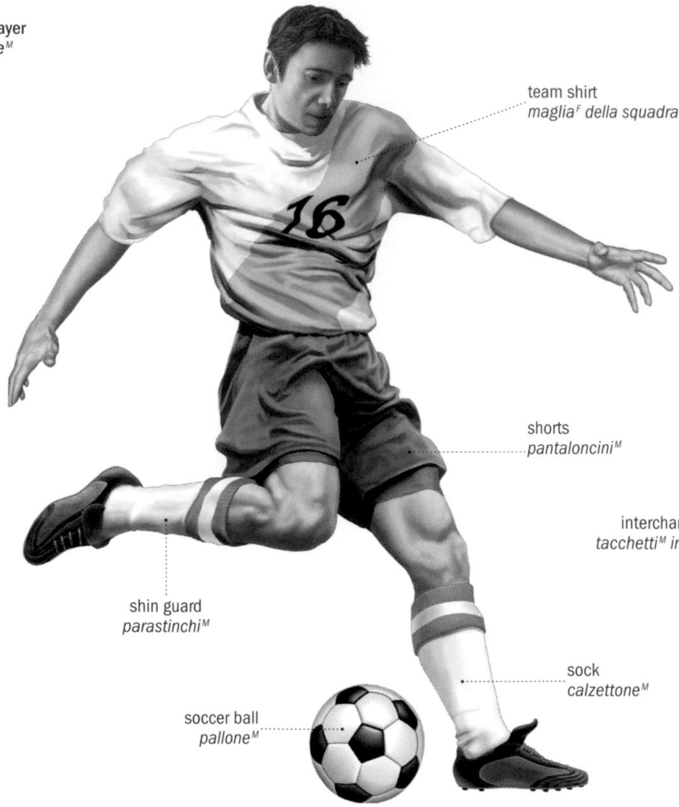

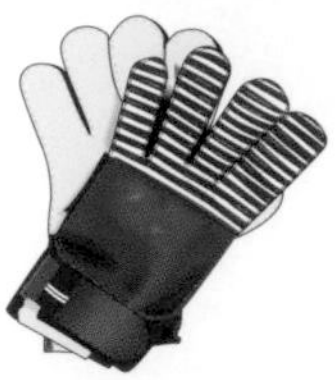

team shirt
maglia^{F} della squadra^{F}
shorts
pantaloncini^{M}
shin guard
parastinchi^{M}
sock
calzettone^{M}
soccer ball
pallone^{M}

goalkeeper's gloves
guanti^{M} del portiere^{M}

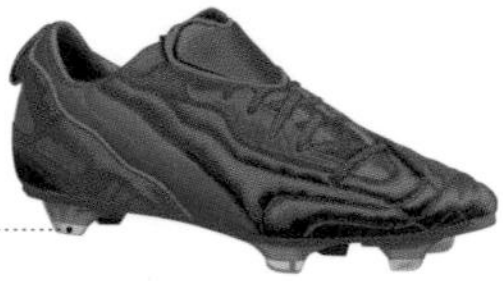

interchangeable studs
tacchetti^{M} intercambiabili

soccer shoe
scarpa^{F}

playing field
campo^{M} di gioco^{M}

center flag
bandierina^{F} centrale
penalty spot
dischetto^{M} del rigore^{M}
goal area
area^{F} di porta^{F}
goal
porta^{F}
penalty area
area^{F} di rigore^{M}
penalty marker
linea^{F} dell'area^{F} di rigore^{M}
penalty arc
lunetta^{F}

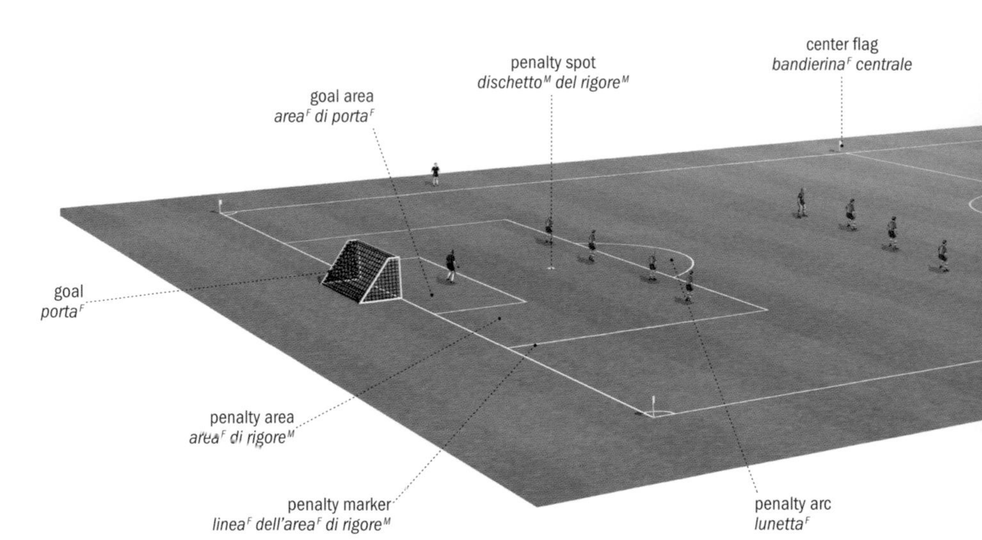

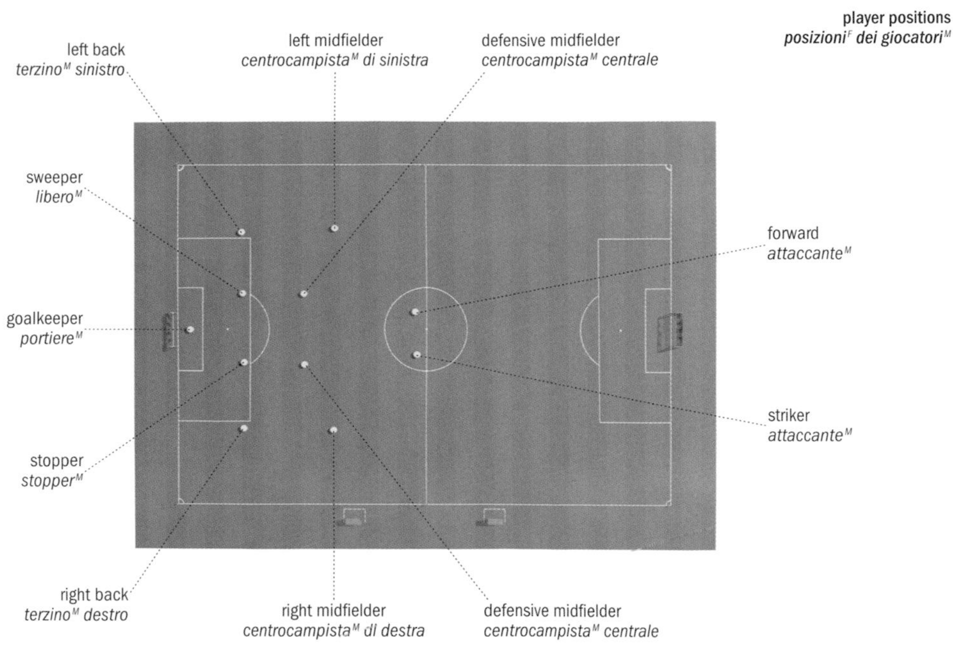
player positions
posizioni^F dei giocatori^M
left back
terzino^M sinistro
left midfielder
centrocampista^M di sinistra
defensive midfielder
centrocampista^M centrale
sweeper
libero^M
forward
attaccante^M
goalkeeper
portiere^M
striker
attaccante^M
stopper
stopper^M
right back
terzino^M destro
right midfielder
centrocampista^M di destra
defensive midfielder
centrocampista^M centrale

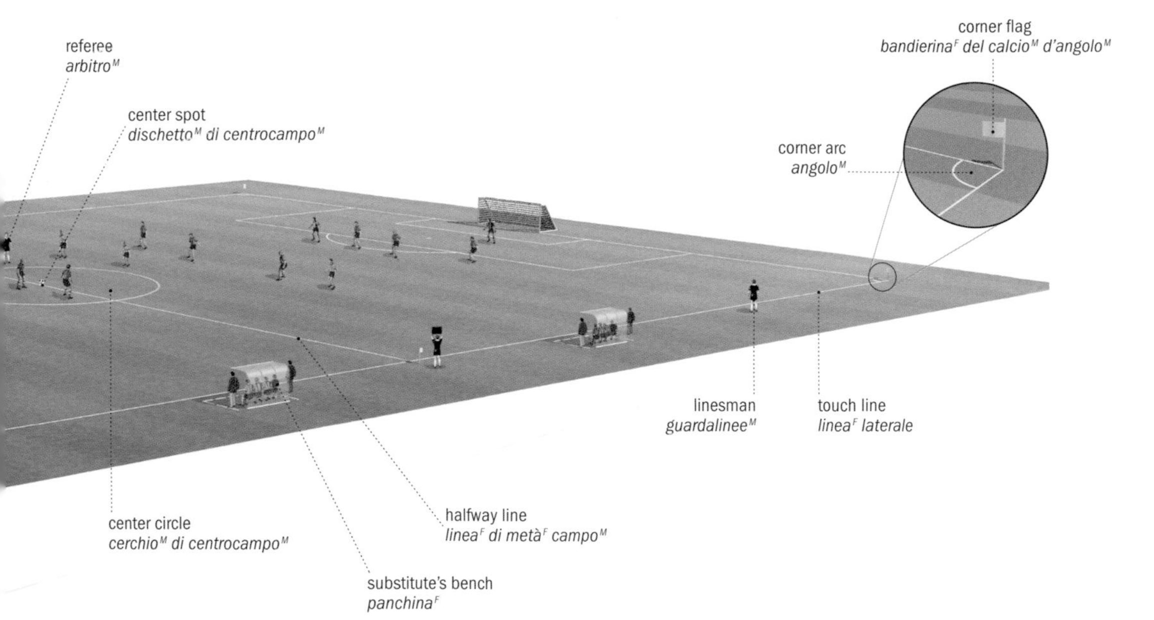
referee
arbitro^M
center spot
dischetto^M di centrocampo^M
corner flag
bandierina^F del calcio^M d'angolo^M
corner arc
angolo^M
linesman
guardalinee^M
touch line
linea^F laterale
center circle
cerchio^M di centrocampo^M
halfway line
linea^F di metà^F campo^M
substitute's bench
panchina^F

ugby

rugby[M]

players' positions
posizioni[F] dei giocatori[M]

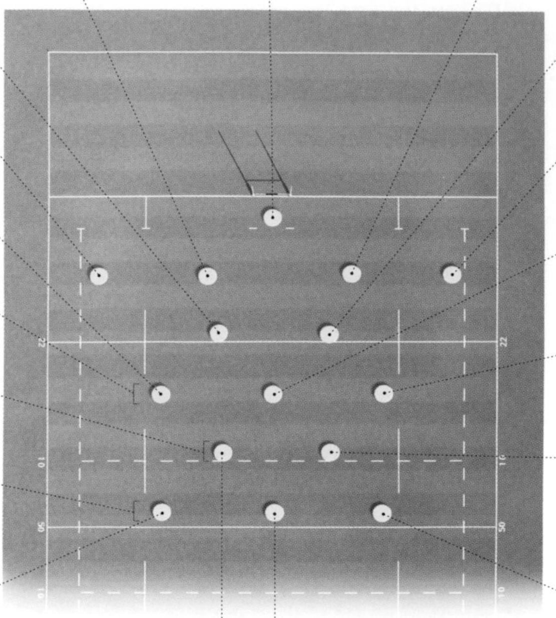

field
campo[M]

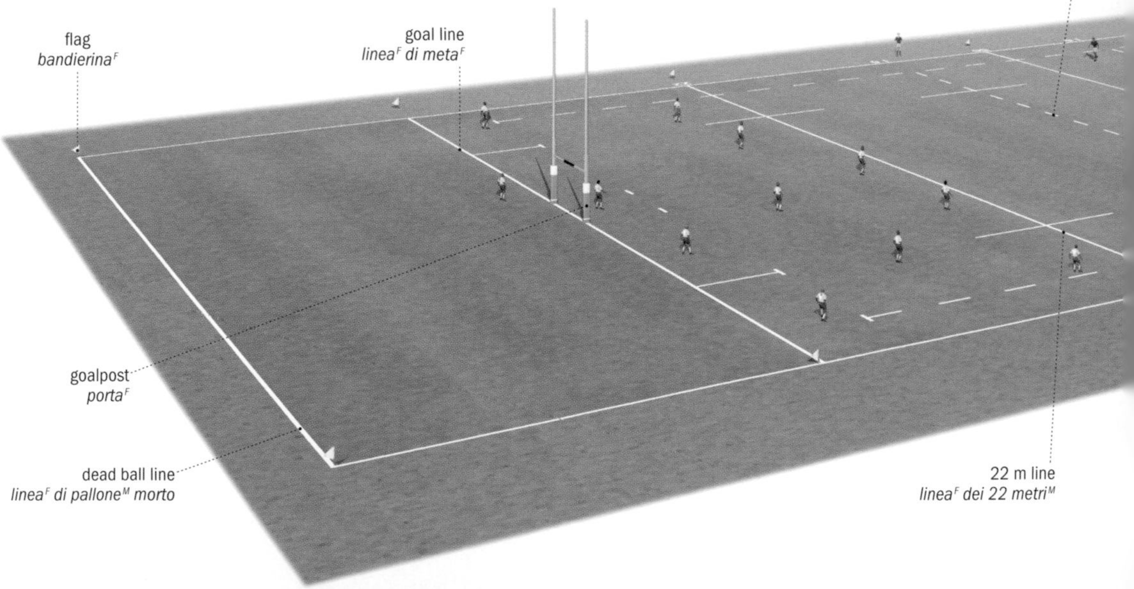

SPORTS AND GAMES

rugby player
giocatore[M]

rugby ball
palla[F] ovale

rugby shirt
maglia[F]

shorts
pantaloncini[M]

sock
calzettono[M]

ruck
mischia[F] spontanea

rugby shoe
scarpa[F]

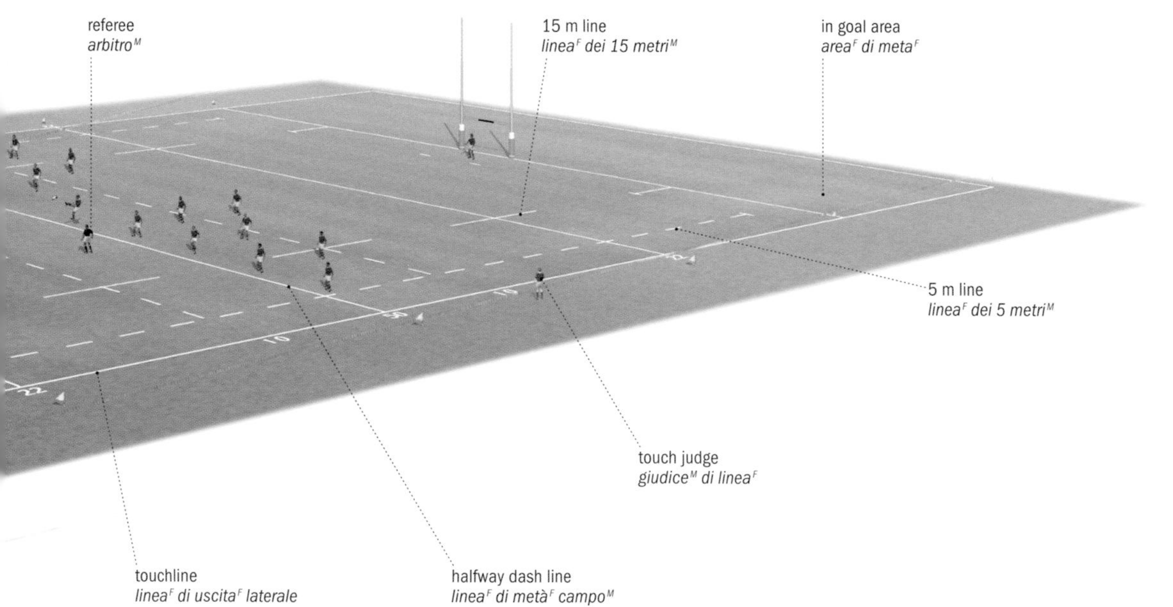

American football

footballᴹ americano

scrimmage: defense
mischiaᶠ: difesaᶠ

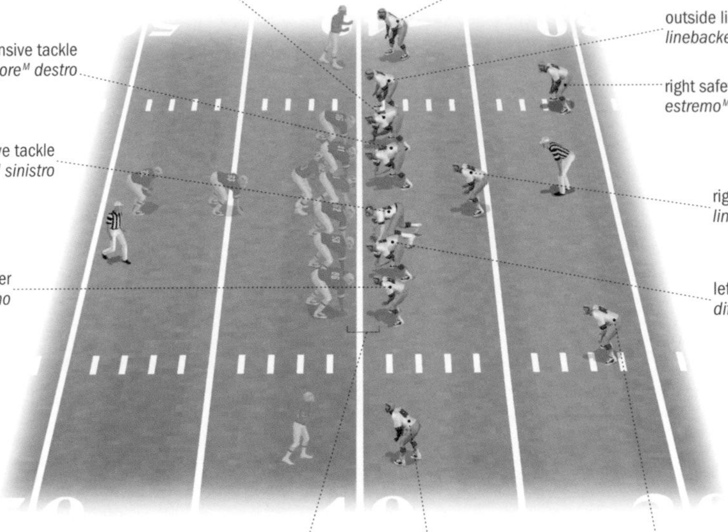

right defensive end
difensoreᴹ alaᶠ destra
right cornerback
terzinoᴹ di destra
outside linebacker
linebackerᴹ esterno
right defensive tackle
placcatoreᴹ destro
right safety
estremoᴹ di destra
left defensive tackle
placcatoreᴹ sinistro
right (strong) safety
linebackerᴹ centrale
inside linebacker
linebackerᴹ interno
left defensive end
difensoreᴹ alaᶠ sinistra
neutral zone
zonaᶠ neutra
left cornerback
terzinoᴹ di sinistra
left (free) safety
estremoᴹ di sinistra

playing field for American football
campoᴹ per footballᴹ americano

inbounds line
lineaᶠ di messaᶠ in giocoᴹ
goal line
lineaᶠ di metaᶠ
fifty-yard line
lineaᶠ di centrocampoᴹ
end zone
areaᶠ di metaᶠ
end line
lineaᶠ di fondoᴹ
yard line
lineaᶠ delle yardsᶠ
sideline
lineaᶠ laterale

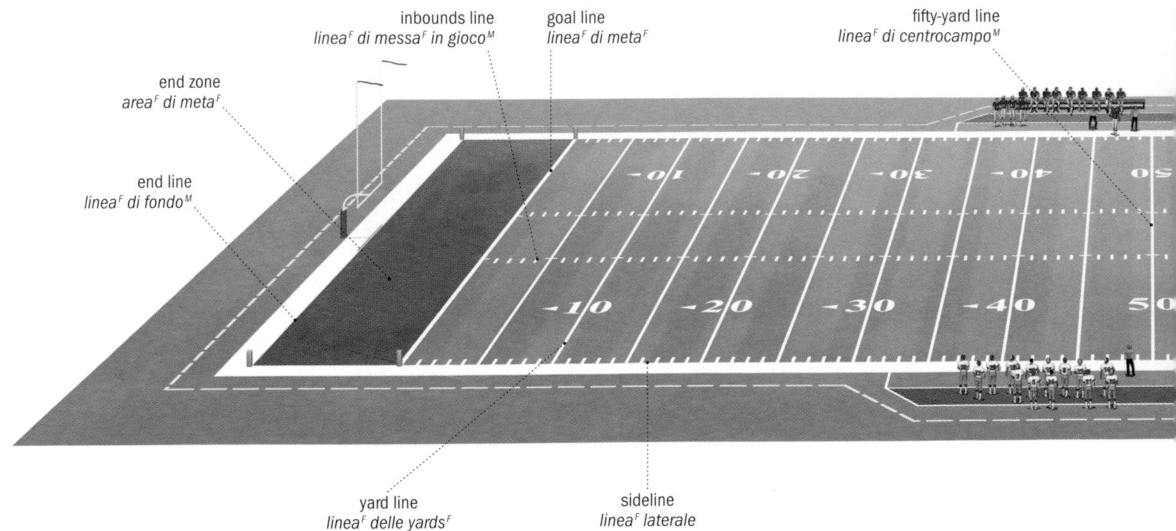

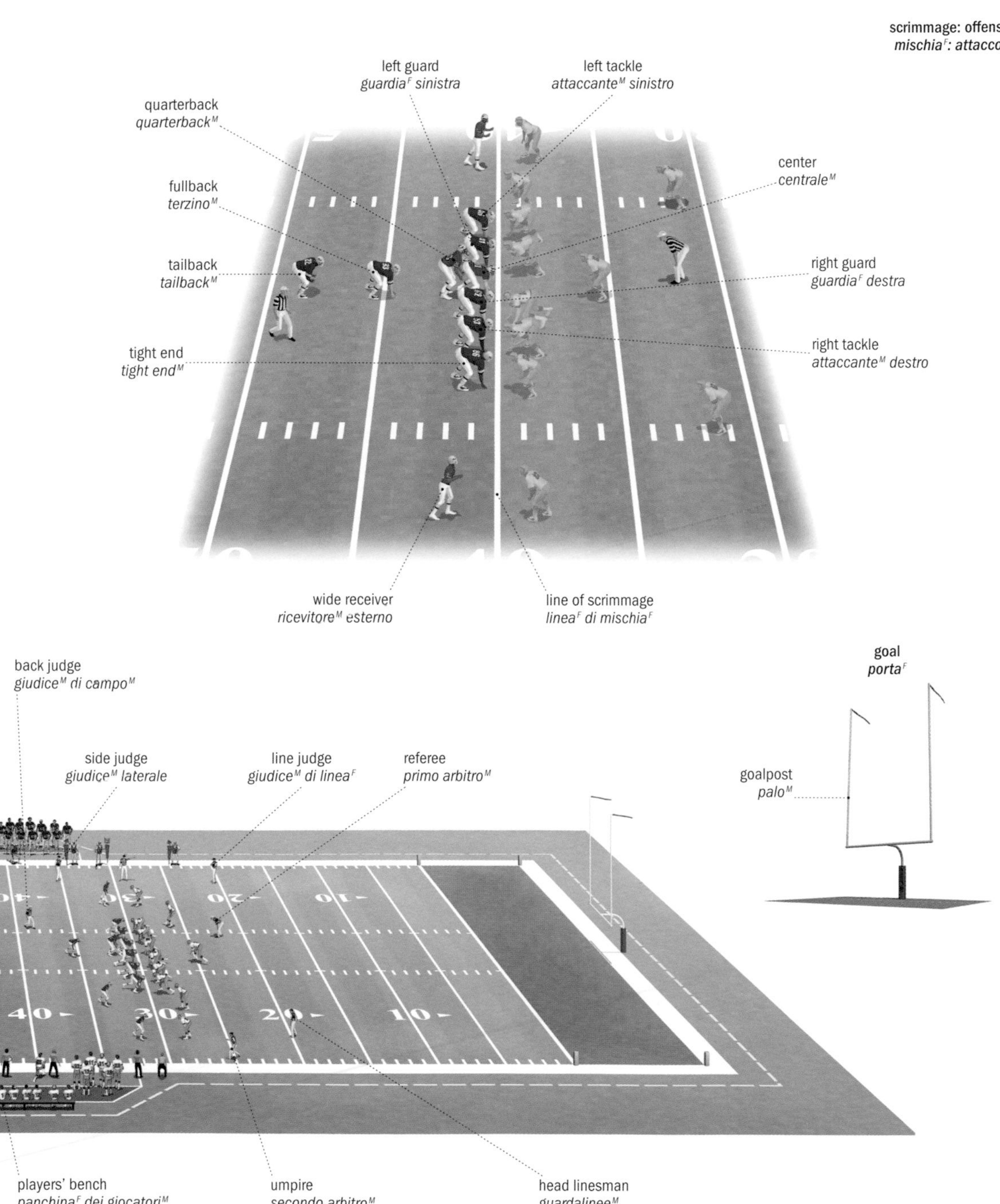
scrimmage: offense
mischia^F: attacco^M
left guard
guardia^F sinistra
left tackle
attaccante^M sinistro
quarterback
quarterback^M
center
centrale^M
fullback
terzino^M
tailback
tailback^M
right guard
guardia^F destra
tight end
tight end^M
right tackle
attaccante^M destro
wide receiver
ricevitore^M esterno
line of scrimmage
linea^F di mischia^F
goal
porta^F
back judge
giudice^M di campo^M
side judge
giudice^M laterale
line judge
giudice^M di linea^F
referee
primo arbitro^M
goalpost
palo^M
players' bench
panchina^F dei giocatori^M
umpire
secondo arbitro^M
head linesman
guardalinee^M

American football

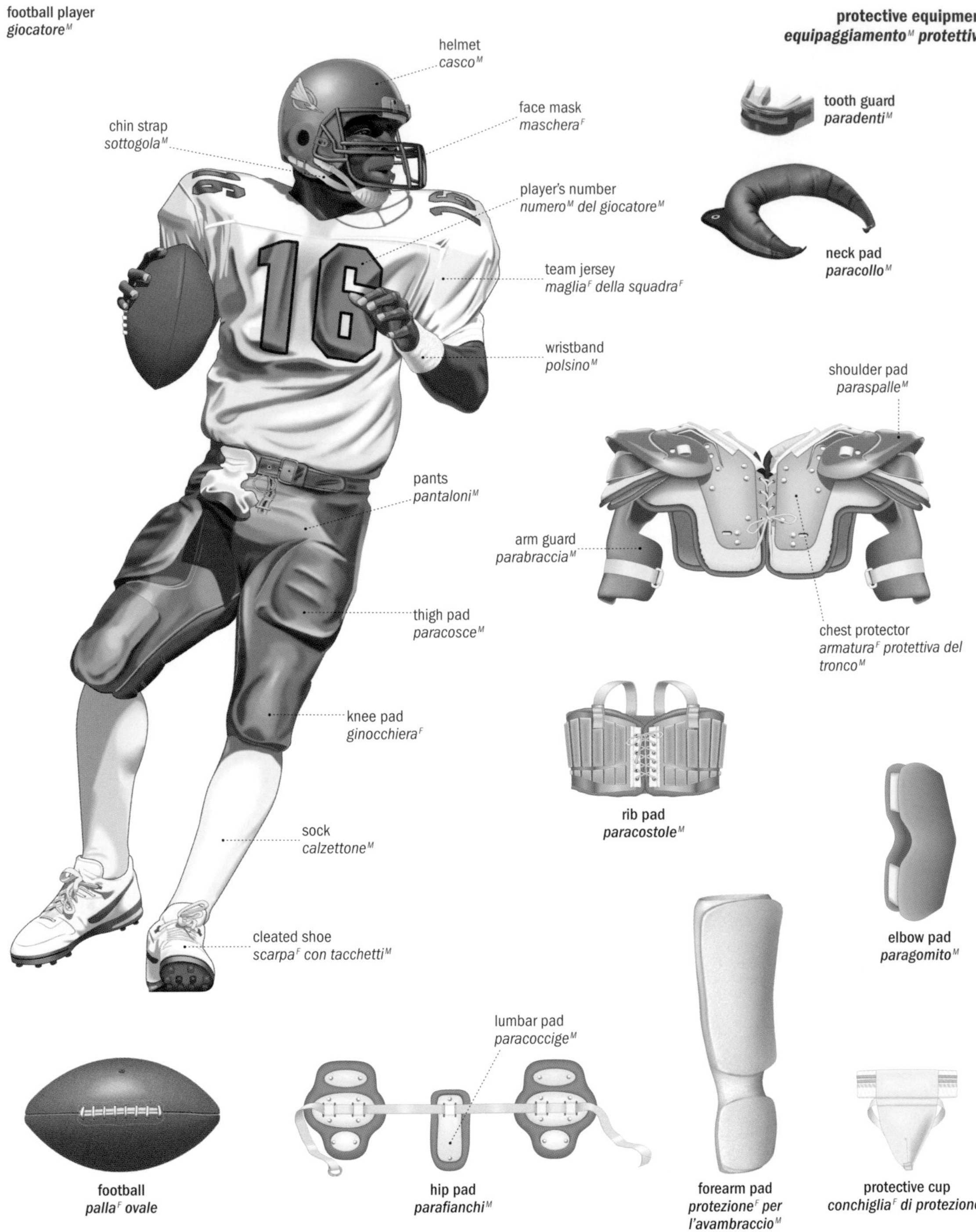

volleyball

pallavolo[F]

court
campo[M]

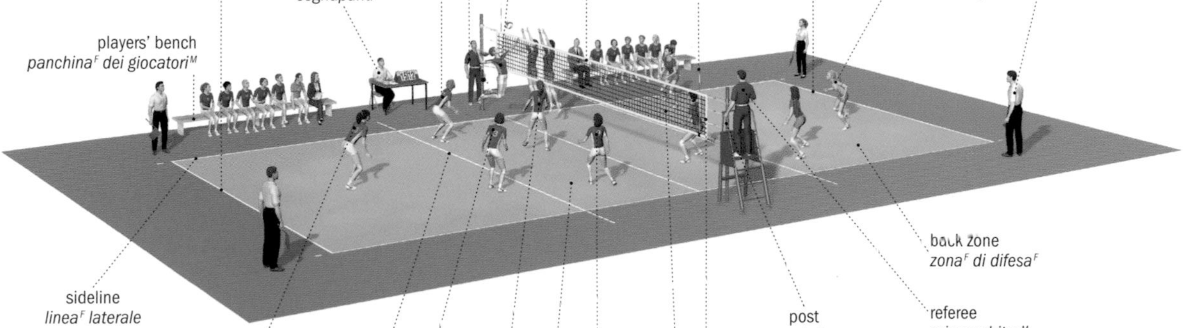
umpire
secondo arbitro[M]
left attacker
attaccante[M] *sinistro*
end line
linea[F] *di fondo*[M]
left back
difensore[M] *sinistro*
white tape
nastro[M] *bianco*
libero
libero[M]
clear space
zona[F] *libera*
scorer
segnapunti[M]
antenna
antenna[F]
linesman
giudice[M] *di linea*[F]
players' bench
panchina[F] *dei giocatori*[M]
back zone
zona[F] *di difesa*[F]
sideline
linea[F] *laterale*
post
palo[M]
referee
primo arbitro[M]
center back
difensore[M] *centrale*
vertical side band
nastro[M] *verticale laterale*
attack line
linea[F] *di attacco*[M]
net
rete[F]
right back
difensore[M] *destro*
right attacker
alzatore[M] *destro*
center attacker
attaccante[M] *centrale*
attack zone
zona[F] *di attacco*[M]

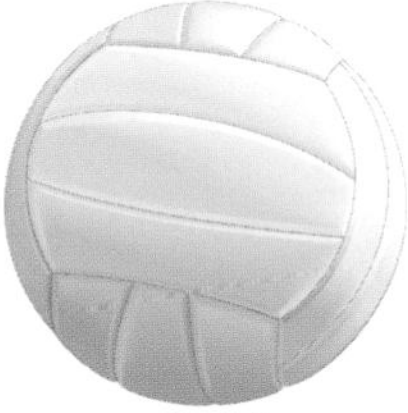

volleyball
pallone[M]

techniques
tecniche[F]

tip
palleggio[M]

bump
bagher[M]

serve
servizio[M]

SPORTS AND GAMES

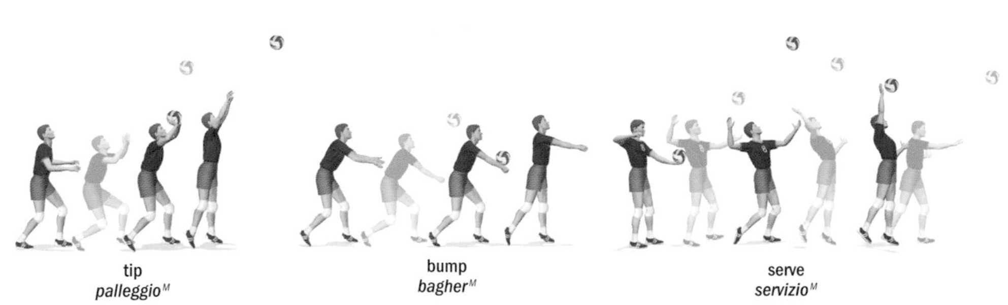

basketball

pallacanestro[F]

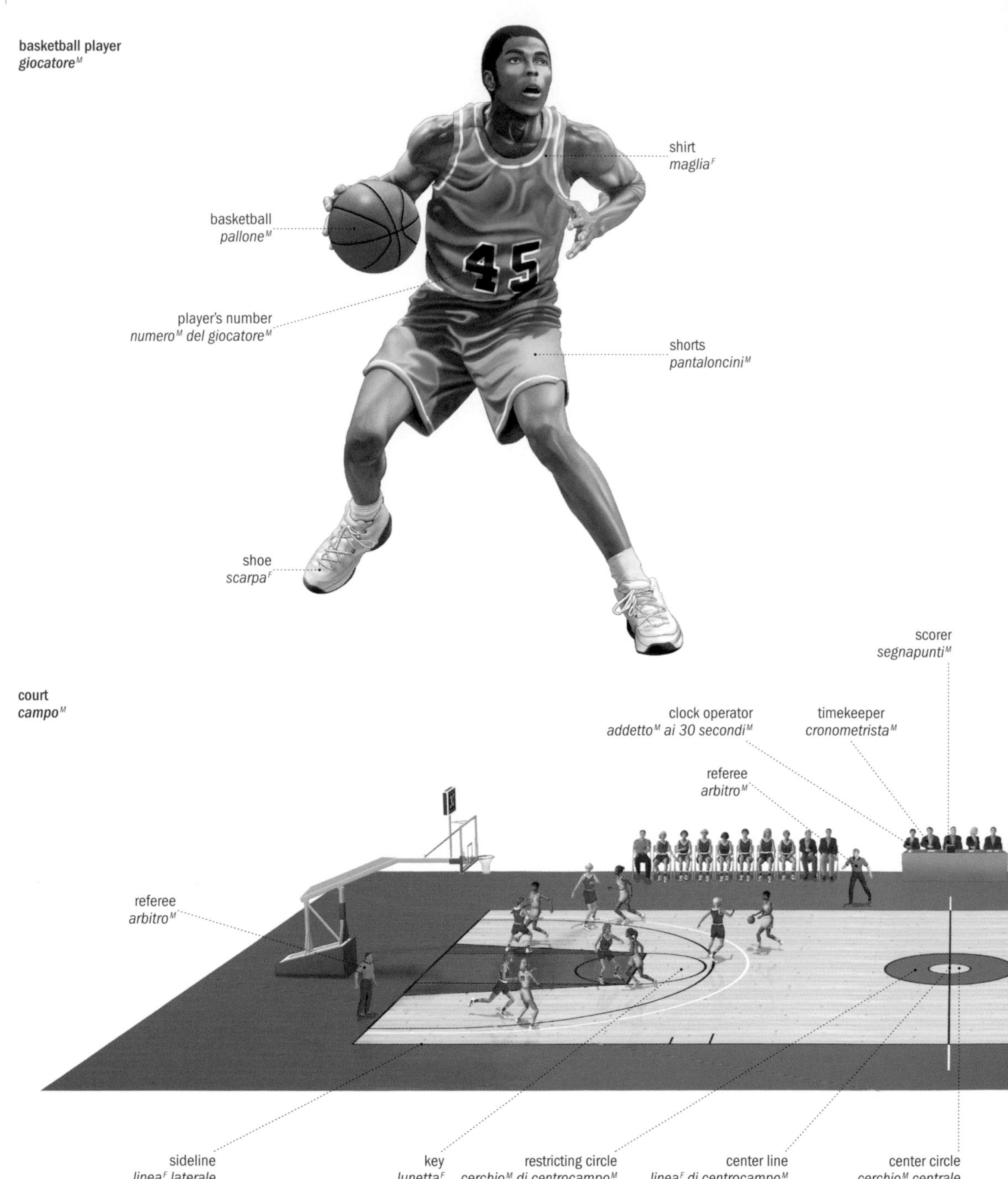

player positions
posizioni^F dei giocatori^M

point guard
playmaker^M
center
pivot^M
guard
guardia^F
left forward
ala^F sinistra
right forward
ala^F destra

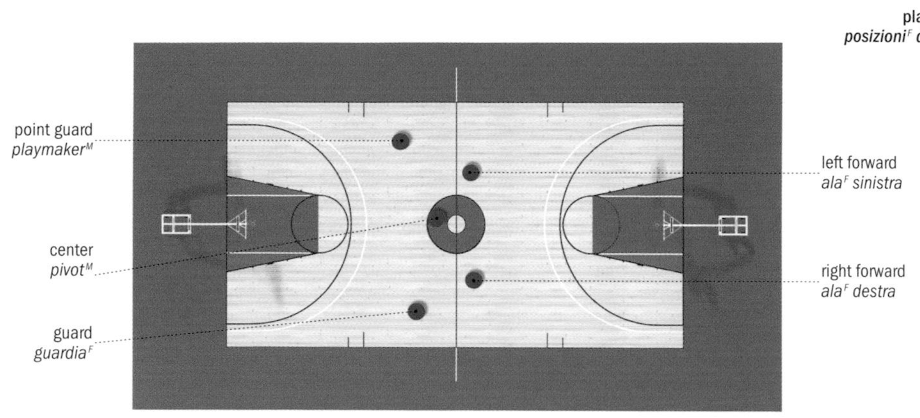

backstop
canestro^M

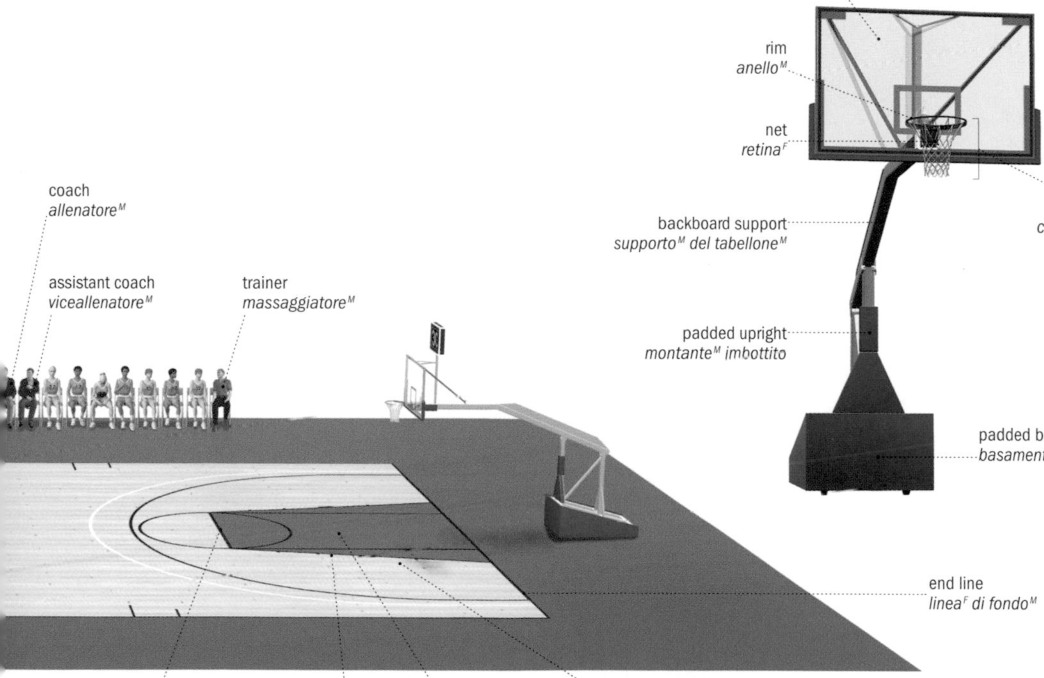

backboard
tabellone^M
rim
anello^M
net
retina^F
basket
canestro^M
backboard support
supporto^M del tabellone^M
padded upright
montante^M imbottito
padded base
basamento^M imbottito
coach
allenatore^M
assistant coach
viceallenatore^M
trainer
massaggiatore^M
end line
linea^F di fondo^M
free throw line
linea^F di tiro^M libero
second space
secondo spazio^M
restricted area
area^F dei tre secondi^M
first space
primo spazio^M

tennis

tennis[M]

court
***campo*[M]**

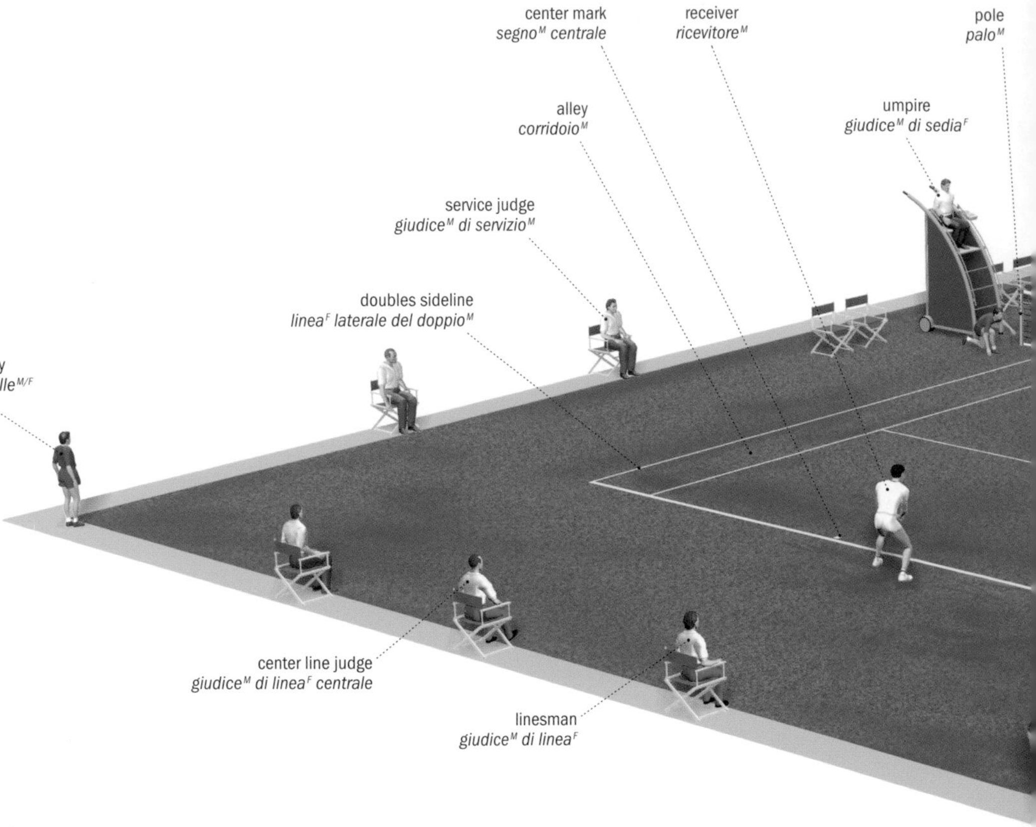

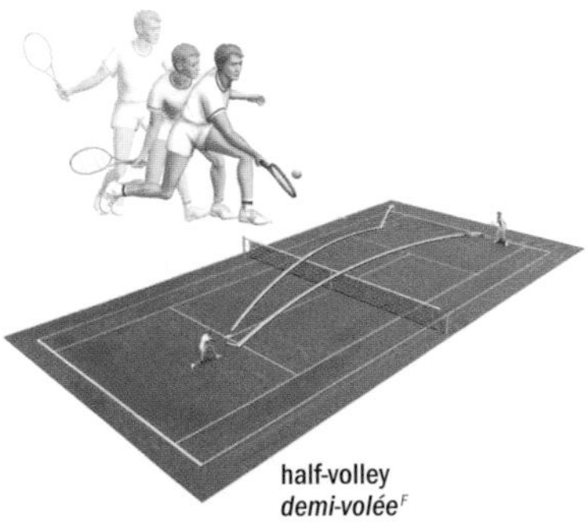

strokes
***colpi*[M]**

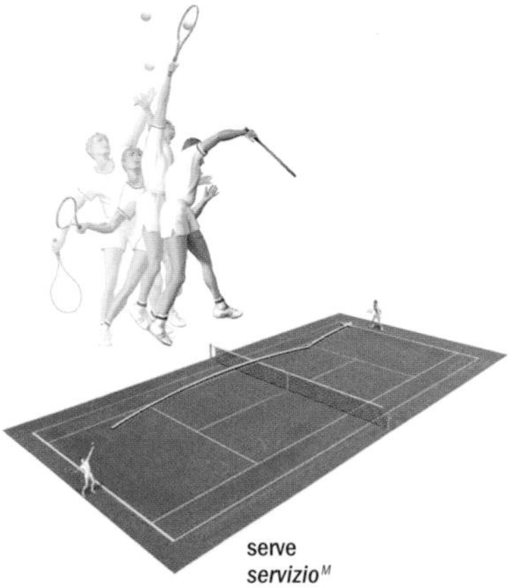

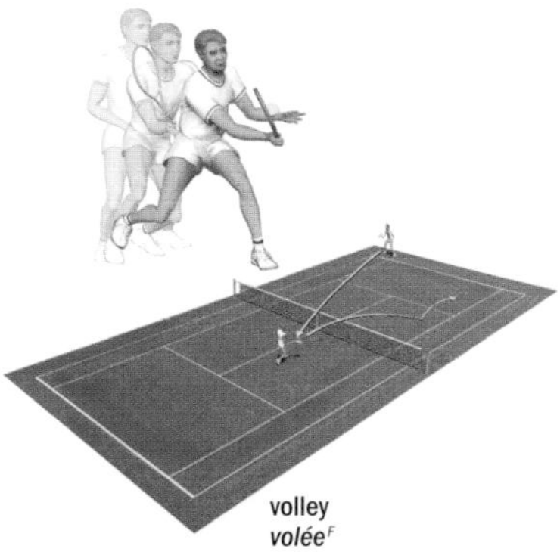

foot fault judge
giudice^M del fallo^M di piede^M

center strap
nastro^M centrale

net band
nastro^M

right service court
rettangolo^M destro di servizio^M

server
battitore^M

left service court
rettangolo^M sinistro di servizio^M

service line
linea^F di servizio^M

baseline
linea^F di fondo^M

singles sideline
linea^F laterale del singolo^M

net judge
giudice^M di rete^F

net
rete^F

forecourt
zona^F di servizio^M

center service line
linea^F centrale di servizio^M

backcourt
fondocampo^M

lob
pallonetto^M

drop shot
smorzata^F

smash
schiacciata^F

tennis

tennis racket
racchetta^{F}

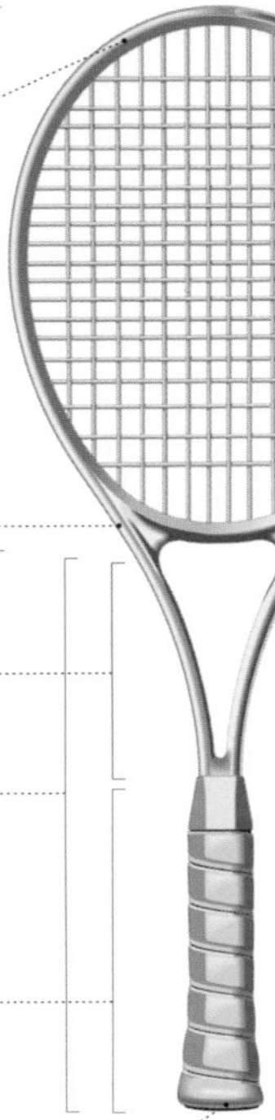

frame
telaio^{M}

head
testa^{F}

shoulder
spalla^{F}

throat
collo^{M}

shaft
fusto^{M}

handle
manico^{M}

butt
fondello^{M}

stringing
incordatura^{F}

tennis ball
palla^{F}

tennis player
tennista$^{M/F}$

polo shirt
polo^{F}

wristband
polsino^{M}

tennis skirt
gonnellino^{M}

sock
calzino^{M}

tennis shoe
scarpa^{F} da tennis^{M}

scoreboard
tabellone^{M} segnapunti

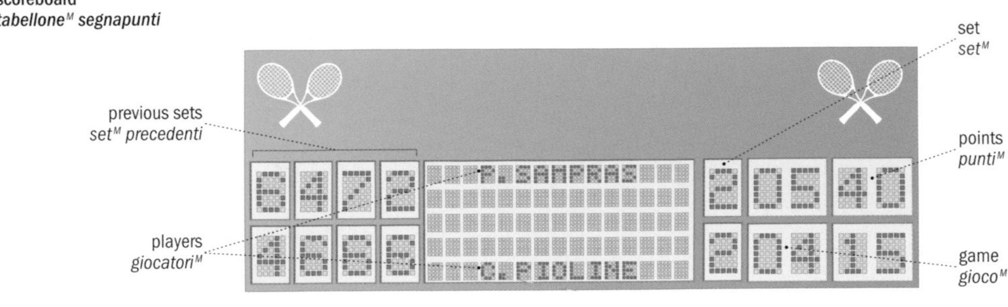

set
set^{M}

previous sets
set^{M} precedenti

points
punti^{M}

players
giocatori^{M}

game
gioco^{M}

playing surfaces
superfici^{F} di gioco^{M}

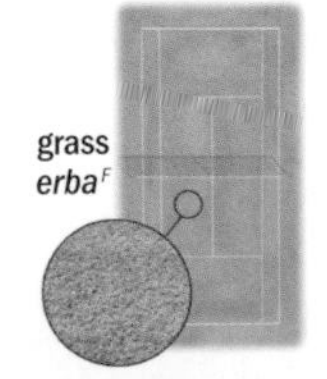

grass
erba^{F}

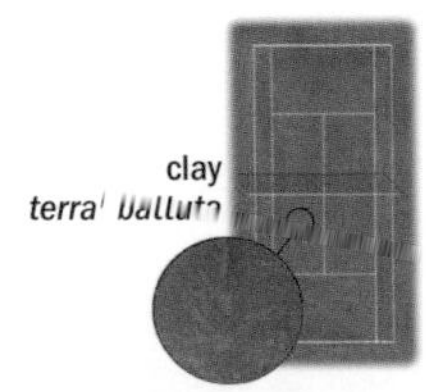

clay
terra^{F} battuta

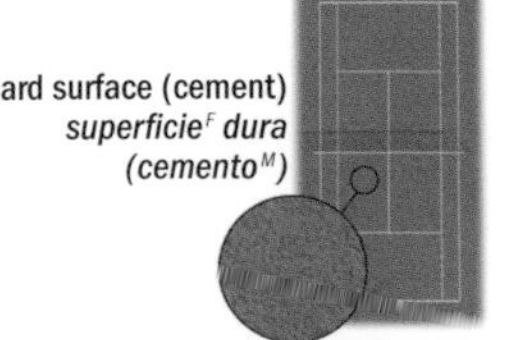

hard surface (cement)
superficie^{F} dura (cemento^{M})

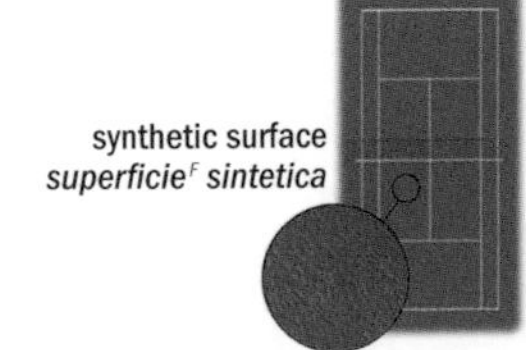

synthetic surface
superficie^{F} sintetica

table tennis

tennis[M] da tavolo[M]

table
tavolo[M]

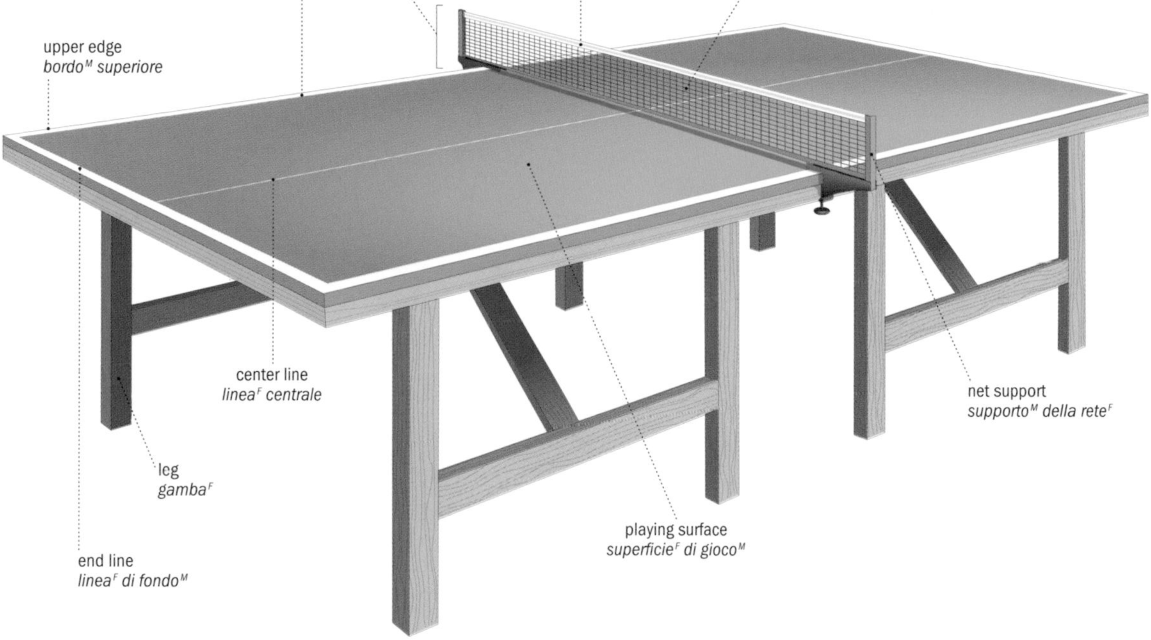

white tape
nastro[M] bianco

mesh
maglia[F]

sideline
linea[F] laterale

net
rete[F]

upper edge
bordo[M] superiore

center line
linea[F] centrale

net support
supporto[M] della rete[F]

leg
gamba[F]

playing surface
superficie[F] di gioco[M]

end line
linea[F] di fondo[M]

table tennis paddle
racchetta[F]

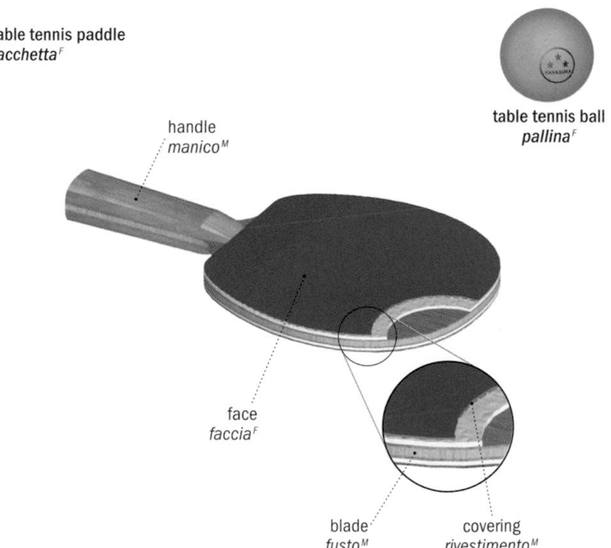

handle
manico[M]

face
faccia[F]

blade
fusto[M]

covering
rivestimento[M]

table tennis ball
pallina[F]

types of grips
tipi[M] di impugnature[F]

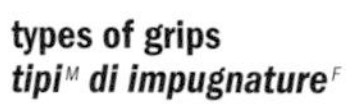

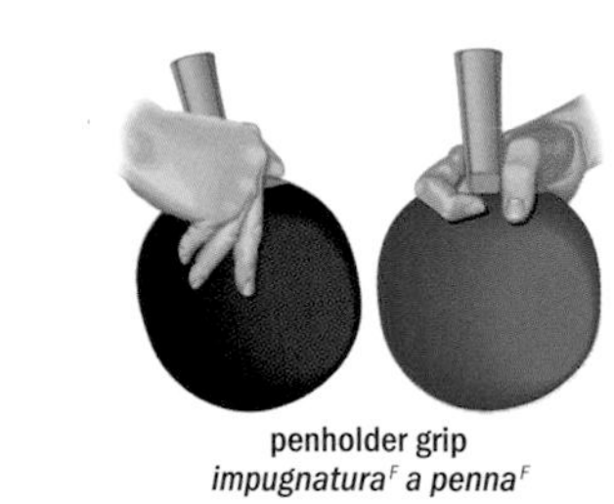

penholder grip
impugnatura[F] a penna[F]

shake-hands grip
impugnatura[F] a stretta[F] di mano[F]

badminton

gioco^M del volano^M

court
campo^M

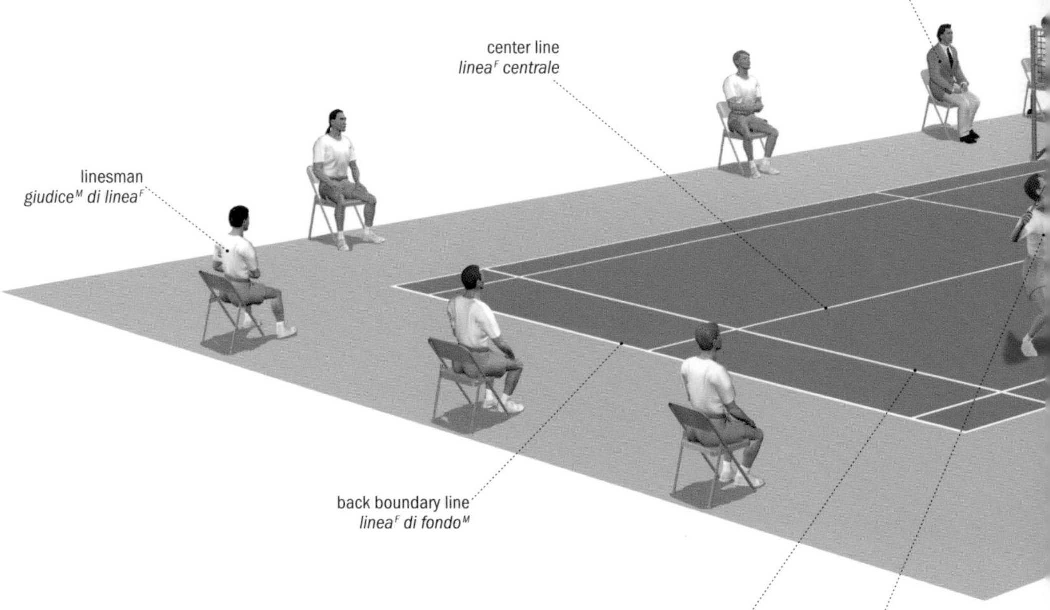

service judge
giudice^M di servizio^M
center line
linea^F centrale
linesman
giudice^M di linea^F
back boundary line
linea^F di fondo^M
long service line
linea^F di servizio^M lungo
server
battitore^M

badminton racket
racchetta^F

frame
telaio^M
handle
manico^M
stringing
incordatura^F
shaft
fusto^M
butt
fondello^M
head
testa^F

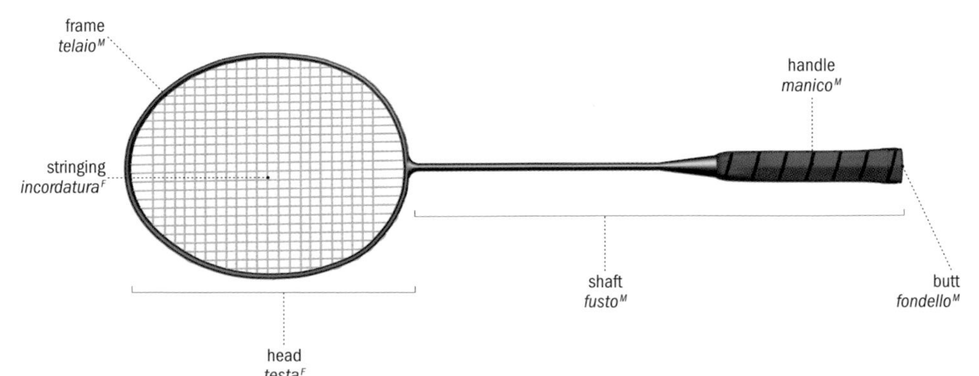

badminton

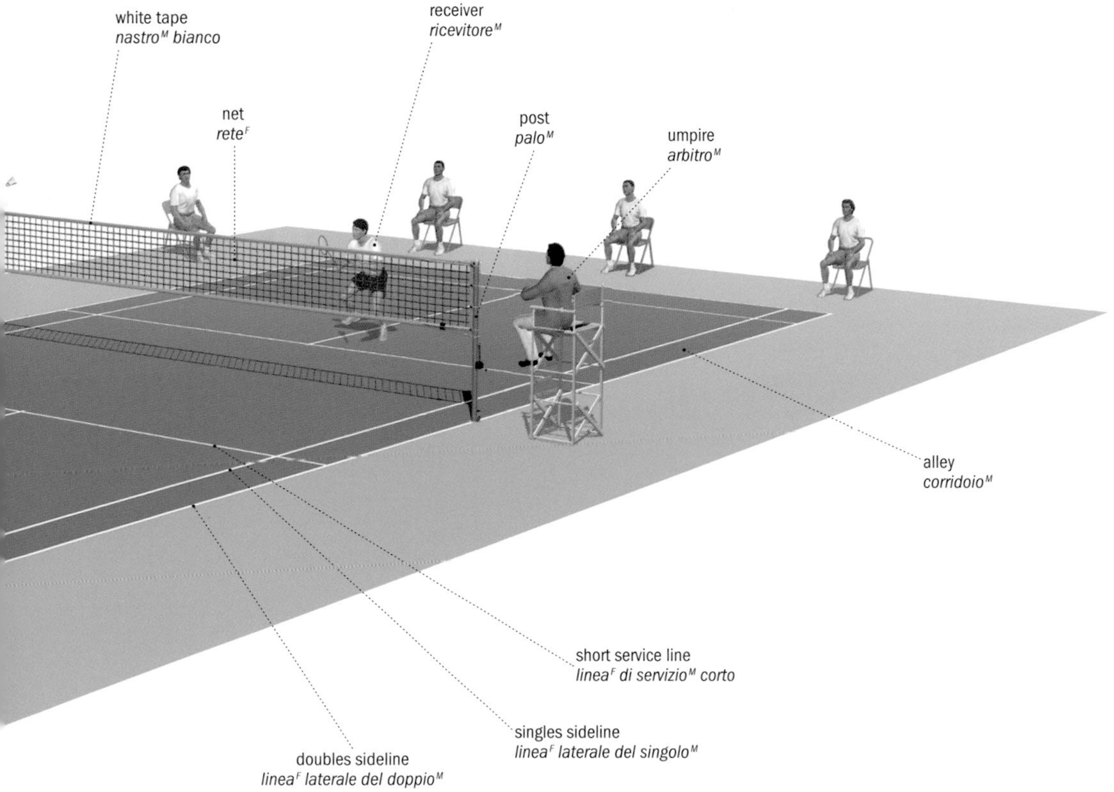

white tape
nastro[M] bianco
receiver
ricevitore[M]
net
rete[F]
post
palo[M]
umpire
arbitro[M]
alley
corridoio[M]
short service line
linea[F] di servizio[M] corto
singles sideline
linea[F] laterale del singolo[M]
doubles sideline
linea[F] laterale del doppio[M]

service zones
zone[F] di servizio[M]

doubles service court
campo[M] di servizio[M] del doppio[M]
singles service court
campo[M] di servizio[M] del singolo[M]

synthetic shuttlecock
volano[M] sintetico

feathered shuttlecock
volano[M] a penne[F] naturali

feather crown
corona[F] di penne[F]
cork tip
mezza sfera[F] di sughero[M]

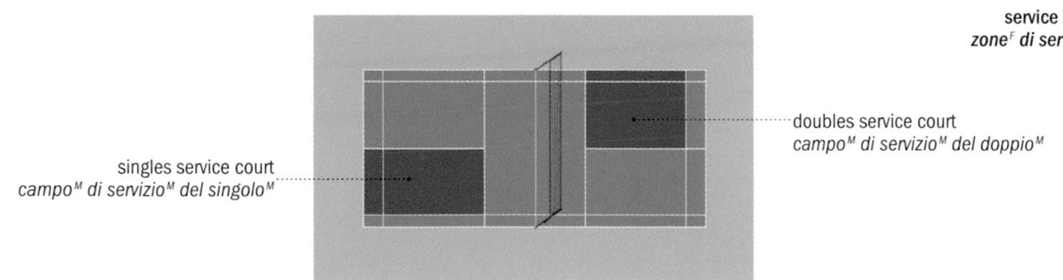

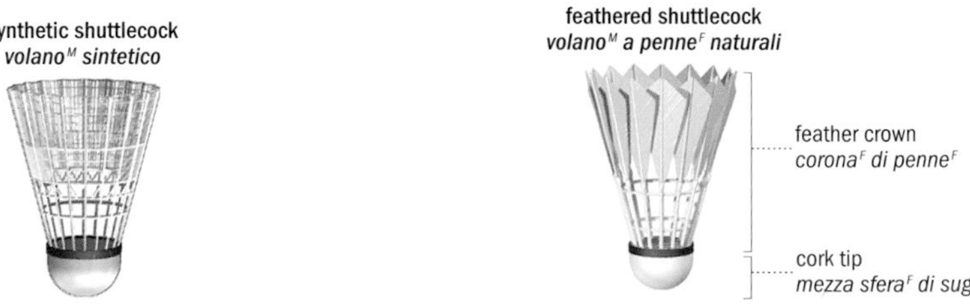

gymnastics

ginnastica[F]

event platform
***pedana*[F]**

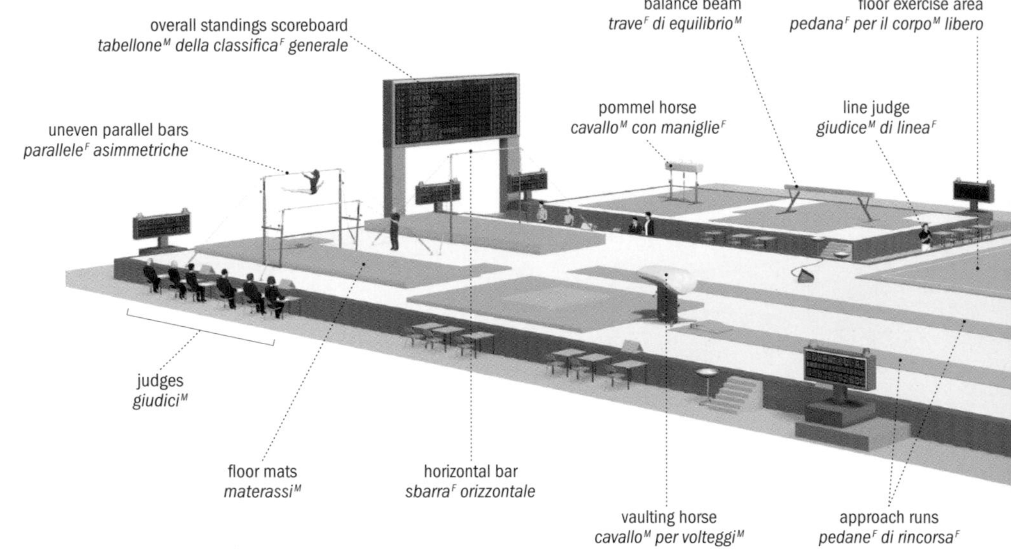

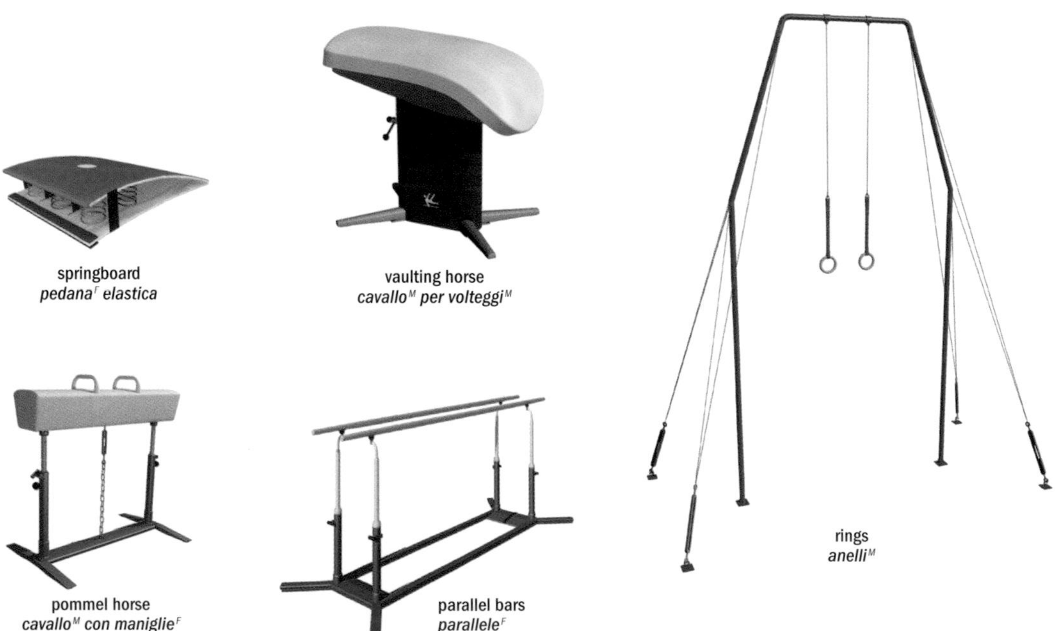

gymnastics

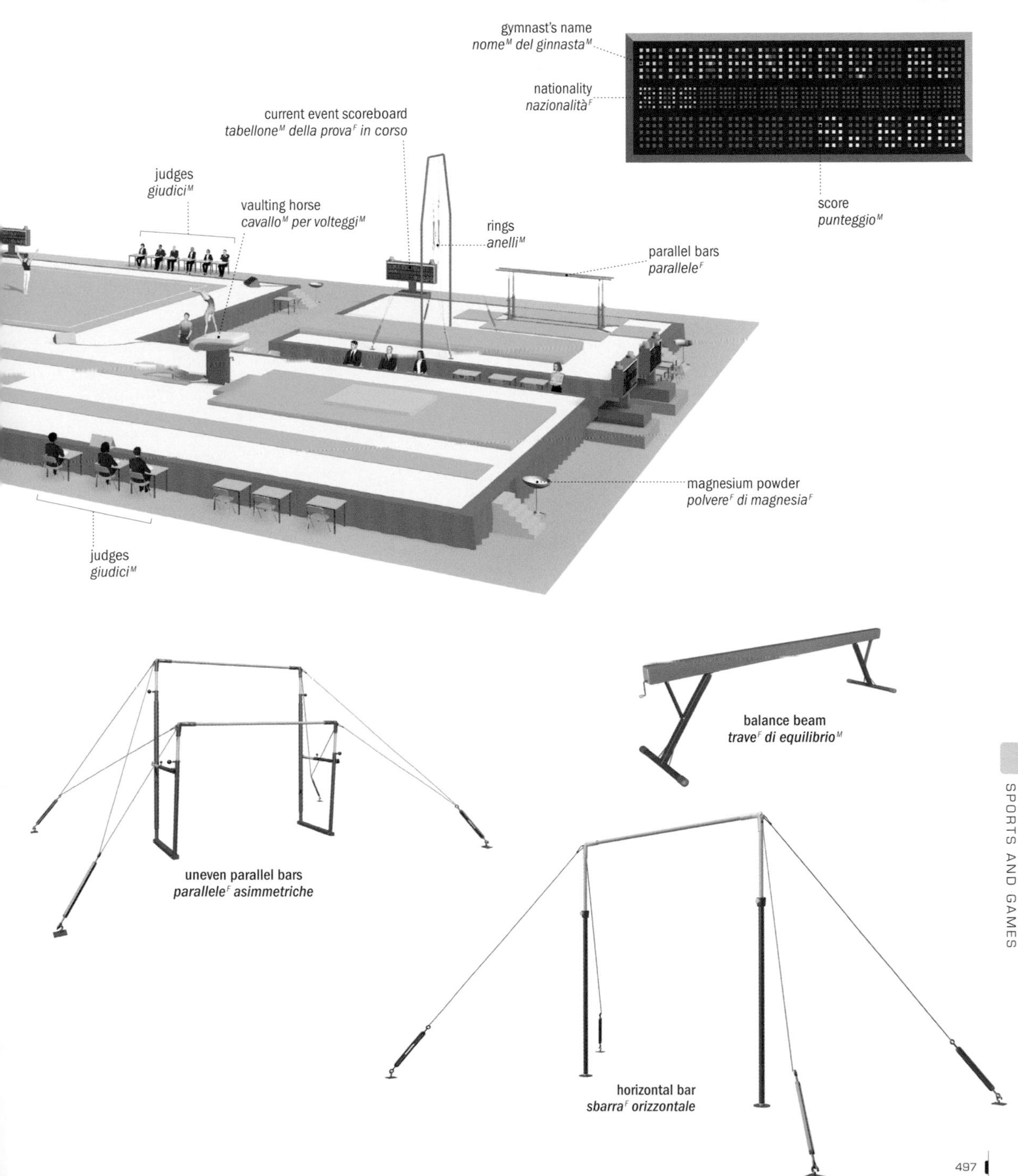
scoreboard
tabellone^M segnapunti
gymnast's name
nome^M del ginnasta^M
nationality
nazionalità^F
current event scoreboard
tabellone^M della prova^F in corso
judges
giudici^M
vaulting horse
cavallo^M per volteggi^M
rings
anelli^M
parallel bars
parallele^F
score
punteggio^M
magnesium powder
polvere^F di magnesia^F
judges
giudici^M
balance beam
trave^F di equilibrio^M
uneven parallel bars
parallele^F asimmetriche
horizontal bar
sbarra^F orizzontale

boxing

pugilato^M

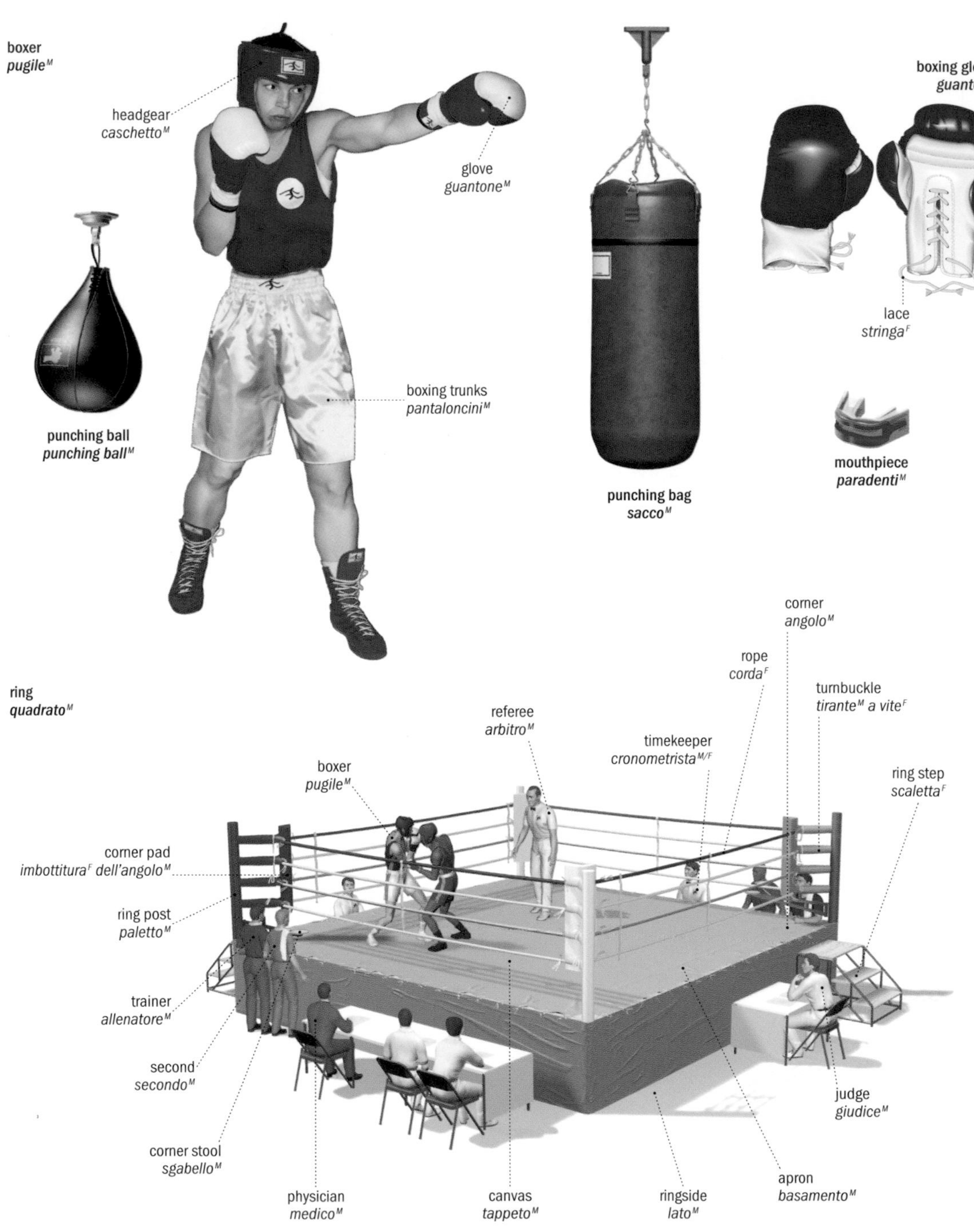

judo

judo^M

mat
tatami^M
scorers and timekeepers
segnapunti^M e cronometristi^M
medical team
staff^M medico
contestant
lottatore^M
safety area
area^F di sicurezza^F
danger area
zona^F di pericolo^M
scoreboard
tabellone^M segnapunti
contest area
area^F di combattimento^M
referee
arbitro^M
judge
giudice^M
examples of holds and throws
esempi^M di prese^F
judogi
judogi^M
jacket
giacca^F
holding
presa^F a terra^F
stomach throw
rovesciata^F all'indietro
sweeping hip throw
spazzata^F d'anca^F
major outer reaping throw
grande falciata^F esterna
major inner reaping throw
grande falciata^F interna
naked strangle
presa^F di strangolamento^M
trousers
pantaloni^M
belt
cintura^F
arm lock
presa^F a croce^F
one-arm shoulder throw
proiezione^F di spalla^F e braccio^M

weightlifting

sollevamento[M] pesi[M]

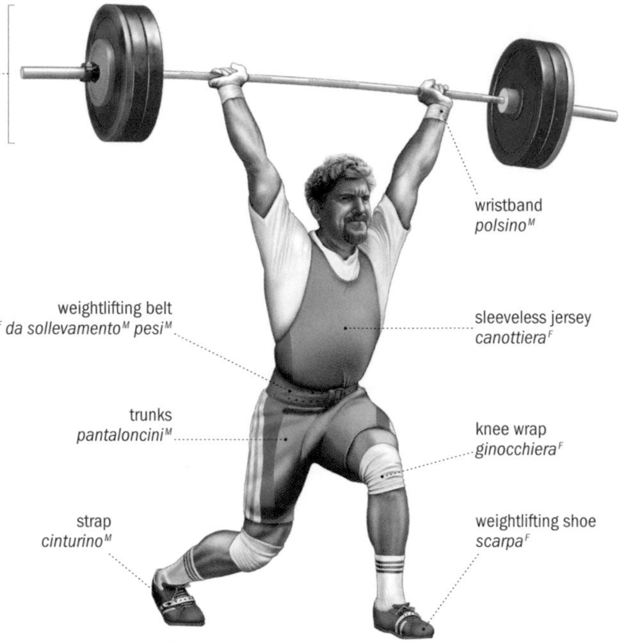

barbell
bilanciere[M]
wristband
polsino[M]
weightlifting belt
cintura[F] da sollevamento[M] pesi[M]
sleeveless jersey
canottiera[F]
trunks
pantaloncini[M]
knee wrap
ginocchiera[F]
strap
cinturino[M]
weightlifting shoe
scarpa[F]

clean and jerk
slancio[M]

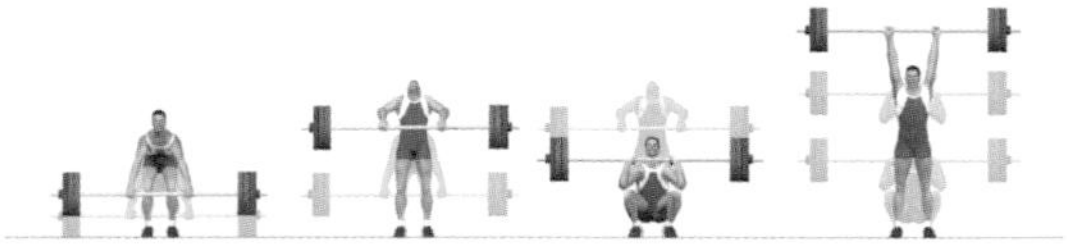

snatch
strappo[M]

fitness equipment

attrezzi[M] ginnici

dumbbells
manubri[M]

bar
impugnatura[F]
weight
peso[M]

handgrips
molle[F] a forbice[F]

ankle/wrist weights
cavigliere[F]/polsiere[F]

jump rope
corda[F]

twist bar
sbarra[F] pieghevole

tension spring
molla[F] di tensione[F]
grip
impugnatura[F]

chest expander
estensore[M]

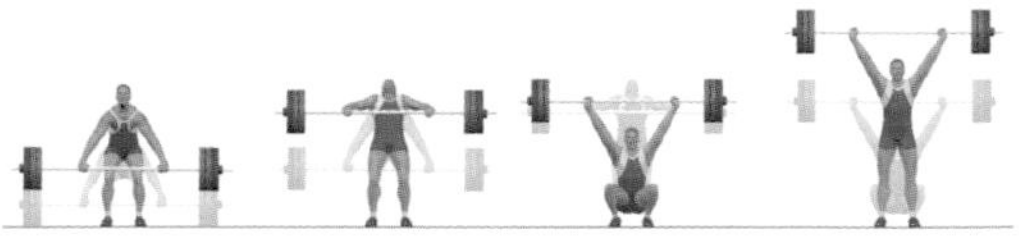

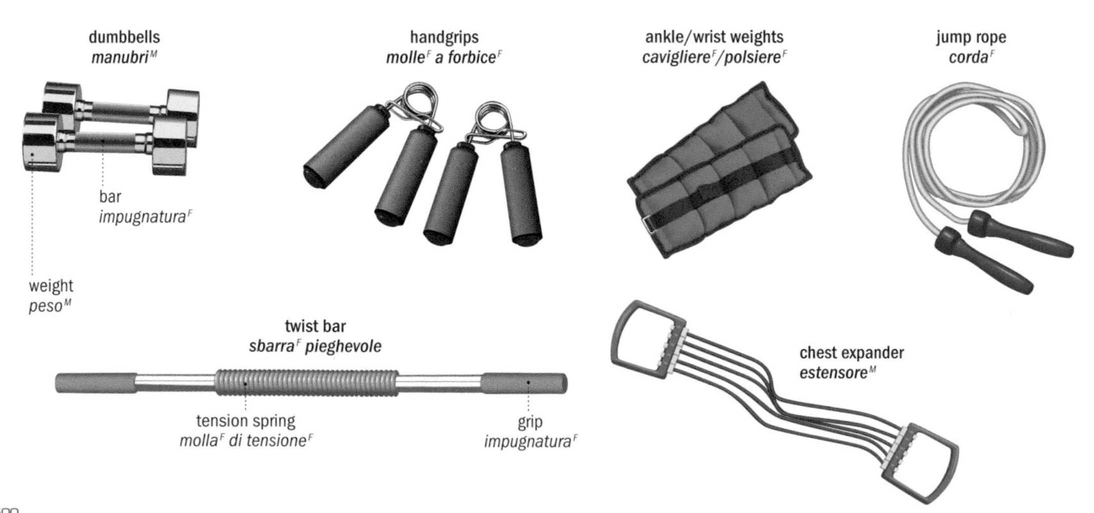

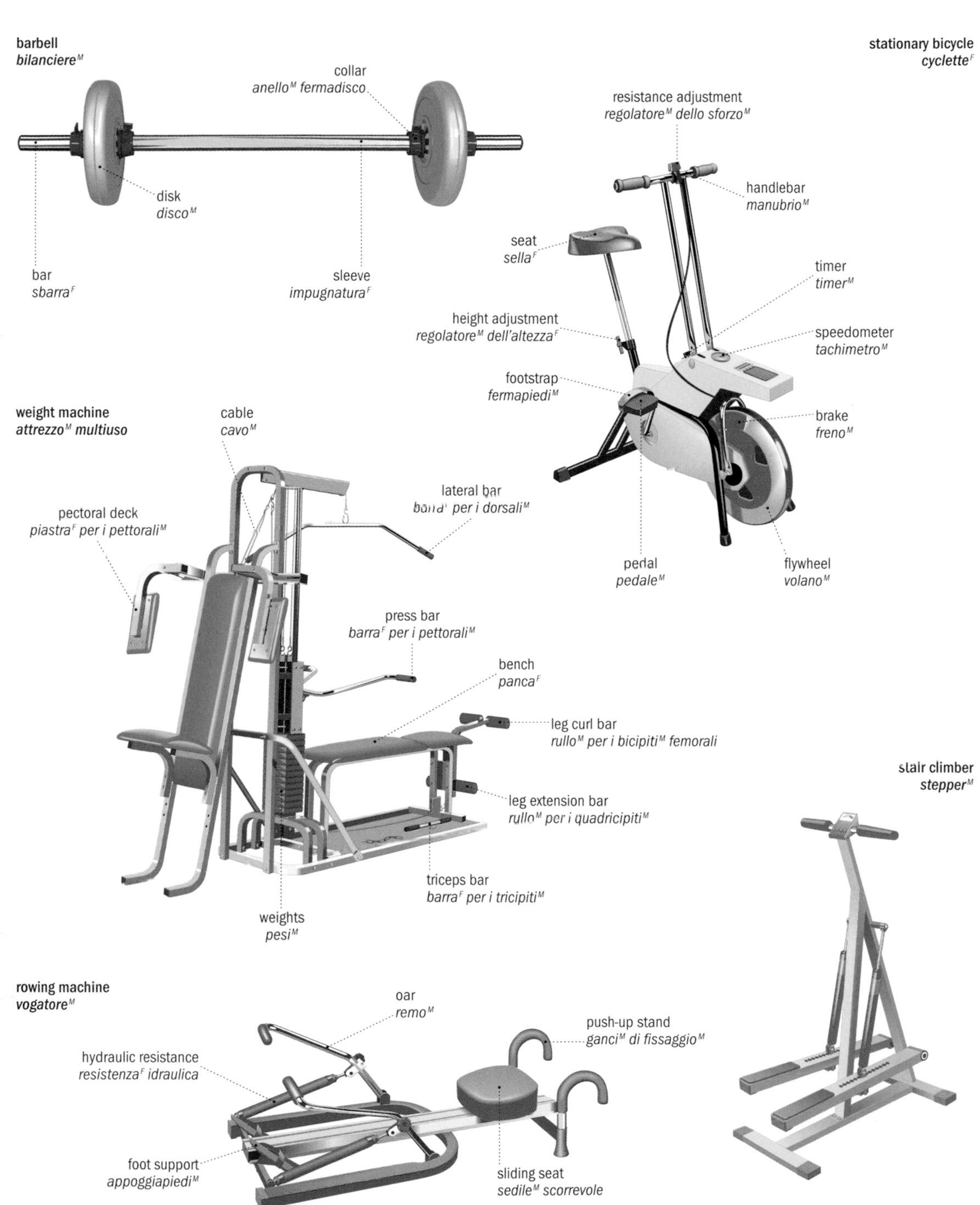
barbell
bilanciere^M
collar
anello^M fermadisco
disk
disco^M
bar
sbarra^F
sleeve
impugnatura^F
stationary bicycle
cyclette^F
resistance adjustment
regolatore^M dello sforzo^M
handlebar
manubrio^M
seat
sella^F
timer
timer^M
height adjustment
regolatore^M dell'altezza^F
speedometer
tachimetro^M
footstrap
fermapiedi^M
brake
freno^M
pedal
pedale^M
flywheel
volano^M
weight machine
attrezzo^M multiuso
cable
cavo^M
lateral bar
barra^F per i dorsali^M
pectoral deck
piastra^F per i pettorali^M
press bar
barra^F per i pettorali^M
bench
panca^F
leg curl bar
rullo^M per i bicipiti^M femorali
leg extension bar
rullo^M per i quadricipiti^M
triceps bar
barra^F per i tricipiti^M
weights
pesi^M
stair climber
stepper^M
rowing machine
vogatore^M
oar
remo^M
push-up stand
ganci^M di fissaggio^M
hydraulic resistance
resistenza^F idraulica
foot support
appoggiapiedi^M
sliding seat
sedile^M scorrevole

billiards

biliardo[M]

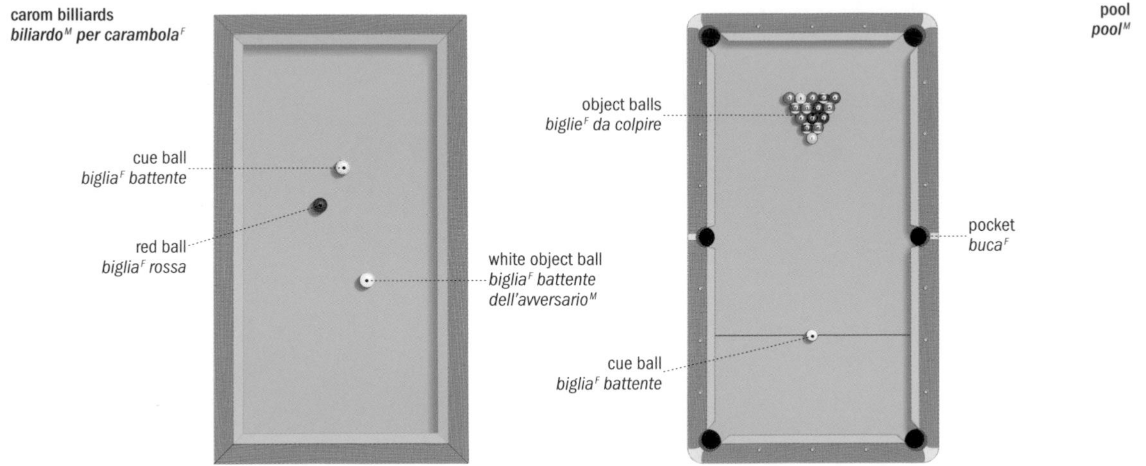

table
tavolo[M]

D
zona[F] di inizio[M] partita[F]

balk line spot
acchito[M] della linea[F] di battuta[F]

pyramid spot
acchito[M] superiore

baize
panno[M]

balk area
rettangolo[M] di battuta[F]

bottom pocket
buca[F] inferiore

center spot
acchito[M] centrale

top pocket
buca[F] superiore

head cushion
sponda[F] inferiore

balk line
linea[F] d'acchito[M]

hook
gancio[M]

billiard spot
acchito[M]

center pocket
buca[F] centrale

rail
sopresponda[F]

foot cushion
sponda[F] superiore

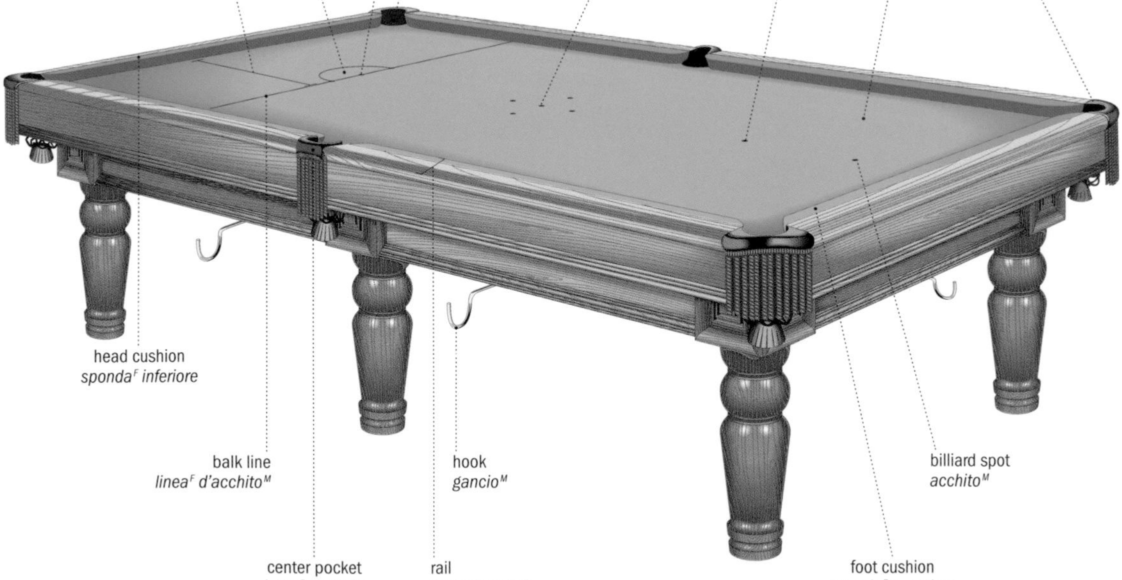

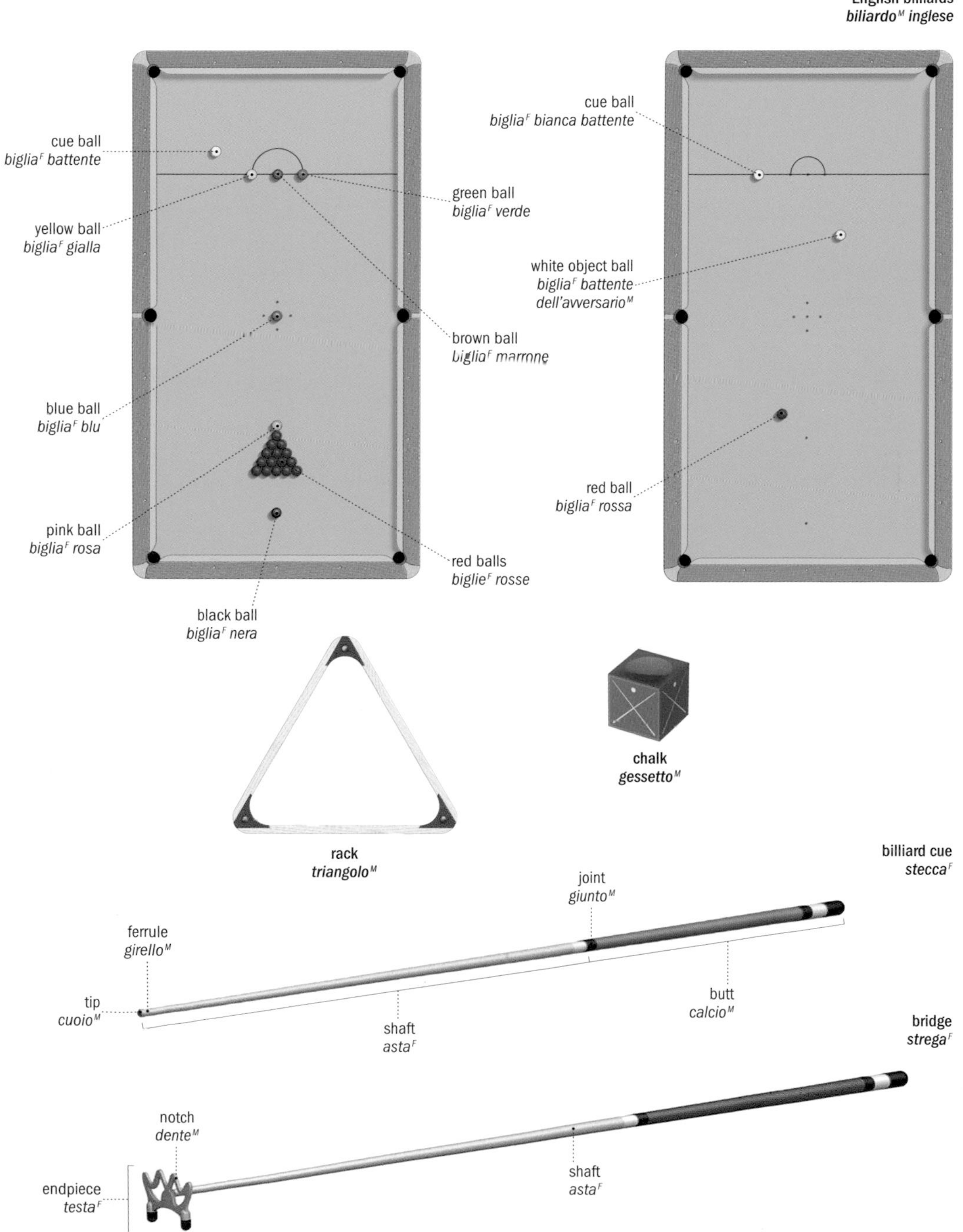
snooker
snooker^M
cue ball
biglia^F battente
yellow ball
biglia^F gialla
green ball
biglia^F verde
brown ball
biglia^F marrone
blue ball
biglia^F blu
pink ball
biglia^F rosa
red balls
biglie^F rosse
black ball
biglia^F nera
English billiards
biliardo^M inglese
cue ball
biglia^F bianca battente
white object ball
biglia^F battente dell'avversario^M
red ball
biglia^F rossa
rack
triangolo^M
chalk
gessetto^M
billiard cue
stecca^F
joint
giunto^M
ferrule
girello^M
tip
cuoio^M
shaft
asta^F
butt
calcio^M
bridge
strega^F
notch
dente^M
endpiece
testa^F
shaft
asta^F

golf

golf^M

course
percorso^M

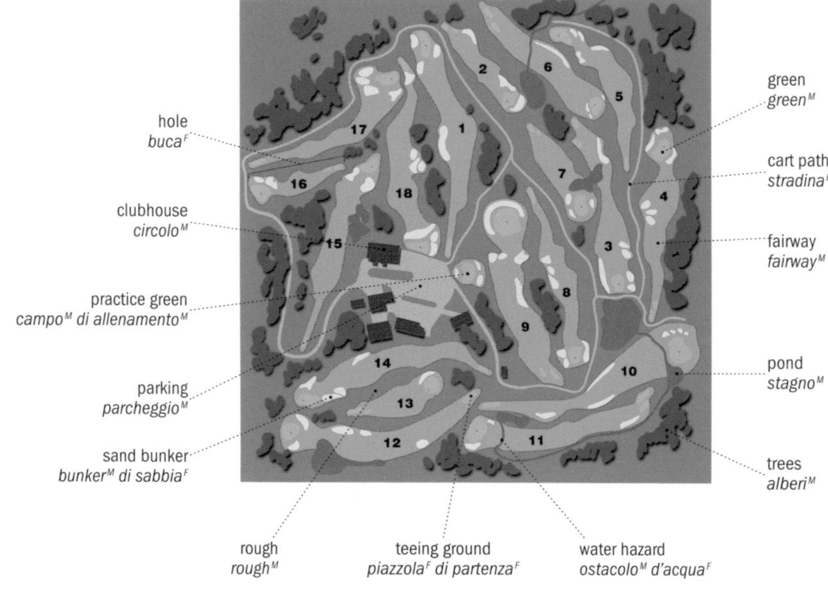

par 5 hole
buca^F par 5

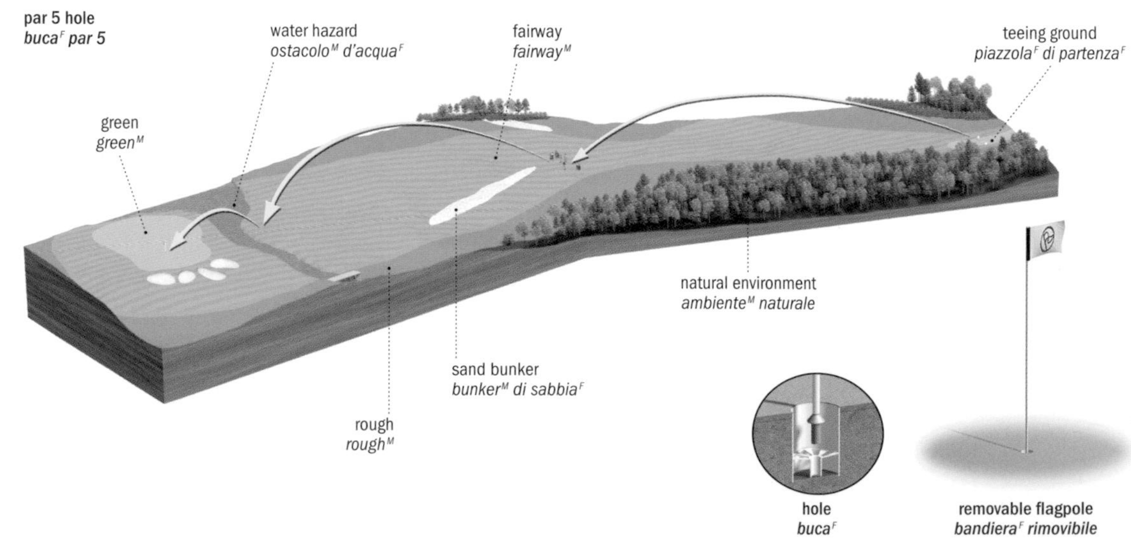

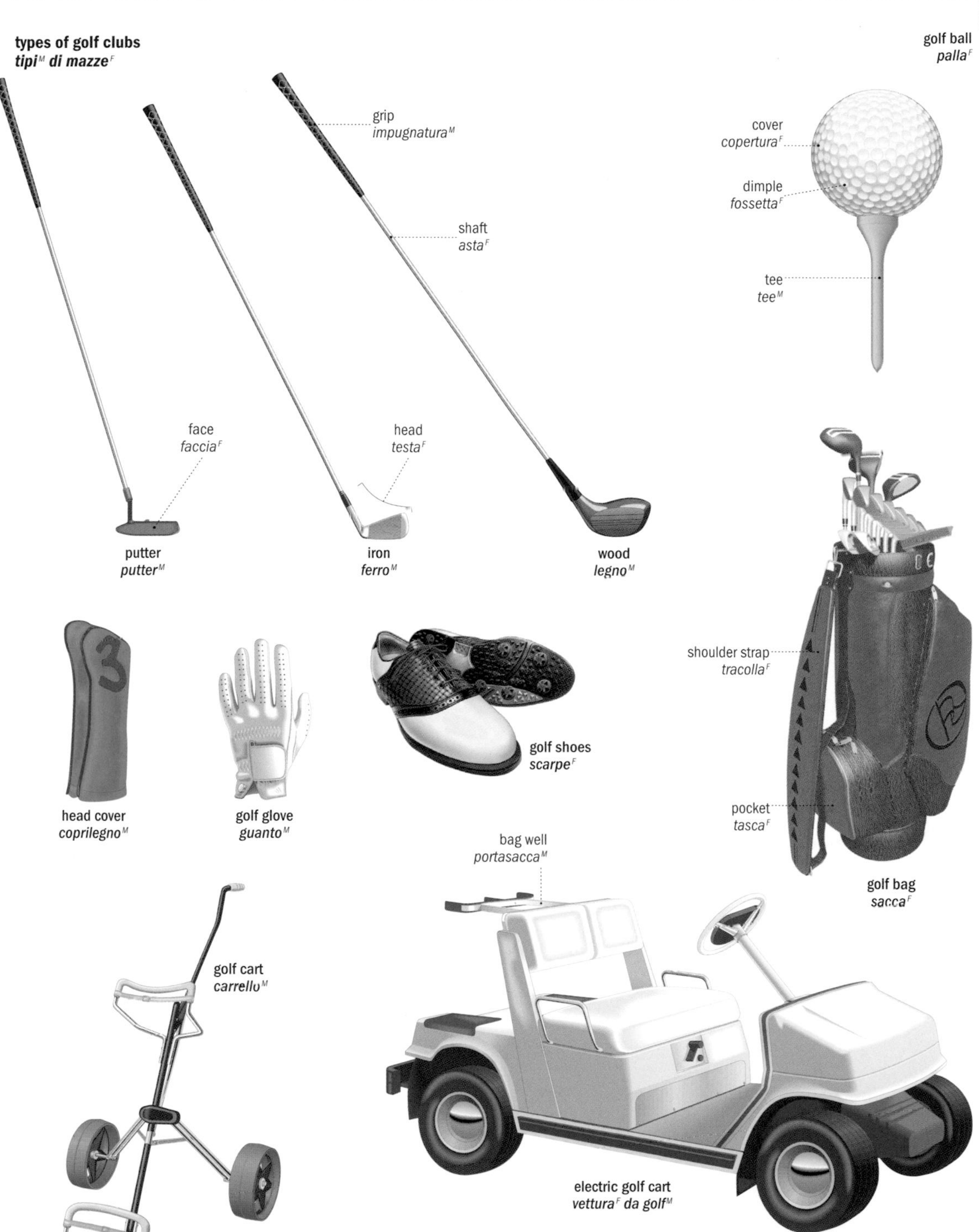
types of golf clubs
tipi^M di mazze^F
grip
impugnatura^M
shaft
asta^F
face
faccia^F
head
testa^F
putter
putter^M
iron
ferro^M
wood
legno^M
golf ball
palla^F
cover
copertura^F
dimple
fossetta^F
tee
tee^M
shoulder strap
tracolla^F
pocket
tasca^F
golf bag
sacca^F
head cover
coprilegno^M
golf glove
guanto^M
golf shoes
scarpe^F
bag well
portasacca^M
golf cart
carrello^M
electric golf cart
vettura^F da golf^M

ice hockey

hockey[M] su ghiaccio[M]

ice hockey player
giocatore[M]

player's stick
bastone[M] del giocatore[M]

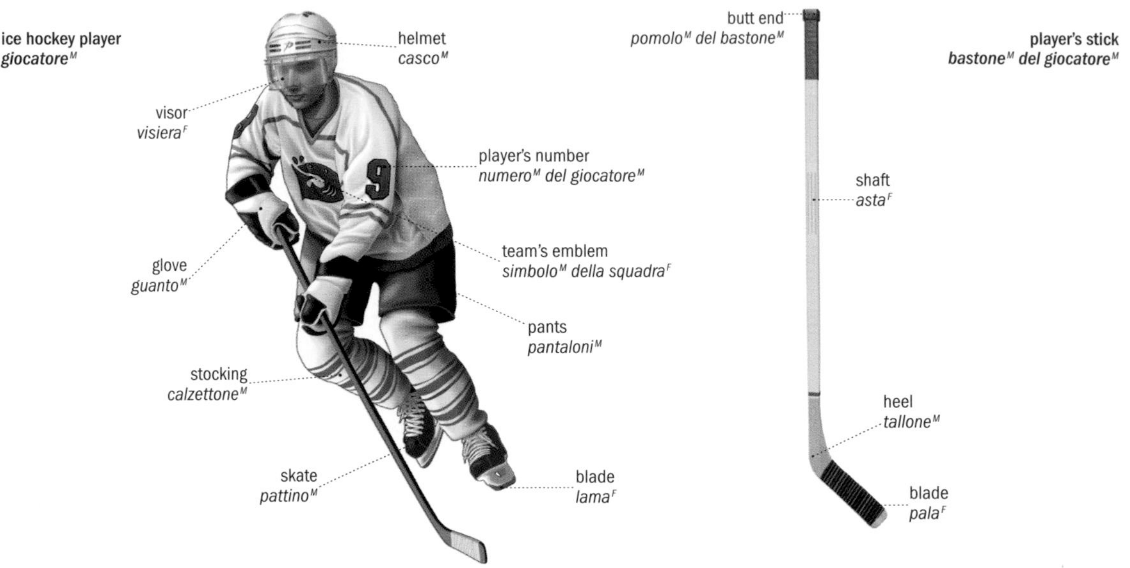

rink
campo[M]

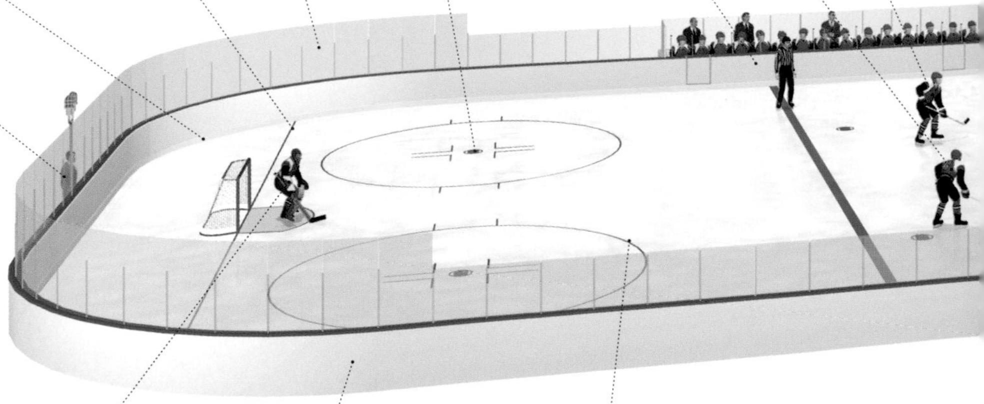

left defense
difensore[M] sinistro

face-off spot
punto[M] di ingaggio[M]

right defense
difensore[M] destro

goal line
linea[F] di porta[F]

glass protector
vetro[M] di protezione[F]

players' bench
panchina[F] dei giocatori[M]

rink corner
angolo[M] della pista[F]

goal judge
giudice[M] di porta[F]

goaltender (goalie)
portiere[M]

boards
balaustre[F]

face-off circle
cerchio[M] di ingaggio[M]

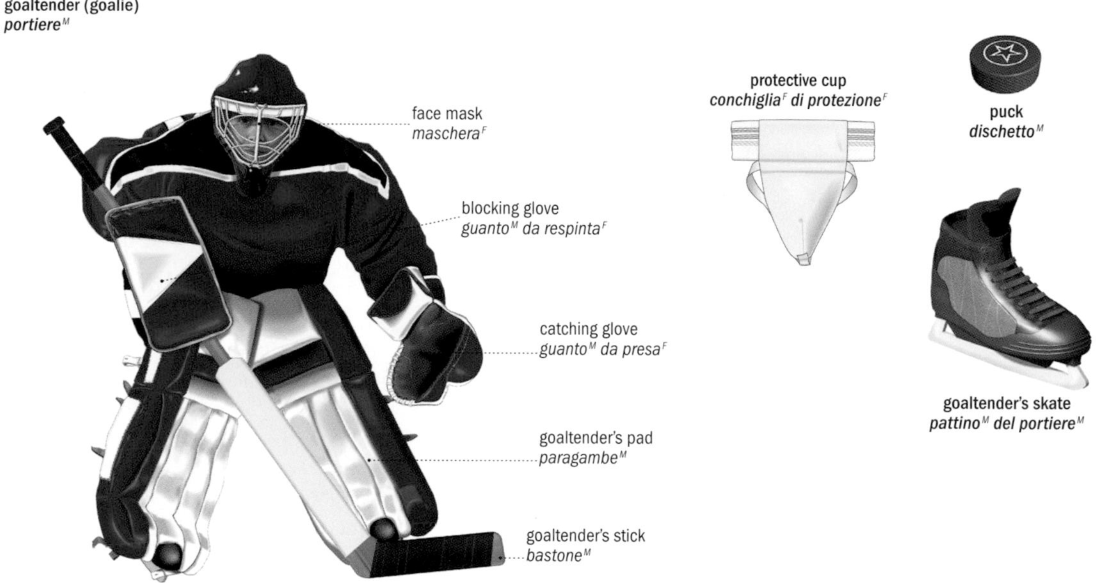

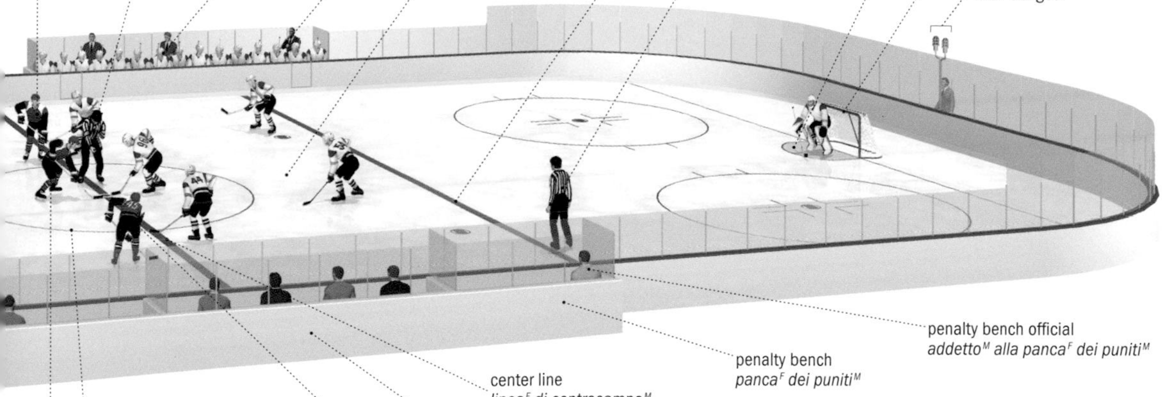

left wing
ala[F] sinistra

coach
allenatore[M]

assistant coach
secondo allenatore[M]

goal crease
area[F] di porta[F]

blue line
linea[F] blu di zona[F]

referee
arbitro[M]

neutral zone
zona[F] neutra

goal
porta[F]

linesman
giudice[M] di linea[F]

goal lights
luci[F] dei goal[M]

penalty bench official
addetto[M] alla panca[F] dei puniti[M]

penalty bench
panca[F] dei puniti[M]

center line
linea[F] di centrocampo[M]

center face-off circle
cerchio[M] di centrocampo[M]

center
centroattacco[M]

right wing
ala[F] destra

officials' bench
panca[F] degli ufficiali[M] di gara[F]

speed skating

pattinaggio^{M} di velocità^{F}

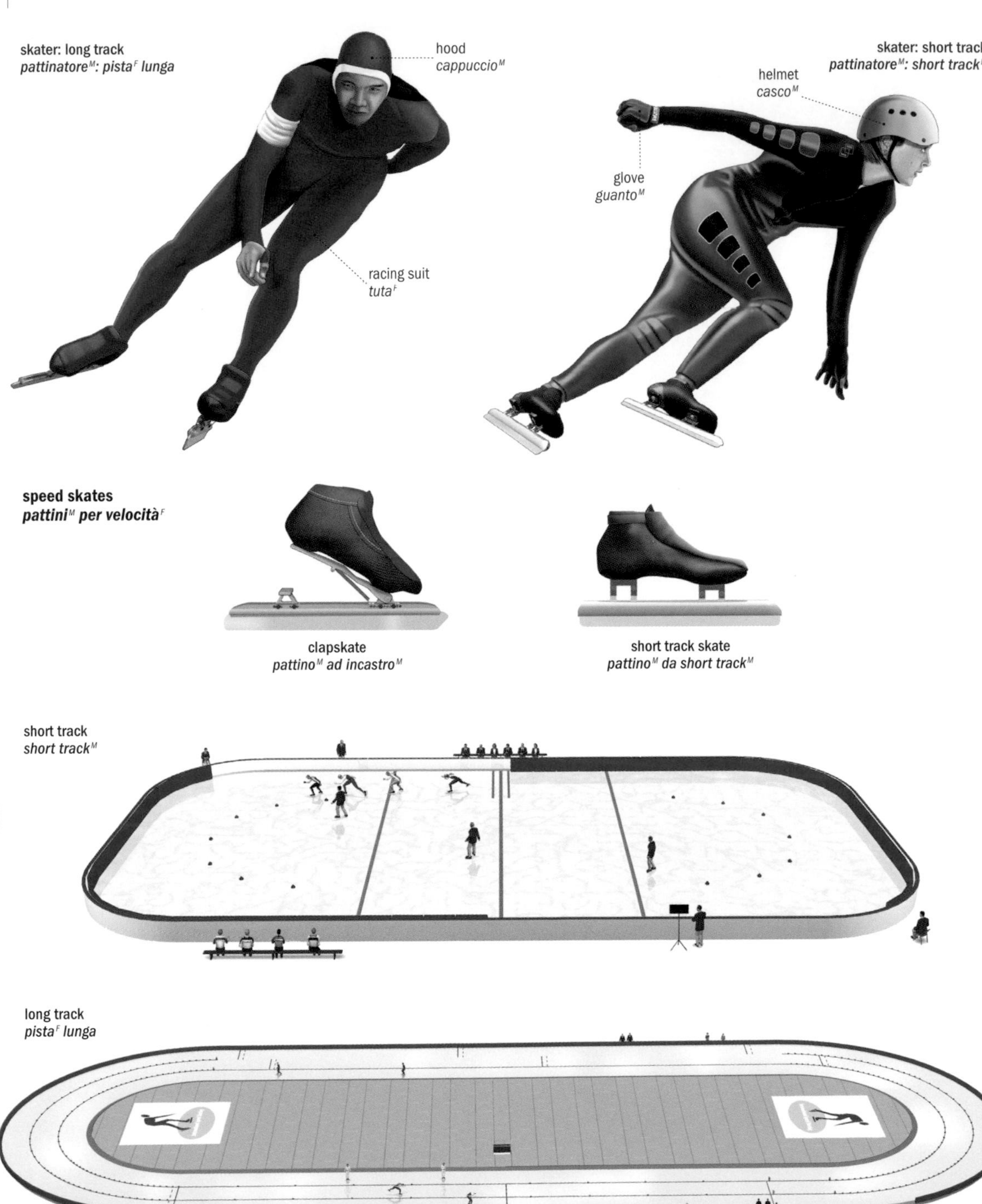

figure skating

pattinaggio^M artistico

figure skate
pattino^M per pattinaggio^M artistico

lining
fodera^F
hook
gancio^M
tongue
linguetta^F
backstay
rinforzo^M posteriore
lace
stringa^F
boot
scarpa^F
eyelet
occhiello^M
heel
tacco^M
sole
suola^F
stanchion
sostegno^M
edge
lamina^F
blade
lama^F
toe pick
punta^F dentellata

dance blade
lama^F per danza^F

free skating blade
lama^F per pattinaggio^M libero

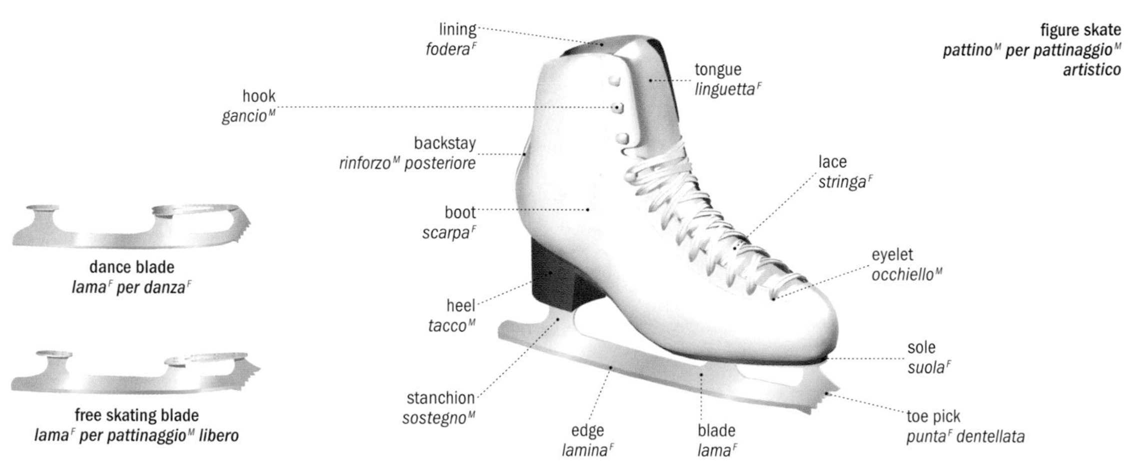

examples of jumps
esempi^M di salti^M

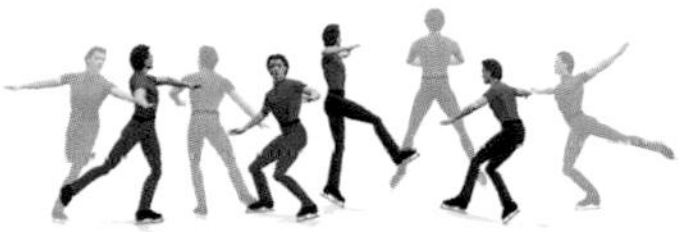

salchow
salchow^M

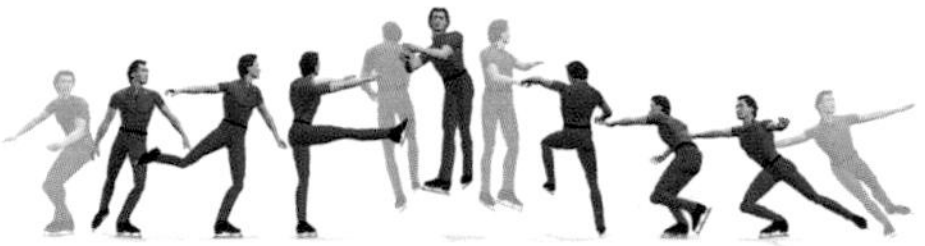

axel
axel^M

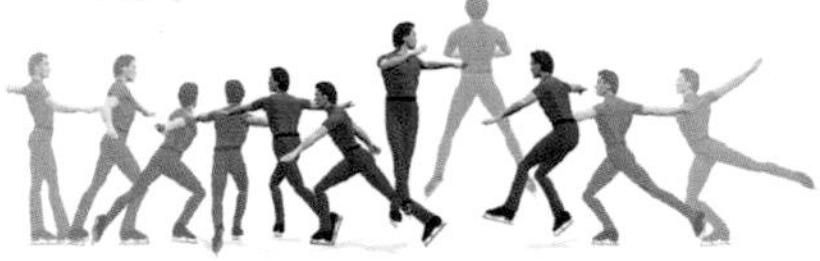

toe loop
loop^M di punta^F

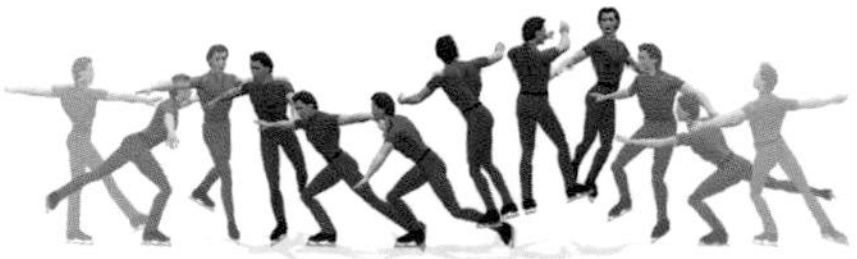

flip
flip^M

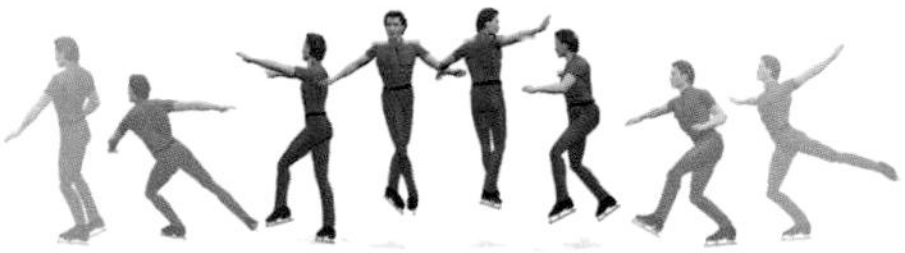

lutz
lutz^M

rink
pista^F di pattinaggio^M

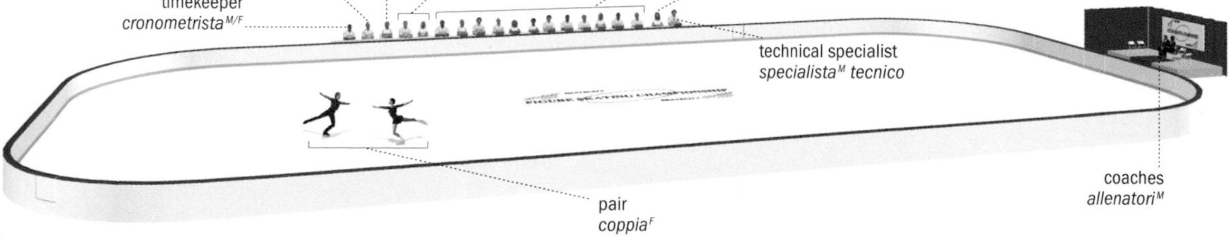

referee
presidente^M di giuria^F
assistant referee
assistente^M del presidente^M di giuria^F
technical delegates
referenti^M tecnici
judges
giudici^M
technical controller
controllore^M tecnico
timekeeper
cronometrista^M/F
technical specialist
specialista^M tecnico
coaches
allenatori^M
pair
coppia^F

SPORTS AND GAMES

alpine skiing

sci[M] alpino

alpine skier
sciatore[M]

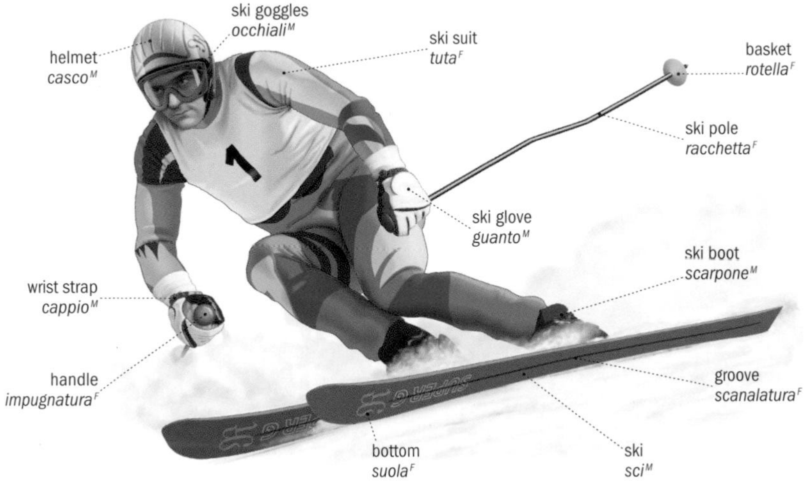

ski goggles
occhiali[M]
helmet
casco[M]
ski suit
tuta[F]
basket
rotella[F]
ski pole
racchetta[F]
ski glove
guanto[M]
ski boot
scarpone[M]
wrist strap
cappio[M]
handle
impugnatura[F]
groove
scanalatura[F]
bottom
suola[F]
ski
sci[M]

ski
sci[M]

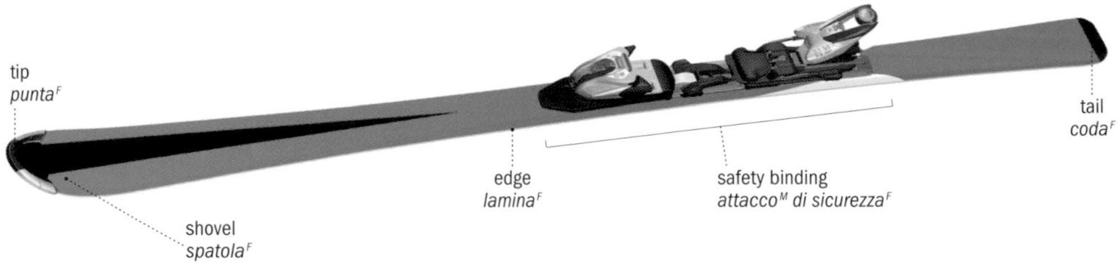

tip
punta[F]
tail
coda[F]
edge
lamina[F]
safety binding
attacco[M] di sicurezza[F]
shovel
spatola[F]

examples of skis
esempi[M] di sci[M]

skiboard
mini sci[M]

slalom ski
sci[M] da slalom[M]

giant slalom ski
sci[M] da slalom[M] gigante

downhill and super-G ski
sci[M] da discesa[F] libera e supergigante[M]

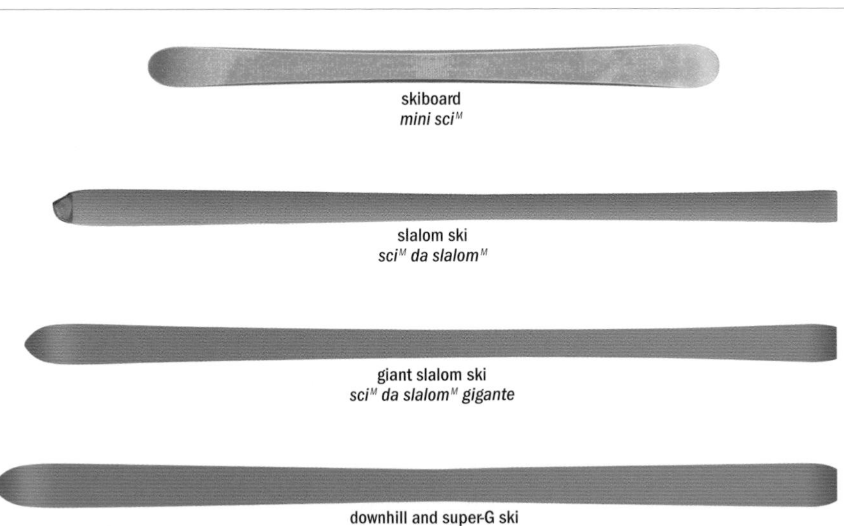

technical events
specialità F

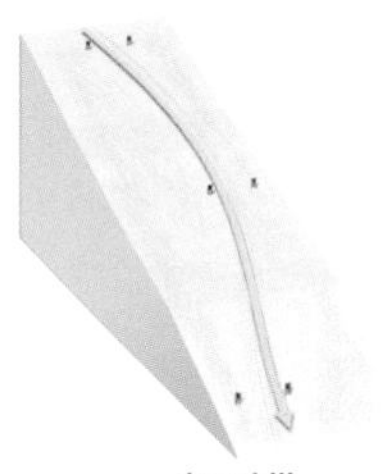

downhill
discesa M *libera*

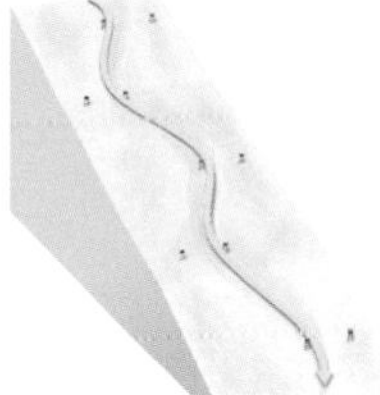

super giant (super-G) slalom
slalom M *supergigante*

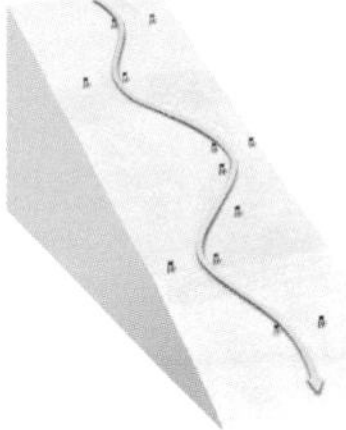

giant slalom
slalom M *gigante*

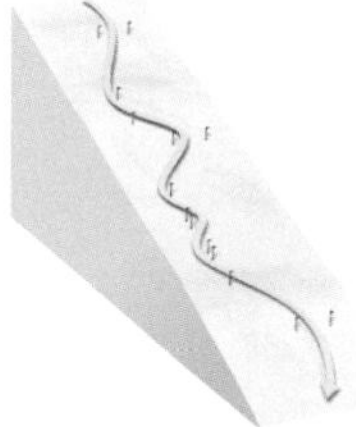

special slalom
slalom M *speciale*

ski boot
scarpone M

safety binding
attacco M *di sicurezza* F

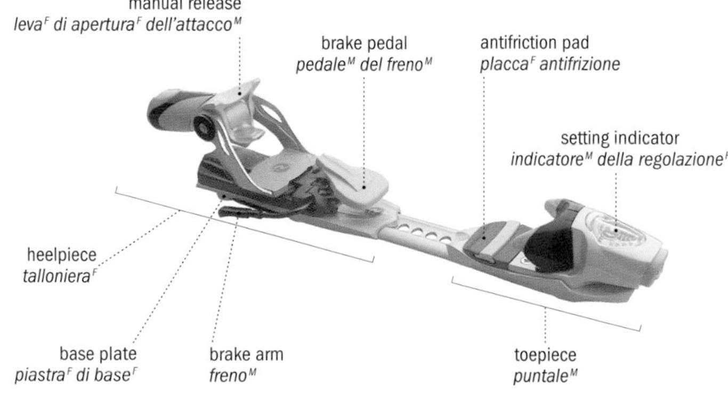

ski resort

stazione[F] sciistica

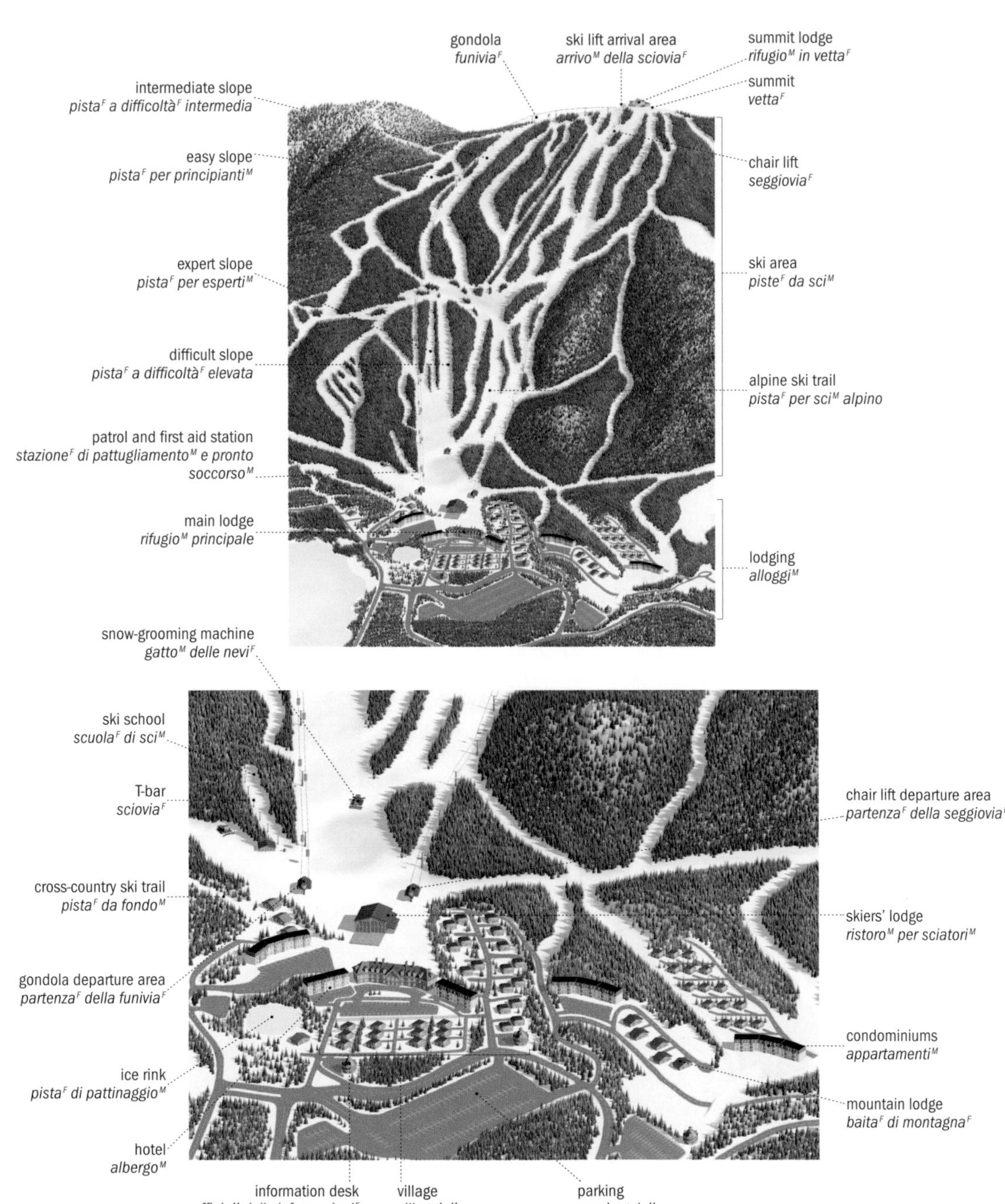

snowboarding

snowboard[M]

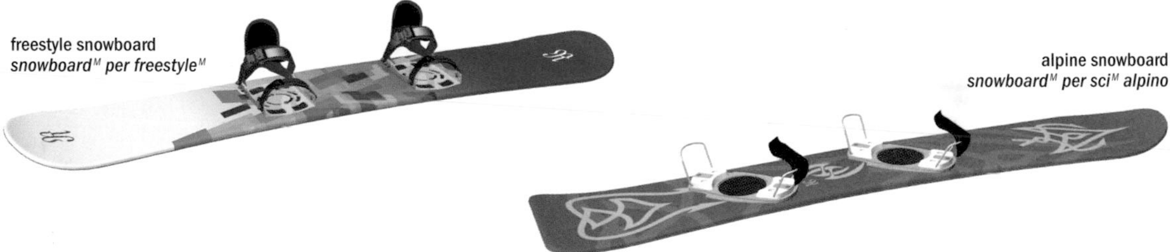

ski jumping

salto[M] con gli sci[M]

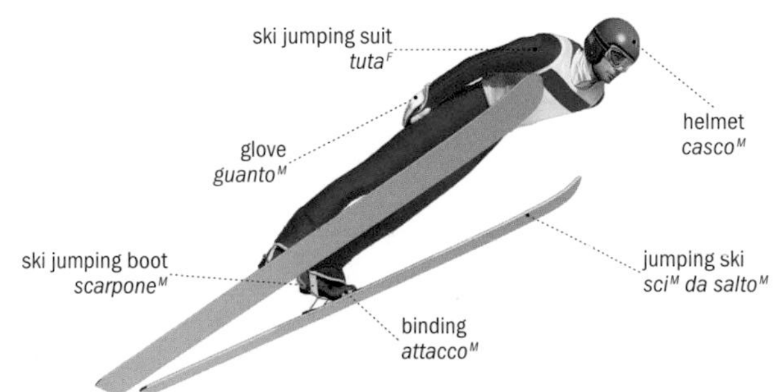

cross-country skiing

sci[M] da fondo[M]

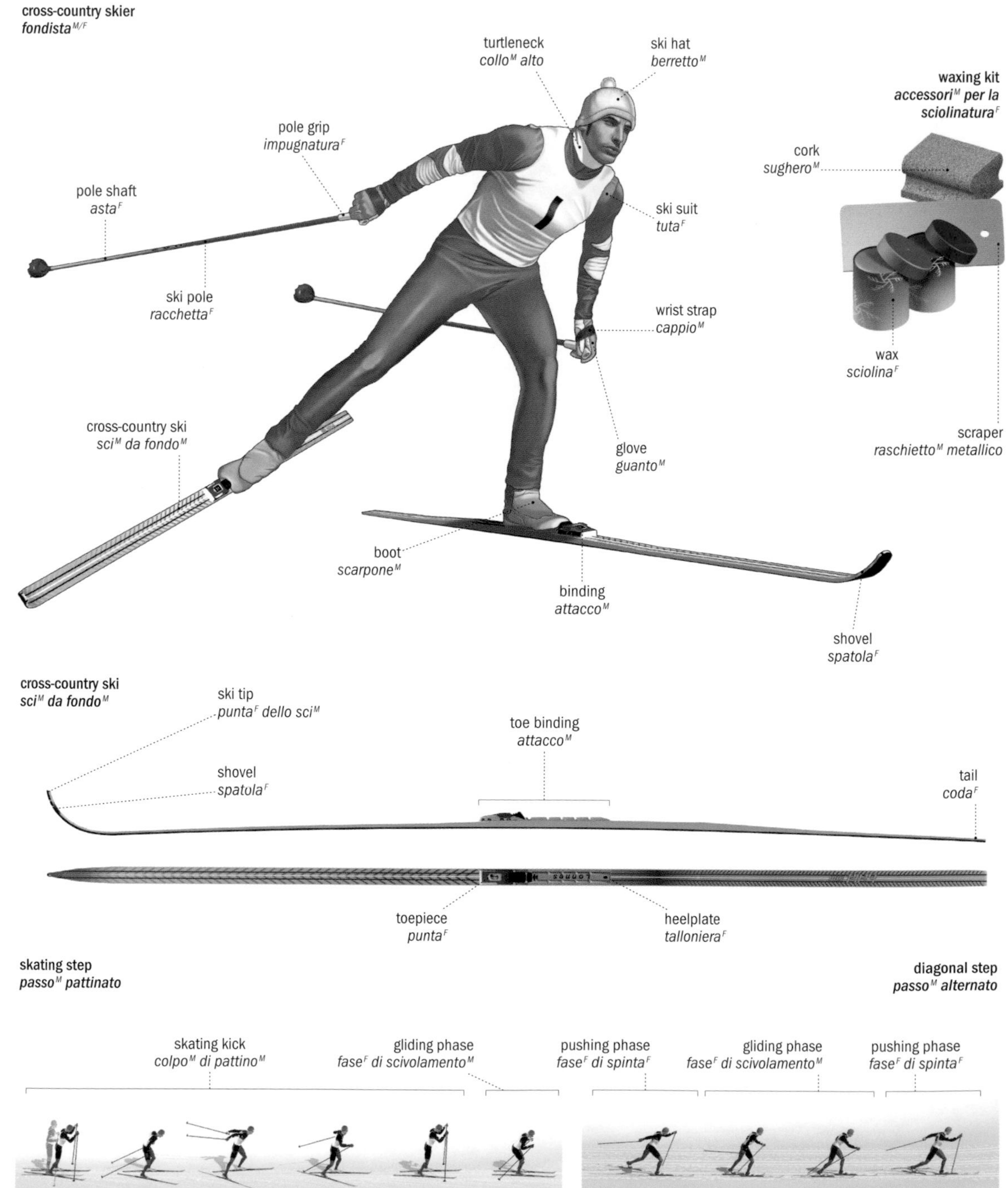

curling

curling[M]

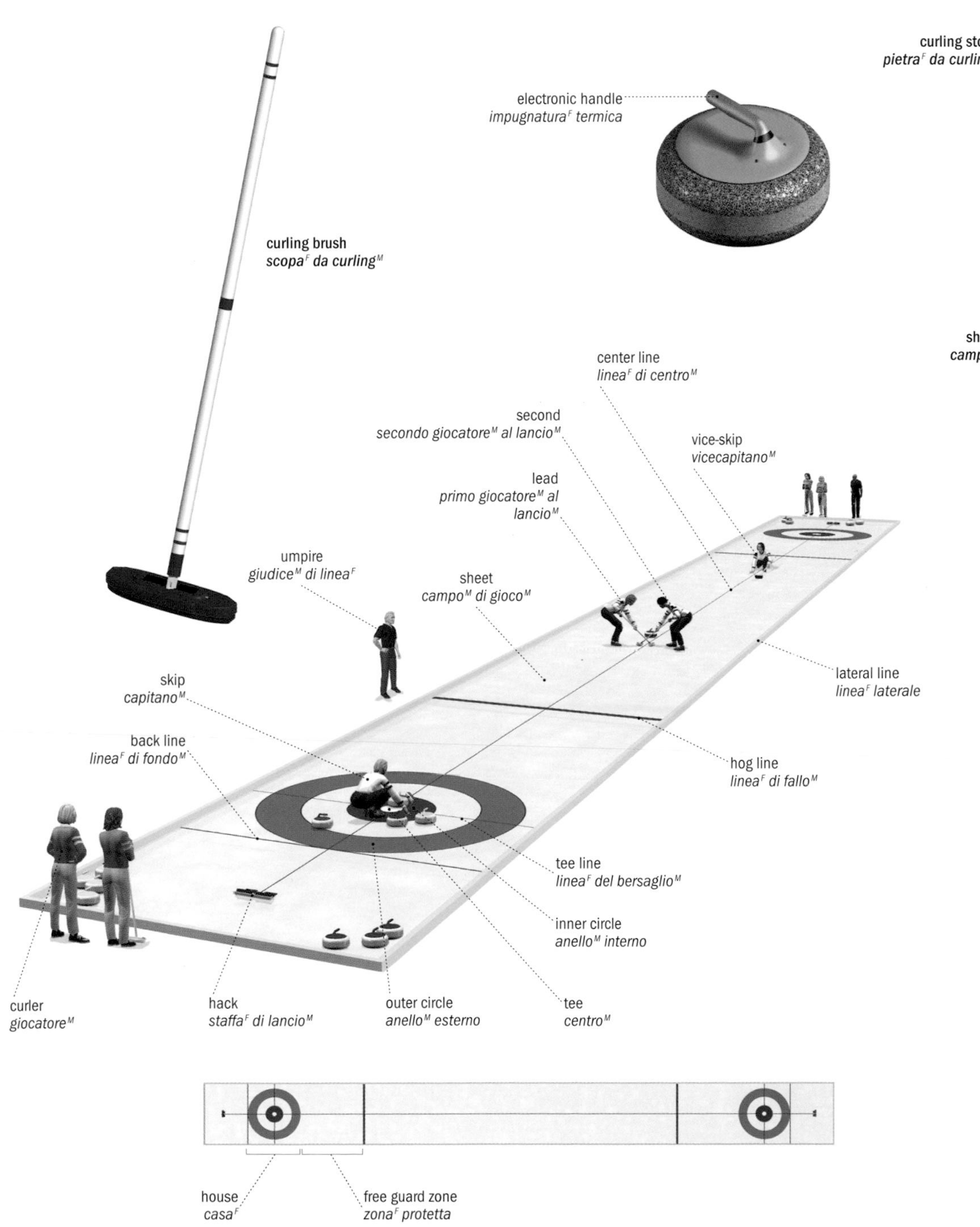

swimming

nuoto^{M}

starting block
blocco^{M} di partenza^{F}

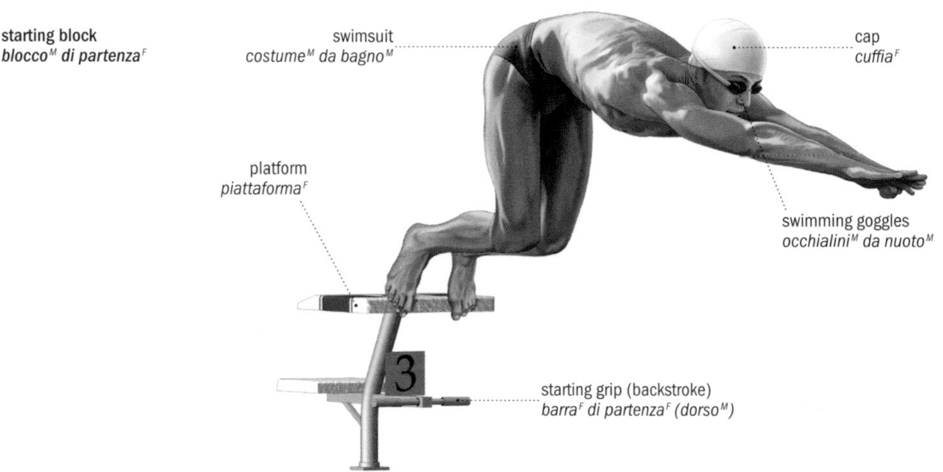

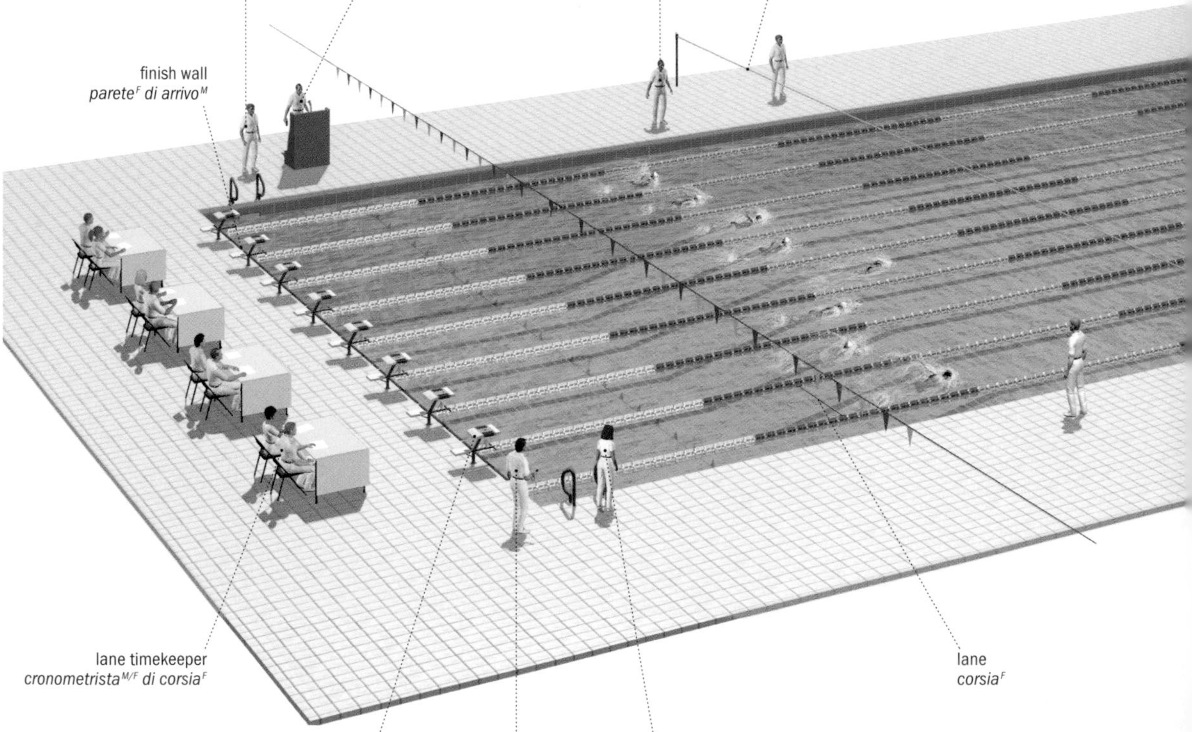

swimsuit
costume^{M} da bagno^{M}
cap
cuffia^{F}
platform
piattaforma^{F}
swimming goggles
occhialini^{M} da nuoto^{M}
3
starting grip (backstroke)
barra^{F} di partenza^{F} (dorso^{M})

referee
arbitro^{M}
starter
starter^{M}
stroke judge
giudice^{M} di stile^{M}
false start rope
fune^{F} di falsa partenza^{F}
finish wall
parete^{F} di arrivo^{M}
lane timekeeper
cronometrista$^{M/F}$ di corsia^{F}
lane
corsia^{F}
starting block
blocco^{M} di partenza^{F}
chief timekeeper
cronometrista$^{M/F}$ capo^{M}
placing judge
giudice^{M} di arrivo^{M}

types of strokes
stili^M di nuoto^M

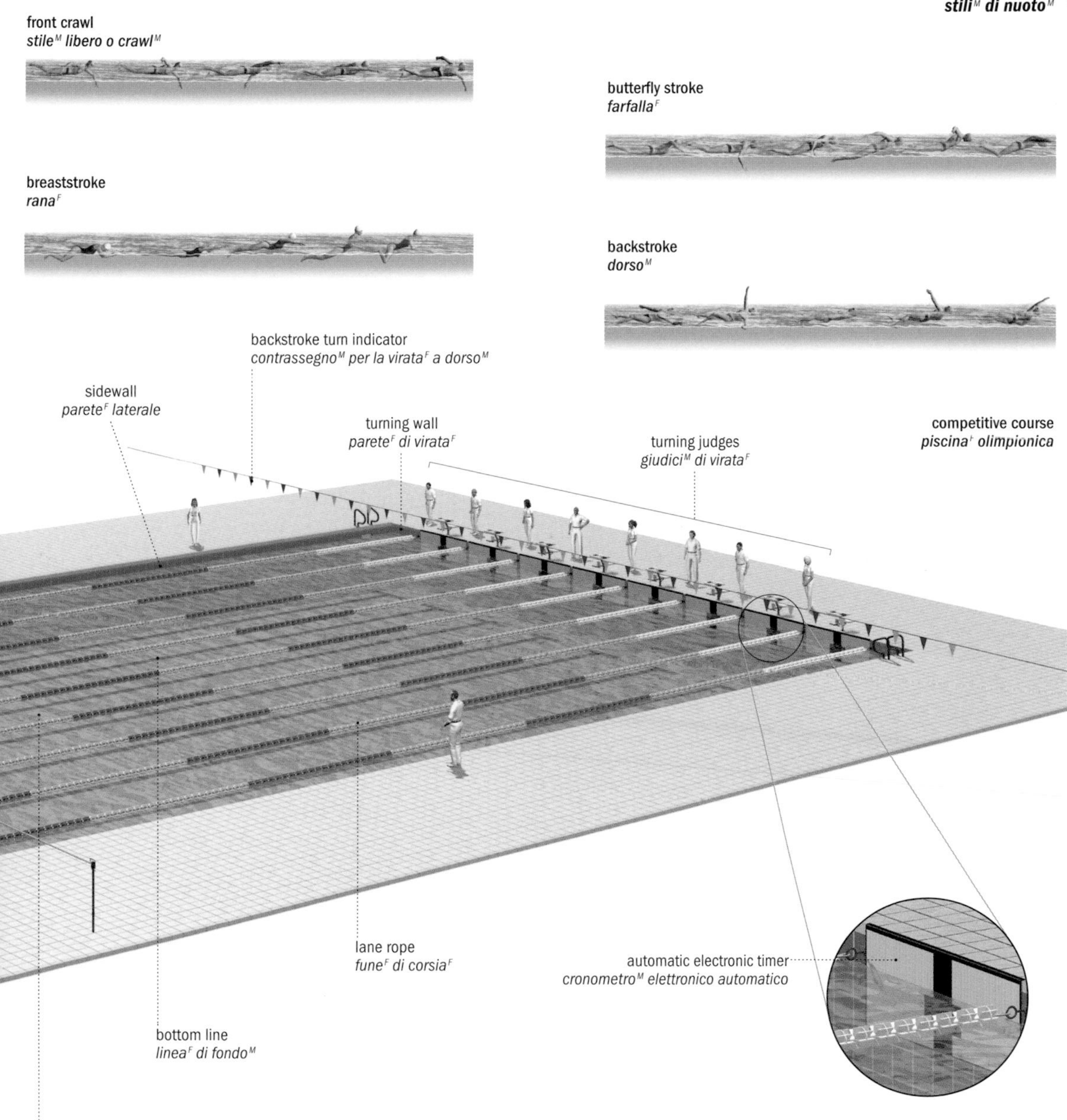

diving

tuffi^M

starting positions
posizioni^F di partenza^F

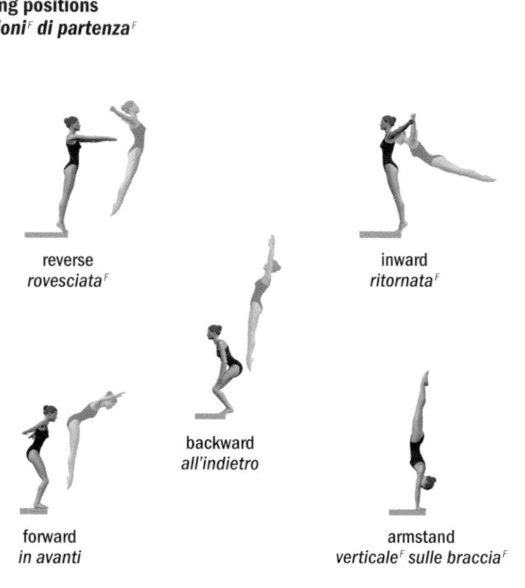

reverse
rovesciata^F
inward
ritornata^F
backward
all'indietro
forward
in avanti
armstand
verticale^F sulle braccia^F

flights
voli^M

tuck position
posizione^F raggruppata
straight position
posizione^F tesa
pike position
posizione^F carpiata

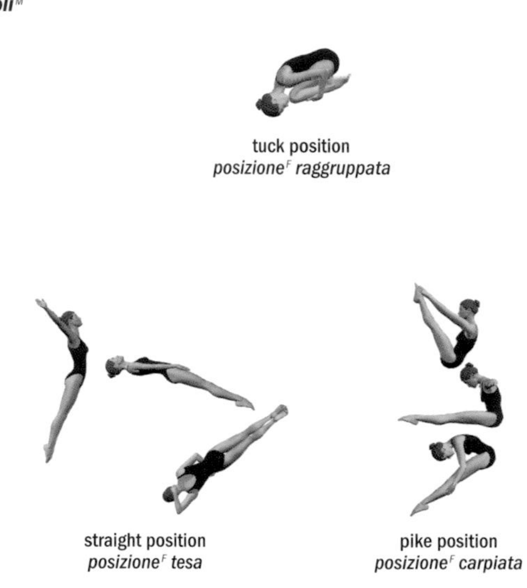

diving installations
strutture^F per i tuffi^M

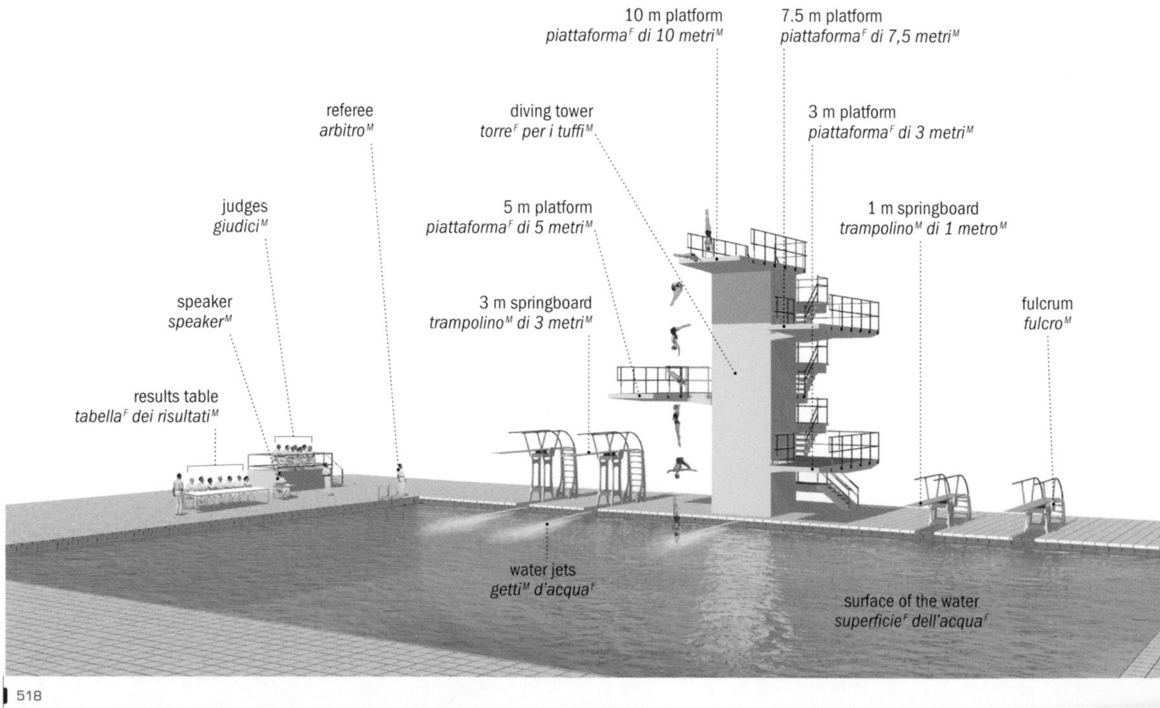

10 m platform
piattaforma^F di 10 metri^M
7.5 m platform
piattaforma^F di 7,5 metri^M
referee
arbitro^M
diving tower
torre^F per i tuffi^M
3 m platform
piattaforma^F di 3 metri^M
judges
giudici^M
5 m platform
piattaforma^F di 5 metri^M
1 m springboard
trampolino^M di 1 metro^M
speaker
speaker^M
3 m springboard
trampolino^M di 3 metri^M
fulcrum
fulcro^M
results table
tabella^F dei risultati^M
water jets
getti^M d'acqua^F
surface of the water
superficie^F dell'acqua^F

sailboard

windsurf[M]

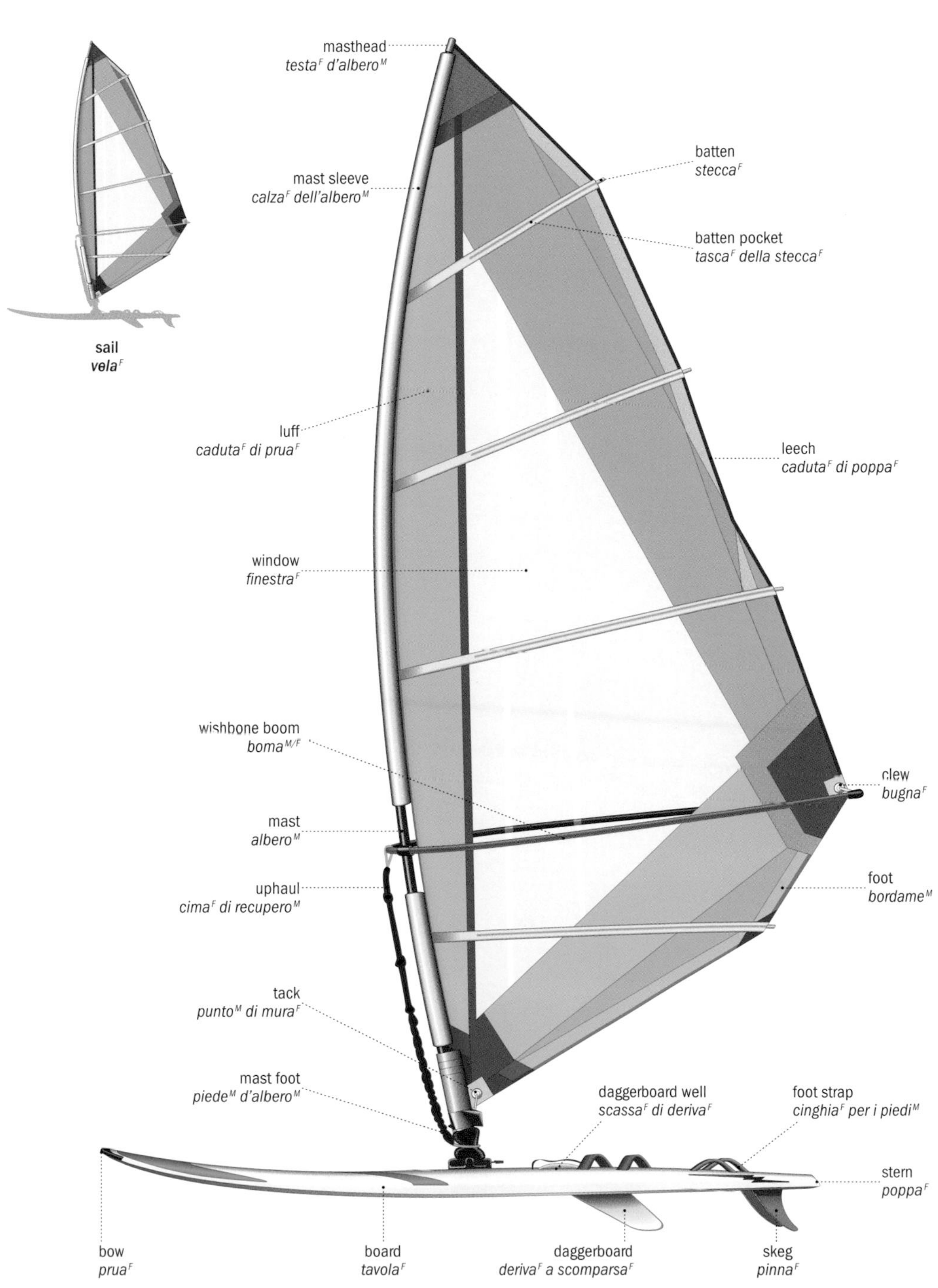

sailing

vela[F]

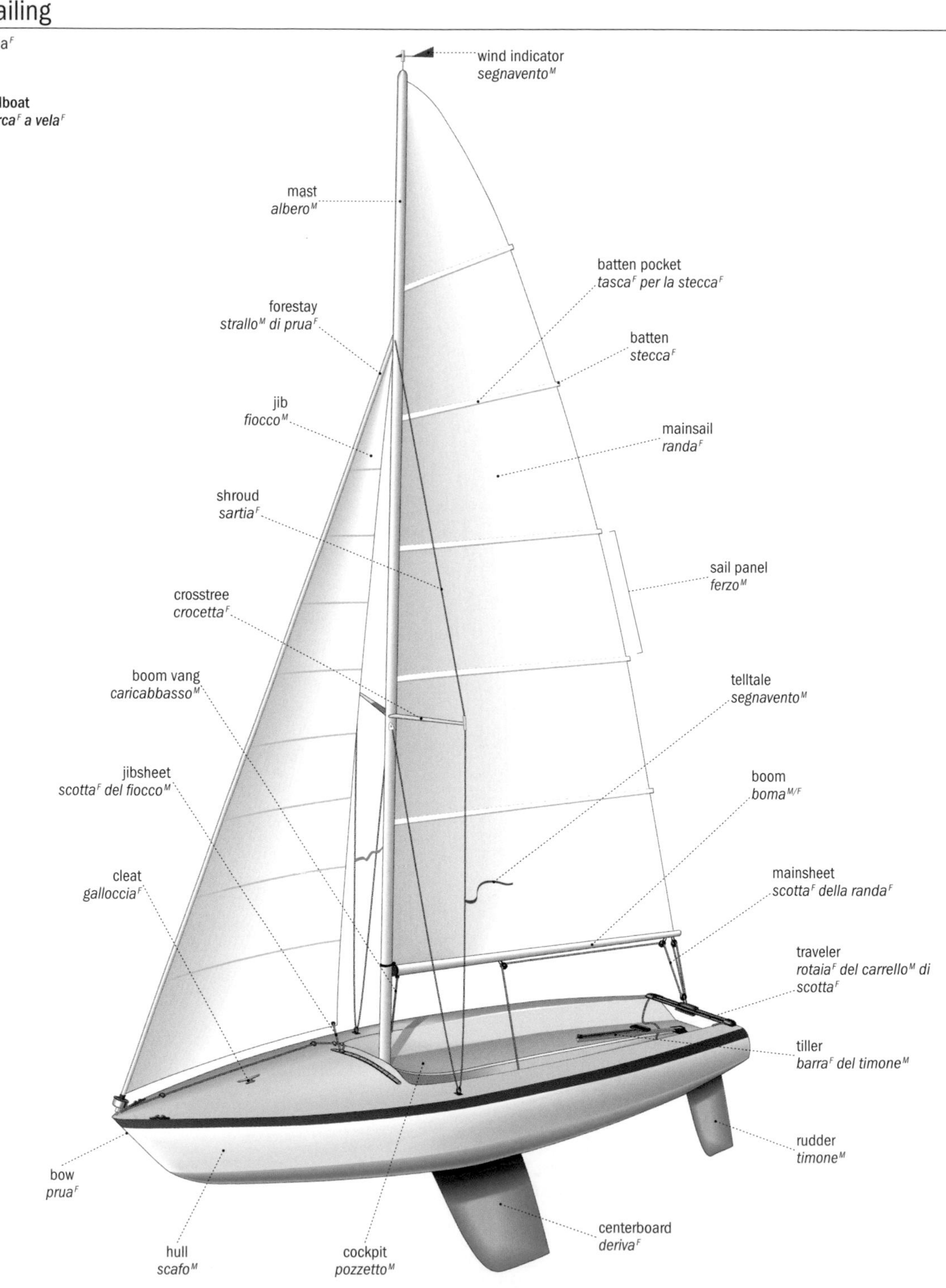

car racing

Formula 1® car
auto^F da formula^F 1

wing
alettone^M
camera
telecamera^F
cockpit
abitacolo^M
radio antenna
antenna^F radio^F
Pitot tube
tubo^M di Pitot
side fairings
carenatura^F laterale
roll structure
struttura^F protettiva
steering wheel
volante^M

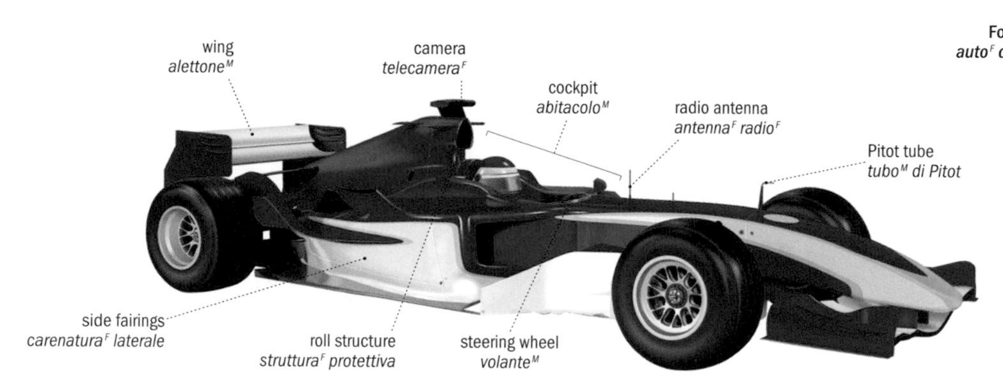

motorcycling

motociclismo^M

motocross and supercross motorcycle
motocicletta^F da motocross^M e supercross^M

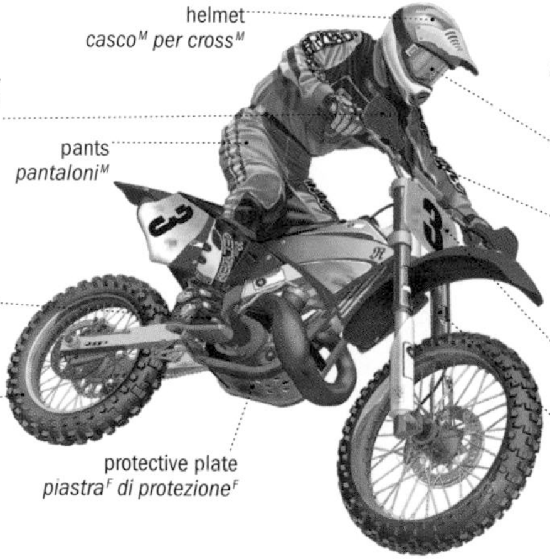

helmet
casco^M per cross^M
hand protector
paramano^M
pants
pantaloni^M
boot
stivale^M
nubby tire
pneumatico^M scolpito
protective plate
piastra^F di protezione^F
protective goggles
occhiali^M protettivi
protective suit
tuta^F protettiva
number plate
numero^M di gara^F
fork
forcella^F

speed grand prix motorcycle and rider
moto^M da Gran premio^M e motociclista^M/F

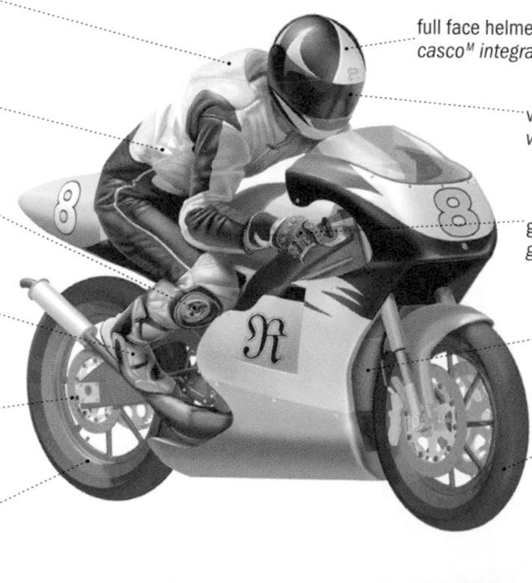

neck support
sostegno^M per il collo^M
racing suit
tuta^F da competizione^F
rub protection
protezione^F antisfregamento
boot
stivale^M
disc brake
freno^M a disco^M
wheel
ruota^F
full face helmet
casco^M integrale
visor
visiera^F
glove
guanto^M
air intake for engine cooling
presa^F d'aria^F per il raffreddamento^M del motore^M
tire
pneumatico^M

skateboarding

skateboard^M

skateboard
skateboard^M

tail
coda^F
truck
attacco^M
nose
punta^F
grip tape
superficie^F antiscivolo
wheel
ruota^F

skateboarder
skater^M/F

knee pad
ginocchiera^F
elbow pad
gomitiera^F
helmet
casco^M
coping
tubo^M metallico

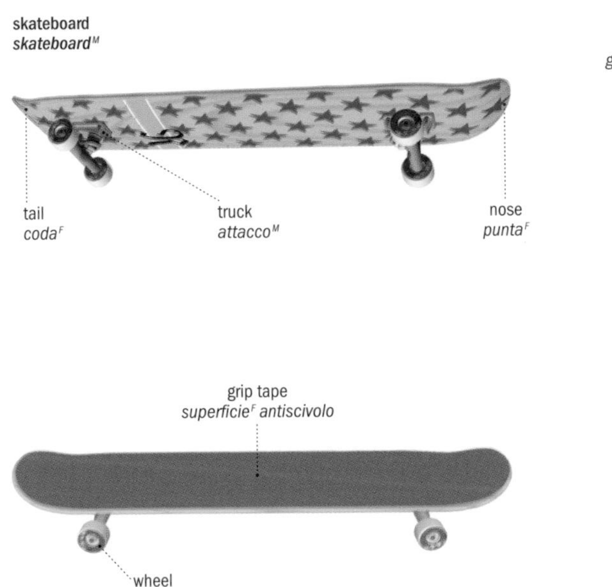

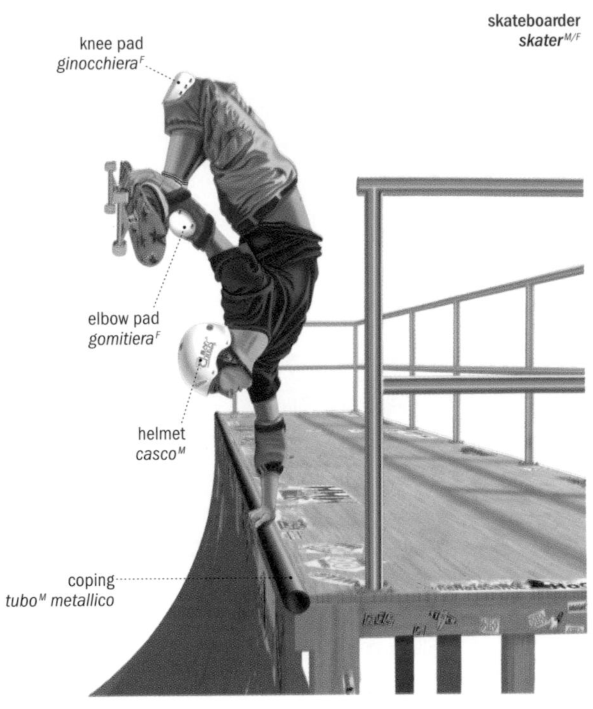

ramp
rampa^F

guard rail
guardrail^M
platform
piattaforma^F
coping
tubo^M metallico
vertical section
superficie^F verticale
flat
piano^M

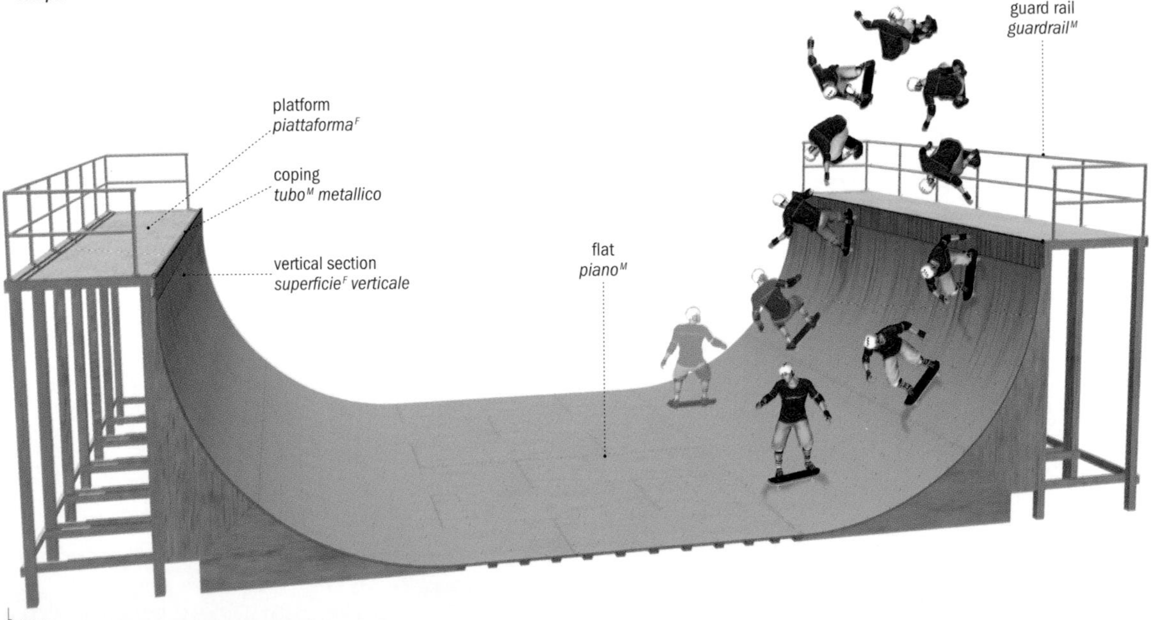

in-line skating

pattinaggio^M in linea^F

camping

campeggio[M]

examples of tents
esempi[M] di tende[F]

two-person tent
tenda[F] a due posti[M]

rainfly
telo[M] esterno

canopy
tettoia[F]

door
porta[F]

guy line
tirante[M]

stake
picchetto[M]

strainer
regolatore[M] del tirante[M]

elastic strainer
elastico[M]

zipper
cerniera[F] lampo

inner tent
tenda[F] interna

family tent
tenda[F] di tipo[M] familiare

window canopy
tenda[F] coprifinestra

living room
zona[F] abitabile

guy line
tirante[M]

elastic strainer
elastico[M]

bedroom
camera[F] da letto[M]

sewn-in floor
fondo[M]

wall
parete[F]

stake loop
asola[F] per il picchetto[M]

canvas divider
divisorio[M] di tela[F]

frame
intelaiatura[F]

screen window
finestra[F] zanzariera

wagon tent
tenda[F] da cucina[F]

wall tent
tenda[F] da campo[M]

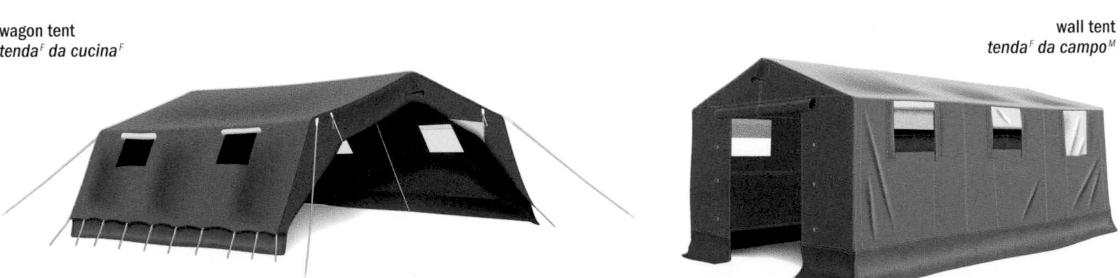

SPORTS AND GAMES

pup tent
tenda^F canadese
rainfly
telo^M esterno
roof pole
palo^M frontale
inner tent
tenda^F interna
elastic strainer
elastico^M
door
porta^F
stake loop
asola^F per il picchetto^M
sewn-in floor
fondo^M
stake
picchetto^M
one-person tent
tenda^F a un posto^M
dome tent
tenda^F a cupola^F
pop-up tent
tenda^F a igloo^M
propane or butane accessories
accessori^M a propano^M o butano^M
lantern
lanterna^F
burner frame
telaio^M del bruciatore^M
globe
globo^M di vetro^M
heater
stufa^F a gas^M
pressure regulator
regolatore^M di luminosità^F
pump
pompa^F
leakproof cap
capsula^F ermetica
tank
bombola^F
double-burner camp stove
fornello^M da campo^M a due fuochi^M
burner
bruciatore^M
tank
bombola^F
wire support
griglia^F
single-burner camp stove
fornello^M da campo^M con un bruciatore^M
control valve
manopola^F di regolazione^F del gas^M
SPORTS AND GAMES

camping

examples of sleeping bags
esempi[M] di sacchi[M] a pelo[M]

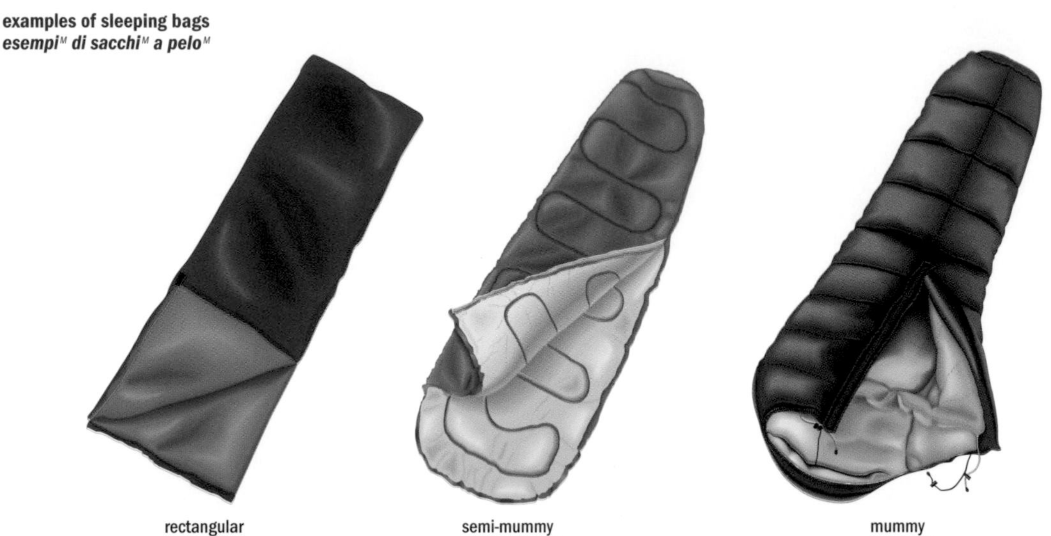

rectangular
rettangolare

semi-mummy
semi-mummia[F]

mummy
mummia[F]

bed and mattress
branda[F] e materassino[M]

folding cot
brandina[F] smontabile

inflator-deflator
gonfiatore[M] a soffietto[M]

air mattress
materassino[M] pneumatico

self-inflating mattress
materassino[M] autogonfiante

foam pad
materassino[M] isolante

inflator
gonfiatore[M]

cutlery set
posate[F]

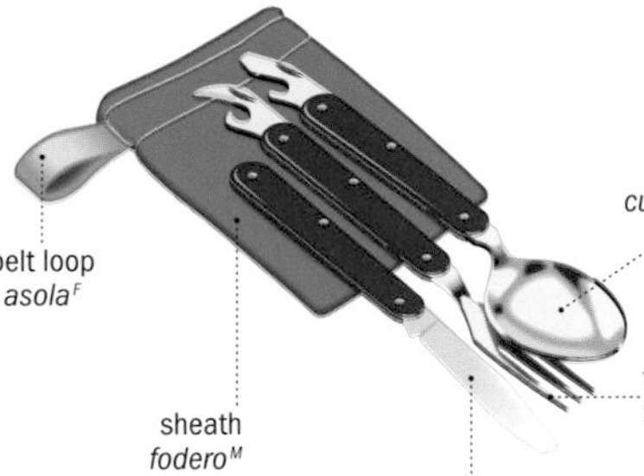

belt loop
asola[F]

sheath
fodero[M]

knife
coltello[M]

spoon
cucchiaio[M]

fork
forchetta[F]

cooking set
set[M] per cucinare

plate
piatto[M]

saucepan
tegame[M]

handle
manico[M]

frying pan
padella[F]

coffee pot
caffettiera[F]

cup
tazza[F]

camping equipment
attrezzature[F] da campeggio[M]

Swiss Army knife
temperino[M] multiuso

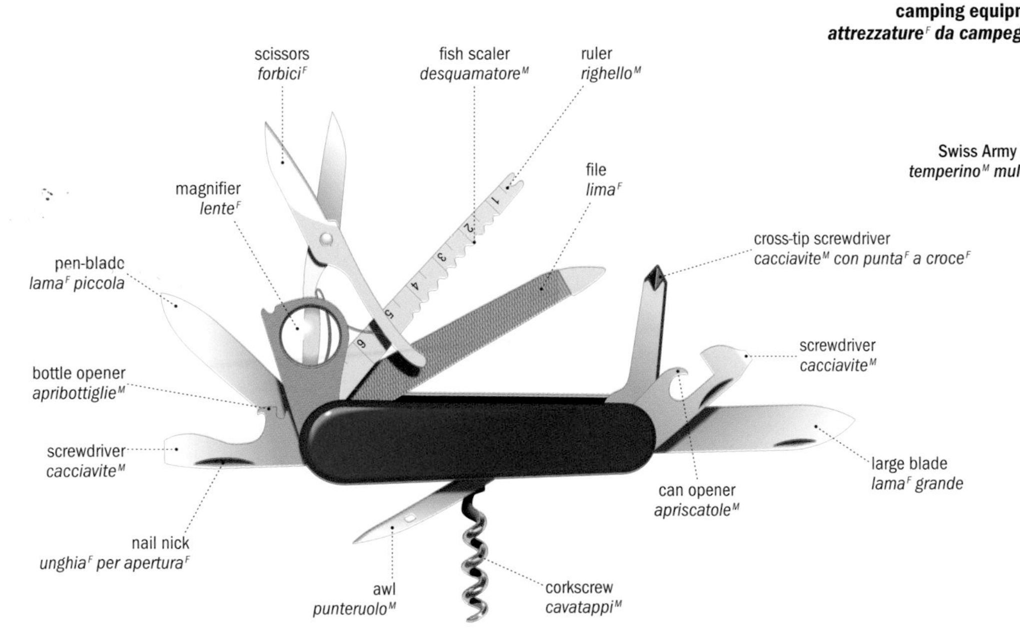

camping

backpack
zaino[M]

top flap
patta[F] di chiusura[F]

shoulder strap
spallaccio[M]

tightening buckle
fibbia[F] di regolazione[F]

side compression strap
cinghia[F] di compressione[F] laterale

front compression strap
cinghia[F] di compressione[F] frontale

strap loop
passacinghia[M]

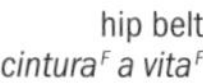

hip belt
cintura[F] a vita[F]

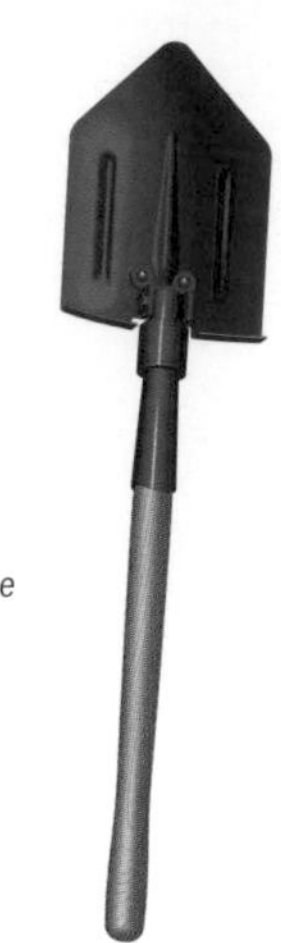

folding shovel
badile[M] pieghevole

hurricane lamp
lampada[F] a petrolio[M]

vacuum bottle
thermos[M]

bottle
bottiglia[F]

stopper
tappo[M]

cup
bicchiere[M]

canteen
borraccia[F]

cooler
frigo[M] portatile

water carrier
contenitore[M] termico

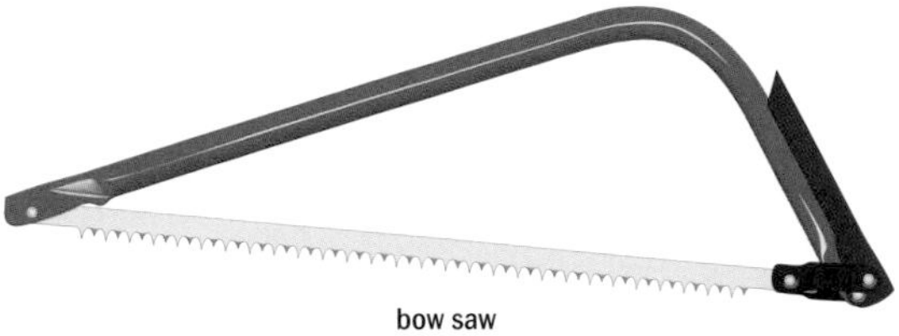

bow saw
sega[F] a mano[F]

knife
coltello[M]

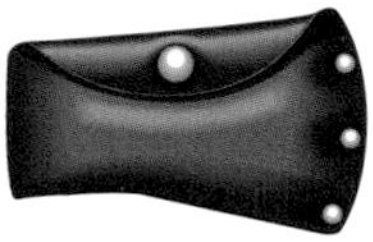

leather sheath
fodero[M] di pelle[F]

sheath
fodero[M]

folding grill
grill[M] pieghevole

hatchet
accetta[F]

magnetic compass
bussola[F] magnetica

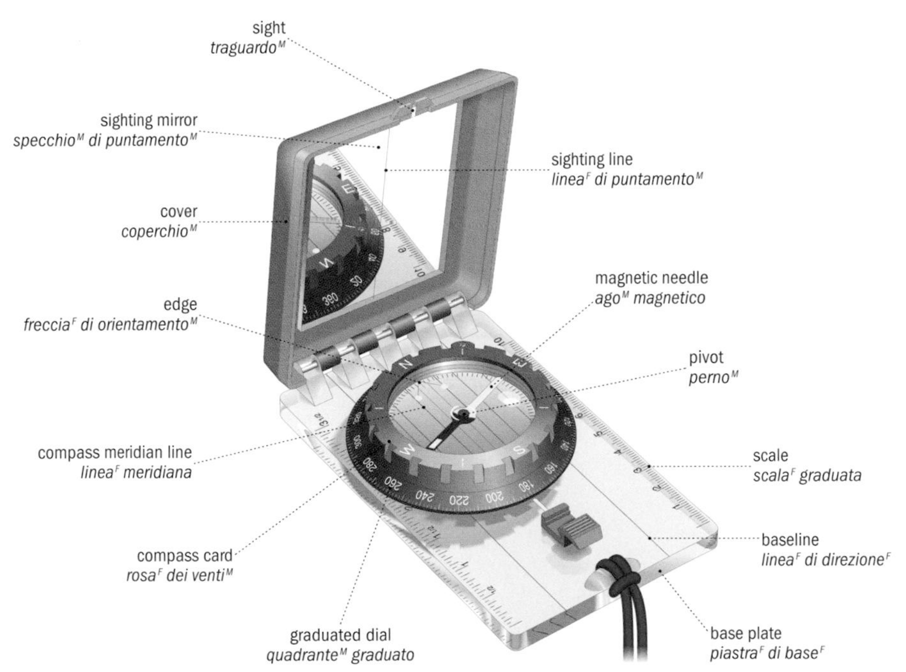

hunting

caccia^F

rifle (rifled bore)
fucile^M a canna^F rigata

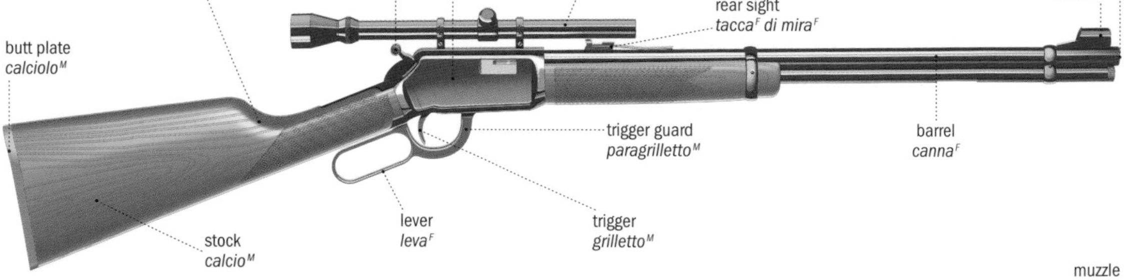

breechblock
blocco^M della culatta^F
muzzle
bocca^F
pistol grip
impugnatura^F a pistola^F
hammer
cane^M
telescopic sight
mirino^M a cannocchiale^M
front sight
mirino^M
rear sight
tacca^F di mira^F
butt plate
calciolo^M
trigger guard
paragrilletto^M
barrel
canna^F
lever
leva^F
trigger
grilletto^M
stock
calcio^M

shotgun (smooth-bore)
fucile^M a canna^F liscia

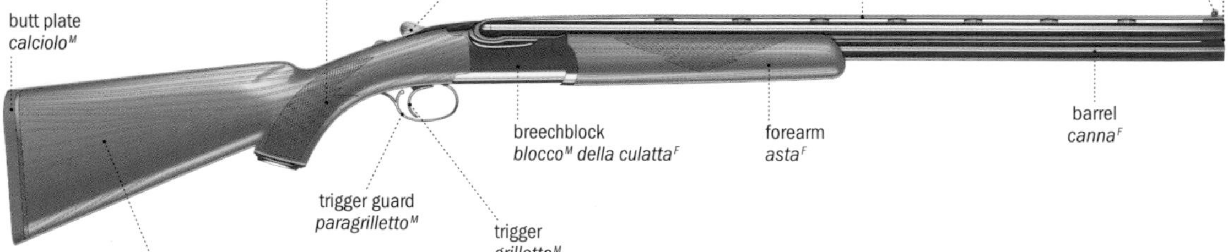

muzzle
bocca^F
hammer
cane^M
ventilated rib
bindella^F ventilata
front sight
mirino^M
pistol grip
impugnatura^F a pistola^F
butt plate
calciolo^M
breechblock
blocco^M della culatta^F
forearm
asta^F
barrel
canna^F
trigger guard
paragrilletto^M
trigger
grilletto^M
stock
calcio^M

cartridge (shotgun)
cartuccia^F per fucile^M a canna^F liscia

crimping
orlatura^F a stella^F
pellets
pallini^M
plastic case
bossolo^M di plastica^F
wad
borra^F
base
fondello^M metallico
charge
carica^F di lancio^M
primer
innesco^M

cartridge (rifle)
cartuccia^F per fucile^M a canna^F rigata

nose
punta^F
core
nucleo^M
bullet
pallottola^F
jacket
incamiciatura^F
case
bossolo^M
propellant
carica^F di lancio^M
primer
innesco^M
cup
fondello^M

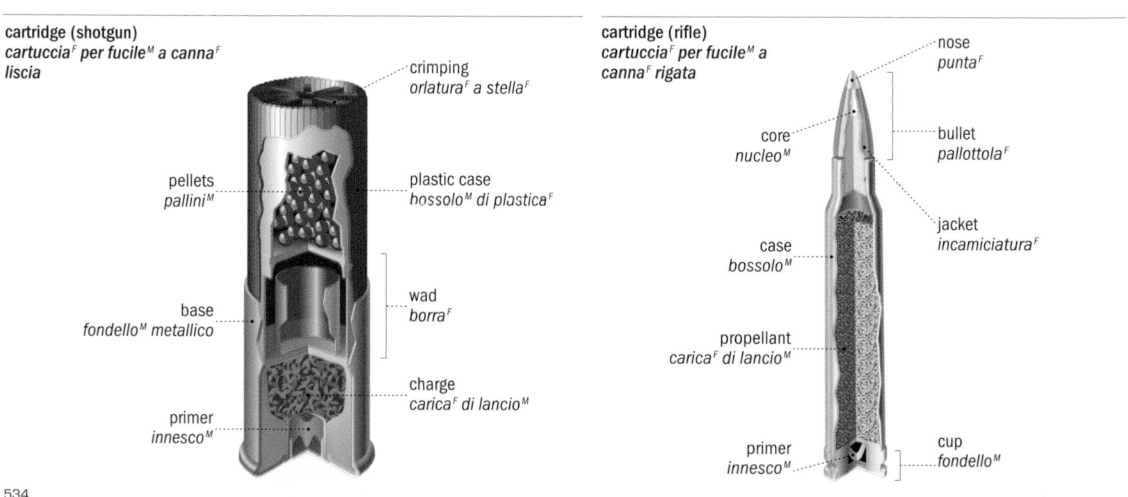

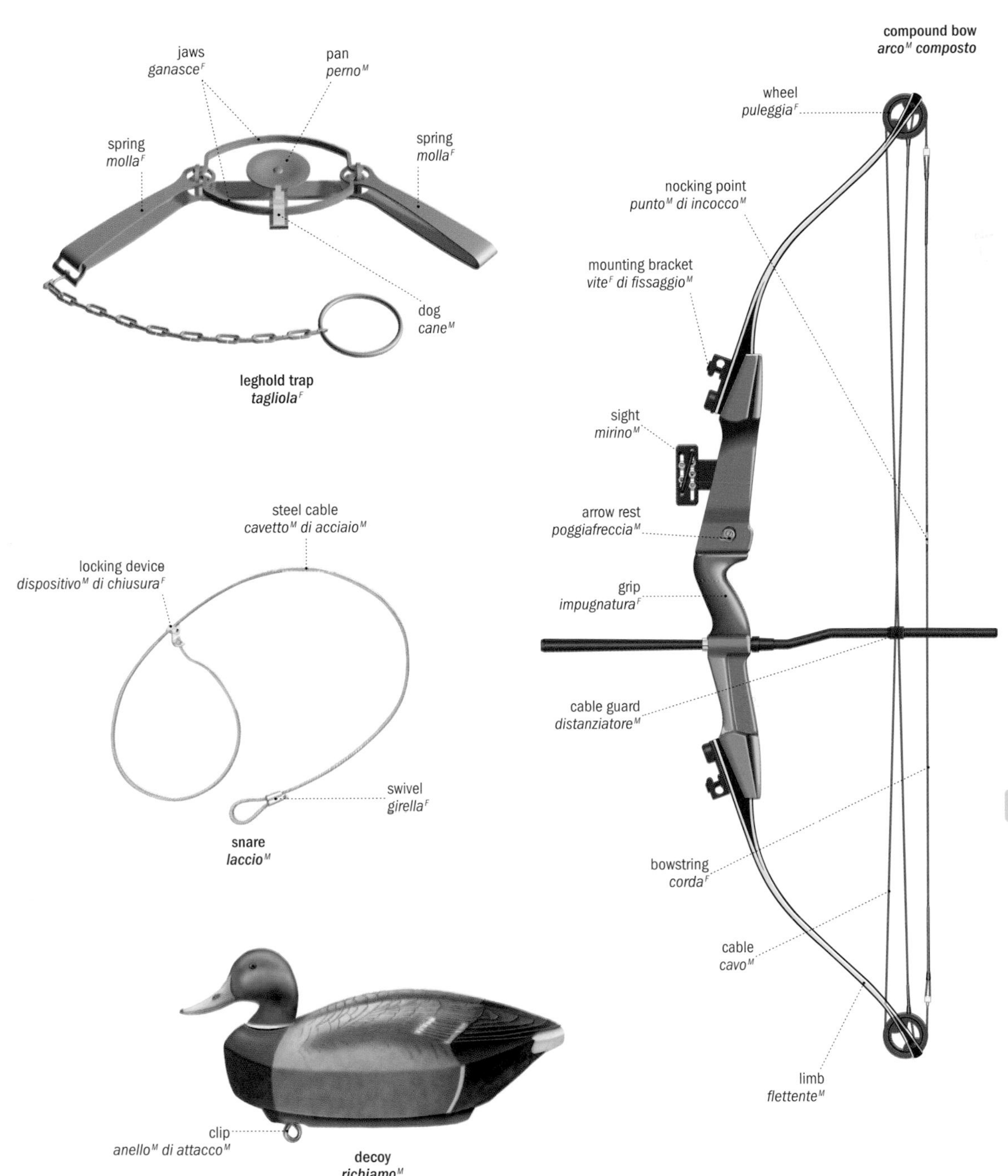

leghold trap
tagliola F

snare
laccio M

decoy
richiamo M

compound bow
arco M ***composto***

fishing

pesca[F]

flyfishing
pesca[F] a mosca[F]

fly reel
mulinello[M]

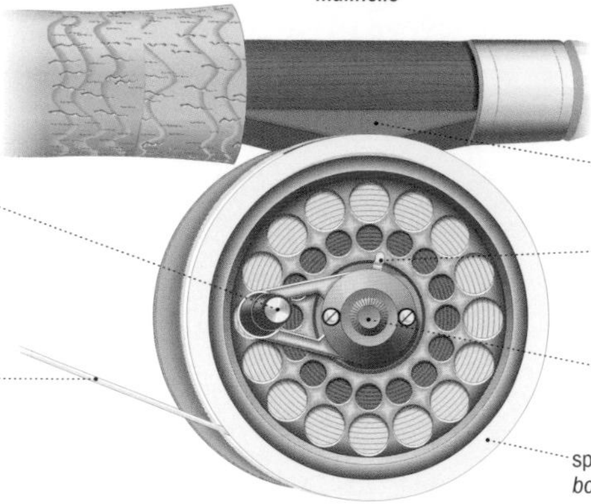

foot
piede[M]
handle
pomello[M]
catch
meccanismo[M] antiritorno
fly line
lenza[F]
drag
frizione[F]
spool
bobina[F]

fly rod
canna[F] da mosca[F]

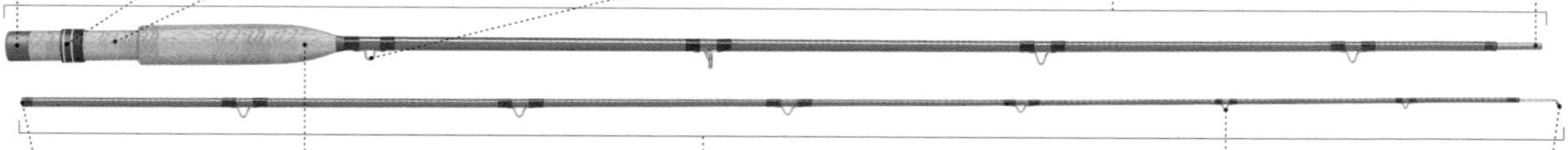

screw locking nut
vite[F] di bloccaggio[M]
butt cap
pomello[M] in gomma[F]
reel seat
alloggiamento[M] del mulinello[M]
keeper ring
anello[M] fermamulinello
butt section
corpo[M]
male ferrule
ghiera[F] maschio
female ferrule
ghiera[F] femmina
handgrip
impugnatura[F]
tip section
cimino[M]
guide
anello[M] guida[F] della lenza[F]
tip-ring
puntalino[M]

artificial fly
mosca[F] artificiale

wing
ala[F]
topping
copertura[F]
ribbing
anelli[M] addominali
veil
velo[M]
cheek
guancia[F]
tail
coda[F]
joint
giunto[M]
tip
punta[F]
head
testa[F]
butt
tacco[M]
shoulder
spalla[F]
fishhook
amo[M]
body
corpo[M]
hackle
penne[F]

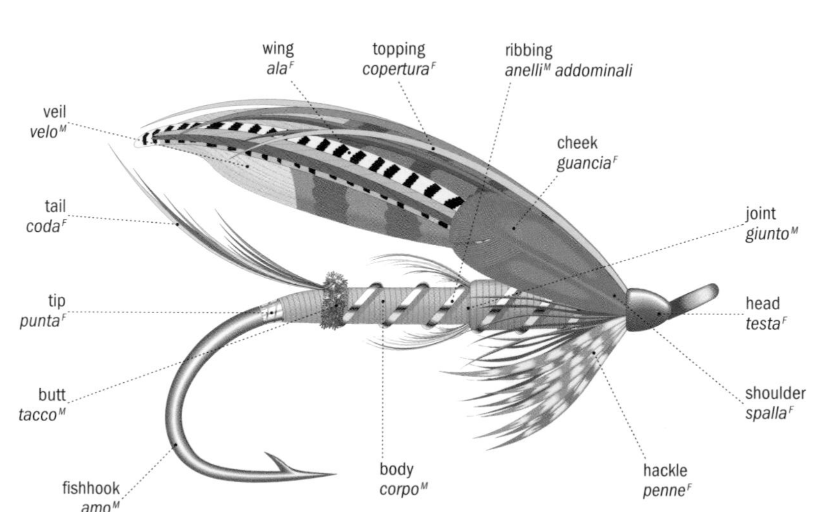

casting
***pesca*[F] *al lancio*[M]**

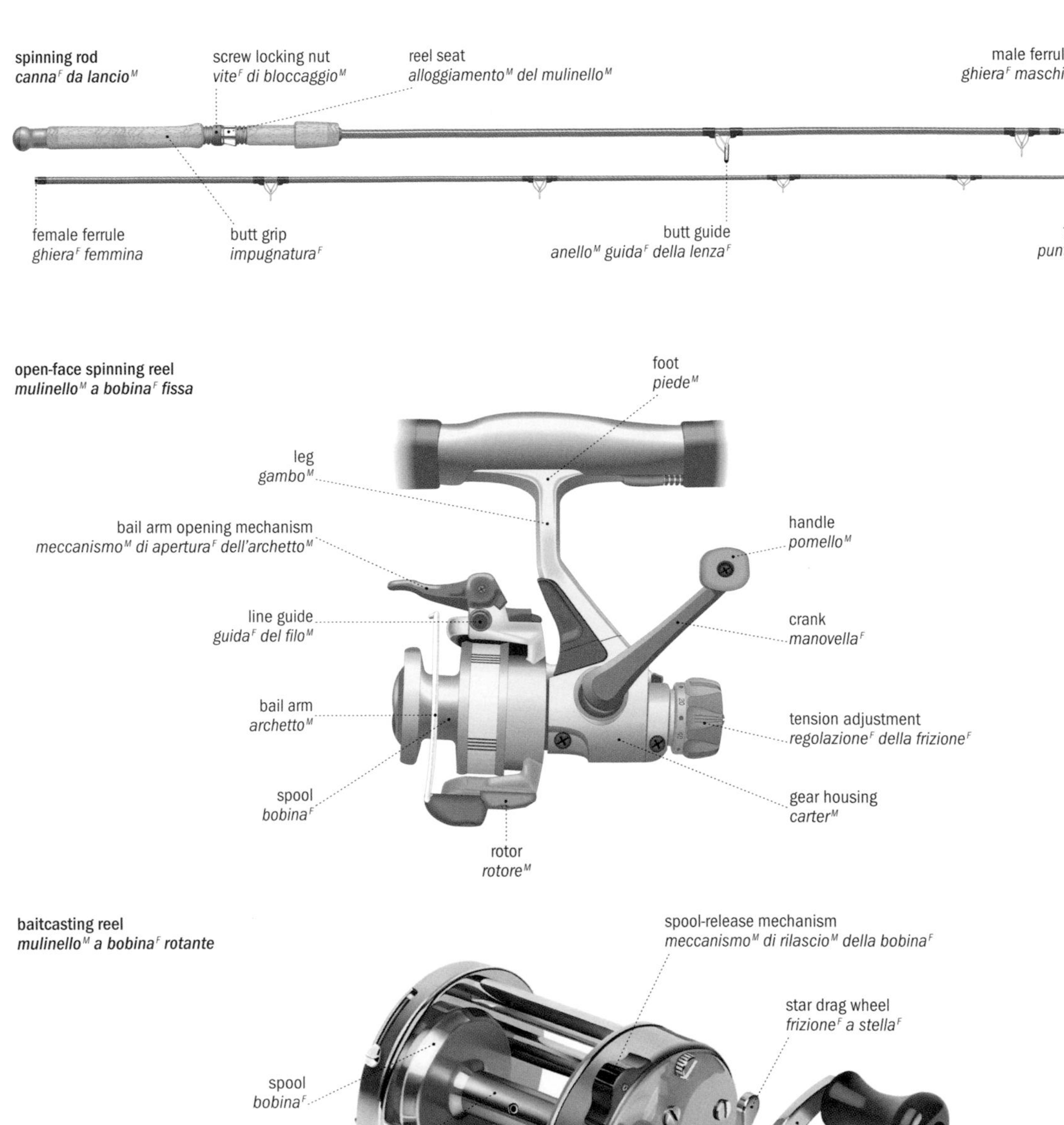

fishing

fishhook
***amo*[M]**

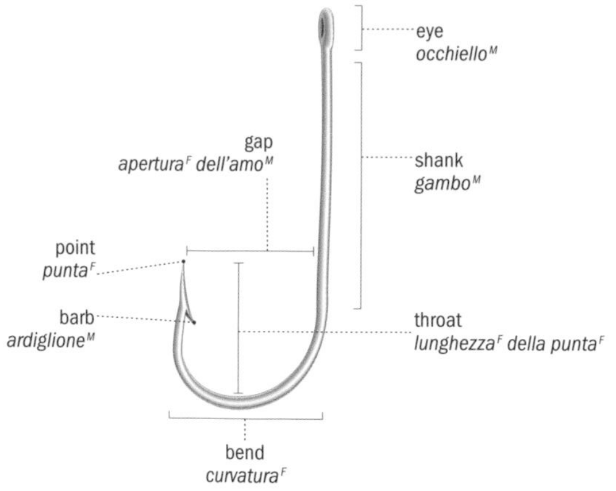

eye
occhiello[M]
shank
gambo[M]
gap
apertura[F] *dell'amo*[M]
point
punta[F]
barb
ardiglione[M]
throat
lunghezza[F] *della punta*[F]
bend
curvatura[F]

float tackle
attrezzatura*[F] *terminale

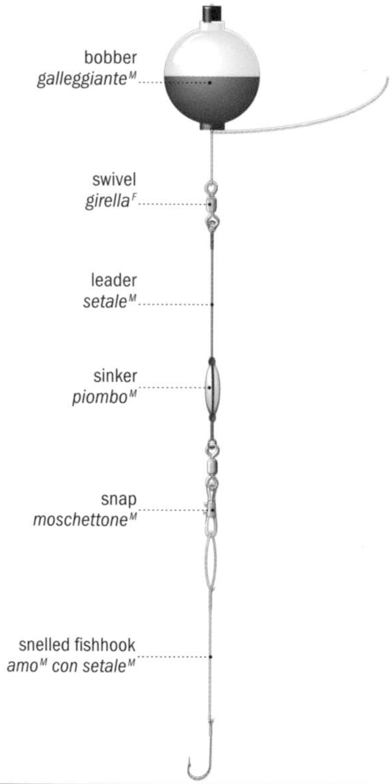

bobber
galleggiante[M]
swivel
girella[F]
leader
setale[M]
sinker
piombo[M]
snap
moschettone[M]
snelled fishhook
amo[M] *con setale*[M]

spinner
cucchiaino*[M] *rotante

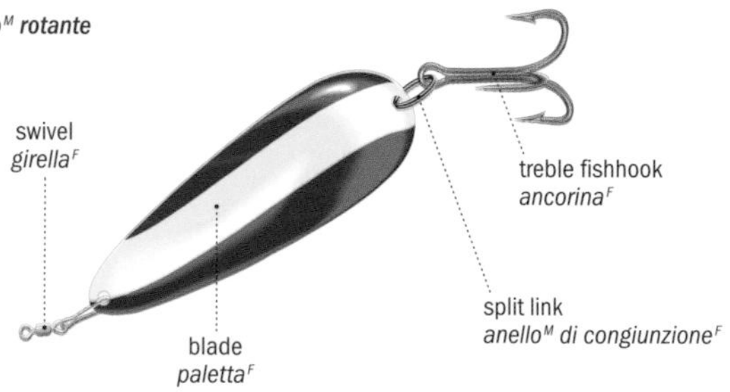

swivel
girella[F]
treble fishhook
ancorina[F]
split link
anello[M] *di congiunzione*[F]
blade
paletta[F]

clothing and accessories
***abbigliamento*[M] *e accessori*[M]**

waders
stivaloni*[M] *impermeabili

tackle box
scatola*[F] *portaesche

creel
***cestino*[M]**

fishing vest
***giubbotto*[M] *da pescatore*[M]**

landing net
***guadino*[M]**

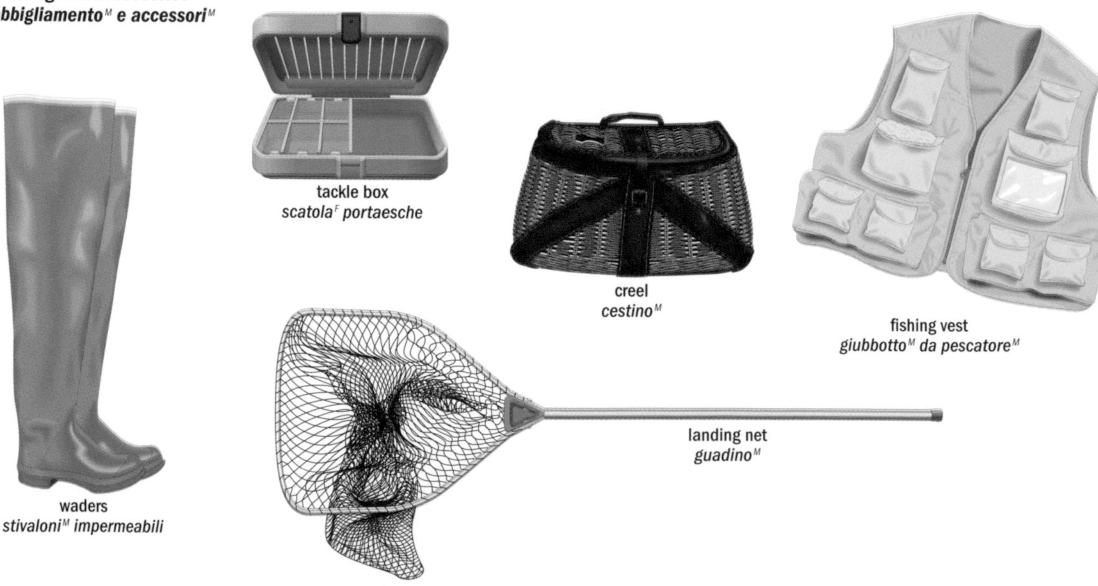

English Index

1 astronomical unit 3
1,500 m starting line 473
1/10 second hand 424
10 m line 482
10,000 m relay starting line 473
100 m hurdles starting line 472
100 m starting line 472
110 m hurdles starting line 472
15 m line 483
200 m starting line 472
22 m line 482
35 mm still camera 10
4 x 400 m relay starting line 473
5 m line 483
5,000 m starting line 472
50 astronomical units 2
50,000 astronomical units 2
800 m starting line 473

A 298
abalone 157
abdomen 67, 68, 70, 71, 78, 92, 94
abdominal aorta 102, 107
abdominal cavity 111, 112
abdominal segment 67
ablutions fountain 447
above-ground swimming pool 184
aboveground pipeline 404
abruptly pinnate 55
ABS 357
absorbed solar radiation 46
absorbent cotton 461
absorbing plate 410
absorption by clouds 46
absorption by Earth's surface 46
absorption of carbon dioxide 54
absorption of water and mineral salts 54
abutment 284, 344
abyssal hill 33
abyssal plain 33
Abyssinian 87
acanthus leaf 200
acceleration lane 343
accelerator cable 237
accelerator control 235
accent mark 299
access door 423
access gallery 407
access road 388
access server 335
access window 333
accessories 356, 372
accessory pocket 352
accessory shoe 314
accidentals 299
accordion 296
accordion bag 276
accordion pleat 253
account identification 443
accumulator 357
accuracy sports 502
ace 468
achene 59, 60
acid rain 47, 48
acid snow 48
acorn nut 223
acorn squash 129
acoustic ceiling 293
acoustic guitar 302
acoustic meatus 115, 116
acrobatic skate 527
acromion 99
acroterion 279
action buttons 471
actor 290
actors' seats 290
actress 291
actuator arm 333
acute angle 428
Adam's apple 92
add key 337
add to memory 337
additive color synthesis 418
adductor longus 96
adductor magnus 97
Aden, Gulf 19, 20
adhesive bandage 461
adhesive disk 75
adhesive tape 461
adipose tissue 113, 114
adjust buttons 329
adjustable channel 222
adjustable clamp 206
adjustable frame 226
adjustable lamp 206
adjustable strap 260
adjustable thermostat 179
adjustable waist tab 244
adjuster 466
adjusting band 324
adjusting buckle 527
adjusting catch 511
adjusting screw 222, 224
adjustment knob 353
adjustment slide 246
administration 445
adobe house 288
Adriatic Sea 18
adult skull, lateral view 100
adventitious roots 52
advertisement 313
advertising panel 378
advertising poster 380
adzuki beans 131
Aegean Sea 18
aerial cable network 316
aerial ladder truck 455
aerocyst 51
aerodynamic brake 412
affluent 32
Afghanistan 452
Africa 14, 20, 34, 451
African Plate 27
Afro pick 268
aft shroud 7
afterbay 406, 407
aftershave 271
agar-agar 123
agglomeration 430
agitator 212
agricultural pollution 47
aileron 392
air bag 354
air bag restraint system 354
air bubbles 339
air communications 317
air compression unit 376
air concentrator 270
air conditioner 361
air conditioner compressor 360
air conditioning equipment 386
air conditioning system 46
air filter 235, 350
air filter pre-cleaner 401
air hole 312
air horn 364
air inlet 367, 395
air inlet control 192
air intake 362, 383
air intake for engine cooling 525
air mass, type 39
air mattress 530
air pollutants 47
air pollution 47
air pre-cleaner filter 398
air pump 346
air relief valve 385
air scoop 523
air shaft 278
air space 79
air temperature 39
air transport 388
air vent 214
air-inlet grille 270
air-outlet grille 270
air-pressure pump 461
air-supply tube 454
aircraft weather station 38
airliner 37
airplane, movements 395
airplanes 394
airport 25, 388, 430
aisle 120, 285
ajowan 139
ala 117
alarm/charge indicator light 337
Alaska, Gulf 16
Albania 450
albatross 80
albumen 79
alcohol bulb 424
alcohol column 424
Aleutian Islands 16
Aleutian Trench 34
alfalfa sprouts 130
alga, structure 51
algae 51
Algeria 451
alkaline manganese-zinc cell 417
alkekengi 132
all-purpose flour 144
all-season tire 358
all-terrain vehicle 369
alley 490, 495
alligator 77
allspice 138
alluvial deposits 32
almonds 133
alphabetical keypad 338
alphanumeric keyboard 346, 442, 443
alphanumeric keypad 327, 330
alpine ski trail 512
alpine skier 510
alpine skiing 510
alpine snowboard 513
Alps 18
Alsace glass 165
altar cross 446
altarpiece 446
alternate 330
alternate: level 3 select 330
alternating-current power cord 336
alternative key (Alt) 330
alternator 350, 360, 413
alternator fan belt 360
alternator warning light 355
alternator/fan belt 350
altitude clamp 8, 9
altitude fine adjustment 8, 9
altitude scale 37
altocumulus 42
altostratus 42
alula 78
aluminum foil 162
aluminum recycling container 49
alveolar bone 101
amaranth 143
Amazon River 17
ambulance 460, 462
ambulatory 285
ambulatory care unit 465
American bacon 156
American corn bread 145
American football 484
American football, playing field 484
American mustard 140
American outlet 198
American plug 198
Americas 448
Amery Ice Shelf 15
ammunition pouch 456
amoeba 66
amorphous solid 414
amount of substance, unit 426
ampere 426
amphibians 75
amphibious firefighting aircraft 394
amphitheater, Roman 281
ampli-tuner 322, 325
amplitude 418
ampulla of fallopian tube 113
anal clasper 67
anal fin 74
analog watch 424
analytical balance 423
anatomy 96
anatomy of a bivalve shell 73
anatomy of a male lobster 71
anatomy, human being 96
anchor 473
anchor pin 357
anchor point 70
anchor-windlass room 383, 387
anchorage block 344
anchovy 159
anconeus 97
Andes Cordillera 17
andirons 193
Andorra 449
andouillette 156
anemometer 413
anesthesia room 464
angles 428
Angola 452
Anik 317
animal cell 66
animal dung 48
animal kingdom 66
anise 142
ankle 92, 94
ankle boot 241
ankle guard 476
ankle length 247
ankle sock 257
ankle/wrist weights 500
annual ring 63
annular eclipse 4
anode 417
anorak 263
ant 69
Antarctic Circle 15, 21, 22
Antarctic Peninsula 15
Antarctic Plate 27
Antarctic Ridge 34
Antarctica 14, 15
antefix 279
antelope 84
antenna 7, 67, 68, 71, 326, 327, 349, 369, 392, 395, 457, 487
antenna terminals 322
antennule 71
anterior adductor muscle 73
anterior chamber 119
anterior end 73
anterior fontanelle 100
anterior horn 109

anterior nasal spine 100
anterior notch 115
anterior root 110
anterior tibial artery 102
anterior view 92, 94, 96
anther 56
anti-torque tail rotor 395
anticline 403
anticollision light 392
antifriction pad 511
Antigua and Barbuda 449
antihelix 115
antilock braking system 357
antireflection coating 410
antiseptic 461
antislip shoe 219
antitragus 115
antivibration handle 235
anus 71, 73, 106, 111, 112
anvil 425
aorta 104, 105
aorta, arch 102, 103, 104
aortic valve 104
apartment building 433
apartment building, high-rise 289
aperture 73
aperture door 7
apex 72, 73, 101, 118
apical foramen 101
apocrine sweat gland 114
apothecium 50
Appalachian Mountains 16
apple 133
apple cider vinegar 141
apple corer 173
apple, section 58
application launch buttons 337
appoggiatura 299
appointment book 338
approach 473
approach ramp 344
approach runs 496
apricot 132
apron 200, 201, 202, 369, 388, 498
apse 285
apsidiole 284, 285
aquatic bird 79
aquatic sports 516
aqueous humor 119
Arabian Peninsula 19
Arabian Sea 19
arachnids 67, 70
arachnoid 109
Aral Sea 19
arame 123
arbor 230
arc 428
arcade 281, 284
arch of aorta 102, 103, 104
arch of foot artery 102
archboard 340
archipelago 24
architecture 278
architecture, elements 286
architrave 279
Arctic 14
Arctic Circle 21, 22
Arctic Ocean 14
arena 281, 472
Arenberg parquet 190
areola 113
Argentina 448
Ariel 3
ark 447
arm 91, 93, 95, 200, 206, 236, 297, 421, 467
arm guard 486
arm lock 499
arm slit 251
arm stump 200
armchair 200
armchairs 200
Armenia 452
armhole 247
armless chair 444
armoire 202
armpit 92, 94
armrest 205, 352, 353, 467
armstand 518
arpeggio 299
arrector pili muscle 114
arrow rest 535
art director 290
art room 444
arteries 102
artichoke 127
article 313
articulated bus 363
articulated joint 363
articulation 355
artificial fly 536
artificial lake 32
artificial satellite 37
arts and architecture 278
arugula 127
asafetida 139
ascending aorta 103
ascending colon 106
ascending passage 278
ascot tie 245
ash layer 28
Asia 14, 19, 34, 452
Asian noodles 147
Asian pear 137
asparagus 125
asphalt 405
asphalt still 405
assist grip 352
assistant camera operator 290
assistant coach 489, 507
assistant director 291
assistant property person 291
assistant referee 509
asteroid belt 3
asthenosphere 26
astigmatism 419
astronautics 10
astronomical observation 7
astronomical observatory 7
astronomical observatory, cross section 7
astronomical unit 3
astronomy 2
Atacama Desert 17
athlete 473
athletic shirt 247
Atlantic cod 161
Atlantic Ocean 14, 15, 18, 20
Atlantic salmon 161
atlas 99
atlas moth 69
Atlas Mountains 20
ATM 442, 443
atmosphere 44, 48
atoll 35
atom 414
atoms 414
atrium 280
attaché case 274
attachment storage area 209
attachments 209
attack line 487
attack zone 487
attitude control thrusters 12
attraction 416
audience 440
audio input/output jack 337
audio jack 329
audio system 354
audiometric examination room 465
auditory meatus, external 100
auditory ossicles 116
auger bit, solid center 228
auricle 116
auricle, ear 115
auriculars 78
Australia 14, 34, 453
Australian-Indian Plate 27
Austria 450
authorized landfill site 47
autoclave 464
automatic dialer index 327
automatic drip coffee maker 181
automatic electronic timer 517
automatic sliding door 286
automatic teller machine 443
automatic teller machine (ATM) 442
automatically controlled door 390
automobile 347
automobile car 377
automobile systems 350, 351
autotrophs 45
autumn 38
autumn squash 129
autumnal equinox 38
auxiliary handle 228
auxiliary tank 365
avenue 25, 433
avocado 128
awl 531
awning channel 361
axe 234
axel 509
axial rib 73
axillary artery 102
axillary bud 53
axillary nerve 108
axillary vein 102
axis 99
axle 527
axle shaft 351
axon 110
axon hillock 110
Azerbaijan 452
azimuth clamp 8, 9
azimuth fine adjustment 8, 9
Aztec temple 283

B

B 298
baboon 91
baby doll 256
back 78, 83, 86, 93, 95, 115, 167, 169, 201, 205, 226, 244, 467
back boundary line 494
back brush 267
back judge 485
back line 515
back of a glove 243
back pocket 246
back ribs 152
back suspension 522
back zone 487
backboard 489
backboard support 489
backcourt 491
backdrop 292
backgammon 469
backguard 212, 213
backhoe 399
backhoe controls 399
backing plate 357
backlighting button 320
backpack 277, 532
backrest 353, 369, 523
backspace 331
backspace key 331
backstay 509
backstop 474, 489
backstroke 517
backstroke turn indicator 517
backward 518
backward bucket 399, 400
bacon 156
bactrian camel 85
badge 456
badger 88
badminton 494
badminton racket 494
Baffin Island 16
bag compartment 209
bag well 505
bagel 144
baggage cart 374
baggage check-in counter 390
baggage claim area 390
baggage compartment 362, 376, 395
baggage lockers 374
baggage racks 383
baggage room 374
bagger 121
bagpipes 296
baguette 144
Bahamas 448
Bahrain 452
Baikal, Lake 19
bail 479
bail arm 537
bail arm opening mechanism 537
bailey 282
baitcasting reel 537
baize 502
bakery 121
baking sheet 172
balaclava 239, 524
balalaika 297
balance beam 496, 497
balance control 322
balancer 303
balcony 189, 293, 447
balcony door 189
baling 49
balk area 502
balk line 502
balk line spot 502
Balkan Peninsula 18
ball 332
ball bearing 312, 413
ball boy 490
ball mount 356
ball peen 220
ball sports 474
ball-cock supply valve 196
ball-peen hammer 220
ballerina slipper 241
ballpoint pen 312
ballroom 387
balsamic vinegar 141
Baltic Sea 18
baluster 191
balustrade 283
bamboo shoot 125
banana 136
band ring 264
band select button 322
Bangladesh 453
bangle 264
banister 191
banjo 296
bank 342, 432, 437, 442
banknote 441
banknote, back 441
banknote, front 441
banner 313
banquette 201
baptismal font 446
bar 273, 293, 309, 432, 436, 438, 469, 500, 501
bar counter 438
bar frame 207
bar line 298
bar nose 235
bar stool 201, 438
barb 538
Barbados 449
barbell 500, 501
barber comb 268
barbican 282
Barbuda 449
Barents Sea 18
bark 63
barley 61, 143
barley: spike 61
barn 122
barometric pressure 39
barometric tendency 39
barrel 269, 270, 312, 471, 534
barrel vault 281
barrette 268
barrier 205, 434
barrier barricade tape 457
barrier beach 35
bartender 438
bartizan 282
basaltic layer 26
base 54, 179, 180, 192, 199, 206, 227, 229, 269, 283, 318, 332, 342, 412, 421, 422, 454, 473, 534
base cabinet 164
base course 342
base of splat 200
base plate 227, 511, 533
baseball 474, 476
baseball, cross section 477
baseboard 191
baseline 491, 533
basement 182, 435
basement window 183
basic source of food 45
basil 142
basilic vein 102
basin wrench 216
basket 178, 181, 211, 212, 489, 510
basket weave pattern 190
basketball 488
basketball player 488
basmati rice 147
bass 160
bass bridge 304
bass clarinet 295
bass clef 298
bass drum 295, 308
bass guitar 303
bass keyboard 296
bass pickup 303
bass register 296
Bass Strait 15
bass tone control 303, 322, 325
bassoon 306
bassoons 295
baster 173
bat 476, 477, 478
bath 194, 439
bath brush 267
bath sheet 267
bath towel 267
bathing wrap 260
bathrobe 256
bathroom 188, 189, 195, 439, 445, 464
bathroom scale 423
bathroom skylight 189
bathtub 189, 195
baton 472
baton holder 456
batsman 478, 479
batten 292, 519, 520
batten pocket 519, 520
batter 475, 476
batter head 308
batter skin 297
batter's helmet 476
battery 221, 350, 359, 411, 416
battery box 365
battery case 359
battery cover 359
battery pack 228
batting glove 476
battlement 282
bay 5, 24
bay filler panel 329
Bay of Bengal 19
bayonet base 199
beach 35
bead 358
beak 90
beaker 171
beam 283, 288, 422
beam balance 422
beam bridge 344
bean bag chair 201
bean thread cellophane noodles 147
beans 130, 131
bearing pad 409
beater 176
beater ejector 176
beaters 176
Beaufort Sea 16
beauty care 121
beaver 82
becquerel 426
bed 204, 342, 530
bed chamber 280
bedrock 27, 54
bedroom 189, 528
bedside lamp 439, 464
bedside table 439, 464
beech 64
beechnut 133
beef cubes 152
beef, cuts 152
beer 120
beer mug 165
beet 129
begonia 56
Belarus 450
belfry 284, 285
Belgian endive 127
Belgium 449
Belize 448
bell 306, 307
bell bottoms 254
bell brace 306
bell tower 285, 446
bellows 296
bellows strap 296
bells 309
belly 83
below-stage 292
belt 225, 246, 248, 499
belt drive 383
belt highway 25
belt loader 402
belt loop 246, 248, 531
bench 201, 379, 437, 501
bench seat 353
bend 273, 538
Bengal, Bay 19
Benin 451

beret 239
bergamot 134
bergère 200
bergschrund 30
Bering Sea 14
Bering Strait 16
Bermuda shorts 254
berries 132
berry fruit 59
bevel 460
bevel square 225
beverage can 163
beverage dispenser 463
Bhutan 453
bib 260, 261
bib necklace 264
biceps brachii 96
biceps femoris 97
biconcave lens 419
biconvex lens 419
bicycle 370
bicycle bag (pannier) 372
bicycle parking 445
bicycle, accessories 372
bicycle, parts 370
bicycles 373
bidet 195
bike carrier 356
bikini 259
bikini briefs 247
bilberries 132
bill 78
bill compartment 274
bill presenter 442
bill-file 341
billfold 275
billhook 234
billiard cue 503
billiard spot 502
billiards 502
billiards, carom 502
billiards, English 503
bills 79
bimah 447
binding 238, 513, 514
binocular microscope 421
biology 426
biosphere 44
biosphere, structure 44
biparous cyme 57
birch 64
bird 78
bird of prey 79
bird's eye chile 139
bird's nest fern 52
bird, morphology 78
birds 78, 80
birth 426
bishop 470
bison 84
bit 221, 403
bits 228
bitt 385
bitter melon 128
bivalve shell 73
bivalve shell, anatomy 73
bivalve shell, morphology 73
Black 470
black 418
black ball 503
black beans 131
black bear 89
black clamp 356
black currants 132
black gram beans 131
black mustard 138
black pepper 138
black pollock 161
black radishes 129
black rye bread 144
black salsify 129
Black Sea 14, 18, 19
black square 470
black stone 470
black tea 148
black-eyed peas 130
blackberries 132
blade 52, 55, 167, 169, 177, 180, 198, 216, 219, 221, 226, 227, 229, 235, 270, 271, 398, 401, 412, 413, 493, 506, 509, 538
blade close stop 270
blade injector 271
blade lift cylinder 398
blade lift fan 383
blade locking bolt 227
blade rotation cylinder 401
blade shifting mechanism 401
blade tilting lock 227
blade tilting mechanism 227
blade-lift cylinder 401
blank 468
blanket 204
blanket sleepers 261
blastodisc 79
blazer 254
blender 176
blending attachment 176
blind spot mirror 362, 363
blinking lights 362
block 215, 305, 473
blocking glove 507
blog 335
blood circulation 102
blood circulation, schema 103
blood factor RH negative 426
blood factor RH positive 426
blood pressure monitor 461
blood sausage 156
blood vessel 104, 114
blood, composition 104
blow pipe 296
blowhole 90
blucher oxford 240
blue 418
blue ball 503
blue beam 318
blue line 507
blue mussels 157
blue-veined cheeses 151
blueberries 132
bluefish 160
blusher brush 266
BMX bike 373
boa 77
board 470, 519
board games 469
boarding room 391
boarding step 395
boarding walkway 389
boards 506
boater 238
boats 382
bobber 538
bobby pin 268
bobeche 207
bodies 347
body 118, 180, 208, 228, 303, 305, 306, 348, 361, 420, 523, 536
body care 267
body flap 13
body of fornix 109
body of nail 114
body side molding 349
body suit 255, 258
body temperature control unit 10
body tube 421
bodysuit 260
bok choy 126
bole 63
bolero 254
Bolivia 448
bolster 167, 169, 204
bolt 222, 223, 224
bolts 223
bongos 309
boning knife 169
bony fish 74
bony fishes 159
book ends 341
bookcase 444
booking hall 374
bookstore 436
boom 364, 399, 400, 520
boom cylinder 399, 400
boom operator 291
boom swing hinge pin 399
boom vang 520
booster parachute 12
booster seat 205
boot 241, 509, 514, 525, 527
bootee 240
bootees 260
booth 438
borage 142
bordeaux glass 165
border 182, 293
borders 292
boreal forest 44
Bosnia and Herzegovina 450
Bothnia, Gulf 18
Botswana 452
bottle 267, 532
bottle opener 170, 531
bottom 510
bottom bracket axle 372
bottom cap 417
bottom deck 404
bottom deckboard 396
bottom line 517
bottom pocket 502
bottom rail 185, 202
bottom-fold portfolio 274
boulevard 25, 433
bow 238, 301, 387, 519, 520
bow door 383
bow loading door 386
bow saw 533
bow thruster 387
bow tie 245
bow-winged grasshopper 69
bowl 167, 177, 180, 400
bowl with serving spout 177
bowler 479
bowling alley 436
bowling crease 479
bowstring 535
box 192, 293
box bag 276
box end wrench 223
box office 294
box spring 204
boxer 498
boxer shorts 247, 263
boxing 498
boxing gloves 498
boxing trunks 498
bra 259
brace 187, 219
bracelets 264
brachial artery 102
brachial plexus 108
brachialis 96
brachioradialis 96, 97
bracket 283
bracket base 202
bract 60
brain 71
brains 154
brake 467, 501, 522
brake arm 511
brake booster 350, 357
brake cable 371
brake caliper 366
brake fluid reservoir 357
brake handle 523
brake lever 371, 522
brake light 352
brake line 357
brake lining 357
brake pad 357
brake pedal 350, 354, 357, 511
brake pressure modulator 357
brake shoe 357
brakes 357
braking circuit 357
braking system 351
branch 62, 63, 65, 125, 194, 416, 460
branch clip 460
branches 63
branching 197
brandy snifter 165
brass section 295
brattice 282
brazier 283
Brazil 448
Brazil nuts 133
bread 144
bread and butter plate 166
bread guide 178
bread knife 169
bread machine 179
break 331
breaker 33
breast 78, 92, 94, 113
breast dart 248
breast pocket 245, 248
breast welt pocket 244
breaststroke 517
breech 306
breech guard 306
breechblock 534
brick carton 163
bricklayer's hammer 216
bridge 25, 273, 297, 301, 302, 303, 381, 420, 503
bridge assembly 303
bridges 344
bridging 187
Brie 151
briefcase 274
briefs 247, 259
brim 238, 239
bristle 271, 272
bristles 219
broad beans 130
broad ligament of uterus 113
broad welt side pocket 251
broad-welt side pocket 248
broadcast satellite communication 316
broadleaved trees 64
broccoli 127
broccoli rabe 127
brochure rack 442
broken line 342, 343
brook 32
brook trout 161
broom 193, 215
brow brush and lash comb 266
brown alga 51
brown ball 503
brown rice 147
brown sugar 149
browser 334
Brunei 453
brush 61, 209, 215, 219, 272
brussels sprouts 126
bubble 367
bubble bath 267
bucket 399
bucket cylinder 399, 400
bucket lever 399
bucket seat 353
buckle 246, 276, 353, 511
buckwheat 61, 143
buckwheat: raceme 61
bud 54
buffalo 84
buffer 287
buffer tank 404
buffet 203, 438
bugle 307
building sewer 194
bulb 125, 199, 217, 385, 416
bulb dibble 231
bulb vegetables 124
bulb, section 54
bulbil 54
bulbocavernous muscle 111
Bulgaria 450
bulge 6
bulk carrier 382
bulk terminal 381
bull's-eye 471
bulldog 86
bulldozer 398
bullet 534
bulletin board 341, 444
bumblebee 69
bump 487
bumper 209, 364, 369, 375
bumper molding 348
bunch 522
bunch of grapes 62
bundle 125
bunk 361
bunker oil 405
bunker silo 122
bunting bag 260
buoy weather station 38
burdock 129
burgundy glass 165
burial 49
Burkina Faso 451
Burma 453
burner 174, 210, 529
burner control knobs 210
burner frame 529
burner ring 174
Burundi 451
bus 435
bus shelter 434
bus station 432
bus stop 434
busbar 407
buses 362
bush 230
bush-cricket 69
bushing 406, 407
business aircraft 394
business district 430, 432
business transactions 335
business wicket 443
butane accessories 529
butcher's counter 120
butt 492, 494, 503, 536
butt cap 536
butt end 506
butt grip 537
butt guide 537
butt plate 534
butt section 536
butt-strap 273
butte 36
butter 150
butter compartment 211
butter cup 163
butter curler 169
butter dish 166
butter knife 168
butter lettuce 126
butterfly 67
butterfly stroke 517
butterfly, morphology 67
buttermilk 150
buttock 93, 95, 111, 112
button 199, 245, 250, 296
button loop 246
button strap 261
buttondown collar 245
buttoned placket 245, 250
buttonhole 248
buttress 284
by-pass taxiway 388

C

C 298
C clef 298
C-clamp 224
cab 398, 399, 400, 401, 523
cabbage 126
cabin 386, 395
cabinet 164, 211, 212, 213, 318
cable 228, 326, 332, 356, 364, 501, 535
cable distributor 316
cable guard 535
cable line 335
cable modem 335
cable sleeve 228
caboose 377
cabriole leg 200
cabriolet 200
cafeteria 445
cage 281
caiman 77
cajun spice seasoning 139
cake mascara 266
cake pan 172
calcaneus 99
calculator 274
calculator, pocket 337
calculator, printing 337
calendar pad 338
calf 84, 93, 95
California, Gulf 16
caliper 357
call button 287
Callisto 2
calyx 56, 59, 60, 107
cambium 63
Cambodia 453
camel 85
Camembert 151
camera 290, 525
camera body 314
camera key 327
camera operator 290
Cameroon 451
camisole 258
camp stove 529
camping 528
camping equipment 531
camping trailers 361
camshaft 360
can opener 170, 180, 531
Canada 448
Canadian bacon 156

canal lock 381
canary melon 135
cancel button 333
candela 426
candle 446
candy thermometer 171
cane pen 312
canine 101
canisters 162
canned goods 121
cannelloni 146
cannon 83
canopy 273, 286, 361, 394, 401, 528
cantaloupe 135
canteen 532
canter 83
cantilever bridge 344
cantilever span 344
canvas 498
canvas divider 528
cap 52, 176, 191, 238, 312, 412, 456, 467, 516
cap iron 229
capacitor 417
cape 24, 251
Cape Horn 17
Cape of Good Hope 20
Cape Verde 451
capillary blood vessel 114
capillary tube 424
capital 23
capitals lock 330
capitals lock key 330
capitulum 57
capon 155
capped tee 193
capsule 51, 467
capsule, section 60
captain's quarters 387
caption 313
capture 470
car 521
car ceiling 287
car coat 251
car cover 356
car dealer 433
car deck 386
car floor 287
car guide rail 287
car racing 524
car safety 287
car wash 346
carafe 181
carambola 137
carapace 71, 76
caraway 138
carbon rod 417
carbon-zinc cell 417
carburetor 366
card case 274
card number 441, 443
card reader 321
card reader slot 442, 443
card slot 320
card-reader slot 346
cardamom 138
cardholder's name 441
cardholder's signature 441
cardiac stomach 71
cardigan 250, 255
cardinal 80
cardoon 125
cards 468
cargo aircraft 394
cargo bay 12
cargo bay door 13
Caribbean Islands 448
Caribbean Plate 27
Caribbean Sea 14, 16
caribou 84
carina 74
carnation 56
carnivores 45
carnivorous mammals 86, 88
carom billiards 502
carp 160
Carpathian Mountains 18
Carpentaria, Gulf 15
carpenter's hammer 220
carpentry material 225
carpentry: drilling tools 228
carpentry: nailing tools 220
carpentry: sawing tools 226
carpentry: screw-driving tools 221
carpentry: shaping tools 229
carpet 190
carriage 396
carrier 369, 370
carrier bag 276
carrot 129
carry-on bag 276
cart path 504
cartilaginous fish 74
cartilaginous fishes 158
cartography 21
carton 163
cartoon 313
cartridge 216, 312, 459
cartridge (rifle) 534
cartridge (shotgun) 534
cartwheel hat 239
carving fork 169
carving knife 169
casaba melon 135
case 225, 265, 304, 424, 534
case fan 329
casement 186
casement window 287
cash dispenser 437, 442
cash register 121
cash supply 443
cashews 133
cashier 121
casing 186, 237
Caspian Sea 14, 19
cassava 124
Cassegrain focus 7
cassette 326, 333
cassette compartment 320, 321
cassette drive 333
cassette holder 323
cassette player 326
cassette player controls 326
cassette tape deck 323
castanets 295, 309
caster 205, 209, 308
castes 68
casting 537
castle 282
casual shoe 241
cat 87
cat's head 87
catalytic converter 351
catalytic reforming plant 405
catamaran 521
catch 536
catcher 474, 475, 476
catcher's glove 476
catching glove 507
category buttons 326
catenary 376
cathedral 284
cathedral ceiling 189
cathedral, plan 285
cathode 417
cathode ray tube (CRT) television 318
Catholic church 446
catwalk 292
caudal fin 74, 90
cauliflower 127
caulking gun 216
cave 31, 35
cavernous body 111
cayenne pepper 139
CD/DVD player 471
CD/DVD-ROM drive 310, 329, 336
CD/DVD-ROM eject button 329
cecum 106
cedar of Lebanon 65
ceiling 193
ceiling collar 193
ceiling fixture 206
ceiling joist 187
celeriac 129
celery 125
celestial bodies 2
celiac trunk 103, 107
cell 67, 281
cell body 110
cell membrane 50, 66
cell wall 50
cello 301
cellos 295
cells 416, 440
cellular telephone, portable 327
Celsius 426
Celsius scale 424
celtuce 126
cement 492
cement screed 190
cementum 101
cemetery 25, 433
censer 446
cent 440
center 293, 428, 470, 485, 489, 507
center attacker 487
center back 487
center back vent 244
center circle 481, 488
center console 354
center electrode 359
center face-off circle 507
center field 475
center fielder 474
center flag 480
center keelson 385
center line 488, 493, 494, 507, 515
center line judge 490
center loudspeaker 321
center mark 490
center pocket 502
center post 202, 349
center service line 491
center span 344
center spot 481, 502
center strap 491
centerboard 520
centerboard boat 521
Central African Republic 451
Central America 14, 16
central brush 365
central column 412
central focusing wheel 420
central incisor 101
central nave 447
central nervous system 109
central pumping station 404
centrifuge module 11
centriole 66
cephalic vein 102
cephalothorax 70, 71
ceramic capacitor 417
cereal 61, 143
cereal products 144
cerebellum 109
cerebropleural ganglion 73
cerebrospinal fluid 110
cerebrum 109
Ceres 2
cervical vertebra 110
cervical vertebrae 99
cervix of uterus 112
Chac-Mool 283
Chad 451
Chad, Lake 20
chain 372
chain brake 235
chain guide 372
chain of dunes 36
chain of neurons 110
chain reaction 415
chain stay 370
chain wheel 522
chain wheel A 372
chain wheel B 372
chainsaw 235
chainsaw chain 235
chair 444, 464
chair lift 512
chair lift departure area 512
chairs 201
chaise longue 201
chalaza 79
chalice 446
chalk 503
chalk board 444
chalk line 225
challah 145
chameleon 77
chamois leather 265
chamomile 148
champagne flute 165
chandelier 207
change room 444
change-sign key 337
changing table 205
channel scan button 319
channel selector 319
channel selector controls 319
chanter 296
chanterelles 123
Chantilly parquet 190
chapati 145
chapel 282
chard 125
charge 534
charge indicator 271
charger 228
charging light 271
charging plug 271
charlotte mold 172
charm bracelet 264
Charon 3
chart room 382
chat room 335
chayote 129
checkbook 274, 275
checkbook/secretary clutch 274
checker 470
checkerboard 470
checkers 469, 470
checkout 121
checkouts 121
checks 441
cheek 83, 86, 94, 220, 536
cheese box 163
cheese counter 121
cheese grater, rotary 170
cheese knife 168
cheeses, blue-veined 151
cheeses, fresh 150
cheeses, goat's-milk 150
cheeses, soft 151
cheetah 89
chef's knife 169
cheliped 71
chemical bond 414
chemical treatment 405
chemise 282
chemistry 414
cherimoya 136
cherries 132
chervil 142
chess 470
chess notation 470
chess pieces 470
chessboard 470
chest 83
chest expander 500
chest freezer 211
chest protector 476, 486
chesterfield 200
chestnuts 133
chevet 285
chèvre cheese 150
chicane 524
chick peas 130
chicken 155
chief timekeeper 516
chiffonier 203
child carrier 372
child safety seat 356
child's skull, lateral view 100
child's tricycle 373
children's clothing 261
children's furniture 205
Chile 448
chile 139
Chile Trench 34
chili powder 139
chimney 183, 193
chimney connection 192
chimney pot 183
chimpanzee 91
chin 78, 94
chin protector 367
chin rest 301
chin strap 486, 522
China 453
China Sea, East 19
China Sea, South 19
Chinese dates 137
chinois 171
chip cover 227
chipmunk 82
chipolata sausage 156
chives 124
chloroplast 50
chocolate 148
choir 284, 285
choir organ manual 305
choker 264
chop 152, 153
chord 299
chorizo 156
choroid 119
Christmas tree 404
chromatin 66
chromosphere 4
chrysalis 67
chuck 221, 228
chuck key 228
chuck, keyless 228
chukka 240
church 433
church, Catholic 446
cicada 69
ciliary body 119
ciliate 55
cilium 66
cinnamon 138
circle, parts 428
circuit 524
circuit breaker 407
circuit vent 194
circular body 296
circular route 25
circular saw 227
circular saw blade 227
circumference 428
circumvallate papilla 118
cirque 5
cirque, glacial 30
cirrocumulus 42
cirrostratus 42
cirrus 42
citron 134
citrus fruit 58
citrus fruits 134
citrus juicer 170, 177
city 23, 430
city bicycle 373
city bus 362
city hall 432
city houses 289
clam 157
clam cleat 521
clamp 198, 226, 269
clamp binder 339
clamp lever 269
clamp spotlight 206
clamping block 425
clamping screw 224
clamping screws 425
clams 157
clapper/the slate 291
clapskate 508
clarinet 306
clarinets 295
clasp 274, 275
classic blouse 255
classified advertisements 313
classroom 444, 445
classroom for students with learning disabilities 444
clavicle 98
claw 71, 76, 78, 82, 220
claw hammer 220
clay 492
clean and jerk 500
clean utility room 462
cleaner height adjustment knob 209
cleaning brush 271
cleanout 197
clear key 337
clear space 487
clear-entry key 337
cleat 520, 521
cleated shoe 486
cleaver 169
clefs 298
clerks' desk 440
clerks' office 440
clew 519
cliff 5, 29, 35
climate control 354
climates of the world 40
climbing plant 230
clinical thermometer 424
clinical thermometers 461
clip 312, 535
clip earrings 264
clipboard 340
clipless pedal 522
clippers 269
clitoris 112
cloakroom 443
cloche 239
clock 444
clock operator 488

clock radio 325
clock timer 178, 210
clog 242
closed stringer 191
closeness setting 271
closet 188, 189, 203
clothing 238
clothing guard 467
clothing store 436
cloud 37, 41
cloud of volcanic ash 28
clouds 42
clouds of vertical development 42
cloudwater 48
cloverleaf 342, 343
cloves 138
club 468
club chair 200
clubhouse 504
clump of flowers 230
clutch 350
clutch housing 368
clutch lever 366, 368
clutch pedal 354
coach 362, 489, 507
coach car 376
coach's box 474
coaches 509
coal storage yard 402
coal-fired thermal power plant 402
coarse adjustment knob 421
coarse salt 141
coastal features 35
coat dress 252
coats 248, 251
cob 61
cobra 77
coccyx 98
cochlea 116
cochlear nerve 116
cockchafer 69
cockles 157
cockleshell 200
cockpit 520, 525
cocktail cabinet 203
cocktail glass 165
cocktail lounge 439
cocoa 148
coconut 133
Cocos Plate 27
coffee 148
coffee beans 148
coffee maker 181
coffee makers 181
coffee mill 180
coffee mug 166
coffee pot 531
coffee shop 432, 437
coffee spoon 168
coil spring 351
coin 441
coin purse 275
coin, reverse 441
coin: obverse 441
cola nuts 133
colander 171
cold air 41
cold coolant 408
cold shed 381
cold storage chamber 120, 121
cold temperate climates 40
cold-water circuit 194
cold-water pipe 194
cold-water supply line 196, 197
collar 53, 244, 245, 248, 262, 271, 501
collar point 245
collar stay 245
collards 126
collateral 110
collection body 365
collet 229
collie 86
Colombia 448
color selection filter 318
color shifting ink 441
color supplement 313
color synthesis 418
color television camera 10
columella 73
columella fold 73
column 31, 207, 279, 313
column of mercury 424
coma 6
comb binding 340
combat sports 498
combination box and open end wrench 223
combination lock 274
combs 268
combustion chamber 360
comet 6
comforter 204
command control dial 314
commercial area 435
commercial concern 335
commercial zone 431
commissure of lips of mouth 116
common carotid artery 102
common coastal features 35
common frog 75
common hair cap moss 51
common iliac artery 102, 107
common iliac vein 107
common nail 220
common periwinkles 157
common peroneal nerve 108
common plaice 161
common polypody 52
common toad 75
communicating ramus 110
communication by telephone 327
communication module 316
communication protocol 334
communication set 380
communication tunnel 13
communications 312
communications volume controls 10
communion rail 446
commuter train 375
Comoros 452
compact 266
compact camera 315
compact disc 326
compact disc player 323, 325, 326
compact disc player controls 326
compact disc player, portable 325
compact disc recorder 325
compact memory card 315
compact videocassette adapter 320
compacting 49
compartment 203, 286
compass 533
compass bridge 382, 386, 387
compass card 533
compass meridian line 533
compass rose 23
compass saw 226
competitive course 517
complex dune 36
complexus 97
compluvium 280
composition of the blood 104
compost bin 231
compound bow 535
compound eye 67, 68
compound leaves 55
compressed-air cylinder 454
compression coupling 197
computer 329, 444
computer programs 457
computer science room 444
computer screen 10
concave lens 419
concave primary mirror 9
concha 115
conchiglie 146
concrete mixer truck 365
condensation 45, 414
condensation of steam into water 408
condenser 402, 421
condenser adjustment knob 421
condenser height adjustment 421
condiments 140
condominiums 289, 512
condor 80
conduction 415
conductor's podium 295
cone 119, 429
conference room 442
confessionals 446
configuration of the continents 14
confined aquifer 402
confirmation key 443
confluence 32
Congo 451
Congo River 20
conic projection 22
conical washer 196
conifer 65
coniferous forest 44
conifers 65
conjunctiva 119
connecting cable 324
connecting gallery 345
connecting rod 360
connection 470
connection pin 417
connection point 198
connective tissue 114
constriction 424
consumer 317
contact 470
contact devices 198
contact lenses 272
contact lever 207
container 176, 383
container car 377
container hold 383
container ship 381, 382
container terminal 381, 430
container-loading bridge 381
containment building 408, 409
contest area 499
contestant 499
continent 33
continental crust 26
continental margin 33
continental rise 33
continental shelf 33
continental slope 33
continents, configuration 14
continuity person 291
continuous beam 344
contrabassoons 295
contractile vacuole 66
control 330
control button 176, 332
control buttons 214
control cable 372
control deck 383
control key 330
control keys 328
control knob 210, 212, 213
control panel 178, 179, 210, 212, 213, 314, 455
control panel: dishwasher 214
control room 293, 406
control stick 395
control tower 388
control tower cab 388
control valve 529
control wheel 455
control: group select 330
controller 471
convection 415
convection current 415
convection zone 4
convective cell 43
convenience food 121
convenience outlet 217
convention center 433
conventional door 286
convergent plate boundaries 27
converging lenses 419
convertible 347
convex lens 419
conveyor 402
conveyor belt 49, 390
Cook Strait 15
cooked ham 156
cookie cutters 172
cooking dishes 179
cooking element 210
cooking plate 179
cooking set 531
cooking surface 179
cooking utensils 174
cooktop 164, 210
cooktop edge 210
cool tip 269
coolant 408
coolant inlet 410
coolant outlet 410
cooler 532
cooling 405
cooling cylinder 420
cooling fan 322, 350, 358, 360
cooling system 351
cooling tower 402
cooling vent 336
coping 526
coping saw 226
Coral Sea 15
coral snake 77
corbel 282
corbel piece 192
cord 208, 209, 217, 235, 237
cord sleeve 218, 229
cordate 55
cordless drill 228
cordless mouse 332
cordless screwdriver 221
core 4, 58, 534
coriander 142
Corinthian column 281
Corinthian pilaster 281
cork 514
cork ball 477
cork tip 495
corkscrew 531
corn 61, 143
corn bread 145
corn flour 144
corn oil 149
corn salad 127
corn syrup 149
corn: cob 61
cornea 119, 419
corner 498
corner arc 481
corner cupboard 203
corner flag 481
corner pad 498
corner stool 498
corner stud 187
corner tower 282
cornerpiece 277
cornet 295, 307
cornice 183, 185, 202, 279
corolla 56
corona 4
corona radiata 112
coronal suture 100
coronet 83
corpus callosum 109
corrective lenses 419
corselette 258
corset 259
cortex 107
corymb 57
Costa Rica 448
costal shield 76
costume 290
cot 460
Côte d'Ivoire 451
cottage cheese 150
cotton applicators 461
cotyledon 53
coudé focus 7
cougar 88
coulomb 426
Coulommiers 151
counsels' assistants 440
counter 262
counter reset button 323
counterjib 397
counterjib ballast 397
countertop 164
counterweight 8, 287, 345, 397, 400, 401
counterweight guide rail 287
country 23, 431
coupler head 377
coupler-tilt tablet 305
coupling guide device 376
coupon booth 443
course 504
court 440, 487, 488, 490, 494
courthouse 432
courtroom 440
courtyard 445, 447
couscous 144
couscous kettle 175
cover 180, 198, 315, 454, 471, 477, 505, 533
coveralls 513
covered parapet walk 282
covering 493
cow 84
cowl 348
Cowper's gland 111
cowshed 122
Coyolxauhqui stone 283
crab 158
crab spider 70
cracked bread 145
cracked rye bread 145
cradle 8, 9
cranberries 132
crane runway 397
cranes 397
cranial nerves 108
crank 170, 224, 372, 537
crank handle 225
crankshaft 360
crash helmet 524
crate 162
crater 5, 28
crater ray 5
crawler tractor 398
crayfish 158
cream 150
cream cheese 150
cream cup 163
creamer 166
crease 246
credit card 441
creel 538
creep 31
crenate 55
crêpe pan 175
crepidoma 279
crescendo pedal 305
crescent wrench 223
crescentic dune 36
crest 29, 33, 418, 477
crest of spillway 406
crevasse 30
crevice tool 209
crew neck 260
crew neck sweater 250, 255
crew quarters 382
crew return vehicle 11
crib 205
cribriform plate of ethmoid 117
cricket 478
cricket ball 478
cricket player 478
cricket shoe 478
crime prevention 456
crimping 534
crisper 211
Croatia 450
crocodile 77
crocus 56
croissant 144
crook 306
crook key 306
crookneck squash 129
crosne 124
cross brace 467
cross head 221
cross rail 201
cross section of a baseball 477
cross section of a hydroelectric power plant 407
cross section of a molar 101
cross section of a reflecting telescope 9
cross section of a refracting telescope 8
cross section of a road 342
cross section of a street 434
cross section of an astronomical observatory 7
cross-country bicycle 522
cross-country cyclist 522
cross-country ski 514
cross-country ski trail 512
cross-country skier 514
cross-country skiing 514
cross-headed tip 221
cross-tip screwdriver 531
crossbar 297, 370
crosshead 396
crossing 284, 285
crossing arm 362
crossover cargo deck line 385
crossover mirror 362
crosspiece 202, 466
crosstree 520
crotch 247
crotch piece 255
Crottin de Chavignol 150
croup 83
crown 63, 78, 101, 238, 239, 302, 308, 424
crown block 403
crucifix 446
crude oil 405
crude-oil pipeline 404

cruise control 354
crus of helix 115
crushed chiles 139
crusher 49, 402
crustaceans 71, 158
crustose lichen 50
crutch 466
crystal button 207
crystal drop 207
crystallization 414
Cuba 448
cube 429
cucumber 128
cue ball 502, 503
cuff 240, 245, 246
culottes 253
cultivated mushrooms 123
cultural organization 335
cumin 138
cumulonimbus 42
cumulus 42
cup 163, 166, 259, 531, 532, 534
cup gasket 459
cupped Pacific oysters 157
cupule 60
curb 434, 524
curler 515
curling 515
curling brush 515
curling iron 269
curling stone 515
curly endive 127
curly kale 126
currant tomatoes 128
currants 132
currency abbreviations 440
currency, name 441
current event scoreboard 497
curry 138
cursor down 331
cursor left 331
cursor movement keys 331
cursor right 331
cursor up 331
curtain 277
curtain wall 282
curved jaw 222
customer service 443
customer's restrooms 438
customer's service entrance 198
customers' cloakroom 438
customers' entrance 438
customs control 391
customs house 381
cut nail 220
cuticle nippers 265
cuticle pusher 265
cuticle scissors 265
cuticle trimmer 265
cutlery basket 214
cutlery set 531
cuts of beef 152
cuts of lamb 153
cuts of pork 153
cuts of veal 152
cutter link 235
cutting blade 176, 180, 341
cutting board 169
cutting edge 167, 169, 270, 398, 399, 400
cutting head 341
cutting tools 234
cuttlefish 157
cyan 418
cycling 522
cyclone 43
cyclone names 43
cylinder 429
cylinder head cover 350
cylinder vacuum cleaner 209
cylindrical projection 22
cymbal 308
cymbals 295, 309
cypress scalelike leaves 65
Cyprus 450
cytopharynx 66
cytoplasm 50, 66, 112
cytoproct 66
cytostome 66
Czech Republic 450

D

D 298
d quark 414
daffodil 56
daggerboard 519
daggerboard well 519
daikon 129
dairy 122
dairy compartment 211
dairy products 120, 150
dairy products receiving area 120
Dalmatian 86
dam 406
damper pedal 304, 311
dance blade 509
dandelion 127
danger area 499
Danish Blue 151
Danish rye bread 145
Danube River 18
dark chocolate 148
dart 471
dartboard 471
darts 471
dashboard 354, 366
dashboard computer 457
dashboard equipment 457
data display 328
data processing 38
data storage devices 333
database 335
date 441
dater 338
dates 132
davit 384
day-care center 437
dead ball line 482
dead bolt 186
deadly poisonous mushroom 52
death 426
debit card 443
debris 43
decagon 429
decanter 165
deceleration lane 343
deciduous forest 44
decimal key 337
deck 313, 344
declination setting scale 8, 9
décolleté bra 259
decomposers 45
decorative articles store 437
decorative braid 260
decoy 535
dedicated line 334
deep end 184
deep fryer 178
deep peroneal nerve 108
deep-sea floor 26
defense counsels' bench 440
defensive midfielder 481
deferent duct 111
deflector 236, 237
deforestation 47
defrost drain 211
degree 428
degree Celsius 426
Deimos 2
delete 328, 331
delete key 331
delicatessen 120, 156
delicious lactarius 123
delivery 479
delivery entrance 435
delta 32, 35
delta distributary 32
delta wing 394
deltoid 96
deluge gun 455
demitasse 166
Democratic Republic of the Congo 451
dendrite 110
Denmark 450
denomination 441
dental alveolus 101
dental care 272
dental floss 272
dental floss holder 272
dentate 55
dentin 101
deodorant 267
deoxygenated blood 104
department store 437
departure time indicator 374
depolarizing mix 417
deposit slot 442
depth adjustment 229
depth of focus 27
depth-of-cut adjustment knob 229
depth-of-field preview button 314
derailleur 370, 372, 522
derby 238
dermis 114
derrick 382, 385, 403, 404
derrick mast 385
descending aorta 103
descending colon 106
descending passage 278
desert 36, 40, 44
desk 439
desk lamp 206
desk tray 338
desktop computer 334
dessert fork 168
dessert knife 168
dessert spoon 168
destination 374
destroying angel 52
detachable control 179
detachable palm rest 330
detergent dispenser 214
dew 41
dew shield 8
diable 175
diagonal buttress 284
diagonal movement 470
diagonal step 514
dial 422, 424
dial/action button 337
diameter 428
diamond 468
diamond interchange 342
diamond point 202
diaper 260
diaphragm 105, 324
dibble 231
dice 468
dice cup 469
die 469
diesel engine compartment 399, 400, 401
diesel lift engine 383
diesel motor compartment 398
diesel oil 405
diesel propulsion engine 383
diesel shop 375
diesel-electric locomotive 377
differential 351
difficult slope 512
diffuser 290
diffuser pin 236
digestive gland 71, 73
digestive system 106
digit 75, 82
digital answering machine 328
digital audio player, portable 326
digital display 423, 461
digital nerve 108
digital pulp 114
digital reflex camera 315
digital thermometer 461
digital versatile disc 319
digital watch 424
Dijon mustard 140
dike 28
dill 142
dimmer switch 198
dimple 505
dinette 164
dining car 376
dining room 188, 280, 386, 438, 439
dinner fork 168
dinner knife 168
dinner plate 166
dinnerware 166
diode 411
Dione 3
dip switch 368
dipper arm 399, 400
dipper-arm cylinder 399, 400
direct disc access buttons 323
direct home reception 316
direct-current power cord 336
direction of electron flow 416, 417
direction of Mecca 447
directional buttons 471
directional sign 379
director 291
director of photography 291
director's chair 200
director's control monitors 290
director's office 443
director's seat 291
directory 334
disc 357
disc brake 350, 357, 366, 525
disc compartment 323
disc compartment control 319, 323
disc skip 323
disc tray 319
discharge outlet 184
discus 472
discus throw 473
dish 179, 321
dish antenna 321
dishwasher 164, 214
dishwasher, control panel 214
disk 6, 333, 501
disk drive 310
diskette 333
disks 177
displacement 418
display 319, 321, 322, 323, 325, 326, 327, 328, 336, 337, 338, 346, 423, 442, 443
display button 326
display cabinet 203
display preparation area 120
display release button 336
display setting 327
disposable camera 315
disposable contact lens 272
disposable diaper 260
disposable fuel cylinder 218
disposable razor 271
distal phalanx 114
distributary, delta 32
distribution by aerial cable network 316
distribution by submarine cable 317
distribution by underground cable network 317
distribution panel 198
distributor cap 350, 360
distributor service loop 198
district 25
ditali 146
ditch 342
divergent plate boundaries 27
diverging lenses 419
diversion tunnel 406
divide key 337
divided by 427
divider 274
dividers 339
diving 518
diving board 184
diving installations 518
diving tower 518
djembe 297
Djibouti 451
Dnieper River 18
do-it-yourself 216
do-it-yourself shop 436
dock 381
docking cradle 337
document folder 339
document-to-be-sent position 328
dodecagon 429
dog 86, 535
dog, morphology 86
dolichos beans 130
dollar 440
dolly 290
dolly tracks 290
dolphin 90
dolphin, morphology 90
domain name 334
dome shutter 7
dome tent 529
domestic appliances 176, 180, 208
domestic pollution 47
Dominica 449
Dominican Republic 449
dominoes 468
donkey 84
door 178, 202, 210, 212, 213, 287, 349, 352, 361, 392, 439, 447, 528, 529
door handle 349
door jamb 185
door lock 349
door open warning light 355
door panel 202
door stop 211
door switch 213
doorknob 185, 186
doors 286
Doric column 281
dormer window 182
dorsal abdominal artery 71
dorsal fin 90
dorsalis pedis artery 102
dorsum of nose 117
dorsum of tongue 118
dose inhaler 467
double bass 301
double basses 295
double bed 439
double boiler 175
double flat 299
double kitchen sink 194
double plate 187
double reed 306
double ring 471
double room 439
double seat 380
double sharp 299
double virgule 334
double-blank 468
double-breasted buttoning 248
double-breasted jacket 244
double-burner camp stove 529
double-decker bus 363
double-edged blade 271
double-edged razor 271
double-leaf bascule bridge 345
double-six 468
double-twist auger bit 228
doubles service court 495
doubles sideline 490, 495
doublet 468
doubling die 469
doubly dentate 55
dough hook 176
Douglas, pouch 112
dousing water tank 408
dovetail 420
down tube 371
downhill 511
downhill bicycle 522
downhill cyclist 522
downhill ski 510
downspout 182
downtown 431, 432
draft arm 400
draft tube 400, 407
drag 536
dragonfly 69
drain 194, 197
drain hose 212, 214
drain valve 404
draining circuit 194
draining spoon 173
Drake Passage 15, 17
draw hoe 233
draw tube 421
drawbridge 282
drawer 164, 202, 203, 205, 210
drawers 247
drawstring 249, 275
drawstring bag 275, 276

dredger 172
dresser 203, 290
dresses 252
dressing room 290, 293
dried chiles 139
drill collar 403
drill pipe 403
drill ship 382
drilling drawworks 403
drilling rig 403
drilling tools 228
drills 228
drink box 163
drinks 120
drip bowl 210
drip molding 349
drip pan 179
drip tray 181
dripping pan 174
drive belt 212
drive chain 370
drive mode 314
drive shaft 351, 383, 395
drive wheel 180
drive wheels 401
driver 524
driver's cab 376, 377
driver's seat 369
driveway 183
driving glove 243
dromedary camel 85
drone 68
drone pipe 296
droop nose 394
drop earrings 264
drop light 217
drop shot 491
drop-leaf 202
drop-waist dress 252
drum 170, 213, 308, 357
drum brake 357
drum sticks 309
drumlin 29
drums 308
drumstick 297
drupelet 59
dry cells 417
dry cleaner 437
dry climates 40
dry dock 381
dry fruits 60, 133
dry gallery 31
dryer 213
dual cassette deck 325
dual seat 367
dual swivel mirror 269
dual-in-line package 417
duck 81, 155
duck egg 155
duffel bag 276
duffle coat 249
dugout 474
dulse 123
dumbbells 500
dump body 401
dump truck 401
dune 35
dunes 36
duo 300
duodenum 106
dura mater 109, 110
durian 137
dust canister 229
dust receiver 208
dust ruffle 204
dust tail 6
dusting brush 209
dustpan 215
Dutch bicycle 373
Dutch oven 175
duty belt 456
duty-free shop 391
DVD 319
DVD burner 333
DVD recorder 319
dynamics propeller 383

E

E 298
e-commerce 335
e-mail 335
e-mail key 330
e-mail software 334
eagle 81
ear 92, 201
ear drum 116
ear flap 238
ear loaf 144
ear protection 458
ear, auricle 115
ear, structure 116
earlobe 115
earphone 324
earphones 325, 326
earpiece 273, 460
earplugs 458
earrings 264
Earth 2, 3, 4, 5, 14
Earth coordinate system 21
earth foundation 342
Earth's atmosphere, profile 37
Earth's crust 26, 27
Earth's crust, section 26
Earth's orbit 4, 5
Earth, structure 26
earthflow 31
earthquake 27
East 23
East China Sea 19
East Pacific Rise 34
East Timor 452
East-Northeast 23
East-Southeast 23
Eastern hemisphere 21
Eastern meridian 22
easy slope 512
eau de parfum 267
eau de toilette 267
eave 283
eccrine sweat gland 114
echinoderms 66
eclipses, types 4, 5
economy and finance 441
Ecuador 448
edge 441, 509, 510, 533
edger 237
edging 230
edible boletus 123
editorial 313
education 444
educational institution 335, 433
eel 159
effluent 32
effusive volcano 28
egg 79, 112
egg beater 172
egg carton 162
egg noodles 147
egg poacher 175
egg slicer 173
egg timer 171
eggplant 128
eggs 155
Egypt 451
Egyptian reed pens 312
eighth note 299
eighth rest 299
ejaculatory duct 111
eject button 315, 323, 471
El Salvador 448
elastic 204
elastic strainer 528, 529
elastic support bandage 461
elastic waistband 249
elastic webbing 246
elasticized leg opening 247
elbow 83, 86, 93, 95
elbow pad 486, 526, 527
elbows 146
electric charge, unit 426
electric current, unit 426
electric drill 228
electric fan motor 358
electric golf cart 505
electric griddle 179
electric grill, indoor 179
electric guitar 303
electric knife 177
electric motor 235, 237
electric potential difference, unit 426
electric range 210
electric razor 271
electric resistance, unit 426
electric steamer 179
electrical box 198
electrical cable 354
electrical circuit, parallel 416
electrical connection 365
electrical system 351
electricity 198, 416
electricity cable 434
electricity meter 198
electricity tools 217
electricity transmission 408
electrolytic capacitors 417
electrolytic separator 417
electromagnetic spectrum 418
electron 414
electron beam 318
electron collector 417
electron flow, direction 416, 417
electron gun 318
electronic ballast 199
electronic control unit 357
electronic drum pad 311
electronic handle 515
electronic instruments 310
electronic organizer 338
electronic payment terminal 121, 443
electronic piano 311
electronic scale 423
electronic viewfinder 320
electronics 417
electronics store 436
elements of a house 185
elements of architecture 286
elephant 85
elevating cylinder 364, 397, 455
elevation 182
elevation adjustment 420
elevation zones 44
elevator 281, 287, 393, 400, 435, 439
elevator car 287
elevon 13
embankment 342
emergency 462
emergency brake 380
emergency physician's office 462
emergency station 345
emergency switch 368
emergency truck 345
emery boards 265
Emmenthal 151
empty set 427
emptying hose 212
enamel 101
enclosure 286
end 331
end aisle display 121
end button 301
end cap 409
end joist 187
end key 331
end line 484, 487, 489, 493
end moraine 30
end piece 111
end plate 409
end stop 226, 521
end zone 484
end/power key 327
endocardium 104
endocarp 57, 58
endoplasmic reticulum 50, 66
endpiece 273, 503
energy 402
energy integration to the transmission network 413
energy release 415
energy, unit 426
energy-saving bulb 199, 411
engaged Corinthian column 281
engaged Doric column 281
engaged Ionic column 281
engagement ring 264
engine 366, 403
engine air intake 362
engine block 360
engine compartment 362, 396, 401
engine control room 384
engine housing 235
engine mounting pylon 393
engine room 386
English billiards 503
English cane 466
English Channel 18
English horn 306
English horns 295
English loaf 145
English mustard 140
enhanced greenhouse effect 46
enoki 123
ENT room 463
entablature 185, 279
enter key 331
enterprise 335
entire 55
entrance 343
entrance door 362, 363
entrance doors 294
entrance for the public 278
entrance hall 188
entrance to the pyramid 278
entrance turnstile 378
entrances for the actors 278
entry 396
environment 44
epaulet 248
epicalyx 59
epicenter 27
epicondyle 99
epidermis 114
epididymis 111
epidural space 110
epiglottis 105, 118
epitrochlea 99
equals 427
equals key 337
Equator 17, 20, 21, 22, 43
Equatorial Guinea 451
equipment 472
equipment compartment 376
equipment storage room 444
erase button 315
eraser 341
erecting lenses 420
Eris 3
Eritrea 451
escalator 294, 378, 435
escape 330
escape key 330
escarole 126
escutcheon 73, 186, 197
esophagus 105, 106
espadrille 242
espresso machine 181
espresso maker 181
Estonia 450
eternal light 447
Ethernet port 336
Ethiopia 451
ethmoid, cribriform plate 117
Eurasia 14
Eurasian Plate 27
euro 440
Europa 2
Europe 14, 18, 34, 449
European experiment module 11
European outlet 198
European plug 198
European robin 80
European Union, flag 441
Eustachian tube 116, 117
Eutelsat 316
euthynteria 279
evacuation route 345
evaporated milk 150
evaporation 45, 414
evening glove 243
event platform 496
ex-voto 446
examination room 463, 465
examples of cat breeds 87
examples of dog breeds 86
examples of shirts 255
examples of utensils for cutting 169
executive length 247
exercise wear 263
exhalation valve 459
exhaust air duct 345
exhaust manifold 350, 360
exhaust pipe 350, 351, 367, 368, 395
exhaust pipe stack 398
exhaust stack 364
exhaust system 351
exhaust tube 199
exhaust valve 360
exhibition center 430
exit 343
exit button 337
exit taxiway 391
exit turnstile 378
exocarp 57, 58, 59
exosphere 37
expandable baton 456
expandable file pouch 274
expander 310
expanding file 340
expansion bolt 221
expansion chamber 424
expert slope 512
expiration date 441
explosive volcano 28
exposure adjustment knob 314
exposure mode 314
expressway 343
extension 202
extension ladder 219
extension pipe 209
extension table 202
extensor carpi radialis brevis 97
extensor carpi radialis longus 97
extensor carpi ulnaris 97
extensor digitorum 97
extensor digitorum brevis 96
extensor digitorum longus 96
exterior dome shell 7
exterior door 185
exterior of a house 182
exterior pocket 274, 276
exterior sign 378
external auditory meatus 100
external ear 116
external floppy disk drive 333
external fuel tank 12
external jugular vein 102
external nose 117
external oblique 96, 97
external tooth lock washer 222
eye 43, 70, 71, 72, 76, 90, 94, 119, 220, 538
eye makeup 266
eye pencil 266
eye protection 458
eye ring 78
eye wall 43
eyeball 75, 119
eyebrow stripe 78
eyebrow tweezers 265
eyeglasses 273
eyeglasses case 275
eyeglasses parts 273
eyelahes 87
eyelash 119
eyelash curler 266
eyelashes 87
eyelet 240, 262, 275, 509
eyelet tab 240
eyelid 76
eyepiece 8, 9, 320, 420, 421
eyepiece holder 8
eyeshadow 266
eyestalk 72

F

F 298
fabric guide 208
façade 285
face 91, 92, 220, 493, 505
face mask 478, 486, 507
face-off circle 506
face-off spot 506
facepiece 459
faceplate 186
facial makeup 266
facsimile (fax) machine 328
factorial 427
factory 430
faculae 4
Fahrenheit scale 424
fairing 366
fairlead 521
fairway 504
falcon 81
Falkland Islands 17
fall front 203
fallopian tube 112
fallopian tubes 113
fallow 122
false rib 99
false start rope 516
false tuck 260
family tent 528
family waiting room 462
fan 213
fan brush 266
fan housing 270
fan trellis 230

fang 70, 76
fantail 412
farmhouse 122
farmhouse bread 145
farmstead 122
farmyard 122
fast-food restaurants 437
fast-forward button 323
fastener binder 339
fats and oils 149
faucet 195
fault 27
feather crown 495
feathered shuttlecock 495
Federated States of Micronesia 453
feed tube 177, 180
feedhorn 321
feet 79
feijoa 137
felt hat 238, 239
female 426
female cone 65
female ferrule 536, 537
female reproductive organs 112
femoral artery 102
femoral nerve 108
femoral vein 102
femur 98
fence 122, 182, 226
fender 348, 364, 370
fennec 88
fennel 125
fenugreek 138
fermata 299
fern 52
fern, structure 52
ferns 52
ferrule 219, 503
ferryboat 381
ferryboat, catamaran 386
fertilizer application 47
fetlock 83
fetlock joint 83
fettucine 146
fibers 215
fibula 98
fibularis brevis 97
fiddlehead 52
fiddleheads 125
field 472, 474, 479, 482
field lens 420
field lens adjustment 421
field line 416
field mouse 82
fielder's glove 477
fielders 479
fifth 298
fifth wheel 364
fifty 427
fifty-yard line 484
fig 137
figure skate 509
figure skating 509
Fiji 453
Fiji Islands 15
filament 56, 199
Filchner Ice Shelf 15
file 229, 334, 531
file format 334
file guides 340
filiform papilla 118
filing box 340
fill opening 208
filler cap 237, 358, 364
filler neck 351
filler tube 196
filleting knife 169
filling inlet 404
filter 184, 210
filter cover 459
filter holder 181
fin 393, 395
final drive 398
financial services 442
finch 80
finderscope 8, 9
fine adjustment knob 421
fine adjustment wheel 425
fine guidance system 7
finely threaded screw 425
finger 114, 477
finger flange 460
finger tip 339
fingerboard 296, 301, 303
fingernail 115
finial 283
finish line 473
finish wall 516
finishing nail 220
Finland 450
fir 65
fir needles 65
fire box 192
fire door 286
fire extinguisher 457
fire extinguisher, portable 454
fire hose 454
fire hydrant 434, 454
fire irons 193
fire prevention 454
fire station 433
fire trucks 455
fire-fighting materials 454
firebrick 192
firebrick back 192
firefighter 454
fireplace 188, 192
fireplace screen 193
FireWire port 336
firn 30
first aid equipment 460
first aid kit 457, 461
first aid manual 461
first aid station 512
first assistant camera operator 290
first base 474
first baseman 474
first dorsal fin 74
first floor 182, 188
first leaves 53
first molar 101
first premolar 101
first quarter 5
first row 482
first space 489
first valve slide 307
first violins 295
first voltage increase 413
first-class cabin 392
fish fork 168
fish knife 168
fish net stocking 257
fish platter 166
fish poacher 174
fish scaler 531
fishes 74
fishes, bony 159
fishes, cartilaginous 158
fishhook 536, 538
fishing 536
fishing vest 538
fission of uranium fuel 408
fission products 415
fissionable nucleus 415
fitness equipment 500
fitted sheet 204
fitting 455
fittings 277
five 427
five hundred 427
five spice powder 139
fixed base 224
fixed bridges 344
fixed distance marking 391
fixed jaw 223, 224, 425
fixture drain 194
fjords 35
flag 482
flag of the European Union 441
flageolets 131
flags 448
flame 415
flame spreader tip 218
flame-resistant driving suit 524
flamingo 81
flank 78, 83
flanker 482
flanking tower 282
flap 244, 275
flap pocket 244, 248
flare 4
flare nut wrench 223
flash tube 420
flashing 193
flashlight 456
flat 299, 526
flat car 377
flat head 221
flat mirror 7
flat oyster 157
flat sheet 204
flat tip 221
flat washer 222
flat-back brush 268
flat-plate solar collector 410
flea 69
fleece jacket 262
flesh 57, 58, 59
fleshy fruit 58, 59
fleshy fruit: pome fruit 58
fleshy fruit: stone fruit 57
fleshy leaf 54
flews 86
flexible boot 513
flexible hose 209
flexible skirt 383
flexible tube 460
flexor carpi ulnaris 96, 97
flies 292
flight 471
flight deck 12, 392, 395
flight information board 391
flight of stairs 191
flights 518
flint 218
flip 509
float 394
float ball 196
float seaplane 394
float tackle 538
floating crane 381
floating head 271
floating ribs 98
floating roof 404
floating-roof tank 404
floodplain 32
floor 193, 412
floor brush 209
floor coverings, textile 190
floor drain 194
floor exercise area 496
floor joist 187
floor lamp 206
floor mat 356
floor mats 496
floorboard 190, 369
florist 437
flour 144
flow tube 410
flower 53, 56
flower bed 183, 230
flower bud 53
flower, inflorescences 57
flower, structure 56
flowering 62
flowers 56
flue 305
flue pipe 305
fluorescent tube 199
flush 468
flush handle 196
flute 228
fluted land 228
fluted shaft 355
flutes 295
fly 69, 246, 247, 260
fly agaric 52
fly front closing 251
fly line 536
fly reel 536
fly rod 536
flyfishing 536
flyhalf 482
flying buttress 284, 285
flywheel 360, 501
FM mode select button 322
foam 33
foam cushion 458
foam monitor 385
foam pad 530
focus 27, 419
focus button 320
focus mode selector 314
focusing knob 8, 9
focusing ring 420
fodder corn 122
fog 41
fog light 352, 364
foie gras 156
foil, aluminum 162
folder 340
folding chairs 201
folding cot 530
folding door 286
folding grill 533
folding nail file 265
folding ramp 386
folding shovel 532
foliage 63
foliate papilla 118
foliose lichen 50
follicle 60
follicle, section 60
following car 522
fondue fork 168
fondue pot 174
fondue set 174
fontanelle 100
food 120
food and kitchen 120
food can 163
food chain 45
food mill 170
food processor 177
food reserves 439
food tray 162
food vacuole 66
food, basic source 45
foot 72, 73, 91, 92, 93, 94, 95, 202, 260, 302, 305, 308, 519, 536, 537
foot cushion 502
foot fault judge 491
foot hole 305
foot protection 459
foot strap 519
foot support 501
football 486
football player 486
football, American 484
footboard 204, 523
footbridge 282, 375, 379
footing 187
footless tights 263
footrest 205, 224, 467
footstool 201
footstrap 254, 501
for filing 339
for opening 170
foramen cecum 118
force, unit 426
fore and aft passage 385
forearm 83, 86, 93, 95, 534
forearm crutch 466
forearm pad 486
forearm support 466
forecastle 383, 387
forecourt 491
forehead 78, 92
foreleg 67, 68
forelimb 75
forelock 83
foremast 385
forest 29
forest fire 47
forestay 520
forewing 67
fork 8, 167, 371, 396, 522, 525, 531
fork arm 396
forked tongue 76
forklift truck 396
forks 168
Former Yugoslav Republic of Macedonia 450
formeret 284
forming food vacuole 66
forms of medications 467
Formula 1® car 525
Formula 3000 car 524
fortified wall 447
forward 481, 518
fossil fuel 46, 48
foul line 474
foul post 475
foundation 187
foundation of tower 344
foundation slip 258
fountain pen 312
four blade beater 176
four-door sedan 347
four-four time 298
four-of-a-kind 468
four-way lug wrench 356
four-way selector 315
fourchette 243
fourth 298
fovea 119
fox 88
foyers 293
fraction 427
fractionating tower 405
frame 187, 192, 202, 204, 219, 224, 226, 248, 274, 277, 297, 309, 367, 396, 401, 410, 411, 412, 425, 460, 476, 492, 494, 522, 527, 528
frame stile 202
framing square 225
France 449
frankfurters 156
free guard zone 515
free margin 114
free skating blade 509
free throw line 489
freestyle snowboard 513
freeway 431
freewheel 372
freezer 164, 211, 438
freezer bag 162
freezer bucket 180
freezer compartment 211
freezing 414
freezing rain 41
freight car 375
freight cars 377
freight expedition 391
freight hold 393
freight reception 391
freight station 375
French bread 144
French horn 307
French horns 295
French press 181
French window 287
frequency display 325
frequency, unit 426
fresco 280
fresh air duct 345
fresh cheeses 150
fret 302, 303
friction strip 218
frieze 202, 279
frog 75, 249, 301
frog, morphology 75
frog-adjustment screw 229
frond 52
front 244, 245
front apron 245
front axle 401
front beam 422
front brake 371
front brake lever 368
front compression strap 532
front cover 333
front crawl 517
front derailleur 370, 372
front desk 439
front door 188
front fascia 348
front fender 366
front foil 387
front footrest 367, 368
front fork 522
front hydraulic brake line 350
front leg 201
front page 313
front picture 313
front pocket 275
front rigid section 363
front shock absorber 369
front sight 534
front tip 208
front top pocket 246
front view 478
front wheel 401, 467
front-end loader 399
front-loading washer 212
frontal 446
frontal bone 98, 100
frontal sinus 117
frontalis 96
frontwall 365
frost 41
frozen food storage 121
frozen foods 121
fruit 57
fruit branch 62
fruit tree 122
fruit vegetables 128
fruition 62
fruits 120, 132
fruits, tropical 136
fruticose lichen 50
fry basket 171
frying pan 175, 531
fuel 408
fuel bundle 409

fuel indicator 355
fuel injector 360
fuel oil 405
fuel pellet 409
fuel tank 235, 364, 377, 395
fulcrum 518
full face helmet 525
full face mask 454
full house 468
full moon 5
fullback 482, 485
fully reflecting mirror 420
fumarole 28
function buttons 319
function display 310
function keys 328, 330, 423
function selectors 327
fungicide 47
fungiform papilla 118
funiculus 59, 60
funnel 171, 318, 386
funnel cloud 43
fur 82, 91
furrow 118
fuse 198, 411
fuselage 393
fusilli 146
futon 204

G

G 298
gable 182, 285
gable stud 187
gable vent 182
gabletop 163
Gabon 451
gaffer 291
Gai-lohn 127
gaits, horse 83
galaxy 6
gallbladder 106
gallery 285, 412
galley 392
Gambia 451
game 154, 492
game board 469
game console 471
game port 329
games 468
gamma rays 418
gantry crane 406, 407
Ganymede 2
gap 538
garage 182
garage door 286
garam masala 139
garbage can 215
garbage collection truck 364
garbage disposal sink 197
garbage disposal unit 197
garden 280
garden cress 127
garden fork 233
garden hose 236
garden line 231
garden path 182
garden sorrel 127
garden spider 70
garden, pleasure 230
garden, public 435
garden, vegetable 122
gardening 216, 230
gardening gloves 232
garlic 124
garlic press 170
garment bag 277
garment strap 277
garrison cap 238
garter 259
garter belt 259
garter snake 77
gas 403, 414
gas line 351
gas main 434
gas pedal 354
gas range 210
gas supply system 351
gas tank 351, 366, 369
gas tank cap 368
gas tank door 349
gasket 214
gaskin 83
gasoline 405
gasoline engine 351, 360
gasoline pump 346
gasoline pump hose 346
gastrocnemius 96, 97
gate 381, 407
gate-leg 202
gate-leg table 202
gather 255
gathered skirt 253
gauntlet 243
gauze roller bandage 461
gear housing 537
gear shift 368
gearbox 350
gearshift lever 350, 354, 367, 369
gelatin capsule 467
generator 370, 402
generator unit 407
Genoa salami 156
gentlemen's restroom 439
gentlemen's restrooms 294
geographical map 444
geography 14
geology 26
geometrical shapes 428
geometry 428
Georgia 452
geothermal and fossil energy 402
geothermal energy 402
geothermal field 402
germ 61
German mustard 140
German rye bread 145
German salami 156
German shepherd 86
Germany 450
germination 53
geyser 28
Ghana 451
ghee 150
gherkin 128
giant slalom 511
giant slalom ski 510
gibbon 91
Gibraltar, Strait 18
gift store 436
gill slits 74
gills 52, 73
ginger 139
ginkgo nuts 133
giraffe 85
girder 187
girdle 259
glacial cirque 30
glacial lake 32
glacier 30, 32, 44
glacier tongue 30
glans penis 111
glass 410, 411
glass bottle 163
glass case 423
glass collection unit 49
glass lens 273
glass protector 506
glass recycling container 49
glass roof 188
glass slide 421
glass sorting 49
glass-fronted display cabinet 203
glassed roof 374, 435
glassware 165
gliding phase 514
global warming 46
globe 444, 529
globular cluster 6
glottis 76
glove 10, 478, 498, 506, 508, 513, 514, 522, 525
glove compartment 354
glove finger 243
glove storage 464
glove, back 243
glove, palm 243
gloves 243
glucose 54
glue 190
glue stick 341
gluteal nerve 108
gluteus maximus 97
gnocchi 146
gnomon 424
go 470
goal 480, 485, 507
goal area 480
goal crease 507
goal judge 506
goal lights 507
goal line 482, 484, 506
goalkeeper 481
goalkeeper's gloves 480
goalpost 482, 485
goaltender (goalie) 506, 507
goaltender's pad 507
goaltender's skate 507
goaltender's stick 507
goat 84
goat's milk 150
goat's-milk cheeses 150
goatfish 159
gob hat 239
Gobi Desert 19
goggles 218, 513, 522
golf 504
golf bag 505
golf ball 505
golf cart 505
golf cart, electric 505
golf clubs, types 505
golf course 430
golf glove 505
golf shoes 505
Golgi apparatus 50, 66
gonad 73
gondola 121, 512
gondola departure area 512
gong 295, 309
goose 81, 155
goose egg 155
goose-neck 191
gooseberries 132
gooseneck 400
gored skirt 253
gorge 31, 32
Gorgonzola 151
gorilla 91
gorilla, morphology 91
Gothic cathedral 284
gour 31
government organization 335
governor tension sheave 287
grab handle 361, 364, 455
gracilis 97
grade slope 182
grader 401
graduated dial 533
graduated scale 422, 423
grain of wheat, section 61
grain terminal 381
Grand Canyon 16
grand gallery 278
granitic layer 26
granivorous bird 79
granulated sugar 149
granulation 4
grape 62
grape leaf 62
grape leaves 126
grape, section 59
grapefruit 134
grapefruit knife 169
grapes 132
grass 492
grassbox 237
grasshopper 69
grassland 44
grate 210
grater 170
gravel bed 524
gravy boat 166
gray matter 109, 110
grease well 179
greases 405
Great Australian Bight 15
Great Barrier Reef 15
Great Dane 86
Great Dividing Range 15
great green bush-cricket 69
great horned owl 81
Great Lakes 16
great organ manual 305
Great Sandy Desert 15
great saphenous vein 102
great scallop 157
Great Victoria Desert 15
greater alar cartilage 117
greater covert 78
greater trochanter 99
Greece 450
Greek bread 144
Greek temple 279
Greek temple, plan 279
Greek theater 278
green 418, 504
green alga 51
green ball 503
green beam 318
green bean 131
green cabbage 126
green coffee beans 148
green gland 71
green light 434
green onion 124
green peas 130
green pepper 138
green russula 123
green sweet pepper 128
green tea 148
green walnut 60
greenhouse 122
greenhouse effect 46
greenhouse effect, enhanced 46
greenhouse effect, natural 46
greenhouse gas 46
greenhouse gas concentration 46
Greenland 16
Greenland Sea 14
Grenada 449
Grenadines 449
grid 318
grid system 22
grille 279, 296, 348, 358
grip 290, 500, 505, 535
grip handle 226
grip tape 526
gripping tools 222
grocery bags 121
groin 92, 94
groove 169, 510
ground 404
ground beef 152
ground electrode 359
ground lamb 153
ground moraine 30
ground pepper 139
ground pork 153
ground terminal 322
ground veal 152
ground wire 198
groundhog 82
grounding prong 198
grow sleepers 260
growth line 72, 73
Gruyère 151
guard 169, 217, 489
guard rail 191, 211, 526
guardhouse 282
guardrail 188, 189, 384
Guatemala 448
guava 137
guide 536
guide bar 235
guide handle 229
guiding tower 345
Guinea 451
guinea fowl 81, 154
guinea pig 82
Guinea, Gulf 20
Guinea-Bissau 451
guitar 302, 303
gulf 24
Gulf of Aden 19, 20
Gulf of Alaska 16
Gulf of Bothnia 18
Gulf of California 16
Gulf of Carpentaria 15
Gulf of Guinea 20
Gulf of Mexico 16
Gulf of Oman 19
Gulf of Panama 17
gum 101, 116
gun 216
gun flap 248
gurnard 159
gusset 274, 276
gusset pocket 255
Gutenberg discontinuity 26
gutter 182
guy line 528
guy wire 412
Guyana 448
guyot 33
gym teachers' office 444
gymnasium 386, 444
gymnast's name 497
gymnastics 496
gynecological examination room 463

H

hack 515
hackle 536
hacksaw 226
haddock 161
hair 93, 95, 114, 301
hair bulb 114
hair clip 268
hair conditioner 267
hair dryer 270
hair follicle 114
hair roller 268
hair roller pin 268
hair shaft 114
hairbrushes 268
haircolor 267
haircutting scissors 270
hairdressing 268
hairdressing salon 436
hairpin 268
hairstylist 290
Haiti 448
half handle 169
half note 299
half rest 299
half-glasses 273
half-mask respirator 459
half-slip 258
half-volley 490
halfway dash line 483
halfway line 481
halibut 161
hall 188, 386, 439
halo 6
halogen desk lamp 206
ham knife 169
hammer 304, 472, 534
hammer loop 225
hammer rail 304
hammer throw 473
hamster 82
hand 91, 93, 95, 115
hand blender 176
hand brake 350
hand cultivator 232
hand fork 232
hand held vacuum cleaner 208
hand miter saw 226
hand mixer 176
hand post 297
hand protector 235, 525
hand rest 332
hand strap 320
hand tools 232
hand truck 396
hand-warmer pocket 249, 251
handbags 275
handcuff case 456
handgrip 366, 369, 466, 536
handgrips 500
handheld computer/personal digital assistant (PDA) 337
handicap spot 470
handle 167, 170, 176, 177, 178, 179, 180, 192, 204, 208, 209, 210, 211, 214, 215, 216, 217, 219, 220, 221, 222, 223, 224, 225, 226, 227, 229, 231, 235, 236, 237, 269, 270, 271, 272, 273, 274, 275, 276, 277, 301, 325, 326, 341, 356, 467, 477, 478, 492, 493, 494, 510, 531, 536, 537
handle, retractable 277
handlebar 501, 523
handlebars 371, 523
handling 396
handrail 287, 363, 380, 385
handsaw 226
handset 327
handset cord 327
hang-up ring 270
hanger bracket 467
hanging basket 230
hanging file 340
hanging glacier 30
hanging pendant 206
hanging stile 185, 186, 202
hank 521
hapteron 51
harbor 381

hard boot 513
hard contact lens 272
hard disk drive 333
hard hat 458
hard palate 116, 117
hard surface 492
hard-shell clams 157
hare 82, 154
harissa 141
harmonica 296
harp 302
harps 295
hasp 277
hastate 55
hat switch 332
hatband 238
hatch 13
hatchback 347
hatchet 454, 533
hawk 216
hayloft 122
hazelnut, section 60
hazelnuts 133
head 6, 67, 72, 78, 93, 95, 103, 111, 125, 220, 221, 223, 229, 271, 272, 301, 302, 303, 309, 492, 494, 505, 536
head cover 505
head cushion 502
head harness 459
head linesman 485
head nurse's office 463
head of femur 99
head of frame 186
head of humerus 99
head protection 458
head tube 371
head, bird 78
headband 324, 458, 459
headbay 406
headboard 204, 205
header 185, 187
headgear 238, 239, 498
heading 313
headland 35
headlight 348, 364, 366, 368, 371, 376, 377, 523
headlight/turn signal 354
headlights 352
headline 313
headphone jack 310, 311, 322, 323, 326
headphones 324
headrest 353
heads 221
headset kit 327
health 460
health and beauty care 121
health organization 335
hearing 115
heart 71, 73, 104, 105, 154, 468
heartwood 63
heat deflecting disc 199
heat energy 46
heat gun 219
heat loss 46
heat production 408
heat ready indicator 269
heat selector switch 270
heat shield 12
heat transfer 415
heat-sealed film 163
heater 529
heating 192
heating duct 213
heating element 213, 214, 218
heating equipment 386
heating grille 380
heating oil 405
heavy duty boot 240
heavy gasoline 405
heavy machinery 398
heavy rainfall 43
hedge 183, 230
hedge shears 234
hedge trimmer 235
heel 93, 95, 169, 226, 229, 240, 247, 262, 301, 302, 477, 506, 509
heel grip 240
heel loop 467
heel rest 176, 208
heel stop 527
heelpiece 511
heelplate 514
height adjustment 501
height adjustment scale 227
helicopter 395
helix 115, 429
helmet 10, 454, 478, 486, 506, 508, 510, 513, 522, 525, 526, 527
helmet ring 10
hemisphere 429
hemispheres 21
hemlath 412
hen 81
hen egg 155
hen house 122
hendecagon 429
hepatic vein 103
heptagon 429
herbal teas 148
herbicide 47
herbivores 45
herbs 142
heron 80
herring 159
herringbone parquet 190
herringbone pattern 190
hertz 426
Hertzian wave transmission 316
Herzegovina 450
heterotrophs 45
hex nut 359
hexagon 429
hexagon nut 223
hidden pocket 274
high altar 446
high beam 352
high beam indicator light 355
high beam warning indicator 368
high card 468
high chair 205
high cloud, type 39
high clouds 42
high frequency antenna cable 394
high jump 473
high wing 394
high-hat cymbal 308
high-pressure area 43
high-pressure center 39
high-rise apartment building 289
high-speed exit taxiway 388
high-speed shaft 413
high-speed train 376
high-tension electricity transmission 413
high-tension electricity transmission tower 402
highball glass 165
highland 5, 40
highland climates 40
highway 25, 343
highway number 25
hijiki 123
hiking boot 242
hill 29
Himalayas 19
hind leg 67
hind leg, honeybee 68
hind limb 75
hind toe 78, 79
hind wing 67
hinge 178, 185, 186, 202, 214, 274, 352, 420, 511
hinge pin 400
hip 93, 95
hip belt 532
hip pad 486
hippopotamus 85
hitch ball 356
hitch pin 304
hitting area 477
hive 122
hobo bag 276
hock 83, 86, 153
hockey 506
hockey skate, in-line 527
hoe 233
hoe-fork 233
hog line 515
hoisin sauce 140
hoisting block 397
hoisting rope 219, 287, 397
holding 499
holding area marking 390
holds and throws 499
hole 504
hollow barrel 460
hologram foil strip 441
holster 456
Holy See (Vatican City) 450
holy water font 446
home 331
home antenna 316
home key 331
home plate 475
home theater 321
home user 335
home-plate umpire 475
homogenized milk 150
Honduras 448
honey 149
honeybee 68
honeybee, hind leg 68
honeybee, middle leg 68
honeybee, morphology 68
honeydew melon 135
hood 192, 209, 249, 260, 261, 348, 364, 508
hooded sweat shirt 262
hoof 83
hook 186, 217, 225, 364, 397, 423, 460, 502, 509
hooker 482
hoop earrings 264
horizontal bar 496, 497
horizontal ground movement 27
horizontal movement 470
horizontal pivoting window 287
horizontal seismograph 27
horizontal stabilizer 393, 395
horizontal-axis wind turbine 413
horn 354, 368, 377, 455
horned melon 136
hornet 69
horny beak 76
hors d'oeuvre dish 166
horse 83, 85
horse, gaits 83
horse, morphology 83
horsefly 69
horseradish 129
horseshoe mount 7
hose 209, 257, 259, 454
hose connector 236
hose nozzle 236
hose trolley 236
hospital 433, 462
hospital bed 464
hot coolant 408
hot pepper 128
hot tub 184
hot-air outlet 192
hot-shoe contact 314
hot-water circuit 194
hot-water heater 194
hot-water pipe 194
hot-water supply line 197
hotel 432, 439, 512
hotel reservation desk 390
hotel rooms 439
hour angle gear 7
house 182, 293, 515
house furniture 200
house, elements 185
house, elevation 182
house, exterior 182
house, frame 187
house, structure 188
houseboat 385
housedress 252
household equipment 215
household products 120
household waste 47, 48
houses, city 289
houses, traditional 288
housing 199, 218, 228, 229, 271
hovercraft 383
hub 70, 341, 371, 413, 467
Hubble space telescope 7, 37
Hudson Bay 16
hull 60, 520, 523
human being 92
human body 92
human denture 101
humerus 98
humid continental-hot summer 40
humid continental-warm summer 40
humid subtropical 40
hummingbird 80
hummus 140
humpback whale 90
Hungary 450
hunting 534
hunting cap 238
hurricane 43
hurricane lamp 532
husk 60, 61
hut 288
hydrant intake 455
hydraulic disc brake 522
hydraulic hoses 396
hydraulic resistance 501
hydraulic shovel 400
hydroelectric complex 406
hydroelectric power plant, cross section 407
hydroelectricity 406
hydrofoil boat 387
hydrologic cycle 45
hydrometer 359
hydrosphere 44
hyena 88
hyperlinks 334
hyperopia 419
hypha 52
hyssop 142

I

Iapetus 3
Iberian Peninsula 18
ice 45
ice breaker 384
ice cream maker 180
ice cream scoop 173
ice cube dispenser 164
ice dispenser 346
ice hockey 506
ice hockey player 506
ice rink 512
iceberg lettuce 126
Iceland 18, 450
icing syringe 172
identification badge 456
identification bracelet 264
identification tag 277
idler wheel 523
igloo 288
igneous rocks 26
ignition switch 354, 368
iguana 77
ileum 106
iliohypogastric nerve 108
ilioinguinal nerve 108
ilium 98
image review button 315
impervious rock 403
impluvium 280
impulse sprinkler 236
in goal area 483
in-ground swimming pool 184
in-line hockey skate 527
in-line skate 527
in-line skating 527
in-line speed skate 527
inbounds line 484
incandescent lightbulb 199
incident neutron 415
incineration 49
incisors 101
incus 116
index 313
index finger 115
index/enlarge button 315
India 453
Indian Ocean 14, 15, 19, 20
indicator board 374
indicator light 454
indicator lights 331
indicators 318
Indonesia 19, 453
indoor electric grill 179
industrial area 431
industrial communications 317
industrial pollution 47
industrial waste 47, 48
industry 335
Indycar® 524
inert gas 199
inferior cymbal 308
inferior dental arch 116
inferior mesenteric artery 107
inferior nasal concha 117
inferior rectus muscle 119
inferior vena cava 102, 103, 104, 107
infield 474
infiltration 45
infinity 427
inflated carrying tire 380
inflated guiding tire 380
inflator 530
inflator-deflator 530
inflorescences, types 57
inflorescent vegetables 127
information booth 437
information counter 390
information desk 442, 463, 512
information spreading 335
infrared port 336, 337
infrared radiation 46, 418
infraspiatus 97
infundibulum of fallopian tube 113
infusions 148
inhalation valve 459
initials of the issuing bank 441
injection well 402
ink 312
inkjet printer 333
inlaid parquet 190
inlet valve 360
inner boot 511, 527
inner circle 515
inner core 26
inner door shell 352
inner hearth 192
inner lip 73
inner planets 3
inner table 469
inner tent 528, 529
inner toe 78
inorganic matter 45
input devices 330
input lights 322
input select button 322
input selector 322
input tray 333
input/output audio/video jacks 322
insectivorous bird 79
insects 67, 69
insert 331
insert key 331
inside 167
inside linebacker 484
inside-leg snap-fastening 260, 261
instant-read thermometer 171
instep 92, 247
instrument panel 355
instrumental groups 300
insulated blade 217
insulated handle 179, 217
insulating material 190, 214
insulation 410
insulator 359
insurance services 442
intake manifold 360
integral 427
integrated circuit 417
Intelsat 317
intensive care unit 464
intensive farming 46, 48
intensive husbandry 46, 47
interchange 431
interchangeable studs 480
interchanges 342
intercostal nerve 108
interior dome shell 7
interior door handle 352
interior door lock button 352
interior pocket 277
intermediate booster station 404
intermediate slope 512
intermodal car 377
internal boundary 23
internal ear 116
internal filum terminale 109
internal iliac artery 102, 103, 107
internal iliac vein 103
internal jugular vein 102
internal modem port 336

internal tooth lock washer 222
international boundary 23
international space station 11
international system of units 426
Internet 334
Internet keys 330
Internet service provider 335
Internet user 334
Internet uses 335
internode 53
interosseus plantaris 96
interrupted projection 22
intersection of two sets 427
intertragic notch 115
intervals 298
interventricular septum 104
interview rooms 440
intestine 71, 73, 103
intravenous stand 464
intrusive filtration 47
intrusive rocks 26
inverted pleat 253
inward 518
Io 2
ion tail 6
Ionic column 281
Iran 452
Iraq 452
Ireland 449
iris 119
Irish moss 123
Irish Sea 18
Irish soda bread 145
iron 505
iron curtain 292
is an element of 427
is approximately equal to 427
is equivalent to 427
is greater than 427
is greater than or equal to 427
is identical to 427
is included in/is a subset of 427
is less than 427
is less than or equal to 427
is not an element of 427
is not equal to 427
is not identical to 427
is not parallel to 428
is parallel to 428
isba 288
ischium 99
island 24, 164, 188, 343
island arc 33
isobar 39
isolation room 462
isoseismal line 27
Israel 452
ISS 11
issuing bank, initials 441
isthmus 24
isthmus of fallopian tube 113
isthmus of fauces 116
Isthmus of Panama 16
Italy 450

J

jaboticabas 137
jack 468
jacket 249, 251, 417, 499, 534
jacket, fleece 262
jackets 244, 254
jackfruit 136
jaguar 89
jalapeño chile 139
jalousie 186
Jamaica 448
jamb 192
janitor's closet 439, 443
Japan 19, 453
Japan Trench 34
Japan, Sea 19
Japanese experiment module 11
Japanese persimmon 137
Japanese plums 133
Jarlsberg 151
Java Trench 34
javelin 472
javelin throw 473
jaw 217, 221, 224, 228, 265
jaws 224, 535
jay 80
jazz band 300
jeans 254
jejunum 106
jerboa 82
jersey 522
Jerusalem artichoke 124
jet fuel 405
jet tip 272
Jew's harp 297
jewelry 264
jewelry store 436
jib 397, 520
jib tie 397
jibsheet 520
jicama 124
jig saw 227
jingle 309
jockey rollers 372
John Dory 161
joint 312, 503, 536
joint filler 216
joist 190
joker 468
Jordan 452
joule 426
joystick 332
joysticks 471
judge 498, 499
judges 496, 497, 509, 518
judges' bench 440
judges' office 440
judo 499
judogi 499
juice sac 58
juicer 180
jump rope 500
jump, steeplechase hurdle 472
jumper 252
jumper cables 356
jumping ski 513
jumps 509
jumpsuit 254, 260, 261
juniper berries 138
Jupiter 2
jurors' room 440
jury box 440
justice 440

K

Kalahari Desert 20
Kamchatka Peninsula 19
Kazakhstan 452
keel boat 521
keep 282
keeper ring 536
kelly 403
kelvin 426
Kenya 451
Kermadec-Tonga Trench 34
kernel 61
kerosene 405
ketchup 141
kettle 29, 180
kettledrum 308
key 296, 304, 306, 307, 488
key case 275
key cutting shop 437
key finger button 306
key grip 290
key guard 306
key lever 306
key lock 274
key signature 299
keybed 304
keyboard 304, 310, 330, 336
keyboard instruments 304
keyboard port 329
keyless chuck 228
keys 311
keystone 284
kick pleat 253
kicker 313
kickstand 367, 369
kidney 73, 103, 154
kielbasa sausage 156
killer whale 90
kilogram 426
kilt 253
kimono 256
king 468, 470
king's chamber 278
king's side 470
kingfisher 80
kingpin 365
kiosk 346, 379
Kiribati 453
kitchen 162, 164, 188, 280, 439, 445
kitchen knife 169
kitchen scale 171
kitchen shears 173
kitchen timer 171
kitchen utensils 169
kiwi 136
knee 83, 86, 92, 94
knee pad 476, 486, 526, 527
knee wrap 500
knee-high sock 257
knickers 254
knife 167, 531, 533
knife pleat 246, 253
knight 470
knit shirt 250
knives 168
knob 202, 229, 477
knob handle 227
knobby tread tire 369
knurled bolt 219
kohlrabi 125
Kola Peninsula 18
kombu 123
kora 297
Korea, North 453
Korea, South 453
Korean Peninsula 19
Kuiper belt 2
kumquat 134
Kuril Trench 34
Kuwait 452
Kyrgyzstan 452

L

label maker 340
labial palp 67, 73
labium majus 112, 113
labium minus 112, 113
lablab beans 130
laboratory 7
laccolith 28
lace 177, 498, 509
lachrymal canal 119
lachrymal caruncle 119
lachrymal gland 119
lactiferous duct 113
ladder 184, 288, 361, 401, 404, 469
ladder pipe nozzle 455
ladders 219
ladies' restroom 439
ladies' restrooms 294
ladle 173
Ladoga, Lake 18
Lady chapel 284, 285
ladybug 69
lagomorphs 82
lagoon 35
lake 5, 24, 29, 32
lake acidification 48
Lake Baikal 19
Lake Chad 20
Lake Eyre North 15
Lake Ladoga 18
Lake Malawi 20
Lake Tanganyika 20
Lake Titicaca 17
Lake Victoria 20
lakes 32
lamb cubes 153
lamb, cuts 153
lambdoid suture 100
lamina 51
lamp 320, 421
lamp oil 405
lamp socket 199
lamprey 159
lanceolate 55
land 228
land pollution 47
land station 38
landfill 431
landfill site 47
landing 189, 191
landing area 472
landing gear 361, 365
landing gear crank 365
landing light 395
landing net 538
landing window 395
landslides 31
lane 433, 472, 516
lane line 473
lane rope 517
lane timekeeper 516
languid 305
lantern 230, 529
Laos 453
lapel 244
lapiaz 31
laptop computer 336
laptop computer: front view 336
laptop computer: rear view 336
larch 65
lard 149
larding needle 173
large blade 531
large intestine 106
large wheel 467
large-screen television set 321
larger spotted dogfish 158
larva 67
larynx 105
lasagna 146
laser beam 420
last quarter 5
latch 178, 277
latch bolt 186
lateral bar 501
lateral brush 365
lateral condyle of femur 99
lateral cutaneous nerve of thigh 108
lateral incisor 101
lateral line 74, 515
lateral moraine 30
lateral semicircular canal 116
lateral view of adult skull 100
lateral view of child's skull 100
lateral-adjustment lever 229
latex glove 460
latex glove case 456
latissimus dorsi 97
latrines 280
Latvia 450
laundry 439
laundry room 188
lava flow 28
lava layer 28
lawn 183, 230
lawn aerator 237
lawn care 237
lawn edger 233
lawn rake 237
leaching 48
lead 313, 515
lead pencil 312
lead screw 228
lead-in wire 199
leader 538
leading bunch 522
leading edge 393
leading motorcycle 522
leaf 51, 53, 54, 55, 125
leaf axil 55
leaf lettuce 126
leaf margins 55
leaf node 53
leaf vegetables 126
leaf, structure 55
leakproof cap 529
leather end 246
leather goods 274
leather goods shop 436
leather sheath 533
leather skin 478
leaves 65
Lebanon 452
lectern 446
ledger 187
ledger line 298
leech 519
leeks 124
left (free) safety 484
left atrium 103, 104
left attacker 487
left back 481, 487
left center 482
left channel 324
left cornerback 484
left defense 506
left defensive end 484
left defensive tackle 484
left field 475
left fielder 474
left forward 489
left guard 485
left kidney 107
left lung 103, 105
left midfielder 481
left pulmonary vein 104
left service court 491
left side 272
left tackle 485
left ventricle 103, 104
left wing 482, 507
leg 70, 76, 91, 93, 95, 202, 204, 205, 231, 247, 308, 493, 537
leg curl bar 501
leg extension bar 501
leg guard 476
leg-warmer 263
leghold trap 535
legume, section 60
legumes 130
lemon 134
lemon balm 142
lemur 91
length, unit 426
lengthwise bulkhead 384
lens 119, 332, 419
lens accessories 314
lens cap 314
lens case 272
lens hood 314
lens release button 314
lens system 420
lenses 314, 419
lentils 130
leopard 89
leotard 263
Lesotho 452
lesser covert 78
letter opener 339
letter scale 339
letters to the editor 313
lettuce 126
leucoplast 50
level crossing 375
leveling foot 212, 213, 214
leveling screw 423
lever 178, 197, 222, 265, 534
lever cap 229
lever corkscrew 170
Liberia 451
libero 487
library 433, 444
license plate light 352
lichen 50
lichen, structure 50
lichens 50
lid 174, 177, 178, 179, 180, 181, 211, 212, 215, 225, 417
Liechtenstein 450
lierne 284
life buoy 387, 457
life raft 383
life support system 10
life support system controls 10
lifeboat 382, 386
lift arm 399
lift bridge 345
lift chain 196
lift door 363
lift span 345
lift-arm cylinder 399
lift-fan air inlet 383
lifting chain 396
lifting hook 403
ligament 73
ligature 306
light 7, 8, 9, 380
light aircraft 394
light bar 455, 457
light bar controller 457
light ray 419
light shield 7
lighted mirror 269
lighthouse 381
lighting 199, 269
lighting cable 361
lighting grid 291
lighting technician 291
lightning 41
lightning arrester 407
lightning rod 183, 413
lights 206, 293
lily 56
lily of the valley 56
lima beans 131
limb 63, 535
limb top 421
lime 134
limit switch 287
limousine 347
limpet 157

linden 148
line 225, 298, 443
line guide 537
line judge 485, 496
line map 378
line of scrimmage 485
linear 55
lineman's pliers 217
linen 204
linen chest 203
linen room 439
lines of latitude 22
lines of longitude 22
linesman 481, 487, 490, 494, 507
lingerie shop 436
lingual tonsil 118
lining 240, 244, 245, 262, 274, 509
lint filter 212
lint trap 213
lintel 192, 285
lion 89
lip 83, 87
lip brush 266
lip makeup 266
lipid droplet 50
lipliner 266
lipstick 266
liqueur glass 165
liquid 414, 415
liquid crystal display 315, 320, 326, 327, 424
liquid crystal display (LCD) television 318
liquid eyeliner 266
liquid foundation 266
liquid mascara 266
liquid/gas separator 359
lists 282
litchi 137
literary supplement 313
lithosphere 26, 44
Lithuania 450
little finger 115
little finger hook 307
liver 103, 106, 154
livestock car 377
living room 188, 528
lizard 77
llama 84
loading dock 435
loading door 192
loading hopper 364
loaf pan 179
loafer 242
loan services 442
lob 491
lobate 55
lobate toe 79
lobby 390, 435, 439, 440, 442
lobe 79
lobe bronchus 105
lobster 71, 158
lobster, morphology 71
local station 316
location of the statue 279
lock 185, 186, 202, 211, 275, 277, 352, 372, 482
lock dial 332
lock nut 425
lock rail 185
lock washer 222
lock-on button 227, 229
locket 264
locking button 208
locking device 209, 219, 535
locking lever 224
locking pliers 222
locking ring 221
locknut 197
locomotive, diesel-electric 377
loculus 58
lodging 512
log carrier 193
log chute 406
log tongs 193
loin 83, 93, 95
loin chop 153
long jump 472
long residue 405
long service line 494
long track 508
long-range jet 392
longan 136
longitudinal dunes 36
loop 245, 250, 262, 343
loose powder 266
loose powder brush 266
loosehead prop 482
lopping shears 234
lore 78
loudspeaker 325, 455
loudspeaker system select buttons 322
loudspeaker terminals 322
loudspeakers 324
lounge 386, 439
louse 69
louver-board 285
louvered window 287
lovage 142
love seat 200, 439
low beam 352
low cloud, type 39
low clouds 42
low fuel warning light 355
low-pressure area 43
low-pressure center 39
low-speed shaft 413
low-tension distribution line 198
lower blade guard 227
lower bowl 181
lower confining bed 402
lower eyelid 75, 87, 119
lower guard retracting lever 227
lower lateral lobe 62
lower lateral sinus 62
lower lip 116, 305
lower lobe 105
lower mandible 78
lower mantle 26
lower radiator hose 358
lower shell 511
lubricant eye drops 272
lubricants plant 405
lubricating oils 405
Luer-Lock tip 460
luff 519
lug 308
lug wrench 356
luggage 276
luggage carrier 277
luggage elastic 277
luggage rack 361, 369, 523
lumbar pad 486
lumbar plexus 108
lumbar vertebrae 99
luminous intensity, unit 426
lunar eclipse 5
lunar features 5
lung 105
lungs 105
lunula 114, 115
lunule 73
lupines 130
lutz 509
Luxembourg 449
Lybia 451
lynx 88
lyre 297
lysosome 66

M

macadamia nuts 133
macaque 91
macaw 80
Macedonia 450
machicolation 282
machine hall 406, 407
machinery shed 122
Mackenzie River 16
mackerel 159
macro lens 314
macronucleus 66
macula 119
Madagascar 20, 452
magazine 313
magenta 418
magma 28, 33
magma chamber 28, 402
magnesium powder 497
magnet 341, 416
magnetic compass 533
magnetic damping system 422
magnetic field 318, 416
magnetic gasket 211
magnetic lid holder 180
magnetic needle 533
magnetic separation 49
magnetic stripe 441
magnetism 416
magnifier 531
magnifying glass 421
main bronchus 105
main circuit vent 194
main cleanout 194
main deck 385
main drain 184
main engine 13
main entrance 435, 445, 465
main frame 400
main landing gear 393
main line 375
main lodge 512
main loudspeaker 321
main rooms 188
main scale 425
main scope tube 420
main sewer 434
main stand 367
main switch 198
main transformer 376
main tube 8, 9
main vent 28
main waiting room 465
Maine coon 87
mainsail 520
mainsheet 520
maintenance 346
maintenance hangar 389
maître d' 438
major inner reaping throw 499
major motions 470
major outer reaping throw 499
makeup 266
makeup artist 290
malanga 129
malar region 78
Malawi 452
Malawi, Lake 20
Malaysia 453
Maldives 453
male 426
male cone 65
male ferrule 536, 537
male reproductive organs 111
male urethra 111
Mali 451
mallet 220, 308
mallets 309
malleus 116
malt vinegar 141
Malta 450
mammary gland 113
man 92
mandarin 134
mandible 67, 74, 98, 100
mandolin 297
mandoline 170
mandown alarm 454
mane 83
maneuvering area 388
maneuvering engine 13
manganese mix 417
mango 137
mango chutney 141
mangosteen 136
manhole 404, 434
manicure set 265
manned maneuvering unit 10
mantel 192
mantel shelf 192
mantid 69
mantle 72, 73
manual jack 361
manual release 511
manual revolving door 286
manual sorting 49
manuals 305
Manx 87
map projections 22
map, physical 24
map, political 23
map, road 25
map, urban 25
map, weather 39
maple 64
maple syrup 149
maquis 44
margarine 149
margin 55
marginal shield 76
Mariana Trench 34
Marie Byrd Land 15
marinade spices 139
marine 40
marine diesel 405
marine mammals 90
maritime communications 317
maritime transport 381
marker 312
marker light 364, 365
marking tools 225
marmoset 91
marrow 154
Mars 2, 3
Marshall Islands 453
marten 88
mascara brush 266
mask 476
mason's trowel 216
masonry drill 228
masonry nail 220
masonry tools 216
mass 27
mass, unit 426
massage glove 267
masseter 96
mast 281, 375, 396, 519, 520
mast foot 519
mast sleeve 519
mast-operating lever 396
master bedroom 189
master cylinder 357
masthead 313, 519
masthead light 383
mastoid fontanelle 100
mastoid process 100
mat 499
material handling 396
mathematics 427
matinee-length necklace 264
mating adaptor 11
matter 414
mattress 204, 205, 460, 530
mattress cover 204
Mauritania 451
Mauritius 452
maxilla 74, 98, 100, 117
maxillary bone 101
meadow 122
mean position 418
meander 32
measurement of length 425
measurement of temperature 424
measurement of thickness 425
measurement of time 424
measurement of weight 422
measuring beaker 171
measuring cup 171
measuring cups 171
measuring devices 424
measuring spoons 171
measuring tools 225
meat 152
meat grinder 170
meat keeper 211
meat thermometer 171
Mecca, direction 447
mechanical mouse 332
mechanical pencil 312
mechanical stage 421
mechanical stage control 421
mechanics 346
medial condyle of femur 99
medial moraine 30
median 343
median lingual sulcus 118
median nerve 108
median strip 434
medical equipment storage room 465
medical gas cylinder 464
medical records 465
medical team 499
medications, forms 467
Mediterranean Sea 14, 18, 20
Mediterranean subtropical 40
medium-format SLR (6 x 6) 315
medium-tension distribution line 198
medulla 107
medulla oblongata 109
meeting room 439, 442, 445
Meissner's corpuscle 114
Melanesia 15
melody strings 296
melon 135
melon baller 173
melons 135
melting 414
meltwater 30
memo pad 338
memorial board 447
memory button 322, 326, 327
memory cancel 337
memory card reader 329, 333
memory recall 337
men's bag 276
men's clothing 244
men's gloves 243
men's headgear 238
men's shoes 240
meninges 109
menorah 447
menu button 315, 319, 320, 326, 329
menu key 327
Mercury 2, 3
mercury bulb 424
mercury thermometer 461
merguez sausages 156
méridienne 200
mesa 36
mesh 205, 493
mesh bag 162
mesh strainer 171
mesocarp 57, 58, 59
mesopause 37
mesosphere 37
metal arm 236
metal counterhoop 308
metal frame 304
metal rod 309
metal sorting 49
metal structure 374
metallic contact grid 410
metamorphic rocks 26
meteorological forecast 38
meteorology 37
meteorology, station model 39
meter 426
metered dose inhaler 467
Mexico 448
Mexico, Gulf 16
mezzanine 293, 378
mezzanine stairs 189
micro compact car 347
microfilament 66
micrometer caliper 425
Micronesia, Federated States 453
micronucleus 66
microphone 320, 327, 328, 332, 337, 456
microphones 457
microscope 421
microscope, binocular 421
microscopes 421
microtubule 66
microwave oven 164, 178
microwave relay station 334
microwaves 418
Mid-Atlantic Ridge 34
mid-calf length 247
Mid-Indian Ridge 34
mid-ocean ridge 33
middle cloud, type 39
middle clouds 42
middle covert 78
middle ear 116
middle finger 115
middle leg 67
middle leg, honeybee 68
middle lobe 105
middle nasal concha 117
middle panel 185
middle phalanx 114
middle piece 111
middle primary covert 78
middle sole 262
middle toe 78
middy 255
MIDI cable 311
MIDI port 329
midrange 324
midrange pickup 303
midrib 51, 55, 60
midriff band 259
mihrab 447
mihrab dome 447
military communications 317
milk 150
milk chocolate 148
milk cup 163

Milky Way 6
millet 61, 143
millet: spike 61
Mimas 3
minaret 447
minbar 447
mini stereo sound system 325
mini-DV camcorder: front view 320
mini-DV camcorder: rear view 320
minibus 363
minivan 347
mink 88
minor surgery room 462
mint 142
minus/negative 427
minute 428
minute hand 424
Miranda 3
mirror 195, 366, 368, 369, 421, 439, 523
miscellaneous articles 341
Mississippi River 16
mist 41
miter box 226
miter latch 226
miter saw, hand 226
miter scale 226
mitochondrion 50, 66
mitral valve 104
mitt 243
mitten 243
mittens 260
mixed forest 44
mixing bowl 176
mixing bowls 172
moat 282
mobile remote servicer 11
mobile unit 316
mobile X-ray unit 462
moccasin 242
mock pocket 251
mode selectors 326
modem 334
moderator 408
modes of payment 441
Mohorovicic discontinuity 26
moistener 339
molar, cross section 101
molars 101
molasses 149
Moldova 450
mole 426
molecule 414
mollusks 72, 157
Monaco 450
money 441
Mongolia 453
mongoose 88
monitor 471
monitor lizard 77
monkfish 160
monohulls 521
mons pubis 112
Montenegro 450
monument 25
Moon 2, 4, 5
Moon's orbit 4, 5
Moon, phases 5
mooring winch 385
moose 85
mop 215
moped 369
moraine 30
mordent 299
morels 123
Morocco 451
morphology of a bird 78
morphology of a bivalve shell 73
morphology of a butterfly 67
morphology of a dog 86
morphology of a dolphin 90
morphology of a female shark 74
morphology of a frog 75
morphology of a gorilla 91
morphology of a honeybee: worker 68
morphology of a horse 83
morphology of a lobster 71
morphology of a perch 74
morphology of a rat 82
morphology of a snail 72
morphology of a spider 70
morphology of a turtle 76
morphology of a univalve shell 73
morphology of a venomous snake: head 76
morphology of an octopus 72
mortadella 156
mortar 170
mosaic 280
mosque 447
mosquito 69
moss 51
moss, structure 51
mosses 51
motion detector 286
motocross motorcycle 525
motor 212, 213, 214, 227, 229, 237
motor car 380
motor end plate 110
motor home 361
motor neuron 110
motor root 109, 110
motor scooter 369
motor sports 524
motor truck 376
motor unit 176, 177, 180, 208, 272, 376
motor vehicle pollution 47
motor yacht 385
motorcycle 366, 368
motorcycle dashboard 368
motorcycle-mounted camera 522
motorcycles 369
motorcycling 525
motto 441
mouflon 84
mountain 29
mountain bike 373
mountain biking 522
mountain lodge 512
mountain mass 24
mountain range 5, 24, 26
mountain slope 29
mountain torrent 29
mounting bracket 535
mounting plate 199
mouse pad 332
mouse port 329
mouse, mechanical 332
mouth 71, 72, 73, 75, 94, 116, 305
mouthparts 68
mouthpiece 306, 307, 311, 467, 498
mouthpiece receiver 307
mouthpipe 307
mouthwash 272
movable bridges 344
movable jaw 223, 224
movable maxillary 76
movable stands 444
movements of an airplane 395
movie theater 294, 386, 432, 436
movies' titles and schedules 294
Mozambique 452
Mozambique Channel 20
mozzarella 150
Mt Everest 37
mud flap 349, 364, 365
mud injection hose 403
mud pit 403
mud pump 403
mudflow 31
muff 276
muffin pan 172
muffler 351, 369
muffler felt 304
muffler pedal 304
mule 84, 242
mullet 160
multi-image jump button 315
multigrain bread 145
multihulls 521
multipack 163
multiple exposure mode 314
multiplied by 427
multiply key 337
multipurpose solution 272
multipurpose tool 217
mummy 530
mung beans 131
Munster 151
muntin 185, 186
muscle fiber 110
muscles 96
museum 433
mushroom 52
mushroom, structure 52
mushrooms 123
music 296
music room 444
music stand 305, 311
music store 436
musical instrument digital interface cable 311
musical instruments, traditional 296
musical notation 298
muskmelon 135
muslin 171
mustard 140
mute 307, 319
muzzle 83, 86, 87, 534
mycelium 52
myelin sheath 110
myocardium 104
myopia 419

N

naan 145
nacelle 413
nacelle, cross-section 413
nail 220
nail bed 114
nail buffer 265
nail care 265
nail cleaner 265
nail clippers 265
nail enamel 265
nail file 265
nail matrix 114
nail nick 531
nail scissors 265
nail set 220
nail shaper 265
nail whitener pencil 265
nailing tools 220
nails 220
naked strangle 499
name of the currency 441
nameplate 228, 313
Namib Desert 20
Namibia 452
naos 279
nape 78, 93, 95
nasal bone 100, 117
nasal cavity 105
nasal fossae 117
NASCAR car 524
nasopharynx 117
national broadcasting network 316
national park 25
nationality 497
natural 299
natural arch 35
natural environment 504
natural greenhouse effect 46
natural sponge 267
Nauru 453
nautical sports 516
nave 285
navel 92, 94
navigation button 319
navigation key 327
navigation light 383, 393
Nazca Plate 27
Neapolitan coffee maker 181
neck 76, 83, 93, 94, 95, 101, 111, 167, 297, 301, 302, 303, 318
neck end 245
neck of femur 99
neck pad 486
neck roll 204
neck strap 458
neck support 525
neckhole 247
necklaces 264
necktie 245
nectarine 132
needle 36, 460
needle hub 460
needle-nose pliers 217
negative contact 410, 411
negative meniscus 419
negative plate 359
negative plate strap 359
negative region 410
negative terminal 359, 416, 417
negligee 256
neon lamp 217
neon tester 217
Nepal 453
Neptune 2, 3
nerve 114
nerve fiber 114
nerve termination 114
nerve, olfactory 117
nervous system 108
nervous system, central 109
nervous system, peripheral 108
nest of tables 202
net 487, 489, 491, 493, 495
net band 491
net judge 491
net support 493
Netherlands 449
nettle 127
network connection 198
network port 329
neurons 110
neutral conductor 198
neutral indicator 368
neutral line 416
neutral zone 484, 507
neutron 414
Nevis 449
New Caledonia 15
new crescent 5
New Guinea 15, 453
new moon 5
new shekel 440
New Zealand 15, 453
newborn children's clothing 260
newel post 191
Newfoundland Island 16
news items 313
newsgroup 335
newspaper 313
newspaper shop 437
newt 75
newton 426
next 328
next/fast-forward button 326
nib 312
Nicaragua 448
nictitating membrane 87
Niger 451
Niger River 20
Nigeria 451
night deposit box 443
nightgown 256
nightingale 80
nightshot button 320
nightwear 256
Nile 20
nimbostratus 42
nipple 92, 94, 113
nitric acid emission 48
nitrogen oxide emission 48
no. 8 482
nocking point 535
node 416
node of Ranvier 110
nonagon 429
nonbiodegradable pollutants 47
nonbreaking space 330
nonreusable residue waste 49
noodles 147
nori 123
normal vision 419
North 23
North America 14, 16, 34
North American Plate 27
North Korea 453
North Pole 21
north pole 416
North Sea 14, 18
North-Northeast 23
North-Northwest 23
Northeast 23
Northern hemisphere 21
Northern leopard frog 75
northern right whale 90
Northwest 23
Norway 450
Norwegian Sea 18
nose 82, 83, 94, 117, 392, 526, 534
nose landing gear 392
nose leather 87
nose of the quarter 240, 262
nose pad 273
nosing 191
nostril 74, 75, 76, 78, 83, 117
notation, musical 298
notch 244, 422, 473, 503
notched double-edged thinning scissors 270
notched edge 270
notched lapel 248
notched single-edged thinning scissors 270
note symbols 299
nozzle 12, 216, 219, 236
nubby tire 525
nuclear energy 408
nuclear energy, production of electricity 408
nuclear envelope 50, 66
nuclear fission 415
nuclear reactor 409
nuclear waste 48
nuclear whorl 73
nucleolus 50, 66, 112
nucleus 6, 50, 66, 110, 112, 414
nucleus splitting 415
number 473
number buttons 326
number key 328, 337
number plate 525
numbering machine 338
numeric keyboard 423
numeric keypad 331, 338
numeric lock 331
numeric lock key 331
nurse 464
nurses' lounge 465
nurses' station (ambulatory emergency) 463
nurses' station (major emergency) 462
nut 222, 223, 301, 302, 303
nutcracker 170
nutmeg 138
nutmeg grater 170
nuts 223
nylon thread 237

O

oak 64
oar 501
oasis 32, 36
oat flour 144
oats 61, 143
oats: panicle 61
Oberon 3
obituaries 313
object 419
object balls 502
objective 421
objective lens 8, 314, 327, 420
oblique fissure 105
oboe 306
oboes 295
observation deck 391
observation post 7
observation room 462, 465
observation window 13
observatory 7
obturator nerve 108
obtuse angle 428
occipital bone 99, 100
occipitalis 97
ocean 5, 24, 45
ocean floor 33
ocean ridges 34
ocean trenches 34
ocean weather station 38
Oceania 14, 15
Oceania and Polynesia 453
oceanic crust 26
oche 471
octave 298
octave mechanism 306
octopus 72, 157
octopus, morphology 72
odd pinnate 55
odometer 355
off-road motorcycle (dirtbike) 369
office 346, 374, 438, 439
office automation 312, 329
office building 381, 432, 435
office tower 435
official signature 441
officials' bench 507
offshore well 404
Ogen melon 135
ohm 426
oil 403
oil drain plug 360
oil pan 235, 360

oil pan gasket 360
oil pollution 48
oil pressure warning indicator 368
oil spill 48
oil terminal 381
oil warning light 355
okapi 84
okra 128
old crescent 5
old-fashioned glass 165
olecranon 99
olfactory bulb 117
olfactory mucosa 117
olfactory nerve 117
olfactory tract 117
olive oil 149
olives 128
Oman 452
Oman, Gulf 19
on-board computer 354
on-deck circle 474
on-off button 180
on-off indicator 269
on-off light 327
on-off switch 177, 180, 181, 206, 208, 209, 218, 269, 270, 271, 272, 314
on-off/volume 326
one 427
one hundred 427
one pair 468
one thousand 427
one-arm shoulder throw 499
one-bar shoe 241
one-person tent 529
one-storey house 289
one-way head 221
onion 124
online game 335
oolong tea 148
Oort cloud 2
Op-Ed article 313
open crate 162
open end wrench 223
open stringer 191
open strings 296
open-air terrace 387
open-face spinning reel 537
opening 243
opening, utensils 170
opera glasses 273
opera house 432
opera-length necklace 264
operating instructions 346
operating mask 459
operating panel 287
operating room 464, 465
operating suite 464
operating table 464
operation keys 442, 443
operator's cab 397
operculum 74
ophthalmology room 463
opisthodomos 279
opposable thumb 91
optic chiasm 109
optic nerve 119
optical mouse 332
optical scanner 121
optical sensor 332
optical sorting 49
optician 437
optics 418
oral cavity 105, 106
oral hygiene center 272
oral irrigator 272
orange 134
orange, section 58
orangutan 91
orbicularis oculi 96
orbiculate 55
orbital-action selector 227
orbiter 12, 13
orchard 122
orchestra 278, 295
orchestra pit 292
orchid 56
order 285
ordinary die 468
oregano 142
organ 305
organ console 305
organ meat 154
Orinoco River 17
ornamental kale 126
ornamental tree 122, 182, 230
ornaments 299
ortho-cane 466
oscillating light 455
oscillating sprinkler 236
ostrich 81
ostrich egg 155
ottoman 201
outboard engine 385
outdoor leisure 528
outer bull 471
outer circle 515
outer core 26
outer lip 73
outer planets 2
outer ring 441
outer table 469
outer toe 78
outfield fence 475
outlet 361
output devices 333
output jack 303
output tray 333
outrigger 397, 400, 455
outside counter 240
outside linebacker 484
outside mirror 348, 362
outside mirror control 352
outside ticket pocket 244
outsole 240, 263
outwash plain 30
oval head 221
ovary 56, 112, 113
ovate 55
oven 164, 210
oven thermometer 171
over-blouse 255
overall standings scoreboard 496
overalls 254, 260, 261
overbed table 464
overcoat 248, 251
overflow 194, 195
overflow protection switch 214
overflow tube 196
overhead frame 401
overhead guard 396
overlay flooring 190
overpass 343, 344
oversized shirt 255
ovule 56
owl 81
ox 85
oxbow 32
oxbow lake 32
oxford shoe 240
oxygen outlet 464
oxygen pressure actuator 10
oxygenated blood 104
oyster 123
oyster fork 168
oyster knife 169
oysters, cupped Pacific 157
ozone layer 37

P

pace 83
Pacific Ocean 14, 15, 19
Pacific Plate 27
Pacific salmon 161
Pacific-Antarctic Ridge 34
Pacinian corpuscle 114
package 163
packaged integrated circuit 417
packaging 162
packaging products 120
packer body 364
packing tape dispenser 341
pad 478
pad arm 273
pad plate 273
padded base 489
padded envelope 339
padded upright 489
paddy field 47
page down 331
page down key 331
page up 331
page up key 331
pagoda 283
pail 215
painkillers 461
paint roller 219
painting 219
pair 509
pajamas 256, 261
Pakistan 452
palatine tonsil 118
palatoglossal arch 116
Palau 453
paling fence 230
pallet truck 396
palm 115, 243, 477
palm grove 36
palm of a glove 243
palm tree 64
palmaris brevis 96
palmaris longus 96
palmate 55
palmette 200
pan 422, 423, 535
pan hook 422
Panama 448
panama 238
Panama, Gulf 17
Panama, Isthmus 16
pancetta 156
pancreas 106
pane 186
panel 185, 246, 259
panoramic window 435
panpipe 297
pantograph 376
pantry 164, 188
pants 246, 254, 263, 476, 486, 506, 525
panty corselette 258
panty girdle 259
panty hose 257
papaya 137
paper clip holder 341
paper clips 341
paper collection unit 49
paper fasteners 341
paper feed button 333, 443
paper feed light 333
paper guide 328
paper punch 340
paper recycling container 49
paper separation 49
paper shredder 341
paper sorting 49
paperboard separation 49
paperboard sorting 49
papilla 114, 119
papillary muscle 104
paprika 139
Papua New Guinea 15, 453
par 5 hole 504
parabolic dune 36
paraffins 405
Paraguay 448
parallel 22
parallel bars 496, 497
parallel electrical circuit 416
parallel port 329
parallelepiped 429
parallelogram 429
paramecium 66
Paraná River 17
parapet 344
parapet walk 282
parboiled rice 147
parcels office 374
parchment paper 162
parietal bone 99, 100
parietal pleura 105
paring knife 169
park 25, 433
parka 249
parking 375, 435, 504, 512
parking area 389, 430, 445
parking brake lever 354
parking lot 381, 390
Parmesan 151
parquet 190
parsley 142
parsnip 129
parterre 293
partial eclipse 4, 5
partially reflecting mirror 420
partition 60, 457
partlow chart 365
partridge 80
parts 200, 201, 204
parts of a bicycle 370
parts of a circle 428
parts of a shoe 240
pascal 426
pass 29
passbook update slot 442
passenger cabin 383, 386, 387, 393
passenger car 376, 380
passenger cars, types 376
passenger liner 386
passenger platform 374
passenger seat 369
passenger station 374, 375
passenger terminal 381, 389, 390
passenger train 374
passenger transfer vehicle 391
passing lane 343
passion fruit 136
passport case 275
passport control 391
pasta 146
pasta maker 170
pastern 83
pastry bag and nozzles 172
pastry blender 172
pastry brush 172
pastry cutting wheel 172
pastry shop 437
Patagonia 17
patch pocket 244, 249, 260
patella 98
patera 200
path 230
pathology laboratory 465
patient 464
patient room 464
patio 182, 230
patio door 164, 188
patrol and first aid station 512
pattypan squash 129
pause 331
pause button 323
pause/break key 331
pause/still button 319
paver 230
pavilion 432
pawn 470
pay phone 294, 437, 438, 463
PC card slot 336
pe-tsai 126
pea 60
pea jacket 251
peach 132
peach, section 57
peacock 81
peak 29, 238, 239, 458
peak-level meter 323
peaked lapel 244
peanut 130
peanut oil 149
pear 133
pear-shaped body 297
peas 130
pecan nuts 133
peccary 84
pectoral deck 501
pectoral fin 74, 90
pectoral limb 103
pectoralis major 96
pedal 302, 308, 370, 372, 473, 501, 522
pedal key 305
pedal keyboard 305
pedal pushers 254
pedal rod 304
pedal with wide platform 522
pedestal 302
pedestrian call button 434
pedestrian crossing 434
pedestrian lights 434
pedicel 59, 62
pediment 279
pedipalp 70
peduncle 56, 57, 58, 59, 62
peeler 169
peg 202, 224, 301, 302
peg box 301
pelerine 251
pelican 80
pellets 534
peltate 55
pelvic fin 74
pelvic limb 103
pen 27, 122, 312
pen holder 274
pen-blade 531
penalty arc 480
penalty area 480
penalty bench 507
penalty bench official 507
penalty marker 480
penalty spot 480
pencil 312, 409
pencil sharpener 341
pencil-point tip 218
pendant 264
penguin 80
penholder grip 493
peninsula 24
penis 92, 111
penne 146
penstock 406, 407
pentagon 429
penumbra shadow 4, 5
pepino 137
pepper shaker 166
pepper spray 456
pepperoni 156
percent 427
percent key 337
perch 160
perch, morphology 74
perching bird 79
percolator 181
percussion instruments 308
percussion section 295
perforated toe cap 240
perforation 243
performance tire 358
performing arts 294
perfume shop 436
pergola 230
pericardium 105
pericarp 60
periodontal ligament 101
peripheral freeway 431
peripheral nervous system 108
peristome 66
peristyle 279, 280
peritoneum 111, 112
permanent pasture 122
peroneus longus 96
peroxide 461
peroxisome 66
perpendicular 428
perpetual snows 29
Persian 87
Persian Gulf 19
personal adornment 264
personal articles 264, 271
personal communications 317
personal computer 329
personal identification number pad 443
personal radio cassette player 325
personal watercraft 523
Peru 448
Peru-Chile Trench 34
peso 440
pesticide 47, 48
pestle 170
pet food 121
pet shop 436
petal 56
petiolar sinus 62
petiole 52, 55
petrochemical industry 405
petrochemicals 405
petroleum trap 403
pew 446
pharmacy 436, 462, 465
pharynx 105, 106
phase conductor 198
phases of the Moon 5
pheasant 81, 154
pheasant egg 155
Philippine Plate 27
Philippine Trench 34
Philippines 19, 453
philtrum 117
phloem 63
Phobos 2
phosphorescent coating 199
photo booth 437
photo credit line 313
photocopier 442
photographer 436
photography 314
photon 420
photoreceptors 119
photoshot button 320
photosphere 4
photosynthesis 54

photovoltaic arrays 11
phyllo dough 145
physical map 24
physician 464, 498
physics 418
pi 428
pia mater 109
piano 295, 304
piccolo 295, 306
pick 233
pickguard 303
pickling onions 124
pickup selector 303
pickup truck 347
pickups 303
pictograms 330
picture tube 318
pie pan 172
pier 285, 344
pierce lever 180
pierced earrings 264
pig 84
pigeon 81, 154
pigsty 122
pika 82
pike 160
pike perch 160
pike pole 454
pike position 518
pile 190
pile carpet 190
pile dwelling 288
pillar 27, 283, 284, 302
pillbox hat 239
pillion footrest 367, 368
pillow 204
pillow protector 204
pillowcase 204
pilot 376, 377
pilot house 385
pin 199, 454
pin base 199
pin block 304
PIN pad 443
pinch 199
pine needles 65
pine nuts 133
pine seed 65
pineal body 109
pineapple 136
pinecone 65
pink ball 503
pink pepper 138
pinna 52, 82
pinnacle 282, 284
pinnatifid 55
pinto beans 131
pip 58, 468
pipe 209, 224
pipe clamp 224
pipe section 193
pipe wrench 216
pipeline 404
pistachio nuts 133
pistil 56
pistol 456
pistol grip 534
pistol grip handle 218, 228
pistol nozzle 236
piston 357
piston head 360
piston lever 216
piston release 216
piston ring 360
piston skirt 360
pit 57, 76
pit lane 524
pita bread 145
pitch 395, 475, 479
pitch and modulation switch 310
pitcher 474, 475
pitcher's mound 475
pitcher's plate 475
pitchfork comb 268
pith 63
Pitot tube 525
pits 524
pituitary gland 109
pivot 217, 270, 271, 533
pivot cab upper structure 400
placing judge 516
plaice 161
plain 24, 32
plan 279, 285
plane 229
plane projection 22
plane surfaces 428
planets 2
planets, inner 3
planets, outer 2
planisphere 14
plano-concave lens 419
plano-convex lens 419
plant 53
plant cell 50
plant litter 54
plant, structure 53
plantain 136
plantaris 97
planting tools 231
plasma 104
plasma membrane 66
plasma television 318
plasmodesma 50
plaster room 463
plastic case 534
plastic film (cellophane) 162
plastic film capacitor 417
plastics sorting 49
plastron 76
plate 178, 269, 531
plate grid 359
plateau 24, 29
platelet 104
platform 219, 363, 379, 390, 423, 516, 526
platform edge 374, 379
platform entrance 374
platform ladder 219
platform number 374
platform shelter 375
platform, 10 m 518
platform, 3 m 518
platform, 5 m 518
platform, 7.5 m 518
platter 166
play 328
play button 319, 323
play/pause button 326
player positions 474, 481, 489
player's number 486, 488, 506
player's stick 506
players 492
players' bench 485, 487, 506
players' positions 482
playing area 471
playing field 480
playing surface 493
playing surfaces 492
playpen 205
pleasure garden 230
pleats 253
plectrum 297
pleural cavity 105
plexus of nerves 101
pliers 222
plug 198, 228, 324, 326
plug adapter 198, 271
plum sauce 141
plumber's snake 216
plumbing 194
plumbing system 194
plumbing tools 216
plums 132
plums, Japanese 133
plunger 216, 460
plus or minus 427
plus/positive 427
Pluto 3
pneumatic armlet 461
pocket 225, 274, 502, 505
pocket calculator 337
pocket handkerchief 244
podcasting 335
podium 283, 435, 444
point 167, 169, 301, 312, 469, 471, 538
point guard 489
point of interest 25
pointed tab end 245
pointer 422, 423
points 492
poisonous mushroom 52
poker 193
poker die 468
Poland 450
polar axis 7
polar bear 89
polar climates 40
polar ice cap 40
polar lights 37
polar tundra 40
polarizing filter 314
Polaroid® camera 315
pole 321, 490
pole grip 514
pole position 524
pole shaft 514
pole vault 472
police car 457
police officer 456
police station 433
political map 23
politics 448
pollen basket 68
pollutants, non-biodegradable 47
polluting gas emission 47
pollution, agricultural 47
pollution, air 47
pollution, domestic 47
pollution, industrial 47
pollution, land 47
pollution, motor vehicle 47
pollution, oil 48
pollution, water 48
polo dress 252
polo shirt 255, 492
polygons 429
Polynesia 453
pome fruits 133
pomegranate 136
pomelo 134
pommel horse 496
poncho 251
pond 230, 504
pons Varolii 109
Pont-l'Évêque 151
poodle 86
pool 184, 502
pop-up tent 529
poplar 64
popping crease 479
poppy 56
poppy seeds 139
porch 183, 285, 447
porch dome 447
porcupine 82
pore 50, 60, 114
pork, cuts 153
Porro prism 420
port 431
port glass 165
port hand 387
portable CD/radio/cassette recorder 326
portable cellular telephone 327
portable compact disc player 325
portable digital audio player 326
portable fire extinguisher 454
portable radio 325
portable shower head 195
portable sound systems 325
portal 285
portal vein 103
porthole 386
portrait 441
Portugal 449
position indicator 287
position light 376, 395
position marker 302, 303
positive contact 410, 411
positive meniscus 419
positive plate 359
positive plate strap 359
positive region 410
positive terminal 359, 416, 417
positive/negative junction 410
post 412, 487, 495
post binder 339
post lantern 207
post mill 412
post office 433, 437
postage meter 339
poster 294
posterior adductor muscle 73
posterior chamber 119
posterior cutaneous nerve of thigh 108
posterior end 73
posterior fontanelle 100
posterior horn 109
posterior root 110
posterior rugae 93, 95
posterior semicircular canal 116
posterior view 93, 95, 97
postern 282
posting surface 341
potato masher 173
potatoes 124
pothole 31
pouch 162
pouch of Douglas 112
poultry 155
poultry shears 173
pound 440
pouring spout 215
powder blusher 266
powder puff 266
powdered milk 150
powdered mustard 140
powdered sugar 149
power adapter 336
power adapter port 336
power and backlight button 337
power button 318, 319, 321, 322, 323, 328, 329, 333, 336
power cable plug 329
power car 376
power cord 177, 227, 229, 269, 271, 322
power indicator 329
power light 333
power mower 237
power plant 406
power plug 326, 337
power source 416
power supply cord 270
power supply fan 329
power switch 311, 315, 329
power train 372
power, unit 426
power-on/paper-detect light 443
power/functions switch 320
practice green 504
prairie 24
prayer hall 447
precipitation 41, 45
precipitation area 39
precision sports 502
prehensile digit 91
premaxilla 74
premolars 101
prepared foods 121
prepuce 111
present state of weather 39
preset button 326
preset tuning button 322
press bar 501
pressed cheeses 151
pressed powder 266
pressure bar 304
pressure change 39
pressure control 272
pressure control valve 461
pressure cooker 174
pressure demand regulator 454
pressure gauge 461
pressure regulator 174, 529
pressure tube 409
pressure, unit 426
pressurized refuge 345
prevailing wind 43
previous 328
previous sets 492
previous/rewind button 326
price per gallon/liter 346
prickly pear 137
prickly sphagnum 51
primaries 78
primary consumers 45
primary covert 78
primary crash sensor 354
primary mirror 7
primary root 53
primate mammals 91
primates 91
prime focus 7
prime focus observing capsule 7
prime meridian 22
primer 534
princess seams 258
princess-seamed dress 252
principal's office 445
Principe 451
print cartridge light 333
print screen 331
print screen/system request key 331
printed circuit 417
printed circuit board 417
printer, ink jet 333
printing calculator 337
printout 423
prism binoculars 420
prisoner's dock 440
privacy curtain 464
private broadcasting network 316
private dressing room 290
proboscis 67
procedure checklist 10
producer 291
product code 423
production designer 290
production of electricity by the generator 408
production of electricity from geothermal energy 402
production of electricity from nuclear energy 408
production of electricity from wind energy 413
production platform 404
production well 402
professional training office 442
profile of the Earth's atmosphere 37
program selector 310
programmable buttons 332
programmable function keys 443
projection booth 294
projection device 365
projection room 294
projection screen 294
projector 294
proleg 67
promenade deck 386
prominence 4
pronaos 279
pronator teres 96
propagation 418
propane 405
propane accessories 529
propane gas cylinder 361
propellant 534
propeller 384, 386, 387
propeller duct 383
propeller shaft 387
property line 182
property person 291
propulsion module 316
proscenium 292
prosciutto 156
prosecution counsels' bench 440
prostate 111
protect tab 333
protection layer 10
protective cup 486, 507
protective equipment 486
protective goggles 522, 525
protective helmet 367, 372
protective plate 525
protective suit 525
protective surround 471
protective window 318
proton 414
protoneuron 110
province 23
pruning saw 234
pruning shears 234
pruning tools 234
pry bar 220
pseudopod 66
psychiatric examination room 462
psychiatric observation room 462
pubis 92, 94
public building 25
public garden 435
puck 507
Puerto Rico Trench 34
pull strap 277
pull tab 163
pulley 219, 360
pulling ring 460
Pullman case 277
pulmonary artery 102, 105
pulmonary trunk 104
pulmonary valve 104
pulmonary vein 102
pulp 58, 101
pulp chamber 101
pulpit 446, 447
pulsed ruby laser 420
pulverizer 402

pump 184, 212, 214, 241, 529
pump and motor assembly 357
pump island 346
pump nozzle 346
pump number 346
pump room 384
pumper 455
pumpernickel 145
pumping station 404
pumpkin 129
punch hole 240, 246, 263
punching bag 498
punching ball 498
pup tent 529
pupil 87, 119
purfling 301, 302
purse 275
purslane 127
push bar 286
push buttons 327
push frame 398
push rim 467
push-button 312
push-up bra 259
push-up stand 501
pusher 170, 180
pushing phase 514
putter 505
pygal shield 76
pyloric stomach 71
pyramid 278, 429
pyramid spot 502
pyramid, entrance 278
Pyrenees 18
python 77

Q

Qatar 452
qibla wall 447
quad cane 466
quadrant 428
quadrilateral 429
quail 81, 154
quail egg 155
quark 414
quarter 240, 262
quarter note 299
quarter rest 299
quarter window 349
quarter-deck 386
quarterback 485
quartet 300
quay 381, 430
quay ramp 381
quayside crane 381
quayside railway 381
queen 68, 468, 470
Queen Maud Land 15
queen's chamber 278
queen's side 470
quiche plate 172
quick ticket system 294
quill 312
quill brush 268
quince 133
quinoa 143
quintet 300

R

rabbi's seat 447
rabbit 82, 154
raccoon 88
race director 522
raceme 57
racing suit 508, 525
rack 174, 210, 214, 473, 503
racket sports 493
raclette 151
raclette with grill 179
radar 382, 383, 386, 387
radar display 457
radar mast 384
radar transceiver 457
radial nerve 108
radial passenger-loading area 389
radial thread 70
radiation 415
radiation zone 4
radiator 350, 358
radiator grille 364
radiator panel 13
radiators 11
radicchio 126
radicle 53, 63
radio 457
radio antenna 382, 384, 386, 387, 525
radio waves 418
radioactive nuclei 415
radioactivity, unit 426
radish 129
radius 98, 428
rafter 187
raglan 251
raglan sleeve 248, 251, 261
rail 202, 502
rail transport 374
railing 189
railroad line 25
railroad shuttle service 390
railroad station 25, 375, 430, 432
railroad track 432
railyard 430
rain 41
rain cap 193
rainbow 41
raincoat 248
rainfly 528, 529
raised handlebar 522
rake 233
rake comb 268
rally car 524
rambutan 137
ramekin 166
ramp 279, 281, 343, 526
rampart 282
random orbit sander 229
range hood 164, 210
rank insignia 456
Ranvier, node 110
ras el hanout 139
raspberries 132
raspberry, section 59
rat 82
rat, morphology 82
ratchet 221
ratchet box end wrench 223
ratchet knob 425
ratchet socket wrench 223
rattlesnake 77
raven 80
ravioli 146
razor clam 157
reach-in freezer 120
reactor 408
reactor building 409
reactor vessel 409
read/write head 333
reading lamp 206
reading light 457
reading mirror 10
reamer 177
rear apron 245
rear beam 422
rear brake 370
rear brake pedal 368
rear bumper 523
rear cargo rack 369
rear derailleur 370, 372
rear fender 369
rear foil 387
rear leg 201
rear light 370
rear propeller 384
rear rigid section 363
rear seat 353
rear shock absorber 367
rear sight 534
rear step 455
rearview mirror 354
récamier 200
receiver 321, 327, 490, 495
receiver volume control 327
receiving area 120
receiving tray 328
receptacle 51, 56, 59
receptacle analyzer 217
reception area 462, 465
reception desk 442
reception hall 447
reception level 439
rechargeable battery pack 320
recharging base 208
reclining back 460
record button 319, 323
record muting button 323
recording level control 323
recording media 319
recording mode 320
recording start/stop button 320
recording tape 319
recovery room 464
rectangle 429
rectangular 530
rectum 106, 111, 112
rectus abdominis 96
rectus femoris 96
recycling 49
recycling bin 49
recycling containers 49
Red 469
red 418
red alga 51
red ball 502, 503
red balls 503
red beam 318
red blood cell 104
red cabbage 126
red clamp 356
red kidney beans 131
red light 434
red onion 124
Red Sea 14, 19, 20
red sweet pepper 128
red whortleberries 132
red-kneed tarantula 70
redfish 161
reed 306
reed pipe 305
reel 236, 319
reel seat 536, 537
reentrant angle 428
referee 481, 483, 485, 487, 488, 498, 499, 507, 509, 516, 518
refill 312
refill tube 196
refinery 404, 431
refinery products 405
reflected solar radiation 46
reflecting cylinder 420
reflecting telescope 9
reflecting telescope, cross section 9
reflector 217, 365, 370, 523
refracting telescope 8
refracting telescope, cross section 8
refrigerated display case 438
refrigerated semitrailer 365
refrigeration unit 365
refrigerator 164, 211, 438
refrigerator car 377
refrigerator compartment 211
refrigerators 438
regular decagon 429
regular dodecagon 429
regular hendecagon 429
regular heptagon 429
regular hexagon 429
regular nonagon 429
regular octagon 429
regular octahedron 429
regular pentagon 429
reinforced toe 459
relay starting line 473
relay station 316
release lever 222
release of oxygen 54
relieving chamber 278
religion 446
remote control 319, 321
remote control sensor 318
remote control terminal 314, 315
remote manipulator system 11, 12
removable flagpole 504
removable hard disk 333
removable hard disk drive 333
renal artery 102, 107
renal hilus 107
renal papilla 107
renal pelvis 107
renal vein 102, 107
reniform 55
repeat button 323
repeat mark 298
repeater 317
reproductive organs, female 112
reproductive organs, male 111
reptiles 76, 77
Republic of the Congo 451
repulsion 416
reservoir 181, 406, 407
reset button 329, 424, 471
reset key 328
resident 464
residential district 431
residue waste, non-reusable 49
resistance adjustment 501
resistors 417
resonator 305, 309, 324
respirator 459
respiratory system 105
respiratory system protection 459
rest area 25
rest symbols 299
restaurant 386, 432, 435, 436, 438
restaurant review 313
restaurant, fast-food 437
restricted area 489
restricting circle 488
restroom 440, 443
restrooms 463, 465
results table 518
resurgence 31
resuscitation room 462
reticle 420
retina 119, 419
retractable handle 274, 277
retractable step 361
return 331
return crease 479
return spring 357
reverse 518
reverse light 352
reversing switch 221, 228
revolving nosepiece 421
revolving sprinkler 236
rewind button 323
Rhea 3
rhinoceros 85
rhizoid 51
rhizome 52
rhombus 429
rhubarb 125
rhythm selector 311
rias 35
rib 125, 273, 301, 302, 401, 458
rib joint pliers 222
rib pad 486
rib roast 152
ribbing 250, 261, 536
ribosome 50, 66
ribs 98
rice 61, 143, 147
rice noodles 147
rice paper 147
rice vermicelli 147
rice vinegar 141
rice: panicle 61
ricotta 150
ridge 29
riegel 30
rifle (rifled bore) 534
rigatoni 146
right (strong) safety 484
right angle 428
right ascension setting scale 8, 9
right atrium 103, 104
right attacker 487
right back 481, 487
right center 482
right channel 324
right cornerback 484
right defense 506
right defensive end 484
right defensive tackle 484
right field 475
right fielder 474
right forward 489
right guard 485
right kidney 107
right lung 103, 105
right midfielder 481
right pulmonary vein 104
right safety 484
right service court 491
right side 272
right tackle 485
right ventricle 103, 104
right wing 482, 507
rillettes 156
rim 273, 366, 371, 489
rim soup bowl 166
rime 41
rinceau 200
rind 58
ring 52, 273, 307, 423, 424, 498
ring binder 339
ring post 498
ring step 498
ringhandle 270
ringing volume control 327
rings 264, 496, 497
ringside 498
rink 506, 509
rink corner 506
rinse-aid dispenser 214
rip fence 227
ripeness 62
ripening 62
ripper 398
ripper cylinder 398
ripper shank 398
ripper tip tooth 398
rise 191
riser 191
rising warm air 43
river 24, 25, 32
river estuary 24, 35
river otter 88
rivet 169, 222
road 25, 430
road bicycle 373
road communications 317
road cycling competition 522
road flare 457
road map 25
road number 25
road racing 522
road system 342
road transport 342, 381
road tunnel 345
road, cross section 342
road-racing bicycle 522
road-racing cyclist 522
roadway 342, 345, 434
roast 152, 153
roasted coffee beans 148
roasting pans 174
Roberval's balance 422
robin 80
rock basin 30
rock candy 149
rock garden 230
rocker arm 360
rocking chair 200, 201
rockslide 31
rocky desert 36
rocky islet 35
Rocky Mountains 16
rod 119
rodent 82
rodents 82
roll 395
roll structure 525
roller 268, 332
roller cover 219
roller frame 219
roller shade 356
rolling pin 172
romaine lettuce 126
Roman amphitheater 281
Roman house 280
Roman metal pen 312
Roman numerals 427
Romania 450
Romano 151
romano beans 131
rompers 261
roof 183, 193, 283, 349, 361
roof pole 529
roof vent 194, 361
rook 470
room number 439
rooms, main 188
rooster 81

root 54, 101, 118, 167
root canal 101
root cap 53
root hairs 53
root of nail 114
root of nose 117
root rib 392
root system 53, 62
root vegetables 129
root-hair zone 63
rope 498
rope necklace 264
Roquefort 151
rose 56, 186, 236, 302
rose window 285
rosemary 142
Ross Ice Shelf 15
rotary cheese grater 170
rotary file 338
rotary system 403
rotary table 403
rotating dome 7
rotating drum 27
rotini 146
rotor 412, 537
rotor blade 395
rotor head 395
rotor hub 395
rotunda 435
rough 504
round brush 268
round head 221
route sign 362, 363
router 229, 334
row 272, 293
rowing machine 501
royal agaric 123
royal flush 468
rub protection 525
rubber 240
rubber boot 454
rubber bulb 460
rubber gasket 197
rubber stamp 338
rubber tip 219, 466
rubber wall 358
rubbing alcohol 461
rubbing strip 358
ruby cylinder 420
ruching 260
ruck 483
rudder 13, 383, 384, 386, 393, 520
rudder blade 384
Ruffini's corpuscle 114
ruffled rumba pants 260
ruffled skirt 253
rug 190
rug and floor brush 209
rugby 482
rugby ball 483
rugby player 483
rugby shirt 483
rugby shoe 483
rule 313
ruler 425, 531
rumba tights 260
rump 78
run 191
rung 219
runner 469
running shoe 262
runway 390
runway center line markings 390
runway designation marking 390
runway side stripe markings 390
runway threshold markings 391
runway touchdown zone marking 391
rupee 440
Russia 450
Russian module 11
Russian pumpernickel 145
rutabaga 129
Rwanda 451
rye 61, 143
rye bread 144
rye: spike 61
Ryukyu Trench 34

S

S-Video output 336
sacral plexus 108
sacristy 446
sacrum 98, 99
saddlebag 369
safari jacket 255
safe 443
safe deposit box 443
safety 454
safety area 499
safety binding 510, 511
safety boot 459
safety cage 473
safety earmuffs 458
safety glasses 458
safety goggles 458
safety handle 237
safety lighting 457
safety line 379
safety niche 345
safety rail 219, 377
safety scissors 265
safety tether 10
safety thermostat 213
safety valve 174, 408
saffron 138
safing sensor 354
sage 142
sagittal section 111, 112
Sahara Desert 20
sail 412, 519
sail cloth 412
sail panel 520
sailbar 412
sailboard 519
sailboat 520
sailing 520
Saint Bernard 86
Saint Kitts and Nevis 449
Saint Lawrence River 16
Saint Lucia 449
Saint Vincent and the Grenadines 449
salad bowl 166
salad dish 166
salad fork 168
salad plate 166
salad spinner 171
salamander 75
salami 156
salchow 509
saline lake 36
salivary gland 118
salivary glands 106
salmon, Atlantic 161
salmon, Pacific 161
salsify 129
salt 141
salt shaker 166
sambal oelek 141
Samoa 453
sampler 310
San Marino 450
sanctuary lamp 446
sand bar 33
sand bunker 504
sand island 35
sand paper 229
sand shoe 365
sandal 241, 242
sandbox 377
sanding disk 229
sanding pad 229
sandy desert 36
Sao Tome and Principe 451
saphenous nerve 108
sapodilla 137
sapwood 63
sardine 159
sarong 253
sartorius 96
sash frame 186
sash window 287
satchel bag 275
satellite 316
satellite earth station 335
satellite radio receiver 326
satellites 2
Saturn 2, 3
saucepan 175, 531
Saudi Arabia 452
sauté pan 175
savanna 44
savanna climate 40
savory 142
savoy cabbage 126
sawing tools 226
saxhorn 307
saxophone 306
scale 74, 76, 79, 225, 298, 424, 460, 533
scale leaf 54
scales 425
scallion 124
scallop 157
scampi 158
Scandinavian cracked bread 145
Scandinavian Peninsula 18
scapula 98, 99
scapular 78
scarlet runner beans 131
scatter cushion 204
scene 278
scenic route 25
schedules 374
schema of circulation 103
schnauzer 86
school 444
school bus 362
Schwann, sheath 110
sciatic nerve 108
science 414
science room 444
scientific air lock 13
scientific calculator 337
scientific instruments 7, 13
scientific symbols 426
scissors 461, 531
scissors crossing 375
sclera 119
score 497
scoreboard 471, 472, 492, 497, 499
scoreboard, current event 497
scoreboard, overall standings 496
scorer 487, 488
scorers 499
scorpion 70
Scotia Plate 27
scouring pad 215
scraper 219, 400, 514
screen 271, 318, 407, 439, 479
screen door 361
screen print 260, 261
screen window 528
screw 221, 301
screw base 199
screw cap 163
screw earring 264
screw locking nut 536, 537
screwdriver 221, 531
screwdriver bit 228
screwdriver, cordless 221
scrimmage: defense 484
scrimmage: offense 485
scroll 301
scroll case 407
scroll foot 200
scroll wheel 332
scrolling 331
scrolling lock key 331
scrotum 92, 111
scrub room 464
scrumhalf 482
scuffle hoe 233
sea 5, 24, 32
sea bag 276
sea bass 160
sea bream 159
sea kale 126
sea lettuce 123
sea level 26, 33, 37
sea lion 90
Sea of Japan 19
sea salt 141
sea-level pressure 39
seafood 121
seal 90
sealing material 417
sealing plug 417
sealing ring 404
seam 243, 244, 478
seam pocket 251
seamount 33
search 335
seasons of the year 38
seat 195, 196, 200, 201, 205, 293, 294, 353, 369, 370, 467, 501, 523
seat belt 353
seat cover 196
seat post 370
seat stay 370
seat tube 370
seat-belt warning light 355
seats 201
seaweed 123
sebaceous gland 114
second 298, 428, 498, 515
second assistant camera operator 290
second base 474
second baseman 474
second dorsal fin 74
second floor 182, 189
second hand 424
second molar 101
second premolar 101
second row 482
second space 489
second valve slide 307
second violins 295
second voltage increase 413
second-level domain 334
secondaries 78
secondary altar 446
secondary consumers 45
secondary mirror 7, 9
secondary road 25
secondary root 53
secondary waiting room 465
secretaries' office 445
secretary 203
secretary's office 443
section 313
section of a bulb 54
section of a capsule: poppy 60
section of a follicle: star anise 60
section of a grape 59
section of a hazelnut 60
section of a legume: pea 60
section of a peach 57
section of a raspberry 59
section of a silique: mustard 60
section of a strawberry 59
section of a walnut 60
section of an apple 58
section of an orange 58
section of the Earth's crust 26
sectional garage door 286
sector 428
security casing 237
security check 391
security grille 442
security guard's work station 463
security thread 441
security trigger 235
security vestibule 440
sedimentary rocks 26
seed 53, 57, 58, 59, 60
seed coat 57, 61
seeder 231
seeding tools 231
seedless cucumber 128
segment 58
segment score number 471
seismic wave 27
seismogram 27
seismograph, vertical 27
seismographic recording 403
seismographs 27
select button 319, 326, 329
selective sorting of waste 49
self-adhesive labels 340
self-contained breathing apparatus 454
self-inflating mattress 530
self-sealing flap 339
self-service meat counter 120
self-stick note 338
self-timer indicator 314
semi-mummy 530
semicircle 428
semicircular canal, lateral 116
semicircular canal, posterior 116
semicircular canal, superior 116
semidetached house 289
semimembranosus 97
seminal vesicle 111
semitendinosus 97
semolina 144
Senegal 451
Senegal River 20
sense organs 114
sense receptor 110
sensitive root 109
sensitivity 314
sensor wiring circuit 357
sensory impulse 110
sensory neuron 110
sensory root 110
sent document tray 328
sepal 56, 58, 59
separate collection 49
separator 359, 384, 402, 417
septal cartilage of nose 117
septic tank 48
septum 60, 117
septum pellucidum 109
sequencer 310
sequencer control 310
serac 30
Serbia 450
serial number 441
serial port 329
serve 487, 490
server 334, 335, 491, 494
service area 25, 389
service box 198
service judge 490, 494
service line 491
service main 434
service module 316
service provider, Internet 335
service road 388
service room 447
service station 346, 433
service table 438
service zones 495
serving cart 202
sesame oil 149
set 291, 492
set dresser 291
set of bells 309
set of utensils 173
set-in sleeve 245
setting indicator 511
settings display button 315
setup 328
seventh 298
sewer 434
sewn-in floor 528, 529
sextet 300
Seychelles 452
shackle 521
shad 160
shade 206
shadow 424
shady arcades 447
shaft 278, 471, 492, 494, 503, 505, 506
shake-hands grip 493
shallot 124, 305
shallow root 63
sham 204
shampoo 267
shank 152, 153, 220, 221, 228, 270, 273, 538
shank protector 398
shaping tools 229
shapka 238
shark, morphology 74
sharp 299
sharpening steel 169
sharpening stone 169
shaving 271
shaving brush 271
shaving foam 271
shaving mug 271
sheath 55, 531, 533
sheath dress 252
sheath of Schwann 110
sheath skirt 253
sheathing 187
shed 182, 230
sheep 84
sheep barn 57, 122
sheepskin jacket 249
sheet 515
sheet lead 521
shekel, new 440
shelf 203, 211, 219
shelf channel 211
shell 60, 72, 73, 79, 277, 308, 404
shell membrane 79
shelter 345
shield bug 69
shift key 330
shift: level 2 select 330
shifter 371, 372
shin guard 480, 513
ships 382
shirt 245, 260, 488

shirttail 245, 255
shirtwaist dress 252
shitake 123
shock absorber 351, 523
shock wave 403
shoe 488, 522, 524
shoe store 437
shoe, parts 240
shoelace 240, 262
shoes 240
shoot 53, 63
shooting star 37
shop 280
shopping bag 276
shopping carts 121
shopping center 431, 436
shopping street 432
shore 33
shore cliff 35
shorelines 35
short glove 243
short service line 495
short sock 257
short track 508
short track skate 508
shortening 149
shorts 254, 261, 263, 313, 473, 480, 483, 488, 522
shortstop 474
shot 472
shot put 472
shotgun (smooth-bore) 534
shoulder 83, 86, 92, 94, 223, 302, 342, 492, 536
shoulder bag 276
shoulder belt 353
shoulder blade 93, 95
shoulder bolt 223
shoulder pad 486
shoulder strap 259, 276, 456, 505, 532
shovel 193, 233, 510, 514
shower 189, 439, 464
shower and tub fixture 194
shower head 195
shower stall 195
shredding 49
shrimp 158
shroud 520
shuffle play 323
shunt 416
shut-off valve 194, 196, 197
shutter 186, 333
shutter release button 314
shutting stile 185
shuttlecock, synthetic 495
Siamese 87
sickle 234
side 167, 293
side back vent 244
side chair 201
side chapel 284
side compression strap 532
side door 380
side fairings 525
side footboard 377
side handrail 380
side hatch 12
side judge 485
side lane 343
side mirror 269
side panel 248
side rail 219, 365
side span 344
side vent 28, 361
side view 478
side-marker light 352
sideline 484, 487, 488, 493
sidewalk 183, 434
sidewall 365, 517
Sierra Leone 451
sieve 171
sifter 172
sight 119, 533, 535
sighting line 533
sighting mirror 533
sigmoid colon 106
signal 375
signal gantry 375
signal lamp 178, 179, 180, 181, 208, 214
signal light 181
signet ring 264
silique, section 60
silk 61
sill 28
sill of frame 186
sill plate 187
silos 381
silverware 167
simple eye 67
simple leaves 55
simple organisms 66
Singapore 453
single bed 439
single reed 306
single room 439
single seat 380
single-breasted jacket 244
single-burner camp stove 529
single-handle kitchen faucet 197
single-leaf bascule bridge 345
single-lens reflex camera 314
singles service court 495
singles sideline 491, 495
singlet 473
sink 164, 194, 195, 197, 439, 464
sinker 538
sinkhole 31
siphon 72
siphonal canal 73
sistrum 309
site 182
site plan 183
sitting room 188
sixteenth note 299
sixteenth rest 299
sixth 298
sixty-fourth note 299
sixty-fourth rest 299
skate 158, 506, 509
skateboard 526
skateboarder 526
skateboarding 526
skater 527
skater: long track 508
skater: short track 508
skating kick 514
skating step 514
skeg 519
skeleton 98
skerry 35
ski 510, 523
ski area 512
ski boot 510, 511
ski glove 510
ski goggles 510
ski hat 514
ski jumper 513
ski jumping 513
ski jumping boot 513
ski jumping suit 513
ski lift arrival area 512
ski pants 254
ski pole 510, 514
ski rack 356
ski resort 512
ski school 512
ski suit 510, 514
ski tip 514
ski, giant slalom 510
ski, jumping 513
skiboard 510
skid 395
skiers' lodge 512
skimmer 173, 184
skin 57, 58, 59, 110, 114
skin surface 114
skip 515
skirt 251
skirt finger 383
skirts 253
skis 510
skull 92
skullcap 238
skunk 88
sky coverage 39
skylight 183, 189
slalom ski 510
slat 205
sled 236
sleeper-cab 364
sleepers 261
sleeping bags 530
sleeping car 376
sleet 41
sleeve 244, 395, 501
sleeve strap 248
sleeve strap loop 248
sleeveless jersey 500
sleigh bells 309
slide 214
sliding door 195, 286
sliding folding door 286
sliding folding window 287
sliding jaw 425
sliding lever 353
sliding rail 353, 521
sliding seat 501
sliding sunroof 349
sliding weight 422
sliding window 287
sling back shoe 241
slip 258
slip joint 222
slip joint pliers 222
slip presenter 346
slip-stitched seam 245
slope 342
sloping cornice 279
slot 167, 178, 221, 274
Slovakia 450
Slovenia 450
slow-burning wood stove 192
slower traffic 343
SLR camera 314
small carton 163
small crate 162
small decanter 165
small hand cultivator 232
small intestine 106
small open crate 162
small saucepan 175
smash 491
smell 116
smelt 159
smock 255
smog 47
smoke baffle 192
smoke detector 454
smoke shop 436
smoked ham 153
smooth hound 158
snack bar 294
snail 72, 157
snail dish 173
snail tongs 173
snail, morphology 72
snake 76, 469
snakes and ladders 469
snap 538
snap fastener 243, 249
snap shackle 521
snap-fastening front 261
snap-fastening tab 249
snap-fastening waist 260
snare 308, 535
snare drum 295, 308
snare head 297, 308
snare strainer 308
snatch 500
snelled fishhook 538
snooker 503
snout 74, 75
snow 41
snow brush 356
snow guard 523
snow peas 130
snow-grooming machine 512
snowblower 365
snowboard 513
snowboard, alpine 513
snowboard, freestyle 513
snowboarder 513
snowboarding 513
snowmobile 523
snowsuit 261
soap dish 195
soba noodles 147
soccer 480
soccer ball 480
soccer player 480
soccer shoe 480
social services 465
social worker's office 463
society 430
sock 257, 480, 483, 486, 492
socket head 221
socket set 223
socket-contact 198
socks 247
sofa 200
sofa bed 204
soft cheeses 151
soft contact lens 272
soft key 327
soft palate 116, 117
soft pedal 304, 311
soft ray 74
soft shell clam 157
soft-drink dispenser 346
softball 477
softball bat 477
softball glove 477
soil 48
soil fertilization 47
soil profile 54
soiled utility room 462, 464
solar array 316
solar cell 337, 410, 411
solar collector 410
solar eclipse 4
solar energy 54, 410
solar panel 7
solar radiation 45, 46, 410, 411
solar reflectors 316
solar shield 10
solar system 2
solar-cell panel 411
solar-cell system 411
solder 218
soldering gun 218
soldering iron 218
soldering tools 218
soldering torch 218
sole 161, 229, 247, 509, 511
soleplate 208
soleus 96
solid 414, 415
solid center auger bit 228
solid line 342
solid rocket booster 12
solids 429
solitaire ring 264
Solomon Islands 453
solvent extraction unit 405
Somalia 451
somen noodles 147
sorghum 61
sorghum: panicle 61
sorting plant 49
sorus 52
sou'wester 239
soufflé dish 172
sound box 297, 302
sound engineer 291
sound field control 322
sound hole 301
sound mode lights 322
sound mode selector 322
sound receiver 460
sound recording equipment 291
sound reproducing system 322
sound stage 290
sound systems, portable 325
soundboard 296, 297, 301, 302, 304
sounding balloon 38
soup bowl 166
soup spoon 168
soup tureen 166
sour cream 150
South 23
South Africa 452
South America 14, 17, 34
South American Plate 27
South China Sea 14, 19
South Korea 453
South Pole 15, 21
south pole 416
South-Southeast 23
South-Southwest 23
Southeast 23
Southeast Indian Ridge 34
Southern hemisphere 21
Southwest 23
Southwest Indian Ridge 34
soy sauce 140
soybean sprouts 131
soybeans 131
space 298, 330, 469
space bar 330
space probe 37
space shuttle 12, 37
space shuttle at takeoff 12
space telescope 7, 37
spacelab 13
spacer 409, 467
spacesuit 10
spade 233, 468
spade bit 228
spadix 57
spaghetti 146
spaghetti squash 129
spaghetti tongs 173
spaghettini 146
Spain 449
spar 392
spare tire 361
spareribs 153
spark plug 359, 360
spark plug body 359
spark plug cable 350, 360
spark plug gap 359
spark plug seat 359
spark plug terminal 359
sparkling wine glass 165
sparrow 80
spatula 173
spatulate 55
speaker 294, 320, 326, 328, 336, 518
speaker cover 324
spear 125
special slalom 511
specimen collection center waiting room 465
specimen collection room 465
speed control 176, 237
speed governor 287
speed grand prix motorcycle 525
speed grand prix rider 525
speed selector 176
speed selector switch 227, 228, 270
speed skate, in-line 527
speed skates 508
speed skating 508
speed-increasing gearbox 413
speedboat 385
speedometer 355, 368, 501
spelt wheat 143
spencer 254
spent fuel storage bay 409
sperm whale 90
spermatozoon 111
sphenoid bone 100
sphenoidal fontanelle 100
sphenoidal sinus 117
sphere 429
sphincter muscle of anus 106
spices 138
spicules 4
spider 70
spider web 70
spider, morphology 70
spike 57, 473
spiked shoe 476
spillway 406
spillway chute 406
spillway gate 406
spinach 127
spinach tagliatelle 146
spinal cord 109, 110
spinal cord, structure 109
spinal ganglion 109, 110
spinal nerve 109, 110
spindle 177, 201, 425
spine of scapula 99
spinner 538
spinneret 70
spinning rod 537
spinous process 110
spiny lobster 158
spiny ray 74
spiracle 67
spiral 221
spiral arm 6
spiral beater 176
spiral cloud band 43
spiral nail 220
spiral notebook 340
spiral rib 73
spiral screwdriver 221
spiral thread 70
spire 285
spirit level 225
spirulina 123
spit 35
spit valve 307
splat 200
splay 285
spleen 103
splenius 97
spline 359
splints 461
split link 538

split peas 130
spoiler 366, 392
spoke 371
sponge-tipped applicator 266
sponson 523
spool 536, 537
spool axle 537
spool-release mechanism 537
spoon 167, 531
spoons 168
spores 52
sport-utility vehicle 347
sporting goods store 437
sports 468
sports area 386
sports car 347
sports complex 431
sports on wheels 526
sports, combat 498
sportswear 262
spot 207
spotlight 290, 455
spotlights 293
spout 180, 181
spout assembly 197
spray arm 214
spray button 208
spray control 208
spray head 197
spray hose 195, 197
spray nozzle 208, 236
sprayer 236
spread collar 245
spreader 273
spring 27, 32, 38, 206, 212, 222, 312, 535
spring balance 423
spring binder 339
spring wing 221
spring-form pan 172
springboard 496
springboard, 1 m 518
springboard, 3 m 518
sprinkler hose 236
sprinklers 408
sprocket 523
sprocket wheel 398
spruce 65
spur 29, 228, 308
squamous suture 100
square 429
square movement 470
square root key 337
square root of 427
square trowel 216
square-headed tip 221
squash 128
squid 157
squirrel 82
Sri Lanka 453
stabilizer fin 386
stabilizer jack 361
stack 35, 382, 402
stacking chairs 201
stadium 431
staff 298
staff change room 465
staff cloakroom 438
staff entrance 438, 445
staff lounge 443, 463
staff room 445
stage 278, 292, 293, 421
stage clip 421
stage curtain 292, 293
stage left 293
stage right 293
stage-house 292
stained glass 285
stained glass window 446
stair 293, 294
stair climber 501
stairs 188, 191, 283, 345, 378, 404, 439
stairways 283
stairwell 189
stairwell skylight 189
stake 230, 528, 529
stake loop 528, 529
stakes 231
stalactite 31
stalagmite 31
stalk 51, 125
stalk vegetables 125
stamen 56, 58
stamp pad 338
stanchion 509
stand 27, 174, 176, 206, 269, 277, 308, 537
standard poker hands 468
stapes 116
staple remover 341
stapler 341
staples 341
star diagonal 8
star drag wheel 537
Star of David 447
starboard hand 387
starch 61
starch granule 50
starling 80
start 469
start button 424
start key 328, 330
start switch 213
starter 237, 516
starter button 368
starter handle 235
starting block 473, 516
starting grid 524
starting grip (backstroke) 516
starting line 473, 524
starting pistol 472
starting positions 518
starting step 191
state 23
states of matter 414
station circle 39
station entrance 378
station model 39
station name 378
station platform 375
station wagon 347
stationary bicycle 501
stationery 337
statue 446
steak 152
steak knife 168
steam 402
steam control knob 181
steam generator 402
steam iron 208
steam nozzle 181
steam pressure drives turbine 408
steamer 175
steamer basket 175
steel 259
steel cable 535
steel casing 417
steel pen 312
steelyard 422
steeplechase hurdle jump 472
steering column 350
steering cylinder 400
steering system 351
steering wheel 350, 354, 385, 525
stem 51, 52, 53, 54, 57, 58, 59, 181, 199, 371, 384, 424
stem bulb 387
stem propeller 384
step 191, 219, 364
step chair 201
step groove 191
step stool 219
stepladder 219
stepladders 219
steppe 40
steps 183, 184, 188, 412
steps in maturation 62
stereo control 326
sterile pad 461
sterilization room 464, 465
stern 386, 519
sternal artery 71
sternomastoid 96
sternum 98
stethoscope 460
stick 301
stifle 83
stigma 56, 60
stile 201
stile groove of sash 186
stile tongue of sash 186
still cameras 315
still water level 33
stills photographer 291
Stilton 151
stimulator tip 272
sting 68
stipule 55
stirrup sock 476
stitch 240, 262
stitches 477
stitching 243
stock 296, 412, 534
stock pot 175
stockade 282
stocking 257, 506
stocking cap 239
stomach 73, 103, 106
stomach throw 499
stone 57
stone for sacrifice 283
stone fruits 132
stone marten 88
stone, curling 515
stoner 173
stool 164
stop 86, 328
stop button 235, 319, 323, 424
stop knob 305
stopper 267, 481, 532
stopwatch 424
storage compartment 361, 364, 455
storage door 211
storage furniture 202
storage tank 405
store 432
store room 438
storeroom 444
stork 80
storm collar 193
storm sewer 434
stormy sky 41
straight 468
straight flush 468
straight jaw 222
straight position 518
straight razor 271
straight skirt 253
straight-up ribbed top 247
straightening iron 269
straightneck squash 129
strainer 177, 180, 528
strainer body 197
strainer coupling 197
strait 24
Strait of Gibraltar 18
strap 265, 424, 477, 500
strap eyelet 315
strap loop 532
strap system 303
strapless bra 259
stratocumulus 42
stratopause 37
stratosphere 37
stratum basale 114
stratum corneum 114
stratum granulosum 114
stratum lucidum 114
stratum spinosum 114
stratus 42
straw 163
strawberries 132
strawberry, section 59
street 25, 433, 435
street light 434
street sweeper 365
strength sports 500
stretcher 202, 460
stretcher area 462
striker 218, 481
string 301, 302
string section 295
stringed instruments 301
stringer 396
stringing 492, 494
strings 297, 304
strip 286
strip door 286
strip flooring with alternate joints 190
strip lights 207
stroke judge 516
strokes 490
strokes, types 517
structure 186
structure of a fern 52
structure of a flower 56
structure of a house 188
structure of a leaf 55
structure of a lichen 50
structure of a moss 51
structure of a mushroom 52
structure of a plant 53
structure of a tree 63
structure of an alga 51
structure of the biosphere 44
structure of the ear 116
structure of the Earth 26
structure of the spinal cord 109
structure of the Sun 4
strut 187, 308, 357, 387, 412
stud 187, 478
studded tire 358
student 444
student's desk 444
students' lockers 445
study 189
study room 445
stump 63, 479
sturgeon 158
style 56, 57, 58, 59, 60
stylobate 279
styloid process 100
stylus 312, 337
subarctic 40
subbase 342
subclavian artery 102
subclavian vein 102
subcutaneous tissue 114
subduction 27
subfloor 187, 190
subgrade 342
subhead 313
sublimation 414
submarine cable 317
submarine canyon 33
submarine line 334
submarine pipeline 404
subsidiary track 375
subsiding cold air 43
subsoil 54
substitute's bench 481
substructure 403
subterranean stream 31
subtract from memory 337
subtract key 337
subtractive color synthesis 418
suburb 431
suburban commuter railroad 375
suburbs 25
subway 378, 435
subway map 379, 380
subway station 378, 432
subway train 378, 380
subwoofers 321
sucker 62, 72
suction hose 455
Sudan 451
sudoriferous duct 114
sugar 149
sugar bowl 166
suit 251
suitcase, upright 277
sulcus terminalis 118
sulfur dioxide emission 48
sulfuric acid emission 48
sum 427
sumac 139
summer 38
summer solstice 38
summer squash 128
summit 29, 512
summit lodge 512
Sun 2, 4, 5, 38
sun deck 385, 387
sun visor 354, 356, 361
Sun, structure 4
sundae spoon 168
sundial 424
sundress 252
sunflower 56
sunflower-seed oil 149
sunglasses 273
sunspot 4
super giant slalom 511
Super-G ski 510
super-G slalom 511
supercooling 414
supercross motorcycle 525
superficial peroneal nerve 108
superior cymbal 308
superior dental arch 116
superior mesenteric artery 102, 107
superior mesenteric vein 102
superior nasal concha 117
superior rectus muscle 119
superior semicircular canal 116
superior vena cava 102, 103, 104
superjumbo jet 394
supermarket 120, 433, 437
supersonic jet 37
supersonic jetliner 394
supervisor's office 445
supply line 194
supply point 198
supply room 464
supply tube 197
support 9, 199, 201
support thread 70
suprarenal gland 107
sural nerve 108
surface course 342
surface element 210
surface insulation 12
surface of the water 518
surface prospecting 403
surface runoff 45
surface-piercing foils 387
surgeon's sink 465
Suriname 448
surround loudspeaker 321
suspended span 344
suspender 344
suspender clip 246
suspenders 246
suspension 380
suspension arm 212, 351
suspension band 458
suspension bridge 344
suspension cable 344
suspension system 351
suspension truck 376
suspensory ligament 119
suture 60, 73
swallow 80
swallow hole 31
Swaziland 452
sweat pants 262
sweat shirt 262
sweat suit 262
sweater vest 250
sweaters 250, 254
Sweden 450
sweeper 481
sweeping hip throw 499
sweet bay 142
sweet pepper 128
sweet potato 124
sweetbreads 154
swell organ manual 305
swell pedals 305
swift 80
swimming 516
swimming goggles 516
swimming pool 386, 517
swimming pool, above-ground 184
swimming pool, in-ground 184
swimming trunks 263
swimsuit 263, 516
swing bridge 344
Swiss Army knife 531
Swiss chard 125
switch 198, 211, 219, 229, 375, 416
switch lock 228
switch plate 198
switch tower 375
switched outlet 322
Switzerland 450
swivel 403, 535, 538
swivel base 224
swivel cord 269
swivel head 224
swivel lock 224
swivel wall lamp 207
swordfish 159
symbols 468
sympathetic ganglion 109
symphony orchestra 295
symphysis pubis 111, 112
synagogue 447
synapse 110
sync cable 337
synthesizer 310
synthetic shuttlecock 495
synthetic sponge 266
synthetic surface 492
Syria 452
syringe 460
syringe for irrigation 460
syrup 467
system buttons 310
system of units 426

T

T-bar 512
T-shirt 263
T-shirt dress 261
T-strap shoe 241
tab 248, 273, 274, 340
Tabasco® sauce 140
tabernacle 446
table 202, 493, 502
table lamp 206
table mixer 176
table salt 141
table tennis 493
table tennis ball 493
table tennis paddle 493
tables 202
tablespoon 168
tablet 467
tablinum 280
tabloid 313
tabulation key 330
tabulation left 330
tabulation right 330
tachometer 355, 368
tack 220, 519
tackle box 538
tackless strip 190
tag 240, 262
tagine 174
tagliatelle 146
tahini 140
tail 71, 76, 82, 83, 86, 90, 111, 393, 510, 514, 526, 536
tail assembly 393
tail boom 395
tail comb 268
tail feather 78
tail of helix 115
tail pipe 351
tail pole 412
tail skid 395
tail stop 224
tailback 485
taillight 352, 367, 368
taillights 352
tailored collar 251
tailpiece 297, 301
tailrace 407
Tajikistan 452
takeover zone 472
talk key 327
talking drum 297
talon 79
talus 99
tamarillo 136
tamarin 91
tamarind paste 140
tambourine 309
tamper 181
tandem bicycle 373
tang 167, 169, 216
Tanganyika, Lake 20
tank 13, 385, 454, 529
tank ball 196
tank body 364
tank car 377
tank farm 404
tank hatch cover 385
tank lid 196
tank sprayer 236
tank top 261, 263
tank truck 364
tanker 381, 384
Tanzania 451
tap connector 236
tape 225
tape counter 323
tape dispenser 341
tape guide 341
tape lock 225
tape measure 225
tape recorder select button 322
tape selector 323
taproot 63
tarantula 70
taro 124
tarragon 142
tarsus 78
Tasman Sea 15
Tasmania 15
taste 116
taste bud 118
taste receptors 118
tasting spoon 173
taxiway 388
taxiway line 389
tea 148
tea bag 148
tea ball 173
tea towel 215
teacher 444
teacher's desk 444
team jersey 486
team shirt 476, 480
team's emblem 506
teapot 166
tear-off calendar 338
teaser comb 268
teaspoon 168
technical controller 509
technical delegates 509
technical events 511
technical room 345
technical specialist 509
technical specifications 358
techniques 487
tectonic lake 32
tectonic plates 27
teddy 258
tee 505, 515
tee line 515
teeing ground 504
teeth 101
Teflon® tape 216
telecommunication antenna 386, 387
telecommunication satellite 335
telecommunication satellites 316
telecommunications by satellite 317
telephone 439
telephone cable 434
telephone index 327, 338
telephone line 334
telephone network 317
telephone set 327
telephone, communication 327
telephony 335
telephoto lens 314
teleport 317
telescope 7
telescope base 7
telescopic boom 397, 455
telescopic corridor 389
telescopic front fork 366, 369
telescopic leg 460
telescopic sight 420, 534
telescoping antenna 325
television 318
television program schedule 313
television set 439, 444
telltale 520
telson 71
temperate forest 44
temperature control 178, 208, 211
temperature indicator 355
temperature of dew point 39
temperature scale 37
temperature selector 178, 212, 213
temperature sensor 358
temple 92, 273, 283
tempo control 311
temporal bone 98, 100
ten 427
Ten Commandments 447
tenderloin roast 152
tendril 62
tennis 490
tennis ball 492
tennis player 492
tennis racket 492
tennis shoe 242, 492
tennis skirt 492
tenor drum 308
tension adjustment 537
tension rod 308
tension rope 297
tension screw 308
tension spring 355, 500
tension-adjusting screw 341
tensor fasciae latae 96
tent trailer 361
tentacle 72
tents 528
tepee 288
teres major 97
teres minor 97
terminal 198, 210, 404
terminal arborization 110
terminal box 411
terminal bronchiole 105
terminal bud 53
terminal cover 320
terminal filament 109
terminal lobe 62
terminal moraine 30
termite 69
terrine 174
tertial 78
tertiary consumers 45
test button 454
testicle 111
testis 71
Tethys 3
textile floor coverings 190
Thailand 453
thallus 50, 51
The Bahamas 448
The Gambia 451
theater 292, 432, 433
theater, Greek 278
thermal energy 402
thermodynamic temperature, unit 426
thermometer 404, 424
thermopause 37
thermosphere 37
thermostat 178
thigh 78, 83, 86, 93, 95, 111, 112
thigh pad 486
thigh-boot 241
thigh-high stocking 257
thimble 425
thinning razor 269
thinning scissors 270
third 298
third base 474
third baseman 474
third finger 115
third floor 182, 189
third molar 101
third row 482
third valve slide 307
thirty-second note 299
thirty-second rest 299
thong 242
thoracic legs 71
thoracic vertebrae 99
thorax 67, 68, 92, 94
thread 221
threaded rod 223
three-blade propeller 394
three-four time 298
three-of-a-kind 468
three-quarter coat 248
threshold 185
throat 78, 224, 492, 538
throat protector 476
throttle control 332
throwing circle 472, 473
thrust device 312
thrust tube 312
thruster 10
thumb 115, 243, 477
thumb hook 307
thumb piston 305
thumb rest 306, 460
thumb tacks 341
thumbscrew 223
thyme 142
tibia 98
tibial nerve 108
tibialis anterior 96
tick 70
ticket clerk 294
ticket collecting booth 378
ticket collector 374
ticket counter 390
tie 273, 299
tie beam 187
tie rod 308
tier 281
tierceron 284
Tierra del Fuego 17
tiers 278
tiger 89
tight end 485
tightening buckle 532
tightening tools 222
tighthead prop 482
tile 12, 279, 280, 283
tiller 520
tilt-back head 176
timber 279, 280
time code 291
time signatures 298
timekeeper 488, 498, 509
timekeepers 499
timer 178, 179, 501
timing belt 360
timpani 295
tine 167
tip 55, 125, 167, 216, 218, 220, 221, 227, 246, 273, 487, 503, 510, 536
tip cleaners 218
tip of nose 117
tip protector 460
tip section 536
tip-ring 536, 537
tipping lever 467
tips 221
tire 349, 358, 364, 371, 522, 525
tire barrier 524
tire pump 370
tire valve 371
tires 358
tissue holder 195
Titan 3
Titania 3
Titicaca, Lake 17
toad 75
toaster 178
Tobago 449
toe 79, 86, 92, 94, 226, 229, 247
toe binding 514
toe clip 370, 372
toe guard 459, 476
toe loop 509
toe pick 509
toe piston 305
toenail scissors 265
toepiece 511, 514
toggle bolt 221
toggle fastening 249
Togo 451
toilet 189, 194, 195, 196, 439, 464
toilet bowl 196
toilet soap 267
toilet tank 195
toilets 437
token 469
tom-tom 308
tomatillos 128
tomato 128
tomato paste 140
tomato sauce 140
tombolo 35
tone control 303
Tonga 453
Tonga Trench 34
tongs 173
tongue 106, 116, 117, 154, 240, 246, 262, 297, 305, 509, 511
tongue sheath 76
tongue, dorsum 118
tonsil 116
tool belt 225
tool box 225
tool holder 229
tool kit 372
tool shelf 219
tool tether 10
tools for loosening the earth 233
tools, electricity 217
tooth 74, 76, 226, 227, 235, 270, 400
tooth guard 486
toothbrush 272
toothbrush shaft 272
toothbrush well 272
toothed jaw 222
toothpaste 272
top 63, 202, 219
top box 369
top cap 417
top coat 251
top deck 404
top deckboard 396
top flap 532
top hat 238
top ladder 455
top lift 240
top of dam 406
top pocket 502
top rail 185, 201, 202, 205
top rail of sash 186
top stitching 246
top-level domain 334
top-loading washer 212
top-stitched pleat 253
top-stitching 260
topping 536
topsoil 54
toque 239
Torah scrolls 447
toric lens 419
tornado 43
torque adjustment collar 228
torque converter 212
Torres Strait 15
tortellini 146
tortillas 145
torus 429
total 423
total eclipse 4, 5
total sale display 346
tote bag 276
toucan 80
touch 114
touch judge 483
touch line 481
touch pad 336
touch pad button 336
touch screen 337
touchline 483
Toulouse sausages 156
touring bicycle 373
touring motorcycle 369
touring tire 358
tow bar frame 361
tow safety chain 361
tow truck 364
towel bar 195
tower 284, 344, 412, 413
tower case 329
tower crane 397
tower ladder 455
tower mast 397
tower mill 412
tower silo 122
towing device 364
towing hitch 361
town houses 289
toy store 436
tracery 285
trachea 105
track 374, 378, 398, 431, 472, 523, 524
track idler 398
track lighting 207
track roller frame 398
track search/fast operation buttons 319, 323
track shoe 473
tractor engine compartment 400
traditional houses 288
traditional musical instruments 296
traffic circle 25, 342
traffic lane 343
traffic lanes 343
traffic lights 434
tragus 115
trailer 361
trailer car 380
trailing edge 392
trailing-edge flap 392
train 374
trainer 489, 498
training set 261
training wall 406
transaction receipt 443
transaction record slot 442
Transantarctic Mountains 15
transept 285
transept spire 284
transfer dispensing machine 379
transfer of heat to water 408

transfer ramp 343
transform plate boundaries 27
transformer 207, 407
transformer (voltage decrease) 402
transformer (voltage increase) 402
transit shed 381
transmission 212
transmission dish 316
transmission system 351
transmission to consumers 402, 413
transmitter 327
transmitting tower 316
transmitting/receiving dish 316
transmitting/receiving parabolic antenna 316
transpiration 45
transport and machinery 342
transport, air 388
transport, maritime 381
transverse bulkhead 384
transverse colon 106
transverse dunes 36
transverse flute 306
transverse process 110
trap 194, 196, 197, 292
trap coupling 197
trapdoor 281
trapeze dress 252
trapezius 96, 97
trapezoid 429
travel agency 436
traveler 520, 521
traveler's check 441
traveling block 403
traveling crane 407
traverse arch 284
trawler 384
tray 205, 219, 225, 231, 277
tread 191, 262
tread design 358
treatment room 463, 465
treble bridge 304
treble clef 298
treble fishhook 538
treble keyboard 296
treble pickup 303
treble register 296
treble tone control 303, 322, 325
tree 63
tree fern 52
tree frog 75
tree pruner 234
tree, structure 63
tree, trunk 63
trees 504
trefoil 285
trench 33
trench coat 248
triage room 463
triangle 295, 309, 429
triangular bandage 461
triangular body 297
triangular fossa 115
triceps bar 501
triceps brachii 97
tricuspid valve 104
trifoliolate 55
trigger 235, 332, 454, 534
trigger guard 534
trigger switch 227, 228, 229
trill 299
trim 277
trim panel 352
trim ring 210
trimaran 521
trimmer 271
trimming 274
Trinidad and Tobago 449
trio 300
trip lever 196, 236
trip odometer 355
tripe 154
triple jump 472
triple ring 471
tripod 8
tripod accessories shelf 8
tripod stand 308
triticale 143
Triton 3
trolley 397
trolley crank 236
trolley pulley 397
trombone 307
trombones 295
Tropic of Cancer 20, 21, 22
Tropic of Capricorn 20, 21, 22
tropical climates 40
tropical cyclone 43
tropical cyclone names 43
tropical forest 44
tropical fruits 136
tropical rain forest 40, 44
tropical wet-and-dry (savanna) 40
tropical yam 124
tropopause 37, 46
troposphere 37
trot 83
trough 33, 39, 418
trousers 499
trout 161
trowel 232
truck 526, 527
truck crane 397
truck tractor 364
trucking 364
trucks 364
truffle 123
trumpet 307
trumpet interchange 342
trumpets 295
trunk 52, 62, 63, 75, 93, 95, 277, 349
trunk, cross section 63
trunks 500
truss structure 11
trussing needle 173
tsetse fly 69
tub 212, 214, 230
tub platform 195
tub rim 212
tuba 295, 307
tube 163, 461
tube retention clip 199
tuber vegetables 124
tubular bells 295, 309
tubular element 210
tubular heater 405
tuck position 518
tug 384
tulip 56
tuna 160
tundra 44
tuner 326
tungsten-halogen lamp 199
tunic 255
tunic dress 252
tuning buttons 322
tuning control 325, 326
tuning controls 318
tuning gauge 308
tuning peg 302, 303
tuning pin 304
tuning ring 297
tuning slide 307
tuning wire 305
Tunisia 451
tunnel 378
turban 239
turbine 402
turbine shaft turns generator 408
turbo-alternator unit 402
turbojet engine 393
turbot 161
Turkey 452
turkey 81, 155
Turkmenistan 452
turmeric 138
turn 299
turn signal 352, 366, 367, 368
turn signal indicator 355, 368
turnbuckle 498, 521
turner 173
turning judges 517
turning wall 517
turnip 129
turnouts 454
turnstile 378
turntable 176, 344, 400, 401
turntable mounting 455
turret 282
turret cap 420
turtle 76
turtle, morphology 76
turtleneck 250, 514
Tuvalu 453
tweeter 324
tweezers 461
twig 53, 63
twin-set 255
twist 228
twist bar 500
twist bit 228
twist drill 228
twist grip throttle 368
twist handle 332
two pairs 468
two-blade propeller 394
two-door sedan 347
two-leaf door 362
two-person tent 528
two-storey house 289
two-two time 298
two-way collar 248
tympanum 75, 279, 285
type of fuel 346
type of high cloud 39
type of low cloud 39
type of middle cloud 39
type of the air mass 39
types of eclipses 4, 5
types of golf clubs 505
types of movements 470
types of passenger cars 376
types of strokes 517
typhoon 43

U

u quark 414
U.S. habitation module 11
U.S. laboratory 11
udon noodles 147
Uganda 451
Ukraine 450
ulna 98
ulnar nerve 108
ultracompact camera 315
ultraviolet radiation 418
umbel 57
umbo 73
umbra shadow 4, 5
umbrella pine 65
umbrella stand 273
umbrellas 273
umbrellas and stick 273
Umbriel 3
umpire 479, 485, 487, 490, 495, 515
unbleached flour 144
under tail covert 78
underarm crutch 466
underarm portfolio 275
underarm rest 466
undergarment 524
underground 281
underground cable network 317
underground chamber 278
underground flow 45
underground passage 375
underground stem 54
underlay 190
underpass 344
undershirt 476
underwater light 184
underwear 247, 258
underwire 259
undressing booth 465
uneven parallel bars 496, 497
ungulate mammals 83, 84
unicellulars 66
uniform 456
uniform resource locator 334
uniform resource locator (URL) 334
union of two sets 427
union suit 247
uniparous cyme 57
unisex headgear 239
unisex shoes 242
unison 298
unit of amount of substance 426
unit of electric charge 426
unit of electric current 426
unit of electric potential difference 426
unit of electric resistance 426
unit of energy 426
unit of force 426
unit of frequency 426
unit of length 426
unit of luminous intensity 426
unit of mass 426
unit of power 426
unit of pressure 426
unit of radioactivity 426
unit of temperature 426
unit of thermodynamic temperature 426
unit price 423
United Arab Emirates 452
United Kingdom 449
United States of America 448
univalve shell 73
univalve shell, morphology 73
university 432
unleavened bread 145
unloading dock 437, 439
up and over garage door 286
uphaul 519
upholstery nozzle 209
upper 511
upper blade guard 227
upper bowl 181
upper confining bed 402
upper cuff 511
upper deck 363, 392
upper edge 493
upper eyelid 75, 87, 119
upper lateral lobe 62
upper lateral sinus 62
upper lip 116, 305
upper lobe 105
upper mandible 78
upper mantle 26
upper shell 511, 527
upper strap 511
upper tail covert 78
upperworks 521
upright 184, 466
upright piano 304
upright suitcase 277
upright vacuum cleaner 209
upstage 292, 293
Ural Mountains 18
Uranus 2, 3
urban map 25
ureter 107
urethra 107, 112
urinary bladder 107, 111, 112
urinary meatus 111
urinary system 107
URL 334
uropod 71
Uruguay 448
USB connector 333
USB key 333
USB port 310, 329, 336
used syringe box 457
usual terms 58, 59
utensils for cutting, examples 169
utensils, kitchen 169
utensils, set 173
uterovesical pouch 112
uterus 112, 113
utility case 276
uvula 116, 117
Uzbekistan 452

V

V-neck 244, 250
V-neck cardigan 250
vacuole 50, 66
vacuum bottle 532
vacuum cleaner attachments 209
vacuum cleaner, cylinder 209
vacuum cleaner, upright 209
vacuum coffee maker 181
vacuum diaphragm 360
vacuum distillation 405
vagina 112, 113
valley 29, 32
valve 60, 73, 307
valve casing 307
valve cover 360
valve seat shaft 196
valve spring 360
vamp 240, 263
van straight truck 365
vane 213
vanilla extract 140
vanity cabinet 195
vanity mirror 354
Vanuatu 453
vapor 415
variable ejector nozzle 394
vastus lateralis 96, 97
vastus medialis 96
vault 284, 443
vaulting horse 496, 497
veal cubes 152
vegetable bowl 166
vegetable brush 173
vegetable garden 122, 182
vegetable kingdom 50
vegetable sponge 267
vegetables 120, 124
vegetables, bulb 124
vegetables, fruit 128
vegetables, inflorescent 127
vegetables, leaf 126
vegetables, root 129
vegetables, stalk 125
vegetables, tuber 124
vegetation 44
vegetation regions 44
vehicle jack 356
vehicle rest area 345
veil 536
vein 55
veins 102
velarium 281
Velcro closure 260
velvet-band choker 264
Venezuela 448
venom canal 76
venom gland 76
venom-conducting tube 76
venomous snake, morphology 76
vent 354
vent brush 268
vent door 365
ventilated rib 534
ventilating circuit 194
ventilating grille 209
ventilator 380
ventral abdominal artery 71
ventral nerve cord 71
Venus 2, 3
verbena 148
vermicelli 147
vermiform appendix 106
vernal equinox 38
vernier 422, 425
vernier caliper 425
vernier scale 425
Versailles parquet 190
vertebral body 110
vertebral column 98, 109
vertebral shield 76
vertical cord lift 208
vertical ground movement 27
vertical movement 470
vertical pivoting window 287
vertical pupil 76
vertical section 526
vertical seismograph 27
vertical side band 487
vertical-axis wind turbine 412
vest 244, 255
vestibular nerve 116
vestibule 116, 280
vial 467
vibrating mudscreen 403
vibrato arm 303
vice skip 515
Victoria, Lake 20
video and digital terminals 315
video entertainment system 471
video monitor 329
video port 329, 336
videocassette 319
videocassette recorder (VCR) 321
videophony 335
videotape operation controls 320
Vietnam 453
view camera 315
viewfinder 315
village 430, 512
vine shoot 62
vine stock 62
vinyl grip sole 261
viola 301
violas 295

violet 56
violin 301
violin family 301
viper 77
visceral ganglion 73
visceral pleura 105
vise 224
visible light 418
vision 419
vision defects 419
visor 367, 459, 506, 525
visor hinge 367
Vistula River 18
vitelline membrane 79
vitreous body 119
vocal cord 105
voice edit buttons 310
voice recorder button 337
voice selector 311
volcanic bomb 28
volcanic island 33
volcanic lake 32
volcano 26, 28
volcano during eruption 28
volcanoes 28
Volga River 18
volley 490
volleyball 487
volt 426
voltage decrease 413
voltage increase 408
voltage tester 217
volume 328
volume control 303, 310, 311, 319, 322, 325
volume display 346
volute 200
volva 52
vulture 80
vulva 94, 113

W

wad 534
waders 538
wadi 36
wading bird 79
waffle iron 178
wagon tent 528
waist 93, 95, 240, 301
waist belt 205
waistband 246, 247, 249
waistband extension 246
waiter's corkscrew 170
waiting area 442
waiting room 463
wakame 123
walk 83
walk-in closet 189
walker 466
walkie-talkie 456
walking aids 466
walking leg 67
walking stick 273, 466
walkway 436
wall 5, 58, 184, 528
wall cabinet 164
wall cloud 43
wall lantern 207
wall sconce 207
wall side 385
wall tent 528
wallet 275, 337
walnut 64, 133
walnut, section 60
waning gibbous 5
wapiti (elk) 84
wardrobe 189, 203, 439
warehouse 430
warm air 41
warm temperate climates 40
warm-air baffle 192
warming plate 181
warning lights 355
warning plate 228
warning track 475
wasabi 141
wash tower 214
washcloth 267
washer 194, 417
washer nozzle 348
washer, front-loading 212
washer, top-loading 212
washers 222
wasp-waisted corset 259
Wassily chair 200
waste basket 341
waste layers 47
waste pipe 196
waste stack 194
waste water 48
waste, selective sorting 49
water 402
water bottle 371
water bottle clip 371
water carrier 532
water chestnut 124
water cools the used steam 408
water dispenser 211
water goblet 165
water hazard 504
water hose 214
water intake 407
water is pumped back into the steam generator 408
water jets 518
water level 181
water level indicator 179
water meter 194
water pitcher 166
water pollution 48
water pressure gauge 455
water service pipe 194
water spider 70
water strider 69
water table 31, 48
water tank 181, 272
water tank area 394
water turns into steam 408
water-level selector 212
water-level tube 208
water-steam mix 402
watercourse 32, 48
watercress 127
waterfall 31, 32
watering can 236
watering tools 236
watering tube 365
watermark 441
watermelon 135
waterproof pants 260
waterspout 43
watt 426
wave 33, 418
wave base 33
wave clip 268
wave height 33
wave length 33
wavelength 418
wax 514
wax bean 131
wax gourd (winter melon) 128
wax seal 196
waxed paper 162
waxing gibbous 5
waxing kit 514
weasel 88
weather map 38, 39
weather radar 38, 392
weather satellite 38
weatherboard 185, 186
web 75, 79, 477
web frame 385
webbed foot 75
webbed toe 79
webbing 353
Webcam 332
Weddell Sea 15
wedding ring 264
wedge 305
wedge lever 229
weeder 232
weeding hoe 233
weekender 277
weeping willow 64
weighing platform 423
weight 422, 423, 500
weight machine 501
weightlifting 500
weightlifting belt 500
weightlifting shoe 500
weights 501
welding tools 218
welt 240, 244
welt pocket 244, 250
West 23
West Coast mirror 363, 364
West Indies 16
West-Northwest 23
West-Southwest 23
Western hemisphere 21
Western meridian 22
whale 90
wheat 61, 143
wheat, grain 61
wheat: spike 61
wheel 231, 277, 364, 522, 525, 526, 527, 535
wheel cover 349
wheel cylinder 357
wheel loader 399
wheel mouse 332
wheel speed sensor 357
wheel stud 357
wheel tractor 399
wheelbarrow 231
wheelchair 467
wheelchair lift 363
wheelhouse 384
whelk 157
whipping cream 150
whisk 172
whisker 82, 87
White 469, 470
white 418
white blood cell 104
white bread 145
white cabbage 126
white chocolate 148
white matter 109, 110
white mustard 138
white object ball 502, 503
white onion 124
white pepper 138
white rice 147
white square 470
white stone 470
white tape 487, 493, 495
white wine glass 165
white-tailed deer 84
whiting 161
whole note 299
whole rest 299
whole-wheat flour 144
wholegrain mustard 140
wholemeal bread 145
whorl 72, 73
wicket 443, 479
wicketkeeper 479
wide receiver 485
wide-angle lens 314
widescreen/data code button 320
wigwam 288
wild boar 84
wild rice 143
Wilkes Land 15
willow 478
winch 287, 364, 521
winch controls 364
wind 47, 48
wind action 45
wind deflector 364
wind direction 39
wind energy 412
wind indicator 520
wind instruments 306
wind speed 39
wind synthesizer controller 311
wind turbine, horizontal-axis 413
wind turbines 412
wind vane 413
windbag 296
windbreaker 249
winding adjustment 420
windmill 412
window 178, 179, 186, 189, 210, 274, 349, 352, 361, 380, 392, 519
window canopy 528
window regulator handle 352
window sill 187
window tab 340
windows 274, 287
windshaft 412
windshield 348, 364, 366, 369, 385, 392, 523
windshield wiper 348, 355
windshield wiper blade 355
wine 120
wine cellar 438
wine steward 438
wine vinegar 141
wing 13, 68, 78, 286, 393, 525, 536
wing covert 78
wing nut 223
wing pallet 396
wing rib 392
wing slat 393
wing strut 394
wing vein 67
wing, bird 78
winglet 393, 394
wings 292
winter 38
winter precipitation 41
winter solstice 38
winter sports 515
winter tire 358
wiper 355
wiper arm 355
wiper switch 354
wire 417
wire beater 176
wire brush 309
wire cutter 217
wire nut 217
wire stripper 217
wire support 529
wishbone boom 519
withers 83, 86
witness stand 440
wok 174
wok set 174
wolf 88
woman 94
women's clothing 251
women's gloves 243
women's headgear 239
women's shoes 241
won ton skins 147
wood 505
wood burning 192
wood chisel 229
wood ear 123
wood flooring 190
wood flooring arrangements 190
wood flooring on cement screed 190
wood flooring on wooden structure 190
wood frog 75
wood ray 63
woodbox 192
woodpecker 80
woods 25
woodwind section 295
woofer 324
Worcestershire sauce 140
work bench and vise 224
work surface 224
worker 68
worm 365
wraparound dress 252
wraparound skirt 253
wrapover top 255
wrenches 216, 223
wrist 86, 93, 95, 115
wrist guard 527
wrist strap 510, 514
wrist-length glove 243
wristband 486, 492, 500
writing brush 312
writing case 275
writing instruments 312

X

X-ray unit, mobile 462
X-rays 418
xylophone 295, 309

Y

Y-tube 460
yak 85
yard line 484
yard-long beans 130
yarn 477
yaw 395
yellow 418
yellow ball 503
yellow light 434
yellow onion 124
yellow sweet pepper 128
yellowjacket 69
Yemen 452
yen 440
yogurt 150
yoke 245, 249, 255
yoked skirt 253
yolk 79
Yucatan Peninsula 16
yurt 288

Z

Zambia 452
zebra 84
zest 58
zester 169
Zimbabwe 452
zinc can 417
zinc-electrolyte mix 417
zipper 249, 261, 265, 277, 528
zither 296
zona pellucida 112
zoom button 320
zoom lens 314, 320
zucchini 128
zygomatic bone 98, 100

Indice dei nomi italiani

A

abat-son 285
abbaino 182
abbellimenti 299
abbigliamento 238
abbigliamento da ginnastica 263
abbigliamento femminile 251
abbigliamento maschile 244
abbigliamento sportivo 262
abbigliamento, negozio di 436
abbottonatura a doppiopetto 248
abbottonatura a polo 250
abbottonatura a pressione 260
abbottonatura anteriore a pressione 261
abbottonatura della cintura 246
abete 65
abete, aghi d' 65
abissino 87
abitacolo 525
abitazioni urbane 289
abiti, esempi di 252
abito a polo 252
abito a T-shirt 261
abito a trapezio 252
abito a tunica 252
abito a vestaglia 252
abito a vita bassa 252
abito da casa 252
ABS, sistema frenante antibloccaggio 357
abside 285
acagiù, noce di 133
acanto, foglia di 200
accappatoio 256
acceleratore, manopola dell' 368
acceleratore, pedale dell' 354
accelerazione, cavo di 237
accelerazione, grilletto di 235
accensione, blocchetto di 354
accensione, interruttore di 336
accensione, pulsante di 213
accensione/spegnimento, spia luminosa di 327
accento 299
accesso, pista di 388
accesso, portello di 385
accesso, strada di 388
accessori 209, 356, 372
accessori a propano o butano 529
accessori dell'obiettivo 314
accessori di bellezza 264
accessori di pulitura 209
accessori per la sciolinatura 514
accessori personali 264
accessori, espulsore degli 176
accessori, scomparto degli 209
accessori, slitta per gli 314
accetta 234, 533
accettazione 462, 465
acchito 502
acchito centrale 502
acchito della linea di battuta 502
acchito superiore 502
acciaio, corpo d' 417
acciaiolo 169
acciarino 218
accidenti 299
acciuga 159
accompagnamento, corde per l' 296
acconciatura, articoli per 268
accoppiamento, adattatore di 11
accordatura, anello d' 297
accordo 299
accordo, asta d' 305
accumulatore 357
acero 64
acero, sciroppo d' 149
aceto balsamico 141
aceto di malto 141
aceto di mele 141
aceto di riso 141
aceto di vino 141
acetosa 127
achenio 59, 60
acidificazione dei laghi 48
acido nitrico, emissione di 48
acido solforico, emissione di 48
acino 62
acino, sezione di un 59
acqua 402, 408
acqua calda, colonna montante dell' 194
acqua calda, rete di distribuzione dell' 194
acqua di disgelo 30
acqua fredda, colonna montante dell' 194
acqua fredda, rete di distribuzione dell' 194
acqua ossigenata 461
acqua, attacco del tubo di alimentazione dell' 236
acqua, bicchiere da 165
acqua, bottiglia dell' 371
acqua, chiave dell' 307
acqua, contatore dell' 194
acqua, corso d' 32, 48
acqua, getti d' 518
acqua, inquinamento dell' 48
acqua, livello dell' 181
acqua, serbatoio dell' 181, 272
acqua, superficie dell' 518
acquasantiera 446
acquascooter 523
acque reflue 48
acquifero artesiano 402
acromion 99
acroterio 279
acuti, ponticello degli 304
acuti, registro degli 296
acuti, tastiera degli 296
Adamo, pomo d' 92
adattatore 198, 271
adattatore di accoppiamento 11
adattatore per videocassette compatte 320
addebito, carta di 443
addetto ai 30 secondi 488
addetto al controllo biglietti 294
addetto alla panca dei puniti 507
addizione 427
addome 67, 68, 70, 71, 78, 92, 94
adduttore lungo 96
Aden, Golfo di 19, 20
Adriatico, Mar 18
aerazione, canale di 278
aerazione, comando dell' 354
aerazione, griglia di 182
aereo da ricognizione meteorologica 38
aereo di linea 37
aerociste 51
aeroplani, esempi di 394
aeroplano anfibio antincendio 394
aeroplano da carico 394
aeroplano leggero 394
aeroplano privato 394
aeroplano, movimenti di un 395
aeroporto 25, 388, 430
affari, quartiere degli 430, 432
affettauova 173
affettaverdure 170
affissione, superficie di 341
affluente 32
affrancatrice 339
affresco 280
Afghanistan 452
Africa 14, 20, 34, 451
agar-agar 123
agarico delizioso 123
agenda 338
agente di polizia 456
agente di sicurezza, postazione dell' 463
agenzia di viaggi 436
aggancio, pulsante di 227
aggetto, manopola di regolazione dell' 229
aghi d'abete 65
aghi di pino 65
aglio 124
agnello, tagli di 153
ago 460
ago magnetico 533
ago per legare 173
agricoltura intensiva 46, 48
agrippina 200
agrume 58
agrumi 134
air bag 354
air bag, sistema di ritenuta degli 354
airone 80
aiuola 183, 230
aiutante 121
aiuto attrezzista 291
aiuto regista 291
ajowan 139
ala 13, 68, 78, 117, 393, 536
ala a delta 394
ala alta 394
ala anteriore 67
ala destra 482, 489, 507
ala poppiera 387
ala posteriore 67
ala prodiera 387
ala semiimmersa 387
ala sinistra 482, 489, 507
alamaro 249
alano 86
alari 193
Alaska, Golfo dell' 16
Albania 450
albatros 80
albergo 432, 439, 512
albergo, camera d' 439
alberi 504
albero 63, 412, 519, 520
albero a bassa velocità 413
albero a camme 360
albero a gomiti 360
albero ad alta velocità 413
albero da frutto 122
albero del derrick 385
albero del radar 384
albero dell'elica 387
albero della vite 62
albero delle pedivelle 372
albero di Natale 404
albero di trasmissione 383
albero di trasmissione longitudinale 351
albero motore 395
albero ornamentale 122, 230
albero prodiero 385
albero, struttura di un 63
albicocca 132
albume 79
alburno 63
alce 85
alchechengi 132
alcol puro 461
alcool, bulbo d' 424
alcool, colonna d' 424
alesatori per la pulizia degli ugelli 218
aletta 244, 275, 393, 394, 460
aletta a molla 221
aletta autoadesiva 339
aletta del parafango 364
aletta parasole 354
aletta staccata 248
aletta, tasca applicata con 245
aletta, tasca interna con 244, 248, 249, 251
aletta, tasca profilata con 244, 248
aletta, taschino con 244
aletta, taschino tagliato con 244
alette 471
alettone 392, 525
alettone parafango 365
Aleutine, Isole 16
alfiere 470
alga bruna 51
alga marina 123
alga rossa 51
alga verde 51
alga, struttura di un' 51
Algeria 451
alghe 51
alghe, esempi di 51
alimentatore 336
alimentatore, ventola dell' 329
alimentazione dell'acqua, tubo di 214
alimentazione dell'aria, tubo di 454
alimentazione, cavo d' 177, 229
alimentazione, cavo di 227, 269, 270, 322
alimentazione, cordone dell' 271
alimentazione, presa di 326, 329
alimentazione, pulsante di 319
alimentazione, sistema di 351
alimentazione, spina di 337
alimentazione, tubo di 197
alimenti e prodotti per animali 121
alimenti, latta per 163
alimenti, rete per 162
alimenti, vaschetta per 162
aliscafo 387
all'indietro 518
allacciamento alla rete 198
allacciamento, esempi di 197
allacciamento, punto di 198
allacciatura con bottoni a pressione 249
allarme, dispositivo di 454
allenatore 489, 498, 507
allenatore, zona dell' 474
allenatori 509
allevamento intensivo 46, 47
alligatore 77
alloggi 512
alloggi dell'equipaggio 382
alloggiamento 199, 286, 337
alloggiamento del bocchino 307
alloggiamento del mulinello 536, 537
alloggiamento del ventilatore 270
alloggiamento della scheda di memoria 320
alloggio del comandante 387
alloro 142
alone 6
alosa 160
Alpi 18
alta pressione, area di 43
altare maggiore 446
altare secondario 446
altare, croce dell' 446
altare, pala dell' 446
alte frequenze, pick-up per 303
alternato 330

alternato: selezione di livello 3 330
alternatore 350, 360, 402, 408, 413
altezza dell'onda 33
altezza, indice di regolazione dell' 227
altezza, regolazione micrometrica dell' 8, 9
alti, regolatore degli 322
altitudine 44
altitudini, scala delle 37
altocumulo 42
altoparlante 320, 326, 328, 336, 380, 455
altoparlanti, bilanciamento degli 322
altopiano 5, 24, 29
altostrato 42
alula 78
alveolo della presa 198
alveolo dentario 101
alzata 191, 212, 213
alzatore destro 487
amanita muscaria 52
amanita virosa 52
amaranto 143
Amazzoni, Rio delle 17
ambiente 44
ambiente naturale 504
ambio 83
ambulanza 460, 462
ameba 66
America Centrale 14, 16
America Meridionale 14, 17, 34
America Settentrionale 14, 16, 34
America, Stati Uniti d' 448
Americhe 448
Amery, Banchisa di 15
amido 61
ammasso globulare 6
amministrazione 445
ammiraglia 522
ammortizzatore 287, 351, 523
ammortizzatore anteriore 369
ammortizzatore posteriore 367
amo 536, 538
amo con setale 538
amo, apertura dell' 538
ampere 426
ampiezza 418
ampolla della tuba di Falloppio 113
ananas 136
anatomia 96
anatomia di un astice machio 71
anatomia di una conchiglia bivalve 73
anatomia patologica, laboratorio di 465
anatra 81, 155
anatra, uovo di 155
ancia 305, 306
ancia doppia 306
ancia semplice 306
ancia, canna ad 305
anconeo 97
ancora a scatto 221
ancoraggio 473
ancorina 538
andature 83
Ande, Cordigliera delle 17
Andorra 449
anelli 264, 496, 497
anelli addominali 536
anello 52, 270, 307, 423, 424, 489
anello a fascia 264
anello a strappo 163
anello centrale esterno da 25 punti 471
anello con sigillo 264
anello d'accordatura 297
anello dei doppi 471
anello dei tripli 471
anello di attacco 535
anello di bloccaggio 332
anello di chiusura 210
anello di congiunzione 538
anello di fidanzamento 264
anello di regolazione 236
anello di regolazione della coppia di serraggio 228
anello di regolazione diottrica 420
anello di sospensione 270
anello di traino 460
anello esterno 515
anello fermadisco 501
anello fermamulinello 536
anello guida della lenza 536, 537
anello interno 515
anello oculare 78
anello, orecchini ad 264
anemometro 413
anestesia, stanza per l' 464
aneto 142
anfibi 75
anfibi, esempi di 75
anfiteatro romano 281
anfora, gonna ad 253
Angola 452
angolare 277
angoli, esempi di 428
angoli, lenzuolo con 204
angoliera 203
angolo 481, 498
angolo acuto 428
angolo concavo 428
angolo della pista 506
angolo di elevazione, regolazione dell' 420
angolo ottuso 428
angolo retto 428
anguilla 159
anice 142
anice stellato 60
anidride carbonica, assorbimento di 54
anidride solforosa, emissione di 48
Anik 317
anima 305
anima, canna ad 305
animali, negozio di 436
animelle 154
annaffiatoio 236
anno 441
anno, stagioni dell' 38
annodatura 245
ano 71, 73, 106, 111, 112
anodo 417
anta, pannello dell' 202
Antartide 14, 15
antefissa 279
antelice 115
antenna 7, 67, 68, 71, 326, 327, 349, 369, 392, 395, 457, 487
antenna ad alta frequenza, cavo dell' 394
antenna di captazione 376
antenna di casa 316
antenna di trasmissione/ricezione 316
antenna emittente 316
antenna parabolica 321
antenna parabolica ricetrasmittente 316
antenna per telecomunicazioni 386, 387
antenna radio 382, 384, 386, 387, 525
antenna telescopica 325
antenne, terminali di collegamento delle 322
antennula 71
antera 56
antiallagamento, dispositivo 214
anticlinale 403
anticollisione, luce 392
Antigua e Barbuda 449
Antille, Isole delle 448
antilope 84
antipastiera 166
antisettico 461
antitrago 115
antivibrazione, impugnatura con sistema 235
aorta 104, 105
aorta addominale 102, 107
aorta ascendente 103
aorta discendente 103
aorta, arco dell' 102, 104
ape 68
ape operaia 68
ape operaia, morfologia di un' 68
ape regina 68
apertura 73, 224, 243, 247
apertura dell'amo 538
apertura per le braccia 251
apertura/chiusura vassoio del disco 319
apice 55, 72, 73, 101, 118
apotecio 50
apparato del Golgi 50, 66
apparato digerente 106
apparato radicale 53, 62
apparato respiratorio 105
apparato urinario 107
apparecchio telefonico 327
appartamenti 512
appartiene a 427
appendice vermiforme 106
applicatore a spugnetta 266
appoggiamano 466
appoggiapiedi 224, 369, 467, 501
appoggiapiedi del guidatore 367, 368
appoggiapiedi del passeggero 367, 368
appoggiatura 299
appoggio del mignolo 307
appoggio del pollice 306, 307
appoggio del polpaccio 511
appoggio, barra d' 219
appoggio, filo d' 70
appoggio, piano di 396
appoggio, piastra d' 229
appoggio, punto d' 70
approssimativamente uguale a 427
apribottiglie 170, 531
apriscatole 170, 180, 531
aptero 51
aquila 81
Arabia Saudita 452
Arabico, Mare 19
arachide 130
arachidi, olio di 149
aracnidi 67
aracnidi, esempi di 70
aracnoide 109
aragosta 158
Aral, Lago di 19
arame 123
arancia 134
arancia, sezione di un' 58
arbitro 479, 481, 483, 488, 495, 498, 499, 507, 516, 518
arbitro capo 475
arborizzazione terminale 110
arca 447
arcata 281, 284
arcata dentale inferiore 116
arcata dentale superiore 116
archetto 301, 425, 460, 537
archetto, meccanismo di apertura dell' 537
archi, famiglia degli 301
architettura 278
architrave 185, 192, 279, 285
archiviazione 339
archivio delle cartelle cliniche 465
archivio, scatola per 340
archivolto 285
arcipelago 24
arco 428
arco aortico 102, 103, 104
arco composto 535
arco diagonale 284
arco insulare 33
arco longitudinale 284
arco naturale 35
arco palatoglosso 116
arco rampante 284, 285
arco trasversale 284
arcobaleno 41
ardiglione 246, 538
area commerciale 435
area d'attesa 442
area dei tre secondi 489
area di alta pressione 43
area di atterraggio 472
area di bassa pressione 43
area di combattimento 499
area di gioco 386, 471
area di meta 483, 484
area di parcheggio 389
area di porta 480, 507
area di precipitazione 39
area di rifornimento 346
area di rigore 480
area di servizio 25, 389
area di sicurezza 499
area di sosta 25
area di sosta dei veicoli 345
area per il ritiro dei bagagli 390
arena 281
areola 113
argani di perforazione 403
argano 287
Argentina 448
argine 342
aria calda 41
aria calda ascendente 43
aria calda, deflettore dell' 192
aria calda, uscita dell' 192
aria compressa, bombola di 454
aria fredda 41
aria fredda discendente 43
aria, compressore dell' 376
aria, filtro dell' 235, 398
aria, inquinamento dell' 47
aria, presa d' 367, 383, 395
aria, temperatura dell' 39
aria, tipo di massa d' 39
Ariele 3
aringa 159
armadietti degli studenti 445
armadio 202, 213, 439
armadio appendiabiti 203
armadio frigorifero 438
armatura di chiave 299
armatura protettiva del tronco 486
Armenia 452
armonica a bocca 296
arnia 122
aromatiche, piante 142
arpa 302
arpe 295
arpeggio 299
arredamento per la casa 200
arresto, blocco d' 229
arresto, pulsante di 229, 424
arresto, tasto di 319, 323
arricciaburro 169
arricciacapelli 269
arricciatura 255
arridatoio 521
arrivo della sciovia 512
arrivo, parete di 516
arrosto 153
arrotolato 152
arte 278
arteria addominale dorsale 71
arteria ascellare 102
arteria brachiale 102
arteria carotide comune 102
arteria dell'arco del piede 102
arteria dorsale del piede 102
arteria femorale 102
arteria iliaca comune 102, 107
arteria iliaca interna 102, 103, 107
arteria mesenterica inferiore 107
arteria mesenterica superiore 102, 107
arteria polmonare 102, 104, 105
arteria renale 102, 107
arteria sternale 71
arteria succlavia 102
arteria tibiale anteriore 102
arteria ventrale 71
arterie 102
arti plastiche, aula di 444
arti sceniche 294
arti toracici 71
articolazione 355
articolazione del nodello 83
articoli da regalo, negozio di 436
articoli di cancelleria 337
articoli di pelletteria 274
articoli per acconciatura 268
articoli personali 264, 271
articoli sportivi, negozio di 437
articoli vari 341
articolo 313
articolo di spalla 313
Artide 14
artiglio 79, 82
arto anteriore 75
arto inferiore 103
arto locomotore 70
arto locomotorio 67
arto posteriore 75
arto superiore 103
ascella 92, 94
ascella fogliare 55
ascensione retta, cerchio graduato dell' 8, 9
ascensore 287, 435, 439
ascensore, cabina dell' 287
asciugacapelli 270
asciugamano 267
asciugamano da bagno 267
asciugatrice 213
Asia 14, 19, 34, 452
asino 84
asola 246, 531
asola per il picchetto 528, 529
asparago 125
aspirapolvere 209
aspirapolvere verticale 209
aspirazione, tubo di 455
Aspirina® 461
assafetida 139
assale 527
assale anteriore 401
asse della bobina 537
asse di trasmissione del motore 177
asse orizzontale, regolazione micrometrica dell' 9
asse polare 7
assegni 441
assegni libretto degli 274
assistente sociale, ufficio dell' 463
assistenti degli avvocati 440
asso 468
assone 110
assorbimento attraverso la superficie terrestre 46
assorbimento attraverso le nuvole 46
assorbimento di acqua e sali minerali 54
assorbimento di anidride carbonica 54
asta 199, 424, 503, 505, 506, 514, 534
asta d'accordo 305
asta del meccanismo a scatto 312
asta di perforazione 403
asta di sostegno 380
asta mobile 425
asta motrice quadra 403
astata 55
astenosfera 26
asteroidi, fascia degli 3
astice 71, 158
astice, morfologia di un 71
astigmatismo 419
astragalo 99
astronautica 10
astronomia 2
astuccio 265
astuccio delle manette 456
astuccio per i guanti di lattice 456
astuccio per occhiali 275
Atacama, Deserto di 17
atlante 99
Atlante, Monti dell' 20
Atlantico, merluzzo dell' 161
Atlantico, Oceano 14, 15, 18, 20
Atlantico, salmone dell' 161
atleta 473
atletica leggera 472
atmosfera 44, 48
atmosfera terrestre, profilo dell' 37
atollo 35
atomi 414
atomizzatore 236
atomo 414
atrio 280, 374, 435, 439, 440, 442
atrio destro 103, 104
atrio sinistro 103, 104
attaccante 481
attaccante centrale 487
attaccante destro 485
attaccante sinistro 485, 487
attacco 199, 273, 485, 513, 514, 526
attacco a baionetta 199
attacco a spina 199
attacco a vite 199
attacco del manubrio 371
attacco del tubo di alimentazione dell'acqua 236
attacco del tubo di scarico 192
attacco della campana 306
attacco di sicurezza 10, 510, 511
attacco per attrezzi 10
attacco, leva di apertura dell' 511
atterraggio, faro di 395
atterraggio, finestrino di 395
attesa, area d' 442
attizzatoio 193
attore 290
attori, ingresso degli 278
attori, sedie degli 290
attrazione 416
attrezzatura 472
attrezzatura elettrica 217
attrezzatura terminale 538
attrezzatura, ripostiglio per l' 444
attrezzature da campeggio 531
attrezzi da muratore 216
attrezzi di brasatura 218
attrezzi di saldatura 218
attrezzi di serraggio 222
attrezzi domestici 215
attrezzi ginnici 500
attrezzi idraulici 216

attrezzi per annaffiare 236
attrezzi per chiodare 220
attrezzi per piccoli lavori di giardinaggio 232
attrezzi per potare e tagliare 234
attrezzi per sagomare 229
attrezzi per seminare e piantare 231
attrezzi per smuovere la terra 233
attrezzi per trapanare 228
attrezzi, cassetta degli 225
attrezzi, kit di 372
attrezzista 291
attrezzo multiuso 501
attrice 291
audio, sistema di registrazione 291
augnatura manuale, sega per 226
augnatura, cassetta ad 226
aula 444, 445
aula di arti plastiche 444
aula di informatica 444
aula di musica 444
aula di scienze 444
aula di tribunale 440
aula per studenti con difficoltà d'apprendimento 444
aumento di tensione 402, 408
auricolare 325
aurora polare 37
Australia 14, 34, 453
Austria 450
auto da formula 1 525
auto da formula 3000 524
auto da formula Indy 524
auto da NASCAR 524
auto da rally 524
autobotte 364
autobus 362, 435
autobus a due piani 363
autobus articolato 363
autobus urbano 362
autobus, fermata dell' 434
autobus, stazione degli 432
autocaravan 361
autocarro a cassone ribaltabile 401
autoclave 464
autogrù 364, 397
autogruista, cabina dell' 397
autolavaggio 346
automobile 347
automobilismo 524
automotrice 376
autopompa 455
autoradio 354
autoreggente, calza 257
autorespiratore 454
autoscala 455
autoscatto, spia luminosa dell' 314
autostrada 25, 343, 431
autostrada, numero di 25
autotrofi, organismi 45
autoveicoli industriali 364
autovetture, ponte per le 386
autunno 38
autunno, equinozio d' 38
avambraccio 86, 93, 95
avambraccio, protezione per l' 486
avanzamento della carta, tasto di 443
avanzamento rapido, tasto di 323
avena 61, 143
avena, farina di 144
avena: pannocchia 61
avenue 25, 433
aviogetto a lungo raggio 392
aviorimessa 389
avocado 128
avvertenze, targhetta delle 228
avviamento, manovella di 235
avviamento, motorino d' 237
avvio, tasto di 328
avvisatore acustico 377
avvisatore acustico a tromba 364
avvocati dell'accusa, banco degli 440
avvocati, assistenti degli 440
avvolgimento, manovella d' 225
avvoltoio 80
axel 509
Azerbaigian 452
azienda 335
azienda commerciale 335
azione del vento 45
azzeramento, pulsante di 424

B

babbuino 91
baby-doll 256
bacca 59
bacce di ginepro 138
baccello 60
bacche 132
bacchetta 301
bacchetta di metallo 309
bacchette 309
bacheca 341, 444
bacinella raccogligocce 210
bacinella raccogligrasso 179
bacino 381, 406, 407
bacino a monte 406
bacino a valle 406, 407
bacino di carenaggio 381
bacino, porta del 381
backgammon 469
backspace 331
bacon americano 156
bacon canadese 156
badile 233
badile pieghevole 532
Baffin, Isola di 16
bagagli 276
bagagli, deposito 374
bagagli, scompartimento 376
bagagliai 383
bagagliaio 362, 393, 395
bagaglio a mano 276
bagher 487
bagno degli uomini 294
bagno delle donne 294
bagno, costume da 263
bagno, lucernario del 189
bagno, slip da 263
bagno, stanza da 439
bagno, vasca da 195
bagnomaria, pentola per cucinare a 175
bagnoschiuma 267
baguette 144
Bahama 448
Bahrein 452
baia 5, 24
Baia di Hudson 16
Baikal, Lago 19
baionetta, attacco a 199
baita di montagna 512
balalaica 297
balaustra 188, 189, 283
balaustra della comunione 446
balaustre 506
balaustro 191
balconata 447
balconcino, reggiseno a 259
balcone 189, 412
balena franca 90
balenottera 90
ballatoi 292
ballerina 241
ballerino 160
ballo, sala da 387
balsamo per capelli 267
Baltico, Mar 18
balze, gonna a 253
bambini, vestiti per 261
banana 136
banana plantain 136
banca 432, 437, 442
banca di emissione, iniziali della 441
banchina 381
banchina di scarico delle merci 437, 439
banchina laterale 342
Banchisa di Amery 15
Banchisa di Filchner 15
Banchisa di Ross 15
banco 444
banco degli avvocati dell'accusa 440
banco degli avvocati difensori 440
banco dei formaggi 121
banco dei giudici 440
banco dei testimoni 440
banco dell'imputato 440
banco della carne fresca 120
banco della carne self-service 120
banco della giuria 440
banco della reception 442
banco delle informazioni 390, 437, 442, 463
banco di registrazione 390
banco di sabbia 33
banco per la prenotazione degli hotel 390
bancomat, sportello 437, 442
bancone del bar 438
banconota: dritto 441
banconota: rovescio 441
banconote, emissione di 442
banconote, scomparto per 274
banda 286
banda magnetica 441
banda nuvolosa a spirale 43
banda olografica 441
banda, tasto di selezione della 322
bande verticali, porta a 286
bandella di rinforzo 277
banderuola 413
bandiera dell'Unione Europea 441
bandiera rimovibile 504
bandiere 448
bandierina 482
bandierina centrale 480
bandierina del calcio d'angolo 481
Bangladesh 453
banjo 296
bar 293, 432, 436, 438
bar, bancone del 438
bar, mobile 203
bar, sgabello da 438
barattoli 162
barba 61
barba, pennello da 271
barbabietola 129
barbacane 282
Barbados 449
barbaforte 129
barbetta 61
barbone 86
barca a chiglia 521
barca a vela 520
barcana 36
barche, esempi di 382
bardana 129
barelle, deposito delle 462
Barents, Mar di 18
barista 438
barra 412, 469
barra collettrice 407
barra d'appoggio 219
barra dei martelletti 304
barra del timone 520
barra di comando 395
barra di partenza 516
barra di pressione 304
barra di traino 361
barra distanziatrice 362
barra per i dorsali 501
barra per i pettorali 501
barra per i tricipiti 501
barra spaziatrice 330
barretta 273
barretta di combustibile 409
barriera 434
barriera di pneumatici 524
basamento 27, 227, 283, 435, 498
basamento del telescopio 7
basamento imbottito 489
baschina, gonna con 253
basco 239
base 164, 174, 176, 179, 180, 192, 197, 206, 229, 269, 277, 296, 308, 332, 412, 421, 422, 454, 473
base del bulbo 54
base del tergale 200
base dell'intelaiatura 186
base di sostegno 202
base fissa 224
base girevole 224
base, piastra di 27, 227
baseball 474
basilico 142
Bass, Stretto di 15
bassa pressione, area di 43
bassa tensione, linea di distribuzione a 198
basse frequenze, pick-up per 303
bassi, bottoniera dei 296
bassi, ponticello dei 304
bassi, registro dei 296
bassi, regolatore dei 322
basso, chiave di 298
bastoncello 119
bastoncino di carbone (catodo) 417
bastone 507
bastone con manico anatomico 466
bastone da passeggio 273, 466
bastone del giocatore 506
bastone estendibile 456
bastone inglese 466
bastone, pomolo del 506
battagliola 384
battente 286
batteria 221, 228, 308, 350, 359, 411, 416
batteria elettronica 311
batteria ricaricabile 320
batteria, contenitore della 359
battistrada, scolpitura del 358
battitoia 297, 308
battitore 475, 476, 478, 479, 491, 494
battuta, zona di 477
baule 277
bauletto 369
bavaglino 260
Beaufort, Mar di 16
beccatello 282
beccheggio 395
becchi lunghi, pinza a 217
becchi, esempi di 79
becco 78
becco corneo 76
beccuccio 180, 181, 215, 268
beccuccio spruzzatore 272
beccuccio, vaschetta con 177
becquerel 426
begonia 56
Belgio 449
Belize 448
bemolle 299
benda elastica 461
Bengala, Golfo del 19
Benin 451
benzina auto 405
benzina avio 405
benzina leggera 405
benzina pesante 405
bequadro 299
bergamotto 134
bergère 200
Bering, Mar di 14
Bering, Stretto di 16
berlina 347
bermuda 254
berretto 238, 456, 514
berretto con pompon 239
berretto da cacciatore 238
berretto impermeabile 239
bersaglio 471
bertesca 282
bestiame, carro 377
betoniera 365
betulla 64
Bhutan 453
biancheria da letto 204
biancheria da notte 256
biancheria intima 247, 258
biancheria intima, negozio di 436
biancheria, loale per la 439
bianchi 470
bianco 418, 469
bibita, bicchiere da 165
bibita, cucchiaio da 168
bibite 120
bibite, distributore di 463
biblioteca 433, 444
bicchiere 176, 532
bicchiere da acqua 165
bicchiere da bibita 165
bicchiere da Bordeaux 165
bicchiere da Borgogna 165
bicchiere da brandy 165
bicchiere da porto 165
bicchiere da vino alsaziano 165
bicchiere da vino bianco 165
bicchierino da liquore 165
bicicletta 370
bicicletta da corsa 373, 522
bicicletta da cross-country 522
bicicletta da downhill 522
bicicletta da turismo 373
bicicletta olandese 373
bicicletta, componenti di una 370
biciclette, esempi di 373
biciclette, parcheggio per le 445
bicipite brachiale 96
bicipite femorale 97
bicipiti femorali, rullo per i 501
bidè 195
bidello, ufficio del 445
bidone carrellato per il riciclaggio del vetro 49
bidone carrellato per il riciclaggio dell'alluminio 49
bidone carrellato per il riciclaggio della carta 49
bidone dei rifiuti 215
biella 360
Bielorussia 450
bietola da coste 125
bietta 301
biglia battente 502, 503
biglia battente dell'avversario 502, 503
biglia bianca battente 503
biglia blu 503
biglia gialla 503
biglia marrone 503
biglia nera 503
biglia rosa 503
biglia rossa 502, 503
biglia verde 503
biglie da colpire 502
biglie rosse 503
biglietteria 294, 390
biglietteria automatica 294
biglietti, distributore automatico di 379
biglietti, vendita dei 378
bigodino 268
bilancia 292
bilancia a molla 423
bilancia a sospensione inferiore 422
bilancia da analisi 423
bilancia da cucina 171
bilancia di precisione 422
bilancia elettronica 423
bilancia pesapersone 423
bilanciamento 303
bilanciamento degli altoparlanti 322
bilanciere 360, 500, 501
bilanciere, placchetta a 305
biliardo 502
biliardo inglese 503
biliardo per carambola 502
bimah 447
binari del carrello 290
binario 207, 374, 378, 431
binario di raccordo 375
binario ferroviario 432
binario morto 375
binario, faretto da 207
binario, numero del 374
bindella ventilata 534
binocolo da teatro 273
binocolo prismatico 420
biologia 426
biosfera 44
biosfera, struttura della 44
birra 120
birra, boccale da 165
biscroma 299
biscroma, pausa di 299
bisonte 84
bistecca 152
bistecca, coltello da 168
bitta 385
bitume 405
blastodisco 79
blazer 254
bloc-notes 338
bloccaggio della base 224
bloccaggio, dispositivo di 209
bloccaggio, ghiera di 221
bloccaggio, leva di 224
bloccaggio, pulsante di 208
bloccaggio, viti di 425
blocchetto 308
blocchetto di accensione 354
blocchetto di avviamento 368
blocco 305, 473
blocco d'arresto 229
blocco del ponticello 303
blocco della culatta 534
blocco delle maiuscole 330
blocco di ancoraggio dei cavi 344
blocco di chiusura 425
blocco di partenza 473, 516
blocco motore 176, 177, 180, 208, 272
blocco numerico 331
blocco operatorio 464
blocco, dispositivo di 219, 226
blog 335

blu 418
boa 77
boa di ricognizione meteorologica 38
bobina 319, 536, 537
bobina, asse della 537
bobina, meccanismo di rilascio della 537
bocca 71, 72, 73, 75, 90, 94, 116, 220, 305, 534
bocca di carico 208
bocca di erogazione 197
boccaglio 467
boccale da birra 165
boccaporto 13
bocchetta 177, 180
bocchetta 186
bocchetta del serbatoio 237
bocchetta di ventilazione 354
bocchetta per fessure 209
bocchetta per tappezzeria 209
bocchette 172
bocchettone di riempimento 351
bocchino 306, 307, 311
body 255, 258, 260, 263
bolero 254
Bolivia 448
bolla, livella a 225
bolle d'aria 339
bollitore 180
boma 519, 520
bomba vulcanica 28
bombetta 238
bombo 69
bombola 454, 529
bombola del gas 218
bombola di aria compressa 454
bombola di gas medicale 464
bombola di gas propano 361
bongos 309
booster, paracadute del 12
bordame 519
Bordeaux, bicchiere da 165
bordo 205
bordo a coste 250, 261
bordo del piano di cottura 210
bordo della scarpetta 511
bordo di attacco 393
bordo di rifinitura 277
bordo di uscita 392
bordo elastico 247
bordo superiore 493
bordone 296
bordoniera 308
bordura 182, 230
Borgogna, bicchiere da 165
borra 534
borraccia 532
borragine 142
borsa a manicotto 276
borsa a soffietto 274
borsa a telaio rigido 276
borsa a tracolla 276
borsa da postino 276
borsa da viaggio 276
borsa della spesa 276
borsa laterale 369
borse 275
borsellino 275
borsello 276
borsone da viaggio 276
boschi, rana dei 75
bosco 25
Bosnia ed Erzegovina 450
bossolo 534
bossolo di plastica 534
Botnia, Golfo di 18
botola 281, 292
Botswana 452
bottega 280
bottiglia 267, 532
bottiglia da tavola 165
bottiglia dell'acqua 371
bottiglia di vetro 163
bottone 199, 245, 250, 296, 301
bottone a pressione 243, 249
bottone della tracolla 303
bottoniera dei bassi 296
boulevard 25, 433
bowling 436
box 524
box doccia 195
boxer 247
bozzello 397, 521
braccia, apertura per le 251
bracciale con ciondoli 264
bracciale con piastrina 264
bracciale pneumatico 461
bracciale tubolare 264
bracciali 264
braccio 83, 91, 93, 95, 206, 236, 270, 297, 333, 397, 412, 421, 467
braccio del tergicristallo 355
braccio del tremolo 303
braccio della forca 396
braccio della pala caricatrice 399
braccio della sospensione 351
braccio della spirale 6
braccio di posizionamento 400
braccio di scavo 400
braccio di sollevamento 364, 399, 400
braccio di sospensione 212, 467
braccio distanziatore 219
braccio manipolatore telecomandato 12
braccio metallico 236
braccio spruzzante 214
braccio telecomandato 11
braccio telescopico 397, 455
braccio, tirante del 397
bracciolo 200, 205, 352, 353, 467
bracciolo, sostegno del 200
brachiale 96
brachioradiale 96, 97
braciere 283
braciola 152, 153
branca 222
branchie 73
branda 530
brandina smontabile 530
brandy, bicchiere da 165
branzino 160
Brasile 448
Brasile, noce del 133
brattea 60
bretella abbottonabile 261
bretella di raccordo 343
bretella di uscita 391
bretella di uscita della pista ad alta velocità 388
bretella regolabile 260
bretelle 246
bricco del latte 166
brick 163
brick a tappo 163
bricolage, negozio di 436
brie 151
brillamento 4
brillantante, serbatoio per il 214
brina 41
broccolo 127
brochure, espositore di 442
brodo, cucchiaio da 168
bronchiolo terminale 105
bronco lobare 105
bronco principale 105
browser 334
bruciatore 210, 529
bruciatore a corona 174
bruciatore, telaio del 529
bruco 67
Brunei 453
Bruxelles, cavolini di 126
buca 502, 504
buca centrale 502
buca inferiore 502
buca par 5 504
buca superiore 502
buccia 57, 58, 59
buccino 157
bue 85
bufalo 84
buffet 438
bugna 519
bulbillo 54
bulbo 125, 199, 385, 387
bulbo d'alcool 424
bulbo del pelo 114
bulbo di mercurio 424
bulbo olfattivo 117
bulbo, base del 54
bulbo, fusto del 54
bulbo, sezione di un 54
Bulgaria 450
bulldog 86
bulldozer 398
bulletta 220
bullone 222, 223, 224, 357
bullone a espansione 221
bullone di spallamento 223
bullone zigrinato 219
bulloni 223
bunker di sabbia 504
Buona Speranza, Capo di 20
Burkina Faso 451
burotica 312
burotica e forniture per l'ufficio 329
burriera 166
burro 150
burro, coltello da 168
burro, scomparto per il 211
Burundi 451
bussola magnetica 533
bussole, set di 223
bussolotto 469
busta imbottita 339
busta portadocumenti 275
bustina 238
bustina di tè 148
bustine trasparenti 274
button-down, collo 245

C

C, morsetto a 224
cabina 386, 398, 399, 400, 401, 443
cabina armadio 189
cabina del gruista 397
cabina dell'ascensore 287
cabina dell'autogruista 397
cabina della torre di controllo 388
cabina di classe turistica 393
cabina di guida 376, 377
cabina di manovra 375
cabina di osservazione del fuoco primario 7
cabina di pilotaggio 12, 385, 392, 395
cabina di prima classe 392
cabina di proiezione 294
cabina di regia 293
cabina passeggeri 395
cabina, guida della 287
cabina, pavimento della 287
cabina, soffitto della 287
cabriolet 200
cacao 148
caccia 534
cacciapietre 376, 377
cacciavite 221, 531
cacciavite automatico 221
cacciavite con batteria incorporata 221
cacciavite con punta a croce 531
cachi 137
caditoia 282
caduta di poppa 519
caduta di prua 519
caffè 148, 432, 437, 445
caffè, chicchi tostati di 148
caffè, chicchi verdi di 148
caffè, cucchiaino da 168
caffè, macchine da 181
caffè, tazza alta da 166
caffè, tazzina da 166
caffettiera 531
caffettiera a filtro 181
caffettiera a infusione 181
caffettiera a pistone 181
caffettiera napoletana 181
caffettiera per espresso 181
caimano 77
calabrone 69
calamaro 157
calamita 341
calamo vegetale 312
calaza 79
calcagno 99, 247
calcagno, rinforzo del 262
calcagno, rinforzo esterno del 240
calcagno, rinforzo interno del 240
calciatore 480
calcio 480, 503, 534
calciolo 534
calcolatrice 274
calcolatrice da tavolo 337
calcolatrice scientifica 337
calcolatrice tascabile 337
caldaia 308
calendario a fogli staccabili 338
calendario da tavolo 338
calibro a corsoio con nonio 425
calice 56, 59, 60, 107, 446
calice da cocktail 165
calice gustativo 118
calicetto 59
California, Golfo di 16
Callisto 2
calore 408
calore, dispersione di 46
calore, produzione di 408
calore, trasferimento di 415
calotta 208, 209, 238, 239, 367, 412
calotta della torretta 420
calotta di sicurezza 237
calotta filtrante 459
calotta polare, della 40
calza 257, 259
calza a rete 257
calza autoreggente 257
calza con reggicalze 476
calza dell'albero 519
calze 247, 257
calzerotto 247, 257
calzettone 257, 480, 486, 506
calzettono 483
calzino 257, 492
calzino corto 247
calzino lungo 247
camaleonte 77
cambio 63
cambio disco 323
cambio, cavo del 372
cambio, leva del 350, 354, 371, 372
cambio, pedale del 367, 368, 369
cambio, scatola del 350
Cambogia 453
Camciatca, Penisola di 19
camembert 151
camera a spirale 407
camera anteriore 119
camera blindata 443
camera d'albergo 439
camera d'aria 79
camera da letto 189, 528
camera da letto principale 189
camera del re 278
camera della regina 278
camera di espansione 424
camera di scarico 278
camera di scoppio 360
camera doppia 439
camera magmatica 28, 402
camera matrimoniale 439
camera posteriore 119
camera pressurizzata 345
camera pulpare 101
camera sotterranea 278
camera, numero della 439
cameraman 290
camerino 290, 293
camerino privato 290
Camerun 451
camicetta classica 255
camicetta incrociata 255
camicette, esempi di 255
camicia 245
camicia da notte 256
camicia, collo a 245
camicia, lembo della 245
camicione 255
camiciotto 255
caminiera 192
camino 183, 188, 192, 193
camino principale 28
camino, ferri per il 193
camion, esempi di 364
cammello 85
cammino di ronda 282
cammino di ronda coperto 282
camomilla 148
camoscio, pelle di 265
campagna 431
campana 306, 307
campana per la raccolta del vetro 49
campana per la raccolta della carta 49
campana, attacco della 306
campane tubolari 295, 309
campanelle 309
campanile 446
campata centrale 344
campata laterale 344
campeggio 528
campeggio, attrezzature da 531
campi solcati 31
campionatore 310
campo 474, 479, 482, 487, 488, 490, 494, 506, 515
campo da golf 430
campo di allenamento 504
campo di gioco 480, 515
campo di servizio del doppio 495
campo di servizio del singolo 495
campo geotermico 402
campo magnetico 318, 416
campo per football americano 484
Canada 448
canale del sifone 73
Canale della Manica 18
canale della radice 101
canale deltizio 32
canale destro 324
canale di aerazione 278
Canale di Drake 15, 17
Canale di Mozambico 20
canale di scarico 407
canale lacrimale 119
canale per le acque meteoriche 434
canale semicircolare laterale 116
canale semicircolare posteriore 116
canale semicircolare superiore 116
canale sinistro 324
canale velenifero 76
canale, chiusa di un 381
canali, tasti di selezione dei 319
cancella 328
cancellazione 331
cancellazione, pulsante di 315
cancelleria, articoli di 337
cancellieri, scrivania dei 440
cancellieri, ufficio dei 440
cancello 202
Cancro, Tropico del 20, 21, 22
candela 359, 360, 426, 446
candela, cavo della 350, 360
cane 86, 534, 535
cane, morfologia di un 86
canestro 489
canino 101
canna 370, 534
canna ad ancia 305
canna ad anima 305
canna da lancio 537
canna da mosca 536
canna della melodia 296
canna di imboccatura 307
canna, zucchero di 149
cannella 138
cannello 296
cannelloni 146
cannocchiale 8
cannocchiale cercatore 8, 9
cannocchiale di mira 420
cannolicchio 157
cannoncino 245
cannone 83
cannone elettronico 318
cannotto reggisella 370
cannuccia 163
canottiera 247, 261, 263, 500
cantalupo 135
cantarello 123
cantina dei vini 438
canyon sottomarino 33
capanna di fango 288
capanna di paglia 288
capannoni delle merci in transito 381
capasanta 157
capelli 93, 95
capelli, pinza per 268
capelli, spazzole per 268
capezzale 204
capezzolo 92, 94, 113
capitale 23
capitano 515
capo 24, 67, 72, 78
Capo di Buona Speranza 20
Capo Horn 17
Capo Verde 451
capocroce 285
capodoglio 90
capolino 57
capomacchinista 290
caposala, ufficio del 463
caposquadra 291
capotasto 301, 302, 303
cappa 164, 192, 210
cappella 282
cappella assiale 284, 285
cappella laterale 284
cappella radiale 284, 285
cappelletto 247
cappello 52, 191, 286, 313

cappello a falda larga 239
cappello da marinaio 239
cappello di feltro 238, 239
cappello terminale 409
cappio 510, 514
cappone 155
cappotti, esempi di 248, 251
cappotto 248, 251
cappotto alla raglan 251
cappotto con pellegrina 251
cappuccio 249, 260, 261, 312, 467, 508
cappuccio di protezione 460
cappuccio, felpa con 262
capra 84
capra, formaggi di 150
capra, latte di 150
Capricorno, Tropico del 20, 21, 22
capsula 51, 467
capsula a depressione 360
capsula di gelatina 467
capsula di risonanza 460
capsula ermetica 529
capsula, sezione di una 60
captazione, antenna di 376
caraffa 165, 166, 181
carambola 137
carapace 71, 76
caratteristiche della costa 35
caratteristiche della Luna 5
carbone, deposito di 402
carburante, condotto del 351
carburante, serbatoio del 235, 351, 366, 369, 377
carburante, serbatoio per il 364
carburante, tipo di 346
carburatore 366
carcassa 228, 229
carciofo 127
cardamomo 138
cardigan 250, 255
cardigan con scollo a V 250
cardii 157
cardinale 80
cardine 352
cardo 125
carena 74
carenaggio, bacino di 381
carenatura 366, 523
carenatura laterale 525
Caribico, Mar 14, 16
carica di lancio 534
carica elettrica, unità di misura della 426
carica, indicatore di 271
caricabatteria 228
caricabbasso 520
caricatore di lamette 271
carico, aeroplano da 394
carico, bocca di 208
carico, piano di 396
carico, piattaforma di 423
carico, tubo di 196
cariosside 61
carne 152
carne, cassetto per la 211
carnivori 45
Caronte 3
carota 129
carpa 160
Carpentaria, Golfo di 15
carpenteria 220, 221, 222, 225, 226, 228, 229
carpo, flessore ulnare del 96, 97
carré 249, 255
carreggiata 343
carrelli 121
carrello 236, 290, 376, 396, 397, 505, 521, 527
carrello a forca per palette di carico 396
carrello anteriore 376, 392
carrello avvolgitubo 236
carrello elevatore 396
carrello portabagagli 277, 374
carrello portavivande 202
carrello principale 393
carrello tenda 361
carrello, binari del 290
carri dei pompieri 455
carri merci, esempi di 377
carriola 231
carro bestiame 377
carro bisarca 377
carro cisterna 377
carro frigorifero 377
carro merci 375
carro pianale 377
carro pianale portacontainer 377
carrozza passeggeri 380
carrozzeria 348, 361, 523
carrozzerie, esempi di 347
carrucola del carrello 397
carta cerata 162
carta da forno 162
carta dei contintinenti 14
carta del tempo 38, 39
carta della rete metropolitana 379, 380
carta di addebito 443
carta di credito 441
carta fisica 24
carta geografica 444
carta più alta 468
carta politica 23
carta stradale 25
carta vetrata 229
carta, guida della 328
carta, numero della 441, 443
carta, pulsante di alimentazione della 333
carta, spia di alimentazione della 333
carte di credito, portafoglio per 274
carte di credito, scomparto per 274
carte, lettore di 442, 443
cartella 275
cartella con linguetta 339
cartella con pressino 339
cartella per documenti 339
cartella sospesa 340
cartelletta 340
cartellino di identificazione 456
cartello indicatore delle stazioni della linea 378
cartello pubblicitario 378, 380
carter 537
cartilagine alare maggiore 117
cartilagine del setto nasale 117
cartoccio 61
cartografia 21
cartone 163
cartone piccolo 163
cartuccia 216, 312
cartuccia per fucile a canna liscia 534
cartuccia per fucile a canna rigata 534
cartuccia, spia della 333
cartucciera 456
caruncola lacrimale 119
carvi 138
casa 182, 515
casa a due piani 289
casa a un piano 289
casa colonica 122
casa galleggiante 385
casa in mattoni cotti 288
casa romana 280
casa, abito da 252
casa, arredamento per la 200
casa, elementi della 185
casa, esterno di una 182
casa, struttura di una 188
casacca 255
casalinghi 120
casatorre 289
cascata 31, 32
caschetto 498
casco 10, 476, 478, 486, 506, 508, 510, 513, 522, 524, 526, 527
casco di protezione 367, 372
casco integrale 525
casco per cross 525
case a schiera 289
case tradizionali 288
casella 469
casella bianca 470
casella nera 470
caserma dei vigili del fuoco 433
Caspio, Mar 14, 19
cassa 121, 218, 271, 303, 304, 424
cassa acustica 294, 324, 325
cassa acustica centrale 321
cassa acustica principale 321
cassa acustica surround 321
cassa armonica circolare 296
cassa armonica piriforme 297
cassa armonica triangolare 297
cassa chiara 295, 308
cassa di risonanza 297, 302
cassa piena 303
cassa portabatteria 365
cassa, registratore di 121
cassaforte 443
cassapanca 203
casse 121
casse acustiche, tasti di selezione delle 322
casse acustiche, terminali di collegamento delle 322
cassero poppiero 386
casseruola 175
cassetta 326, 333
cassetta ad augnatura 226
cassetta aperta 162
cassetta degli attrezzi 225
cassetta di pronto soccorso 457, 461
cassetta di sicurezza 443
cassetta filtro 181
cassetta piccola 162
cassetta, coperchio della 196
cassetta, vano 321
cassetta, vano della 323
cassette di deposito per bagagli 374
cassettiera 203
cassetto 164, 202, 203, 205, 210
cassetto per la carne 211
cassetto per la verdura 211
cassiera 121
cassone 231, 400
cassone ribaltabile, autocarro a 401
cassone di compattazione 364
cassone di raccolta dei rifiuti 365
cassone per legna da ardere 192
cassone ribaltabile 401
castagna d'acqua 124
castagne 133
caste 68
castello 282, 383
castello di prua 387
castello motore 393
castoro 82
catamarano 521
catarifrangente 365, 370, 523
catena 370, 372
catena alimentare 45
catena di dune 36
catena di neuroni 110
catena di sicurezza 361
catena di sollevamento 396
catena montuosa 5, 24, 26
catena trinciante 235
catena, freno della 235
catena, guida della 235, 372
catodo 417
cattedra 444
cattedrale 284
cattedrale gotica 284
cattedrale, pianta della 285
cattura 470
cavalcavia 343, 344
cavalletta 69
cavalletta verde 69
cavalletto centrale 367
cavalletto laterale 367, 369
cavallo 83, 85, 247, 255, 470
cavallo con maniglie 496
cavallo per volteggi 496, 497
cavallo, morfologia di un 83
cavatappi 531
cavatappi a leva 170
cavatappi da cameriere 170
cavatorsoli 173
cavea 278, 281
cavetto di acciaio 535
cavi di accoppiamento 356
cavi, blocco di ancoraggio dei 344
cavia 82
cavicchiera 301
cavicchio 301, 302, 303
caviglia 92, 94, 302, 304
cavigliera 304
cavigliere/polsiere 500
cavità addominale 111, 112
cavità nasale 105
cavità orale 105, 106
cavità pleurica 105
cavo 228, 326, 332, 356, 364, 418, 501, 535
cavo d'alimentazione 177, 229
cavo del cambio 372
cavo del freno 371
cavo dell'antenna ad alta frequenza 394
cavo dell'elettricità 434
cavo della candela 350, 360
cavo di accelerazione 237
cavo di alimentazione 227, 269, 270, 322
cavo di alimentazione a corrente alternata 336
cavo di alimentazione a corrente continua 336
cavo di collegamento 324
cavo di interfaccia digitale per strumenti musicali (MIDI) 311
cavo di messa a terra 198
cavo di raccordo per luci di segnalazione 361
cavo di sincronizzazione 337
cavo di sollevamento 397
cavo di sospensione 344
cavo elettrico 354
cavo telefonico 434
cavo, manicotto del 228
cavolfiore 127
cavolini di Bruxelles 126
cavolo bianco 126
cavolo marittimo 126
cavolo ornamentale 126
cavolo rapa 125
cavolo riccio 126
cavolo rosso 126
cavolo verza 126
cavolo verzotto 126
cazzuola da muratore 216
ceci 130
cedro 134
cedro del Libano 65
cefalo 160
cefalotorace 70, 71
cella 67, 281
cella frigorifera 120, 121
cella solare 337, 410, 411
celle 440
celle solari, pannello di 411
celle solari, sistema a 411
cellula animale 66
cellula convettiva 43
cellula del succo 58
cellula vegetale 50
cellula, membrana della 50, 66
cellula, parete della 50
Celsius, grado 426
Celsius, scala 424
cemento 101
cemento, sottofondo di 190
ceneri vulcaniche, nube di 28
ceneri, strato di 28
cent 440
centina 392
centina di radice alare 392
cento 427
Centrafricana, Repubblica 451
centrale 485
centrale elettrica 406
centrale idroelettrica, sezione trasversale di una 407
centrale termoelettrica a carbone 402
centrifuga 180, 212
centrifuga scolainsalata 171
centriolo 66
centro 293, 428, 470, 471, 515
centro commerciale 431, 436
centro della città 431, 432
centro della ragnatela 70
centro di alta pressione 39
centro di bassa pressione 39
centro prelievi, sala d'attesa del 465
centroattacco 507
centrocampista centrale 481
centrocampista di destra 481
centrocampista di sinistra 481
ceppo 63
ceramica, condensatore di 417
cercafase 217
cerchia annuale 63
cerchio 366, 371
cerchio centrale 488
cerchio del battitore successivo 474
cerchio di centrocampo 481, 488, 507
cerchio di ingaggio 506
cerchio di serraggio 308
cerchio di stazione 39
cerchio graduato dell'ascensione retta 8, 9
cerchio graduato della declinazione 8, 9
cerchio, parti di un 428
cerchione 349
cereali 61, 143
Cerere 2
cerfoglio 142
cerimolia 136
cerniera 73, 178, 185, 186, 202, 214, 420
cerniera della visiera 367
cerniera lampo 265, 277, 528
cerniera regolabile 222
cerotto 461
cerotto adesivo 461
cervella 154
cervelletto 109
cervello 71, 109
cervo dalla coda bianca 84
cesoie 234
cesoie da giardino 234
cespo 125
cespuglio 230
cestella 68
cestello 177, 178, 180, 211, 212, 214
cestello di refrigerazione 180
cestello per friggere 171
cestello per la cottura a vapore 175
cestello per le posate 214
cestino 341, 538
cetriolino 128
cetriolo 128
cetriolo senza semi 128
Chac-Mool 283
chanel, scarpa 241
charleston 308
charlotte, stampo per 172
châssis: dorso 329
châssis: vista frontale 329
chat room 335
chayote 129
chela 71
chelicero 70
chemisier 252
cherosene 405
Chesterfield, divano 200
chiamata automatica, tasti di 327
chiamata, pulsante di 287
chiamata, tasto di 327
chiambrana 186
chiasma ottico 109
chiave 306
chiave a bussola a cricchetto 223
chiave a croce 356
chiave a forchetta doppia 223
chiave a rullino 223
chiave combinata 223
chiave del chiver 306
chiave del mandrino 228
chiave dell'acqua 307
chiave di basso 298
chiave di contralto 298
chiave di violino 298
chiave di volta 284
chiave poligonale a cricco 223
chiave poligonale doppia 223
chiave poligonale doppia ad anello aperto 223
chiave regolabile da lavandino 216
chiave USB 333
chiave, leva della 306
chiave, serratura a 274
chiavi 216, 223, 298, 311
chiavi di tensione 308
chiavi, negozio per la riproduzione delle 437
chiavi, protezione delle 306
chiavistello a scatto 186
chiavistello senza scatto 186
chicchi di caffè tostati 148
chicchi di caffè verdi 148
chicco di grano, sezione di un 61
chiesa 433, 446
chimica 414
chinois 171
chiocciola 72, 157
chiocciola per nastro adesivo 341
chiocciola, morfologia di una 72
chiocciole, molle per 173
chiocciole, tegamino per 173
chiodi di garofano 138
chiodi, esempi di 220
chiodo 220, 473
chiodo a spirale 220
chiodo comune 220

chiodo da muratore 220
chiodo di finitura 220
chiodo troncato 220
chioma 6, 63
chiosco 346
chirurgia minore, sala per operazioni di 462
chirurgo, lavandino del 465
chitarra acustica 302
chitarra basso 303
chitarra elettrica 303
chiusa di un canale 381
chiusura 274, 275
chiusura a occhiello 277
chiusura a scatto 178
chiusura in rilievo 163
chiusura lampo 249, 261
chiusura metallica a pressione 274
chiusura, anello di 210
chiusura, blocco di 425
chiusura, cordoncino di 275
chiusura, dispositivo di 535
chiusura, valvola di 196
chiver 306
chiver, chiave del 306
chorizo 156
chutney al mango 141
Ciad 451
Ciad, Lago 20
ciak 291
ciambella 144
ciano 418
cibi pronti 121
cicala 69
ciccioli 156
ciclismo 522
ciclismo su strada 522
ciclismo su strada, gara di 522
ciclista 522
ciclo idrologico 45
ciclomotore 369
ciclone 43
ciclone tropicale 43
cicloni tropicali, denominazione dei 43
cicogna 80
cieco 106
cieletti 292
cieletto 293
cielo tempestoso 41
cielo, copertura del 39
ciglia 66, 87
ciglio 66, 119
Cile 448
ciliato 55
ciliegie 132
cilindretto 357
cilindro 238, 429, 460
cilindro del braccio di scavo 400
cilindro del braccio di sollevamento 399, 400
cilindro della pala caricatrice 399, 400
cilindro dello scarificatore 398
cilindro di raffreddamento 420
cilindro di riflessione 420
cilindro di rotazione della lama 401
cilindro di rubino 420
cilindro di sollevamento 364, 397, 399, 455
cilindro di sollevamento della lama 398, 401
cilindro direzionale 400
cilindro principale 357
cima 29, 63, 219
cima bipara 57
cima di recupero 519
cima unipara 57
cimasa 202
cime di rapa 127
cimice rigata 69
ciminiera 402
cimino 536
cimitero 25, 433
Cina 453
cinema 294, 386, 432, 436
cinescopio 318
Cinese Meridionale, Mar 14, 19
Cinese Orientale, Mar 19
cinghia del mantice 296
cinghia del ventilatore 360
cinghia della ventola 350
cinghia di compressione frontale 532
cinghia di compressione laterale 532
cinghia di distribuzione 360
cinghia di tramissione 212
cinghia per i piedi 519
cinghiale 84
cinghietta posteriore di regolazione 458
cingolo 398, 523
cinquanta 427
cinque 427
cinque spezie, miscela di 139
cinquecento 427
cinta muraria 282
cintura 225, 246, 248, 499
cintura a vita 532
cintura da sollevamento pesi 500
cintura di Kuiper 2
cintura di ritenuta 205
cintura di servizio 456
cintura di sicurezza 353
cintura portautensili 225
cintura ventrale 353
cintura, abbottonatura della 246
cintura, passante della 248
cinturino 273, 424, 477, 500
cinturino a T, scarpa con 241
cinturino della manica 248
cinturino regolabile 244
cinturino, scarpa con 241
cioccolato 148
cioccolato al latte 148
cioccolato bianco 148
cioccolato fondente 148
ciondoli, bracciale con 264
ciotola 176
ciotole per mescolare 172
cipolla 236
cipolla bianca 124
cipolla d'inverno 124
cipolla di Spagna 124
cipolla rossa 124
cipolla verde 124
cipolline 124
cipresso, foglie squamiformi del 65
cipria compatta 266
cipria in polvere 266
cipria in polvere, pennello da 266
cipria, piumino da 266
Cipro 450
circo 5
circo glaciale 30
circolazione del sangue 102
circolazione, schema della 103
circolo 504
Circolo Polare Antartico 15, 21, 22
Circolo Polare Artico 21, 22
circonferenza 428
circonvallazione 25
circuito 524
circuito di distribuzione 198
circuito elettrico dei sensori 357
circuito elettrico parallelo 416
circuito frenante 350, 357
circuito integrato 417
circuito integrato inscatolato 417
circuito stampato 417
circuito stampato, scheda del 417
cirro 42
cirrocumulo 42
cirrostrato 42
cisterna 364, 385
cisterna, carro 377
cisterna, nave 384
cistifellea 106
citofaringe 66
citopigio 66
citoplasma 50, 66, 112
citostoma 66
città 23, 430
Città del Vaticano 450
città, centro della 431, 432
città, pianta di 25
city bike 373
ciuffo 83
clacson 354, 368
clarinetti 295
clarinetto 306
clarinetto basso 295
classifica generale, tabellone della 496
classificatore a soffietto 340
clavicola 98
clessidra per uova alla coque 171
climatizzazione, sistema di 46
climi aridi 40
climi del mondo 40
climi di montagna 40
climi polari 40
climi temperati caldi 40
climi temperati freddi 40
climi tropicali 40
clip, orecchini a 264
clitoride 112
cloche 239
cloroplasto 50
cobra 77
coccige 98
coccinella 69
cocco, noce di 133
coccodrillo 77
cocktail, calice da 165
coclea 116
cocomero 135
Cocos, placca delle 27
coda 71, 76, 82, 83, 86, 90, 111, 393, 510, 514, 526, 536
coda dell'elice 115
coda di polvere 6
coda ionica 6
coda, pattino di 395
coda, trave di 395
codetta 199
codice del prodotto 423
codice temporale 291
codolo 167, 169, 216, 228, 471
codrione 78
cofano anteriore 348, 364
cofano posteriore 349
coincide con 427
cola, noce di 133
colapasta 171
colata di fango 31
colata lavica 28
colbacco 238
colibrì 80
colino 171
colla in stick 341
collana 264
collana a cinque giri 264
collana lunga 264
collana lunga alla vita 264
collane 264
collant 257
collante 190
collare 193, 229, 273
collare del solaio 193
collare di chiusura del casco 10
collare tagliafuoco 193
collarino di velluto 264
collegamenti ipertestuali 334
collegamento elettrico 365
collegamento, cavo di 324
colletto 53, 101, 245, 271
colletto, punta del 245
collettore di alimentazione 360
collettore di elettroni 417
collettore di scarico 194, 350, 360
collettore principale 194
collettore solare piatto 410
collibia 123
collie 86
collina 29
collina abissale 33
collo 76, 83, 93, 94, 95, 111, 167, 240, 244, 248, 262, 318, 492
collo a camicia 245
collo a uomo 251
collo alto 514
collo button-down 245
collo d'oca 191, 400
collo del femore 99
collo del piede 92
collo dell'utero 112
collo, sostegno per il 525
colloquio, sale di 440
collutorio 272
Colombia 448
colon ascendente 106
colon discendente 106
colon sigmoideo 106
colon trasverso 106
colonna 31, 207, 279, 302, 313
colonna centrale 412
colonna d'alcool 424
colonna di frazionamento 405
colonna di mercurio 424
colonna di ventilazione 194
colonna montante dell'acqua calda 194
colonna montante dell'acqua fredda 194
colonna principale di scarico 194
colonna principale di ventilazione 194
colonna vertebrale 98, 109
colore 468
colori, sintesi dei 418
colpi 490
colpo di pattino 514
coltelli da cucina, esempi di 169
coltelli, esempi di 168
coltello 167, 176, 531, 533
coltello da bistecca 168
coltello da burro 168
coltello da cucina 169
coltello da dessert 168
coltello da formaggio 168
coltello da ostriche 169
coltello da pane 169
coltello da pesce 168
coltello da pompelmo 169
coltello da prosciutto 169
coltello da tavola 168
coltello elettrico 177
coltello miscelatore 176
coltello per affettare 169
coltello per disossare 169
coltivatore 233
columella 73
columella, piega della 73
comandi del retroescavatore 399
comandi del verricello 364
comandi della videocassetta 320
comandi di sintonia 318
comando a distanza, presa per il 314, 315
comando del tavolino traslatore 421
comando del tergicristallo 354
comando del tiraggio 192
comando zoom 320
comando, ponte di 382, 383, 386, 387
comando, quadro di 178, 179, 210, 212, 213, 214
combinazione 247
combinazione, serratura a 274
combinazioni del poker 468
combustibile 408
combustibile esaurito, vasca di deposito del 409
combustibile fossile 46, 48
combustibile per motori diesel 405
combustibile per motori diesel marini 405
combustibile, barretta di 409
combustibile, pastiglia di 409
combustione lenta, stufa a 192
cometa 6
comignolo 183
commessura labiale 86, 116
commutatore delle luci 368
comò 203
comodino 439, 464
comodino, lampada da 439
Comore 452
compact disc 326
compattatore 364
compattazione 49
compensazione dell'esposizione, pulsante di 314
complesso scolastico 433
complesso sportivo 431
completo da ginnastica 261
compluvio 280
componenti di una bicicletta 370
composizione del sangue 104
composta, contenitore della 231
compressa 467
compressore del climatizzatore 360
compressore dell'aria 376
computer 444
computer da tavolo 334
computer di bordo 354, 457
computer portatile 336
computer portatile: dorso 336
computer portatile: vista frontale 336
computer tascabile 337
computer, programmi del 457
comunicazione via telefono 327
comunicazione, modulo di 316
comunicazione, tunnel di 13
comunicazioni 312
comunicazioni aeree 317
comunicazioni industriali 317
comunicazioni marittime 317
comunicazioni militari 317
comunicazioni private 317
comunicazioni stradali 317
comunione, balaustra della 446
conca 115
conca di concrezione 31
conca nasale inferiore 117
conca nasale media 117
conca nasale superiore 117
concentrato di pomodoro 140
concentrazione di gas serra 46
concessionaria di automobili 433
conchiglia 72, 73, 200
conchiglia bivalve 73
conchiglia bivalve, anatomia di una 73
conchiglia bivalve, morfologia di una 73
conchiglia di protezione 486, 507
conchiglia univalve 73
conchiglia univalve, morfologia di una 73
conchiglie 146
concime organico 48
condensatore 402, 421
condensatore a pellicola plastica 417
condensatore di ceramica 417
condensatore, manopola di regolazione del 421
condensatori elettrolitici 417
condensazione 45, 414
condilo laterale del femore 99
condilo mediale del femore 99
condimenti 140
condimento alle spezie cajun 139
condizionatore 361
condominio 433
condor 80
condotta dell'acquedotto 434
condotta fognaria 434
condotta fognaria principale 434
condotta forzata 406, 407
condotto 278
condotto del carburante 351
condotto dell'aria di scarico 345
condotto dell'aria pulita 345
condotto di alimentazione 194
condotto di riscaldamento 213
conduttore di fase 198
conduttore di messa a terra 404
conduttore neutro 198
conduttura del gas 434
conduttura dell'acqua calda 197
conduttura dell'acqua fredda 197
conduzione 415
conferma, tasto di 443
confessionale 446
confezionamento, prodotti per 120
confezione in cartone per uova 162
confezione multipla 163
confezioni 162
confezioni farmaceutiche di medicinali 467
confine di proprietà 182
confine internazionale 23
confine interno 23
confluente 32
congelatore 164, 438
congelatore orizzontale 211
congelatore, scomparto del 211
congiuntiva 119
Congo 451
Congo, Fiume 20
Congo, Repubblica Democratica del 451
congressi, palazzo dei 433
conifera 65
conifere, esempi di 65
conifere, foresta di 44
coniglio 82, 154
connessione, spinotto di 417
connettore USB 333
cono 65, 119, 429, 460
cono avventizio 28
cono d'ombra 4, 5
cono di emergenza 110
cono di penombra 4, 5
cono di spremitura 177
cono femminile 65
cono maschile 65
console 471
console centrale 354
console dell'organo 305
consumatori primari 45
consumatori secondari 45
consumatori terziari 45
contachilometri parziale 355
contachilometri totale 355

contagiri 355, 368
container 383
containers, deposito per 430
contaminuti 171, 178, 179, 210
contanti, rifornimento di 443
contatore 323
contatore dell'acqua 194
contatore elettrico 198
contatore, tasto di azzeramento del 323
contatto 470
contatto caldo 314
contatto negativo 410, 411
contatto positivo 410, 411
contatto, dispositivi di 198
contatto, leva di 207
contenitore della batteria 359
contenitore della composta 231
contenitore delle siringhe usate 457
contenitore in calcestruzzo 408, 409
contenitore per filo interdentale 272
contenitore per il riciclaggio 49
contenitore termico 532
contenitori per la raccolta differenziata 49
contenuto in 427
continentale umido - estate calda 40
continentale umido - estate torrida 40
continente 33
continenti, carta dei 14
conto, tasti di identificazione del 443
contorno 441
contrabbassi 295
contrabbasso 301
contrafforte 284
contralto, chiave di 298
contrappeso 8, 287, 345, 397, 400, 401
contrappeso, guida del 287
contrassegno per la virata a dorso 517
controbraccio 397
controfagotti 295
controferro 229
controllo 330
controllo biglietti, addetto al 294
controllo dei passaporti 391
controllo del campo audio 322
controllo del sequencer 310
controllo del tempo 311
controllo del volume 310, 311
controllo dell'accelerazione 332
controllo della velocità di crociera 354
controllo di sicurezza 391
controllo: selezione di gruppo 330
controllore 374
controllore tecnico 509
controporta attrezzata 211
contropunta 425
controstecca 273
controtelaio 186
controvento 187
conurbazione 430
convertitore 321
convertitore catalitico 351
convertitore di coppia 212
convezione 415
convezione, corrente di 415
convogliatore 402
Cook, Stretto di 15
coordinate terrestri, sistema di 21
coperchio 174, 177, 178, 179, 180, 181, 198, 211, 212, 215, 225, 303, 315, 333, 359, 417, 454, 471, 533
coperchio del sedile 196
coperchio della cassetta 196
coperchio delle punterie 350, 360
coperchio di protezione dell'obiettivo 314
coperchio inferiore 417
coperchio protettivo 333
coperchio superiore 417
coperta 204
coperta, ponte di 385
copertura 273, 505, 536
copertura boccaporto della cisterna 385
copertura del cielo 39
copiglia 454
coppa da spumante 165
coppa del reggiseno 259
coppa dell'olio 235, 360
coppa dell'olio, guarnizione della 360
coppa inferiore 181
coppa superiore 181
coppetta 207
coppetta per l'insalata 166
coppetta per latte/panna 163
coppia 468, 509
coppia di serraggio, anello di regolazione della 228
coppia, convertitore di 212
copricapi 238
copricapi femminili 239
copricapi maschili 238
copricapi unisex 239
copricerniera 273
coprifiltro 459
copriguanciale 204
coprilegno 505
coprimaterasso 204
copriprese 320
copripunta 273
copritrice primaria 78
copritrice primaria media 78
copritrice secondaria mediana 78
Coralli, Mar dei 15
corda 301, 302, 498, 500, 535
corda di tensione 297
corda vocale 105
cordata 55
corde 297, 304
corde per l'accompagnamento 296
corde per la melodia 296
corde, strumenti a 301
cordiera 297, 301, 308
Cordigliera delle Ande 17
cordolo 434, 524
cordoncino 249
cordoncino di chiusura 275
cordone 208, 209, 217, 235, 237
cordone del microtelefono 327
cordone dell'alimentazione 271
cordone litorale 35
cordone nervoso ventrale 71
cordone, manicotto del 218, 229
cordone, supporto del 208
Corea, Repubblica Democratica Popolare di 453
Corea, Repubblica di 453
coriandolo 142
corimbo 57
cornamusa 296
cornea 119, 419
cornetta 295, 307
corni 295
corni inglesi 295
cornice 185, 202, 279
cornice inclinata 279
cornicione 183
corno 307
corno anteriore 109
corno inglese 306
corno posteriore 109
coro 284, 285
coroide 119
corolla 56
corona 4, 83, 101, 302, 308, 344, 424, 441
corona di penne 495
corona radiata 112
coronamento 406
corpi celesti 2
corpo 118, 180, 228, 270, 305, 306, 312, 420, 536
corpo calloso 109
corpo cavernoso 111
corpo cellulare 110
corpo ciliare 119
corpo cilindrico 471
corpo d'acciaio 417
corpo del fornice 109
corpo dell'unghia 114
corpo della macchina fotografica 314
corpo della valvola 307
corpo di guardia 282
corpo isolante 359
corpo libero, pedana per il 496
corpo stradale 342
corpo umano 92
corpo vertebrale 110
corpo vitreo 119
corpo, cura del 267
corpuscolo di Meissner 114
corpuscolo di Pacini 114
corpuscolo di Ruffini 114
corrente di convezione 415
corrente di fondazione 187
corrente elettrica, unità di misura della 426
corrente orizzontale 187
corrente, doppio 187
corrente, presa di 217
corrente, regolatore di 199
corrente, sorgente di 416
corridoio 490, 495
corridoio di discesa 278
corridoio di salita 278
corridoio di sicurezza 440
corridoio telescopico 389
corrimano 191, 287, 363, 385
corrimano di spinta 460
corsa, bicicletta da 373
corsa, direttore della 522
corsa, scarpa da 262
corsetto 259
corsia 120, 434, 472, 516
corsia dei box 524
corsia di accelerazione 343
corsia di decelerazione 343
corsia di entrata 343
corsia di marcia normale 343
corsia di sorpasso 343
corsia di traffico lento 343
corsia di uscita 343
corsia laterale 343
corso d'acqua 32, 48
corso d'acqua sotterraneo 31
corteccia 63
cortile 122, 282, 445, 447
cortina 282
corvo 80
coscia 83, 86, 93, 95, 111, 112
costa 33, 125, 167, 169
costa a rias 35
costa assiale 73
Costa d'Avorio 451
Costa Rica 448
costa spirale 73
costa, caratteristiche della 35
costate 152
coste, bordo a 250, 261
costine 152
costole 98
costole false 99
costole fluttuanti 98
costolette 153
costolone dorsale 284
costolone intermedio 284
costruttore, targhetta del 228
costume 290
costume da bagno 263, 516
costumista 290
cotiledone 53
cotone idrofilo 461
cottage cheese 150
cotton fioc® 461
cottura a vapore, cestello per la 175
cottura, piano di 164, 179, 210
cottura, piastra di 179
cottura, piatti di 179
coulisse 249
coulomb 426
coulommiers 151
coupé 347
Cowper, ghiandola di 111
Coyolxauhqui, pietra di 283
cranio 92
cratere 5, 28
cratere, scia luminosa del 5
cravatta 245
credenza 203
credenza con vetrina 203
credito, carta di 441
cremagliera 473
crenato 55
crepaccio 30
crepaccio terminale 30
crêpe, padella per 175
crepidine 279
crescione 127
crescione d'orto 127
cresta 29, 33, 418
cric 356
cricchetto 221
cricco, chiave poligonale a 223
criceto 82
cricket 478
crimine, prevenzione del 456
crinale 29
crine 301
criniera 83
crisalide 67
cristalleria 165
cristallino 119, 419
cristallizzazione 414
cristallo di sicurezza 318
cristallo, goccia di 207
Croazia 450
croce dell'altare 446
croce di sant'Andrea 187
croce, punta a 221
croce, testa a 221
crocetta 520
crociera 284, 285
crocifisso 446
croco 56
croissant 144
croma 299
croma, pausa di 299
cromatina 66
cromosfera 4
cronometrista 488, 498, 509
cronometrista capo 516
cronometrista di corsia 516
cronometristi 499
cronometro 424
cronometro elettronico automatico 517
crosne 124
cross, motocicletta da 369
crosta continentale 26
crosta oceanica 26
crosta terrestre 26, 27
crosta terrestre, sezione della 26
crostacei 71, 158
crostata, stampo per 172
crottin de chavignol 150
cruschello di segale, pane 145
cruscotto 366, 368
cruscotto, equipaggiamento del 457
Cuba 448
cubia 383, 387
cubicolo 280
cubo 429
cuccetta 364
cucchiai dosatori 171
cucchiai, esempi di 168
cucchiaino da caffè 168
cucchiaino da tè 168
cucchiaino rotante 538
cucchiaio 167, 531
cucchiaio da assaggio 173
cucchiaio da bibita 168
cucchiaio da brodo 168
cucchiaio da dessert 168
cucchiaio da tavola 168
cucchiaio forato 173
cucina 120, 162, 164, 188, 280, 439, 445
cucina a gas 210
cucina di bordo 392
cucina elettrica 210
cucina, bilancia da 171
cucina, coltello da 169
cucina, forbici da 173
cucina, robot da 177
cucina, strofinaccio da 215
cucina, utensili da 169
cucitrice 341
cucitura 243, 244, 477, 478
cucitura a princesse 258
cucitura a sottopunto 245
cucitura, tasca inserita nella 251
cuffia 324, 516
cuffia, presa per 310, 311, 326
cuffie 326
cuffie di sicurezza 458
culatta, blocco della 534
cumino 138
cumulo 42
cumulonembo 42
cuneo 224, 305
cuoio 478, 503
cuore 71, 73, 104, 105, 154
cuore del legno 63
cuori 468
cupola 60
cupola rotante 7
cupola sul mihrab 447
cupola sul porticato 447
cupola, portellone della 7
cupola, volta esterna della 7
cupola, volta interna della 7
cura del corpo 267
cura del prato 237
cura intensiva, unità di 464
curcuma 138
curling 515
curling, pietra da 515
curling, scopa da 515
curry 138
cursore 246
cursore a destra 331
cursore a sinistra 331
cursore in alto 331
cursore in basso 331
curva 306
curva, rinforzo della 306
curvatura 273, 538
cuscinetti antirumore 458
cuscinetto a sfere 413
cuscino 204
cuscino a rullo 204
cuscus 144
cuscus, pentola per 175
custodia 337
custodia a pareti di vetro 423
cute 110, 114
cute, superficie della 114
cuticole, forbicine per 265
cuticole, tronchesina per 265
cyclette 501

D

dadi 223, 468
dado 222, 223, 469
dado cieco 223
dado comune 468
dado da poker 468
dado del raddoppio 469
dado di fissaggio 197
dado di serraggio 197
dado esagonale 223, 359
dalmata 86
dama 470
Danimarca 450
danish blue 151
Danubio, Fiume 18
danza, lama per 509
data base 335
data di scadenza 441
datario 338
dati tecnici 358
dati, elaborazione dei 38
datteri 132
davanti 244, 245
David, stella di 447
deambulatore 466
deambulatorio 285
deasfaltizzazione, impianto di 405
decagono regolare 429
decimi di secondo, lancetta dei 424
declinazione, cerchio graduato della 8, 9
décolleté, reggiseno 259
décolleté, scarpa 241
decompositori, organismi 45
decoratore scenico 291
decorazione a trifoglio 285
deflettore 236, 237
deflettore del fumo 192
deflettore dell'aria calda 192
deflusso superficiale 45
deforestazione 47
degenza postoperatoria, stanza di 464
degenza, stanza di 464
Deimos 2
delfino 90
delfino, morfologia di un 90
delimitazione, nastro di 457
della calotta polare 40
della tundra polare 40
delta 32, 35
deltoide 96
demi-volée 490
denaro 441
dendrite 110
denominazione dei cicloni tropicali 43
densimetro 359
dentato 55
dentatura nell'uomo 101
dente 74, 76, 226, 227, 235, 244, 270, 398, 400, 503
dente del giudizio 101
dente dello scarificatore 398
dente di leone 127

dente velenifero 76
denti 101
denti, spazzolino da 272
denti, spazzolino elettrico da 272
dentifricio 272
dentina 101
deodorante 267
depositi alluvionali 32
deposito bagagli 374
deposito dei cereali 381
deposito dei containers 381
deposito del materiale medico 465
deposito del materiale sporco 464
deposito del materiale sterile 464
deposito del petrolio 381
deposito delle barelle 462
deposito delle rinfuse 381
deposito di carbone 402
deposito per containers 430
deposito, fessura per il 442
deragliatore 522
deragliatore anteriore 370, 372
deragliatore posteriore 370, 372
deriva 393, 395, 520, 521
deriva a scomparsa 519
derivazione 416
derma 114
derrick 382, 385
derrick, albero del 385
desertico 40
deserto 36, 44
Deserto dei Gobi 19
Deserto del Kalahari 20
Deserto del Namib 20
Deserto del Sahara 20
Deserto di Atacama 17
deserto roccioso 36
deserto sabbioso 36
deserto, volpe del 88
designer di produzione 290
desquamatore 531
dessert, coltello da 168
dessert, cucchiaio da 168
dessert, forchetta da 168
destinazione 374
detersivo, vaschetta per il 214
detriti 43
di montagna 40
diaframma 105, 324
diagramma di carico 365
diamante 474
diamante, punta di 202
diametro 428
dicco 28
didascalia 313
dieci 427
dieci comandamenti 447
diesis 299
dietro 244
difensore ala destra 484
difensore ala sinistra 484
difensore centrale 487
difensore destro 487, 506
difensore sinistro 487, 506
difensori 479
difesa 484
difetti della vista 419
differenziale 351
diffusione di informazioni 335
diffusore 290
diffusore della fiamma 218
diga 406
digiuno 106
diminuzione di tensione 402, 413
dinamo 370
diodo 411
Dione 3
directory 334
direttore artistico 290
direttore d'orchestra, podio del 295
direttore della corsa 522
direttore della fotografia 291
direttore, ufficio del 443
direzione del flusso di elettroni 416, 417
direzione del vento 39
direzione della Mecca 447
direzione e forza del vento 39
discarica 431
discarica autorizzata 47
discesa libera 511
discesa, corridoio di 278
dischetto 507
dischetto del rigore 480
dischetto di centrocampo 481
dischi 177
dischi, negozio di 436
disco 6, 321, 333, 357, 472, 501
disco abrasivo 229
disco abrasivo, supporto del 229
disco adesivo 75
disco deflettore del calore 199
disco del freno 366
disco versatile digitale (DVD) 319
disco, freno a 525
disco, vano del 323
discontinuità di Gutenberg 26
discontinuità di Mohorovicic 26
disegno stampato 260, 261
disgelo, acqua di 30
disinnesto del pistone 216
dispensa 164, 188, 439
dispersione di calore 46
display 314, 319, 321, 322, 323, 325, 326, 327, 328, 336, 337, 338, 346, 423, 442, 443
display a cristalli liquidi 315, 320, 326, 327
display del radar 457
display delle frequenze 325
display delle funzioni 310
display digitale 423, 461
display, pulsante di apertura del 336
display, regolatore del 327
dispositivi di contatto 198
dispositivi di entrata 330
dispositivi di memorizzazione dei dati 333
dispositivi di uscita 333
dispositivo antiallagamento 214
dispositivo di agganciamento 377
dispositivo di bloccaggio 209
dispositivo di blocco 219, 226
dispositivo di blocco dell'inclinazione della lama 227
dispositivo di blocco dell'interruttore 228
dispositivo di chiusura 535
dispositivo di fissaggio del tubo 199
dispositivo di regolazione 511, 527
dispositivo di rimorchio 364
dispositivo di smorzamento magnetico 422
disposizione 182
distanza tra le puntine 359
distanziatore 467, 535
distillazione sotto vuoto 405
distintivo 456
distributore automatico d'acqua 211
distributore automatico di biglietti 379
distributore del ghiaccio 346
distributore di bibite 346, 463
distributore di ghiaccio in cubetti 164
distributore via cavo 316
distribuzione del fertilizzante 47
distribuzione della vegetazione 44
distribuzione, quadro di 198
distruggidocumenti 341
ditale in gomma 339
ditali 146
dito 75, 79, 82, 86, 114, 477
dito anulare 115
dito del guanto 243
dito del piede 92, 94
dito esterno 78
dito indice 115
dito interno 78
dito lobato 79
dito medio 78, 115
dito mignolo 115
dito palmato 79
dito posteriore 78, 79
dito prensile 91
divanetto 201
divani 200
divano 200
divano a due posti 200, 439
divano Chesterfield 200
divano posteriore 353
divano-letto 204
diverso da 427
divisa di pronto intervento 454
divisione 427
divisori 339
divisori alfabetici per schedario 340
divisorio 457
divisorio di tela 528
djembè 297
Dnepr, Fiume 18
do 298
doccetta 197
doccia 189, 195, 439, 464
doccia a telefono 195
doccia orale 272
doccia, box 195
dodecagono regolare 429
dogana 381, 391
dolcevita, maglione 250
dolci, miscelatore per 172
dolci, pennello per 172
dolci, stampini per 172
dolichi 130
dolina 31
dollaro 440
Dominica 449
Dominicana, Repubblica 449
dominio di livello superiore 334
dominio di secondo livello 334
dominio, nome del 334
domino 468
dondolo, sedia a 200, 201
donna 94, 468
donna, scarpe da 241
donnola 88
dopobarba 271
doppia coppia 468
doppia piastra di registrazione 325
doppiamente dentato 55
doppio bemolle 299
doppio corrente 187
doppio diesis 299
doppio lavello 194
doppio slash 334
doppio-sei 468
doppio-zero 468
doppione 468
doppiopetto, abbottonatura a 248
doppiopetto, giacca a 244
Dorsale Medio-Atlantica 34
Dorsale Medio-Indiana 34
Dorsale medio-oceanica 33
Dorsale Pacifico-Antartica 34
Dorsale Pacifico-Orientale 34
Dorsale Sud Occidentale Indiana 34
Dorsale Sud Orientale Indiana 34
dorsali oceaniche 34
dorsali, barra per i 501
dorso 78, 83, 86, 115, 167, 215, 226, 516, 517
dorso del guanto 243
dorso del naso 117
dorso della lingua 118
dotto deferente 111
dotto eiaculatore 111
dotto galattoforo 113
dotto sudoriparo 114
dotto velenifero 76
Douglas, tasca di 112
dragoncello 142
Drake, Canale di 15, 17
drenaggio, tubo di 212, 214
drenaggio, valvola di 211
dritta 387
drive per cassette 333
dromedario 85
drumlin 29
drupa 57
drupe 132
drupeola 59
due metà, tempo di 298
dulse 123
duna 35
duna complessa 36
duna parabolica 36
dune longitudinali 36
dune trasversali 36
dune, catena di 36
dune, esempi di 36
duo 300
duodeno 106
dura madre 109, 110
durian 137
duty free 391

E

e-commerce 335
eau de toilette 267
echinodermi 66
eclissi anulare 4
eclissi di Luna 5
eclissi di Sole 4
eclissi parziale 4, 5
eclissi totale 4, 5
economia 441
Ecuador 448
edicola 379, 437
edificio del reattore 409
edificio per uffici 432, 435
edificio pubblico 25
editing del suono, tasti per l' 310
editoriale 313
effetto serra 46
effetto serra naturale 46
effetto serra, incremento dell' 46
effigie 441
Egeo, Mare 18
Egitto 451
eglefino 161
El Salvador 448
elaborazione dei dati 38
elastici stringitesta 459
elastico 204, 247, 528, 529
elastico ferma abiti 277
elastico regolabile per il capo 459
elefante 85
elementi architettonici 286
elementi della casa 185
elemento della canna fumaria 193
elemento di combustibile 409
elemento di cottura 210
elemento riscaldante 213, 214, 218
elettricità 198, 408, 413
elettrodo centrale 359
elettrodo di massa 359
elettrodo negativo 359
elettrodo positivo 359
elettrodomestici 176, 208
elettrodomestici vari 180
elettrone 414
elettroni, collettore di 417
elettroni, direzione del flusso di 416, 417
elettronica 417
elettronica, negozio di 436
elevatore 281, 400
elevatore a nastro 402
elevatore per sedie a rotelle 363
elevone 13
elica 228, 384, 386, 387, 429
elica bipala 394
elica di propulsione 383
elica di prua 384
elica posteriore 384
elica tripala 394
elica, albero dell' 387
elica, mantello d' 383
elice 115
elice, coda dell' 115
elice, radice dell' 115
eliche 146
elicottero 395
elmetto 458
elmo 454
emergenza, freno di 380
Emirati Arabi Uniti 452
emisferi 21
emisfero meridionale 21
emisfero occidentale 21
emisfero orientale 21
emisfero settentrionale 21
emissario 32
emissione dello scontrino 346
emissione di acido nitrico 48
emissione di acido solforico 48
emissione di anidride solforosa 48
emissione di banconote 442
emissione di gas inquinanti 47
emissione di ossido d'azoto 48
emittenti, tasti di ricerca 319
emmental 151
endecagono regolare 429
endocardio 104
endocarpo 57, 58
energia 402
energia eolica 412
energia eolica, produzione di elettricità da 413
energia fossile 402
energia geotermica 402
energia nucleare 408
energia nucleare, produzione di elettricità da 408
energia solare 54, 410
energia termica 46, 402
energia, rilascio di 415
energia, unità di misura dell' 426
enneagono regolare 429
enti sanitari 335
entrata principale 188
epeira 70
epicarpo 58
epicentro 27
epicondilo 99
epidermide 114
epididimo 111
epifisi 109
epiglottide 105, 118
epistrofeo 99
epitroclea 99
Equatore 17, 20, 21, 22, 43
equilibratore orizzontale 395
equilibrio, posizione d' 418
equinozio d'autunno 38
equinozio di primavera 38
equipaggiamento del cruscotto 457
equipaggiamento protettivo 486
equipaggio, alloggi dell' 382
equivalente a 427
erba 492
erba cipollina 124
erba medica 130
erbicida 47
erbivori 45
Eris 3
Eritrea 451
erogatore del tubo della scala 455
erogazione, bocca di 197
eruzione, vulcano in 28
esagono regolare 429
esame audiometrico, stanza per l' 465
esame psichiatrico, stanza per 462
escape 330
escavatore idraulico 400
esempi di abiti 252
esempi di aeroplani 394
esempi di alghe 51
esempi di anfibi 75
esempi di angoli 428
esempi di aracnidi 70
esempi di becchi 79
esempi di biciclette 373
esempi di camicette 255
esempi di camion 364
esempi di carri merci 377
esempi di carrozzerie 347
esempi di chiodi 220
esempi di coltelli 168
esempi di coltelli da cucina 169
esempi di conifere 65
esempi di cucchiai 168
esempi di dune 36
esempi di felci 52
esempi di finestre 287
esempi di fiori 56
esempi di foglie 65
esempi di forchette 168
esempi di giacche e pullover 254
esempi di gonne 253
esempi di gruppi strumentali 300
esempi di insetti 69
esempi di lagomorfi 82
esempi di latifoglie 64
esempi di licheni 50
esempi di linee di costa 35
esempi di mammiferi carnivori 88
esempi di mammiferi marini 90
esempi di mammiferi ungulati 84
esempi di mecchie e punte da trapano 228
esempi di motociclette e ciclomotore 369
esempi di muschi 51

esempi di occhiali 273
esempi di pantaloni 254
esempi di pieghe 253
esempi di pneumatici 358
esempi di porte 286
esempi di prese 499
esempi di primati 91
esempi di raccordo 342
esempi di rettili 77
esempi di roditori 82
esempi di sacchi a pelo 530
esempi di salti 509
esempi di sci 510
esempi di sedie 201
esempi di simboli di valute 440
esempi di tavoli 202
esempi di tende 528
esempi di uccelli 80
esempi di vulcani 28
esempi di zampe 79
esocarpo 57, 58, 59
esofago 105, 106
esosfera 37
espadrille 242
espansione fissa 425
espansione mobile 425
espansione, bullone a 221
espansione, camera di 424
espositore di brochure 442
espositore di fine corsia 121
espressione, pedali d' 305
espulsione, pulsante di 315
espulsione, tasto di 323
espulsore degli accessori 176
essere umano 92
Est 23
Est Nord-Est 23
Est Sud-Est 23
estate 38
estate, solstizio d' 38
estensore 500
estensore breve delle dita 96
estensore comune delle dita 97
estensore lungo delle dita 96
estensore radiale breve del carpo 97
estensore radiale lungo del carpo 97
estensore ulnare del carpo 97
esterno centro (giocatore) 474
esterno centro (posizione) 475
esterno destro 474
esterno destro (posizione) 475
esterno di una casa 182
esterno sinistro 474
esterno sinistro (posizione) 475
estintore 457
estintore portatile 454
estirpatore 232
Estonia 450
estratto conto, fessura di
aggiornamento dell' 442
estratto di vaniglia 140
estrazione dell'aria, tubo di 199
estremità del braccio 421
estremità della guida 235
estremo 482
estremo di destra 484
estremo di sinistra 484
estuario 24, 35
eterotrofi, organismi 45
etichetta portaindirizzo 277
etichettatrice 340
etichette autoadesive 340
Etiopia 451
ettagono regolare 429
Eurasia 14
euro 440
Europa 2, 14, 18, 34, 449
Eustachio, tuba di 116, 117
Eutelsat 316
euthynteria 279
evacuazione, percorso di 345
evaporazione 45, 414
evidenziatore 312
ex voto 446
expander 310
eye-liner 266
Eyre, Lago 15

F

fa 298
faccetta 228
faccetta scanalata 228
faccia 92, 493, 505
facciata 285
facole 4
faggio 64
faggiola 133
fagiano 81, 154
fagiano, uovo di 155
fagioli 131
fagioli adzuki 131
fagioli borlotti 131
fagioli cannellini 131
fagioli di Lima 131
fagioli di Spagna 131
fagioli mungo 131
fagioli mungo neri 131
fagioli mungo, spaghetti di 147
fagioli neri 131
fagioli pinti 131
fagioli romani 131
fagiolino 131
fagiolino giallo 131
fagiolo asparagio 130
fagiolo dall'occhio nero 130
fagiolo egiziano 130
faglia 27
fagotti 295
fagotto 306
Fahrenheit, scala 424
fai da te 216
faina 88
fairway 504
falange, seconda 114
falange, terza 114
falcetto 234
falco 81
falda 248
falda freatica 48
falda larga, cappello a 239
falesia 35
falesia costiera 35
Falkland, Isole 17
Falloppio, tuba di 112
Falloppio, tube di 113
falsa partenza, fune di 516
falsa zampa 67
falsa zampa anale 67
falsabraca 282
falso puntone 187
famiglia degli archi 301
familiari, sala d'attesa dei 462
fanale 377
fanale anteriore 371, 376
fanale di testa 376
fanale di testa dell'albero 383
fanale posteriore 367, 368, 370
fango, colata di 31
fante 468
faraglione 35
faraona 81, 154
fard in polvere 266
fard, pennello da 266
faretto a pinza 206
faretto da binario 207
faretto orientabile 207
farfalla 67, 517
farfalla, morfologia di una 67
farina 144
farina di avena 144
farina di mais 144
farina integrale 144
farina non trattata 144
farina semplice 144
faringe 105, 106
farmacia 436, 462, 465
faro 381
faro di atterraggio 395
faro fendinebbia 352, 364
faro subacqueo 184
farro 143
fascetta 265
fascia 301, 302, 360
fascia degli asteroidi 3
fascia di chiusura 511
fascia di cuoio 246
fascia di regolazione 324
fascia di sospensione 458
fascia elastica 249
fascia lata, tensore della 96
fascia laterale 349
fascia protettiva della fronte 459
fascia reggibraccio 461
fascia sopracigliare 78
fascia stringitesta 458
fasciatoio 205
fascio blu 318
fascio elettronico 318
fascio rosso 318
fascio verde 318
fascione anteriore 348
fase di scivolamento 514
fase di spinta 514
fase, conduttore di 198
fasi della Luna 5
fast food 437
fattore Rh negativo 426
fattore Rh positivo 426
fattoria 122
fattoriale 427
fauci, istmo delle 116
fave 130
fazzoletto da taschino 244
fede nuziale 264
federa 204
Federazione Russa 450
fegato 103, 106, 154
feijoa 137
felce 52
felce arborea 52
felce, struttura di una 52
felci, esempi di 52
felpa 262
felpa con cappuccio 262
feltro, cappello di 238, 239
femminella 62
femminile 426
femore 98
femore, collo del 99
femore, condilo laterale del 99
femore, condilo mediale del 99
femore, testa del 99
fendinebbia, faro 352, 364
fenicottero 81
feritoia 178
fermacampioni 341
fermacapelli 268
fermagli 341
fermaglio 246, 312
fermapiedi 370, 372, 501
fermaporta 211
fermata dell'autobus 434
fermo a molla 273
fermo del nastro 225
fermo della lama 270
fermo di testa 521
ferodo 357
ferretto 259
ferri per il camino 193
ferro 229, 505
ferro da stiro a vapore 208
ferrovia 25
fertilizzante, distribuzione del 47
fertilizzazione del suolo 47
ferzo 520
fessura 93, 95, 167, 274, 305
fessura di aggiornamento dell'estratto
conto 442
fessura di registrazione della
transazione 442
fessura per il deposito 442
fessura per la scheda PC 336
fessure branchiali 74
fessure, bocchetta per 209
fettuccine 146
fiala 467
fiamma 415
fiancata 467
fianco 78, 83, 93, 95, 358
fianco esterno 191
fianco interno 191
fiato, strumenti a 306
fibbia 246, 248, 276, 353
fibbia di regolazione 532
fibra muscolare 110
fibra nervosa 114
fico 137
fico d'India 137
fidanzamento, anello di 264
fienile 122
fieno greco 138
Figi 453
Figi, Isole 15
fila 272, 293
filamento 56, 199
Filchner, Banchisa di 15
file 334
file, formato del 334
filettatura 301, 302
filetto 152, 221, 313
filiere 70
filigrana 441
Filippine 19, 453
Filippine, Fossa delle 34
filo 167, 169, 225, 417
filo conduttore 199
filo d'appoggio 70
filo da giardino 231
filo della lama 270
filo di nylon 237
filo di sicurezza 441
filo di tracciamento 225
filo interdentale 272
filo interdentale, contenitore per 272
filo per saldatura 218
filo radiale 70
filo spirale 70
filone francese 144
filone strato 28
filtro 117, 184, 210, 459
filtro dell'aria 235, 350, 398
filtro dello scarico 197
filtro per il tè 173
filtro per lanugine 212, 213
filtro polarizzatore 314
filtro, cassetta 181
filtro, macchina da caffè a 181
filum terminale esterno 109
filum terminale interno 109
finanza 441
fine 331
fine corsa, interruttore di 287
finecorsa 226
finestra 186, 189, 477, 519
finestra a battenti 287
finestra a battenti con apertura
all'interno 287
finestra a bilico orizzontale 287
finestra a bilico verticale 287
finestra a gelosia 287
finestra a ghigliottina 287
finestra a libro 287
finestra del seminterrato 183
finestra di accesso 333
finestra di controllo 178, 179, 210
finestra panoramica 435
finestra scorrevole 287
finestra zanzariera 528
finestra, traversa inferiore di 187
finestra, traversa superiore di 187
finestre, esempi di 287
finestrino 349, 352, 361, 380, 392
finestrino di atterraggio 395
finestrino di osservazione 13
finitura, chiodo di 220
Finlandia 450
finocchio 125
finta 251
fiocco 238, 520
fioraio 437
fiordi 35
fiore 53, 56
fiore del pinnacolo 283
fiore, struttura di un 56
fiori 468
fiori, esempi di 56
fiori, macchia di 230
fioritura 62
fiosso 240
firma del titolare 441
firma ufficiale 441
fisarmonica 296
fisica: elettricità e magnetismo 416
fisica: ottica 418
fissaggio del tubo, dispositivo di 199
fissione dell'uranio 408
fissione nucleare 415
fiume 24, 25, 32
Fiume Congo 20
Fiume Danubio 18
Fiume Dnepr 18
Fiume Mackenzie 16
Fiume Mississippi 16
Fiume Niger 20
Fiume Orinoco 17
Fiume Paranà 17
Fiume San Lorenzo 16
Fiume Senegal 20
Fiume Vistola 18
Fiume Volga 18
flacone 467
flap 392
flash, tubo a 420
flauti 295
flauto di Pan 297
flauto traverso 306
flessometro 225
flessore ulnare del carpo 96, 97
flettente 535
flip 509
floema 63
floppy disk 333
fluido vettore caldo 408
fluido vettore freddo 408
fluido vettore, ingresso del 410
fluido vettore, uscita del 410
flusso sotterraneo 45
flûte 165
Fobos 2
foca 90
focolare 192
fodera 240, 244, 245, 262, 274, 509
fodera del guanciale 204
fodero 531, 533
fodero di pelle 533
foglia 51, 53, 54, 55, 125
foglia carnosa 54
foglia di acanto 200
foglia, struttura di una 55
fogliame 63
foglie composte 55
foglie semplici 55
foglie squamiformi del cipresso 65
foglie, esempi di 65
fogliolina arrotolata 52
foie-gras 156
follicolo 60
follicolo pilifero 114
follicolo, sezione di un 60
fondale 292
fondale oceanico 33
fondazione 342
fondazione del pilone 344
fondazione naturale 342
fondazione, corrente di 187
fondazione, muro di 187
fondello 318, 492, 494, 534
fondello metallico 534
fondina 456
fondista 514
fondo 528, 529
fondo abissale 26
fondo dell'onda 33
fondo protettivo 471
fondo refrattario 192
fondo, pista da 512
fondocampo 491
fondotinta fluido 266
fonduta, forchetta da 168
fonduta, servizio da 174
fonduta, tegame per 174
fonendoscopio 460
fontana per le abluzioni 447
fontanella anteriore 100
fontanella mastoidea 100
fontanella posteriore 100
fontanella sfenoidale 100
fonte alimentare primaria 45
fonte battesimale 446
fonte del servizio 313
football americano 484
forame cieco 118
forbice sfoltitrice a doppia lama
dentellata 270
forbice sfoltitrice a lama singola
dentellata 270
forbici 461, 531
forbici da cucina 173
forbici da parrucchiere 270
forbici di sicurezza 265
forbici per unghie dei piedi 265

forbici tagliasiepi 234
forbicine per cuticole 265
forbicine per unghie 265
forca 396
forca, braccio della 396
forcella 8, 371, 522, 525
forcella anteriore 522
forcella inferiore 370
forcella superiore 370
forcella telescopica anteriore 366, 369
forchetta 167, 531
forchetta da dessert 168
forchetta da fonduta 168
forchetta da insalata 168
forchetta da ostriche 168
forchetta da pesce 168
forchetta da tavola 168
forchette, esempi di 168
forchettone 169
forcina 268
forcone 233
foresta 29
foresta boreale 44
foresta di caducifoglie 44
foresta di conifere 44
foresta mista 44
foresta pluviale tropicale 44
foresta temperata 44
foresta tropicale 44
foreste, incendio delle 47
formaggi a pasta dura 151
formaggi a pasta molle 151
formaggi di capra 150
formaggi erborinati 151
formaggi freschi 150
formaggio cremoso 150
formaggio fresco di capra 150
formaggio, coltello da 168
formato del file 334
formazione professionale, ufficio di 442
forme geometriche 428
formica 69
formina da forno 166
formula 1, auto da 525
formula 3000, auto da 524
formula Indy, auto da 524
fornellino 174
fornello da campo a due fuochi 529
fornello da campo con un bruciatore 529
fornice, corpo del 109
fornitore del servizio Internet 335
forno 164, 210
forno a microonde 164, 178
forno tubolare 405
forno, teglia da 172
foro 240, 243, 246, 263
foro apicale 101
foro del piede 305
foro di risonanza 301
forti precipitazioni 43
forum 335
forza del vento 39
forza, linea di 416
forza, unità di misura della 426
foschia 41
Fossa del Giappone 34
Fossa delle Aleutine 34
Fossa delle Curili 34
Fossa delle Filippine 34
Fossa delle Marianne 34
Fossa delle Ryukyu 34
Fossa di Giava 34
Fossa di Kermadec-Tonga 34
Fossa di Puerto Rico 34
fossa oceanica 33
Fossa Perù-Cile 34
fossa settica 48
fossa triangolare 115
fossato 282, 342
fosse nasali 117
fosse oceaniche 34
fossetta 76, 505
foto in prima pagina 313
fotocamera 35 mm 10
fotocopiatrice 442
fotografia 314
fotografia, direttore della 291
fotografo 436
fotografo di scena 291
fotone 420
fotorecettori 119
fotosfera 4
fotosintesi 54
fototessere, macchina per 437
fovea 119
foyer 293
fragola, sezione di una 59
fragole 132
frana 31
francesina 241
Francia 449
Francoforte, salsiccia di 156
frangente 33
frangia, scopa a 215
frangizolle 237
frantumatore 402
frantumatrice 49
frattazzo 216
frazione 427
freccetta 471
freccette 471
freccia di orientamento 533
freestyle, snowboard per 513
fregio 279
freni 357
freno 467, 501, 511, 522
freno a disco 350, 357, 525
freno a disco idraulico 522
freno a disco, pinza del 366
freno a mano 350
freno a mano, leva del 354
freno a tamburo 357
freno a tampone 527
freno aerodinamico 412
freno anteriore 371
freno anteriore, leva del 368
freno della catena 235
freno di emergenza 380
freno posteriore 370
freno posteriore, pedale del 368
freno, cavo del 371
freno, disco del 366
freno, leva del 371, 523
freno, pedale del 350, 354, 357
freno, tubazione del 357
frequenza, unità di misura della 426
frequenze, display delle 325
fresatrice verticale 229
friggitrice 178
frigo portatile 532
frigoriferi 438
frigorifero 164, 211, 438
frigorifero, scomparto del 211
fringuello 80
frizione 350, 536
frizione a stella 537
frizione, leva della 366, 368
frizione, pedale della 354
frizione, regolazione della 537
frizione, scatola della 368
fronda 52
fronde arrotolate 125
frontale 96, 191
fronte 78, 92
frontone 279
frullatore 176
frullatore a immersione 176
frullatore elettrico a mano 176
frullino 172
frumento 143
frusta 172, 176
frusta a quattro bracci 176
frusta a spirale 176
frusta ad anello 176
fruste 176
frutta 120
frutteto 122
frutti 57, 132
frutti secchi 60, 133
frutti tropicali 136
fruttificazione 62
frutto carnoso 58, 59
frutto carnoso: mela 58
frutto del jack 136
frutto, albero da 122
fucile a canna liscia 534
fucile a canna rigata 534
fuco 68
fuga, via di 524
fulcro 518
full 468
fulmine 41
fumaiolo 382, 386
fumarola 28
fumo, deflettore del 192
fumo, rilevatore di 454
fune di corsia 517
fune di falsa partenza 516
fune di sollevamento 219, 287
funghi 123
fungicida 47
fungo 52
fungo coltivato 123
fungo velenoso 52
fungo velenoso e mortale 52
fungo, struttura di un 52
funicolo 59, 60
funivia 512
funivia, partenza della 512
funzionamento, pannello di 287
funzione, selettori di 327
funzione, tasti 328, 423, 442
funzioni, display delle 310
fuoco 27, 419
fuoco Cassegrain 7
fuoco coudé 7
fuoco primario 7
fuoco primario, cabina di osservazione del 7
fuoco, profondità del 27
Fuoco, Terra del 17
fuoristrada 347
fuoriuscita di idrocarburi 48
furgone 365
fuseau 254
fusibile 198, 411
fusilli 146
fusione 414
fusoliera 393
fusto 53, 125, 273, 492, 493, 494
fusto del bulbo 54
futon 204

G

gabbia 281, 308
gabbia del palcoscenico 292
gabbia di protezione 217, 473
gabbia, lampada portatile a 217
Gabon 451
Gai-lohn 127
galassia 6
galleggiante 196, 394, 538
galleggiante, valvola del 196
galleria 285, 345, 378
galleria di collegamento 345
galleria di derivazione 406
galleria di ispezione 407
galleria secca 31
galleria, prima 293
galleria, seconda 293
galletta di segale 145
galletta scandinava 145
gallette di riso 147
galletto 223
gallina 81
gallina, uovo di 155
gallo 81
galloccia 520, 521
galoppo 83
galoscia 240
gamba 83, 91, 93, 95, 202, 204, 205, 247, 493
gamba a capriolo 200
gamba anteriore 201
gamba posteriore 201
gamba telescopica 460
gambale 478, 511, 527
gambaletto 257
gamberetto 158
gambero di acqua dolce 158
Gambia 451
gambo 51, 52, 181, 220, 221, 537, 538
gambo a innesto dello spazzolino 272
gambo filettato 223
ganasce 224, 535
ganascia 217, 224, 265, 357
ganascia curva 222
ganascia dentata 222
ganascia diritta 222
ganascia fissa 223, 224
ganascia mobile 223, 224
ganci di fissaggio 501
gancio 186, 217, 225, 364, 397, 423, 460, 502, 509, 511
gancio del manganello 456
gancio del piatto 422
gancio di chiusura 277
gancio di sollevamento 403
gancio di traino 361
gancio per l'impasto 176
ganglio cerebropleurale 73
ganglio simpatico 109
ganglio spinale 109, 110
ganglio viscerale 73
Ganimede 2
gara di ciclismo su strada 522
gara, numero di 525
garage 182
garage, porta basculante del 286
garage, porta sezionale del 286
garam masala 139
garitta 282
garofano 56
garrese 83, 86
garretto 83, 86
garza sterile 461
gas 403, 405, 414
gas di scarico delle automobili, inquinamento da 47
gas inerte 199
gas inquinanti, emissione di 47
gas serra 46
gas serra, concentrazione di 46
gas, manopola di regolazione del 529
gasolio 405
gastrocnemio 96, 97
gastronomia 156
gatti, razze di 87
gatto 87
gatto del Maine 87
gatto dell'isola di Man 87
gatto delle nevi 512, 523
gatto, testa di 87
gattone 285
gattuccio 226
gattuccio stellato 158
gelatiera 180
gelato, porzionatore per 173
gelone 123
gemma 54
gemma apicale 53
gemma ascellare 53
gemma fiorale 53
gemma terminale 53
generatore 408
generatore di vapore 402
generatore, gruppo del 407
generi alimentari 120
gengiva 101, 116
genitali femminili, organi 112
genitali maschili, organi 111
Genova, salame di 156
geografia 14
geologia 26
geometria 428
Georgia 452
geotermica 402
gerboa 82
Germania 450
germe 61
germinazione 53
germogli di soia 131
germoglio 53
germoglio di bambù 125
gessetto 503
getti d'acqua 518
geyser 28
Ghana 451
ghepardo 89
gheriglio 60
ghettina con ruches 260
ghi 150
ghiacciaio 30, 32, 44
ghiaccio 45
ghiandaia 80
ghiandola di Cowper 111
ghiandola digestiva 71, 73
ghiandola lacrimale 119
ghiandola mammaria 113
ghiandola salivare 118
ghiandola sebacea 114
ghiandola sudoripara apocrina 114
ghiandola sudoripara eccrina 114
ghiandola surrenale 107
ghiandola velenigena 76
ghiandole salivari 106
ghiera 219
ghiera di bloccaggio 221, 425
ghiera di tenuta 197
ghiera femmina 536, 537
ghiera maschio 536, 537
giacca 251, 499
giacca a doppiopetto 244
giacca a un petto 244
giacca a vento 249
giacca alla marinara 251
giacca avento 263
giacca in pile 262
giacche 244
giacche e pullover, esempi di 254
giacche, esempi di 251
giaccone 251
giacconi, esempi di 248
giaguaro 89
giallo 418
Giamaica 448
Giapeto 3
Giappone 19, 453
Giappone, Fossa del 34
Giappone, Mar del 19
giardinaggio 216, 230
giardinaggio, guanti da 232
giardiniere, sega da 234
giardino 230, 280
giardino pubblico 435
giardino roccioso 230
giardino, filo da 231
giarrettiera 259
Giava, Fossa di 34
giavellotto 472
gibbone 91
Gibilterra, Stretto di 18
Gibuti 451
giglio 56
gilè 244, 250, 255
ginco, noce di 133
ginnasta, nome del 497
ginnastica 496
ginnastica, abbigliamento da 263
ginnastica, completo da 261
ginocchiera 476, 486, 500, 526, 527
ginocchio 83, 86, 92, 94
giocatore 483, 486, 488, 506, 515
giocatore, bastone del 506
giocatore, numero del 486, 488, 506
giocatore: battitore 478
giocatori 492
giocatori, panchina dei 474, 485
giocatori, posizioni dei 474, 481, 482, 489
giocattoli, negozio di 436
giochi 468
giochi con la racchetta 493
giochi da tavola 469
giochi di carte 468
gioco 492
gioco del volano 494
gioco online 335
gioco, area di 386
giogo 422
giogo anteriore 422
giogo di supporto 8, 9
giogo posteriore 422
gioielleria 436
gioielli 264
Giordania 452
giornale 313
giornale, nome del 313
Giove 2
giraffa 85
giraffista 291
girasole 56
giratubi 216
girella 535, 538
girello 503
giro 72
giro della spira 73
giro embrionale 73
girocollo 260, 264
girocollo, maglia 255
girocollo, maglione 250
giubbotto da pescatore 538
giudice 498, 499
giudice del fallo di piede 491
giudice di arrivo 516
giudice di campo 485
giudice di linea 483, 485, 487, 490, 494, 496, 507, 515
giudice di linea centrale 490
giudice di porta 506
giudice di rete 491
giudice di sedia 490

giudice di servizio 490, 494
giudice di stile 516
giudice laterale 485
giudici 496, 497, 509, 518
giudici di virata 517
giudici, banco dei 440
giudici, ufficio dei 440
giudizio, dente del 101
giuggiola 137
giunto 503, 536
giunto a compressione 197
giunto scorrevole 222
giunto scorrevole, pinza a 222
giunzione a linguetta del telaio 186
giunzione positivo-negativa 410
giunzione scanalata del telaio 186
giurati, stanza dei 440
giuria, banco della 440
giustizia 440
giustizia, palazzo di 432
Glaciale Artico, Mar 14
glande 111
globo di vetro 529
globo oculare 75, 119
globulo bianco 104
globulo rosso 104
glottide 76
glucosio 54
gnocchi 146
gnomone 424
go 470
Gobi, Deserto dei 19
gocce oftalmiche lubrificanti 272
goccia di cristallo 207
gocciolatoio 185, 186, 349
gola 31, 32, 78, 305
golf 504
golf, campo da 430
golf, vettura da 505
golfo 24
Golfo del Bengala 19
Golfo del Messico 16
Golfo dell'Alaska 16
Golfo di Aden 19, 20
Golfo di Botnia 18
Golfo di California 16
Golfo di Carpentaria 15
Golfo di Guinea 20
Golfo di Oman 19
Golfo di Panama 17
golfo mistico 292
Golfo Persico 19
Golgi, apparato del 50, 66
gombo 128
gomiti 146
gomitiera 526, 527
gomito 83, 86, 93, 95
gomma 341
gomma di tenuta del grembiule 383
gomma, guarnizione di 197
gomma, piedino di 219
gommino 460
gonade 73
gonfiatore 530
gonfiatore a soffietto 530
gong 295, 309
gonna 251
gonna a balze 253
gonna a portafoglio 253
gonna a teli 253
gonna ad anfora 253
gonna arricciata 253
gonna con baschina 253
gonna diritta 253
gonna pantalone 253
gonne, esempi di 253
gonnelino scozzese 253
gonnellino 492
gorgonzola 151
gorilla 91
gorilla, morfologia di un 91
gracile 97
gradi 456
gradino 191, 219, 364
gradino di accesso 395
gradino posteriore 455
gradino rientrabile 361
gradino, larghezza del 191
gradino, lunghezza del 191
grado 428
grado Celsius 426
gramigna crestata 126
Gran Deserto Sabbioso 15
Gran Deserto Vittoria 15
gran dorsale 97
granaio 122
grancassa 295, 308
granchio 158, 220
Grand Canyon 16
grande adduttore 97
Grande Baia Australiana 15
Grande Barriera Corallina 15
Grande Catena Divisoria 15
grande complesso 97
grande copritrice secondaria 78
grande falciata esterna 499
grande falciata interna 499
grande galleria 278
grande gluteo 97
grande labbro 112, 113
grande pettorale 96
grande rotondo 97
grande safena 102
grande trocantere 99
Grandi Laghi 16
grandi magazzini 437
grano 61
grano saraceno 61, 143
grano, chicco di 61
grano: spiga 61
granturismo 347
granulazione 4
granulo d'amido 50
granulo lipidico 50
grappolo d'uva 62
grassella 83
grassi 149
grassi lubrificanti 405
grasso alimentare 149
grattugia 170
grattugia per noce moscata 170
grattugiaformaggio 170
Grecia 450
green 504
grembiule 383
grembiule, gomma di tenuta del 383
Grenada 449
griffa 221, 228
griglia 174, 210, 271, 318, 324, 358, 359, 407, 529
griglia dei ripiani 211
griglia del radiatore 364
griglia del riscaldamento 380
griglia di aerazione 182, 380
griglia di contatto metallica 410
griglia di illuminazione 291
griglia di partenza 524
griglia di sicurezza 442
griglia di uscita dell'aria 270
griglia di ventilazione 209
griglia elettrica 178
griglia elettrica per interni 179
griglia per casco 476
griglia per raclette 179
griglia terminale 409
grill pieghevole 533
grilletto 235, 332, 454, 534
grilletto di accelerazione 235
grilletto di sicurezza 235
grillo 521
Groenlandia 16
Groenlandia, Mar di 14
gronda 283
grondaia 182
groppa 83
grotta 31, 35
groviera 151
gru 384, 397
gru a ponte 407
gru a portale 381, 406, 407
gru a torre 397
gru mobile a braccio 381
gru su pontone 381
gruccia 466
gruista, cabina del 397
gruppetto 299
gruppi strumentali, esempi di 300
gruppo 470, 522
gruppo del generatore 407
gruppo del turbo-alternatore 402
gruppo dell'elettropompa 357
gruppo delle sospensioni 351
gruppo dello sterzo 351
gruppo di testa 522
gruppo frigorifero 365
guadino 538
guaiava 137
guaina 55
guaina della lingua 76
guaina di Schwann 110
guaina mielinica 110
guancia 83, 86, 94, 220, 536
guanciale 204
guanciale, fodera del 204
guanti 243
guanti da donna 243
guanti da giardinaggio 232
guanti da uomo 243
guanti del portiere 480
guanti di lattice, astuccio per i 456
guanto 10, 476, 477, 478, 505, 506, 508, 510, 513, 514, 522, 525
guanto alla scudiera 243
guanto corto 243
guanto da guida 243
guanto da presa 507
guanto da respinta 507
guanto da sera 243
guanto del difensore 477
guanto di crine 267
guanto di lattice 460
guanto lungo 243
guanto, dito del 243
guanto, dorso del 243
guanto, palmo del 243
guantone 498
guantoni 498
guardalinee 481, 485
guardaroba 188, 203, 443
guardaroba dei clienti 438
guardaroba del personale 438
guardia 169, 489
guardia destra 485
guardia giurata, stanzino della 443
guardia sinistra 485
guardolo 240
guardrail 526
guarnizione 214, 260, 404
guarnizione conica 196
guarnizione della coppa dell'olio 360
guarnizione di gomma 197
guarnizione magnetica 211
Guatemala 448
guepière 259
gufo reale 81
guglia 36, 284, 285
guida 214, 396
guida del contrappeso 287
guida del filo 537
guida del nastro 341
guida della cabina 287
guida della carta 328
guida della catena 235, 372
guida di appoggio 226
guida di scorrimento 521
guida fine, sistema di 7
guida parallela 227
guida per il pane 178
guida, cabina di 376
guida, guanto da 243
guida, leva di manovra della 396
guida, ruota di 380
Guinea 451
Guinea Bissau 451
Guinea Equatoriale 451
Guinea, Golfo di 20
guscio 60, 79, 277
gusto 116
Gutenberg, discontinuità di 26
Guyana 448
guyot 33

H

Haiti 448
hall 439
handicap, punto di 470
hard disk estraibile 333
harissa 141
hat switch 332
hertz 426
hijiki 123
Himalaya 19
hockey su ghiaccio 506
home 331
home theatre 321
Honduras 448
Horn, Capo 17
hovercraft 383
Hubble, telescopio spaziale 7
Hudson, Baia di 16
Huitzilopochtli, tempio di 283
hummus 140
humus 54

I

identificazione, cartellino di 456
idrante a colonna 454
idrante antincendio 434
idrante, presa dell' 455
idraulica 194, 197
idrocarburi, fuoriuscita di 48
idroelettricità 406
idrosfera 44
idrovolante a due galleggianti 394
iena 88
ifa 52
igiene orale 272
igloo 288
igname 124
iguana 77
ileo 98, 106
illuminazione 199
illuminazione, griglia di 291
ilo renale 107
imballaggio 49
imbarco, passerella di 389
imbardata 395
imboccatura, canna di 307
imbottitura dell'angolo 498
imbuto 171, 318
immagine, raddrizzatori di 420
immagini, pulsante di visualizzazione delle 315
immagini, pulsante per il salto di 315
immersione, frullatore a 176
impalcato 344
imparipennata 55
impastatrice 176, 179
impasto, gancio per l' 176
impennaggio verticale 393
impermeabile 248
impianto di climatizzazione 386
impianto di deasfaltizzazione 405
impianto di estrazione con solventi 405
impianto di produzione dei lubrificanti 405
impianto di raffreddamento 351
impianto di reforming catalitico 405
impianto di smistamento 49
impianto di trivellazione 403
impianto elettrico 351
impianto frenante 351
impianto hi-fi di riproduzione del suono 322
impianto idraulico 194
impianto idroelettrico 406
impieghi di Internet 335
impluvio 280
importo da pagare 346
imposta 186
impostazioni 328
impostazioni, pulsante di visualizzazione delle 315
impugnatura 170, 176, 177, 180, 208, 217, 221, 226, 227, 229, 235, 237, 269, 271, 272, 301, 460, 467, 477, 478, 500, 501, 505, 510, 514, 535, 536, 537
impugnatura a penna 493
impugnatura a pistola 218, 228, 534
impugnatura a stretta di mano 493
impugnatura con sistema antivibrazione 235
impugnatura di sicurezza 237
impugnatura laterale 228
impugnatura rotante 332
impugnatura sagomata 269
impugnatura termica 515
impulsi, irrigatore a 236
impulso sensoriale 110
impuntura 240, 243, 246, 260, 262
imputato, banco dell' 440
in avanti 518
inalatore dosimetrico 467
incamiciatura 534
incandescenza, lampadina a 199
incasso, scatola da 198
incavo 167
incendi, prevenzione degli 454
incendio delle foreste 47
incenerimento 49
incernieramento, perno di 400
inchiostro 312
inchiostro a colori cangianti 441
incisivi 101
incisivo centrale 101
incisivo laterale 101
incisura anteriore 115
incisura intertragica 115
incocco, punto di 535
incordatura 492, 494
incremento dell'effetto serra 46
incudine 116
India 453
Indiano, Oceano 14, 15, 19, 20
indicatore del livello d'acqua 179
indicatore del livello dell'acqua 208
indicatore del livello di carburante 355
indicatore del piano 287
indicatore della pressione dell'acqua 455
indicatore della regolazione 511
indicatore della temperatura del liquido di raffreddamento 355
indicatore di carica 271
indicatore di destinazione 379
indicatore di direzione 352
indicatore di direzione, comando dell' 354
indicatore di linea 362, 363
indicatore di temperatura 269
indicatore generale degli orari 374
indicazione del valore 441
indicazioni di tempo 298
indice 313, 422, 423
indice di regolazione dell'altezza 227
indice, pulsante per l' 315
Indie Occidentali 16
indivia riccia 127
Indonesia 19, 453
industria 335
industria petrolchimica 405
infermiera 464
infermieri, postazione degli 462, 463
inferriata 279
infiltrazione 45, 47
infilzacarte 341
infinito 427
infiorescenze, tipi di 57
inforcamento, tasca di 396
informatica, aula di 444
informazioni, banco delle 390, 437, 442, 463
informazioni, diffusione di 335
infradito 242
infraspinato 97
infundibolo della tuba di Falloppio 113
infusi 148
ingaggio, cerchio di 506
ingaggio, punto di 506
ingegnere del suono 291
inghiottitoio 31
ingranaggio di trascinamento 180
ingranaggio per il moto orario 7
ingrandimento, pulsante per l' 315
ingressi uscite audio/video 322
ingresso 188
ingresso al marciapiede 374
ingresso alla piramide 278
ingresso degli attori 278
ingresso dei clienti 438
ingresso del fluido vettore 410
ingresso del personale 438, 445
ingresso del pubblico 278
ingresso dell'alimentazione dell'utente 198
ingresso della stazione 378
ingresso delle merci 435
ingresso principale 435, 445, 465
ingresso, porte d' 294
ingresso, selettore di 322
ingresso/uscita audio 337
inguine 92, 94
iniettore 360
iniziali della banca di emissione 441
innesco 534
inquinamento agricolo 47
inquinamento da gas di scarico delle automobili 47
inquinamento del suolo 47
inquinamento dell'acqua 48
inquinamento dell'aria 47
inquinamento domestico 47
inquinamento industriale 47
inquinamento petrolifero 48
inquinanti atmosferici 47
inquinanti non biodegradabili 47

insalata belga 127
insalata riccia 126
insalata, coppetta per l' 166
insalata, forchetta da 168
insalatiera 166
insegna esterna 378
insegnante 444
inserimento 331
inserimento dei documenti da trasmettere, punto di 328
inserto 313
inserzione pubblicitaria 313
insetti 67
insetti, esempi di 69
insieme vuoto 427
integrale 427
integrazione di energia alla rete di trasmissione 413
intelaiatura 192, 528
intelaiatura, base dell' 186
intelaiatura, parte superiore dell' 186
Intelsat 317
intensità luminosa, unità di misura dell' 426
interbase 474
interiora 154
Internet 334
interno gamba con abbottonatura a pressione 260, 261
internodo 53
interosseo plantare 96
interramento 49
interruttore 177, 180, 181, 198, 206, 208, 209, 211, 218, 219, 229, 269, 270, 271, 272, 311, 319, 416
interruttore a grilletto 227, 228, 229
interruttore automatico 407
interruttore d'alimentazione 328
interruttore del portello 213
interruttore di accensione 314, 315, 318, 320, 322, 323, 329, 333, 336
interruttore di accensione e del volume 326
interruttore di avviamento 368
interruttore di emergenza 368
interruttore di fine corsa 287
interruttore generale 321
interruttore principale 198
interruttore, dispositivo di blocco dell' 228
interruttore, placca dell' 198
interruzione 331
intersezione 427
intersuola 262
intervalli 298
intervista 313
intestino 71, 73, 103
intestino crasso 106
intestino tenue 106
inverno 38
inverno, solstizio d' 38
invertitore 221, 228
invio 331
invito, scalino d' 191
involucro 192, 225
involucro di zinco (anodo) 417
io 2
ipermetropia 419
ipersostentatore 13
ipersostentatore sul bordo di attacco 393
ipofisi 109
ippoglosso 161
ippopotamo 85
Iran 452
Iraq 452
iride 119
Irlanda 449
Irlanda, Mar d' 18
irrigatore a impulsi 236
irrigatore oscillante 236
irrigatore rotativo a pioggia 236
isba 288
ischio 99
Islanda 18, 450
isobara 39
isola 24, 164, 343
Isola di Baffin 16
isola di Man, gatto dell' 87
Isola di Terranova 16
isola vulcanica 33
isolamento, stanza di 462
isolamento, tappo di 417
isolante 410
isolante termico 12
Isole Aleutine 16
Isole delle Antille 448
Isole Falkland 17
Isole Figi 15
Isole Marshall 453
Isole Salomone 453
isolotto roccioso 35
isolotto sabbioso 35
ispezione, tappo di 197
Israele 452
issopo 142
istituzioni educative 335
istmo 24
istmo della tuba di Falloppio 113
istmo delle fauci 116
Istmo di Panama 16
istruzione 444
istruzioni per l'uso 346
Italia 450
iurta 288

J

jaboticaba 137
jarlsberg 151
jazz-band 300
jeans 254
jet supersonico 37, 394
jicama 124
jolly 468
joule 426
joystick 332, 471
judo 499
judogi 499

K

Kalahari, Deserto del 20
Kazakistan 452
kelvin 426
Kenya 451
Kermadec-Tonga, Fossa di 34
ketchup 141
kilogrammo 426
kimono 256
Kirghizistan 452
Kiribati 453
kit con cuffia dotata di microfono 327
kit di attrezzi 372
kiwano 136
kiwi 136
Kola, Penisola di 18
kombu 123
kora 297
Kuiper, cintura di 2
kumquat 134
Kuwait 452

L

la 298
labbra, pennellino per 266
labbra, trucco per le 266
labbro 83, 87
labbro esterno 73
labbro inferiore 116, 305
labbro interno 73
labbro superiore 116, 305
laboratorio 7
laboratorio americano 11
laboratorio di anatomia patologica 465
laboratorio spaziale 13
laccio 262, 535
laccio di pelle 246
laccolite 28
Ladoga, Lago 18
laghetto 230
laghi 32
laghi, acidificazione dei 48
lago 5, 24, 29, 32
lago artificiale 32
Lago Baikal 19
Lago Ciad 20
Lago di Aral 19
lago di meandro abbandonato 32
Lago Eyre 15
lago glaciale 32
Lago Ladoga 18
Lago Malawi 20
lago salato 36
Lago Tanganica 20
lago tettonico 32
Lago Titicaca 17
Lago Vittoria 20
lago vulcanico 32
lagomorfi 82
lagomorfi, esempi di 82
laguna 35
lama 84, 167, 169, 177, 180, 216, 219, 221, 226, 227, 235, 270, 271, 341, 398, 401, 506, 509
lama dentellata 270
lama di sega circolare 227
lama dritta 270
lama grande 531
lama isolata 217
lama per danza 509
lama per pattinaggio libero 509
lama piccola 531
lama, cilindro di rotazione della 401
lama, cilindro di sollevamento della 398, 401
lama, dispositivo di blocco dell'inclinazione della 227
lama, fermo della 270
lama, filo della 270
lama, meccanismo di spostamento della 401
lama, regolatore dell'inclinazione della 227
lama, vite di blocco della 227
lamelle 52
lametta a due tagli 271
lamette, caricatore di 271
lamina 51, 52, 55, 509, 510
lamina assorbente 410
lamina cribrosa dell'etmoide 117
lampada 320, 421
lampada a braccio regolabile 206
lampada a petrolio 532
lampada a risparmio energetico 411
lampada a sospensione 206
lampada a stelo 206
lampada al neon 217
lampada alogena al tungsteno 199
lampada alogena da tavolo 206
lampada da comodino 439
lampada da lettura 206
lampada da notte 464
lampada da parete 207
lampada da parete con braccio estensibile 207
lampada da tavolo 206
lampada del presbiterio 446
lampada per saldare 218
lampada portatile a gabbia 217
lampada provacircuiti 217
lampadario 207
lampade in serie 207
lampadina 217, 416
lampadina a incandescenza 199
lampadina a risparmio di energia 199
lampeggiante 455, 457
lampeggiante, sistema di controllo del 457
lampeggiatore anteriore 366, 368
lampeggiatore posteriore 367, 368
lampione 207, 230, 434
lampione da parete 207
lampone 132
lampone, sezione di un 59
lampreda 159
lanceolata 55
lancetta dei decimi di secondo 424
lancetta dei minuti 424
lancetta dei secondi 424
lancia 236
lancia antincendio 455
lancia antincendio schiumogena 385
lanciatore 474, 475, 479
lancio 475, 479
lancio del disco 473
lancio del giavellotto 473
lancio del martello 473
lancio del peso 472
lanterna 529
lanugine, filtro per 212, 213
Laos 453
lapide commemorativa 447
lardatoio 173
lardo 149
larghezza del gradino 191
larice 65
laringe 105
lasagne 146
laser a rubino pulsato 420
lastrico, pietra da 230
latifoglie, esempi di 64
latitudine 22
lato 167, 293, 498
lato del re 470
lato della regina 470
lato destro 272
lato di destra 293
lato di sinistra 293
lato sinistro 272
latrine 280
latta per alimenti 163
latte 150
latte di capra 150
latte evaporato 150
latte in polvere 150
latte omogeneizzato 150
latte, bricco del 166
latteria 122
latticello 150
latticini 120
latticini, scomparto per i 211
lattina 163
lattuga asparago 126
lattuga cappuccina 126
lattuga iceberg 126
lattuga marina 123
lattuga romana 126
lava, strato di 28
lavabiancheria a carica frontale 212
lavabiancheria a carica verticale 212
lavabo 194
lavaggio, torre di 214
lavagna 444
lavallière 245
lavanderia 188, 439
lavanderia a secco 437
lavandino 195, 439, 464
lavandino del chirurgo 465
lavaparabrezza, ugello del 348
lavastoviglie 164, 214
lavatrice 194
lavello 164, 197
lavello con tritarifiuti 197
lavello, doppio 194
lavoro, piano di 164, 224
leccarda 174, 179
LED indicatore del livello di picco 323
legabagagli elastico 277
legame chimico 414
legamento 73
legamento largo dell'utero 113
legamento periodontale 101
legamento sospensore 119
legatura 299, 306
leggio 305, 311, 446
legna da ardere, cassone per 192
legno 505
legume, sezione di un 60
legumi 130
legumiera 166
lembo 255
lembo anteriore 245
lembo della camicia 245
lembo posteriore 245
lemure 91
lente 273, 531
lente a contatto monouso 272
lente a contatto morbida 272
lente a contatto rigida 272
lente biconcava 419
lente biconvessa 419
lente concava 419
lente convessa 419
lente di campo 420
lente di ingrandimento 421
lente obiettivo 420
lente piano-concava 419
lente piano-convessa 419
lente torica 419
lenti 419
lenti a contatto 272
lenti convergenti 419
lenti divergenti 419
lenti, sistema di 420
lenticchie 130
lenza 536
lenzuolo 204
lenzuolo con angoli 204
leone 89
leone marino 90
leopardo 89
lepre 82, 154
lepre fischiante 82
lesena corinzia 281
lesena dorica 281
lesena ionica 281
Lesotho 452
lettere al direttore 313
lettiga 460
lettino 460
lettino a sponde 205
lettino pieghevole con fasciatoio 205
letto 204, 361
letto d'ospedale 464
letto matrimoniale 439
letto singolo 439
letto ungueale 114
letto, biancheria da 204
letto, vagone 376
Lettonia 450
lettore audio digitale portatile 326
lettore CD 329, 336
lettore CD portatile 325
lettore CD/DVD 471
lettore CD/DVD-ROM 310
lettore di carte 346, 442, 443
lettore di compact disc 323, 325, 326
lettore di compact disc, tasti del 326
lettore di scheda di memoria 329, 333
lettore di schede 321
lettore DVD-ROM 329, 336
lettura, luce di 457
lettura, specchio di 10
leucoplasto 50
leva 178, 197, 222, 265, 534
leva del cambio 350, 354, 371, 372, 522
leva del freno 371, 522, 523
leva del freno a mano 354
leva del freno anteriore 368
leva del pedale 304
leva del pistone 216
leva della chiave 306
leva della frizione 366, 368
leva della pinza 269
leva di apertura dell'attacco 511
leva di bloccaggio 224
leva di bloccaggio dell'altezza 8, 9
leva di bloccaggio dell'asse orizzontale 8, 9
leva di contatto 207
leva di manovra della guida 396
leva di regolazione laterale 229
leva di sbloccaggio 222
leva di scatto 196
leva di scorrimento 353
leva di serraggio 224, 229
leva per togliere il paralama inferiore 227
levapunti 341
levetta 170
levetta dello sciacquone 196
Libano 452
libellula 69
Liberia 451
libero 481, 487
Libia 451
libreria 436, 444
libretto degli assegni 274
libretto, scala a 219
lichene 50
lichene crostoso 50
lichene fogliaceo 50
lichene fruticoso 50
lichene, struttura di un 50
licheni, esempi di 50
Liechtenstein 450
lima 229, 531
limetta 134, 265
limetta di cartoncino vetrato 265
limetta pieghevole 265
limite del campo 475
limone 134
limousine 347
lince 88
linea 298
linea aerea di alimentazione 376
linea blu di zona 507
linea cablata 335
linea centrale 493, 494
linea centrale di servizio 491
linea continua 342
linea d'acchito 502

linea dedicata 334
linea dei 10 metri 482
linea dei 15 metri 483
linea dei 22 metri 482
linea dei 5 metri 483
linea del battitore 479
linea del bersaglio 515
linea del traguardo 473
linea dell'area di rigore 480
linea della corsia 473
linea della fila di attesa 443
linea delle yards 484
linea di accrescimento 72, 73
linea di attacco 487
linea di centro 515
linea di centrocampo 484, 488, 507
linea di demarcazione 479
linea di direzione 533
linea di distribuzione a bassa tensione 198
linea di distribuzione a media tensione 198
linea di fallo 515
linea di fondo 484, 487, 489, 491, 493, 494, 515, 517
linea di forza 416
linea di fuoricampo 474
linea di fuoricampo, palo della 475
linea di lancio 471
linea di messa in gioco 484
linea di meta 482, 484
linea di metà campo 481, 483
linea di mira, regolazione della 420
linea di mischia 485
linea di pallone morto 482
linea di partenza 473, 524
linea di partenza degli 800 metri piani 473
linea di partenza dei 100 metri piani e dei 100 metri ostacoli 472
linea di partenza dei 10000 metri piani e della staffetta 4 x 400 metri 473
linea di partenza dei 110 metri ostacoli 472
linea di partenza dei 1500 metri piani 473
linea di partenza dei 200 metri piani 472
linea di partenza dei 400 metri piani, dei 400 metri ostacoli 473
linea di partenza dei 5000 metri piani 472
linea di partenza della staffetta 4 x 100 metri 473
linea di porta 506
linea di puntamento 533
linea di rimando 479
linea di rullaggio 389
linea di servizio 491
linea di servizio corto 495
linea di servizio lungo 494
linea di sicurezza 379
linea di tiro libero 489
linea di uscita laterale 483
linea ferroviaria locale 375
linea ferroviaria principale 375
linea isosismica 27
linea laterale 74, 481, 484, 487, 488, 493, 515
linea laterale del doppio 490, 495
linea laterale del singolo 491, 495
linea meridiana 533
linea neutra 416
linea sottomarina 334
linea telefonica 334
linea tratteggiata 342, 343
linea, aereo di 37
linea, giudice di 490, 494, 496
lineare 55
linebacker centrale 484
linebacker esterno 484
linebacker interno 484
linee di costa, esempi di 35
lingua 106, 116, 117, 154
lingua biforcuta 76
lingua di cervo 52
lingua di terra 35
lingua glaciale 30
lingua, dorso della 118
lingua, guaina della 76
linguella 243
linguetta 240, 248, 262, 274, 297, 340, 509
linguetta con finestra 340
linguetta di protezione 333
linguettone 511
liquido 414, 415
liquido cefalorachidiano 110
liquido dei freni, serbatoio del 357
liquore, bicchierino da 165
lira 297
liscio 55
lisciviazione 48
lisosoma 66
lista di controllo delle procedure 10
lista serratura 304
listarella 211
listello 412
listello rompitratta 186
litchi 137
litosfera 26, 44
litri erogati 346
littorine 157
Lituania 450
livella a bolla 225
livellatrice 401
livello base del moto ondoso 33
livello del mare 26, 33, 37
livello dell'acqua 181
livello dell'acqua, indicatore del 208
livello dell'acqua, selettore del 212
livello di carburante, indicatore del 355
livello di mare calmo 33
livello superiore, dominio di 334
livello, vite di 423
lizza 282
lobato 55
lobo 79, 115
lobo inferiore 105
lobo laterale inferiore 62
lobo laterale superiore 62
lobo medio 105
lobo superiore 105
lobo terminale 62
locale delle pompe 384
locale per la biancheria 439
locale tecnico 345
locomotiva diesel-elettrica 377
loculo 58
lombo 83, 93, 95
longan 136
longherone 392
longherone laterale 365
longitudine 22
lontra comune 88
lonza 153
loop di punta 509
lottatore 499
lubrificanti, impianto di produzione dei 405
lucchetto 372
luccio 160
luce 7, 8, 9, 269, 380
luce anticollisione 392
luce della targa 352
luce di arresto 352
luce di ingombro laterale 352, 364, 365
luce di lettura 457
luce di navigazione 383, 393, 395
luce di posizione 352, 376
luce di posizione posteriore 352
luce di retromarcia 352
luce di sicurezza 457
luce gialla 434
luce perpetua 447
luce rossa 434
luce rotante 455
luce verde 434
luce visibile 418
lucernario 183
lucernario del bagno 189
lucernario della tromba delle scale 189
lucertola 77
luci 206
luci abbaglianti, spia delle 368
luci anteriori 352
luci dei goal 507
luci delle sorgenti 322
luci intermittenti 362
luci pedonali 434
luci posteriori 352
luci, commutatore delle 368
luci, tecnico delle 291
lucidaunghie 265
lucioperca 160
Luer-Lock, punta 460
Luna 2, 4, 5
Luna calante 5
Luna crescente 5
Luna gibbosa calante 5
Luna gibbosa crescente 5
Luna nuova 5
Luna piena 5
Luna, caratteristiche della 5
Luna, eclissi di 5
Luna, fasi della 5
Luna, orbita della 4, 5
lunetta 240, 480, 488
lunghezza d'onda 418
lunghezza del gradino 191
lunghezza dell'onda 33
lunghezza della punta 538
lunghezza, misura della 425
lunghezza, unità di misura della 426
lunotto laterale 349
lunula 73, 114, 115
lupino 130
lupo 88
Lussemburgo 449
lutz 509

M

macaco 91
macadamia, noce di 133
macao 80
macchia 44
macchia di fiori 230
macchia solare 4
macchina compatta 315
macchina da caffè a filtro 181
macchina della polizia 457
macchina fotografica a lastre 315
macchina fotografica reflex (6x6) 315
macchina fotografica reflex digitale: dorso 315
macchina fotografica reflex monoculare: vista frontale 314
macchina fotografica usa e getta 315
macchina fotografica, corpo della 314
macchina per espresso 181
macchina per fare la pasta 170
macchina per fototessere 437
macchina ultracompatta 315
macchine da caffè 181
macchine fotografiche 315
macchine pesanti 398
macchine, sala 384, 386
macchinetta 269
macchinista 290
macinacaffè 180
macinato 152, 153
Mackenzie, Fiume di 16
macronucleo 66
macula 119
Madagascar 20, 452
magazzino 430, 438, 444
magazzino dei surgelati 121
magazzino frigorifero 381
magenta 418
maggese 122
maggiolino 69
maggiore di 427
maggiore o uguale a 427
maglia 483, 488, 493, 522
maglia della squadra 476, 480, 486
maglia dentata 235
maglia girocollo 255
maglietta 473
maglietta alla marinara 255
maglietta intima 260
maglione dolcevita 250
maglione girocollo 250
maglioni 250
magma 28, 33
magnesia, polvere di 497
magnete 416
magnete fermacoperchio 180
magnetismo 416
maiale 84
maiale, tagli di 153
mais 61, 143
mais foraggero 122
mais, farina di 144
mais, olio di 149
mais, pane americano di 145
mais, sciroppo di 149
mais: pannocchia 61
maître 438
maiuscola 330
malanga 129
Malawi 452
Malawi, Lago 20
Malaysia 453
Maldive 453
Mali, Repubblica del 451
mallo 60
Malta 450
malto, aceto di 141
mammiferi carnivori 86
mammiferi carnivori, esempi di 88
mammiferi marini 90
mammiferi marini, esempi di 90
mammiferi ungulati 83
mammiferi ungulati, esempi di 84
mandarino 134
mandibola 67, 74, 98, 100
mandibola inferiore 78
mandibola superiore 78
mandolino 297
mandorla 57
mandorle 133
mandrino 228
mandrino autoserrante 228
mandrino, chiave del 228
manette, astuccio delle 456
manganello, gancio del 456
mango 137
mangostano 136
mangusta 88
manica 244
manica a giro 245
manica alla raglan 248, 251, 261
Manica, Canale della 18
manichetta antincendio 454
manico 167, 215, 216, 219, 220, 223, 236, 270, 271, 272, 273, 274, 275, 276, 277, 297, 301, 302, 303, 341, 492, 493, 494, 531
manico a scomparsa 274
manico isolato 217
manicotto 395
manicotto del cavo 228
manicotto del cordone 218, 229
manicotto di attacco dello scalpello 403
manicotto inferiore del radiatore 358
manicotto, borsa a 276
manicure 265
manicure, set per 265
manifesto 294
maniglia 178, 179, 185, 186, 204, 209, 210, 211, 214, 225, 277, 325, 326, 349, 361, 455
maniglia di salita 364
maniglia di spinta 286
maniglia di traino 277
maniglia fissa 352
maniglia interna 352
maniglia isolata 179
maniglia laterale 380
maniglia retrattile 277
maniglie, cavallo con 496
manioca 124
manipolazione a distanza, sistema di 11
mannaia 169
mano 91, 93, 95, 115
mano, scudo di protezione della 235
manometro 461
manopola 192, 210, 243, 267, 366, 369
manopola alzacristalli 352
manopola del volume 325
manopola dell'acceleratore 368
manopola della messa a fuoco 8, 9
manopola della sintonia 326
manopola di controllo 471
manopola di regolazione del condensatore 421
manopola di regolazione del gas 529
manopola di regolazione dell'aggetto 229
manopola di regolazione dell'altezza 209
manopola di regolazione dello schienale 353
manopola di sintonizzazione 325
manopole 260
manopole di comando dei bruciatori 210
manovella 224, 236, 356, 537
manovella d'avvolgimento 225
manovella del supporto 365
manovella di avviamento 235
manovra, motore di 13
mansardato, piano 189
mantella 251
mantello 72, 73
mantello d'elica 383
mantello del pistone 360
mantello inferiore 26
mantello superiore 26
mantice a soffietto 296
mantide religiosa 69
manto di usura 342
manuale del grand'organo 305
manuale dell'organo espressivo 305
manuale dell'organo positivo 305
manuale di pronto soccorso 461
manuale, pistoncino del 305
manuali 305
manubri 500
manubrio 371, 501, 523
manubrio rialzato 522
manubrio, attacco del 371
manzo, tagli di 152
mappamondo 444
Mar Adriatico 18
Mar Baltico 18
Mar Caribico 14, 16
Mar Caspio 14, 19
Mar Cinese Meridionale 14, 19
Mar Cinese Orientale 19
Mar d'Irlanda 18
Mar dei Coralli 15
Mar del Giappone 19
Mar di Barents 18
Mar di Beaufort 16
Mar di Bering 14
Mar di Groenlandia 14
Mar di Norvegia 18
Mar Glaciale Artico 14
Mar Mediterraneo 14, 18, 20
Mar Nero 14, 18, 19
Mar Rosso 14, 19, 20
maracuja 136
marciapiede 183, 375, 379, 390, 434
marciapiede dei viaggiatori 374
marciapiede, ingresso al 374
marciapiede, margine del 379
mare 5, 24, 32
Mare Arabico 19
mare calmo, livello di 33
Mare del Nord 14, 18
Mare di Tasmania 15
Mare di Weddell 15
Mare Egeo 18
mare, livello del 26, 33, 37
mare, orecchia di 157
mare, passera di 161
mare, pressione a livello del 39
mare, tartufo di 157
margarina 149
margine 55
margine anteriore 73
margine continentale 33
margine del marciapiede 379
margine fogliare 55
margine libero 114
margine posteriore 73
Marie Byrd, Terra di 15
marinaio, sacca da 276
marino 40
marmitta 29, 351
marmotta 82
Marocco 451
Marte 2, 3
martelletti, barra dei 304
martelletto 304
martello 116, 472
martello a penna tonda 220
martello da carpentiere 220
martello da falegname 220
martello da muratore 216
martin pescatore 80
martinetto idraulico 361
martora 88
mascara compatto 266
mascara liquido 266
mascara, spazzolino per 266
mascella 74, 98, 100, 117
mascellare mobile 76
maschera 454, 476, 478, 486, 507
maschera a pieno facciale bifiltro 459
maschera forata 318
mascherina 296, 348, 459
mascherina chirurgica 459
mascherina perforata 240

maschile 426
maschio 282
maschio della messa a terra 198
massa 27
massa d'aria, tipo di 39
massa, unità di misura della 426
massaggiatore 489
massetere 96
massetto 187
massiccio montuoso 24
mastice di tenuta 196
matematica 427
materassi 496
materassino 205, 460, 530
materassino autogonfiante 530
materassino isolante 530
materassino pneumatico 530
materasso 204, 205
materia 414
materia inorganica 45
materia, stati della 414
materiale antincendio 454
materiale isolante 190, 214, 417
materiale medico, deposito del 465
materiale pulito, ripostiglio del 462
materiale sporco, deposito del 464
materiale sporco, ripostiglio del 462
materiale sterile, deposito del 464
materiale vario 225
materiali metallici, smistamento dei 49
materiali, movimentazione dei 396
matita 312
matita occhi 266
matita sbiancante per unghie 265
matite per il contorno delle labbra 266
matrice ungueale 114
matterello 172
mattone refrattario 192
maturazione 62
maturazione, stadi di 62
maturità 62
Mauritania 451
Maurizio 452
mazza 308, 476, 477, 478
mazze 309
mazze, tipi di 505
mazzo 125
mazzuolo 220, 297
meandro 32
meandro abbandonato 32
meandro abbandonato, lago di 32
meato auditivo 115, 116
meato uditivo esterno 100
meato urinario 111
Mecca, direzione della 447
meccanismo a scatto 312
meccanismo antiritorno 536
meccanismo dell'ottava 306
meccanismo di apertura dell'archetto 537
meccanismo di rilascio della bobina 537
meccanismo di spostamento della lama 401
mecchia 228
mecchia a doppia elica 228
mecchia a lancia 228
mecchia a tortiglione 228
mecchia elicoidale 228
mecchie e punte da trapano, esempi di 228
medaglione 264
media tensione, linea di distribuzione a 198
mediano di apertura 482
mediano di mischia 482
medicinali, confezioni farmaceutiche di 467
medico 464, 498
medico di guardia, ufficio del 462
medico interno 464
medie frequenze, pick-up per 303
Mediterraneo, Mar 14, 18, 20
Meissner, corpuscolo di 114
mela 133
mela cotogna 133
mela, sezione di una 58
Melanesia 15
melanzana 128
melassa 149
mele, aceto di 141
melissa 142
melodia, canna della 296
melodia, corde per la 296
melograno 136
melone amaro 128
melone giallo canario 135
melone invernale 129, 135
melone mieloso 135
melone Ogen 135
melone retato 135
meloni 135
membrana 309
membrana cellulare 50, 66
membrana del timpano 116
membrana interdigitale 75, 79
membrana nittitante 87
membrana nucleare 50, 66
membrana plasmatica 66
membrana testacea 79
membrana vitellina 79
memorizzazione dei dati, dispositivi di 333
memorizzazione, tasto di 322, 327
meningi 109
menisco convergente 419
menisco divergente 419
menorah 447
mensola 192, 283, 302
mensola portaccessori 8
mensola portautensili 219
mensolone 192
menta 142
mento 78, 94
mento, protezione del 367
mentoniera 301
menu 319
menu, pulsante del 315
merci, banchina di scarico delle 437, 439
merci, ingresso delle 435
merci, scalo 375, 430
Mercurio 2, 3
mercurio, bulbo di 424
mercurio, colonna di 424
merguez 156
meridiana 424
meridiano fondamentale 22
meridiano occidentale 22
meridiano orientale 22
méridienne 200
merlano 161
merlano nero 161
merluzzo dell'Atlantico 161
mesa 36
mesocarpo 57, 58, 59
mesopausa 37
mesosfera 37
messa a fuoco, manopola della 8, 9
messa a fuoco, selettore della 314
messa a terra, maschio della 198
messa a terra, terminale della 322
messaggio precedente 328
messaggio successivo 328
Messico 448
Messico, Golfo del 16
mestolo 173
meta, area di 484
meta, linea di 484
metallo, bacchetta di 309
meteorologia 37
metodi di pagamento 441
metro 426
metropolitana 378, 380, 435
metropolitana, stazione della 378, 432
metropolitana, treno della 378
mezza sfera di sughero 495
mezzanino 378
mezzi occhiali 273
mezzo di pronto intervento 345
mezzo manico 169
mezzoguanto 243
mi 298
micelio 52
microfilamento 66
microfoni 457
microfono 320, 327, 328, 332, 337, 456
micrometro a vite 425
Micronesia 453
micronucleo 66
microonde 418
microonde, forno a 178
microscopi 421
microscopio 421
microscopio binoculare 421
microtelefono 327
microtelefono, cordone del 327
microtubulo 66
microvettura compatta 347
MIDI (cavo di interfaccia digitale per strumenti musicali) 311
midollo 63, 154
midollo allungato 109
midollo spinale 109, 110
midollo spinale, struttura del 109
midrange 324
miele 149
migale del Messico 70
miglio 61, 143
miglio: spiga 61
mihrab 447
mihrab, cupola sul 447
mille 427
milza 103
Mimas 3
minareto 447
minbar 447
mini impianto hi-fi 325
mini sci 510
miniaspiratutto 208
minibus 363
minima 299
minima, pausa di 299
minore di 427
minore o uguale a 427
minuti, lancetta dei 424
miocardio 104
miopia 419
mira, cannocchiale di 420
Miranda 3
mirino 315, 534, 535
mirino a cannocchiale 534
mirino elettronico 320
mirtilli 132
mirtilli palustri 132
mirtilli rossi 132
miscela di cinque spezie 139
miscela di manganese (catodo) 417
miscela di sostanze depolarizzanti 417
miscela di zinco ed elettroliti (anodo) 417
miscelatore 197
miscelatore per dolci 172
miscelatore vasca/doccia 194
mischia 484, 485
mischia spontanea 483
mischia, linea di 485
Mississippi, Fiume 16
misura del peso 422
misura del tempo 424
misura della lunghezza 425
misura della temperatura 424
misura dello spessore 425
misurini 171
mitili 157
mitocondrio 50, 66
mitra 193
mobile 318
mobile bar 203
mobile portaccessori 195
mobili contenitori 202
mobili per bambini 205
mocassino 242
mocassino classico 242
modalità FM, tasto di selezione della 322
modanatura 348
modellatore aperto 258
modellatore sgambato 258
modello di stazione 39
modem 334
modem cablato 335
moderatore 408
modo di acquisizione 314
modo di esposizione, tasto per il 314
modo di registrazione 320
modo, selettori di 326
modulatore della pressione dei freni 357
modulazione dell'altezza e del timbro del suono 310
moduli fotovoltaici 11
modulo abitativo americano 11
modulo centrifugo 11
modulo di comunicazione 316
modulo di propulsione 316
modulo di servizio 316
modulo di sperimentazione europeo 11
modulo di sperimentazione giapponese 11
modulo russo 11
moffetta 88
Mohorovicic, discontinuità di 26
molare, sezione trasversale di un 101
molari 101
Moldavia 450
mole 426
molecola 414
molla 27, 206, 212, 222, 312, 460, 535
molla della valvola 360
molla di richiamo 357
molla di tensione 355, 500
molla sturatrice per scarichi 216
molla, aletta a 221
molle 173, 193
molle a forbice 500
molle per chiocciole 173
molle per spaghetti 173
molle, rete a 204
molletta 268
molletta fermavetrino 421
molluschi 72, 157
molo 430
moltiplica, ruota della 522
moltiplicatore 413
moltiplicazione 427
Monaco, Principato di 450
mondo, climi del 40
moneta: diritto 441
moneta: rovescio 441
Mongolia 453
monitor 329
monitor della pressione sanguigna 461
monitori di controllo del regista 290
monoblocco 360
monoscafi 521
monovolume 347
montagna 29
montagna sottomarina 33
montagna, climi di 40
Montagne Rocciose 16
montante 184, 186, 187, 219, 281, 349
montante centrale 185, 202
montante d'angolo 187
montante del telaio 202
montante del timpano 187
montante dell'ala 394
montante della ferratura 185
montante della serratura 185
montante imbottito 489
montante verticale 201, 202
montatura 273
montatura a ferro di cavallo 7
monte di lancio 475
monte di Venere 112
Monte Everest 37
Montenegro 450
montgomery 249
Monti Appalachi 16
Monti Carpazi 18
Monti dell'Atlante 20
Monti Transantartici 15
Monti Urali 18
montone 249
monumento 25
moquette 190
mordente 299
more 132
morena di fondo 30
morena frontale 30
morena laterale 30
morena mediana 30
morena terminale 30
morfologia di un astice 71
morfologia di un cane 86
morfologia di un cavallo 83
morfologia di un delfino 90
morfologia di un gorilla 91
morfologia di un persico 74
morfologia di un polpo 72
morfologia di un ragno 70
morfologia di un ratto 82
morfologia di un serpente velenoso: testa 76
morfologia di un uccello 78
morfologia di un'ape: operaia 68
morfologia di una chiocciola 72
morfologia di una conchiglia bivalve 73
morfologia di una conchiglia univalve 73
morfologia di una farfalla 67
morfologia di una rana 75
morfologia di una tartaruga 76
morfologia di uno squalo femminile 74
morsa 224
morsa serratubi 224
morsettiera 411
morsetto 198, 221, 226
morsetto a C 224
morsetto nero 356
morsetto regolabile 206
morsetto rosso 356
morsetto terminale a spina 359
mortadella 156
mortaio 170
morte 426
mosaico 280
mosca 69
mosca artificiale 536
mosca tse-tse 69
moschea 447
moschettiera, stivale alla 241
moschettone 521, 538
mosse principali 470
moto da Gran premio 525
moto ondoso, livello base del 33
motocicletta 366
motocicletta con telecamera 522
motocicletta da cross 369
motocicletta da motocross 525
motocicletta da supercross 525
motocicletta da turismo 369
motocicletta di testa 522
motocicletta: vista dall'alto 368
motociclette e ciclomotore, esempi di 369
motociclismo 525
motociclista 525
motofalciatrice 237
motore 212, 213, 214, 227, 229, 237, 366, 403
motore a benzina 351, 360
motore di manovra 13
motore di traino, vano del 400
motore diesel del ventilatore di sostentamento 383
motore diesel di propulsione 383
motore diesel, vano del 398, 399, 400, 401
motore elettrico 235, 237, 358
motore fuoribordo 385
motore principale 13
motore, asse di trasmissione del 177
motore, blocco 176, 177, 180, 208
motore, rivestimento del 235
motore, vano 396
motore, vano del 401
motore, yacht a 385
motori diesel marini, combustibile per 405
motori diesel, combustibile per 405
motorino d'avviamento 237
motoscafo da diporto 385
motosega 235
motrice 364, 380
motto 441
mountain bike 373, 522
mountain bike da cross 373
mouse a rotella 332
mouse meccanico 332
mouse ottico 332
mouse senza fili 332
mouse, tappetino del 332
movimentazione 396
movimentazione dei materiali 396
movimenti del terreno 31
movimenti di un aeroplano 395
movimento a L 470
movimento diagonale 470
movimento orizzontale 470
movimento orizzontale del suolo 27
movimento verticale 470
movimento verticale del suolo 27
movimento, rilevatore di 286
Mozambico 452
Mozambico, Canale di 20
mozzarella 150
mozzo 341, 371, 413, 467
mozzo del rotore 395
mucca 84
mucosa olfattiva 117
muffola 243
muflone 84
mughetto 56
mulinello 536
mulinello a bobina fissa 537
mulinello a bobina rotante 537

mulinello, alloggiamento del 536, 537
mulino a pilastro 412
mulino a torre 412
mulino a vento 412
mulo 84
multiscafi 521
mummia 530
municipio 432
munster 151
mura fortificate 447
murata 385
muro di fondazione 187
muro di fondo 292, 293
muro di sponda 406
muschi, esempi di 51
muschio 51
muschio d'Irlanda 123
muschio, struttura di un 51
muscoli 96
muscolo adduttore anteriore 73
muscolo adduttore posteriore 73
muscolo bulbocavernoso 111
muscolo erettore del pelo 114
muscolo papillare 104
muscolo retto inferiore 119
muscolo retto superiore 119
museo 433
musica 296
musica, aula di 444
muso 75, 83, 86, 87, 91, 392
muso abbassabile 394
mussolina 171
mutande 247
mutandina 259
mutandina con ruches 260
mutandina elastica 259
mutandina impermeabile 260
mutandoni 247
muting 323
Myanmar 453

N

n. 8 avanti 482
nacchere 295, 309
Namib, Deserto del 20
Namibia 452
naos 279
narice 74, 75, 76, 78, 83, 117
nascita 426
nasello 273
nashi 137
naso 82, 83, 94
naso esterno 117
naso, dorso del 117
naso, punta del 117
naso, radice del 117
nasofaringe 117
nastratrice 341
nastro 225, 238, 491
nastro adesivo, chiocciola per 341
nastro bianco 487, 493, 495
nastro centrale 491
nastro di delimitazione 457
nastro di Teflon® 216
nastro magnetico 319
nastro trasportatore 49, 390
nastro verticale laterale 487
nastro, fermo del 225
nastro, selettore del 323
natica 93, 95, 111, 112
Nauru 453
navata centrale 285, 447
navata laterale 285
nave cisterna 384
nave da perforazione 382
nave da ricognizione meteorologica 38
nave per il trasporto delle merci 382
nave portacontainer 381, 382
nave traghetto 386
navetta per il trasbordo dei passeggeri 391
navetta spaziale 12, 37
navetta spaziale al decollo 12
navi, esempi di 382
navicella 413
navicella, sezione trasversale di una 413
navigazione, luce di 383, 393
navone 129
Nazca, placca di 27
nazionalità 497
nebbia 41
nebulizzatore 236
necrologia 313
nefridio 71
negozio 432
negozio di abbigliamento 436
negozio di animali 436
negozio di articoli da regalo 436
negozio di articoli sportivi 437
negozio di biancheria intima 436
negozio di bricolage 436
negozio di dischi 436
negozio di elettronica 436
negozio di giocattoli 436
negozio di oggettistica 437
negozio di scarpe 437
negozio per la riproduzione delle chiavi 437
nembostrato 42
neon, lampada al 217
neonati, vestiti per 260
Nepal 453
neri 470
nero 418
Nero, Mar 14, 18, 19
nervatura 55, 401, 458
nervatura alare 67
nervatura centrale 51, 55, 60
nervi cranici 108
nervo 114
nervo ascellare 108
nervo cocleare 116
nervo cutaneo laterale della coscia 108
nervo cutaneo posteriore della coscia 108
nervo digitale 108
nervo femorale 108
nervo gluteo 108
nervo ileoinguinale 108
nervo ileoipogastrico 108
nervo intercostale 108
nervo ischiatico 108
nervo mediano 108
nervo olfattivo 117
nervo ottico 119
nervo otturatorio 108
nervo peroniero comune 108
nervo peroniero profondo 108
nervo peroniero superficiale 108
nervo radiale 108
nervo safeno esterno 108
nervo safeno interno 108
nervo spinale 109, 110
nervo tibiale 108
nervo ulnare 108
nervo vestibolare 116
nervoso centrale, sistema 109
nervoso periferico, sistema 108
nervoso, sistema 108
nespole del Giappone 133
nettarina 132
Nettuno 2, 3
neurone motorio 110
neurone sensoriale 110
neuroni, catena di 110
neutrone 414
neutrone incidente 415
nevato 30
neve 41
neve acida 48
nevi perenni 29
nevischio 41
newton 426
Nicaragua 448
nicchia di sicurezza 345
Niger 451
Niger, Fiume 20
Nigeria 451
Nilo 20
nocciola, sezione di una 60
nocciole 133
nocciolo 57
noce 64, 133
noce del Brasile 133
noce di acagiù 133
noce di cocco 133
noce di cola 133
noce di ginco 133
noce di macadamia 133
noce di pecan 133
noce moscata 138
noce, sezione di una 60
nodello 83
nodo 53, 167, 169, 416
nodo di Ranvier 110
nome del dominio 334
nome del ginnasta 497
nome del giornale 313
nome del titolare 441
nome della stazione 378
nome della valuta 441
non appartiene a 427
non coincide con 427
non parallelo a 428
nonio 422, 425
nonio, scala graduata del 425
Nord 23
Nord Nord-Est 23
Nord Nord-Ovest 23
Nord, Mare del 14, 18
Nord-Est 23
Nord-Ovest 23
nori 123
Norvegia 450
Norvegia, Mar di 18
notazione degli scacchi 470
notazione musicale 298
note, valori di durata delle 299
notizie 313
notizie in breve 313
notte, camicia da 256
nottolino a scatto 425
nube 41
nube a proboscide 43
nube alta, tipo di 39
nube bassa, tipo di 39
nube di ceneri vulcaniche 28
nube di Oort 2
nube media, tipo di 39
nubi 42
nubi a sviluppo verticale 42
nubi alte 42
nubi basse 42
nubi medie 42
nuca 78, 93, 95
nuclei radioattivi 415
nucleo 4, 6, 50, 66, 110, 112, 414, 534
nucleo esterno 26
nucleo fissile 415
nucleo interno 26
nucleo, membrana del 50
nucleo, scissione del 415
nucleolo 50, 66, 112
numeratore 338
numeri romani 427
numero 473
numero del binario 374
numero del giocatore 486, 488, 506
numero della camera 439
numero della carta 441, 443
numero della pompa 346
numero di autostrada 25
numero di gara 525
numero di serie 441
numero di strada 25
nuoto 516
nuoto, stili di 517
Nuova Caledonia 15
Nuova Zelanda 15, 453
nuovo shekel 440
nuvola 37
nuvole, assorbimento attaverso le 46
nuvole, parete di 43

O

oasi 32, 36
Oberon 3
obiettivi 314
obiettivo 8, 314, 327, 332, 421
obiettivo grandangolare 314
obiettivo macro 314
obiettivo zoom 314
obiettivo, accessori dell' 314
obiettivo, coperchio di protezione dell' 314
obiettivo, lente 420
obiettivo, pulsante di sblocco dell' 314
obliquo esterno dell'addome 96, 97
oblò 386
oboe 306
oboi 295
oca 81, 155
oca, uovo di 155
occhi, trucco per gli 266
occhiali 273, 510, 513, 522
occhiali da sole 273
occhiali di protezione 218
occhiali di protezione con ripari laterali 458
occhiali di protezione panoramici 458
occhiali protettivi 522, 525
occhiali, astuccio per 275
occhiali, esempi di 273
occhiali, mezzi 273
occhiali, parti degli 273
occhialini da nuoto 516
occhiello 240, 248, 262, 275, 313, 509, 538
occhiello per la tracolla 315
occhio 43, 70, 71, 72, 76, 90, 94, 119, 220, 312
occhio composto 67, 68
occhio semplice 67
occhio, orbicolare dell' 96
occhio, parete dell' 43
occhione di traino 356
occipitale 97
Oceania 14, 15, 453
oceano 5, 24, 45
Oceano Atlantico 14, 15, 18, 20
Oceano Indiano 14, 15, 19, 20
Oceano Pacifico 14, 15, 19
oculare 8, 9, 320, 420, 421
offerta, prodotti in 121
officina di riparazione dei locomotori diesel 375
officina meccanica 346
oftalmologia, sala di 463
oggetto 419
ohm 426
okapi 84
olecrano 99
oleodotti, rete di 404
oleodotto 404
oleodotto di superficie 404
oleodotto sottomarino 404
olfatto 116
oli 149
olii lubrificanti 405
olio combustibile leggero 405
olio combustibile per stufe 405
olio combustibile pesante 405
olio d'oliva 149
olio di arachidi 149
olio di mais 149
olio di semi di girasole 149
olio di sesamo 149
olio, tappo di scarico dell' 360
oliva auricolare 460
oliva, olio d' 149
olivetta 249
olivi 128
Oman 452
Oman, Golfo di 19
ombelico 30, 92, 94
ombra 424
ombrella 57
ombrelli 273
ombrelli e bastone 273
ombretto 266
omero 98
omero, testa dell' 99
onda 33, 418
onda d'urto 403
onda sismica 27
onda, altezza dell' 33
onda, fondo dell' 33
onda, lunghezza d' 418
onda, lunghezza dell' 33
onde hertziane, trasmissione a 316
onde radio 418
Oort, nube di 2
Opera 432
opera morta 521
opercolo 74
opilione 69
opistodomo 279
orangotango 91
orari 374
orari dei film 294
orari, tabellone degli 374
orata 159
orbicolare 55
orbicolare dell'occhio 96
orbita della Luna 4, 5
orbita della Terra 4, 5
orbiter 12, 13
orca 90
orchestra 278
orchestra sinfonica 295
orchidea 56
ordinata rinforzata 385
orecchia di mare 157
orecchie, tappi per le 458
orecchini 264
orecchini a clip 264
orecchini a perno 264
orecchini a vite 264
orecchini ad anello 264
orecchini pendenti 264
orecchio 92
orecchio di Giuda 123
orecchio esterno 116
orecchio interno 116
orecchio medio 116
orecchio, struttura dell' 116
organi di senso 114, 115, 119
organi di trasmissione 372
organi genitali femminili 112
organi genitali maschili 111
organismi autotrofi 45
organismi decompositori 45
organismi eterotrofi 45
organismi semplici 66
organizer 338
organizzazione culturale 335
organizzazione governativa 335
organo 305
organo di raccordo 364
origano 142
Orinoco, Fiume 17
orlatura a stella 534
orlo 238
orlo della vasca 212
ormeggio, verricello di 385
orologio 444
orologio analogico 424
orologio contaminuti 178
orologio digitale 424
orso bruno 89
orso polare 89
ortaggi 124
ortaggi da bulbo 124
ortaggi da foglia 126
ortaggi da frutto 128
ortaggi da fusto 125
ortaggi da infiorescenza 127
ortaggi da radice 129
ortaggi da tubero 124
ortica 127
orto 122, 182
orzo 61, 143
orzo: spiga 61
ospedale 433, 462
ospite 267
osservatorio 7
osservatorio astronomico 7
osservatorio astronomico, sezione trasversale di un 7
osservazione astronomica 7
osservazione psichiatrica, stanza per 462
osservazione, finestrino di 13
osservazione, punto di 7
osservazione, stanza di 462, 465
ossicini dell'udito 116
ossido d'azoto, emissione di 48
ossigeno, presa dell' 464
ossigeno, produzione di 54
ossigeno, regolazione della pressione dell' 10
osso alveolare 101
osso frontale 98, 100
osso mascellare 101
osso nasale 100, 117
osso occipitale 99, 100
osso parietale 99, 100
osso sfenoide 100
osso temporale 98, 100
osso zigomatico 98, 100
ossobuco 152
ostacolo d'acqua 504
ostrica 157

ostrice 157
ostriche, coltello da 169
ostriche, forchetta da 168
otorinolaringoiatria, sala di 463
ottaedro regolare 429
ottagono regolare 429
ottava 298
ottava, meccanismo dell' 306
ottavino 295, 306
ottico 437
otturatore 329
ovaia 112, 113
ovario 56
ovata 55
Ovest 23
Ovest Nord-Ovest 23
Ovest Sud-Ovest 23
ovile 57, 122
ovolo buono 123
ovulo 56, 112
oxford, scarpa 240
ozono, strato di 37

pacchetto 163
Pacifico, Oceano 14, 15, 19
Pacifico, placca del 27
Pacifico, salmone del 161
Pacini, corpuscolo di 114
padella 531
padella doppia 175
padella per crêpe 175
padella per friggere 175
padella per rosolare 175
padiglione 116, 305, 432
padiglione auricolare 82, 115
paese 23, 430
Paesi Bassi 449
pagamento elettronico, terminale per il 121
pagina precedente 331
pagina successiva 331
pagliaccetto 258, 261
paglietta 238
pagnottella inglese 145
pagoda 283
pak-choi 126
Pakistan 452
pala 213, 412, 413, 478, 506
pala ausiliaria 412
pala caricatrice anteriore 399
pala caricatrice posteriore 399
pala caricatrice, braccio della 399
pala caricatrice, cilindro della 399
pala del rotore 395
pala del timone 384
pala dell'altare 446
palafitta 288
palanchino 220
palato duro 116, 117
palato molle 116, 117
Palau 453
palazzo dei congressi 433
palazzo di giustizia 432
palazzo in condominio 289
palazzo residenziale 282
palchetto 293
palcoscenico 278, 292, 293
palcoscenico, gabbia del 292
palestra 386, 444
palestra, ufficio della 444
paletta 167, 173, 193, 215, 302, 303, 538
paletta di carico ad alette 396
paletta riempigiunti 216
palette di carico, carrello a forca per 396
paletto 498
paliotto 446
palizzata 230, 282
palla 476, 477, 478, 492, 505
palla di filo 477
palla di sughero 477
palla ovale 483, 486
palla, sezione di una 477
pallacanestro 488
pallavolo 487
palleggio 487
pallina 493
pallini 534
pallone 480, 487, 488
pallone sonda 38
pallonetto 491
pallottola 534
palma 64
palmare breve 96
palmare lungo 96
palmata 55
palmeto 36
palmetta 200
palmo 115, 243
palmo del guanto 243
palo 321, 485, 487, 490, 495
palo della linea di fuoricampo 475
palo frontale 529
palombo liscio 158
palpebra 76
palpebra inferiore 75, 87, 119
palpebra superiore 75, 87, 119
palpo 73
palpo labiale 67
pampino 62, 126
Panama 448
panama 238
Panama, Golfo di 17
Panama, Istmo di 16
panca 446, 501
panca degli ufficiali di gara 507
panca dei puniti 507
panca dei puniti, addetto alla 507
pancetta 156
panchina 201, 379, 437, 481
panchina dei giocatori 474, 485, 487, 506
panciera 259
pancreas 106
pane 144
pane azzimo 145
pane bianco 145
pane chapati indiano 145
pane di mais americano 145
pane di segale danese 145
pane di segale tedesco 145
pane e burro, piattino per 166
pane ebraico 145
pane greco 144
pane integrale 145
pane irlandese 145
pane multicereali 145
pane naan indiano 145
pane nero di segale 144
pane pita 145
pane, coltello da 169
pane, guida per il 178
pane, stampo per 179
panetteria 121, 437
panna 150
panna acida 150
panna da montare 150
pannello 185, 259, 352
pannello dell'anta 202
pannello di celle solari 411
pannello di comando 455
pannello di copertura 348
pannello di funzionamento 287
pannello di mezzo 185
pannello di protezione 369
pannello divisorio 274, 277
pannello solare 7, 316
panno 502
pannocchia 61
pannolino 260
pannolino usa e getta 260
pantacollant 263
pantaloncini 261, 473, 480, 483, 488, 498, 500, 522
pantaloncini da ciclista 263
pantaloncini da corsa 263
pantaloni 246, 263, 476, 486, 499, 506, 525
pantaloni a zampa di elefante 254
pantaloni alla pescatora 254
pantaloni alla zuava 254
pantaloni felpati 262
pantaloni, esempi di 254
pantografo 376
papaia 137
papalina 238
papavero 56, 60
papavero, semi di 139
papilla 114
papilla circumvallata 118
papilla filiforme 118
papilla foliata 118
papilla fungiforme 118
papilla ottica 119
papilla renale 107
papillon 245
paprika 139
Papua Nuova Guinea 453
Papuasia-Nuova Guinea 15
parabraccia 486
parabrezza 348, 364, 366, 369, 385, 392, 394, 523
paracadute 287
paracadute del booster 12
paracoccige 486
paracollo 486
paracosce 486
paracostole 486
paradenti 486, 498
parafango 348, 349, 364, 370
parafango anteriore 366
paraffine 405
parafianchi 486
parafulmine 183, 407, 413
parafuoco 193
paragambe 507
paragola 476
paragomito 486
paragrilletto 534
Paraguay 448
paralama inferiore 227
paralama inferiore, leva per togliere il 227
paralama superiore 227
parallele 496, 497
parallele asimmetriche 496, 497
parallelepipedo 429
parallelo 22
parallelo a 428
parallelogramma 429
paraluce 8, 314
paralume 206
paramano 525
paramecio 66
paramezzale centrale 385
Paranà, Fiume 17
paraneve 523
paraorecchi 238
parapetto 191, 282, 344, 377
parapetto, pilastro del 191
parapunta 476
parasole 356
parasole, aletta 354
paraspalle 486
parastinchi 476, 480, 513
paratia longitudinale 384
paratia trasversale 384
paratoia 407
paratoia dello sfioratore 406
paratrucioli 227
paraurti 364, 369
paraurti posteriore 369, 523
parcheggio 375, 381, 390, 430, 435, 445, 504, 512
parcheggio per le biciclette 445
parco 25, 433
parco nazionale 25
parete 5, 58, 184, 528
parete anteriore 365
parete cellulare 50
parete dell'occhio 43
parete della qibla 447
parete di arrivo 516
parete di nuvole 43
parete di virata 517
parete inferiore 404
parete laterale 365, 404, 517
parete superiore 404
parete, lampada da 207
parete, lampione da 207
pareti di vetro, custodia a 423
paripennata 55
parka 249
parmigiano 151
parquet 190
parquet a listelli 190
parquet a listoni 190
parquet a mosaico 190
parquet a spina di pesce 190
parquet a tessitura di vimini 190
parquet Arenberg 190
parquet Chantilly 190
parquet su sottofondo di cemento 190
parquet su struttura lignea 190
parquet Versailles 190
parquet, tipi di 190
parrucchiere 290, 436
parrucchiere, forbici da 270
parte anteriore del quartiere 240, 262
parte inferiore del tronco 63
parte intermedia 111
parte superiore dell'intelaiatura 186
parte terminale 111
partenza 469
partenza della funivia 512
partenza della seggiovia 512
partenza, griglia di 524
partenza, piazzola di 504
partenza, pulsante di 424
parti 200, 201, 204
parti boccali 68
parti degli occhiali 273
parti di un cerchio 428
parti di una scarpa 240
pascal 426
pascolo 122
passacavo 521
passacinghia 532
passaggio a livello 375
passaggio a soffietto 363
passaggio pedonale 434, 436
passamontagna 239
passante 245, 246, 250
passante del cinturino 248
passante della cintura 248
passascotte 521
passata di pomodoro 140
passavanti 385
passaverdure 170
passeggeri, carrozza 380
passeggeri, sala 383, 386, 387
passeggeri, terminal satellite dei 389
passeggeri, treno 374
passeggiata, ponte di 386
passera di mare 161
passerella 282, 292, 379
passerella di imbarco 389
passerotto 80
passo 29, 83
passo alternato 514
passo d'uomo 404
passo pattinato 514
pasta 146
pasta di tamarindo 140
pasta sfoglia 145
pasta won ton 147
pasta, macchina per fare la 170
pasticceria 437
pastiglia 357
pastiglia di combustibile 409
pastinaca 129
pastoia 83
pastore tedesco 86
Patagonia 17
patata americana 124
patate 124
patella 157
patera 200
patio 182, 230
patio, porta del 188
patta 246, 260
patta di chiusura 532
pattinaggio artistico 509
pattinaggio di velocità 508
pattinaggio in linea 527
pattinaggio libero, lama per 509
pattinatore 508, 527
pattini per velocità 508
pattino 395, 506
pattino a rotelle 527
pattino acrobatico 527
pattino ad incastro 508
pattino da hockey 527
pattino da short track 508
pattino da velocità 527
pattino del portiere 507
pattino di coda 395
pattino distanziatore 409
pattino per pattinaggio artistico 509
pattino, colpo di 514
pausa 323, 331
pausa di biscroma 299
pausa di croma 299
pausa di minima 299
pausa di semibiscroma 299
pausa di semibreve 299
pausa di semicroma 299
pausa di semiminima 299
pausa, tasto di 323
pause, valori di durata delle 299
pavimenti, spazzola per 209
pavimento 193
pavimento della cabina 287
pavimento, rivestimenti in tessuto per 190
pavone 81
paziente 464
pe-tsai 126
pecari 84
pecora 84
pecorino romano 151
pedale 302, 305, 308, 370, 372, 473, 501, 522
pedale ad ampio appoggio 522
pedale del cambio 367, 368, 369
pedale del crescendo 305
pedale del freno 350, 354, 357, 511
pedale del freno posteriore 368
pedale del piano 304, 311
pedale dell'acceleratore 354
pedale della frizione 354
pedale della sordina 304
pedale di risonanza 304, 311
pedale di sollevamento 467
pedale senza fermapiedi 522
pedale, leva del 304
pedale, pistoncino del 305
pedali d'espressione 305
pedaliera 305
pedana 423, 496, 523
pedana di lancio 472, 473
pedana elastica 496
pedana per il corpo libero 496
pedane di rincorsa 496
pedata 191
pediera 204
pedine 469
pedipalpo 70
pedivella 372
pedivelle albero delle 372
pedone 470
pedula 242
peduncolo 52, 56, 57, 58, 59, 62
peli radicali 53
pelle armonica 297
pelle di camoscio 265
pelle, laccio di 246
pellegrina 251
pelletteria 436
pelletteria, articoli di 274
pellicano 80
pelliccia 82, 91
pellicola d'alluminio 162
pellicola plastica, condensatore a 417
pellicola sigillata a caldo 163
pellicola trasparente 162
pelo 114
pelo, muscolo erettore del 114
peltata 55
pelvi renale 107
pendenti 264
pene 92, 111
penisola 24
Penisola Antartica 15
Penisola Arabica 19
Penisola Balcanica 18
Penisola Coreana 19
Penisola dello Yucatan 16
Penisola di Camciatca 19
Penisola di Kola 18
Penisola Iberica 18
Penisola Scandinava 18
penna a sfera 312
penna con pennino metallico 312
penna copritrice 78
penna copritrice inferiore della coda 78
penna copritrice superiore della coda 78
penna d'oca 312
penna stilografica 312
penna timoniera 78
penna tonda 220
pennatifida 55
penne 146, 536
pennellino per labbra 266
pennello 219

pennello a ventaglio 266
pennello da barba 271
pennello da cipria in polvere 266
pennello da fard 266
pennello per dolci 172
pennello per scrivere 312
pennello, spazzola a 209
pennino 27, 312
pensile 164
pensilina 375, 434
pentagono regolare 429
pentagramma 298
pentola 175
pentola a pressione 174
pentola a vapore 175
pentola a vapore elettrica 179
pentola per cucinare a bagnomaria 175
pentola per cuscus 175
pepaiola 166
pepe bianco 138
pepe della Giamaica 138
pepe di Cayenna 139
pepe macinato 139
pepe nero 138
pepe rosa 138
pepe verde 138
peperoncini secchi 139
peperoncino 128, 139
peperoncino in polvere 139
peperoncino rosso 139
peperoncino tritato 139
peperoncino, spray al 456
peperone giallo 128
peperone rosso 128
peperone verde 128
pepino 137
per aprire 170
pera 133
percento 427
percorso 504
percorso di evacuazione 345
percussione, strumenti a 295, 308
peretta per ingrassare 173
perforatore 340
pergola 230
pericardio 105
pericarpo 60
peristilio 279, 280
peristoma 66
peritoneo 111, 112
perlina di cristallo 207
pernice 80
perno 217, 270, 271, 533, 535
perno di agganciamento 365
perno di ancoraggio 357
perno di incernieramento 400
perno di incernieramento della pala caricatrice 399
perno oscillante 355
perno, orecchini a 264
perone 98
peroneo breve 97
peroneo lungo 96
perossisoma 66
perpendicolare 428
persiana 186
persiano 87
persico 160
persico trota 160
Persico, Golfo 19
persico, morfologia di un 74
personal computer 329
personale, ingresso del 445
personale, stanza del 463
Perù 448
Perù-Cile, Fossa 34
pesalettere 339
pesca 132, 536
pesca a mosca 536
pesca al lancio 537
pesca, sezione di una 57
pescatora, pantaloni alla 254
pesce 121
pesce cappone 159
pesce cartilagineo 74
pesce osseo 74
pesce rospo 160
pesce San Pietro 161
pesce spada 159
pesce, coltello da 168
pesce, forchetta da 168
pesce, piatto per il 166
peschereccio 384
pesci 74
pesci cartilaginei 158
pesci ossei 159
pesciera 174
pesi 501
peso 422, 423, 440, 472, 500
peso, misura del 422
pestello 170
pesticida 47, 48
petalo 56
petroliera 381
petrolio 403
petrolio greggio 405
pettine 157
pettine a coda 268
pettine a forchetta 268
pettine afro 268
pettine da barbiere 268
pettine per cotonare 268
pettine rado 268
pettini 268
pettinino per ciglia e spazzolino per sopracciglia 266
pettirosso 80
petto 78, 83
pettorali, barra per i 501
pettorali, piastra per i 501
pettorina 260, 261
pettorina di protezione 476
pezzi 470
pi greco 428
pia madre 109
pialla 229
piana da dilavamento glaciale 30
piana inondabile 32
pianella 242
pianerottolo 189, 191
pianeti 2
pianeti esterni 2
pianeti interni 3
piano 202, 412, 526
piano a scomparti 225
piano della reception 439
piano di appoggio 396
piano di caricamento 435
piano di carico 396
piano di cottura 164, 179, 210
piano di cottura, bordo del 210
piano di lavoro 164, 224
piano di lavoro a morsa 224
piano elettronico 311
piano mansardato 182, 189
piano stradale 342
piano superiore 363
piano, indicatore del 287
piano, pedale del 304, 311
piano, primo 182, 189
pianoforte 295
pianoforte verticale 304
pianta 53, 183
pianta del tempio greco 279
pianta della cattedrale 285
pianta di città 25
pianta ornamentale 182
pianta rampicante 230
pianta, struttura di una 53
piantabulbi 231
piantana per fleboclisi 464
piantatoio 231
piante aromatiche 142
pianterreno 182, 188
piantone del volante 350
pianura 24, 32
pianura abissale 33
piastra 178, 208, 269, 309
piastra costale 76
piastra d'appoggio 229
piastra di base 27, 227, 511, 533
piastra di cottura 179
piastra di protezione 525
piastra di registrazione 323
piastra di supporto 199
piastra elettrica 179, 210
piastra marginale 76
piastra negativa 359
piastra neurale 76
piastra per i pettorali 501
piastra portaforche 396
piastra positiva 359
piastra riscaldante 181
piastra sopracaudale 76
piastra stiracapelli 269
piastrella 12
piastrina 104, 186
piastrina, bracciale con 264
piastrone 76
piattaforma 219, 363, 516, 526
piattaforma continentale 33
piattaforma della vasca 195
piattaforma di 10 metri 518
piattaforma di 3 metri 518
piattaforma di 5 metri 518
piattaforma di 7,5 metri 518
piattaforma di carico 423
piattaforma di produzione 404
piattaforma girevole 176, 455
piattaforma, scala con 219
piatti 295, 309
piatti di cottura 179
piattino per pane e burro 166
piatto 179, 308, 422, 423, 531
piatto da portata 166
piatto del lanciatore 475
piatto della casa-base 475
piatto fondo 166
piatto frutta / insalata 166
piatto inferiore 308
piatto per il pesce 166
piatto piano 166
piatto portaceppi 357
piatto superiore 308
piatto, gancio del 422
piazzale 388
piazzola di partenza 504
picche 468
picchetto 528, 529
picchetto, asola per il 528, 529
picchio 80
picciolo 55, 57, 58, 59
piccione 81, 154
picco 29
piccola copritrice secondaria 78
piccola forca a mano 232
piccoli annunci 313
piccolo labbro 112, 113
piccolo rotondo 97
piccolo tegame 175
piccone 233
piccozza 454
picea 65
pick-up 303
pick-up per alte frequenze 303
pick-up per basse frequenze 303
pick-up per medie frequenze 303
pick-up, selettore dei 303
pickup 347
pidocchio 69
piede 72, 73, 91, 92, 93, 94, 95, 202, 231, 247, 260, 302, 305, 536, 537
piede a voluta 200
piede d'albero 519
piede di appoggio 365
piede palmato 75
piede, dito del 92, 94
piede, foro del 305
piedino 153, 308
piedino di gomma 219
piedino regolabile 212, 213, 214
piedino snodato antiscivolo 219
piedritto 285
piega 246
piega a coltello 253
piega della columella 73
piega impunturata 253
piega invertita 253
piega piatta 246
piega sovrapposta 253
piegaciglia 266
pieghe, esempi di 253
pietra affilacoltelli 169
pietra bianca 470
pietra da curling 515
pietra da lastrico 230
pietra di Coyolxauhqui 283
pietra focaia 218
pietra nera 470
pietra sacrificale 283
pigiama 256, 261
pigiamino 261
pigiamino a due pezzi 260
pigiatore 170
pila 344
pila a carbone-zinco 417
pila alcalina a manganese-zinco 417
pilastro 27, 283, 284, 412
pilastro corinzio 281
pilastro del parapetto 191
pile 416
pile a secco 417
pilone 344, 375
pilone destro 482
pilone sinistro 482
piloriza 53
pilota 524
pilotaggio, cabina di 12, 385, 392, 395
pinguino 80
pinna 519
pinna anale 74
pinna caudale 74, 90
pinna dorsale 90
pinna pelvica 74
pinna pettorale 74, 90
pinna stabilizzatrice 386
pinnacolo 282, 284
pinnacolo, fiore del 283
pinnula 52
pino domestico 65
pino, aghi di 65
pinoli 133
pinolo 65
pinza 269, 357
pinza a becchi lunghi 217
pinza a giunto scorrevole 222
pinza a scatto 222
pinza del freno a disco 366
pinza multiuso 217
pinza per capelli 268
pinza regolabile 222
pinza universale 217
pinza, faretto a 206
pinze 222
pinzette 461
pinzette per sopracciglia 265
piogge acide 47, 48
pioggia 41
pioggia congelantesi 41
pioggia, irrigatore rotativo a 236
piolo 219, 479
piombo 538
pioppo 64
piramide 278, 429
piramide, ingresso alla 278
Pirenei 18
piscina 184, 386
piscina fuori terra 184
piscina interrata 184
piscina olimpionica 517
piselli 130
piselli mangiatutto 130
piselli secchi spaccati 130
pisello 60
pista 390, 472, 524
pista a difficoltà elevata 512
pista a difficoltà intermedia 512
pista da fondo 512
pista di accesso 388
pista di pattinaggio 509, 512
pista di rincorsa 473
pista di rullaggio 388
pista lunga 508
pista per esperti 512
pista per principianti 512
pista per sci alpino 512
pistacchi 133
piste da sci 512
pistillo 56
pistola 216, 456
pistola dello starter 472
pistola di erogazione 346
pistola per sverniciatura 219
pistola turapori 216
pistola, impugnatura a 218, 228
pistola, polverizzatore a 236
pistola, saldatore a 218
pistoncino 357
pistoncino del manuale 305
pistoncino del pedale 305
pistone 307, 360
pistone, disinnesto del 216
pistone, leva del 216
pitone 77
Pitot, tubo di 525
pittogrammi 330
più o meno 427
piumino da cipria 266
pivot 489
placca africana 27
placca antartica 27
placca antifrizione 511
placca caribica 27
placca del Pacifico 27
placca dell'interruttore 198
placca delle Cocos 27
placca di Nazca 27
placca di Scozia 27
placca euroasiatica 27
placca filippina 27
placca indoaustraliana 27
placca motrice 110
placca nordamericana 27
placca sudamericana 27
placcatore destro 484
placcatore sinistro 484
placche convergenti 27
placche divergenti 27
placche tettoniche 27
placche trasformi 27
placchetta a bilanciere 305
placchetta del portanasello 273
plafoniera 206
plancia 354
planisfero 14
plantare 97
plasma 104
plasmodesma 50
plastica, smistamento della 49
platea 293
playmaker 489
plesso brachiale 108
plesso dentale 101
plesso lombare 108
plesso sacrale 108
plettro 297
pleura parietale 105
pleura viscerale 105
plissé 253
Plutone 3
pluviale 182
pneumatici, barriera di 524
pneumatici, esempi di 358
pneumatico 349, 358, 364, 371, 522, 525
pneumatico chiodato 358
pneumatico granturismo 358
pneumatico invernale 358
pneumatico per tutte le stagioni 358
pneumatico scolpito 369, 525
pneumatico sportivo 358
podcasting 335
podio 283, 444
podio del direttore d'orchestra 295
poggiafreccia 535
poggiamano 227, 297, 332
poggiamano amovibile 330
poggiapiedi 205
poggiatesta 353
poker 468
poker, combinazioni del 468
polacchina 241
Polaroid® 315
pole position 524
poliambulatorio 465
poligoni 429
Polinesia 453
polipodio comune 52
politica 448
politrico comune 51
polizia, agente di 456
polizia, macchina della 457
polizia, stazione di 433
pollaio 122
pollice 115, 243, 477
pollice opponibile 91
pollice, appoggio del 307
pollo 155
pollone 63
polmone destro 103, 105
polmone sinistro 103, 105
polmoni 105
polo 250, 255, 492
polo negativo 359, 416, 417
Polo Nord 21
polo nord 416
polo positivo 359, 416, 417
Polo Sud 15, 21
polo sud 416

polo, abito a 252
Polonia 450
polpa 57, 58, 59, 101
polpaccio 93, 95
polpastrello 114
polpo 72, 157
polpo, morfologia di un 72
polsiera 527
polsino 245, 486, 492, 500
polso 86, 93, 95, 115
poltrona 200
poltrona da salotto 200
poltrona sacco 201
poltrona Wassily 200
poltroncina del paziente 464
poltroncina per bambini 205
poltrone 200
polvere di magnesia 497
polverizzatore 402
polverizzatore a pistola 236
pomello 202, 536, 537
pomello della sicura 352
pomello in gomma 536
pomelo 134
pomi 133
pomo 201, 477
pomo d'Adamo 92
pomodorini a grappolo 128
pomodoro 128
pomodoro, passata di 140
pomolo 229
pomolo del bastone 506
pompa 184, 212, 214, 370, 529
pompa della benzina 346
pompa di circolazione del fango 403
pompa per gli pneumatici 346
pompa, numero della 346
pompa, tubo della 346
pompe, locale delle 384
pompelmo 134
pompelmo, coltello da 169
pompetta ad aria 461
pompieri, carri dei 455
poncho 251
pont-l'évêque 151
ponte 25, 420
ponte a cantilever 344
ponte a travata 344
ponte di caricamento per containers 381
ponte di comando 382, 383, 386, 387
ponte di coperta 385
ponte di passeggiata 386
ponte di Varolio 109
ponte girevole 344
ponte levatoio 282
ponte luce 293
ponte pedonale 375
ponte per le autovetture 386
ponte ribaltabile a due ali 345
ponte ribaltabile a un'ala 345
ponte segnali 375
ponte sollevabile 345
ponte sospeso 344
ponte superiore 392
ponti fissi 344
ponti mobili 344
ponticello 273, 297, 301, 302, 303
ponticello degli acuti 304
ponticello dei bassi 304
ponticello, blocco del 303
pool 502
poppa 386, 519
porcellana 127
porcile 122
porcino 123
porcospino 82
poro 50, 60
poro sudoriparo 114
porri 124
Porro, prisma di 420
porta 202, 287, 361, 380, 439, 447, 479, 480, 482, 485, 507, 528, 529
porta a bande verticali 286
porta a due battenti 362
porta a fisarmonica 286
porta a infrarossi 336, 337
porta a libro 286
porta a un battente 286
porta a zanzariera 361
porta antincendio 286
porta automatica 390
porta basculante del garage 286
porta del bacino 381
porta del laboratorio a tenuta stagna 13
porta del modem interno 336
porta del mouse 329
porta del patio 188
porta dell'elevatore 363
porta della tastiera 329
porta di entrata 362, 363
porta di prua 383
porta di rete 329
porta di rete telefonica 317
porta esterna 185
porta Ethernet 336
porta FireWire 336
porta giochi 329
porta girevole manuale 286
porta MIDI 329
porta parallela 329
porta per l'alimentatore 336
porta scorrevole 195, 286
porta scorrevole automatica 286
porta seriale 329
porta sezionale del garage 286
porta USB 310, 329, 336
porta video 329, 336
porta, area di 507
porta-finestra 164, 189
portabagagli 361, 523
portabatteria, cassa 365
portabici 356
portabiti 277
portablocco 275, 340
portablocco, tavoletta 340
portabottiglia 371
portacalcolatrice 274
portacarte a soffietto 274
portaceppi 193
portachiavi 275
portacipria 266
portafermagli 341
portafiltro 181
portafoglio 275
portafoglio per carte di credito 274
portaindirizzo, etichetta 277
portalampada 199
portale 285
portalenti 272
portamartello 225
portamine 312
portamonete 275
portanasello 273
portanasello, placchetta del 273
portaobiettivi a revolver 421
portaoculare 8
portaoggetti 421
portaombrelli 273
portapacchi 369, 370
portapacchi posteriore 369
portapassaporto 275
portapenne 274
portarotolo 195
portasacca 505
portasapone 195
portasci 356
portasciugamano 195
portassegni 274, 275
portata, piatto da 166
portatabulati 339
portautensili 229
porte d'ingresso 294
porte, esempi di 286
portello 212, 213, 392
portello di apertura 7
portello, interruttore del 213
portellone della cupola 7
portellone dello scomparto di carico 13
portellone laterale 12
portellone prodiero di carico 386
porticato 447
portico 183, 285
portico coperto 447
portiera 349, 352
portiera, telaio interno della 352
portiere 479, 481, 506, 507
portiere, pattino del 507
portiere, stanzino del 439
porto 431
porto marittimo 381
porto, bicchiere da 165
Portogallo 449
porzionatore per gelato 173
posate 531
posate, cestello per le 214
posateria 167
posizionamento, braccio di 400
posizionamento, tubo di 400
posizione carpiata 518
posizione d'equilibrio 418
posizione della statua 279
posizione raggruppata 518
posizione tesa 518
posizione, luce di 376
posizione, tasto di 302, 303
posizioni dei giocatori 474, 481, 482, 489
posizioni di partenza 518
post-it 338
posta elettronica 335
posta elettronica, software di 334
postazione degli infermieri (pronto soccorso ambulatoriale) 463
postazione degli infermieri (pronto soccorso principale) 462
postazione dell'agente di sicurezza 463
posti a sedere 293
posti, divano a due 200
postierla 282
postino, borsa da 276
posto a sedere 294
potenza elettrica, unità di misura della 426
potenziale elettrico, unità di misura della differenza di 426
pouf 201
pozzetto 520
pozzetto d'ispezione 434
pozzo 31
pozzo di iniezione 402
pozzo di produzione 402
pozzo off-shore 404
prateria 24, 44
prato 122, 183, 230
prato, cura del 237
precipitazione 45
precipitazione, area di 39
precipitazioni 41
precipitazioni invernali 41
precipitazioni, forti 43
prelievi, sala dei 465
premascellare 74
premolari 101
prendisole 252
preparazione chirurgica, stanza per la 464
prepuzio 111
presa a croce 499
presa a terra 499
presa audio 329
presa cuffie 323
presa d'acqua 407
presa d'aria 362, 365, 367, 383, 395, 523
presa d'aria del motore 362
presa d'aria del ventilatore di sostentamento 383
presa d'aria laterale 361
presa d'aria per il raffreddamento del motore 525
presa d'aria posteriore 270
presa d'aria sul tetto 361
presa d'uscita 303
presa dell'idrante 455
presa dell'ossigeno 464
presa di alimentazione 326, 329
presa di corrente 217, 361
presa di corrente commutata 322
presa di ricarica 271
presa di strangolamento 499
presa europea 198
presa per cuffia 310, 311, 322, 326
presa per il comando a distanza 314, 315
presa per ricarica 208
presa per spina americana 198
presa, alveolo della 198
presa, tester di 217
presbiterio, lampada del 446
prese digitali 315
prese video 315
prese, esempi di 499
preside, ufficio del 445
presidente di giuria 509
presidente di giuria, assistente del 509
pressacaffè 181
pressatore 180
pressione a livello del mare 39
pressione alta, centro di 39
pressione atmosferica 39
pressione bassa, centro di 39
pressione dei freni, modulatore della 357
pressione sanguigna, monitor della 461
pressione, bottone a 249
pressione, pentola a 174
pressione, regolatore della 272
pressione, regolatore di 174
pressione, unità di misura della 426
pressione, variazione di 39
prevenzione degli incendi 454
prevenzione del crimine 456
previsioni meteorologiche 38
prezzemolo 142
prezzo per litro/gallone 346
prezzo unitario 423
prima base 474
prima base (posizione) 474
prima galleria 293
prima linea 482
prima maglia 476
prima pagina 313
prima pagina, foto in 313
prima pinna dorsale 74
primati 91
primati, esempi di 91
primavera 38
primavera, equinozio di 38
prime foglie 53
primi violini 295
primo 428
primo arbitro 485, 487
primo assistente cameraman 290
primo aumento di tensione 413
primo giocatore al lancio 515
primo molare 101
primo piano 182, 189
primo premolare 101
primo quarto 5
primo spazio 489
princesse 252
princesse, cucitura a 258
Principato di Monaco 450
prisma astronomico 8
prisma di Porro 420
proboscide 67
processo mastoideo 100
processo spinoso 110
processo stiloideo 100
processo trasverso 110
procione 88
prodotti caseari 150
prodotti cerealicoli 144
prodotti di fissione 415
prodotti di raffinazione 405
prodotti in offerta 121
prodotti per confezionamento 120
prodotti petrolchimici 405
prodotto, codice del 423
produttore 291
produzione di calore 408
produzione di elettricità 412
produzione di elettricità da alternatore 408
produzione di elettricità da energia eolica 413
produzione di elettricità da energia nucleare 408
produzione di ossigeno 54
produzione, designer di 290
produzione, segretaria di 291
profilo del suolo 54
profilo dell'atmosfera terrestre 37
profilo dello spacco 245
profilo sbieco 260
profondità del fuoco 27
profondità di campo, pulsante di controllo della 314
profondità, regolatore di 229
profumeria 436
profumeria e igiene personale 121
profumo 267
programma, selettore di 310
programmatore 212, 213
programmi del computer 457
programmi televisivi 313
proiettore 290, 294, 348, 364, 366, 368, 523
proiettore abbagliante e anabbagliante 352
proiettore orientabile 455
proiettori 293
proiettori, comando dei 354
proiezione cilindrica 22
proiezione conica 22
proiezione di spalla e braccio 499
proiezione interrotta 22
proiezione piana 22
proiezione, cabina di 294
proiezione, sala di 294
proiezione, schermo di 294
proiezioni cartografiche 22
prolunga 202
prolunga, tubo rigido di 209
promontorio 35
pronao 279
pronatore rotondo 96
pronto intervento, mezzo di 345
pronto soccorso 462, 512
pronto soccorso, cassetta di 457, 461
pronto soccorso, manuale di 461
pronto soccorso, stazione di 345
pronto soccorso, strumenti per il 460
propagazione 418
proprietà, confine di 182
propulsione, modulo di 316
propulsore 10
propulsore di prua 387
propulsori per il controllo direzionale 12
proscenio 292
prosciutto 156
prosciutto affumicato 153
prosciutto cotto 156
prosciutto, coltello da 169
prospetto 182
prospezione terrestre 403
prostata 111
proteggicavo 217
protezione antisfregamento 525
protezione antiurto 209
protezione del dente 398
protezione del mento 367
protezione delle chiavi 306
protezione per gli occhi 458
protezione per i piedi 459
protezione per l'avambraccio 486
protezione per la testa 458
protezione per le orecchie 458
protezione per le vie respiratorie 459
protezione posteriore 7
protezione, gabbia di 217
protezione, occhiali di 218
protezione, piastra di 525
protezione, schermo di 474
protocollo di comunicazione 334
protone 414
protoneurone 110
protuberanza 4
prova in corso, tabellone della 497
prova, pulsante di 454
provacircuiti, lampada 217
provincia 23
prua 384, 387, 519, 520
prua, castello di 387
prua, elica di 384
prua, porta di 383
prua, propulsore di 387
prugne 132
prugne, salsa di 141
pseudopodio 66
pubblico 440
pubblico, ingresso del 278
pube 92, 94
pugilato 498
pugile 498
pulce 69
puleggia 219, 360, 535
puleggia di tensione del regolatore 287
pulisci unghie 265
pulitura, accessori di 209
pullman 362
pulpito 446, 447
pulsante 312
pulsante del menu 315
pulsante del registratore vocale 337
pulsante del touch pad 336
pulsante del vaporizzatore 208

pulsante di accensione 213
pulsante di aggancio 227
pulsante di alimentazione 319, 337
pulsante di alimentazione della carta 333
pulsante di annullamento 333
pulsante di apertura del display 336
pulsante di arresto 229, 235, 424
pulsante di azzeramento 424
pulsante di bloccaggio 208
pulsante di cancellazione 315
pulsante di chiamata 287
pulsante di chiamata pedonale 434
pulsante di compensazione dell'esposizione 314
pulsante di controllo 332
pulsante di controllo della profondità di campo 314
pulsante di controluce 337
pulsante di espulsione 315, 471
pulsante di espulsione del CD 329
pulsante di espulsione del DVD-ROM 329
pulsante di partenza 424
pulsante di prova 454
pulsante di reset 329, 471
pulsante di sblocco dell'obiettivo 314
pulsante di scatto 314
pulsante di uscita 337
pulsante di visualizzazione delle immagini 315
pulsante di visualizzazione delle impostazioni 315
pulsante per il salto di immagini 315
pulsanti di avvio delle applicazioni 337
pulsanti di azione 471
pulsanti direzionali 471
pulsanti programmabili 332
puma 88
Pumpernickel russo 145
punching ball 498
pungiglione 68
punta 125, 167, 169, 208, 216, 218, 220, 221, 226, 227, 229, 246, 301, 312, 460, 469, 471, 510, 514, 526, 534, 536, 538
punta a croce 221
punta a testa quadra 221
punta da muro 228
punta del colletto 245
punta del naso 117
punta dello sci 514
punta dentellata 509
punta di centratura 228
punta di diamante 202
punta elicoidale 228
punta fredda 269
punta Luer-Lock 460
punta per piastra 304
punta piana 221
punta, lunghezza della 538
puntale 221, 240, 262, 466, 511
puntale di protezione 459
puntale rinforzato 459
puntalino 536, 537
punte, tipi di 221
punteggio 497
punterie, coperchio delle 350, 360
punteruolo 531
punti 492
punti metallici 341
puntine da disegno 341
puntine, distanza tra le 359
punto 468
punto coronato 299
punto d'appoggio 70
punto di alimentazione 198
punto di allacciamento 198
punto di handicap 470
punto di incocco 535
punto di ingaggio 506
punto di inserimento dei documenti da trasmettere 328
punto di interesse 25
punto di mura 519
punto di osservazione 7
puntone 412
punzone 220
pupilla 87, 119
pupilla verticale 76
putter 505

Q

Qatar 452
qibla, parete della 447
quadrante 422, 424, 428
quadrante a cristalli liquidi 424
quadrante graduato 533
quadrato 429, 498
quadri 468
quadricipiti, rullo per i 501
quadrilatero 429
quadripode 466
quadro degli strumenti di controllo 355
quadro delle temperature 208
quadro di comando 178, 179, 210, 212, 213, 214
quadro di distribuzione 198
quaglia 81, 154
quaglia, uovo di 155
quantità di sostanza, unità di misura della 426
quarantottore 277
quark d 414
quark u 414
quarta 298
quarterback 485
quartetto 300
quartiere 25, 240, 262
quartiere degli affari 430, 432
quartiere fieristico 430
quartiere residenziale 431
quartiere, parte anteriore del 240, 262
quattro quarti, tempo di 298
quercia 64
quinoa 143
quinta 298
quinte 292
quintetto 300

R

rabarbaro 125
rabbino, seggio di 447
raccattapalle 490
racchetta 492, 493, 494, 510, 514
racchetta, giochi con la 493
raccoglierba 237
raccogligocce, bacinella 210
raccoglipolvere 229
raccoglitore a molla 339
raccoglitore ad anelli 339
raccolta del vetro, campana per la 49
raccolta della carta, campana per la 49
raccolta differenziata 49
raccolta differenziata, contenitori per la 49
raccolta, vaschetta di 181
raccordo 312, 455
raccordo a losanga 342
raccordo a quadrifoglio 342, 343
raccordo a rotatoria 342
raccordo a T 193
raccordo a tromba 342
raccordo a Y 460
raccordo, esempi di 342
racemo 57, 200
rachide 62
raclette 151
raclette, griglia per 179
radar 382, 383, 386, 387
radar meteorologico 38, 392
radar, albero del 384
radar, display dei 457
raddrizzatori di immagine 420
radiatore 13, 350, 358
radiatore, griglia del 364
radiatore, manicotto inferiore del 358
radiatori 11
radiazione 415
radiazione infrarossa 46, 418
radiazione solare 45, 46, 410, 411
radiazione solare assorbita 46
radiazione solare riflessa 46
radiazione ultravioletta 418
radicchio 126
radice 54, 101, 118, 167
radice a fittone 63
radice anteriore 110
radice del naso 117
radice dell'elice 115
radice dell'unghia 114
radice filettata 359
radice laterale 53
radice motoria 109, 110
radice posteriore 110
radice principale 53
radice quadrata di 427
radice secondaria 53
radice sensoriale 109, 110
radice superficiale 63
radichetta 53, 63
radici avventizie 52
radio 98, 457
radio portatile 325
radio, antenna 384, 525
radioattività, unità di misura della 426
radioregistratore con compact disc 326
radiosveglia 325
radiotelefono portatile 456
rafano giapponese 129
raffinazione, prodotti di 405
raffineria 404, 431
raffreddamento 405
raffreddamento del motore, presa d'aria per il 525
raffreddamento, cilindro di 420
raganella 75
raggi gamma 418
raggi X 418
raggio 371, 428
raggio laser 420
raggio luminoso 419
raggio midollare 63
raggio molle 74
raggio spinoso 74
ragnatela 70
ragnatela, centro della 70
ragno 70
ragno acquatico 70
ragno, morfologia di un 70
ragno-granchio 70
ralla di rotazione 400, 401
rally, auto da 524
rambutan 137
rami 63
ramificazione collaterale 110
ramo 62, 63, 65, 416
ramo comunicante 110
ramo con frutti 62
ramo primario 63
ramo secondario 63
ramoscello 53
rampa 279, 281, 343, 344, 526
rampa ad anello 343
rampa di accesso 386
rampa di scale 191
rampicante, pianta 230
rampone 454
rana 75, 517
rana comune 75
rana dei boschi 75
rana leopardo 75
rana, morfologia di una 75
randa 520
Ranvier, nodo di 110
rapa 129
ras el hanout 139
rasatura 271
raschietto 219
raschietto metallico 514
rasoio a mano libera 271
rasoio di sicurezza 271
rasoio elettrico 271
rasoio sfoltitore 269
rasoio usa e getta 271
rastrello 233
rastrello scopa 237
ratto 82
ratto, morfologia di un 82
ravanello 129
ravenelli neri 129
ravioli 146
razza 158
razze canine 86
razze di gatti 87
razzo a propellente solido 12
razzo illuminante 457
re 298, 468, 470
re, camera del 278
re, lato del 470
Rea 3
reattore 408
reattore nucleare 409
reattore, recipiente del 409
reazione a catena 415
rebbio 167
recensione gastronomica 313
reception 439
reception, banco della 442
reception, piano della 439
recettore sensoriale 110
recettori gustativi 118
recinto 122
recinzione 122, 475
recipiente del reattore 409
recipiente graduato 171
redine 78
redingote 251
referenti tecnici 509
refill 312
reforming catalitico, impianto di 405
refrattario, mattone 192
refrigerante 408
refrigerazione, cestello di 180
reggicalze 259
reggicoperchio 274
reggilibri 341
reggiseno 259
reggiseno a balconcino 259
reggiseno a bustino 259
reggiseno décolleté 259
reggiseno, coppa del 259
reggiseno, sottoveste con 258
regia, cabina di 293
regina 470
Regina Maud, Terra della 15
regina, camera della 278
regina, lato della 470
regione auricolare 78
regione malare 78
regione pilifera 63
regista 291
regista, sedia da 200
regista, sedia del 291
registratore di cassa 121
registratore di compact disc 325
registratore di DVD 333
registratore DVD 319
registratore, tasto di selezione del 322
registrazione notturna, tasto di 320
registrazione sismografica 403
registrazione, banco di 390
registrazione, tasto di 323
registrazione, tasto di avvio/arresto 320
registro degli acuti 296
registro dei bassi 296
registro, tasto di 305
regno animale 66
Regno Unito di Gran Bretagna e Irlanda del Nord 449
regno vegetale 50
regolatore 466
regolatore degli alti 322
regolatore dei bassi 322
regolatore dei toni alti 325
regolatore dei toni bassi 325
regolatore del display 327
regolatore del getto di vapore 208
regolatore del tirante 528
regolatore del volume di ricezione 327
regolatore dell'altezza 501
regolatore dell'inclinazione della lama 227
regolatore della pressione 272
regolatore della velocità 237
regolatore delle testine 271
regolatore dello sforzo 501
regolatore di corrente 199
regolatore di luminosità 529
regolatore di pressione 174
regolatore di profondità 229
regolatore di velocità 176, 287
regolatore di volume 322
regolatore staccabile 179
regolatore, puleggia di tensione del 287
regolazione dei toni 303
regolazione dei toni alti 303
regolazione dei toni bassi 303
regolazione del diaframma 421
regolazione del livello sonoro delle comunicazioni 10
regolazione del sistema di sopravvivenza 10
regolazione del vapore 181
regolazione del volume 303
regolazione dell'altezza, manopola di 209
regolazione dell'angolo di elevazione 420
regolazione della frizione 537
regolazione della linea di mira 420
regolazione della pressione dell'ossigeno 10
regolazione della temperatura corporea 10
regolazione dello specchietto retrovisore esterno 352
regolazione in altezza del condensatore 421
regolazione laterale, leva di 229
regolazione micrometrica dell'altezza 8, 9
regolazione micrometrica dell'asse orizzontale 8, 9
regolazione, anello di 236
regolazione, dispositivo di 511
regolazione, indicatore della 511
regolazione, vite di 222, 229
religione 446
remigante primaria 78
remigante secondaria 78
remigante terziaria 78
remo 501
rene 73, 103
rene destro 107
rene sinistro 107
reniforme 55
renna 84
reostato 198
replo 60
reptazione 31
Repubblica Ceca 450
Repubblica Centrafricana 451
Repubblica del Mali 451
Repubblica Democratica del Congo 451
Repubblica Democratica Popolare di Corea 453
Repubblica di Corea 453
Repubblica di San Marino 450
Repubblica Dominicana 449
Repubblica Ex Jugoslava di Macedonia 450
Repubblica Sudafricana 452
repulsione 416
reset, tasto di 328
residuo lungo 405
resistenza elettrica, unità di misura della 426
resistenza idraulica 501
resistenze 417
respingente 375
respiratorio, apparato 105
rete 487, 491, 493, 495
rete a molle 204
rete di distribuzione dell'acqua calda 194
rete di distribuzione dell'acqua fredda 194
rete di oleodotti 404
rete di scarico 194
rete di trasmissione, integrazione di energia alla 413
rete di ventilazione 194
rete per alimenti 162
rete stabilizzante 190
rete telefonica 317
rete trasmittente nazionale 316
rete trasmittente privata 316
rete, supporto della 493
reticolato geografico 22
reticolo 420
reticolo endoplasmatico 50, 66
retina 119, 205, 419, 489
retro benna 400
retroescavatore 399
retroescavatore, comandi del 399
rettangolare 530

rettangolo 429
rettangolo destro di servizio 491
rettangolo di battuta 502
rettangolo sinistro di servizio 491
rettili 76
rettili, esempi di 77
retto 106, 111, 112
retto dell'addome 96
retto della coscia 96
revers 244, 248
revers a punta 244
revolver, portaobiettivi a 421
rialzo continentale 33
rianimazione, sala di 462
riavvolgimento, tasto di 323
ribalta 202, 203
ribes 132
ribes nero 132
ribosoma 50, 66
ricarica, presa di 271
ricarica, presa per 208
riccio 301
ricerca 335
ricerca traccia/riproduzione rapida 319, 323
ricetrasmettitore radar 457
ricettacolo 51, 56, 59
ricevimento merci 391
ricevitore 321, 327, 474, 475, 476, 490, 495
ricevitore auricolare 324
ricevitore esterno 485
ricevitore radio satellitare 326
ricevuta della transazione 443
ricezione privata diretta 316
richiamo 535
riciclaggio 49
riciclaggio del vetro, bidone carrellato per il 49
riciclaggio dell'alluminio, bidone carrellato per il 49
riciclaggio della carta, bidone carrellato per il 49
riciclaggio, contenitore per il 49
ricognizione meteorologica, aereo da 38
ricognizione meteorologica, boa di 38
ricognizione meteorologica, nave da 38
ricotta 150
riduttore 270
riempimento, tubo di 196
rifiuti domestici 47, 48
rifiuti industriali 47, 48
rifiuti non riciclabili 49
rifiuti nucleari 48
rifiuti, bidone dei 215
rifiuti, smistamento selettivo dei 49
rifiuti, strati di 47
riflessione parziale, specchio a 420
riflessione totale, specchio a 420
riflessione, cilindro di 420
riflettore 217
riflettori solari 316
rifornimento di contanti 443
rifugio 345
rifugio in vetta 512
rifugio principale 512
rigatoni 146
righello 425, 531
righello, scala graduata del 425
rigonfiamento 6
rilascio di energia 415
rilegatura con spirale 340
rilevatore di fumo 454
rilevatore di movimento 286
rimessa 122, 182, 230
rimorchi 361
rimorchi, carro pianale per il trasporto di 377
rimorchiatore 384
rimorchio 380
rimorchio, dispositivo di 364
rinario 87
rincorsa, pedane di 496
rinforzo a crociera 467
rinforzo del calcagno 262
rinforzo della curva 306
rinforzo esterno del calcagno 240
rinforzo interno del calcagno 240
rinforzo per serratura 185
rinforzo posteriore 509
rinforzo, bandella di 277
rinfuse, deposito delle 381
ringhiera 189
rinoceronte 85
Rio delle Amazzoni 17
ripetitore 317
ripetizione, tasto di 323
ripiani, griglia dei 211
ripiano 203, 211, 219
ripostiglio per il materiale pulito 462
ripostiglio per il materiale sporco 462
ripostiglio per l'attrezzatura 444
ripresa 248
riprese, set delle 290
riproduttore a cassette 326
riproduttore a cassette, tasti del 326
riproduttori portatili 325
riproduzione 323, 328
riproduzione casuale 323
riproduzione, tasto di 319, 323
riquadro 274
risaia 47
riscaldamento 192
riscaldamento a legna 192
riscaldamento, comando del 354
riscaldamento, condotto di 213
riscaldamento, griglia del 380
riso 61, 143, 147
riso basmati 147
riso bianco 147
riso integrale 147
riso nero selvatico 143
riso parboiled 147
riso, aceto di 141
riso, gallette di 147
riso, spaghetti di 147
riso, vermicelli di 147
riso: pannocchia 61
risonanza, cassa di 297, 302
risonatore 309, 324
risorgiva 31
risparmio di energia, lampadina a 199
ristorante 386, 432, 435, 436, 438
ristorante, vagone 376
ristoro per sciatori 512
risultati, tabella dei 518
risvolto 246
ritmo, selettore del 311
ritornata 518
ritornello 298
rivestimenti in tessuto per pavimento 190
rivestimento 187, 417, 493
rivestimento antiriflettente 410
rivestimento del motore 235
rivestimento esterno 477
rivestimento fluorescente 199
rivetto 169, 222
rivista 313
rizoide 51
rizoma 52
robe-manteau 252
robot da cucina 177
rocce ignee 26
rocce intrusive 26
rocce metamorfiche 26
rocce sedimentarie 26
roccia impermeabile 403
roccia in posto 54
roditore 82
roditori 82
roditori, esempi di 82
rognone 154
rollio 395
Romania 450
romano 422
rombo 161, 429
rompigetto, vite 236
rompighiaccio 384
roncola 234
rondella 417
rondella di tenuta 359
rondine 80
rondone 80
roquefort 151
rosa 56, 302
rosa dei venti 23, 533
rosetta 186
rosetta a dentatura esterna 222
rosetta a dentatura interna 222
rosetta elastica 222
rosetta piatta 222
rosette 222
rosmarino 142
rosone 285
rospo comune 75
Ross, Banchisa di 15
rossetto 266
rosso 418, 469
Rosso, Mar 14, 19, 20
rostro 74
rotaia del carrello di scotta 520, 521
rotaia di scorrimento 353, 397
rotatoria 25
rotazione, sistema a 403
rotella 510, 527
rotella centrale di messa a fuoco 420
rotella di comando 337
rotella di regolazione 425
rotella orientabile 308
rotella tagliapasta 172
rotellina di scorrimento 332
rotoli della Torah 447
rotolo di benda garzata 461
rotonda 435
rotore 412, 537
rotore anticoppia 395
rotore, mozzo del 395
rotore, pala del 395
rotore, testa del 395
rotula 98
rough 504
roulotte 361
router 334
rovesciata 518
rovesciata all'indietro 499
Ruanda 451
rubinetto 195
rubinetto di arresto 197
rubinetto di regolazione della pressione 454
rubinetto generale 194
rubino pulsato, laser a 420
rubino, cilindro di 420
rubrica telefonica 327, 338
ruches 260
ruches, ghettina con 260
rucola 127
Ruffini, corpuscolo di 114
rugby 482
rugiada 41
rugiada, temperatura di 39
rullaggio, linea di 389
rullaggio, pista di 388
rulli dei cingoli, telaio dei 398
rullini tenditori 372
rullino 223, 332
rullo 219, 268, 269
rullo per i bicipiti femorali 501
rullo per i quadricipiti 501
rullo, cuscino a 204
rullo, supporto del 219
runner 469
ruota 231, 277, 364, 522, 525, 526, 527
ruota anteriore 401
ruota della moltiplica 522
ruota dentata A 372
ruota dentata B 372
ruota dentata motrice 523
ruota di guida 380
ruota di scorta 361
ruota di spinta 467
ruota folle 523
ruota girevole 205
ruota libera 372
ruota motrice 398
ruota orientabile 209
ruota piena o gonfiabile 467
ruota pivotante 467
ruota portante 380
ruota tendicingolo 398
ruote motrici 401
rupe 29
rupia 440
ruscello 32
ruspa 400

S

sabbiera 377
sacca 505
sacca a tracolla 276
sacca da marinaio 276
saccatura 39
sacchetti 121
sacchetto 162
sacchetto per freezer 162
sacchetto, scomparto del 209
sacchi a pelo, esempi di 530
sacco 296, 477, 498
sacco, poltrona 201
sacrestia 446
sacro 98, 99
Sahara, Deserto del 20
sahariana 255
Saint Kitts e Nevis 449
Saint Lucia 449
Saint Vincent e Grenadine 449
sala 293, 386
sala d'attesa 463
sala d'attesa dei familiari 462
sala d'attesa del centro prelievi 465
sala d'attesa principale 465
sala d'attesa secondaria 465
sala da bagno 464
sala da ballo 387
sala da pranzo 188, 386, 438, 439
sala degli infermieri 465
sala dei prelievi 465
sala del personale 443
sala della preghiera 447
sala di controllo 406
sala di imbarco 391
sala di ingresso 188, 447
sala di proiezione 294
sala di rianimazione 462
sala di servizio 447
sala di sterilizzazione 465
sala gessi 463
sala macchine 384, 386, 406, 407
sala nautica 382
sala operatoria 464, 465
sala passeggeri 383, 386, 387
sala per conferenze 442
sala per i cocktail 439
sala per operazioni di chirurgia minore 462
sala per riunioni 439, 442, 445
salamandra 75
salame di Genova 156
salame di Tolosa 156
salame tedesco 156
salchow 509
saldatore a pistola 218
saldatore elettrico 218
saldatura, filo per 218
sale di colloquio 440
sale fino 141
sale grosso 141
sale marino 141
salice piangente 64
saliera 166
salita, corridoio di 278
salmerino di fontana 161
salmone del Pacifico 161
salmone dell'Atlantico 161
salmone rosso 161
salone 386, 390
salopette 254, 260, 261
salopette a tutina 260
salopette con bretelle incrociate 261
salotto 188, 439
salotto, poltrona da 200
salsa di prugne 141
salsa di soia 140
salsa hoisin 140
salsa Tobasco® 140
salsa Worcestershire 140
salsefica 129
salsiccia alle cipolle 156
salsiccia di Francoforte 156
salsiccia di trippa 156
salsiccia kielbasa 156
salsiccia piccante 156
salsiera 166
saltatore 513
salti, esempi di 509
salto con gli sci 513
salto con l'asta 472
salto in alto 473
salto in lungo 472
salto triplo 472
salute 460
salvagente 387, 457
salvatacchi 240
salvataggio, scialuppa di 382, 386
salvataggio, zattera di 383
salvia 142
sambal oelek 141
Samoa 453
San Lorenzo, Fiume 16
San Marino, Repubblica di 450
sanbernardo 86
sandalo 241, 242
sandalo indiano 242
sangue deossigenato 104
sangue ossigenato 104
sangue, circolazione del 102
sangue, composizione del 104
sanguinaccio 156
santoreggia 142
São Tomé e Príncipe 451
sapone da barba, tazza per 271
saponetta 267
sapotiglia 137
saracco 226
sarchiello 233
sarchiello a mano 232
sarchio 233
sardina 159
sarong 253
sartia 520
sartorio 96
sassofono 306
satellite 316
satellite artificiale 37
satellite meteorologico 38
satellite per le telecomunicazioni 335
satelliti 2
satelliti per telecomunicazioni 316
Saturno 2, 3
savana 40, 44
saxhorn 307
sbadacchio 187
sbarra 205, 501
sbarra orizzontale 496, 497
sbarra pieghevole 500
sbuccialimoni 169
sbucciatore 169
scacchi 470
scacchi, notazione degli 470
scacchiera 470
scacciapensieri 297
scadenza, data di 441
scaffale 121
scafo 511, 520, 523
scaglia 74
scala 188, 225, 288, 293, 294, 298, 361, 412, 468, 469
scala a libretto 219
scala a pioli 404
scala aerea 455
scala Celsius 424
scala con piattaforma 219
scala delle altitudini 37
scala delle temperature 37
scala di accesso al piano mansardato 189
scala estensibile 219
scala esterna 183
scala Fahrenheit 424
scala graduata 226, 422, 423, 424, 425, 460, 533
scala graduata del nonio 425
scala graduata del righello 425
scala mobile 294, 378, 435
scala reale 468
scala reale massima 468
scala sgabello 219
scaldabagno 194
scaldamuscoli 263
scale 191, 219, 283, 345, 378, 404, 439
scale a libretto 219
scale, rampa di 191
scale, tromba delle 189
scaletta 184, 401, 498
scaletta laterale 377
scalfo 247
scalinata 283
scalini 184
scalino d'invito 191
scalo ferroviario 381
scalo merci 375, 430
scalogno 124
scalpello 403
scalpello da falegname 229

scalpello dello scarificatore 398
scambio 375
scamiciato 252
scampo 158
scanalatura 169, 228, 359, 510
scanner ottico 121
scapo 114
scapola 93, 95, 98, 99
scapola, spina della 99
scapolare 78
scappamento 351
scappamento, tubo di 367, 368, 369
scaricatore 184
scarichi, molla sturatrice per 216
scarico 184, 194
scarico, camera di 278
scarico, colonna principale di 194
scarico, rete di 194
scarico, tappo di 194
scarico, tubo di 194, 196, 212, 395, 398, 401
scarificatore 398
scarificatore, cilindro dello 398
scarificatore, dente dello 398
scarificatore, scalpello dello 398
scarola 126
scarpa 473, 478, 480, 483, 488, 500, 509, 522, 524, 527
scarpa a collo alto 240
scarpa chanel 241
scarpa con cinturino 241
scarpa con cinturino a T 241
scarpa con tacchetti 476, 486
scarpa da corsa 262
scarpa da tennis 242, 492
scarpa décolleté 241
scarpa oxford 240
scarpa stringata 240
scarpa, parti di una 240
scarpata 5, 182, 342
scarpata continentale 33
scarpe 240, 505
scarpe da donna 241
scarpe da uomo 240
scarpe unisex 242
scarpe, negozio di 437
scarpetta interna 511, 527
scarpetta, bordo della 511
scarponcino 240, 260
scarponcino di sicurezza 459
scarpone 240, 510, 511, 513, 514
scarpone morbido 513
scarpone rigido 513
scassa di deriva 519
scatola a doppia linea di connessione 417
scatola da incasso 198
scatola degli ingranaggi del moltiplicatore 413
scatola del cambio 350
scatola della frizione 368
scatola di servizio 198
scatola per archivio 340
scatola per formaggio 163
scatola portaesche 538
scatola portaprisma 421
scatolame 121
scatto, ancora a 221
scatto, chiavistello a 186
scatto, chiavistello senza 186
scatto, chiusura a 178
scatto, pulsante di 314
scavamelone 173
scavo, braccio di 400
scena 278
scena, fotografo di 291
scheda del circuito stampato 417
scheda di memoria 315
scheda PC, fessura per la 336
schedario rotativo 338
schedario, divisori alfabetici per 340
scheletro 98
schema della circolazione 103
schermo 7, 318, 439, 479
schermo del computer 10
schermo di proiezione 294
schermo di protezione 474
schiaccianoci 170
schiacciapatate 173
schiacciata 491
schiena 93, 95
schienale 201, 205, 353, 369, 467, 523
schienale reclinabile 460
schienale, manopola di regolazione dello 353
schiniere 476
schiuma 33
schiuma da barba 271
schiumaiola 173
schizzetto 460
schnauzer 86
Schwann, guaina di 110
sci 510, 523
sci alpino 510
sci alpino, pista per 512
sci alpino, snowboard per 513
sci da discesa libera 510
sci da fondo 514
sci da salto 513
sci da slalom 510
sci da slalom gigante 510
sci da supergigante 510
sci, esempi di 510
sci, piste da 512
sci, scuola di 512
scia luminosa del cratere 5
scia, punta dello 514
sciacquone 195
sciacquone, levetta dello 196
scialuppa di salvataggio 382, 386
sciatore 510
scienza 414
scienze, aula di 444
scimpanzé 91
sciolina 514
sciolinatura, accessori per la 514
sciovia 512
sciovia, arrivo della 512
sciroppo d'acero 149
sciroppo di mais 149
scissione del nucleo 415
scissura obliqua 105
scivolamento, fase di 514
scivolo della banchina 381
scivolo dello sfioratore 406
scivolo per tronchi d'albero 406
sclera 119
scocca 237, 361
scodella 166
scoglio 35
scoiattolo 82
scolainsalata, centrifuga 171
scollo 247
scollo a V 244, 250
scolpitura del battistrada 358
scompartimento bagagli 376
scomparto 203
scomparto degli accessori 209
scomparto del congelatore 211
scomparto del frigorifero 211
scomparto del sacchetto 209
scomparto della strumentazione 376
scomparto di carico 12
scomparto di carico, portellone dello 13
scomparto per banconote 274
scomparto per carte di credito 274
scomparto per i guanti 464
scomparto per i latticini 211
scomparto per il burro 211
scomparto portadocumenti 274
scontrino 423
scooter 369
scopa 193, 215
scopa a frangia 215
scopa da curling 515
scopa, rastrello 237
scorpione 70
scorrimento 331
scorza 58
scorzetta 58
scorzonera 129
scossalina 193
scotta del fiocco 520
scotta della randa 520
scotta, rotaia del carrello di 520, 521
Scozia, placca di 27
scrivania 439
scrivania dei cancellieri 440
scroto 92, 111
scudo di protezione della mano 235
scudo termico 12
scuola 444
scuola di sci 512
scuolabus 362
scutello 73
secchiello con cordoncino 275
secchiello piccolo con cordoncino 276
secchio 215
seconda 298
seconda base 474
seconda base (posizione) 474
seconda falange 114
seconda galleria 293
seconda linea 482
seconda linea destra 482
seconda linea sinistra 482
seconda pinna dorsale 74
secondi violini 295
secondi, lancetta dei 424
secondo 428, 498
secondo allenatore 507
secondo arbitro 485, 487
secondo assistente cameraman 290
secondo aumento di tensione 413
secondo giocatore al lancio 515
secondo livello, dominio di 334
secondo molare 101
secondo premolare 101
secondo spazio 489
secrétaire 203
sedano 125
sedano di monte 142
sedano rapa 129
sede della valvola di tenuta 196
sedia 201
sedia a dondolo 200, 201
sedia a rotelle 467
sedia a sdraio 201
sedia con braccioli 444
sedia da regista 200
sedia del regista 291
sedia pieghevole 201
sedia scala 201
sedia senza braccioli 444
sedie degli attori 290
sedie impilabili 201
sedie, esempi di 201
sedile 195, 196, 200, 201, 205
sedile doppio 380
sedile scorrevole 501
sedile singolo 380
sedile: vista anteriore 353
sedile: vista laterale 353
sedili 201
seduta 353, 467
seduta del divano posteriore 353
sega a mano 533
sega circolare 227
sega circolare, lama di 227
sega da giardiniere 234
sega per augnatura manuale 226
segale 61, 143
segale, galletta di 145
segale, pane danese di 145
segale, pane nero di 144
segale, pane tedesco di 145
segale: spiga 61
seggio del rabbino 447
seggiolino per bambini 356, 372
seggiolone 205
seggiovia 512
seggiovia, partenza della 512
seghetto 226
seghetto alternativo 227
seghetto da traforo 226
segmento addominale 67
segnalatore di pericolo 454
segnale dell'area di attesa 390
segnale di distanza fissa 391
segnale di identificazione della pista 390
segnale di zona di contatto 391
segnali dell'asse della pista 390
segnali della soglia della pista 391
segnali laterali 390
segnalino 469
segnapunti 487, 488, 499
segnavento 520
segno centrale 490
segretaria di produzione 291
segretaria, ufficio della 443
segreteria scolastica, ufficio della 445
segreteria telefonica digitale 328
selettore dei pick-up 303
selettore dei programmi 314
selettore del livello dell'acqua 212
selettore del livello di registrazione 323
selettore del movimento orbitale 227
selettore del nastro 323
selettore del ritmo 311
selettore del timbro 311
selettore della messa a fuoco 314
selettore della modalità audio 322
selettore della temperatura 178, 270
selettore della velocità 270
selettore di ingresso 322
selettore di programma 310
selettore di velocità 176, 227, 228
selettore quadridirezionale 315
selettore stazioni 326
selettore stereo/mono 326
selettori di funzione 327
selettori di modo 326
selezione 319
selezione dei canali 319
sella 369, 370, 501, 523
sella biposto 367
sella del guidatore 369
sella del passeggero 369
selvaggina 154
semaforo 375, 434
seme 53, 57, 58, 59, 60
semi di girasole, olio di 149
semi di papavero 139
semi di soia 131
semi-mummia 530
semiasse 351
semibiscroma 299
semibiscroma, pausa di 299
semibreve 299
semibreve, pausa di 299
semicerchio 428
semicroma 299
semicroma, pausa di 299
semimembranoso 97
semiminima 299
semiminima, pausa di 299
seminatoio a mano 231
seminterrato 182
seminterrato, finestra del 183
semirimorchio frigorifero 365
semisfera 429
semitendinoso 97
semolino 144
senape americana 140
senape bianca 138
senape di Digione 140
senape in granuli 140
senape in polvere 140
senape inglese 140
senape nera 60, 138
senape tedesca 140
Senegal 451
Senegal, Fiume 20
seno 92, 94, 113
seno frontale 117
seno laterale inferiore 62
seno laterale superiore 62
seno peziolato 62
seno sfenoidale 117
sensibilità 314
sensore del telecomando 318
sensore di collisione principale 354
sensore di sicurezza 354
sensore di temperatura 358
sensore di velocità delle ruote 357
sensore ottico 332
sepalo 56, 58, 59
separatore 359, 384, 402, 417
separatore elettrolitico 417
separatore liquido/gas 359
separazione del cartone 49
separazione della carta 49
separazione magnetica 49
séparé 438
seppia 157
sequencer 310
sequencer, controllo del 310
seracco 30
serbatoi di stoccaggio 404
serbatoio 13, 181
serbatoio a tetto galleggiante 404
serbatoio ausiliario 365
serbatoio del carburante 235, 351, 366, 369, 377, 395
serbatoio del liquido dei freni 357
serbatoio dell'acqua 181, 272
serbatoio dell'acqua di raffreddamento 408
serbatoio dell'acqua, vano del 394
serbatoio di stoccaggio 405
serbatoio di stoccaggio temporaneo 404
serbatoio esterno del combustibile 12
serbatoio per il brillantante 214
serbatoio per il carburante 364
serbatoio, bocchetta del 237
serbatoio, sportello del 349
serbatoio, tappo del 364, 368
Serbia 450
serie, lampade in 207
serie, numero di 441
serpente 76, 469
serpente a sonagli 77
serpente corallo 77
serpente giarrettiera 77
serpente velenoso: testa, morfologia di un 76
serpenti e scale 469
serpentina 210
serra 122
serraggio, leva di 224, 229
serraggio, vite di 224
serratura 185, 186, 202, 211, 275, 277, 349, 352
serratura a chiave 274
serratura a combinazione 274
server 334, 335
server d'accesso 335
servizi assicurativi 442
servizi di credito 442
servizi finanziari 442
servizi sociali 465
servizio 487, 490
servizio corto, linea di 495
servizio da fonduta 174
servizio da wok 174
servizio del doppio, campo di 495
servizio del singolo, campo di 495
servizio di assistenza ai clienti 443
servizio di babysitteraggio 437
servizio di navetta 390
servizio Internet, fornitore del 335
servizio lungo, linea di 494
servizio manutenzione 346
servizio mobile a distanza, unità di 11
servizio pacchi 374
servizio, cintura di 456
servizio, fonte del 313
servizio, giudice di 490, 494
servizio, linea centrale di 491
servizio, linea di 491
servizio, modulo di 316
servizio, stazione di 433
servizio, tavolo di 438
servizio, zona di 491
servizio, zone di 495
servofreno 350, 357
sesamo, olio di 149
sesta 298
sestetto 300
set 291, 492
set delle riprese 290
set di bussole 223
set di utensili 173
set per cucinare 531
set per manicure 265
set precedenti 492
setaccio 171, 172
setale 538
setola 271, 272
setole 215, 219
settima 298
setto 60, 117
setto interventricolare 104
setto nasale, cartilagine del 117
setto pellucido 109
settore 428
Seychelles 452
sezione degli archi 295
sezione degli ottoni 295
sezione dei legni 295
sezione della crosta terrestre 26
sezione di un acino 59
sezione di un bulbo 54
sezione di un cannocchiale 8
sezione di un lampone 59
sezione di un telescopio 9
sezione di un'arancia 58
sezione di una fragola 59
sezione di una mela 58
sezione di una nocciola 60
sezione di una noce 60
sezione di una palla 477
sezione di una pesca 57
sezione rigida anteriore 363
sezione rigida posteriore 363
sezione sagittale 111, 112
sezione trasversale di un molare 101
sezione trasversale di un osservatorio astronomico 7
sezione trasversale di un tronco 63

sezione trasversale di una centrale idroelettrica 407
sezione trasversale di una navicella 413
sezione trasversale di una strada 342, 434
sezione variabile, ugello a 394
sfagno pungente 51
sfera 312, 332, 429
sfera, penna a 312
sfera, supporto della 356
sfiatatoio 90, 214
sfiato 194
sfiato, valvola di 385
sfintere anale 106
sfioratore 406
sfioratore, paratoia dello 406
sfioratore, scivolo dello 406
sfioratore, soglia dello 406
sgabello 164, 201, 498
sgabello alto 201
sgabello da bar 438
sgambatura elasticizzata 247
sgombro 159
shampoo 267
shekel, nuovo 440
shiitake 123
short track 508
shorts 254
si 298
siamese 87
sicurezza 454
sicurezza, cassetta di 443
sicurezza, corridoio di 440
sicurezza, griglia di 442
sicurezza, grilletto di 235
sicurezza, impugnatura di 237
sicurezza, linea di 379
sicurezza, luce di 457
sicurezza, termostato di 213
sicurezza, valvola di 174
siepe 183, 230, 472
Sierra Leone 451
sifone 72, 194, 196, 197
siliqua, sezione di una 60
silo orizzontale 122
silo verticale 122
silos 381
simboli 468
simboli scientifici 426
simbolo della squadra 506
sinagoga 447
sinapsi 110
sinfisi pubica 111, 112
Singapore 453
sinistra 387
sintesi additiva 418
sintesi dei colori 418
sintesi sottrattiva 418
sintetizzatore 310
sintetizzatore a fiato 311
sintoamplificatore 325
sintoamplificatore: dorso 322
sintoamplificatore: vista frontale 322
sintonia, comandi di 318
sintonia, manopola della 326
sintonia, tasti di selezione della 322
sintonia, tasto di preselezione della 322
sintonizzatore 326
sintonizzazione, manopola di 325
sipario 292, 293
sipario tagliafuoco 292
Siria 452
siringa 460
siringa per decorazioni 172
siringhe usate, contenitore delle 457
sismografi 27
sismografo orizzontale 27
sismografo verticale 27
sismogramma 27
sistema a celle solari 411
sistema a rotazione 403
sistema di alimentazione 351
sistema di climatizzazione 46
sistema di controllo del lampeggiante 457
sistema di coordinate terrestri 21
sistema di guida fine 7
sistema di lenti 420
sistema di manipolazione a distanza 11
sistema di registrazione audio 291
sistema di ritenuta degli air bag 354
sistema di sopravvivenza 10
sistema di trasmissione 351
sistema idraulico 396
sistema internazionale di unità di misura 426
sistema nervoso 108
sistema nervoso centrale 109
sistema nervoso periferico 108
sistema solare 2
sistema stradale 342
sistema, tasti di 310
sistemi dell'automobile 351
sistemi dell'automobile: componenti principali 350
sistro 309
skateboard 526
skater 526
skimmer 184
slalom gigante 511
slalom speciale 511
slalom supergigante 511
slancio 500
slip 247, 259
slip da bagno 263
slitta 236
slitta di fissaggio 420
slitta per accessori 314
Slovacchia 450
Slovenia 450
smalto 101
smalto per unghie 265
smerigliatrice eccentrica 229
sminuzzamento 49
smistamento dei materiali metallici 49
smistamento del cartone 49
smistamento del vetro 49
smistamento della carta 49
smistamento della plastica 49
smistamento manuale 49
smistamento ottico 49
smistamento selettivo dei rifiuti 49
smog 47
smorzamento magnetico, dispositivo di 422
smorzata 491
smottamento 31
snack bar 294
snocciolatore 173
snodo 511
snooker 503
snowboard 513
snowboard per freestyle 513
snowboard per sci alpino 513
snowboardista 513
sobborghi 25
società 430
soffietto 274, 276
soffietto, borsa a 274
soffietto, mantice a 296
soffietto, portacarte a 274
soffietto, tasca applicata a 255
soffitto a due spioventi 189
soffitto acustico 293
soffitto della cabina 287
soffitto, travetto del 187
softball 477
software di posta elettronica 334
soggiorno 188
soglia 185
soglia dello sfioratore 406
soglia glaciale 30
sogliola 161
soia, germogli di 131
soia, salsa di 140
soia, semi di 131
sol 298
solaio 193
solaio, collare del 193
solarium 385, 387
solco 118
solco mediano 118
solco terminale 118
Sole 2, 4, 5, 38
Sole, eclissi di 4
sole, occhiali da 273
Sole, struttura del 4
soleo 96
soletta 247
soletta antiscivolo 261
solidi 429
solidificazione 414
solido 414, 415
solido amorfo 414
solitario 264
sollevacuticole 265
sollevamento pesi 500
sollevamento, braccio di 399, 400
sollevamento, catena di 396
sollevamento, cavo di 397
sollevamento, cilindro di 397, 455
sollevamento, fune di 287
solstizio d'estate 38
solstizio d'inverno 38
soluzione multiuso 272
solventi, impianto di estrazione con 405
Somalia 451
sommatoria 427
sommelier 438
sonagli 309
sonda spaziale 37
sopracciglia, pinzette per 265
soprafusione 414
soprasponda 502
soprastruttura 342
sopravveste a grembiule 255
sopravvivenza, regolazione del sistema di 10
sopravvivenza, sistema di 10
sordina 304, 307, 319
sordina, pedale della 304
sorgente 32
sorgente di corrente 416
sorgenti, luci delle 322
sorgenti, tasto di selezione delle 322
sorgo 61
sorgo: pannocchia 61
soro 52
sospensione 351, 380
sospensione posteriore 522
sospensione, braccio di 212
sospensione, lampada a 206
sospensioni, gruppo delle 351
sostanza bianca 109, 110
sostanza corticale 107
sostanza grigia 109, 110
sostanza midollare 107
sostegno 201, 509
sostegno del bracciolo 200
sostegno dell'ala 387
sostegno per il collo 525
sostegno, base di 202
sotterraneo 281, 435
sottocasco 524
sottofondo 187, 190
sottofondo di cemento 190
sottofondo di cemento, parquet su 190
sottogola 486, 522
sottogonna 258
sottopalco 292
sottopassaggio 375
sottopunto, cucitura a 245
sottostruttura 403
sottosuolo 54
sottotitolo 313
sottotuta 524
sottoveste 258
sottoveste con reggiseno 258
sottovia 344
sottrazione 427
spacco centrale 244
spacco laterale 244
spadice 57
spaghetti 146
spaghetti all'uovo 147
spaghetti asiatici 147
spaghetti di fagioli mungo 147
spaghetti di riso 147
spaghetti soba 147
spaghetti somen 147
spaghetti udon 147
spaghetti, molle per 173
spaghettini 146
Spagna 449
spalla 83, 86, 92, 94, 284, 302, 344, 492, 536
spallaccio 532
spallamento 223
spalliera 230
spalliera ad arco 230
spallina 248, 259, 456
spartitraffico 343, 434
sparviero 216
spatola 173, 510, 514
spatola metallica 355
spatolata 55
spaziatore 409
spazio 298, 330
spazio epidurale 110
spazio unificatore 330
spazzaneve a turbina 365
spazzata d'anca 499
spazzatrice 365
spazzola 173, 209, 215, 272
spazzola a dorso piatto 268
spazzola a pennello 209
spazzola antistatica 268
spazzola da bagno 267
spazzola da neve con raschietto 356
spazzola di gomma 355
spazzola metallica 309
spazzola per la schiena 267
spazzola per pavimenti 209
spazzola per tappeti e pavimenti 209
spazzola ragno 268
spazzola rotante centrale 365
spazzola rotante laterale 365
spazzola rotonda 268
spazzole per capelli 268
spazzolino da denti 272
spazzolino da denti elettrico 272
spazzolino di pulizia 271
spazzolino per mascara 266
spazzolino, gambo a innesto dello 272
speaker 518
specchietto 523
specchietto anteriore di accostamento 362
specchietto di cortesia 354
specchietto per il punto cieco 362, 363
specchietto retrovisore 354, 363, 366, 368, 369
specchietto retrovisore esterno 348, 362, 364
specchio 195, 421, 439
specchio a riflessione parziale 420
specchio a riflessione totale 420
specchio di lettura 10
specchio di puntamento 533
specchio doppio girevole 269
specchio laterale 269
specchio luminoso 269
specchio piano 7
specchio primario 7
specchio primario concavo 9
specchio secondario 7, 9
specialista tecnico 509
specialità 511
specialità gastronomiche 120
spedizione merci 391
spelafili 217
spelucchino 169
spencer 254
sperlano 159
spermatozoo 111
sperone 29
spesa, borsa della 276
spessore 224
spessore, misura dello 425
spettro elettromagnetico 418
spezie 138
spezie cajun, condimento alle 139
spezie marinate 139
spezzatino 152, 153
spia 269
spia cinture di sicurezza non allacciate 355
spia dei proiettori abbaglianti 355
spia dell'indicatore di direzione 355, 368
spia della batteria 355
spia della cartuccia 333
spia della posizione di folle 368
spia della pressione dell'olio 355, 368
spia della riserva di carburante 355
spia delle luci abbaglianti 368
spia di accensione 443
spia di alimentazione 329, 333
spia di alimentazione della carta 333
spia di allarme 337
spia di messa in carica 337
spia di rilevamento della carta 443
spia luminosa 178, 179, 180, 181, 208, 214, 454
spia luminosa dell'autoscatto 314
spia luminosa di accensione/spegnimento 327
spia luminosa di carica 271
spia porte aperte 355
spiaggia 35
spicchio 58
spicole 4
spider 347
spie 355
spie della modalità audio 322
spie luminose 318, 331
spiga 57, 144
spillone 268
spina 228, 326
spina americana, presa per 198
spina americana 198
spina della scapola 99
spina di alimentazione 337
spina europea 198
spina nasale anteriore 100
spinacio 127
spingicuticole 265
spingistantuffo 460
spinotto 198, 199, 324
spinotto di connessione 417
spinotto di messa a terra 198
spinta, fase di 514
spinta, maniglia di 286
spinta, telaio di 398
spinterogeno 350, 360
spirale 221
spirale, braccio della 6
spirulina 123
splenio 97
spogliatoio 444, 465
spogliatoio del personale 465
spoiler 364, 366, 392
spolverino 172
sponda inferiore 502
sponda protettiva 205
sponda superiore 502
spore 52
sporgenza 191
sport 468
sport a motore 524
sport acquatici 516
sport con la palla 474
sport di combattimento 498
sport di forza 500
sport di precisione 502
sport invernali 515
sport nautici 516
sport su rotelle 526
sporta 276
sportello 178, 210, 423, 443
sportello automatico 442, 443
sportello bancomat 437, 442
sportello commerciale 443
sportello del serbatoio 349
sportello di carico 192
sportello notturno 443
spostamento 418
spray al peperoncino 456
spremiaglio 170
spremiagrumi 170
spremiagrumi elettrico 177
spremitura, cono di 177
sprone 245
spruzzatore 236
spruzzatori 408
spugna abrasiva 215
spugna naturale 267
spugna sintetica 266
spugna vegetale 267
spugnetta 339
spugnetta, applicatore a 266
spugnola 123
spumante, coppa da 165
squadra 225
squadra falsa 225
squadra, simbolo della 506
squama 76, 79
Sri Lanka 453
stabilimento industriale 430
stabilizzatore 393, 397, 400, 455, 523
staccionata 182
stadera 422
stadi di maturazione 62
stadio 431, 472
staff medico 499
staffa 116, 254
staffa di lancio 515
staggio 219
stagioni dell'anno 38
stagno 504
stalagmite 31
stalattite 31
stalla 122
stame 56, 58
stampa 331
stampante a getto di inchiostro 333
stampella canadese 466
stampini per dolci 172
stampo per charlotte 172
stampo per crostata 172
stampo per pane 179
stanga 231

stanghetta 273, 298
stantuffo 460
stanza da bagno 188, 189, 195, 439
stanza degli insegnanti 445
stanza degli studenti 445
stanza dei giurati 440
stanza del personale 463
stanza del triage 463
stanza di degenza 464
stanza di degenza postoperatoria 464
stanza di isolamento 462
stanza di osservazione 462, 465
stanza di sterilizzazione 464
stanza per esame psichiatrico 462
stanza per l'anestesia 464
stanza per l'esame audiometrico 465
stanza per la preparazione chirurgica 464
stanza per le terapie 465
stanza per le visite mediche 465
stanza per osservazione psichiatrica 462
stanza per visite ginecologiche 463
stanze principali 188
stanzino del portiere 439
stanzino della guardia giurata 443
starter 516
starter, pistola dello 472
stati della materia 414
Stati Uniti d'America 448
station wagon 347
stato 23
stato presente del tempo 39
statua 446
statua, posizione della 279
stazione degli autobus 432
stazione dei viaggiatori 374, 375, 381
stazione della metropolitana 378, 432
stazione di pattugliamento 512
stazione di polizia 433
stazione di pompaggio 404
stazione di pompaggio intermedia 404
stazione di pompaggio principale 404
stazione di pronto soccorso 345
stazione di servizio 346, 433
stazione di superficie 38
stazione di trasformazione 406, 407
stazione ferroviaria 25, 375, 430, 432
stazione locale 316
stazione ripetitrice 316
stazione ripetitrice a microonde 334
stazione sciistica 512
stazione spaziale internazionale 11
stazione terminale 404
stazione terrestre per le telecomunicazioni 335
stazione, cerchio di 39
stazione, ingresso della 378
stazione, modello di 39
stazione, nome della 378
stecca 259, 273, 503, 519, 520
stecche 461
stella cadente 37
stella di David 447
stelo 51, 54, 221
stelo, lampada a 206
stemma 477
stepper 501
steppico 40
stereo/mono, selettore 326
sterilizzazione, sala di 465
sterilizzazione, stanza di 464
sterlina 440
sterno 98
sternocleidomastoideo 96
sterzo, gruppo dello 351
stigma 56, 60, 67
stile libero o crawl 517
stili di canna 312
stili di nuoto 517
stilo 56, 57, 58, 59, 60, 312, 337
stilo di piombo 312
stilo metallico romano 312
stilobate 279
stilton 151
stimolatore gengivale 272
stinco 153
stipite 185, 192
stipola 55
stiva per i containers 383
stivale 241, 305, 525
stivale alla moschettiera 241
stivale di gomma 454
stivaloni impermeabili 538
stoccaggio temporaneo, serbatoio di 404
stoccaggio, serbatoi di 404
stoccaggio, serbatoio di 405
stomaco 73, 103, 106
stomaco cardiaco 71
stomaco pilorico 71
stop 86, 323, 328
stopper 481
storione 158
stornello 80
strada 25, 345, 430, 435
strada di accesso 388
strada di servizio 388
strada panoramica 25
strada secondaria 25
strada, numero di 25
strada, sezione trasversale di una 342
stradina 504
strallo 412
strallo di prua 520
strappo 500
strati di rifiuti 47
strato 42
strato basale 114
strato basaltico 26
strato corneo 114
strato di base 342
strato di ceneri 28
strato di collegamento 342
strato di lava 28
strato di ozono 37
strato granitico 26
strato granulare 114
strato impermeabile 190
strato inferiore confinante 402
strato lucido 114
strato protettivo 10
strato spinoso 114
strato superficiale del suolo 54
strato superiore confinante 402
stratocumulo 42
stratopausa 37
stratosfera 37
strega 503
stretto 24
Stretto di Bass 15
Stretto di Bering 16
Stretto di Cook 15
Stretto di Gibilterra 18
Stretto di Torres 15
stringa 240, 477, 498, 509
striscia antiabrasiva 358
striscia di gioco 479
striscia di sfregamento 218
striscia di sicurezza 374
strofinaccio da cucina 215
strombatura 285
strozzascotte 521
strozzatura 301, 424
strumentazione scientifica 13
strumenti a corde 301
strumenti a fiato 306
strumenti a percussione 295, 308
strumenti a tastiera 304
strumenti di misura 424
strumenti di misurazione e tracciamento 225
strumenti elettronici 310
strumenti musicali tradizionali 296
strumenti per il pronto soccorso 460
strumenti scientifici 7
strumenti scrittori 312
struttura 186, 187
struttura del midollo spinale 109
struttura del Sole 4
struttura dell'orecchio 116
struttura della biosfera 44
struttura della Terra 26
struttura di un albero 63
struttura di un fiore 56
struttura di un fungo 52
struttura di un lichene 50
struttura di un muschio 51
struttura di un'alga 51
struttura di una casa 188
struttura di una felce 52
struttura di una foglia 55
struttura di una pianta 53
struttura esterna 211, 212
struttura lignea, parquet su 190
struttura metallica 374
struttura protettiva 525
strutture per i tuffi 518
struzzo 81
struzzo, uovo di 155
studente 444
studenti, armadietti degli 445
studenti, stanza degli 445
studio 189
stufa a combustione lenta 192
stufa a gas 529
stufe, olio combustibile per 405
sturalavandini 216
sub woofer 321
subartico 40
subduzione 27
sublimazione 414
subtropicale mediterraneo 40
subtropicale umido 40
suburbio 431
Sud 23
Sud Sud-Est 23
Sud Sud-Ovest 23
Sud-Est 23
Sud-Ovest 23
Sudafricana, Repubblica 452
Sudan 451
sufflè, tegamino per 172
sughero 514
sumac 139
suola 240, 263, 509, 510, 511
suolo 48
suolo, fertilizzazione del 47
suolo, inquinamento del 47
suolo, movimento orizzontale del 27
suolo, movimento verticale del 27
suolo, profilo del 54
suolo, strato superficiale del 54
suoneria, regolatore della 327
suono, ingegnere del 291
superfici 428
superfici di gioco 492
superficie antiscivolo 526
superficie dell'acqua 518
superficie della cute 114
superficie di affissione 341
superficie di gioco 493
superficie dura (cemento) 492
superficie freatica 31
superficie sintetica 492
superficie terrestre, assorbimento attraverso la 46
superficie verticale 526
superficie, stazione di 38
superjumbo 394
supermercato 120, 433, 437
superstrada 343
supplemento a colori 313
supplemento letterario 313
supporti di registrazione 319
supporti per camminare 466
supporto 9, 199, 269, 308
supporto anteriore retrattile 361
supporto del cordone 208
supporto del disco abrasivo 229
supporto del rullo 219
supporto del tabellone 489
supporto della rete 493
supporto della sfera 356
supporto elastico 324, 458
supporto per il braccio 466
supporto per il tallone 467
supporto retrattile 365
supporto sottoascellare 466
supporto stabilizzatore 361
supporto, piastra di 199
supporto, telaio di 401
surgelati 121
surgelati, magazzino dei 121
Suriname 448
surriscaldamento globale 46
sutura 60, 73
sutura coronale 100
sutura coronaria 100
sutura lambdoidea 100
sutura squamosa 100
sverniciatura, pistola per 219
svettatoio 234
Svezia 450
svincolo 431
Svizzera 450
Swaziland 452

T

T-shirt 263
tabaccheria 436
tabella dei risultati 518
tabellone 489
tabellone degli arrivi e delle partenze 391
tabellone degli orari 374
tabellone della classifica generale 496
tabellone della prova in corso 497
tabellone segnapunti 471, 472, 492, 497, 499
tabellone, supporto del 489
tabernacolo 446
tablino 280
tabloid 313
tabulazione a destra 330
tabulazione a sinistra 330
tacca 422, 473
tacca di mira 534
tacchetti intercambiabili 480
tacchetto 262, 478
tacchino 81, 155
tacco 240, 509, 536
tachimetro 355, 368, 501
tafano 69
Tagikistan 452
tagli di agnello 153
tagli di maiale 153
tagli di manzo 152
tagli di vitello 152
taglia fissa 403
taglia mobile 403
tagliabasette 271
tagliabiscotti 172
tagliabordi 233, 237
tagliacarte 339
tagliacuticole 265
tagliafili 217
tagliasiepi 235
tagliasiepi, forbici 234
tagliatelle verdi 146
tagliente 180, 228, 398, 399, 400
tagliere 169
taglio 221
taglio addizionale 298
tagliola 535
tahini 140
Tailandia 453
tailback 485
tailleur 251
tajina 174
tallo 50, 51
tallonatore 482
tallone 93, 95, 169, 226, 229, 262, 301, 302, 358, 477, 506
tallone d'appoggio 176
tallone di appoggio 208
talloniera 511, 514
tamarillo 136
tamarindo , pasta di 140
tamarino 91
tamburello 309
tamburo 170, 213, 357, 425
tamburo parlante 297
tamburo rotante 27
tamburo tenore 308
tamia 82
tampone 338
tandem 373
Tanganica, Lago 20
tangenziale 25, 431
Tanzania 451
tappeti e pavimenti, spazzola per 209
tappetino 356
tappetino del mouse 332
tappeto 190, 498
tappezzeria, bocchetta per 209
tappi per le orecchie 458
tappo 176, 267, 358, 532
tappo a vite 163
tappo del serbatoio 364, 368
tappo di isolamento 417
tappo di ispezione 197
tappo di scarico 194
tappo di scarico dell'olio 360
targhetta del costruttore 228
targhetta delle avvertenze 228
taro 124
tarso 78
tartaruga 76
tartaruga, morfologia di una 76
tartufo 123
tartufo di mare 157
tasca 172, 225, 274, 505
tasca anteriore 246
tasca applicata 244, 249, 260
tasca applicata a soffietto 255
tasca applicata con aletta 245
tasca della stecca 519
tasca di Douglas 112
tasca di inforcamento 396
tasca esterna 274, 276
tasca finta 251
tasca frontale 275
tasca inserita nella cucitura 251
tasca interna 277
tasca interna con aletta 244, 248, 249, 251
tasca nascosta 274
tasca per la stecca 520
tasca portaoggetti 352
tasca posteriore 246
tasca profilata 250
tasca profilata con aletta 244, 248
tasca tagliata in verticale 251
tasca vescicouterina 112
taschino 248
taschino con aletta 244
taschino tagliato con aletta 244
taschino, fazzoletto da 244
Tasmania 15
Tasmania, Mare di 15
tassello 202
tasso 88
tasti del cursore 331
tasti del lettore di compact disc 326
tasti del riproduttore a cassette 326
tasti di accesso diretto 323
tasti di categorie 326
tasti di chiamata automatica 327
tasti di comando 214, 328
tasti di identificazione del conto 443
tasti di regolazione 329
tasti di regolazione del volume 319
tasti di ricerca emittenti 319
tasti di selezione dei canali 319
tasti di selezione della sintonia 322
tasti di selezione delle casse acustiche 322
tasti di sistema 310
tasti funzione 319, 328, 330, 423, 442, 443
tasti funzione programmabili 443
tasti Internet 330
tasti numerici 326
tasti per l'editing del suono 310
tastiera 296, 301, 303, 304, 310, 327, 330, 336
tastiera alfanumerica 330, 346, 442, 443
tastiera degli acuti 296
tastiera numerica 328
tastiera, strumenti a 304
tastierina per il codice di identificazione personale (PIN) 443
tastierino alfabetico 338
tastierino alfanumerico 327
tastierino numerico 331, 338, 423
tasto 296, 304, 306
tasto Alt 330
tasto Avvio 330
tasto backspace 331
tasto Control 330
tasto del menu 329
tasto delle maiuscole 330
tasto di addizione 337
tasto di arresto 319, 323
tasto di arresto e di scorrimento 331
tasto di avanzamento della carta 443
tasto di avanzamento rapido 323
tasto di avvio 328
tasto di avvio registrazione 320
tasto di azzeramento 337
tasto di azzeramento del contatore 323
tasto di azzeramento ultimo dato 337
tasto di blocco delle maiuscole 330
tasto di blocco numerico 331
tasto di cambio segno 337
tasto di cancellazione 331
tasto di cancellazione della memoria 337
tasto di chiamata 327
tasto di comando 176
tasto di conferma 443
tasto di divisione 337
tasto di espulsione 323

tasto di memorizzazione 322, 327
tasto di messa a fuoco 320
tasto di moltiplicazione 337
tasto di navigazione 319, 327
tasto di pagina giù 331
tasto di pagina su 331
tasto di pausa 323
tasto di pausa/fermo immagine 319
tasto di percentuale 337
tasto di posizione 302, 303
tasto di preselezione 326
tasto di preselezione della sintonia 322
tasto di punto decimale 337
tasto di radice quadrata 337
tasto di registrazione 319, 323
tasto di registrazione notturna 320
tasto di registro 305
tasto di reset 328
tasto di riavvolgimento 323
tasto di richiamo della memoria 337
tasto di ripetizione 323
tasto di riproduzione 319, 323
tasto di selezione 326, 329
tasto di selezione del registratore 322
tasto di selezione della banda 322
tasto di selezione della modalità FM 322
tasto di selezione delle sorgenti 322
tasto di somma in memoria 337
tasto di sottrazione 337
tasto di sottrazione in memoria 337
tasto di tabulazione 330
tasto di uguale 337
tasto di visualizzazione 326
tasto email 330
tasto Esc 330
tasto Fine 331
tasto fine chiamata/interruttore 327
tasto foto 320
tasto Home 331
tasto Ins 331
tasto Invio 331
tasto macchina fotografica 327
tasto memoria 326
tasto menu 320, 326, 327
tasto numerico 337
tasto pausa 331
tasto per il modo di esposizione 314
tasto per le esposizioni multiple 314
tasto play 319
tasto precedente/indietro veloce 326
tasto programmabile 327
tasto retroilluminazione 320
tasto riproduzione/pausa 326
tasto schermo panoramico/inserimento data 320
tasto stampa 331
tasto stop 319
tasto successivo/avanti veloce 326
tatami 499
tavola 469, 519
tavola armonica 296, 297, 301, 302, 304
tavola di rotazione 403
tavola esterna 469
tavola interna 469
tavola, coltello da 168
tavola, cucchiaio da 168
tavola, forchetta da 168
tavola, vasellame da 166
tavoletta 190
tavoletta portablocco 340
tavoli, esempi di 202
tavolini sovrapponibili 202
tavolino da letto 464
tavolino traslatore 421
tavolino traslatore, comando del 421
tavolo 202, 493, 502
tavolo a cancello 202
tavolo allungabile 202
tavolo di servizio 438
tavolo operatorio 464
tavolo, lampada da 206
tazza 531
tazza alta da caffè 166
tazza da tè 166
tazza graduata 171
tazza per sapone da barba 271
tazzina da caffè 166
tè 148
tè nero 148
tè oolong 148
tè verde 148
tè, bustina di 148
tè, cucchiaino da 168
tè, filtro per il 173
tè, tazza da 166
teatro 292, 432, 433
teatro greco 278
teatro, binocolo da 273
tecniche 487
tecnico delle luci 291
tee 505
tegame 175, 531
tegame per fonduta 174
tegame per uova in camicia 175
tegamino per chiocciole 173
tegamino per sufflè 172
teglia con fondo staccabile 172
teglia da forno 172
teglia per torta 172
teglie da forno 174
tegola 279, 280, 283
tegumento del seme 57
tegumento seminale 61
teiera 166
tela 412
telaio 186, 200, 201, 202, 204, 224, 226, 274, 277, 297, 309, 367, 396, 400, 401, 410, 411, 412, 466, 492, 494, 522, 527
telaio dei rulli dei cingoli 398
telaio del bruciatore 529
telaio di spinta 398
telaio di supporto 401
telaio interno della portiera 352
telaio metallico 304
telaio per tenda esterna 361
telaio regolabile 226
telaio rigido, borsa a 276
telaio, giunzione a linguetta del 186
telaio, giunzione scanalata del 186
telaio, montante del 202
telaio, traverso superiore del 186
telecamera 290, 525
telecamera a colori 10
telecomando 319, 321
telecomando, sensore del 318
telecomunicazioni via satellite 317
telecomunicazioni, satelliti per 316
telefax 328
telefonia 335
telefono 439
telefono cellulare 327
telefono pubblico 294, 437, 438, 463
teleobiettivo 314
telescopio 7, 9
telescopio spaziale Hubble 7, 37
telescopio, basamento del 7
telescopio, sezione di un 9
televisione 318, 439, 444
televisore a cristalli liquidi 318
televisore a grande schermo 321
televisore a tubo catodico 318
televisore al plasma 318
teli, gonna a 253
telo di spugna con cappuccio 260
telo esterno 528, 529
telone proteggiauto 356
telson 71
temperamatite 341
temperatura corporea, regolazione della 10
temperatura del liquido di raffreddamento, indicatore della 355
temperatura dell'aria 39
temperatura di rugiada 39
temperatura termodinamica, unità di misura della 426
temperatura, indicatore di 269
temperatura, misura della 424
temperatura, selettore della 178
temperature, scala delle 37
temperino multiuso 531
tempia 92
tempio azteco 283
tempio di Huitzilopochtli 283
tempio di Tlaloc 283
tempio greco 279
tempio greco, pianta del 279
tempo di due metà 298
tempo di quattro quarti 298
tempo di tre quarti 298
tempo libero all'aria aperta 528
tempo, carta del 38, 39
tempo, controllo del 311
tempo, indicazioni di 298
tempo, misura del 424
tempo, stato presente del 39
tenda a cupola 529
tenda a due posti 528
tenda a igloo 529
tenda a un posto 529
tenda canadese 529
tenda coprifinestra 528
tenda da campo 528
tenda da cucina 528
tenda di tipo familiare 528
tenda interna 528, 529
tende, esempi di 528
tendenza barometrica 39
tendicollo 245
tendina divisoria 464
tendina parasole avvolgibile 356
tennis 490
tennis da tavolo 493
tennis, scarpa da 242
tennista 492
tensione, aumento di 402, 408
tensione, chiavi di 308
tensione, corda di 297
tensione, diminuzione di 402, 413
tensione, primo aumento di 413
tensione, secondo aumento di 413
tensore della fascia lata 96
tentacolo 72
tentacolo oculare 72
tenuta, mastice di 196
tenuta, valvola di 196
tepee 288
terapie, stanza per le 463, 465
tergale 200
tergale, base del 200
tergicristallo 348, 355
tergicristallo, comando del 354
terminal dei passeggeri 389, 390
terminal satellite dei passeggeri 389
terminale 198, 210, 273
terminale della messa a terra 322
terminale di messa a terra 198
terminale di pagamento elettronico 443
terminale di scarico 351
terminale per il pagamento elettronico 121
terminali di collegamento delle antenne 322
terminali di collegamento delle casse acustiche 322
terminazione nervosa 114
termini comuni 58, 59
termite 69
termometri clinici 461
termometro 404, 424
termometro a lettura istantanea 171
termometro a mercurio 461
termometro clinico 424
termometro del forno 171
termometro digitale 461
termometro per carne 171
termometro per zucchero 171
termopausa 37
termosfera 37
termostato 178, 208, 211, 212, 213
termostato di sicurezza 213
termostato regolabile 179
terna 399
Terra 2, 3, 4, 5, 14
terra battuta 492
Terra del Fuoco 17
Terra della Regina Maud 15
Terra di Marie Byrd 15
Terra di Wilkes 15
terra, lingua di 35
Terra, orbita della 4, 5
terra, spinotto di messa a 198
Terra, struttura della 26
terra, terminale di messa a 198
Terranova, Isola di 16
terrapieno 342
terrazza 391
terrazza scoperta 387
terremoto 27
terrina 174
terza 298
terza base 474
terza base (posizione) 474
terza falange 114
terza linea 482
terzino 485
terzino destro 481
terzino di destra 484
terzino di sinistra 484
terzino sinistro 481
tesa 238, 239
tessuto adiposo 113, 114
tessuto connettivo 114
tessuto elastico 246
tessuto sottocutaneo 114
testa 6, 93, 95, 103, 111, 220, 221, 223, 229, 272, 492, 494, 503, 505, 536
testa a croce 221
testa bombata 221
testa concava 221
testa d'albero 519
testa del femore 99
testa del martinetto elevatore 396
testa del rotore 395
testa dell'omero 99
testa di gatto 87
testa di iniezione del fango 403
testa di taglio 341
testa non svitabile 221
testa orientabile 224
testa piatta 221
testa quadra, punta a 221
testa ribaltabile 176
testa tonda 221
testata 313
testatina 313
teste, tipi di 221
tester di presa 217
testicoli 71
testicolo 111
testiera 204, 205
testimone 36, 472
testimone, zona del passaggio del 472
testimoni, banco dei 440
testina 271, 301
testina di lettura/scrittura 333
testina rotante 271
Teti 3
tetto 183, 193, 283, 349, 361, 401
tetto a vetro 188
tetto di vetro 435
tetto galleggiante 404
tettoia 528
tettoia vetrata 374
tettuccio 361
tettuccio apribile 349
tettuccio di protezione 396
thermos 532
tibia 78, 98
tibiale anteriore 96
Tifone 43
tight end 485
tiglio 148
tigre 89
timbro di gomma 338
timbro, selettore del 311
timer 501
timo 142
timone 13, 383, 384, 386, 412, 520
timone di direzione 393
timone di profondità 393
timone, barra del 520
timone, pala del 384
timoneria 384
Timor Orientale 452
timpani 295
timpano 75, 182, 279, 285, 308
timpano, montante del 187
tinello 188
tintura per capelli 267
tipi di eclissi 4, 5
tipi di infiorescenze 57
tipi di mazze 505
tipi di movimenti 470
tipi di parquet 190
tipi di punte 221
tipi di teste 221
tipi di vagoni passeggeri 376
tipo di carburante 346
tipo di nube alta 39
tipo di nube bassa 39
tipo di nube media 39
tirante 196, 262, 308, 344, 528
tirante a vite 308, 498
tirante del braccio 397
tirante della cordiera 308
tirante, regolatore del 528
tisane 148
Titania 3
Titano 3
Titicaca, Lago 17
titolare, firma del 441
titolare, nome del 441
titoli dei film 294
titolo 313
titolo a caratteri cubitali 313
Tlaloc, tempio di 283
tocco 239
Togo 451
toilette 437, 440, 443, 445, 463, 465
toilette degli uomini 439
toilette delle donne 439
toilette per i clienti 438
Tolosa, salame di 156
tom tom 308
tomaia 240, 263
tomatilli 128
tombolo 35
Tonga 453
toni alti, regolatore dei 325
toni alti, regolazione dei 303
toni bassi, regolatore dei 325
toni bassi, regolazione dei 303
toni, regolazione dei 303
tonno 160
tonsilla 116
tonsilla linguale 118
tonsilla palatina 118
top 258
topinambur 124
topo campagnolo 82
toque 239
torace 67, 68, 92, 94
Torah, rotoli della 447
torcia 456
tornado 43
tornelli di entrata 378
tornelli di uscita 378
toro 429
torre 284, 412, 413, 470
torre a traliccio 397
torre angolare 282
torre campanaria 285
torre di controllo 388
torre di controllo, cabina della 388
torre di fiancheggiamento 282
torre di guida 345
torre di lavaggio 214
torre di perforazione 403, 404
torre di raffreddamento 402
torre per i tuffi 518
torre per uffici 435
torre trasmittente 316
torrente montano 29
Torres, Strettodi 15
torretta 282, 284, 285, 400
torretta, calotta della 420
torsolo 58
torta, teglia per 172
tortellini 146
tortiera 172
tortilla 145
tostapane 178
totale 423
touch pad 336
touch pad, pulsante del 336
touch screen 337
trabeazione 185, 279
tracciamento, filo di 225
trachea 105
tracolla 276, 320, 505
tracolla, borsa a 276
tracolla, bottone della 303
traforo 285
traghetto 381
trago 115
traguardo 533
tralcio 62
traliccio, torre a 397
tramoggia di caricamento 364
trampoliere, uccello 79
trampolino 184
trampolino di 1 metro 518
trampolino di 3 metri 518
transatlantico 386
transazione, fessura di registrazione della 442
transazione, ricevuta della 443
transazioni commerciali 335
transetto 285
trapano elettrico 228
trapano senza fili 228
trapezio 96, 97, 429
trapezio, abito a 252
trapiantatoio 232

MASTERPLOTS
FIFTEEN-VOLUME
COMBINED EDITION

Volume One
Abbe-Barb

Masterplots

DIGESTS OF WORLD LITERATURE

FIFTEEN-VOLUME COMBINED EDITION

VOLUME ONE

ABBE-BARB

Edited by FRANK N. MAGILL Story Editor DAYTON KOHLER

CURTIS BOOKS
A division of
The Curtis Publishing Company
Philadelphia . New York

THE WORK ALSO APPEARS UNDER THE TITLE OF

MASTERPIECES OF WORLD LITERATURE IN DIGEST FORM

PREFACE

The array of literature represented in this fifteen-volume set is drawn from the vast reservoir of literary achievements which has been accumulating since the legendary beginnings of Western civilizations. All the great literature is not here; perhaps all that is here is not great. But these works are representative of the places and the times from which they sprang and they have helped to tint the fabric which makes up the composite imprint of our culture. Romance and adventure, laughter and illusion, dreams and desperate hopes, fear and angry resentment — these things have prodded men's minds as they walked toward our century. Their insight is our heritage.

Along with this heritage, our generation has fallen heir to a Busy Age. Never in history has there been so much competition for the attention of the average individual. But although ours is a Busy Age, unparalleled technological advancements have made it an age in which the chances for enlightenment and cultural development, at all levels, have never before been approached even remotely. Out of this increased "exposure" must surely come a more intellectually alert society. From such a society we may reasonably expect an acceleration of our cultural development. It is in the light of all these circumstances that a work such as MASTERPLOTS can have a place and a purpose.

The fifteen-volume Combined Edition of MASTERPLOTS comprises a collection of digests and essay-reviews covering 1,510 titles from world literature. This work is not an anthology or a collection of "reprints." The two million words of material it contains were newly written expressly for this set. Two styles are employed: the synopsis and the essay-review. 1,287 of the entries are handled as synopses, 223 as essay-reviews. Most of the essays are devoted to poetry, philosophy, and other types of literature that have no plots to summarize.

Designed primarily for reference, the format of MASTERPLOTS is styled and standardized to afford maximum information in the quickest time. Each of the digests is preceded by carefully checked, concisely stated reference data which furnish at a glance the type of work, authorship, type of plot, time of plot, locale, and first publication date. Following this will be found a list of principal characters and their relationships, often a highly useful feature. Next is the *Critique,* a short, incisive critical analysis of the original book. Finally there is the plot-summary, given as a well-rounded story and devoid of quotations from the original work. Editorial comments having been confined to the *Critique,* the reader is afforded an uninterrupted opportunity to study the action, characterizations, and development of the theme as the plot-story progresses. For clarity, a character is usually referred to by one designated name throughout the digest. Stories are arranged alphabetically by title. They average twelve to fifteen hundred words in length, though some exceed twenty-five hundred words.

In contrast to the plot-summaries, the 223 essay-reviews sometimes include quotations from the original works to illustrate salient points. This is especially true of those critical articles dealing with poetry. It will be noted that some novels and plays are handled as essay-reviews instead of plot-summaries. Sometimes such a procedure was followed so that a general discussion of the author's other work could be included in the article dealing with a specific title. In a few cases the essay-review method was employed in compliance with the wishes expressed by authors or copyright owners who preferred to be represented in essay-reviews rather than plot-summaries.

A total of 753 authors are presented in the fifteen-volume Combined Edition of MASTERPLOTS. The range is from Homer and Hesiod to the present day and such wide author representation assures the reference value of MASTERPLOTS. In keeping with the interest ratio, however, later writers predominate. More than one-third of the authors included were active in the twentieth century. Forty-one are winners of the Nobel Prize in Literature. A complete Author Index appears at the end of Volume Fifteen.

Of primary importance from the beginning was the selection of titles intended for inclusion in MASTERPLOTS. Interests and requirements vary, but almost any worth-while literary work will influence in some measure the writings that follow it and for this reason a number of titles of historical significance were chosen regardless of whether they still enjoy a wide audience today. In almost every case living authors were consulted about their own books which were under consideration. Because the relative merit of contemporary writing is likely to be a subject of some controversy, the assistance of authors themselves concerning their own works was valuable.

Consultations with specialists here and abroad have resulted in the inclusion of titles which are important but which are often overlooked when standard book lists are compiled. For example, a number of excellent but little-known Spanish and Latin American works are represented, some of which have been translated into English only recently. We have also drawn, to a small degree, on the vast reservoir of Oriental literature, an area of world culture long neglected by Western readers. However, we are now in an age of world-wide cultural intercourse, a force that —happily—transcends temporary political considerations, and as the wisdom, the humanity, the delights of Oriental literature come to the attention of the mass Western audience, interest in this field is sure to widen.

Actual preparation of this work required an enormous amount of active assistance from a carefully selected staff that included scores of English Faculty associates chosen from dozens of universities and colleges throughout the United States. I wish to express my appreciation for the able and cheerful assistance received from these staff members, some of whom have been active in the project continuously since its inception.

Throughout the preparation of this work the cooperation of authors, publishers, agents, and literary trustees has been solicited and I wish to acknowledge the assistance received from these sources. Copyright notices and credit lines appear as footnotes accompanying the appropriate titles.

This Preface would be incomplete without special reference to Story Editor Dayton Kohler's masterful survey of world literature entitled "Books and Reading," which appears on pages xxxi-lxi in the front part of this volume. Professor Kohler's brief, lucid treatment of his subject is superior to any we have seen. It is "must" reading for all those who are interested in a concise, erudite guide to the major currents of world literature from Homer to the most recent Nobel Prize winner.

PREFACE

Some will find in the pages of MASTERPLOTS a pleasant renewal of an old acquaintance, a chance meeting with an almost forgotten literary friend. Others may wish to pursue further an interest encountered here for the first time. In either case, this work will have served its purpose.

FRANK N. MAGILL

COMPLETE LIST OF CONTENTS

Abbé Constantine, The — *Halévy*
Abe Lincoln in Illinois — *Sherwood*
Abraham and Isaac — *Unknown*
Abraham Lincoln — *Sandburg*
Absalom, Absalom! — *Faulkner*
Absalom and Achitophel — *Dryden*
Absentee, The — *Edgeworth*
Acharnians, The — *Aristophanes*
Adam Bede — *G. Eliot*
Addresses — *Lincoln*
Admirable Crichton, The — *Barrie*
Adolphe — *Constant*
Aeneid, The — *Virgil*
Aesop's Fables — *Aesop*
Against the Grain — *Huysmans*
Age of Innocence, The — *Wharton*
Agnes Grey — *A. Brontë*
Ajax — *Sophocles*
Al filo del agua — *Yáñez*
Alcestis — *Euripides*
Alchemist, The — *Jonson*
Aleck Maury, Sportsman — *Gordon*
Alice Adams — *Tarkington*
Alice in Wonderland — *Carroll*
All Fools — *Chapman*
All for Love — *Dryden*
All Men Are Brothers — *Shih Nai-an*
All Quiet on the Western Front — *Remarque*
All the King's Men — *Warren*
All's Well That Ends Well — *Shakespeare*
Almayer's Folly — *Conrad*
Amadís de Gaul — *Lobeira*
Ambassadors, The — *H. James*
Amelia — *Fielding*
American, The — *H. James*
American Tragedy, An — *Dreiser*
Amphitryon — *Plautus*
Amphitryon 38 — *Giraudoux*
Anabasis — *Perse*
Anabasis, The — *Xenophon*
Anatomy of Melancholy, The — *Burton*
And Quiet Flows the Don — *Sholokhov*
Andersen's Fairy Tales — *Andersen*
Andria — *Terence*
Andromache — *Euripides*
Andromache — *Racine*
Ángel Guerra — *Pérez Galdós*
Anna Christie — *O'Neill*
Anna Karenina — *Tolstoy*
Anna of the Five Towns — *Bennett*
Annals of Tacitus, The — *Tacitus*
Annals of the Parish — *Galt*
Annals of the Roman People — *Livy*
Anthony Adverse — *Allen*
Antigone — *Sophocles*
Antiquary, The — *Scott*
Antony and Cleopatra — *Shakespeare*
Apologia pro Vita Sua — *Newman*
Apology for the Life of Colley Cibber, Comedian, An — *Cibber*
Apostle, The — *Asch*
Apple of the Eye, The — *Wescott*
Appointment in Samarra — *O'Hara*
Arabian Nights' Entertainments, The — *Unknown*
Arbitration, The — *Menander*
Arcadia — *Sidney*
Argenis — *Barclay*
Arme Heinrich, Der — *Hartmann von Aue*
Arne — *Björnson*
Arrowsmith — *S. Lewis*
Ars Poetica — *Horace*
Artamène — *Scudéry*

Artamonov Business, The — *Gorky*
As I Lay Dying — *Faulkner*
As You Like It — *Shakespeare*
Ash Wednesday — *T. S. Eliot*
Ashes — *Zeromski*
At the Sign of the Reine Pédauque — *France*
Atala — *Chateaubriand*
Atalanta in Calydon — *Swinburne*
Aucassin and Nicolette — *Unknown*
Autobiography of Benjamin Franklin, The — *Franklin*
Autobiography of Benvenuto Cellini, The — *Cellini*
Autocrat of the Breakfast-Table, The — *Holmes*
Awakening of Spring, The — *Wedekind*
Axe, The — *Undset*

Babbitt — *S. Lewis*
Bacchae, The — *Euripides*
Back to Methuselah — *Shaw*
Bambi — *Salten*
Barabbas — *Lagerkvist*
Barber of Seville, The — *Beaumarchais*
Barchester Towers — *Trollope*
Barnaby Rudge — *Dickens*
Baron Münchausen's Narrative — *Raspe*
Barren Ground — *Glasgow*
Barry Lyndon — *Thackeray*
Bartholomew Fair — *Jonson*
Batouala — *Maran*
Bay of Silence, The — *Mallea*
Beach of Falesá, The — *Stevenson*
Beauchamp's Career — *Meredith*
Beaux' Stratagem, The — *Farquhar*
Beaver Coat, The — *Hauptmann*
Beggars' Bush, The — *Fletcher* and *Massinger*
Beggar's Opera, The — *Gay*
Bel-Ami — *Maupassant*
Bell for Adano, A — *Hersey*
Ben Hur: A Tale of the Christ — *Wallace*
Benito Cereno — *Melville*
Beowulf — *Unknown*
Bérénice — *Racine*
Betrothed, The — *Manzoni*
Between the Acts — *Woolf*
Bevis of Hampton — *Unknown*
Beyond Good and Evil — *Nietzsche*
Beyond Human Power, II — *Björnson*
Big Sky, The — *Guthrie*
Biglow Papers, The — *Lowell*
Billy Budd — *Melville*
Birds, The — *Aristophanes*
Black Arrow, The — *Stevenson*
Black Lamb and Grey Falcon — *R. West*
Black Valley — *Wast*
Bleak House — *Dickens*
Blithedale Romance, The — *Hawthorne*
Blood Wedding — *García Lorca*
Blot in the 'Scutcheon, A — *R. Browning*
Bohemians of the Latin Quarter, The — *Murger*
Bondman, The — *Massinger*
Bonds of Interest, The — *Benavente*
Book of Songs — *Heine*
Boris Godunov — *Pushkin*
Bourgeois Gentleman, The — *Molière*
Bouvard and Pécuchet — *Flaubert*
Bracknels, The — *Reid*
Braggart Soldier, The — *Plautus*
Brand — *Ibsen*
Brave New World — *A. Huxley*
Bread and Wine — *Silone*
Bride of Lammermoor, The — *Scott*
Brideshead Revisited — *Waugh*
Bridge, The — *Crane*
Bridge of San Luis Rey, The — *Wilder*
Britannicus — *Racine*
Broad and Alien Is the World — *Alegría*
Broken Jug, The — *Kleist*
Brothers, The — *Terence*
Brothers Ashkenazi, The — *Singer*
Brothers Karamazov, The — *Dostoevski*
Brushwood Boy, The — *Kipling*
Brut, The — *Layamon*

COMPLETE LIST OF CONTENTS

Buddenbrooks — *Mann*
Bulwark, The — *Dreiser*
Bussy D'Ambois — *Chapman*

Cabala, The — *Wilder*
Cabin, The — *Blasco Ibáñez*
Cadmus — *Folk tradition*
Caesar and Cleopatra — *Shaw*
Caesar or Nothing — *Baroja*
Cain — *Byron*
Cakes and Ale — *Maugham*
Caleb Williams — *Godwin*
Call of the Wild, The — *London*
Camille — *Dumas,* fils
Campaspe — *Lyly*
Candida — *Shaw*
Candide — *Voltaire*
Canterbury Tales, The — *Chaucer*
Cantos — *Pound*
Captain Horatio Hornblower — *Forester*
Captain Singleton — *Defoe*
Captains Courageous — *Kipling*
Captain's Daughter, The — *Pushkin*
Captives, The — *Plautus*
Carmen — *Mérimée*
Carmina — *Catullus*
Case of Sergeant Grischa, The — *Zweig*
Cass Timberlane — *S. Lewis*
Caste — *Robertson*
Castle, The — *Kafka*
Castle of Fratta, The— *Nievo*
Castle of Otranto, The — *Horace Walpole*
Castle Rackrent — *Edgeworth*
Casuals of the Sea — *McFee*
Catiline — *Jonson*
Cavalleria Rusticana — *Verga*
Cawdor — *Jeffers*
Cecilia — *Burney*
Celestina — *Rojas*
Cenci, The — *P. B. Shelley*
Cesar Birotteau — *Balzac*
Chainbearer, The — *Cooper*
Changeling, The — *Middleton* and *Rowley*
Charles Demailly — *The Goncourts*
Charles O'Malley — *Lever*
Charterhouse of Parma, The — *Stendhal*
Chaste Maid in Cheapside, A — *Middleton*
Chéri — *Colette*
Cherry Orchard, The — *Chekhov*
Chevalier of the Maison Rouge, The — *Dumas,* père
Children of God — *Fisher*
Children of Herakles, The — *Euripides*
Children of the Ghetto — *Zangwill*
Chita — *Hearn*
Chousans, The — *Balzac*
Christmas Carol, A — *Dickens*
Chronicle of the Conquest of Granada, A — *Irving*
Chronicles of Froissart — *Froissart*
Cicero's Orations — *Cicero*
Cid, The — *Corneille*
Cinna — *Corneille*
Cinq-Mars — *Vigny*
Circle of Chalk, The — *Unknown*
Clarissa Harlowe — *S. Richardson*
Claudius the God — *Graves*
Clayhanger Trilogy, The — *Bennett*
Cligés — *Chrétien de Troyes*
Cloister and the Hearth, The — *Reade*
Closed Garden, The — *J. Green*
Clouds, The — *Aristophanes*
Cocktail Party, The — *T. S. Eliot*
Collected Poems — *de la Mare*
Collected Poems, 1934-1952 — *Thomas*
Collegians, The — *Griffin*
Colomba — *Mérimée*
Comedy of Errors, The — *Shakespeare*
Commentaries — *Caesar*
Compleat Angler, The — *Walton*
Comrades — *Strindberg*
Comus — *Milton*
Confessions — *Augustine*
Confessions — *Rousseau*

Confessions of an English Opium Eater — *De Quincey*
Confessions of Felix Krull, Confidence Man — *Mann*
Confidence Man, The — *Melville*
Coningsby — *Disraeli*
Conjure Woman, The — *Chesnutt*
Connecticut Yankee at King Arthur's Court, A — *Twain*
Conquistador — *MacLeish*
Conscious Lovers, The — *Steele*
Consolation of Philosophy, The — *Boethius*
Consuelo — *Sand*
Copperhead, The — *Frederic*
Coriolanus — *Shakespeare*
Corsican Brothers, The — *Dumas,* père
Cossacks, The — *Tolstoy*
Count of Monte-Cristo, The — *Dumas,* père
Counterfeiters, The — *Gide*
Countess of Charny, The — *Dumas,* père
Country Doctor, A — *Jewett*
Country Doctor, The — *Balzac*
Country House, The — *Galsworthy*
Country of the Pointed Firs, The — *Jewett*
Country Wife, The — *Wycherley*
Courtesan, The — *Aretino*
Courtship of Miles Standish, The — *Longfellow*
Cousin Bette — *Balzac*
Cousin Pons — *Balzac*
Coxcomb, The — *Beaumont* and *Fletcher*
Cradle Song, The — *Martínez Sierra*
Cranford — *Gaskell*
Cream of the Jest, The — *Cabell*
Crime and Punishment — *Dostoevski*
Crime of Sylvestre Bonnard, The — *France*
Crisis, The — *W. Churchill*
Crisis, The — *Paine*
Critic, The — *Sheridan*
Critique of Pure Reason — *Kant*
Crock of Gold, The — *Stephens*
Crome Yellow — *A. Huxley*
Crotchet Castle — *Peacock*
Cruise of the Cachalot, The — *Bullen*
Cry, The Beloved Country — *Paton*
Cudjo's Cave — *Trowbridge*
Cupid and Psyche — *Folk tradition*
Custom of the Country, The — *Wharton*
Cyclops, The — *Euripides*
Cymbeline — *Shakespeare*
Cyrano de Bergerac — *Rostand*

Daisy Miller — *H. James*
Dame Care — *Sudermann*
Damnation of Theron Ware, The — *Frederic*
Dance of Death, The — *Strindberg*
Dangerous Acquaintances — *Laclos*
Daniel Deronda — *G. Eliot*
Daphnis and Chloë — *Longus*
Dark Journey, The — *J. Green*
Dark Laughter — *S. Anderson*
Darkness at Noon — *Koestler*
David Copperfield — *Dickens*
David Harum — *Westcott*
De rerum natura — *Lucretius*
Dead Fires — *Lins do Rêgo*
Dead Souls — *Gogol*
Dear Brutus — *Barrie*
Death Comes for the Archbishop — *Cather*
Death in Venice — *Mann*
Death of a Hero — *Aldington*
Death of a Salesman — *Miller*
Death of Ivan Ilyich, The — *Tolstoy*
Death of the Gods, The — *Merejkowski*
Death of the Heart, The — *Bowen*
Death of Virgil, The — *Broch*
Debit and Credit — *Freytag*
Decameron, The — *Boccaccio*
Decline and Fall — *Waugh*
Deephaven — *Jewett*
Deerslayer, The — *Cooper*

COMPLETE LIST OF CONTENTS

Defense of the Constitutions, A — *J. Adams*
Deirdre — *Stephens*
Deirdre of the Sorrows — *Synge*
Delphine — *Staël*
Delta Wedding — *Welty*
Desire Under the Elms — *O'Neill*
Destiny Bay — *Byrne*
Devil's Elixir, The — *Hoffmann*
Devotion of the Cross, The — *Calderón*
Diable boiteau, Le — *Le Sage*
Dialogue des héros de roman — *Boileau-Despréaux*
Dialogues of Plato, The — *Plato*
Diana of the Crossways — *Meredith*
Diary — *Evelyn*
Diary — *Pepys*
Diary of a Country Priest, The — *Bernanos*
Digby Grand — *Whyte-Melville*
Disciple, The — *Bourget*
Divan, The — *Hāfiz*
Divine Comedy, The — *Dante*
Divine Fire, The — *M. Sinclair*
Divine Love and Wisdom — *Swedenborg*
Doctor Faustus — *Mann*
Doctor Faustus — *Marlowe*
Doctor in Spite of Himself, The — *Molière*
Dr. Jekyll and Mr. Hyde — *Stevenson*
Doctor Pascal — *Zola*
Doctor Thorne — *Trollope*
Dodsworth — *S. Lewis*
Doll's House, A — *Ibsen*
Dombey and Son — *Dickens*
Dominique — *Fromentin*
Don Carlos — *Schiller*
Don Flows Home to the Sea, The — *Sholokhov*
Don Juan — *Byron*
Don Juan — *Molière*
Don Juan Tenorio — *Zorilla*
Don Quixote de la Mancha — *Cervantes*
Don Segundo Sombra — *Güiraldes*
Doña Barbara — *Gallegos*
Doña Perfecta — *Pérez Galdós*
Double-Dealer, The — *Congreve*
Down There — *Huysmans*
Downfall, The — *Zola*
Dracula — *Stoker*
Dragon Seed — *Buck*
Dream of the Red Chamber — *Tsao Hsueh-chin*
Drink — *Zola*
Drums — *Boyd*
Drums Along the Mohawk — *Edmonds*
Duchess of Malfi, The — *Webster*
Duino Elegies — *Rilke*
Dunciad, The — *Pope*
Dynasts, The — *Hardy*

Earth — *Zola*
East of Eden — *Steinbeck*
Eastward Ho! — *Chapman* with *Jonson*
Ebony and Ivory — *L. Powys*
Ecclesiazusae, The — *Aristophanes*
Edmund Campion — *Waugh*
Education of Henry Adams, The — *H. Adams*
Edward the Second — *Marlowe*
Effi Briest — *Fontane*
Egmont — *Goethe*
Egoist, The — *Meredith*
Elective Affinities — *Goethe*
Electra — *Euripides*
Emigrants, The — *Bojer*
Emigrants of Ahadarra, The — *Carleton*
Émile — *Rousseau*
Emilia Galotti — *Lessing*
Eminent Victorians — *Strachey*
Emma — *Austen*
Emperor Jones, The — *O'Neill*
Endymion — *Lyly*
Enemy of the People, An — *Ibsen*
Enoch Arden — *Tennyson*
Enormous Room, The — *Cummings*
Enquiry Concerning Human Understanding, An — *Hume*

Epic of Gilgamesh, The — *Unknown*
Epigrams of Martial — *Martial*
Epinicia, The — *Pindar*
Epitaph of a Small Winner — *Machado de Assis*
Erec and Enide — *Chrétien de Troyes*
Erewhon — *Butler*
Essais — *Montaigne*
Essay Concerning Human Understanding, An — *Locke*
Essays — *Bacon*
Essays: First and Second Series — *Emerson*
Essays of Elia *and* Last Essays of Elia — *Lamb*
Esther Waters — *G. Moore*
Ethan Frome — *Wharton*
Ethics — *Spinoza*
Eugene Aram — *Bulwer-Lytton*
Eugene Onegin — *Pushkin*
Eugenie Grandet — *Balzac*
Eunuch, The — *Terence*
Euphues and His England — *Lyly*
Euphues, the Anatomy of Wit — *Lyly*
Evan Harrington — *Meredith*
Evangeline — *Longfellow*
Eve of St. Agnes, The — *Keats*
Evelina — *Burney*
Every Man in His Humour — *Jonson*
Every Man out of His Humour — *Jonson*
Everyman — *Unknown*
Exemplary Novels — *Cervantes*
Exiles — *Joyce*

Fable, A — *Faulkner*
Fables — *La Fontaine*
Faerie Queene, The — *Spenser*
Fair Maid of Perth, The — *Scott*
Faithful Shepherdess, The — *Fletcher*
Fall of the House of Usher, The — *Poe*
Family at Gilje, The — *Lie*
Family Reunion, The — *T. S. Eliot*
Far Away and Long Ago — *Hudson*
Far From the Madding Crowd — *Hardy*
Farewell to Arms, A — *Hemingway*
Father, The — *Strindberg*
Father Goriot — *Balzac*
Fathers and Sons — *Turgenev*
Faust — *Goethe*
Federalist, The — *Hamilton, Madison,* and *Jay*
Felix Holt, Radical — *G. Eliot*
Fêtes Galantes and Other Poems — *Verlaine*
Fields, The — *Richter*
File No. 113 — *Gaboriau*
Financier, The — *Dreiser*
Finn Cycle, The— *Unknown*
Finnegans Wake — *Joyce*
Fisher Maiden, The — *Björnson*
Five Women Who Loved Love — *Ibara Saikaku*
Flowers of Evil — *Baudelaire*
Foma Gordyeeff — *Gorky*
Fool of Quality, The — *Brooke*
For Whom the Bell Tolls — *Hemingway*
Forsyte Saga, The — *Galsworthy*
Fortitude — *Hugh Walpole*
Fortress, The — *Hugh Walpole*
Fortunata and Jacinta — *Pérez Galdós*
Fortunes of Nigel, The — *Scott*
Fortunes of Richard Mahony, The — *H. H. Richardson*
Forty Days of Musa Dagh, The — *Werfel*
Four Quartets — *T. S. Eliot*
Framley Parsonage — *Trollope*
Frankenstein — *M. Shelley*
Fraternity — *Galsworthy*
French Revolution, The — *Carlyle*
Friar Bacon and Friar Bungay—*R. Greene*
Frithiof's Saga — *Tegnér*
Frogs, The — *Aristophanes*
Fruit of the Tree, The — *Wharton*
Funeral, The — *Steele*

Gambler, The — *Dostoevski*
Garden, The — *Strong*
Gardener's Dog, The — *Vega*

COMPLETE LIST OF CONTENTS

Gargantua and Pantagruel — *Rabelais*
Gaucho: Martín Fierro, The — *Hernández*
"Genius," The — *Dreiser*
Gentleman Dancing Master, The — *Wycherley*
Gentleman Usher, The — *Chapman*
Georgia Scenes — *Longstreet*
Germinal — *Zola*
Germinie Lacerteux — *The Goncourts*
Gettysburg — *Singmaster*
Ghosts — *Ibsen*
Giants in the Earth — *Rölvaag*
Gil Blas of Santillane — *Le Sage*
Gilded Age, The — *Twain* and *Warner*
Glass Key, The — *Hammett*
Glass Menagerie, The — *T. Williams*
Goat Song — *Werfel*
Gods Are Athirst, The — *France*
Gold Bug, The — *Poe*
Golden Ass of Lucius Apuleius, The — *Apuleius*
Golden Bowl, The — *H. James*
Golden Boy — *Odets*
Gondoliers, The — *Gilbert*
Gone With the Wind — *M. Mitchell*
Good Companions, The — *Priestley*
Good Earth, The — *Buck*
Goodbye, Mr. Chips — *Hilton*
Gorboduc — *Norton* and *Sackville*
Grand Hotel — *Baum*
Grandissimes, The — *Cable*
Grandmothers, The — *Wescott*
Grapes of Wrath, The — *Steinbeck*
Great Expectations — *Dickens*
Great Galeoto, The — *Echegaray*
Great Gatsby, The — *Fitzgerald*
Great Meadow, The — *Roberts*
Great Testament, The — *Villon*
Great Valley, The — *Johnston*
Green Bay Tree, The — *Bromfield*
Green Grow the Lilacs — *Riggs*
Green Mansions — *Hudson*
Green Mountain Boys, The — *Thompson*
Grettir the Strong — *Unknown*
Gringa, La — *Sánchez*
Growth of the Soil — *Hamsun*
Grüne Heinrich, Der — *Keller*
Guard of Honor — *Cozzens*
Guest the One-Eyed — *Gunnarsson*
Gulliver's Travels — *Swift*
Guy Mannering — *Scott*
Guy of Warwick — *Unknown*
Guzman de Alfarache — *Alemán*

Hajji Baba of Ispahan — *Morier*
Hakluyt's Voyages — *Hakluyt*
Hamlet, The — *Faulkner*
Hamlet, Prince of Denmark — *Shakespeare*
Handful of Dust, A — *Waugh*
Handley Cross — *Surtees*
Handy Andy — *Lover*
Hangman's House — *Byrne*
Hard Times — *Dickens*
Harmonium — *W. Stevens*
Harp of a Thousand Strings — *Davis*
Harp-Weaver and Other Poems, The — *Millay*
Havelok the Dane — *Unknown*
Hazard of New Fortunes, A — *Howells*
Headlong Hall — *Peacock*
Heart Is a Lonely Hunter, The — *McCullers*
Heart of Darkness — *Conrad*
Heart of Midlothian, The — *Scott*
Heart of the Matter, The — *G. Greene*
Heartbreak House — *Shaw*
Heat of the Day, The — *Bowen*
Heaven's My Destination — *Wilder*
Hedda Gabler — *Ibsen*
Heimskringla, The — *Sturluson*
Helen — *Euripides*
Henry Esmond — *Thackeray*
Henry the Eighth — *Shakespeare*
Henry the Fifth — *Shakespeare*
Henry the Fourth, Part One — *Shakespeare*

Henry the Fouth, Part Two — *Shakespeare*
Henry the Sixth, Part One — *Shakespeare*
Henry the Sixth, Part Two — *Shakespeare*
Henry the Sixth, Part Three — *Shakespeare*
Herakles Mad — *Euripides*
Hercules and His Twelve Labors — *Folk tradition*
Hereward the Wake — *C. Kingsley*
Hero of Our Time, A — *Lermontov*
Herself Surprised — *Cary*
Hesperides — *Herrick*
High Wind Rising, A — *Singmaster*
Hill of Dreams, The — *Machen*
Hillingdon Hall — *Surtees*
Hippolytus — *Euripides*
Historia calamitàtum — *Abélard*
History of Colonel Jacque, The — *Defoe*
History of England, The — *Macaulay*
History of Mr. Polly, The — *Wells*
History of New York, By Diedrich Knickerbocker, A — *Irving*
History of the Conquest of Mexico — *Prescott*
History of the Decline and Fall of the Roman Empire, The — *Gibbon*
History of the Peloponnesian War — *Thucydides*
History of the Persian Wars, The — *Herodotus*
Hiza-Kurige — *Jippensha Ikku*
H. M. S. Pinafore — *Gilbert*
Holy Terrors, The — *Cocteau*
Honest Whore, Part One, The — *Dekker*
Honest Whore, Part Two, The — *Dekker*
Honey in the Horn — *Davis*
Hoosier Schoolmaster, The — *Eggleston*
Horace — *Corneille*
Horse's Mouth, The — *Cary*
Horseshoe Robinson — *Kennedy*
House by the Churchyard, The — *Le Fanu*
House by the Medlar Tree, The — *Verga*
House in Paris, The — *Bowen*
House of Atreus, The — *Aeschylus*
House of Gentlefolk, A — *Turgenev*
House of Mirth, The — *Wharton*
House of the Seven Gables, The — *Hawthorne*
House With the Green Shutters, The — *G. Douglas*
How Green Was My Valley — *Llewellyn*
Howards End — *Forster*
Huasipungo — *Icaza*
Huckleberry Finn — *Twain*
Hudibras — *Butler*
Hugh Wynne, Free Quaker — *S. W. Mitchell*
Human Comedy, The — *Saroyan*
Humphry Clinker — *Smollett*
Hunchback of Notre Dame, The — *Hugo*
Hunger — *Hamsun*
Huon de Bordeaux — *Unknown*
Hyde Park — *Shirley*
Hypatia — *C. Kingsley*
Hypochondriac, The — *Molière*

I, Claudius — *Graves*
I Speak for Thaddeus Stevens — *Singmaster*
Iceland Fisherman, An — *Loti*
Ides of March, The — *Wilder*
Idiot, The — *Dostoevski*
Idylls of the King, The — *Tennyson*
If Winter Comes — *Hutchinson*
Iliad, The — *Homer*
Imaginary Conversations — *Landor*
Imitation of Christ, The — *Thomas à Kempis*
Importance of Being Earnest, The — *Wilde*
In Dubious Battle — *Steinbeck*
In the Wilderness — *Undset*
Inazuma-byôshi — *Santô Kyôden*

COMPLETE LIST OF CONTENTS

Independent People — *Laxness*
Indian Summer — *Howells*
Indiana — *Sand*
Inês de Castro — *Ferreira*
Informer, The — *O'Flaherty*
Innocent Voyage, The — *R. Hughes*
Inspector General, The — *Gogol*
Interpretation of Dreams, The — *Freud*
Intruder in the Dust — *Faulkner*
Invisible Man, The — *Wells*
Iolanthe — *Gilbert*
Ion — *Euripides*
Iphigenia in Aulis — *Euripides*
Iphigenia in Tauris — *Euripides*
Israel Potter — *Melville*
It Is Better than It Was — *Calderón*
It Is Worse than It Was — *Calderón*
Italian, The — *Radcliffe*
Itching Parrot, The — *Fernández de Lizardi*
Ivanhoe — *Scott*

Jack of Newberry — *Deloney*
Jack Sheppard — *Ainsworth*
Jalna — *de la Roche*
Jane Eyre — *C. Brontë*
Jason and the Golden Fleece — *Folk tradition*
Java Head — *Hergesheimer*
Jean-Christophe — *Rolland*
Jennie Gerhardt — *Dreiser*
Jerusalem Delivered — *Tasso*
Jew of Malta, The — *Marlowe*
Jewess of Toledo, The — *Grillparzer*
Joanna Godden — *Kaye-Smith*
John Brown's Body — *Benét*
John Halifax, Gentleman — *Mulock*
John Inglesant — *Shorthouse*
Jonathan Wild — *Fielding*
Jorrocks' Jaunts and Jollities — *Surtees*
Joseph Andrews — *Fielding*
Joseph Vance — *De Morgan*
Journey to the End of the Night — *Céline*
Journey's End — *Sherriff*
Jovial Crew, A — *Brome*
Jude the Obscure — *Hardy*
Judith Paris — *Hugh Walpole*
Julius Caesar — *Shakespeare*
Jungle, The — *U. Sinclair*
Jungle Books, The — *Kipling*
Juno and the Paycock — *O'Casey*
Jurgen — *Cabell*
Justice — *Galsworthy*

Kalevala, The — *Lönnrot*
Kapital, Das — *Marx*
Kate Fennigate — *Tarkington*
Kenilworth — *Scott*
Kidnapped — *Stevenson*
Kim — *Kipling*
King and No King, A — *Beaumont* and *Fletcher*
King John — *Bale*
King John — *Shakespeare*
King Lear — *Shakespeare*
King of the Golden River, The — *Ruskin*
King of the Mountains, The — *About*
King Paradox — *Baroja*
King Solomon's Mines — *Haggard*
King, the Greatest Alcalde, The — *Vega*
Kingdom of God, The — *Martínez Sierra*
Kings in Exile — *Daudet*
King's Row — *Bellamann*
Kipps — *Wells*
Knight of the Burning Pestle, The — *Beaumont*
Knights, The — *Aristophanes*
Kreutzer Sonata, The — *Tolstoy*
Kristin Lavransdatter — *Undset*

Lady from the Sea, The — *Ibsen*
Lady into Fox — *Garnett*
Lady of the Lake, The — *Scott*
Lady Windermere's Fan — *Wilde*
Lady's Not for Burning, The — *Fry*
L'Aiglon — *Rostand*
Lalla Rookh — *T. Moore*

L'Amorosa Fiammetta — *Boccaccio*
Last Athenian, The — *Rydberg*
Last Chronicle of Barset, The — *Trollope*
Last Days of Pompeii, The — *Bulwer-Lytton*
Last of Summer, The — *O'Brien*
Last of the Barons, The — *Bulwer-Lytton*
Last of the Mohicans, The — *Cooper*
Last of the Vikings, The — *Bojer*
Last Puritan, The — *Santayana*
Last Tycoon, The — *Fitzgerald*
Late George Apley, The — *Marquand*
Late Mattia Pascal, The — *Pirandello*
Lavengro — *Borrow*
Lay of the Last Minstrel, The — *Scott*
Lazarillo de Tormes — *Unknown*
Leaves of Grass — *Whitman*
Legend of Good Women, The — *Chaucer*
Legend of Sleepy Hollow, The — *Irving*
Legend of the Moor's Legacy — *Irving*
Legend of Tyl Ulenspiegel, The — *Coster*
Letters from an American Farmer — *Crèvecœur*
Letters from the Underworld — *Dostoevski*
Letters of Walpole, The — *Horace Walpole*
Letters to His Son — *Chesterfield*
Leviathan — *Hobbes*
Liber Amoris — *Hazlitt*
Lieh Kuo Chih — *Feng Meng-lung*
Life and Death of Mr. Badman, The — *Bunyan*
Life in London — *Egan*
Life Is a Dream — *Calderón*
Life of Nelson — *Southey*
Life of Samuel Johnson, LL.D., The — *Boswell*
Life on the Mississippi — *Twain*
Life With Father — *C. Day*
Ligeia — *Poe*
Light in August — *Faulkner*
Liliom — *Molnar*
Link, The — *Strindberg*
Lion of Flanders, The — *Conscience*
Little Clay Cart, The — *Shudraka*
Little Dorrit — *Dickens*
Little Foxes, The — *Hellman*
Little Minister, The — *Barrie*
Little Women — *Alcott*
Lives of the Caesars — *Suetonius*
Liza of Lambeth — *Maugham*
Long Journey, The — *Jensen*
Long Night, The — *Lytle*
Longest Journey, The — *Forster*
Look Homeward, Angel — *Wolfe*
Looking Backward — *Bellamy*
Lord Jim — *Conrad*
Lorna Doone — *Blackmore*
Lost Horizon — *Hilton*
Lost Illusions — *Balzac*
Lost Lady, A — *Cather*
Lost Weekend, The — *Jackson*
Love for Love — *Congreve*
Love in a Wood — *Wycherley*
Love's Labour's Lost — *Shakespeare*
Loving — *H. Green*
Lower Depths, The — *Gorky*
Loyalties — *Galsworthy*
Lucien Leuwen — *Stendhal*
Luck of Roaring Camp, The — *Harte*
Lusiad, The — *Camoëns*
Lysistrata — *Aristophanes*

Mabinogion, The — *Unknown*
Macbeth — *Shakespeare*
McTeague — *Norris*
Madame Bovary — *Flaubert*
Mademoiselle de Maupin — *Gautier*
Madras House, The — *Granville-Barker*
Madwoman of Chaillot, The — *Giraudoux*
Maggie: A Girl of the Streets — *Crane*
Magic Mountain, The — *Mann*
Magnalia Christi Americana — *Mather*
Magnificent Obsession, The — *L. C. Douglas*
Mahabharata, The — *Unknown*

COMPLETE LIST OF CONTENTS

Maid of Honour, The — *Massinger*
Maid's Tragedy, The — *Beaumont* and *Fletcher*
Main Street — *S. Lewis*
Main-Travelled Roads — *Garland*
Major Barbara — *Shaw*
Malcontent, The — *Marston*
Maltese Falcon, The — *Hammett*
Man Against the Sky, The — *Robinson*
Man and Superman — *Shaw*
Man of Feeling, The — *Mackenzie*
Man of Mode, The — *Etherege*
Man Who Was Thursday, The — *Chesterton*
Man With a Bull-Tongue Plow — *Stuart*
Man Without a Country, The — *Hale*
Manette Salomon — *The Goncourts*
Manfred — *Byron*
Manhattan Transfer — *Dos Passos*
Manon Lescaut — *Prévost*
Man's Fate — *Malraux*
Mansfield Park — *Austen*
Marble Faun, The — *Hawthorne*
Marching On — *Boyd*
Mardi — *Melville*
Maria Chapdelaine — *Hémon*
Maria Magdalena — *Hebbel*
Marianne — *Marivaux*
Marius the Epicurean — *Pater*
Market Harborough — *Whyte-Melville*
Marmion — *Scott*
Marriage à la Mode — *Dryden*
Marriage of Figaro, The — *Beaumarchais*
Marse Chan — *Page*
Martin Chuzzlewit — *Dickens*
Master Builder, The — *Ibsen*
Master of Ballantrae, The — *Stevenson*
Mastro-don Gesualdo — *Verga*
Max Havelaar — *Multatuli*
Maxims, The — *La Rochefoucauld*
Mayor of Casterbridge, The — *Hardy*
Mayor of Zalamea, The — *Calderón*
Measure for Measure — *Shakespeare*
Medea — *Euripides*
Meditations — *Marcus Aurelius*
Meek Heritage — *Sillanpää*
Melmoth the Wanderer — *Maturin*
Member of the Wedding, The — *McCullers*
Memoirs — *Casanova*
Memoirs of a Cavalier, The — *Defoe*
Memoirs of a Fox-Hunting man — *Sassoon*
Memoirs of a Midget — *de la Mare*
Memoirs of a Physician — *Dumas,* père
Memoirs of an Infantry Officer — *Sassoon*
Menaechmi, The — *Plautus*
Menteur, Le — *Corneille*
Merchant of Venice, The — *Shakespeare*
Merry Wives of Windsor, The — *Shakespeare*
Messer Marco Polo — *Byrne*
Metamorphoses, The — *Ovid*
Micah Clarke — *Doyle*
Michael and His Lost Angel — *Jones*
Mid-Channel — *Pinero*
Middlemarch — *G. Eliot*
Midsummer Night's Dream, A — *Shakespeare*
Mikado, The — *Gilbert*
Mill on the Floss, The — *G. Eliot*
Mill on the Po, The — *Bacchelli*
Ministry of Fear, The — *G. Greene*
Minna von Barnhelm — *Lessing*
Mirror for Witches, A — *Forbes*
Misanthrope, The — *Molière*
Miscellanies — *Cowley*
Miser, The — *Molière*
Misérables, Les — *Hugo*
Miss Julie — *Strindberg*
Miss Lonelyhearts — *N. West*
Miss Ravenel's Conversion — *De Forest*
Mr. Britling Sees It Through — *Wells*
Mr. Facey Romford's Hounds — *Surtees*
Mr. Midshipman Easy — *Marryat*
Mister Roberts — *Heggen*
Mr. Sponge's Sporting Tour — *Surtees*
Mr. Weston's Good Wine — *T. F. Powys*

Mrs. Dalloway — *Woolf*
Mrs. Dane's Defence — *Jones*
Mistress of the Inn, The — *Goldoni*
Mithridate — *Racine*
Moby Dick — *Melville*
Mock Astrologer, The — *Calderón*
Modern Chivalry — *Brackenridge*
Modern Comedy, A — *Galsworthy*
Modern Instance, A — *Howells*
Modern Midas, A — *Jókai*
Moll Flanders — *Defoe*
Monk, The — *M. G. Lewis*
Monkey— *Wu Ch'eng-en*
Monsieur Beaucaire — *Tarkington*
Monsieur d'Olive — *Chapman*
Monsieur Lecoq — *Gaboriau*
Mont-Oriol — *Maupassant*
Month in the Country, A — *Turgenev*
Moon and Sixpence, The — *Maugham*
Moonstone, The — *Collins*
Morte d'Arthur, Le — *Malory*
Mother, The — *Deledda*
Mother — *Gorky*
Mourning Becomes Electra — *O'Neill*
Much Ado About Nothing — *Shakespeare*
Murder in the Cathedral — *T. S. Eliot*
Mutiny on the Bounty — *Nordhoff* and *Hall*
My Ántonia — *Cather*
My Life and Hard Times — *Thurber*
Mysteries of Paris, The — *Sue*
Mysteries of Udolpho, The — *Radcliffe*
Mysterious Island, The — *Verne*
Mystery of Edwin Drood, The — *Dickens*

Naked Year, The — *Pilnyak*
Nana — *Zola*
Napoleon of Notting Hill, The — *Chesterton*
Narrative of Arthur Gordon Pym, The — *Poe*
Narrative of the Life of David Crockett, A — *Crockett*
Nathan the Wise — *Lessing*
Native Son — *Wright*
Nausea — *Sartre*
Nazarene, The — *Asch*
Nest of Simple Folk, A — *O'Faoláin*
New Atlantis — *Bacon*
New Grub Street, The — *Gissing*
New Héloïse, The — *Rousseau*
New Way to Pay Old Debts, A — *Massinger*
Newcomes, The — *Thackeray*
Nibelungenlied, The — *Unknown*
Nicholas Nickleby — *Dickens*
Nick of the Woods — *Bird*
Niels Lyhne — *Jacobsen*
Nigger of the Narcissus, The — *Conrad*
Night Flight — *Saint-Exupéry*
Night in the Luxembourg, A — *Gourmont*
Nightmare Abbey — *Peacock*
Nineteen Eighty-Four — *Orwell*
No Name — *Collins*
No Trifling With Love — *Musset*
Nocturne — *Swinnerton*
Northanger Abbey — *Austen*
Northern Lass, The — *Brome*
Nostromo — *Conrad*
Notes on the State of Virginia — *Jefferson*

O Pioneers! — *Cather*
Oblomov — *Goncharov*
Ode to Aphrodite — *Sappho*
Odyssey, The — *Homer*
Oedipus at Colonus — *Sophocles*
Oedipus Tyrannus — *Sophocles*
Of Human Bondage — *Maugham*
Of Mice and Men — *Steinbeck*
Of Time and the River — *Wolfe*
Old and the Young, The — *Pirandello*
Old Bachelor, The — *Congreve*
Old Curiosity Shop, The — *Dickens*
Old Fortunatus — *Dekker*
Old Maid, The — *Wharton*
Old Man and the Sea, The — *Hemingway*

COMPLETE LIST OF CONTENTS

Old Mortality — *K. A. Porter*
Old Mortality — *Scott*
Old St. Paul's — *Ainsworth*
Old Wives' Tale, The — *Bennett*
Old Wives' Tale, The — *Peele*
Oldtown Folks — *Stowe*
Oliver Twist — *Dickens*
Omoo — *Melville*
On Liberty — *Mill*
On the Origin of Species — *Darwin*
Ordeal of Richard Feverel, The — *Meredith*
Oregon Trail, The — *Parkman*
Orfeo — *Politian*
Orlando — *Woolf*
Orlando Furioso — *Ariosto*
Orlando Innamorato — *Boiardo*
Orley Farm — *Trollope*
Oroonoko — *Behn*
Orphan, The — *Otway*
Orpheus and Eurydice — *Folk tradition*
Othello — *Shakespeare*
Other One, The — *Colette*
Our Mutual Friend — *Dickens*
Our Town — *Wilder*
Our Village — *Mitford*
Overcoat, The — *Gogol*
Ox-Bow Incident, The — *Clark*

Pamela — *S. Richardson*
Parade's End — *F. M. Ford*
Paradise Lost — *Milton*
Paradise Regained — *Milton*
Parallel Lives — *Plutarch*
Parliament of Fowls, The — *Chaucer*
Parzival — *Wolfram von Eschenbach*
Passage to India, A — *Forster*
Passion Flower, The — *Benavente*
Paterson — *W. C. Williams*
Path to Rome, The — *Belloc*
Pathfinder, The — *Cooper*
Patience — *Gilbert*
Patrician, The — *Galsworthy*
Patriot, The — *Fogazzaro*
Paul Bunyan — *J. Stevens*
Peace, The — *Aristophanes*
Peasants, The — *Reymont*
Peder Victorious — *Rölvaag*
Pedro Sánchez — *Pereda*
Peer Gynt — *Ibsen*
Peg Woffington — *Reade*
Pelle the Conqueror — *Nexö*
Pélléas and Mélisande — *Maeterlinck*
Peñas Arriba — *Pereda*
Pendennis — *Thackeray*
Penguin Island — *France*
Pensées — *Pascal*
People of Juvik, The — *Duun*
People, Yes, The — *Sandburg*
Pepita Jiménez — *Valera*
Peregrine Pickle — *Smollett*
Pericles, Prince of Tyre — *Shakespeare*
Persian Letters — *Montesquieu*
Persians, The — *Aeschylus*
Persuasion — *Austen*
Peter Ibbetson — *G. du Maurier*
Peter Pan — *Barrie*
Peter Simple — *Marryat*
Peter Whiffle — *Van Vechten*
Phèdre — *Racine*
Philaster — *Beaumont* and *Fletcher*
Philippics, The — *Demosthenes*
Philoctetes — *Sophocles*
Philosophiae Naturalis Principia Mathematica — *Newton*
Philosophy of Art — *Taine*
Phineas Finn — *Trollope*
Phineas Redux — *Trollope*
Phoenician Women, The — *Euripides*
Phormio — *Terence*
Physical Basis of Life, The — *T. H. Huxley*
Pickwick Papers — *Dickens*
Picture of Dorian Gray, The — *Wilde*
Pierre — *Melville*
Pilgrimage — *D. Richardson*
Pilgrimage of Charlemagne, The — *Unknown*

Pilgrim's Progress, The — *Bunyan*
Pillars of Society, The — *Ibsen*
Pilot, The — *Cooper*
Pioneers, The — *Cooper*
Pirates of Penzance, The — *Gilbert*
Pit, The — *Norris*
Plague, The — *Camus*
Plaideurs, Les — *Racine*
Plain Dealer, The — *Wycherley*
Platero and I — *Jiménez*
Playboy of the Western World, The — *Synge*
Plough and the Stars, The — *O'Casey*
Plumed Serpent, The — *D. H. Lawrence*
Plutus — *Aristophanes*
Poem of the Cid — *Unknown*
Poems, Chiefly in the Scottish Dialect — *Burns*
Poetical Works of Edward Taylor, The — *Taylor*
Poetics, The — *Aristotle*
Poetry of Auden, The — *Auden*
Poetry of Bashô, The — *Bashô*
Poetry of Blake, The — *Blake*
Poetry of Bryant, The — *Bryant*
Poetry of Carducci, The — *Carducci*
Poetry of Christina Rossetti, The — *C. Rossetti*
Poetry of Dante Gabriel Rossetti, The — *D. G. Rossetti*
Poetry of Donne, The — *Donne*
Poetry of Drayton, The — *Drayton*
Poetry of Emily Dickinson, The — *Dickinson*
Poetry of Freneau, The — *Freneau*
Poetry of Frost, The — *Frost*
Poetry of Gray, The — *Gray*
Poetry of Hopkins, The — *Hopkins*
Poetry of Horace, The — *Horace*
Poetry of Lanier, The — *Lanier*
Poetry of Lewis, The — *C. D. Lewis*
Poetry of Lindsay, The — *Lindsay*
Poetry of Lovelace, The — *Lovelace*
Poetry of Mallarmé, The — *Mallarmé*
Poetry of Marvell, The — *Marvell*
Poetry of Ronsard, The — *Ronsard*
Poetry of Spender, The — *Spender*
Poetry of Stefan George, The — *George*
Poetry of Theocritus, The — *Theocritus*
Poetry of Yeats, The — *Yeats*
Point Counter Point — *A. Huxley*
Polyeucte — *Corneille*
Poor People — *Dostoevski*
Poor White — *S. Anderson*
Porgy — *Heyward*
Portrait of a Lady, The — *H. James*
Portrait of the Artist as a Young Man, A — *Joyce*
Possessed, The — *Dostoevski*
Pot of Gold, The — *Plautus*
Power — *Feuchtwanger*
Power and the Glory, The — *G. Greene*
Power of Darkness, The — *Tolstoy*
Pragmatism — *W. James*
Prairie, The — *Cooper*
Praise of Folly, The — *Erasmus*
Precious Bane — *Webb*
Prejudices: Six Series — *Mencken*
Prelude, The — *Wordsworth*
Pride and Prejudice — *Austen*
Prince, The — *Machiavelli*
Prince and the Pauper, The — *Twain*
Prince of Homburg, The — *Kleist*
Princess of Clèves, The — *Lafayette*
Prisoner of Zenda, The — *Hope*
Private Life of the Master Race, The — *Brecht*
Private Lives — *Coward*
Private Papers of Henry Reycroft, The — *Gissing*
Professor, The — *C. Brontë*
Professor's House, The — *Cather*
Prometheus Bound — *Aeschylus*
Prometheus Unbound — *P. B. Shelley*
Promised Land, The — *Pontoppidan*
Proserpine and Ceres — *Folk tradition*
Purple Dust — *O'Casey*
Purple Land, The — *Hudson*

COMPLETE LIST OF CONTENTS

Pygmalion — *Shaw*

Quality Street — *Barrie*
Queen's Necklace, The — *Dumas,* père
Quentin Durward — *Scott*
Quo Vadis? — *Sienkiewicz*

Rainbow, The — *D. H. Lawrence*
Raintree County — *Lockridge*
Ralph Roister Doister — *Udall*
Ramayana, The — *Valmiki*
Rameau's Nephew — *Diderot*
Rape of Lucrece, The — *Shakespeare*
Rape of the Lock, The — *Pope*
Rasselas — *Johnson*
Ravenshoe — *H. Kingsley*
Rebecca — *D. du Maurier*
Rebel Generation, The — *Ammers-Küller*
Recruiting Officer, The — *Farquhar*
Red and the Black, The — *Stendhal*
Red Badge of Courage, The — *Crane*
Red Room, The — *Strindberg*
Red Rover, The — *Cooper*
Redburn — *Melville*
Redskins, The — *Cooper*
Relapse, The — *Vanbrugh*
R. E. Lee — *Freeman*
Remembrance of Things Past — *Proust*
Remembrance Rock — *Sandburg*
Renée Mauperin — *The Goncourts*
Republic, The — *Plato*
Resurrection — *Tolstoy*
Return, The — *de la Mare*
Return of the Native, The — *Hardy*
Revenge of Bussy D'Ambois, The — *Chapman*
Revenger's Tragedy, The — *Tourneur*
Revolt of the Angels, The — *France*
Revolt of the Masses, The — *Ortega*
Reynard the Fox — *Unknown*
Rhadamistus and Zenobia — *Crébillon*
Riceyman Steps — *Bennett*
Richard the Second — *Shakespeare*
Richard the Third — *Shakespeare*
Right You Are — If You Think So — *Pirandello*
Rime of Petrarch, Le — *Petrarch*
Rime of the Ancient Mariner, The — *Coleridge*
Ring and the Book, The — *R. Browning*
Ring Round the Moon — *Anouilh*
Rip Van Winkle — *Irving*
Rise of Silas Lapham, The — *Howells*
Rivals, The — *Sheridan*
River of Earth — *Still*
Rivet in Grandfather's Neck, The — *Cabell*
Roan Stallion — *Jeffers*
Rob Roy — *Scott*
Robin Hood's Adventures — *Unknown*
Robinson Crusoe — *Defoe*
Roderick Random — *Smollett*
Rogue Herries — *Hugh Walpole*
Roman Actor, The — *Massinger*
Romance of a Schoolmaster, The — *Amicis*
Romance of Leonardo da Vinci, The — *Merejkowski*
Romance of the Forest, The — *Radcliffe*
Romance of the Three Kingdoms — *Lo Kuan-chung*
Romantic Comedians, The — *Glasgow*
Romantic Ladies, The — *Molière*
Romany Rye, The — *Borrow*
Rome Haul — *Edmonds*
Romeo and Juliet — *Shakespeare*
Romola — *G. Eliot*
Room With a View, A — *Forster*
Rory O'More — *Lover*
Rosmersholm — *Ibsen*
Roughing It — *Twain*
Roxana — *Defoe*
Rubáiyát of Omar Khayyám, The — *FitzGerald*
Rule a Wife and Have a Wife — *Fletcher*
R. U. R. — *Capek*

Saint, The — *Fogazzaro*

Saint Joan —*Shaw*
St. Peter's Umbrella — *Mikszáth*
St. Ronan's Well— *Scott*
Sakuntala — *Kalidasa*
Salammbô — *Flaubert*
Samson Agonistes — *Milton*
Sanctuary — *Faulkner*
Sandford and Merton — *T. Day*
Sanine — *Artsybashev*
Sappho — *Daudet*
Sappho — *Grillparzer*
Saragossa — *Pérez Galdós*
Sartor Resartus — *Carlyle*
Satanstoe — *Cooper*
Satires — *Juvenal*
Satiromastix — *Dekker*
Satyricon, The — *Petronius*
Scarlet Letter, The — *Hawthorne*
Scepticism and Animal Faith — *Santayana*
School for Husbands, The — *Molière*
School for Scandal, The — *Sheridan*
School for Wives, The — *Molière*
Scornful Lady, The — *Beaumont* and *Fletcher*
Scottish Chiefs, The — *J. Porter*
Sea and the Jungle, The — *Tomlinson*
Sea of Grass, The — *Richter*
Sea Wolf, The — *London*
Seagull, The — *Chekhov*
Season in Hell, A — *Rimbaud*
Second Mrs. Tanqueray, The — *Pinero*
Second Shepherds' Play, The — *Unknown*
Second World War, The — *W. S. Churchill*
Secret Agent, The — *Conrad*
Sejanus — *Jonson*
Selected Poems — *Ransom*
Self-Tormentor, The — *Terence*
Sense and Sensibility — *Austen*
Sentimental Education, A — *Flaubert*
Sentimental Journey, A — *Sterne*
Seven Against Thebes — *Aeschylus*
Seven Gothic Tales — *Dinesen*
Seven Pillars of Wisdom — *T. E. Lawrence*
Seven Short Plays — *Gregory*
Seven Who Fled, The — *Prokosch*
Seven Who Were Hanged, The — *Andreyev*
Seventeen — *Tarkington*
Shadows on the Rock — *Cather*
She — *Haggard*
She Stoops to Conquer — *Goldsmith*
Sheep Well, The — *Vega*
Sheltered Life, The — *Glasgow*
Shih Ching, The — *Confucius*
Shirley — *C. Brontë*
Shoemaker's Holiday, The — *Dekker*
Short Stories of Katherine Mansfield — *Mansfield*
Short Stories of O. Henry — *Henry*
Shropshire Lad, A — *Housman*
Sickness unto Death, The — *Kierkegaard*
Siege of Rhodes, The — *Davenant*
Sign of Four, The — *Doyle*
Silas Marner — *G. Eliot*
Silent Woman, The — *Jonson*
Simplicissimus the Vagabond — *Grimmelshausen*
Sir Charles Grandison — *S. Richardson*
Sir Gawain and the Green Knight — *Unknown*
Sir John van Olden Barnavelt — *Fletcher* and *Massinger*
Sir Roger de Coverley Papers, The — *Addison, Steele,* and *Budgell*
Sister Carrie — *Dreiser*
Sister Philomène — *The Goncourts*
Six Characters in Search of an Author — *Pirandello*
Skin of Our Teeth, The — *Wilder*
Sleepwalkers, The — *Broch*
Slipknot, The — *Plautus*
Small House at Allington, The — *Trollope*
Small Souls — *Couperus*

Smoke — *Turgenev*
Snake Pit, The — *Undset*
Snow-Bound — *Whittier*
So Red the Rose — *Young*
Sohrab and Rustum — *Arnold*
Soldier's Fortune, The — *Otway*
Son Avenger, The — *Undset*
Sonezaki Shinjû — *Chikamatsu Monzaemon*
Song of Bernadette, The — *Werfel*
Song of Hiawatha, The — *Longfellow*
Song of Roland, The — *Unknown*
Song of Songs, The — *Sudermann*
Song of the Lark, The — *Cather*
Song of the World — *Giono*
Sonnets from the Portuguese — *E. B. Browning*
Sons and Lovers — *D. H. Lawrence*
Sorrows of Young Werther, The — *Goethe*
Sotileza — *Pereda*
Sound and the Fury, The — *Faulkner*
South Wind — *N. Douglas*
Spanish Friar, The — *Dryden*
Spanish Gipsy, The — *Middleton*
Spanish Tragedy, The — *Kyd*
Spoilers, The — *Beach*
Spoils of Poynton, The — *H. James*
Spoon River Anthology — *Masters*
Spy, The — *Cooper*
Star of Seville, The — *Unknown*
State Fair — *Stong*
Steppenwolf — *Hesse*
Stoic, The — *Dreiser*
Stone Desert — *Wast*
Story of a Bad Boy, The — *Aldrich*
Story of a Country Town, The — *Howe*
Story of an African Farm, The — *Schreiner*
Story of Burnt Njal, The — *Unknown*
Story of Gösta Berling, The — *Lagerlöf*
Story of the Guitar — *Kao Tse-ch'eng*
Strange Interlude — *O'Neill*
Strange Stories from a Chinese Studio — *P'u Sung-ling*
Street Scene — *Rice*
Strife — *Galsworthy*
Studs Lonigan: A Trilogy — *Farrell*
Study in Scarlet, A — *Doyle*
Study of History, A — *Toynbee*
Summa Theologica — *Aquinas*
Sun Also Rises, The — *Hemingway*
Sunken Bell, The — *Hauptmann*
Suppliants, The — *Aeschylus*
Suppliants, The — *Euripides*
Suppositi, I — *Ariosto*
Surry of Eagle's-Nest — *Cooke*
Swallow Barn — *Kennedy*
Swiss Family Robinson, The — *Wyss*

Tale of Genji, The — *Murasaki*
Tale of Two Cities, A — *Dickens*
Tales of Ise — *Arihara no Narihira*
Tales of Soldiers and Civilians — *Bierce*
Tales of Uncle Remus — *Harris*
Talisman, The — *Scott*
Tamar — *Jeffers*
Tamburlaine the Great — *Marlowe*
Taming of the Shrew, The — *Shakespeare*
Taps for Private Tussie — *Stuart*
Taras Bulba — *Gogol*
Tarr — *W. Lewis*
Tartarin of Tarascon — *Daudet*
Tartuffe — *Molière*
Task, The — *Cowper*
Tempest, The — *Shakespeare*
Temple, The — *Herbert*
Temple Beau, The — *Fielding*
Temptation of Saint Anthony, The — *Flaubert*
Tenant of Wildfell Hall, The — *A. Brontë*
Tender Is the Night — *Fitzgerald*
Tess of the d'Urbervilles — *Hardy*
Thaddeus of Warsaw — *J. Porter*
Thebais, The — *Statius*

There Are Crimes and Crimes — *Strindberg*
Thérèse — *Mauriac*
Thin Man, The — *Hammett*
Thirty-Nine Steps, The — *Buchan*
This Above All — *Knight*
Three Black Pennys, The — *Hergesheimer*
Three-Cornered Hat, The — *Alarcón*
Three Men in a Boat — *Jerome*
Three Musketeers, The — *Dumas,* père
Three Sisters, The — *Chekhov*
Three Soldiers — *Dos Passos*
Through the Looking Glass — *Carroll*
Thus Spake Zarathustra — *Nietzsche*
Thyestes — *Seneca*
Time Machine, The — *Wells*
Time of Man, The — *Roberts*
Timon of Athens — *Shakespeare*
'Tis Pity She's a Whore — *J. Ford*
Titan, The — *Dreiser*
Titus Andronicus — *Shakespeare*
To Be a Pilgrim — *Cary*
To the Lighthouse — *Woolf*
Tobacco Road — *Caldwell*
Toilers of the Sea, The — *Hugo*
Tom Brown's School Days — *T. Hughes*
Tom Burke of Ours — *Lever*
Tom Cringle's Log — *M. Scott*
Tom Jones — *Fielding*
Tom Sawyer — *Twain*
Tom Thumb the Great — *Fielding*
Tono-Bungay — *Wells*
Tower of London, The — *Ainsworth*
Town, The — *Faulkner*
Town, The — *Richter*
Track of the Cat, The — *Clark*
Traitor, The — *Shirley*
Travels in Arabia Deserta — *Doughty*
Travels of Marco Polo, The — *Polo*
Travels With a Donkey — *Stevenson*
Treasure Island — *Stevenson*
Tree Grows in Brooklyn, A — *B. Smith*
Tree of the Folkungs, The — *Heidenstam*
Trees, The — *Richter*
Trial, The — *Kafka*
Trial by Jury — *Gilbert*
Trick to Catch the Old One, A — *Middleton*
Trickster, The — *Plautus*
Trilby — *G. du Maurier*
Tristan and Isolde — *Gottfried von Strassburg*
Tristram — *Robinson*
Tristram Shandy — *Sterne*
Triumph of Death, The — *D'Annunzio*
Troilus and Cressida — *Shakespeare*
Troilus and Criseyde — *Chaucer*
Trojan Women, The — *Euripides*
True History, The — *Lucian*
Truth Suspected — *Ruiz de Alarcón*
Turcaret — *Le Sage*
Turn of the Screw, The — *H. James*
Twelfth Night — *Shakespeare*
Twenty Thousand Leagues Under the Sea — *Verne*
Twenty Years After — *Dumas,* père
Two Gentlemen of Verona — *Shakespeare*
Two Noble Kinsmen, The — *Shakespeare*
Two Years Before the Mast — *Dana*
Typee — *Melville*

Ugly Duchess, The— *Feuchtwanger*
Ulysses — *Joyce*
Unbearable Bassington, The — *Saki*
Uncle Silas — *Le Fanu*
Uncle Tom's Cabin — *Stowe*
Uncle Vanya — *Chekhov*
Under Fire — *Barbusse*
Under the Greenwood Tree — *Hardy*
Under the Yoke — *Vazov*
Under Two Flags — *Ouida*
Under Western Eyes — *Conrad*
Underdogs, The — *Azuela*
Undine — *La Motte-Fouqué*
Unfortunate Traveller, The — *Nash*
U. S. A. — *Dos Passos*
Utopia — *More*

Vanessa — *Hugh Walpole*
Vanity Fair — *Thackeray*
Vathek — *Beckford*
Venetian Glass Nephew, The — *Wylie*
Venice Preserved — *Otway*
Venus and Adonis — *Shakespeare*
Vicar of Bullhampton, The — *Trollope*
Vicar of Wakefield, The — *Goldsmith*
Vicomte de Bragelonne, The — *Dumas,* père
Victory — *Conrad*
Vile Bodies — *Waugh*
Village, The — *Bunin*
Village, The — *Crabbe*
Villette — *C. Brontë*
Vindication of Natural Society, A — *Burke*
Violent Land, The — *Amado*
Virgin Soil — *Turgenev*
Virginia Comedians, The — *Cooke*
Virginian, The — *Wister*
Virginians, The — *Thackeray*
Visión de Anáhuac — *Reyes*
Vision of William, Concerning Piers the Plowman, The — *Langland*
Vita Nuova, The — *Dante*
Vivian Grey — *Disraeli*
Volpone — *Jonson*
Volupté — *Sainte-Beuve*
Voyage of the Beagle, The — *Darwin*

Waiting for Godot — *Beckett*
Walden — *Thoreau*
Wallenstein — *Schiller*
Wanderer, The — *Alain-Fournier*
Wandering Jew, The — *Sue*
Wandering Scholar from Paradise, The — *Sachs*
War and Peace — *Tolstoy*
War of the Worlds, The — *Wells*
Warden, The — *Trollope*
Washington Square — *H. James*
Wasps, The — *Aristophanes*
Waste Land, The — *T. S. Eliot*
Waverley — *Scott*
Waves, The — *Woolf*
Way of All Flesh, The — *Butler*
Way of the World, The — *Congreve*
Wealth of Nations, The — *A. Smith*
Weavers, The — *Hauptmann*
Web and the Rock, The — *Wolfe*
Westward Ho! — *C. Kingsley*
What Every Woman Knows — *Barrie*
What Maisie Knew — *H. James*
When the Mountain Fell — *Ramuz*
When We Dead Awaken — *Ibsen*
Where Angels Fear to Tread— *Forster*
White Company, The — *Doyle*
White Devil, The — *Webster*
White-Jacket — *Melville*
Wickford Point — *Marquand*
Wieland — *Brown*
Wild Ass's Skin, The — *Balzac*
Wild Duck, The — *Ibsen*
Wilhelm Meister's Apprenticeship — *Goethe*
Wilhelm Meister's Travels — *Goethe*
William Tell — *Schiller*
Wind in the Willows, The — *Grahame*
Windsor Castle — *Ainsworth*
Winesburg, Ohio — *S. Anderson*
Wings of the Dove, The — *H. James*
Winter's Tale, The — *Shakespeare*
Winterset — *M. Anderson*
With Fire and Sword — *Sienkiewicz*
Within the Gates — *O'Casey*
Wolf Solent — *J. C. Powys*
Woman Hater, The — *Beaumont* and *Fletcher*
Woman in White, The — *Collins*
Woman Killed With Kindness, A — *Heywood*
Woman of Rome, The — *Moravia*
Woman's Life, A — *Maupassant*
Woman's Prize, The — *Fletcher*
Women Beware Women — *Middleton*
Women of Trachis, The — *Sophocles*
Woodlanders, The — *Hardy*

Woodstock — *Scott*
Works and Days — *Hesiod*
Works of Jonathan Edwards — *Edwards*
World as Will and Idea, The — *Schopenhauer*
World Enough and Time — *Warren*
World of the Thibaults, The — *Martin du Gard*
World's Illusion, The — *Wassermann*
Woyzeck — *Büchner*
Wreck of the Grosvenor, The — *Russell*
Wuthering Heights — *E. Brontë*
Yearling, The — *Rawlings*
Years, The — *Woolf*
Yemassee, The — *Simms*
You Can't Go Home Again — *Wolfe*
You Know Me Al — *Lardner*
Youma — *Hearn*
Yvain — *Chrétien de Troyes*

Zadig — *Voltaire*
Zaïre — *Voltaire*
Zarco, El — *Altamirano*
Zuleika Dobson — *Beerbohm*

Books and Reading

A Survey of World Literature

by
DAYTON KOHLER
Story Editor of
MASTERPLOTS

I

AN INTRODUCTION TO READING

"Each of us, then, makes his own illusion of the world—illusion poetic, sentimental, joyous, melancholy, foul, or dismal—according to his nature. And the writer has no mission other than to reproduce faithfully this illusion, with all the processes of art he has learned."

GUY DE MAUPASSANT

There are many roads into the world of books, but the way of fiction is probably the most common. The reason is plain. The novel and the short story come closer to the experience of the modern reader than any other form of contemporary writing. They are to us what epic poetry was to the Greeks and Romans, what stage drama was to the Elizabethans. Then, too, the appeal of the story, whether told as poem, play, history, biography, or novel, is primitive and strong.

Mankind's delight in stories has never been limited to any period or place. It is as timeless and universal as the art of the storyteller, which stretches in an unbroken line back to the unrecorded oral beginnings of literary history. Men and women of earlier times were moved by the same impulse that makes us, before we turn the page, anticipate the next chapter of a good novel. The craftsmanship of structure, realistic character portrayal, evocation of atmosphere and setting, and the writers' strategy with symbol and language can add much to our appreciation of the art of fiction, but always it is the story, a time sequence of events relating fiction to life, which first captures our interest and then compels a sense of recognition and belief.

But the appeal of fiction may go deeper. We all live, perhaps more intensely than we realize, in our imaginings and emotions. Aware of our own difficulties in the uncertain business of living, we are all the more interested in other men and their problems, and stories provide a sort of life extension course by which we try to vary or lengthen our own lives.

We begin a story with the hope that it will be faithful, in Hawthorne's words, "not merely to the possible, but to the probable and ordinary in man's experience." When the writer adds perspective and meaning to that experience and gives it beauty of form, his story becomes a record of human interest and permanent value. And what is true of the story is true of all other types of literature as well. Lyric poetry, the essay, philosophy, each in its own way, touch our imagination and emotions and satisfy our sense of belief.

The aim of all literature is truth. There are, however, two kinds of truth. One we call factual. It is the material of the daily newspaper, a scientific treatise, history, biography. Many able novelists, from Daniel Defoe to John Dos Passos, have reshaped this body of observed and proved fact into the form of fiction. The other is inner or imaginative truth. It, too, is grounded in the physical world, but its vision is inward and downward, not outward. Less concerned with the appearances of things than it is with deeper realities of human personality and conduct, this is the kind of truth we find in literature that we call creative. It is more than the thing which seems true merely because it conforms to our knowledge of the world. We do not need to believe in men six inches tall, for example, in order to understand Swift's criticism of human society in *Gulliver's Travels*. In the same way, modern disbelief in ghosts and witches takes away nothing from our appreciation of *Hamlet* and *Macbeth*. Whether realistic or romantic, imaginative truth penetrates deeply into the experience of the individual or the race. The result is a fuller interpretation of life as we know it.

Books which continue to gratify our sense of truth over a long period of time we call classics. The name is unfortunate, suggesting classroom lectures and dusty library shelves, but we have no other. Age, however, does not make a classic, for time quickly sends to the rubbish pile the outdated books of every literature. A book is a classic because it tells us something so undeniably true that it becomes part of our experience as we read, because it presents a character who seems to embody in one person a significant phase of human personality or fate. Ulysses is immortal as the far-seeking wanderer. Chaucer's Wife of Bath has the earthy vitality of life itself. Hamlet is for all time the tragic hero broken under a load of duty too heavy for the spirit to sustain. Don Quixote will ride forever as the romantic idealist tilting against windmills. Jean Valjean is society's outcast who shows man's inhumanity to man. Huck Finn's adventures reveal a boy's world, the restless energy of a young nation, the goodness and shoddiness of human nature. Books can do no more than vary timeless themes of birth and striving, endurance and death, but they can make life more real, more understandable. Although the conditions of men change, man does not, and so the classic is capable of renewing its meaning for each generation.

We read for a variety of reasons: for relief from boredom, for information, for culture, for pleasure. All of these aims are in some measure justified by the pressures and necessities of the world we live in today. But, as W. Somerset Maugham has pointed out, no reading is of lasting value unless it gives us pleasure. Many people, unfortunately, think of pleasurable reading in terms of "light" fiction, escapist books which offer only temporary release from daily routine or commonplace surroundings. The enjoyment we get from good reading is a quality more positive than simple diversion, for which there is nowadays no need of books at all. Reading for information serves a practical but limited purpose. All on one factual level, it adds to our store of information without enriching personality. Much so-called cultural reading is no more than genteel snobbery. Culture is for use; its ends are goodness and truth. There are no absolute values in literature, and the only real meaning a book can have is the meaning it holds for its reader. We should read our books as we eat a good dinner, with appreciation and zest, not take them in prescribed doses, like a tonic. Reading for pleasure is an exercise which enables us to live with our whole bodies as well as our minds.

In one of his essays Robert Louis Stevenson describes his experience when he read Dumas' *Vicomte de Bragelonne* for the first time: "I carried the thread of that epic into my slumbers, I woke with it unbroken, I rejoiced to plunge into the book at breakfast, it was with a pang that I must lay it down and turn to my own labors; for no part of the world has ever seemed to me so charming as these pages, and not even my friends are quite so real, perhaps quite so dear, as D'Artagnan."

This is what we mean by the true magic of reading. Not all of us are so temperamentally constituted that we can read with the same thoroughgoing gusto, but every reader comes, at one time or another, upon some book which in substance or style seems written for his particular delight. No one can say what this book will be. For one it may be the essays of Montaigne, who has been called the first modern man, for another the passionate search for truth and beauty in the poetry of John Keats, for still another one of the great novels—*Pickwick Papers, Father Goriot, Moby Dick, War and Peace, Wuthering Heights*. No matter what the starting point, the world of books will never again be a dreary, uncharted wasteland. A few lines of type, a chance reference, and we are off with Tom Jones on the highroad to London, riding with D'Artagnan to save the honor of a queen, at our ease with Hazlitt over a supper of bread, cheese, and ale in an old English inn, or embarking with Ishmael on the bedlam voyage of the *Pequod*.

Books can never be a substitute for life.

They can, as we have already seen, add much to our knowledge of the world and the people in it. For instance, we may be certain that a neighbor's wife is carrying on a secret love affair with the golf professional at the country club, but we can never understand her motives and feelings as clearly as we know those of Emma Bovary. Or a poem like Edwin Arlington Robinson's "Miniver Cheevy" may give us better insight into the true nature of an impractical, tippling, day-dreaming friend. In real life our knowledge of people is usually limited to what they say and do; we can only guess at the vital inner life which lies, like the submerged portion of an iceberg, below the surface. The novelist and the poet, however, go beneath externals of speech and action to show life at its source, in the hidden world of thought and feeling.

Reading makes us citizens of the world at large. Sam Weller, Soames Forsyte, Becky Sharp, Emma Bovary, Raskolnikov, Mrs. Proudie, and a thousand other figures from the world's literature belong to all ages and all countries. Like Chaucer's Canterbury Pilgrims and the boarders in Balzac's Pension Vauquer, they are a part of all humanity. To know them is to cross national and racial boundaries and to shed our complacency and provincialism at the same time.

Great books not only record and interpret life for us but also console our griefs, expose our vices, redeem our weaknesses. When we read wisely, we are always in the process of becoming. No one could read Thoreau's *Walden* and remain insensible to his own natural environment. Poetry shows us that in our daily lives we think in imagery and talk in figurative language. Books teach us how to live more completely within ourselves. Proust's *Remembrance of Things Past* contains a revealing episode. There the narrator, a grown man, dips a small cake into a cup of tea. The taste of this morsel brings back childhood memories of a tea-moistened cake his aunt had given him years before at Combray, and with this recollection all the impressions of that time return. "In that moment all the flowers in our garden and in M. Swann's park, and the water lilies on the Vivonne, and the good people of the village and their little dwellings and the church and all Combray and its surroundings, came into being, both town and gardens, from my cup of tea."

We are all like Proust's narrator, but we may need the example of a discerning writer before we can realize our own resources of memory and imagination.

The trivial writer offers entertainment and asks little except our time in return. The serious writer, on the other hand, may make greater demands on his readers. Although some poems and novels must be read with disciplined, attentive minds, the qualities which make for hard or easy reading are no test of literary value. The final test for any book is what we get out of it, according to our tastes and capacities. One of the greatest pleasures in reading is the discovery of the unexpected or purposeful in a work we once took for granted. Sometimes a book leads us into strange bypaths. Browning's *The Ring and the Book,* for example, is on one level a murder melodrama laid in seventeenth-century Italy. So complex is his poem, however, so rich and varied its background, that if we were to follow all the threads of interest in his story we would find ourselves reading many volumes on painting, literature, science, religion, history, psychology, law, architecture, and costume. To master such a work gives us a feeling of power as well as pleasure.

Since there are no absolute values in literature, it follows that all reading must be selective. But the *what* of reading is often as perplexing as the *why* and *how.* No one can read everything. It has been estimated that one would have to read more than twenty volumes a day to keep up with books published each year. Even Dr. Bookworm could not exhaust the shelves of a fair-sized library in a normal lifetime. For most readers some kind of guide is necessary; without a sense of direction we flounder among books past or present and are likely to fall back on whatever is currently popular.

We should learn at the outset to distrust the book whose chief recommendation is its popularity. Public favor is too fickle to mark any book for survival, as the forgotten, unread titles on the best seller lists of the last fifty years will show. If we cannot rely on our own judgment, mistrust the enthusiasms of our friends, and rebel against the dictates of our teachers, there are other aids for our guidance. Reviews in newspapers and magazines will keep us informed on new books as they appear. There are also scholarly lists of many kinds—Ten Books to Take to a Desert Island, the Twenty Best Novels, One Hundred Great Books, all compiled as if some virtue existed in round numbers. We need only consult these lists, however, to discover how widely literary experts disagree, and their differences of critical opinion may throw us back upon our own resources.

Probably the best course for the reader who has some half-defined idea of what he wants to read, or thinks he should read, would be to examine a comprehensive book of literary synopses. If the condensed versions are presented objectively along with some background information on the book and its writer, they become an excellent basis for appraisal and selection. From such a book pick out a group of titles which in substance and treatment seem to suit your taste or mood. Then sample. Since tastes differ, there is little point in reading a book which does not promise an adequate return for your effort.

Perhaps a preference for humor and the oddities of human character has led you to the novels of Charles Dickens, but on closer inspection you find his sentimentality and melodramatic plots distasteful. Try Thackeray, whose satire may be a proper corrective, or Jane Austen. If you tire of the novel of manners, read *Wuthering Heights,* a story of human passion as wild and bleak as its Yorkshire moorland setting. From Tennyson's lyricism turn to the philosophical poems of Wordsworth or the psychological portraits of Browning. If you prefer something more modern, you may find what you are looking for in Hemingway, who in *The Sun Also Rises* and *A Farewell to Arms* expresses the violence and despair of his generation. Somewhere along the line you will find those books which make reading a true pleasure, and your literary perspectives will have widened considerably in the meantime. An adventure story like *Treasure Island* may lead you to Melville or Conrad. Conrad may take you to the French novelists whom he acknowledged as his masters or to Henry James, his contemporary, who in turn may carry us back to Hawthorne, another writer concerned with man's moral problems. Stephen Vincent Benet's fine narrative poem of the Civil War, *John Brown's Body,* may send us to Sandburg's biography of Lincoln or Freeman's life of Lee. Eugene O'Neill's *Mourning Becomes Electra* may stir our curiosity about the plays of Aeschylus. Literary paths cross and recross and we are free to choose our reading wherever they may lead.

The brief survey of reading that follows is selective as well. There has been no attempt to make a complete outline of world literature and much has necessarily been omitted. This survey is intended only to relate certain literary works to their periods and to indicate whenever possible why they have stirred the imaginations and emotions of their readers.

II
A SURVEY OF READING

GREECE AND ROME

Life in ancient Greece must have been intensely absorbing and rewarding, for on that small, rocky peninsula at the edge of a continent the Greeks made for themselves a place of many beginnings. Surrounded by barbarian tribes, they came into history with the assets of every civilized people: inquiring, imaginative minds and a beautiful and precise language. Knowing nothing of the past, they created an enduring body of folk tradition. Ignorant of geography, they sailed their ships into the unknown Mediterranean. They loved games and relished learning. Their gods they made in their own image—expedient, quarrelsome, witty, wise. Their small city states were models of government upon which our own is based.

The time, the place, and the people were right for a great civilization. During the Age of Pericles, for example, more men of genius lived in Athens than the world has seen since in any other place at one time. There the Greeks brought to perfection a literature and a style of architecture which have left deep imprints on the arts for more than two thousand years. They discovered principles and invented systems, and so laid the foundations of philosophy, natural science, mathematics, medicine. It has been truly said that the Western world goes back to Greece for everything but its religious faith.

The Greeks were a practical, realistic people, never mystics. In their need to understand the world they lived in they created myths to account for origins of things and to explain why life must be as it is. Stories like those of Pandora's box, Cupid and Psyche, Orpheus and Eurydice, Icarus, goat-footed Pan, the rape of Proserpine, are never childish; they are filled with beauty and wisdom. Also in the oral tradition were later tales of legendary heroes and tribal history, such as the labors of Hercules, the expedition of the seven against Thebes, the quest of the Argonauts, Theseus and the killing of the Minotaur. Out of this background of myth and heroic legend came the two great Homeric epics, the *Iliad* and the *Odyssey*.

Whether Homer was one man or ten is a secret lost in the shadowy past. What is more important, the two stories told in his name survive, as fresh and vivid as they were thousands of years ago. To citizens of Greek towns that had known assault and siege the *Iliad* was a great poem of battles. Beginning in the tenth year of the war with Troy, it tells of Achilles' terrible wrath and the death of Hector. It is a tale of violence and doom, compassion and grief, the earthly and the divine, for Homer is one of the few writers capable of making the gods seem at home in the human world, at the same time lifting men almost to the stature of gods.

The *Iliad* is the tragic epic of man's ambition for conquest and glory. The *Odyssey* is romantic comedy dealing with his desire for peace and home. Crafty Ulysses is a hero who emerges triumphant over every disastrous circumstance during his ten years of wandering after the fall of Troy, and his reward at the end is the comfort of his own hearth and the love of Penelope, his faithful spouse.

The Greeks prized their other poets—Hesiod, Sappho, Pindar, Theocritus, and all the singers of the *Greek Anthology*—but Homer was their master writer. To them his poems were more than heroic epics richly told. They were a storehouse of literature, history, religious tradition, social custom, moral instruction. Because he touched on whatever is universal in human thought and deed, Homer remains a poet for all moods and all ages.

Aeschylus, first of the Greek writers of tragedy, called his plays "morsels from the banquet of Homer," but this statement we must credit in part to the patriotic feelings of an Athenian who wished to be remembered only as one who had fought at Marathon. His work is filled with pride of country, poetic grandeur, tragic insight. Of his seven surviving plays the most interesting are the three relating to the descendants of Atreus. *Agamemnon, The Libation-Bearers,* and *The Furies* tell on one level a story of faithlessness, murder, revenge, and expiation. On another level this trilogy is a tremendous fable of a moral order overthrown and then reëstablished. Equally powerful is *Prometheus Bound,* the story of the titan who stole fire from the gods and gave it to mankind.

These plays have a bold and austere quality we do not find in the work of his successor and rival, Sophocles. A superior craftsman, especially in *Oedipus the King, Electra,* and *Antigone,* Sophocles is more restrained in his treatment of the problem of evil and divine retribution. He is the humanist among Greek playwrights. Even mocking Aristophanes paid him high tribute when he showed Sophocles in the underworld, as gentle among the shades as he had been in life.

Euripides, third of the tragic dramatists, lived in a later age. Faith in the gods was waning in his day, and skepticism and speculative philosophy had begun to weaken traditional morality. Lacking the religious fervor of Aeschylus and the moral serenity of Sophocles, he came closer to realistic studies of personality. *Alcestis* and *The Trojan Women* are stories of devoted, suffering womanhood. In *Medea* and *The Bacchae* he made fatal flaws of character the secret of man's tragic destiny.

Behind all of these plays is deep concern with the fate that pursues mankind, a subject of perennial interest to writers of all periods. Thomas Hardy, William Butler Yeats, Eugene O'Neill, and Robinson Jeffers are among modern writers who have found in Greek drama the themes and symbols of their own novels, poetry, and plays.

The lighter side of Greek nature found expression in comedy. Aristophanes is a master of irreverence and satire. Demagogues and political quackery are nothing new under the sun, and it is not necessary to know Athenian politics in order to enjoy his plays. Whether he is ridiculing politics in *The Knights* and *Lysistrata,* philosophy in *The Clouds,* or artistic rivalry in *The Frogs,* there is a serious purpose beneath his hilarity and bite. He is pleading for a return to the private and public morality of the earlier democracy.

Among the glories of Greece were the great minds it produced, thinkers and philosophers like Socrates, Plato, and Aristotle. Our knowledge of Socrates we get chiefly from the writings of Plato, his pupil and friend. What we owe most to Socrates is his method of teaching, the dialogue of questions and answers going deeply into the heart of a problem. Plato gave form to abstract thought. His conception of the ideal state, as outlined in *The Republic,* may seem outdated in our day of conflicting ideologies, but his views on love, friendship, and ethics are among the world's permanent possessions. A good beginning for the interested reader would be *The Apology* and *Phaedo,* dialogues dealing with the trial and death of Socrates.

Aristotle has been called "the master of those who know." No abstract speculator, he broke with Plato's idealism and translated thought into action. Churchmen and scholars of the Middle Ages called him "The Philosopher" and found in his writings not only the wisdom of a way of life but also the principles of Christian conduct. From him the modern world has inherited theology, logic, biology, rhetoric, politics, literary criticism, and even the terms that philosophers use today.

The Greeks, vitally interested in every form of human activity, found their first historian in Herodotus. His history of the wars between Greeks and Persians is more than a chronicle of events, for he was a student of mankind who poured into his books a flood of informative detail, anecdote, and hearsay, bringing life and drama to his pages. He is the great storyteller among historians, and his picture of the Greek state against a wider background of world culture gives us history in its proper perspective. Thucydides was a more sober, and at times sounder, writer. His *History of the Peloponnesian War* is largely an eyewitness account of the struggles between Athens and Sparta. Xenophon wrote also as a participant in the events he describes. He was a general in the famous army of ten thousand Greeks during their retreat from Persia, as told in his *Anabasis.*

If Herodotus is the father of history, then Plutarch stands in the same relationship to biography. Living in a world dominated by the Roman Empire, he was able to make comparisons between great men of both civilizations. His method in *Lives of the Noble Grecians and Romans* was to place two figures side by side—Alexander and Caesar, Alcibiades and Coriolanus, Demosthenes and Cicero—and then subject them to the tests of Greek philosophy. Modern scholars may deplore his carelessness with dates and scientific detail, but our knowledge of many of his subjects remains almost as he presented them. Plutarch, in fact, answered his later critics when he wrote: "Nay, a slight thing, like a phrase or a jest, often makes a greater revelation of character than battles where thousands fall." The *Lives* is still one of the great source books in history and literature. Shakespeare is only one of many writers who have borrowed from the first and one of the best of biographers.

Although Greek literature was to supply Latin writers with their best models, no two peoples were ever less alike than the Greeks and the Romans. The Greek genius was for the arts of beauty and daily living, that of the Romans for conquest, law, and engineering. One aspect of the Latin character is clearly revealed in Caesar's *Gallic War,* once the property of every schoolboy. The book is more than an account of military campaigns and the administration of conquered tribes; it is a classic example of forceful, incisive prose. In Caesar, as in many Roman writers, the style reflects the energy and practicality of the race.

The history of Greece began with Homer, but Rome had known more than five hundred years of history before her first writers appeared. Then, at the end of the third century B.C., Plautus and Terence wrote comedies adapted chiefly from Menander, a Greek comic poet, just as Seneca, several hundred years later, imitated the tragic drama of Athens. Certainly Romans had no literature they could call their own until the period of Vergil, Ovid, Horace, Cicero, and Lucretius, in the first century B.C.

Vergil wished for his country a literature as great as that of Greece. Toward this end he wrote the *Aeneid,* its theme borrowed in part from the Homeric epics. His story of the wanderings of Aeneas and the founding of Rome shows deep reverence for the past. But Vergil was a gentle poet who also loved country life and rustic virtues, as he described them in his *Eclogues* and the *Georgics,* and his epic lacks the stirring clash of arms and vivid pageantry we find in the *Iliad.* Perhaps the autumnal serenity of his verse made him all the more loved by the Romans. He was one of the few pagan writers esteemed by scholars and churchmen of the Middle Ages.

Horace is another beloved classic poet. Urbane, temperate, humorous, he expresses the spirit of Roman society in its Golden Age. At the other extreme from his gentle philosophy are Martial's caustic wit and Juvenal's savage pessimism and satire. Among Latin poets, however, Lucretius fills a place of his own. *On the Nature of Things* is a long philosophical poem unlike anything else in classic literature. In it he examines natural phenomena, religion, science, philosophy, and in the process he anticipates several scientific discoveries of the past hundred years. A man centuries ahead of his time, he has gained in our own day the recognition he deserves.

Cicero survives as the most famous of Latin prose writers. Lawyer, politician, and a master of eloquence, he shaped a lasting prose style which even in translation is powerful in clarity and rhythm. Fifty-seven of his speeches have been preserved, along with fragments of many others. His treatises on friendship and old age and his collection of letters have influenced many later writers, among them Montaigne, Sir Francis Bacon, Jonathan Swift.

The leading historians of the Roman Empire were Livy and Tacitus. Livy wrote the history of Rome from its founding to the fall of Carthage. Much of his material he drew from Polybius, a Greek historian who had lived through the period of the Punic Wars. The effectiveness of Tacitus as the historian of his own age lies in his powers of analysis, his excellent character sketches, and his lucid, ironic style. Suetonius presents a different and more scandalous picture of Roman history and life in his *Lives of the Twelve Caesars*. His account is one of imperial baseness and intrigue.

What Suetonius did with historical characters, Petronius, friend of the Emperor Nero, did in prose fiction. His *Satyricon* is a sly, unvarnished tale of magnificence and vice, a shameless comedy of manners laying bare a decadent society that had lost all sense of shame. Several generations later Lucius Apuleius wrote *The Golden Ass,* a satirical story of witchcraft and picaresque adventure. *Daphnis and Chloë* belongs to the same period, a romantic idyl of pastoral life and young love attributed to Longus, a Greek writer of the Hellenistic revival.

Under happier circumstances these tales might have speeded the development of the novel, but by the second century Roman culture had grown stagnant and the empire was crumbling from within. Only two other literary works stand out in the closing centuries of Roman rule and the long twilight of Greek culture. One of these is the *Meditations* of Marcus Aurelius, an emperor influenced by the Stoic philosopher, Epictetus. Written in Greek, the *Meditations* reveals the inner thoughts of a wise and humane ruler who believed that virtue is its own reward and that the ways of the gods, inscrutable to man, are just. The other is *On the Consolation of Philosophy,* by Boethius, who has been called the last Roman writer. This work, which bridges the gap between pagan philosophy and Christian belief, was a favorite book among scholars and writers of the Middle Ages.

Through the writings of St. Jerome, St. Augustine, St. Ambrose, and others, Latin survived as the language of the medieval Church. But in the centuries which followed the fall of Rome the great Greek and Latin classics were to have little influence on literature or thought. Their revival came only with the beginning of the Italian Renaissance in the fifteenth century.

It would be impossible to pass from the classic world without some consideration of the Bible as a literary work. For the Bible is an anthology of fine literature—myth, history, biography, poetry, short stories, letters, prophecy—as well as a tremendous religious document. In *Joseph and His Brothers,* Thomas Mann has shown that the Joseph story is the outline of a novel perfect in construction. Milton went directly to the Bible for his subject in *Paradise Lost.* Certainly no other book has had a more profound or far-reaching influence on human conduct and belief. Here again we are partly indebted to Greece and Rome. At Alexandria, in the second century B.C., Jewish scholars began the Greek translation of the Old Testament known as the Septuagint. The New Testament was written entirely in Hellenistic Greek. When St. Jerome prepared the Latin translation of the Bible—the Vulgate—he worked with Greek texts as well as Hebrew and Aramaic manuscripts. Wycliff's translation was made from the Vulgate. The Authorized, or King James, Version was prepared from Hebrew and Greek texts. Published in 1611, it has in large measure determined English prose style. So the Bible as most of us know it today is a religious and literary heritage transmitted through the great cultures of the past.

THE MIDDLE AGES

The Middle Ages is the name historians gave to the period between the pillage of Rome by the Visigoths in 410 and the fall of Constantinople in 1453. These dates are convenient but hardly accurate, for we know that the return to barbarism began with the recall of the Roman legions and that the Renaissance had its roots planted deeply in the feudal system which replaced the authority of Rome.

The Middle Ages were the Dark Ages. The period was one of wars, famine, pestilence, and gross superstition. Aside from the monasteries, there was no place where a writer could work, and there were few men who would have been capable of reading his manuscript. But the age was not as benighted as was once supposed. In the Arab universities at Damascus, Cairo, and Cordova the Greek philosophers and scientists were studied as carefully as the Koran. It is said that the tutor of St. Thomas Aquinas was a Moor, and in the second half of the Middle Ages many French and English scholars studied in the Moorish schools. In England and Ireland, less ravaged by turmoil after the collapse of Rome, there were famous scholars like the Venerable Bede or the Irish monks Charlemagne summoned to his court when he planned to revive the schools. The Benedictine monks collected classic manuscripts and preserved them in their libraries. Medieval scholasticism, dry and schematic as it was, did more than keep learning alive. The schools produced both a Friar Bacon and a François Villon.

The period was also one of great faith which gave meaning and dignity to men's lives. During the Middle Ages man's hope of forgiveness and salvation inspired the building of magnificent cathedrals and sent knightly Europe on crusades to reclaim Jerusalem from the Saracens. It was only natural that this same faith should find expression in literature. St. Augustine was both a father of the Church and a profound thinker. In his *Confessions* he wrote an intimate and revealing autobiography. *The City of God,* written to refute the charge that the sack of Rome was punishment by the gods because of the spread of Christianity, is a religious treatise over which theologians have been disputing ever since. In it he wrote: "The greatest city in the world has fallen in ruin, but the City of God abideth for ever." His argument established the tradition of spiritual and temporal power for the medieval Church. Although St. Augustine lived in the fifth century, he is as much a citizen of the Middle Ages as St. Francis of Assisi, St. Bonaventure, and St. Thomas Aquinas.

Meanwhile, out of the pine forests and frost-rimed harbors of the North, a new type of literature was emerging, tales of Germanic tribal heroes that come down to us in the Anglo-Saxon poem *Beowulf* and the German *Nibelungenlied,* stories of heroic adventure, enchantments and strange monsters, bloody family feuds. From the same sources at a later date came the Scandinavian eddas and sagas, long chronicles in verse or prose of legendary Viking days and the early history of Iceland and Norway.

As the ideals of the chivalric code began to change the old, rough feudal life, metrical romances dealing with King Arthur and other chivalric heroes followed the primitive, vigorous Germanic stories of the earlier period. In France troubadours sang graceful poems in praise of their loves and created the knightly cult of woman-worship. Most famous of the French romances were *The Song of Roland* and *Aucassin and Nicolette.*

By the thirteenth century medieval society was almost as formalized in its literature as it was in its social structure. For the knight and his lady there were the courtly romances sung by minstrels and troubadours; for the churchman, stories of saints and martyrs and collections of moral tales like those in the *Gesta Romanorum;* for the artisan and peasant, folk ballads and beast fables in which they satirized the clergy and nobility; for scholars, chronicles like those of Froissart and Commines.

The figure of Dante towers high above all other writers of the fourteenth century. *The Divine Comedy*—in Dante's day it was simply the *Commedia,* a story with a happy ending—is his master work, a long poem revealing the whole mind and spirit of the Middle Ages. In it the poet records the splendor and faith of the medieval Church, the idealism of chivalry, the scope of philosophy and science in his day. The framework of the story is simple. Dante, lost in the darkness of a deep wood, is rescued by Vergil, who guides the younger poet through Hell, Purgatory, and Heaven. The poem may be read for story, for poetic imagery, for allegorical interpretation. No other literary work has the scope and depth of Dante's narrative poem, and no other writer has ever expressed so vividly man's need for wisdom and spiritual guidance.

Geoffrey Chaucer is the great figure in English literature of the Middle Ages. *The Canterbury Tales* is a work of realism and humor that has not staled with time. *Troilus and Criseyde,* although written in verse, is our earliest example of the psychological novel. When Chaucer assembled his thirty-two pilgrims at the Tabard Inn at Southwark and set them on their way with gaiety and gusto, he was representing almost the whole of medieval society. But his people are never types. They are as strongly individualized as the stories they tell. And what stories! Chaucer is worth knowing. If the Middle English in which he wrote confuses you, read him in one of the excellent modern versions now available. There is no better introduction to English literature than the characters and tales of the Canterbury pilgrims.

Some of his stories Chaucer borrowed from Boccaccio, his Italian contemporary. Boccaccio lived and wrote in the Middle Ages, but his work points unmistakably toward the Renaissance. Author of various books, including a biography of Dante, he is best known for *The Decameron,* a collection of one hundred court and tavern tales retold in his graceful, lively prose. The stories range from the bawdy and the grotesque to the poetic and the pathetic. They are told, supposedly, by young men and women who have retired to a country villa to escape a plague. In *The Decameron,* however, the writer directs our interest to the stories and not, as Chaucer does, to their tellers. The collection demonstrated for Boccaccio's time the possibilities of fiction in prose. He is one of the forerunners of the modern novel.

Sir Thomas Malory performed the same service in English literature when he collected all the stories of King Arthur and his knights of the Round Table and retold them in *Le Morte d'Arthur.* Malory's tales, written in quaint, simple prose, still mean for most readers the romantic side of medieval life. The book is historically important, as it was one of the first printed by Caxton on his press at Westminster.

One last figure, and the most picturesque of all, stands between the old medieval world and the new. He is François Villon, scholar, poet, tosspot, gallows bait, associate of thieves and drabs. In his poetry he paints a realistic picture of the Paris underworld of violence and sin. His work also reveals his touching devotion to his aged mother and his adoration of the Virgin. Medieval and modern, he is the spiritual ancestor of Baudelaire. It has been said with justification for the claim that Villon, Rabelais, and Montaigne shaped French literature between them.

THE RENAISSANCE

The Renaissance was a period of rebirth, in art, science, and literature.

Again the change had come more slowly than men realized at the time. Artists of the Renaissance knew the earlier paintings of Cimabue and Giotto. Writers had before them the examples of Dante, Boccaccio, Chaucer, and Petrarch's sonnets. Medieval alchemists had never changed lead into gold, but they had made other discoveries adding to man's knowledge of his world. Coster in Holland and Gutenberg in Germany had invented the printing press and ended forever the slow process of copying books by hand. Marco Polo had traveled to Cathay and returned to Venice to stir men's imaginations with accounts of strange lands beyond the boundaries of Europe. And everywhere men were growing restless under the feudal domination of Church and state.

Perhaps the deciding impulse came when Constantinople fell to the Turks in 1453. Greek scholars, taking with them to Italy a knowledge of classic literature that Western Europe had almost forgotten, gave medieval man a new sense of continuity with the past. Suddenly, it seemed, a new age was dawning. It was Shakespeare's "brave new world," in which anything was possible.

Columbus, Vasco da Gama, the Cabots, Magellan, Sir Francis Drake, and all the great navigators and freebooting captains of the age widened men's physical horizon and claimed new lands beyond the seas for their sovereigns. Meanwhile men were exploring new frontiers of the mind as well as unknown continents. Galileo invented the telescope and Copernicus changed man's conception of the world when he viewed the earth as only one small dot in a universe of stars and planets. Painters learned from Greek sculpture the singleness of body and spirit. Da Vinci, Michelangelo, Raphael, and Titian were pioneers and masters in the greatest period of painting the world has ever known. Men began also to assert the right to worship as they pleased. Martin Luther and the Reformation are as much a part of the Renaissance as Michelangelo's *Last Judgment* or Shakespeare's plays.

It is against this larger background that the literature of the period must be viewed, for to the Renaissance man scholarship, art, science, statecraft, poetry, and philosophy were one unit of human thought and activity, not divided into separate departments as we know them today. Da Vinci was, among other things, a painter, musician, inventor, architect, mathematician, chemist, and botanist. Michelangelo wrote beautiful sonnets. Spenser, Sidney, and Raleigh were poets as well as soldiers. Benvenuto Cellini, sculptor and goldsmith, painted indelibly his own swaggering portrait in his *Autobiography,* in which he showed the age more vividly alive than Vasari revealed it in *Lives of the Painters.*

Italy, having inherited the relics of Greek and Roman civilizations, was the first country to feel the stirrings of the new age. At Florence, Lorenzo de Medici, patron of poets and artists, gathered about him a notable group of writers. There Machiavelli, Florentine diplomat, studied the career of the Medici and as the result of his observations wrote *The Prince,* a realistic treatise on statecraft. Ludovico Ariosto, at Ferrara, wrote *Orlando Furioso,* based on the French *Song of Roland.* In the same court Torquato Tasso completed his heroic poem, *Jerusalem Delivered,* a story of the Crusades.

In 1494 there was born at Chinon, France, a writer whose name is inseparably connected with the Renaissance spirit. François Rabelais, scholar and physician, poured his deep wisdom and racy humor into his two tales, *Gargantua* and *Pantagruel.* These books are a blend of seriousness and ribald laughter, and their humor still rings true after four centuries. A lusty rebel against medieval asceticism and scholastic dogma, Rabelais wrote in such fashion that the phrase "Rabelaisian wit" has passed into common usage.

A very different writer, but typical in his own fashion, is Michel de Montaigne, who tried to express in his essays what he felt as a man. "I am my book," he declared, and his writing covers a wide segment of human experience, all recorded with critical skepticism and complete intellectual honesty. His gifts to French literature are the frankness and irony of the Gallic spirit.

In England the Renaissance reached its peak during the reign of Queen Elizabeth. The sixteenth century was an age of great names and titles—Sir Thomas More's *Utopia,* Sidney's *Astrophel and Stella,* Spenser's *The Shepherd's Calendar* and *The Faerie Queene,* Bacon's essays, the plays of Christopher Marlowe, master of the resounding line—but Shakespeare stands far above his contemporaries. Like Homer and Dante, he is the poet of his own place and of all the world as well. It would require a book to analyze the many aspects of his genius. We read him for the entertaining stories he tells. Most of them, we know, were borrowed from other sources, from playwrights of his own day, from Holinshed's *Chronicles,* from Plutarch's *Lives,* but we can still admire the creative skill of a writer able to take a slight or threadbare story and shape it into a work of art. We read him for his matchless poetry, the sheer beauty of language we find even in his poorer plays. We read him for characters who seem as various as life itself—braggart Falstaff, noble Othello, perplexed Hamlet, ambitious Macbeth, tragic Lear, Malvolio, Prospero, Brutus, Dogberry, Pistol, Romeo, Shylock, Rosalind. The list is almost endless. We read him because he brings history dramatically before us, for the sweeping range of his thought, for the lyrics scattered through his plays. He stands at the center of Elizabethan England, but, as Ben Jonson wrote of him, "He was not of an age, but for all time."

While Shakespeare was at work on his tragedies, Miguel de Cervantes, an old Spanish soldier imprisoned for debt, began to write the first part of *Don Quixote,* published in 1605. This novel is more than the great book of the Spanish Renaissance—it is universal. The old Don is noble in his illusions, dignified in disaster. Beside him in his quest for adventure rides his lazy, shrewd, devoted squire. They are among the immortal characters of fiction. Perhaps Cervantes began his book, as some critics assert, with the intention of laughing antiquated chivalry out of Spain. Whatever his purpose, he produced a work which is both realistic and romantic and our one great example of the comic novel. The two parts of *Don Quixote* and the plays of Lope de Vega and Calderón mark the Golden Age of Spanish literature.

THE SEVENTEENTH CENTURY

When Shakespeare died in 1616, his laurels passed to Ben Jonson, whom the next generation ranked as the better playwright. One of Jonson's contributions to the theater was his revival of classical tragedy. More pleasing to modern taste, however, are his great comedies of humors—*Every Man in His Humour, The Silent Woman, Volpone, The Alchemist*—satires on the men and foolish foibles of his day. In Jonson's time the English stage seemed as brilliant as ever, but we know now that its light was little more than the afterglow of the bright Elizabethan day. The romances and tragi-comedies of Beaumont and Fletcher and the poetic violence of Webster are good, but the thinning vitality runs out in the sentimental melancholy of Ford and Shirley's artificiality. The closing of the theaters by law in 1642 ended officially the great decades of Elizabethan drama.

The translators of the Bible and Sir Francis Bacon wrote the most notable prose of the period. Bacon, like Montaigne, made all knowledge his province and natural experience his guide in the study of mankind. His essays he called "certain brief notes, set down curiously rather than significantly" on a wide range of topics. Many of his pithy sentences have passed into proverbial usage: "To choose time is to save time." "Silence is the virtue of fools." "Hope is a good breakfast, but it is a bad supper." A voluminous writer, he made his most important contributions to scientific thought in his *Advancement of Learning* and *Novum Organum,* in which he set forth his theory of inductive reasoning.

In the seventeenth century, an age of religious controversy and wars all over Europe, England was to reap the bitter fruits of the Reformation. Expansion of trade during the Renaissance had created a new, prosperous middle class. Industrious, thrifty, tenacious of rights, dissenting in religious views, this class owed nothing to the tradition of the medieval Church and little to the spirit of Renaissance humanism. In England the rebellion that began in 1642 was social, political, and religious warfare—middle class against the nobility, Parliamentarian against Royalist, Puritan against Established Church.

Today we see that the confusion and strife of the period were signs of painful readjustment to forces and drifts set in motion by Renaissance individualism. But to men of that time it seemed, as John Donne wrote, as if the world were "all in peeces, all cohearance gone, All just supply, and all relation." Few writers of the period escaped being swept along by the cross-currents of the time. Among prose writers, Milton's *Areopagitica,* Hobbes' *Leviathan,* Taylor's *Holy Living and Holy Dying,* Dryden's *Absalom and Achitophel,* Fuller's *Holy and Profane States,* and Locke's *Of Civil Government* reflect the religious and political sentiments of the age. Herrick, Lovelace, Suckling, and Waller were Royalist poets.

In John Milton, Puritanism found its great spokesman. Time has drained away much of the Puritan dogma from *Paradise Lost;* what remains in this greatest of English epics is spiritual exhaltation that dramatizes the conscience of a man and the conscience of his century. Writing to "justify the ways of God to man," Milton's majestic poem is a testament to faith and the same austere but sublime certainties in man's struggle between good and evil that we find in the work of Aeschylus and Sophocles. Pagan and Puritan were moved alike by the spectacle of divine redress redeeming mankind.

John Bunyan stands out as the great amateur among English storytellers. Setting out to write a simple parable of human life and Christian conduct, he produced a fervent allegory whose worldwide appeal is indicated by its translation into more than one hundred languages and dialects. This tinker and unlicensed preacher who learned the art of writing from his Bible is a master of eloquent prose. *Pilgrim's Progress* is a pious tale, an adventure story, a realistic novel. Many readers will be entertained also by the naïveté and disarming simplicity of Bunyan's autobiography, *Grace Abounding to the Chief of Sinners.*

With the Restoration of Charles II in 1660 the English stage had a brief but brilliant revival. Restoration comedy is witty and artificial, often shocking in its lack of moral taste. Written to please dissolute courtiers of a profligate court, it has had little popularity or influence beyond its own period. William Wycherley's *The Country Wife* and *A Plain Dealer* and William Congreve's *The Way of the World* are far superior to other plays of the time.

A Restoration work certain to find many readers in the long future is Samuel Pepys' *Diary*. Pepys is one of the truth tellers of our literature, and the diary he kept from 1660 to 1669 gives us our most intimate picture of men, manners, and morals in the days of the Merry Monarch.

The seventeenth century was rich in scientific writing. Descartes published *An Essay on Method;* Kepler formulated his mathematical laws of astronomy, and Newton in his *Principia* outlined his findings in physics, including the law of gravitation.

While English drama was declining, the French theater was entering its classic age. French drama was an outgrowth of the luxury and magnificence of the court during the long reign of Louis XIV, whose "L'état, c'est moi" created monarchial absolutism and prepared the way for the French Revolution. Pierre Corneille and Jean Racine wrote notable plays which have had a continued popularity in France, where the neo-classical elements of their dramas seem to satisfy Gallic passion for precision and form. A playwright more universal in his appeal is Molière, whose *Tartuffe,* and *The Misanthrope* are comedies of rich fun and good-natured satire. He has been called the Cervantes among playwrights.

When we look back on the seventeenth century, we are most likely to be attracted to its minor works: Donne's metaphysical poems, Herrick's lovely lyrics, La Fontaine's *Fables,* Madame de Sévigné's *Letters,* La Rochefoucauld's ironic *Reflections,* and Walton's *Compleat Angler,* the best book ever written on the "Contemplative Man's Recreation." These writers often seem closer to the true spirit of the age than the major figures who voiced its confusion and fury.

THE EIGHTEENTH CENTURY

The eighteenth century was an age of great prose. This is not to say that its poetry was inferior—only that its poets were few. Early in the period Alexander Pope polished the heroic couplet to epigrammatic perfection and in *The Rape of the Lock* and his *Essay on Man* made poetry a vehicle for social criticism and philosophic speculation. In the closing decades of the century Robert Burns brought poetry back to the simplicity of common things when he wrote of the sorrows, joys, and loves of the Scottish peasant.

But prose is the language of thought, and the eighteenth century has been aptly called the Age of Reason. It was a time when many men believed a perfect social order possible by systematizing all knowledge, thought, and activity. If science could be explained rationally, they argued, the same laws could be extended to society, government, religion, and the arts. Deism became the characteristic religious tendency, its essence the attempt to rationalize faith by reason and evidence. Constitutionalism became the ideal principle of government and *laissez faire* the dominant theory in trade and industry. To understand the underlying temper of the time, read its philosophers and scientists—Montesquieu's *The Spirit of the Laws,* Voltaire's treatises and his devastating satire in *Candide,* Rousseau's *The Social Contract,* Adam Smith's *An Inquiry into the Nature and Causes of the Wealth of Nations*—and you will see why the typical figures of the century are Franklin, Jefferson, Thomas Paine, Edmund Burke, Samuel Johnson. The age was trying to give order and meaning to what the Renaissance had promised and the seventeenth century had preserved.

The literature of the age reflects that common-sense point of view which sets a premium on truth. "The value of any biography depends on its being true," declared Dr. Samuel Johnson, and Boswell's biography of the great lexicographer is for all time a model of the factual and the real. Johnson's essays and his novel, *Rasselas,* are little read today, his dictionary is no more than a literary landmark; but the man himself, burly, slovenly, opinionated, yet great in spirit and revealingly human, lives in Boswell's work. The same deep and informed passion for truth makes Edward Gibbon's *The Decline and Fall of the Roman Empire* one of the greatest histories of all time.

Their purpose "to expose the false arts of life, to pull off the disguises of cunning, vanity, and affectation," Richard Steele and Joseph Addison reclaimed the essay from philosophy and science, gave it characters and the interests of the everyday world, made it familiar and entertaining as a picture of life. Good-humored, they stand at the opposite pole from Jonathan Swift, for whom the way to truth was the method of satire. *Gulliver's*

Travels is a classic of fantastic adventure and a savage indictment of civilized society, a story to entertain children and a moral lesson for older readers. It can be two different books in one because Swift masked his unpleasant truths about man, his pettiness, grossness, stupidity, and appalling animalism, within a framework of travel adventure in strange lands.

The development of the English novel, in fact, grew out of the truth-telling impulse of its creators. For most of us, probably, the first novel compelling our sense of belief is one we read in childhood—*Robinson Crusoe.* Daniel Defoe was a citizen of the country called by the derisive French a nation of shopkeepers, and his middle-class practicality and interest in factual detail are apparent in all of his books. *Moll Flanders* and *The Journal of the Plague Year* have one quality in common: both are fiction. His use of real names and places, his autobiographical method, even his stripped clarity of style, are devices to convince us of the truth of his narratives.

What Defoe did for the seamier side of human character, Samuel Richardson did for its virtues. His intention being "to promote the cause of religion and virtue," he told in *Pamela* and *Clarissa Harlowe* stories of high-minded and good young women. But he was less successful in portraying a noble young man in *Sir Charles Grandison.* His novels are awkward in their letter form and heavy with analysis of character, but they are models for sentimental fiction from his day to the vogue of the latest serial queen.

Henry Fielding, lawyer and playwright, believed that Richardson's moral views were conventional and shallow. In protest, he began a burlesque of *Pamela* in his own *Joseph Andrews,* but he forgot his fun-making purpose when Parson Adams walked into the pages of his novel. Fielding's masterpiece is *Tom Jones,* the realistic story of a hearty, vigorous young man of eighteenth-century England. This work is one of the world's great novels, filled as it is with the writer's robust humor and deep, mellow philosophy of life. Fielding's novels have the realism and shrewd insights we find in Hogarth's paintings.

A writer similar in material but without Fielding's warm sympathies is Tobias Smollett. His humor is crude and boisterous, his view of life critical and coarse. For all that, *Roderick Random, Peregrine Pickle,* and *Humphry Clinker* present a clear picture of the social life of the time.

Lawrence Sterne is a unique figure in the history of the novel. In one sense *Tristram Shandy* is not a novel at all but an elaborate cock-and-bull story in which Sterne allows his foibles and whimsical nature to lead him into all kinds of digressions on any topic that comes into his head. His biographical novel becomes a picaresque of the mind, wayward, witty, with flashes of sly sentiment and deep feeling. But his characters live. Uncle Toby, Corporal Trim, Mr. Shandy, and Parson Yorick are as real as Parson Adams and Tom Jones. *A Sentimental Journey* is in the same vein, a narrative unlike any other travel book ever written, entertaining because it reflects Sterne's own delight in the oddities of human character and experience.

Like the previous age, the eighteenth century has its literary residues, lesser works that still provide entertainment. Goldsmith's *She Stoops to Conquer* and Sheridan's *The Rivals* and *The School for Scandal* are delightful comedies. René Le Sage's *Gil Blas* is one of the earliest and best of picaresque novels; it is difficult to explain why it is not more widely known today. Then there are the comedies of Beaumarchais on which popular operas have been based—*The Barber of Seville* and *The Marriage of Figaro.* Fanny Burney's *Evelina* is dated now, but Goldsmith's *The Vicar of Wakefield* still holds its cheerful sentiment for many readers. Mention must also be made of John Gay's *The Beggar's Opera,* forerunner of the buoyant merriment of Gilbert and Sullivan.

THE NINETEENTH CENTURY

A literary colossus, Johann Wolfgang von Goethe stands astride the neo-classicism of the eighteenth-century and nineteenth-century romanticism. Emerging from the Storm and Stress period of German literature, he became our last example of the universal mind. His influence began in 1774, when *The Sorrows of Young Werther* infected a whole generation with pleasurable melancholy. He wrote plays as popular as those of Schiller, his friend and contemporary, and lyrics as lovely as those of Heine. His *Wilhelm Meister's Apprenticeship* is one of the great novels. But the true measure of his genius is *Faust,* the story of man's thirst for all knowledge and all power, reckless of consequences, regardless of moral and religious law. Perhaps the widespread interest which in 1949 attended his two hundredth anniversary will reclaim Goethe from awe-stricken neglect. He is the only modern writer to challenge the statures of Shakespeare, Dante, and Homer.

In general, the literary history of the nineteenth century is the story of romanticism in retreat and the triumph of the commonplace. The literature of the age we view in clearer perspective, for its great names were those we studied in high school and college, its titles the books we found on library shelves when we were children. Closer to these writers in time, we have a better understanding of their problems and achievements.

The age, which began with the Napoleonic Wars as an aftermath of the French Revolution, saw the peace muddled by the Congress of Vienna, knew disillusionment, and lived through financial panics, has more than surface resemblances to our own cycle of World Wars, the Russian Revolution, the Treaty of Versailles, dictators, depression, and spiritual bankruptcy. Today we know that the writers of the Romantic Age were not always romantic and that the great Victorians were not as full of sweetness and light as they seemed to their readers.

But for a time, at least, English romanticism spoke in its poets: Wordsworth, who found intimations of immortality in the beauty of nature and the heart of man; Coleridge, poet of imagination and dream; visionary Shelley; Byron, eternity's pilgrim and society's critic; Keats, who found life's joys and sorrows in the world of the senses.

It spoke also in the essays of Charles Lamb and Thomas De Quincey, and in that strange offshoot, the Gothic romance. Horace Walpole in *The Castle of Otranto* and Mrs. Radcliffe in *The Mysteries of Udolpho* created a literary fashion, a spine-tingling fiction of ghosts, sleepwalkers, ruined castles, dismal crypts, birds of ill omen, plots of abduction and murder. This literature was to cross the Atlantic and reach its final flowering in Edgar Allan Poe's poems and his *Tales of the Grotesque and Arabesque.*

In a Hampshire village a quiet spinster turned her back on terror and stormy passion and in *Pride and Prejudice* brought the novel of manners to a point of perfection it has not achieved since. Perhaps *Emma,* or *Persuasion,* is a better novel in construction and detail, but her story of the five Bennett sisters will always hold first place among Jane Austen's readers. For her the materials of fiction were not the clash of events in that uncertain time. She took her subjects from provincial society, the only life she knew. A country dance or a strawberry tea was to her an occasion filled with dramatic possibilities, but she created great effects with her small cast and single scene. Her shrewd observations of life, ironic wit, and agreeable good sense make her a writer whose popularity is not likely to fade.

At the same time Sir Walter Scott was creating the historical novel, perhaps the most lasting contribution of English romanticism to world literature. Scott's style seems awkward to us now and his fiction weighted with excessive detail, but he has never been surpassed in sheer storytelling ability or the variety of characters we find in his books. Pick any six titles from his long list of novels—*Guy Mannering, The Heart of Midlothian, Old Mortality, Ivanhoe, Kenilworth, Quentin Durward.* Each is an invitation to renew old pleasures in Scott's stirring pictures of the past.

Tennyson and Browning began their careers as romantics; they ended them as chief poetic spokesmen of the Victorian Age. Tennyson summed up its indecisions, hopes, and fears when he published *In Memoriam* in 1850. Browning's master work did not appear until 1868. *The Ring and the Book* is a long narrative poem pointing toward the modern psychological novel. Poetry interpreted the age; the essay criticized it in the work of Matthew Arnold, John Ruskin, Thomas Carlyle.

The parade of books which were to affect the contemporary world began in mid-century. John Stuart Mill published his *Principles of Political Economy* in 1848, the year in which Marx and Engels issued their *Communist Manifesto.* Charles Darwin's *Origin of Species* appeared in 1859, *The Descent of Man* in 1871. Marx spoke out again with the first volume of *Das Kapital* in 1867. In the next year Huxley's *The Physical Basis of Life* disturbed many readers. The next decade brought Henry George's *Progress and Poverty.* The 1880's saw the publication of Nietzsche's *Thus Spake Zarathustra* and *Beyond Good and Evil.* By 1890 only the writings of William James, Sigmund Freud, Henri Bergson, and Albert Einstein were needed to complete seasonal changes in the intellectual climate of our time.

The lasting effects of these world movers were still hidden in the future, however, when Charles Dickens published *Pickwick Papers* in 1836. This early work contains all the qualities we continue to associate with his name: the vivid characterizations, droll humor, pathos, a mastery of scene and situation. Today we know that his books sin against almost every canon of the novel, but we still read him because he carries us forward with a creative vitality that seldom loosens his hold upon our sense of belief. Again we can pick our titles at random—*David Copperfield,* the immortal *Pickwick, A Tale of Two Cities, Great Expectations.* In them Dickens remains the most popular of nineteenth-century writers.

Thackeray's *Vanity Fair* we read for the character of Becky Sharp in a novel which has unfortunately overshadowed the greater art of his historical masterpiece, *Henry Esmond.* Of George Eliot we are no longer quite so sure. *Adam Bede, Silas Marner, Middlemarch* and *Romola* are impressive monuments to her fame, but we miss in her moral seriousness and critical point of view the saving grace of humor which redeems Dickens' melodrama and sentimentality. Yet *Middlemarch* remains, as Virginia Woolf has pointed out, one of the few novels ever written for adult minds.

A writer more to the modern taste is Anthony Trollope, restored to popularity after several decades of neglect. Trollope is another of the great truth tellers. With reckless haste that paid little heed to niceties of style he turned out scene after scene of English provincial life, and as a result the social and cultural picture of his age stands before us today as meaningful and whole as it was when the ink dried on his page. Because he hurried to get everything in, his Barchester *is* nineteenth-century England. In novels like *The Warden* and *Barchester Towers* we recognize it for what it was, a very real and self-contained world.

Trollope presents his Slopes and Proudies with keen awareness of their social and moral values but without mocking irony. For that we go to George Meredith's *The Ordeal of Richard Feverel* and *The Egoist.* Meredith asks much of his readers, who must realize that his poised humor and subtle, figurative style are a comic mask over a view of life that was essentially tragic.

From art as discipline we turn to the world of the Brontës, where everything is natural and free. The heroine of Charlotte Brontë's *Jane Eyre* owes nothing to the conventions of Victorian society as she tells her own story with frankness and passion that brought new insights into English fiction. *Wuthering Heights,* by Emily Brontë, is a work of pure genius. Charlotte called her sister's novel a "wild" book, and it is that. Heathcliff and Catherine Earnshaw are human beings in speech and form, but their natures are as wild and stormy as nature itself. The brooding spirit of the Yorkshire moors sweeps into Emily Brontë's prose, filling it with harsh poetry. The result is a book that stands high among the world's great novels.

On the continent, meanwhile, novelists had carried realism to a point where no English writer of the time dared venture. The realists had not won their place without a struggle. Victor Hugo's *Les Miserables* and *The Hunchback of Notre Dame* keep alive the romantic spirit of his work. Few characters in fiction are as well known as D'Artagnan, Athos, Porthos and Aramis, the gallant heroes Alexandre Dumas immortalized in *The Three Musketeers, Twenty Years After,* and *The Vicomte de Bragelone.* Stendhal, author of *The Charterhouse of Parma* and *The Red and the Black,* is another writer marked for survival. Realism came into its own, however, when Gustave Flaubert wrote *Madame Bovary* and *A Sentimental Education.* Honoré de Balzac, most fertile of French novelists, wrote more than ninety novels and tales in his tremendous Human Comedy. Here, again, we pick our titles at random—*Father Goriot, Cousin Bette, Eugénie Grandet.* Guy de Maupassant, master of the short story, is the connecting link between Flaubert's realism and the naturalism of Émile Zola, who in *Nana, The Downfall,* and *The Land* carried realism to its farthest edge in his attempt to make fiction an exact transcription of life.

Nikolai Gogol, author of *Dead Souls,* is one of the fathers of the Russian novel, which reached its peak in the work of Ivan Turgenev, Fyodor Dostoevski, and Count Leo Tolstoy. Turgenev is the great critic of his society in *Smoke* and *Fathers and Sons,* a master of form and a writer of deep humanitarian spirit. Dostoevski's province is the black night of the human soul in the world of the outcast and the oppressed. In *Crime and Punishment, The Idiot,* and *The Brothers Karamazov* he plumbs the depths of man's shame and guilt. Tolstoy brought his passion for reform into much of his fiction. *War and Peace* stands far above his other novels, just as it towers over all fiction of the past or present. A story of the Napoleonic Wars, its vast enclosures of time and space seem to hold the whole of human experience within its pages. Anton Chekhov is the fourth of the great nineteenth-century Russians. Best known for his short stories, he wrote in *The Cherry Orchard* and *The Seagull* plays which convey the same terse, impressionistic pictures of Russian life.

Neither Robert Louis Stevenson's revival of romance in *Treasure Island* and *Kidnapped* nor Rudyard Kipling's brilliantly vigorous short stories—good as these writers are—measure up to European literature at the end of the nineteenth century. The only English writer to stand beside his continental contemporaries is Thomas Hardy. In novels like *The Return of the Native, The Mayor of Casterbridge,* and *Tess of the d'Urbervilles* he explored tragic relationships between character and environment. The individual, good or bad, against the vast, imponderable forces of the universe is Hardy's vision of life, and this spectacle he treats with detached awareness of the parts played by tragic circumstance and the irony of fate in the lives of men. In his work we feel that an Aeschylus or Sophocles has been reborn in a modern writer.

The nineteenth century in Europe closed with a revival of dramatic literature. Henrik Ibsen brought realism and social problems into the theater in *The Doll's House* and *Ghosts,* plays which prepared the way for George Bernard

Shaw and John Galsworthy. Bitterness and pessimism also marked the plays of August Strindberg. Maxim Gorky dramatized sheer human misery in *The Lower Depths.* The novel, the short story, and the drama were now realistic. Europe had entered the twentieth century.

More important to American readers, however, is the fact that the nineteenth century saw the development of our national literature. The early beginnings had been tentative and far apart. Benjamin Franklin's *Autobiography,* written without thought of publication, has become one of our permanent possessions, but it is an exception. The writings of Thomas Paine and Philip Freneau belong only to the period of the Revolution; the Connecticut wits are as dated as Michael Wigglesworth's *The Day of Doom;* the novels of Charles Brockden Brown are no more than titles in literary histories. But if William Cullen Bryant had written nothing but "Thanatopsis" and "To a Waterfowl" he would still be remembered, for he was our first true poet, finding food for moral reflection in the woods and fields of the American landscape. Washington Irving wrote the folklore of a new continent in "Rip Van Winkle" and "The Legend of Sleepy Hollow." Lover of legend and tradition, a writer perfect in the short flight, he bridged the gap between the old world and the new in *The Sketch Book* and *Bracebridge Hall.*

James Fenimore Cooper brought into American fiction a knowledge of rivers and woods and the wild, free life of the frontier. He wrote our best novel of the Revolutionary War in *The Spy* and our first true sea novel in *The Pilot,* but his fame is even more secure in the Leatherstocking Tales—*The Deerslayer, The Last of the Mohicans, The Pathfinder, The Pioneers,* and *The Prairie.* The figure of the lone hunter in the American wilderness possessed Cooper's imagination, and in his novels, carelessly written as they are, he gives us our heroic picture of pioneer life. There was a time when Cooper was read chiefly for his thrilling stories of escape and pursuit. Nowadays we know that his values run deeper. There is almost a prophetic quality in his writing; long before the actual frontier disappeared he dramatized the fate of the Indian and the frontiersman in that short interval between wilderness life and an expanding industrial society. Beneath their blood-and-thunder plots the Leatherstocking Tales reflect Cooper's interest in the westward movement and the social tensions it created.

The American renaissance came suddenly in New England. For a good picture of that spacious time read Van Wyck Brooks' *The Flowering of New England,* a book neither biography, chronicle, nor analysis, but a mixture of all three. The opening chapters on Ticknor and Everett, scholars of genius who gave the age its taste for learning, and the closing chapters on Holmes and Lowell—the lesser men of the period—enclose the book in a frame of reference. Everywhere else is the passionate stir of a new day. The background is of two parts: first the clear New England landscape of hills and meadows, quiet villages, orchards, and dark sea, a region marked by the trades and traits of its people; then the indoor world of the library, where men studied the philosophies of Greece and the Orient and poets discovered in lays of the troubadours and roaring sagas the literature of a romantic past. Against this background the great writers come to life, and as they move—Longfellow, Prescott, Emerson, Hawthorne, Thoreau, Whittier, Holmes, Lowell, and many others—through an age that begins in Gilbert Stuart's Boston and ends in Concord with the death of Thoreau, Brooks distills into flowing, luminous prose the essence of their work.

Something in the keen, bracing atmosphere of Concord seemed for a time to lift men above themselves. There Ralph Waldo Emerson, social rebel and ethical thinker, wrote his poems and essays to set forth his doctrine of self-knowledge and self-reliance. He preached no formal philosophy, only a transcendental belief in the possible in man, but he brought the democratic ideal into our intellectual and moral life. There Henry David Thoreau went into the woods in quiet protest against growing materialism in the society about him, and the record of his experience he wrote in *Walden* has become twentieth-century man's text in essential living. Nathaniel Hawthorne was never far from Concord in spirit. Working in solitude, he explored his regional and ancestral past. Out of his brooding concern for the Puritan spirit and the problem of evil came *The Scarlet Letter* and *The House of the Seven Gables* as well as the allegorical short stories, all works of quiet but sure art.

At Cambridge, meanwhile, Longfellow and Lowell lived in a mellower, more scholarly atmosphere. *Evangeline* and *The Courtship of Miles Standish* have the same academic echoes we hear in *The Vision of Sir Launfal* and *The Biglow Papers*. Oliver Wendell Holmes was a Boston wit. At Amesbury, not far off, Whittier preserved in *Snow-Bound* and other poems a nostalgic picture of rural New England already passing.

There were other great figures in America's Golden Day. In the South, Edgar Allan Poe had expressed in musical verse the mysteries of love and death, and he had brought the short story to its finished form in his tales of imagination and the supernatural. West of Boston, Herman Melville, having written *Typee* and *Omoo* among other books of seafaring adventure, was ready to publish *Moby Dick*. His own generation read *Moby Dick* for information and romance. Today we read it as a fable of man's self-destroying pursuit of natural evil in the world, the white whale a symbol of all the forces creating rage and hatred in man's long history. The novel is a reflection of America's unquiet mind, its magnificent hopes, despair, and defiance.

Walt Whitman published the first edition of *Leaves of Grass* in 1855. The decade was already one of stress when he spoke out bravely in the face of the gathering storm. Many of his poems are weakened by bombast and fustian, but at his best his work is filled with eloquence and beauty. It is a saddening commentary on our way of life to say that Whitman is our only great poet of democratic beliefs and institutions, a writer who spoke for himself, his country, and his time. Only Carl Sandburg in *The People, Yes* has echoed Whitman's vision of the greatness and simple dignity possible in the life of Western Man.

Mark Twain was in many ways Whitman's common, democratic man. He was born at the end of an era, and in his best books—*Huckleberry Finn, Tom Sawyer, Life on the Mississippi*—he looked back to a place and a way of life the Civil War had ended forever. The Mark Twain who looked toward the future was the tired, disgusted pessimist of *The Man That Corrupted Hadleyburg* and *The Mysterious Stranger*. His Hannibal is a place of idyl and myth, the enchanted world of boyhood in a young nation, between the forest and the river. All the life of America moved up and down the Mississippi in those years; Huck Finn and Nigger Jim are only a part of its restless humanity. Although the river offered tranquillity and freedom, its currents sometimes flowed into violence or into backwaters where a clear-eyed boy could see whatever was shoddy or soiled in human character. Twain was a curiously uneven writer. Much of his clowning as a public entertainer has already worn thin, but the virility and hearty laughter and sane pessimism are in the durable American grain, the drawling voice of the frontier in protest against mediocrity and conformity.

William Dean Howells, Twain's contemporary and friend, had the even temperament Twain lacked, but he was not sufficiently a rebel to break with the genteel tradition of most American writing after the Civil War. Admirer of Balzac and Zola, he created in his own novels only a domestic realism which has been called "the romance of the commonplace." *The Rise of Silas Lapham* is his most representative book.

On this side of the Atlantic the new realism first made itself heard in the novels of Stephen Crane and Frank Norris. Crane's *Maggie: A Girl of the Streets* was the shocking book of the mauve decade, a novel Howells thought "too honest" for readers of the 90's. Crane's great book is *The Red Badge of Courage,* a vividly realistic story of war from the point of view of a soldier in the ranks. Norris, a more somber writer, wrote *McTeague* and in *The Octopus* and *The Pit* completed two novels of a planned trilogy on American economic life, before his death at thirty-two.

Henry James, who wrote at the end of the nineteenth century and the beginning of the twentieth, belongs to British literature as well as American. An expatriate almost all of his life, he wrote on English and European society from the viewpoint of a sensitive American. His themes are the artist in a materialistic society and the American who is always a pilgrim to old world tradition and sometimes its victim. James' craftsmanship is so scrupulous and exquisite in detail that he has become one of the great influences on the technique of the novel, so that his fame, at least as a writer's writer, seems assured. *The Portrait of a Lady* is the best novel of his early period. *The Wings of the Dove, The Ambassadors,* and *The Golden Bowl,* written shortly after the turn of the century, are more complex in structure but more revealing as art. His novelette, *The Turn of the Screw,* is one of the great psychological horror stories in the language.

A few more names and we finish with the nineteenth century. These include Emily Dickinson, who wrote distilled lyrics on love, death, immortality, in the hidden privacy of her Amherst garden; Sidney Lanier, belated romantic; Bret Harte, whose tales of the gold rush created the vogue of the local color story; and Sarah Orne Jewett, who in *The Country of the Pointed Firs* re-created a picture of New England life after its great days had passed.

THE TWENTIETH CENTURY

When twentieth-century science invented the atomic bomb, it made fate more planetary than personal; otherwise our cares and concerns seem very much as they were a generation ago. Our attitudes toward our problems change more quickly —that is all. We have had the boob-baiting satire of the generation represented by H. L. Mencken in the essay and by Sinclair Lewis in the novel, the private anguish of Hemingway and others of the lost generation, and the proletarian dialectics of John Dos Passos and James T. Farrell in the depression 30's. Nowadays we are told that ours is the Age of Anxiety, but the telling has a familiar sound. Most of it was said, and more emphatically, by the major prophets of the Victorian Age. So while we wait to learn the mid-century *Zeitgeist,* the voices to whom we listen are mostly those from the recent past.

Looking back to the beginning of the century, for example, we know that Henry Adams and Theodore Dreiser speak to us more truly than Booth Tarkington and Winston Churchill, the popular writers of the period. *The Education of Henry Adams* is more than one man's examination of himself in relation to his background and his age. Adams viewed with detached appraisal a modern society which "ran in every conceivable and inconceivable direction," but without ethical purpose or significance. His importance is historical if nothing else, for he was the first serious writer to consider philosophically the relationship between modern man and the mechanical symbols of his civilization.

When Stuart Sherman complained that Dreiser "has chosen only to illustrate the unrestricted flow of temperament," he was pointing unknowingly to the trait which makes Dreiser a modern. There is a primitive, monolithic quality in his writing, "something grey and bleak and hurtful, that has been in the world perhaps forever," as Sherwood Anderson once wrote. Into his long, unwieldy novels and cumbersome short stories he poured all the accumulated facts resulting from his patient brooding over the activities and psychology of the animal man. In his world the divine fury of Aeschylus becomes the inward compulsions of nature and the external drives of a competitive society. *Sister Carrie, Jennie Gerhardt, The Financier,* and *The Titan* brought the American novel close to Balzac's achievement in his Human Comedy. *An American Tragedy* is documentary analysis of social morality. If *The Bulwark* and *The Stoic,* published after Dreiser's death, are less powerful than his earlier fiction, they gain serenity as the last words of a writer who dedicated his art to a search for truth concerning human behavior. There are no tricks in his novels; his artlessness is the secret of his simple and often terrifying sincerity.

Edith Wharton maintained for the novel its last hold upon a traditional society. Born into a Jamesian world of wealth and culture, she arrived on the scene too late to sustain its values and so became the historian of its disintegration as the old aristocracy of dignity and breeding was giving way to a new plutocracy of easy money and vulgar display. Having known what the traditional society once stood for, she let her characters stand or fall by its old-fashioned but recognizable standards. Her titles (*The House of Mirth, The Age of Innocence*) reveal the ironic temper of her art. Critic of the society she knew best, she made few excursions beyond her own fashionable world. One of these is *Ethan Frome,* a starkly realistic, almost timeless tragedy of New England life.

These three writers stand out among the literary cross-currents of the time. Local color, carrying over from the nineteenth century a minor art based on landscape, created effects as diverse as Owen Wister's sagebrush stereotype ("When you call me that, smile.") and brisk tales in which O. Henry recreated New York as Baghdad-on-the-Subway. Regionalism took on firmer outlines in Ellen Glasgow's novels. "What the South needs," she declared, "is blood and irony." *Barren Ground, The Romantic Comedians,* and *The Sheltered Life* are among the social chronicles and novels of manners that grew out of her determination to write about the South not sentimentally, as a stricken province, but as a part of the larger world. But writers were not satisfied to get America stated; they also wanted to remake it. When Upton Sinclair exposed the evils of the meatpacking industry in *The Jungle,* he assumed leadership of a group of writers who stood for political, social, and economic reforms. James Branch Cabell took the way of evasion and mockery. His romances of mythical Poictesme are escapes into ironic fantasy and nose-thumbing gestures toward Comstockery and Mrs. Grundy.

Suddenly America was reading its new poets: the psychological portraiture of Edwin Arlington Robinson's character studies; the pastoral meditations and narratives of Robert Frost, Yankee farmer and poet-sage; Carl Sandburg's American scene of prairie wheat fields, Chicago, steel mills, and the laboring life; Vachel Lindsay's chants of salvation in ragtime. These writers were already well established when T. S. Eliot published *The Waste Land* in 1922. Most influential poem of its period, *The Waste Land* presents in historical and literary image a contrast between the heroic past and an ignoble present.

Revolt from the village had already begun. In *Winesburg, Ohio,* Sherwood Anderson viewed with poetic perception the quiet bravery and longings of repressed, inarticulate lives. Edgar Lee Masters wrote as a poet in *Spoon River Anthology,* but his brief chronicles of drabness and disillusionment belong to the tradition of prose rather than to poetry.

The country roads of village fiction led inevitably to *Main Street.* Sinclair Lewis gave us an America of small-town smugness, stupidity, and sham, of billboards, realtors' conventions, adding machines, corner drug stores, filling stations, telephone operators, the movies, suburbia, high-pressure salesmanship, pepped-up religion, boosters' clubs, commercialized medicine. Critics might protest that the strident tones and confusion of his novels showed no depths of wisdom and repose, but we read *Main Street* and *Babbitt* as soon as they appeared. Lewis' people were two-dimensional caricatures, paper-thin, but they were close enough to the real to let us see ourselves and our neighbors. Although we realize now that Lewis loved best what he satirized most, he did succeed in doing perfectly what Mark Twain had attempted in *The Gilded Age*. His novels show America talking loud and acting big to conceal the poverty of spirit beneath its gadget-minded civilization.

One true artist of the period stood apart from literary cliques and fashions. Willa Cather was the last of a generation of writers who lived through the passing of the frontier, who saw the land of the homesteader transformed into a countryside of tidy farms and cramped, ugly towns; and she found in pioneer virtues her own values as an artist. Her first important novels—*O Pioneers!*, *The Song of the Lark*, *My Antonia*—enclosed vast areas of prairie, hills, and sky in a world rich and sustaining with homely realism. *A Lost Lady* belongs to a later period. Its theme, like that of *The Professor's House*, is decay, the spectacle of a way of life that was once great and spacious giving place to a new way that is paltry and crude. Having written the elegy of the frontier, Miss Cather found in more traditional societies realities of the spirit which have been almost overwhelmed in the complexities and confusion of the present. *Death Comes for the Archbishop*, a story of the Southwest, is an American masterpiece reclaiming a significant segment of our national past.

But Willa Cather's concern for lasting values offered little comfort, in the period between the wars, to young writers facing realities of disaster from want and destruction by war. By that time the Jamesian pilgrim had become the drifter, a rootless generation looking for emotional release in Paris night life or in the hot violence of Spain. To the young expatriates who drift between Left Bank cafés and Spanish fiestas in Ernest Hemingway's *The Sun Also Rises*, life has become the physical sensations of drink, sport, lovemaking, and the bullfight. The tragic love story and the disastrous retreat from Caporetto in *A Farewell to Arms* told us how the old values had been lost. The sense of retrieval which Hemingway expressed in an inferior novel, *To Have and Have Not*, found complete affirmation in *For Whom the Bell Tolls*, a novel of the Spanish civil war. Master of a stripped prose style that conveys the immediate realities of experience, Hemingway is important as the spokesman and technical innovator of his generation. His short stories, ranging from familiar anthology pieces like "The Killers" to the less familiar but more impressive "The Snows of Kilimanjaro," are probably the best being written today.

The 1930's gave us John Dos Passos, James T. Farrell, Thomas Wolfe, John Steinbeck, and William Faulkner. Dos Passos' best-known work is *U.S.A.*, a trilogy made up of *The 42nd Parallel*, *1919*, and *The Big Money*. This novel attempts to show, through the experiences of a dozen or so representative characters, the vast and complicated structure of American life between 1900 and 1930 and to trace the slow cleavage of its social and economic system, which by the depression years had created a nation divided between the possessors and the dispossessed. The note of social protest is loud in everything Dos Passos has written between *Manhattan Transfer*, a kaleidoscopic picture of New York life, and his recent novels of the New Deal era. To create the effect of contemporary life in *U.S.A.*, he hit upon three time-fixing devices: Newsreel, The Camera Eye, and a series of impressionistic biographies. Farrell is a realist more in the tradition of Zola. His Studs Lonigan trilogy and the series of novels dealing with Danny O'Neill are purely objective studies of life on Chicago's mean streets.

Thomas Wolfe's four novels— *Look Homeward, Angel* and *Of Time and the River, The Web and the Rock* and *You Can't Go Home Again*—present in the experiences of two different heroes a thinly disguised autobiography of Wolfe himself. Whether the hero's name is Eugene Gant or George Webber, he is the same undisciplined personality, a reflecting screen for his author's exuberance and confusion and despair. Wolfe's virtues as a writer are as great as his faults: on one side an unsurpassed realism of sense impressions, an expert command of language, the dream of lost time, the marvelous reporting, the vivid character sketches; on the other his failure to achieve form, the impassioned rhetoric and hymns to death and time that stand outside the framework of the novels, the overpowering egoism. His books make life seem the thing he said it was, a common haze of loneliness and groping shot through with private fantasy and furious outbreak against a materialistic society.

Wolfe's novels, diffuse in form, are in spirit all of one piece. Steinbeck is a more uneven writer. He has veered from primitive mysticism to the issues of class conflict, from sentimental exploitation of Whitman's dear love of comrades to quaintly humorous idealization of the simple life. His one really fine performance is *The Grapes of Wrath,* a bitter saga of migration and hardship in the experiences of a dispossessed dustbowl family lured to California during the depression and there betrayed by economic exploitation.

William Faulkner is another writer who has followed his own course. His subject is the destruction of the old order in the South and the further corruption of the descendants of that order by a ruthless and competitive industrial society; and his novels, experimental in form, poetic in style, are haunted alike by the beginnings of Southern culture and the threat of its extinction. Most of his fiction has for background imaginary Yoknapatawpha County in Mississippi. The Yoknapatawpha novels—*The Sound and the Fury, As I Lay Dying, Light in August, Absalom, Absalom!,* and *Intruder in the Dust* are among the best—elaborate a tremendous myth of Southern life and history. *The Sound and the Fury* tells of social and moral decay in a family of gone-to-seed aristocrats. *Light in August* and *Intruder in the Dust* reflect racial problems. *Absalom, Absalom!,* key novel of the series, brings together all of Faulkner's themes: the old order in the South, chattel slavery and the evils it engendered, the poor white, miscegenation, fratricide, community shame and guilt, social decay.

F. Scott Fitzgerald is a writer whose posthumous reputation has added greatly to his stature. During the 1920's he created three fashions in fiction: the younger generation novel, the college novel, and the gangster novel. *This Side of Paradise* has the wit and brilliance of a rebellious talent. *The Great Gatsby,* mature in theme and construction, is the story of one man's education in the emotional erosion and waste the boom period imposed upon the human spirit. *Tender Is the Night* is another picture of the lost generation, grown older and sadder but little wiser, and still lost.

In spite of recent vulgarization, regional and historical novels make up an interesting and varied body of work: the blend of realism and folk poetry in *The Time of Man* and *The Great Meadow,* by Elizabeth Madox Roberts of Kentucky; Glenway Wescott's stories of rural life in Wisconsin in *The Apple of the Eye* and *The Grandmothers;* Walter D. Edmonds' re-creation of Erie Canal days in *Rome Haul;* Elsie Singmaster's stories of the Pennsylvania German country; novels of the West by H. L. Davis, Vardis Fisher, Walter Van Tilburg Clark, and A. B. Guthrie; Conrad Richter's remarkable trilogy of pioneer life in *The Trees, The*

Fields, and *The Town;* Carl Sandburg's panorama of American history in *Remembrance Rock.* A list of books out of the ordinary in theme or treatment would include E. E. Cummings' *The Enormous Room,* a story of life in a French military prison; Pearl Buck's *The Good Earth;* Elinor Wylie's *The Venetian Glass Nephew;* Katherine Anne Porter's *Pale Horse, Pale Rider* and her short stories in *Flowering Judas;* Thornton Wilder's *The Bridge of San Luis Rey,* and Erskine Caldwell's tall-story exaggeration in *Tobacco Road.*

The vitality and techniques of the American novel have greatly influenced contemporary world literature. In England, on the other hand, the century has seen a decline in the tradition of the novel. Signs of change are most apparent in the work of H. G. Wells, who made the novel a literary packsack in which to peddle his views on science, education, religion, history, politics, and war. He began his career as a writer of pseudo-scientific romances like *The Time Machine* and *The War of the Worlds,* both still readable, and he ended it with didactic studies excellent for social and political analysis but of little value as fiction. *Tono-Bungay,* a satire on modern business practices, and *Mr. Britling Sees It Through,* a study of a rational, liberal-minded Englishman in wartime, will probably be read after his Utopian novels have been forgotten.

Polish-born Joseph Conrad was unequaled in his generation for technical and aesthetic effects which are only now being properly evaluated. He has been called a novelist of the sea, a romanticist, a realist, a writer of atmosphere, and a philosopher in fiction. His own experiences as a sailor provided many of the plots and exotic settings of his novels, but he is more than a writer of sea stories in the Marryat tradition, for his novels take shape around the moral issues of courage, love, fidelity, honor. Man he saw in conflict with powers of evil—savagery in *Almayer's Folly,* cowardice in *Lord Jim,* greed in *Nostromo,* lawlessness in *Victory,* madness in *Heart of Darkness.* To him, as he showed in *The Nigger of the Narcissus,* the sea was the testing ground of human character and action. He stated his literary creed in his preface to the same novel, when he wrote: "My task which I am trying to achieve is, by the power of the written word, to make you hear, to make you feel—it is, before all, to make you see."

John Galsworthy's deep humanitarian sympathies and impartial realism set the pattern for his novels and plays. What he did, quite simply, was ask the English upper middle class to re-examine its social structure and morality. In his novels the forces of conflict are always social, between the conservative group to whom property means goods acquired and possessed, a symbol of class responsibility and position, and the rebellious artist or lover of beauty. The three novels of *The Forsyte Saga—The Man of Property, In Chancery* and *To Let*—present a family whose collective life is dominated by things. This trilogy is both family chronicle and a social history of English life between the Victorian Age and the period immediately following World War I, in which Galsworthy analyzes with patient, scrupulous detail not only the acquisitive instincts of his ruling class but also its clannishness, stubborn pride, inverted sentimentalism, and indifference to the arts. *A Modern Comedy,* made up of *The White Monkey, The Silver Spoon,* and *Swan Song,* continues the story of the Forsytes in order to show postwar forces at work among the younger generation. Soames Forsyte, the man of property, is the central character giving unity to the whole work, a frank materialist whose life is nevertheless touched with greatness because he stands for order and recognized values in a world drifting toward no values whatever. He became so real to Galsworthy's readers that when *Swan Song* was published a London newspaper appeared with the heading, "Death of Soames Forsyte."

Although Arnold Bennett wrote a number of novels about the manufacturing district he called the Five Towns, *The Old Wives' Tale* is his greatest achievement in fiction. Time is the real theme of this novel, which relates the life stories of two sisters, Constance and Sophia Baines. Everything contributes to a sense of time passing. It condemns Constance to meek endurance of provincial routine and tedium. It carries Sophia to Paris and a precarious existence there, as well as to the accumulation of a modest fortune. In the end she goes back to the town of her birth, where the sisters end their days together as time rounds out its circle. *The Old Wives' Tale* is a cleanly built, powerfully realistic novel giving the impression of life itself. The Clayhanger tetrology and *Riceyman Steps* are other fine novels by Bennett, each as detailed and painstakingly realistic as a painting of the Dutch school.

The contemporary British novel reflects a variety of aims and means if not a great tradition. D. H. Lawrence wrote as a social prophet who wished to bring back to everyday existence a closer relationship between man and nature, an understanding of life less of the intellect than of the five senses. *Sons and Lovers,* a study of human personality thwarted by possessive mother love, is a powerful psychological novel written in vigorous, poetic prose. *The Rainbow* and *Women in Love* uncover subconscious tensions in sexual relationships to show that many moderns are lost in the confusion of their own emotions. W. Somerset Maugham is an unsparing realist and expert craftsman whose best novel, *Of Human Bondage,* is the partly autobiographical story of a young man who learns through disillusionment and hardship the limitations of his nature and talent. *The Moon and Sixpence* provides an exotic South Seas background for a grimly realistic study of self-centered genius in a novel based on the life of Paul Gauguin. *Cakes and Ale* is a wickedly satirical portrait of literary genius in shirt sleeves. Hugh Walpole was a more traditional writer. *Fortitude* is a modern version of *David Copperfield. The Herries Chronicle,* his most ambitious work, carries an English family through more than two hundred years of social and political history. Virginia Woolf experimented daringly with technique in her attempt to convey the true nature of reality. In prose as delicate and impressionistic as that of Katherine Mansfield in her short stories, Mrs. Woolf went even beyond Joyce in her use of symbols to make objects in the outer world correspond to inward states of thought and feeling. In *Mrs. Dalloway* and *To the Lighthouse* she was most successful in piercing the "luminous halo" of experience to show the fleeting, fragmentary interior life of her people. *Orlando* is fantasy on themes of English history and literature. *The Waves,* most intricate of her novels, attempts to record impressions of memory and sensation simultaneously in the lives of six different characters. Like Wells, Aldous Huxley has used the novel as a vehicle of ideas. Unlike Wells, however, he has no faith in science as a cure for mankind's ills. In *Brave New World* he satirizes with the savagery of a modern Swift all concepts of a scientific Utopia. *Crome Yellow* and *Point Counter Point* show modern man divided between the sensualism of his animal impulses and the frustration of his intellectual processes. The wisdom and insight of E. M. Forster are illustrated in *A Passage to India,* a study of racial tensions. *Memoirs of a Midget,* by Walter de la Mare, combines poetic fantasy and realistic social criticism.

One of the most remarkable and influential novels of modern times is James Joyce's *Ulysses,* a novel that records the events of a single day in the lives of a small group of Dubliners. In telling his story, Joyce has given his stream-of-consciousness technique a kind of order by superimposing his characters and the events of their day upon a structure of Homeric myth. Thus *Ulysses,* beneath its confusion of incident and subjective probings, parallels the story of the *Odyssey,* so that Leopold Bloom, frustrated advertising salesman, is recognizable as Ulysses, his earthy wife Molly as Penelope, and Stephen Dedalus, a young writer, as Telemachus. Joyce's bewildering system of cross-references, parodies, and parallels makes a first reading of this novel a bewildering experience for the uninitiated, for his purpose is not only to reproduce the sights, sounds, and smells of his scene but also to reveal the memories, desires, and emotions of his people. Standing, as it does, between his more objective and beautifully written autobiographical novel, *A Portrait of the Artist as a Young Man,* and the later, nightmare dream-world of *Finnegan's Wake, Ulysses* considerably enlarged the technical resources and scope of the novel. There are only a few contemporary novelists who have not borrowed either directly or indirectly from Joyce's symbolism and technique.

Evelyn Waugh and Graham Greene are the outstanding figures among younger novelists. Waugh at his best has powers of comic invention and satire reminiscent of a younger and less didactic Shaw. Under his hilarious improvisations in *Decline and Fall* and *Vile Bodies,* however, a serious writer is at work, whose theme is the shoddiness of fashionable Mayfair and the vicious frivolity of over-civilized society. *A Handful of Dust* shows class and country on the brim of a moral abyss. From these not-so-funny comedies of morals Waugh has turned in *Brideshead Revisited* and later novels to themes just as devastating but leavened by an undercurrent of religious significance. Graham Greene, who has written entertaining melodramas in *Stamboul Train, The Ministry of Fear,* and *It's a Battlefield,* and more realistic novels in *Brighton Rock, The Power and the Glory,* and *The Heart of the Matter,* carries an almost militant Christianity into the themes and style of his books. He writes always with an acute sense of surrounding evil and man's eternal conflict with a malignant universe.

In the drama George Bernard Shaw looms above all other playwrights of his own and later generations, just as Eugene O'Neill occupies the foremost place in the American theater. Shaw's wit and moral fury in such plays as *Candida, Man and Superman, Back to Methuselah, Heartbreak House,* and *Saint Joan* have lifted doctrine to the level of art and stripped away sentimentality and bourgeois morality from the English stage. Ireland's William Butler Yeats is still the giant among English poets of the last half century. The Sitwells—Edith, Osbert, and Sacheverell —represent aesthetic trends of the present time, and W. H. Auden and Stephen Spender speak for a more intellectual and critical school of poets trying to express in their verse the anxiety and turmoil of our industrial civilization.

Except for a few writers whose work holds immediate, topical interest, as in the case of the French Resistance group or the current Existentialists, the continental writers with whom we are most familiar are those whose established reputations make them available in excellent translations. The number of good books out of Europe seems all the more remarkable when we consider the wars, putsches, and purges which have ravaged the continent for more than two generations.

From France we have had the sophisticated satires of the writer who signed his country's name to his novels. Although Anatole France began his career in the 1880's, he did not publish *Penguin Island, The Gods Are Athirst,* and *The Revolt of the Angels* until the early decades of the present century. Roger Martin du Gard gave us an important domestic chronicle in *The Thibaults.* André Gide, eminent stylist and neo-classicist, is the author of *The Counterfeiters. Man's Fate* and *Man's Hope,* by André Malraux, reflect modern ideological issues. François Mauriac, author of *Thérèse,* is a deeply religious writer. Jules Romains presents a panoramic view of modern history in the series of novels called *Men of Good Will.* Albert Camus has brought new techniques into French fiction. Antoine de Saint-Exupéry has given us our only classic examples of the literature of flight in *Night Flight* and *Wind, Sand and Stars.* There is also American-born Julian Green, whose somber work, particularly in *The Closed Garden* and *The Dark Journey,* is Gallic in theme and treatment as well as language.

The most important writer in modern French literature, however, is Marcel Proust. His *Remembrance of Things Past* traces with subjective realism and profound psychological analysis the decay of French bourgeois society. In form *Remembrance of Things Past* is a novel without plot or crisis, unfolding with every lavish detail that Proust could invoke. From the dream-trance reverie which introduces Proust's themes and characters to that long last sentence with its slow echoes of the word *time,* the novel is art distilled out of the processes of memory and time itself, the structure being dictated entirely by the movement of memory and the illusion of the way time passes, or seems to pass, recurs, or seems to recur. The story begins against the idyllic setting of Combray, when the narrator was a child. It ends with a scene in which Proust collects his corrupt and aging people for the last time at a reception in the Faubourg Saint-Germain, and shows us a death's-head in every chair. It is an indecent spectacle of the end of an age, the will to death of an effete society, as revealed by an introspective storyteller whose observations and perceptions we follow from childhood to disillusioned middle age.

Close to Proust in stature stands Thomas Mann, German author who has now become an American citizen, a writer whom many regard as the greatest man of letters in the world today. Mann's international reputation rests chiefly upon his four great novels. *Buddenbrooks,* published in 1901, preceded *The Forsyte Saga* as a novel carrying the story of a single family through several generations. In this book the author traces the decline and dissolution of a wealthy mercantile family of Lübeck, where he himself had been born into the society he describes. *The Magic Mountain* is a symbolic and philosophical novel that attempts to take in the whole range of contemporary thought. To a sanatorium high in the Alps come diseased people from many countries. They are the citizens of a sick world, and their stories reflect the ills of an age and a continent. *Joseph and His Brothers* is an ambitious retelling of the Bible story in the light of anthropology, modern psychology, and historical perspectives. *Doctor Faustus* is another novel of modern Europe, in which a German musician symbolically sells his soul to the devil in return for two decades of creative genius. It is an allegory of moral and political crisis told with smoky medieval overtones of doom and damnation.

Franz Kafka is another writer who has imposed his vision of illusion and reality upon the twentieth-century consciousness. *The Castle* is a strange fable of spiritual quest, an inverted *Pilgrim's Progress* through the modern world in which science has established everything except the guideposts leading to human salvation. *The Trial* reads more like a modern *Book of Job,* for in it divine justice is as inscrutable and difficult to fathom as divine grace.

Norwegian literature has given us two novelists of wide range and power. Knut Hamsun is best known for *Growth of the Soil,* the story of a peasant farmer around whose land a small community grows, its growth paralleling the development of civilization itself. In *Kristin Lavransdatter* and *The Master of Hestviken,* Sigrid Undset created against the background of the past a fictional world of solid reality, so that these historical novels make the remote medieval age as real as the present. Her men and women live in a violent and picturesque time, yet they are true to the everyday experiences of life which have been common to men in all ages. When Sigrid Undset brought realism and modern psychology into the historical novel, she made the first important contribution to this form since the days of Scott. Another outstanding woman novelist was

Selma Lagerlöf of Sweden. Her most popular book, *The Story of Gösta Berling,* appeared at the end of the nineteenth century, but she did important work, in *Jerusalem* and *The Ring of the Lowenskölds,* during the present period. Her contemporary, Verner von Heidenstam, was a poet and novelist of strongly romantic and nationalistic temperament. Another Swedish writer who has achieved a world reputation in recent years is Pär Lagerkvist, a poet, dramatist, and novelist concerned with the problem of faith in a world of cosmic malevolence and human guilt. Special mention should also be made of Johan Bojer and Olav Duun, Norwegian novelists whose work had deep roots in peasant life; Johannes V. Jensen, author of *The Long Journey,* and Isak Dinesen, a writer in the Gothic tradition, of Denmark, and Halldór Laxness and Gunnar Gunnarsson, Icelandic novelists. The promising career of Kaj Munk, Danish playwright, was cut short when he was killed by the Nazis in 1944.

Under the Soviet regime the tremendous scope and vitality of Russian literature in the nineteenth century has been curbed by the masters in the Kremlin. Maxim Gorky continues to hold his place of importance among Russian writers whose careers began before the Red Revolution. Of the novelists who have received official approval, the best known outside Russia are Boris Pilnyak, Konstantin Fedin, Leonid Leonov, Ilya Ehrenburg, and Mikhail Sholokhov, and of these Sholokhov is the only writer who approaches the stature of the generation of Turgenev, Dostoevski, and Tolstoy. His epic work is *The Silent Don,* which, ironically enough, deals with counter-revolutionary activities of stubbornly independent Cossacks in the period between 1912 and 1922. A rather special work is Vladimir Dudintsev's *Not by Bread Alone.* Published during the brief period of seeming liberalism in 1957, this novel aroused considerable excitement both inside Russia and abroad when it appeared. An even greater furor arose over Boris Pasternak's *Doctor Zhivago* in 1958. The only long work of fiction by one of the leading Russian poets of the century, this novel in the great moral tradition of Russian literature presents a vivid picture of a disordered revolutionary age which, through loneliness, violence, cruelty, and fear, involves a whole society in the common ruin. The impact of this novel outside Russia has led to the translation of Pasternak's poems and also to interest in two other poets of the early revolutionary period, Sergey Esenin and Vladimir Mayakovsky.

In Italy the collapse of Fascist dictatorship was marked by a tremendous resurgence of literary activity. During the period of political domination of the arts only Riccardo Bacchelli achieved a critical stature matching that of the older generation of writers represented by Giovanni Verga, Luigi Pirandello, and Grazia Deledda. Although *Fontamara* had established the international reputation of Ignazio Silone, that bitter indictment of man's inhumanity to man had been written in exile; at home, Alberto Moravia had been the object of official censorship. But after the war a new generation of writers in the realistic tradition made their influence felt in such works as Moravia's *The Woman of Rome, Two Adolescents, Conjugal Love,* and *The Conformist;* Elsa Morante's *House of Liars;* Vasco Pratolini's *A Tale of Poor Lovers* and *A Hero of Our Time;* Giuseppe Berto's *The Sky Is Red* and *The Brigand;* Elio Vittorini's *In Sicily* and *The Twilight of the Elephant;* and Carlo Levi's *Christ Stopped at Eboli.* These writers in no sense comprised a school or another Italian Renaissance, but in these books and later ones they continue to attract the attention of readers abroad. Meanwhile the older classics have not been neglected. Alessandro Manzoni's *The Betrothed* has appeared in a new translation for English-speaking readers, and *Le Confessioni di un ottuagenario,* Ippolito Nievo's long chronicle of the struggle for Italian independence, is now available under a new title, *The Castle of Fratta.* The same theme of national freedom serves as the framework of *The Leopard,* by Giuseppe di Lampedusa. This story of the rise of Garibaldi and the unification of Italy was hailed as a masterpiece when it appeared in 1959. In the same year Salvatore Quasimodo, a controversial figure among modern Italian poets, was awarded the Nobel Prize for literature.

Greece is another nation now in the process of an active literary revival. The leading figures of the movement were Kostis Palamis and Constantine Kavafis in poetry and Nikos Kazantzakis in prose. Three of Kazantzakis' novels—*Zorba the Greek, The Greek Passion,* and *Freedom or Death,* as well as his epic retelling of the *Odyssey*—have been widely translated. Other novelists who have found an English-speaking audience are Stratis Myrivalis and Elias Venezis.

In Spain, on the other hand, the deaths of Jacinto Benavente y Martínez, José Ortega y Gasset, Pío Baroja y Nessi, and Juan Ramón Jiménez have left no figures of comparable stature in the fields of drama, philosophy, fiction, and poetry. Among the younger novelists Camilo José Cela, author of *The Hive,* and José María Gironella, who has written a trilogy of the Spanish Civil War, are the most outstanding.

The situation is quite different in Latin America, where in the past three decades Spanish American literature, having shed much of the revolutionary concerns of Mariano Azuela and Martín Luis Guzmán, the Parnassianism of Rubén Dario, and the provincialism of such writers as José Hernández, Rómulo Gallegos, Ricardo Palma, and Hugo Wast, has come of age. Two important influences on this new literature were Gabriela Mistral, Chilean poet and Nobel Prize winner, and Alfonso Reyes, Mexican poet, critic, essayist, and short story writer, who by their examples and their work helped to realign Hispano-American letters with the cultural tradition of the past and the rich, meaningful resources of the present beyond the limits of the national experience. Writers of the new generation have added the techniques of Joyce, Hemingway, Faulkner, and Eliot to their own native materials and models. The result is writing that is experimental, fresh, and indigenous without being provincial: in Argentina the novels and tales of Eduardo Mallea and Jorge Luis Borges; in Chile the poetry of Pablo Neruda; in Ecuador the novels and plays of Jorge Icaza; in Peru the novels of Ciro Alegría; in Mexico the verse of Octavio Paz and Alí Chumacero, the short stories of Francisco Rojas González, and Juan José Arreola, and the novels of Agustín Yáñez, Carlos Fuentes, Juan Rulfo, and Jorge López Paez. The late Xavier Villarrutia still remains an important figure in the Mexican theater, as does Florenzio Sánchez in Argentina and Uruguay. Eunice Odio, born in Costa Rica, is a poet of individual temperament and great talent. Although contemporary Brazilian literature has not produced a writer of the stature of Joaquim Maria Machado de Assís, Manuel Bandeira and Carlos Drummond de Andrade in poetry, Nelson Rodrigues in drama, and Jorge Amado and José Lins do Rego in the novel have made important contributions to the national literary tradition.

In Japan, since the end of World War II, a new literary tradition seems to be taking shape, a grafting of Western techniques and influences upon the older forms of Japanese literature. In present-day Japan the *Kabuki* theater and the classical *Noh* dramas still flourish; the change is most apparent in poetry and fiction. Both forms reveal a fusion of native and Western traditions. Of the novelists now known outside Japan, Junichiro Tanizaki is possibly the least affected by Occidental influences. His *Some Prefer Nettles* is regarded as a modern classic, and *The Makioka Sisters* is a beautifully presented study of the old merchant culture destroyed by the war. One of the most popular of contemporary writers is Yukio Mishima, whose *Confessions of a Mask, The Sound of Waves,* and *The Temple of the Golden Pavilion,* as well as a collection of his plays, are now available in translation. His range includes both the pastoral and the deeply psychological. Like Osamu Dazai and Jiro Osaragi, he also reflects in some of his novels the cultural tensions of a nation trapped by history between the power of the past and the processes of change. Another traditionalist is Yasunari Kawabata, author of *Snow Country*. *Fires on the Plain*, by Shohei Ooka, is a tragically compelling novel dealing with Japanese resistance in the Philippines during World War II. In *The Heiké Story*, Eiji Yoshikawa turned away from the confusion of the present to give an account of twelfth century history in his chronicle of the warring Genji and Heiké clans. The novel suggests Lady Murasaki Shikibu's *The Tale of Genji* in theme and treatment, but in Yoshikawa's work the events of the medieval past are viewed through the modern sensibility.

China, wracked by internal strife, war with Japan, and ideological domination throughout the present century, has produced no writing of any real significance; however, a number of the celebrated Chinese classics have recently been translated. These include Shih Nai-an's *Shui Hu Chuan (All Men Are Brothers)*, Tsao Hsueh-chin's *Hung Lou Meng (Dream of the Red Chamber)*, and the *Chin P'ing Mei*, now attributed to Hsü Wei.

In India another active literary movement, partly nationalistic, partly regional, partly social, is now in progress, and the time has passed when the native literature spoke to Western readers chiefly through the poems of Rabindranath Tagore and Mohammed Iqbal. Although E. M. Forster's *A Passage to India* remains the dominant image of Anglo-Indian life, writers in all fifteen major languages of Indian and in English are now attempting to create their own image of that vast and varied land. In some ways the situation is like that which existed in Ireland at the turn of the century, for many of the new Indian writers, particularly in the field of the novel, are engaged in creating a national literature in English. Of the novelists, R. K. Narayan has almost achieved classic dimensions. His fictional world is Malgudi, an imaginary town in South India, and within this setting, as in *The Guide, Swami and Friends, The Financial Expert,* and *The Man-Eater of Malgudi*, he shows himself a master of themes and moods that range from the tragic to the farcical. A writer of completely somber effect is Kamala Markandaya, whose *Nectar in a Sieve* presents dramatically the poverty, ignorance, and squalor of millions of Indian peasants. Another novel, *Some Inner Fury*, deals with the more familiar theme of Anglo-Indian relationships. The background picture of India's struggle for power, especially the influence of Gandhi on ideals of leadership, makes Anand Lall's *The House at Adampur* an impressive first novel. Politics is again the theme of Nayantara Sahgal's *A Time to Be Happy*. R. Prawer Jhabvala, although not a native Indian, is able through marriage and association to present with intimate knowledge the witty yet sympathetic pictures of Indian social life shown in *Amrita* and *The Nature of Passion*.

When we read or discuss these writers of our time, we are on more familiar but less certain ground. Contemporary judgments are likely to be more contemporary than final, however, and it is impossible to tell which books of the past sixty years speak only for a generation and which are the classics of the future.

To tell completely the story of the world's literature would require a book of many pages. This survey, as was stated at the beginning, is no more than tentative, an attempt to indicate the pleasurable reading of various literary ages. There have been many omissions, as the reader undoubtedly discovered for himself. But since every reader must eventually revise any reading list according to his own findings, this brief survey is not aimed at completeness or finality. Its usefulness is therefore limited to its stated purpose—an introduction to reading.

MASTERPLOTS
FIFTEEN-VOLUME
COMBINED EDITION

Volume One
Abbe-Barb

THE ABBÉ CONSTANTIN

Type of work: Novel
Author: Ludovic Halévy (1834-1908)
Type of plot: Sentimental romance
Time of plot: 1881
Locale: France
First published: 1882

Principal characters:
ABBÉ CONSTANTIN, a French priest
JEAN REYNAUD, his godson
MRS. SCOTT, an American
MISS PERCIVAL, her sister

Critique:

This tale has long been a favorite book for use in French classes. The story is full of pleasant places and pleasant people. There is little if any conflict; the one character who might possibly be considered the villain is too polite to offer much resistance to the plans of the hero and heroine. The novel was crowned by the French Academy.

The Story:

The kindly old curé, Abbé Constantin, stopped before the chateau of Longueval to look at posters which proclaimed that the chateau and its surroundings were to be sold at auction either in four pieces, or as a unit. The abbé, like the rest of the neighborhood, smiled at the idea that anyone might be able to buy the entire estate; more than two million francs was too large a sum for anyone to have. As he walked along by the old estate, he thought of all the delightful days he had spent with the old marchioness and her family. He dreaded the thought of a new owner who might not ask him to dinner twice a week, who might not contribute generously to the poor, who might not attend all the services of his little church. The abbé was too old to desire a change.

He walked on to the little house where Madame de Lavardens lived with her son Paul. Paul had not turned out well. His mother gave him a generous allowance to spend every year. After spending his money within three months in Paris, he stayed the rest of the year with his mother in the country. At the de Lavardens home, the abbé learned that Madame de Lavardens was hoping that her agent had secured at least one part of the estate for her. She was awaiting news of the auction, and she invited the abbé to wait with her and her son to hear what had happened.

When the agent arrived, he informed them that Mrs. Scott, a wealthy American, had bought the whole estate. The abbé's heart sank. An American! She would be a Protestant—no doubt a heretic. His hopes for his little church grew weak. No longer would the hothouses of the estate keep his altar full of flowers; no longer would the poor be relieved by the charity of the chateau. With a gloomy heart he went home to supper.

Jean Reynaud, the abbé's godson, was his guest at supper that night. Jean's father had been an officer in the same regiment in which the abbé had been chaplain, and the two had been the best of friends. When Jean's father had been killed, the abbé had taken care of Jean as if he were his own son. The boy had insisted on following his father in a military career. Jean's kindness was well-known in the area. He gave a yearly income to the destitute families of two men who had been killed on the same day as his father, and he was always doing charitable deeds for the abbé's poor.

On his arrival Jean set about cutting garden greens for the salad. He was startled when he looked up and saw two beautifully but simply dressed young women who asked to see the abbé. They introduced themselves as Mrs. Scott and Miss Percival, her sister. In a flurry of excitement the old abbé came out to meet his unexpected guests, and to his great pleasure they announced that they were Catholics of French-Canadian blood. When each of the women gave the abbé a thousand francs to give to the poor, the happy man almost burst into tears. The inhabitants of the chateau were still to be a blessing for the town.

Jean, overcome by the beauty of the two women, could not decide who was the more handsome. Miss Percival was the younger and more vivacious, but the serene charm of Mrs. Scott was equally attractive. The women told the abbé the story of their lives; of their poverty as children, of the lawsuit which their dying father had made them promise never to give up, and of the final success of the suit and the millions that became theirs because of it. Mrs. Scott said that she and her husband intended to spend much time in France at their new home. When the ladies left, the abbé and Jean were profuse in their praise.

This meeting was the first of many. The ladies had grown tired of social gaiety during their stay in Paris, and Miss Percival had become disgusted with the great number of men, thirty-four in all, who had proposed marriage to her, for she knew that it was her money, not herself, they were after. The women hoped to spend a quiet few weeks in the chateau, with the abbé and Jean as their only visitors. During the visits Jean fell in love with Miss Percival. He was upset when Paul de Lavardens insisted on being introduced.

Miss Percival knew at once that Paul's proposal would be number thirty-five. He was polite and made conversation easily, but he did not have the qualities she had come to admire in Jean. The more she saw of Jean the more she liked him, and it was not long before she realized that she was in love with the young officer.

At the first ball held at the chateau, Jean's manner showed Miss Percival that he loved her. But he said nothing, for he believed that army life would not be a happy one for her. As he had neither social graces nor the wealth which could be substituted for them, he did not dare to dance with her at the ball for fear he would blurt out his love. When she approached him to ask for a dance, he left abruptly.

Jean's regiment went away for twenty days. When he returned, he realized that he loved Miss Percival more than ever. Finally he decided that his only course was to be transferred to a regiment stationed in another area. On the night he was to leave he sent his excuses to the chateau and went to explain his actions to the abbé, who listened to his story with deep interest. Suddenly there was a knock on the door and Miss Percival walked in. She apologized for her intrusion, but said that she had come to confess to the abbé. She asked Jean not to leave, but to stay and hear her.

She announced that she loved Jean and felt sure that he loved her. Jean had to admit that it was true. She said she knew he had not dared to ask her to marry him because of her wealth. Consequently she was forced to ask him to marry her. The abbé commending her action, they became engaged.

When the marriage ceremony for the happy couple was performed in the little church, a fine new organ played the music for the service. It was Miss Percival's marriage gift to the church. The abbé was happy; the sale of the old chateau had brought more good to the town than it had known before.

ABE LINCOLN IN ILLINOIS

Type of work: Drama
Author: Robert E. Sherwood (1896-1955)
Type of plot: Historical chronicle
Time of plot: 1831-1861
Locale: New Salem and Springfield, Illinois
First presented: 1938

Principal characters:
MENTOR GRAHAM, a schoolmaster
ABE LINCOLN
ANN RUTLEDGE, Abe's early love
JUDGE BOWLING GREEN, Justice of the Peace
NINIAN EDWARDS, a politician
JOSHUA SPEED, a merchant
WILLIAM HERNDON, Abe's law clerk
MARY TODD, Abe's wife
STEPHEN A. DOUGLAS, Abe's political opponent
SETH GALE, Abe's friend
JIMMIE GALE, Seth's young son

Critique:

Robert Sherwood saw in the struggles of Abe Lincoln a symbol of democracy in action. The playwright was able to stick fairly close to the facts of Lincoln's life in working out his allegory of the growth of the democratic spirit, but in several scenes he was forced to invent fictitious characters or incidents to make his point. Whether the play be viewed as history or allegory, it remains as authentically American as its leading character.

The Story:

In the summer of 1831, when Abe Lincoln was twenty-two years old, he arrived in New Salem, Illinois, at that time a frontier village of fifteen log cabins. Shortly afterward the lanky young man opened a general store in partnership with a friend named Berry. Their stock included whiskey. Berry continued to tap the keg until he drank up all their liquid assets, and the store went bankrupt. Abe voluntarily assumed all the obligations for the partnership and went into debt for about fifteen hundred dollars.

At that time Abe boarded with Mentor Graham, the neighborhood schoolmaster, who began the task of teaching the young backwoodsman the rudiments of grammar. He awakened in Abe an interest in great oratory as well as a love for poetry. Graham sensed his pupil's extreme melancholy and preoccupation with death as well as his marked disinclination to do anything which required much effort. He advised Abe to go into politics, declaring wryly that there were only two professions open to a man who had failed at everything else—schoolteaching and politics.

Abe's opportunity came a year later while he held the job of local postmaster. A young politician, Ninian Edwards, a vigorous opponent of President Jackson, appeared at the Rutledge tavern in New Salem. He was looking for a possible candidate for the State Assembly. Edwards so much admired Abe's deft handling of several quarrelsome Jackson supporters that he offered Abe the candidacy.

In making his offer he was supported by Abe's two loyal and influential friends in Salem, Joshua Speed, a merchant, and Judge Bowling Green, the justice of the peace. But Abe, who had been considering going farther west, refused. Then several circumstances arose to change his mind. Seth Gale, the friend with whom

Abe had planned to make the trip, received news that his father was sick and he had to return to his native state of Maryland at once. And Ann Rutledge, daughter of the local tavernkeeper, with whom Abe had been secretly in love, received a letter from New York State to the effect that a young man named McNeil, with whom Ann had been in love, would not be able to return to New Salem. When Abe declared his devotion, Ann, disillusioned with her former lover, encouraged him. As a consequence, Abe sent word by his friend Judge Bowling Green that he would be a candidate for the State Assembly.

Fate brought about another, more disastrous, turn in Abe's fortunes. Ann Rutledge fell suddenly ill of a fever, and nothing that the doctor or Abe did could save her. After Ann's death, Abe became completely obsessed by a feeling of melancholia from which none of his friends could rouse him. He opened a Springfield law office with his friend, Judge Stuart, but he refused to take much interest in politics, in spite of the urgings of his clerk, William Herndon, who was a firebrand Abolitionist. Although Abe disliked slavery, he failed to see that the Abolitionists were helping their cause by threatening to split the country.

Knowing that something must be done to pull Abe out of his lethargy, his old political mentor, Ninian Edwards, introduced him to his ambitious sister-in-law, Mary Todd. Mary saw immediately that Lincoln was a man she could inspire to great things. Her aristocratic sister, Elizabeth, could not understand what Mary saw in this raw-boned frontiersman, but Mary saw in him the satisfaction of her own frustrated yearnings. They became engaged.

But Abe had not forgotten Ann Rutledge. On the day of his wedding to Mary Todd, he pleaded with his friend, Joshua Speed, to deliver to Mary a letter he had written to tell her that he did not love her. Speed insisted that Abe go to Mary himself and explain that he was afraid of her, of the demands she would make upon him. After he had humiliated Mary Todd with his explanation, Abe drifted back to the prairie frontier once more.

One day he encountered his old friend, Seth Gale, with whom he had once planned to go west. Seth had set out from Maryland with his wife and child, and was headed for Oregon. But his child, Jimmie, was ill, and Seth felt that if his son died neither he nor his wife would have the courage to continue the journey. In a flash of insight, Abe saw in his friend's predicament a symbol of the plight of the country as a whole. The Dred Scott Decision had made it possible to extend slavery in the West, a circumstance that would be fatal to those who, like Seth Gale, were trying to build a new country there. That vision crystallized Abe's purpose in life; and when he offered up a prayer to the Almighty for the life of little Jimmie, he was thinking of the country as a whole. Filled with a new purpose, he pocketed his pride and went back to Mary Todd. Still believing in him, she accepted Abe without a moment's hesitation.

From that day on his career followed one straight line, culminating in his nomination for the presidency. There were his debates with Stephen A. Douglas, who was to be his opponent in the election that followed. Within his own party there were political considerations which Lincoln handled with dignity and tact. But most important of all, there was his own life with Mary Todd. In the years since their marriage she had borne him four sons, one of whom had died, and through those years she had grown more tense and irritable, until the home life of the Lincolns became almost intolerable. Abe patiently endured her tirades in their own home, but when Mary began criticizing him in public, he resisted. On the night of his election she had one of her tantrums, and Abe was forced to send her home on the very eve of her triumph.

With his election to the highest office in the land, Lincoln's troubles increased. The old melancholia returned, the old preoccupation with death. On an eventful day in 1861, standing on the rear platform of the train which was to take him from Springfield to Washington, he tried to express to his old neighbors and friends his ideals for the future of America. As the presidential train pulled out he could hear his well-wishers singing the last strains of "John Brown's Body"—"His soul goes marching on!"

ABRAHAM AND ISAAC

Type of work: Drama
Author: Unknown
Type of plot: Biblical story
Time of plot: Biblical antiquity
Locale: Beersheba
First presented: Fifteenth century

Principal characters:
ABRAHAM
ISAAC, his son
DEUS, God
ANGELUS, the Angel
THE DOCTOR, a commentator

Critique:

One of the fifteenth-century mystery plays performed by guild members in various towns in England, *Abraham and Isaac* tells the biblical story of Abraham's willingness to sacrifice his son. The Brome version is distinguished from others by its greater length and its fuller development of the characters of Abraham and Isaac. The mystery plays, although often simple in both plot and design, helped to provide the background and tradition from which Elizabethan drama later emerged. The play is in verse, sometimes written in five-line stanzas rhyming *abaab* and sometimes in eight-line stanzas with alternate rhymes, these stanzas often ending in a shortened line. At other times the poetry conforms to no clear rhyming or stanzaic pattern. It is difficult to determine whether the play was originally written in a more careful poetic pattern, now lost through successive copyings and oral repetition, or whether it was originally written in a form close to the present version.

The Story:

Abraham, offering a prayer of Thanksgiving to God, counted his blessings—his land, his peaceful life, his children—and told of his delight in his favorite child, Isaac. He stood, while praying, in a field near his home in Beersheba. After the prayer he called to Isaac to return to their home.

God, in Heaven, summoned an Angel and told him that He intended to test Abraham's steadfastness by asking him to sacrifice Isaac, and he ordered the Angel to announce his wish to Abraham. Meanwhile, Abraham prayed again, asking God what gift or offering might please Him most. The Angel then appeared and told Abraham that God had commanded the sacrifice of Isaac as an indication of Abraham's love for the Lord.

Abraham immediately experienced great inward conflict. He kept repeating that Isaac was the most loved of all his children, that he would rather sacrifice anything else of his, including his own life, than to offer up Isaac. At the same time he was aware that God's will must be obeyed and that the sacrifice, no matter how painful, must be made. Abraham then called Isaac, who had been praying, and told him that they must perform a sacrifice for the Lord. Isaac declared his willingness to help. Abraham felt his heart breaking as they walked toward Mount Vision to make the sacrifice.

On their arrival at the mount, Isaac asked why Abraham seemed so concerned. The boy began to quake at the sight of the sharp sword in his father's hand because, aware of his father's acute misery, he guessed that he was to be the offering in the sacrifice to the Lord. Abraham then tried to explain to Isaac that they must follow God's commandment, having no other choice. But Isaac prayed to his father, asking him to spare his life and wishing his mother were there to intercede for him. Isaac also wondered what crimes he had committed that his life should be demanded by God. Abraham, in his misery, explained that God's will must simply be obeyed. At last Isaac understood and yielded to God's will. He asked, however, that Abraham not tell his mother he had been killed. Instead, she was to believe that he had gone into another land.

Resigning himself to death, Isaac asked for his father's blessing. Abraham gave his blessing, lamented further, and proceeded to bind Isaac's hands. Abraham then repeated his hope that he could be sacrificed in Isaac's place, but the brave Isaac reminded him that God must be obeyed and asked that the killing be done quickly. Abraham covered Isaac's face with a cloth and made ready to lift his sword.

But just as he was about to strike Isaac, the Angel appeared and took the sword from his upraised hand. The Angel said that Abraham had proved his willingness to obey God's command, an act which fully displayed Abraham's mind and heart. Therefore, the Angel continued, Abraham would not be compelled to sacrifice his son, but might substitute a young ram, tied nearby, for the offering. Abraham was overjoyed and after the Angel's departure gave thanks to God for Isaac's deliverance. Isaac, too, welcomed his reprieve, but only did so after Abraham had assured him that God would regard the ram as a worthy substitute. Isaac, at his father's bidding, ran to bring the ram. Returning with it, Isaac expressed his happiness that the beast, rather than he, was to be sacrificed. When Abraham offered up the ram, Isaac still showed a great fear of Abraham's sword and did not wish to look at it.

After the sacrifice, God again spoke to Abraham, acknowledging his goodness and promising that his family would multiply. Abraham then returned with Isaac to their home, recounting on the way his pleasure that his favorite child had been spared. Isaac was also grateful, but realistically he mentioned his fear and stated that he never wanted to see the hill again. Both thanked God and both showed great relief to be returning home together. Abraham praised the gentleness and understanding of his young son.

(At that point the Doctor appeared on the scene to make the moral of this happening explicit. The Doctor brought out the fact that the story showed how one should follow God's commandments without quarreling. The Doctor asked how many would be willing to smite their children if God so commanded. He thought that several might do so, though their women would wail and protest. But, the Doctor continued, God would mend everything for those truly willing to follow his commandments, for those who served God faithfully would be certain to benefit from their loyalty.)

ABRAHAM LINCOLN

Type of work: Biography
Author: Carl Sandburg (1878-)
Time: 1809-1865
Locale: Kentucky, Illinois, Washington, D. C., and areas of the Civil War campaigns
First published: ***The Prairie Years,*** **1926;** ***The War Years,*** **1939**

Carl Sandburg's *Abraham Lincoln* is a monumental work on a monumental theme, the life, works, and times of a symbolic American of history and legend. There is nothing of its kind, ancient or modern, with which it may adequately be compared. Among Civil War biographies its closest counterpart is Douglas Southall Freeman's *R. E. Lee* (q.v.), but even on this common ground point of view and the use of salient detail create vastly different effects of organization and presentation. In the Freeman biography Lee holds the center of the stage at all times, and the background panorama of people and events, even the battles and campaigns of the war, are shown only as they throw light on Lee's personality and labors. Sandburg, on the other hand, sets Lincoln against a tremendous movement of history as he tells simultaneously, on different levels, the story of a man, a war, an age, and a people. In the end the qualities which set this work apart seem appropriate and significant. Lincoln, that ungainly, complex, humorous, melancholy, and sadly serene man, was also one of the great solitaries.

When *The War Years* appeared in 1939, more than one reviewer commented on the happy conjunction of the perfect writer and the perfect subject. In Sandburg's case there is more truth in this critical generalization than in most, for he brought to his tremendous task a greater familiarity with the regional and folk aspects of Lincoln's life than anyone had possessed since Lincoln's own day. In the late nineteenth century there was still no wide gap between Sandburg's boyhood in Galesburg, Illinois, and Lincoln's growing years in the Sangamon River country. Familiar with New Salem, Vandalia, Springfield, and other landmarks of Lincoln's early life, the Swedish immigrant's son had known the men and women of Lincoln's day and had listened to their stories. Poet, fabulist, folklorist, and singer of the American dream, Sandburg felt in time that the Lincoln story had become a part of himself, not in the sense of blind hero worship but as evidence of the believable reality and fulfilled promise of American life.

More than thirty years of preparation, research, and writing went into the two divisions of *Abraham Lincoln*. At first Sandburg had in mind a story of Lincoln as the prairie lawyer and politician, but as his investigations continued he realized that his book was outgrowing its projected length and purpose. His increasing desire to tell all the facts of Lincoln's life as they existed in books already published, documentary records, or in the memories of men and women finally led him to divide his material into two parts, the first the story of the country boy and lawyer-politician, the second an account of Lincoln in the White House.

The Prairie Years was published in 1926. In these two volumes Sandburg deals with the more legendary aspects of the Lincoln story: boyhood days and backwoods life; a young man's journeys down the Mississippi; a masculine schooling, mostly self-taught, in grammar, mathematics, surveying, debate, and law; the years of clerking in grocery stores and working at odd jobs; military service in the Black Hawk War; his relations with Ann Rutledge, Mary Owens, Mary Todd; his law practice, and his early political career. This material is presented with a wealth of anecdote—stories about Lincoln and by him—so that it resembles at times an anthology of Lincoln lore. This period of Lincoln's life lends itself at times to fabulous or lyric treatment of which Sandburg the poet takes full advantage. There are passages that read like poetry, sentences and paragraphs that celebrate the beauty of nature and the mystery and wonder of life. Yet these occasional flights of poetic fancy are held firmly within bounds by realistic portrayal and strict regard for fact. In these volumes Sandburg's Lincoln emerges as a man of the people but no hero in the ordinary sense. Circumstances had shaped him into a man of vision and resource, but he was also a troubled, threatened, doubted man when he left Springfield in 1861 on the eve of his inauguration as President of the United States.

The War Years was published in four volumes thirteen years later. In the meantime Sandburg had traveled widely to gather material from every available source, read extensively in histories, biographies, newspapers, pamphlets, diaries, letters, and handbills, looked at pictures and cartoons, collected memorabilia of every sort, and written steadily while he studied, pondered, and re-created—in effect, relived—Lincoln's life during the Civil War period. The result, in the opinion of historians and critics, is a biography not likely soon to be surpassed of a man linked inseparably to his country's history and the folk imagination of all time.

Sandburg makes no attempt to gloss over the dark years of 1861-1862. Lincoln, who had incurred ridicule by arriving in Washington in a military cape and a Scotch plaid cap—in disguise, his enemies jeered—found himself hated in the South, handicapped by his Cabinet and the Congress, and faced with the crisis of Fort Sumter. Having taken over the leadership which William Henry Seward, Secretary of State, had tried at first to withhold from the chief executive, Lincoln then proceeded to display a temporizing attitude which history finds hard to explain. His declaration at the end of 1862—"Fellow-citizens, we cannot escape history."—is open to various interpretations. But Lincoln was to ride out of the storm of public disfavor. The Emancipation Proclamation, the turn of the tide at Gettysburg, the appointment of Ulysses S. Grant to the high command, and the Gettysburg Address mark what Sandburg calls the "Storm Center" of the war years. Although the mid-term elections of 1863 were against Lincoln and his own party was prepared to abandon him for the sake of political expediency, he won the campaign of 1864 in the face of the bitterest opposition of his enemies and the apathy of his party. From this time on Sandburg shows the tide in full flood—the aggressive final phase of the war, Sherman's march to the sea, the passing of the Thirteenth Amendment, the surrender at Appomattox, and the night at Ford's Theater on April 14, 1865. The end of the story is starkly, movingly, eloquently told with a poet's power of words and the historian's respect for truth.

In handling the massive reportage of *Abraham Lincoln,* Sandburg never pretends to be more than a storyteller, a recorder. Ever since the publication of *The Prairie Years* critics had tried to find a term to describe his method as a biographer, since his work could not be judged by any of the accepted schools from Herodotus to Lytton Strachey. *The War Years,* with all its vast accumulation of fact piled on fact, detail on detail, gave them the answer. Sandburg's method is the way of the old chronicles and sagas in telling the stories of folk and tribal heroes. This biography is a work which expands within the consciousness of the reader because of its continuous addition and multiplication of concrete and evocative details—battle summaries, character sketches, anecdotes, letters, quotations of every kind—all presented without analysis or interpretation so that in the end they shape themselves to their own pattern and carry their own weight of meaning.

Nothing is too vast or too commonly known to be glossed over without patient attention to every living detail; nothing is too trivial to be included. Never has there been such a summoning of witnesses to testify to a man and his age.

Foreign diplomats, members of the Cabinet and the Congress, military men of the North and the South, Tolstoy, Ibsen, Hawthorne, Mrs. Mary Chesnut, that shrewd, ardent Secessionist, and hundreds of obscure men and women appear briefly, make their gesture or have their say, and then disappear. His enemies make their insults and accusations; his detractors voice their ridicule; his friends speak in his praise. All leave behind them something that adds to our understanding of Lincoln, something more important than the opinions of politicians or the decisive outcomes of battles and accounts of military campaigns in creating the illusion of life itself.

These details, great and small, are the background setting against which Lincoln looms with increasing stature as his story unfolds. Against this backdrop of history he appears as a man all too human in his weaknesses and failures, just as he appears greater than other men in the strength, wisdom, and sad serenity of his last months. "Unfathomable" is the adjective Sandburg most frequently applies to him. Many writers have tried to analyze Lincoln. It remained for Sandburg simply to show the man, letting him speak and act for himself. This also was the method of the anonymous writers of the ancient sagas.

The War Years, more somber in tone, offers less opportunity than *The Prairie Years* for bardic song. Occasionally, however, the poet breaks in on the biographer and historian. One such passage occurs after the account of the Gettysburg Address when Lincoln, a wet towel over his tired eyes, was on his way back to Washington, and a moonlit hush had fallen over the battlefield and the new-made graves. Then in Whitmanesque measures Sandburg speaks his requiem for the buried dead in the silent cemetery as he looks out over the land and into the homes where the son, the husband, or the father is missing from his familiar place and the clocks of time and destiny tick on. Again, at the beginning of the chapter titled "The Calendar Says Good Friday," he employs another poetic passage to set the mood for coming tragedy. Nowhere, however, is he more moving than in the solemn intensity of the three simple sentences that bring the Lincoln story to its irrevocable close.

Sandburg's *Abraham Lincoln* is the biography of an American whose true story lends itself to the spirit of legend, a pageant of history, a poet's dream, a national myth. It is a story that is vast, implicative, at times contradictory. It is the stubborn, time-defying stuff of life itself, a story in which Sandburg finds in Lincoln's life the meaning of all America. But it is a poet's biography only in the sense that every true poet is a biographer providing insights to human experience. Unfortunately, not all biographers are poets. Carl Sandburg, to our enrichment, is the rare writer who is both. If America has an epic, it is this story of a national hero re-created from the testimony of the men and women of Lincoln's time.

ABSALOM, ABSALOM!

Type of work: Novel
Author: William Faulkner (1897-1962)
Type of plot: Psychological realism
Time of plot: Nineteenth century
Locale: Mississippi
First published: 1936

Principal characters:
Thomas Sutpen, owner of Sutpen's Hundred
Ellen Coldfield Sutpen, his wife
Henry, and
Judith, their children
Rosa Coldfield, Ellen's younger sister
Goodhue Coldfield, Ellen's and Rosa's father
Charles Bon, Thomas Sutpen's son by his first marriage
Quentin Compson, Rosa Coldfield's young friend
Shreve McCannon, Quentin's roommate at Harvard

Critique:

This novel is the most involved of William Faulkner's works, for the narrative is revealed by recollections years after the events described have taken place. Experience is related at its fullest expression; its initial import is recollected and its significance years thereafter is faithfully recorded. The conventional method of story-telling has been discarded. Through his special method Faulkner is able to re-create human action and human emotion in its own setting. Sensory impressions gained at the moment, family traditions as powerful stimuli, the tragic impulses—these focus truly in the reader's mind so that a tremendous picture of the nineteenth-century South, vivid down to the most minute detail, grows slowly in the reader's imagination. *Absalom, Absalom!* is a novel of tremendous and tragic import.

The Story:

In the summer of 1910, when Quentin Compson was preparing to go to Harvard, old Rosa Coldfield insisted upon telling him the whole infamous story of Thomas Sutpen, whom she called a demon. According to Miss Rosa, he had brought terror and tragedy to all who had dealings with him.

In 1833 Thomas Sutpen had come to Jefferson, Mississippi, with a fine horse and two pistols and no known past. He had lived mysteriously for a while among people at the hotel, and after a short time he disappeared. Town gossip was that he had bought one hundred square miles of uncleared land from the Chickasaws and was planning to turn it into a plantation.

When he returned with a wagon load of wild-looking Negroes, a French architect, and a few tools and wagons, he was as uncommunicative as ever. At once he set about clearing land and building a mansion. For two years he labored and during all that time he hardly ever saw or visited his acquaintances in Jefferson. People wondered about the source of his money. Some claimed that he had stolen it somewhere in his mysterious comings and goings. Then for three years his house remained unfinished, without windowpanes or furnishings, while Thomas Sutpen busied himself with his crops. Occasionally he invited Jefferson men to his plantation to hunt, entertaining them with liquor, cards, and savage combats between his giant slaves—combats in which he himself sometimes joined for the sport.

At last he disappeared once more, and when he returned he had furniture and furnishings elaborate and fine enough to make his great house a splendid showplace. Because of his mysterious actions, sentiment in the village turned against him. But this hostility subsided somewhat when Sutpen married Ellen Coldfield, daughter of the highly respected Goodhue Coldfield.

Miss Rosa and Quentin's father shared some of Sutpen's revelations. Because Quentin was away in college many of the things he knew about Sutpen's Hundred had come to him in letters from home. Other details he had learned during talks with his father.

He learned of Ellen Sutpen's life as mistress of the strange mansion in the wilderness. He learned how she discovered her husband fighting savagely with one of his slaves. Young Henry Sutpen fainted, but Judith, the daughter, watched from the haymow with interest and delight. Ellen thereafter refused to reveal her true feelings and ignored the village gossip about Sutpen's Hundred.

The children grew up. Young Henry, so unlike his father, attended the university at Oxford, Mississippi, and there he met Charles Bon, a rich planter's grandson. Unknown to Henry, Charles was his half-brother, Sutpen's son by his first marriage. Unknown to all of Jefferson, Sutpen had got his money as the dowry of his earlier marriage to Charles Bon's West Indian mother, a wife he discarded when he learned she was partly of Negro blood.

Charles Bon became engaged to Judith Sutpen but the engagement was suddenly broken off for a probation period of four years. In the meantime the Civil War began. Charles and Henry served together. Thomas Sutpen became a colonel.

Goodhue Coldfield took a disdainful stand against the war. He barricaded himself in his attic and his daughter, Rosa, was forced to put his food in a basket let down by a long rope. His store was looted by Confederate soldiers. One night, alone in his attic, he died.

Judith, in the meanwhile, had waited patiently for her lover. She carried his letter, written at the end of the four-year period, to Quentin's grandmother. About a week later Wash Jones, the handyman on the Sutpen plantation, came to Miss Rosa's door with the crude announcement that Charles Bon was dead, killed at the gate of the plantation by his half-brother and former friend. Henry fled. Judith buried her lover in the Sutpen family plot on the plantation. Rosa, whose mother had died when she was born, went to Sutpen's Hundred to live with her niece. Ellen was already dead. It was Rosa's conviction that she could help Judith.

Colonel Thomas Sutpen returned. His slaves had been taken away, and he was burdened with new taxes on his overrun land and ruined buildings. He planned to marry Rosa Coldfield, more than ever desiring an heir now that Judith had vowed spinsterhood and Henry had become a fugitive. His son, Charles Bon, whom he might, in desperation, have permitted to marry his daughter, was dead.

Rosa, insulted when she understood the true nature of his proposal, returned to her father's ruined house in the village. She was to spend the rest of her miserable life pondering the fearful intensity of Thomas Sutpen, whose nature, in her outraged belief, seemed to partake of the devil himself.

Quentin, during his last vacation, had learned more of the Sutpen tragedy. He now revealed much of the story to Shreve McCannon, his roommate, who listened with all of a Northerner's misunderstanding and indifference.

Quentin and his father had visited the Sutpen graveyard, where they saw a little path and a hole leading into Ellen Sutpen's grave. Generations of opossums lived there. Over her tomb and that of her husband stood a marble monument from Italy. Sutpen himself had died in 1869. In 1867 he had taken young Milly Jones, Wash Jones' granddaughter When she bore a child, a girl, Wash Jones had killed Thomas Sutpen.

Judith and Charles Bon's son, his child by an octoroon woman who had brought her child to Sutpen's Hundred when he was eleven years old, died in 1884 of smallpox. Before he died the boy had married a Negro woman and they had had an idiot son, Jim Bond. Rosa Coldfield had placed headstones on their graves and on Judith's she had caused to be inscribed a fearful message.

In that summer of 1910 Rosa Coldfield confided to Quentin that she felt there was still someone living at Sutpen's Hundred. Together the two had gone out there at night, and had discovered Clytie, the aged daughter of Thomas Sutpen and a Negro slave. More important, they discovered Henry Sutpen himself hiding in the ruined old house. He had returned, he told them, four years before; he had come back to die. The idiot, Charles Bon, watched Rosa and Quentin as they departed. Rosa returned to her home and Quentin went back to college.

Quentin's father wrote to tell him the tragic ending of the Sutpen story. Months later, Rosa sent an ambulance out to the ruined plantation house, for she had finally determined to bring her nephew Henry into the village to live with her, so that he could get decent care. Clytie, seeing the ambulance, was afraid that Henry was to be arrested for the murder of Charles Bon many years before. In desperation she set fire to the old house, burning herself and Henry Sutpen to death. Only the idiot, Charles Bon, the last surviving descendant of Thomas Sutpen, escaped. No one knew where he went, for he was never seen again. Miss Rosa took to her bed and there died soon afterward, in the winter of 1910.

Quentin told the story to his roommate because it seemed to him, somehow, to be the story of the whole South, a tale of deep passions, tragedy, ruin, and decay.

ABSALOM AND ACHITOPHEL

Type of work: Poem
Author: John Dryden (1631-1700)
Time: Late seventeenth century
Locale: London
First published: 1681

Principal characters:
DAVID, King of Israel
ABSALOM, his illegitimate son
ACHITOPHEL, chief of the rebels

Dryden claimed that *Absalom and Achitophel* was carefully planned to promote political reform. To gain this end, Dryden used satire, the true aim of which he defined as "the amendment of vices by correction." The particular vices he wanted corrected were those of the Whigs of his day, who were seeking to secure the succession of the Duke of Monmouth, illegitimate son of Charles II, to his father's throne. Second, realizing that direct satire might defeat its purpose by incurring resentment, Dryden chose to attack the Whigs by casting them as characters in the Biblical story of Absalom's revolt against David. Third, to dull the edge of the satire even more and thus increase its effectiveness proportionately, he cast it in verse, "for there's a sweetness in good verse, which tickles even while it hurts."

The poem is loosely organized, but several main divisions can be noted. The first of these, an account of the political situation in Israel (England), opens with a joking reference to David's (Charles II's) virility, which though wasted on a barren queen, produced a host of illegitimate progeny, of which by far the fairest and noblest was Absalom (Duke of Monmouth). David's kingly virtues were equally strong but unappreciated by a great number of Jews (Whigs), who because of a perverse native temperament wanted to rebel. Although David had provided no cause for rebellion, as the wiser Jews (Tories) pointed out, a cause was found in the alleged Jebusite (Catholic) plot to convert the nation to the Egyptian (French) religion. The plot miscarried, but it did create factions whose leaders were jealous of David and opposed his reign.

The second section consists of a portrait of Achitophel, the chief of these leaders (the Earl of Shaftesbury, leader of the Whigs), and an account of his efforts to persuade Absalom to seize the throne. Dryden characterized Achitophel as a brilliant wit touched by the madness of ambition. Unwilling to be remembered only for his distinguished career as a judge, he "Resolv'd to ruin or to rule the State," using the king's alleged sympathy for the Jebusites as an excuse for rebellion. Achitophel first used flattery to win over Absalom, proclaiming that the nation was clamoring for him—a "second Moses." At first Absalom resisted, pointing out that David was a wise and just king, and that David's brother (the Duke of York) was the legal heir. These halfhearted objections Achitophel met with sophistry. David's mildness, he claimed, had deteriorated into weakness; the public good demanded Absalom's strength; the rightful heir was planning to murder Absalom; David himself secretly wanted Absalom to be king and would support his claim as heir to the throne. To these specious arguments Absalom succumbed, whereupon Achitophel proceeded to organize all the Jewish malcontents into a single seditious party.

The third section of the poem lists the motives of these misguided patriots, opportunists, republicans, and religious fanatics. In a series of satiric character studies Dryden ridiculed their chieftains. In the character of Zimri, which Dryden considered "worth the whole poem," he poked fun at the fickleness and "extremity" of Buckingham, Shaftesbury's lieutenant in the Whig Party. Shimei represented the Sheriff of London, who had betrayed the king's interests, and Corah, the notorious Titus Oates, who had fabricated many of the details of the Catholic plot.

The next section of the poem describes Absalom's nation-wide tour, planned by Achitophel to gauge the extent of the people's support for their plan to exclude the legal heir from the throne and to establish Absalom's right to the succession by law. Traveling up and down the land, Absalom craftily represented himself as the people's friend, opposed to Egyptian domination, the Jebusite plot, and a senile king, but powerless to act because of his loyalty to the crown and the lawful succession. The Jews, always easy to delude, proclaimed Absalom a new messiah.

A long tirade follows in which Dryden attacked the Jews' naïve support of Absalom and their willingness to overthrow legally instituted authority. Though not a believer in absolute monarchy, Dryden was a conservative who upheld the supremacy of established law over the voice of the people. He feared that the government would quickly deteriorate into anarchy if the people were given the power to make and break kings at will by changing the order of the succession. Dryden, like all the conservatives of his time, feared the judgment of the people, and, therefore, any movement toward democracy.

In the next section Dryden sketched portraits of David's supporters—the Tory leaders. Here, of course, there was no satiric intent. Barzillai (the Duke of Ormond) was lavishly praised as the noblest adherent to David's cause and one of Israel's true heroes. Two members of the clergy, namely Zadoc (the Archbishop of Canterbury) and the Sagan of Jerusalem (the Bishop of London), were commended for their services to the crown. Other loyalists, praised for their services in Sanhedrin (Parliament), include Adriel (the Earl of Mulgrave), Jotham (the Marquis of Halifax), Hushai (Laurence Hyde), and Amiel (Edward Seymour). These loyal chieftains who defied the powerful rebel faction ultimately convinced David that concessions to the people would but feed their leaders' ambition, and that Absalom was being used as a tool by the treacherous Achitophel.

The last section of the poem consists of a long speech in which David finally reasserted the royal prerogative. Realizing that his enemies had been scoffing at his moderation and clemency as a sign of weakness and fear, he resolved to show his strength. David, regretting that Absalom would be compelled to suffer, expressed his willingness to forgive at the sign of repentance, but he refused to condone disloyalty. The Sanhedrin's attempt to change the line of succession he denounced, scorning their deceitful claim that they were trying to protect him from a scheming brother. Finally, he stated his reluctance to resort to force but declared his readiness to use it to defend the supremacy of established law over both Sanhedrin and king. In the last lines of the poem, heaven clapped its thunder in approval of David's words and the new era which they heralded.

Absalom and Achitophel failed, of course, to reform the Whigs; their attempts to put the Duke of Monmouth rather than the Duke of York on the throne were defeated only some fifteen years after the publication of the poem, which is remembered for its literary, not historical, significance.

THE ABSENTEE

Type of work: Novel
Author: Maria Edgeworth (1767-1849)
Type of plot: Social criticism
Time of plot: Early nineteenth century
Locale: England and Ireland
First published: 1812

Principal characters:
LORD CLONBRONY, an absentee landlord
LADY CLONBRONY, his affected, ambitious wife
LORD COLAMBRE, their son
GRACE NUGENT, a cousin
MISS BROADHURST, an heiress
ARTHUR BERRYL, Lord Colambre's friend
COUNT O'HALLORAN, an Irish gentleman
SIR TERENCE O'FAY, an impecunious nobleman
LADY DASHFORT, a designing noblewoman
LADY ISABEL, her daughter
MR. MORDICAI, one of Lord Clonbrony's creditors
MR. BURKE, an honest estate agent
NICHOLAS GARRAGHTY, a dishonest estate agent

Critique:

The Absentee, published in the second series of Miss Edgeworth's "Tales of Fashionable Life," is a novel of protest against the system of landlordism under which the owners of Irish estates disported themselves in fashionable London society while their tenants lived in misery and squalor, at the mercy of agents who were often unscrupulous and concerned only with their own interests. The Irish scenes of this novel are as fresh and vivid as those in the earlier *Castle Rackrent,* and the picture of London society, a world of thriftless absentees, wealthy snobs, fortune hunters, and match-making mothers, is excellent in critical and satirical detail. In this work the writer displayed a talent for caricature as well as deep regional feeling. Her vulgar Lady Clonbrony, Nicholas Garraghty, the dishonest agent, and Sir Terence O'Fay, an impecunious sponger, suggest later figures in the work of Surtees and Dickens.

The Story:

Lord Clonbrony was an absentee landlord. The owner of large but encumbered Irish estates, he lived in England because Lady Clonbrony, an extravagant, ambitious woman, would have nothing to do with Ireland or the Irish. People of wealth and position laughed at her and the silly determination with which she aped English manners and speech. Lord Clonbrony they ignored. A respected peer in Dublin and a good landlord when he had lived on his own estates, he was a nobody in his wife's fashionable world, and so he associated with questionable and dissipated companions like Sir Terence O'Fay. Little was known about Lord Colambre, the Clonbrony heir, except that he was a student at Cambridge and a young man of considerable expectations from a distant relative. A cousin, Grace Nugent, was well thought of because of her beauty and good manners.

Lady Clonbrony was anxious to have her son marry Miss Broadhurst, a young woman of much sense and large fortune. Although Lady Clonbrony and Mrs. Broadhurst did their best to promote the match, the young people, while friendly, were not drawn to each other, Lord Colambre because he was too much attracted by Grace's amiability and charm, Miss Broadhurst because she respected his feelings for his cousin.

In execution of a commission for Arthur Berryl, a Cambridge friend, Lord

Colambre went to the establishment of Mr. Mordicai, a coachmaker and money-lender. There he overheard some talk which revealed that his father's financial affairs were not in good order. Questioned, Lord Clonbrony admitted that his situation was grave but that he relied on Sir Terence, often his intermediary with his creditors, to prevent legal action against him. The father reflected with some bitterness that there would be no need for such expediency if landowners would live on their own estates and kill their own mutton.

Lord Colambre saw for himself the results of reckless borrowing when Sir John Berryl, the father of his friend, was taken suddenly ill. Mordicai, demanding immediate payment of a large debt, attempted to have the sick man arrested and thrown into prison. Only Lord Colambre's presence and firm words of rebuff kept the money-lender from carrying out his intention. Mordicai left with threats that Lord Colambre would someday regret his insults. Sir John Berryl died that night, leaving his family almost penniless.

Deeply concerned for his own family's welfare, Lord Colambre decided to visit Ireland and see for himself the state of his father's affairs. Lady Clonbrony used every possible argument to dissuade her son, and Sir Terence suggested that the young man could best help his father by marrying a woman as wealthy as Miss Broadhurst. When Lord Colambre left suddenly for Ireland, his mother, refusing to give up her matrimonial plans for her son, allowed her friends to believe that he had gone to attend to private business in connection with his marriage settlement. Since many people expected him to marry Miss Broadhurst, that story satisfied the Clonbrony creditors for the time being.

Arriving in Dublin, Lord Colambre met Sir James Brooke, a British official well informed on Irish affairs, and the two men became good friends. The young nobleman, pleased with everything he heard and saw, was unable to understand his mother's detestation of the Irish. He tried to meet Nicholas Garraghty, his father's agent, but the man was away on business. Instead, he was entertained by the agent's sister, a silly, affected woman named Mrs. Raffarty.

He also met Lady Dashfort, who saw in him a possible husband for her widowed daughter, Lady Isabel. Although he heard no good reports of Lady Dashfort or her daughter, he became a frequent visitor in their home. At last, interested in securing an alliance for her daughter, Lady Dashfort proposed that he accompany her to Killpatrickstown, where she was going to visit Lord and Lady Killpatrick. It was her intention to show him Irish life at its worst, so that he would have no desire to live on the Clonbrony estates after his marriage to Lady Isabel. Aware of his affection for Grace, Lady Dashfort arranged matters so that Lady Killpatrick asked her to exhibit her genealogical table, which had been prepared as evidence in a lawsuit. She did so with seeming reluctance, on the grounds that she was ashamed of her remote connection with the scandalous St. Omars. She then revealed that Grace's mother had been a St. Omar.

Lord Colambre wrote to his mother to ask the truth. She replied that the girl's mother had been a St. Omar but that she had taken the name Reynolds after an affair with a gentleman of that name. When the Reynolds family refused to acknowledge her child, she had married a Mr. Nugent, who had generously given the daughter his own name. The young man realized that this disclosure put a bar between Grace and himself.

Through the Killpatricks, Lord Colambre met Count O'Halloran, regarded by his neighbors as an oddity because of his learning, his fondness for animals, and his liking for the Irish. When the count returned the visit, Lady Dashfort took issue with him because he criticized the improper conduct of an English officer with whom both were acquainted. Lady

Dashfort's lack of good manners and moral sense, and the further revelation of Lady Isabel as a malicious flirt, showed the two women to Lord Colambre in their true light. He decided to leave the Dashforts and continue his tour alone.

Count O'Halloran prevailed upon him, however, to accompany that gentleman to Oranmore. There Lord Colambre found a family of taste and breeding, interested in affairs of the day and the welfare of their tenants. Stimulated by the example of Lord and Lady Oranmore, he planned to go immediately to his father's estate, but incognito, so that he could observe more accurately the conditions of the tenantry and the conduct of the estate agents.

He found the village of Colambre neat and prosperous, well looked after by Mr. Burke, the agent. After a dinner with the Burkes, the agent showed him over the estate with evident pride in all he had accomplished. He regretted, however, that the absentee owner took no interest in the land or the tenants, aside from the revenues derived from them. Burke's fears that Lord Clonbrony was displeased with his management were confirmed by the arrival of a letter in which his lordship dismissed the agent and directed him to turn over his accounts to Nicholas Garraghty.

Lord Colambre went next to Clonbrony. From a driver he learned that the tenants hated and feared Nicholas Garraghty, the factor, and Dennis Garraghty, his brother and assistant. The carriage breaking down, Lord Colambre spent the night with Mrs. O'Neill, a widow whose niece had been named after Grace Nugent. The next day the young nobleman was present when Dennis Garraghty refused to renew a lease promised to Mrs. O'Neill's son Brian. The arrival of Mrs. Raffarty and her identification of Lord Colambre caused Garraghty quickly to change his mind. Disgusted by the man's methods of doing business and by the unkempt, poverty-stricken appearance of the village, Lord Colambre wrote to his father and asked him to have no further dealings with the Garraghtys.

During the voyage back to England Lord Colambre's ship was delayed by a storm, so that the Garraghtys arrived in London ahead of him. He returned, however, in time to confront the agent and his brother with a report on their transactions. Hearing his son's story, Lord Clonbrony would have dismissed them on the spot if he had possessed the cash necessary to settle their entangled accounts. Lord Colambre then asked his father and Sir Terence for a full accounting of the distressed nobleman's obligations. In return, he proposed to settle the debt with the inheritance he would receive when he came of age, a date only a few days off, if his father would end all business relations with the Garraghtys and go to Ireland to live. Lord Clonbrony welcomed the proposal, but his wife, when she heard of it, treated the idea with scorn. She was already displeased with her son because he had not pressed his suit upon Miss Broadhurst and the heiress was to marry his friend, Sir Arthur Berryl. When Lord Colambre expressed pleasure over his friend's good fortune, Lady Clonbrony retired in disgust.

Under persuasion by every member of her family, Lady Clonbrony at last ungraciously agreed to return to Ireland. Meanwhile Lord Colambre, busy with his father's accounts, discovered that many of the London bills had been deliberately overcharged and that Nicholas Garraghty was in reality his lordship's debtor, not his creditor, as the agent had claimed. With some ready money sent by Lady Berryl, the former Miss Broadhurst, through her husband, Lord Colambre was able to settle his father's most pressing debts and Sir Terence was able to reclaim Mordicai's bond at a discount. Garraghty having been dismissed in disgrace, Mr. Burke was appointed agent of the Colambre and Clonbrony estates.

On the day he came of age Lord Colambre's first duty was to execute a bond for five thousand pounds in Grace's name, that amount of her own inheritance having been lent to her guardian years before. The young man's secret regret was that he could not offer his heart with his cousin's restored property.

Count O'Halloran, arriving in London, called on Lord Colambre. When the young nobleman confided his true feelings for Grace and told his friend something of her story, the count recalled a Captain Reynolds whom he had known in Austria. Dying, the officer had told of his secret marriage with a Miss St. Omar and had entrusted to the count a packet of private papers, among them a marriage certificate. The count had given the papers to the English ambassador and they had passed in turn into the keeping of Sir James Brooke, the executor of the ambassador's estate. Acting on this information, Lord Colambre went to Sir James and obtained the papers, which had never been carefully examined. When he presented them to the dead officer's father, old Mr. Reynolds accepted with delight the proof of his granddaughter's legitimacy and declared his intention to make her his heiress. Because Grace had never known of the shadow cast on her birth, Lady Berryl was delegated to tell her the whole story, a task which that friendly young woman performed with great delicacy and tact.

Acquainted with the true state of affairs, Lady Clonbrony offered no objections to her son's marriage with Grace. Lord Clonbrony and his wife returned to Ireland and there, in due time, Grace became Viscountess Colambre, much to the satisfaction of Lady Clonbrony, who saw so happily fulfilled her hopes that her son would marry an heiress.

THE ACHARNIANS

Type of work: Drama
Author: Aristophanes (c. 448-c. 385 B.C.)
Type of plot: Social satire
Time of plot: The time of the Peloponnesian War, 431-404 B.C.
Locale: Athens
First presented: 425 B.C.

Principal characters:
DICAEOPOLIS, a peace-loving citizen
AMPHITHEUS, his friend
EURIPIDES, the playwright
LAMACHUS, a general
AMBASSADORS TO THE ALLIES OF ATHENS
THE ACHARNIANS, a chorus of charcoal burners

Critique:

The Acharnians is the earliest known comedy of Aristophanes and, deservedly, his first prize-winner. Thematically, it is the most inclusive of his plays; in it we find his powerful wit and satire against militarism and war, his contempt for petty politicians and informers, his delight in earthy sex play, and his spirited spoofing of Euripides—qualities which make it the most personal of Aristophanes' works. When Dicaeopolis speaks directly to the audience in the parabasis, he does so with the voice of Aristophanes eloquently asserting his intellectual honesty and independence and declaring that he will always fight for the cause of peace and justice in his comedies.

The Story:

Dicaeopolis, waiting for the assembly to convene, sat musing, making figures in the dust, pulling out his loose hairs, and longing for peace. He was fully prepared to harass and abuse the speakers if they talked of anything but peace with Sparta. Immediately after the citizens had gathered, his friend Amphitheus began to complain of hunger because of the wartime diet. He was saved from arrest only by the intervention of Dicaeopolis.

The assembly then listened to a series of fantastic claims made by the pompous ambassadors to Athens' allies, each speech punctuated by a scoffing aside from Dicaeopolis, who knew full well that the entire alliance was wasting away from the effects of the Peloponnesian War. The high point of absurdity was reached when the last of the ambassadors ushered in a few scraggly, miserably dressed troops, introducing them as a Thracian host sent to assist in the war. Dicaeopolis, knowing of the assembly's willingness to adjourn upon the slightest provocation, then brought about the end of the session by claiming to have felt a drop of rain.

Finding himself unable to bring about the end of the war, Dicaeopolis determined to effect a personal, separate peace. Amphitheus, his own ambassador, returned from the enemy with three bottles of wine—the first five years old, the second ten years old, and the third thirty years old. The first two tasted vile, but the last was rich with a bouquet of nectar and ambrosia. Drinking it down, Dicaeopolis personally accepted and ratified a thirty-year peace. The Acharnians, whose vineyards had been ravaged by the enemy, having got wind of this traitorous act, arrived in pursuit of Amphitheus just as Dicaeopolis was leaving his house to offer up a ritual prayer to Bacchus in thanks for the peace that allowed him to resume once more a normal existence with his wife. Upon hearing his prayer, the Acharnians began to stone him as he tried in vain to persuade them that peace was good. Threatened with further violence, Dicaeopolis seized a covered basket of coals and announced that it was an Acharnian child, a hostage, which he would disembowel if he were not permitted to plead his cause. When the Acharnians agreed, he asked further to be allowed to dress properly for the occasion.

Dicaeopolis then went to the house of Euripides to borrow the costume of Telephus, the most unfortunate and pathetic of all the heroes of Euripides' tragedies. The great playwright, in the midst of composing a new tragedy, was hardly in the mood to be disturbed, but Dicaeopolis could not resist the opportunity to tease him about his wretched heroes and about the fact that his mother had sold vegetables. Finally the irate Euripides gave him the miserable costume and turned him out.

The eloquent plea for peace that Dicaeopolis delivered to the Acharnians was so moving that the chorus was divided on the issue. At that moment Lamachus, a general dressed in full armor, arrived on the scene. He declared that nothing could dissuade him from eternal war on the Spartans and their allies. Dicaeopolis countered with a proclamation that his markets were henceforth open to all the enemies of Athens, but not to Lamachus.

Shortly thereafter a starving Megarian appeared in Dicaeopolis' market place with his two daughters, who had agreed with their father that it would be better to be sold than to die of hunger. After disguising them as pigs by fitting them with hoofs and snouts, the Megarian stuffed them into a sack and offered them to Dicaeopolis as the finest sows he could possibly offer to Aphrodite. Dicaeopolis, aware of the deception, nevertheless accepted them in exchange for a supply of garlic and salt. The next trader was a fat, thriving Boeotian with a tremendous supply of game birds, animals, and fish. All he asked in exchange was some item of Athenian produce not available in Boeotia. Careful bargaining revealed, however, that the only such item was an informer—a vessel useful for holding all foul things, a mortar for grinding out lawsuits, a light for looking into other people's accounts. At last the bargain was made, and the next meddling informer to enter the market place and threaten Dicaeopolis with exposure to the authorities was seized, bound, and carefully packed in hay for the Boeotian to carry home.

Suddenly General Lamachus was ordered to take his battalions to guard the borders against invasion during the forthcoming Feast of the Cups. At the same time the priest of Bacchus ordered Dicaeopolis to prepare for joyous participation in the feast. The chorus wished them both joy as Lamachus donned his heavy armor and Dicaeopolis dressed in festival clothes, as Lamachus unhooked his spear and Dicaeopolis unhooked a sausage. After the feast Lamachus was carried in, hurt in a fall in a ditch before encountering the enemy; and Dicaeopolis entered, hilariously drunk and supported by two voluptuous courtesans. The blessings of peace were emphasized by the fact that, in the end, Lamachus the militarist was carried off to the surgeon while Dicaeopolis was conducted before the judges to be awarded the wineskin of victory.

ADAM BEDE

Type of work: Novel
Author: George Eliot (Mary Ann Evans, 1819-1880)
Type of plot: Domestic romance
Time of plot: 1799
Locale: England
First published: 1859

Principal characters:
ADAM BEDE, a carpenter
SETH BEDE, his brother
MARTIN POYSER, proprietor of Hall Farm
MRS. POYSER, his wife
DINAH MORRIS, her niece, a Methodist preacher
HETTY SORREL, another niece
CAPTAIN ARTHUR DONNITHORNE, the young squire

Critique:

This novel of English pastoral life probably shows George Eliot's quality as a novelist better than any other of her works, with the possible exception of *Middlemarch.* When George Eliot was writing of the peasants, the artisans, the yeomen, the clergy, and the squires of Warwickshire, she was writing out of memories of her own childhood, and her characters come to life as people she had known. Moreover, she superimposes upon them an awareness of fate, not majestic as in Hardy, but growing out of her convictions that there is a cause and effect relationship in human behavior as there is in the rest of nature.

The Story:

In the village of Hayslope at the close of the eighteenth century, there lived a young carpenter named Adam Bede. Tall and muscular, Adam was respected by everyone as a good workman and an honest and upright man. Even the young squire, Captain Arthur Donnithorne, knew Adam and liked him, and Adam in turn regarded the squire as his best friend.

Adam was, in fact, so good a workman that his employer, Mr. Jonathan Burge, the builder, would have welcomed him as his son-in-law and partner. But Adam had no eyes for Mary Burge; his only thoughts were of distractingly pretty Hetty Sorrell, niece of Mrs. Poyser, whose husband, Martin, ran the Hall Farm. Hetty, however, cared nothing for Adam. She was interested only in Captain Donnithorne, whom she had met one day in her aunt's dairy.

No one in Hayslope thought Hetty would make Adam a good wife, least of all Adam's mother, Lisbeth, who would have disapproved of any girl who threatened to take her favorite son from her. Her feelings of dependence upon Adam were intensified after her husband, Matthias Bede, drowned in Willow Brook while on his way home from the village inn.

In the meantime, Adam's brother Seth had fallen in love with the young Methodist preacher, Dinah Morris. Dinah was another niece of Mrs. Poyser, as unlike her cousin Hetty as Adam was unlike Seth. Hetty resembled nothing so much as a soft, helpless kitten, but Dinah was firm and serious in all things. One evening while she and Seth were walking home together from the village green, he had proposed marriage. Dinah sadly declined, saying she had dedicated her life to preaching the gospel.

When funeral services for Matthias Bede were held in Hayslope Church on the following Sunday, the thoughts of the congregation were on many things other than the solemn occasion they were attending. Adam's thoughts of Hetty blended with memories of his father.

Hetty's thoughts were all of Captain Donnithorne, who had promised to make his appearance. She was disappointed, however, for Donnithorne had already departed with his regiment. When he returned on leave, the young squire celebrated his twenty-first birthday with a great feast to which nearly all of Hayslope was invited. Adam was singled out as a special guest to sit at Donnithorne's table. Adam's mother was both proud and jealous lest her son be getting more and more out of her reach.

One August night, exactly three weeks after the Donnithorne party, Adam was returning home from his work on the Donnithorne estate when he saw two figures in close embrace. They were Donnithorne and Hetty Sorrel. When Adam's dog barked, Hetty hurried away. Donnithorne, embarrassed, tried to explain that he had met the girl by chance and had stolen a kiss. Adam called his friend a scoundrel and a coward. They came to blows, and Donnithorne was knocked senseless. Adam, frightened that he might have killed the young squire in his rage, revived him and helped him to a nearby summerhouse. There he demanded that Donnithorne write a letter to Hetty telling her that he would not see her again.

The next day Donnithorne sent the letter to Hetty in Adam's care, thus placing the responsibility for its possible effect upon Adam himself. Adam gave her the letter while they were walking the following Sunday. When, in the privacy of her bedchamber, she read the letter, Hetty was in despair. Her dreams shattered, she thought only of finding some way out of her misery. Then in November Adam was offered a partnership in Mr. Burge's business, and he proposed to Hetty. Mr. and Mrs. Poyser were delighted to find that their niece was to marry the man they so much admired.

But the wedding had to be delayed until two new rooms could be added to the Bede house. In February, Hetty told her aunt she was going to visit Dinah Morris at Snowfield. Actually, however, she was determined to find Donnithorne. When she arrived at Windsor, where he was supposed to be stationed, she found that his regiment had been transferred to Ireland. Now in complete despair Hetty roamed about until in a strange village, and in the house of a widow named Sarah Stone, her child by Donnithorne was born. Frightened, Hetty wandered on, leaving her baby to die in a wood. Later, tortured by her conscience, she returned to find the child gone.

When his grandfather died, Donnithorne returned to Hayslope to discover that Hetty was in prison, charged with the murder of her child. He did everything in his power to free her, and Dinah Morris came to her prison cell and prayed with her to open up her heart and tell the truth. Finally poor Hetty broke down and confessed everything that had happened since she left Hayslope. She had not intended to kill her baby; in fact, she had not actually killed the child. She had considered taking her own life. Two days later, Donnithorne, filled with shame and remorse, brought a reprieve. Hetty's sentence was committed to deportation. A few years later she died on her way home. Donnithorne went to Spain.

Dinah Morris stayed with the Poysers often now, and gradually she and Adam were drawn to each other. But Dinah's heart was still set on her preaching. She left Hall Farm and went back to Snowfield. Adam Bede found his only satisfaction toiling at his workbench. Then one day his mother spoke again of Dinah and her gentle ways. Adam could wait no longer. He went to find her.

ADDRESSES

Type of work: Formal speeches
Author: Abraham Lincoln (1809-1865)
First delivered: 1838-1865

Abraham Lincoln, sixteenth President of the United States and author of the Gettysburg Address, has come to be recognized as a creative speaker with an individual and appealing style. He had a perceptive sense of humor and an awareness of human dignity and of the tragedy which occurs with the loss of it. His arguments were logically respectable and responsive to the problems of his times. Although he always retained a directness of statement and feeling which reflected the conditions of his boyhood in Kentucky and Indiana, he was by no means a merely homespun speaker or writer; his poetic phrasing and imagery, Biblical allusions, and rhetorical devices all testify to the fact that he was a well-educated and intelligent man who could speak to any kind of audience in a manner and with the diction appropriate to the occasion.

But Lincoln was not perfect. If it is relevant to state the fact of his imperfection, the reason is that Lincoln's compassion and understanding and his contribution to the creation of American democracy as we know it have so impressed his fellow citizens that sometimes romantic legends lead us to believe that he never spoke without winning assent and admiration from those whom he addressed. But since he was human and to err is human, and since he was sometimes called upon to speak when there was no great problem to resolve or attack, he was on occasion ineffective in what he said.

Once the legend of Lincoln's perfection is dispelled, the fact of his greatness as a man, a President, and a speaker emerges. The Gettysburg Address of 1863 was no isolated phenomenon; the ideas, the sentiments, the clear eloquence had all been heard before, but never with such economy and depth.

"The Perpetuation of Our Political Institutions," one of the earliest of Lincoln's speeches, was an address given to the Young Men's Lyceum of Springfield, Illinois, on January 27, 1838. Lincoln began by recalling the political and social legacy bequeathed the American people of the nineteenth century by their fathers, and he asked how the task of maintaining the liberties transmitted to them might best be performed. He argued that the danger of loss came not from abroad but only from Americans themselves: "If destruction be our lot, we must ourselves be its author and finisher." Lincoln then referred to several violent instances of mob action and argued that such disregard for law could result in the loss of the legacy of freedom. Although the passion of revolution had helped Americans achieve their liberty, it was necessary to let reason and a reverence for law prevail.

In this early speech there is ample evidence of Lincoln's power, a power partly literary and partly spiritual. The young speaker reflected his sense of his role, as a citizen, to transmit the American heritage. Like his contemporaries, he placed his faith in reason, law, the orderly processes of government, and a sense of human dignity; but he added to this conventional faith his own clear conviction and commitment, applying the principles of democracy to the immediate danger he found about him. His philosophy of government was conservative; he did not speak for abolition—but what he conserved were the principles needed in critical times. His character, not the particular strain of his politics, was already the most persuasive element in his addresses; the demands of the Presidency in a time of civil war were to realize the nobility of that character.

At the close of the Republican State Convention at Springfield, Illinois, on

June 16, 1858, Lincoln delivered an acceptance of the senatorial nomination. This speech marked the beginning of the campaign that was to involve him in the series of debates with Stephen A. Douglas. After referring to the increase in slavery agitation, Lincoln declared:

> In my opinion, it will not cease, until a crisis shall have been reached, and passed—
>
> "A house divided against itself cannot stand."
>
> I believe this government cannot endure, permanently half slave and half free.
>
> I do not expect the Union to be dissolved—I do not expect the house to fall—but I do expect it will cease to be divided.
>
> It will become all one thing, or all the other.

Lincoln went on to discuss the Nebraska Bill, which allowed the people of any state or territory to determine whether slavery was to be allowed in their state or territory, the Dred Scott Decision, and the opinions of Senator Douglas. Lincoln maintained that Douglas cared nothing about halting the advance of slavery, and he implied that Douglas' policy tended to divide the Union.

In the first Lincoln-Douglas debate at Ottawa, Illinois, on August 21, 1858, Douglas referred to Lincoln's acceptance speech and quoted Lincoln's remarks concerning the "house divided against itself." He argued that the founders of the nation had believed it possible for the union to exist with both free and slave states, and he suggested that Lincoln could hardly disagree with such men as Washington, Jefferson, Franklin, and Hamilton. He endorsed the Dred Scott Decision, declaring that if Lincoln's opinions prevailed "black settlements" would "cover your prairies." "I am in favor of confining citizenship to white men, men of European birth and descent," Douglas asserted, "instead of conferring it upon Negroes, Indians, and other inferior races."

Lincoln replied by correcting a number of misrepresentations made by Senator Douglas, and in order to counter the charge that he was an abolitionist he quoted from a speech he had made at Peoria, Illinois, in 1854. Although he stated that he had no intention of introducing political and social equality between the white and the black races, he added that "notwithstanding all this, there is no reason in the world why the Negro is not entitled to all the natural rights enumerated in the Declaration of Independence—the right to life, liberty, and the pursuit of happiness." Even when, for the sake of politics, Lincoln agreed with Douglas that the black man was not his equal, he qualified his admission: "I agree with Judge Douglas that he [the Negro] is not my equal in many respects—certainly not in color, perhaps not in moral or intellectual endowment." Then, although the "perhaps" made a world of difference, Lincoln closed that particular subject: "But in the right to eat the bread, without the leave of anybody else, which his own hand earns, he is my equal, and the equal of Judge Douglas, and the equal of every living man."

Even now, more than a hundred years after the debates, the speeches by Douglas and Lincoln bring the living man before the imagination. Douglas is the clever, urbane debater; but Lincoln is at least as clever, and he has the words to reach all minds and to express sentiments which make up the American ideal. In debate, Lincoln was as relentless as his opponent in the attempt to win his points, but he was never vicious, even when he was not as candid as a man could be. His homely sense of humor remained an invaluable instrument in his bag of rhetorical devices. Immediately after considering Douglas' charge that he was an abolitionist, Lincoln passed on to the question of whether he had ever been a grocery-keeper. He said, "I don't know that it would be a great sin if I had been; but he is mistaken. Lincoln never kept a grocery anywhere in the world. It is true that Lincoln did work the latter part of one winter in a little still-house up at the head of a hollow."

At Springfield, Illinois, in his last speech of the campaign of 1858, Lincoln repeated that he admitted the right of the South to reclaim its fugitives and that he denied the right of Congress to interfere with the states. He declared that he had found the campaign painful, particularly because former friends accused him of wishing to destroy the union. Then he concluded that some had charged him with ambition, but that he would gladly withdraw if he could be assured of "unyielding hostility" to the spread of slavery. The candor and intensity of this brief speech make it one of Lincoln's most moving addresses.

Lincoln's courage became most evident with his address at Cooper Union in New York on February 27, 1860. He took issue with Douglas' claim that the authors of the Constitution understood the "question" as well as the men of his own day. He agreed with Douglas that the fathers of the Constitution understood the issue, but he disagreed with Douglas' assertion that they sided with Douglas' view that the Constitution forbids federal control of slavery. Lincoln argued strongly against any interpretation of the Constitution which would have permitted the extension of slavery to the Free States and the territories. He referred to the secessionist threat to destroy the union if a Republican president were elected, and he urged that the Republicans do their part to maintain peace. He concluded, "Let us have faith that right makes might, and in that faith, let us, to the end, dare to do our duty as we understand it."

Later in the year, in May, Lincoln was nominated for the office of President by the Republican Party; although he had been defeated in his senatorial campaign against Douglas, his speeches had brought him into national prominence. In February, 1861, after having been elected to the Presidency in November of the preceding year, Lincoln said farewell to the people of Springfield, Illinois, with a few poignant sentences in which he asked for the assistance of "that Divine Being" who had attended Washington. The Civil War began in April.

Lincoln's inaugural addresses, his message to Congress on July 4, 1861, and his annual messages to Congress presented the facts of the national crisis with clarity and compassion. The Gettysburg Address of November 19, 1863, brought all of Lincoln's sincere idealism into focus and related it to the grief of a nation. His addresses will continue to remain a cherished part of the American heritage and a significant segment of the world's literature.

THE ADMIRABLE CRICHTON

Type of work: Drama
Author: James M. Barrie (1860-1937)
Type of plot: Humorous satire
Time of plot: Early twentieth century
Locale: Loam House, Mayfair; a desert island
First presented: 1903

Principal characters:
THE EARL OF LOAM
LADY MARY,
LADY CATHERINE, and
LADY AGATHA, his daughters
THE HON. ERNEST WOOLLEY, his nephew
WILLIAM CRICHTON, his butler

Critique:

One of the best of Barrie's comedies, *The Admirable Crichton* contains a more definite theme than Barrie generally put into his plays. His satirical portrait of an English aristocrat with liberal ideas is the most skillful that has been done on the subject. Lord Loam, like many liberals, is a kind of social Jekyll and Hyde, accepting the doctrine of the rights of man in theory, but holding tightly to his vested interests in practice.

The Story:

Once every month, the philanthropic Earl of Loam gave expression to his views on human equality by forcing his servants to have tea with him and his family in the great hall of Loam House in Mayfair. It was a disagreeable experience for everyone concerned, especially for his butler, Crichton, who did not share his master's liberal views. Lord Loam alone enjoyed the occasion, for he was the only one who remained completely himself. He ordered his daughters and his nephew about and treated them exactly as he treated his servants on the remaining days of the month.

Lady Mary, his oldest daughter, was a spirited young woman who resented her father's high-handed methods with his family. Her indignation reached a climax one day when Lord Loam announced that his three daughters were to have but one maid among them on a yachting trip on which the family was about to embark. Lady Mary was furious, but she assumed that her maid, Fisher, would go along. When Fisher learned that she was expected to look after the two younger sisters in addition to Lady Mary, she promptly resigned, and the two maids attending Catherine and Agatha followed suit. Lord Loam was left without any servants for his projected cruise, for his valet also resigned. Although it hurt his pride deeply, Crichton finally agreed, out of loyalty to his master, to act as his valet on the trip. Moreover, he persuaded Tweeny, the housemaid upon whom he had cast a favorable eye, to go along as maid to Lord Loam's daughters.

The cruise ended unhappily when the yacht was pounded to pieces during a violent storm in the Pacific, and the party was cast away on a tropical island. All reached shore except Lord Loam. The other survivors had watched him throw away his life in a frantic but vain attempt to get into the lifeboat first.

On the island all tried to preserve as much as possible the class distinction which had prevailed in England. But the attempt was unsuccessful. Crichton alone knew exactly what he was doing, and it was upon him that the others had to depend. So Crichton, the servant, became on the island the natural leader, and he ruled his former superiors with a gentle but a firm hand. For example, he found the epigrams of the Hon. Ernest, which had seemed so brilliant in England, a bit trying; as a consequence, Crichton adopted the policy of submitting Ernest to a severe ducking whenever he came forth with an epigram. The aristocrats worried over the rising authority of their former butler and the decline in their own prestige. When Lord Loam finally appeared, after washing ashore with some wreckage, they urged him to take a stand of authority. Lord Loam's only recourse was to remove his little party to another section of the island apart from Crichton. But hunger, which the aristocrats by their own efforts could not assuage, brought them meekly back. Crichton became the acknowledged leader of them all.

Crichton took full advantage of his newly acquired authority. Having none of the earl's ideas about equality, he found no necessity for pretending that on the island his former betters were his equals in any sense. Each was kept in his place and required to do his own work according to the needs of the camp.

Under Crichton's rule the aristocrats were happy for perhaps the first time in their lives. The hard physical labor made something approaching a man out of Ernest, and the task of helping to prepare Crichton's food and waiting on him at the table turned Lord Loam's snobbish daughters into attractive and useful women. Lord Loam, dressed in animal skins, was merely a harmless and rather genial old man with no particular talents, whom everyone called Daddy. But the greatest change occurred in Lady Mary. She alone realized that in any environment Crichton was superior to them all, and that only the conventions of so-called civilized society had obscured that fact. Consequently she fell in love with the butler and did everything in her power to make herself his favorite. Crichton, attracted to the beautiful Lady Mary, considered making her his consort on the island. He indulged in the fancy that in some past existence he had been a king and she a Christian slave. But when a ship appeared on the horizon, Crichton realized that his dreams were romantic nonsense. On their return to England he again would be a butler, and she would be Lady Mary.

It was as Crichton had expected. After the rescue Lord Loam and his family returned to their old habits of thought and behavior. Crichton was again the butler. The Hon. Ernest wrote a book about their experiences on the island and made himself the hero of their exploits. Crichton was barely mentioned. Lady Mary reluctantly renewed her engagement to the rather asinine Lord Brocklehurst, whose mother was greatly worried over what had happened on the island and not sure that a daughter of Lord Loam was a fit wife for her son.

But Lady Mary still recognized Crichton's superiority, and told him so frankly. Crichton was shocked. Her views might have been acceptable on the island, he said, but not in England. When she expressed the radical view that something might be wrong with England, Crichton told her that not even from her would he listen to a word of criticism against England or English ways.

ADOLPHE

Type of work: Novel
Author: Benjamin Constant (1767-1830)
Type of plot: Psychological romance
Time of plot: Late eighteenth and early nineteenth centuries
Locale: Germany and Poland
First published: 1815

Principal characters:
ADOLPHE, the narrator
ELLÉNORE, his mistress

Critique:

From one point of view it may be said that the modern psychological novel sprang full-blown from the brain of Benjamin Constant; from other points of view, however, *Adolphe* is too much of a sport in nineteenth-century literature to shed much light on the historical development of the novel. The work might be described as a little seventeenth-century tragedy written in lucid eighteenth-century prose about a nineteenth-century situation by a twentieth-century analytical consciousness. The brevity and the apparently effortless progression of the story result in a deceptive simplicity. Ostensibly about an unhappy love affair—from the first fixation of an abundant and unattached vitality, through the luminous point of love, to the final disillusionment, or dissolution—*Adolphe* represents a remorseless survey of a familiar modern interior waste land whose most marked characteristic is gradual emotional atrophy.

The Story:

Having creditably completed his studies at Göttingen in spite of a somewhat dissipated life, Adolphe was expected, after a preliminary period of travel, to take his place in the governmental department of which his father was the head. The hopes entertained by his father, the minister of a German Electorate, inclined him to leniency regarding his son's indiscretions, but because of an inherent timidity shared by father and son—a timidity combined, on the part of the father, with a defensive outward coldness—no real sympathy was possible between the two. The constraint generated by this relationship had a considerable effect on Adolphe's character, as did a period he spent as the protégé of a woman much older than he whose strong and unconventional opinions made on him an indelible impression. This period, spent in long, passionately analytical conversations, culminated with the woman's death.

On leaving the university, Adolphe went to the small German principality of D——. At first he was welcomed at court, but eventually he attracted to himself the malicious judgments of those who resented the mannered frivolity, alternating with scathing frankness, which stemmed from his profound indifference to the available society. The woman who had formed his mind had bequeathed to him an ardent dislike of mediocrity and all its expressions, and he found it difficult to reconcile himself with the artificiality of society and the necessity for arbitrary convention. Moreover, his only interest at that time was indulgence in passionate feelings which lead to contempt for the ordinary world.

One thing which did impress him was the spectacle of a friend's joy at making a conquest of one of the less mediocre women of the court. His friend's reaction not only developed in Adolphe the regrets connected with piqued vanity, but also other, more confused emotions related to newly discovered aspects of his desire to be loved. He could discover in himself no marked tastes, but on making the acquaintance of Count P——, Adolphe soon determined to attempt establishing a liaison with the woman who had shared the count's life for ten years and whose two illegitimate children had been acknowledged by their father. Ellénore was a spirited woman who came from a good Polish family ruined in her childhood by political troubles. Her history was one of untiring devotion to the count and constant conflict between her respectable sentiments and her position in society—a position which had gradually become sanctioned, however, through the influence of her lover.

Adolphe did not think of himself as being in love, but as fulfilling obligations to his self-esteem; yet he found his thoughts increasingly occupied with Ellénore's person as well as his project and, unable to make a verbal declaration, he finally wrote to her. His inner agitation and the conviction he sought to express rebounded, however, and his imagination became wholly entangled when Ellénore refused to receive him. Becoming perfectly convinced of his love, he finally succeeded in overcoming her resistance to his suit. When the count was called away on urgent business, Adolphe and Ellénore basked for a few weeks in the charm of love and mutual gratitude. But Adolphe began almost immediately to be annoyed at the new constraint imposed on his life by this attachment, rewarding though he found it. The idea that it could not last calmed his fears, and he wrote to his father upon Ellénore's importunings, asking permission to postpone his return for six months. When his father gave the desired consent, Adolphe was immediately confronted again by all the drawbacks involved in his remaining at D——. He was irritated at the prospect of prolonging the deceptions required by his affair; of continuing the profitless life he led under Ellénore's exacting domination; above all, of making her suffer by compromising her position, for the count had become suspicious on his return.

Adolphe's resentment led to a quarrel with Ellénore in which were made the first irreparable statements that once spoken, cannot be recalled. The quarrel and the forced intimacy which followed it only increased Ellénore's anxiety and ardor, and she decided to break with Count P—— when he ordered her not to see Adolphe. Adolphe could not summon the courage to reject her sacrifice, even though it caused him great anguish and destroyed in a moment the social respect which Ellénore had acquired through years of effort. His sense of duty increasing as his love weakened, he was willing to fight a duel at the slightest disparaging remark about her; yet he himself wronged her in inconsequential social conversation. When the time came for him to leave, he promised to return, fearing her violent grief. Moreover, he discovered that the arrival of the break he had longed for filled him with keen regret, almost with terror. He wrote regular letters to her, each begun with the intention of indicating his coldness, but always ended with words calculated to restore her confidence in his passion. Meanwhile, he relished his independence.

Having understood from Adolphe's letters that it would be difficult for him to leave his father, Ellénore decided to join him. He wrote advising her to postpone her coming, with the consequence that her indignation was aroused and her arrival hastened. Adolphe had resolved to meet her with a show of joy, concealing his real feelings, but she sensed the deception immediately and reproached him, putting his weakness in such a miserable light that he became enraged. Finally, the two turned on each other in a violent scene.

On returning to his father's house, Adolphe learned that his father had been informed of Ellénore's arrival and had taken steps to force her to leave the town. His father's concern with Adolphe's future was undoubtedly genuine, but it unfortunately took the form of adherence to the standard values of a corrupt society and could only have the effect of strengthening the bond between the lovers. Adolphe made hurried arrangements and carried Ellénore off precipitately, smothering her with passion. Always astute, she detected contradictions in his actions and told him that he was moved by pity rather than by love—thereby revealing something which he would have preferred not to know and giving him a new preoccupation to conceal.

When the two reached the frontier, Adolphe wrote to his father with some bitterness, holding him responsible for the course he had been forced to take. His father's reply was notable for its generosity; he repeated everything Adolphe had said and ended by saying that although Adolphe was wasting his life, he would be allowed complete freedom. In the absence of the necessity to defend Ellénore, Adolphe's impatience with the tie became even more pronounced.

The two settled for a time in Bohemia where Adolphe, having accepted the responsibility for Ellénore's fate, made every effort to restrain himself from causing her suffering. He assumed an artificial gaiety and with the passing of time once again came intermittently to feel some of his feigned sentiment. When alone, however, his old unrest gripped him and he made vague plans to flee from his attachment.

At this point Adolphe learned of a fresh sacrifice which Ellénore had made, the refusal of an offer from Count P—— to settle her again in suitable circumstances. Adolphe, grasping at this opportunity, told her that he no longer loved her, but at the sight of her violent grief he pretended that his attitude was all a ruse. Another possibility of escape occurred after Ellénore's father had been reinstated in his property in Poland: she was notified that he had died and that she had been made the sole heir. Because the will was being contested, Ellénore persuaded Adolphe to accompany her to Poland. Meanwhile, their relationship continued to deteriorate.

Letters came from Adolphe's father asserting that since Adolphe could no longer be considered Ellénore's protector there was no longer any excuse for the life he was leading. The father had recommended Adolphe, the letters said, to Baron T—— (a friend of the father's and the minister from their country to Poland) and wished Adolphe to call on him. When the young man did so, Baron T—— assumed the father's role and attempted to separate Adolphe and Ellénore. Adolphe spent a night wandering in the country, engaged in confused meditations in which he told himself that his mind was recovering from a long degradation.

Ellénore made another futile effort to penetrate the closed sanctuary of his mind, but a new alignment of forces emerged as Adolphe succumbed more and more to the influence of Baron T——. He continued to procrastinate in putting a definite end to the relationship, but he wrote incriminating letters which the baron forwarded to Ellénore. At last she became fatally ill. Adolphe was finally freed by her death, which produced in him a feeling of great desolation.

THE AENEID

Type of work: Poem
Author: Publius Vergilius Maro (70-19 B.C.)
Type of plot: Heroic epic
Time of plot: The period immediately following the Trojan War
Locale: The Mediterranean region
First transcribed: Augustan manuscript

Principal characters:

AENEAS, Trojan hero destined to found the Roman race
DIDO, Queen of Carthage, in love with Aeneas
ANNA, her sister
ASCANIUS, son of Aeneas
ANCHISES, father of Aeneas
VENUS, goddess of love and beauty, mother of Aeneas
JUNO, queen of the gods and enemy of the Trojans
CUMAEAN SIBYL, prophetess who leads Aeneas to Hades
LATINUS, king of the Latins, whom Aeneas defeats in battle
LAVINIA, his daughter
TURNUS, Latin hero ambitious for the Latin throne and hand of Lavinia
EVANDER, Arcadian king, ally of Aeneas
PALLAS, his son

Critique:

This poem is the distinguished Latin epic which celebrates the glory of Rome in great poetry. It records the traditional story of the establishment of the Roman race and thus traces the lineage of the Romans back to Aeneas and Troy. It has already stood the test of time and will go down in history as one of the world's great epics.

The Story:

Aeneas, driven by storm to the shores of Libya, was welcomed gladly by the people of Carthage. Because Carthage was the favorite city of Juno, divine enemy of Aeneas, Venus had Cupid take the form of Ascanius, son of Aeneas, so that the young god of love might warm the heart of proud Dido and Aeneas come to no harm in her land. At the close of a welcoming feast Aeneas was prevailed upon to recount his adventures.

He described the fall of his native Troy at the hands of the Greeks after a ten-year siege, telling how the armed Greeks had entered the city in the belly of a great wooden horse and how the Trojans had fled from their burning city, among them Aeneas with his father Anchises and young Ascanius. Not long afterward, Anchises had advised setting sail for distant lands. Blown by varying winds, the Trojans had at length reached Buthrotum, where had been foretold a long and arduous journey before Aeneas would reach Italy. Having set sail once more, they had reached Sicily. There Anchises, who had been his son's sage counselor, had died and had been buried. Forced to leave Sicily, Aeneas had been blown by stormy winds to the coast of Libya. Here he ended his tale, and Dido, influenced by Cupid disguised as Ascanius, felt pity and admiration for the Trojan hero.

The next day Dido continued her entertainment for Aeneas. During a royal hunt a great storm drove Dido and Aeneas to the same cave for refuge. There they succumbed to the passion of love. Aeneas spent the winter in Carthage and enjoyed the devotion of the queen. But in the spring he felt the need to continue his destined course. When he set sail, the sorrowing Dido killed herself. The light of her funeral pyre was seen far out at sea.

Again on the shores of Sicily, Aeneas bade his men refresh themselves with food, drink, and games. First of all there was a boat race in which Cloanthus was the victor. The second event was a foot race, won by Euryalus. Entellus engaged Dares in a boxing match, which Aeneas stopped before the obviously superior Entellus achieved a knock-out. The final contest was with bow and arrow. Eurytion and Acestes made spectacular showings and to each was awarded a handsome prize. Following the contests, Ascanius and the other young boys rode out to engage in war games. Meanwhile, the women were grieving the lost guidance of Anchises, and at the instigation of Juno set fire to the ships. Aeneas, sustained by the gods, bade his people repair the damage. Once more the Trojans set sail.

Finally, they reached the shores of Italy, at Cumae, famous for its sibyl. The sibyl granted Aeneas the privilege of visiting his father in the underworld. After due sacrifice, the two of them began their descent into Hades. At length they reached the river Styx and persuaded the boatman Charon to row them across. Aeneas saw the spirits of many people he had known in life, including the ill-fated Dido. Then they came to the beginning of a forked road. One path led to the regions of the damned; the other led to the land of the blessed. Following this latter road, they came at last to Anchises, who showed Aeneas in marvelous fashion all the future history of Rome, and commanded him to found his kingdom at the place where he would eat his tables. On his return to the upper regions Aeneas revisited his men and proceeded to his own abode.

Again the Trojans set sail up the coast of Italy, to the ancient state of Latium, ruled over by Latinus. On the shore they prepared a meal, laying bread under their meat. As they were eating, Ascanius jokingly observed that in eating their bread they were eating their tables. This remark told Aeneas that here was the place Anchises had foretold. Next day the Trojans came to the city of King Latinus on the Tiber. Latinus had been warned by an oracle not to give his daughter Lavinia in marriage to any native man, but to wait for an alien, who would come to establish a great people. He welcomed Aeneas as that man of destiny.

A Latin hero, Turnus, became jealous of the favor Latinus showed Aeneas, and stirred up revolt among the people. Juno, hating Aeneas, aided Turnus. One day Ascanius killed a stag, not knowing that it was the tame favorite of a native family. There grew from the incident such a feud that Latinus shut himself up in his house and ceased to control his subjects. Meanwhile Aeneas made preparations for battle with the Latins under Turnus.

In a dream he was advised to seek the help of Evander, whose kingdom on the Seven Hills would become the site of mighty Rome. Evander agreed to join forces with Aeneas against the armies of Turnus and to enlist troops from nearby territories as well. Now Venus presented Aeneas with a fabulous shield made by Vulcan, for she feared for the safety of her son.

When Turnus learned that Aeneas was with Evander, he and his troops besieged the Trojan camp. One night Nisus and Euryalus, two Trojan youths, entered the camp of the sleeping Latins and slaughtered a great many of them before they were discovered and put to death. The enraged Latins advanced on the Trojans with fire and sword and forced them into open battle. When the Trojans seemed about to beat back their attackers, Turnus entered the fray and put them to flight. But the thought of Aeneas inspired the Trojans to such bravery that they drove Turnus into the river.

Aeneas, warned in a dream of this battle, returned and landed with his allies on the shore near the battlefield, where he encountered Turnus and his armies. Evander's troops were being routed when Pallas, Evander's beloved son, began to urge them on and himself rushed into the fight, killing many of the enemy before he was slain in combat with

Turnus. Aeneas sought to take the life of Turnus, who escaped through the intervention of Juno.

Aeneas decreed that the body of Pallas should be sent back to his father with appropriate pomp during a twelve-day truce. The gods had watched the conflict from afar; now Juno relented at Jupiter's command, but insisted that the Trojans must take the Latin speech and garb before their city could rule the world.

Turnus led his band of followers against Aeneas in spite of a treaty made by Latinus. An arrow from an unknown source wounded Aeneas, but his wound was miraculously healed. The Trojan hero reëntered the battle, was again wounded, but was able to engage Turnus in personal combat and strike him down. Aeneas killed his enemy in the name of Pallas and sacrificed his body to the shade of his dead ally. No longer opposed by Turnus, Aeneas was now free to marry Lavinia and establish his long-promised new nation. This was Rome, the mistress of the ancient world.

AESOP'S FABLES

Type of work: Didactic fiction
Author: Aesop (fl. sixth century B.C.?)
First published in English: 1484

A mid-nineteenth-century French lawyer, M. L. Hervieux, wanting his daughters to know something of Roman literature, decided to translate some of the animal stories which had been put into Latin verse by Phaedrus, a Macedonian servant freed by Emperor Augustus. The trouble was to find a definitive edition of the work. Years later, after visiting most of the important libraries of Europe, M. Hervieux published *Les fabulistes latins* in two volumes and fifteen hundred pages, attributing only sixty-seven fables to this Greek who translated into Latin verse the Greek prose of Demetrius Phalereus of the third century B.C. In the third century of the Christian era, Valerius Babrius, Latin tutor to the son of Emperor Alexander Severus, had also put into Greek verse the fables in Latin prose by Nicostratus, a hanger-on at the court of Marcus Aurelius. Three quarters of the fables set down by Nicostratus were attributed to Aesop.

Some scholars believe that Aesop was as much a fable as his fables. Of course, there is a *Life of Aesop,* written by a certain Planudes Maximus, a thirteenth-century Byzantine monk who prefaced his collection of fables in Latin prose with what he claimed was a true biography of their author. According to the Byzantine monk, Aesop was a slave born in Samos and killed in Delphi in the sixth century B.C. One statue shows him as deformed and animal-like as the characters of his tales.

History does provide a few details. There is reference to a "noble statue" of him that once existed in Athens, the work of Lysippus, but that may have been as much a creation of the imagination as the sturdy, brown-clad figure in Velázquez' painting. Herodotus, writing less than a century after Aesop was supposed to have flourished, in describing the lovely courtesan Rhodopis, who lived about 550 B.C., mentioned (II,134) the fact that the girl was a slave of Iadmon of Samos, and added: "Aesop, the maker of fables, was a fellow slave." Also, Herodotus recorded the payment of an indemnity paid by the Delphians to the grandson of Iadmon for the murder of Aesop, supposedly because some fable symbolizing the misdeeds of one citizen had angered the others.

Aristotle, in his *Rhetoric,* II, xx, is the authority for Aesop's use of a fable in oratory, as he defended a demagogue accused of embezzling. The slave told of a fox who was infested by fleas but refused to let a hedgehog remove them: "These have already taken their fill of me and do not continue to suck my blood. If you remove them, others less satiated will come to extract what blood I have left." The story was a hint to the Samians to let his client continue in office, since he had already made his fortune.

Also tagged with Aesop's name is the story of the frogs who asked for a king and were sent a stork who gobbled them up, a fable intended to dissuade the citizens of Athens from deposing Pisistratus. But when researchers seek in Greek manuscripts other fables that can definitely be attributed to Aesop, they find hardly a dozen, of which that of the nightingale is the oldest. True, seven collections were ascribed to Aesop, but without proof, and usually their content goes still farther back into antiquity, to early Indian tellers of tales or even to Egyptian poets of the fourteenth century B.C.

One explanation of the infrequent references to the Greek beast-fables is that they were so well known that nobody bothered to mention them. The interesting thing is that Aesop has been called "Father of the Animal Fable," even though the form had existed centuries before his assumed time.

Seventy years ago, Joseph Jacobs, an English investigator engaged in cataloguing fables attributed to Aesop, gave as good an answer as any. Before the time of Aesop, these stories, regarded as jokes, were told for amusement. Aesop, by his use of them, as Aristotle acknowledged, raised them in dignity to the ranks of serious oratorical material, worthy of use when a life was at stake and, if deductions about the cause of his death be correct, taken seriously enough to cause the death of their author.

Ninety-seven of the fables attributed to Aesop composed the first book printed in English with initial letters, printed by William Caxton at Westminster in 1484. Only one perfect copy remains, in the possession of the Queen of England. Others, damaged, are found in the Bodleian Library and the British Museum. The rest were probably as popular as Aesop's fables today and were read to pieces. The tales were equally popular in other lands. In 1496, the Infante Henrique made a Spanish translation that inspired Tomás Iriarte (1750-1791) and his contemporary Samaniego to versify fables memorized by every Spanish school child. Marie de France, at the beginning of the thirteenth century, put more than a hundred of them into French, antedating what has probably been the most elegant form in which they have ever appeared, the twelve books of *Fables* written in verse by Jean de La Fontaine (1668-1694).

"Esope, man of Greece," explained William Caxton in 1484, "subtyll and ingenyous, techeth in his fables how men ought to kepe and rewle them well. And to thende that he shold shewe the lyf and customes of al maner of men, he induceth the byrdes, the trees, and the bestes spekynge to thende that the men may know wherfore the fables were found . . . the whiche yf thou rede them, they shalle aguyse and sharpe thy wytte and shal gyve to thee Cause of Joye." Then follow the fables, in their crude Gothic type and quaint spelling, each illustrated by a grotesque woodcut.

First comes the fable of the cock and the precious stone, in which the bird, discovering a diamond in the filth, saw no possible use for it. The fable writer ends with the implication that those who see no wisdom in "this fayre and playsaint book," are as stupid as the cock. The second tells of the wolf who accused the lamb of enough crimes for an excuse to eat him. The fifth deals with the greedy dog crossing the stream with meat in his mouth and trying to snap up also the piece he saw reflected in the water.

Part II begins with the famous fable of the frogs who asked Jupiter for a king and ends with the story of the frog who tried to swell up to equal the size of the ox. Book III contains the fable of the nightingale to whose nest the "sperehawk" came with the demand that the songster entertain him; otherwise, he would eat one of the little birds. But a hunter came by and caught the marauder. This story follows a set form. It begins: "He that oppresseth the Innocent shalle have an evyle end, whereof Esope reherceth to us such a fable." At the end the story restates the moral: "And therefore he that doth harm and letteth the Innocent is worthy to dye of evylle dethe, as Cayn dyd which slewe his broder Abel."

This is the formula of all the fables in this ancient volume, the forerunner of so many editions that have appeared throughout the centuries with or without their morals stated, to delight readers who know nothing about Aesop himself and care even less.

AGAINST THE GRAIN

Type of work: Novel
Author: Joris Karl Huysmans (Charles Marie Georges Huysmans, 1848-1907)
Type of plot: Exotic romance
Time of plot: Nineteenth century
Locale: Paris
First published: 1884

Principal character:
JEAN DES ESSEINTES, an aesthete

Critique:

Huysmans, profoundly influenced by Baudelaire and Mallarmé, is perhaps the outstanding prose writer of the decadent school. His writing has the characteristics of the movement: detailed, sensuous description and precise, erudite vocabulary. *Against the Grain* (*À Rebours*) is a novel in which almost nothing happens; what one learns of the action is through retrospect. Most of the book is concerned with the hero's library, his taste in interior decoration, his illusions, and the complete decadence which stems directly from his conception of Catholicism.

The Story:

The Des Esseintes were an old family. In the Chateau de Lourps the portraits of the ancestors were those of rugged troopers and stern cavalry men. But the family had followed a familiar pattern; through two hundred years of intermarriage and soft indulgence the men had become increasingly effeminate. Now the only remaining Des Esseintes was Jean, a man of thirty. By a kind of atavism, Jean resembled in looks his first grandsire. The resemblance was in looks only.

Jean had had an unhappy childhood. His father, living in Paris most of the time, visited Jean briefly at school once in a while when he wished to give moral counsel. Occasionally he went to see his wife at the chateau. Jean was always present at those hushed interviews in which his mother took little interest. Jean's mother had a strange dread of light. Passing her days in her shaded boudoir, she avoided contact with the world.

At the Jesuit school Jean became a precocious student of Latin and acquired a fair knowledge of theology. At the same time he was a stubborn, withdrawn child who refused all discipline. The patient fathers let him follow his own bent, for there was little else they could do. Both his parents died while he was young; at his majority he came into complete control of his inheritance.

In his contacts with the world Jean went through two phases. At first he lived a wild, dissolute life. For a time he was content with ordinary mistresses. His first love was Miss Urania, an American acrobat. Because she was strong and healthy Jean yearned for her as an anemic young girl might long for a Hercules. But Miss Urania was quite feminine, even prudish in her embraces. Their liaison prematurely hastened his impotence.

Another mistress was a brunette ventriloquist. One day he purchased a tiny black sphinx and a chimera of polychrome clay. Bringing them into the bedchamber, he prevailed on her to imitate Flaubert's famous dialogue between the Sphinx and the Chimera. His mistress, however, was sulky at having to perform offstage.

After that phase Jean began to be disgusted with people. He saw that men brought up in parochial schools, as he was, were timid and boring. Men who had been educated in the public schools were more courageous but even more boring. In a frantic effort to find companionship, he wildly sought out the most carnal pastimes and the most perverted pleasures.

Jean had never been strong, and from childhood he had been afflicted with scrofula. Now his nerves grew weaker. The back of his neck always pained him; his hand trembled when he lifted a light object. In a burst of despairing eccentricity he gave a farewell dinner to his lost virility. The meal was served on a black table to the sound of funeral marches. The waitresses were nude Negresses. The plates were edged in black; the menu included dark bread, meat with licorice sauce, and wine served in dark glasses.

At thirty Jean decided to withdraw from the world. Having concluded that artistry was much superior to nature, he vowed that in his retreat he would be completely artificial. He found a suitable house in a remote suburb of Paris and made elaborate preparations for his retirement.

The upper floor was given over to his two elderly servants, who had to wear felt coverings on their shoes at all times. The downstairs he reserved for himself. The walls were paneled in leather like book binding, and the only color for ceilings and trim was deep orange. In his dining-room he simulated a ship's cabin and installed aquariums in front of the windows. The study was lined with precious books. With great art he contrived a luxurious bedroom which looked monastically simple.

Among his paintings Jean treasured two works of Moreau which depicted Salomé and the head of John the Baptist. He pondered long over the meaning of the scenes. History being silent on the personality of Salomé, Jean decided that Moreau had recreated her perfectly. To him she was the incarnation of woman.

His library was his chief concern. Among the Latin writers he had no love for the classicists: Vergil, for example, he found incredibly dull. But he took great delight in Petronius, who had brought to life Roman decadence under Nero. He loved ardently a few of the French sensualists, Verlaine and Baudelaire among them. He had also a small collection of obscure Catholic writers whose refinement and disdain for the world suited his own temperament.

For months his life was regular and satisfying. He breakfasted at five and dined at eleven. About dawn he had his supper and went to bed. Because of his weak stomach he was most abstemious in his diet.

After a time his old ailments came back to plague him. He could eat or drink very little and his nerves pained him. After weeks of torture he fainted. When his servants found him, they called a neighborhood doctor who could do little for him. At last Jean seemed to recover, and he scolded the servants for having been so concerned. With sudden energy he made plans to take a trip to England.

His luggage having been packed, he took a cab into Paris. To while away the hours before train time, he visited a wine cellar frequented by English tourists and had dinner at an English restaurant. Realizing afresh that the pleasure of travel lies only in the anticipation, he had himself driven home that same evening and thus avoided the banality of actually going somewhere.

At one stage of his life Jean had loved artificial flowers. Now he came to see that it would be more satisfying to have real flowers that looked artificial. He promptly amassed a collection of misshapen, coarse plants that satisfied his aesthetic needs.

But Jean's energy soon dissipated. His hands trembled, his neck pained him, and his stomach refused food. For weeks he dreamed away his days in a half-stupor. Thinking of his past, he was shocked to realize that his wish to withdraw from the world was a vestige of his education under the Jesuits. Finally he became prey to hallucinations. He smelled unaccountable odors, and strange women kept him company.

One day he was horrified to look into his mirror. His wasted face seemed that of a stranger. He sent for a doctor from Paris. After the physician had given him injections of peptone, Jean returned to something like normal. Gradually the doctor began injecting cod liver oil and other nourishing food into his veins. For a while Jean was entranced with the notion of getting all his sustenance through injections. One more activity would thus be unnecessary.

Then the doctor sent his little artificial world crashing; he ordered Jean to leave his retreat and go live a normal social life in Paris. Otherwise his patient would be in danger of death or at least of a protracted illness with tuberculosis. Jean, more afraid of his illness than he was of the stupid world, gave the necessary orders and glumly watched the movers begin their work.

THE AGE OF INNOCENCE

Type of work: Novel
Author: Edith Wharton (1862-1937)
Type of plot: Social criticism
Time of plot: Late nineteenth century
Locale: New York City
First published: 1920

Principal characters:
NEWLAND ARCHER, a young attorney
MAY WELLAND, his fiancée
COUNTESS ELLEN OLENSKA, her cousin

Critique:

This novel is an incisive but oblique attack on the intricate and tyrannous tribal customs of a highly stratified New York society with which the author herself was familiar. Her psychological probing of the meaning and motivation behind the apparent façade of her characters' social behavior shows her to be a true disciple of Henry James. The method is indeed that of James, but Edith Wharton's style is clearer and less involved. Here is a well-made novel, the work of a craftsman for whom form and method are perfectly welded, and the action results inevitably from the natures of the characters themselves.

The Story:

Newland Archer, a handsome and eligible young attorney engaged to lovely May Welland, learned that the engagement would be announced at a party to welcome his fiancée's cousin, Countess Ellen Olenska. This reception for Ellen constituted a heroic sacrifice on the part of the many Welland connections, for her marriage to a ne'er-do-well Polish count had not improved her position so far as rigorous and straight-laced New York society was concerned. The fact that she contemplated a divorce action also made her suspect, and, to cap it all, her rather bohemian way of living did not conform to what her family expected of a woman who had made an unsuccessful marriage.

Newland Archer's engagement to May was announced. At the same party Archer was greatly attracted to Ellen. Before long, with the excuse that he was making the cousin of his betrothed feel at home, he began to send her flowers and call on her. To him she seemed a woman who offered sensitivity, beauty, the promise of a life quite different from that he could expect after his marriage to May.

He found himself defending Ellen when the rest of society was attacking her contemplated divorce action. He did not, however, consider breaking his engagement to May, but constantly sought reasons for justifying what was to the rest of his group an excellent union. With Ellen often in his thoughts, May Welland's cool beauty and correct but unexciting personality began to suffer in Archer's estimation.

Although the clan defended her against all outsiders, Ellen was often treated as a pariah. Her family kept check on her, trying to prevent her from indulging in too many bohemianisms, such as her strange desire to rent a house in a socially unacceptable part of town. The women of the clan also recognized her as a dangerous rival, and ruthless Julius Beaufort, whose secret dissipations were known by all, including his wife, paid her marked attention. Archer found himself hating Julius Beaufort very much.

Convincing himself that he was seeing too much of Ellen, Archer went to St. Augustine to visit May, who was vacationing there with her mother and her hypochondriac father. In spite of her cool and conventional welcome and her gentle rebuffs to his wooing, her beauty reawakened in him a kind of affection, and he pleaded with her to advance the date of their wedding. May and her parents refused because their elaborate preparations could not be completed in time.

Archer returned to New York. There, with the aid of the family matriarch, Mrs. Manson Mingott, he achieved his purpose, and the wedding date was advanced. This news came to him in a telegram sent by May to Ellen, which Ellen read to him just as he was attempting to advance the intimacy of their relationship. Archer left Ellen's house and found a similar telegram from May to himself. Telling his sister Janey that the wedding would take place within a month, he suddenly realized that he was now protected against Ellen and himself.

The ornate wedding, the conventional European honeymoon which followed, and May's assumption of the role of the proper wife, soon disillusioned Archer. He realized that he was trapped, that the mores of his society, helped by his own lack of courage, had prepared him, like a smooth ritual, for a rigid and codified life. There was enough intelligence and insight in Archer, however, to make him resent the trap.

On his return to New York, he continued to see Ellen. The uselessness of his work as junior attorney in an ancient law firm, the stale regimen of his social life, and the passive sweetness of May did not satisfy that part of Archer which set him apart from the rest of his clan.

He proposed to Ellen that they go away together, but Ellen, wise and kind, showed him that such an escape would not be a pleasant one, and she indicated that they could love each other only as long as he did not press for a consummation. Archer agreed. He further capitulated when, urged by her family, he advised Ellen, as her attorney and as a relative, not to get a divorce from Count Olenski. She agreed, and Archer again blamed his own cowardice for his action.

The family faced another crisis when Julius Beaufort's firm, built upon a framework of shady financial transactions. failed, ruining him and his duped customers. The blow caused elderly Mrs. Mingott to have a stroke, and the family rallied around her. She summoned Ellen, a favorite of hers, to her side, and Ellen, who had been living in Washington, D. C., returned to the Mingott house to stay. Archer, who had not met Ellen since he advised her against a divorce, began seeing her again, and certain remarks by Archer's male acquaintances along with a strained and martyrlike attitude which May had adopted, indicated to him that his intimacy with Ellen was known among his family and friends. The affair came to an end, however, when Ellen left for Paris, after learning that May was to have a baby. It was obvious to all that May had triumphed, and Archer was treated by his family as a prodigal returned. The rebel was conquered. Archer made his peace with society.

Years passed. Archer dabbled in liberal politics, interested himself in civic reforms. His children, Mary and Dallas, were properly reared. May died when Archer was in his fifties. He lamented her passing with genuine grief. He watched society changing, and saw the old conservative order give way, accepting and rationalizing innovations of a younger, more liberal generation.

One day his son Dallas, about to be married, phoned him and proposed a European tour, their last trip together. In Paris, Dallas revealed to his father that he knew all about Ellen Olenska and had arranged a visit to her apartment. But when they arrived, Archer sent his son ahead, to pay his respects, while he remained on a park bench outside. A romantic to the end, incapable of acting in any situation which made demands on his emotional resources, he sat and watched the lights in Ellen's apartment until a servant appeared on the balcony and closed the shutters. Then he walked slowly back to his hotel. The past was the past; the present was secure.

AGNES GREY

Type of work: Novel
Author: Anne Brontë (1820-1849)
Type of plot: Sentimental romance
Time of plot: Mid-nineteenth century
Locale: England
First published: 1847

Principal characters:
Agnes Grey, a young governess
Edward Weston, a curate, later Agnes' husband
Mary Grey, Agnes' sister
Richard Grey, Agnes' father
Mrs. Grey, Agnes' mother
Mrs. Murray, owner of Horton Lodge, Agnes' second employer
Rosalie Murray, her older daughter
Matilda Murray, her younger daughter
Mr. Hatfield, Rector at Horton, Rosalie's suitor
Sir Thomas Ashby, later Rosalie's husband
Harry Meltham, and
Mr. Green, Rosalie's other suitors
Nancy Brown, an old widow at Horton
Mrs. Bloomfield, owner of Wellwood, Agnes' first employer
Tom Bloomfield, her oldest child
Mary Ann Bloomfield, her older daughter
Fanny Bloomfield, her younger daughter
Uncle Robson, Mrs. Bloomfield's brother

Critique:

This novel, written in the first person, is the account of the tribulations of a poor governess trying to achieve respectability and independence in nineteenth-century England. Agnes Grey, a governess because of economic necessity, finds the people among whom she works either bleak or frivolous representatives of the upper classes. They are neither understanding nor helpful, and Agnes, saddled with impossibly arrogant charges, is not a great success as a governess. Fortified by a loving though poor family and by an irreproachable character, she eventually marries the sterling and attractive clergyman. Agnes is the sentimental heroine, and the plot is not to be distinguished from that of the conventional sentimental romance. The good and the true ultimately triumph; the evil and the frivolous are ultimately unhappy. In spite of Agnes' pious sentiments, however, the novel is marked by sharp observations of contemporary life and a gentle and penetrating sarcasm in some of Agnes' comments on her employers. Anne Brontë never became an important novelist, but this novel suggests her ability lay more in the direction of Jane Austen than in that of her sister Emily.

The Story:

Mrs. Grey, a squire's daughter, had offended her family by marrying for love a poor parson in the north of England. She bore him six children, but only two, Mary and Agnes, survived. Nevertheless, the Greys were happy with their humble, educated, pious life in their small house and garden.

Mr. Grey, never wholly at his ease because his wife had been forced to give up carriages and fine clothes in order to marry him, attempted to improve their fortunes by speculating and investing his patrimony in a merchant's sea voyage. But the vessel was wrecked, everything was lost, and the Greys were soon left penniless. In addition, Mr. Grey's health, never robust, began to fail more perceptibly under the strain of his guilt for bringing his family close to ruin. Mary and Agnes, reared in the sheltered atmosphere of a clergyman's household, had spent their time reading, studying, and working in the garden. When the family situation became desperate, however, Mary began to try to sell her drawings to help with the household expenses, and Agnes, the younger daughter, decided to become a governess.

Overcoming the qualms her family felt at the idea of her leaving home, Agnes found a situation and, on a bleak and windy autumn day, arrived at Wellwood, the home of the Bloomfield family. She was received rather coldly by Mrs. Bloomfield and told that her charges, especially Tom, a seven-year-old boy, were noble and splendid children. She soon found that the reverse was true. Tom was an arrogant and disobedient little monster whose particular delight was to pull the legs and wings off young sparrows. Mary Ann, his six-year-old sister, was given to tantrums of temper and refusal to do her lessons. The children were frightened of their father, a peevish and stern disciplinarian, and the father, in turn, blamed Agnes when the children, as frequently happened, got out of control.

Agnes found it impossible to teach the children anything because all her efforts to discipline them were undermined by Mrs. Bloomfield, who felt that her angels must always be right. Even four-year-old Fanny lied consistently and was fond of spitting in people's faces. For a time, Agnes was heartened by Mr. Bloomfield's mother's visit, but the pious old lady turned out to be a hypocrite who sympathized with Agnes verbally and then turned on her behind her back.

Matters became a great deal worse with the visit of Uncle Robson, Mrs. Bloomfield's brother, who encouraged young Tom to torture small animals. One day, after he had collected a whole brood of young birds for Tom to torture, Agnes crushed them with a large stone, choosing to kill them quickly rather than to see them suffer a slow, cruel death. The family felt she had deprived Tom of his normal, spirited pleasure. Shortly after this incident she was told that her services would no longer be required; the Bloomfields felt that she had not disciplined the children properly or taught them very much.

Agnes spent a few months with her family at home before taking up her next post. She found the Murrays, the owners of Horton Lodge, more sophisticated, wealthier, and less bleak and cruel than the owners of Wellwood; but they were still hardly the happy, pious, warm family that Agnes had hoped to encounter. Her older charge, Rosalie, was sixteen, very pretty, interested only in flirting and in eventually making the most suitable marriage possible; her younger charge, Matilda, fourteen, was interested only in horses and stables. Although they treated her with politeness, neither girl had any respect for the learning and piety that Agnes had to offer. If Agnes' work was less unpleasant than it had been at Wellwood, it was equally futile.

After living at Horton Lodge for nearly a year, Agnes returned home for a month for her sister's wedding. During this time, the Murrays had given Rosalie a coming-out ball, after which she began to exercise her charms on the young men at Horton. Agnes was shocked, when she returned, to find Rosalie flirting with all the men and summarizing the marital possibilities of each with such a hardened and materialistic eye. In the meantime a new curate had come to Horton. Edward Weston was a sober and sincere churchman, neither climbing nor pompous like the rector, Mr. Hatfield. Edward Weston and Agnes, attracted to each other, found many opportunities to meet in their sympathetic visits to Nancy Brown, an old widow who was almost blind. At first Rosalie found Weston both dogmatic and dull, but Agnes found him representative of the true piety and goodness which she believed were the qualities of a clergyman. Rosalie, continuing to play the coquette, conquered first the unctuous rector, Mr. Hatfield, and then after Mr. Hatfield had proposed and been quickly rejected, turned her charms on Mr. Weston. Although Agnes was fiercely jealous of Rosalie's flirtation, she never really acknowledged her own growing love. Finally, Rosalie accepted Sir Thomas Ashby; his home, Ashby Park, and his fortune were the largest in the vicinity of Horton.

Shortly after Rosalie's marriage, before Agnes had the opportunity to see much of Edward Weston, she was called home by the death of her father. She and her mother decided to start a school for young ladies in the fashionable watering place of A——. Although Agnes returned to Horton Lodge for another month, she did not see Weston before she resignedly left to rejoin her mother. Although the school began to prosper after a few months, Agnes still seemed weary and depressed, and she welcomed an invitation from Rosalie, now Lady Ashby, to visit Ashby Park. She found Rosalie disappointed in her marriage to a grumbling, boorish man who ignored her and who, after a honeymoon on the Continent, had forbidden her the frivolous pleasures of London and European society. Agnes also learned from Rosalie that Weston had left Horton a short time before.

A few days after Agnes returned to her mother and the school, she was walking along the water front one morning when she was surprised by Weston. He had secured a living in a nearby village. He promptly began calling on Agnes and her mother and as time passed gained Agnes' love and her mother's esteem. One day, while walking with Agnes to the top of a high hill, he proposed. As husband, father, clergyman, and manager of a limited income, he was in after years the perfect mate for virtuous and worthy Agnes.

AJAX

Type of work: Drama
Author: Sophocles (495?-406 B.C.)
Type of plot: Classical tragedy
Time of plot: The Trojan War
Locale: Phrygia, before Troy
First presented: c. 440 B.C.

Principal characters:
AJAX, a Greek warrior
ODYSSEUS, a Greek leader
TECMESSA, Ajax's female captive
TEUCER, Ajax's half-brother
EURYSACES, son of Ajax and Tecmessa

Critique:

The age-old problem of individual versus group prerogative is masterfully presented in this play. One finds it tempting to sympathize with Ajax for his devotion to his consort and his son, the love and admiration he commands from his followers, and the courage he displays before the walls of Troy. It is inevitable, however, that his ungovernable pride should bring about his ruin. His downfall, the tragic hero's dissolution as a man because of unbearable humiliation and shame, is one of the most touching and disturbing in literature. Sophocles achieved this terrible spectacle by unusual cogency of action, a remarkable delineation of character, and a judicious point of view.

The Story:

Odysseus, chosen by Greek leaders in the Trojan War to replace the dead Achilles as the chief warrior of the Greek forces, paced up and down before the tent of Ajax, who had been slighted by the selection of Odysseus. The goddess Athena, appearing above the tent, told Odysseus that Ajax, covered with blood, was in his tent. Her words confirmed Odysseus' suspicions that it had indeed been Ajax who had slaughtered all of the Greeks' livestock and their shepherd dogs. Athena explained that she had cast a spell over Ajax, who, in his hurt pride, had vowed to murder Menelaus and Agamemnon, the Greek commanders, as well as Odysseus. Under her spell Ajax had committed the horrible slaughter in the belief that the animals he slew were the hated leaders who had opposed his election to the place of the late Achilles.

When Tecmessa, Ajax's Phrygian captive, revealed to his followers what the great warrior had done, they lamented his downfall and questioned the dark purposes of the gods. Certain that Ajax would be condemned to die for his transgressions, his warriors prepared to retire to their ships and return to Salamis, their homeland.

Ajax, recovered from the spell, emerged from his tent and clearly revealed to his friends that he was a shamed and broken man. Sick in mind at the thought of the taunts of Odysseus, he wished only to die. Even in his abject misery, however, he was sure that had Achilles personally chosen his successor he would have named Ajax. The despairing man tried to find some means of escape from the consequences of his deed. The alternative to death was to return to Salamis and his noble father, Telamon; but he knew that he could never shame Telamon by facing him. His friends, alarmed at his deep gloom and sensing tragedy, advised him to reflect; Tecmessa urged him to live for her sake and for the sake of their little son, Eurysaces. At the mention of the name of his beloved son, Ajax called for the boy. Solemnly he gave Eurysaces his great shield and directed that the child be taken to Salamis, so that he might grow up to avenge his father's disgrace. After dismissing Tecmessa and his son, he remained in his tent alone to clear his troubled thoughts. His followers, meanwhile, resumed their lament over their disgraced leader.

Apparently reconciled to his fate, Ajax emerged at last from his tent and declared that he was ready to recognize authority, to revere the gods, and to bury his sword with which he had brought disgrace and dishonor upon himself. His decision, he said, had been dictated by his affection for Tecmessa and Eurysaces. This apparent change brought forth cheers of rejoicing from his countrymen; they thanked the gods for what appeared to be Ajax's salvation.

In the meantime the Greeks taunted Teucer, Ajax's half-brother, for his kinship with one demented. Calchas, the Greek prophet, warned Teucer that unless Ajax were kept in his tent a full day, no one would again see Ajax alive, since the proud warrior had twice offended the goddess Athena in the past. But Ajax had already left his tent in order to bury his sword. Teucer and the men of Salamis, in alarm, hastened in search of their leader.

Ajax planted his sword, a gift from Hector, the great Trojan warrior, hilt-down in the earth. After he had asked the gods to inform Teucer of his whereabouts so that he might receive a proper burial, he fell upon his sword. Heavy underbrush partly concealed his body where it lay.

Tecmessa was the first to discover her dead lord; in sorrow she covered him with her mantle. Teucer was summoned. Tecmessa and the men of Salamis could not refrain from mentioning the dire part played by Athena in the tragedy of Ajax and the pleasure Menelaus and Agamemnon would feel when they heard of Ajax's death. Fearing foul play, Teucer ordered Tecmessa to bring Eurysaces immediately. Teucer himself was in a dilemma. He knew that the Greeks detested him because of his kinship with Ajax. He feared also that Telamon would suspect him of being responsible for Ajax's death, so that he might be Telamon's heir.

While Teucer pondered his own fate, Menelaus appeared and told him that Ajax could not receive proper burial because he had been a rebel, offensive to the gods. Teucer maintained that Ajax had not been subject to Spartan Menelaus, nor to anyone else, for he had come to Troy voluntarily at the head of his own men from Salamis; therefore he deserved burial. Seeing that Teucer held firm, Menelaus went away. Teucer dug a grave while Tecmessa and Eurysaces stood vigil over the body. The men of Salamis sang a dirge over their dead leader.

Agamemnon, King of Mycenae, appeared and rebuked Teucer, the son of a slave, for his audacity in defying the will of Menelaus. Agamemnon insulted the memory of Ajax by saying that he had been stronger than he was wise. Teucer, bitterly recalling Ajax's many heroic deeds in behalf of the Greek cause, reminded Agamemnon of the many blots on the escutcheon of the Atridae, Agamemnon's royal house. Teucer defended his own blood by pointing out that although his mother, Hesione, was a captive, she was nevertheless of noble birth.

Odysseus resolved the dispute by declaring that no Greek warrior should be denied burial. He himself had hated Ajax, but he admitted that Ajax had been both noble and courageous. He shook hands with Teucer in friendship, but Teucer, lest the gods be offended, refused his offer to assist in the burial. Thus Ajax, whose pride had brought him to an early death, received proper burial and the death ceremonies of a warrior hero.

AL FILO DEL AGUA

Type of work: Novel
Author: Agustín Yáñez (1904-)
Time: Spring, 1909-spring, 1910
Locale: Near Guadalajara, Mexico
First published: 1947

Principal characters:
DON DIONISIO, the parish priest
MARÍA, and
MARTA, his nieces
PADRE ISLAS, and
PADRE REYES, assistant priests
DAMIÁN LIMÓN, a young man who had been to the United States
MICAELA RODRÍGUEZ, a spoiled girl
VICTORIA, a young widow, visiting from Guadalajara
GABRIEL, a young man reared by Don Dionisio
LUIS GONZAGA PÉREZ, a seminary student
MERCEDES TOLEDO, another young girl
LUCAS MACÍAS, a soothsayer

Al filo del agua is a Spanish phrase with two meanings, one literal, the other figurative. Literally, it signifies the moment that the rain begins. However, it is in its figurative sense that it takes on meaning as the title of this book: the imminence of something that is about to happen. The event about to take place was brought on by a growing dissatisfaction with the political situation and the unnaturalness of the environment imposed by the Church as reflected by life in a small town in Mexico.

In 1910, Porfirio Díaz had been dictator of Mexico for more than thirty years. He had ruled with an iron hand and only now had the dream of political freedom and social improvement begun to filter through to the many semi-isolated towns of Mexico. The same few families had always been the social leaders and political bosses in the communities and Díaz' thirty-odd years of rule had done nothing to lessen this strangle hold or to improve the lot of the common man. Education was nonexistent except for the privileged few, and superstition was rampant.

Another force which held the people in its grip was the Church, a circumstance especially true in rural areas where the long arm of Juarez' 1859 Reform Laws seldom reached. These laws had greatly reduced the political power of the Church, and such things as processions and public religious festivities were forbidden. In the small towns, however, with the ever-present threat of arrest hanging over their heads, the priests often continued their regular clerical activities in spite of the law.

Agustín Yáñez has painted against this background a series of character studies portraying the effects of a narrow and rigid as well as dull and conventional life on people of different ages, with varying degrees of education and exposure to outside influences. (These influences, being outside ones and therefore bad, make up a long and varied list, and include such things as Free Masonry, bright clothing, strangers, uncensored written material, fun, spiritualists, people who had been to the United States; the list could go on and on.) Yáñez creates a sense of monotonous semi-gloom with the sure hand of an artist who has experienced this kind of life himself at one time or another. The fictitious, but very typical, town in which the action takes place is set in the state of Jalisco, of which the author is a native.

Each morning the church bells in this town call the people out of their beds as early as four o'clock to begin another dreary, quiet, prayerful day. Life is very serious. The women wear dark somber colors and do not leave the house except to go to church or to do necessary errands. There is no visiting except in the case of extreme illness or a death in the house of a neighbor. There is little laughter, dancing, or singing. Strangers and strangeness are not only suspect, but already condemned. Nonconformity, even in small things, starts tongues wagging. At the end of each unvarying day, the church bells send the people to bed, an act which for many means the onset of sleepless hours or wrestling with guilty consciences and with wondering when and in what form God's wrath will be brought down upon their heads.

With this daily pattern providing the atmosphere, broken only by funerals, special fiesta days, and an occasional scandal, the action in the story begins as the people are preparing for their Lenten and Easter activities. The panorama of people and events proceeds on through the year, displaying the special religious days of June, the expected deaths, illnesses, and bad luck of August, the celebration of patriotic holidays in September, the scandalous pranks of the students home for vacation in November, the Christmas season with its festivities, and continues on into the New Year, at which time the people are awaiting the appearance of Halley's Comet. This event is being anticipated so intently by Lucas Macías, the soothsayer, that the rest of the people do well to prepare for trouble, for Lucas has from the start associated the appearance of this comet with the stepping onto the scene of Francisco Madero, the man who is to lead the revolution against the tyranny of Díaz.

The person who can most nearly be described as the main character is Don Dionisio, the stern and upright, but just and compassionate parish priest. He alone touches in some way upon the lives of all the other characters in the book. His main ecclesiastical help comes from two assistant priests who present a vivid contrast to each other, one, Padre Reyes, being liberal and forward-looking, the other, Padre Islas, narrow and conservative beyond belief. Although Padre Reyes is much more likable, it is Padre Islas, scurrying along the street from church to home so as to avoid meeting his parishioners on a personal basis, who wields more influence on the lives of the townspeople, for it is he who directs the organization to which all the unmarried girls belong. Into their minds he instills the urgent need to stay pure by remaining single, and he imbues them with a sense of guilt for even thinking wholesome thoughts connected with the opposite sex. This narrow man will never use the chapel of the Holy Family, but always the chapel of the Virgin Mary, and Padre Reyes, the other assistant, is not above teasing him by asking if he thinks María and Juan will make a nice couple, or if he is aware that Mercedes is just about ready to make someone a good wife. These questions are calculated to enrage Padre Islas. Padre Reyes, with his modern ideas about such things as life insurance—too far removed from the imaginations of the people to be noticed—is largely ignored, while Padre Islas is revered as a saint beyond the temptations and afflictions of ordinary man. Great is the disillusionment when the good Father Islas is found collapsed on the floor of the church in a fit of epilepsy, which results in his having to be removed permanently from the priesthood. The archbishop had chosen wisely when Don Dionisio was made head priest, with the authority for making final decisions, for he approaches the problems of his parishioners with the best elements of the philosophies of his two assistants—an urgent sense of responsibility for their souls accompanied by a forgiving and understanding heart.

Two other personalities who present a study in contrasts are María and Marta, the orphaned nieces of Don Dionisio, who has reared them since they were very small. At the time the story begins, they are in their twenties, unmarried, and on the verge of taking opposite paths in life. Marta, the contented, with her love for children, her work in the hospital, and other gentle occupations, is the ideal end product of the social and religious forces at work in her environment. María, the rebellious, who has always read forbidden literature (*The Three Musketeers* and newspapers from the capital) behind her uncle's back, and who finally runs away with a woman of very questionable reputation to follow the revolutionary army, is a creature of reaction against this unnatural environment.

What happened to María happens, with variations, to nearly all the young people who have had contact in any way with the outside world. Luis Gonzaga Pérez, a young and talented seminary student, is unable to reconcile his inhibitions concerning the opposite sex with his natural desires, and at the end of the novel he is drawing lewd pictures on the walls of his room in the insane asylum.

Damián Limón, young son of a fairly prosperous landowner, leaves home, like the prodigal son, and goes to the United States to work. Upon his return home, when criticized for going to such a sinful place where Mexicans are treated like dogs, he counters by stating that at least they are paid in money instead of in promises, as in Mexico. Damián becomes scandalously involved in a flagrant love affair and kills the girl, after having just caused his father to have a fatal heart attack over an argument about his father's will. A corrupt political boss has a disgracefully light sentence placed upon him and, at the end of the story, he rides away to join the ranks of the revolutionaries.

The parents of Micaela Rodríguez, a spoiled only child, make the mistake of taking her to Mexico City for a few months. There she sees the parties, pretty clothes, and merriment of the capital's young people. Never again is she satisfied to stay in her dreary home town and, failing to force her parents to move away to a gayer place, she threatens vengeance on the environment that binds her and shocks the town to its roots with her shameless flirting and indecent dress. She ends up being stabbed by a jealous lover, but dies forgiving him and putting the blame for her death on her own actions.

Doubt seems to be the villain that causes the downfall of these unfortunate young people. They have tasted of the world, compared it with their narrow surroundings, and found them wanting. Being few in number, these unlucky ones have fallen under the weight of a relentless social system that brooks no questioning.

But the time is near at hand when many doubters will join together with enough force to make a crack in this teetering wall of hypocrisy, a crack which will ever become wider as education and enlightenment seep through. And in this thought is captured the essence of the title, *Al filo del agua.*

Agustín Yáñez has given us an unprejudiced and intricately detailed view of life in a Mexican town just after the turn of the century. The purpose of the book is not a call to arms to reform, but to present an understanding, not necessarily sympathetic, but always touching story.

ALCESTIS

Type of work: Drama
Author: Euripides (480-406 B.C.)
Type of plot: Classical tragedy
Time of plot: Remote antiquity
Locale: Pherae, in ancient Greece
First presented: 438 B.C.

Principal characters:
Apollo, god of the sun
Admetus, King of Pherae
Alcestis, his wife
Thanatos, Death
Hercules, son of Zeus and friend to Admetus

Critique:

Composed by Euripides as the fourth play of a tragic tetrology performed at the Feast of Dionysius in 438 B.C., *Alcestis* has characteristics of both the tragedy and the satyr play. Although this was a rare but not unique form among Attic playwrights, *Alcestis* is the only surviving example. Consistent with Euripidean technique, the conclusion of the drama results from the intervention of a heavenly power that resolves the conflict, in this case the character of Hercules.

The Story:

Phoebus Apollo had a son, Asclepius, who in time became a god of medicine and healing. Asclepius transgressed divine law by raising a mortal, Hippolytus, from the dead, and Zeus, in anger, killed Apollo's son with a thunderbolt forged by the Cyclops. Apollo then slew the Cyclops, a deed for which he was condemned by Zeus to leave Olympus and to serve for one year as herdsman to Admetus, King of Pherae in Thessaly.

Some time after Apollo had completed his term of service, Admetus married Alcestis, daughter of Pelias, King of Iolcus. But on his wedding day he offended the goddess Artemis and so was doomed to die. Apollo, grateful for the kindness Admetus had shown him in the past, prevailed upon the Fates to spare the king on the condition that when his hour of death should come, they should accept in ransom the life of whoever would consent to die in his place.

None of Admetus' kin, however, cared to offer themselves in his place. Then Alcestis, in wifely devotion, pledged herself to die for her husband. Finally the day arrived when she must give up her life.

Concerned for the wife of his mortal friend, Apollo appealed to Thanatos, who had come to take Alcestis to the underworld. But Thanatos rejected his pleas, warning the god not to transgress against eternal judgment or the will of the Fates. Apollo declared that there was one powerful enough to defy the Fates who was even then on his way to the palace of Admetus. Meanwhile Alcestis prepared for her approaching death. On the day she was to die she dressed herself in her rich funeral robes and prayed before the hearth fire to Vesta, goddess of the hearth, asking her to be a mother to the two children she was leaving behind, to find a helpmate for the boy, a gentle lord for the girl, and not to let them follow their mother's example and die before their time. After her prayers, she placed garlands of myrtle on each altar of the house and at each shrine prayed tearlessly, knowing that death was coming. Then in her own chamber she wept as she remembered the happy years she and Admetus had lived together. There her children found her, and she said her farewells to them. The house was filled also with the sound of weeping servants, grieving for the mistress they loved. Admetus also wept bitterly, begging Alcestis not to leave him. But the condition imposed by the Fates had to be met. While he watched, her breath grew fainter, and her cold hand fell languidly. Before she died, she asked him to promise that he would always care tenderly for their children and that he would never marry again.

At that moment Hercules arrived at the palace of Admetus, on his way to slay the wild horses of Diomedes in Thrace as the eighth of his twelve labors. Admetus concealed from Hercules the news of Alcestis' death so that he might keep the son of Zeus as a guest and carry out the proper rites of hospitality. Hercules, ignorant of what had taken place before his arrival in Pherae, spent the night carousing, drinking wine, and singing, only to awaken in the morning and discover that Alcestis had died hours before he came and that his host had purposely deluded him in order to make his stay in Pherae as comfortable as possible. In gratitude for Admetus' thoughtfulness and in remorse for having reveled while the home of his friend was deep in sorrow, he determined to ambush Thanatos and bring Alcestis back from the dead.

Since no labor was too arduous for the hero, he set out after Thanatos and Alcestis. Overtaking them, he wrestled with Thanatos and forced him to give up his victim. Then he brought Alcestis, heavily veiled, into the presence of sorrowing Admetus, and asked the king to protect her until Hercules returned from Thrace. When Admetus refused, Hercules insisted that the king at least peer beneath the woman's veil. Great was the joy of Admetus and his household when they learned that the woman was Alcestis, miraculously returned from the grave. Pleased with his efforts, doughty Hercules set out once more to face the perilous eighth labor which awaited him in Thrace, firm in the knowledge that with him went the undying gratitude of Admetus and the gentle Alcestis.

THE ALCHEMIST

Type of work: Drama
Author: Ben Jonson (1572?-1673)
Type of plot: Comedy of manners
Time of plot: Early seventeenth century
Locale: London
First presented: 1610

Principal characters:
FACE, a butler
SUBTLE, a swindler posing as an alchemist
DOL COMMON, their partner
LOVEWIT, owner of the house and Face's master
SIR EPICURE MAMMON, a greedy knight
DAME PLIANT, a young widow

Critique:

The Alchemist marked the peak of Ben Jonson's artistic career. Despite a somewhat huddled denouement, the play is a masterpiece of construction. As far as is known, the plot—which Samuel Taylor Coleridge declared one of the three most perfect in existence, the other two being Sophocles' *Oedipus the King* and Fielding's *Tom Jones*—was original with Jonson. In this play, Jonson, the artist superseded Jonson the moralist: as a highly entertaining and dramatic satire on human greed, *The Alchemist* displays none of the sermonizing which marks, more or less, Jonson's other plays.

The Story:

Master Lovewit having left the city because of plague, his butler, Jeremy, known as Face to his friends of the underworld, invited Subtle, a swindler posing as an alchemist, and Dol Common, a prostitute, to join him in using the house as a base of operations for their rascally activities. Matters fared well for the three until a dispute arose between Face and Subtle over authority. Dol, seeing their moneymaking projects doomed if this strife continued, rebuked the two men and cajoled them back to their senses.

No sooner had Face and Subtle become reconciled than Dapper, a gullible lawyer's clerk given to gambling, called, by previous arrangement with Face, to learn from the eminent astrologer, Doctor Subtle, how to win at all games of chance. Dapper, in the hands of the two merciless rascals, was relieved of all his ready cash, in return for which Subtle predicted that Dapper would have good luck at the gaming tables. In order to gull Dapper further, Subtle told him to return later to confer with the Queen of Fairy, a mysterious benefactress who could promote Dapper's worldly success.

Abel Drugger, an ambitious young druggist who had been led on by Face, was the next victim to enter the house. To his delight, he learned from Subtle, who spoke in incomprehensible pharmaceutical and astrological jargon, that he would have a rich future.

Next arrived Sir Epicure Mammon, a greedy and lecherous knight, with his friend Pertinax Surly, a man versed in the ways of London confidence men. Having been promised the philosopher's stone by Subtle, Mammon had wild visions of transforming all of his possessions into gold and silver, but he was completely taken in by the duplicities of Subtle and Face. Subtle further aroused Mammon's greed by describing at length, in the pseudo-scientific gibberish of the alchemist-confidence man, the processes which led to his approximate achievement of the mythical philosopher's stone. Surly, quick to see what was afoot, scoffed at Subtle and at the folly of Mammon.

During the interview Mammon caught sight of Dol, who appeared inadvertently, and was fascinated. Thinking quickly,

Face told Mammon that Dol was an aristocratic lady who, being mad, was under the care of Doctor Subtle but who in her moments of sanity was most affable. Before he left the house Mammon promised to send to the unprincipled Subtle certain of his household objects of base metal for the purpose of having them transmuted into gold.

The parade of victims continued. Elder Ananias of the Amsterdam community of extreme Protestants came to negotiate for his group with Subtle for the philosopher's stone. Subtle, with Face as his assistant, repeated his extravagant jargon to the impressionable Ananias, who, in his greed, declared that the brethren were impatient with the slowness of the experiment. Subtle, feigning professional indignation, frightened Ananias with a threat to put out forever his alchemist's fire.

Drugger reappeared to be duped further. Subtle and Face were delighted when he told them that a wealthy young widow had taken lodgings near his and that her brother, just come into an inheritance, had journeyed to London to learn how to quarrel in rakish fashion. The two knaves plotted eagerly to get brother and sister into their clutches.

Ananias returned with his pastor, Tribulation Wholesome. Both Puritans managed to wink at moral considerations as Subtle glowingly described the near completion of the philosopher's stone. Prepared to go to any ends to procure the stone, Ananias and Tribulation contracted to purchase Mammon's household articles, which, Subtle explained, he needed for the experiment; the proceeds of the sale would go toward the care of orphans for whom Subtle said he was responsible.

Subtle and Face also plotted to sell these same household articles to the young widow, who, having just moved to London, was probably in need of such items. In the meantime Face met in the streets a Spanish Don—Surly in clever disguise—who expressed a desire to confer with Subtle on matters of business and health.

Dapper returned to meet the Queen of Fairy. At the same time Drugger brought to the house Master Kastril, the angry young man who would learn to quarrel. Kastril was completely taken in. Subtle, promising to make him a perfect London gallant, arranged to have him instructed by Face, who posed as a city captain. Kastril was so pleased with his new acquaintances that he sent Drugger to bring his sister to the house.

Kastril having departed, Dol, Subtle, and Face relieved Dapper of all of his money in a ridiculous ritual in which Dapper was to see and talk to the Queen of Fairy. During the shameless proceedings Mammon knocked. Dapper, who had been blindfolded, was gagged and hastily put into a water closet at the rear of the house. Mammon entered and began to woo Dol, whom he believed to be a distracted aristocratic lady. Face and Subtle, in order to have the front part of the house clear for further swindles, shunted the amorous pair to another part of the house.

Young Kastril returned with his widowed sister, Dame Pliant; both were deeply impressed by Subtle's manner and by his rhetoric. When the Spanish Don arrived, Subtle escorted Kastril and Dame Pliant to inspect his laboratory. By that time both Subtle and Face were determined to wed Dame Pliant.

Face introduced the Spaniard to Dame Pliant, who, in spite of her objections to Spaniards in general, consented to walk in the garden with the Don.

Meanwhile, in another part of the house, Dol assumed madness. Subtle, discovering the distraught Mammon with her, declared that Mammon's moral laxity would surely delay completion of the philosopher's stone. Following a loud explosion, Face reported that the laboratory was a shambles. Mammon despondently left the house, and Subtle simulated a fainting spell.

In the garden Surly revealed his true identity to Dame Pliant and warned the young widow against the swindlers. When, as Surly, he confronted the two rogues, Face, in desperation, told Kastril that Surly was an impostor who was trying to steal Dame Pliant away. Drugger entered and, being Face's creature, insisted that he knew Surly to be a scoundrel. Then Ananias came to the house and all but wrecked Subtle's plot by talking indiscreetly of making counterfeit money. Unable to cope with the wily rascals, Surly departed, followed by Kastril.

Glad to be rid of his callers, Subtle placed Dame Pliant in Dol's care. But they were once more thrown into confusion when Lovewit, owner of the house, made an untimely appearance. Face, quickly reverting to his normal role of Jeremy, the butler, went to the door in an attempt to detain his master long enough to permit Subtle and Dol to escape.

Although warned by his butler that the house was infested, Lovewit suspected that something was amiss when Mammon and Surly returned to expose Subtle and Face. Kastril, Ananias, and Tribulation confirmed their account. Dapper, having managed to get rid of his gag, cried out inside the house. Deciding that honesty was the only policy, Face confessed everything to his master and promised to provide him with a wealthy young widow as his wife, if Lovewit would have mercy on his servant.

In the house, meanwhile, Subtle concluded the gulling of Dapper and sent the young clerk on his way, filled with the belief that he would win at all games of chance. Subtle and Dol then tried to abscond with the threesome's loot, but Face, back in Lovewit's good graces, thwarted them in their attempt. They were forced to escape empty-handed by the back gate.

Lovewit won the hand of Dame Pliant and in his good humor forgave his crafty butler. When those who had been swindled demanded retribution, they were finally convinced that they had been mulcted as a result of their own selfishness and greed.

ALECK MAURY, SPORTSMAN

Type of work: Novel
Author: Caroline Gordon (1895-)
Type of plot: Fictional biography
Time of plot: Late nineteenth, early twentieth centuries
Locale: Virginia, Tennessee, Mississippi, Missouri
First published: 1934

Principal characters:
ALECK MAURY, a Southern sportsman
JAMES MORRIS, his uncle
VICTORIA, his aunt
JULIAN, his cousin
MR. FAYERLEE, owner of Merry Point
MRS. FAYERLEE, his wife
MOLLY FAYERLEE, their daughter, Aleck's wife
RICHARD, and
SARAH (SALLY), Aleck's and Molly's children
STEVE, Sarah's husband

Critique:

This novel tells of Aleck Maury, who devoted his life to his twin enthusiasms for gun and rod. To him, hunting and fishing were the very breath of life; everything else was secondary, including his career as a teacher of Latin and Greek. The book is a series of incidents which, when put together, describe Aleck Maury and make him seem real.

The Story:

Aleck Maury's love for hunting and fishing began in childhood. At the age of eight, Rafe, a Negro handyman at the Maury household, took Aleck coon hunting. Not long after, a mill owner named Jones took the boy fishing and encouraged his lifelong love for that sport. Aleck was always happiest when he was out in the fields. One of five children, he was reared by his oldest sister after his mother died. Until he was ten years old, he was educated at home by his father, who put great stress upon the classics and taught his children nothing else.

At the age of ten, Aleck went to live at Grassdale with his Uncle James and Aunt Victoria Morris and their son, Julian. There his education was to be broadened under the tutelage of Aunt Victoria, who was a learned woman. Aleck's life at Grassdale was pleasant, centering chiefly about sport.

When Aleck was graduated from the University of Virginia, he had a classical education but no plans for making a living. He tried several jobs. He cleared out a dogwood thicket for a set sum of money, worked on a construction project on the Missouri River, in the city engineer's office in Seattle, and as a day laborer on a ranch in California. While working at the ranch, he contracted typhoid fever and was sent back east as far as Kansas City, to stay with some relatives there. At last through the efforts of his family Aleck became a tutor at Merry Point, the home of Mr. Fayerlee, near Gloversville, Tennessee.

Aleck, living with the Fayerlees, became the local schoolmaster for the children of most of the landowners in the area. Aleck's first interest, however, was not in the school or the students he taught, but in the possibilities for fishing and hunting.

During his stay with the Fayerlees, Aleck fell in love with Molly Fayerlee, and in 1890 they were married. They continued to live on with the Fayerlees and Aleck continued to teach school. During his first year of marriage Aleck acquired the pup Gyges, a small but thoroughbred bird dog. He trained Gy from a pup and became greatly attached to him. The next fall Aleck's son Richard was born. Two years later a daughter Sarah, nicknamed Sally, was born. They all continued to live at Merry Point.

When Richard was seven, Aleck was offered the presidency of a small seminary in Mississippi, and over the protestations of the Fayerlee family the Maurys left Merry Point. On the way, while spending the night in Cairo, Aleck lost Gy. The dog was never heard of again. They continued their journey to Oakland and the seminary. When Aleck arrived, he found that the school was running smoothly under the able direction of Harry Morrow, his young assistant, who was interested in administration rather than teaching. A few months after arriving at Oakland, Aleck acquired an untrained two-year-old pointer named Trecho from his friend, William Mason. Once again Aleck started the slow, arduous training of a good hunting dog.

When Richard was fifteen, Aleck tried to interest him in the joys of his own life, hunting and fishing, but his son, although he was a splendid swimmer and wrestler, had little interest in his father's fondness for field and stream. That summer Richard, while swimming in the river with a group of his companions, was drowned. The boy had been Molly's favorite and his loss was almost more than she could bear. Aleck thought it would be best for all concerned to leave for different surroundings.

He decided after some correspondence with friends that he would start a school in Gloversville, and the family moved back there. Settled in the small Tennessee town, Aleck found much time for fishing and hunting. He met Colonel Wyndham and from him learned a great deal about casting, flies, and the techniques to be used for catching various fish. Finally he began to grow tired of the same pools and the same river, and it was with pleasure that he accepted Harry Morrow's offer of a job on the faculty of Rodman College at Poplar Bluff, Missouri, of which Morrow had just been made president.

Aleck's main reason for accepting the position was the possibility it offered for fishing in the Black River. Thus once again, after ten years in Gloversville, the Maury family was on the move to newer fishing grounds. Sally, however, did not accompany them, but went to a girls' school in Nashville. The faithful Trecho was also left behind, for he had been destroyed at the age of twelve because of his rheumatism.

At Rodman Aleck had only morning classes, a schedule which left him free to fish every afternoon. This pleasant life—teaching in the morning, fishing in the afternoon—continued for seven years. Then Molly died after an emergency operation. Mrs. Fayerlee and Sally arrived too late to see her alive. The three of them took her back to be buried in the family plot at Merry Point.

Aleck returned to Poplar Bluff and continued teaching there for a few years, but at last he resigned his position and went to live at Jim Buford's, near Gloversville, where he spent the next two years restocking Jim's lakes with bream and bass. Later he decided to go to Lake Harris in Florida to try the fishing; but he found it disappointing because of the eel grass which kept the fish from putting up a fight. About that time he received a letter from Sally, who had married and gone touring abroad with her husband. The letter informed him that she and her husband were soon to return home and that they hoped to find a quiet place in the country on some good fishing water, where Aleck would go to live with them. Aleck wrote and suggested that they start their search for a house near Elk River.

Four weeks later he meet Sally and Steve at Tullahoma, only to learn that Steve and Sally, who had arrived the day before, had already discovered the place they would like to have. They told him it was the old Potter house, close to the river. When Aleck saw the big, clapboard house, however, all his dreams about a white cottage disappeared, and when he looked at the river he decided that it would probably be muddy about half the year. Seeing his disappointment, Steve and Sally promised to continue their attempt to find a more ideal house, but at the end of the day's search they decided that they still liked the old Potter house the best. That night Aleck boarded a bus bound for Caney Fork, the place where he really wanted to live, and he went to stay at a small inn located there. The fishing was always good at Caney Fork.

ALICE ADAMS

Type of work: Novel
Author: Booth Tarkington (1869-1946)
Type of plot: Social criticism
Time of plot: Early twentieth century
Locale: A small Midwestern town
First published: 1921

Principal characters:
ALICE ADAMS, a small-town girl
VIRGIL ADAMS, her father
MRS. ADAMS, his wife
WALTER ADAMS, his son
MILDRED PALMER, Alice's friend
ARTHUR RUSSELL, the Palmers' relative
MR. LAMB, of Lamb and Company

Critique:

Alice Adams is a rather simply told story containing one plot and concerning itself with one central character. The novel is the vehicle through which Tarkington expounds his philosophy of life and his gentle satire on small town manners and morals.

The Story:

Alice Adams had been reared in a town in which each person's business was everybody's business, sooner or later. Her father, Virgil Adams, worked for Lamb and Company, a wholesale drug factory in the town, where he also obtained a job for his son Walter. Alice had been one of the town's young smart set while she was in high school, but when the others of the group had gone to college Alice had remained behind because of economic reasons. As time passed she felt increasingly out of things. To compensate for a lack of attention, Alice often attracted notice to herself by affected mannerisms.

Alice had been invited to a dance given by Mildred Palmer, who, according to Alice, was her best friend. Walter had also been invited so as to provide her with an escort. Getting Walter to go out with Alice, however, was a process which took all the coaxing and cajoling that Mrs. Adams could muster. On the night of the dance Alice departed in a made-over formal, carrying a homemade bouquet of wild violets, and with an unwilling escort who was driving a borrowed flivver. The party itself turned out no better than its inauspicious beginning. Alice was very much a wallflower except for the attentions of Frank Dowling, a fat, unpopular boy. Toward the end of the evening Mildred Palmer introduced Alice to a new young man, Arthur Russell, a distant relative of the Palmers. It was rumored that Mildred and Arthur would become engaged in the near future. Alice asked Arthur to find her brother, whom she had not seen since the second dance. When Arthur found Walter shooting dice with the Negro waiters in the cloakroom, Alice was mortified.

A week later Alice accidently met Arthur Russell and he walked home with her. During their walk Alice learned that Arthur had asked for an introduction to her at the dance. Flattered, Alice built up for herself a background which did not exist. Arthur asked for permission to call on her.

But Arthur failed to appear the next evening. Several nights later, after Alice had helped with the dishes, she was sitting on the front porch when Arthur finally came to call. To hold his interest, Alice asked him to promise not to listen to any gossip about her. As time went on, she repeated her fear that someone would talk about her. Her protestations were something Arthur could not understand.

For many years Mrs. Adams had been trying to convince her husband to leave his job at Lamb and Company and go into business for himself. Her idea was that he could start a factory to manufacture glue from a formula he and another young man at Lamb and Company had discovered years before. Meanwhile the other man had died and the only people who knew the formula were Mr. Lamb and Mr. Adams. Mr. Lamb had lost interest in the formula. Mr. Adams felt that his wife's scheme was dishonest, and in spite of her nagging he refused to do as she wished. But after Mr. Lamb's granddaughter failed to invite Alice to a dinner party she was giving, Mrs. Adams convinced her husband that the true reason was their own poor economic status. In that way she finally won his grudging agreement to her plan.

Without delay, Mr. Adams began to organize his new business. Walter refused to join him because Mr. Adams would not give him three hundred dollars immediately. But Mr. Adams needed all his money for his new project. He sent Mr. Lamb a letter of resignation, telling of his intention to start a glue factory. He expected some sort of action or at least an outburst on Mr. Lamb's part when he read the letter, but nothing was forthcoming. He went ahead with his arrangements and began to manufacture his glue.

Alice's mother decided the time had come to invite Arthur to dinner, and Alice agreed with great reluctance. An elaborate meal was prepared; a maid was hired to serve, and Mr. Adams was forced into his dress suit. But the dinner was a dismal failure, and everyone, including Arthur, was extremely uncomfortable. Arthur had more reason than the rest for being so, for he had heard Mr. Adam's venture discussed in the most unfavorable light. He had also heard some uncomplimentary remarks about Alice. Before dinner was over, a friend named Charley Lohr came to speak to Mr. Adams. When both her mother and father failed to return to the table, Alice and Arthur went out to the porch. She soon dismissed him, knowing that something had come between them. When she went into the house, Charley Lohr informed her that her brother had been caught short in his accounts and had skipped town.

Mr. Adams decided to get a loan from the bank the first thing in the morning in order to pay back what Walter had taken. However, when he went to his factory in the morning, he discovered that the building which had been erected across the street from his was in reality another glue factory, one started by Mr. Lamb. His hopes of obtaining money on his factory were shattered. Then Mr. Lamb rode up to gloat over his retaliation. Mr. Adams angrily accused Mr. Lamb of waiting until Walter got into trouble before announcing his new factory and thereby making Mr. Adams' property practically worthless. He worked himself into such a state that he had a stroke.

Mr. Lamb, feeling sorry for Mr. Adams, offered to buy him out, and Mr. Adams was forced to agree. Now there was no income in the family. Mrs. Adams decided to take in boarders, and Alice finally made up her mind to enroll in Frincke's Business College. She had lost more than Arthur Russell; she had lost her daydreams as well.

ALICE IN WONDERLAND

Type of work: Imaginative tale
Author: Lewis Carroll (Charles Lutwidge Dodgson, 1832-1898)
Type of plot: Fantasy
Time of plot: Victorian England
Locale: The dream world of an imaginative child
First published: 1865

Principal characters:
ALICE
THE WHITE RABBIT
THE DUCHESS
THE QUEEN OF HEARTS

Critique:

Adults will view this book as a gentle satire on education, politics, literature, and Victorian life in general, seen through the eyes of Alice, a child who is the product of a confusing environment. The book is written with charming simplicity. There are poetic parodies on Wordsworth and Southey which are amusing to the point of hilarity, as well as ingenuous observations on the status of powerful female rulers. Through all her puzzling adventures in the dream world, Alice remains the very essence of little girlhood. Children read this book with delight, finding in Alice a heroine who aptly represents their own thoughts and feelings about growing up.

The Story:

Alice was quietly reading over her sister's shoulder when she saw a White Rabbit dash across the lawn and disappear into its hole. She jumped up to rush after him and found herself falling down the rabbit hole. At the bottom she saw the White Rabbit hurrying along a corridor ahead of her and murmuring that he would be late. He disappeared around a corner, leaving Alice standing in front of several locked doors.

On a glass table she found a tiny golden key which unlocked a little door hidden behind a curtain. The door opened upon a lovely miniature garden, but she could not get through the doorway because it was too small. She sadly replaced the key on the table. A little bottle mysteriously appeared. Alice drank the contents and immediately began to grow smaller, so much so that she could no longer reach the key on the table. Next, she ate a piece of cake she found nearby and soon she began to grow to such enormous size that she could only squint through the door. In despair, she began to weep tears as big as raindrops. As she sat there crying, the White Rabbit appeared, bewailing the fact that the Duchess would be angry if he kept her waiting.

The White Rabbit dropped his fan and gloves. Alice picked them up and as she did so she began to grow smaller. Again she rushed to the garden door, but she found it shut and the golden key once more on the table out of reach.

Then she fell into a pool of her own tears! Splashing along, she encountered a mouse who had stumbled into the pool. Alice tactlessly began a conversation about her cat Dinah, and the mouse became speechless with terror. Soon the pool of tears was filled with living creatures, birds and animals of all kinds. An old Dodo suggested that they run a Caucus Race to get dry. Having asked what a Caucus Race was, Alice was told that the best way to explain it was to do it. Whereupon the animals ran themselves quite breathless and finally became dry.

Afterwards, the mouse told a "Tail" to match its own appendage. Alice was asked to tell something, but the only thing she could think of was her cat Dinah. Frightened, the other creatures went away, and Alice was left alone.

The White Rabbit appeared once

more, this time hunting for his gloves and fan. Catching sight of Alice, he sent her to his home to get him a fresh pair of gloves and another fan. In the Rabbit's house she found the fan and gloves and also took a drink from a bottle. Instantly she grew to a giant size, and was forced to put her leg up the chimney and her elbow out of the window in order to keep from being squeezed to death.

She managed to eat a little cake and shrink herself again. As soon as she was small enough to get through the door, she ran into a nearby wood where she found a caterpillar sitting on a mushroom. The caterpillar was very rude to Alice and he scornfully asked her to prove her worth by reciting "You Are Old, Father William." Alice did so, but the words sounded very strange. Disgusted, he left her after giving her some valuable information about increasing or decreasing her size. She broke off pieces of the mushroom and found to her delight that by eating from the piece in her left hand she could become taller, and from the piece in her right hand, smaller.

She came to a little house among the trees. There a footman, who looked very much like a fish, presented to another footman, who closely remembled a frog, an invitation for the Duchess to play croquet with the Queen. The two amphibians bowed to each other with great formality, tangling their wigs together. Alice opened the door and found herself in the chaotic house of the Duchess. The cook was stirring a large pot of soup and pouring plenty of pepper into the mixture. Everyone was sneezing except the cook and a Cheshire cat which sat on the hearth grinning. The Duchess herself held a sneezing, squalling baby, and sang to it a blaring lullaby. Alice, in sympathy with the poor child, picked it up and carried it out into the fresh air, whereupon the baby turned slowly into a pig, squirmed out of her arms, and waddled into the forest.

Standing in bewilderment, Alice saw the grinning Cheshire cat sitting in a tree. He was able to appear and disappear at will, and after exercising his talents, he advised Alice to go to a tea party given by the Mad Hatter. The cat vanished, all but the grin. Finally that, too, disappeared, and Alice left for the party.

There Alice found she had to deal with the strangest people she had ever seen—a March Hare, a Mad Hatter, and a sleepy Dormouse. All were too lazy to set the table properly; dirty dishes were everywhere. The Dormouse fell asleep in its teacup; the Mad Hatter told Alice her hair needed cutting; the March Hare offered her wine and then told her there was none. They asked her foolish riddles that had no answers. Then, worse, they ignored her completely and carried on a ridiculous conversation among themselves. She escaped after the Dormouse fell asleep in the middle of a story he was telling.

Next she found herself in a garden of talking flowers. Just as the conversation was beginning, some gardeners appeared with paint brushes and began to splash red paint on a rose bush. Alice learned that the Queen had ordered a red bush to be placed in that spot, and the gardeners had made a mistake and planted a white one. Now they were busily and fearfully trying to cover their error before the Queen arrived. But the poor gardeners were not swift enough. The Queen caught them in the act, and the wretched gardeners were led off to be decapitated. Alice saved them by shoving them down into a large flower pot, out of sight of the dreadful Queen.

A croquet game began. The mallets were live flamingoes, and the balls were hedgehogs which thought nothing of uncurling themselves and running rapidly over the field. The Duchess cornered Alice and led her away to the seaside to introduce her to the Mock Turtle and the Gryphon.

While engaged in a Lobster Quadrille, they heard the news of a trial. A thief had stolen some tarts. Rushing to the courtroom where a trial by jury was already in session, Alice was called upon to act as a witness before the King and Queen of Hearts. But the excited child upset the jury box and spilled out all its occupants. After replacing all the animals in the box, Alice said she knew nothing of the matter. Her speech infuriated the Queen, who ordered that Alice's head be cut off. The whole court rushed at her, and Alice defiantly called them nothing but a pack of cards. She awoke from her dream as her sister brushed away some dead leaves blowing over her face.

ALL FOOLS

Type of work: Drama
Author: George Chapman (c. 1559-1634)
Type of plot: Romantic comedy
Time of plot: Sixteenth century
Locale: Italy
First presented: c. 1604

Principal characters:
RINALDO, a young gentleman
VALERIO, his friend
GOSTANZO, Valerio's father
MARC ANTONIO, Rinaldo's father
FORTUNIO, Rinaldo's brother
CORNELIO, a jealous husband
GRATIANA, Valerio's wife
BELLANORA, Valerio's sister, loved by Fortunio
GAZETTA, Cornelio's wife

Critique:

All Fools is one of Chapman's best comedies. A successful adaptation to the English stage of material from two Terentian comedies, it lacks the weakness in plot construction that mars several of his plays. Delightful comic situations are developed through his deft handling of the complicated intrigue. The major characters, although based on traditional types, are individualized; and their actions, except in the final act, are skillfully motivated.

The Story:

Gostanzo fancied himself a man of true worldly wisdom. He loved money, relished his neighbor's misfortunes, and was unhampered by any petty scruples about honesty. Aware of the temptations that might lead a young man to become a waster, he had taken great care in rearing his son Valerio. He had lectured the boy on the importance of thrift and, to teach him responsibility, made him an overseer. But Valerio was also a man of worldly wisdom. Although he put on the appearance of industry and innocence in front of his father, he was well acquainted with the gentlemanly activities of dicing, drinking, and wenching. He had, as the result of these pursuits, accumulated a respectable number of debts. To cap his sins, he had now married Gratiana, a girl with beauty but no dowry.

Fortunio was a young man of quite different character. Without parading his virtue, he led an upright life and was a dutiful son. In love with Valerio's sister Bellanora, he was not permitted to court her because Gostanzo was seeking a wealthier son-in-law. Fortunio's brother Rinaldo, having experienced the fickleness of women, was through with love and now devoted himself exclusively to cozenage of others.

One day, when Rinaldo, Fortunio, Valerio, and Gratiana were together talking, they sighted Gostanzo coming their way, and all but Rinaldo rushed off. In answer to Gostanzo's questions, Rinaldo said that Gratiana was the wife of Fortunio, who dared not tell his father of the marriage; Gostanzo believed the lie. Although he promised to keep it secret, he nevertheless revealed it the minute he was alone with Marc Antonio, the father of Fortunio and Rinaldo. Acting on Rinaldo's suggestion, Gostanzo recommended that Fortunio and Gratiana be installed in his home. Marc Antonio accepted this offer, not because he was angry with his son, but because Gostanzo had convinced him that Fortunio was in danger of falling victim to greater evils. With the restraining influence of the strict Gostanzo and the good example of Valerio, he might still be saved.

Rinaldo's scheming thus enabled Valerio and his wife to live in the same house, and it also gave Fortunio a chance to pursue his courtship of Bellanora. When Gratiana was brought to Gostanzo's home, the old man told Valerio to kiss her, but the crafty youth feigned shyness. The father, gratified by this manifestation of a strict upbringing, congratulated himself on being a much better parent than the easy-going Marc Antonio.

Later, however, Gostanzo found Valerio embracing and kissing Gratiana. The old man, still not suspecting the true state of affairs, thought merely that his son was a fast learner. He decided that, to avoid mischief, Gratiana and Fortunio would have to leave his house. When he told Rinaldo of this development, Rinaldo suggested that his father be told that Gratiana was really Valerio's wife and that Marc Antonio now take her into his house. Rinaldo further advised that, in order to make the ruse effective, Valerio be permitted to visit her there. The plan met with the ready assent of Gostanzo, who, being innocently gulled, was happy in the thought that he would be gulling Marc Antonio.

Meanwhile, Rinaldo, encouraged by his success in this project, had been directing his genius to a new endeavor, a plan intended to gull Cornelio, an inordinately jealous husband who was an easy mark for a trickster and whose wife Gazetta complained that he brought home gallants and then upbraided her for being in their company. Rinaldo's accomplice in his scheme was Valerio, who had been angered at Cornelio for making fun of his singing. Valerio had little difficulty in awakening the jealousy in Cornelio. With the help of a page who defended Gazetta on the grounds that women's wantonness was a result of weakness and not design, he so infuriated Cornelio that the jealous husband attacked and wounded his wife's supposed lover.

When Marc Antonio was told that Valerio, not Fortunio, was married to Gratiana, he made merry with Gostanzo for his blind pride. The latter, unable to tolerate gloating other than his own, declared that the plot had been contrived for entertainment. When they met Valerio, Gostanzo feigned extreme anger with him and threatened to disown his son. Valerio, playing the penitent, protested his devotion to his father and avowed his love of Gratiana. Gostanzo, believing the whole affair a joke, dissembled an appearance of being softened and gave his blessing to the match.

Cornelio, meanwhile, had procured a notary and was proceeding with the divorce of his wife. A nosebleed, which he took as an omen, caused him to suspend action just as he was preparing to sign the final papers. After the notary left, a friend explained to him that he had been tricked into his jealousy by Rinaldo and Valerio. Cornelio resolved to repay them with a deception of his own.

When Cornelio found Rinaldo, he told this master trickster that Valerio had been arrested for debts. Since Valerio had been dodging the officials for some time, Rinaldo believed the lie and, having gone on bond for Valerio, he felt that some immediate action was unnecessary. At Cornelio's suggestion, he took Gostanzo with him to the Half Moon Tavern, where Cornelio said Valerio was being held before being taken to prison. Valerio was at the tavern, but not as a captive. Instead, he was engaged in his usual pursuits of drinking and playing dice.

When Gostanzo saw his son's true nature and also learned that Valerio really was married to Gratiana, he threatened, this time in earnest, to disown the boy and to settle his estate on his daughter. But this plan was rejected when he discovered that Bellanora had married Fortunio. The old man, frustrated in his efforts to control events, decided to accept them. Finally, when Cornelio revealed that his jealousy had been feigned in order to restrain his wife's high spirits, the reconciliations were complete and happiness reigned in the Half Moon Tavern.

ALL FOR LOVE

Type of work: Drama
Author: John Dryden (1631-1700)
Type of plot: Romantic tragedy
Time of plot: First century B.C.
Locale: Alexandria, Egypt
First presented: 1677

Principal characters:
MARK ANTONY, one of the Roman triumvirate
VENTIDIUS, his faithful general
DOLABELLA, Antony's friend
OCTAVIA, Antony's wife
CLEOPATRA, Queen of Egypt
ALEXAS, Cleopatra's eunuch

Critique:

Having written rhymed heroic dramatic verse with great success, Dryden turned to a study of Shakespeare and other great playwrights of the English Renaissance. He had only admiration for Shakespeare's great tragedies, but, influenced by the French neo-classicists, he felt that the Elizabethan playwrights had not shown sufficient discipline in construction or in the observance of the classical unities of time, place, and action. *All for Love, Or, The World Well Lost,* his answer as it were to these shortcomings, is an adaptation in the neo-classic manner—but not uncomfortably so—of Shakespeare's *Antony and Cleopatra.* Dryden's Antony occasionally slips into pompous rhetoric, however, and his Cleopatra never becomes the exciting personality of Shakespeare's Egyptian queen. Unity of action, unity of place, dignity of expression, and well-conceived characters especially mark this play as a great piece of dramatic literature. The difference between *All for Love* and *Antony and Cleopatra* is not simply the difference between Dryden and Shakespeare; Dryden excelled himself here.

The Story:

After his humiliating defeat at Actium, Mark Antony retired to Alexandria, Egypt, where he remained in seclusion for some time in the temple of Isis. He avoided meeting his mistress, Cleopatra, the Queen of Egypt, whose cowardice had largely caused the defeat. Meanwhile the Romans, under Octavius, Maecenas, and Agrippa, had invaded Egypt, where, having laid siege to Alexandria, they calmly awaited Antony's next move.

Serapion, a patriot and a priest of Isis, became alarmed at a sudden rising of the Nile and by prodigious disturbances among the royal tombs; these events seemed to presage disaster for Egypt.

Ventidius, Antony's trusted and highly successful general in the Middle East, came at this time to Alexandria to aid his commander. Serapion and Alexas, Cleopatra's loyal, scheming eunuch, tried to encourage citizens and troops with a splendid birthday festival in Antony's honor. Ventidius, in Roman fashion, scorned the celebration. He told Antony's Roman soldiers not to rejoice, but to prepare to defend Antony in his peril.

Antony, clearly a ruined man, at last came out of his seclusion. While he cursed his fate and lamented the day that he was born, Ventidius, in concealment, overheard the pitiful words of his emperor. Revealing his presence, he attempted to console Antony. Both men wept; Antony marveled that Ventidius could remain faithful to a leader who had brought a large part of the Roman Empire to ruin through his love for Cleopatra.

Ventidius offered to Antony his twelve legions, which were stationed in Lower Syria, but his stipulation that these legions would not fight for Cleopatra plunged doting Antony into renewed gloom. When Ventidius mentioned the name of Cleopatra lightly, Antony took offense and cursed the general as a traitor. After this insult Antony, his mind filled with misgivings, guilt, and indecision, hastened to assure Ventidius of his love for him. He promised to leave Cleopatra to join the legions in Syria.

The word that Antony was preparing to desert her left Cleopatra in a mood of anger and despair. Meanwhile Charmion, her maid, went to Antony and begged the Roman to say farewell to her mistress. Antony refused, saying that he did not dare trust himself in Cleopatra's presence.

Not daunted by Antony's refusal, Alexas then intercepted him as he marched out of Alexandria. The eunuch flattered the Romans and presented them with rich jewels from Cleopatra. As Antony was with difficulty clasping a bracelet around his arm, Cleopatra made her prepared appearance. Antony bitterly accused her of falseness and of being the cause of his downfall. The two argued. In desperation, Cleopatra told Antony that as her friend he must go to Syria, but that as her lover he must stay in Alexandria to share her fate. Antony wavered in his determination to leave when Cleopatra told him that she had spurned Octavius' offer of all Egypt and Syria if she would join his forces, and he elected to stay when she represented herself as a weak woman left to the mercy of the cruel invaders. Antony declared, in surrendering again to Cleopatra's charms, that Octavius could have the world as long as he had Cleopatra's love. Ventidius was overcome with shame and pity at Antony's submission.

Cleopatra was triumphant in her renewed power over Antony, and Antony himself seemed to have recovered some of his former magnificence when he was successful in minor engagements against the troops of Octavius. While Octavius, biding his time, held his main forces in check, Ventidius, still hopeful of saving Antony, suggested that a compromise might be arranged with Maecenas or with Agrippa.

Dolabella, the friend whom Antony had banished because he feared that Cleopatra might grow to love the young Roman, came from Octavius' camp to remind Antony that he had obligations toward his wife and two daughters. Then Octavia and her two young daughters were brought before Antony, Octavia, in spite of Antony's desertion, still hoping for reconciliation with her husband. When Antony accused her of bargaining with her brother Octavius, Octavia, undismayed, admitted that Octavius was prepared to withdraw from Egypt at the news that a reconciliation had been effected between his sister and Antony. Octavia's calm dignity affected Antony greatly, and when his two small daughters embraced him, he declared himself ready to submit to the will of Octavia. Cleopatra, entering upon this family reunion, exchanged insults with the momentarily triumphant Octavia.

Still afraid to face Cleopatra for the last time, Antony prevailed upon Dolabella to speak his farewell to Cleopatra. Dolabella, aspiring to Cleopatra's favors, accepted the mission with pleasure. But Alexas, knowing of Dolabella's weakness and ever solicitous of the welfare of Egypt, advised Cleopatra to excite Antony's jealousy by pretending to be interested in Dolabella. After Ventidius and Octavia had secretly overheard the conversation between Dolabella and Cleopatra, Ventidius, now unwittingly a tool of Alexas, reported to Antony Cleopatra's apparent interest in the young Dolabella. Octavia confirmed his report, and Alexas suggested to the raging Antony that Cleopatra was capable of perfidy. Antony's passionate reaction to this information convinced Octavia that her mission was a failure and she returned to the Roman camp. Antony meanwhile, accused Cleopatra and Dolabella of treachery. Ignoring their earnest denials, he banished them from his presence.

Cleopatra, cursing the eunuch's ill advice, attempted unsuccessfully to take her own life with a dagger. Antony ascended a tower in Alexandria harbor to watch an impending naval engagement between the Egyptian and Roman fleets. To his horror he saw the two fleets join and the entire force advance to attack the city. Antony realized now that his end was near; furthermore, his heart was broken by the belief that Cleopatra was responsible for the treachery of the Egyptian fleet. When Alexas brought false word that Cleopatra had retired to her tomb and had taken her life, Antony, no longer desiring to live, fell on his own sword. The faithful Ventidius killed himself. Cleopatra came to the dying Antony and convinced him, before he died, that she had remained steadfast in her love for him. Then, to cheat Octavius of a final triumph, she dressed herself in her royal robes and permitted herself to be bitten by a poisonous asp. Her maids, Iras and Charmion, killed themselves in the same manner. Serapion entered to find that Cleopatra had joined her Antony in death.

ALL MEN ARE BROTHERS

Type of work: Novel
Author: Shih Nai-an (fl. fourteenth century)
Type of plot: Picaresque romance
Time of plot: Thirteenth century or earlier
Locale: China
First transcribed: Possibly the fourteenth or fifteenth century

Principal characters:
Shih Chin, The Nine Dragoned
Lu Ta, later Lu Chi Shen, The Tattooed Priest
Ling Ch'ung, The Leopard Headed
Ch'ai Chin, The Little Whirlwind
Yang Chi, The Blue-Faced Beast
Chu T'ung, The Beautiful Bearded
Lei Heng, The Winged Tiger
Ch'ao Kai, The Heavenly King
Wu Yung, The Great Intelligence
Kung Sun Sheng, Dragon in the Clouds
Sung Chiang, The Opportune Rain
Wu Sung, The Hairy Priest
Wang The Dwarf Tiger
Tai Chung, The Magic Messenger
Li K'uei, The Black Whirlwind
Lu Chün I, The Jade Ch' Lin

Critique:

All Men Are Brothers translated by Pearl Buck, was published in the United States in 1933. She supplied the present English title, which is a translation of a saying by Confucius because she felt that the Chinese title, the *Shui Hu Chuan* (literally, "water margins novel"), conveyed little meaning. The stories which make up the plot originated many years before the novel as a whole was composed and probably have some basis in fact. The version chosen by the translator is the shortest, omitting the spurious chapters telling of the robbers' downfall. It runs to well over 1,200 eventful pages, and the reader is likely to be appalled by the enormous number of characters he must keep in mind; 108 named chieftains form the band at the close of the book. The plot outline which follows can convey very little of the extraordinary bloodthirstiness of these "good fellows," who slaughter entire households of their enemies, who occasionally indulge in cannibalism, and whose reasons for becoming outlaws are not always noble. But the characters are vividly portrayed; the story is always interesting, and all is presented with the greatest realism and vigor. Long attributed to Shih Nai-an, many scholars now claim that Lo Kuan-chung may well be the author, or that the real author is unknown.

The Story:

To escape the persecution of evil Commander Kao, a military instructor fled to the borders. On the way he instructed a village lord's son, Shih Chin, in warlike skills. Later Shih Chin became friendly with the robbers of Little Hua Mountain. Discovery of this alliance forced Shih Chin to flee.

He fell in with Captain Lu Ta and Li Chung. Lu Ta, after killing a pig butcher who was persecuting a girl, escaped capture by becoming priest Lu Chi Shen. But his violence and intemperance forced the abbot to send him to another temple.

On the way he made peace between a village lord and the robbers of Peach Blossom Mountain, now led by Li Chung.

Shih Chin joined the robbers of Little Hua Mountain. Lu Chi Shen went on to his temple, where he became a friend of military instructor Ling Ch'ung. Because Commander Kao's son lusted for Ling Ch'ung's wife, Ling Ch'ung was falsely accused of murder, branded, and exiled to Ch'ang Chou. His guards were prevented by Lu Chi Shen from carrying out their secret orders to kill Ling Ch'ung. Again on his way, Ling Ch'ung was hospitably received by Lord Ch'ai Chin.

In Ch'ang Chou, Ling Ch'ung accidentally escaped a death trap and killed his three would-be assassins. Again he encountered Ch'ai Chin, who sent him to take refuge in Liang Shan P'o, a robbers' lair headed by ungracious Wang Lun.

Warrior Yang Chi, after killing a bully, was branded and sent to be a border guard. His skill delighted Governor Liang of Peking, who kept and promoted him and even selected him to transport rich birthday gifts to Liang's father-in-law. To rid the way of robbers, Chu T'ung and Lei Heng were sent out ahead of the party carrying the treasures. Lei Heng captured drunken Liu T'ang and took him to Lord Ch'ao Kai, but the lord arranged his release on privately discovering that Lei Heng had come to seek him; Lei Heng brought the news of the birthday gifts, which he, Ch'ao Kai and a teacher, Wu Yung, then plotted to steal. Magician Kung Sun Sheng and the three Juan brothers joined them.

The plotters cleverly drugged Yang Chi and his disguised soldiers and stole the treasure. Yang Chi in despair left the others, who resolved to throw the guilt on him. Yang Chi fell in with Lu Chi Shen; they went to Double Dragon Mountain and, overcoming the robber chief who refused to admit them, became the leaders of the band.

When Ch'ao Kai was discovered to have been one of the robbers, plans were made to catch him; but with the aid of scribe Sung Chiang and of robber-catcher Chu T'ung, Ch'ao Kai and the others escaped to Liang Shan P'o. Ling Ch'ung killed the ungracious Wang Lun, and Ch'ao Kai was made the chief. Ling Ch'ung discovered that his wife had killed herself to escape the advances of Commander Kao's son. The robbers vanquished two groups sent against them.

Sung Chiang's connection with the robbers was discovered by his unfaithful mistress. Enraged at her blackmail threats, he killed her and escaped to Ch'ai Chin's village. There he met Wu Sung, who was on his way to see his older brother after a long absence.

Wu Sung killed a tiger and was greatly fêted. He was of heroic size; his brother was puny and small. The latter's wife tried unsuccessfully to seduce Wu Sung. In Wu Sung's absence, she took a lover and with his help killed her husband. Wu Sung returned, and killed the pair. Though generally pitied, he was branded and exiled.

After an eventful journey, Wu Sung defended his jailer's son against a usurper and so offended the tyrant that he plotted with General Chang to accuse Wu Sung falsely of a crime. Wu Sung killed the plotters and joined those at Double Dragon Mountain.

Sung Chiang, going to visit a military magistrate, Hua Yung, was captured by the robbers of the Mountain of Clear Winds, but they recognized and welcomed him. One of them, lustful Wang The Dwarf Tiger, captured the wife of a civil magistrate, Liu Kao. Thinking to please Hua Yung, Sung Chiang persuaded Wang to release her. Later the woman, a troublemaker, identified Sung Chiang as one of the robbers. Sung Chiang and Hua Yung escaped to the Mountain of Clear Winds, and Liu Kao was killed.

General Ch'ing Ming came against these robbers and was captured. Their plot to force him to join their band was successful. Liu Kao's wife, recaptured, was executed. Sung Chiang promised to get a wife for the disappointed Wang

The Dwarf Tiger. The whole band decided to join those at Liang Shan P'o, but Sung Chiang was summoned home for the burial of his father. The report of his father's death turned out to be, however, a trick to keep Sung Chiang from turning outlaw. Persuaded to stand trial for his mistress' murder, he was branded and exiled. The trip was very eventful, involving many near escapes in encounters with robbers who later proved friendly. At his destination Sung Chiang became a friend of his gaoler, Tai Chung, who possessed magic enabling him to walk three hundred miles a day. Another friend, violent but loyal Li K'uei, caused much trouble which Sung Chiang was able to smooth over. One day Sung Chiang became drunk and wrote revolutionary verses on a wall. Tai Chung, sent to a distant city to get execution orders, went instead to Liang Shan P'o, where a letter was forged, freeing Sung Chiang. But a mistake made in the seal resulted in Tai Chung's death sentence also. Both were freed from the execution grounds by the robbers. All went back to Liang Shan P'o, enlarging their group with additional robbers recruited along the way.

Sung Chiang set out to bring his father and brother to the robbers' lair. He was miraculously saved from capture by a temple goddess who gave great prophecies. The robbers took the Sung family to the lair. Kung Sun Sheng and Li K'uei went out to get their old mothers.

On his journey Li K'uei killed a false robber who pretended to be himself, but the impostor's wife escaped. Li K'uei's mother, on the return journey, was killed by tigers. Li K'uei killed the tigers but when he went to receive the reward money, the impostor's wife identified him and he was captured. Another of the band freed him, however, and they returned to Liang Shan P'o.

Shih Hsiu opened a meat shop with the help of Official Yang Hsiung. Shih Hsiu discovered adultery between Yang Hsiung's wife and a priest. They killed the adulterers and escaped. Later they fell in with a thief, Shih Ch'ien, who caused a row and was captured in the village of Chu. In Liang Shan P'o the robbers planned warfare against the Chu village; the others were at last victorious. Li K'uei, ignoring a pact between the robbers and the Hu village, killed all the members of the Hu household except the female warrior, The Ten-Foot Green Snake, who had previously been captured by the robbers. Later she joined the robbers and married Wang The Dwarf Tiger.

Robber-catcher Lei Heng, after killing a courtesan, was allowed to escape to Liang Shan P'o by Robber-catcher Chu T'ung, who was, consequently, exiled. However, he pleased the magistrate, who liked to have Chu T'ung look after his little son. By killing the little boy the robbers forced Chu T'ung to join them.

Li K'uei and Ch'ai Chin went to right a wrong; Ch'ai Chin was captured and the robbers attempting to free him were repelled by their enemies' magic. Kung Sun Sheng, now a hermit, was sent for; his magic finally enabled the robbers to overcome the enemy and free Ch'ai Chin.

A fresh advance planned by Commander Kao against the robbers resulted in many useful additions to Liang Shan P'o when enemy leaders were captured and persuaded to change allegiance. The robbers of Double Dragon, Peach Blossom, and Little Hua Mountains, after some difficulties of capture and escape, joined those at Liang Shan P'o.

A stolen horse intended for Sung Chiang had been stolen again by the Chun family. Instructor Shi Wen Kung, now possessor of the horse, boasted that he would destroy the robbers. Chief Ch'ao Kai, while leading his men, was mortally wounded. Dying, he asked that whoever should capture Shi Wen Kung be named the new chief. A long period of mourning followed.

Rich and respected Lu Chün I was enticed to Liang Shan P'o in hopes that he would join them. Returning, he was arrested and imprisoned as a robber. His steward, now in possession of his wife and goods, plotted to have Lu Chün I killed. Many events followed, including the near death of Sung Chiang, but finally the city was taken. The prisoners were freed and the adulterers killed. Lu Chün I refused Sung Chiang's offer to make him the chief.

The robbers captured additional soldiers sent against them and added many of the leaders to their ranks. Ch'ao Kai's death was finally avenged in the conquest of the Chun family and of Shi Wen Kung, whose actual captor was Lu Chün I, who still refused to become the chief. Since all the robbers wished Sung Chiang to remain the leader, he prepared a test. He and Lu Chün I each led a group against one of the two cities remaining to be taken. The first to take his city would be the chief. After some reverses, Sung Chiang was successful. He then went to the aid of Lu Chün I, who had been twice vanquished by warrior Chang Ch'ing. This general, finally overcome, was persuaded to join the outlaws. Sung Chiang received a heavenly message in the form of a miraculous stone tablet which listed all thirty-six greater and seventy-two lesser chieftains who made up the robber band. All swore undying loyalty, wishing to be united forever, life after life.

ALL QUIET ON THE WESTERN FRONT

Type of work: Novel
Author: Erich Maria Remarque (1897-
Type of plot: Social criticism
Time of plot: World War I
Locale: Germany and France
First published: 1928

Principal characters:
PAUL BÄUMER,
ALBERT KROPP,
MÜLLER,
TJADEN,
HAIE WESTHUS, and
STANISLAUS KATCZINSKY (KAT), German soldiers

Critique:

All Quiet on the Western Front is a powerful novel reflecting the disillusionment that followed World War I. Written in the first person with short, simple sentences, this outstanding book makes clear the common soldier's reactions to shellfire, hunger, fear, sickness, and danger. There is no show of heroism in the story. Yet the hero, Paul Bäumer, engenders the essence of heroism. He is symbolic of any boy who must become a soldier.

The Story:

Just out of school, little more than nineteen years old, Paul Bäumer and his companions were in the front lines of the army. Albert Kropp, Müller, Leer, Tjaden, Haie Westhus, the farmer Detering, and Stanislaus Katczinsky, called Kat, the forty-year-old food plunderer, were part of the second company in the front lines, where Corporal Himmelstoss contrived cruel and inhuman assignments and punishments for his men. Tjaden hated him a little more than the others did. Kemmerich had his leg shot off. When he died, Müller got his boots.

The boys wanted to get back at Himmelstoss, but they knew that it would do them no good to complain about him. One night, when they caught Himmelstoss alone, they threw a sheet over his head and gave him a sound thrashing. Tjaden never forgot his own satisfaction in that accomplishment.

During the bombardments Paul saw men cry like babies or do other things for which they were later ashamed. When the trenches were quiet the men sat in groups talking about what they would do when the wai ended. Paul always felt bewildered during such discussions because, having been drafted so young, he had no occupation to which he could return.

Himmelstoss was reprimanded for his treatment of the men, and they knew about it. They could not directly disobey him because that would be insubordination, but they could jeer at him and insult him. Tjaden was called before a court-martial for his insults, and given a three-day open confinement. He thought his punishment worth the pleasure of insulting the corporal.

The company moved closer to the front. At first the men sat in the trench and waited, fighting rats and playing cards. The recruits were frightened, and Paul and the old-timers kept an eye on them. One young recruit went mad and climbed out of the trench; he had to be tied down to keep him from committing suicide. There was a retreat and then another attack, with the trenches nearly flattened under the bombardment. After one attack a man lay dying somewhere on the field. They could hear his cries

---

but could not find him. When the second company was relieved, there were only thirty-two men left from the original company of two hundred.

Relief came to Paul and the others. Good food and rest was all they needed. They met some friendly French girls. At night they took food with them for a bribe and sneaked across the river to the girls' house. The girls helped them to forget the war.

Paul was given a fourteen-day leave. He went home to see his sister Erna and his mother, who was sick in bed. His mother had saved from her own small rations his favorite food. He felt strange there in his home. Erna told him that their mother had cancer. One day he met in the street an officer who demanded a salute. Paul went home and took off his uniform. People asked too many questions about the war, questions which he could not answer.

At the end of his leave Paul went to a training camp for four weeks. On his last Sunday in the camp Paul's father and sister came to see him. They told him that his mother was in the hospital.

Finding his old company, Paul anxiously looked for his comrades. He found Kat, Tjaden, and Kropp. Haie had been killed. Paul shared with his friends the moldy cake he had brought from home. The men were given new uniforms. They had periods of extra drill. It was rumored that they were going to Russia. Then they heard that the kaiser was coming. After he inspected them and had watched a review, the new uniforms were taken from the men.

During an attack Paul found himself alone in a shell hole. Panicky and lonely, he crawled out of the hole to find his friends. Caught by machine-gun fire, he crawled into another hole. When a French soldier leaped into the hole, Paul stabbed him. After what seemed many hours Paul noticed that the man was still alive. He tried to relieve the dying man's pain. After the man died, Paul's conscience tormented him. When he was able to crawl from the shell hole, he found Müller and Kat, who fed him and comforted him by telling him that he had committed no crime.

Paul, Kat, Müller, Albert, and Tjaden were detailed to guard a heavily bombarded village where an important supply dump was located. They spent three weeks eating, drinking, and wandering about. Enemy fire continued to molest them. Albert and Paul were wounded. In the hospital they bribed a doctor to let them stay together. They were taken to a Catholic hospital, where the cleanliness almost made Paul sick. His broken leg refused to heal. Albert lost his leg. After a while Paul was able to hobble around on crutches, but he could not bear Albert's jealous gaze. Paul recovered and went home for a short while. His mother was still living. Soon he returned to his company.

The war dragged on. Müller was killed and Paul inherited Kemmerich's boots. Dysentery, typhus, influenza, and violent death dogged them constantly. Kat was wounded while he and Paul were in a trench together. Paul carried his friend through the lines. Just as he brought him to safety, Kat was killed when a piece of shrapnel struck him in the head.

The summer of 1918 passed. Paul was lonely and philosophical. He stayed in a convalescent ward after he had been slightly gassed. The meaning of the war loomed dismally before him. No one will ever know, he thought, what the war had done to him and the other soldiers.

In October, 1918, on a day when the army communiqué reported that all was quiet on the western front, a stray bullet hit Paul, and he died.

ALL THE KING'S MEN

Type of work: Novel
Author: Robert Penn Warren (1905-)
Type of plot: Social criticism
Time of plot: Late 1920's and early 1930's
Locale: Southern U.S.A.
First published: 1946

Principal characters:
JACK BURDEN, a journalist and political lackey
WILLIE STARK, a political boss
SADIE BURKE, his mistress
ANNE STANTON, a social worker
ADAM STANTON, her brother
JUDGE IRWIN

Critique:

All the King's Men, after a sluggish beginning, races smoothly to its inevitable ending. Warren's literary style is excellent. It is so good that the reader is likely to regret reaching the final pages of the book. Although the rise of Willie Stark is ostensibly the theme of the novel, the real issue is the character of Jack Burden, a caustic-tongued, brilliant journalist, whose self-examination becomes a symbol of the era that is treated in the book. From the opening description of Sugar Boy's drive through the country highway until the last pages when Jack Burden realizes his self-destruction and, phoenix-like, rises from the ruins of his past to make a new life with Anne Stanton, the plot is gripping and real.

The Story:

When Governor Willie Stark tried to intimidate old Judge Irwin of Burden's Landing, the judge stood firm against the demagogue's threats. As a result, Willie ordered Jack Burden to find some scandal in the judge's past that could ruin the elderly man.

Jack had met Willie back in 1922, when Willie, the county treasurer, and Lucy Stark, his schoolteacher wife, were fighting against a corrupt building contractor who was constructing the new schoolhouse. Sent by his newspaper, the *Chronicle,* to investigate, Jack found Willie and Lucy both out of jobs but still fighting against graft. Two years later the fire escape of the school collapsed during a fire drill and Willie became a hero.

Willie then ran in the Democratic primary race for governor. There were two factions, those of Harrison and MacMurfee. Because it was to be a close election, someone proposed that Willie be used as a dummy candidate to split the rural MacMurfee followers. Tiny Duffy and some other men convinced Willie that he could save the state. By then Willie had become a lawyer and politically ambitious man. Jack covered the campaign.

Aiding Willie was Sadie Burke, a clever, energetic woman with political skill. Inadvertently she revealed Harrison's plan to Willie. Crushed and gloomy at this news, Willie rallied his spirits and offered to campaign for MacMurfee, who was elected.

Willie practiced law for a few years until 1930 when he ran for governor with the assistance of Sadie Burke, who became his mistress, and Tiny Duffy, who was Willie's political jackal.

Meanwhile Jack had quit his job on the *Chronicle.* Reared by a mother who had remarried since Ellis Burden had deserted her, Jack had become a faithless, homeless cynic whose journalism career meant nothing to him as an ideal. He had, in his youth, played with Anne and Adam Stanton. Adam was now a famous surgeon, and Anne, still unmarried, had become a welfare worker.

Jack was in love with Anne, but time had placed a barrier between him and the girl with whom he had fallen in love during the summer after he had come home to Burden's Landing from college. He had been twenty-one then, she seventeen. But Jack's youthful cynicism, which later took possession of him completely, spoiled him in Anne's eyes.

When Jack went to work for Governor Willie Stark, Jack's mother was deeply pained and Judge Irwin was disgusted, but Jack cared little for their opinions.

By 1933 Willie was on the verge of losing his wife, who could not stand her husband's political maneuvers and his treatment of their son Tom. Willie assured Jack that Lucy knew nothing about Sadie Burke. Lucy remained with Willie through his reëlection in 1934 and then retired to her sister's farm. She appeared with Willie in public only for the sake of his reputation.

Jack began to dig into Judge Irwin's past. Delving into the judge's financial transactions during the time when he was attorney general under Governor Stanton, Jack learned that a power company had been sued by the government for a large sum. As a bribe to the attorney general the company fired one of its men to give a highly paid job to Irwin. Later this man, Littlepaugh, committed suicide after writing the facts in a letter to his sister. Still living, Miss Littlepaugh told Jack the story.

The issue of the Willie Stark six-million-dollar hospital demanded use of this scandal which Jack had uncovered. Willie told Jack that he wanted Adam Stanton to head the new hospital. It would, Jack knew, be a ridiculous offer to the aloof and unworldly young doctor, but he made an effort to convince Adam to take the post. Adam flatly refused. A few days later Anne sent for Jack. She wanted Adam to take the position. Jack showed Anne the documents proving Judge Irwin's acceptance of a bribe and Governor Stanton's attempt to cover up for his friend. Knowing that Adam would want to protect his father's good name, Anne showed the evidence to him. He then said he would head the hospital. Later Jack wondered how Anne had known about the plans for the hospital because neither he nor Adam had told her.

Jack's suspicions were confirmed when Sadie Burke, in a torrent of rage, told him that Willie had been betraying her. Jack knew then that Anne Stanton was the cause.

Disillusioned, he packed a suitcase and drove to California. This journey to the West and back completed, Jack, his torment under control, went back to work for Willie.

One of MacMurfee's men tried to bribe Adam to use influence in selecting a man named Larson as the builder of the medical center. When Adam, outraged, decided to resign, Anne phoned Jack for the first time since he had learned of her affair with Willie. Anne and Jack decided to get Adam to sign a warrant against the man who had tried to bribe him. Jack also warned Anne that as a witness she would be subject to public scrutiny of her relationship with Willie, but she said she did not care. Jack asked her why she was associating with Willie. She said that after what Jack had told her about Governor Stanton's dishonesty in the past she did not care what happened to her. Later, Jack persuaded Adam not to bring suit.

After Willie's political enemy, MacMurfee, tried to blackmail him because of a scandal concerning Tom Stark, Willie ordered Jack to use his knowledge to make Judge Irwin throw his weight against MacMurfee's blackmail attempt. When Jack went to Burden's Landing to confront Judge Irwin with the evidence that Jack had obtained from Miss Littlepaugh, the old man shot himself.

In the excitement following the suicide, Jack's mother told him that he had caused his father's death. Belatedly, Jack discovered the reason for Ellis Burden's desertion. In his will Judge Irwin left his estate to his son, Jack Burden.

Only one way seemed left to handle MacMurfee. Willie decided to give the building contract for the hospital to MacMurfee's man, Larson, who in turn would suppress the scandal about Tom. Duffy made the arrangements.

Tom Stark was a football hero. One Saturday during a game his neck was broken. Adam reported that Tom would remain paralyzed. This news had its effect on Willie. He told Duffy that the hospital deal was off. Turning to Lucy once more, he dismissed Sadie Burke and Anne Stanton.

Duffy, driven too far by Willie, phoned Adam and told him that Anne had been responsible for his appointment. Adam, having known nothing of his sister's relationship with the governor, went to her apartment to denounce her. Then, in the hall of the state building, Adam shot Willie and was killed immediately afterward by Willie's bodyguard.

Piece by piece the tangled mess of Jack's life began to take new meaning. He separated himself from every particle of his past with the exception of two people: his mother, whose devotion to Judge Irwin over all the years had given her a new personality in Jack's eyes, and Anne Stanton, whom he married.

ALL'S WELL THAT ENDS WELL

Type of work: Drama
Author: William Shakespeare (1564-1616)
Type of plot: Romantic comedy
Time of plot: Sixteenth century
Locale: France and Italy
First presented: c. 1602

Principal characters:
The King of France
Bertram, Count of Rousillon
The Countess of Rousillon, his mother
Helena, the Countess' ward
Parolles, a scoundrel, Bertram's follower
A Widow of Florence
Diana, her daughter

Critique:

More serious and dramatic than most of the Shakespearian comedies, *All's Well That Ends Well* is thought to have been revised several times before its first publication in the Folio of 1623. It is not a smooth piece of work. Parts of it are farce-comedy; other parts are marked by a seriousness of insight that is not always compatible with the general tone. Shakespeare's purpose was to portray the blindness brought about by prejudices formed without reason. Yet he gave sound basis for Bertram's refusal to see the good in Helena. Twice she humiliated him and forced him into unwanted situations. It took all of Shakespeare's skill to bring about a happy ending in the face of such odds.

The Story:

Bertram, the Count of Rousillon, had been called to the court to serve the King of France, who was ill of a disease that all the royal physicians had failed to cure. In the entire country the only doctor who might have cured the king was now dead. On his deathbed he had bequeathed to his daughter Helena his books and papers describing cures for all common and rare diseases, among them the one suffered by the king.

Helena was now the ward of the Countess of Rousillon, who thought of her as a daughter. Helena loved young Count Bertram and wanted him for a husband, not a brother. Bertram considered Helena only slightly above a servant, however, and would not consider her for a wife. Through her knowledge of the king's illness, Helena at last hit upon a plot to gain the spoiled young man for her mate, in such fashion as to leave him no choice in the decision. She journeyed to the court and, offering her life as forfeit if she failed, gained the king's consent to try her father's cure on him. If she won, the young lord of her choice was to be given to her in marriage.

Her sincerity won the king's confidence. She cured him by means of her father's prescription and as her boon asked for Bertram for her husband. That young man protested to the king, but the ruler kept his promise, not only because he had given his word but also because Helena had won him over completely.

When the king ordered the marriage to be performed at once, Bertram, although bowing to the king's will, would not have Helena for a wife in any but a legal way. Pleading the excuse of urgent business elsewhere, he deserted her after the ceremony and sent messages to her and to his mother saying he would never belong to a wife forced upon him. He told Helena that she would not really be his wife until she wore on her finger a ring he now wore on his and carried in her body a child that was his. And these two things would never come to pass, for he would never see Helena again. He was encouraged in his hatred for Helena by his follower, Parolles, a scoundrel and a coward who would as soon betray one person as another. Helena had reproached him for his vulgar ways and he wanted vengeance on her.

Helena returned to the Countess of Rousillon, as Bertram had commanded. The countess heard of her son's actions with horror, and when she read the letter he had written her, restating his hatred for Helena, she disowned her son, for she loved Helena like her own child. When Helena learned that Bertram had said he would never return to France until he no longer had a wife there, she sadly decided to leave the home of her benefactress. Loving Bertram, she vowed that she would not keep him from his home.

Disguising herself as a religious pilgrim, Helena followed Bertram to Italy, where he had gone to fight for the Duke of Florence. While lodging with a widow and her daughter, a beautiful young girl named Diana, Helena learned that Bertram had seduced a number of young Florentine girls. Lately he had turned his attention to Diana, but she, a pure and virtuous girl, would not accept his attentions. Then Helena told the widow and Diana that she was Bertram's wife, and by bribery and a show of friendliness she persuaded them to join her in a plot against Bertram. Diana listened again to his vows of love for her and agreed to let him come to her rooms, provided he first gave her a ring from his finger to prove the constancy of his love. Bertram, overcome with passion, gave her the ring, and that night, as he kept the appointment in her room, the girl he thought Diana slipped a ring on his finger as they lay in bed together.

News came to the countess in France and to Bertram in Italy that Helena had died of grief and love for Bertram. Bertram returned to France to face his mother's and the king's displeasure, but first he discovered that Parolles was the knave everyone else knew him to be. When Bertram held him up to public ridicule, Parolles vowed he would be revenged on his former benefactor.

When the king visited the Countess of Rousillon, she begged him to restore her son to favor. Bertram protested that he really loved Helena, though he had not recognized that love until after he had lost her forever through death. His humility so pleased the king that his confession of love, coupled with his exploits in the Italian wars, won him a royal pardon for his offense against his wife. Then the king, about to betroth him to another wife, the lovely and wealthy daughter of a favorite lord, noticed the ring Bertram was wearing. It was the ring given to him the night he went to Diana's rooms; the king in turn recognized it as a jewel he had given to Helena. Bertram tried to pretend that it had been thrown to him in Florence by a high-born lady who loved him. He said that he had told the lady he was not free to wed, but that she had refused to take back her gift.

At that moment Diana appeared as a petitioner to the king and demanded that Bertram fulfill his pledge to recognize her as his wife. When Bertram tried to pretend that she was no more than a prostitute he had visited, she produced the ring he had given her. That ring convinced everyone present, especially his mother, that Diana was really Bertram's wife. Parolles added to the evidence against Bertram by testifying that he had heard his former master promise to marry the girl. Bertram persisted in his denials. Diana then asked for the ring she had given to him, the ring which the king thought to be Helena's. The king asked Diana where she had gotten the ring. When she refused to tell on penalty of her life, he ordered her taken to prison. Diana then declared that she would send for her bail. Her bail was Helena, now carrying Bertram's child within her, for it was she, of course, who had received him in Diana's rooms that fateful night. To her Diana gave the ring. The two requirements for becoming his real wife being now fulfilled, Bertram promised to love Helena as a true and faithful husband. Diana received from the king a promise to give her any young man of her choice for her husband, the king to provide the dowry. And so the bitter events of the past made sweeter the happiness of all.

ALMAYER'S FOLLY

Type of work: Novel
Author: Joseph Conrad (Teodor Józef Konrad Korzeniowski, 1857-1924)
Type of plot: Romantic realism
Time of plot: Late nineteenth century
Locale: Dutch East Indies
First published: 1895

Principal characters:

ALMAYER, an unsuccessful trader of Dutch ancestry
MRS. ALMAYER, his Malay wife
NINA, his half-caste daughter
DAIN MAROOLA, Nina's Malay lover
LAKAMBA, Rajah of Sambir, Almayer's enemy

Critique:

Almayer's Folly is a good example of Conrad's carefully constructed stories. Laid in the Far East, as many of his novels are, the story is played out against the inscrutable mystery of nature. The theme of the meeting of East and West has long found varied treatment in English literature.

The Story:

By marrying Lingard's adopted daughter, a Malay, Almayer had inherited that prosperous merchant's business and his plans for amassing a huge fortune in gold from rich mines up the Pantai River. Almayer and his wife had one daughter, Nina, a beautiful girl, who had been sent to Singapore, where for ten years she was educated as a European. She returned home to Sambir unexpectedly at the end of that time, for she could not bear to be treated as a half-caste in a white community. Unsuccessful in business, Almayer nursed dim hopes that he could find a gold mine and, his fortune made, take Nina to Amsterdam to spend his last days in prosperous retirement.

News that the English were to have control of the Pantai River caused Almayer to start building a new house in his compound, not far removed from the one in which he was living. He wanted a house fine enough to receive the British. When the project was abandoned and the Dutch were left in nominal power, Almayer stopped work on his new house. A company of Dutch seamen christened the structure "Almayer's Folly."

The native rajah, named Lakamba, had a compound across the river from Almayer's home. There he lived with his women and his slaves and his principal aide, Babalatchi. Lakamba kept close watch on Almayer when he would leave for several days at a time with a few of his men. But Almayer gave up his trips after a time and settled down to empty daydreams on his rotten wharf. His native wife despised him.

Nina's presence in Sambir offered another problem for Almayer, for the young men of the settlement were eyeing her with interest.

One day the handsome son of a Malayan rajah came sailing up the river in a brig and wanted to trade with Almayer. His name was Dain Maroola. At length, after conversations with Lakamba and long conferences with Almayer, Dain got what he was after, gunpowder. Meanwhile he had fallen passionately in love with Nina. One night she came into the women's room in her father's house and discovered her mother counting out the money Dain had been giving her in payment for Nina. Mrs. Almayer had been arranging meetings between Nina and Dain, and giving them warning at the approach of Almayer. Mrs. Almayer wished her daughter to remain native. She had a deep distrust of white men and their ways.

Dain went away, promising that he would return to help Almayer in locating the hidden gold mine. When he did return, he saw Almayer for just a moment and then hurried to see Lakamba. He told the rajah that his brig had fallen into the hands of the Dutch and that he had narrowly escaped with one slave. Most of his men had been killed. And in a day or two the Dutch would be up the Pantai looking for him.

After this interview Lakamba told Babalatchi he must poison Almayer before the Dutch arrived. Now that Dain knew where the gold treasure was, Almayer was no longer needed. If allowed to live, he might reveal his secret to the white men.

Next morning the body of a Malay was found floating in the river. The head was smashed beyond recognition, but it wore an anklet and a ring that had belonged to Dain. Almayer was overcome with grief, for Dain was his last hope of finding the gold. The Dutch officers who came looking for Dain told how he had escaped from his brig and how, as the Dutch approached it, the gunpowder it carried ignited and blew up the boat, killing two of the Dutch. Almayer promised his visitors that after they had dined he would deliver Dain into their hands.

Meanwhile Babalatchi was telling Lakamba the true story of Dain. Nina had been waiting for the young Malay on the night of his conference with Lakamba, and she had taken him to a secluded clearing farther up the river. There he was now hiding. The corpse that had floated down the river was that of his slave, who had died when the canoe overturned. Mrs. Almayer had suggested that Dain put his anklet and ring on the body and let it float down the river. Lakamba and Babalatchi planned Dain's escape from his Dutch enemies. Knowing that Dain would not leave without Nina, Babalatchi and Mrs. Almayer plotted to get her away from Almayer, who was drinking with the Dutch. After some persuasion Almayer did lead his guests to the grave of the man recovered from the river. The Dutch took the anklet and ring as proof that Dain was dead. Then they left for the night.

Nina, willing to go with Dain, felt an urge to see her father once more before she left, but her mother would not let her go into the house where her father lay in a drunken sleep. Nina went to the clearing where Dain was hiding. Soon afterward a slave girl awakened Almayer and told him where Nina was. Almayer was panic-stricken. He traced Nina to Dain's enclosure and begged her to come back to him, but she would not. She did not want to run the risk of insults from white people. With Dain she would be a ranee, and she would be married to a Malay, a brave warrior, not a lying, cowardly white man. Almayer threatened to send his servant to tell the Dutch where Dain was.

While they argued, Babalatchi came up and cried out that the slave girl had revealed Dain's hiding place to the Dutch, who were now on their way to capture the young Malay. Babalatchi, astounded when Dain announced that he would stay with Nina, left them to their fate. After he had gone, Almayer said he would never forgive Nina, but he offered to take the two to the mouth of the river. So in heavy darkness the fugitive lovers escaped their pursuers.

On an island at the mouth of the river Dain, Nina, and Almayer awaited the canoe that would take the lovers to Lakamba's hidden boat. After the two had gone, Almayer covered up Nina's footprints and returned to his house up the river. His compound was deserted. Mrs. Almayer with her women had gone to Lakamba for protection, taking Dain's gift of money with her. Almayer found the old rusty key to his unused office. He went inside, broke up the furniture, and piled it in the middle of the room. When he came out he threw the key into the river and sat on his porch until the flames began to billow from his office. He was burning down his old house.

He lived out the rest of his days in "Almayer's Folly." Finally he began the practice of smoking opium in an effort to forget his daughter Nina. When he died, the opium had given his eyes the look of one who indeed had succeeded in forgetting.

AMADÍS DE GAUL

Type of work: Novel
Author: Vasco de Lobeira (c. 1360-c. 1403)
Type of plot: Chivalric romance
Time of plot: First century
Locale: France, England, and the rest of Europe
First published: 1508

Principal characters:
AMADÍS OF GAUL
KING PERIÓN, his father
PRINCESS ELISENA, his mother
GALAOR, another son of King Perión
LISUARTE, King of Great Britain
BRISENA, his queen
ORIANA, their daughter
URGANDA, an enchantress
ARCALAUS, a magician

Critique:

"The best of all books of this kind and unique in its art" was the description of *Amadís de Gaul* put by Cervantes into the mouth of Don Quixote. It had many competitors. Besides thirteen other versions in fifty years, dozens of other romantic tales of knights-errant were written after the fifteenth-century Garci Ordóñez (or Rodríguez) de Montalvo, Mayor of Medina del Campo, found a three-volume novel in Portuguese by Lobeira, and, according to his testimony, "corrected the original—corrupt and composed in old style—and took out superfluous words and substituted others more polished and elegant," thus producing a piece of effulgent Renaissance prose. Scholars have disputed the identity of the Lobeira who wrote the version found by Montalvo, a manuscript reportedly seen in the library of the Duke of Alveiro as late as 1750, but destroyed, perhaps, along with the library, in the Lisbon earthquake of 1755. João de Lobeira flourished between 1258 and 1285. Vasco de Lobeira, knighted in the battle of Aljubarrota in 1385, could not have been born until after 1350, the year in which a book containing a reference to Amadís was circulated in Seville. If Vasco de Lobeira was the author of Montalvo's source, he must have based the work on an earlier story. But regardless of who wrote the first long prose novel with a single hero in modern European literature, Montalvo rewrote it and, adding a fourth part, produced the only surviving version of this long-drawn-out tale with an unreal plot believable only to those who lived in a rapidly expanding and newly explored world where anything might be credible. Certainly the Montalvo version is superior to its many sequels in which giants became taller, wild beasts fiercer, and magicians more powerful. Glorifying the ideals of chivalry, the story had great influence on the manners and thinking, and of course the literature, of its time.

The Story:

Not many years after the passion of Christ there lived in Lesser Britain a Christian king named Garinter. His older daughter was married to the King of Scotland. The younger daughter, Elisena, found none of her suitors attractive until the day her father brought home King Perión of Gaul, whom Garinter had watched defeat two powerful knights and kill a lion. The scheming of Elisena's attendant, Darioleta, allowed the young people to meet secretly in the royal garden. King Perión departed ten days later without knowing the results of their nights of love.

When Elisena's son was born, Darioleta concealed her mistress' indiscretion by putting him into an ark, along with his father's sword and ring, and a parchment declaring the boy to be "the timeless Amadís, son of a king." She set the ark afloat in the river beside the palace; it drifted out to sea where it was found by a knight, Gandales, who was on a voyage to Scotland. Gandales, who brought up the foundling with his son Gandalín, called the boy "Child of the Sea."

Gandales, riding through the woods when the boy was three, rescued Urganda, an enchantress who was being pursued by a knight. The grateful witch, after prophesying that the adopted boy would become the flower of knighthood, the most honorable warrior in the world, promised to aid him should he ever need her help.

When the boy was seven, King Languines of Scotland and his queen saw him and offered to bring him up at court. Five years later King Lisuarte and Queen Brisena paused in Scotland on their way to claim the throne of England. Until all was safe, they asked permission to leave behind their daughter Oriana. King Languines appointed the "Child of the Sea" to be her squire.

The two children fell so deeply in love with each other that never again did they fall out of love, but they dared not let others know of their feelings. To be worthy of Oriana, Amadís determined to be knighted, and when King Perión visited Scotland to seek help against his enemy, King Abies of Ireland, Oriana asked her father's old friend to knight Amadís. The young knight then rode away in search of fame through adventures.

Urganda met him in the forest and gave him a lance with which he rescued King Perión from Irish knights. Though neither was aware of the blood relationship between them, Amadís swore always to aid King Perión in time of danger. Then followed a series of fantastic and extraordinary adventures, among them the encounter with haughty Galpano, whose custom was to stop and rob all who passed through his realm. Amadís defeated the bully and his two brothers, though in the battles he was so severely wounded that he had to be nursed back to health by a friendly noble.

Meanwhile, King Perión had married Elisena. Although they lamented their lost son, they took pleasure in a second son, Galaor. When King Abies sent an expedition against Gaul, Amadís overcame the Irish champion. In the celebration festivities at King Perión's court, the identity of Amadís was discovered through the ring he wore and King Perión proudly acknowledged his long-lost son.

Amadís remained melancholy, thinking himself unworthy to aspire to the daughter of the King of England. He did briefly visit her at Vindilisora (Windsor), only to be called away to rescue his brother Galaor. That summons was a trick of the enchanter Arcalaus, who cast a spell over the knight and disarmed him. When the villain appeared in the armor of Amadís and riding his horse, Oriana almost died. Only the timely news of further feats of arms by Amadís told her he was still alive, and so she was restored to health.

Tireless in his villainy, Arcalaus caused King Lisuarte to disappear and abducted Oriana. Amadís and his brother, knighted by Amadís, rescued the princess, but in the absence of the king, the traitor Barsinan tried to seize Brisena and usurp the throne. Amadís, dressed in rusty armor, defeated the rebel; and when Oriana's father reappeared twelve days of feasting followed. Amadís, however, was no nearer to winning the hand of his beloved in spite of his great service to the king.

Continuing to seek knightly fame, Amadís and his friends sailed for the Firm Island, settled by Apolidón, son of the King of Greece, who had taken refuge there after eloping with the daughter of Emperor Siudan of Rome. Here was an enchanted arch through which only faithful lovers could pass. Beyond it was a marriage chamber guarded by invisible knights. After his arrival in that land Amadís received a note from Oriana, who had believed the lying charges of unfaithfulness made against him by a malignant dwarf. She had signed herself as a damsel pierced through the heart by the sword of Amadís.

His ecstasy of grief upon reading the note and his withdrawal, under the name of Beltenebros (The Fair Forlorn One) to the hermitage at the Poor Rock, convinced Oriana that she had wronged him. However, there was nothing she could do to right matters, for King Lisuarte had given her in marriage to the Emperor of Rome.

When a fleet from Rome took her away, Amadís, calling himself The Greek Knight, defeated it and returned Oriana to her father, asking only that she be protected against further misalliances. King Lisuarte decided to punish such effrontery by an attack on Firm Island, a decision that ranged the knights of the world on two sides. King Lisuarte enlisted the help of the Emperor of Rome. Amadís visited the Emperor of Constantinople and sent a messenger to the King of Bohemia. Arcalaus, hating both Amadís and King Lisuarte, encouraged King Aravigo to march with his army and prey on both sides.

When the hosts assembled for the battle, King Gasquilán of Sweden sent a personal challenge to Amadís to meet him in single combat between the lines. The king's overthrow was the signal for a general onslaught that lasted for two days, until at last the death of the Emperor of Rome disheartened and routed his army.

Out of affection for Oriana, Amadís did not pursue the defeated host, but King Aravigo took this opportunity to plunder the followers of King Lisuarte. A hermit, who had been trying to bring about peace among the combatants, sent the youthful Esplandián to take the news of King Lisuarte's distress to Amadís. The hero marched at once to the rescue of King Lisuarte, a kindness that wiped out the enmity between them. The marriage of Oriana and Amadís was solemnized on Firm Island. Afterward the couple passed under the Arch of True Love into the magic bridal chamber.

THE AMBASSADORS

Type of work: Novel
Author: Henry James (1843-1916)
Type of plot: Psychological realism
Time of plot: About 1900
Locale: Paris, France
First published: 1903

Principal characters:
CHADWICK NEWSOME (CHAD), an American expatriate
LAMBERT STRETHER, his friend
MARIA GOSTREY, an acquaintance of Strether
COMTESSE DE VIONNET, in love with Chadwick Newsome
MRS. POCOCK, Chadwick's married sister
MAMIE POCOCK, Mrs. Pocock's husband's sister

Critique:

Henry James put great emphasis on the construction and form of his novels, and *The Ambassadors* is one of his best in point of construction. There are no loose ends; the entire story is neatly gathered together. The importance of this novel in Henry James' work is that in it he at last conquered his embarrassment over people from America. His earlier novels had displayed the people of his native land as rather barbaric in their appreciation of Europe. But in Lambert Strether and Chadwick Newsome, James portrayed two Americans who had the intelligence to realize in Paris what they had missed in the bleak and narrowed existence of their earlier lives in New England.

The Story:

Lambert Strether was engaged to marry Mrs. Newsome, a widow. Mrs. Newsome had a son Chadwick, whom she wanted to return home from Paris and take over the family business in Woollett, Massachusetts. She was especially concerned for his future after she had heard that he was seriously involved with a Frenchwoman. In her anxiety she asked Strether to go to Paris and persuade her son to return to the respectable life she had planned for him.

Strether did not look forward to his task, for the young man had ignored all his mother's written requests to return home. Nor did Strether know what hold Chadwick's mistress might have over him or what sort of woman she might be. He strongly suspected that she was a young girl of unsavory reputation. Strether realized, however, that his hopes of marrying Mrs. Newsome depended upon his success in bringing Chad back to America, where his mother could see him married to Mamie Pocock.

Leaving his ship at Liverpool, Strether journeyed across England to London. On the way he met Miss Gostrey, a young woman who was acquainted with some of Strether's American friends, and she promised to aid Strether in getting acquainted with Europe before he left for home again. Strether met another old friend, Mr. Waymarsh, an American lawyer living in England, whom he asked to go with him to Paris.

A few days after arriving in Paris, Strether went to Chad's house. The young man was not in Paris, and he had temporarily given the house over to a friend, Mr. Bilham. Through Bilham, Strether got in touch with Chad at Cannes. Strether was surprised to learn of his whereabouts, for he knew that

Chad would not have dared to take an ordinary mistress to such a fashionable resort.

About a week later Strether, Miss Gostrey, and Waymarsh went to the theater. Between the acts of the play, the door of their box was opened and Chad entered. He was much changed from the adolescent college boy Strether remembered. He was slightly gray, although only twenty-eight.

Both Strether and Chad Newsome pleased each other on sight. Over coffee after the theater, the older man told Chad why he had come to Europe. Chad answered that all he asked was an opportunity to be convinced that he should return.

A few days later Chad took Strether and his friends to a tea where they met Mme. and Mlle. de Vionnet. The former, who had married a French count. turned out to be an old school friend of Miss Gostrey. Strether was at a loss to understand whether Chad was in love with the comtesse or with her daughter Jeanne. Since the older woman was only a few years the senior of the young man and as beautiful as her daughter, either was possibly the object of his affections.

As the days slipped by it became apparent to Strether that he himself wanted to stay in Paris. The French city and its life were much calmer and more beautiful than the provincial existence he had known in Woollett, and he began to understand why Chad was unwilling to go back to his mother and the Newsome mills.

Strether learned that Chad was in love with Mme. de Vionnet, rather than with her daughter. The comtesse had been separated from her husband for many years, but their position and religion made divorce impossible. Strether, who was often in the company of the Frenchwoman, soon fell under her charm. Miss Gostrey, who had known Mme. de Vionnet for many years, had only praise for her and questioned Strether as to the advisability of removing Chad from the woman's continued influence.

One morning Chad announced to Strether that he was ready to return immediately to America. The young man was puzzled when Strether replied that he was not sure it was wise for either of them to return, that it would be wiser for them both to reconsider whether they would not be better off in Paris than in New England.

When Mrs. Newsome, back in America, received word of that decision on the part of her ambassador, she immediately sent the Pococks, her daughter and son-in-law, to Paris along with Mamie Pocock, the girl she hoped her son would marry. They were to bring back both Strether and her son.

Mrs. Newsome's daughter and her relatives did not come to Paris with an obvious ill-will. Their attitude seemed to be that Chad and Strether had somehow drifted astray, and it was their duty to set them right. At least that was the attitude of Mrs. Pocock. Her husband, however, was not at all interested in having Chad return, for in the young man's absence Mr. Pocock controlled the Newsome mills. Mr. Pocock further saw that his visit was probably the last opportunity he would have for a gay time in the European city, and so he was quite willing to spend his holiday going to theaters and cafés. His younger sister, Mamie, seemed to take little interest in the recall of her supposed fiancé, for she had become interested in Chad's friend, Mr. Bilham.

The more Strether saw of Mme. de Vionnet after the arrival of the Pococks, the more he was convinced that the Frenchwoman was both noble and sincere in her attempts to make friends with her lover's family. Mrs. Pocock found it difficult to reconcile Mme. de Vionnet's aristocratic background with the fact that she was Chad's mistress.

After several weeks of hints and genteel pleading, the Pococks and Mamie went to Switzerland, leaving Chad to make a decision whether to return to America. As for Mr. Strether, Mrs. Newsome had advised that he be left alone to make his own decision, for the widow wanted to avoid the appearance of having lost her dignity or her sense of propriety.

While the Pococks were gone, Strether and Chad discussed the course they should follow. Chad was uncertain of his attitude toward Mamie Pocock. Strether assured him that the girl was already happy with her new love, Mr. Bilham, who had told Strether that he intended to marry the American girl. His advice, contrary to what he had thought when he had sailed from America, was that Chadwick Newsome should remain in France with the comtesse, despite the fact that the young man could not marry her and would, by remaining in Europe, lose the opportunity to make himself an extremely rich man. Chad decided to take his older friend's counsel.

Waymarsh, who had promised his help in persuading Chad to return to America, was outraged at Strether's changed attitude. Miss Gostrey, however, remained loyal, for she had fallen deeply in love with Strether during their time together in Paris. But Strether, realizing her feelings, told her that he had to go back to America alone. His object in Europe had been to return Chad Newsome to his mother. Because he had failed in that mission and would never marry Mrs. Newsome, he could not justify himself by marrying another woman whom he had met on a journey financed by the woman he had at one time intended to marry. Only Mme. Vionnet, he felt, could truly appreciate the irony of his position.

AMELIA

Type of work: Novel
Author: Henry Fielding (1707-1754)
Type of plot: Domestic realism
Time of plot: 1740's
Locale: England
First published: 1751

Principal characters:
Captain Booth, a soldier
Amelia, his wife
Elizabeth Harris, her sister
Sergeant Atkinson, her foster brother
Dr. Harrison, Booth's benefactor
Miss Matthews, a woman of the town
Colonel James, Booth's former officer

Critique:

As Fielding declared in his introduction to *The History of Amelia,* he satirized nobody in the novel. Amelia, the long-suffering wife of every generation, is charming and attractive. The foibles of her husband still ring true. Dr. Harrison is a man each reader would like to know. Some of the interest of the novel lies in Fielding's accurate presentation of prison life and the courts. Having been a magistrate for many years, he was able to present these scenes in a most modern and realistic way, for aside from presenting the virtuous character of Amelia, Fielding wanted his novel to interest people in prison and legal reform. Although the novel lacks the extravagant humor of his earlier novels, the plot presents many amusing characters and complex situations.

The Story:

One night the watchmen of Westminster arrested Captain William Booth, seizing him during his attempt to rescue a stranger who was being attacked by two ruffians. The footpads secured their own liberty by bribing the constables, but Booth, in spite of his protests, was hailed before an unjust magistrate. The story he told was a straightforward one, but because he was penniless and shabbily dressed the judge dismissed his tale and sentenced him to prison. Booth was desperate, for there was no one he knew in London to whom he could turn for aid. His plight was made worse by his reception at the prison. His fellow prisoners stripped him of his coat, and a pickpocket made off with his snuffbox.

While he was smarting from these indignities, a fashionably dressed young woman was brought through the gates. Flourishing a bag of gold in the face of her keepers, she demanded a private room in the prison. Her appearance and manner reminded Booth of an old friend of questionable background, a Miss Matthews whom he had not seen for several years. But when the woman passed him without a sign of recognition, he believed himself mistaken.

Shortly afterward a guard brought him a guinea in a small parcel, and with the money Booth was able to redeem his coat and snuffbox. The rest of the windfall he lost in a card game. Booth was penniless once more when a keeper came to conduct him to Miss Matthews, for the woman was indeed she. Seeing his wretched condition as he stood by the prison gate, she had sent him the mysterious guinea.

Reunited under these distressing circumstances, they proceeded to relate the stories of their experiences. Miss Matthews told how she had been committed to await sentence for a penknife attack on a soldier who had seduced her under false promises of marriage.

Booth, in turn, told this story. He had met a Miss Amelia Harris, a beautiful girl whose mother at first opposed her daughter's marriage to a penniless soldier. The young couple eloped but were later, through the efforts of Dr. Harrison, a wise and kindly curate, reconciled with Amelia's mother. Booth's regiment was ordered to Gibraltar, shortly before a child was to be born to Amelia. He left reluctantly, leaving Amelia in the care of her mother and her older sister, Elizabeth. At Gibraltar Booth earned the good opinion of his officers by his bravery. Wounded in one of the battles of the campaign, he was very ill, and Amelia, learning of his condition, left her child with her mother and sister and went to Gibraltar to nurse her sick husband. Then Amelia, in her turn, fell sick. Wishing to take her to a milder climate, Booth wrote to Mrs. Harris for money, but in reply received only a rude note from Elizabeth. He hoped to get the money from his army friend, Major James, but that gentleman was away at the time. Finally he borrowed the money from Sergeant Atkinson, his friend and Amelia's foster brother, and went with his wife to Montpelier. There the couple made friends with an amusing English officer named Colonel Bath and his sister.

Joy at the birth of a second child, a girl, was dampened by a letter from Dr. Harrison, who wrote to tell them that old Mrs. Harris was dead, and that she had left her property to Amelia's sister. The Booths returned home, to be greeted so rudely by Elizabeth that they withdrew from the house. But for the help of Dr. Harrison, they would have been destitute. Harrison set Booth up as a gentleman farmer and tried to help him make the best of his half-pay from the Army. But because of several small mistakes, Booth made enemies among the surrounding farmers. Dr. Harrison was traveling on the continent at the time and in his absence Booth was reduced almost to bankruptcy. He came to London to try his fortunes anew. He preceded Amelia, found modest lodgings, and wrote her where they were. It was at this point that another misfortune landed him in prison. At the end of Booth's story, Miss Matthews sympathized with his unfortunate situation, congratulated him on his wife and children, and paid the jailer to let Booth spend the next few nights with her in her cell.

Booth and Miss Matthews were shortly released from prison. The soldier wounded by Miss Matthews having completely recovered, charges against her were dropped. Miss Matthews also secured the release of Booth, and the two were preparing to leave prison when Amelia arrived. She had come up from the country to save him, and his release was a welcome surprise for the distressed wife. The Booths set themselves up in London. Shortly afterward, Booth met his former officer, now Colonel James, who in the meanwhile had married Miss Bath and grown quickly tired of her. Mrs. James and Amelia resumed their old friendship. Booth, afraid that Miss Matthews would inform Amelia of their affair in prison, told Colonel James of his difficulties and fears. The colonel gave him a loan and told him not to worry. Colonel James was himself interested in Miss Matthews, but he was unable to help Booth by his intercession. Miss Matthews continued to send Booth reproachful and revealing letters which might at any time have been intercepted by Amelia.

While walking in the park one day, the Booths met Sergeant Atkinson. He joined their household to help care for the children, and soon he started a half flirtation with a Mrs. Ellison, Booth's landlady.

Mrs. Ellison proved useful to the Booths, for a lord who came also to visit her advanced money to pay some of Booth's debts. Meanwhile Miss Matthews had spitefully turned Colonel James against Booth. Colonel Bath, hearing his brother-in-law's poor opinion of Booth, decided that Booth was neither an officer nor a gentleman, and challenged him to a duel. Colonel Bath believed in nothing so much as a code of honor, and when, in the duel, Booth had run him through, without serious injury, the colonel was so much impressed by Booth's gallantry that he forgave him and brought about a reconciliation between James and Booth.

During this time Mrs. Ellison had been trying to arrange an assignation between Amelia and the nobleman who had given Booth money to pay his gambling debts. Amelia was innocently misled by her false friends. But the nobleman's plan to meet Amelia secretly at a masquerade was thwarted by another neighbor, Mrs. Bennet. This woman, who had been a boarder in Mrs. Ellison's house, had also met the noble lord, had encountered him at a masquerade, and had drunk the drugged wine he provided. To prevent Amelia's ruin in the same manner, Mrs. Bennet came to warn her friend. Then she informed Amelia that she had recently married Sergeant Atkinson, whom Amelia had thought in love with Mrs. Ellison. But Amelia's joy at learning of both the plot, which she now planned to escape, and of the marriage, was marred by the news that Booth had again been put into prison for debt, this time on a warrant of their old friend Dr. Harrison.

Amelia soon discovered that Dr. Harrison had been misled by false rumors of Booth's extravagance, and had put him in jail in order to stop his rash spending of money. Learning the truth, Dr. Harrison had Booth released from prison.

On the night of the masquerade Amelia remained at home but sent Mrs. Atkinson dressed in her costume. At the dance Mrs. Atkinson was able to fool not only the lord but also Colonel James. The complications of the affair were many, almost every relationship being misunderstood. Booth fell in with an old friend and lost a large sum of money to him. Again he became worried about being put in jail. Then he became involved in a duel with Colonel James over Miss Matthews, whom Booth had visited only at her insistence. Before the duel could take place, Booth was again imprisoned for debt, and Dr. Harrison was forced to clear his name with Colonel James. Finally James forgave Booth, and Miss Matthews promised never to bother him again.

Called by chance into a strange house to hear the deathbed confession of a man named Robinson, Dr. Harrison learned that Robinson had at one time been a clerk to a lawyer named Murphy who had made Mrs. Harris' will. He learned also that the will which had left Amelia penniless was a false one prepared by Elizabeth and Murphy. Dr. Harrison had Robinson write a confession so that Amelia could get the money that was rightfully hers. The lawyer Murphy was quickly brought to trial and convicted of forgery.

Booth's troubles were now almost at an end. With Dr. Harrison he and Amelia returned home to confront Elizabeth with their knowledge of her scheme. Elizabeth fled to France, where Amelia, relenting, sent her an annual allowance. Booth's adventures had finally taught him not to gamble, and with his faithful Amelia he settled down to a quiet and prosperous life blessed with many children and the invaluable friendship of Dr. Harrison and the Atkinsons.

THE AMERICAN

Type of work: Novel
Author: Henry James (1843-1916)
Type of plot: Psychological realism
Time of plot: Mid-nineteenth century
Locale: Paris, France
First published: 1877

Principal characters:
CHRISTOPHER NEWMAN, an American
MR. TRISTRAM, a friend
MRS. TRISTRAM, his wife
M. NIOCHE, a shopkeeper
MLLE. NIOCHE, his daughter
MADAME DE BELLEGARDE, a French aristocrat
CLAIRE DE CINTRÉ, Madame de Bellegarde's daughter
MARQUIS DE BELLEGARDE, Madame de Bellegarde's older son
VALENTIN DE BELLEGARDE, Madame de Bellegarde's younger son
MRS. BREAD, Madame de Bellegarde's servant

Critique:

In this novel Henry James shows the interreaction of two cultures, the American and the French. His primary interest is not in the action; his aim is to analyze the various psychological situations created by the events of the plot. The author scrutinizes the inner lives of his characters and writes about them in an urbane and polished style uniquely his own.

The Story:

In 1868 Christopher Newman, a young American millionaire, withdrew from business and sailed for Paris. He wanted to loaf, to develop his aesthetic sense, and to find a wife for himself. One day, as he wandered in the Louvre, he made the acquaintance of Mlle. Nioche, a young copyist. She introduced him to her father, an unsuccessful shopkeeper. Newman bought a picture from Mlle. Nioche and contracted to take French lessons from her father.

Later, through the French wife of an American friend named Tristram, he met Claire de Cintré, a young widow, daughter of an English mother and a French father. As a young girl, Claire had been married to Monsieur de Cintré, an evil old man. He had soon died, leaving Claire with a distaste for marriage. In spite of her attitude, Newman saw in her the woman he wished for his wife. But an American businessman was not the person to associate with French aristocracy. On his first call, Newman was kept from entering Claire's house by her elder brother, the Marquis de Bellegarde.

True to his promise, M. Nioche appeared one morning to give Newman his first lesson in French. Newman enjoyed talking to the old man. He learned that Mlle. Nioche dominated her father and that he lived in fear that she would leave him and become the mistress of some rich man. M. Nioche assured Newman that he would shoot her if she did. Newman took pity on the old man and promised him enough money for Mlle. Nioche's dowry if she would paint some more copies for him.

Newman left Paris and traveled through Europe during the summer. When he returned to Paris in the autumn he learned that the Tristrams had been helpful; the Bellegardes were willing to receive him. One evening Claire's younger brother, Valentin, called on Newman and the two men found their opposite points of view a basis for friendship. Valentin envied Newman's liberty to do as he pleased; Newman wished himself acceptable to the society in which the Bellegardes moved. After they had become good friends, Newman told Valentin that he wished to marry his sister and asked Valentin to plead his cause. Warning Newman that his social position was against him, Valentin promised to help the American as much as he could.

Newman confessed his wish to Claire, and asked Madame de Bellegarde, Claire's mother, and the marquis for permission to be her suitor. The permission was given, grudgingly. The Bellegardes needed money in the family.

Newman went to the Louvre to see how Mlle. Nioche was progressing with her copying. There he met Valentin and introduced him to the young lady.

Mrs. Bread, an old English servant of the Bellegardes, assured Newman that he was making progress with his suit. He asked Claire to marry him and she accepted. Meanwhile, Valentin had challenged another man to a duel in a quarrel over Mlle. Nioche. Valentin left for Switzerland with his seconds. The next morning Newman went to see Claire. Mrs. Bread met him at the door and said that Claire was leaving town. Newman demanded an explanation. He was told that the Bellegardes could not allow a commercial person in the family. When he arrived home, he found a telegram from Valentin stating that he had been badly wounded and asking Newman to come at once to Switzerland.

With this double burden of sorrow, Newman arrived in Switzerland and found Valentin near death. Valentin guessed what his family had done and told Newman that Mrs. Bread knew a family secret. If he could get the secret from her, he could make them return Claire to him. Valentin died the next morning.

Newman attended the funeral. Three days later he again called on Claire, who told him that she intended to enter a convent. Newman begged her not to take this step. Desperate, he called on the Bellegardes again and told them that he would uncover their secret. Newman arranged to see Mrs. Bread that night. She told him that Madame de Bellegarde had killed her invalid husband because he had opposed Claire's marriage to M. de Cintré. The death had been judged natural, but Mrs. Bread had in her possession a document which proved that Madame de Bellegarde had murdered her husband. She gave this paper to Newman.

Mrs. Bread left the employ of the Bellegardes and came to keep house for Newman. She told him that Claire had gone to the convent and refused to see anyone, even her own family. The next Sunday Newman went to mass at the convent. After the service he met the Bellegardes walking in the park and showed them a copy of the paper Mrs. Bread had given him.

The next day the marquis called on Newman and offered to pay for the document. Newman refused to sell. He offered, however, to accept Claire in exchange for it. The marquis refused.

Newman found he could not bring himself to reveal the Bellegardes' secret. On the advice of the Tristrams he traveled through the English countryside and in a melancholy mood went to some of the places he had planned to visit on his honeymoon. Then he went to America. Restless, he returned to Paris and learned from Mrs. Tristram that Claire had become a nun.

The next time he went to see Mrs. Tristram, he dropped the secret document on the glowing logs in her fireplace and told her that to expose the Bellegardes now seemed a useless and empty gesture. He intended to leave Paris forever. Mrs. Tristram told him that he probably had not frightened the Bellegardes with his threat, because they knew that they could count on his good nature never to reveal their secret. Newman instinctively looked toward the fireplace. The paper had burned to ashes.

AN AMERICAN TRAGEDY

Type of work: Novel
Author: Theodore Dreiser (1871-1945)
Type of plot: Social criticism
Time of plot: Early twentieth century
Locale: Kansas City, Chicago, and Lycurgus, New York
First published: 1925

Principal characters:
Clyde Griffiths
Roberta Alden, his mistress
Samuel Griffiths, Clyde's wealthy uncle
Sondra Finchley, society girl whom Clyde loves

Critique:

An American Tragedy is probably Dreiser's best novel. The title itself is, of course, significant. Dreiser believed that Clyde's downfall was due to the American economic system and he presents a strong indictment against that system. If Clyde had had the privileges of wealth and social position, he would never have been tempted to a moral decision and his consequent ruin. The novel is a powerful document on the theme of social inequality and lack of privilege.

The Story:

When Clyde Griffiths was still a child, his religious-minded parents took him and his brothers and sisters around the streets of various cities, where they prayed and sang in public. The family was always very poor, but the fundamentalist faith of the Griffiths was their hope and mainstay throughout the storms and troubles of life.

Young Clyde was never religious, however, and he always felt ashamed of the existence his parents were living. As soon as he was old enough to make decisions for himself, he decided to go his own way. At sixteen he got a job as a bellboy in a Kansas City hotel. There the salary and the tips he received astonished him. For the first time in his life he had money in his pocket, and he could dress well and enjoy himself. Then a tragedy overwhelmed the family. Clyde's sister ran away, supposedly to be married. Her elopement was a great blow to the parents, but Clyde himself did not brood over the matter. Life was too pleasant for him; more and more he enjoyed the luxuries which his job provided. He made friends with the other bellhops and joined them in parties that centered around liquor and women. Clyde soon became familiar with drink and brothels.

One day he discovered that his sister was back in town. The man with whom she had run away had deserted her, and she was penniless and pregnant. Knowing his sister needed money, Clyde gave his mother a few dollars for her. He promised to give her more; instead he bought an expensive coat for a girl in the hope that she would yield herself to him. One night he and his friends went on a party in a car that did not belong to them. Coming back from their outing, they ran over a little girl. In their attempt to escape, they wrecked the car. Clyde fled to Chicago.

In Chicago he got work at the Union League Club, where he eventually met his wealthy uncle, Samuel Griffiths. The uncle, who owned a factory in Lycurgus, New York, took a fancy to Clyde and offered him work in the factory. Clyde went to Lycurgus. There his cousin, Gilbert, resented this cousin from the Middle West. The whole family, with the exception of his uncle, considered

Clyde beneath them socially, and would not accept him into their circle. Clyde was given a job at the very bottom of the business, but his uncle soon made him a supervisor.

In the meantime Sondra Finchley, who disliked Gilbert, began to invite Clyde to parties she and her friends often gave. Her main purpose was to annoy Gilbert. Clyde's growing popularity forced the Griffiths to receive him socially, much to Gilbert's disgust.

In the course of his work at the factory Clyde met Roberta Alden, with whom he soon fell in love. Since it was forbidden for a supervisor to mix socially with an employee, they had to meet secretly. Clyde attempted to persuade Roberta to give herself to him, but the girl refused. At last, rather than lose him, she consented and became his mistress.

At the same time Clyde was becoming fascinated by Sondra. He came to love her and hoped to marry her, and thus acquire the wealth and social position for which he yearned. Gradually he began breaking dates with Roberta in order to be with Sondra every moment that she could spare him. Roberta began to be suspicious and eventually found out the truth.

By that time she was pregnant. Clyde went to drug stores for medicine that did not work. He attempted to find a doctor of questionable reputation. Roberta went to see one physician who refused to perform an operation. Clyde and Roberta were both becoming desperate, and Clyde saw his possible marriage to the girl as a dismal ending to all his hopes for a bright future. He told himself that he did not love Roberta, that it was Sondra whom he wished to marry. Roberta asked him to marry her for the sake of her child, saying she would go away afterward, if he wished, so that he could be free of her. Clyde would not agree to her proposal and grew more irritable and worried.

One day he read in the newspaper an item about the accidental drowning of a couple who had gone boating. Slowly a plan began to form in his mind. He told Roberta he would marry her and persuaded her to accompany him to an isolated lake resort. There, as though accidentally, he lunged toward her. She was hit by his camera and fell into the water. Clyde escaped, confident that her drowning would look like an accident, even though he had planned it all carefully.

But he had been clumsy. Letters that he and Roberta had written were found, and when her condition became known he was arrested. His uncle obtained an attorney for him. At his trial, the defense built up an elaborate case in his favor. But in spite of his lawyer's efforts, he was found guilty and sentenced to be electrocuted. His mother came to see him and urged him to save his soul. A clergyman finally succeeded in getting Clyde to write a statement—a declaration that he repented of his sins. It is doubtful whether he did. He died in the electric chair, a young man tempted by his desire for luxury and wealth.

AMPHITRYON

Type of work: Drama
Author: Titus Maccius Plautus (c. 254-184 B.C.)
Type of plot: Farce
Time of plot: The Heroic Age
Locale: Thebes
First presented: c. 185 B.C.

Principal characters:

AMPHITRYON, a Theban general
ALCMENA, his wife
JUPITER, and
MERCURY, Roman gods
SOSIA, Amphitryon's slave

Critique:

Amphitryon is closely akin to many of the other Plautine plays in that it is a comedy of mistaken identity. It has long been believed that a lost Greek play was the original of Plautus' comedy, but no definite proof is available. *Amphitryon* has had a great influence on modern drama throughout the Western world, and there have been numerous translations, adaptations, and imitations. Such great dramatists as John Dryden, in England, and Molière, in France, made use of its theme and structure. Shakespeare's *Comedy of Errors,* taken largely from Plautus' *The Menaechmi,* owes something also to *Amphitryon.* In very recent times a production of the story as adapted by Jean Giraudoux was successful as a stage play under the title *Amphitryon* 38.

The Story:

Amphitryon, a Theban, joined the army of Thebes to fight against the Teloboans. When he left for the wars, his wife Alcmena, daughter of Electryon, was pregnant. Nevertheless, in the absence of Amphitryon, Jupiter fell in love with Alcmena and decided that he must enjoy her favors. Disguising himself as Amphitryon, Jupiter appeared to Alcmena as her husband, just returned from a battle with the Teloboans. Alcmena was unable to penetrate the disguise of the impostor and welcomed Jupiter as her husband. Because Jupiter wished to enjoy Alcmena as long as possible, he had the sun, moon, and stars remain fixed, and so the night he spent with Alcmena was long enough for her to conceive and be ready to bring forth a child by Jupiter at the same time she gave birth to the child by her husband.

In the meantime Amphitryon's ship returned to Thebes. Because it was still night Amphitryon's slave, Sosia, fearfully walking the streets of the sleeping town, tried to console himself with the pleasantness of the news he was bringing to its citizens. He thought how well his master, Amphitryon, had handled the war with the Teloboans, how the enemy had refused to arbitrate the dispute over lands, how the battle had been joined, and how Amphitryon had been awarded the golden cup of Pterela as a token of the valor displayed in the battle.

While Sosia soliloquized, Mercury, disguised as Sosia, was listening to every word. Mercury had assumed the disguise to aid his father, Jupiter, in the latter's scheme to make love to Alcmena. As Sosia came through the streets to Amphitryon's house, Mercury, in the guise of Sosia, was guarding the house and the inmates against any disturbance. When Sosia saw Mercury he was afraid, but he went up to the door and tried to enter. Mercury, as Sosia, told him to be gone and beat him with his fists. When Sosia cried out that he was a slave named Sosia who belonged to the household, he received another drubbing.

Sosia, confused, then asked the stranger who he was. Merucry replied that he was

Sosia, a slave of the household. Looking closely, Sosia saw that the person in front of him was dressed and looked exactly like himself. When Sosia went on to ask questions about the household, Mercury answered each one satisfactorily. Sosia asked about his own conduct during the battle; Mercury replied that he had been drinking. Knowing that the answer was correct and sure that someone had stolen his very identity, Sosia ran off to the ship, leaving Mercury to chuckle over the ruse which would prevent Amphitryon from spoiling Jupiter's night with Alcmena.

Eventually Jupiter took leave of Alcmena, after telling her that he had to return to his army, lest the men become bitter because their leader absented himself while they could not. When she grew sad at the thought of his departure, the god, to propitiate her, gave her the golden cup of Pterela which Amphitryon had received as a token of merit in the war. As he left, Jupiter ordered the night to move on in its regular course.

Amphitryon was furious when Sosia returned to the ship. He thought that the slave must be mad or, at the very least, drunk, and he refused to believe that anyone could have stolen the identity of Sosia, as the slave declared. Amphitryon, anxious to discover what was happening, set out for his home immediately, taking Sosia with him. By the time the real Amphitryon and Sosia arrived at the house Jupiter and Mercury had departed. Alcmena was surprised to see her husband return in so short a time. She feared that he was simply testing her fidelity.

Amphitryon, greeting his wife as a husband would after an absence of months, was unable to understand what Alcmena meant when she rebuked him for leaving her a short time before on a pretext of returning to his army. When she told Amphitryon that he had spent the night with her, Amphitryon became suddenly and decidedly angry. Then she mentioned the golden cup of Pterela, which she had received from Jupiter during his visit in disguise. Amphitryon declared she could not have the cup, for he had it under seal in his possession. But when he opened the chest in which he had put the cup, it was missing; the gods had stolen it to give to Alcmena.

In spite of the evidence produced to show that it was he who had been with his wife, Amphitryon was exceedingly angry and accused his wife of losing her honor by breaking her marriage vows. Alcmena, entirely innocent of any such intent and still believing that her husband had visited her earlier, was hurt and furious at the charges he made. Amphitryon, wishing to be fair but wanting to get to the bottom of the matter, went to get Alcmena's kinsman, Naucrates, who had been with him all night on board the ship. He also told Alcmena that he would divorce her unless she could prove her innocence.

Alcmena was upset at the charges heaped upon her by Amphitryon and made plans to leave the house. Jupiter, sorry for the trouble he had caused, prepared to help her. He appeared to Alcmena in disguise and softened somewhat her anger against Amphitryon. Speaking as Amphitryon, he apologized for the charges made against Alcmena's honesty and virtue.

Amphitryon was unable to find Naucrates and returned to his home. Warned by Mercury, Jupiter appeared as Amphitryon, and a riotous scene, with both men seeming to be Amphitryon, followed, an argument broken off when word came that Alcmena was about to give birth to a child. As Amphitryon prepared to leave, Jupiter struck him unconscious with a thunderbolt. With Jupiter's aid Alcmena painlessly gave birth to two sons, one by Amphitryon and the other by Jupiter. One child was so active that he could hardly be held on his cot to be bathed, and the waiting-women reported that within a few minutes of his birth the baby had strangled two large snakes that entered the room. The voice of Jupiter called out to Alcmena and told her that the lusty lad, Hercules, was his and the other child

Amphitryon's.

After the waiting-women had gone, Jupiter himself appeared to Amphitryon and told the husband what had happened. When he warned Amphitryon not to be harsh toward his wife for producing a child by a god, Amphitryon, faced with no other choice, promised to obey all that the god commanded.

AMPHITRYON 38

Type of work: Drama
Author: Jean Giraudoux (1882-1944)
Time: The Heroic Age
Locale: In and about Amphitryon's palace, Thebes
First presented: 1929

Principal characters:
JUPITER, master of the gods
MERCURY, his half-son
AMPHITRYON, a general of Thebes
ALKMENA, his wife
SOSIE, their servant

It is a fact that much influence was exerted on the written works of Jean Giraudoux by the physical productions of all but two of his plays in the theater of actor-director Louis Jouvet. Such a close and mutually advantageous association of managers or directors with a favorite playwright (or vice versa) has become an established pattern in the modern theater. Where highly personal directorial techniques and positive artifice exist in director and author, the published product is likely to contain much that the playwright never conceived in the original manuscript. The result is as it should be, not only living theater, but an art form embodying a power of ideas. In the partnership between Jouvet and Giraudoux, the actor respected and hallowed the poet. The happy circumstance of complete understanding between the writer's temperament and spirit and the actor's interpretative powers insured a rarity in the theater: Giraudoux wrote in a prose style that is practically verse, and the words roll from the tongues of actors with an ease and fluency that many writers strive for but few attain. *Amphitryon* 38, the second production of the Giraudoux-Jouvet collaboration, conclusively established Giraudoux as a playwright of great wit and dexterity.

The recasting of Greek myths into modern molds has long fascinated playwrights. Giraudoux's *Amphitryon* 38 may or may not be the thirty-eighth version of that legend. The whimsical title, implying that legends and myths belong to time, sets the mood for the capricious events of the play.

The Amphitryon legend tells us that Jupiter impersonated Amphitryon and gained admission to the bed of his wife Alkmena. From this encounter Hercules was born. On this familiar framework Giraudoux draws fresh character, weaves new plot structure, and imbues the play with wit and ideas impossible in the original. The result is a mixture of theology, high comedy, satire, farce, and matrimonial and political commentary.

Basking on a cloud and spying on their victim, Jupiter and Mercury lay plans for the seduction of Alkmena as if preparing for a tasty banquet. In order to remove Amphitryon from his bedchamber, Mercury suggests that Jupiter have the friendly Athenians declare war on Thebes. Amphitryon, a stalwart general of the Theban army, will hurry to engage the enemy. Mercury will then take the place of Sosie, a servant, and tell Alkmena that Amphitryon will momentarily desert the battle and return to her bed that very night. Jupiter, of course, will impersonate Amphitryon and partake of the delectable Alkmena.

Giraudoux's writings have long been concerned with the causes of war; opportunities for comment on the high level planning of war appear early in *Amphitryon* 38 and in most of his other plays. Giraudoux leaves the sordid, clinical reporting of battle for his colleagues; he himself, in play after play, shows us the causes of conflict, frequently a startlingly inhuman cause which frighteningly illustrates the workings of political power.

Jupiter arrives before the palace of Alkmena amidst a great clanging noise, for he has forgotten the laws of gravity in his descent. With the help of Mercury he goes through some difficulty in transforming himself from the guise of a god to that of a mortal. Giraudoux sets for himself the difficult task of showing Jupiter the god and Jupiter the mortal simultaneously, a device of dual identity he uses in many of his works.

Mercury has already prepared the faithful wife for the return of Amphitryon, to whom she has promised fidelity or suicide if she knowingly deceives him Jupiter whets his appetite for love by demanding admission to her bed as a lover, not as a huband. It is not enough to love within the union of marriage—the added fillip is to be the tantalizingly illegal husband-seducer. With guileless logic, Alkmena swears fidelity to her husband-wife vows and refuses to open her gates and admit the false husband Jupiter to her chambers as a lover. As her husband, however, he gains easy entry through the gates which had been unlocked all the while.

Mercury thoughtfully holds back the dawn until Jupiter consummates the union, but he takes the precaution of informing the universe that Jupiter has made another mortal conquest so that the proper celestial eruptions will signify the seduction. He also practices a caprice of his own and has the real Amphitryon leave the battle and return to Alkmena the next day. This is only fair, for Jupiter, as has been his practice, will reveal his true identity to Alkmena with the coming of dawn and take leave of her in a burst of ego-satisfying, celestial glory.

But Mercury and Jupiter have underestimated the power of Alkmena. Giraudoux shows us here, as he does in other plays, his strong conviction that the female possesses a brand of intellect of an extraordinary nature; mere feminine wiles and physical beauty are but a means to an end, for the true power of logic and incisiveness belong in the female mind. Alkmena, without deliberation, but because she is a woman, is more than a match for Jupiter. When dawn finally arrives, she is found on her patio placidly eating breakfast fruit, while Jupiter, the traditional ravisher of innocent womanhood, lolls in the drowsy sensuality of her bed. When he joins her, he tries to reveal his true identity, but he is thwarted at every turn by Alkmena's charming and unclouded humanistic approach to divinity. There is a clarity and lack of religious fervency here that might pass for naïveté. But Giraudoux has more in mind than mere flippancy; Alkmena's childlike reasoning is the embodiment of utter simplicity and faithfulness in the kind, matter, and form of the gods. It is a perfectly satisfying and workable theology, uncluttered by the implementalia of animistic practices.

Jupiter, having satisfied his desires, and knowing that if his true identity is revealed Alkmena will kill herself and his unborn seed, now wishes to whet his holy ego by paying a formal celestial visit to Alkmena, thereby legalizing their secret union. Mercury makes the official proclamation of the impending visit, and Leda, Queen of Sparta, who has had some previous knowledge of heavenly unions, pays a duty call on Alkmena. In the scene between the two women Giraudoux epitomizes his own simplicity and clarity of style. With wit and candor, Leda describes her encounter with the heavenly swan. There is no pretense or pomposity here, only statement of fact which becomes a kind of understatement that runs through all of Giraudoux's plays and is particularly apparent in his female characterizations. The expected is avoided, humor for its own sake and wit as a result of syntax. The comedy is the result of character rather than situation, but the situation produces the character.

Alkmena, having discovered that Leda longs for another encounter with Jupiter, persuades the queen to take her place in the bedchamber. Jupiter will visit her in the form of Amphitryon, for he has a habit of appearing in the form most desired by his earthly mates. Leda agrees, and the real

Amphitryon arrives, is mistaken for Jupiter masquerading, and is sent into the palace. Only when Jupiter himself appears to Alkmena does she realize her mistake.

The resolution of the provocative situation is brought about by the resourceful Alkmena. Will Jupiter forego the celestial visit for which she is so evidently unprepared, and remain only friends with her? Jupiter quickly agrees to this strange relationship and assures the suspicious Alkmena that he has never visited her before—as her lover. Jupiter then gives his blessing to Alkmena and Amphitryon and bids them name their unborn child Hercules. As a twinkling afterthought, he offers to be godfather to the child.

Amphitryon 38 may appear to the casual reader or spectator to be comedy that is witty, satirical, and playfully suggestive. In order to appreciate Giraudoux fully, it is necessary to look further for the social and political playwright. Giraudoux does not obscure his point, nor does he burden his audience with a message. Rather, he tantalizes with ideas craftily derived from situation, character, and language that joins the comedy of manners and the comedy of ideas.

ANABASIS

Type of work: Poem
Author: St.-John Perse (Alexis St.-Léger Léger, 1887-)
Time: The past
Locale: The East
First published: 1924

Principal characters:
The Conqueror-Prince
A Woman
The Mariner

If the distinction between traditional poetry and modern poetry is that the traditional attempts to tell about experiences and emotions (*has* its own subject matter) whereas the modern attempts to present experiences and emotions directly (*is* its own subject matter), then St.-John Perse can be said to be both a traditional and a modern poet at the same time. His five long works—*Éloges, Anabasis, Exile, Winds,* and the recent and magnificent *Seamarks*—have been called "epics of the soul." But each has a more definite, a more tangible, subject matter than the soul itself. *Éloges,* for example, is about childhood; *Seamarks* is a poem in praise of the sea, a majestic symbol enclosing the beginning, perhaps the end, of life.

There is always a coherent system of solid reality behind what T. S. Eliot calls Perse's "logic of the imagination." The modernist surface of the poems may present what seem at first glance to be fascinatingly juxtaposed but apparently disconnected images, brilliantly phrased but completely gratuitous declamations, catalogues of wonderful but bewilderingly selected things. Below the surface, however, is a firm foundation of experience, as systematized and coherent as that of *The Knight's Tale* or *Madame Bovary.*

In Perse's *Anabasis* this concreteness is perhaps more clearly seen, more palpably felt, than in any of his other poems. *Anabasis* is, first of all, a modern poem, reminiscent in its technique of Rimbaud and of the French Symbolist school in general. Relying on the "logic of imagination" rather than on the logic of discourse, it attempts to present experience directly. But as we discover (through the impact of the images and through our resultant awareness of their symbolic meanings) the nature of the experience being presented, we realize that we are being told *about* an experience, as well. Something is happening in an epic more than in the figurative sense of the word, and it is happening somewhere—in time and in a certain place.

The place is important for at least two reasons. It is the East, not the romanticized Orient, not specifically the Far East or the Near East, but the wide expansive East of the great conquerors like Alexander, Tamerlane, Genghis Khan; the East of ancient ceremony, the age-old source of knowledge. As such, it is important symbolically, for the experience presented is in one sense the experience of knowledge—of awareness, of contact with (or, perhaps more accurately, of a return to) reality. A theme that runs through the poem is the theme of power, the power of knowledge—

> The Sun is unmentioned but his power is amongst us
> and the sea at morning like a presumption of the mind.

> Et le soleil n'est point nommé, mais sa puissance est parmi nous
> et la mer au matin comme une présomption de l'esprit.

There is also a recurrence of ceremony.

The language is important for the clarity and immediacy of imagery that it allows the poet. His scene is not the romantic East in any vague or misty sense. For the East is familiar to St.-John Perse as fact. It must be remembered that Perse the poet is also Alexis St.-Léger Léger, a leading French diplomat until the time of the German occupation during World War II. As a diplomat he had spent the early part of his career in China. There, undoubtedly, the keen senses of the poet Perse took in the sights, sounds, and ceremonial ways of that ancient land, the poet's sensibilities transmuting them into images that make up the texture of *Anabasis* and give the poem its strong feeling of reality of the East that underlines its theme of contact with the real:

> Milch camels, gentle beneath the shears, sewn with mauve
> scars, let the hills march forth under the facts of the harvest sky
> —let them march in silence over the pale incandescence of the
> plain;

> Chamelles douces sous la tonte, cousues de mauves
> cicatrices, que les collines s'acheminent sous les données
> du ciel agraire—qu'elles cheminent en silence sur les in-
> candescences pâles de la plaine;

or

> Through
> the gate of living chalk we see the
> things of the plain: living
> things,
> excellent things!

> Par la
> porte de craie vive on voit les choses
> de la plaine: choses
> vivantes, ô choses
> excellentes!

> sacrifice of colts on the tombs of children, purification of
> widows among the roses and consignments of green birds in the
> courtyards to do honour to the old men;

> des sacrifices de poulains sur des tombes d'enfants,
> des purifications de veuves dans les roses et des rassemble-
> ments d'oiseaux verts dans les cours en l'honneur des vieil-
> lards;

> many things on the earth to hear and to see, living
> things among us!

> beaucoup de choses sur la terre à entendre et à voir,
> choses vivantes parmi nous!

Anabasis stands firmly on the substrata of the poet's life in still another way; and again these facts work themselves up to the symbolic surface of the poem. It is a story of a quest and of conquest and of the continuing cycle of these things, for after two conquests the poem ends at the beginning of a new search. The quest, the military advance into the new country, from which the poem derives its name, is at its basic level the search for reality. (Eliot's note, that the title is not an allusion to Xenophon but is used in a literal sense, bears repetition.) The quest is the Rimbaudian search, but with a significant difference: For Perse, there is no descent into hell; there is sufficient reality for him above ground. To capture it, he must return to ancient ways and ceremonies; but the reality is there.

In this princeliness the essential difference between Perse and Rimbaud can be found. The poem begins, "Sur trois grandes saisons m'établissant avec honneur,/j'augure bien du sol où j'ai fondé ma loi":

> I have built myself, with honor and dignity have I
> built myself on three great seasons, and it
> promises well, the soil whereon I have established my Law.

The poet is the Prince, the lawgiver, the conqueror, the founder of cities. As the Prince, Perse can do in this poem the very things that Rimbaud had to leave his poetry to do. Just as there need be no descent, so there need be no flight from poetry into action. Perse's life has been a life of action; for him there has been only the necessity of distilling the experience of the action into poetry. Born on a family-owned Caribbean island, he had been educated as an aristocrat whose destiny was to serve his state. His diplomatic career had been one of authority and responsibility, of power, decision, and restraint. These also go into the distillation. The poem is powerful yet restrained and it is about power, the conquest of those "living things, excellent things."

Thus, while Rimbaud had to descend into hell to find himself and had then to fly to primitivism to find reality, Perse knows himself already as the Prince and knows from experience, not so much the primitive, but the ceremonial and ancient. With these he turns to poetry to find the reality of that experience. Aside from obvious technical similarities—and in technique Perse owes much to Rimbaud, particularly in his use of "poetic prose," which is really poetry measured in terms of paragraphs rather than in terms of lines—the two are alike in their search but different in their means of searching. In this respect, it is Perse who is the true poet: the maker, serene, detached, anonymous.

In this sense, *Anabasis* is a poem by the Prince and is about the quest and conquest by the poet as the Prince. It is divided into ten parts. These parts were indicated in the original merely by Roman numerals, but later they were given titles (actually brief synopses) by Lucien Fabre. Part I, following the beautiful introductory "Song" ("Under the bronze leaves a colt was foaled") ("Il naissait un poulain sous les feuilles de bronze") deals with the "arrival of the Conqueror at the site of the city which he is about to build." The dominating symbols here are those of power, knowledge, and humanity: the Sun, salt, and thirst:

"Him who has not praised thirst and
drunk the water of
the sands from a sallet
I trust him little in the commerce of
the soul. . . ."

"Qui n'a, louant la soif, bu l'eau
des sables dans un
casque,
je lui fais peu crédit au commerce
de l'âme. . . ."

The next three parts—"Tracing the plan of the city," "Consultation of augurs," and "Foundation of the city"—are quieter: ceremony and the business of living take the place of power:

Come, we are amazed at you, Sun!
You have told us such
lies!

Va! nous nous étonnons de toi, Soleil!
Tu nous as
dit de tels mensonges!

Gradually blended with the ceremony are discontentment and lust. The city is good, and it has its own beauty,

. . . more beauty
than a ram's skin painted red!

. . . plus beau
qu'une peau de belier peinte en rouge!

But the sense of reality is dulled by its busyness and shoddy ways.

In Part V, "Restlessness towards further explorations and conquests," the symbols of knowledge and power begin to serve as counterpoint to those of city and ceremony. They reassert themselves more in Parts VI and VII—"Schemes for foundation and conquest" and "Decision to fare forth"—in which a new, erotic theme is added. Now the lust felt in the second part assumes new meaning. Love joins power, knowledge, humanity; the

"scented girls, who shall soothe us
with a breath, silken
webs"

"parfumées, qui nous apaiseront d'un
souffle, ces
tissus"

join the Sun, the Law, and Salt as dominant symbols. These symbols give way for a time to those of desolation and dryness in Part VIII, "March through the desert"; but they rise with new strength in the penultimate section, "Arrival at the threshold of a great new country." Here the erotic theme reaches its climax in a song reminiscent of the Song of Solomon in its voluptuous grandeur. It is spoken by one of the women (perhaps the Princess) of the city which the Prince is about to capture, and with its note of physical union the triumphant union of all the themes and symbols is announced. The poet-prince, victorious over reality, sees the "living things, excellent things" in a state of full awareness in the final section of the poem. Ceremony, the occupations of the men of the city, serve with love, law, power to make awareness of reality complete, triumph unconditional.

The first half of the final section is called "Acclamation, festivities, repose." The second adds, "Yet the urge towards departure, this time with the mariner." There is still more "out in the vast spaces" where the mariner plots the way. This is the reality of the earth, but there is one more conquest to be made.

There is more for the Prince, but the poem, with its look to the heavens, is complete. The reader has watched the conquest and participated in it; he has been told about an experience and has had it presented directly, thanks to the Prince's knowledge and power.

THE ANABASIS

Type of work: History
Author: Xenophon (c. 430-c. 354 B.C.)
Time: 401-399 B.C.
Locale: Persia, Babylon, Armenia, Paphlagonia, Thrace
First transcribed: Fourth century B.C.

Principal personages:
XENOPHON, the narrator
CYRUS, son of King Darius of Persia
ARTAXERXES, the older son of Darius
TISSAPHERNES, a Persian general
CLEARCHUS, a Spartan exile, a general under Cyrus
CHIRISOPHUS, a Spartan mercenary captain
AGASIAS, a Stymphalian captain in the Greek army
PROXENUS, a Theban mercenary captain under Cyrus

The *Anabasis* is Xenophon's personal account of one of the most amazing marches in history, the march of a Greek army numbering ten thousand men from Babylon to the Black Sea. Xenophon played a leading role in the march and was, in effect, supreme commander of the army, although he refused the actual title. This account of the Persian expedition begins with the recital of Cyrus' effort to wrest the Persian throne from his brother Artaxerxes, but its principal part is concerned with the march from Babylon after the death of Cyrus at the battle of Cunaxa. The narrative is lively and vivid; it presents a great historical event from the perspective of a humane leader who organized his troops and maintained discipline by combining intelligence with the methods of Greek democratic leadership.

After the death of King Darius of Persia, his son Artaxerxes took possession of the throne. Cyrus, the younger son, with the support of his mother, Parysatis, began to build up an army to wrest control of Persia from his brother. By pretending to need troops to fight the Persian general Tissaphernes and the Pisidians, Cyrus acquired armies from the Peloponnese, the Chersonese (under the Spartan exile Clearchus), the Thessalians (under Aristippus), the Boeotians (under Proxenus), the Stymphalians (under Sophaenetus), and the Achaeans (under Socrates, the mercenary).

Cyrus marched from Sardis to Tarsus, gathering the elements of his army. At Tarsus the troops under Clearchus refused to move forward, arguing that they had not been hired to fight against the king. Clearchus dealt with the mutiny by first enlisting the loyalty of the men to himself (by pretending he would stay with them and not with Cyrus) and then by supporting Cyrus' claim that the enemy was not the king, but Abrocomas, one of the king's commanders.

By marches averaging fifteen miles a day Cyrus brought his army from Tarsus to Issus, the last city in Cilicia, where he was joined by ships from the Peloponnese. The march continued through the gates of Cilicia and Syria without opposition.

When Cyrus arrived at the city of Myriandrus, Xenias the Arcadian and Pasion the Megarian deserted the army. Cyrus refused to pursue or punish them, declaring that they had served him well in the past.

The army moved on to the Euphrates and the city of Thapsacus. Here the word was finally given to the Greek soldiers that the campaign was to be against King Artaxerxes. At first the soldiers refused to go further without more pay, but when Menon led his forces across the Euphrates in order to set a good example and to win Cyrus' favor, and when Cyrus promised to give each soldier additional pay, the Greeks crossed the river in force, making the crossing on foot. Since the Euphrates was usually too high for such a passage, the army was encouraged by this good sign.

When they reached the Arabian desert, Cyrus forced the troops to long marches in order to bring them to water and fodder. He kept discipline by ordering important Persians to help with the wagons when the road was difficult. A quarrel between the soldiers of Menon and Clearchus was halted by Cyrus' warning that they would all be destroyed if they fought among themselves.

Orontas, a Persian under Cyrus, attempted to transfer his army to the king's forces, but Cyrus learned of the plan by intercepting a letter from Orontas to the king. At a trial held in Cyrus' tent Orontas was condemned to death. He was never seen again.

Cyrus moved through Babylonia and prepared for battle with King Artaxerxes, but when the king's forces failed to take a stand at a defensive ditch which had been dug, Cyrus proceeded with less caution.

The two armies met at Cunaxa, and the Greeks put the opposing Persian forces to flight. Cyrus, with six hundred Persian cavalry, charged the center of the Persian line in order to reach the king; but after wounding King Artaxerxes, Cyrus was himself killed by a javelin blow. The cavalrymen with Cyrus were killed, except for the forces under Ariaeus, who hastily retreated.

While the main Greek armies under Clearchus and Proxenus were pursuing the Persians, the king's troops broke into Cyrus' camp and seized his mistresses, money, and property. Tissaphernes then joined the king's force and attacked the Greeks, but again the Greeks put the Persians to flight.

Phalinus, a messenger from King Artaxerxes, attempted to force Clearchus to surrender, but the Spartan, regarding the Greeks as victors, refused. The Greeks then allied themselves again with Ariaeus, who had been second to Cyrus, and pledged their support of him. When Ariaeus refused to attempt further battle against the king, the joint decision was to take a longer route back, putting as much distance as possible between their forces and the king's army.

The Greeks began their march and by accident came close to the king's army, frightening it into retreat. A truce was then arranged, and the king transferred supplies to the Greeks. Finally a treaty was made which provided safe conduct for the Greek army, with Tissaphernes as escort.

Many of the Greek leaders suspected Tissaphernes of treachery, but Clearchus, reassured by a conference with the Persian general, went to Tissaphernes with four of his generals and twenty of his captains in order that those who had been slandering the Persian commander could be named. Then, at a signal from the treacherous Tissaphernes, the Persians massacred the captains and took the generals as prisoners. The generals—Clearchus, Proxenus, Menon, Agias, and Socrates—were taken to the king and beheaded. Ariaeus was discovered to have been involved with Tissaphernes in this act of treachery.

After the capture of the generals, Xenophon, who had accompanied the Greek army at the urging of his friend Proxenus, bolstered the courage of the Greeks and urged that new generals and captains be appointed. The army responded to this decisive act of leadership.

Mithridates, a Persian commander who had been with Cyrus, returned to the Greeks and pretended to be friendly, but he suddenly attacked them and had to be driven back. The Greeks were then pursued by Tissaphernes and harassed by attacks from the Carduchi as they crossed the mountains to Armenia. Hearing that Tiribazus, the governor of Western Armenia who had promised the Greeks safe passage, planned to attack them, the Greek generals ordered a raid on Tiribazus' camp and then quickly resumed the march across snow-covered plains. The soldiers suffered from snow-blindness, frostbite, and bulimia.

To encourage the soldiers, Xenophon often worked and marched with the men. He arranged to procure guides from the Armenians and conceived the idea of capturing the mountain pass beyond the Phasis River by climbing it at night. Chirisophus and Xenophon were the principal leaders of the march.

In the country of the Taochi the Greeks were delayed by an attack from a fortification out of which large boulders were rolled down a hill, but when the stones were exhausted and as the opposing forces—including women and children—began to leap from the walls, the Greeks took possession. Finally, after fighting the Chalybes, the Greeks came within sight of the sea on their arrival at Trapezus.

Chirisophus was sent to secure ships, and the Greeks, now numbering eighty-six hundred troops of their original ten thousand, went on plundering expeditions for supplies. When Chirisophus was delayed, the available ships were loaded with the sick and wounded and with women, children, and baggage, while the rest of the army continued by land. After battling their way through the country of the barbarous Mossynoici, the Greeks arrived in the Euxine. There Xenophon considered founding a city, but he rejected the idea when the others opposed him. Some of the generals were critical of Xenophon's disciplinary measures, but he was able to defend himself against their charges.

The Greeks bought food and also plundered supplies from the Paphlagonians. During their stay in that territory the captains went to Xenophon and asked him to be commander-in-chief of the army, but after reflection and sacrifices to the gods he decided that it would be better both for himself and the army if the command were either kept divided or given to some other man. When Chirisophus was elected commander-in-chief, Xenophon willingly accepted a subordinate position.

By this time the Greeks had enough ships to carry all their men, and they sailed along the Paphlagonian coast from Harmene, the port of Sinope, to Heraclea, a Greek city in the country of the Maryandyni. The army then split into three parts because of a disagreement about demanding supplies from Heraclea. The Arcadians and Achaeans, who favored the demand, formed one body; Chirisophus, no longer in supreme command, headed a second body of troops; and Xenophon commanded the remainder. The Arcadians landed in Thrace and attacked some villages. When they got into difficulties, they were rescued by Xenophon and his force. At Port Calpe the three armies were reunited.

Many Greeks were killed by the Bithynians while hunting for supplies, but the Greek forces finally achieved victory over them. A quarrel involving Cleander, the Spartan governor of Byzantium, and Agasias, a Greek captain who had rescued one of his men from arrest by Dexippus, a traitorous Greek acting by Cleander's order, was settled by Xenophon's diplomacy.

Eventually the army crossed the straits from Asia to Byzantium. After some difficulty with Anaxibius, a Spartan admiral at Byzantium, the Greeks joined forces with King Seuthes of Thrace and participated in numerous raids on Thracian villages for supplies. When King Seuthes withheld pay from the Greeks, Xenophon was blamed but after a long inquiry, during which Xenophon was accused of being too much concerned with the welfare of the ordinary soldier, King Seuthes finally gave the Greeks the money due them.

Xenophon then led the army out of Thrace by sailing to Lampsacus, marching through the Troad, and crossing Mount Idea to the plain of Thebe. When the army reached Pergamon in Mysia, Xenophon conducted a partially successful raid against the Persian Asidates. He then turned the Greek army over to Thibron, the Spartan commander, who used the Greeks to war against Tissaphernes and Pharnabazus, a Persian governor.

THE ANATOMY OF MELANCHOLY

Type of work: Philosophical and scientific treatise
Author: Robert Burton (1577-1640)
First published: 1621

The seventeenth century found men beset by intellectual ferment, even intellectual confusion. Ideas and theories, old and new, clamored for attention and consideration because science had not yet begun to classify, assimilate, accept, and reject what man found in the world about him. More than that, each man attempted, in an age before specialization, to master all, or as much as he could, of human knowledge. Such was the age in which Robert Burton, who styled himself Democritus, Jr., wrote *The Anatomy of Melancholy,* which in many ways exemplifies the times in which it was written.

Burton was more than an educated man; he was a learned man who gave his life to learning, and much of his vast hoard of erudition found its way into his book. Ostensibly a study on melancholy, his work, before it was finished, absorbed into its pages most of the learning of Burton's time, either through his examination of everything he could associate with melancholy or through his many digressions.

The Anatomy of Melancholy is difficult to categorize. Its organization is complex, almost incoherent. An outline for each of the three "partitions" of the book, complicated though each is, does not indicate all that Burton managed to cram into the pages. The device seems really to be Burton's way of following a "scientific" convention of the times. Perhaps the best way to categorize the book is to regard it as an informal and heterogeneous collection of essays on man's dissatisfaction with the universe, as the seventeenth century saw it, and on ways in which that dissatisfaction could be cured. In that sense, at least, the book is a treatise on psychology, although the digressions Burton made are so numerous and involved that the reader sometimes wonders whether the author may not have lost his way.

Burton assuredly had no special theme or thesis he was attempting to prove. One critic has said that all *The Anatomy of Melancholy* proves is that a seventeenth-century classical education could produce an astounding amount of recondite learning. While Burton presented no set of principles, scientific or otherwise, to be proved, he did bring to his work a tremendous zest for learning as he found it in the books he read. This sense of gusto often puts the modern reader at a disadvantage, for Burton larded his paragraphs heavily, perhaps no English writer more so, with tags of Latin prose and poetry, and nowadays too few readers have a knowledge of Latin which enables them to read even tags in that language. The quotations are from countless authorities, many of them long since almost forgotten. A typical page, for example, cites Leo Afer, Lipsius, Zuinger, Seneca, Tully, Livy, Rhasis, Montaltus, Celsus, and Comesius. It is the host of references, allusions, and quotations that makes Burton's style seem heavy. Actually, he wrote in the tradition of Francis Bacon, studiously striving for a plain, even colloquial and racy, style. Like Bacon, too, he frequently begins a topic with an allusion, an anecdote, or a quotation as a springboard and from such a start often moves to whimsy and humor.

Sections of *The Anatomy of Melancholy* are famous for various reasons. The opening letter, a foreword to the reader, is well known for its satirical tone and its catalogue of the follies of mankind. Humor and whimsy account for the popularity of the sections on marriage and bachelorhood, on the "love of learning or overmuch study," and on the nature of spirits. The last "partition," ostensibly on melancholy growing out of love and religion, has many short synopses of world-famous stories. One contemporary critic has shown that if Elizabethan literature had somehow been lost during the intervening centuries, we could reconstruct a good bit of its nature from a study of *The Anatomy of Melancholy* alone.

The pervading tone of the book is satirical, but Burton's satire is always realistic, reflecting the point of view of an objective, even detached, observer of human folly. He begins the first "partition" with a contrast between man as he was in the Garden of Eden and man as he has been since the Fall. The result of man's transgression, according to Burton, is that mankind has since suffered a universal malady, a melancholy that affects both mind and body. Since he regards man as a whole, from a humanistic point of view, he proceeds to mingle sympathetically both religion and science. Much of the learning and many of the notions and theories which found their way into the book are nowadays of historical interest only, such as the analysis of the four humors, the discussion of the understanding and the will (as the seventeenth century used those terms), and the discussion of the nature of angels and devils. Still amusing, however, are his discussions of old age, diet, heredity, exercise, and constipation. While admitting that none is a panacea, Burton offers various cures for melancholy, including prayer, practice of the arts, the study of geography, coffee, traditional games, and moderate amounts of wine and other drink.

Like many another learned man in history, the writer often found himself discoursing on subjects on which there is perhaps no answer. Thus it is in his critique on marriage, which he delivers under the heading of "Cure of Love-Melancholy," that Burton, who himself never married, first quotes twelve reasons in favor of marriage, taking them from Jacobus de Voragine. Those arguments in favor of marriage include statements that a wife is a comfort and assistance in adversity, that she will drive away melancholy at home, that she brings an additional supply of the "sweet company of kinsmen," and that she enables a man to have fair and happy children. Immediately following these arguments, Burton himself adds an equal number as an Antiparodia. He suggests that a wife will aggravate a man's misery in adversity, will scold a man at home, bring a host of needy relatives, and make him a cuckold to rear another man's child. At the last, all Burton can say is that marriage, like much of life, is filled with chance: " 'Tis a hazard both ways I confess, to live single or to marry."

A sound observer of human nature, Burton also showed sympathetic understanding for his fellow beings. Living in an age when religious beliefs held a strong hold on men's and women's emotions, reinforced by fears of a physical Satan and Calvinistic doctrines of predestination and the depravity of man, he advocated that people afflicted by religious melancholy turn from contemplation of the more awful aspects of God and religion to such aspects of God as His infinite mercy and love. He even advocated recreation of an honest sort as an antidote to too much religion. In this, as in other ways, Burton was a man who stood out as being ahead of his time, a rare tribute to a man in any age.

AND QUIET FLOWS THE DON

Type of work: Novel
Author: Mikhail Sholokhov (1905-)
Type of plot: Historical chronicle
Time of plot: 1913-1918
Locale: Tatarsk, Russia
First published: 1928

Principal characters:
GREGOR MELEKHOV, a Cossack
PIOTRA, Gregor's brother
NATALIA, Gregor's wife
AKSINIA ASTAKHOVA, Gregor's mistress
BUNCHUK, a revolutionary leader

Critique:

Inasmuch as this novel has been so frequently mentioned by the Russians as proof that great art can be produced under their form of government, the book deserves careful consideration. The Russians are quite right in being proud of Sholokhov. *And Quiet Flows the Don* is a good book, free of any propaganda and standing on its own merit as a novel. The book is doubly successful, both as historical narrative and as an interesting story of people living during a difficult period in history.

The Story:

The Melekhov family lived in the small village of Tatarsk, in the Don basin of Tsarist Russia. Gregor, the oldest son, had a love affair with Aksinia, wife of his neighbor, Stepan Astakhova. Stepan was away serving a term in the army. In an effort to make his son settle down, Gregor's father arranged a marriage with Natalia Korshunov. Because Gregor never loved Natalia, their relationship was a cold one. Soon Gregor went openly to Aksinia and the affair became the village scandal.

When he heard the gossip, Gregor's father whipped him. Humiliated and angry, Gregor left home. With Aksinia he became the servant of the Listnitsky family, well-to-do landowners who lived outside the village of Tatarsk. When Aksinia bore him a daughter, Gregor's father relented enough to pay a visit before Gregor left for the army.

In the meantime, Gregor's wife, Natalia, tried to commit suicide because Gregor did not return her love. She went back to her own home, but the Melekhovs asked her to come to them. She was glad to do so. When Gregor returned to Aksinia, on his first leave from the army, he discovered that she had been unfaithful to him with Eugene Listnitsky, the young officer-son of his employer. Aksinia's daughter had died, and Gregor felt nothing but anger at his mistress. He fought with Eugene and whipped Aksinia as well. Then he returned to his own home, and there he and Natalia became reconciled. During the time he served in the army, Natalia bore him twins, a boy and a girl.

In the war against the Central Powers, Gregor distinguished himself. Wounded, he was awarded the Cross of St. George and so he became the first Chevalier in the village. While in the army, he met his brother, Piotra, and his enemy, Stepan Astakhova, who had sworn to kill him. Nevertheless, on one occasion he saved Stepan's life during an attack.

Discontent was growing among the soldiers. Bolshevik agitators began to talk against the government and against a continuance of the war. In Eugene Listnitsky's company an officer named Bunchuk was the chief agitator. He deserted before Listnitsky could hand him over to the authorities.

Then the provisional government of Kerensky was overthrown and a Soviet Socialist Republic was established. Civil war broke out. The Cossacks, proud of their free heritage, were strongly nationalistic and wanted an autonomous government for the Don region. Many of them joined the counter-revolutionists, under such men as Kornilov. Many returned to their homes in the Don basin. Gregor, joining the revolutionary forces, was made an officer of the Red Army.

Meanwhile the revolutionary troops in Rostov were under attack. Bunchuk, the machine gunner, was prominent in the battle and in the administration of the local revolutionary government. He fell in love with a woman machine gunner, Anna Poodko, who was killed during an attack. The counter-revolutionary troops were successful, and the Red Army troops had to retreat.

Gregor returned to the village and resumed the ordinary life he had led before the war. Soon news came that revolutionary troops were advancing on the village. When his neighbors prepared to flee, Gregor refused to do so. Stories of burning, looting, and rape spread through the countryside. A counter-revolutionary officer attempted to organize the villagers against the approaching enemy troops. He named Gregor as commander, but the nomination was turned down in anger because all the village knew that Gregor sympathized with the Reds, had fought with them. Instead, Gregor's brother Piotra was named commander.

The village forces marched out, Gregor going with them. When they arrived at their destination, they found that the revolutionary troops had already been defeated and that the leaders had been captured. Gregor asked what would happen to them. He was told they would be shot. Then Gregor came face to face with Podtielkov, his old revolutionary leader. When the latter accused him of being a traitor and opportunist, all of Gregor's suppressed feelings of disgust and nationalism burst forth. He reminded Podtielkov that he and other Red leaders had ordered plenty of executions, and he charged that Podtielkov had sold out the Don Cossacks. The revolutionists died prophesying that the revolution would live. Gregor went back to his Cossack village.

ANDERSEN'S FAIRY TALES

(SELECTIONS)

Type of work: Tales
Author: Hans Christian Andersen (1805-1875)
Type of plots: Folk tradition
Time of plots: Indeterminate
Locale: Denmark
First published: At intervals, 1835-1872

Principal characters:
KAREN, who owned the red shoes
THE UGLY DUCKLING
THE SNOW QUEEN
KAY, a little boy
GERDA, a little girl
THE SHEPHERDESS, a china figure
THE CHIMNEYSWEEP, her lover
THE EMPEROR
A TIN SOLDIER
A POOR SOLDIER

Critique:

Hans Christian was a dreamy little boy whose thoughts were very much like those of many of the characters in his fairy tales. When his father died and his mother remarried, he asked to go to Copenhagen to make his fortune. Because a soothsayer had told his mother that Hans would be Denmark's pride, she let him go. When he tried to enter the theater, he had little success. However, influential men realized he was a poet and befriended him until his publications began to attract attention. By the time Hans Christian Andersen died, he was Denmark's most beloved countryman. His tales may be fantastic, running through many moods, but they merely reflect his own character which was equally fantastic, though lovable.

The Stories:

THE RED SHOES

Karen was a little girl so poor that she had to go barefoot in winter. An old mother shoemaker felt sorry for her and made Karen a clumsy pair of shoes out of pieces of red felt. When Karen's mother died, the girl had to wear the red shoes to the funeral. An old lady, seeing Karen walking forlornly behind her mother's coffin, pitied her and took the child home. The old lady thought the red shoes ugly and burned them.

One day Karen saw the queen and the little princess. The princess was dressed all in white, with beautiful red morocco shoes.

When the time came for Karen's confirmation, she needed new shoes. The old lady, almost blind, did not know that the shoes Karen picked out were red ones just like those the princess had worn. During the confirmation Karen could think of nothing but her red shoes.

The next Sunday, as Karen went to her first communion, she met an old soldier with a crutch. After admiring the red shoes, he struck them on the soles and told them to stick fast when Karen danced. During the service she could think only of her shoes. After church she started to dance. The footman had to pick her up and take off her shoes before the old lady could take her home.

At a ball in town Karen could not stop dancing. She danced out through the fields and up to the church. There an angel with a broad sword stopped her and told her she would dance until she became a skeleton, a warning to all other vain children.

She danced day and night until she came to the executioner's house. There she tapped on the window and begged him to come out and cut off her feet. When he chopped off the feet, they and the little red shoes danced off into the forest. The executioner made Karen wooden feet and crutches and taught her a psalm, and the parson gave her a home.

Karen thought she had suffered enough to go to church, but each time she tried she saw the red shoes dancing ahead of her and was afraid. One Sunday she stayed at home. As she heard the organ music, she read her prayer book humbly and begged help from God. Then she saw the angel again, not with a sword but with a green branch covered with roses. As the angel moved the branch, Karen felt that she was being carried off to the church. There she was so thankful that her heart broke and her soul flew up to heaven.

THE UGLY DUCKLING

A mother duck was sitting on a clutch of eggs. When the largest egg did not crack with the rest, an old matriarchal duck warned the setting fowl that she might as well let that egg alone; it would probably turn out to be a turkey. But the egg finally cracked, and out of it came the biggest, ugliest duckling ever seen in the barnyard. The other ducklings pecked it and chased it and made it so unhappy that it felt comfortable only when it was paddling in the pond. The mother duck was proud only of the very fine paddling the ugly duckling did.

The scorn heaped on his head was so bitter that the duckling ran away from home. He spent a miserable winter in the marsh.

When spring came he saw some beautiful white swans settle down on the water. He moved out to admire them as they came toward him with ruffled feathers. He bent down to await their attack, but as he looked in the water he saw that he was no longer a gray ugly duckling but another graceful swan. He was so glad then that he never thought to be proud, but smiled when he heard some children say that he was the handsomest swan they had ever seen.

THE SNOW QUEEN

A very wicked hobgoblin once invented a mirror that reflected everything good as trivial and everything bad as monstrous; a good thought turned into a grin in the mirror. His cohorts carried it all over the earth and finally up to heaven to test the angels. There many good thoughts made the mirror grin so much that it fell out of their hands and splintered as it hit the earth. Each tiny piece could distort as the whole mirror had done.

A tiny piece pierced Kay through the heart and a tiny grain lodged in his eye. Kay had been a happy little boy before that. He used to play with Gerda in their rooms high above the street, and they both admired some rose bushes their parents had planted in boxes spanning the space between their houses. With the glass in his eye and heart, however, Kay saw nothing beautiful and nothing pleased him.

One night he went sledding in the town square. When a lady all in white drove by, he thought her so beautiful that he hitched his sled behind her sleigh as she drove slowly around the square. Suddenly her horses galloped out of the town. The lady looked back at Kay and smiled each time he tried to loosen his sled. Then she stopped the sleigh and told Kay to get in with her. There she wrapped him in her fur coat. She was the Snow Queen. He was nearly frozen, but he did not feel cold after she kissed him, nor did he remember Gerda.

Gerda did not forget Kay, and at last she ran away from home to look for him. She went to the garden of a woman learned in magic and asked all the flowers if they had seen Kay, but the flowers knew only their own stories.

She met a crow who led her to the prince and princess, but they had not heard of Kay. They gave her boots and a muff, and a golden coach to ride in when they sent her on her way.

Robbers stopped the golden coach. At the insistence of a little robber girl, Gerda was left alive, a prisoner in the robber's house. Some wood pigeons in the loft told Gerda that Kay had gone with the Snow Queen to Lapland. Since the reindeer tethered inside the house knew the way to Lapland, the robber girl unloosed him to take Gerda on her way.

The Lapp and the Finn women gave Gerda directions to the Snow Queen's palace and told her that it was only through the goodness of her heart that Kay could be released. When Gerda found Kay, she wept so hard that she melted the piece of mirror out of his heart. Then he wept the splinter from his eye and realized what a vast and empty place he had been in. With thankfulness in her heart, Gerda led Kay out of the snow palace and home.

THE SHEPHERDESS AND THE SWEEP

In the middle of the door of an old wooden parlor cupboard was carved a ridiculous little man with goat's legs, horns on his head, and a beard. The children called him Major-general-field-sergeant-commander-Billy-goat's-legs. He always looked at the china figure of a Shepherdess. Finally he asked the china figure of a Chinaman, who claimed to be her grandfather, if he could marry the Shepherdess. The Chinaman, who could nod his head when he chose, nodded his consent.

The Shepherdess had been engaged to the china figure of a Chimneysweep. She begged him to take her away. That night he used his ladder to help her get off the table. The Chinaman saw them leave and started after them.

Through the stove and up the chimney went the Shepherdess and the Chimneysweep. When she saw how big the world was, the Shepherdess began to cry, and the Chimneysweep had to take her back to the parlor. There they saw the Chinaman broken on the floor. The Shepherdess was distressed, but the Chimneysweep said the Chinaman could be mended and riveted.

The family had the Chinaman riveted so that he was whole again, but he could no longer nod his head. When the Major-general-field-sergeant-commander-Billy-goat's-legs asked again for the Shepherdess, the Chinaman could not nod, and so the Shepherdess and the Chimneysweep stayed together and loved each other until they were broken to pieces.

THE EMPEROR'S NEW CLOTHES

Once there was a foolish Emperor who loved clothes so well that he spent all of the kingdom's money to buy new ones. Two swindlers, who knew the Emperor's weakness, came to town with big looms. They told the people they wove the most beautiful cloth in the world but that it had a magical property. If someone unworthy of his post looked at it, the cloth became invisible.

The Emperor gave them much gold and thread to make him a new outfit. The swindlers set up their looms and worked far into the night. Becoming curious about the materials, the Emperor sent his most trusted minister to see them. When the minister looked at the looms, he saw nothing; but, thinking of the magical property of the cloth, he decided that he was unworthy of his post. Saying nothing to the swindlers, he reported to the Emperor, praising the colors and pattern of the cloth as the swindlers had described it.

Others, looking at the looms, saw nothing and said nothing. Even the Emperor saw nothing when the material was finished and made into clothes, but he also kept silent. He wore his new clothes in a fine procession. All the people called out that his new clothes were beautiful, all except one little boy who said that the Emperor did not have on any clothes at all.

Then there was a buzzing along the line of march. Soon everyone was saying that the Emperor wore no clothes. The Emperor, realizing the truth, held himself stiffer than ever until the procession ended.

THE STEADFAST TIN SOLDIER

A little boy had a set of twenty-five tin soldiers made out of the same tin spoon. Since there was not quite enough tin, one soldier had only one leg, but he stood as solidly as those with two legs.

The one-legged soldier stood on a table and looked longingly at a paper castle, at the door of which stood a paper dancer who wore a gauze dress. A ribbon over her shoulder was held in position by a spangle as big as her face.

One morning the little boy put the one-legged soldier on a window sill. When the window opened, the soldier fell three stories to the ground. There he stuck, head down between two stones, until some boys found him. They made a paper boat for the soldier and sailed it down the gutter. After a time the boat entered a sewer. Beginning to get limp, it settled deeper into the water. Just as the soldier thought he would fall into the water, a fish swallowed him.

When the fish was opened, the soldier found himself in the same house out of which he had fallen. Soon he was back on his table looking at the dancer. For no reason the boy threw him into a roaring fire. Suddenly a draft in the room whisked the dancer off the table and straight to the soldier in the fire. When the fire burned down, the soldier had melted to a small tin heart. All that was left of the dancer was her spangle, burned black.

THE TINDER BOX

A soldier was walking along the highroad one day when a witch stopped him and told him that he could have a lot of money if he would climb down a hollow tree and bring her up a tinder box. Thinking that was an easy way to get money, he tied a rope around his waist and the witch helped him to climb down inside the tree.

He took along the witch's apron, for on it he had to place the dogs that guarded the chests of money. The first dog, with eyes as big as saucers, guarded a chest full of coppers. The soldier placed the dog on the apron, filled his pockets with coppers, and walked on.

The next dog, with eyes as big as millstones, guarded silver. The soldier placed the dog on the apron, emptied his pockets of coppers, and filled them with silver.

The third dog had eyes as big as the Round Tower. He guarded gold. When the soldier had placed the dog on the apron, he emptied his pockets of silver and filled them, his knapsack, his cap and his boots with gold. Then he called to the witch to pull him up.

When she refused to tell him why she wanted the tinder box, he cut off her head and started for town. There he lived in splendor and gave alms to the poor, for he was good-hearted.

He heard of a beautiful princess who was kept locked up because of a prophecy that she would marry a common soldier. Idly he thought of ways to see her.

When his money ran out, and he had no candle, he remembered that there was a piece of candle in the tinder box. As he struck the box to light the candle, the door flew open and the dog with eyes like saucers burst in, asking what the soldier wanted. When he asked for money, the dog brought it back immediately. Then he found that he could call the second dog by striking the box twice, and the third dog by striking it three times. When he asked the dogs to bring the princess, she was brought to his room.

The king and queen had him thrown into prison when they caught him. There he was helpless until a little boy to whom he called brought the tinder box to him.

When the soldier was about to be hanged, he asked permission to smoke a last pipe. Then he pulled out his tinder box and hit once, twice, three times. All three dogs came to rout the king's men and free the soldier. The people were so impressed that they made the soldier king and the princess his queen.

ANDRIA

Type of work: Drama
Author: Terence (Publius Terentius Afer, c. 190-159 B.C.)
Type of plot: Comedy
Time of plot: Second century B.C.
Locale: Athens
First presented: 166 B.C.

Principal characters:
SIMO, a wealthy Athenian
PAMPHILUS, Simo's son
GLYCERIUM, beloved of Pamphilus
DAVUS, slave of Pamphilus
CHREMES, another wealthy Athenian, friend of Simo
CRITO, a traveler from Andros
CHARINUS, a suitor for the daughter of Chremes

Critique:

Although *Andria* was Terence's first play, it shows those characteristics for which this dramatist was noted throughout his career. As in all his plays, the action is closely knit, with no digressions, and the comedy is of a more serious turn than the popular slapstick humor. The language is natural. Actually, the plot was not new. Terence admitted that he had adapted his drama from two plays by Menander, the Greek dramatist who wrote *The Lady of Andros* and *The Lady of Perinthos.* The whole story turns, like so many Greek and Latin comedies, on the theme of mistaken identity. The modern reader will undoubtedly compare it to Shakespeare's *Comedy of Errors,* which in turn was freely adapted from *The Menaechmi* of Plautus. Nor have modern authors ceased to adapt from Terence's *Andria.* It was the basis of Baron's *L'Andrienne,* Sir Richard Steele's *The Conscious Lovers,* and Thornton Wilder's novel, *The Woman of Andros.*

The Story:

One day Simo confided in a servant that he had been pleased with his son Pamphilus until that very afternoon, when he had discovered that his son was in love with Glycerium, the sister of a courtesan who had recently died. Simo, who wished to marry his son to the daughter of his friend Chremes, saw in his son's love for Glycerium a threat to his plans.

Later Simo encountered his son's slave, Davus, and threatened him with severe punishment. Simo was afraid that Davus, a clever fellow, would help Pamphilus thwart his father's plans for his future. Davus immediately saw that some scheme would have to be put into action quickly if the love between Pamphilus and Glycerium were to end in marriage, even though Glycerium was already pregnant by Pamphilus.

Pamphilus' own scheme was to acknowledge the expected infant and then claim that Glycerium was actually an Athenian whose father had been shipwrecked on Andros and who had been reared by the family of the courtesan as a foster child. But Davus laughed at the story and felt that no one would believe it.

Pamphilus, warned that his father wanted him to marry that very day, was greatly troubled. He was put at ease, however, when Davus heard that the approaching marriage to Chremes' daughter had been refused by the girl's father, for Chremes had also learned of the affair between Pamphilus and the courtesan's sister. Davus told Pamphilus to agree to the marriage for the time being. Before long, he added, some way out of the predicament might be found.

Charinus met Davus and Pamphilus and told them that he was in love with Chremes' daughter. Pamphilus said he had no desire to marry the girl and that Charinus was welcome to her. Not knowing the true reason for Pamphilus' assent,

Charinus was thrown into despair within the hour, when he heard Pamphilus agree to marry Chremes' daughter.

Later, while Simo, the father, and Davus stood before the door of Glycerium's residence, they heard the servants send for a midwife. Simo was angry, thinking that Davus was trying to trick him into believing that Glycerium was having a child by his son. A short time later Glycerium was delivered of a baby boy. When Simo heard the news, he still thought Davus was trying to trick him and refused to believe what he heard.

Meanwhile Pamphilus waited patiently, believing that no marriage with Chremes' daughter had been arranged. While he waited, however, his father met Chremes on the street, and they agreed once more to marry their children to one another.

When Davus reported the latest development to Pamphilus, the young man was furious, for it now seemed certain he would never be able to marry the woman he loved. Glycerium, from her confinement bed, sent for Pamphilus to learn what progress he was making in his plans to marry her.

Davus, to prevent the marriage between Pamphilus and Chremes' daughter, had Glycerium's maidservant lay the infant on a bed of verbena in front of Simo's door. Chremes came up the street and saw the child. Davus, pretending that he did not see Chremes, began to argue with Glycerium's servant. During the argument the fact that the child was the son of Pamphilus and Glycerium was shouted aloud. Chremes stormed into Simo's house to withdraw again his offer of marriage between Pamphilus and his daughter.

Soon afterward Crito, a cousin of the dead courtesan, came looking for the house of his dead cousin. As soon as he found it, he asked the maidservant if Glycerium had found her parents in Athens. Davus, looking after Pamphilus' interests, overheard the conversation and entered the house after them.

When Davus left the house a few minutes later, he met Simo, who ordered the slave chained and thrown into a dungeon. While Chremes and Simo were talking over the delayed wedding, Pamphilus also left the house. After some argument the young man convinced his father that Crito had proof that Glycerium was an Athenian and Pamphilus would have to marry her because they had had a child. Pamphilus re-entered the house where Glycerium was lodged and emerged presently with Crito.

Chremes immediately recognized Crito as an acquaintance from Andros. Simo was finally convinced that Crito was an honorable man from that island. Crito then told how Phania, a citizen of Athens, had been shipwrecked on Andros and had died there. With the man had been a little girl, whom the dying man said was his brother's daughter. Chremes then broke into the story to exclaim that Glycerium must be his own daughter, because Phania had been his brother. When Chremes asked what the girl's name had been, Crito said that her name had been changed to Glycerium from Pasibula, the name of Chremes' daughter.

Everyone congratulated Chremes on finding his long-lost child. Pamphilus reminded his father that there could be no barrier to the marriage since Glycerium, too, was a daughter of Chremes and, according to the law, Pamphilus would have to marry her as her seducer. Chremes, overjoyed, declared that he would give a dower of ten talents to the bride.

Davus was freed from the dungeon, and Pamphilus told him all that had occurred. While they spoke, Charinus entered, happy that the other daughter of Chremes was now free to be his bride. The father gave ready consent to Charinus' suit and said that his only objection had been a desire to have his family united with Simo's. In addition, he promised that Charinus would receive a large dowry as well as a wife.

ANDROMACHE

Type of work: Drama
Author: Euripides (c. 485-c. 406 B.C.)
Type of plot: Tragedy of intrigue
Time of plot: About a decade after the Trojan War
Locale: The temple of Thetis in Thessaly
First presented: c. 426 B.C.

Principal characters:
ANDROMACHE, Hector's widow, slave to Neoptolemus
HERMIONE, wife of Neoptolemus and daughter of Menelaus
MENELAUS, King of Sparta
PELEUS, Neoptolemus' grandfather
MOLOSSUS, son of Andromache and Neoptolemus
ORESTES, Agamemnon's son
THETIS, goddess and dead wife of Peleus
CHORUS OF PYTHIAN MAIDENS

Critique:

Andromache is one of Euripides' most poorly constructed plays; both the plot line and the focus on personalities undergo a radical shift in the middle. It moves, not by development out of the original situation, but by accretion, and new characters are introduced with no preparation whatsoever. The first half of the play concerns Hermione's foiled plot against her rival, Andromache; the second deals with Orestes' treacherous murder of his rival, Neoptolemus; and there is only a very tenuous connection between the two. Written shortly after the outbreak of the war between Athens and Sparta, the play seems to be strongly motivated by Euripides' intense hatred of Spartan characteristics as they are shown in the arrogance of Hermione, the treachery of Orestes, and the criminal brutality of Menelaus. Although flawed, *Andromache* nevertheless has a certain hardness and brilliance that are fascinating.

The Story:

After the death of Hector and the fall of Troy, Andromache had been given as a special prize to Neoptolemus, son of Achilles. As his slave and concubine, she had borne a son, Molossus, thereby arousing the jealous wrath of Hermione, the barren wife of Neoptolemus. Fearing Hermione's hatred and sensing impending doom, Andromache sought sanctuary in the sacred grounds of the temple of Thetis, after secretly sending her son to a neighbor for safekeeping.

Hermione appeared at the temple and accused Andromache of seeking to oust her, taunted her for bearing a son to Hector's slayer, and threatened her with death. Andromache protested that as an aging woman and a helpless slave she would be mad to compete with Hermione and that she herself had gracefully accepted Hector's illegitimate children rather than let herself be corrupted by jealousy. Hermione, unmoved by these arguments, left the temple after threatening that she would find bait that would lure Andromache from her sanctuary.

She was true to her word, for soon afterward Menelaus arrived leading Molossus by the hand. The Spartan king warned that he would kill the boy on the spot if Andromache would not emerge and offer up her own life instead. Once again Andromache argued with a Spartan, pointing out that murder would surely pollute his reputation and that Neoptolemus would never condone the death of his only son. But Menelaus was adamant, and Andromache emerged from the sanctuary to learn that both she and her son were marked for slaughter. But before the order for execution could be carried out, the aged Peleus appeared and in response to her supplication commanded that her bonds be loosened. Furious with Menelaus, Peleus denounced Spartan cowardice and treachery and ordered the king to leave Thessaly at once and to take his barren daughter with him. Menelaus, however, announced that he was leaving with his army only in order to vanquish a city hostile to Sparta, after which he would return to confront Neoptolemus himself and settle the matter of his daughter's status in Thessaly.

After everyone had left the temple, a terribly distraught Hermione entered carrying a sword with which she intended to commit suicide. After her nurse had wrested the sword from her, Hermione, in great anguish, lamented the horrible deed she had plotted and chanted her fear that Neoptolemus would banish her. Suddenly Orestes appeared, claiming that he was merely passing through on his way to the oracle at Dodona, and Hermione threw herself at his feet. Because Orestes had once been betrothed to Hermione and had always loved her, he revealed that he had actually come to carry her off; he was prepared to murder her husband even if the deed involved sacrilegious treachery. Hermione's taunts at Andromache were now ironically being fulfilled upon herself.

After the desperate pair had fled, Peleus appeared. Before he could question the chorus about the fearful rumors he had heard, a messenger brought sad news. Peleus' grandson, Neoptolemus, was dead; he had been horribly murdered and mutilated by Orestes and his brigands while praying to the gods in the temple of Phoebus. The body of Neoptolemus was then carried in on a bier and bereaved old Peleus lamented the end of his line, for the only son of his only son was now dead. Throwing his scepter on the ground, the distraught king resolved to grovel in the dust until his death. At that moment the dim form of the divine Thetis, the goddess who had once been his wife, appeared hovering in mid-air. She commanded her husband to cease his mourning and take the body of Neoptolemus to be buried at the Pythian altar as a reproach to the Spartans. She further commanded that he take Andromache and Neoptolemus' son to Helenus, whom Andromache would marry so that the line of Peleus could continue. After this mission Peleus himself would be converted into a god and live with Thetis in the halls of Nereus forever. Peleus consented, moralizing that every prudent man should take heed to marry a wife of noble stock and give his daughter to a good husband.

ANDROMACHE

Type of work: Drama
Author: Jean Baptiste Racine (1639-1699)
Type of plot: Neo-classical tragedy
Time of plot: Shortly after the close of the Trojan War
Locale: Epirus
First presented: 1667

Principal characters:
ANDROMACHE, widow of Hector and captive of Pyrrhus
PYRRHUS, King of Epirus and son of Achilles
ORESTES, son of Agamemnon and spurned suitor of Hermione
HERMIONE, daughter of Helen and affianced bride of Pyrrhus
PYLADES, Orestes' friend and companion

Critique:

The appearance of *Andromache* on the stage was one of the great events of the French theater for 1667 and for all time. This play has been acted more times than any other drama by Racine. Its dramatic simplicity is outstanding. Each of the four leading characters is dominated by a single emotion. Orestes loves Hermione to distraction; Hermione is overwhelmed by Pyrrhus; Pyrrhus is madly in love with Andromache; Andromache can think only of the dead Hector and their child, Astyanax. Suffering of an emotional kind drives the four characters into a maze of spite, love, hate, and vengeance. At the end only Andromache is left—Pyrrhus and Hermione are dead, and Orestes has gone mad. The distinction is important, for Racine killed off the three who were led by their personal passions, but he saved the sole character whose unselfish grief was for others.

The Story:

Orestes, son of the Greek leader, Agamemnon, journeyed to Epirus to tell Pyrrhus, King of Epirus, that the Greeks were fearful of Astyanax, the young son of Hector and Andromache, who might someday try to avenge the fall of Troy. Because of their fear, they had sent Orestes to request that Pyrrhus put Astyanax to death.

Pyrrhus had fallen in love with Andromache, however, and at first, afraid of losing her love, he refused to grant the request. To Orestes, who had long loved Hermione, betrothed of Pyrrhus, the news of Pyrrhus' love for Andromache was welcome. Orestes thought he saw in the situation a chance for him to win Hermione for his wife. Orestes' friend Pylades was amazed, for Orestes had previously sworn that his love for Hermione had degenerated into hate because she spurned him.

When Pyrrhus refused to kill Astyanax or turn the child over to the Greeks, Orestes threatened him. Pyrrhus swore that he would make Epirus a second Troy before he permitted the death of Astyanax. Pyrrhus, hoping that his decision would lead her to forget her dead husband, told Andromache what he had done, but she made no response to his overtures. Angered, Pyrrhus told her that unless she married him the child would die.

Meanwhile Hermione, spurned by Pyrrhus, was trying to decide whether she loved or hated the king, and whether she wanted to flee with Orestes. When Pyrrhus, rebuffed by Andromache, went to her, they decided that they were still in love. Reconciled to Hermione, Pyrrhus promised to love only her and to give Astyanax to the Greeks.

But Hermione, changing her mind, prepared to flee with Orestes to inflict punishment on Pyrrhus, after Orestes told her that Pyrrhus had renewed his suit of Andromache. Pyrrhus returned while they spoke and announced that he was ready to give over the boy to the Greeks because Andromache had again spurned his love and aid.

Convinced that Pyrrhus had decided to

marry Hermione only to keep her from her Greek lover, Orestes plotted to carry off the girl. Pylades, his friend, agreed to help in the abduction. When Hermione met Orestes, she spoke only of her approaching marriage to Pyrrhus, whom she still loved. While they talked, Andromache entered the room and begged Hermione to protect Astyanax, whom Pyrrhus had determined to kill. Andromache reminded Hermione that Hector had championed Helen, Hermione's mother, when the Trojans had wished to murder her. Hermione refused to listen and scorned Andromache's request.

Andromache then pleaded with Pyrrhus, but he told her that her plea came too late. At last, when Andromache vowed to kill herself, her vow and tears moved the vacillating Pyrrhus, who once again told her that he would marry her instead of Hermione and champion the boy against the Greeks. But Andromache refused to save her son by marrying her captor and former enemy. After a conference with her waiting-woman, she decided to consult her husband's ghost. The result of that conference was a decision to marry Pyrrhus, thus bringing Astyanax under Pyrrhus' protection, and then to kill herself.

Hermione, furious when she learned that on the following day Pyrrhus intended to marry Andromache, sent for Orestes and told him that she wanted his help in avenging herself on the king. Without promising herself to Orestes, she asked him to kill Pyrrhus during the wedding ceremony.

At first Orestes demurred. Not wishing to become an assassin, he wanted to declare war on Pyrrhus and earn glory on the battlefield. But at Hermione's urging he finally agreed to the murder. She told him that it would be easy to commit the crime, because the king's guards had been sent to watch over Astyanax and none had been ordered to guard the nuptial ceremonies. She finally added that after the murder she would become Orestes' bride.

After Orestes left, Pyrrhus came once more to Hermione. Hoping that the king had changed his mind again, she sent her serving-woman to tell Orestes not to act until he had further word from her. But Pyrrhus had come to tell her only that he intended to marry Andromache, come what would. Hermione vowed she would have revenge.

This was her message to Orestes. Finally Orestes arrived to inform her that the deed was done; Pyrrhus had died at the hands of Orestes' soldiers.

Hermione, turning on Orestes, declared that she disowned such savagery and would have no more to do with him because he had killed the man she loved. When Orestes argued with her that she had persuaded him to commit the murder for her sake, her only defense was that she had been distraught at having her love spurned by Pyrrhus and that Orestes should not have listened to her. When she rushed out of the room, Pylades came with the Greek warriors to warn Orestes that if they were to escape the wrath of Pyrrhus' subjects they must take ship and sail away from Epirus at once. The people, they said, were obeying Andromache as their queen. And Hermione was dead; she had run into the temple and thrown herself on Pyrrhus' body, after stabbing herself with mortal wounds.

Hearing that news, Orestes turned mad and fainted in his agony. His men quickly took him away and made their escape from Epirus.

ÁNGEL GUERRA

Type of work: Novel
Author: Benito Pérez Galdós (1843-1920)
Type of plot: Political and religious tragedy
Time of plot: Late nineteenth century
Locale: Madrid and Toledo
First published: 1890-1891

Principal characters:
ÁNGEL GUERRA, a widower
DOÑA SALES, his mother
ENCARNACIÓN ("CIÓN"), his seven-year-old daughter
LORENZA ("LERÉ"), Doña Sales' nurse
ARÍSTIDES GARCÍA BABEL, an embezzler
FAUSTO GARCÍA BABEL, his dishonest brother
DULCENOMBRE ("DULCE") BABEL, Ángel's sometime mistress
PADRE CASADO, a priest

Critique:

Pérez Galdós, a great figure in Spanish literature of the late nineteenth century, wrote thirty novels in addition to the forty-six in his series called National Episodes. *Ángel Guerra* belongs to a group of about eight that present a picture of religious faith and the results of fanaticism on Spanish life. This group includes some of his best, *Doña Perfecta* (1876), *Gloria* (1876-1877), *The Family of León Roch* (1879), and *The Crazy Woman in the House* (1892). *Ángel Guerra* is the story of a politician and a mystic, a character whose names, "Angel" and "War," were intended to present his dual personality. By environment he was made a rebel who hated his mother, yet received from her the wealth that meant his personal freedom. Not only does the novel depict the working of fate, but it also presents a philosophy of religion and the influence of a deeply religious atmosphere on a man who was essentially destructive and modern. Besides the intermingling of human and religious love, the novel contains a realistic touch in having violence and crime cure idealism. As always, in the novels of this great local color artist, the painting of the background is unforgettable: the summer houses in the suburbs of Toledo, the narrow cobbled streets of the city, and the noble, austere cathedral.

The Story:

Ángel Guerra, thirty and a widower, father of an adored daughter Encarnación, had spent an unhappy childhood. An idealist, he had turned to the revolutionists, thinking that if everything were overthrown life could be improved in the rebuilding. His mother, Doña Sales, disapproved of him and treated him like a child, even after he was married. An extremely rich woman, she tried to starve her liberal-minded son into submission to her wishes, but she managed only to drive him into the company of advocates of violence, the Babels.

The Babel household contained an unsavory group. With Babel lived his brother, Captain Agapito, an ex-slaver, and his children, drunken Matías and slippery Policarpo. Babel's family was as bad. Arístides, an embezzler, had fled from Cuba; Fausto had been dismissed from the post office for peculation; and Dulcenombre had love affairs from which the whole family profited. She became attracted to Ángel and lived with him for a year in order to escape her family, but he was too poor to marry her.

At last the crimes of the Babels sent Ángel also into hiding, with a wounded hand that Dulce bandaged. After a month of skulking he went home to find his mother, Doña Sales, dying. Leré, the twenty-year-old tutor of "Ción," was nursing her. At first she and Dr. Maquis refused to let Ángel see the sick woman, but finally he was allowed to be with her during her dying moments. She left him a comfortable fortune, but when he tried to use it selfishly the convent-trained Leré shamed him into carrying out his mother's desires with it.

Troubles mounted for Ángel. Dulce, his mistress, became ill. Ción died. Leré announced she was entering a convent in Toledo. In his loneliness, Ángel followed her, and when Dulce came looking for him he had already gone. Following the advice of her uncle, Captain Agapito, she sought solace in alcohol.

Ángel had both rich and poor relatives in Toledo. He became a boarder at the home of Teresa Pantoja, along with two priests. Leré was already working for one of the nursing orders. Discussing life with her, and moved by his loneliness, his affection for her, and the religious atmosphere of Toledo, Ángel also found himself seeking the comfort of the Church.

The appointment of one Babel to a government post in Toledo brought the whole family, including Dulce, to that city. To escape them, Ángel went to live with wealthy relatives in the outskirts of Toledo. Leré demanded that he marry Dulce or never see her again. Going to discuss the situation with Dulce, Ángel found her disgustingly drunk. In a quarrel that followed, he almost killed Arístides. Again, at Leré's bidding, he went to Arístides to ask forgiveness. He learned that Dulce's illness had cured her of her liking for alcohol and that she was planning to enter a convent.

Ángel's many conversations with Leré caused considerable gossip, with the result that the Mother Superior called the girl in for questioning. Although she was declared innocent, the lack of trust so angered Ángel that he declared his intention of founding a convent to be put in Leré's charge. She declared that she would accept his plan only if he became a priest. Ángel agreed.

Padre Casado, a clear-sighted priest, whose preference for farming instead of books had prevented his advance in the Church, prepared Ángel for taking holy orders. One night, while he and Leré were nursing an ailing priest, Ángel felt desire for the girl. Later he confessed his carnal thoughts to Padre Casado, who could not understand any sexual attraction to a woman in plain nun's clothing. They also discussed Ángel's plans for the convent, and his philosophy for improving mankind by a Christian revolution.

Ángel tried to prove his theories when Arístides, again caught in crime, and Fausto, also fleeing justice, begged him for help and he hid them. Joined by Policarpo, they demanded money for a flight to Portugal. Ángel was stabbed during a quarrel over his refusal. Although badly wounded, he would not give the police the name of his assailant.

Leré came to nurse Ángel. The dying man had no regrets. Like Don Quixote, he felt that the approach of death restored his reason and also solved his problems. He would not have made a good priest, he declared. He apportioned his wealth, designating most for Leré's project, some for relatives and servants, before he died. Leré, stifling her sorrow, returned to the convent where she was assigned to nurse another patient.

ANNA CHRISTIE

Type of work: Drama
Author: Eugene O'Neill (1888-1953)
Type of plot: Social realism
Time of plot: Early twentieth century
Locale: Johnny the Priest's saloon, New York City, and Provincetown harbor
First presented: 1921

Principal characters:

CHRIS CHRISTOPHERSON, captain of the barge, *Simeon Winthrop*
ANNA, his daughter
MAT BURKE, a stoker
MARTHY OWEN, a prostitute

Critique:

O'Neill claims rightfully that the ending of his play was not intended to be a happy one. The play illustrates O'Neill's idea that the forces which control our destinies and which seemingly lie outside ourselves are really within. O'Neill agrees with Galsworthy in maintaining that man's character is his fate and in *Anna Christie* he proves it.

The Story:

Old Chris Christopherson looked upon the sea as the symbol of a malignant fate. True, he was now skipper of the coal barge, *Simeon Winthrop,* but in his younger days he had been an able seaman and bosun on the old windjammers and had visited every port in the world. As far back as he knew, the men of his family in Sweden had followed the sea. His father died aboard ship in the Indian Ocean, and two of his brothers were drowned. Nor was the curse of the sea confined to the men in the family. After the news of her husband's and her sons' deaths, Chris' mother had died of a broken heart. Unable to bear the loneliness of being a sailor's wife, his own wife had brought their young daughter, Anna, to America to live with some cousins on a farm in Minnesota. Here Anna's mother had died, and the girl was brought up by her relatives.

Chris had not seen his daughter for almost twenty years. One day while he was having a drink at Johnny the Priest's saloon near South Street in New York City, he received a postcard from St. Louis telling him that Anna was on her way to New York.

This news threw Chris into something of a panic, for living on the barge with him was an ancient prostitute named Marthy. Chris decided to get rid of the woman. Being a kind-hearted soul and genuinely fond of Marthy, he disliked the idea of turning her out. But Marthy said that Chris had always treated her decently, and she would move on to someone else.

When Marthy caught a glimpse of Chris's daughter, she was shocked. Anna was twenty years old and pretty in a buxom sort of way. But her painted face and cheap showy clothes were telltale evidence of what she was—a prostitute. Marthy wondered what Chris' reaction was going to be.

In his eyes, however, Anna was the innocent child he had always imagined her to be, and he was even hesitant about ordering wine to celebrate their reunion. Life on the barge was an entirely new experience for Anna Christopherson. She came to love the sea and to respond to its beauty with the same intensity with which her father responded to its malignance. With the soothing effect of her new environment, and the presence of her father's gentleness and simplicity, Anna began to lose some of her hardness and to build up some faith in men.

One night, while the *Simeon Winthrop* was anchored in the outer harbor of Provincetown, Massachusetts, Chris heard cries for help. He pulled aboard the barge four men from a boat which had been drifting for five days after the wreck of their ship. One of the men, an Irishman named Mat Burke, took an immediate fancy to Anna, and even in his weakened condition he made it clear that he intended to have Anna for his own.

Mat Burke represented everything in life that Chris hated. In the first place, he was a stoker on a steamship, an occupation the old windjammer sailor regarded as beneath contempt. Secondly, Burke followed the sea and so was connected in the old Swede's mind with inevitable tragedy. But lastly, and most important from Chris' viewpoint, Mat was obviously in love with Anna and wanted to take her away from him. But to Anna Mat represented all that she had always wanted in life. At first she was naturally suspicious of his Irish glibness, but she soon began to see that underneath his voluble exterior there were some genuine convictions, a basic core of integrity which gave her as a woman a sense of security, as well as, in the light of her own past, a gnawing fear.

Her father and Mat were mortal enemies from the start. This conflict reached its climax one day in the cabin when Chris, goaded on by the Irishman's taunts, came at Mat with a knife, intending to kill him. Anna came in as Mat overpowered the old man. She realized that they were fighting over her as if she were a piece of property which must belong to one or the other.

This situation was so close to her previous experience with men that she made them both listen to a confession of the truth about herself, of which apparently neither of them had been aware. She informed her father that his romantic picture of her idyllic life on the Minnesota farm was untrue from beginning to end, that she had been worked relentlessly by her relatives, and that at sixteen she had been seduced by one of her cousins. At last she had gone to St. Louis and entered a bawdy house, where her experience with men did not differ greatly from what she had known on the farm. She informed Mat that for the first time in her life she had realized what love might be. But Mat, having neither intelligence nor imagination enough to appreciate Anna's sincerity, angrily called her names and left the barge in disgust. Chris followed him, and the two men proceeded to get drunk. Anna waited on the *Simeon Winthrop* for two days, hoping that Mat would return. Finally she prepared to go to New York and resume her old profession.

Her father was the first to return with the news that to save her from going back to the old life he had signed on the *Londonderry,* a steamer to Capetown, Africa, and had made arrangements for his pay to be turned over to Anna. When Mat returned, Anna felt sure he had come back merely to kill her. He was bruised and bloody from waterfront fights. He too had signed on the *Londonderry,* and the irony of her father and Mat on the same boat struck Anna as funny. Finally she made Mat see that she had hated the men who had bought her and that all she wanted was the assurance of one man's love.

Chris was glad that Anna and Mat were reconciled, were going to be married and be happy, for he now realized that much of Anna's past misery was his own fault. But at the same time he wondered what tricks the malignant sea would play on Anna and Mat in the future.

ANNA KARÉNINA

Type of work: Novel
Author: Count Leo Tolstoy (1828-1910)
Type of plot: Social criticism
Time of plot: Nineteenth century
Locale: Russia
First published: 1875-1877

Principal characters:
ANNA KARÉNINA
ALEXEI KARÉNIN, her husband
COUNT VRONSKY, her lover
STEPAN OBLONSKY, her brother
KITTY SHTCHERBATSKY, Stepan's sister-in-law
KONSTANTINE LEVIN, in love with Kitty

Critique:

Anna Karénina, one of Tolstoy's masterpieces, is distinguished by its realism. The novel contains two plots: the tragedy of Madame Karénina, in love with a man who is not her husband, and the story of Konstantine Levin, a sensitive man whose personal philosophy is Tolstoy's reason for writing about him. The story of Anna is an absorbing one and true; the person of Levin reflects Tolstoy's own ideas about the Russian society in which he lived. Thus the book is a closely knit plot of a woman bound in the fetters of the Russian social system and a philosophy of life which attempts to untangle the maze of incongruities present in this society.

The Story:

Anna Karénina, the sister of Stepan Oblonsky, came to Moscow in an attempt to patch up a quarrel between her brother and his wife, Dolly. There she met the handsome young Count Vronsky, who was rumored to be in love with Dolly's younger sister, Kitty.

But Konstantine Levin, of an old Muscovite family, was also in love with Kitty, and his visit to Moscow coincided with Anna's. Kitty refused Levin, but to her chagrin she received no proposal from the count. Indeed, Vronsky had no intention of proposing to Kitty. His heart went out to Anna the first time he laid eyes on her, and when Anna returned to her home in St. Petersburg, he followed her.

Soon they began to be seen together at soirees and at the theater, apparently unaware of gossip which circulated about them. Karénin, Anna's husband, became concerned. A coldly ambitious and dispassionate man, he felt that his social position was at stake. One night he discussed these rumors with Anna and pointed out the danger of her flirtation, as he called it. He forbade her to entertain Vronsky at home, and cautioned her to be more careful. He was not jealous of his wife, only worried over the social consequences of her behavior. He reminded her of her duty to her young son, Seryozha. Anna said she would obey him, and there the matter rested.

But Anna was unable to conceal her true feelings when Vronsky was injured in a race-track accident. Karénin upbraided her for her indiscreet behavior in public. He considered a duel, separation, divorce, but rejected all of these courses. When he finally decided to keep Anna under his roof, he reflected that he was acting in accordance with the laws of religion. Anna continued to meet Vronsky in secret.

Levin had returned to his country estate after Kitty had refused him, and there he busied himself in problems of agriculture and peasant labor. One day he went into the fields and worked with a scythe along with the serfs. He felt that he was beginning to understand the old primitive philosophy of their lives. He planned new developments, among them a cooperative enterprise system. When he heard that Kitty was not married after all, and that she had been ill but was soon returning to Moscow, he resolved to seek her hand once more. Secretly, he knew she loved him. His pride, as well as hers, had kept them apart.

Accordingly, Levin made the journey to Moscow with new hope that soon Kitty would be his wife.

Against her husband's orders, Anna Karénina sent for Vronsky and told him that she was with child. Aware of his responsibilities to Anna, he begged her to petition Karénin for a divorce so that she would be free to marry him. Karénin informed her coldly that he would consider the child his and accept it so that the world should never know his wife's disgrace, but he refused to think of going through shameful divorce proceedings. Karénin reduced Anna to submission by warning her that he would take Seryozha away if she persisted in making a fool of herself.

The strained family relationship continued unbroken. One night Karénin had planned to go out, and Anna persuaded Vronsky to come to the house. As he was leaving, Karénin met Vronsky on the front steps. Enraged, Karénin told Anna that he had decided to get a divorce and that he would keep Seryozha in his custody. But divorce proceedings were so intricate, the scandal so great, the whole aspect of the step so disgusting to Karénin that he could not bring himself to go through with the process. As Anna's confinement drew near, he was still undecided. After winning an important political seat, he became even more unwilling to risk his public reputation.

At the birth of her child, Anna became deathly ill. Vronsky, overcome with guilt, attempted suicide, but failed. Karénin was reduced to a state of such confusion that he determined to grant his wife any request, since he thought her to be on her deathbed. The sight of Vronsky seemed to be the only thing that restored her. After many months of illness, she went with her lover and baby daughter to Italy, where they lived under strained circumstances. Meanwhile, Levin proposed once more to Kitty, and after a flurry of preparations they were married.

Anna Karénina and Vronsky returned to Russia and went to live on his estate. It was now impossible for Anna to return home. Although Karénin had not gone through with divorce proceedings, he considered himself separated from Anna and was everywhere thought to be a man of fine loyalty and unswerving honor, unjustly imposed upon by an unfaithful wife. Sometimes Anna stole into town to see Seryozha but her fear of being discovered there by her husband cut these visits short. After each visit she returned bitter and sad. She became more and more demanding toward Vronsky, with the result that he spent less time with her. She took little interest in her child. Before long she convinced herself that Vronsky was in love with another woman. One day she could not stay alone in the house. She found herself at the railway station. She bought a ticket. As she stood on the platform gazing at the tracks below, the thunder of an approaching train roared in her ears. Suddenly she remembered a man run over in the Moscow railroad station on the day she and Vronsky met. Carefully measuring the distance, she threw herself in front of the approaching train.

After her death, Vronsky joined the army. He had changed from a handsome, cheerful man to one who welcomed death; his only reason for living had been Anna.

For Levin and Kitty life became an increasing round of daily work and everyday routine, which they shared with each other. Levin knew at last the responsibility wealth imposed upon him in his dealings with the peasants. Kitty helped him to share his responsibility. Although there were many questions he could never answer satisfactorily to himself, he was nevertheless aware of the satisfying beauty of life, its toil, leisure, pain, and happiness.

ANNA OF THE FIVE TOWNS

Type of work: Novel
Author: Arnold Bennett (1867-1931)
Type of plot: Domestic realism
Time of plot: Late nineteenth century
Locale: Rural England
First published: 1902

Principal characters:
EPHRAIM TELLWRIGHT, a miser
ANNA, his older daughter
AGNES, his younger daughter
HENRY MYNORS, Anna's suitor
WILLIE PRICE, in love with Anna
BEATRICE SUTTON, Anna's friend

Critique:

Anna of the Five Towns was the first of Bennett's novels dealing with the pottery region of the Five Towns. It is primarily a novel of character, but Anna changes so slightly that the reader is hardly aware of any development in her attitudes or actions. In fact, her tragedy occurs because she cannot change her original nature. But in spite of certain weaknesses, the story has touches of Bennett's great writing skill and human insight and is worth the time of all Bennett lovers. The novel is also Bennett's most detailed study of the repressive effects of Wesleyanism, which affects all his characters in one degree or another.

The Story:

Ephraim Tellwright was a miser, one of the wealthiest men in any of the Five Towns, a group of separate villages joined by a single road. He was a former preacher, concerned more with getting congregations in good financial shape, however, than with the souls of his parishioners. Although he had made money from rentals and foreclosures, in addition to marrying money, he lived in the most frugal way possible and gave his two daughters nothing but the barest essentials. Both of his wives had died, the first giving him his daughter Anna and the second producing Agnes before her death. Mr. Tellwright was usually amiable. As long as his meals were on time, no money was wasted, and the house was never left alone and unguarded, he paid little attention to his daughters.

Anna loved her father even though she could never feel close to him. Agnes, much younger, followed her sister's lead. The two girls were especially close, since their father ignored them most of the time.

On Anna's twenty-first birthday her father called her into his office and told her that she would that day inherit almost fifty thousand pounds from her mother's estate. He had invested the original sum wisely until it had grown to a fortune. Anna, who had never owned one pound to call her own, could not comprehend an amount so large. Accustomed to letting her father handle all business affairs, she willingly gave him control of her fortune. The income from the stocks and rentals was deposited in the bank in her name, but she gave her father her checkbook and signed only when he told her to. The money made little difference in Anna's life; it simply lay in the bank until her father told her to invest it.

One result of the money, however, was unhappy for Anna. Among her properties was a run-down factory owned by Titus Price. Because Price was continually behind in his rent, Mr. Tellwright forced Anna to keep demanding something on account. Knowing that the property would never rent to anyone else, the old miser never put Price out but kept hounding him for as much as the man could pay. Anna usually had to deal with Willie Price, the son, and she always left the interview with a feeling of guilt. Although the sight of Willie's embarrassment left her unhappy, she always demanded his money because she was afraid to face her father without it.

A teacher in the Sunday School in which Anna taught was Henry Mynors, a pillar in the church and a successful man in the community. Anna, attracted to him, tried to join in his religious fervor, but she could not quite bring herself to repent and to accept God publicly. She felt repentance to be a private matter, not one to be dragged out in meeting. Henry was patient with her, however. When the townspeople said that he was interested mainly in her money, Anna refused to believe the gossip. Henry began to call on her occasionally, combining his courtship with business with Mr. Tellwright. The miser persuaded Anna to invest some of her money in Henry's business, after arranging first for a large share of the profits and a high interest. Anna, caring little for the money, liked to be associated with Henry and spent much time with him.

After Anna had received her fortune, she was invited for the first time to the house of Mrs. Sutton, the social leader of the town. Mrs. Sutton's daughter Beatrice and Anna became friends. There was talk that Beatrice and Henry Mynors had once been engaged. The Suttons took Anna and Henry to the Isle of Man on a vacation, and Anna thought there could never again be such luxurious living. She had had to take ten pounds of her own money without her father's knowledge in order to get clothes for the trip, and the miser had berated her viciously when she told him what she had done. Being with Henry and the Suttons, however, helped her forget his anger. When the vacation was marred by Beatrice's serious illness, Anna won a permanent place in the Suttons' affection by her unselfish and competent nursing.

After Beatrice had recovered, Anna and Henry returned home. Before they left the island Henry proposed to Anna and she accepted. Later her father gave his consent because Henry knew the value of money. Young Agnes was enchanted by the romantic aspects of the courtship, and Anna was happy in her quiet love for Henry. But her joy at being engaged was soon clouded by the news that old Mr. Price, Willie's father, had hanged himself. Anna felt that she and her father were to blame because they had hounded him for his rent. Henry assured her that Mr. Price was in debt to many people and that she need not feel guilty. Nevertheless, Anna worried a great deal about the suicide and about Willie.

Later Willie confessed to her that a bank note he had given in payment had been forged. The confession seemed to reduce Willie to nothing. Anna, realizing that he and his father had been driven to desperation, tried to protect Willie and his father's reputation by taking the forged note from her father's office. When she told Mr. Tellwright that she had burned the note, he was so furious with her that he never forgave her.

Because Willie was planning to make a fresh start in Australia, Henry arranged to buy the Price house for them to live in after he and Anna were married. Although Anna was sure she could never be happy in a house the miserable Prices had owned, she was docile and let Henry make all the arrangements.

When Anna told her father that she needed one hundred pounds to pay for her linens and her wedding clothes, Mr. Tellwright denounced her for a spendthrift. Handing over the checkbook, he told her not to bother him again about her money. Henry, pleased at the turn of events, was full of plans for the use of Anna's fortune. Then there was more bad news about Mr. Price. Before his death he had defrauded the church of fifty pounds. Anna tried to cover up for him so that Willie would never know, but someone told the secret. Willie, ready to leave for Australia, heard of the theft. When he told Anna goodbye, he was like a whipped child. As Anna looked into his eyes for the last time, she knew suddenly that he loved her and that she loved him. She let him go, however, because she felt bound by her promise to Henry. She had been dutiful all her life; it was too late for her to change.

Willie was never heard from again. Had anyone in Five Towns happened to look into an abandoned pitshaft, the mystery of Willie would have been solved. The meek lad had found his only way to peace.

THE ANNALS OF TACITUS

Type of work: History
Author: Cornelius Tacitus (c. 55-c. 120)
Time: 14-69
Locale: The Roman Empire
First transcribed: c. 119

Principal personages:
TIBERIUS, Augustus Caesar's stepson and successor
GERMANICUS (NERO CLAUDIUS DRUSUS),Tiberius' brother
AGRIPPINA (MAJOR), Germanicus' wife and Caligula's mother
DRUSUS, Tiberius' son
DRUSUS, Germanicus' son
CALIGULA, Tiberius' successor
CLAUDIUS, Caligula's uncle and his successor
MESSALINA, Claudius' first wife
AGRIPPINA (MINOR), Claudius' niece and second wife
BRITANNICUS, Claudius' son, killed by Nero
NERO, Agrippina's son and Claudius' successor
POPPAEA, Nero's wife
AELIUS SEJANUS, Tiberius' favorite
PISO, leader of a conspiracy against Nero

Cornelius Tacitus is by an accident of fate the sole surviving historian of his day; all the writings of his contemporaries and immediate predecessors are lost. It may be that the fates were guided by standards of literary aesthetics rather than scientific accuracy, for though Tacitus' facts and interpretations have from time to time been severely criticized, he has always been admired for his lucid, morally-charged narrative style. The *Annals* are not merely a skillful prose account of a half-century of Roman history, but also a compassionate evaluation of the horrors of imperial despotism. In fact, the earliest extant manuscript is entitled *Ab excessu divi Augusti* (although in Book IV, the writer refers to his work as *Annals*).

Obviously, Tacitus saw in Roman history a gradual decline from a primitive Golden Age when no laws were necessary to times when laws became a necessity and, finally, an abominable evil. As the *Annals* proceed from the reign of Tiberius to those of Claudius and Nero (a section dealing with Caligula is lost, as are the last books) the tyranny becomes more cruel, the populace and patricians grow more submissive, the opportunists and informers become more despicable, and the dwindling number of virtuous men find themselves more helpless.

In these matters, Tacitus is by no means taciturn; in fact, so great are the horrors depicted in the *Annals* that until the atrocities of twentieth-century politics and war recapitulated them on a horrendously magnified scale, civilized men were inclined to view Tacitus' account as grossly exaggerated, beyond the possible depths of human nature.

Tacitus is modest about his aims, though the grave irony of his remarks should not go unnoticed:

> The matter upon which I am occupied is circumscribed, and unproductive of renown to the author—a state of undisturbed peace, or only interrupted in limited degree, the sad condition of affairs in the city, and a prince indifferent about extending the bounds of the empire. Not unprofitable, however, will it be to investigate matters which, though unimportant in a superficial view, frequently give the first impulse to events of magnitude. . . . I have only to record the mandates of despotism, incessant accusations, faithless friendships, the ruin of innocence; the one unvarying repetition of causes terminating in the same event, and presenting no novelty from their similarity and tiresome repetition. (IV, 32-33)

In general, Tacitus presents not a sustained history, but a chronological depiction of selected events—some thoroughly detailed over several chapters and others sketched in lightly, continually referred to but not described extensively in any one place. It has been conjectured that the original *Annals* consisted of three hexads, the pattern employed by Vergil, Statius, Polynus, and Cicero; but there is no concrete evidence that there were two books written after XVI, and the loss of Books VII-X prevents us from being absolutely certain they fitted with Books XI-XII to constitute a middle hexad. At any rate, the *Annals,* as they now stand, can be conveniently arranged by subject matter—the reign of Tiberius is the concern of the first six books, of Claudius in books XI-XII, and of Nero in the final four books. This is not to say that the focus of attention is concentrated on the three emperors. In dealing with Tiberius, for example, Tacitus devotes the opening forty-nine chapters to the first year (more space than to any other year of the entire history), beginning with the jockeying for power after the death of Augustus. Since Tiberius never led troops in battle after he became emperor, the narrative shifts to Tiberius' son Drusus (Chapters 16-30) quelling the Pannonian mutiny and to Germanicus (most of Chapters 31-71) campaigning on the Rhine. These two men, logical heirs to the throne, were the objects of the intrigues of the utterly unscrupulous Aelius Sejanus, Tiberius' favorite. Jealous of Germanicus' successes, Tiberius had him recalled and sent to the East as king in Armenia, where he died in A.D. 19, probably at the hands of Piso under orders from Tiberius. Piso's trial ended abruptly with his unexplained murder, though Tacitus hints that Tiberius arranged that as well. Drusus, then, dominated the sons of Germanicus (Nero, another Drusus, and Caligula) as heir-apparent, but Tiberius openly preferred Sejanus—"a stranger was called in as coadjutor in the government; nay, how little was wanting to his being declared colleague." This Sejanus, "whose heart insatiably lusted for supreme domination," then dispatched Drusus with a slow poison that made him appear a victim of disease, and set out to marry Livia, his widow and the sister of Germanicus. There remained, however, Agrippina, widow of Germanicus, and her three sons. Sejanus contrived open enmity between Agrippina and Tiberius and skillfully arranged for the emperor to retire to Capri from Rome in A.D. 27. There, while Sejanus plotted his rise to power, the ruler "indulged his cruel and libidinous disposition . . . in the secrecy of a retired situation." One of the most tantalizing lacunae of the *Annals* deals with Agrippina's hopeless struggle for the rights of her sons and the final conflict between Sejanus and the emperor, a struggle leading to Sejanus' execution.

The first hexad ends with Tiberius at the age of seventy-eight, when he had outlived all the intriguers who surrounded him and relinquished "nothing of his libidinous excesses." His end was dramatic, and Tacitus relishes the irony. Assured by Tiberius' physician that his death was imminent,

> Caligula in the midst of a great throng of persons, paying their gratulations, was already going forth to make a solemn entrance on the sovereignty, when suddenly a notice came, "that Tiberius had recovered his sight and voice, and had called for some persons to give him food to restore him." The consternation was universal: the concourse about Caligula dispersed in all directions . . . Caligula himself stood fixed in silence —fallen from the highest hopes, he now expected the worst. Macro [Caligula's right hand man], undismayed, ordered the old man to be smothered with a quantity of clothes. . . . (VI, 51)

The dramatic technique is magnificent. Caligula is left as a monstrous legacy to Rome. However, the extant history resumes in Book XI with Claudius' succession to the purple. The new emperor is depicted as a cut above his predecessors: he dignified the theater, augmented the alphabet, restrained predatory creditors, increased the Senate, and incorporated new provinces into the Empire. But the intrigues flourished, centering upon Claudius' wife Messalina, who was concerned at the way in which freedmen (especially Narcissus and Pallas) had gained the actual power. Messalina, knowing she was about to be murdered by Claudius' agents, committed suicide: "Tidings were then carried to Claudius 'that Messalina was no more'; without inquiring whether by her own or another's hand, [he] called for a cup of wine and proceeded in the feast." Tacitus brilliantly achieves a sense of horror at the moral corruption of the Empire with just such detail and understatement. Book XII opens with the contest among the freedmen concerning the choice of a new wife for Claudius. Pallas prevailed with his suggestion of Agrippina, despite the fact that she was the daughter of Claudius' brother Germanicus. The horrendous narrative continues to delineate debauchery and chaos. Nero destroyed the emperor's son Britannicus, and Agrippina afterward poisoned Claudius in order to secure the succession for her own son, Nero. Book XIII tells of Agrippina's struggles for power, first against the freedwoman Acte and then against Poppaea, Nero's wife—murders and counter-murders and abortive palace revolts that went on while Nero engaged in his orgiastic debauches. Book XIV opens with Poppaea's vigorously dramatic reproach against Nero for his cowardice in not destroying his mother, who had desperately clung to life and power by incestuously lavishing her own body on her son. Tacitus handles Nero's attempts on Agrippina's life with almost grotesque comedy. First, she was put to sea in a faulty vessel, but she swam ashore while another woman, hoping to save herself by claiming to be the emperor's mother, was slain. Finally, brute force was resorted to and she was slain in bed: ". . . to the centurion, as he was drawing his sword to dispatch her, she presented her womb, and with a loud voice, 'Strike your sword into my belly,' she cried, and was instantly dispatched." Thus, Tacitus vivifies an important dramatic scene with a stroke of realism.

Nero, struck with remorse and apparently unaware of the extent to which Roman society had degenerated to his own low level, feared to return to the capital. Matricide during the Republic would have seemed the destruction of morality's basis, the family. But Nero's entry into Rome was triumphant and he thenceforth "abandoned himself to all his inordinate passions which, though insufficiently controlled, had been somewhat checked by his reverence for his mother, such as it was." Throughout his career "Nero wallowed in all sorts of defilements, lawful and unlawful: and seemed to leave no atrocity which could add to his pollution," including one which Tacitus describes with great disgust—a mock-marriage "with all the solemnities of wedlock" to a homosexual. The height of his inhuman cruelty was the great fire of Rome, in which he madly reveled and from which he gained enormous profits. The most sustained episode of the final books concerns the conspiracy in A.D. 65 of Piso and eighteen other leaders to assassinate Nero and set up Piso as emperor.

Piso gave no promise of better government, since he was almost as addicted to sensuous pleasure as Nero himself, but some change was obviously necessary. The conspiracy had difficulty settling on a method, and before it could get under way the plot was inadvertently revealed when Epicharis, a freedwoman, attempted to solicit one of Nero's naval officers, Volusius Proculus, who alerted Nero. One of the rare cases of personal virtue was Epicharis' refusal to betray the conspirators, despite the horrible torture she endured. In their haste the conspirators betrayed themselves, and in panic Nero began wholesale slaughters. Chapters 37-70 constitute a steady series of death scenes—Epicharis, Seneca, Subrius Flavus, Lucan (who died reciting his verses), and others—each presented with vivid detail. Piso, himself, though urged to stir up a popular revolt, chose to sever his veins and "left a will full of odious flattery to Nero, in tenderness to his wife, a depraved woman and void of every recommendation but personal beauty."

The deaths of those close to Nero continued. Poppaea died "by a fit of passion in her husband, who gave her a violent blow with his foot when she was pregnant; for I cannot believe he poisoned her as some have stated." Her funeral was sumptuous; she was embalmed with spices rather than cremated as was the custom, but her death was "rejoiced at by those who recollected her . . . lewdness and cruelty." An account of the last two years of Nero's life is missing, and the *Annals,* ending in mid-sentence, suggest that this section was lost.

Such are the main lines of Tacitus' history, but the text abounds in frequent digressions tracing in close detail the fortunes of the Roman Empire and its provinces and outposts so vividly that some authorities suggest that he must have had a host of reliable sources in the form of autobiographies and diaries. However, the *Annals* are clearly the personal document of a writer with sincerity, intelligence, courage, and enormous artistry. In a very real sense, Tacitus was an Existentialist in his view of social corruption replacing traditional morality. Convinced that human effort is absurd, he was sustained, however, by a faith in human solidarity and unity in suffering. The gravity of his tragic vision is relieved by a deeply felt compassion for suffering mankind, and he has left in the *Annals* one of the greatest histories of all time.

ANNALS OF THE PARISH

Type of work: Novel
Author: John Galt (1779-1839)
Type of plot: Social chronicle
Time of plot: 1760-1810
Locale: Scotland
First published: 1821

Principal characters:
THE REVEREND MICAH BALWHIDDER, minister at Dalmailing
LORD EAGLESHAM, the minister's friend and patron
BETTY LANSHAW, the first Mrs. Balwhidder
LIZY KIBBOCK, the second Mrs. Balwhidder
MRS. NUGENT, a widow, the third Mrs. Balwhidder
MR. CAYENNE, an industrialist
LADY MACADAM, a high-spirited old lady in the parish

Critique:

John Galt was important to his own time both as a settler in Canada and as a novelist who presented Scottish life in fiction. As both a novelist and a leader in the Canada Company, he has, however, been largely forgotten. In the field of fiction Galt was so far overshadowed by Sir Walter Scott in his own time that he never became widely known outside of Britain, and the neglect has continued, unfortunately, to this time. A Scot himself, Galt wrote in the *Annals of the Parish* about the Scotland he and his parents had known, and he wrote lovingly. His humane feeling and the love he gave to his own country can be marked on almost every page he wrote. In this novel the strongest and most sympathetically portrayed character is of the Scottish Presbyterian clergyman of strict Calvinist persuasion. Hardly less important are the descriptions of the new class of industrialists.

The Story:

As a young man just out of divinity school at the University of Glasgow, and but recently accepted for the ministry, the Reverend Micah Balwhidder was appointed to the charge of the established Presbyterian church in the village of Dalmailing, in western Scotland. Because he had been appointed by a great landowner, without their approval, the people of Dalmailing tried to prevent Mr. Balwhidder from taking his post. On the Sunday Mr. Balwhidder was installed, the ministers officiating had to enter the church through a window, because the door had been nailed fast. Nor did they try to go to the church without a guard of soldiers.

Immediately after being installed, Mr. Balwhidder began a series of visits to his parishioners, as he believed a good Calvinistic clergyman should do. He was rebuffed at door after door, until Thomas Thorl, the minister's most outspoken opponent, relented and accepted him. The rest of the parish followed within a matter of weeks. Soon after the excitement died down, Mr. Balwhidder married his first wife, Betty Lanshaw, a cousin with whom he had grown up; he believed strongly that a minister should be married to accomplish his best work.

During the first few years of his ministry, during the 1760's, Mr. Balwhidder fought earnestly against two habits among his parishioners, smuggling and drinking. He felt that both were sinful. In the end, however, he became reconciled to tea as a beverage, for he thought it better for his people to drink that instead of spirituous liquors. His main objection to smuggling was that it encouraged lawlessness among his people and resulted in the appearance of illegitimate children.

One of the chief problems in Dalmailing, so far as the minister was concerned, was the Malcolm family, composed of Mrs. Malcolm, a widow, and her five children. The minister always tried to help them succeed, for they were hard-working folk who had known better days. The first ray of success for them came when Charles Malcolm was made an officer in the merchant marine, an event which gladdened Mr. Balwhidder's heart. In that same year the first Mrs. Balwhidder died. Her death saddened the whole parish, for everyone had come to love her.

In the following year, 1764, Mr. Balwhidder tried to write a doctrinal book. He found, however, that he had too much to do to keep his house and servants in order and so he decided to look about for another wife, and none too soon, for one of his maidservants was with child. Some of the village gossips blamed the minister, although the actual father admitted his part in the affair. As soon as a year and a day had passed after his first wife's death, Mr. Balwhidder married Lizy Kibbock, the daughter of a very successful farmer in the parish.

The second Mrs. Balwhidder immediately set out to augment her husband's stipend. She purchased cattle and hogs and set up a regular dairy. Within a year she had sufficient income from her projects so that the minister's pay could be put into the bank. Her husband approved heartily of her industry, not only because he himself was made comfortable but because the industry of his wife encouraged greater efforts on the part of other women in the parish. In that year three coal mines were opened in the parish, bringing new prosperity to the people.

In 1767 a great event occurred in the village's history. Lord Eaglesham, after being thrown in a muddy road which ran through the village, resolved to have a fine highway built to prevent a second occurrence. The new road made transportation much easier for the villagers. The event also caused the lord and Mr. Balwhidder to become friends, for at the time of the accident the clergyman had lent Lord Eaglesham some dry clothes. Through the nobleman's influence Mr. Balwhidder was on many occasions able to help the people of his village.

Scandal threatened the pulpit in 1772, when a visitor from another parish, Mr. Heckletext, was invited to speak. Shortly after his sermon the church session learned that he was the father of an illegitimate child by one of the village girls. It was a bitter lesson for Mr. Balwhidder, who resolved never again to permit a man to speak from his pulpit until he had thoroughly investigated the stranger's habits and character.

The 1770's were disturbing times for the minister of Dalmailing. Mr. Balwhidder was a peace-loving man who hated to see his young parishioners enlist to fight against the rebellious colonists in America. More especially, he hated to hear of the battles in which some of them were killed. The greatest blow given him by the war was the death of the widow Malcolm's son, who died a hero in a naval battle with the French. Mr. Balwhidder, who looked upon the fatherless Malcolm family as his particular charge, grieved as much as if the boy had been his own son.

He was also in difficulties with Lady MacAdam, an older woman who had been at court in England and France in her youth. A spirited woman who wanted to have a good time in life and to dictate to other people, she was beside herself when she learned that her son, an officer in the Royal Scots regiment, was in love with the oldest Malcolm girl. She mistreated the girl shamefully, refusing even to listen to the minister's remonstrations. Using his own judgment, he finally had to marry the young people against her wishes. She soon became reconciled, however, after the marriage had taken place.

After the close of the American Revolution, a loyal American who had returned to Britain settled in Dalmailing. This man, Mr. Cayenne, had a temper as fiery as his name. The weaving mill he set up near the village brought prosperity to the parish, but it also brought troubles. During the 1790's the weavers who settled there were in favor of the French Revolution, while Mr. Balwhidder and his more conservative parishioners were all against it. Aside from their political differences, the weavers also belonged to different faiths, a fact which gave the minister grave concern, for he disliked any other church to set itself up as long as the Presbyterian Church was the official church of the land. He fought a lengthy but losing battle against churches which preached other doctrines than his own. It was the one problem which he felt he could not solve, for the tide of history was against him.

In 1796, Mr. Balwhidder again became a widower. Still of the opinion that to serve his people best he ought to be a married man, he took another wife a year later. His third wife was Mrs. Nugent, a widow of good reputation.

As the years passed the minister's two children, a son and a daughter, grew up and were married. Finally, in 1810, the church authorities decided that Mr. Balwhidder who had served his parish for fifty years, should have some help. But he had become so deaf and so forgetful that he himself decided to retire. He preached a farewell sermon to his crowded church and then set himself to write into a book the annals of the parish he had served so long.

ANNALS OF THE ROMAN PEOPLE

Type of work: History
Author: Livy (Titus Livius, 59 B.C.-A.D. 17)
Time: 753-9 B.C.
Locale: Rome, Spain, Carthage, Greece, Macedonia
First transcribed: c. 26 B.C.-A.D. 14

Livy undertook a great task. In his *Ab urbe condita libri,* he was attempting to narrate the history of nearly eight centuries, from the time of Romulus and Remus to the reign of Tiberius. The work occupied 142 books, of which barely a quarter have been preserved: Books I-X and XXI-XLV, along with some fragments of several others. Even so, this material is enough to fill six volumes in one English translation and thirteen in another.

Titus Livius Patavinus (from his birthplace, Padua), was originally a teacher of rhetoric and apparently, from casual references in his writing, a friend of the Emperor Augustus. Perhaps the emperor, as part of his program to glorify Rome, suggested that Livy stop teaching and write a history of the city. The project represented a challenge. His only sources were traditions, the official temple annals listing the consuls and the chief events of each year, and personal records, frequently exaggerated, kept by the famous families. Like Herodotus, however, Livy was always attracted to a colorful story. Macaulay declared in disgust: "No historian with whom we are acquainted has shown so complete indifference to the truth."

But probably a truthful chronicle was not what Livy set out to produce. In addition to his patriotic duty, he wanted by his dramatic power and the charm of his style to impress the sophisticated readers of Rome. Accuracy came second. He was no soldier in his battles, no statesman in recording the problems of government; even as a geographer he was most hazy. In an epoch when research was unknown, he was no critical historian. When he found two conflicting accounts, he was likely to chose the more colorful, or include both and let the reader be the judge.

The *Annals* were issued in "decades," or units of ten, a volume at a time, the first between 27 and 25 B.C., at the time Vergil was writing his *Aeneid.* The work did what the author intended: painted vividly the grandeur of Rome, even though, like an artist, he sometimes changed details for better composition. Whatever his faults as a historian, Livy the novelist, the dramatist, the orator, left unforgettable pages for readers of later generations.

It is a wonder that so much of his work has come down to us, for he had many enemies. Pope Gregory I, for example, ordered all available copies burned because of the superstitions they contained, and other Church fathers were also to blame for the hundred books that have disappeared, including those about Livy's own times. More than one modern historian has wished he could exchange the first ten books for those in which Livy set down what he had seen. Few, however, would willingly give up the books dealing with the sixteen years of the Punic Wars, the story of the life and death struggle between Rome and Carthage.

"It would be a satisfaction to me," declared Livy in the preface to the first decade of his *Annals,* "that I have contributed my share to perpetuate the achievements of a people, the lords of the world." He determined "neither to affirm nor refute" the traditions antedating the founding of Rome, even though they were "more suited to the fiction of poetry than to the genuine record of history." In writing them down, however, his aim was to acquaint the Romans of his day with the lives and customs of ancestors who might serve as examples in the present low moral status of Rome, "when we can neither endure our vices nor their remedies."

He began by repeating the legend of Aeneas, who led the Trojans to Latium and married Lavinia. He listed the petty chiefs who followed, making no changes in the story of Romulus and Remus and their wolf nurse. He related briefly the account of the founding of Rome, April 21, 753 B.C., when the ceremonies ended with the quarrel between the brothers and the death of Remus. By inviting in the discontented from the neighboring tribes, Romulus populated the city, then provided wives by kidnaping the Sabine women who came as guests to a feast.

In the remaining books of the first decade, which carries the story through 460 years, Livy paid special attention to Rome's virtuous and exemplary citizens: Cincinnatus, summoned from his plow to drive back the Aequians; Virginius, protecting his daughter Virginia from lustful decemvir Appius Claudius; Camillus, returning from exile to fight the Gauls; Manlius, defending the capitol; and the patriotic Curtius, riding his horse into a chasm in the Forum to preserve his city. The decade ends when the defeat of the Samnites left Rome the master of Italy.

The next ten books have been lost. Only because they were summarized in an epitome does the world know Livy's account of what happened between 294 and 219 B.C.

At the beginning of the next decade, Books XXI-XXX, Livy declared: "I am about to relate the most memorable of all wars that were ever waged, the war which the Carthaginians under Hannibal maintained against the Roman people." As far as ancient history goes, he was undoubtedly right. It was a war between the Indo-Germanic and the Semitic races for world dominion. The two were not only equally matched, but they were also familiar with the enemy's war tactics and potential power; and their hatred for each other, as the historian pointed out, was as strong as their armies.

Livy never minimized the exploits of twenty-six-year-old Hannibal, who became the outstanding figure in his book. What details he could not find recorded of the crossing of the Alps by ninety thousand infantry, twelve thousand cavalry, and thirty-seven elephants, he made up from his imagination.

Scipio the father, having failed to stop the Carthaginians in Gaul, tried again on the plains of Italy, but one defeat after another brought terror to the imperial city. After Trebia and Lake Trasimene, the delaying tactics of Fabius Maximus succeeded in holding back the invaders for a time, but the impatience of another consul, Varro, resulted in the culminating Roman disaster at Cannae (216 B.C.). Had Hannibal taken advantage of his victory, he could easily have entered Rome.

Book XXV deals with another phase of the struggle. Marcellus, besieging Syracuse, was held at bay for three years by the craft of a seventy-four-year-old mathematician, Archimedes, with his invention of the catapult and the grappling hooks that lifted the prows of Roman ships trying to attack the breakwater, and sank them. Ultimately, however, the Romans found the weak spot in the defenses and captured the island.

On another battlefront, a second Scipio, later to be called Africanus, was trying to keep Spain from being used as the Carthaginians' European headquarters. A comparison of the version by Livy with another by Polybius shows the superiority of Livy's technique. Though Scipio could not immobilize Hasdrubal entirely or prevent his departure with reinforcements for his brother in Italy, the delay did contribute to the Carthaginian defeat on the Metaurus River, a Roman victory that was quickly neutralized by the death of Marcellus in a clash with Hannibal. Eventually, however, Roman might prevailed when Scipio carried the war into Africa. Although Hannibal was recalled for the defense of Carthage, his veterans were no match for the Roman legionaries at the Battle of Zama (202 B.C.), and defeated Carthage was literally wiped from the map.

An additional fifteen books of Livy's history survive, dealing with Roman expansion in Greece and Asia and ending when Macedonia became a Roman province. But this story is an anticlimax. No longer were the soldiers fighting for the life of Rome, but the plunder they hoped to acquire, so that the reader does not follow the story with the same interest. But even in these pages, the storytelling ability of Livy is still apparent. It is easy to understand why he was called the greatest prose writer of the Augustine Age.

ANTHONY ADVERSE

Type of work: Novel
Author: Hervey Allen (1889-1949)
Type of plot: Picaresque romance
Time of plot: Late eighteenth and early nineteenth centuries
Locale: Western Europe, Africa, North America
First published: 1933

Principal characters:
Anthony Adverse
Don Luis, Marquis da Vincitata, husband of Anthony's mother
Maria, Anthony's mother
Mr. Bonnyfeather, Anthony's grandfather
Faith Paleologus, Mr. Bonnyfeather's housekeeper
Angela Guiseppe, Anthony's mistress
Florence Udney, Anthony's first wife
Dolores de la Fuente, Anthony's second wife
Vincent Nolte, Anthony's friend, a banker

Critique:

Anthony Adverse is the story of a soldier of fortune whose ramblings carry him over a large part of Europe, to Africa, and to North America. The book contains a wealth of incident, as well as mention of historical personages. The characters, however, are subordinate to the plot. The novel is also interesting because its various sections represent different types of romantic fiction.

The Story:

The pretty young Marquise Maria da Vincitata, daughter of a Scottish merchant of Leghorn, fell in love with young Denis Moore within a year of her marriage and met with him secretly in France while her husband was taking a cure for his gout. Don Luis, the arrogant Marquis da Vincitata, discovering the intrigue, spirited his wife away and killed her gallant, luckless lover when he started out in pursuit. Maria's baby was born high up in the Alps. After his wife had died in childbirth, Don Luis took the child to Leghorn, where he stealthily deposited the infant at the Convent of Jesus the Child. The only tokens of its parentage were a cape and a statue of the Madonna which had belonged to Maria.

The boy, christened Anthony by the nuns, lived at the convent until he was ten. Then he was delivered to a prominent merchant of the town, Mr. Bonnyfeather, to become his apprentice.

Bonnyfeather and his housekeeper had no trouble recognizing the cape and the doll as possessions of the merchant's daughter, Maria. Although Anthony was given the surname Adverse and was not told of his relationship to his benefactor, he was carefully educated with the tacit understanding that he would one day inherit the flourishing Bonnyfeather business.

Anthony matured early. Seduced by the housekeeper, Faith Paleologus, he also had a brief affair with the cook's daughter, Angela. He was attracted, too, by the English consul's daughter, Florence Udney, but was not encouraged by her mother, who was unaware that Anthony had any expectations.

Anticipating the eventual arrival of Napoleon's army in Leghorn, Mr. Bonnyfeather quietly liquidated his business, sent his money abroad, and made plans to retire. He arranged passage for his grandson on the American ship *Wampanoag,* under Captain Jorham. Anthony was to sail to Cuba to collect some money on a long-overdue account.

The *Wampanoag* stopped first at Genoa. There Anthony visited Father Xavier, a Jesuit, who had been his guardian at the convent. Mr. Bonnyfeather had given the priest the right to decide whether the time had come to tell Anthony he was the merchant's heir. It was from the priest's lips that Anthony learned of his origin and prospects.

When the *Wampanoag* reached Havana Anthony discovered that his creditor, Gallego, was in Africa as a slave trader. With the aid of the captain-general, Don Luis de la Casas, a plan was devised whereby Anthony would sail to Africa as a government agent. There he would impound a cargo of Gallego's slaves, bring them to Cuba for sale, and split the proceeds with the captain-general, thus satisfying the Bonnyfeather debt. Strongly attracted by Don Luis' young relation, Dolores de la Fuente, the young man finally agreed to stay in Africa and to ship several additional cargoes of slaves, for the enrichment of the captain-general and the increase of his own hopes that he might one day marry Dolores.

The trip aboard the *Ariostatica* was a trying one. Father François, a monk who was being shipped to Africa because he had tried to give aid and comfort to the slaves, fell ill of yellow fever and nearly died. Anthony, forced to rule the crew and its captain with an iron hand, was able to put down a mutiny as the ship sailed up the Rio Pongo to the Gallego establishment. There he learned that Gallego had died a few months before, leaving his factor, Ferdinando, in charge.

Anthony took over the trade station and for three years shipped cargoes of human freight to Cuba to be sold there. To the sorrow of Father François, he took the half-breed Neleta, Ferdinando's sister, as his mistress. But he was not able completely to reconcile himself to trading in human bodies.

While Anthony was absent from the trading station, Father François was captured by a native witch doctor, Mnombibi, and crucified. Upon his return, Anthony found the priest pinioned to his own cross. With the knowledge that Mr. Bonnyfeather was dead, and that Captain Bittern of the *Unicorn* was waiting in the Rio Pongo to bear him back to Leghorn, Anthony decided to leave the trading station. He left Neleta behind.

Don Luis, Marquis da Vincitata, arrived in Leghorn at the same time. They were both there on business, the marquis to close up the Casa Bonnyfeather, of which he was landlord, and Anthony to receive the merchant's will from Vincent Nolte, a banker with whom he had been friendly in his youth. Vincent suggested that Anthony take advantage of an offer made by M. Ouvrard, a French financier who was planning to supply the bankrupt Spanish government with French food and money, in return for silver from Mexican mines. Anthony was to take charge of the shipments, which would arrive at New Orleans from Vera Cruz, and to reinvest profitably as much of the money as he could. The rest was to be shipped to Florence Udney's husband, David Parish, in Philadelphia, and from there on to Europe.

Traveling to Paris to make arrangements, Vincent and Anthony were waylaid in the Alps by Don Luis, who tried to force their coach over a cliff. His plans were thwarted, however, and his own carriage and coachman plunged into the deep gorge. At the time Don Luis was traveling with Faith Paleologus, whom he had made his mistress. The two had dismounted to watch the destruction of Anthony and his friend. After their plot failed, they were left to descend the mountain on foot.

In Paris Anthony met Angela for the first time in many years. She had borne him a son, and had become a famous singer and the mistress of Napoleon. She refused to marry Anthony and follow him to America, but she did give him his son. At her entreaty, Anthony left the child with Vincent's childless cousin, Anna.

Anthony's affairs prospered in New Orleans. He was able to invest the silver profitably, to form a bank, and to build a handsome plantation for himself. When David Parish died of heart failure, Anthony married Florence. Their daughter, Maria, was three, when the plantation house caught fire one night while Anthony was away. His wife and daughter were burned to death.

Burdened by his sorrow, Anthony started west. Captured by a tribe of Indians, he escaped, only to fall into the hands of soldiers from Santa Fé. There he was brought before the governor, Don Luis, and sentenced to go to Mexico City in a prison train. That same day Don Luis had a stroke and died. Faith, his wife by that time, prepared to return to Spain.

Anthony spent two years in the Hospital of St. Lazaro before Dolores, widow of a wealthy landowner, found him and arranged for his freedom. Later they were married and went to live in the village of San Luz. Dolores bore him two children. All went well until an ax slipped one day and caught Anthony in the groin while he was felling a tree. He bled to death before he was found.

Many years later, long after the village had been deserted by Dolores and her people, a group of migrants on their way to Santa Fé came to its site. The little Madonna, which Anthony had carried with him through life, still stood in a chapel in the ruins of San Luz. Mary Jorham, the young niece of a Captain Jorham, found the image, but she was not allowed to keep it because her parents thought it a heathen idol. Instead, it served as a fine target for a shooting match. It was splintered into a thousand pieces.

ANTIGONE

Type of work: Drama
Author: Sophocles (495?-406 B.C.)
Type of plot: Classical tragedy
Time of plot: Remote antiquity
Locale: The city of Thebes
First presented: 440 B.C.

Principal characters:
CREON, tyrant of Thebes
ANTIGONE, daughter of Oedipus
ISMENE, her sister
HAEMON, son of Creon
TIRESIAS, a prophet

Critique:

Although the main problem of this play would be unimportant today, the discussions of the responsibilities of a ruler are as pertinent now as in ancient Greece. The characters of the play move to their tragic ends with highly dramatic speeches, while the moral and philosophical problems of the plot are displayed through the chorus and soliloquies. When first presented, the play was so successful with Athenian audiences that Sophocles was made a general in the war against Samos. Recent presentations of the play have been well received by both audience and critic.

The Story:

Polynices and Eteocles, sons of the cursed family of King Oedipus, led two armies against each other before the gates of Thebes, and both brothers were killed in single combat with each other. Creon, their uncle, and now the tyrant ruler of the city, ordered that Eteocles be given full funeral rites, but that Polynices, who had attacked the city, be left unburied and unmourned. Anyone who broke this decree would be punished with death.

Antigone and Ismene, the sisters of Polynices and Eteocles, discussed this order, and with grief for the unburied brother tearing at her heart, Antigone asked Ismene to aid her in giving him burial. When Ismene refused to help in so dangerous a task, Antigone went defiantly to bury Polynices.

Shortly afterward, Creon learned from a sentry that the body had been buried. Angrily he ordered the sentry to find the perpetrator of the deed. The sentry returned to the grave and uncovered the body. During a dust storm Antigone came to look at the grave and, finding it open, filled the air with lamentation. Her cries attracted the attention of the guard, who captured her and took her to Creon.

Questioned by Creon, she said that to bury a man was to obey the laws of the gods, even if it were against the laws of a man. Her reply angered Creon. Antigone must die. Ismene tried to soften Creon's heart toward her sister by reminding him that Antigone was engaged to his son, Haemon. But Creon remained firm.

Haemon incurred his father's anger by arguments that Creon should soften his cruel decree because of popular sympathy for Antigone. Creon said that he cared nothing for the ideas of the town, and Haemon called his answer foolish. As a punishment, Creon ordered that Antigone be killed before Haemon's eyes. Haemon fled with threats of revenge. Creon ordered that Antigone be walled up in a cave outside Thebes and left there to die for her crime against his law.

When Antigone was led out of the city, the people of Thebes followed her, lamenting her fate. She was thrust into the cave. All this while, Polynices' body lay unburied outside the walls. The prophet Tiresias warned Creon that the gods had not been pleased with his action, and that the body should be buried. He foretold that before long Haemon would die if his father did not bury Polynices and rescue Antigone from the cave.

Creon, realizing that Tiresias' prophesies had never proved false, hurried to avert the fate the prophet had foretold. Quickly he ordered a tomb prepared for Polynices, and he himself set off to release Antigone. But the will of the gods could not be changed so easily. When he reached the cave, he heard his son's voice within, crying out in grief. Creon entered and saw that Antigone had hanged herself with a rope made from her own dress. Haemon, sword in hand, rushed at his father as if to attack him, but instead he spat on the old man. He then fell on his sword and killed himself in sorrow over Antigone's death. The news of these events quickly traveled back to the city, and Creon's wife, hearing of so many misfortunes, died by her own hand.

On returning to Thebes with the body of his son, Creon learned of his wife's death. Seeing that his life could no longer have meaning, he had himself led out of the city into exile. He was, himself, the final victim of his harsh tyranny.

THE ANTIQUARY

Type of work: Novel
Author: Sir Walter Scott (1771-1832)
Type of plot: Domestic romance
Time of plot: Late eighteenth century
Locale: Scotland
First published: 1816

Principal characters:
JONATHAN OLDBUCK OF MONKBARNS, the antiquary
LOVEL, an illegitimate son of unknown parents
SIR ARTHUR WARDOUR, a baronet, Oldbuck's friend
MISS ISABELLA WARDOUR, his daughter
EDIE OCHILTREE, a beggar
HECTOR M'INTYRE, Oldbuck's nephew
THE EARL OF GLENALLAN, present head of a powerful family
DOUSTERSWIVEL, a magician

Critique:

Not one of the most popular of Scott's novels, *The Antiquary* is nevertheless a respected member of the Waverley group and the novel most nearly contemporary to Scott's own time. Although it is a romance, it is also a novel of manners. Scott admitted that when necessary he sacrificed the plot in order to describe more clearly the manners of the characters, particularly those of the lower social classes. His characterizations of the Scottish peasants are much more vivid than are those of the upper classes. But the touch of magic that was Scott's is evident everywhere in this novel, as it is in all he wrote.

The Story:

When old Jonathan Oldbuck of Monkbarns first met young Lovel, he was impressed by the young man's good manners and conduct; but he was also mystified by the little he could learn of Lovel's past. It was obvious that Lovel was not the boy's real name and that there was something in his history of which he was ashamed.

From his good friend Sir Arthur Wardour, Oldbuck at last learned something of Lovel's history. The young man was the illegitimate son of unknown parents. Although a benefactor had settled a large estate on him, he lived in solitude and disgrace because of his questionable ancestry. To make matters worse, he was in love with Sir Arthur's daughter, Isabella. Though the girl loved him, she would not accept him because she knew her father would not permit an alliance with a man of unknown and illegitimate origins. Even after Lovel had saved her life and that of her father, when they were trapped by the tides, she gave him no more than the thanks due him for his bravery.

Sir Arthur was in serious financial straits, in debt to dozens of tradesmen and friends, among them Oldbuck. In order to restore his fortune, he had fallen into a plot prepared by one Dousterswivel, an evil magician who had promised his aid in finding valuable minerals on Sir Arthur's property. Sir Arthur, forced to put up money before Dousterswivel would work his magic, had already borrowed one hundred pounds from Oldbuck, who suspected that Dousterswivel was the crook that he was.

Before the magician could attempt to work his magic, Oldbuck's nephew, Captain Hector M'Intyre, came home for a visit. A hot-headed young man, he accused Lovel of lying about the little he told of his past. Hector challenged Lovel to a duel, and although Lovel did everything he could to prevent it the duel was fought. Lovel wounded Hector fatally, or so it appeared, and was forced to flee the country on a boat provided by a friend. Hector did recover, but Lovel did not hear the news until much later. He had been aided in his flight by Edie Ochiltree, a beggar who knew all the secrets of the countryside. While Edie hid Lovel in a cave, they overheard Dousterswivel trying to convince Sir Arthur that he could find buried treasure in that cave, if Sir Arthur would put up the necessary money. Edie used that knowledge to good account.

When Sir Arthur asked Oldbuck for another hundred pounds to give to Dousterswivel so that he would get the treasure from the cave, Oldbuck insisted that they go to the cave and dig for the treasure. Although the magician tried to prevent the excursion, Oldbuck would not be denied. Everyone present was completely surprised when, after much digging, old Edie the beggar stuck a pick into the ground and hit a chest. When the chest was opened, the bewildered spectators found a fortune in coin; Sir Arthur was saved from disaster. Edie, in an attempt to pay back Dousterswivel, tricked him into digging for hours for more treasure that Edie said was also buried in the cave. He also arranged with a friend to have a specter appear and frighten the magician half to death.

About the same time there occurred another event which was to have great influence upon Oldbuck, Sir Arthur, and their friends. An old woman in the neighborhood sent for the Earl of Glenallan, head of a wealthy and powerful family. Before she died, the old woman wanted to clear her conscience of a terrible wrong she had done the earl when he was a young man. The earl had been in love with a girl whom his mother hated, primarily because of her family. The earl had secretly married the girl before his mother, in a spiteful attempt to break up the romance, told her son that the girl was his own sister. Because of certain letters and the perjured testimony of servants, including the old woman telling the story, the earl had believed his mother's story. His wife had taken her own life, but before she died she had given birth to a male child. A servant had whisked the child away, and the old woman did not know whether he had lived or died. The earl, who had lived a life of misery because of the horrible crime he thought he had committed in marrying his own sister, was joyful at the news given him by the old crone, even though he grieved at the useless death of the girl he loved. He told the story to Oldbuck and asked his help in determining whether the child had lived.

While Oldbuck and the Earl of Glenallan were conducting their investigation, news came that the French were about to raid the Scottish coast. Hector, who was now fully recovered from the wound suffered at Lovel's hands, prepared to gather troops and meet Major Neville, an officer in charge of local defense. Lovel had not been heard from since the duel, and there were rumors that he had died at sea. Then old Edie brought the joyful news that the ship carrying Lovel had put in to shore and that all aboard were safe. From his remarks to Oldbuck, the old gentlemen learned that the money found in the cave on Sir Arthur's land had been buried there by Lovel and Edie after they had overheard the conversation between Dousterswivel and Sir Arthur. Lovel, hearing of Sir Arthur's financial difficulties, had taken that way of helping Isabella's father without embarrassing the old gentleman by offering him money outright.

When Major Neville appeared to take charge of the garrison, everyone was amazed to see that he was in reality Lovel. Lovel, or rather Major Neville, brought word that there would be no battle. A watchman had mistaken a bonfire for a signal that the French were coming. As they all stood talking, the Earl of Glenallan noted the young man's marked resemblance to his dead wife. Then the mystery was solved. Through old papers and the words of old servants of the Glenallan family, the earl learned that without doubt Lovel was his son. While a baby, the boy had been cared for by the earl's brother and, unknown to the earl, had inherited his uncle's fortune.

Lovel was restored to his rightful place, and within a month he and Isabella Wardour were married. From that time on all the friends lived in peace and prosperity and joy.

ANTONY AND CLEOPATRA

Type of work: Drama
Author: William Shakespeare (1564-1616)
Type of plot: Romantic tragedy
Time of plot: About 30 B.C.
Locale: Egypt and various parts of the Roman Empire
First presented: 1606-1607

Principal characters:
MARK ANTONY,
OCTAVIUS CAESAR, and
LEPIDUS, triumvirs, ruling Rome
ENOBARBUS, and
EROS, Antony's friends
SEXTUS POMPEIUS, leader of the party opposed to Octavius Caesar
CLEOPATRA, Queen of Egypt
OCTAVIA, Caesar's sister and Antony's wife
CHARMIAN, and
IRAS, Cleopatra's attendants

Critique:

In his tragedies Shakespeare rose to dramatic heights seldom equaled. Although critics may argue to determine the greatest of his tragedies, surely *Antony and Cleopatra* is among the top few. Its scope is staggering; it covers the whole Roman Empire and the men who ruled it. Only a genius could match the greatness of the scenes with such beauty of poetry and philosophy. Here a man born to rule the world is brought to ruin by his weaknesses and lusts. Deserted by friends and subjects, he is denied even a noble death, but must attempt suicide. Even that he bungles. The tragedy is grimly played out; honor and nobility die, as well as the man.

The Story:

After the murder of Julius Caesar, the Roman Empire was ruled by three men, the noble triumvirs, Mark Antony, Lepidus, and Octavius, Caesar's nephew. Antony, having been given the Eastern sphere to rule, had gone to Alexandria and there he had seen and fallen passionately in love with Cleopatra, Queen of Egypt. She was the flower of the Nile, but a wanton who had been the mistress of Julius Caesar and of many others. Antony was so filled with lust for her that he ignored his own counsel and the warnings of his friends, and as long as possible he ignored also a request from Octavius Caesar that he return to Rome. Sextus Pompeius, son of Pompey the Great, and a powerful leader, was gathering troops to seize Rome from the rule of the triumvirs, and Octavius Caesar wished to confer with the other two, Antony and Lepidus. At last the danger of a victory by Sextus Pompeius, coupled with the news that his wife Fulvia was dead, forced Antony to leave Egypt and Cleopatra and journey to Rome.

Pompeius was confident of victory so long as Antony stayed in Egypt, for Antony was a better general than either Lepidus or Octavius. When Pompeius heard that Antony was headed toward Rome, his hope was that Octavius and Antony would not mend their quarrels but would continue to fight each other as they had in the past. Lepidus did not matter; he sided with neither of the other two, and cared little for conquest and glory. Pompeius faced disappointment, however, for Antony and Octavius mended their quarrels in the face of common danger. To seal their renewed friendship, Antony married Octavia, the sister of Octavius; through her, each general would be bound to the other. Thus it seemed that Pompeius' scheme to separate Antony and Octavius would fail. His last hope was that Antony's lust would send him back to Cleopatra; then he and Octavius would battle each other and Pompeius would conquer Rome. To stall for time, he sealed a treaty with the triumvirs. Antony, with his wife, went to Athens on business for the Empire. There word reached him that Lepidus and Octavius had waged war in spite of the treaty they had signed, and Pompeius had been killed. Octavius' next move was to seize Lepidus on the pretext that he had aided Pompeius. Now the Roman world had but two rulers, Octavius and Antony.

But Antony could not resist the lure of Cleopatra. Sending Octavia, his wife, home from Athens, he hurried back to Egypt. His return ended all pretense of friendship between him and Octavius. Each man prepared for battle, the winner to be the sole ruler of the world. Cleopatra joined her forces with those of Antony. At first Antony was supreme on the land, but Octavius ruled the sea and lured Antony to fight him there. Antony's friends and captains, particularly loyal Enobarbus, begged him not to risk his forces on the sea, but Antony, confident of victory, prepared to match his ships with those of Octavius at Actium. But in the decisive hour of the great sea fight Cleopatra ordered her fleet to leave the battle, and sail for home. Antony, leaving the battle and his honor and his glory, followed her. Because he had set the example for desertion, many of his men left his forces and joined the standard of Octavius.

Antony was sunk in gloom at the folly of his own actions, but his lust had made him drunk with desire, and everything, even honor, must bow to Cleopatra. She protested that she did not know that Antony would follow her when she sailed away. Antony had reason enough to know she lied, but he still wanted the fickle wanton at any cost.

Octavius sent word to Cleopatra that she might have all her wishes granted if she would surrender Antony to Octavius. Knowing that Octavius was likely to be the victor in the struggle, she sent him a message of loyalty and of admiration for his greatness. Although Antony had seen her receive the addresses of Octavius' messenger, and even though he ranted and stormed at her for her faithlessness, she was easily able to dispel his fears and jealousy and make him hers again. After a failure to sue for peace, Antony decided to march again against his enemy. At this decision even the faithful Enobarbus left him and went over to Octavius, for he thought Antony had lost his reason as well as his honor. But Enobarbus too was an honorable man who shortly afterward died of shame for deserting his general.

On the day of the battle victory was in sight for Antony, in spite of overwhelming odds. But once more the flight of the Egyptian fleet betrayed him. His defeat left Octavius master of the world. Antony was like a madman, seeking nothing but revenge on treacherous Cleopatra. When the queen heard of his rage, she had word sent to him that she was dead, killed by her own hand out of love for him. Convinced once more that Cleopatra had been true to him, Antony called on Eros, his one remaining follower, to kill him so that he could join Cleopatra in death. But faithful Eros killed himself rather than stab his beloved general. Determined to die, Antony fell on his own sword. Even that desperate act was without dignity or honor, for he did not die immediately and he could find no one who loved him enough to end his pain and misery. While he lay there, a messenger brought word that Cleopatra still lived. He ordered his servants to carry him to her. There he died in her arms, each proclaiming eternal love for the other.

When Octavius Caesar heard the news of Antony's death, he grieved. Although he had fought and conquered

Antony, he lamented the sorry fate of a great man turned weakling, ruined by his own lust. He sent a messenger to assure Cleopatra that she would be treated royally, that she should be ruler of her own fate. But the queen learned, as Antony had warned her, that Octavius would take her to Rome to march behind him in his triumphant procession, where she, a queen and mistress to two former rulers of the world, would be pinched and spat upon by rabble and slaves. To cheat him of his triumph, she put on her crown and all her royal garb, placed a poisonous asp on her breast, and lay down to die. Charmian and Iras, her loyal attendants, died the same death. Octavius Caesar, entering her chamber, saw her dead, but as beautiful and desirable as in life. There was only one thing he could do for his one-time friend and the dead queen: he ordered their burial in a common grave, together in death as they had wished to be in life.

APOLOGIA PRO VITA SUA

Type of work: Autobiography
Author: John Henry Newman (1801-1890)
First published: 1864

This long essay, also known as *History of My Religious Opinions,* is the famous reply written by John Henry Newman in answer to the attack made upon him by Charles Kingsley (1819-1875). The years 1833 to 1841 had seen the publication of the *Tracts for the Times,* to which Newman had been a contributor; these tracts, which gave their name to the "Tractarian Movement" or "Oxford Movement," were the spearhead of the great theological controversy of the middle years of the century. Newman and his friends were eager to return the Anglican Church to something like its position during past centuries; they valued tradition and hierarchy; they wished to go back to the severe, authoritarian faith of the past, from which they believed the Church of England had lapsed. In a word, they were the "High Church" party; and some idea of the rift that was created within the Church can be gleaned from Trollope's Barchester novels. In 1845, Newman left the Anglican Church for the Roman; two years later he was ordained priest in that communion.

In January, 1864, Kingsley, an Anglican clergyman of what was known as the "Broad Church" party and a popular novelist, attacked Newman in a magazine article, in which he stated that "Truth, for its own sake, has never been a virtue with the Roman clergy. Father Newman informs us that it need not, and on the whole ought not to be. . . ." To this article, Newman replied in a pamphlet in February of that year, whereupon Kingsley wrote still another pamphlet entitled "What, then, does Dr. Newman mean?" in which he accused Newman of having "gambled away" his reason, of having a "morbid" mind, and of not caring about "truth for its own sake." It was in answer to this pamphlet that *Apologia pro Vita Sua* was written.

Newman divided his work into chapters, each dealing with a crucial period in his life. The first gives the story of his youth and his education up to his thirty-second year, by which time he was a Fellow of Oriel College, Oxford, and had been ordained in the Anglican Church. By his own account, he emerges as an extraordinarily precocious lad, preoccupied at a very early age with religious questions. He resembled, indeed, the hero of his own novel *Loss and Gain*—which phrase might be applied as a description of his career. The modern reader will smile at Newman's decision, reached at the age of fifteen, that celibacy was the only course for him; yet his prodigious intellect shines through his very modest account of his youth. He tells us of his reading; but the real influences were his friends Hurrell Froude and the older John Keble (1792-1866). It was Froude, with his love for tradition and for the external beauty of the Roman Church, who began to soften Newman's insular dislike of that institution.

The year 1830 was a momentous one for Newman. The revolution that deposed Charles X of France distressed him; the Whig victory in England distressed him even more. He had a violent hatred of Liberalism, and everywhere it seemed triumphant. The "Tractarian Movement" was largely a counterattack. Newman himself claimed that the movement had begun to stir as far back as 1828, when he was Vicar of St. Mary's, Oxford; but the date of its beginning is usually set in July of 1833, when Keble preached a famous sermon at Oxford against the errors of the Whig government in Church policy. The *Tracts for the Times,* written by Newman and his friends, stated their position. As Newman saw it, the Whigs must be opposed and the Church of England returned to the position of authority it had held during the early seventeenth century. He considered himself as belonging to neither the "High" nor the "Low" Church party; he was merely anti-

Liberal. He explained his position as based on: (1) dogma (he had no use for "religion as a mere sentiment"; there must be positive beliefs); (2) a visible Church with sacraments and rites and the Episcopal system; (3) anti-Romanism. Such was the general point of view of the Oxford Movement. Newman, incidentally, had very little to say about ritual, usually associated with the High Church position. He was interested in theology, not liturgics.

Newman admitted frankly that in the vast amount of writing he did during these years he had attempted to refute many of the tenets of Romanism. What he was seeking for himself was a basis in reason for his beliefs; for the Anglican Church, he was seeking a theology of its own that would make it more than a *via media*. These investigations led him to a consideration of the common heritage of Romanism and Anglicanism and to the question of how much of the Roman belief could be accepted by an Anglican. He began to be convinced that in English history the real objection to Rome had been political rather than theological; that Romanism and Anglicanism had, after all, not been so far apart as was generally believed. Inevitably, he began to find a difference between Roman dogmas, which he could accept, and Roman practice, which he often could not. He confessed that, for a long time, the stumbling block had been the Roman veneration of the Virgin and prayers to the saints. But he was obviously drawing closer to Rome.

It was Tract XC, published in 1841, that brought the storm on Newman's head and led to his final break with the Church of England. In this tract he examined the question of how far the Thirty-Nine Articles, on which the Church rests, were capable of a Roman interpretation. Immediately he was accused of everything from "traducing the Reformation" to planning to build a monastery near Oxford. He himself was feeling grave doubts about Anglicanism, derived mainly from his reading on the abstruse doctrines of the Monophysites. When he could no longer conscientiously maintain his clerical position, he resigned his living of St. Mary's in September of 1843. As he explained, he had spent the years from 1835 to 1839 trying, in his writings, to benefit the Church of England at the expense of the Church of Rome and the years from 1839 to 1843 trying to benefit the Church of England without prejudice to the Church of Rome. In 1843 he began to despair of the Church of England.

The years between 1843 and 1845 were spent, according to Newman, in retirement. He had now reached the crossroads but was as yet unable to make his final decision. He had already retracted the "hard things" he had said against Rome, the things he had felt compelled to say in defense of the Anglican Church. He made a point of seeing no Roman Catholics; his struggle was purely an inward one. Though he still felt that the Church of England was a branch of the true Church, though he still deplored the "Mariolatry" of Rome, he was convinced that Rome was more in accord with the early Church. His horror of Liberalism also played its part; he very genuinely felt that the spirit of Liberalism was the spirit of Antichrist. As he now saw the situation, on the one hand there was Liberalism leading inevitably to atheism; on the other, Anglicanism leading to Rome. He still remained in lay communion with the Church of England during this difficult period, but more and more often he found himself asking this question: "Can I be saved in the English Church?" When he was compelled to answer in the negative, he made the great decision and was received into the Roman Communion in 1845. Two years later he was ordained priest.

In the concluding section of the essay Newman defended himself against the jibes that were hurled at him after his conversion. It was said that by submitting to Rome he had abdicated his power of personal judgment and that he was now compelled to accept dogmas which might, at any moment, be changed. His reply was that the Roman doctrines were not difficult for him, that historically the Church had not suppressed freedom of intellect. He felt that an infallible Church had been intended by the Creator to preserve religion—especially in an age of increasing skepticism. Lastly—and this is the most famous part of the essay—he advanced the idea that a conflict between authority and private judgment is beneficial to the man whose ideas are being tested.

Though the *Apologia* won Newman a resounding victory over Kingsley, the work is not easy reading. The difficulty does not lie in the style, for no one has written more clearly and simply than he. But he wrote for readers who were familiar with Church history and with theological problems, so that most readers in our age of religious ignorance and indifference lack the knowledge to grasp many of his arguments. It is difficult today to understand his dilemma. Yet the *Apologia* remains a powerful and sincere work. Some, naturally, have seen in Newman, as Kingsley must have done, only a man whose habit of mind made him take refuge in an authoritarian Church which would solve his spiritual problems for him. Others, taking the opposite view, would agree with Ramon Fernandez that "In him intelligence and faith act as mutual brakes and yet no attentive reader can accuse him of the slightest artifice."

AN APOLOGY FOR THE LIFE OF COLLEY CIBBER, COMEDIAN

Type of work: Autobiography
Author: Colley Cibber (1671-1757)
Time: Late seventeenth and early eighteenth centuries
Locale: England
First published: 1740

Principal personages:
COLLEY CIBBER, actor, playwright, producer
WILLIAM CONGREVE, playwright
SIR JOHN VANBRUGH, architect and playwright
JOHN GAY, poet, author of *The Beggar's Opera*
JOSEPH ADDISON, essayist and author of the successful *Cato*
SIR RICHARD STEELE, essayist and playwright
ALEXANDER POPE, author of *The Dunciad*

To read Colley Cibber's *Apology* is to recapture intimate views of London theatrical, social, and literary life during the last decade of the seventeenth and the first quarter of the following century, as observed by a successful actor and theatrical manager, a playwright of sorts, and a man of shrewd insight into his own foibles and those of his fellows.

Published ten years after his retirement from the stage (1730) and his acceptance of the poet laureateship, this autobiography is a frank and engaging account of his childhood experiences as the son of a well-known sculptor, his schoolboy activities, his early days as a stage-struck youth, his long career in the theater, and his candid and unprejudiced observations of people and events. For this is an *apology,* not in the sense of an acknowledgment of wrongdoing, mistake, or regrettable circumstance, but as an explanation of the life of a man who was regularly and closely connected with the theater; who knew and talked with many of the most influential people of his day; who was acquainted with political actions, backstage gossip, and the infinite variety of public life and private in his time. Cibber was attempting, as he expressed it in the first chapter, to present "as true a picture of myself as natural vanity will permit me to draw," since "a man who has pass'd above forty years of his life upon a theatre, where he has never appear'd to be himself, may have naturally excited the curiosity of his spectators to know what he really was, when in no body's shape but his own. . . ." He also proposed to include "the theatrical history of my own time, from my first appearance on the stage to my last exit."

Following a simple chronological pattern of development, Cibber devotes the first three chapters of his autobiography to matters of his parents and family. His father had emigrated from Holstein many years before the Restoration in 1660; his mother was a member of the Colley family, formerly of some prominence in Rutlandshire. His education was regrettably limited to a few years in a free school. Early in life, he says he was possessed of a "giddy negligence," an inconsistency of character, and these qualities persisted, he admits, frequently to his own embarrassment. But Cibber notes that Pope's selection of him as the heir to the throne of folly in *The Dunciad* was done not so much to satirize Cibber as it was to give publicity to the poem, for an attack on the laureate was likely to gain increased sales for any publication. Thus, with remarkable good nature, Cibber transforms Pope's malicious defamation into a device for "profit to himself." This was both a successful and extraordinary outcome for any controversy with Alexander Pope, "the wasp of Twickenham."

Cibber's attempts to gain entrance to Winchester proving fruitless, he next tried the life of a trooper in the Revolution of 1688. His father sought preferment for his lively and mercurial son in various ways, but by 1690, Cibber succumbed to the "allurements of a theatre," and so his long stage career began.

In the remaining portion of the book, chapters IV through XVI, Cibber intermingles autobiographical details and anecdotes with factual accounts of the history of the London stage from its restoration in 1660 until his retirement in the 1730's; with personal reminiscences and valuable word-portraits of actors and actresses, playwrights, managers; with first-hand experiences with the licensing acts and Masters of Revels. For example, before recounting his early days in the theater, Cibber sets forth, swiftly but convincingly, his own "short view of the stage" from its rebirth in 1660 until the time he became an actor in 1690. To this he adds an account of the greatest players of the time, describing them in vivid and satisfying detail, evaluating their performances, enumerating their best roles. His highest praise goes to Betterton and Mrs. Bracegirdle, for Cibber knew them all, regarded them closely as a student of acting, and valued their talents shrewdly as a stage manager. He writes of his own first appearance in a significant acting role as the chaplain in Otway's *The Orphan,* of the first prologue he composed, of his first play, the successful *Love's Last Shift.* This play led to his long acquaintanceship with Sir John Vanbrugh, an architect turned playwright. Cibber frankly admits that Gay's *The Beggar's Opera* was a "vast success" and that his attempt to offset this portrayal of highwaymen, thieves, and receivers of stolen goods with a comedy in praise of virtue, *Love in a Riddle,* was a resounding failure. In this instance, his middle-class morality seems to have blurred Cibber's judgment, for the charm and delightful raciness of Gay's ballad-opera have made it a favorite for countless generations, while no one but an avid student of the history of English comedy has ever heard of *Love in a Riddle.*

Cibber traces the complex and curious history of the rival acting companies, of the rise to great popularity of Italian opera, of his ultimate assumption of a position of authority as actor-manager. He pauses to comment upon the building of a new theater, the Hay Market, and its weaknesses acoustically. He remarks upon the actor-manager's difficulties with gentlemen who sought to master the intricacies of theater operation, of the intense rivalries and jealousies of actors and actresses, of the origin of actor's benefits. He admits freely his own inadequacies as a tragic actor, for his voice was unsuited to heavy roles; however, he does assert his success as a villain. He comments on the unfortunate public attitude toward the profession of acting; he even offers good advice to would-be playwrights, suggesting that they always pay particular attention to their plotting.

No doubt it is this union of the frank appraisal of a man who recognizes his own mistakes and strong points with his shrewd observations of personages and events that gives Cibber's book its continuing vigor, its essential charm. He can look upon the self-seeking defections of actors with charity, for he realizes intimately the insecurity of their profession and excuses their failure to fulfill certain obligations as understandable. He perceives that well-meaning patrons of the theater could not possibly understand all the implications of their amateurish decisions, and so he deals with them gently, despite all the trouble they caused him as an actor-manager. In short, Cibber is both a professional in the theater and a devoted, though not always gifted, master craftsman in the art of the drama. His youthful passion for the stage and acting and writing plays and refurbishing old dramas seems never to have left him. His lifelong interest in matters theatrical seldom wavers; hence his desire to record important happenings in dramatic history, his awareness of the significance of minor occurrences, and his appraisal of the people concerned with these events large and small combine to give this account remarkable value.

If the test of excellence in autobiographical writing is the author's ability not only to set down his views of people, events, and circumstances accurately and with satisfying detail, but also to portray his own qualities with rich revealing honesty, then Colley Cibber's *Apology* deserves recognition. For Cibber's enthusiasm for the stage and its people is intensely absorbing; his zeal to make his readers understand the development of English acting, the facts of play production during his time, and the history of the theater in those lively years is genuine and almost incomparable. Moreover, his sincerity, his good humor, his vanity, his strong armor against insult and vitriolic attack, his keen sense of justice, and his wholesome absorption in the "allurements of a theatre," make this autobiography a record unique in theatrical writings. Cibber the playwright, manager, actor, play-doctor, poet laureate is dead long since save for specialists in theatrical matters. But Colley Cibber the apologist and commentator on dramatic history is still intensely human, vivid, and readable.

THE APOSTLE

Type of work: Novel
Author: Sholem Asch (1880-   )
Type of plot: Religious chronicle
Time of plot: Shortly after the Crucifixion
Locale: The Roman Empire
First published: 1943

Principal characters:
SAUL OF TARSHISH, afterwards known as Paul
JOSEPH BAR NABA OF CYPRUS, Saul's friend, an early convert
REB ISTEPHAN, a famous Jewish preacher
SIMON BAR JONAH, called Peter
REB JACOB, Joseph's son

Critique:

The Apostle is a faithful attempt to chronicle the life of the two great apostles, Peter and Paul. Adhering carefully to the history of the period, the author has presented a sympathetic portrait of the struggles of the early Christians. His knowledge of contemporary events gives the reader a vivid picture of the life of the period shortly after the Crucifixion.

The Story:

It was seven weeks after the crucifixion of Yeshua of Nazareth by Pontius Pilate. All the poor of Jerusalem, who had found in Jeshua their Messiah, had gone into hiding; but the word was spreading. Little by little the story was told, of Yeshua who had come back after his death, of the Messiah who had appeared to his disciples. The matter was hotly argued on all sides. The pious Jews could not believe in a Messiah who had been killed; the Messianists devoutly affirmed their faith.

Saul of Tarshish and Joseph bar Naba came upon a street preacher, a rustic Galilean, who told with great conviction of Yeshua's return after he had been entombed. Cries of belief and of repugnance interrupted his talk. Saul himself spoke with great bitterness against this Messiah, for he had no patience with the gentle Yeshua who was hanged.

The agitation rapidly spread. One of the most vigorous upholders of Yeshua was Reb Istephan. He had a gift for moving men's souls, and more and more Jews became persuaded. Joseph bar Naba himself had known Yeshua in his lifetime, and when Joseph heard Reb Istephan he was convinced. Joseph became a Messianist. This conversion disgusted Saul, and in sorrow and bitterness he turned away from his friend Joseph.

Then a dramatic incident took place. Simon, the first of Yeshua's disciples, healed Nehemiah the cripple in the name of the Nazarene. Many were much impressed by the cure, but others resented Simon's use of the Messiah's name. As a result his enemies had their way, and Simon was imprisoned by the High Priest to await trial. Then another miracle happened! Simon and his follower Jochanan had been securely locked in a dungeon, but in the morning they were walking the streets again. It was said that they had passed directly through the stone walls — with the help of Yeshua.

The resentment against the wild Galileans grew among the rulers, while the humble folk followed Simon with trust. The High Priest again brought Simon to trial; but Simon spoke so well in defense of his doctrine that he was freed. And now the tumult increased. The ignorant folk, seeing Simon released, concluded that there was official sanction for the new cult; hence more joined the followers of Yeshua.

Saul was greatly incensed. He believed that the Messiah was yet to come, that the disciples were corrupting Jerusalem. He went to the High Priest and secured appointment as official spy. In his new job Saul tracked down the humble Messianists and sentenced them to the lash. Growing in power, Saul the Zealot finally took Reb Istephan prisoner for preaching the new faith. With grim pleasure Saul led the way to the stoning pit and watched Istephan sink beneath the flung rocks. As he died, the preacher murmured a prayer for the forgiveness of his tormentors. Saul was vaguely troubled.

Then the Messianists were much heartened. Reb Jacob ben Joseph, Yeshua's younger brother, came to Jerusalem to head the humble cult, and Saul could do little against this pious and strict Jew. By chance the High Priest heard of more Messianists in Damascus Saul volunteered to investigate and hurried to his new field. But on the way a vision appeared to him and said, "Saul, Saul, why dost thou persecute me?" Saul then recognized Yeshua for his Lord and as he was commanded he went on to Damascus, although he was still blinded by the heavenly apparition. A follower of the new religion baptized him and restored his sight. The penitent Saul hurried away from the haunts of man. In all he waited seven years for his mission.

Finally as he prayed in his mother's house, the call came. Joseph bar Naba asked Saul to go with him to Antioch to strengthen the congregation there. At last Saul was on the way to bring the word of the Messiah to others. He left for Antioch with Joseph and the Greek Titus, Saul's first convert.

Now Simon had founded the church at Antioch among the Greeks. The perplexing question was, could a devout Jew even eat with the gentiles, let alone accept them into the church? In Jerusalem Jacob held firmly to the law of the Torah: salvation was only for the circumcised. Simon vacillated. In Jerusalem he followed Jacob; among the Greeks he accepted gentiles fully. Joseph had been sent by the elders of Jerusalem to Antioch to apply the stricter rule to the growing Messianic church.

Saul at first met with much suspicion. The Messianists remembered too well Saul the Zealot who had persecuted them. But little by little the apostle won them over. Yeshua appeared to Saul several times, and he was much strengthened in the faith. At last Saul found his true mission in the conviction that he was divinely appointed to bring the word of Yeshua to the gentiles. He worked wonders at Antioch and built a strong church there, but his acceptance of gentiles cost him Joseph's friendship. As a symbol of his new mission Saul became Paul and began his years of missionary work.

To Corinth, to Ephesus, to Cyprus—to all the gentiles went Paul. Everywhere he founded a church, sometimes small but always zealous. With him much of the time went Lukas, the Greek physician. Lukas was an able minister and a scholar who was writing the life of Yeshua.

The devout Jews in Jerusalem were greatly troubled by this strange preacher who accepted the gentiles. Finally they brought him up for trial. Paul escaped only by standing on his rights as a Roman citizen. As such he could demand a trial before Caesar himself. Paul went to Rome as a captive, but he rejoiced, for he knew the real test of Christianity would be in Rome. Already Simon was there, preaching to the orthodox Jews.

The evil Nero made Paul wait in prison for two years without a hearing, and even then only the intervention of Seneca freed the apostle. For a short time Simon and Paul worked together, one among the Jews and the other among the gentiles. They converted many, and the lowly fervently embraced the promise of salvation.

To give himself an outlet for his

fancied talents as an architect, Nero burned Rome and planned to rebuild a beautiful city. But the crime was too much even for the Romans. To divert suspicion from himself, Nero blamed the Christians. He arrested thousands of them, and on the appointed day opened the royal carnage. Jews and Christians hour after hour were gored by oxen, torn by tigers, chewed by crocodiles. At the end of the third day many Romans could no longer bear the sight, but still Nero sat on. It was so strange: the Christians died well, and with their last breath they forgave their persecutors.

Simon, only a Jew, was crucified afterward; Paul, born a Roman citizen, was beheaded. With them to the execution went Gabelus the gladiator, who had accepted Christianity. But the deaths of Simon and Paul were in reality the beginning. The martyrdom of the early Christians was the foundation stone of the Christian church.

THE APPLE OF THE EYE

Type of work: Novel
Author: Glenway Wescott (1901-)
Type of plot: Regional romance
Time of plot: Twentieth century
Locale: Rural Wisconsin
First published: 1924

Principal characters:
HANNAH MADOC, a primitive
JULE BIER, Hannah's lover
SELMA, Jule's wife
ROSALIA, Jule's and Selma's daughter
MIKE, Rosalia's lover
DAN STRANE, Rosalia's cousin

Critique:

This novel tells of the background and youth of Dan Strane in rural Wisconsin, and the story of Hannah Madoc reveals the set of values against which the author measures his characters. Jule himself believed in Hannah's goodness, but he was too weak to break away from his own social ties to marry the girl he really loved. The emphasis upon sex in the story is typical of a young boy's wonder at the difference between religious doctrines and the natural functions of man's true personality.

The Story:

When her drunken father came home one night and swung at her with a broom handle, patient, hard-working Hannah Madoc pushed him off the porch in self-defense. He died a few days later, leaving his daughter orphaned and penniless, and Hannah went to work in Mrs. Boyle's store. There she waited on customers during the day and served the men liquor in the evening.

One night Jule Bier saw her behind the store counter. Ever since the death of his wife and the piling up of debts, old Mr. Bier had struggled to make enough money from his farm to give Jule a chance in life. Cold and calculating, the elder Bier had sent Jule to work as a hired hand on the neighborhood farms. Jule began to court Hannah during long walks at night; he took her to neighborhood dances, and they went for rides in his buggy. Hannah soon tired of the attentions of other men. When Mr. Boyle attempted to make love to her, she quit her job to go to work on a farm near Jule's home.

Old Mr. Bier sent Jule to court Selma Duncan, the oldest daughter of a wealthy farmer. Blindly obeying his father, Jule proposed to the girl and was accepted. Then he realized what he had done. Facing Hannah, he was bewildered by her grief, only half aware of his own.

Leaving the neighborhood of Sheboygan, Hannah went to Fond du Lac, where she became a prostitute and lost in a few years her beauty and vitality. At last Jule went to Fond du Lac to bring his former sweetheart back to her home. Hannah ended her years in bitter sterility, answering a call for help from a neighbor, nursing a sick calf, or taking care of someone's children when their mother became ill. She died, prematurely aged and broken, as the result of a fall.

Jule and Selma had one daughter, Rosalia. Selma's sister, Mrs. Strane, had a son, Dan, who was a boy of fourteen when Rosalia was in her early twenties. Mike, a young man with a keen zest for life, worked on Jule's farm. Because his mother was so tight-lipped and because she tried to instill in him a chastity of ignorance and abstinence, Dan had developed an adolescent feeling of frustration and curiosity. He longed to know what sex was, how it affected people, but at the same time he was overcome by an inbred feeling of shame. It was Mike who cleared the way for Dan after they became friends. Mike, who believed that life should be full of experience both physical and mental, made life's processes a wonderful thing, not obscene and dirty, as Dan's mother had led the boy to believe. Breaking away from the mother who had been his idol, Dan replaced her with his new friend, Mike. Mike, in love with Rosalia, shared his deeper feelings with his young friend. Dan had grown up.

Mike loved Rosalia and he desired her, but at first Rosalia resisted his love-making. One afternoon he seduced her. Rosalia's subsequent tears frightened him, but soon she learned to hide her terror of love. She told Mike that they ought to get married to redeem their sin, but Mike's suggestion that Selma might not approve quieted the frightened girl. Mike was not certain that he wanted to marry Rosalia. When Jule quietly told Mike that he had noticed Rosalia's and Mike's love and that he would not object to the marriage if Mike wanted it, Mike felt trapped. He quit his job with Jule and left the Bier farm.

Dan was inconsolable. Having looked upon his cousin and Mike as perfect lovers, he could not understand why Mike should leave. Rosalia brooded, her sense of guilt increasing after Mike's departure. Although she hid her feelings from her parents, Dan knew enough of her affair with Mike to be curious about Rosalia's feelings. But he could learn nothing from her. Rosalia herself was not as calm as she appeared to be. The punishment for love was a child. She felt a surge of emotion within her, and it seemed permanently a part of her. She concluded that she must be with child. It was inevitable; she had sinned and this was to be her harvest. Deserted by her lover-husband, she could not bear to think of her shame. She told some neighbors that she was going to run off to meet Mike, and one night during a snowstorm she left her home.

No one had heard from Rosalia or Mike. Dan and Selma waited through the winter. Once, when Dan went to visit his aunt in Milwaukee, he looked for Mike, but he did not find him. In the spring a neighbor brought the news to Jule that Rosalia's body had been found in the swamp. Fearing that the news would kill the already ailing Selma, Jule made the neighbor and Dan promised to tell no one about Rosalia's body. They buried the girl in the swamp.

All summer Dan worked on his father's farm. He had begun to hate the memory of Mike ever since he had helped Jule bury the body of Rosalia. A hundred times over Dan killed Mike in effigy. In the fall Selma died, and Dan went to live with Jule. The kindly, patient man, who had seen so much of life, won Dan's affections.

Jule wanted Dan to tell him all he knew about Rosalia and Mike. The wonderful understanding of the old man impressed his nephew. Mike had done the best he knew how, Jule maintained. In turn, he told Dan about Hannah Madoc. If Hannah had been Rosalia's mother instead of Selma, Jule said, Rosalia would not have been destroyed through fear. Hannah knew how to handle life. Religious people were always trying to make life better than it was, but life should be accepted at its simple, natural values. Dan accepted his uncle's views.

Dan's father had never understood his son. Having completed his high school education, Dan was becoming restless. His father, realizing that Dan was not cut out for farm work, suggested that he go to college. With high hopes that he would find more answers to his questioning of life, Dan prepared to enter the state university.

APPOINTMENT IN SAMARRA

Type of work: Novel
Author: John O'Hara (1905-   )
Type of plot: Naturalism
Time of plot: 1930
Locale: Pennsylvania
First published: 1934

Principal characters:
JULIAN ENGLISH, a car dealer
CAROLINE, his wife
HARRY REILLY, a rich man
AL GRECCO, the bootlegger's handyman

Critique:

This novel is in the tradition of the roaring twenties; it deals with prohibition, bootleggers, easy morals. In style it recalls F. Scott Fitzgerald, who is mentioned in the book. The character analysis is somewhat in the manner of Lewis' *Babbitt*. *Appointment in Samarra* goes beyond mere pandering to sensationalism, however, in that it sustains a theme of moral judgment, as implied by the title. The lives led by these people can have no fruitful or important end.

The Story:

Julian English was thirty, a congenial seller of cars, popular with the country club set. He had the right connections with Ed Charney, the local bootlegger, and consequently was always well supplied with liquor. He and Caroline had been married four years. They were both natives of Gibbsville and had an assured social position. They had no children.

Just before Christmas they went to a party at the country club. As usual, Julian had had too much to drink. He sat idly twirling his highball and listening to Harry Reilly's stories. Harry was a rich Irish Catholic and definitely a social climber. Actually, Julian hated Harry, although Harry had lent him twenty thousand dollars the previous summer to bolster his Cadillac agency. But that loan did not give Harry the right to make passes at Caroline, Julian thought darkly.

Harry told stories in paragraphs. He always paused at the right time. Julian kept thinking how fitting it would be if he stopped the stories by throwing his drink in Harry's face. Julian grew bored. On impulse he did throw his drink in Harry's face. A big lump of ice hit Harry in the eye.

On the way home Julian and Caroline quarreled furiously. Julian accused his wife of infidelity with Harry, among other people. Caroline said that Julian always drank too much and chased women as well. More important, Harry had a mortgage on the car agency and a good deal of influence with the Catholics, and he was a man who could hold a grudge.

Al Grecco was a little man who as Ed Charney's handyman had a certain standing in the town. He liked Julian because Julian was the only one of the social set who was really friendly. Al grew up on the wrong side of the tracks. Before he was finally sentenced to a year in prison he had been arrested several times. When he got out he worked in a poolroom for a while until his boss died. The widow wanted Al to stay on as manager, but he went to work for Charney. Now he delivered bootleg booze, ran errands, and kept an eye on the torch singer at the Stage Coach, a country inn owned by Charney. Helene Holman, the singer, was Charney's girl, and if she were not carefully watched, she might out of sheer good-heartedness extend her favors to other men.

On Christmas Day Julian woke up with a hangover. As was his custom, he quarreled with the cook. At Caroline's suggestion he went to Harry Reilly's house to apologize. Although Reilly's sister was sympathetic, she brought down word that Harry would not see him; he had a black eye and still nursed a grouch.

Julian's father and mother came for Christmas dinner. The father, a staid, successful surgeon, was suspicious of his son. He always looked for evidence of moral weakness in Julian, for his own father had committed suicide after embezzling a fortune. He was afraid that the English inheritance was stained. Dinner was a trying time.

Caroline and Julian had supper at the club. The usual crowd was there. Julian was unmercifully ribbed in the locker room. In a dismal mood he sat drinking by himself while he waited for a chance to see Father Creedon and ask him to patch up his affair with Harry. The old priest was sympathetic and made light of the incident. After agreeing that Harry was a bore, he promised to send Julian some good Irish whiskey.

Ed Charney was a good family man who spent Christmas Day with his wife and son. He intended to go out to the Stage Coach only in the evening. Then his son became suddenly ill. It looked as if he would have to stay home. Mindful of Helene's weaknesses, he telephoned Al Grecco to go out to the inn and keep watch on her. It was Christmas night and she would be drinking too much. Al did not care for the assignment, but he dutifully went out to the inn and sat down with Helene.

The country club set began to drift in. Froggy Ogden, who was Caroline's one-armed cousin, was the oldest man there; he seemed to feel a responsibility for Julian, who was still drinking. In a spirit of bravado Julian danced several times with Helene, even though Al warned him of Charney's anger. Finally, carried away by the music and too many drinks, Julian and Helene left the dance floor. Caroline and Froggy found Julian in a stupor in the back of a sedan and took him home.

The day after Christmas Caroline went to her mother and announced her intention to divorce Julian. Her mother found it difficult to listen to her daughter; she believed herself above the foibles of the younger generation. Caroline thought herself a heroine in an old-fashioned melodrama. But she was determined not to go back to Julian. After meeting him on the street and quarreling again, she canceled the big party they were to have given that evening.

Al Grecco, as he backed out of the garage with a case of Scotch, had decided to kill Ed Charney. When Charney had phoned him, he had tried to excuse his lack of vigilance: he protested that he had only let Helene dance. But Ed in a rage had said some things that Al could not accept.

Determined to look businesslike, Julian went to his office at the auto agency. He sat importantly at his desk and wrote figures on a piece of scratch paper. The only conclusion he could reach was that he needed more money. One of his salesmen came in to try to lay down the law. He asserted that Julian's difficulties were gossiped about strenuously in the little town of Gibbsville. The offense to Charney was particularly grave: he had been a good friend to the agency and had helped them sell cars to other bootleggers.

Julian left the office in no cheerful mood. He wandered into his club for lunch. Since it was the day after Christmas, the dining-room was deserted except for some elderly lawyers and Froggy. Avoiding his wife's cousin, Julian sat down in a far corner of the room. After picking up his plate, Froggy followed him and began to reproach him for his conduct with the torch singer. He told Julian he had always distrusted him and had warned Caroline about his conduct many times. When Froggy invited him outside to fight, Julian refused because he could not hit a one-armed man. Froggy became more insulting, so that the lawyers came to their table to interfere. Julian was intensely angered when they seemed to side with Froggy. Turning quickly, he hit one of the lawyers full in the mouth and dislodged his false teeth.

Julian went home and fell asleep. About ten o'clock a society reporter awoke him when she came to get a story about the canceled party. After several drinks, he tried to seduce her but with no success. As soon as she left, Julian went to the garage, closed the door, and started the motor. He was pronounced a suicide by the coroner.

THE ARABIAN NIGHTS' ENTERTAINMENTS

(SELECTIONS)

Type of work: Tales
Author: Unknown
Type of plots: Adventure romances
Time of plots: The legendary past
Locale: India, China, Persia, Arabia
First transcribed: Fifteenth century

Principal characters:
SHAHRIAR, Emperor of Persia and India
SCHEHERAZADE, his bride
THE FISHERMAN
THE KING OF THE BLACK ISLES, half man, half marble
SINDBAD THE SAILOR, a wanderer from Baghdad
THE SULTAN OF INDIA
HOUSSAIN,
ALI, and
AHMED, his sons
PERIEBANOU, Ahmed's wife
ALI BABA, a woodcutter in Persia
CASSIM, his brother
MORGIANA, his slave
ALADDIN, a good-for-nothing boy in China

Critique:

The Arabian Nights' Entertainments is the title usually used in English to designate a group of tales more properly called *The Thousand and One Nights.* These stories, adapted and formalized by bazaar storytellers, had their origins in many lands throughout the East and were handed down by word of mouth for hundreds of years. Some present interesting parallels. In the story of "The Three Sisters" a baby is put in a basket to float down a river, a circumstance reminiscent of the Biblical account of Moses in the bulrushes. In Sindbad's various journeys by sea there are similarities to the wanderings of Ulysses as related by Homer, in one instance a close parallel to the Cyclops story. Some of the characters have been drawn from history. But whether the source is folklore, religious tradition, or history, the tales have a timeless quality appealing, from legendary times to the present, to authors of every sort. Stories of Robin Hood have the same flavor. More recently, Gilbert and Sullivan used the "sisters and the cousins and the aunts" grouping such as Aladdin employed to impress the sultan that he had plenty of followers to back his cause as suitor for the hand of the princess. Most scholars believe that the collection took its present form in Cairo in the fifteenth century; it was introduced to the Western World in a translation by Antoine Galland, published in Paris in 1704. Traditionally there were a thousand and one stories told by Scheherazade to her emperor-husband, but in extant manuscripts the tales are not always the same. Practically all modern editions contain only a small portion of the complete collection. Those most frequently reprinted have become minor classics of the world's literature.

The Stories:

Convinced by the treachery of his brother's wife and his own that all women were unfaithful, Shahriar, Emperor of Persia and India, vowed that he would marry a new wife every day and have her executed the next morning. Only Scheherazade, wise as well as beautiful, had the courage to try to save the young women of Persia. On the night of her marriage to Shahriar, she began to tell him a tale which fascinated him so much that he stayed her death for one more night so that he could learn the end of the story. Scheherazade told him stories for one thousand and one nights. At that time, convinced of her worthiness and goodness, he bade her live and made her his consort.

One tale Scheherazade told was "The History of the Fisherman and the Genie": A poor Mussulman fisherman drew from the sea in his nets a strange box with a seal on top. When he pried off the top, a huge genie appeared and threatened him with death, offering the poor man no more than his choice in the manner of his death. The fisherman begged for his life because he had done the genie a favor by releasing him, but the genie declared that he had vowed death to the man who opened the box. Finally the fisherman exclaimed that he could not believe anything as huge and terrible as the genie could ever have been in a space so small. Dissolving into a cloud of smoke, the genie shrank until he could slip back into the box, whereupon the fisherman clamped on the lid. Throwing the box back into the sea, he warned all other fishermen to beware if it should ever fall into their nets.

Another story was "The History of the Young King of the Black Isles": A fisherman caught four beautiful fish, one white, one red, one blue, and one yellow. They were so choice that he took them to the sultan's palace. While the fish were being cooked, a beautiful girl suddenly appeared and talked to the fish, after which they were too charred to take to the sultan. When the same thing happened two days in a row, the sultan was called. After asking where the fish came from, he decided to visit the lake. Nearby he found a beautiful, apparently deserted palace. As he walked through the beautiful halls, he found one in which a king was sitting on a throne. The king apologized for not rising, explaining that his lower half was marble.

He was the King of the Black Isles. When he had learned that his queen was unfaithful to him, he had nearly killed her blackamoor lover. In revenge the queen had cast a spell over her husband, making him half marble. Daily she whipped him, then had him dressed in coarse goat's hair over which his royal robes were placed. In the meantime, while she had kept her lover barely alive, she had changed her husband's town and all its inhabitants into the lake full of fish.

The king told the sultan where the queen's lover was kept. There the sultan went, killed the lover, and put himself in the blackamoor's place. The queen, overjoyed to hear speaking the one she had kept from the edge of death so long, hastened to do all the voice commanded. She restored the king to his human form and the lake to its previous state as a populous town. The four colors of fish indicated the four different religions of the inhabitants.

When the queen returned to the sultan, whom she mistook for her lover, he killed her for her treachery. Thereafter he took home with him the King of the Black Isles, and rewarded the fisherman who had led him to the magic lake.

Shahriar was vastly entertained by "The History of Sindbad the Sailor": A poor porter in Baghdad, resting before the house of Sindbad, bewailed the fact that his lot was harder than that of Sindbad. Overhearing him, Sindbad invited the porter to dine with him. During the meal he told of the hardships he had suffered in order to make his fortune.

On his first voyage, to India by way of the Persian Gulf, Sindbad's ship was becalmed near a small green island. The sailors climbed upon the island, only to find that it was really a sea monster which heaved itself up and swam away. Sindbad was the only man who did not get back to the ship. After days of clinging to a piece of driftwood, he landed on an island where some men were gathered. They led him to a maharajah who treated Sindbad graciously.

When he had been there some time his own ship came into port, and he claimed his bales of goods, to the astonishment of the captain, who thought he had seen Sindbad killed at sea. Then Sindbad sailed home in the ship in which he had set out.

The porter was so impressed with the first tale that he came again to hear a second. On his second voyage Sindbad was left asleep on an island where the sailors had rested. There he found a huge roc's egg. Knowing that the parent bird would return to the nest at dusk, he waited. When it came, he used his turban to tie himself to the bird's leg. In the morning the bird flew to a place surrounded by mountains. There Sindbad freed himself when the bird descended to pick up a serpent. The place seemed deserted, except for large serpents. Diamonds of great size were scattered throughout the valley.

Sindbad remembered that merchants were said to throw joints of meat into the diamond valley, from which big eagles carried the joints to their nests close to shore. At the nests the merchants frightened away the birds and recovered diamonds which had stuck to the meat. Sindbad collected some large diamonds. Then with his turban he fastened a piece of meat to his back and lay down. An eagle picked him up and carried him to its nest. When he was dropped into a nest, the merchant who claimed the nest was indignant and accused Sindbad of stealing his property. Sindbad offered him some choice diamonds. In return the merchant was glad to take the adventurer back to civilization.

On his third voyage Sindbad was wrecked on an island inhabited by cannibal dwarfs and huge black creatures with only one eye in the middle of their foreheads. Sindbad and his friends blinded one black giant, but two others helped the blind one to chase the sailors. By the time the giants and a large serpent had overtaken them, only Sindbad was lucky enough to escape.

Sindbad sailed from a port in Persia on his fourth voyage. He and his friends were shipwrecked on an island inhabited by black cannibals who fattened the sailors before killing them. Sindbad refused the food, grew too thin to interest the black men, and finally found his way to the shore. There he met white men who took him to their kingdom. To please the king, Sindbad made a fine saddle. In appreciation the king married Sindbad to a beautiful girl. In that country a man or woman was buried alive if the spouse died. When Sindbad's wife died, he was put in a tomb with a small amount of bread and water. As he ate the last of his food he heard an animal snuffling, then running away. Following the sound, he found himself on the shore and hailed a ship which carried him home.

Sindbad used his own ship on his fifth voyage. After his sailors had broken open a roc's egg, the parent rocs hurled tremendous stones on the ship and broke it to pieces. Sindbad came under the power of the Old Man of the Sea and escaped only after making the old man so intoxicated that he loosed his death grip on Sindbad. Again Sindbad found a ship to take him home; he did much profitable trading on the way.

All his companions on the sixth voyage succumbed on a beautiful but lifeless coast. Sindbad, expecting to die, built a raft which he put in an underground river to drift where it would. When he reached the kingdom of Serendib, he had to be revived. He found the country exceedingly rich and the people kind. When he asked to be allowed to go home, the king sent him there with rich presents for Sindbad's ruler, the Caliph Harun-al-Rashid of Baghdad.

Sindbad made his seventh and final voyage to take gifts from the caliph to the King of Serendib. He carried them safely, but his return trip was delayed when corsairs seized his ship and sold the sailors into slavery. Sindbad, sold to an ivory merchant, was ordered to shoot an elephant a day. Annoyed at Sindbad's persistence, an elephant picked him up and took him to an elephant burial ground, to which Sindbad and his owner returned many times to gather ivory. As a reward, the merchant sent Sindbad home with rich goods.

Another diverting tale was "The History of Prince Ahmed": Houssain, Ali, and Ahmed, sons of the Sultan of India, were all in love with the Princess Nouronnihar, their father's ward. To determine who should be the bridegroom, the sultan sent them out to find the most extraordinary things they could. Whoever brought back the rarest object would win the hand of the princess.

Houssain found a magic carpet which would transport him wherever he wished. Ali found an ivory tube containing a glass which would show any object he wished to see. Ahmed found an artificial apple, the odor of which would cure any illness.

The three princes met before they journeyed home. As they displayed their gifts, Houssain, looking through the tube, saw the princess apparently at the point of death. They all jumped on his magic carpet and were whisked to her bedroom, where Ahmed used his magic apple to revive her. The sultan could not determine which article was the most unusual, for all had been of use to effect the princess' recovery. He suggested an archery contest. Prince Ali shot farther than Houssain, but Ahmed's arrow could not be found. The sultan decided in favor of Ali. Houssain retired to become a dervish. Ahmed, instead of attending the wedding, went in search of his arrow, which he found at the foot of a mountain, much farther away than he could have shot. Looking around, he found a door into the mountain. When he passed through the door, he found a fairy called Periebanou, who pleased him so much that he married her.

When Ahmed went to visit his father, he refused to discuss where or how he lived, but he appeared to be so rich that the courtiers grew jealous and persuaded the sultan that it was dangerous to have his son so powerful a neighbor. The sultan asked Ahmed to perform unreasonable tasks, made possible only by Periebanou's help; but while fulfilling one request her brother became so annoyed with the sultan that he killed him. Ahmed became sultan and afterward dealt kindly with his brothers.

Scheherazade pleased her lord also with "The History of Ali Baba and the Forty Thieves": Ali Baba was a Persian woodcutter. One day, to hide from a band of strange horsemen, he climbed a tree under which they halted. When the leader cried, "Open, Sesame!" to a rock nearby, a door opened through which the men carried their heavy packs. After the men left, Ali Baba used the secret word to investigate the cave. He found such riches there that the gold he took could never be missed.

He and his wife were content with that amount, but his brother Cassim, to whom he had told his story, was greedy for more wealth. Without telling Ali Baba, Cassim went to the cave. He was so excited by the gold that he forgot the password and could not get out. The robbers found and murdered him.

The robbers tried to find Ali Baba in order to kill him and so keep the secret of their hoard. The leader brought his men, hidden in oil jars, to Ali Baba's house, but a beautiful slave, Morgiana, went in search of oil, discovered the ruse, and killed the bandits. Again the captain, disguised as a merchant, entered the house, but Morgiana saw through his disguise and killed him.

To reward Morgiana, Ali Baba not only made her a free woman, but he also gave her to his son in marriage. Ali Baba was then the only one who knew the secret of the cave. He used the hidden wealth in moderation and passed the secret on to his posterity.

No less pleasing was "The History of Aladdin, or the Wonderful Lamp": Aladdin was a youthful vagabond who lived in China. An African magician, sensing that Aladdin would suit his plans, and pretending to be the boy's rich uncle, took him to a secret place to get a magic lamp. Passing through halls stored with treasures, Aladdin filled his gown with so many things that he could not give the magician the lamp at the moment he wanted it, and the magician sealed him up in the earth. By chance Aladdin rubbed a ring which the magician had given him. A genie appeared and escorted him home.

When Aladdin showed his mother the lamp, she tried to clean it to sell. As she rubbed, another genie appeared from whom Aladdin asked food. The food appeared on silver trays that Aladdin sold one by one to a Jewish chapman. When an honest jeweler stopped Aladdin one day and asked to buy the silver, Aladdin began to realize the great riches he had at his finger tips, enough to win him the sultan's daughter as his wife.

Because the grand vizier wanted his own son to marry the princess, he suggested many outrageous demands which the sultan made upon Aladdin before he could be considered a suitor. The genies produced slaves, costumes, jewelry, gold, and chargers in such profusion that the sultan gladly accepted Aladdin's suit. Overnight Aladdin had the genie build a magnificent palace next to the sultan's.

Life went smoothly until the African magician, while Aladdin was away, persuaded the princess to trade the old lamp for a new one. Then the magician transported the great palace to Africa. When Aladdin came home, the sultan threatened him with arrest, but allowed him forty days in which to find the palace with the princess therein. Rubbing his ring by chance and summoning its genie, Aladdin asked to be carried wherever his palace was. The princess was overjoyed to see him. After he had killed the magician by a ruse, he ordered the genie of the lamp to transport the palace back to China. There, after disposing of the magician's brother, who had followed them, Aladdin and the princess lived happily ever after.

THE ARBITRATION

Type of work: Drama
Author: Menander (342-291 B.C.)
Type of plot: Comedy of manners
Time of plot: Fourth century B.C.
Locale: A suburb of Athens
First presented: c. 310 B.C.

Principal characters:

CHARISIUS, a young Athenian
PAMPHILA, his wife
SMICRINES, miserly father of Pamphila
ONESIMUS, Charisius' slave
CHAERESTRATUS, Charisius' friend and neighbor
SYRISCUS, a charcoal burner
DAVUS, a goatherd
HABROTONON, a pretty harp-playing slave
SOPHRONA, a nurse

Critique:

What Aristophanes was to the great age of Greek comedy, Menander was to New Comedy, that form characterized by the abandonment of the chorus and the intervention of the gods and by its concern with domestic problems of ordinary mortals. Tradition made Menander author of a hundred plays, of which about eighty titles are still known, but for centuries all trace of his writings, except for a few fragments, was lost. In the late nineteenth century papyri recovered from Egyptian tombs enabled students to get a better idea of Menander's writing. Still more recent discoveries provided almost complete versions of two of his comedies: *The Girl with the Shorn Locks,* about a soldier-lover who mistreated his mistress and almost lost her, but won her back by marrying her, and the *Arbitration*. Actually, the title refers only to one amusing scene in this comedy of a harsh father, a knavish slave, and a slave girl with a heart of gold. The play contains stock material and situations. The nurse, even to her name, is a type, as are the servant and the avaricious father. But Menander's clever plotting is shown in his use of the miser as the arbitrator whose decision regarding the fate of his own grandson brings trouble to him and provides material for the picaresque servant's amusing insults. The action is lively and the dialogue amusing, especially in the scene in which the two slaves, Onesimus and Habrotonon, outmaneuver each other.

The Story:

Pamphila, the daughter of a respected but miserly Athenian citizen, had been ravished by a drunken young man of ordinarily good behavior during the night festival of the Tauropolia. The only clue she had to his identity was a signet ring which he had left in her possession. A short time later Pamphila was married to her ravisher, a young Athenian named Charisius, and Smicrines, her father, provided a good dowry for his idealistic but rather priggish son-in-law. Pamphila, who soon learned to love her husband, gave birth to her child during his absence and, acting on the advice of her nurse Sophrona, exposed the infant and with the baby a pouch containing assorted tokens, including the ring. Charisius, learning of the birth from his prying servant Onesimus, decided that the child could not be his. Instead of repudiating Pamphila, however, he left home and began to waste his substance in rich feasts given at the home of his friend Chaerestratus, who lived next door. Pamphila was distracted because the husband she loved had deserted her for the company of hired dancing girls and harp players.

So matters stood when Smicrines came to investigate reports of Charisius' conduct; he had heard that his son-in-law was spending every night for a hired harp player a sum sufficient to feed a slave for a month. Just before his arrival a conceited, loud-mouthed cook, Carion, on his way to prepare a meal in the house of Chaerestratus, vainly questioned Charisius' servant Onesimus about his master; the cook also wanted to know why Charisius neglected his wife and paid twelve drachmas a night to be entertained by the lovely, harp-playing slave, Habrotonon. While Carion and Onesimus were talking, the musician was delivered by her master. The slave dealer managed to persuade bemused Charisius that he owed money for several previous nights' entertainment. Charisius paid, but wily Onesimus recovered the overpayments for himself.

When Smicrines appeared, Onesimus managed to befuddle the anxious, angry father with the story that it was Chaerestratus who was giving the parties and that Charisius attended only to protect his friend's possessions and good name.

After Smicrines had gone into his son-in-law's house, two of Chaerestratus' tenants appeared to pay their rent. They were Davus, a goatherd, and Syriscus, a charcoal burner accompanied by his wife carrying a baby. While they waited they argued over another matter. A month earlier Davus had come upon a baby exposed in the hills. His first impulse had been to adopt the foundling, but later, having calculated the cost of rearing a child, he was returning the infant to the place where he had found it when Syriscus offered to adopt the baby in place of his own child who had just died. Now Syriscus, having learned that Davus had kept the trinkets left beside the baby, claimed them because they might some day help to identify the child's parents. **Davus had refused to give up the tokens,** but he had agreed to let someone else decide the matter. Smicrines, reappearing from the house of Charisius, was persuaded to listen to the story and give his decision. Deciding that the trinkets ought to go with the baby, he ordered Davus to give Syriscus the pouch containing them.

While Syriscus and his wife were looking over the contents of the pouch, Onesimus recognized the signet ring that his master had lost at the time of the Tauropolia festival a year before. The slave borrowed it to show his master, then hesitated because to return it would be to accuse Charisius of having fathered the abandoned baby. Habrotonon came came along about that time, saw the ring, heard the story, and concocted a scheme of her own. She would learn the truth by wearing the ring and seeing if Charisius recognized it. In that case, she would claim that she had been the girl he had ravished and so rescue the child from the life of a slave. Onesimus knew very well that her chief purpose was to win her own freedom.

Smicrines reappeared, determined to demand the return of his daughter and her dowry. The neighbors tried to dissuade him by saying that everything would turn out all right. As the party ended, broken up by Habrotonon and her claim that the child was hers, Onesimus infuriated the miser by congratulating him on bringing happiness to everybody by his arbitration.

Pamphila begged her father not to meddle with her marriage; she had no desire for another husband, she declared. If Charisius was infatuated with a harpist, that was only a temporary estrangement. At her father's announcement that his current love was the mother of his child, Pamphila fainted.

Regaining consciousness, she accused her nurse Sophrona of causing all the trouble by preventing her confession to Charisius after the birth of the child. While they argued, Habrotonon happened by and recognized Pamphila as the girl who had been Charisius' companion of a year earlier. She told the patrician so when he came to keep his promise to arrange for her freedom. At first he regarded the story as another of her lies. To save himself, Onesimus also accused her of having invented the story. Habrotonon maintained stoutly that it was true, and she declared that she would rather see the child looked after properly than win her own freedom.

Chaerestratus, who had always admired the lovely slave, began questioning her about her own early history, but she remembered nothing of her infancy, not even her name. Then the sight of a small silver cup with an indecipherable inscription among the trinkets of Syriscus caused her to comment that she had once possessed a similar cup. Smicrines, seeing the cup for the first time, identified it as having once belonged to his oldest daughter, who had been kidnapped by the slave traders during the siege of the city some years before. Sophrona, recognizing the harp player as Smicrines' long-lost daughter Clearista, stirred the girl's recollection by using her baby name of "grasshopper."

Chaerestratus, who had loved the girl from the first, now asked to marry her, and when he showed miserly Smicrines how he could get his daughter back without spending money in court trials, he got both the girl and her father's blessing. Rascally Onesimus, instead of getting the beating he deserved, was probably given his freedom.

ARCADIA

Type of work: Novel
Author: Sir Philip Sidney (1554-1586)
Type of plot: Pastoral romance
Time of plot: Classical antiquity
Locale: Arcadia, in Greece
First published: 1590

Principal characters:
PRINCE PYROCLES (ZELMANE), son of Evarchus, King of Macedon
PRINCE MUSIDORUS (DORUS), Duke of Thessalia, Pyrocles' friend, Evarchus' nephew
BASILIUS, Duke of Arcadia
GYNECIA, his wife
PAMELA, his older daughter
PHILOCLEA, his younger daughter
PHILANAX, Arcadian general, Basilius' friend
DAMETAS, Basilius' chief herdsman
MISO, his wife
MOPSA, his daughter
EVARCHUS, King of Macedon

Critique:

Although the original version of this work was intended by Sidney as an entertainment for his sister Mary, Countess of Pembroke, and her friends (the tale was originally titled *The Countess of Pembroke's Arcadia*), this light pastoral story holds a significant place in the development of the English novel, for it serves as a bridge between the delicately written Italian romances and the more sturdy prose tales of the later Elizabethan period in England. The original *Arcadia* was revised and considerably enlarged by Sidney into an unfinished version which was published in 1590. The "old" *Arcadia,* although not published in its complete and original form until 1926, clearly shows the complete primary intention of its author. It has a rustic charm and coherence of plot not nearly so evident in the more ambitious later version. The presence of occasional passages of poetry and of the four eclogues, largely in the form of poetry, which are inserted among the five "books" of the romance is a carryover from the earlier continental romances; but the plot, skillfully handled for its time, and the philosophical asides of the author pointed the way toward a more serious genre of fiction to follow.

The Story:

Basilius, the powerful Duke of Arcadia, a quiet and peaceful province of Greece, ruled his faithful subjects happily and well. Being overcome by an ungovernable curiosity to learn what the future held for him, his wife Gynecia, and his beautiful daughters Pamela and Philoclea, he went to consult the Oracle at Delphos. There he was told that his older daughter, Pamela, would be stolen from him; his younger daughter would engage in an unsuitable love affair; his wife would commit adultery; and a foreign ruler would sit upon his throne—all within a year.

Basilius told the prophecy to his friend Philanax, whom he left in charge of the country while he, in an effort to escape the destiny foretold by the Oracle, took his wife and daughters into a secluded part of the country to live for the year. Basilius lived in one of two lodges with his wife and Philoclea; in the other he put Pamela under the care of Dametas, a rude shepherd of whose honesty Basilius had a high opinion.

Shortly after the duke's retirement, two young princes, Pyrocles and Musidorus, arrived in Arcadia. Young men of great courage, personal beauty, and integrity, who had been reared together in close friendship, they had been swept ashore at Lydia after experiencing a shipwreck and many strange adventures as well as performing many acts of daring and honor.

Pyrocles saw a picture of Philoclea, learned of her enforced retirement, and fell in love with her. Determined to see the princess face to face, he told Musidorus of his love and of his plan to disguise himself as a chivalric Amazon and in woman's guise to approach Philoclea. For a name, he took that of his lost lady, Zelmane.

After a lengthy debate, in which Musidorus attempted to convince his friend of the folly of love, Pyrocles still remained firm in his intention; and the two princes traveled to the place of the duke's retirement, Pyrocles in his disguise as an Amazon. While Musidorus waited in a nearby wood, Pyrocles, now Zelmane, sat down and sang a melancholy song which awakened Dametas, who hastened to the duke's lodge to tell him of a strange woman who had arrived in the vicinity.

Basilius, upon seeing Pyrocles in his disguise, fell in love with the supposed Amazon. His true identity still unsuspected, he was introduced to the duke's family and invited to remain with them for a while. Soon a young shepherd appeared. He was Musidorus, who had fallen in love with Pamela on sight and assumed a disguise of his own. After telling his contrived tale of being sent by a friend to serve Dametas, Musidorus, under the name Dorus, was taken by the chief herdsman as a servant.

Zelmane saved Philoclea from a savage lion, but in doing so he was discovered by Gynecia, the duke's wife, to be a man; she immediately fell in love with him. Dorus, meanwhile, saved Pamela from a bear. Before long both princesses began to become enamored of the disguised princes.

The Arcadian shepherds, as was their custom, met and exchanged poetic songs for their own entertainment and that of the duke's family and his guests. The songs, often accompanied by dancing, chiefly concerned the gods and the human passions. This occasion only increased the intensity of the tangle of love relationships that had so rapidly developed.

After the pastoral festival, Gynecia and Basilius both declared their love for Zelmane, and Philoclea was puzzled greatly by the strange passion she felt for the person she thought a woman. In the meantime Dorus pretended to be in love with Mopsa in order to be near Pamela, who in this manner became aware of his affection for her. He also managed, by subtle stories and poems, to reveal his true station to her.

Pyrocles, distressed by the advances of Basilius, revealed his true identity to Philoclea, who at first embraced him joyously but then became ashamed of her sudden show of affection. Gynecia, suspecting this attachment, was overcome with jealousy.

While Gynecia, having sent Philoclea home from a meeting with Pyrocles, was starting to tell the disguised prince of the depth of her love, they were attacked by some roving ruffians. Pyrocles, Basilius, and then Dorus with the aid of some shepherds drove off the attackers. This was only the prelude to an uprising by the citizens of a nearby Arcadian village, who had become enraged by the duke's seeming unconcern about his country. In an impassioned speech, however, Pyrocles convinced them of their error and stirred in them a renewed loyalty to Basilius. This triumph was celebrated by another pastoral entertainment, largely taken up with a poetic debate between Reason and Passion. Once more, the poems, dances, and stories served to increase the depth of the emotions felt by the royal party.

Dorus then told his friend of his moderate success with Pamela, whom he had urged to flee with him to Thessalia. Pyrocles, sharing Dorus' sorrow over their separation, decided to press his suit of Philoclea and to rid himself of the importunate demands of Basilius and Gynecia. When they renewed their entreaties, Pyrocles, still in his disguise and fearing to deny them outright, gave them hopeful but obscure answers.

Meanwhile, Dorus, having tricked Dametas and his family into leaving the lodge, had escaped with Pamela to a forest on the way to Thessalia. There they were set upon by a band of ruffians.

The false Zelmane, hard pressed by Gynecia's declarations, was forced to pretend a deep passion for her, a situation which so distressed Philoclea that she kept to her room in the lodge, in profound sorrow. In order to be free to execute a plan to be alone with Philoclea, Pyrocles moved from the lodge to a dark cave not far away. He then took the duke and his wife aside separately and made an assignation with each at the same time in the cave.

When Basilius met Gynecia, who had dressed like Zelmane, in the cave, he failed to recognize his wife. Gynecia, ashamed of her actions, embraced him lovingly. Back at the lodge, Pyrocles, now in his own person, crept into Philoclea's room and, after a brief time, won her over and stayed the night.

Dametas, realizing that he had been tricked, began a search for Pamela. Entering the duke's lodge by a secret entrance, he discovered Philoclea and Pyrocles asleep. He left hastily to inform the local citizens of the treachery.

In the cave Gynecia, angered at her husband's praise of Zelmane, revealed her identity. Basilius, ashamed, repented his weakness, pledged renewed love to his wife, and drank a long draught from a cup of a mysterious beverage standing close by. The liquid was a potion, believed by Gynecia to be a love philter, which the duchess had brought to give to Zelmane. After drinking it, Basilius fell to the ground and appeared to die.

The duke's death being discovered, Philanax, with a troop of soldiers, imprisoned Gynecia, Pyrocles, and Philoclea.

The rogues who had attacked Dorus and Pamela, the remnant of the rebellious band which had earlier caused much trouble, overwhelmed the lovers and captured them. While in captivity, Musidorus revealed his actual name and rank. A short time later some of Philanax's soldiers, sent to search for Pamela, came upon the band and their prisoners. Recognizing the princess, the soldiers returned the entire group to Philanax, who put the lovers under restraint.

There was now a great turmoil, and many opinions and beliefs were exchanged as to the real guilt in the death of the duke and the disgrace of the princesses.

Hearing that Evarchus, King of Macedon, had arrived in Arcadia to visit the duke, Philanax persuaded him to be the judge in the trial of the five people involved. Gynecia admitted her guilt and begged to be executed. Then Evarchus, not recognizing his son and his nephew because they had been away for such a long time, condemned the two princes to death and the princesses to milder punishments. Even after learning the true identity of the young men, Evarchus refused, from a deep sense of justice, to alter his verdict.

At that point Basilius, who had swallowed only a powerful sleeping potion, awoke. The young lovers and the duchess were promptly forgiven. Basilius pondered on how accurately the Oracle's prophecy had been fulfilled and how happily events had turned out. The princes and their loves, soon wed, assumed the high stations for which their rank fitted them.

ARGENIS

Type of work: Prose romance
Author: John Barclay (1582-1621)
Type of plot: Pseudo-classical heroic allegory
Time of plot: The Hellenistic era
Locale: Sicily and the Western Mediterranean
First published: 1621

Principal characters:

POLIARCHUS, the name assumed by Astioristes, Prince of France
ARGENIS, Princess of Sicily
MELEANDER, King of Sicily, her father
ARCHOMBROTUS, the name assumed by Hyempsal, Prince of Mauritania, during his sojourn in Sicily
HYANISBE, Queen of Mauritania
RADIROBANES, King of Sardinia
LYCOGENES, a Sicilian noble, leader of the rebellion against Meleander
ARSIDAS, a Sicilian noble, Governor of Messana, a friend to Poliarchus
GELANORUS, a French noble sojourning in Sicily in the guise of Poliarchus' servant
SELENISSA, a Sicilian matron, Argenis' nurse and companion
TIMOCLEA, a Sicilian matron, a friend to Poliarchus and, later, Argenis' companion
NICOPOMPUS, a Sicilian courtier-poet of pro-monarchial sentiments

Critique:

John Barclay, the son of a Scot, was born in France, died in Italy, and wrote in Latin. His last work, *Argenis,* finished only a month before his death, became immediately popular and remained so for two centuries. Seven years after its publication it had been honored by three translations into English (the first, by Ben Jonson, in 1623, is, unfortunately, not extant), and as late as the nineteenth century it received the high praise of Samuel Taylor Coleridge. Its original popularity was not due entirely to its artistic merits, however, for it was as satire that it first caught the fancy of readers on both sides of the Channel. Barclay had already a reputation as a satirist, but in *Argenis* the objects of his attacks are generalized behind a screen of allegory. The story of the love of Poliarchus and Argenis is supposed to represent the wars and intrigues in France before the Concordat under Henry IV. As revealed by the *Clovis* published in the edition of 1623, Sicily, the scene of the action, stands for France, with Argenis a personified symbol of the throne contested during the religious wars and Poliarchus and Archombrotus representing different aspects of Henry of Navarre (later Henry IV). Meleander is Henry III; Mauritania is England; Hyanisbe, Elizabeth; and Radirobanes, the rapacious and deceitful Philip of Spain. The whole work is aimed at opponents of the monarchical system. Although interest in the work as satire lasted only as long as the controversy over the divine right of kings remained a vital issue, *Argenis* was long praised for the grandeur of its expression, the nobility of its theme, the heroic stature of its characters. Today, however, only its historical interest remains; it stands with Honoré d'Urfé's *L'Astrée* as an interesting transitional work between the Greek-influenced prose romances of the sixteenth century on the one hand, and the interminable French romances of La Calprenède and Mlle. de Scudéry on the other.

The Story:

Before the Mediterranean world had ever come under the dominance of Rome, a young adventurer from Africa landed on the shores of Sicily and was met by a distraught lady who begged him to assist her friend, who was being attacked by thieves. The young man, who gave his name as Archombrotus, sped to the rescue only to find that his help was not needed: the lady's friend had dispatched the thieves singlehanded. The three returned to the lady's house where Archombrotus learned that the lady was Timoclea, a respected Sicilian matron, and that her friend was young Poliarchus, also a stranger to Sicily, who had distinguished himself in the service of King Meleander against a rebel army led by the traitorous noble, Lycogenes. Poliarchus, having urged more forceful resistance to the rebellion, had been banished when the over-cautious king declared a truce. Meleander, Archombrotus learned, had a beautiful daughter, Argenis; Archombrotus concluded immediately that Poliarchus was in love with her.

While engaged in their discussion, they noticed signal fires blazing on the surrounding hilltops. Timoclea explained that these were beacons fired to warn the people that a traitor was at large. Presently a servant entered with word that Poliarchus was the one accused of treachery; the "thieves" had been Lycogenes' ambassadors, and the king had interpreted his defense as an attempt to break the truce. Timoclea, loyal to her guest, hid him immediately in a cave on her estate and then sent for his friend Arsidas, the Governor of Messana. Arsidas arrived promptly, and he and Poliarchus' servant, Gelanorus, devised a plan whereby it was given out that Poliarchus had been drowned after a fall from his horse. Arsidas hastened to Argenis to tell her, secretly, the truth so that she should not be distracted by false news of Poliarchus' death.

Meanwhile, rustics on Timoclea's estate mistook Archombrotus for Poliarchus, seized him, and carried him off to the king. Meleander, realizing their mistake, took Archombrotus into his council but praised the peasants for their loyalty. At the same time, Arsidas arranged to have Argenis see Poliarchus. As a priestess of Pallas presiding over the sacrifice to celebrate the truce, she was to insist that the common people be allowed to worship the goddess beforehand, and Poliarchus was to come before her in the dress of a peasant. Thus the lovers were briefly united. Poliarchus then fled with Arsidas to Italy. Argenis, throwing herself into a frenzy, claimed that the goddess would not honor the sacrifice or the truce.

Enraged, Lycogenes resumed the war, and Meleander fled with his train to the fortified seaport of Epercte. On the way he was almost drowned when his coach, driven by a rebel spy, plunged into the river, but he was saved by Archombrotus, who was thus made secure in his favor.

The war going badly for the king, Archombrotus convinced him that their only hope lay in the return of the champion Poliarchus. The king sent a precious brooch to Poliarchus as a peace offering; however, spies of Lycogenes poisoned the brooch, and the rebel sent his own messenger with a letter warning Poliarchus that the brooch was fatal. If the king's messenger arrived first, Poliarchus would be dead; if Lycogenes', he would become an enemy of the king—either way, Lycogenes would no longer have to fear him.

But Poliarchus and his servant Gelanorus had already left for Sicily. Shipwrecked off the coast, they were rudely hauled aboard a pirate craft. The two routed the pirates and turned the ship over to its rightful owner.

Discovering among the pirate treasure jewels and letters belonging to Queen Hyanisbe of Mauritania, Poliarchus immediately ordered the ship to Mauritania so that he could return the royal property. The queen was delighted, for the letters concerned the whereabouts of her knight-errant son. She ordered a celebration which would have continued indefinitely had not Poliarchus been anxious to return to his beloved. But in spite of his anxiety, he was forced to stay when smitten by an attack of the ague. Gelanorus was dispatched with letters in his stead.

In the meantime, at Epercte, Meleander's situation was becoming untenable.

When matters seemed hopeless, the tremendous fleet of Radirobanes, King of Sardinia, arrived to help defend the rights of the monarch against rebel upstarts. The combined forces of Meleander and Radirobanes routed the army of Lycogenes, and Archombrotus slew the rebel leader in single combat.

The rebellion ended, Archombrotus became the king's favorite. Having fallen in love with Argenis, during the siege, and with Poliarchus gone, he thought himself the foremost claimant for her hand. But Radirobanes also announced his claim to the hand of the princess. Meleander was in a quandary. Archombrotus was his favorite, but both gratitude and the armed fleet in the harbor lent weight to Radirobanes' cause. Meleander solved the problem by leaving the decision up to Argenis. The Sardinian ruler advanced his plea; the Sicilian princess rebuffed him. Radirobanes then gained the confidence of Argenis' nurse and companion, Selenissa, who in nightly installments told him the following story:

Lycogenes had also demanded Argenis and, being refused, had threatened to abduct her. To forestall his design, Meleander had his daughter, along with Selenissa and certain young ladies of her court, placed in an inaccessible and heavily guarded castle. While they were thus secluded, a beautiful stranger who gave her name as Theocrine came to Selenissa and begged sanctuary. Admitted to the castle, she shared the chamber of the princess. When Lycogenes' men stormed the castle, Theocrine seized a sword and put the attackers to flight. The supposed Theocrine was in reality Poliarchus, who, having heard of the beauty of Argenis, had used that disguise to be near her. When he begged forgiveness, Argenis immediately fell in love with him. He had then disappeared, to return later in Meleander's service. The king, convinced that Theocrine was warlike Pallas, had dedicated his daughter to the service of that beautiful, austere goddess.

Despairing of winning the princess by fair means, Radirobanes planned to blackmail her into acceptance of his proposal, but Selenissa persuaded him that abduction would be the better course. But Argenis, having overheard part of Selenissa's betrayal, feigned an illness that kept her inaccessible, thereby frustrating Radirobanes' plans. Thwarted, Radirobanes returned with his fleet to Sardinia, leaving with Meleander a letter informing him of the true identity of Theocrine and demanding payment of three hundred talents for his aid. When Meleander confronted his daughter with the information he had received, she denied any untoward dealings in the affair. Meleander, only half believing her, demanded that she marry Archombrotus. Selenissa, seeing the damage she had done, killed herself, and Timoclea succeeded her as chief lady of the household.

Meanwhile, Poliarchus, having recovered from his illness, had returned in disguise to Sicily. Seeing no chance of amicable dealings with Meleander, he asked Argenis to delay her marriage to Archombrotus while he found some means to settle the matter. Then he sailed away. Weeks passed and he failed to return. Finally Argenis sent Arsidas to find him, with letters pleading for his return.

Arsidas' ship was wrecked, however, and he was rescued and taken aboard the leading ship of a great war fleet. Gobrias, the captain, received Arsidas hospitably and informed him that the fleet belonged to the King of France, who was preparing to attack Sicily. The king himself was commanding the flagship, which was leading the second half of the fleet.

To entertain his guest, Gobrias told him the strange history of the French ruler, King Astioristes—how his mother had kept his birth a secret so that he would not be murdered in a rebellion that was going on at the time, how he had been reared by foster parents, had proved himself a hero in battle, and had finally been revealed as the true prince; how he had heard of the beauty of the Sicilian princess, Argenis, and had sojourned in Sicily under the name of Poliarchus to win her, and how now—as king, the old king having died in his absence—he was sailing to claim her.

Arsidas immediately identified himself as Poliarchus' friend and offered his assistance. Gobrias was delighted, but before the two halves of the fleet could establish a rendezvous, a terrible storm came up, driving each part to a different point on the African coast. The flotilla commanded by the French king found safety in the harbor of Mauritania, and once again Astioristes, the one-time Poliarchus, was entertained by Hyanisbe. His arrival was most fortunate, for Radirobanes was threatening Mauritania. Hyanisbe had sent for her son, Hyempsal, who was at the court of King Meleander in Sicily, but he had not yet returned. When the Sardinian troops arrived, they were repulsed by the French. Poliarchus and Radirobanes met in single combat, and the Sardinian ruler was slain. Disheartened, his followers were routed, but Poliarchus was injured and again confined in Mauritania.

Returning belatedly to his mother's defense, Hyempsal turned out to be Archombrotus. Hyanisbe was dismayed when she found that her son and her protector were enemies; but when she learned the cause of their quarrel she was relieved and she wrote to Meleander a letter which, she promised, would end their difficulties.

While Astioristes was recovering from his wounds, Hyempsal led a successful expedition to Sardinia. Then the two returned to Sicily and presented Hyanisbe's sealed letter to Meleander. The message proved as effective as Hyanisbe had promised. Hyempsal, it was revealed, was the son of Meleander and the king's secret first wife, Hyanisbe's sister. Thus he was both the heir to the Sicilian throne and Argenis' half-brother. Since there was now no obstacle to the marriage of Argenis and Astioristes, Meleander gave them his blessing, the wedding took place at once, and an epithalamium was written by the courtier-poet Nicopompus.

DER ARME HEINRICH

Type of work: Poem
Author: Hartmann von Aue (c. 1170–between 1210 and 1220)
Type of plot: Didactic romance
Time of plot: Late twelfth century
Locale: Germany
First transcribed: Between 1192 and 1202

Principal characters:
Heinrich von Aue, a Swabian knight
A Peasant Girl

Critique:

Hartmann von Aue, a knight in the service of a Swabian nobleman and one of the first truly German writers, received his education in monastery schools. Later he traveled in France and translated many French poems into Middle High German. The death of his much admired master in 1195 was the chief reason for his participation in a crusade in Palestine, possibly in 1197. This experience revealed the basic conflict of his life, the struggle to choose between the pen and the sword. The presence of secular and religious elements in *Der arme Heinrich* mirrors the author's dilemma as knight and poet in one person. Regardless of the existence of other legends embodied in the story, *Der arme Heinrich* is considered one of the earliest forms of original German literature. The poem shows the influence of martyr legends popular at the time, especially in the inspired speech of the heroine, a simple peasant girl. The writer also displays remarkable ability for characterization and gives the reader a vivid picture of medieval life and thinking. Hartmann von Aue is regarded as the founder of the German court epic, surpassed only by that master of the chivalric romance, Wolfram von Eschenbach (c. 1170-c. 1220).

The Story:

Heinrich von Aue, a Swabian knight, was a fortunate man. Wealthy and of noble birth, he was known throughout the land for his high standard of honor. Fulfillment of his obligations as a knight was his goal; nothing but purest virtue and upright truth marked his life.

Suddenly, however, all his happiness was blighted by a terrible disaster: Heinrich became leprous. As in the case of Job in ancient times, his physical appearance deteriorated rapidly; but he did not have the patience of Job. All his life seemed a curse to him, and his pride left him without friends. His cheerful nature vanished; he detested even the light of day. Only one thing kept him alive, the hope of a cure for his terrible disease.

Trying to find a cure for his malady, he searched out the most famous doctors in all Europe. The school of Montpellier was known for its able doctors and so he went hopefully to that place, only to learn that there was no medicine to heal him. Disappointed, he traveled to Salerno, where he talked to many skilled physicians. At last he met a master who told him that he could be healed, yet the cure itself would be of such a nature that it would be impossible to achieve it; therefore the doctor preferred not to talk about it.

Desperately, Heinrich begged the doctor to reveal his remedy. After some hesitation the physician yielded and told the knight that he could be cured only by the heart's blood of a virgin who would submit willingly, out of love, to a fatal operation.

Heinrich, realizing the hopelessness of his situation, returned sadly to Swabia. All his worldly belongings he gave to the poor and to the monks. Of his land and estates, he kept no more than a clearing in a wood where a poor but contented peasant lived. When Heinrich decided to live in his house in the wood, the peasant and his family did all they could to ease the suffering of the leprous man. Loving the knight, they were concerned for his health because they realized that they would never find such a good master again. The young daughter of the peasant was, in particular, deeply moved by Heinrich's suffering.

One day the peasant asked why the doctors had been unable to help his master. Heinrich told him of the visit to Salerno and described the impossible cure of which the doctor had spoken. The young girl overheard this tale. Late that same evening she told her parents that she wanted to be the virgin who could save their master's life. Her parents were horrified when they heard her request, and her father threatened physical punishment if she dared to mention the subject again. But the next evening the girl began to talk once more of her desire to help the leprous knight. She spoke in such a convincing manner that her parents did not interrupt her but listened in amazement as their daughter begged with heart-moving words to be allowed to gain the eternal life which would be assured her. She spoke also of the uncertainty her earthly life offered, of the catastrophe which could befall the whole family if their master should die and a harsh ruler scourge the countryside. At last she was able to convince her parents that her service to God and her master would be the only honorable thing to do, and sorrowfully they gave their consent to her intended sacrifice.

Very early the next morning she told the unbelieving Heinrich of her willingness to offer herself for his cure. He warned her that she should not talk lightly about such a subject and assured her that she would soon forget her impulsive idea. After the parents confirmed the seriousness of their daughter's wish, Heinrich took a long time to consider her offer. Finally he too yielded to her pleas.

Beautiful clothes and furs and a fine horse were bought for the girl, and at last she and Heinrich set out on their journey to Salerno. When the doctor there heard from Heinrich that the girl was willing to sacrifice herself in that fashion, he doubted the knight's words and took the girl aside to implore her to speak the truth by telling him whether she was ready of her own free will to face so horrible a fate. Impressed by her sincerity and beauty, the doctor declared that he would be much happier not to take her heart's blood. Still the girl remained steadfast and begged the doctor to proceed with the operation at once.

Sitting in a neighboring room, Heinrich heard the doctor sharpening his knife. The knight peered through a small hole in the wall and saw the girl tied to a table. For the first time he realized how beautiful she was, and he bitterly accused himself of trying to circumvent the judgment of God by sacrificing the girl's beauty to his ugliness. At the very last moment he was able to stop the doctor before an incision had been made. Although the girl implored him not to become weak and called him a coward, a man without the courage of a true knight, Heinrich disregarded her insults and left with her for home.

During the journey back the grace of God touched Heinrich and rapidly his leprosy disappeared; he and the girl had passed the test given to them by God. Heinrich looked younger and handsomer than ever before. The rumor of his miraculous cure having spread throughout the countryside, Heinrich's vassals came to meet the travelers two days before they arrived at their destination. The happy parents of the girl were the first to meet them, and all thanked God for her deliverance and the knight's cure.

In spite of the peasant girl's low birth, the council of knights agreed that the hand of God had surely chosen her to become Heinrich's wife. All in the land, rich and poor, rejoiced when Heinrich and the girl were wed.

ARNE

Type of work: Novel
Author: Björnstjerne Björnson (1832-1910)
Type of plot: Pastoral romance
Time of plot: Early nineteenth century
Locale: Norway
First published: 1858

Principal characters:
NILS, a tailor
MARGIT, his wife
ARNE, their son
BAARD BÖEN, Nils' enemy
ELI, Baard's daughter

Critique:

Arne is best described as a pastoral story, but the discerning reader will find it also an allegory of the life of Norse peasants. He will read of their devotion to personal honor, their ability to translate memory into action of word or deed. He will read of a man as wicked as Nils and feel that Nils was in a sense a martyr to evil spirits. He will leave the story of Arne with a sense of completion, for the restless and tragic searching of Nils' life is in a sense fulfilled when the daughter of his enemy marries his son.

The Story:

Arne was born on the hillside farm of Kampen. He was the son of Margit, betrayed one night when she attended a dance. The man said to be the child's father was Nils, the tailor, who in his free time fiddled for country dances. Arne's grandmother was a frugal widow who saved what she earned so that her daughter and her grandson might not want for lack of a man to look after them. In the meantime the fiddler-tailor, Nils, drank more and tailored less so that his business fell off.

By the time Arne was six he knew a local song written about the wild behavior of his father. His grandmother insisted that Arne be taught his origin. Not long afterward Nils suffered a broken back in a barn fight with Baard Böen. About the same time the old grandmother, who felt that her days were numbered, warned her daughter against wasting the money saved for her use.

When the grandmother died, Arne's mother brought Nils home to be nursed. The next spring Margit and Nils were married and Nils recovered enough to help with some of the farm work. At first Nils was gloomy and morose because he was no longer able to join the fiddlers and the dancers at weddings, and he drank heavily. As his strength returned he began to fiddle once more. Arne went along to merry-makings to carry his fiddle case. By this companionship Nils weaned Arne away from Margit by degrees. Occasionally the boy was remorseful, but his father's hold grew stronger as time passed.

Finally, during a scene of drunken violence, Nils died. Arne and his mother took the blame for his death partly upon themselves. Arne became aloof from the villagers; he tended his cattle and wrote a few songs.

He became more and more shy. At a wedding, interpreting one of the folk tales as referring to him, he told a wild story, part truth, part fancy, about his father's death. Then he rushed from the house. He had had too much brandy, and while he lay in the barn recovering, his mother told him she had once found Nils there in the same condition—on the occasion of Arne's christening.

Arne began to take a new interest in old legends and ballads. As he listened to stories told by an old man of the village, he found himself making up tales of his own. Sometimes he wandered alone in the forest and sang songs as they came into his head.

From a distance he observed Eli Böen and her good friend, the pastor's daughter. He began to sing love songs. Arne did some carpentering and his work took him into the village more often. That winter Böen sent for Arne to do some carpentering. Arne's mother was disturbed because it had been Böen who had caused Nils to break his back years before. At first Böen's wife refused to speak to Arne. Eli Böen, who was attentive to him in the beginning, later ignored him. One day Arne brought word that the pastor's daughter was leaving the village. Eli fainted when she heard the news, for the two girls had been close friends.

Baard Böen tried to explain to Arne what had happened years before between Nils and himself. But he did not manage to make himself clear, and after many years he himself was not sure of the cause of their long-standing quarrel.

Eli's mother became friendly with Arne at last and she asked him to sing for Eli, who seemed to be recovering from her illness. While he sang, he and Eli felt a deep intimacy spring up between them. The next day, his work completed, Arne took his tools and left. From that time on he thought more and more about Baard Böen's daughter.

Arne had a friend, Kristian, who had gone to America. Now Kristian began to write urging Arne to join him, but Margit hid the letters as they came. Finally she went to the pastor for advice. He felt that Arne must be allowed to live his own life as he saw fit.

The farm was beautiful when spring came. On one of his rambles Arne came upon Eli and thought her more beautiful than he had ever seen her before. Margit took heart from his fondness for the girl. One midsummer evening she discovered Eli in the village and asked her to go for a walk. She took the girl to her homestead and showed her about, from the stables to the chest in which Arne kept the many gifts that were to belong to his bride, among them a hymn book with a silver clasp. On the clasp Eli saw her own name engraved.

Presently Arne appeared and later he walked with Eli back to her own home. They realized now that they were completely in love.

Shortly afterward they were married. Children stood by the church bearing bits of cake. Baard Böen, remembering his long-ago feud with Arne's father, marveled at this wedding of his daughter and the son of his old enemy.

ARROWSMITH

Type of work: Novel
Author: Sinclair Lewis (1885-1951)
Type of plot: Social criticism
Time of plot: Early twentieth century
Locale: United States and West Indies
First published: 1924

Principal characters:
MARTIN ARROWSMITH, a medical scientist
LEORA, his wife
DR. MAX GOTTLIEB, a scientist
GUSTAVE SONDELIUS, a scientist
TERRY WICKETT, Martin's friend
JOYCE LANYON, a young widow
DR. ALMUS PICKERBAUGH, a public health reformer

Critique:

Arrowsmith is one of the novels in which Sinclair Lewis has attempted to point out the insufficiencies and complacencies of American life. What *Babbitt* did for the American businessman, *Arrowsmith* was intended to do for the American doctor. The thesis of *Arrowsmith* would appear to be that the only decent way for a physician to serve mankind is by research. Using Martin Arrowsmith as his example, Lewis has tried to show that the progressive doctor is not appreciated in private practice; that the field of public health is politically corrupt; that the fashionable clinic is often a commercial enterprise; that even the best institutes of research are interested chiefly in publicity.

The Story:

Martin Arrowsmith was the descendant of pioneers in the Ohio wilderness. He grew up in the raw red-brick town of Elk Mills, in the state of Winnemac, a restless, lonely boy who spent his odd hours in old Doc Vickerson's office. The village practitioner was a widower, with no family of his own, and he encouraged Martin's interest in medicine.

At twenty-one Martin was a junior preparing for medical school at the University of Winnemac. Continuing on at the medical school, he was most interested in bacteriology and research and the courses of Professor Max Gottlieb, a noted German scientist. After joining a medical fraternity, he made many lifelong friends. He also fell in love with Madeline Fox, a shallow, pseudo-intellectual who was taking graduate work in English. To the young man from the prairie, Madeline represented culture. They became engaged.

Martin spent many nights in research at the laboratory, and he became the favorite of Professor Gottlieb. One day Gottlieb sent him to the Zenith City Hospital on an errand. There Martin met an attractive nurse named Leora Tozer. He soon became so interested in Leora that he became engaged to her as well. Thus young Martin Arrowsmith found himself engaged to two girls at the same time. Unable to choose between them, he asked both Leora and Madeline to lunch with him. When he explained his predicament, Madeline stalked angrily from the dining-room and out of his life. Leora, amused, remained. Martin felt that his life had really begun.

Through his friendship with Gottlieb, Martin became a student instructor in bacteriology. Leora was called home to North Dakota. Because of Leora's absence, trouble with the dean, and too much whiskey, Martin left school during the Christmas holidays. Traveling like a tramp, he arrived at Wheatsylvania, the town where Leora lived. In spite of the warnings of the dull Tozer family, Martin and Leora were married. Martin went back to Winnemac alone. A married man now, he gave up his work in bacteriology and turned his attention to general study. Later Leora joined him in Mohalis.

Upon completion of his internship, Martin set up an office in Wheatsylvania with money supplied by his wife's family. In the small prairie town Martin made friends of the wrong sort, according to the Tozers, but he was fairly successful as a physician. He also made a number of enemies. Meanwhile Martin and Leora moved from the Tozer house to their own home. When Leora's first child was born dead, they knew that they could never have another child.

Martin had again become interested in research. When he heard that the Swedish scientist, Gustave Sondelius, was to lecture in Minneapolis, Martin went to hear his lecture. In that way Martin became interested in public health as a means of controlling disease. Back in Wheatsylvania, still under the influence of Sondelius, he became acting head of the Department of Public Health. Because Martin, in his official capacity, found a highly respected seamstress to be a chronic carrier of typhoid and sent her to the county home for isolation, he became generally unpopular. He welcomed the opportunity to join Dr. Almus Pickerbaugh of Nautilus, Iowa, as the Assistant Director of Public Health, at a considerable increase in salary.

In Nautilus he found Dr. Pickerbaugh to be a public-spirited evangelist with little knowledge of medicine or interest in scientific control of disease. The director spent his time writing health slogans in doubtful poetic meter, lecturing to clubs, and campaigning for health by means of Better Babies Week, Banish the Booze Week, and Tougher Teeth Week. Martin was gradually drawn under the influence of the flashy, artificial methods used by his superior. Although he tried to devote some time to research, the young doctor found that his job took up all his time. While Dr. Pickerbaugh was campaigning for election to Congress, Martin investigated the most sanitary and efficient dairy of the town. He found that the dairy was spreading disease through a streptococcus infection in the udders of the cows. Against the advice of Dr. Pickerbaugh, Martin closed the dairy and made many enemies for himself. Despite his act, however, he was made Acting Director of Public Health when Dr. Pickerbaugh was elected to Congress.

In his new capacity, Martin hired a competent assistant in order to have more time for research in bacteriology. Largely because he fired a block of tenements infested with tuberculosis, Martin was asked to resign. For the next year he worked as staff pathologist of the fashionable Rouncefield Clinic in Chicago. Then publication of a scientific paper brought him again to the attention of his old friend and professor, Max Gottlieb, now located at the McGurk Institute in New York. Dr. Arrowsmith was glad to accept the position Gottlieb offered him.

At the McGurk Institute Martin devoted his whole time to research, with Gottlieb as his constant friend and adviser. He worked on staphylococcus germs, producing first a toxin, then an antitoxin. Under the influence of Gottlieb and Terry Wickett, his colleague at McGurk, Martin discovered the X Principle, a bacterial infection which might prove to be a cure for disease. Although Martin wanted to postpone publication of his discovery until he was absolutely certain of its value, the directors of the institute insisted that he make his results public at once. Before his paper was finished, however, it was learned that the same principle had already been discovered at the Pasteur Institute, where it was called a bacteriophage. After that disappointment, Martin began work on the possibility of preventing and curing bubonic plague with the phage, as the new antitoxin was called.

Meanwhile Gustave Sondelius had come to the McGurk Institute. He became so interested in Martin's work that he spent most of his time helping his young friend. When a plague broke out on St. Hubert, an island in the West Indies, Martin and Sondelius were asked to go there to help in the fight against the epidemic. Accompanied by Leora they sailed for the island of St. Hubert. Before leaving, Martin had promised Gottlieb that he would conduct his experiment deliberately by refusing to treat some of the plague cases with phage, so that the effects of the treatment could be tabulated.

The plague spread daily on the tropical island. Sondelius was stricken and he died. Martin was often away from his laboratory as he traveled between villages. During one of his trips Leora lighted a half-smoked cigarette she found on a table in his laboratory. The tobacco had been saturated with germs from an overturned test tube. Leora died of the plague before Martin's return.

Martin forgot to be the pure scientist. He gave the phage to all who asked for it. Although his assistant continued to take notes to carry on the research, Martin was no longer interested in the results. When the plague began to abate, he went back to New York. There, lonely and unhappy, he married Joyce Lanyon, a wealthy young widow whom he had met on St. Hubert. But the marriage was not a success. Joyce demanded more of his time than he was willing to take from research; he felt ill at ease among her rich and fashionable friends. When he was offered the assistant directorship of McGurk Institute, he refused the position. In spite of Joyce's protests, he went off to join his old friend, Terry Wickett, at a rural laboratory in Vermont, where they intended to experiment on a cure for pneumonia. At last, he believed, his work—his life—was really beginning.

ARS POETICA

Type of work: Poem on critical theory
Author: Horace (Quintus Horatius Flaccus, 65-8 B.C.)
First transcribed: 13-8 B.C.

To Horace, this poem was the last of his Epistles, but almost at once his contemporaries began referring to it as *Ars Poetica* (*The Art of Poetry*) and by "poetry" they meant any field of literary composition. Horace addressed it to his friend Lucius Calpurnius Piso, famous for his battles in Thrace, and to his two sons. Apparently the older son yearned for a career as dramatist or epic poet. Whether he was deterred, and kept his work unpublished for nine years, or whether his assassination while a praetor in Spain was the reason, no writing has survived bearing his name.

While not a formal treatise or abstract discussion, like the similarly named composition of Aristotle, the 476 lines of this unsystematic letter in verse influenced Joachim du Bellay (c. 1524—1560) in writing the manifesto of the Pleiad, and a century later inspired Boileau's *L'Art poétique* (1674) and Pope's *Essay on Criticism* (1711). Some of Horace's suggestions, like the classical five-act division of the drama, are no longer important, but today's writers still can learn much from the rest of the poem. The double purpose of literature, a mingling of "the useful with the sweet," has been quoted through the centuries in every literary movement.

One would be amused rather than impressed, begins Horace, by the painting of a creature with a horse's body and a man's head, with limbs from every sort of animal, adorned with feathers from a variety of birds. Yet poets combine just such outlandish elements, adding "purple patches" where they are entirely out of place in order to give color and brilliance to pompous openings in portions of their writing. Therefore he begins his *Art of Poetry* with a plea for simplicity and unity.

Addressing Piso and his sons directly, Horace confesses that most poets are misled by what looks like truth. When striving for brevity, the poet becomes unintelligible. Attempts to write smoothly result in loss of vigor and spirit. Aiming at grandeur, he becomes bombastic. Only when he is guided by art can a writer avoid some errors without committing worse ones. The remedy, therefore, is to select subjects equal to one's ability and to use appropriate language. Old words, properly used, seem new; new words, borrowed from the Greeks, may also have a place. Man is admired for making over nature when he builds harbors or drains marshes. Usage, then, should maintain or change the material and rules of speech.

Homer, according to Horace, showed the writer how to handle the deeds of kings and sad tales of war. No one is sure who invented the elegiac couplet, but Archilochus devised the iambus, used in tragic and comic drama; and since it was born of rage, it is designed to record man in action. The Muses gave the lyric for singing about victories, lovers, and gay banquets. All these meters have their specific uses and the poets would do well to employ them only in their appropriate places, though sometimes a writer of comedy may borrow from other forms of poetic art or an author of tragedies set aside his sesquipedalian words in favor of shorter ones to touch the hearts of his audience.

Feeling is the true test of literary worth, for beauty of writing is not enough. Unless a writer feels, he cannot make his audience feel. One style of writing goes with a gloomy face; another sort goes with an angry one, or a playful one. Nature first makes us reveal our feelings physically; then with the tongue for an interpreter she voices the emotions of the heart. There is also a difference in language between the gods and men, between old men and young, between merchants and farmers, among Colchians, Assyrians, and Thebans.

Either follow tradition or be consistent in your inventions, Horace advises. Achilles on the stage must be hot-tempered, appealing to the sword rather than to the law. Follow tradition and make Medea haughty, Ino tearful, and Ixion perjured. If the writer presents original characters, he must keep them consistent: do not let them be too bombastic or promise too much out of prudent fear that the mountain in labor will bring forth no more than a ridiculous mouse.

If the writer wishes the applause of his audience, he must paint accurately the characteristics of the four ages of man. The young boy is unsettled and changing; the beardless youth is fond of horses and dogs, boastful, scornful of advice; in middle age, man is ambitious but cautious; and the old man is surrounded by discomfort. Do not, therefore, attribute the wrong qualities to a stage of human life.

In touching lightly on the rules laid down by classical dramatists, Horace believed in the superiority of showing action rather than telling about it; but there are, he adds, things too horrible to be seen. He comments on the number of actors—only three—and the place of the chorus. He comments on the rules and restraints of satyric drama. Then, after an appeal that Greek, not Roman, tastes be followed in selecting verse forms, he embarks on a history of the theater.

Slightly confused, he gives Thespis credit for inventing the tragedy and traveling in a cart to put on plays in which the faces of actors were stained by dregs of wine. Then came Aeschylus, with the invention of the raised stage, the mask, and the buskins. Old comedy followed, soon to degenerate into license, and the chorus lost its role of abuse.

Roman playwrights, he continues, tried all forms of drama, but most were not successful because they were careless. Horace adjures his student reader to condemn any literary composition that has not been erased and amended. Even genius cannot discard rules. Characterizing himself, he says that he is too lazy to be a genius; he will perform his duty and criticize.

Answering the question of what to write, Horace declares that knowledge is the basis of good writing and that moral philosophy will supply matter. Life and manners should also occupy a writer's attention. The purpose of the poet should be to benefit and entertain. "He has received the votes who has mingled the useful and the sweet, by instructing and delighting the reader at the same time."

People do not always expect perfection from a poet. Some faults can be pardoned, for even Homer failed at times, though usually he excelled in his craft. But continued carelessness is unforgivable, and eternally second-rate material cannot be tolerated. A person who cannot play the game should keep off the field unless he craves the jeers of the spectators. If you write something, he told Piso's son, let the censor of plays see it; then show it to your father and me. Afterward, keep it in your desk for nine years. What you have not published, you can always destroy.

The final eighty lines of the poem deal with generalities. In the early days, says Horace, Orpheus represented the dignity of poets who, by their wisdom, distinguished between public and private property, divine and earthly things, lore and law. By their songs, they won honor. Homer and Tyrtaeus inspired men to battle; oracles guided men by their verses. It is a question for debate whether a poet is born or made, but at any rate, without art and study even a genius will fail.

The best of writers need criticism, but they should avoid mere flatterers. One good critic used to mark, for improvement and reworking, lines in poems submitted to him, and if the would-be poet defended his mistakes, the critic had no more to do with him. The honest critic puts black marks before poor verses as Aristarchus did to Homer. Self-willed poets will not like such treatment, comments Horace, but in that case they are not worth trying to save. They are probably mad, each one, like a bear, clawing at an innocent bystander. Such a poet will be your death, reading you his poetry.

ARTAMÈNE

Type of work: Novel
Author: Madeleine de Scudéry (1607-1701)
Type of plot: Sentimental romance
Time of plot: 500 B.C.
Locale: Asia Minor
First published: 1646-1653

Principal characters:
ARTAMÈNE, the Great Cyrus
CYAXARES, King of Cappadocia, then of Media
MANDANE, his daughter
PHILIDASPES, King of Assyria, in love with Mandane
THE KING OF PONTUS, in love with Mandane
ANAXORIS, in reality Aryante, Prince of the Massagetae, Thomyris' brother, in love with Mandane
PRINCE MAZARE OF SACIA, in love with Mandane
THOMYRIS, Queen of Scythia
SPARGAPISES, Thomyris' son
ARAMINTA, Princess of Pontus
SPITHRIDATES, in love with Araminta
PANTHEA, Queen of Susiana
MARTÉSIE, Mandane's maid of honor
METROBATE, a traitor

Critique:

Some books seem to have a universal value that transcends the time in which they were written. Others seem to be particularly representative of their epoch, and eventually stand as a milestone in the development of a genre. *Artamène, ou le grand Cyrus* belongs to the latter category. It consists of ten volumes, each in two books. In spite of its length, it has a remarkable unity of interest, if not of plot. The story is centered around the pursuit of Mandane by Cyrus, Mandane being constantly abducted by various other suitors. The author indulges in lengthy stories within the story. These successive stories are ingeniously knitted together, one character being introduced casually in one, and being caught up with later in another. The organization of the novel is such that it is actually quite difficult to read only parts of it and still understand it. This type of novel was expected to provide a pastime, in the literal sense of the word. Although this may seem ironic in view of its length, *Artamène* fulfilled this purpose. It provided noble sentiments together with a little learning. It is still possible to understand why it was such a great success.

The Story:

Cyrus, son of the King of Persia, had been given away as a child to a shepherd, who was ordered to kill the infant because his grandfather had been told by an omen that his grandson would eventually kill him. Instead, the shepherd had reared the boy to manhood and now, under the name of Artamène, he was the best general of Cyaxares, King of Cappadocia. He was also secretly in love with Mandane, Cyaxares' daughter.

The kings of Cappadocia and of Pontus had decided to settle a dispute between themselves by a combat, using two hundred men on each side. Artamène had been given the command of the Cappadocian warriors, to the great disappointment of his explosive rival, Philidaspes. Although all the odds were against him, Artamène was the only survivor and won the victory for the Cappadocians.

He discovered, however, that Philidaspes was also in love with Mandane. They had a violent fight and Cyaxares, unaware of the real cause of the quarrel, had them both put in prison.

There were other great battles fought, and Artamène, now out of prison, was again victorious. Then he disappeared and was believed dead. This was the occasion for Mandane to confess her love for him to her confidante, Martésie, a thing she had never dared do before. Eventually Artamène returned. He accidentally learned that Philidaspes was actually the prince of Assyria, heir to the throne of his mother Nitocris, and that he was plotting to take Mandane away. The King of Pontus had also become a new rival for the love of Mandane. To make matters worse, Thomyris, Queen of Scythia, who had never loved before, had fallen in love with Artamène the moment she saw him when he was sent on a mission to her court.

Philidaspes, now King of Assyria, had succeeded in taking Mandane to Babylon, where he pleaded with her to love him or at least to let him hope that she would, some day, accept his suit.

Meanwhile, Artamène, sent in pursuit of Mandane, had laid siege to mighty Babylon, but Philidaspes managed to escape to Sinope with Mandane and Mazare, the chivalrous prince of Sacia. Sinope was set afire and while the Assyrian king was locked up in a tower, Mazare took Mandane away to sea. A shipwreck brought her to the fortress of the King of Pontus.

When Cyaxares arrived at Sinope and failed to find his daughter, he also discovered that Artamène was in love with her. However, he still did not know the hero's real identity, and he was about to have him executed when the army assaulting the castle rescued Artamène and proclaimed him as Cyrus.

When Cyrus set out to get Mandane back, Philidaspes insisted on a paradoxical alliance in order to rescue their common love. They besieged Sardis and captured two hostages, Panthea, the wife of Abradantes, one of the enemy rulers, and Araminta, the sister of the Queen of Pontus. Unfortunately this action provoked Mandane's jealousy, and in a letter she accused Cyrus of using her as a mere pretext to further his ambition. She was particularly jealous of Araminta, whose lover Spithridates resembled Cyrus and could easily have been mistaken for him. Cyrus, with his best paladins, managed to enter Sardis, but Mandane was gone, carried away by the King of Pontus, and perhaps not unwillingly. The hunt for Mandane had to be resumed. Philidaspes stole away to search for Mandane by himself.

Cyrus then learned that the King of Pontus had taken Mandane to Cumae, a place protected by marshes and open to the sea on which she had so often been taken away from him. Meanwhile, the Queen of Corinth, who had conceived a romantic but platonic admiration for Cyrus, sent her fleet to help him. Martésie wrote that Mandane was at last no longer jealous, for Panthea had killed herself over the dead body of her husband, and Araminta had been taken away against her will by Prince Phraortes. Spithridates was desperate.

Cumae was captured and the lovers met at last. A certain Anaxoris had been instrumental in keeping Mandane from being carried away from Cumae. When Philidaspes turned up again to keep watch on Cyrus, he later entrusted Anaxoris with his secret, asking him to take care of Mandane should anything happen to him. Anaxoris, however, was actually Aryante, the prince of the Massagetae, and brother of Thomyris, the formidable Scythian queen. Aryante surrendered Mandane to his sister, and Cyrus went to fight Thomyris.

Spargapises, the son of Thomyris, considering himself disgraced because he had not been recognized when he was captured in battle, killed himself. Thomyris then threatened Cyrus by declaring that she would deliver Mandane's dead body to him unless he surrendered unconditionally. Aryante, not wishing to have Mandane murdered or to have Cyrus near her, sent him a message begging him not to surrender. A tremendous battle followed in which Cyrus set fire to some forests between the two armies. The unfortunate Spithridates, clad in a suit of armor given to him by Cyrus, was mistaken for Cyrus and was killed. His head was taken to Thomyris. Unfortunately, she was not the only one who was mistaken. Cyrus' troops gave up the fight and he was seized by an ally of Thomyris, but his captor later allowed him to escape because of his admiration for his noble prisoner. Cyrus escaped, but only after many difficulties. Thomyris then ordered Mandane killed, but a maid of honor was mistaken for her and killed in her place. Meanwhile, the queen's allies were preparing to desert her. When Cyrus' faithful friends arrived, she fled.

Now Cyrus and Mandane were free to wed, except that an ancient law stated that a prince or princess could not marry a foreigner. But an oracle declared that he who had conquered every kingdom in Asia could not be considered a foreigner in any of them. Thus, to the satisfaction of all concerned, the last obstacle to their union was cleared away.

THE ARTAMONOV BUSINESS

Type of work: Novel
Author: Maxim Gorky (Aleksei Maksimovich Peshkov, 1868-1936)
Type of plot: Family chronicle
Time of plot: c. 1862-1918
Locale: Russia
First published: 1925

Principal characters:
ILIA ARTAMONOV, the father
PETER ARTAMONOV, his oldest son
NIKITA ARTAMONOV, his hunchbacked son
ALEXEY ARTAMONOV, an adopted son
NATALIA BAIMAKOV, Peter's wife
ULIANA BAIMAKOV, widow of the late mayor and Ilia's mistress
ILIA, Peter's first son
YAKOV, Peter's second son
TIKHON VIALOV, a worker in the Artamonov factory

Critique:

Aleksei Maksimovich Peshkov, whose pseudonym was Maxim Gorky (the bitter one), was the son of poor parents and received no formal education. By the time he was nine years old he was earning his own living. During his long wanderings across Russia he educated himself and gained knowledge of all types of people. About 1900 he became a Marxist and was arrested for revolutionary activities. He was exiled in 1906 to Capri, but was permitted to return in 1913. In 1918 he joined the Bolshevik revolution and became one of the best-known writers of Communist Russia. His novels first excited Russian intellectuals but were popular with the masses after the revolution. In spite of his predominantly political influence he was not able to eliminate elements of romanticism in his novels, as is shown in his presentation of the pre-revolution characters of the *The Artamonov Business*. The author is here still far away from a purely socialistic novel, and he does not attempt to discard the strong influence which orthodox Christianity exercised on his heroes. As a description of the social climate in one particular Russian town before the revolution the novel is successful in its effects; however, if the writer intended also to make a plea for the revolutionary cause, it is not, on this thematic level, wholly convincing.

The Story:

A year or so after the liberation of the Russian serfs Ilia Artamonov arrived with his two sons, Peter and Nikita, and Alexey, his nephew and adopted son, in the little town of Dromov along the Vataraksha River. Ilia Artamonov had served as a bailiff to a prince, and the nobleman had recommended him highly to the authorities. Without giving the mayor of Dromov, Evgeny Baimakov, a chance for objections, Artamonov announced that he planned to build a linen factory and that he considered the mayor's daughter Natalia a good wife for his oldest son. Artamonov, disregarding the resentment his dictatorial behavior provoked in the town, went ahead with plans for the factory and preparations for Peter's marriage. The mayor, who died before the wedding, advised his wife Uliana to let Artamonov have his way. But Peter's marriage to the mayor's daughter and the prospect of employment for many citizens did not reduce the enmity felt toward the intruders.

When Uliana Baimakov became Ilia's mistress, she decided to live with the Artamonovs on the other side of the river where the factory was located. Ilia tried to be a strict but humane superior to his men. Among his workers, Tikhon Vialov was the most able, although he begged not to be promoted because he did not want to supervise others. Meanwhile, Nikita, the hunchback, had fallen in love with Natalia, and when he overheard an unkind remark she made about him, he tried to hang himself. The attempt failing, Nikita entered a monastery.

The factory developed rapidly under Ilia's direction. Peter was the second in charge. Alexey, unhappy at the factory, wanted to join the army, but Ilia refused to give him permission to enlist.

When Natalia bore her first child, the baby died after five months. Another girl, Elena, followed. Then a much desired son, also named Ilia, was born. Alexey married a woman nobody in the family liked or understood.

During the transportation of a heavy steam boiler Ilia senior suffered a hemorrhage and died soon afterward. As time passed, Peter's only true happiness was his son. Against his wife's wishes he let Ilia attend a good secondary school away from Dromov. While Peter devoted his time almost exclusively to the factory, Alexey made the necessary business trips to trade fairs and to Moscow. Although Natalia gave birth to a second boy, Yakov, Ilia remained Peter's favorite.

In spite of all efforts to prepare Ilia as Peter's successor as the factory director, his son showed a completely different attitude. He liked to talk to Vialov, the philosopher among the workers, whom Peter despised; and he also formed a close friendship with an uneducated child of a worker. When Ilia, after completing his schooling, announced his desire to become a historian, his father objected because he still wanted Ilia to take over the factory. Ilia refused and left Dromov without receiving any financial assistance from his father. Thereafter Peter became an unhappy man; his wife could not please him, and he tried to find distraction with a local prostitute.

Often Peter had difficulty in controlling his temper, and one day he accidentally killed Ilia's former playmate. Vialov, too, irritated him with philosophizing whenever he had a question to ask. Hoping to find some spiritual guidance, Peter finally decided to visit his brother Nikita in the monastery. Nikita explained that he had failed in his efforts to become a good monk. Although he considered himself unworthy, the monastery valued him highly because he was able to give visiting pilgrims some comfort with patient ears and empty phrases.

When Peter failed to find peace of mind with Nikita, he attended a trade fair in a nearby city. Alexey had told him so many exciting stories about city life that he hoped to find distraction there. After a series of extended drinking sprees and orgiastic behavior with prostitutes, he was finally discovered by Alexey, who had heard from a friend of the family about Peter's disgraceful behavior. Back home, Peter heard rumors that his son had become a member of a revolutionary extremist party. He also detected unusual new ideas in Alexey's son Miron. Only his younger son, Yakov, seemed unconcerned about the new ideas that were spreading among workers. Yakov was not good-looking; however, Peter considered his interests, mainly girls, more normal than all the ideas expressed by the others, ideas which he believed a threat to the factory.

The rapid growth of the factory had brought a large settlement of workers to Dromov, along with many hardship cases. Peter tried to show his interest in his workers by building a new hospital or arranging a big party for them.

Alexey died suddenly. A telegram was sent to summon Nikita, but he had left the monastery. Only Vialov knew his address. After the funeral Nikita and Vialov were seen together frequently. Peter's feelings grew against all people who did not think primarily of the factory, and when Nikita died four days before the outbreak of World War I, he had no kind word for his dying brother.

When Peter grew too old for most of the factory work and Yakov took over in his place, Yakov also became concerned over the growing signs of unrest among the workers. One worker, who spied for him in the factory, became his oppressor. Early in the war many workers were drafted. Some returned, crippled, to the factory. Yakov's fear of being killed by his workers increased rapidly. With his mistress Pauline, a girl of easy virtue and expensive tastes, he planned to go away. Trying to avoid suspicion, he let Pauline leave Dromov first. His own plan was to meet her in Moscow with all the money he could raise. But he never arrived in Moscow. Reports reached Dromov that he had been robbed, killed, and thrown from the train.

Peter, who had tried to ignore all rumors about uprisings and a new way of life for the workers, lived in a state of semicoma and asked constantly the whereabouts of Ilia and Yakov. He failed to realize what was going on around him until one day, he felt a sharp sense of hunger and realized that he was in his garden house. Outside he saw a soldier. When Peter called for his wife, only Vialov came. He explained that Peter was a prisoner.

At first Peter thought Vialov was jeering at him. Later he believed that he had been taken prisoner because someone had learned the truth about the death of Ilia's former playmate. Vialov tried in vain to inform him about the revolution which had taken place and to explain that he was still alive only because of Ilia's influence. Peter thought Vialov had gone mad. When Natalia arrived with a cucumber and a piece of bread, Peter considered himself insulted that she dared offer him such meager food when he was so hungry. Angrily he threw the food away and with abusive words asked her to leave him alone.

AS I LAY DYING

Type of work: Novel
Author: William Faulkner (1897-1962)
Type of plot: Psychological realism
Time of plot: Early twentieth century
Locale: Mississippi
First published: 1930

Principal characters:
ADDIE BUNDREN, a dying old woman
ANSE BUNDREN, her husband
CASH,
DARL,
JEWEL, and
VARDAMAN, their sons
DEWEY DELL, their daughter

Critique:

Centered around the effect of Addie Bundren's death and burial on the members of her family, this novel has a powerful unity not always found in Faulkner's longer works. The author tells the simple story through the eyes and minds of each of his characters. This method of shifting the multiple points of view binds the Bundrens into a homogeneous group beset by the tragedy of Addie's death and the frustrations connected with her burial, yet each character emerges clearly with his own secrets, his own emotional abnormality.

The Story:

Addie Bundren was dying. She lay propped up in a bed in the Bundren farmhouse, looking out the window at her son Cash as he built the coffin in which she was to be buried. Obsessed with perfection in carpentry, Cash held up each board for her approval before he nailed it in place. Dewey Dell, Addie's daughter, stood beside the bed, fanning her mother as she lay there in the summer heat. In another room Anse Bundren, Addie's husband, and two sons, Darl and Jewel, discussed the possibility of the boys' making a trip with a wagonload of lumber to earn three dollars for the family. Because Addie's wish was that she be buried in Jefferson, the town where her relatives lay, Anse was afraid the boys might not get back in time to carry her body to the Jefferson graveyard. He finally approved the trip and Jewel and Darl set out.

Addie died while the two brothers were gone and before Cash could finish the coffin. When it was obvious that she was dying, a Dr. Peabody was summoned, but he came too late to help the sick woman. While Dr. Peabody was at the house, Vardaman, the youngest boy, arrived home with a fish he had caught in the river; his mother's death somehow became entangled in his mind with the death of the fish and, because Dr. Peabody was there when she died, Vardaman thought the doctor had killed her.

Meanwhile a great rainstorm came up. Jewel and Darl, with their load of lumber, were delayed on the road by a broken wagon wheel. Cash kept working through the rain, trying to finish the coffin. At last it was complete and Addie was placed in it, but the crazed Vardaman, who once had almost smothered in his crib, tried to let his mother out by boring holes through the top of the coffin.

After Jewel and Darl finally got back with the wagon, neighbors gathered at the Bundren house for the funeral service, which was conducted by Whitfield, the minister. Whitfield had once been a lover of Addie's after her marriage, and Jewel, the son whom she seemed to favor, had been fathered by the minister.

Following the service, Anse, his family, and the dead Addie started out for Jefferson, normally one hard day's ride away. The rainstorm, however, had so swollen the river that the bridge had been broken up and could not be crossed by wagon. After trying another bridge, which had also been washed out, they drove back to an old ford near the first bridge. Three of the family—Anse, Dewey Dell, and Vardaman, with the assistance of Vernon Tull, a neighboring farmer—got across the river on the ruins of the bridge. Then Darl and Cash attempted to drive the wagon across at the obliterated ford, with Jewel leading the way on his spotted horse. This horse was Jewel's one great possession; he had earned the money to purchase it by working all day at the Bundren farm and then by working all night clearing ground for a neighbor. When the wagon was nearly across, a big log floating downstream upset the wagon. As a result, Cash broke his leg and nearly died; the mules were drowned; the coffin fell out, but was dragged to the bank by Jewel; and Cash's carpenter's tools were scattered in the water and had to be recovered one by one.

Anse refused the loan of anyone's mules, insisting that he must own the team that carried Addie to the grave. He went off to bargain for mules and made a trade in which he offered, without Jewel's consent, to give the spotted horse as part payment. When Jewel found out what his father had done, he rode off, apparently abandoning the group. Later it turned out that he had put the spotted horse in the barn of Snopes, who was dickering with Anse. And so they got their new mules and the trip continued.

By the time they arrived in Mottson, a town on the way to Jefferson, Addie had been dead so long that buzzards followed the wagon. In Mottson they stopped to buy cement to strengthen Cash's broken leg. The police and citizens, whose noses were offended, insisted that the wagon move on, but they bought the cement and treated the leg before they would budge. While they were in the town, Dewey Dell left the wagon, went to a drugstore, and tried to buy medicine which would abort the illegitimate child she carried, for she had become pregnant by a man named Lafe, with whom she had worked on the farm. The druggist refused to sell her the medicine.

Addie Bundren had been dead nine days and was still not buried. The family spent the last night before their arrival in Jefferson at the house of a Mr. Gillespie, who allowed them to put the odorous coffin in his barn. During the night Darl, whom the neighbors had always thought to be the least sane of the Bundrens, set fire to the barn. Jewel rescued the coffin by carrying it out on his back. Anse later turned Darl over to the authorities at Jefferson; they sent him to the asylum in Jackson.

Lacking a spade and shovel to dig Addie's grave, Anse stopped at a house in Jefferson and borrowed these tools. The burial finally took place. Afterward Dewey Dell again tried to buy her medicine at a drugstore. One of the clerks pretended to be a doctor, gave her some innocuous fluid, and told her to come back that night for further treatment. The further treatment took the form of a seduction in the basement of the drugstore.

Cash's broken leg, encased in cement, had by now become so infected that Anse took him to Dr. Peabody, who said that Cash might not walk for a year. Before starting on the trip home, Anse bought himself a set of false teeth that he had long needed. He then returned the borrowed tools. When he got back to the wagon he had acquired not only the new teeth but also a new Mrs. Bundren, the woman who lent him the tools.

AS YOU LIKE IT

Type of work: Drama
Author: William Shakespeare (1564-1616)
Type of plot: Pastoral romance
Time of plot: The Middle Ages
Locale: The Forest of Arden in medieval France
First presented: 1599-1600

Principal characters:
THE BANISHED DUKE
FREDERICK, his brother and usurper of his dominions
OLIVER, older son of Sir Rowland de Boys
ORLANDO, younger son of Sir Rowland de Boys
ADAM, a servant to Oliver
TOUCHSTONE, a clown
ROSALIND, daughter of the banished duke
CELIA, daughter of Frederick

Critique:

Shakespeare took most of the plot of this play from a popular novel of the period, *Rosalynde,* by Thomas Lodge. What he added was dramatic characterization and wit. *As You Like It* is a comedy compounded of many elements, but the whole is set to some of Shakespeare's loveliest poetry. Kindliness, good fellowship, good-will—these are the elements of *As You Like It,* and Shakespeare shows how much they are worth.

The Story:

A long time ago the elder and lawful ruler of a French province had been deposed by his younger brother, Frederick. The old duke, driven from his dominions, fled with several faithful followers to the Forest of Arden. There he lived a happy life, free from the cares of the court and able to devote himself at last to learning the lessons nature had to teach. His daughter Rosalind, however, remained at court as a companion to her cousin Celia, the usurping Duke Frederick's daughter. The two girls were inseparable, and nothing her father said or did could make Celia part from her dearest friend.

One day Duke Frederick commanded the two girls to attend a wrestling match between the duke's champion, Charles, and a young man named Orlando, the special object of Duke Frederick's hatred. Orlando was the son of Sir Rowland de Boys, who in his lifetime had been one of the banished duke's most loyal supporters. When Sir Rowland died, he had charged his oldest son, Oliver, with the task of looking after his younger brother's education, but Oliver had neglected his father's charge. The moment Rosalind laid eyes on Orlando she fell in love with him, and he with her. She tried to dissuade him from an unequal contest with a champion so much more powerful than he, but the more she pleaded the more determined Orlando was to distinguish himself in his lady's eyes. In the end he completely conquered his antagonist, and was rewarded for his prowess by a chain from Rosalind's own neck.

When Duke Frederick discovered his niece's interest in Sir Rowland's son, he banished Rosalind immediately from the court. His daughter Celia announced her intention of following her cousin. As a consequence, Rosalind disguised herself as a boy and set out for the Forest of Arden, and Celia and the faithful Touchstone, the false duke's jester, went with her. In the meantime, Orlando also found it necessary to flee because of his brother's harsh treatment. He was accompanied by his faithful servant, Adam, an old man who willingly turned over his life savings of five hundred crowns for the privilege of following his young master.

Orlando and Adam also set out for the

Forest of Arden, but before they had traveled very far they were both weary and hungry. While Adam rested in the shade of some trees, Orlando wandered into that part of the forest where the old duke was, and came upon the outlaws at their meal. Desperate from hunger, Orlando rushed upon the duke with a drawn sword and demanded food. The duke immediately offered to share the hospitality of his table, and Orlando blushed with shame over his rude manner. Moreover, he would not touch a mouthful until Adam had been fed. When the old duke found that Orlando was the son of his friend, Sir Rowland de Boys, he took Orlando and Adam under his protection and made them members of his band of foresters.

In the meantime, Rosalind and Celia also arrived in the Forest of Arden, where they bought a flock of sheep and proceeded to live the life of shepherds. Rosalind passed as Ganymede, Celia, as a sister, Aliena. In this adventure they encountered some real Arcadians—Silvius, a shepherd, and Phebe, a dainty shepherdess with whom Silvius was in love. But the moment Phebe laid eyes on the disguised Rosalind she fell in love with the supposed young shepherd and would have nothing further to do with Silvius. As Ganymede, Rosalind also met Orlando in the forest, and twitted him on his practice of writing verses in praise of Rosalind and hanging them on the trees. Touchstone, in the forest, displayed the same willfulness and whimsicality he showed at court, even to his love for Audrey, a country wench whose sole appeal was her unloveliness.

One morning, as Orlando was on his way to visit Ganymede, he saw a man lying asleep under an oak tree. A snake was coiled about the sleeper's neck, and a hungry lioness crouched nearby ready to spring. He recognized the man as his own brother, Oliver, and for a moment Orlando was tempted to leave him to his fate. But he drew his sword and killed the snake and the lioness. In the encounter he himself was wounded by the lioness. Because Orlando had saved his life, Oliver was duly repentant, and the two brothers were joyfully reunited.

His wound having bled profusely, Orlando was too weak to visit Ganymede, and he sent Oliver instead with a bloody handkerchief as proof of his wounded condition. When Ganymede saw the handkerchief the supposed shepherd promptly fainted. The disguised Celia was so impressed by Oliver's concern for his brother that she fell in love with him, and they made plans to be married on the following day. Orlando was so overwhelmed by this news that he was a little envious. But when Ganymede came to call upon Orlando, the young shepherd promised to produce the lady Rosalind the next day. Meanwhile Phebe came to renew her ardent declaration of love for Ganymede, who promised on the morrow to unravel the love tangle of everyone.

In the meantime, Duke Frederick, enraged at the flight of his daughter, Celia, had set out at the head of an expedition to capture his elder brother and put him and all his followers to death. But on the outskirts of the Forest of Arden he met an old hermit who turned Frederick's head from his evil design. On the day following, as Ganymede had promised, with the banished duke and his followers as guests, Rosalind appeared as herself and explained how she and Celia had posed as the shepherd Ganymede and his sister Aliena. Four marriages took place with great rejoicing that day—Orlando to Rosalind, Oliver to Celia, Silvius to Phebe, and Touchstone to Audrey. Moreover, Frederick was so completely converted by the hermit that he resolved to take religious orders, and he straightway dispatched a messenger to the Forest of Arden to restore his brother's lands and those of all his followers.

ASH WEDNESDAY

Type of work: Poem
Author: T. S. Eliot (1888-)
First published: 1930

After the publication of *The Waste Land,* in 1922, had established his reputation as a major poet, T. S. Eliot wrote one important poem, "The Hollow Men" (1925), which seemed at that time to be a postlude to its predecessor but which now appears more as a prelude to *Ash Wednesday.* In any case, it should be read as a connecting link between the two longer poems. Its theme is the emptiness of modern intellectualism, which amounts only to

> Shape without form, shade without colour,
> Paralysed force, gesture without motion.

It is another aspect of the Waste Land, desiccated and meaningless, inhabited only by the empty and futile hollow men.

Ash Wednesday marks an important point in the author's poetic development, for it sprang directly from his acceptance of the Anglo-Catholic faith. This biographical aspect of the poem, even more than its theme, influenced its reception by Eliot's former admirers and caused a schism among them that gave an interesting insight into the modern mind.

The tone of the poem is the humility appropriate to Ash Wednesday, the first day of the penitential season of Lent; its theme is the dilemma of the modern man who wants to believe and who yet cannot bring himself to do so because of his dry, sterile intellectuality. This theme is stated in the first of the six parts: the poet, turning his irony upon himself, describes this characteristically modern predicament of a man caught in the web of his own intellectualizing but who can yet know that he must

> . . . pray that I may forget
> These matters that with myself I too much discuss
> Too much explain,

and that at this stage of religious experience the proper prayer is

> Teach us to sit still.

Throughout this opening section sound the echoes of the Penitential Office: "Turn thou us, O good Lord, and so shall we be turned" as well as of Guido Cavalcanti's poem, "In Exile at Sarzana."

The second part is based on a reminiscence of the Valley of Dry Bones described by Ezekiel, the language of which it echoes. Eliot once said in a lecture that the three white leopards could be taken as representing the World, the Flesh, and the Devil. They have fed on the body of the speaker, but Ezekiel was told to prophesy that these bones should live again, that "I [the Lord] shall put my spirit in you, and ye shall live, and I shall place you in your own land." There is also the figure of the Lady, who seems to play a role analogous to that of Beatrice as an intermediary; she is dressed in white, the color of Faith. The speaker, then, having been stripped of everything, has learned resignation; but through the intercession of the Lady and the prophecy of Ezekiel he has found hope.

The third section, with its description of the spiral stairway, obviously recalls Dante's winding ascent of the Purgatorial Mount. There seems to be no direct connection with any particular canto of the *Purgatorio,* only a linking of the journey of purgation with the penitential spirit of Lent. There is also the glimpse through the window of a scene suggestive of sensual pleasure that distracts the pilgrim from his journey. Dante is again recalled in the fourth section, this time by the Earthly Paradise and the Divine Pageant at the end of the *Purgatorio*. Again there are echoes: of St. Paul's *Epistle to the Ephesians* and of the "Salve Regina."

For the fifth section Eliot made use of a sermon by Lancelot Andrews that he had already quoted in an essay on the Bishop: ". . . the Word of an Infant? The Word and not be able to speak a word?"—an elaborate play upon the word (speech), the Word (the Logos, the most abstruse of Christian doctrines), and the Word made Flesh.

The last section, doubling back upon the opening lines of the poem, suggests a scene in a confessional ("Bless me father") during which the beauty of the natural world intrudes into the mind of the speaker and distracts him from his proper meditation. Thus, the world seeks to draw us back to itself. Then, appropriately, the poem ends with words taken, with one slight change, from the Penitential Office for Ash Wednesday in the Book of Common Prayer:

> And let my cry come unto Thee.

Thus, the poem deals with various aspects of a certain stage in religious experience: "Lord, I am not worthy"; it is a poem of spiritual, as Cavalcanti's was one of physical, exile. The dweller in the Waste Land who "cannot drink/there, where trees flower, and springs flow" must find his way back through penitence, with the humble prayer: "Suffer me not to be separated."

This is a simpler poem than *The Waste Land,* though Eliot used much the same technical devices of ellipsis and echoes. It rises to heights of verbal beauty unequaled in any other contemporary verse. Its reception, however, was curious and not without irony. To many readers of the 1920's, Eliot had become the spokesman for the disillusionment of the now famous "lost generation"—a statement that he himself characterized as "nonsense." 1930, with its Marxian enthusiasm for proletarian literature, was probably the high point of the secular humanism of our time; Bertrand Russell's *A Free Man's Worship* was dominant. It was among the adherents to this secular humanism that Eliot's greatest admirers were to be found. For him to become a member of the Anglican Church and to write a poem with a deeply religious theme was to them a grievous shock. Some of them flatly refused to believe in his sincerity; his membership in the Church of England must be a pose, a kind of romantic, aesthetic Catholicism. To others, to whom religion was a retreat from reality, a "failure of nerve," he was a lost leader, a writer whose significant work had ended with "The Hollow Men." Yet it might not be an exaggeration to claim that the publication of *Ash Wednesday* marked the beginning of the swing from the intellectual Left to Right, with the consequent decline of the secular humanist attitude.

ASHES

Type of work: Novel
Author: Stefan Żeromski (1864-1925)
Type of plot: Historical romance
Time of plot: 1796-1812
Locale: Poland and Spain
First published: 1904

Principal characters:
RAPHAEL OLBROMSKI, a Pole
CHRISTOPHER CEDRO, his friend
HELEN, beloved of Raphael
PRINCE GINTULT, a nobleman
ELIZABETH, his sister
NARDZEVSKI, Raphael's uncle

Critique:

Much of this work is in the German romantic tradition. Żeromski describes nature in great detail and devotes long sections to philosophical speculations engendered by contemplation of nature. The tragic love affair of Helen and Raphael and the frequent unconnected sequences of action are reminiscent of Goethe. In contrast, the scenes descriptive of some of the Napoleonic campaigns are precise and realistic. As a historical novel, *Ashes* ranks high, and as an author Żeromski was acknowledged a master by Conrad.

The Story:

When he was very young, Raphael Olbromski paid a short visit to his uncle's secluded estate. Nardzevski, fond of his nephew, initiated him into the art of hunting. The fierce old man was a firm adherent to feudal times and treated his peasants as serfs. Casper, his huntsman, was his only intimate. Raphael's visit came to a sudden end with the arrival of an Austrian official.

The Austrian lectured Nardzevski severely on the necessity of paying the new taxes and modifying his treatment of his peasants, but the old man had no intention of truckling to the Austrians. To emphasize his attitude, he practiced his pistol marksmanship in the dining hall. Defiantly Nardzevski ordered his steward to summon all the peasants in the morning and to arrange for a public flogging of a miscreant. Raphael never learned what happened afterward because early in the morning he was bundled into a sleigh and sent home.

A great sleighing party one winter attracted all the gentry. Raphael, mounted on a spirited horse, followed Helen's sleigh closely. The party stopped to dance at Raphael's poor house, and his aristocratic father staged a big celebration. During the affair Raphael managed to tell Helen that he would come to her window some midnight. The party lasted for two days, but Raphael missed much of it because he slept in a drunken stupor.

At school Raphael was no student, but he was a leader. One evening he and Christopher stole a rowboat and went out into the ice-packed Vistula. When they tried to land, the thin shore ice broke and the boys were soaked. As they went on toward school, they sank into a bog. They were nearly frozen before Raphael took vigorous measures. He tore off his clothes and those of the weakened Christopher, and the boys pummeled each other to get warm. Then, quite naked, they ran back to school, to be caught as they tried to slip inside. Christopher fell ill with fever, and Raphael as the leader was sentenced to be chastised. When the beadle tried to carry out the punishment, Raphael drew a knife, wounded the beadle, and escaped.

His father, when he arrived home in disgrace, imprisoned him in a small room and forbade the family to speak to him. Later he had to spend months working with the peasants. One night Raphael took a fine mare from the barn and rode through a storm to Helen's house. When a watchman came upon them in an outbuilding, Helen got back to her bedroom safely, but Raphael barely escaped ahead of the fierce watchdogs.

A storm came up. Raphael was followed by four wolves. When his horse stumbled, the wolves were on him. Three brought down the horse; Raphael killed the fourth with his hands. Gravely wounded, he was found by an old peasant and taken home. When he recovered, he was cast out of the family and sent to live with his older brother Peter, who had been cast out years before.

Peter, in poor health from war wounds, lived quietly. Raphael spent delightful months in idleness until the arrival of Prince Gintult, an old comrade of Peter's. Peter and the prince had angry words on the treatment of peasants, and as the result of the quarrel Peter had a hemorrhage and died. With no home and melancholy with memories of Helen, who had been taken out of the country, Raphael went to stay with the prince.

In the noble household Raphael was half family, half guest. The prince gave him money for clothes and others gave him errands to run. Raphael was particularly attracted to the prince's sister Elizabeth, a haughty young girl. One day, while they were riding in a group, Elizabeth's horse ran away. Raphael rescued her and made the mistake of kissing her as he held her in his arms. She slashed his face with her whip.

The prince suddenly departed on a voyage to Venice and Paris, after paying Raphael's lodging in a school for a year. Raphael studied fairly well and spent his time profitably. When he was forced to return home, his stern father outfitted him in work clothes and for four years he worked on the farm. His release came with an offer of a position from Prince Gintult.

In Warsaw, Raphael served as secretary to the prince, who was writing a vague philosophical treatise on Freemasonry. In order to continue the work on the secret lodge, Raphael was taken into the Masons; soon afterward he was accepted in society. Through the lodge, he met Helen again.

Abruptly Raphael and Helen fled to the country to enjoy their love. One night they slept in a cave in the mountains. Although Raphael was armed, brigands overpowered him as he slept and bound him while they had their sport with Helen. She escaped their clutches at last and jumped over a cliff.

While he was searching for Helen's body and tracking the brigands, Raphael was arrested by a patrol. He did not dare give his right name or mention Helen for fear of defiling her memory, and while in prison he had a long siege of fever. More than a year passed before he was released.

Penniless and tramping aimlessly about the country, Raphael fell in with his old friend Christopher. The reunited friends spent happy months on Christopher's estate. Then a soldier who had been with Napoleon for twelve years fired their imagination, and they decided to leave that Austrian-dominated part of Poland and join the emperor. Aided by Elizabeth, who was now married and living near the border, they made a daring escape across the frontier.

Christopher, as an enlisted man, crossed Europe with Napoleon and took part in the Spanish campaign. His most vivid impressions were those of the siege of Saragossa, where he distinguished himself for valor and saved a young girl from soldiers who sacked a convent and raped the nuns. He was thrilled when Napoleon abolished the Inquisition. After he had been wounded, he saw the emperor at close hand.

Raphael saw action in Poland, where the Austrian legions were too strong for Napoleon's forces. Once the Poles were preparing to demolish a church, held by the enemy. Prince Gintult, fighting as a civilian, attempted to save the church by interfering with the cannoneers, and Raphael helped him. For his deed the prince was cut down by an officer's sword. In the confusion Raphael carried the wounded nobleman away to his father's house.

When the fighting died down, Raphael was discharged. He went to live at his uncle's old estate, and for a time he was happy there. He rebuilt the barns demolished by the soldiers and cleared land. Then he began building a house. Just as he was finishing, Christopher arrived. Invalided out of the army, but well again, he was impatient for action. Reluctant to leave his home, Raphael objected at first; but finally he agreed to accompany his friend. In the middle of August, 1812, the Polish Corps was united with the Grand Army, and Raphael returned to serve the emperor. At Orsha, Napoleon reviewed his hordes of Polish, Dutch, Italian, and German soldiers.

AT THE SIGN OF THE REINE PÉDAUQUE

Type of work: Novel
Author: Anatole France (Jacques Anatole Thibault, 1844-1924)
Type of plot: Humorous satire
Time of plot: Eighteenth century
Locale: France
First published: 1893

Principal characters:
JACQUES MÉNÉTRIER, a young scholar
MAÎTRE JÉRÔME COIGNARD, an abbot
CATHERINE, a temptress
JAEL, a Jewess
MONSIEUR D'ASTARAC, a philosopher

Critique:

At the Sign of the Reine Pédauque (*La Rôtisserie de la Reine Pédauque*) was the first of France's many works to exhibit in full his peculiar talents. This tale is gusty in outline and overlaid with vast erudition in philosophy and in ancient history. In plot the novel is reminiscent of *Tom Jones* but the treatment is pure Gallic. France's humor is always subtle and at times wicked. In the Abbé Jérôme he has created a memorable character, the fluent, scoundrelly cleric who becomes a sympathetic creation.

The Story:

Jacques Ménétrier's father was a merry cook and his mother a long-suffering, plain woman. The father spent several hours each night at a nearby tavern in the company of Jeannette, the hurdy-gurdy woman, and Catherine, the lace maker. Both ladies helped him relive his lusty youth.

When Jacques was six, he was stationed all day long in the chimney corner to turn the spitted roasts. His time was not altogether wasted, however, for he learned his letters at the same time from a beggar Capuchin, Brother Ange. The good Brother Ange ate well at the common table in return for his services, and in secret he sighed for Catherine.

After a drunken brawl, Brother Ange was imprisoned, and Maître Jérôme Coignard, a Greek and Latin scholar, became Jacques' tutor. As he grew to young manhood he progressed rapidly under the scholar's teachings.

Jeannette, complaisant with all, initiated Jacques into the mysteries of love, but, perversely, Jacques was attracted to Catherine, who made fun of Jacques' beardless chin and refused to take him seriously. Jacques and his father were greatly discomfited when she ran away with Brother Ange.

One evening a tall, gaunt philosopher entered abruptly, crying that he saw a salamander in the fireplace. Vigorously stirring the ashes, he asked the company if they saw anything. Only Jacques thought he saw the outlines of a beautiful woman in the smoke. The philosopher was much pleased with Jacques' discernment.

When Monsieur d'Astarac, their strange visitor, learned that the Maître Jérôme could read Greek easily, he arranged to have the abbot and Jacques come live with him.

At the ruined estate of the philosopher, the two friends were astonished by the rich library. In spite of crumbling walls and overgrown grounds, d'Astarac was evidently wealthy as well as learned. Maître Jérôme was set to work translating the ancient works of Zosimus the Panopolitan, with Jacques as his helper. According to d'Astarac, the only other inhabitant of the estate was Mosaïde, a

---

learned Jew over a hundred years old. The Jew lived mysteriously withdrawn in a separate cottage, where he worked on old Hebrew manuscripts.

After several tranquil months Jacques went for an evening walk into Paris. Brother Ange came up and whispered that a lady was eagerly awaiting him in her carriage. At the rendezvous Jacques found Catherine seated in an elegant coach. Astonished at her magnificence, Jacques learned that she was now the mistress of de la Guéritaude, a tax collector. Then they kissed fervently and made an appointment for later that night.

On Jacques' arrival, the house where Catherine lived was in disturbance. She, half-dressed, was shrieking at the door and lackeys were pursuing Brother Ange with spears. De la Guéritaude had surprised her with her monk. Jacques comforted Catherine ardently, but when de la Guéritaude returned he rudely shoved Jacques into the street and slammed the door.

Soon afterward d'Astarac summoned Jacques to a private conference in a secret laboratory, where he told the young man that he would reveal some of the mysteries of philosophy. The spirit world consisted of sylphs, males who helped philosophers, and salamanders, beautiful females in search of human lovers. Since Jacques was well on his way to being a philosopher and since he had little to do with carnal women, d'Astarac would show him how to summon a salamander. Guiltily thinking of Catherine, Jacques agreed to try.

D'Astarac helped him open a crystal ball filled with stardust. Feeling overwhelmed, Jacques sank down and d'Astarac left him. After a few minutes Jacques looked up to see in front of him a voluptuous, dark-haired woman. Although she resisted his advances for a time, she accepted him as her lover, and they spent the night together.

Jacques soon learned that she was no salamander; she was Jael, niece of Mosaïde. The fierce old Jew kept her secluded, hiding her from Christian eyes, but Jael came frequently to his room despite the uncle's vigilance. One early morning Maître Jérôme saw her leaving and traced her to Mosaïde's cottage. Although Jael slipped inside unseen, Mosaïde saw the abbot from his window and cursed him in Hebrew and Spanish. Not to be outdone, Maître Jérôme cursed the Jew in French and Latin.

That evening, as Maître Jérôme and Jacques passed Catherine's house, she greeted Jacques with great affection from her doorway. Someone inside slapped her sharply and pulled her inside. It was the noble d'Anquetil, Catherine's new lover. He invited them in, pleased that he had Jacques for a rival instead of the begging Capuchin.

The four spent an agreeable evening at the card table. Maître Jérôme always won. Catherine sat snuggled close to d'Anquetil, and while vowing eternal fidelity to him pressed Jacques' foot under the table. Suddenly there was a thunderous rapping outside. De la Guéritaude had returned, furious at being locked out of the house he rented for Catherine.

The four revelers brawled with the tax collector, injuring him gravely and killing one of his lackeys. Jacques, Maître Jérôme, and d'Anquetil fled to d'Astarac's estate for safety. Jacques put the nobleman in his own room and went to talk with the philosopher, although it was almost morning. Unfortunately, Jael came visiting, and before she could flee d'Anquetil was smitten with her charms.

D'Anquetil, who had hired carriages so that they could flee the police, wanted to take Jael with him. To Jacques' horror, Jael agreed after being promised a set of silver plate and a monthly income. In the morning d'Anquctil and Jael set off in a closed coupé, followed by Maître Jérôme and a morose Jacques.

During the journey Jacques reproached Jael for her easy switch of lovers, but she took a practical view of the matter. A set of silver plate could not be ignored. One night at an inn Jael left d'Anquetil's room to visit Jacques, who was thereafter somewhat more content.

From Jael, Jacques learned that Mosaïde was not a hundred years old, but barely sixty; and instead of being a famous scholar, he was a banker who had fled Spain after killing a Christian. Furthermore, Mosaïde was Jael's lover.

Shocked by these disclosures, Jacques was uneasy at the sight of a mysterious carriage which followed them closely. His apprehensions were justified one night when they ran into a bridge and broke a wheel. Jacques, d'Anquetil, and Jael waited for repairs in a nearby dell, while Maître Jérôme searched the wreckage for bottles of wine.

In the darkness Mosaïde, who had been following the runaways, fell upon the abbot and wounded him mortally, for the jealous Jew thought that Maître Jérôme had stolen Jael. The monk died in a neighboring village, where he had been carried for medical aid. Jacques, mourning his tutor and friend, returned to his parents in Paris.

Later Jacques went to pay a visit to d'Astarac. When he arrived at the estate, he saw the big house blazing fiercely. The philosopher was burned to death in the fire, and Mosaïde drowned in a swamp as he tried to run away. Gradually, the memory of Jael becoming less poignant, Jacques found his true vocation. He became a bookseller and supported his father and mother in dignity in their old age.

ATALA

Type of work: Novel
Author: François René de Chateaubriand (1768-1848)
Type of plot: Philosophical romance
Time of plot: Early eighteenth century
Locale: Louisiana
First published: 1801

Principal characters:
ATALA, an Indian maiden
CHACTAS, beloved of Atala
FATHER AUBRY, a missionary

Critique:

A tale of passionate but pure love, *Atala* is another of the stories of the Noble Savage which began to find such favor in the early nineteenth century. Against a background of the primitive American wilderness, the two lovers and the gentle priest wage a winning battle against sin and paganism. Simplicity and complexity of character are vividly contrasted, the two meeting in Christian faith in the goodness of God. *Atala* was the first of Chateaubriand's romances to be published, and the book had a tremendous vogue in its own day. The novel was originally planned as part of a much longer work, *The Natchez,* based on Chateaubriand's travels on the American frontier and influenced by his romantic philosophy.

The Story:

Chactas was an old, blind, and wise Indian of the tribe of Natchez, whose hunting ground was in the territory of Louisiana. Because of his great age and deep wisdom gained through countless years of tragic misfortune, Chactas was the patriarch of the tribe. Thus it was that when a young Frenchman named René presented himself for membership in the tribe in the year 1725, it was Chactas who questioned him to determine his fitness to join the Natchez nation. Finding René fixed in his determination to become a savage, Chactas accepted him. As the Indians prepared for a beaver hunt, Chactas—even though he was blind—was made the leader of the party. One night as they lay in their canoes Chactas recited to René the story of his adventures.

When Chactas had lived but seventeen summers, his father was killed in battle and he himself was taken prisoner by the enemy and led away by the Spaniards to St. Augustine. There he was befriended by an old Castilian named Lopez and his sister. The two white people cared for the young savage and tried to educate him as their son. But after thirty moons had passed, Chactas tired of this civilized life and begged Lopez to allow him to return to his people. Lopez, knowing the dangers awaiting a lonely youth in the forests, tried to dissuade Chactas at first. At last, seeing that the youth was firm in his resolve, the old man sent him away with his blessing.

The warning given by the good Lopez soon proved right. Chactas, having lost his way in the woods, was captured by an enemy tribe and taken to their village to await death by burning. Because of his youth and bravery, the women of the tribe took pity on him. One night, as he sat by the campfire, he heard a rustling and then felt the presence of a woman beside him. In low tones she told him that she was Atala, daughter of the chief and his dead wife. She asked Chactas if he were a Christian, and when he told her that he had not forsaken the gods of his father, she departed.

For many days the tribe marched, taking Chactas with them, and each night Atala visited him by the fire. One night, after Chactas had been tied to a tree, Atala appeared and told his guard that she would watch the prisoner for a time. Since she was the daughter of the chief, the guard gladly gave her his place. Quickly she untied the cords and gave Chactas his freedom. But he as quickly placed the cords in her hand, telling her that he wanted to be chained to her forever. She cried out in anguish that their religions separated them. She also seemed to have some other terrible secret that she feared he would learn. Atala begged him to flee without her, but Chactas said that he would rather die by fire than leave her. Neither would change, and so Atala tied Chactas again, hoping that soon he would change his mind. Each night they slipped off into the woods together, but Chactas did not possess her, for her God helped her to deny her passion for her beloved. She prayed that the savage boy might give himself to her God so that one barrier to their love would be broken.

One night her father's warriors discovered them together. Chactas was returned to the camp and placed under heavy guard. The tribe marched on and came at last to the place where Chactas was to be burned at the stake. From far and near Indians gathered to witness his torture and death at a Feast of the Dead. Chactas was prepared for his ordeal in the manner of savages, his body being painted and then laid on the ground, with guards lying across the ropes so that they might feel the slightest movement of the prisoner's body. But in spite of the great precautions, Atala again freed him by a ruse, and they made their escape into the forest. Although they were pursued, the Indians were so drunk from celebrating the Feast of the Dead that the pursuit was only half-hearted, and the lovers had little trouble in eluding them.

But the wilderness almost conquered the fugitives, who were ill-prepared for the hardships they now had to endure. Their fates joined, Atala proclaimed her love for Chactas but said that they could never marry. Although she gave their differences in religion as the only reason, Chactas felt that there was more she feared to tell him. At last, upon his urging, she told him her secret. She was not the daughter of the chief, but the illegitimate child of a white man and the chief's wife. When Chactas learned that the white man was his old friend Lopez, he loved her as a sister as well as a lover. It was through Lopez that she had gained her Christian faith, transmitted to her by her mother.

A terrible storm drove them to the shelter of a tree, and while in that refuge they saw approaching a dog and an old hermit. The hermit was a missionary, Father Aubry, who took them to his grotto and gave them food and shelter. Chactas feared to go, for he was not a Christian, but Father Aubry said that he was one of God's children and made him welcome. When he promised to instruct Chactas in Christianity so that he and Atala could be married, the girl paled at his words.

They learned that Father Aubry had spent almost his entire life among the savages, even though he could have had a more comfortable life in Europe. A good man, he considered it a privilege and not a sacrifice to endure the hardships and dangers of the wilderness. Atala and Chactas became a part of the little community of Christian savages over whom the good priest presided. After a time Chactas began to feel the spirit of God in his heart.

One day, returning from a pilgrimage with Father Aubry, Chactas found Atala apparently dying from a mysterious fever. Then they learned what her true secret had been. On her deathbed Atala's mother had taken the girl's vow that she would always remain a virgin. Her own sin had made her want to protect her daughter, and Atala, knowing nothing of real love, had given her vow which could never be broken. When Father Aubry told the lovers that the bishop in Quebec could release her from her vow, Chactas' heart grew light. In real anguish Atala then told them that she had taken poison because she had believed Chactas forever denied to her. There were no remedies for the poison, and so, after receiving the blessing of the priest and the promise of Chactas that he would embrace the Christian religion so that they could be joined in heaven, the poor virgin expired.

With the priest's aid Chactas buried his beloved. Then he said goodbye to Father Aubry and once more began his wanderings. Many years passed before he received baptism in the faith of his beloved Atala.

And many years more were to pass before the daughter of René, whom Chactas had adopted, took the bones of Atala and Father Aubry and Chactas to the land of the Natchez for burial. Chactas and Father Aubry had been killed by savage enemies. The daughter of René told a curious traveler that he should not grieve. The three friends were together with God.

ATALANTA IN CALYDON

Type of work: Poem
Author: Algernon Charles Swinburne (1837-1909)
Type of plot: Classical tragedy
Time of plot: Remote antiquity
Locale: Ancient Greece
First published: 1865

Principal characters:
Œneus, King of Calydon
Althæa, his wife
Meleager, their son
Atalanta, a virgin huntress
Chorus

Critique:

Atalanta in Calydon, typical of the Victorian treatment of Greek tragedy, was the first of Swinburne's longer works to attract marked critical notice. As in the case of Swinburne's other poetic dramas, it was not written for stage presentation, but for reading. One of the Pre-Raphaelites, Swinburne was criticized for using too much intensity and too violent colors in his poetry. In this poem his intensity and violence are very much the essence of the passionate and soul-stirring description of the characters' fateful existence.

The Story:

Œneus, father of Meleager, had offended Artemis, goddess of the hunt, by offering sacrifices to all the gods except her. As a punishment for his negligence Artemis had sent into Calydon a wild boar that ravaged the land and the crops.

Althæa, embittered by the curse, refused to pay homage to Artemis and raged against the gods. Althæa was a woman of strong will and determination. Years before, when her son Meleager was born, she had had a strange dream concerning his birth. In the dream three spinning women, the Fates, had visited Althæa and had promised for Meleager strength, good fortune, and a bounteous life until the brand on the hearth burned out. On hearing the last part of the prophecy, Althæa had sprung from her bed, grasped the burning brand, and beaten and trampled the heat from it with her bare hands and feet. Then, to guard Meleager's life, she had hidden the brand.

Again she had dreamed that the heatless brand burst into flame as a bud bursts into flower; and with this strange phenomenon Death had come to blow charred ash from the brand into her breast, but there Love had quenched the flame. The omen presaged for Althæa the security of her family; but in spite of her great pride she was not unmindful of the lots which the gods might cast for mortals. These thoughts were in her mind as she went to arm Meleager for the boar hunt. Never had there been born so strong a man of royal birth as Meleager.

The Chorus, reviewing the life span of man, summed up this existence as a passing between a sleep and a sleep.

The warriors of Arcadia were to join the Calydonians in the hunt, and Meleager and Althæa discussed the qualities and characteristics of these men, among them the valiant sons of Leda, Althæa's sister. Meleager described Toxeus and Plexippus, Althæa's brothers, as undoing their deeds with too much talk. Althæa counseled her son against too great pride in earthly accomplishments and advised him to submit his soul to fate. The Chorus admonished Meleager to follow his mother's counsel.

Meleager, recounting the many tumultuous battles he had experienced, pointed out to his mother that in all these frays he had never seen evidence of the infallible gods to whom she and the Chorus would have him submit.

Œneus reported the coming of the Arcadians and said that among them was a woman armed for the hunt. Although Œneus wished to have this woman shown great respect because of her favor from the gods, he warned Meleager against becoming infatuated with her beauty. Althæa, recalling the prophecies of the Fates regarding Meleager's career, added to her husband's warning against earthly love. Again imploring her son to give himself to fate, she told him that he would not die as ordinary men die and that his death would be her death as well. Meleager declared his boundless love for his mother and expressed respect for her teaching. Ever faithful to Zeus, the sole determiner of things, he prepared for the hunt.

The Chorus, philosophizing on Love, saw her blind as a flame, covered by earth for hiding, and fronted by laughter to conceal the tears of desire. According to the portent of the Chorus, man and maid would go forth; the maid's name, Fate; the man's, Death. The Chorus lamented also the meagerness of life's span. This futility, an evil blossom born of sea foam and blood froth, had come into existence with Aphrodite, goddess of love. Before, there had been joy upon the earth, but Aphrodite's influence had resulted in suffering, evil, and devastation.

In the hunt, as predicted, Meleager met the Arcadian maiden. She was Atalanta, the virgin priestess of Artemis, whom Œneus had neglected in his sacrifices and who had sent the wild boar to ravage Calydon. Atalanta invoked Artemis to favor Meleager that he might be victorious in the hunt. Meleager, confessing his love for Atalanta, was taunted by his uncles, Toxeus and Plexippus, for his woman-tonguedness. Althæa pleaded for peace among her kinsmen lest words become snakes and poison them against each other.

The hunt proceeded. According to a message sent by Œneus to Althæa, the expedition demanded energy, courage, and hunting strategy. The boar, crazed by the chase and by the numerous wounds inflicted, charged Meleager, who with all daring and skill slew the animal, thereby ridding Calydon of its curse. Althæa offered praise to the gods. A messenger who had brought the message to Althæa added that pride in earthly accomplishments would bring about destruction.

The Chorus, chanting a song of thanksgiving to the gods, was hushed by the messenger, who ordered them to change their songs to wails of pity because Toxeus and Plexippus had been slain.

Althæa, lamenting the death of her brothers, found comfort in the thought that Meleager would avenge them. The messenger questioned whether her son should slay himself. When Althæa threatened him for his ambiguity, the messenger bluntly informed her that Meleager had slain his uncles.

After the boar had been killed, Toxeus and Plexippus requested that the head and the hide be kept as a monument in Calydon; but Meleager, enamoured of Atalanta, gave her the spoils of the hunt. Pleased with this token of his devotion, Atalanta laughed. The Calydonians construed her reaction as a taunt and sought to destroy her. In furious fighting to protect the maiden, Meleager killed his uncles. Althæa recalled her brothers' kindnesses in their childhood, anticipated her sister's scorn for Meleager's crime, and accepted her fate as a victim of many curses.

The Chorus, endeavoring to comfort Althæa in the loss of her brothers, was rebuked. Had Toxeus and Plexippus died in sacrifice or battle, Althæa maintained, their lives would not have been in vain; but knowing that they had been slain by her son, she could never become reconciled to their deaths or to his crime.

In Meleager's deed, caused by excessive earthly pride and undue desire for attainment, Althæa sensed her error in taking the burning brand from the fire at the time of his birth. Stoically she thrust the brand into the fire that it might be consumed at last. Althæa suffered with torment and anguish as the Chorus described the burning, which resulted in Meleager's death after his return from the hunt.

Meleager reviewed his existence without remorse and besought Œneus and Althæa not to let his name die among men. He described his passing as an empty night harvest in which no man gathers fruit. Althæa died of sorrow. Atalanta, hailing Meleager's greatness, returned to Arcadia. Œneus ruled alone in Calydon.

AUCASSIN AND NICOLETTE

Type of work: Tale
Author: Unknown
Type of plot: Chivalric romance
Time of plot: Twelfth century
Locale: Provence, in France
First transcribed: Fourteenth-century manuscript

Principal characters:
COUNT GARIN DE BEAUCAIRE
AUCASSIN, his son
NICOLETTE, a slave girl

Critique:

Aucassin and Nicolette is considered by many scholars to be the masterpiece of the romances of chivalry. It is written in what is called the *chante-fable,* or song-story style—a prose tale containing verse passages which are sung by a minstrel. In it are found certain Oriental elements and much folklore.

The Story:

Count Bougars de Valence and Count Garin de Beaucaire were at war. Count Garin had one son, Aucassin, who was so smitten by love that he would neither accept the duties of knighthood nor participate in his father's quarrel, unless his father consented to his love for Nicolette. She was a slave girl, bought by a captain of the town from the Saracens and reared as his own daughter. Count Garin agreed to the marriage of Aucassin to any daughter of a king or count, but not to Nicolette. He went to see the captain and told him to send Nicolette away. The captain said that he would keep Nicolette out of sight, and so she was imprisoned in the high chamber of a palace with an old woman to keep her company.

Rumors sped through the countryside: Nicolette was lost; Nicolette had fled the country; Nicolette was slain by order of Count Garin.

Meanwhile the war between the two counts grew more fierce, but Aucassin still refused to fight. Father and son then made a covenant; Aucassin would go into the battle, and if God willed that he should survive, the count must agree to allow him two or three words and one kiss from Nicolette. Aucassin rode into the fray, but thoughts of Nicolette so distracted him that he was captured. Then Aucassin reflected that if he were slain, he would have no chance at all to see Nicolette. Therefore he laid his hand on his sword and began fighting with all his strength. He killed ten knights and wounded seven and took Count Bougars prisoner. But when Count Garin refused to keep the covenant, Aucassin released Count Bougars. Aucassin was cast into a dungeon.

Nicolette, knowing her companion to be asleep, escaped from her prison by a rope made of bed linen and went to the castle where Aucassin lay. While they exchanged lovers' vows, the guards came searching for Nicolette, as her escape had been discovered. But a friendly sentinel warned Nicolette of their coming. She leaped into the moat and, bruised and bleeding, climbed the outer wall.

Nicolette fell asleep in a thicket near the castle. Next day she saw some shepherds eating their lunch at a fountain nearby. She asked them to take a message to Aucassin, saying there was a beast in the forest and that he should have this beast and not part with one of its limbs for any price. Nicolette built herself a lodge within the forest and waited to prove her lover's faith.

Aucassin was taken from his prison and allowed to attend a great feast, but he had no joy in it. A friendly knight offered his horse to Aucassin and suggested that he ride into the forest. Aucassin was only too happy for a chance to get away. He met the shepherds by the fountain and heard what Nicolette had told them. Aucassin prayed God that he would find his quarry.

He rode in all haste through the thorny forest. Toward evening he began to weep because his search had been fruitless. He met a huge, ugly fellow, leaning on a terrible cudgel. Aucassin told him that he mourned for a white hound he had lost. The burly fellow scornfully replied that he had lost his best ox and had searched fruitlessly for three days without meat or drink. Aucassin gave the man twenty sols to pay for the beast. They parted and went their separate ways.

Aucassin found the lodge built by Nicolette and rested there that night. Nicolette heard Aucassin singing and came to him. The next day they mounted Aucassin's horse and journeyed until they came to the seas. Aucassin and Nicolette embarked upon a ship. A terrible storm carried them to Torelore. First Aucassin fought with the king of that strange land and then freed the king of his enemies. He and Nicolette lived happily in Torelore until Saracens besieged the castle and captured all within it. Aucassin was put in one ship and Nicolette in another. A storm scattered the ships, and that in which Aucassin was a prisoner drifted ashore at Beaucaire. He was now the Count of Beaucaire, his parents having died.

Nicolette was in the ship bearing the King of Carthage, who was her true father. They did not recognize each other because Nicolette had been but a child when she was stolen. But when she saw the walls of Carthage memory came back to her, and she revealed her identity in a song. The king gave her great honor and desired to marry her to a king of the Saracens, but Nicolette remained steadfast in her love for Aucassin. She disguised herself as a minstrel and took ship for Provence, where she traveled from castle to castle until she came to Beaucaire.

In the great hall Nicolette sang of her adventures. When Aucassin heard her song, he took her aside and inquired concerning Nicolette. He asked her to return to the land where Nicolette lived and bring her to him. Nicolette returned to the captain's house and there she clothed herself in rich robes and sent for Aucassin. And so at last they were wedded and lived long years with great joy.

THE AUTOBIOGRAPHY OF BENJAMIN FRANKLIN

Type of work: Autobiography
Author: Benjamin Franklin (1706-1790)
Time: 1706-1757
Locale: Boston, London, Philadelphia
First published: 1791; first printed in Paris, as *Mémoires*

Principal personages:
Benjamin Franklin
Josiah Franklin, his father
James Franklin, his brother and first employer
Sir William Keith, Governor of Pennsylvania
Mr. Denham, a merchant
Mr. Meredith, Franklin's partner in the print shop
Alexander Hamilton
Governor Morris

Addressing himself to his "Dear Son," Benjamin Franklin first began in Twyford, England, at the age of sixty-five, to set down reminiscences of his early days. For years he had been collecting data about his ancestors, who had lived in Ecton, Northamptonshire, as far back as 1555, the oldest date of the town records; and he thought that his son William Franklin (1731-1813) would someday be interested in the "circumstances" of his father's life, just as Franklin had delighted in anecdotes relating to his family.

The work was composed in installments, the first section, dealing with Franklin's first twenty-four years, the product of a week of leisure in England in 1771. Then, because of his political activities abroad and at home, he had no further opportunity to continue his task until the urgings of friends persuaded him to resume his writing in 1783. The final section was probably written between November, 1789, and April, 1790. Titled *Mémoires,* it was first printed in France in 1791. No complete text appeared until 1868.

In spite of the lengthy period of composition, only Franklin's life before July, 1757, is covered, with a few comments on his activities in the following year. But the failure to complete the *Autobiography* beyond his fifty-first year does not mean that Franklin failed to write of his activities over the next thirty years. Some of his most important diplomatic missions are reported in individual compositions, such as the sample he showed to Jefferson of the "history of my life" that he said he was preparing. They cover "Negotiations in London for Effecting a Reconciliation between Great Britain and the American Colonies" and the "Journal of the Negotiations for Peace with Great Britain from March 21st to July 1st, 1782."

In addition, this indefatigable letter writer filled his correspondence (in many ways the most interesting part of his writing) with details and sketches. Some of the most complete are the letters to his wife, whom he addressed as "My dear Child." By combining the correspondence chronologically, a biographer can obtain Franklin's personal reactions to practically everything that happened to him. These letters show Franklin as the first real American who stood apart from European influences.

The Franklin family, whose ancestors had lived in the Northamptonshire village of Ecton from the time they assumed a surname originally signifying a middle-class landowner, was transplanted to Boston about 1682, when Benjamin's father Josiah brought his wife and several children to Massachusetts. After his wife's death, the older Franklin remarried. Benjamin, born of the second marriage, was the youngest son of seventeen children.

Fond of study and quickly learning to

read, Benjamin was destined for the ministry until his father, a tallow-candler and soap-boiler by trade, began calculating the cost of education and the pitiable salary received by most ministers. So the boy was taken out of school to learn a trade. After a brief period as his father's assistant he was, at the age of twelve, apprenticed to his half brother James, a printer. In his brother's shop he saw his first writing in print, topical ballads written to be sold in the streets.

He continued to read: *The Pilgrim's Progress,* Plutarch's *Parallel Lives,* essays by Defoe, Burton, and Mather. A volume of the *Spectator,* acquired by chance, revealed to him the importance of style and, like Robert Louis Stevenson at a later date, he taught himself by rewriting and comparing sentences. From this printshop came the fifth—Franklin mistakenly says the second—newspaper in America, the *New England Courant,* to which Franklin became an anonymous contributor.

Quarrels with his brother eventually sent the seventeen-year-old apprentice to Philadelphia looking for employment. His arrival early in the morning, with three-penny-worth of rolls in his mouth and under his arms as he walked up Market Street past the home of Miss Read, whom he was to marry later, was Philadelphia's first sight of one of its most distinguished citizens.

Neither Bradford nor Keimer, the only printers in Philadelphia, was very advanced. After the boy found a place in Keimer's shop, his wide reading and his ability to talk and to listen brought him many friends. Finally Governor Keith offered to send him to England to buy type and equipment for a shop of his own. Arriving in London, he learned that Keith, whose credit was not good, had provided nothing but promises. To support himself, Franklin found work in a printing house. After eighteen months he was happy to accept the offer of a merchant who wanted him to take back to America a consignment of merchandise. Back in Philadelphia, he worked for a time in Keimer's shop; then, finding a partner in Hugh Meredith, he and the Welsh Pennsylvanian set up their own establishment. They prospered and in 1729 Franklin became the sole proprietor, having bought out Meredith, whose drinking habits were distasteful to the temperate, frugal Franklin. He branched out as a stationer. In 1730 he founded the *Pennsylvania Gazette* and also married Miss Read. At this point the first section of the *Autobiography* ends.

In 1784, in Passy, France, Franklin again began to write his story, this time addressed more generally to the reading public than to his son. With friends interested in scientific and intellectual matters he had in 1743 founded a Junto for their mutual exchange of ideas and intellectual improvement; this was later to become the American Philosophical Society. The members sponsored a library for the use of the public.

Now that he had educated himself, Franklin sought moral perfection. He set down twelve virtues, then added a thirteenth, Pride, at the suggestion of critical friends. But he had reason to be proud. He had learned to speak fluent French, Spanish, and Italian. His civic spirit, born when he was appointed postmaster of Philadelphia, induced him to reorganize the fire department, start a movement to pave and light the streets, and to establish an academy which later became the University of Pennsylvania. The death of a son from smallpox caused him to argue for inoculation against the disease. He invented an improved form of heating stove and offered it free for general use, only to learn that he had brought wealth to one stove manufacturer. Meanwhile, beginning in 1732, he published *Poor Richard's Almanack,* the usual collection of agricultural and astronomical data to which he added a compendium of practical wisdom and moral maxims. This venture also brought him wealth and enabled him to retire from active business in 1748.

His thoughts about defense caused him to campaign for the establishment of a militia, but this man who so candidly confessed his "errata," his mistakes, was too well acquainted with himself to accept the appointment as their colonel. Other civic improvements, when initiated by others, needed his approval before his fellow citizens would adopt them. He extended his influence beyond his own city to the whole colony, and to other colonies. Yale and Harvard awarded honorary degrees to this self-taught scholar, and he was elected to membership in cultural and scientific societies at home and abroad.

Braddock sought Franklin's advice in campaigning against the Indians, only to disregard it with disastrous results. After selling out his shop to his foreman, he occupied his time with philosophical concerns and scientific experiments, particularly those relating to electricity. His theories, when ignored or contradicted abroad, led to his experiments with lightning in 1752.

Having represented Pennsylvania at the Albany Congress of 1754, he was chosen to represent it in protests to the English crown. His arrival in England, July 27, 1757, is the last date in his story of himself.

THE AUTOBIOGRAPHY OF BENVENUTO CELLINI

Type of work: Autobiography
Author: Benvenuto Cellini (1500-1571)
Type of plot: Chronicle of adventure and art
Time of plot: 1500-1562
Locale: Italy and France
First published: Sixteenth-century manuscript

Principal characters:
BENVENUTO CELLINI, goldsmith, artist, sculptor
POPE CLEMENT VII
POPE PAUL III
FRANCIS I, King of France
COSIMO DE' MEDICI, Duke of Florence
BANDINELLO, a rival sculptor

Critique:

The Autobiography of Benvenuto Cellini, written 1558-1562 and circulated in manuscript form until printed in 1730, is perhaps the finest document left to moderns from the period of the Italian Renaissance. In its pages we view intimately, through the eyes of an artistic and adventurous contemporary, the men, women, princes, dukes, and popes of the sixteenth century. In addition, we see the artists who produced some of the great pictures and sculpture which we take more or less for granted. In Cellini's backward glances we can feel some measure of the pangs and troubles and joys that went into those art works and the climate of culture which produced them. To judge Cellini and his contemporaries by twentieth-century standards is common enough to bear comment. It suffices to say that no one can appreciate Cellini as a man and as an artist who does judge by current standards. He was a product of his time, and on that basis he must be judged as an author, a man, and an artist.

The Story:

At the age of fifty-eight Benvenuto Cellini began to set down his memoirs. He related first a fictional version of the founding of Florence by his ancestors and then began the story of his life.

Benvenuto, destined by his father to be a musician, was as a lad taught to play the flute and sing by note. But lessons in music from his father failed to interest him, and at the age of fifteen Cellini apprenticed himself to a goldsmith. Cellini said of himself that he had a natural bent for the work and in a few months he had surpassed men long in the trade.

As an apprentice and, later, as a journeyman goldsmith, Cellini on his travels through Italy did fine work and acted the part of a bravo. He became an excellent swordsman and handler of the poniard, as he proved when he killed an enemy in a street brawl.

In 1527 the Constable of Bourbon marched on Rome and besieged Pope Clement VII in his fortress. Cellini, then in Rome and in sympathy with the pope, served the pontiff valiantly as an artillerist and as a goldsmith, having been commissioned by the besieged prelate to melt down much jewelry and turn it into a more transportable form. Later he boasted that during the siege he had killed the Constable of Bourbon and wounded the Prince of Orange.

After the siege was lifted and a truce declared, Cellini returned to Florence and killed his brother's murderer. He later went to Mantua. Ill with fever in that city, he returned to Florence. When Pope Clement declared war on that city, however, Cellini left his shop and trade to enter the papal service. While in Rome he made a medallion of tremendous size for the papal cope, a work which was the beginning of his fortunes. It was a splendid button, pleasing greatly the pontiff for whom it was made. From then on, during Clement's life, Cellini did much work for the papacy.

Cellini's career under Pope Clement was a stormy one. His fiery temper often caused him no end of trouble; for example, he received the commission of the papal mint and then lost it because of his foolhardy and unmannerly actions.. He killed another enemy in a quarrel but was lucky enough to be pardoned by his patron.

Cellini's great commission from Pope Clement was for a gold chalice. The chalice was never finished, for Clement died too soon. During the last years of his life, however, the chalice was a matter of contention between the pope and his goldsmith. Cellini, an independent and temperamental workman, often got into trouble because of the slowness with which he worked. And the pope, according to Cellini's account, often forgot that gold was needed to make the vessel.

Upon the accession of Cardinal Farnese as Pope Paul III, Cellini went into his service for a time. But Cellini was away from Rome a great deal, at one time taking service with Cosimo de' Medici, Duke of Florence. Upon his return Cellini was imprisoned on a charge of homicide. The pope granted him a safe-conduct for a time, but eventually he was imprisoned. Only after many difficulties did he receive a pardon for the slaying.

Cellini came to the notice of Emperor Charles V when that monarch visited Rome and was presented by the pope with a Book of Hours bound into a gold cover encrusted with jewels, the work of Cellini. A short time later Cellini was sent for by Francis I, King of France, but before he could leave Rome he was accused of theft and thrown into prison by the pope's *bargello,* or police force. Cellini cleared himself of the charge, but he had made so many enemies that he was kept in prison for many months and suffered, at times, cruel punishment.

Action on Cellini's behalf by King Francis only served to make his lot harder. At last Cellini managed to escape by using bed sheets to lower himself from the prison tower and to get himself over the prison walls. Having broken his leg in his flight, he was recaptured. Released after a long period of confinement, he found asylum with a French cardinal and finally with the aid of Cardinal d'Este of Ferrara made his way to France.

In France, with King Francis as his patron, the goldsmith and artist turned to sculpture. He executed an amazing statue of Jupiter for the king and also constructed the large statue of the nymph of Fontainebleau. But Cellini made an enemy of Madame d'Etampes, the king's mistress, who made his career difficult and his life dangerous, and the Cardinal of Ferrara did not fulfill the promises he had made. Cellini's amorous adventures also got him into many difficulties.

In desperation, and with some hopes of a better future, Cellini left France and returned to his native Florence in 1545, there to find protection under the patronage of Cosimo de' Medici.

In Florence he made an enemy of the Duchess of Florence and a famous sculptor, Bandinello, whose work Cellini reviled in public and to the sculptor's face. As in France, a woman's enmity, the dislike of fellow artists, the pettifogging of minor officials, and small commissions used up Cellini's valuable time in Florence. Nevertheless, while there, in the years after 1545, Cellini did his greatest work, a bronze Perseus of which he was extremely proud.

Following the completion of that statue, Cellini went to work on other pieces, including a tremendous crucifix with a mausoleum at its base, to hold his body when he had died.

While working in Florence for the duke, Cellini bought some farm land which, failing to bring him the revenues he had been promised, embroiled him in a long and upsetting litigation. That trouble, plus the enmity of the duchess, finally drove him from Florence. In 1562, while the duke and his family were away on a journey, Cellini left Florence and headed for Pisa. With that final entry, the departure for Pisa, Cellini ended his memoirs, though he lived for eight more years.

THE AUTOCRAT OF THE BREAKFAST-TABLE

Type of work: Informal essays
Author: Oliver Wendell Holmes (1809-1894)
Time: 1857-1858
Locale: Boston
First published: 1858

Principal characters:
The Autocrat
The Schoolmistress,
The Divinity-Student,
The Old Gentleman, and
The Young Fellow Called John, the Autocrat's fellow boarders
The Landlady
The Landlady's Daughter
Benjamin Franklin, the Landlady's son
The Professor, and
The Poet, friends of the Autocrat who, though never present, contribute to the discussion

At one point in the recounting of his breakfast-table experiences, the Autocrat observed that, since medieval times, the reputation of Aristotle had passed through two stages and was then (one hundred years ago) entering its third. First came the period of idolization when everything attributed to the Greek sage was accepted not only as scientifically sound but as absolute and ultimate truth. Then came the period of critical examination, the stage at which his scientific inaccuracies were discovered and, as a result, all of his ideas belittled and discredited. Finally, in Dr. Holmes' time, there was the third stage, the enlightened period when the scientific inaccuracies were excused, being viewed in historical perspective as unavoidable, and the value of his philosophical insights reasserted.

On a smaller time scale, the reputation of Oliver Wendell Holmes, along with that of the Cambridge-Boston group as a whole (as opposed to that of the Concord group), has gone through the first two of these stages but shows no signs, as yet, of entering the third. Although few, and certainly never Dr. Holmes himself, actually believed that Boston was "The Hub of the Universe," Harvard Yard and the eastern end of Beacon Street (including the first eight doors on Arlington Street so as to take in the offices of the *Atlantic Monthly*) were for better than half a century regarded as the dual nerve center, as it were, the cerebrum and cerebellum, of American culture. A Cambridge-born Harvard Professor of Anatomy, a member of the Saturday Club, a resident of Beacon Street, Dr. Holmes did not merely share in such regard; he helped to create it. It was he, in fact, who coined the term, "The Hub." (But the original statement, as it appeared in Chapter VI of *The Autocrat of the Breakfast-Table,* was made, not by a Bostonian, but an outlander whose remark was, "Boston State-House is the hub of the solar system.") As lecturer, poet, novelist, biographer, and, most of all, perhaps, as the author of *The Autocrat of the Breakfast-Table* and later *The Professor at the Breakfast-Table* (1860) and *The Poet at the Breakfast-Table* (1872), Dr. Holmes helped to establish in the public mind a concept of Bostonian wit, sensibility, and culture.

Gradually—not suddenly as did the Wonderful One-Hoss Shay (Chapter XI of *The Autocrat*)—the reputations of many of the New England writers seemed autumnal and dry, and a season of critical neglect set in. Today, however, the situation has somewhat changed. Hawthorne has been resurrected by the

New Critics; the cautiously radical Emerson has been turned into a spokesman for the Neo-conservatives; and Thoreau is a pet nonconformist in these conformist times. The Concordians have entered their third stage, but not the Cambridge-Bostonians. Yet, while it is no doubt true that the poetry of the Cambridge-Boston group is a mixture of neoclassic moralizing combined with a nostalgic and academic romanticism, it should be remembered that Longfellow had a gift for storytelling, that Lowell was a sprightly satirist, and that Holmes possessed wit, urbanity, a background of knowledge, and a tolerant, all-encompassing view of life, the like of which has not appeared in English letters on either side of the Atlantic since his death.

It can be argued that in regard to Holmes such qualities did not produce the reputation, but are deduced from it, that the alleged wit and urbanity are really provincial smugness, and that what passes for a tolerant and total life-view is in reality a carefully cultivated dilettantism. Such arguments have been made, but they neglect both the facts provided by history and the literary evidence provided by *The Autocrat of the Breakfast-Table*. The facts show that Holmes was learned in both science and humane letters and that he was one of the foremost advocates of technological progress in the nineteenth-century United States. One English critic has said that he, rather than Emerson, deserves the title, the "American Montaigne."

It is on an objective reading of *The Autocrat of the Breakfast-Table* that the case for Holmes must finally rest. *The Autocrat* appeared originally in the first twelve issues of the *Atlantic Monthly* (1857-1858) and was published in book form directly after this appearance. Its plan is simple enough: the Autocrat lives in a Beacon Hill boarding house; the essays are, we are told, reports, somewhat condensed, and interlarded with the Autocrat's comments, of the conversations that take place each morning at the breakfast table of this remarkable establishment, a table at which is found a most heterogeneous collection of boarders. Each has his say occasionally, but his main purpose is to provide a sounding board for the wit and philosophizing of the Autocrat. There is conversation, but mostly (as it is finally reported, in any case) there is monologue. The varied responses of the boarders allow Holmes' wit to play over a wide range of subjects, to jump easily from point to point, and to juxtapose ideas that have no apparent relevance.

The result may seem chaotic at first. One is carried along by the bubbling cleverness easily enough, but apparently to no particular place. For example, the topics of the first chapter are, in order of appearance: (1) the algebraic classification of minds; (2) the value of mutual admiration societies; (3) the meaninglessness of brute fact; (4) the typing of various kinds of speakers; (5) the dangers of specialized learning; (6) an attack on the use of puns (Holmes deplores the use of them here but cannot always resist them; later, for example, he speaks of the landlady's economically-minded poor relation as standing by her guns, "ready to repel boarders"); (7) the poverty of pure logic as opposed to common sense; (8) the foibles of young poets; (9) the superiority of men of family over self-made men, "*other things being equal*" (Holmes' italics); (10) the rendering of a pair of poems. Holmes makes these points interesting in themselves, but there seems to be little connection between one and another. As the reader continues, however, he becomes aware that certain ideas are recurrent; that certain themes are announced, dropped, but repeated later with variations; that there are psychological connections in the apparently chance juxtapositions of ideas—that the whole thing develops in a geometric, not in an arithmetic, progression.

The effect is produced by a means that

is at the same time modern and metaphysical. Holmes was a Proper Bostonian, a Victorian American, and it has been said that his sympathies lay with the eighteenth century, that he was at heart a Neo-Johnsonian. This assertion is in some respects valid. But if his conscious affinities turned back one hundred years, his unconscious ones turned back two. Andrew Lang notes "a fleeting resemblance to Sir Thomas Browne," a resemblance based on "a community of professional studies," but this similarity between Holmes and the author of *Religio Medici* and *Urn Burial* is not explained simply by the fact that both were medical men. Holmes possessed the "divided sensibility" found also in the metaphysical school; and Browne, it is now acknowledged, was a metaphysical poet writing in prose. This division in Holmes, obscured as it is by his neoclassical pose, has been too often neglected.

He was divided along a different axis from Browne's, for he lived under different conditions; but the division is still there. First was the religious division: Holmes had disavowed the Puritanism of his fathers, but the scars of his youthful indoctrination were never completely gone. More important, perhaps, at least as far as its reflection in *The Autocrat of the Breakfast-Table* is concerned, is his divided allegiance between Brahminism, which stood for all the deeply rooted things that meant the good life to him, on the one hand, and science, which meant technology and, with it, the unleashing of those forces, human and mechanical, that would destroy Brahminism, on the other. The division could not exercise itself in Holmes' poetry because the moralizing-romantic tradition was too binding. But when Holmes found in his hands a form free from restrictions and with which he could experiment as he wished, his divided sensibility found expression in the essay through the use of what are very close to metaphysical techniques.

First, there is the juxtaposition of topics. The most extreme, and the one that most strongly anticipates the modern reflection of the metaphysical, is Chapter IX, in which Holmes presents a series of childhood reminiscences—the stuff of poems:

> Many times I have come bearing flowers such as my garden grew; but now I offer you this poor, brown, homely growth, you may cast it away as worthless. And yet—and yet—it is something better than flowers; it is a *seed-capsule.*

There is also the shift in prose styles—from the colloquial or the scientific to the lofty and poetic—a device that harks back to the style of Browne. But most important are the similitudes—the similes, the metaphors, the extended analogies. *The Autocrat of the Breakfast-Table* is full of them. But the important thing is that they are functional, not decorative; they are the very fabric of the work. Holmes uses them to bring into focus the two parts of his divided world. Science and beauty stand for the two parts of the key dichotomy, represented in character by Holmes' own two alter egos, the Professor and the Poet, and playing their dual parts in all of the analogies:

> We get beautiful effects from wit—all the prismatic colors—but never the object as it is in fair daylight. A pun, which is a kind of wit, is a different and much shallower trick in mental optics; throwing the *shadows* of two objects so that one overlies the other. Poetry uses the rainbow tints for special effects, but always keeps its essential object in the purest white light of truth.

Through the interplay of these two conflicting worlds, by means of analogy and opposition of character, the themes of the work are brought out. They appear as questions, not as answers, for awareness of the divided world permits no dogmatic assertions. What is love and what is beauty? How are human communication and expression achieved? What, after all, is really important? And how can it be found—by sculling beneath the bridges of the Charles, by searching for seed capsules of poetry in one's memory, or by counting the rings of an elm that stood when Shakespeare was a boy?

To bring out these questions in a meaningful way is a decided literary achievement. Not that *The Autocrat of the Breakfast-Table* is entirely a great literary work. Holmes cannot maintain his metaphysical detachment. He becomes too concerned with his characters and they begin to lose their reflecting qualities. He becomes too concerned with love: in the end the Autocrat and the Schoolmistress degenerate into the principal figures of a rather sentimental romance. So there are weaknesses, true; but they are not the weaknesses for which the "Genteel Tradition" is usually condemned. Only half of Holmes was in that tradition anyway. In respect to that other half, he deserves to have his reputation advanced to its third stage.

THE AWAKENING OF SPRING

Type of work: Drama
Author: Frank Wedekind (1864-1918)
Type of plot: Psychological realism
Time of plot: Nineteenth century
Locale: Germany
First presented: 1891

Principal characters:
MELCHIOR GABOR, an intelligent high school boy
MORITZ STIEFEL, his friend
WENDLA BERGMANN, a schoolgirl, aged fourteen
MRS. BERGMANN, her mother
MRS. GABOR, and
MR. GABOR, Melchior's parents
MARTHA, and
THEA, schoolgirls
ILSE, a young prostitute and model
RENTIER STIEFEL, Moritz' father
A MUFFLED GENTLEMAN

Critique:

In *The Awakening of Spring,* Wedekind presents a plot stripped to its naturalistic essentials: the suffering inflicted on the very young when their burgeoning native, erotic consciousness confronts the deadly, adult, hypocritical unconsciousness of the society to which they are answerable. The plot is, however, only the crude skeleton for a powerful anti-naturalistic dramaturgy which relies on its own intractable poetic logic. Within a loose episodic structure, scenes are articulated by means of ironic parallel actions, and an unsubtle but dramatically effective use of symbolic references. Dramatic tension depends not upon the formal plot revelations, but on swift modulations of response elicited in the spectator by the mixture of satire and tragedy; caricature yields to lyrical statement, the horrific yields to the commonplace, the commonplace to that realm of parable inhabited by the existential absurd—or rather haunted, in this case, by the figure of the muffled gentleman, to whom the play is dedicated.

The Story:

Wendla hung up again in the closet the long, grown-up dress which her mother had just completed, protesting that she did not see why next year would not be soon enough to put on such a penitential garment. Mrs. Bergmann acquiesced with motherly affection to her daughter's wish to continue wearing, for the present, the freer, familiar clothes of childhood, remarking at the same time on the fact that Wendla had retained her childhood grace without a trace of the gawkiness usual to her age. Mrs. Bergmann was not without misgivings, even while she cherished that appearance of innocence and grace, and she expressed her uneasiness in various equivocating substitutes for her real fears, all of which Wendla gaily laughed away.

Melchior Gabor, Moritz Stiefel, and their classmates broke up their games to go prepare their homework. Moritz and Melchior, walking home in the spring night, became involved in a discussion of the meaninglessness of the exam system and the sexual phenomena of adolescence which they were beginning to experience. For Moritz, the mysterious sexual pressures were a great burden, partly because they hindered his already desperate attempts to meet the rigid demands made upon him by school and parents. Though a poor student, and excessively timid, he possessed an acute sensitivity in certain areas which went unrecognized by all but Melchior, who was his closest friend and, unlike Moritz, an extremely promising student. The ease with which Melchior dealt with his schoolwork left him time not only for metaphysical speculation, but for a scholarly acquisition of the facts of reproduction, which he now offered to impart. Moritz accepted Melchior's offer on the condition that the facts be in written form and slipped into his books where he could come upon them as if by chance.

On a blustery spring day not long afterward, Wendla, Thea, and Martha also exchanged confidences on the subjects of parental tyranny, love, marriage, and children, embellishing their remarks with the gaudy and arbitrary imagination of childish ignorance. The talk turned to boys of their own age, and to the peculiar behavior which they sometimes exhibited. Wendla disclosed that Melchior had once told her he believed in nothing. Mention of the spring floods revealed the fact that Melchior had come near drowning in one of the swollen streams, but was saved by his ability as a swimmer.

In another gathering of the schoolboys, it was revealed that Moritz had illicitly entered the staff common room (repository of all records), driven by the desire to learn whether he was to be promoted. When Moritz appeared, dazed by his own boldness but relieved by the knowledge of a provisional remove, he was taunted by the boys for his statement that he would have shot himself had he not received it.

Melchior and Wendla met by chance in the woods, where Wendla had gone to gather woodruff for her mother and had stopped to daydream by a brook. Melchior persuaded her to sit down and asked if she enjoyed going among the poor to take them food and money, errands on which she was often sent by her mother. Wendla's answer, that it gave her pleasure, began an argument on the reality of virtue and selflessness.

Wendla also confessed that she daydreamed of being a poor beggar child, beaten by a cruel father, although she herself had never been beaten. She picked a switch and begged Melchior to strike her, to show her how such punishment felt. The boy at first refused; then, as she persisted in her request, he threw the stick aside and pummeled her with his fists before he ran away into the wood, crying out in anguish.

Moritz found himself again on the verge of school failure. While reading *Faust* with Melchior, he related his grandmother's story of the headless queen, a tale which had been haunting him during his studying. It told of a fabulously beautiful queen unfortunately born without a head who was one day conquered by a king who happened to be provided with two heads that argued constantly. The court wizard gave one to the queen, on whom it proved surpassingly becoming, and the two were married with great joy, the heads now being on the best of terms. Melchior's mother entered with tea and words of encouragement for Moritz. Noticing the *Faust,* she wondered if they ought to be reading it, saying elliptically, however, that she preferred to place her trust in Melchior rather than in pedagogical principles. Realizing that she was thinking of the Gretchen episode, they became annoyed, Melchior because everyone insisted on acting as if the world turned on nothing but obscenities, Moritz because he had begun to fear that it actually did. He had received Melchior's sex essay which affected him like a series of dim recollections. He was disposed to exalt the satisfaction experienced by the woman, and regarded that of the man as insipid.

Meanwhile, Wendla persistently interrogated her mother on the subject of her sister's latest baby. She mocked her mother's giggling fairy tales by pretending to see a ridiculous vision outside the window. At Wendla's insistence, Mrs. Bergmann was forced to begin telling her daughter how babies come about, but finally she managed to evade the issue by saying that the things required were marriage and an enormity of love which Wendla was too young to comprehend.

A short time later Wendla went looking for Melchior and, disarmed by his intensity and his tortured insistence that there is no such thing as love, she remained with him in the hayloft, where she conceived a child.

Moritz finally reached the end of his resources and, at the brink of suicide over the realization that he was about to fail, wrote to Mrs. Gabor for a loan which would enable him to leave home. She, considering it her duty to refuse, appealed to his common sense and better nature. At dusk, in a parting soliloquy pervaded by his unfailing wry humor but mixed with self-pity, he concluded that life was not his responsibility. The Headless Queen beckoned. Life was a matter of taste. His only regret was in not having known sexual fulfillment, the most human experience of all. When Ilse, a young model with an insatiable appetite for life, appeared to tempt him with tales of her warm, carefree, animal existence, he wavered but then rejected the opportunity she offered.

Moritz' suicide precipitated an investigation on the part of the school officials. Melchior, charged with indecency on the basis of the notes on sex discovered among Moritz' books, became the scapegoat.

At the funeral service Moritz was condemned for his crime against man and God by the adults in attendance. Rentier Stiefel comforted himself by repeating he had never cared for the boy from a child; he was no son of his. The pastor urged with consummate coarseness that he seek comfort in the arms of his wife. While the reaction of the schoolboys at the funeral was largely one of curiosity as to the exact manner of the suicide, Martha and Ilse brought to the grave a profusion of flowers. Ilse had discovered the suicide pistol and concealed it.

Mrs. Gabor, meeting with indignation her husband's determination to send Melchior to the reformatory, defied anyone to perceive moral corruption in what the boy had written; but she was unable to stand up to the discovery that Wendla was pregnant, and Melchior responsible.

Shortly after her discovery of the cause of her illness, Wendla succumbed to the combined concoctions of Dr. Von Brausepulver and Mother Schmidt for inducing abortion. After her death, Melchior, hounded by society and by his own self-contempt, managed to return to look at her grave. As he wandered enviously among the graves, he encountered Moritz Stiefel, with his head under his arm, who attempted to persuade Melchior to join him in his life among the dead, which he pictured as a fabulous if grotesque freedom. While Melchior hesitated, a muffled gentleman appeared to take Moritz to task for his attempt, his lack of a head, and his general crumbling condition. He accused Moritz of charlatanism and asked Melchior to submit himself to his care. Melchior, contending that he could not entrust himself to a masked unknown, subjected the muffled gentleman to questions regarding his moral position. Moritz admitted that he had been boasting and urged Melchior to accompany the muffled gentleman, who was, in any event, alive. The two alive withdrew together while Moritz returned to warm himself with putrefaction.

THE AXE

Type of work: Novel
Author: Sigrid Undset (1882-1949)
Type of plot: Historical chronicle
Time of plot: Late thirteenth century
Locale: Norway
First published: 1925

Principal characters:
OLAV AUDUNSSON, master of Hestviken
STEINFINN TORESSON, his foster father
INGEBJÖRG JONSDATTER, Steinfinn's wife
INGUNN, Steinfinn's daughter, betrothed to Olav
TORA, another daughter
ARNVID FINNSSON, Steinfinn's kinsman
KOLBEIN TORESSON, Steinfinn's half-brother
TEIT, an Icelander, a clerk

Critique:

The Axe is the first volume of a tetralogy—the others are *The Snake Pit, In the Wilderness,* and *The Son Avenger* —published under one title, *The Master of Hestviken.* These four books together make up a great historical chronicle, a great religious novel, and a novel of character. In this story of thirteenth-century Norway, Sigrid Undset presents a massive picture of human conflicts which are universal and timeless. As a study of man's faith, the novel shows a world poised between the old pagan spirit and Christian belief and practice. Olav Audunsson, her chief character, is the medieval man, virile yet innocent and meek in his simple goodness. *The Axe* tells the story of a murder which he never dared confess without the certainty of harming others, a crime which was to burden his conscience and influence his actions for the rest of his days.

The Story:

The troubles of the Steinfinnssons began when Tore Toresson sent his youngest son to the royal bodyguard at Bergen. There Steinfinn Toresson saw Ingebjörg Jonsdatter, who had come from Denmark with young Queen Ingebjörg, and he fell in love with her. But King Magnus had already promised the girl to his friend, Mattias Haraldsson. Steinfinn was in the Orkneys that winter. The next summer he went to Bergen and stole Ingebjörg out of the king's court.

Although Tore was displeased with his son, he gave the couple the manor at Frettastein, where they lived as if in lawful wedlock. After a time the queen reconciled all concerned, and Steinfinn and Ingebjörg held their wedding at the royal court in Oslo. Ingunn, their first child, was three when her parents were wed.

Meanwhile Mattias Haraldsson had gone into foreign lands, so that Steinfinn had little thought of his ill will. When Steinfinn and Ingebjörg had been married about seven years, however, Mattias came one night with his men, bound Steinfinn, and shamed him before his household. After Mattias rode home to his own manor, young Olav Audunsson cut his foster father's bonds. Steinfinn swore that he would not sleep with his wife until he could show the world that she was his without Mattias' leave.

But Steinfinn had no revenge at that time, for Mattias sailed again to foreign lands. Meanwhile life grew slack and somber at Frettastein. Steinfinn was much in the company of Kolbein, his grim half-brother, and Ingebjörg lived in a house apart with her women and her two small sons, Hallvard and Jon. Ingunn and Tora, the older daughters, would have been left to themselves if it had not been for Olav Audunsson, Steinfinn's foster son.

Olav's father had been Audun Ingolfsson of Hestviken; his mother had died at his birth. One summer, when Steinfinn met Auden at the Thing, the man from Vik said that he was soon to die. There was much drinking that night, and it seemed good sport to betroth little Ingunn to Olav. Next morning Steinfinn would have cried quits on the agreement, but Audun held him to his word. So Olav grew up at Frettastein. An aged kinsman managed his estate at Hestviken.

All his life Olav remembered a day just past his sixteenth year. The edge of his ancient Viking ax, Kin-fetch, being blunted, he took it to an armorer in Hamar. Ingunn stole away from the house to go with him, and the two rowed up the fjord under sunny skies. Later he never knew whether his deep feeling of pleasure came from a sudden, disturbing sense of Ingunn's loveliness, the summer light over the town, or the vesper service he and Ingunn went to before they started home through the dark; but he always thought that day the happiest of his life.

Arnvid Finnsson, Ingunn's cousin, brought word that Mattias was at Birid, and two days later Steinfinn and his kinsmen, Olav among them, rode away. There was great merriment at Frettastein when they returned. Mattias and his housecarls had been taken by surprise, and Steinfinn had killed his enemy in fair fight. Steinfinn, badly wounded, laughed at his own hurts. After he and Ingebjörg went to their loft-room, the dancing and drinking continued, and some became wanton. Half-tipsy, Olav went with Ingunn to her loft.

That night Ingebjörg died suddenly in her sleep and Steinfinn's wounds reopened. From that time on he grew steadily weaker. While he lay dying, Arnvid asked him to declare the marriage of Ingunn and Olav but he refused, saying the settlement had never been clearly drawn. After Steinfinn's death Olav found among his own gear the betrothal ring he had given Ingunn many years before. He suspected Kolbein of that sly attempt to repudiate the betrothal.

Arnvid stayed on at Frettastein for a time. That fall Olav spent many nights with Ingunn in her loft. When Arnvid finally learned how matters stood, he advised Olav to lay the case before Bishop Thorfinn in Hamar and to claim that he had only fulfilled a marriage contract which Ingunn's kinsmen had broken. Bishop Thorfinn was a stern man but just, and he saw that Olav had some right in the wrong he had done. All might have gone well for the lovers if the Kolbeinssons had not quarreled with Arnvid and Olav in the convent guest house at Hamar. At last, unable to endure their taunts, Olav raised Kin-fetch and struck down Einar Kolbeinsson.

Proclaimed an outlaw, Olav fled to Sweden, and Ingunn went to stay with Arnvid at Micklebö. There she was taken with an illness so strange that Arnvid's mother accused the Kolbeinssons of witchcraft. After her recovery the girl went to live with her aunt, the Lady Magnhild of Berg. Olav, meanwhile, had gone to his mother's kinsmen in Denmark. Tora married Haakon Gautsson and came to visit at Berg, where her first child was born. Ingunn wished for a husband and child of her own, but she grew stubborn when her relatives talked of marrying her to any of the young men who came wooing.

Four years later Olav returned in the train of Earl Alf Erlingsson, Queen Ingebjörg's liegeman. On promise of penance and payment of blood-atonement to Kolbein for Einar's slaying, the Steinfinnssons acknowledged him as Ingunn's betrothed. Then the queen died and her son proclaimed Alf and all his men outlaws. Word came that Olav had followed Alf to Sweden. Once more Ingunn was left to wait at Berg.

One summer Teit, an Icelander, came on business to the manor. Mistaking Ingunn for a servant, he was not abashed when he learned that she was a daughter of the house. Ingunn liked the clerk's pert speech and merry ways. At last, out of weakness and pity, she let him stay with her in the house she shared with her aged grandmother. When Olav, no longer an outlaw, came home in the spring, she was carrying Teit's child.

Olav was dismayed when he learned how things were with Ingunn, but he felt bound to her by every tie between them in the past. Bitter because he could not part from her, he offered to claim that he had gone secretly to Berg during his outlawry and that the child was his. Shamed, Ingunn refused so unseemly an offer.

Olav was staying with the Preaching Friars in Hamar. Teit, believing that Olav no longer wanted Ingunn, proposed to Olav that he accompany the Icelander when he went to Arnvid to plead for Ingunn's hand. As Olav prepared for the journey, Kin-fetch, hanging on the wall, rang—old superstition said that when the ax sang, death would follow. That night, at the *sæter* where they stopped to rest, Olav killed Teit and burned the hut. Although he knew he could never confess his deed without shaming Ingunn, he felt that her secret was safe.

When Ingunn's child, a boy, was born, Lady Magnhild gave it to a foster mother, a forester's wife. A short time later Olav went to claim his bride. After years of waiting it was a sorry bridal ale they drank at their wedding feast.

BABBITT

Type of work: Novel
Author: Sinclair Lewis (1885-1951)
Type of plot: Social satire
Time of plot: The 1920's
Locale: Zenith, fictional Midwestern town
First published: 1922

Principal characters:
GEORGE F. BABBITT, a middle-aged real estate broker
MYRA, his wife
TED, their son
VERONA, their daughter
PAUL RIESLING, Babbitt's friend
ZILLA, Paul's shrewish wife

Critique:

Babbitt is a pungent satire about a man who typifies complacent mediocrity. George F. Babbitt, as standardized as his electric cigar lighter, revels in his own popularity, his ability to make money, his fine automobile, and his penny-pinching generosity. Babbitt worships gadgets. He praises prohibition and drinks bootleg whiskey, bullies his wife, ogles his manicurist. Though he is constantly discontented with the life he leads, he is thoroughly satisfied with George F. Babbitt. Because his character is grounded in realism, Babbitt is one of the most convincing characters in American literature.

The Story:

George F. Babbitt was proud of his house in Floral Heights, one of the most respectable residential districts in Zenith. Its architecture was standardized; its interior decorations were standardized; its atmosphere was standardized. Therein lay its appeal for Babbitt.

He bustled about in a tile and chromium bathroom in his morning ritual of getting ready for another day. When he went down to breakfast, he was as grumpy as usual. It was expected of him. He read the dull real estate page of the newspaper to his patient wife, Myra. Then he commented on the weather, grumbled at his son and daughter, gulped his breakfast and started for his office.

Babbitt was a real estate broker who knew how to handle business with zip and zowie. Having closed a deal whereby he forced a poor businessman to buy a piece of property at twice its value, he pocketed part of the money and paid the rest to the man who had suggested the enterprise. Proud of his acumen, he picked up the telephone and called his best friend, Paul Riesling, to ask him to lunch.

Paul Riesling should have been a violinist, but he had gone into the tar-roofing business in order to support his shrewish wife, Zilla. Lately she had made it her practice to infuriate doormen, theater ushers, or taxicab drivers, and then ask Paul to come to her rescue and fight them like a man. Cringing with embarrassment, Paul would pretend he had not noticed the incident. Later, at home, Zilla would accuse him of being a coward and a weakling.

So sad did Paul's affairs seem to Babbitt that he suggested a vacation to Maine together—away from their wives. Paul was skeptical, but with magnificent assurance Babbitt promised to arrange the trip. Paul was humbly grateful.

Back in his office Babbitt fired a salesman who was too honest. When he got home, he and his wife decided to give a dinner party, with the arrangements taken bodily from the contents of a woman's magazine, and everything edible disguised to look like something else.

The party was a great success. Babbitt's friends were exactly like Babbitt. They all became drunk on prohibition-period gin, were disappointed when the cocktails ran out, stuffed themselves with food, and went home to nurse headaches.

The next day Babbitt and Myra paid a call on the Reislings. Zilla, trying to enlist their sympathy, berated her husband until he was goaded to fury. Babbitt finally told Zilla that she was a nagging, jealous, sour, and unwholesome wife, and he demanded that she allow Paul to go with him to Maine. Weeping in self-pity, Zilla consented. Myra sat calmly during the scene, but later she criticized Babbitt for bullying Paul's wife. Babbitt told her sharply to mind her own business.

On the train, Babbitt and Paul met numerous businessmen who loudly agreed with each other that what this country needed was a sound business administration. They deplored the price of motor cars, textiles, wheat, and oil; they swore that they had not an ounce of race-prejudice; they blamed Communism and socialism for labor unions which got out of hand. Paul soon tired of the discussion and went to bed. Babbitt stayed up late, smoking countless cigars, and telling countless stories.

Maine had a soothing effect upon Babbitt. He and Paul fished and hiked in the quiet of the north woods, and Babbitt began to realize that his life in Zenith was not all it should be. He promised himself a new outlook on life, a more simple, less hurried way of living.

Back in Zenith, Babbitt was asked to make a speech at a convention of real estate men which was to be held in Monarch, a nearby city. For days he tried to write a speech about the good life, as he now thought of it. But at the convention he scrapped his speech, declaimed loudly that real estate was a great profession, that Zenith was God's own country—the best little spot on earth—and to prove his statements quoted countless statistics on waterways, textile production, and lumber manufacture. The speech was such a success that Babbitt instantly won recognition as an orator.

Babbitt was made a precinct leader in the coming election. His duty was to speak to small labor groups about the inadvisability of voting for Seneca Doane, a liberal, in favor of a man named Prout, a solid businessman who represented the conservative element. Babbitt's speeches helped to defeat Doane. He was very proud of himself for having Vision and Ideals.

On a business trip to Chicago, Babbitt spied Paul Reisling sitting at dinner with a middle-aged but pretty woman. Later, in his hotel room, Babbitt indignantly demanded an explanation for Paul's lack of morality. Paul told Babbitt that he could no longer stand living with Zilla. Babbitt, feeling sorry for his friend, swore that he would keep her husband's secret from Zilla. Privately, Babbitt envied Paul's independence.

Babbitt was made vice-president of the Booster's Club. He was so proud of himself that he bragged loudly when his wife called him at the office. It was a long time before he understood what she was trying to tell him; Paul had shot his wife.

Babbitt's world collapsed about him. Though Zilla was still alive, Paul was in prison. Babbitt began to question his ideas about the power of the dollar. Paul was perhaps the only person Babbitt had ever loved. Myra had long since become a habit. The children were too full of new ideas to be close to their father. Babbitt felt suddenly alone. He began to criticize the minister's sermons. He no longer visited the Athletic Club, rarely ate lunch with any of his business acquaintances.

One day a pretty widow Mrs. Judique, came to his office. She became his mistress, and Babbitt joined her circle of Bohemian friends. He drank more than he had ever drunk in his life. He spent money wildly. Two of the most powerful men in town requested that he join the Good Citizen's League—or else. Babbitt refused to be bullied. For the first time in his life he was a human being. He actually made friends with his arch-enemy, Seneca Doane, and discovered that he liked his liberal ideas. He praised Doane publicly. Babbitt's new outlook on life appealed to his children, who at once began to respect him as they never had before. But Babbitt became unpopular among his business-boosting friends. When he again refused to join the Good Citizen's League, he was snubbed in the streets. Gradually Babbitt found that he had no real resources within himself. He was miserable.

When Myra became ill, Babbitt suddenly realized that he loved his colorless wife. He broke with Mrs. Judique. He joined the Good Citizen's League. By the time Myra was well again, there was no more active leader in the town of Zenith than George F. Babbitt. Once more he announced his distrust of Seneca Doane. He became the best Booster the club ever had. His last gesture of revolt was private approval of his son's elopement. Outwardly he conformed!

THE BACCHAE

Type of work: Drama
Author: Euripides (480-406 B.C.)
Type of plot: Classical tragedy
Time of plot: Remote antiquity
Locale: Thebes, in Boeotia
First presented: c. 405 B.C.

Principal characters:
DIONYSUS, god of the vine
PENTHEUS, King of Thebes
CADMUS, grandfather of Pentheus and former king
TIRESIAS, a Theban seer
AGAVE, Pentheus' mother

Critique:

In this sinister drama, Euripides would seem to have attempted the impossible; that is, to condemn religious excess and at the same time to accept the myth of a man who died for disapproving of religious excess. It has been said that *The Bacchae,* posthumously staged, was a recantation, marking Euripides' acceptance of the nature-worship aspects of the Dionysiac cult. If so, the play can still be interpreted as a warning against excess. In this drama Euripides was also an accurate observer of Nature. As half-man, half-god, Dionysus is exasperating in his divine self-sufficiency; as a symbol of certain aspects of brute Nature, he is terrifying.

The Story:

Visited by Zeus, Semele, daughter of Cadmus, the King of Thebes, conceived a child. While she was still carrying her unborn child, she prayed to see Zeus in all his regal splendor. Zeus accordingly appeared to her in the form of a bolt of lightning; Semele was killed instantly. Zeus took the prematurely born child he had fathered and placed him within himself.

In its proper time the child was born again and was named Dionysus. When he grew up and became the god of revelry and wine, men established a cult for his worship. The cult of Dionysus spread throughout western Asia, but it had not yet gained a real foothold in Europe. Dionysus, the god-man whom his devotees associated with the vine and with the ecstasies derived from the juice of the grape, decided that Thebes, home of his ancestors, would be the logical place for the beginning of his cult in the West. At first Theban resistance to Dionysiac behavior balked his efforts, and many Thebans refused to believe that he was a son of Zeus. Pentheus, grandson of Cadmus and cousin of Dionysus, ruled as King of Thebes. Dreading the disorders and madness induced by the new cult, he stubbornly opposed its mysteries, which hinged largely upon orgiastic and frenzied Nature-rites.

A group of Eastern women, devotees of Dionysus, called upon the Theban women to join them in the worship of their beloved god. During the ceremonies blind Tiresias, an ancient Theban prophet, summoned old Cadmus, now withdrawn from public life, to the worship of Dionysus. Performing the frenzied rites, the two old men miraculously regained youthful vigor.

Pentheus, enraged because some of his people had turned to the new religion, imprisoned all women who were caught carrying any of the Bacchic symbols, wine, an ivy crown, or a staff. He rebuked his aged grandfather and accused Tiresias of responsibility for the spread of the cult in Thebes. Tiresias championed Dionysus, declaring that wine provided men with a temporary release from the harshness and miseries of life. The Theban maidens, he said, were exalted and purified by the Bacchic ecstasies. Old Cadmus seconded the words of Tiresias and offered to place an ivy wreath on Pentheus' brow. Pentheus brushed it aside and ordered some of his soldiers to destroy Tiresias' house; others he directed to seize a mysterious stranger, a priest of Dionysus, who had a remarkable influence over Theban women.

When the stranger, Dionysus in disguise, was brought before the king, all the Theban women who had been jailed suddenly and mysteriously found themselves free in a forest where they were engaged in worship of Dionysus. Meanwhile, in the city, Pentheus asked the prisoner his name and his country. Dionysus answered that he was from Lydia, in Asia Minor, and that he and his followers had received their religion from Dionysus. He refused, however, to tell his name. When Pentheus asked to know more about the strange religion, Dionysus said that this knowledge was reserved for the virtuous only. Pentheus impatiently ordered a soldier to cut off Dionysus' curls, which the prisoner had said were dedicated to his god. Then Pentheus seized Dionysus' staff and ordered him to be imprisoned. Dionysus, calm in spite of these humiliations, expressed confidence in his own welfare and pity at the blindness of Pentheus. Before the guards took Dionysus to be imprisoned in the royal stables, he predicted catastrophe for Pentheus. The king, unmindful of this prophecy, directed that the female followers of Dionysus be put to practical womanly labors.

From his place of imprisonment Dionysus called out encouragement to his devotees. Then he invoked an earthquake which shook the foundations of Pentheus' fortress. Flames danced on Semele's tomb. Dionysus appeared, mysteriously freed from his prison, and rebuked his followers for any doubts and fears they had expressed. He had cast a spell on Pentheus, who in his mad frenzy mistook a bull for Dionysus and chained the animal in its stall while the god-man looked on. Another earth tremor tumbled the royal fortress in ruins.

Pentheus, enraged at seeing Dionysus free, ordered his guards to shut the gates of the city. At the same time a messenger reported that many Theban women, among them Agave, mother of Pentheus, were on nearby Mount Cithaeron observing Dionysiac rites that were partly a dignified and beautiful Nature-worship, partly the cruel slaughter of cattle. A battle had taken place between the women and Boeotian peasants, but the frenzied women, although victorious over the peasants, did not harm them. Pentheus ordered the immediate suppression of the cult. Dionysus offered to lead the women back to the city, but he declared that if he did so the women would only grow more devoted to the man-god.

When Pentheus imperiously demanded that his orders be obeyed, Dionysus cast over him a spell which made the king express a desire to see the women at their worship. In a trance, he resisted only feebly when Dionysus dressed him in woman's clothes in order that he might not be detected by the women, who were jealous of the secrecy of their cult. Pentheus, in fact, was almost overcome by Dionysus' charms as the god led him to Mount Cithaeron.

On the mountain Pentheus complained that he could not see the rites because of the thick pine forest. Dionysus immediately bent a large pine tree to the ground, set Pentheus in its topmost branches, and gently let the tree return to its upright position. At that moment the man-god disappeared, but his voice boomed out to his ecstatic devotees that a great enemy of the cult was hidden in the tall tree. The women, wild with fury, felled the tree, Pentheus with it. Agave, in a Dionysiac frenzy, stood over her son. He frantically threw off his feminine dress and pleaded with her to recognize him, but in her Bacchic trance she imagined him to be a lion. With prodigious strength she tore off his left arm at the shoulder. Her sisters, Ino and Autonoë, joined her and together the three women broke Pentheus' body to pieces. Agave placed his severed head on her wand and called upon the revelers to behold the desert-whelped lion's head that she had taken.

Cadmus and his attendants carried the maimed body of his grandson back to the city. When Agave displayed her bloody trophy, the old man could only feel the deepest pity for his daughter in her blind excess. When Agave awoke from her trance and recognized the head of her beloved son on her wand, she was bewildered and grief-stricken. Cadmus, mourning the violence that had occurred, urged all men to comply with the wishes of the Olympian deities.

Dionysus returned in his divine form and prophesied that Cadmus and his wife, Harmonia, transformed into dragons, would overcome many Grecian lands before they died. He showed no sympathy for Agave, who cried out that she had been guilty of sinning against him. He doomed her and her sisters to wander without respite until death overtook them.

BACK TO METHUSELAH

Type of work: Drama
Author: Bernard Shaw (1856-1950)
Time: The past and the future
Locale: The Garden of Eden, Mesopotamia, the British Isles
First presented: 1922

Principal characters:

ADAM
EVE
CAIN
THE SERPENT
CONRAD BARNABAS, a biologist
FRANKLYN BARNABAS, his brother, a theologian
WILLIAM HASLAM, a rector, later Archbishop of York
A PARLOR MAID, later Mrs. Lutestring, Domestic Minister
JOSEPH P. B. B. BARLOW, an elderly gentleman
BADGER BLUEBIN, Commonwealth Prime Minister
A HE-ANCIENT
A SHE-ANCIENT
LILITH, mother of mankind

Back to Methuselah is Shaw's only major drama of ideas which falls flat as a play. It is true that both *Man and Superman* and *Major Barbara* contain lengthy speeches which contribute little to the action, but Shaw's mastery of idiosyncrasy and dialogue compensates for those stretches of verbosity and often justifies them. *Back to Methuselah,* however, has no such redeeming stylistic touches. For the most part, the dialogue is declamation and the characters are orators. Worst of all, talk takes the place of action—ninety thousand words of talk in the play itself and thirty thousand in the preface which Shaw the essayist wrote to explain the dramatist's ninety thousand.

The play does have moments in which theatricalism relieves the tedium of the talk. In one scene, for example, a make-believe sibyl appears to the accompaniment of lightning and thunder. In another, a full-grown girl is hatched from an egg. In still another, characters appear on a simulated television screen. But all these devices are so obviously contrived that they fail to delight.

Properly speaking, *Back to Methuselah* is not a play at all. A far more appropriate designation is the subtitle Shaw gave it: *A Metabiological Pentateuch.* It is a pentateuch because it consists of five separate plays which add new information to the Bible. It is *biological* because the information concerns evolution. It is *meta*biological because the concept of evolution expounded in the play transcends the conventional theory of Darwin. *Back to Methuselah* is Shaw's attempt to explain the theory of Creative Evolution to a public unwilling or unable to read biological treatises. That the public might be unwilling or unable to sit through a play which takes two or three evenings to perform apparently did not worry him.

Yet *Back to Methuselah* is an important play: a work important in the development of modern drama because it stretched the drama of ideas as far as it could go and important in the body of Shavian drama because it contains the core of Shaw's philosophy.

The theme of the play and the central tenet of Shaw's belief and teaching is that man does not live long enough but that he could if he would. As soon as man has lived long enough to acquire the knowledge and experience to solve some of the problems of life, life ends. The knowledge and experience are wasted. Life itself is wasted. Such waste, in Shaw's belief, is shameful, for all that man must do to avoid it is resolve to live longer. What man wants, he can have, whether it be an extra head, arm, leg, or additional years of life. This is the secret of Creative Evolution: species acquire new characteristics not through random mutations which are confirmed or rejected in the struggle for existence but through the recognition that new characteristics are needed and then the desire, conscious or unconscious, for their development. A disciple of Lamarck and Samuel Butler, Shaw believed that man could create his own evolution. In *Back to Methuselah* he attempts to show how and why.

Creative Evolution, according to Shaw, was one of the mysteries which the Serpent explained to Eve in the Garden of Eden—the setting of "In the Beginning," the first part of the pentateuch. Paradoxically, the great problem of life in the Garden was not how to extend life but how to end it. Faced with the horrible prospect of living forever, Adam longs to die and yet is unwilling to end life on earth. The Serpent solves the dilemma for him by explaining to Eve the doctrine of creative imagination. All they need to do to die is to will to die; to ensure the perpetuation of life, to create new life. The secret of creation is one the Serpent is only too willing to whisper in Eve's ear.

The second act, which takes place a few centuries later, is a variation on this theme of life and death. It is actually a debate on the purpose of life, with Adam, Eve, and Cain taking three different views. Adam contends that the purpose of life is to live, quietly working to pass away the years. Cain, the inventor of murder, believes that to live bravely, daring death and dying gloriously is the goal of man. Eve, believing that there is something nobler than either working or fighting, scoffs at both. Though she has not yet discovered just what it is, she has hope that man will find and cherish it.

By 1919—the date of "The Gospel of the Brothers Barnabas," the second part of the pentateuch—the triumph of Cain's apostles of death and destruction has shortened man's life span to its current length. But Franklyn and Conrad Barnabas have rediscovered the Serpent's secret of Creative Evolution and have settled on three hundred years as the ideal life span. Their task is to convince enough people that extending life is possible, then let nature do the rest. Although they are notably unsuccessful in persuading two politicians, Burge and Lubin, to adopt "Back to Methuselah" as the Liberal Party slogan, they remain confident that someone will soon live for three hundred years.

By 2170, the date of "The Thing Happens," the miracle has been accomplished. The Archbishop of York and Mrs. Lutestring, both of whom had been exposed to the Barnabas gospel, have lived 283 and 274 years respectively. Except for their ages, both are typical Shavian heroes in that they are so superior to a conventional society that society rejects and despises them. Their plight is more ironic than that of most Shavian heroes because by 2170 England is a Utopia, albeit a bureaucratic Utopia, administered by Chinese men and African women. When confronted with the prospect of a race of supermen, the rulers of the Utopia can only contemplate their own impotence.

By 3000, the date of "Tragedy of an Elderly Gentleman," the rulers' worst fears have materialized: the new race has expropriated the British Isles for its own use and banished ordinary mortals. The thematic significance of this section of the play is drawn from the contrast between the new race and the old. From Baghdad, the new capital of the British Commonwealth, comes a politician posing as a statesman to seek counsel from the supermen. The supermen are so contemptuous of the politician's intellect that they present the advice, which itself is humiliating, through a humbug oracle. True to form, the politician ignores it, fabricates his own counsel, and departs. An elderly gentleman, a member of the delegation, decides to remain behind, but he is so feeble in contrast to one of the super beings that he dies upon meeting her gaze.

By 31,920, the ordinary human race is extinct. Children are hatched from eggs at the age of seventeen and live indefinitely. "As Far As Thought Can Reach," the fifth and last section of the play, sketches the development of the new human being, who, after a four-year accelerated intellectual and physical growth devoted to playing, dancing, and mating, becomes an "Ancient," one who devotes himself to pure thought and whose goal is existence as pure, disembodied thought.

That this goal will be reached is affirmed by Lilith, the mother of Adam and Eve, in the closing speech of the play. In fact, the only reason Lilith has permitted the human race to evolve is that it has been striving toward such a goal. But, Lilith concludes, the attainment of the goal is merely a step in a greater plan, the nature of which even she knows nothing.

In such a fashion Shaw finally reaches the conclusion that life, some form of life, will endure. Admittedly, the conclusion is not a profound one, but the insistence that man can forge his own destiny and create his own form of life is well worth considering if only because it is the underlying assumption of every one of Shaw's major plays.

BAMBI

Type of work: Novel
Author: Felix Salten (1869-1945)
Type of plot: Pastoral allegory
Time of plot: Indefinite
Locale: The woods
First published: 1929

Principal characters:
BAMBI, a deer
THE OLD PRINCE, a stag who befriends Bambi
BAMBI'S MOTHER
FALINE, Bambi's cousin
GOBO, her brother

Critique:

Bambi is one of the few successful attempts to humanize animals in fiction. A fairy tale for children, but an allegory for adults, the book tells the story of a deer who learns that he must travel alone if he is to be strong and wise.

The Story:

Bambi was born in a thicket in the woods. While he was still an awkward young fawn, his mother taught him that he was a deer. He learned that deer did not kill other animals, nor did they fight over food as jaybirds did. He learned, too, that deer should venture from their hiding places to go to the meadow only in the early morning and late in the evening and that they must rely on the rustle of last year's dead leaves to give them warning of approaching danger. On his first visit to the meadow Bambi had a conversation with a grasshopper and a close look at a butterfly.

One evening Bambi and his mother went to the meadow again. On his second visit he was introduced to the hare, an animal with big, soft eyes and flopping ears. Bambi was not impressed. The little deer was considerably happier to meet his cousins, Gobo and Faline, and their mother, Ena. The two families were about to separate when two stags with spreading antlers on their heads came crashing out of the forest. Bambi's mother explained that the larger, statelier stag was Bambi's father.

As he grew older, Bambi learned the sounds and smells of the forest. Sometimes his mother went off by herself. Missing her one day, Bambi started out to look for her and came upon his cousins in the meadow. Faline suggested that both their mothers might have gone to visit their fathers. Bambi decided to continue his search by himself. As he stood at the edge of a clearing, he saw a creature he had never seen before. The creature raised what looked like a stick to its face. Terrified, Bambi ran back into the woods as fast as he could go. His mother appeared suddenly, and they both ran home to their glade. When they were safe again, Bambi learned that he had seen a Man.

On another day he began to call for his mother. Suddenly a great stag stood before him. Coldly he asked Bambi why he was crying, and told him that he ought to be ashamed of himself. Then he was gone. The little deer did not tell his mother of his experience, nor did he call her any more. Later he learned that he had met the Old Prince, the biggest and wisest stag in the forest. One morning Bambi was nibbling in the meadow with his mother when one of the stags came out of the forest. Suddenly there was a crash. The stag leaped into the air and then fell dead. Bambi raced away after his mother. All he wanted was to go deeper and deeper into the forest until he could feel free of that new danger. He met the Old Prince again. When Bambi asked him who Man was, the stag only replied that he would find out for himself. Then he disappeared.

The forest gradually changed as summer passed into fall and then into winter. Snow fell, and grass was not easy to find. All of the deer became more friendly during the cold months. They would gather to talk and sometimes even one of the stags would join them. Bambi grew to admire the stags. He was especially interested in Ronno, the stag who had escaped after a hunter had wounded him in the foot. The constant topic of conversation was Man, for none of the deer could understand the black stick he carried. They were all afraid of it.

As the winter dragged on, the slaughter of the weaker animals in the forest began. A crow killed one of the hare's children. A squirrel raced around with a neck wound a ferret had given him. A fox murdered a pheasant. A party of hunters came into the woods with their noise-making sticks and killed many of the animals. Bambi's mother and his cousin Gobo were not seen again.

That spring Bambi grew his first pair of antlers. With his mother gone, he had to spend most of his time alone. The other stags drove him away when he tried to approach them, and Faline was shy with him. Deciding one day that he was not afraid of any of the stags, Bambi charged at what he thought was one of his tormentors in a thicket. The stag stepped aside, and Bambi charged past him. It was the Old Prince. Embarrassed, the young deer began to tremble when his friend came close to him. With an admonishment to act bravely, the older deer disappeared into the woods.

A year later Bambi met Faline again, and once more they played as they had when they were very young. Then an older stag named Karus appeared and tried to block Bambi's way. When Bambi attacked him, Karus fled, as did the stag named Ronno, who had been pursuing Faline.

Faline and Bambi ventured into the meadow one day and there saw a stranger nibbling the grass. They were surprised when he came skipping up to them and asked if they did not know him. It was Gobo. Hunters had caught him and kept him until he was full-grown. Then he had been sent back to join his family in the forest. His mother was delighted to see him once more.

Gobo explained his absence to an admiring audience, and praised Man for his kindness. While he was talking, the Old Prince appeared and asked Gobo about the strip of horsehair around his neck. Gobo answered that it was a halter. The Old Prince remarked pitingly that he was a poor thing, and vanished.

Gobo would not live as the other deer in the forest did. He insisted on going about during the day and sleeping at night. He had no fear about eating in the meadow, completely exposed. One day, when a hunter was in the woods, Gobo declared that he would go talk to him. He walked out into the meadow. Suddenly there was a loud report, Gobo leaped into the air and then dashed into the thicket, where he fell mortally wounded.

Bambi was alone when he met the Old Prince for the first time since Gobo's death. They were walking together when they found a hare caught in a noose. Carefully the Old Prince managed to loosen the snare with his antlers. Then he showed Bambi how to test tree branches for a trap. Bambi realized for the first time that there was no time when Man was not in the woods.

One misty morning, as Bambi stood at the edge of the clearing, a hunter wounded him. He raced madly for the forest, and in its protection lay down to rest. Soon he heard a voice beside him, urging him to get up. It was the Old Prince. For an hour the veteran led Bambi through the woods, crossing and recrossing the place where he had lain down, showing him the herbs which would stop his bleeding and clear his head. He stayed with Bambi until the wound had healed.

Before he went off to die, the old stag showed Bambi a poacher who had been killed. He explained that man, like animals, must die. Bambi understood then that there is someone even more powerful than Man.

Walking through the forest one day, Bambi spied a brother and sister fawn crying for their mother. As the Old Prince had spoken to him so many years before, he asked them if they could not stay by themselves. Then, as his friend had done, he vanished into the forest.

BARABBAS

Type of work: Novel
Author: Pär Lagerkvist (1891-   )
Type of plot: Realistic symbolism
Time of plot: First century
Locale: Palestine, the Near East, Rome
First published: 1949

Principal characters:
BARABBAS, the robber freed in Christ's stead
A GIRL, unnamed, formerly intimate of Barabbas
SAHAK, a fellow slave of Barabbas, an Armenian Christian
THE ROMAN GOVERNOR
MARY
PETER
LAZARUS

Critique:

Barabbas in surface and in details of action and characterization seems a very realistic historical novel. In this fable, however, Lagerkvist has created a symbolic story which treats a primitive man's unwitting search for God. His portrait of the criminal Barabbas' emerging conscience patterns the emergence of Christian doctrine from the superstition and bewilderment which, the author implies, were the first reactions of the populace to the Crucifixion. The symbolic meaning of Barabbas' story is probably to be extended to include the blind search of all men of all times for belief. In 1951, two years after the appearance of this novel, Lagerkvist was awarded the Nobel Prize for literature.

The Story:

At Golgotha, Barabbas, watching the Crucifixion from which he had suddenly been saved, was startled by the words uttered by the figure on the cross: "My God, my God, why hast thou forsaken me?" Even stranger to him was the darkness which seemed to come over the world. As he was leaving the scene he was also disturbed by the look of silent reproach directed at him by the dead man's mother.

Back in Jerusalem, he met and walked with a young girl, whom he had known before. The girl, who had a harelip, went with him to a dive where some of his low companions were gathered. Barabbas and the people there discussed Barabbas' rescue and the strange rabbi who had made such extreme claims and yet permitted himself to be crucified like any criminal. Barabbas was considerably relieved that the people in the café did not believe in the rabbi's divinity, though he was rather troubled that they had not even noticed the darkness which had for a while hung over the land. The young girl having left the dive, Barabbas indulged, as a kind of escape from his worries, in a drunken debauch with one of the patrons of the café—a fat, crude woman.

Later Barabbas met a red-bearded follower of Christ who expected Christ to rise from the dead the next day. He explained some of Christ's teachings to Barabbas, but shamefacedly admitted that before the end he had denied Christ. The girl with the harelip, to whom Barabbas also talked about Christ, said that she had met Him. She was wilder in her predictions than was the red-bearded man; she expected the millennium and divine miracles any day. Superstition did not blur everything, however, for she told Barabbas that Christ's message was one of love. Barabbas thereupon went to the grave, and watched all night, but saw nothing. The next day, however, the stone was gone from the entrance. He believed that the followers of Christ had taken the body; the girl thought He had risen.

Barabbas asked the followers of Christ about these events, but found little satisfaction in their answers. He could not understand One who used His power by refraining from using it. Barabbas was later taken to a man who had been dead four days and had been raised again by this rabbi. This man told Barabbas that death was nothing; it was there, but it signified nothing. He added that after one had experienced death, life also was as nothing. As Barabbas further questioned the followers of Christ, it became clear that though they were believers they were quite confused as to the meaning of all these happenings. When the followers learned Barabbas' identity, as sooner or later they did, they naturally hated him.

About this time Barabbas became estranged from his fellows in the low life of Jerusalem—so much so that he left off his sensual life. The fat woman, his sometime lover, thought that Christ's soul had possessed Barabbas. One day, by accident, Barabbas was present at a church meeting and heard a rather disappointing sermon by the red-bearded man who had denied Christ. The snuffling testimony of witness given by the harelipped girl he found even more distasteful; yet later, when a blind man denounced the girl as a Christian, Barabbas knifed the first person who stoned her. She died a humble martyr, but one who saw Christ as she died. Barabbas carried her body to the grave of a baby she had had: Barabbas had been the father of that child.

A short time later Barabbas left Jerusalem and returned to the robber band which he had at one time led. The robbers were distressed by his seeming character change: formerly the boldest of all, he had become apathetic. So bold had he been that years ago he had fought and killed and supplanted the bandit leader; thus he had come by the scar on his face. What none of the characters knew was that Eliahu, whom Barabbas had killed, was his own father. Sensing that he no longer fitted in with the robber band, Barabbas silently stole away from the camp.

For an indeterminate period Barabbas wandered the face of the earth. Later he was enslaved and put to mining for the Romans. There he met Sahak, a slave who was thrilled by the knowledge that Barabbas had seen Christ. Without revealing to Sahak the true nature of that relation, Barabbas increased the details of Sahak's belief by telling him things about Christ. Some of these were lies, such as that he had seen an angel come down from the sky on the night that he had watched outside Christ's tomb. After a time Barabbas apathetically suffered Sahak to enter into Christian observances with him. He even permitted Sahak to draw Christ's symbol on his slave's disk, and for a time he prayed with him. Years later a new mine overseer, attracted to Christianity but mystified by its doctrine of love, noticed the two slaves, bound to each other by a chain. The overseer, having talked to them about Christianity, was moved to secure positions above ground for the two men. Though still slaves, Sahak and Barabbas were at any rate free of the deadly conditions of primitive mining.

Matters soon changed when the Roman governor of the territory learned through another slave that both men were Christians. Sahak refused to renounce his faith. Barabbas, who by this point would have liked to believe in Christ but could not, readily renounced his. He let the governor scratch through the sign that Sahak had put on his disk. He then had to witness Sahak's crucifixion, but he himself was rewarded. He was relieved when no miraculous occurrences accompanied the death of Sahak.

When the pagan but kindly Roman governor retired to Rome, he took Barabbas with him. Once Barabbas went to the catacombs to see a Christian religious service, but no worshipper was there. In the darkness of the catacombs he felt terribly alone. He also felt that, as he had dreamed one night, he was still chained to Sahak, just as he had been during the days when he had pretended to believe.

After he had left the place of the dead, he smelled fire; flames were everywhere. He thought that Christ had returned to save the world, the first step of which would be to destroy Rome—for Rome felt that Christ was the enemy. Barabbas seized a burning brand and began to set everything afire that he could; he thought, wildly, that he was helping the Christians and his Saviour.

Thrown into prison with the Christians, Barabbas learned that there had been no service in the catacombs because the followers had been forewarned that an attack was to be made on them. The fires were probably set by agents or spies to discredit further the Christians.

The Christians in the prison naturally denied that Barabbas, who had been caught red-handed, was one of them. When they protested to the jailer, the man showed as evidence Barabbas' disk, which still had the Christian symbol dimly scratched on it. A venerable old man among the Christians turned out to be one whom Barabbas had met before, the man who had denied Christ. Now he explained to Barabbas that it was Caesar who had set the fires, not Christ; it had been Caesar, therefore, whom Barabbas had helped by trying to burn Rome. Christ's message was still that of love.

To the others the old man added that they must not condemn Barabbas, though he was the Acquitted One. He continued that Barabbas was unhappy, and he had to wear his crossed-out disk. The others were also weak and full of faults; their belief had come from God. They must not condemn a man who had no god in whom to believe.

Soon the Christians were led out in pairs to be crucified, but Barabbas was taken alone. When death was coming, he spoke rather ambiguously into the darkness, saying that he delivered up his soul "to thee."

THE BARBER OF SEVILLE

Type of work: Drama
Author: Pierre Augustin Caron de Beaumarchais (1732-1799)
Type of plot: Romantic comedy
Time of plot: Eighteenth century
Locale: Seville, Spain
First presented: 1775

Principal characters:
FIGARO, the barber of Seville
COUNT ALMAVIVA, a Grandee of Spain
BARTHOLO, a doctor
ROSINE, his ward
DON BAZILE, Rosine's singing-master

Critique:

Although the plot of *The Barber of Seville* has been used many times by dramatists and composers, Beaumarchais seems to have a fresh approach to the story. It is on this gentle comedy that Rossini's famous opera is based. The play is fast-moving and brisk. It has all the necessary ingredients for a romantic comedy: intrigue, wit, clear-cut characterizations, satire, and a well-defined plot. Indeed, the plot is more important than the actors themselves, even though Figaro, the barber, has become famous in the literature of all countries. Beaumarchais' style served as a model for many dramatists who followed him.

The Story:

Count Almaviva was so much in love with Rosine, the ward of Dr. Bartholo, that even though he had never spoken to her he had left Madrid and the pleasure of the court in order to be near her in Seville. Because her guardian desired to marry her, he kept the young girl locked in her room. To help him in his suit the count enlisted the aid of Figaro, the barber and apothecary of Bartholo.

A note Rosine threw from her window convinced the count that she returned his love. At Figaro's suggestion, the count then disguised himself as a soldier seeking quarters for the night. He called himself Lindor, the name Figaro had used in telling Rosine of her unknown lover. When Bartholo, suspicious of everyone who might come near Rosine, refused to give the disguised count lodging, the count managed to slip a note to Rosine before Bartholo ordered him from the house. Bartholo forced Rosine to show him the note, but she cleverly tricked him into reading another letter which she had received from her cousin. Still his suspicions were not allayed.

His first plan having failed, the count, with the help of Figaro, disguised himself as a student. Calling himself Alonzo, he told Bartholo that he had been sent by Don Bazile, Rosine's music teacher. His story was that Don Bazile was ill and had asked Alonzo to take his place. Bazile was a party to Bartholo's plot to force Rosine to marry him the next day. Figaro, having learned of this plot, had given the count the information so that he could pretend to help Bartholo. The count gave Bartholo a letter which he claimed would help Bartholo in his suit. They would tell her that another woman had given it to Bartholo, a woman with whom the count was supposed to be in love.

The count thought that by pretending to help Bartholo he could be alone with

Rosine and tell her his plans to rescue her from the old man. But again Bartholo would not leave them alone together until Figaro managed to trick him into leaving the room. Then Figaro stole the key to Rosine's room from the old man's key ring. When Bartholo returned to the room, the music lesson seemed to be in progress. Then Don Bazile himself was announced. It took all of Figaro's ingenuity to keep him from revealing Alonzo as an impostor. Figaro and the count at last managed to get Don Bazile out of the house before Bartholo began to suspect the truth. But Bartholo, suspicious of everyone, sneaked behind the count and Rosine and overheard enough to make him decide to investigate Don Bazile's strange behavior and apparent bewilderment.

Don Bazile confessed that he knew nothing of his supposed illness and had never before seen the so-called Alonzo. This confirmation of his suspicions made Bartholo uneasy. Although he feared that Alonzo was the count's friend, he did not suspect that Alonzo was the count himself. He told Don Bazile to arrange to have the notary come at once to perform his marriage with Rosine.

Immediately afterward he went to the young girl's room and showed her the letter the count had given him. Instead of the help the count expected from the letter, however, it worked against him. Bartholo told Rosine also that her young lover would pretend to rescue her, but in reality he planned to sell her to the count. Since Rosine too did not know the real identity of the man she called Lindor, she believed Bartholo and promised to marry him at once. She also told him of Alonzo's plan to steal into her room that night and carry her off. Bartholo left her to arrange for the police to come and apprehend the kidnaper.

While Bartholo was gone, the count and Figaro climbed up a ladder and entered Rosine's room. Thinking him to be Lindor, she scorned the count and accused him of a plot to sell her to the count. The count then threw aside his disguise. He told her he was the Count Almaviva, that in his love for her he had followed her hopelessly for the past six months. Rosine was so overcome that she fainted. When she was revived, she told them of her loss of faith and of her promise to marry Bartholo. She told them also of Bartholo's knowledge of the plan to carry her away. Already the ladder had been removed from her window and the police were on the way.

When all looked blackest, Don Bazile appeared with a notary, as Bartholo had instructed him to do. The notary knew only that he was to perform a marriage here and another marriage at the home of Figaro. Here he was to marry Bartholo and a young lady named Rosine. At Figaro's he was to marry Count Almaviva and a young lady named Rosine. By some clever and rapid talking, the count and Figaro were able to convince the notary that he was merely confused. Don Bazile was more difficult, but he finally decided the money the count slipped into his hand was more important than his loyalty to Bartholo. He signed the marriage contract as a witness just before Bartholo burst into the room with many policemen and a justice of the peace.

Bartholo ordered the justice of the peace to arrest the count, but that civil servant was too much impressed with Count Almaviva's high position to risk offending him. Bartholo, anxious to marry his ward, then ordered the count out of the house. When he learned that the count and Rosine had just been married, and that the contract was legally signed, he was infuriated and tried in vain to keep Rosine from leaving with her husband. By threatening Bartholo with a demand for an exact accounting of his ward's property, an exposé which Bartholo dared not allow, the justice of the peace was able to persuade the old man to sign the marriage certificate, thus giving his consent to the marriage of Rosine. Bartholo could not understand how his plans had failed. Figaro told him that youth and love could always defeat an old man's schemes.